SEVENTH EDITION

GUIDE TO

REFERENCE BOOKS

by CONSTANCE M. WINCHELL

Reference Librarian, Columbia University

Based on the GUIDE TO REFERENCE BOOKS, *Sixth Edition, by Isadore Gilbert Mudge*

Chicago, 1951

AMERICAN LIBRARY ASSOCIATION

PREFACE

The history of the *Guide to Reference Books* now covers almost half a century. It was in 1902 that the American Library Association first published the *Guide to the Study and Use of Reference Books* by Alice Bertha Kroeger. This pioneer work achieved an immediate success and was soon adopted as a textbook in library schools and training classes. Annual supplements for 1903–1907 were printed in the *Library Journal*; and in the fall of 1908, a second edition, revised and considerably enlarged, was issued. Miss Kroeger died in 1909, and in 1910 the Publishing Board of the American Library Association asked Isadore Gilbert Mudge to continue the *Guide*. Thus began a connection which lasted for almost thirty years, and included the preparation of the editions of 1917, 1923, 1929, and 1936 with intervening supplements. Miss Mudge became the outstanding authority on reference books, and her *Guide* has been known and consulted in libraries throughout the world. She was particularly well-fitted for the work by her long experience both as a teacher and as a reference librarian—at the University of Illinois, at Bryn Mawr College, at Simmons College, and finally at Columbia University where she was Reference Librarian from 1911–1941 and Associate Professor in the School of Library Service from 1926–1938. Her thorough familiarity with reference books and reference techniques, her clear thinking, her wide knowledge and remarkable memory, and her deep interest in the subject and in the student or research worker, all combined to impress her influence on succeeding generations of students, colleagues—all who used her book. Probably no other one person has con-

tributed so much to raising the standards of reference collections and reference service in the libraries of this and other countries.

Miss Mudge prepared the first supplement to the sixth edition, *Reference Books of 1935–1937*, which was published in 1939. After her retirement in 1941, the Editorial Committee of the American Library Association asked the present writer to prepare the succeeding supplements, covering 1938–1940, 1941–1943, and 1944–1946.

It had been evident for some time that a completely new edition was needed, and in 1945 the Editorial Committee appointed a subcommittee to ascertain the desires and requirements of the library profession in this regard. This subcommittee, of which Professor Margaret Hutchins of the Columbia University School of Library Service was chairman, sent out questionnaires to library schools and to public, college, university, special and reference libraries; and on the basis of the replies received made a report to the Editorial Committee. Guided by this report, the Editorial Committee decided that: (1) a basic volume should be published to include the basic reference works in all fields and to be followed by a series of supplementary volumes in specialized fields; (2) the basic volume should be prepared by one general editor assisted by an advisory committee; (3) the general pattern of the sixth edition should be followed with the addition of more titles, more annotations, and a strengthening of some sections, particularly Science and Applied Science.

Accordingly, the present editor was asked to undertake the revision, and through the interest and cooperation of Dr. Carl M. White, Director of Libraries, was given a year's leave of absence from her position as Reference Librarian of Columbia University. To help in setting up policies and to serve in an advisory capacity, the following committee was appointed by the Editorial Committee: Mr. Louis Kaplan, Associate Librarian of the University of Wisconsin, to represent reference librarians; Miss Norma Cass, Head of the Reference Department of the University of Kentucky Library, to represent teachers of reference; and Mr. Wyllis E. Wright, Librarian of Williams College, to represent catalogers.

PURPOSE

The techniques and fundamental principles of reference work remain more or less constant through the years, but the number of reference works published grows apace and, as a consequence, more titles are listed in each succeeding edition of this book. From this mass of material, the librarian must select those works best suited to the purposes and clientele of his particular library; the research worker must seek out those books which will help him in searching for facts or for the literature of his specialized subject; and the student must have selected, for his study, representative works in both general and special fields.

This edition, like its predecessors, is planned to serve (1) as a selection aid for the librarian; (2) as a reference manual for the library assistant, research worker, or other user of library resources; and (3) as a textbook for the student who, either in library school, training class, or college course in bibliography, is beginning a systematic study of reference books.

The needs of these types of users have influenced the organization and make-up of this volume in that the requirements of the first two groups have made the manual more comprehensive than it might have been if intended for a school textbook only, while the introductions to separate sections and many of the annotations have been provided particularly for the library school student.

SELECTION OF TITLES

This seventh edition, although definitely based on the sixth edition and incorporating much of the same material and many of the same titles, is completely revised, reorganized, and enlarged.

An attempt has been made to develop and balance the various sections, to add new materials, to omit superseded works, to give descriptive and evaluative annotations for a greater number of entries, and to provide a more detailed index.

The sixth edition contained some 4000 entries; this one includes approximately 5500. The additions include works published since 1936 and older works not listed in the sixth edition which serve to round out the basic collections in various fields. The sixth edition should still be used for titles omitted from this edition and for some historical annotations to which cross references have been made.

The selection of titles was made with a large general reference library in mind and those works, including many scholarly works in English and foreign languages, are listed which might be included in a large general reference collection or with which general reference assistants should be familiar.

It is obvious that a work of this kind cannot be all-inclusive. Each section includes a selection of basic reference materials available in that particular field. For additional titles and more specialized works it will be necessary to consult the manuals, guides, and bibliographies in the various subject fields.

While care has been taken to ensure as great accuracy as possible, it is recognized that in a compilation of this kind, including, as it does, titles in many different languages, errors will doubtless be found. The compiler would be glad to have these called to her attention.

ARRANGEMENT

The over-all arrangement in this edition differs to some extent from that used in the sixth edition. In accordance with the suggestions of the Subcommittee, it was decided to follow the Dewey classification but to omit the Dewey number. However, without the Dewey classification numbers to show the reason for the arrangement there seemed to be little logic in the sequence of headings within some classes. This was particularly true in the Social Sciences and the Fine Arts. Therefore, although the general structure follows the Dewey system, there has been rearrangement of the material within classes to follow a more clearly defined pattern. Wherever subdivisions by countries are used, the United States is listed first, with other countries following it in alphabetical order.

In this edition the arrangement by subject approach has been used throughout, that is, bibliographies, indexes, dictionaries, biographies, etc., are listed with the individual subjects so that *Index Medicus* is under Medicine rather than Periodical Indexes, and *Who's Who in American Art* is under Fine Arts instead of Biography.

While types of reference works vary in the different subject fields and not all types are available for all subjects, the same categories recur in many of the subject divisions and subdivisions of this *Guide*. With some slight variations and with additions or omissions as seemed advisable under each subject, the categories are listed in this order: (1) Guides and manuals; (2) Bibliographies; (3) Indexes and abstracts; (4) Encyclopedias; (5) Handbooks; (6) Dictionaries of special terms; (7) Annuals and directories; (8) Histories; (9) Biographical works; (10) Atlases and collections of illustrations; (11) Serial publications.

CODE NUMBERS

To facilitate the finding of titles, each entry has been assigned a code number. The code numbers were formed by giving a letter to each section and numbering the entries consecutively within the section. When, in the revision of the manuscript, titles were omitted or added, the code numbers were altered to conform, i.e., in some cases numbers have been cancelled, and in others, small letters *a, b, c, etc.* have been added to the numbers in order to insert additional titles. The code numbers are intended solely as an aid in finding titles and have no other significance.

CROSS REFERENCES

Under subjects, a moderate number of cross references call attention to closely allied headings and to individual works listed under other subjects. Cross references by code number are used for titles to which references are made. The detailed author, title, and subject index should be an aid in locating specific books or particular types of material.

PRICES

Prices are given for American and English publications, and for foreign works when post-war listings were found. However, as prices change so frequently, these will serve only as an indication of price range, and individual titles should always be rechecked before quoting or ordering.

SERIAL ENTRIES

Annuals and other serial publications are listed with open entries. In this connection, the war years presented a special problem as many works were forced to suspend publication during that period. In some cases publication has been resumed; in others, it seems reasonably sure that no more will be published; in still others, the outcome is uncertain. The disadvantage of the open entry is that it does not indicate whether the last volume received is 1939 or 1949 or somewhere in between. Where it seems probable that the series is dead, the entry is closed; in other cases, wherever possible, an indication is given of the price of the last volume received by 1948, 1949, or occasionally 1950. Unfortunately, however, it is not possible to assume that an open entry means that postwar issues have been received, although in most cases this is probably true.

For works published in parts, an attempt has been made to list all parts received through 1949, followed by the notation (*In progress*). Because of postwar conditions it was not always possible to procure parts of foreign works, even though they were listed in trade bibliographies; therefore, the listings are not as complete as it was hoped that they might be.

CLOSING DATE

Because the manuscript as a whole was completed early in 1950, the year 1949 was, in most cases, the closing date for listing new works and new editions. In a few instances, where new titles were received early in 1950, it was possible to insert them. Occasionally, new editions have been listed when, as in the case of *Chambers's Encyclopaedia,* the work has been so thoroughly revised as to make the listing of the earlier edition actually misleading. For the most part, however, titles issued in 1950 have not been added.

ACKNOWLEDGMENTS

This kind of an undertaking is extremely rewarding because so many people are interested in its development and betterment and are anxious to be of assistance. Many have proffered aid, others have responded wholeheartedly when asked for opinions, and all have given most generously of their time and specialized knowledge. Among those who have been helpful, my thanks go especially: to the members of the Advisory Committee for their cooperation in the establishment of general policies and for the reading of special parts—particularly to Norma Cass, who read the entire manuscript, section by section; to Richard S. Angell, Chief, Cataloging Division, Copyright Office, Library of Congress; Ruth C. Eisenhart, Chief Cataloger, Union Theological Seminary, New York; Hazel Gay, Librarian, American Museum of Natural History; Isaac Goldberg, Administrative Secretary, Hebrew Union College Library, Cincinnati; Dr. Frederick C. Grant, Professor of Biblical Theology, Union Theological Seminary; Dr. Lucy W. Markley, former Librarian, Union Theological Seminary; Dr. Eleanor B. Marr, Professor of Chemistry, Hunter College; Ralph H. Phelps, Librarian, Engineering Societies Library, New York; Dr. W. W. Rockwell, Librarian Emeritus, Union Theological Seminary; Margaret Inglis Smith, Chief Reference Librarian, University of Michigan; John N. Waddell, Reference Assistant, New York Public Library; to the following members of the staff of the Columbia University Libraries: *Art and Architecture:* Mary W. Chamberlin, Assistant Librarian in charge of Fine Arts Library; Corinne W. Spencer, former Associate Librarian, Avery Library of Architecture; *Business:* Janet Bogardus, Librarian, and Alice Day Hoffman, Reference Librarian, Business Library; *East Asia and Near East:* Howard P. Linton, Librarian, East Asiatic Collections; Isaac Mendelsohn, Curator, Near East Collections; *Education:* Clara Esther Derring, Supervising Librarian, Reference Department, Teachers College Library; *Engineering, Mathematics, and the Physical Sciences:* William S. Budington, Librarian, Engineering and Physical Sciences Libraries; Ben C. Driver, Reference Assistant, Physics Library; S. T. Serghiesco, Librarian, Mathematics Library; Martha R. Thomas, former Librarian, Chemistry Library; *Law:* Miles O. Price, Law Librarian; Harry Bitner, Associate Librarian, and Margaret Hall, former Reference Librarian, Law Library; Florence K. Ferner, Reference Librarian, International Law Library; *Library Service:* Darthula Wilcox, Librarian, School of Library Service;

Medicine and the Biological Sciences: Thomas P. Fleming, Professor of Library Service and Librarian of Biological Sciences; Estelle Brodman, former Associate Librarian, Medical Library; Amy L. Hepburn, Librarian, Natural Sciences Libraries; *Music:* Catharine K. Miller, former Librarian, Music Library; *Rare Books:* Roland Baughman, Head of Special Collections, Alice H. Bonnell, Assistant Librarian, Special Collections; to the library assistants in all of the libraries where I have worked; and to the pages who handled hundreds of volumes.

Particular thanks are due to those good friends who spent many hours wielding paste-brushes when it was found that the material needed to be reorganized, a process which required weeks of cutting and pasting; to Ardis Lodge, Librarian in charge of General Reference Division, in the Reference Department at the University of California at Los Angeles, who spent a year in the Reference Department at Columbia as an exchange assistant, and who read the entire manuscript and made many helpful suggestions; to Jean Macalister, Associate Reference Librarian at Columbia, who read galley and page proof with a critical but friendly eye, and to whom I owe more than I can say; to Louise P. Bull, who served as my personal assistant during the first year of preparation and who did far more than I had any right to expect; and to the editorial staff at American Library Association Headquarters, especially Everett O. Fontaine, Chief of the Publishing Department and Pauline J. Love, Editor of Publications, for their cooperation, patience, and long-suffering.

It would be impossible to express adequately my appreciation of the unstinted cooperation of the members of the Reference Staff of Columbia University Library during the long months and years of preparation. They rearranged schedules, assumed extra duties, and shouldered added responsibilities with the greatest cheerfulness and efficiency; they protected me from interruptions and yet kept me well-informed; and besides seeing that the work of the Department ran smoothly, they found time to help me in gathering and examining material. For all of this, and much more, my unbounded gratitude goes to Jean Macalister, Jane Davies, Keith Dowden, Bruce Harlow, Olive Johnson, Mary Lou Lucy, Carl Reed, Lucy Reynolds Eddy, and to all other members of that loyal staff.

And finally, a special word to my family and to the friends who have encouraged and sustained me; to my Mother, who spent many lonely evenings while I labored; to Dollie B. Hepburn, for her continual encouragement; and to Isadore Gilbert Mudge, who as teacher, colleague, and friend has been a constant source of inspiration and because of whom I dared to attempt this work. Without their help a compilation such as this could never have been completed.

April 1951.   C. M. W.

ABBREVIATIONS AND TRANSLATIONS

❦ *The following list includes only the principal bibliographical abbreviations used in this book for which some explanation or translation seems needed. Shortened forms of publishers' names, signs or abbreviations used to indicate money, and some other abbreviations which are practically self-explanatory, e.g., Acad., Assoc., Inst., Soc., etc., have not been included here.*

aarg (Swed.) aargang: *annual volume*
Abt. (Ger.) Abteilung: *part*
Afd. (Dan.) Afdeling: *part*
afl. (Dutch) aflevering: *part*
A.L.A.: *American Library Association*
ampl. (It.) ampliata: *enlarged*
Aufl. (Ger.) Auflage: *edition*
augm. (Fr.) augmenté: *enlarged*
aum. (Sp.) aumentado: *enlarged*
Ausg. (Ger.) Ausgabe: *printing, edition*
avd. (Nor.) avdeling: *part, volume*

Balt.: *Baltimore*
Bd. (Dan.) Bind, (Ger.) Band: *volume*
bd. (Nor.) bind, (Swed.) band: *volume*
bearb. (Ger.) bearbeitet: *compiled, edited*
begr. (Ger.) begründet: *established*
Bost.: *Boston*
Bull.: *Bulletin*
Burt. (Lettish) Burtricā: *part*

c.: *copyright*
ca.: *circa*
Camb.: *Cambridge, England*
Camb., Mass.: *Cambridge, Massachusetts*
Chic.: *Chicago*
cm.: *centimeters*
col.: *columns, colored*
comp.: *compiled*
compl.: *completed, completely*
Cong.: *Congress*
corr. (Fr.) corrigé, (Sp.) corregido: *corrected*

d. (Ger.) der: *the*
deel (Dutch): *volume, part*
doc.: *document*
druk (Dutch): *printing, copy, edition*

ea.: *each*
ed.: *edition, editor*
éd. (Fr.) édition: *edition*
ed. (It.) edizione, (Sp.) edición: *edition*
Eng.: *English*
erweit. (Ger.) erweiterte: *enlarged*
estab. tip. (Sp.) establecimiento tipografico:
    publishing company

f. (Ger.) für: *for*
facsim.: *facsimile*
fasc. (Fr.) fascicule: *part, number*

gänzl. (Ger.) gänzlich: *entire, complete*
Gosudarst. (Russ.) Gosudarstvo: *state*
Govt. Prt. Off.: *Government Printing Office*

Harv. Univ. Pr.: *Harvard University Press*
Hft. (Dan.) Hefte, (Ger.) Heft: *part, number*
hft. (Nor.) hefte: *part, number*
Hlbbd. (Ger.) Halbband: *half binding*
hrsg. (Ger.) herausgegeben: *published, edited*

il.: *illustrated, illustrations*
imp., impr. (Fr.) imprimé, imprimerie, imprimeur:
    printed, printing, printing firm, printer
imp., impr. (Sp.) imprenta, impresión:
    printing office, impression, edition
Imp. Nat. (Fr.): *Imprimerie Nationale*
incompl.: *incomplete*
Internat.: *International*
Introd.: *Introduction*
izdat. (Russ.) izdatel': *publisher*

jaarg. (Dutch) jaargang: *annual volume*
Jahrg. (Ger.) Jahrgang: *annual publication*

l.: *leaves*
Lfg. (Ger.) Lieferung: *number, part*
Lib.: *Library*
libr. (Fr.) librairie, (It.) libreria: *library*
livr. (Fr.) livraison: *part, issue*
Lond.: *London*

n. (It.) numero: *number*
Nachtr. (Ger.) Nachtrag: *appendix, supplement*
n.d.: *no date*
neubearb. (Ger.) neubearbeitet: *revised*
n.F. (Ger.) neue Folge: *new series*
nouv. (Fr.) nouveau, nouvelle: *new*
n.p.: *no publisher, no place*
Nr. (Dan., Ger.) Nummer: *number*
nr. (Nor.) nummer: *number*
n.s.: *new series*
núm. (Sp.) número: *number*
numb.: *numbered*
N.Y.: *New York*

o.a. (Swed.) och andra: *and others*
omarb. (Swed.) omarbetad: *revised*
o.p.: *out of print*
Ox.: *Oxford*

p.: *page*
pa.: *paper*
Phila.: *Philadelphia*
Pr.: *Press*
Pref.: *Preface*
prel.: *preliminary*
priv. pr.: *privately printed*
priv. pub.: *privately published*
pt. (Fr.) partie: *part*
Pub.: *Publication, Publishers, Public, published*
pub. (Fr.) publié: *published, publication*

réd. (Fr.) rédigé: *edited, compiled*
redig. (Swed.) redigerad: *edited*
ref. (Fr.) refondue: *reorganized*
repr.: *reprinted*
rev. (Sp.) revisado: *revised*
revid. (Swed.) reviderad: *revised*
rif. (It.) rifatta: *restored, repaired*

riv. (It.) riveduto: *revised*

sec. (Sp.) sección: *section*
sér. (Fr.) série: *series*
sess.: *session*
Stat. Off.: *His Majesty's Stationery Office*
subs.: *subscription*
suppl. (Fr.) supplément: *supplement*

t. (Fr.) tome, (Sp.) tomo: *volume*
T., Th. (Ger.) Teil, Theil: *part*
tidskr. (Swed.) tidskrift: *periodical*
tip. (It.) tipografia: *printing firm*
tr.: *translated, translator*
tr. (Swed.) tryckt: *printed*
tr. (Fr.) traduit: *translated*
trad. (Sp.) traducido: *translated*

u. (Ger.) und: *and*
u.A. (Ger.) und Andere: *and others*
übers. (Ger.) übersetzt: *translated*
udarb. (Dan.) udarbeidet: *prepared*
Udg. (Dan.) Udgave: *edition*
uit. (Dutch) uitgaaf: *publication*
uitg. (Dutch) uitgegeven: *published*
ung. (Ger.) ungarische: *Hungarian*
umgearb. (Ger.) umgearbeitete: *revised*
Univ.: *University*
Univ.-Buchdr. (Ger.) Universitäts-Buchdrukerei: *university press*
uppl. (Swed.) upplaga: *edition*
utarb. (Nor.) utarbeidet: *prepared*
utg. (Nor.) utgave: *edition*

v. (It.) volume: *volume*
v. (Ger.) von: *from*
veränd. (Ger.) verändert: *revised*
verb. (Ger.) verbesserte: *improved*
verm. (Ger.) vermehrte: *enlarged*
vollst. (Ger.) vollständig: *completely*
v.p.: *various paging*

Wash.: *Washington, D.C.*
wesentl. (Ger.) wesentlich: *essential, main*

TABLE OF CONTENTS

❧ *This table of contents lists only a few of the subdivisions of some sections. To locate specific subjects see index.*

REFERENCE WORK AND REFERENCE BOOKS

ISADORE GILBERT MUDGE

The following introduction is reprinted from the sixth edition of GUIDE TO REFERENCE BOOKS *for it still expresses adequately, although briefly, the essential points every student and reference worker should know about reference work and the study of reference books.*

REFERENCE DEPARTMENT

The Reference Department of a library is that part of the system which is charged especially with the task of aiding readers in their use of the library, particularly in their use of the resources and books within the library walls as distinguished from the withdrawal of books for home reading. In a large library such a department will have its own staff, often of considerable size, with a chief reference librarian, several reference assistants, often with specialized work, minor desk attendants, pages, etc. In a somewhat smaller library one trained reference assistant may handle the whole work, while in the still smaller library all reference work may have to be done by the librarian or a general assistant. Whatever the size of the library, it will have questions of one sort or another brought to it by its readers and these must be answered in so far as the resources of the library permit. Much of the reputation of the library in its community will depend upon the success with which it handles its reference questions.

Reference work is often spoken of as if it consisted only of the actual use of reference books in answering questions for readers. In its widest and best development, however, the work of a reference department covers everything necessary to help the reader in his inquiries, including the selection of an adequate and suitable collection of reference books; the arrangement and maintenance of the collection in such a way that it can be used easily and conveniently; the making of such files, indexes and clipping collections as are needed to supplement the library catalog and the book collection; the training of a capable staff of reference assistants and their supervision in such a way as to insure skilful and pleasant service and good teamwork; the provision of posted signs, printed directions, lists and bulletins to help the reader who can profit by such guides; expert aid in the use of the catalog and other records; suggestions as to books to be used for special purposes; instruction of individuals, groups, or classes in the use of reference books and reference methods; and constant work in answering individual questions, in helping individual readers to find some elusive fact, or in correcting some wrong method of research on the part of an inexperienced reader. While a large part of this work will be administrative and advisory, with the purpose of helping the reader to help himself, there will always be included, also, a considerable amount of actual research work in looking up questions, both those that come in by mail or telephone, and those which readers, even with some advice and assistance, have found too difficult. A live reference department is not limited to work within its own walls, but through interlibrary loan, telephone reference work, knowledge of outside specialists—either individuals, institutions or learned societies, government or public service bureaus etc.—from whom help can be obtained, can often open up many profitable sources of information to its readers and investigators. In libraries connected with educational institutions, either colleges and universities or secondary schools, the work of the reference department will often include a regular course of lectures and class work on the use of books and libraries. Such a course, especially if it is a required course for freshmen or other beginning students, not merely an elective course for advanced students, can be of great assistance in increasing the intelligent and effective use of library resources.

REFERENCE BOOKS

However varied the work of a reference department may be, the reference book is the basis of its work. The most important element in the equipment of such a department is an adequate and live collection of reference books and the most important asset of a reference assistant is a knowledge of reference books and experience in using the right book at the right time and in the right way. The possession of the right books and the knowledge of how to use them are two things essential to the success of a reference department, and the latter is no less important than the former. The ignorant assistant can render comparatively useless the finest collection of reference books, while the skilled assistant, who knows how to get from each book all the varied kinds of information that it is planned to give, can show astonishing results even when limited to only a few basic books.

From the point of view of use, books may be divided into two groups: those which are meant to be read through for either information or enjoyment, and those which are meant to be consulted or referred to for some definite piece of information. Books of this second class are called reference books, and are usually comprehensive in scope, condensed in treatment and arranged on some special plan to facilitate the ready and accurate finding of information. This special arrangement may be alphabetic, as in the case of most dictionaries or encyclopedias; chronological, as in historical outlines and similar compends; tabular, as in the case of statistical abstracts; regional, as in atlases; classified or systematic as in the case of some bibliographies, technical handbooks, etc. As such books are used for the finding of single definite facts, some alphabetical approach to the fact is usually needed, and if the book is not itself arranged alphabetically it is usually provided with a detailed alphabetical index. Works which follow any of these indicated arrangements are reference books, pure and simple, and are not used for consecutive reading. There are other books, however, which, while intended primarily to be read through for either information or pleasure, are so comprehensive and accurate in their treatment and so well provided with indexes that they serve also as reference books. Examples of such books are the *Cambridge History of American Literature*, anthologies such as Stevenson's *Home Book of Verse*, standard histories such as the *Cambridge Modern History*, and many of the textbooks and treatises used in college work. The reference department of a large library will necessarily contain both formal reference books and these "borderland" books as well, but the student of reference books will naturally devote most of his attention to the formal reference books, both because they are fundamental and because they need careful study before all their uses can be learned. Later, however, in doing actual reference work, he should realize that the formal reference books constitute only a part, though a very important one, of his collection of reference material and that the treatment of some reference questions will involve first the use of some standard reference book in the reference collection, then reference from that to some book in the stack to which the formal reference book has furnished a clue, or even to some source of information outside the library.

HOW TO STUDY REFERENCE BOOKS

Only constant and practical use of a reference book will make a student thoroughly familiar with its character and use, but the following suggestions will help him in his preliminary examination of the book.

1. Examine title page carefully for information as to
   a) scope of work as indicated in title
   b) author's name
   c) author's previous record (often indicated by list of degrees, positions, titles of earlier works, etc.)
   d) publisher
   e) date of publication. Check date of publication by reference to copyright date and date of preface; while these dates offer no

absolute guarantee of the date of information in the book they sometimes help in determining this, especially in cases where they are considerably earlier than the imprint date.

2. Read preface or introduction for
   a) further information as to scope of work
   b) special features claimed
   c) limitations, if any
   d) comparison with other books on same subject.

3. Examine book itself for
   a) arrangement
   b) kind of entry
   c) cross references, i.e., extent to which included, whether given in main work or in separate list, etc.
   d) supplementary lists, noting number and kind and how connected with main work
   e) indexes, noting fullness and exactness of reference
   f) quality and kind of articles, noting whether they are popular or scientific, signed or unsigned, impartial or biased, and especially whether they are equipped with satisfactory bibliographical references in the form of either appended bibliographies, references throughout the text or bibliographical footnotes. Several articles should be read carefully, compared with similar articles in other books. The student should, if possible, look up some subjects upon which he has either some special knowledge or means of securing accurate information. However important the form and convenience of arrangement of a reference book may be, the trustworthiness of its information is of still greater importance, and a knowledge of its comparative accuracy or inaccuracy is fundamental to any real knowledge of the book.

4. In examining both preface and articles note any evidence of lack of impartiality; e.g., if the book deals with a controversial subject, religious, political, etc., does it represent only one side; or, in the case of a biographical work, are the selection of names, kind and length of article, etc., determined in any way by the desire to secure subscribers.

5. In studying the arrangement of a book, note the possibility of variation in books which follow the same general arrangement; e.g., in a work arranged alphabetically, note what rules for alphabetizing have been followed. Among encyclopedias, for example, the *Britannica*[1] and the *Americana* follow different rules, and the student who does not observe that fact may miss the article for which he is looking. The alphabetizing of words containing an umlauted vowel is a possible source of confusion in many books, and in foreign reference books, in general, one should always remember points in which the foreign alphabetizing differs from the English. A fuller discussion of some of these points will be found on page 80 of this *Guide*.

6. If the work in question purports to be a new edition, note carefully the extent of revision claimed for it and check this by comparison with earlier editions. New or revised editions often present very special difficulties, and the examination should be extended enough to determine whether the revision is
   a) so complete and thorough that it supersedes the earlier work
   b) thorough, but with the omission of some material included in the earlier work which is still useful, in which case the two editions may have to be used together, or
   c) so insufficient and superficial that the earlier edition is still to be preferred.
   A reference worker needs such information about a book for two purposes:
   1) to decide whether or not the book should be purchased
   2) to be able to explain to readers who ask for a so-called new edition why its purchase was not considered advisable.

---

[1] In sixth edition *New International* was cited.

GUIDE TO REFERENCE BOOKS

REFERENCE MATERIALS FOR SPECIAL SUBJECTS

A working reference collection, large or small, will include reference books in specialized subject fields as well as comprehensive works such as general bibliographies, encyclopedias, dictionaries, and indexes. For special subjects there are certain recognized types of reference materials. The principal ones are: (1) Guides and manuals; (2) Bibliographies; (3) Indexes and abstracts; (4) Encyclopedias; (5) Handbooks; (6) Dictionaries of special terms; (7) Annuals and directories; (8) Histories; (9) Biographical works; (10) Atlases and collections of illustrations; (11) Serial publications.

1. GUIDES AND MANUALS. Guides and manuals to the literature of the subject are usually prepared for students or research workers as aids to finding bibliographies and other reference materials in the field, e.g. Parke, *Guide to the Literature of Mathematics and Physics* (N67) and Coman, *Sources of Business Information* (L407).

2. BIBLIOGRAPHIES. Of fundamental importance, bibliographies of the subject are usually of two kinds: (a) basic bibliography, comprehensive up to a fixed date; (b) current bibliography, recording the literature of a given period, frequently one year at a time. In some cases a current bibliography connects exactly with the basic work and gives a comprehensive record for the whole field, e.g., Nickles, *Geologic Literature of North America* (N236) which covers publications to 1918, and is continued from 1919 by current bibliographies cumulating decennially. Together these furnish a full record of the literature of the subject.

Reference bibliographies are useful for: (a) verification of incorrect or incomplete titles; (b) finding what material exists on a given topic; (c) an estimate of the value of a book or article, which may be given by an annotation or by reference to a critical review; (d) an abstract or digest of a particular book or article or note of its contents or plot; (e) information on the fundamental or best books on a subject; (f) a statement of the various forms or editions in which a work appears, or historical or bibliographical data about a famous or rare book or edition; (g) biographical data about an author.

Not all bibliographies will furnish information on all of these points; therefore, different types are needed in the reference collection. For most reference purposes, the comprehensive bibliography, which records books, periodical articles, and other analytical material, is the most useful. Within its stated limits it should give full and definite information about each item included, and should be so arranged and indexed that works can be found quickly by author, or by broad or specific subject. If the bibliography is to serve as a critical guide to the literature, annotations or other indications of standing should be given. Frequently this type of information is best found in the selective bibliography which lists outstanding books and articles for a given subject.

3. INDEXES AND ABSTRACTS. Indexes and abstracts may be of periodicals, publications of learned societies, book reviews, or composite books including essays, poetry, plays, short stories, etc. To the reference worker, the importance of a good index, whether it be to an individual book, to a separate periodical, or to a group of periodicals or books, can not be overestimated. Indexes of various kinds are required

in all reference collections. *See* page 253 for a brief discussion on the place of the abstract journal in reference work.

4. ENCYCLOPEDIAS. The *Encyclopaedia of the Social Sciences* (L14) is an outstanding example of an encyclopedia of a subject or group of related subjects. In a well-made work of this kind, the editors and contributors will be specialists and their special knowledge will be evident in the choice of subjects, length and authority of articles, fullness and selection of bibliographies, etc.

5. HANDBOOKS. Handbooks are compilations of miscellaneous information which, in some fields, are particularly important as reference aids, e.g., in branches of engineering there are handbooks which, although prepared primarily for the practicing engineer, are useful for answering reference questions in a library. Literary, historical, and statistical handbooks are needed in libraries of all sizes.

6. DICTIONARIES OF SPECIAL TERMS. Dictionaries of special terms are of two types: (a) The dictionary of terms in one language supplements the general dictionaries of the language by more specific definitions and differentiations of terms and by many special and technical terms omitted from the general dictionary, e.g., Dorland, *American Illustrated Medical Dictionary* (P301). Its main purpose is exact definitions, but it may supply some encyclopedic information, illustrations, and bibliographical references. (b) The bilingual or polyglot dictionary of foreign terms such as De Vries, *French-English Science Dictionary* (N33) or the *Lanz Aviation Dictionary in Nine Languages* (P94), supplements the general bilingual dictionary with the technical terminology of a particular field. Its main use is as an aid in translations, in the reading of technical articles in a foreign language, and in correspondence involving the use of technical terms.

7. ANNUALS AND DIRECTORIES. Annuals and directories vary considerably in different subject fields. They may be mainly (a) records of current developments in the subject; (b) statistical compilations; (c) directories of persons, institutions, firms, or official bodies; or (d) a combination of any or all of these.

8. HISTORIES. Histories of a subject give the main facts and names in its development, often contain biographical and bibliographical information, and, if provided with detailed indexes, may serve to some extent as encyclopedias of the subject. Good examples are Garrison, *Introduction to the History of Medicine* (P329) and Sarton, *Introduction to the History of Science* (N61).

9. BIOGRAPHICAL WORKS. Biographical works, both retrospective and current, supplement the general biographical dictionaries with information about persons connected with a particular subject, e.g., *Baker's Biographical Dictionary of Musicians* (Q247) and Cattell and Ross, *Leaders in Education* (L768).

10. ATLASES AND COLLECTIONS OF PLATES OR ILLUSTRATIONS. Special atlases and collections of illustrations are useful when maps and illustrations are needed for graphic representation of a subject. Examples are Wright and Filson, *Westminster Historical Atlas of the Bible* (K105), Goode and Shannon, *Atlas of English Literature* (R287), and Parmentier, *Album Historique* (V38) or the volumes of plates in the *Cambridge Ancient History* (V83).

11. SERIAL PUBLICATIONS. Much of the important work in subject fields is reported in the specialized journals of the subject. In some cases these journals will be indexed in the general or special periodical indexes or abstracts, but the reference assistant should always be aware of the possibility of unindexed journals. Periodicals as such are not included in this *Guide* but they will be needed frequently in reference work to supplement the more formal reference materials.

BIBLIOGRAPHY

❧ Bibliographies, general and special, are basic materials in a reference collection. In this edition of the *Guide* subject bibliographies are listed with their subjects and only the more general works are treated below. Some of the general bibliographies do, of course, have subject significance which is indicated in other sections of this book by means of cross references or through the index. Bibliographies are so important in reference work that throughout this *Guide*, with few exceptions, they are listed first whether or not the subhead "Bibliography" appears.

General bibliographies are important in any except the very small library and are especially necessary in university and research libraries. They give a wide, though never complete, survey of the mass of printed material in many fields and lead to the answering of questions through the listing of specific books, or actually answer questions involving data about particular books. General bibliographies of a highly selective character, especially if they have descriptive and evaluative notes, e.g., *Standard catalog for public libraries* (A551), are useful for questions for which only a few good books, rather than the whole literature of a subject, are needed.

National and trade bibliographies furnish the record of printing output in a given country and often give descriptions and supply verifications which cannot be found in the less complete bibliographies. In addition they have a very special use for questions connected with book purchase since they usually give prices.

Bibliographies of bibliography show the existence of materials in particular subjects or on specific authors, and bibliographies of incunabula and other book rarities are indispensable for descriptions of rare items and for locating copies of them.

A special type of reference book needed for the intelligent use of bibliographies is a dictionary of bibliographical terms and abbreviations without which the reading of condensed bibliographical descriptions is sometimes difficult; and, for the interpretation as well as the making of such specialized descriptions, manuals of bibliographical and cataloging practice are necessary.

GENERAL WORKS
Guides and manuals

Bowers, Fredson. Principles of bibliographical description. Princeton, Princeton Univ. Pr., 1949. 505p. il. **A1**

A full, detailed treatment of analytical bibliography as applied to the description of books. Covers the principles of describing incunabula, and English and American books from the sixteenth to the twentieth centuries. Most of the principles would be applicable to printing in other countries. Complements McKerrow's *Introduction to bibliography* (A3).

Esdaile, Arundell. A student's manual of bibliography. Lond., Allen & Unwin and the Library Assoc., 1932. 383p. il. **A2**

A useful manual covering such subjects as: papyrus, vellum, paper; printing, type faces; illustration, binding, collation; description of books; classes and examples of bibliography; arrangement of bibliographies, etc.

McKerrow, Ronald B. An introduction to bibliography for literary students. Ox., Clarendon Pr., 1927. 359p. **A3**

A survey of the mechanical side of book production which is of particular interest to students of the literature of the fifteenth and sixteenth centuries. Covers the making of the printed book, the early printing press, paper and decoration, bibliographical technique, formats of books, meaning of "edition," "impression," etc., evidence as to edition, dating editions, variations in copies, cancels, etc. The appendix includes notes on early printing presses, types, abbreviations, etc.

Mudge, Isadore Gilbert. Bibliography. Chic., Amer. Lib. Assoc., 1915. 25p. (preprint of Manual of library economy, ch. 24) o.p. **A4**

5

A brief, clear statement on kinds of bibliographies and standards and use of bibliographies in libraries.

Schneider, Georg. Handbuch der Bibliographie. 4. gänzl. veränd. u. stark verm. Aufl. Leipzig, Hiersemann, 1930. 674p. **A5**

An important guide to general bibliography, national bibliography, bibliographies of incunabula, newspapers, society publications, etc.; lists of biographical dictionaries. Includes comment and annotations. A basic work.

The first three editions (1923–26) contained an introductory theoretical-historical treatment of bibliography, which has been omitted in the fourth edition. An English translation of this portion of the third edition is available under the title *Theory and history of bibliography*, tr. by R. R. Shaw (N.Y., Columbia Univ. Pr., 1934. 306p.).

Stein, Henri. Manuel de bibliographie générale; bibliotheca bibliographica nova. Paris, Picard, 1897. 895p. **A6**

(1) Universal bibliographies; (2) national and regional bibliographies; (3) subject bibliographies. Appendices contain: (1) alphabetical list of places having printing presses before the nineteenth century, arranged by the modern names, with indication of the Latin name of each place, the date of establishment of its press, and references to sources of information; (2) indexes of periodicals; (3) printed catalogs of libraries.

There is a useful subject index, but no author index. As the subject index includes the Latin names of places listed in appendix 1, it serves also as a dictionary of Latin and medieval geography.

The main list and appendices 2 and 3 were continued by the lists of new bibliographies, indexes and catalogs given in each number of *Le Bibliographe moderne,* 1897–1931, edited by Henri Stein.

Van Hoesen, Henry Bartlett and **Walter, Frank Keller.** Bibliography, practical, enumerative, historical; an introductory manual. N.Y., Scribner, 1928. 519p. il. **A7**

Prepared as a textbook for upperclassmen and graduate students, attempts to "indicate the scope, functions, and methods of bibliographical work of all kinds and topics, and [to] describe or enumerate the fundamental works . . ."

The chapters deal with the bibliographies and reference works in special fields and are followed by a bibliographical appendix and topical index.

Bibliography

Arnim, Max. Internationale Personalbibliographie, 1800–1943. 2. verb. und stark verm. Aufl. Leipzig, Hiersemann, 1944- . Bd.1- . (In progress) **A10**

Bd.1, A-K, 706p.

A revised edition of a useful bibliography which was first published in 1936 covering the years, 1850–1935. This edition has been extended to cover the first half of the nineteenth century as well as more recent years. It indexes bibliographies contained in books, periodicals, biographical dictionaries, academic annuals, festschriften, etc. In many cases the references lead to biographical as well as bibliographical information. It is international in

scope with the emphasis on German names. However, it will be necessary to consult the first edition for many names which have been dropped from the second for political reasons. Identification in this edition is simplified by the addition of occupations and frequently the date of death.

Besterman, Theodore. A world bibliography of bibliographies and of bibliographical catalogues, calendars, abstracts, digests, indexes, and the like. 2d ed. rev. and greatly enlarged throughout. Lond., priv. pub. by the author, 1947–49. 3v. **A11**

v.1-2, A-Z; v.3, Index.

1st ed. 1939–40. 2v.

A classified bibliography of 63,776 separately published bibliographies of books, manuscripts, and patent abridgements. International in scope but somewhat uneven in its treatment of various classes. Volume 3 is an index of authors, editors, translators, titles of anonymous and serial publications, libraries, archives and patents. "Bibliographies which would appear in the index under the same heading as in the text are excluded, unless they appear in the text under more than one heading."

Bibliografiíà russkoǐ bibliografiǐ. Leningrad, 1944- . v.1- . (Gosudarstvennaíà ordena trudovogo krasnogo znameni publichnaíà biblioteka im M. E. Saltykova-Shchedrina. Trudy. t.1) **A12**

t.1, Sokurova, M. V. Obshchie bibliografiǐ knig grazhdanskoǐ pechati, 1708–1937.

Bibliographic index; a cumulative bibliography of bibliographies, 1937- . N.Y., Wilson, 1938- . Service basis. **A13**

v.1, 1937–1942 (pub. 1945); v.2, 1943–1946 (pub. 1948).

Published in three forms: (1) permanent cumulated volumes; (2) annual volumes to supplement the permanent volumes ending in a 4-year cumulation; (3) current issues published quarterly in June, Sept., Dec., with annual cumulation in March.

An alphabetical subject arrangement of separately published bibliographies and bibliographies included in books and periodicals. One thousand to 1500 periodicals including many in foreign languages are examined regularly. An extensive and useful list.

Bohatta, Hanns and **Funke, Walter.** Internationale Bibliographie der Bibliographie; ein Nachschlagewerk. Frankfurt am Main, Klostermann, 1939–49. T.1, Lfg.1-8 (652p.) (In progress) RM 6.40 per Lfg. **A14**

A classified bibliography of bibliographies. T.1 covers general and national bibliography and subject bibliography with author and subject indexes. T.2 will cover Personalbibliographie.

Courtney, William Prideaux. Register of national bibliography; with a selection of the chief bibliographical books and articles printed in other countries. Lond., Constable, 1905–12. 3v. **A15**

v.1-2 list the bibliographies published before 1905; v.3 is a supplement containing about 10,000 additional references principally to bibliographies published 1905–1912.

A useful handbook to bibliographies on all subjects, international in scope. Arranged alphabetically by the subjects of the bibliographies listed; refers not only to bibliographies in book form, but also to lists in periodicals and to other analytical material.

Index bibliographicus, catalogue international des bibliographies courantes. 2. éd., mise à jour et considérablement augm., publ. par Marcel Godet et Joris Vorstius. Berlin, de Gruyter, 1931. 420p. **A16**

A classified list, arranged by the decimal classification, of 1900 current bibliographies, including lists which are purely bibliographical and lists included as a regular feature in periodicals, etc.

Internationale Bibliographie des Buch- und Bibliothekswesens, mit besonderer Berücksichtigung der Bibliographie, 1904–12, 1922–39. Leipzig, Harrassowitz, 1905–40. 13v. and n.F. 1–14. **A17**

First series, 1904–12, 1922–25, had title: Bibliographie des Bibliotheks- und Buchwesens and appeared as Beihefte zum *Zentralblatt für Bibliothekswesen,* 29, 31-32, 34, 36-37, 39-40, 42, 51, 54, 56, 58. None issued for 1913–21. The new series covers 1926- .

A comprehensive record of books and periodical articles in different languages on various aspects of bibliography, library science and library history. Each volume is in two main parts: (1) Bibliography; (2) Libraries, with many subdivisions and a general alphabetical index of authors and titles. Part 1 of each volume contains a list of new bibliographies in four large classes: (1) general and national bibliography; (2) subject bibliography; (3) regional and local bibliography; (4) individual bibliography: each class subdivided for smaller topics in its field.

Principal editors: 1904–12, Albert Hortzschansky; 1925- , Joris Vorstius and others.

Møller, Arne J. Dansk Bibliografier, udvalg af Danske bibliografiske Arbejder. København, Levin og Munksgaards, 1929. 28p. **A18**

Northup, Clark Sutherland. Register of bibliographies of the English language and literature. New Haven, Yale Univ. Pr., 1925. 507p. (Cornell studies in English, 9) **A19**

Not so limited as its title indicates; includes also many related bibliographies of other subjects and so serves to a certain extent as a general bibliography of bibliography.

Petzholdt, Julius. Bibliotheca bibliographica; kritisches Verzeichniss der das Gesammtgebiet der Bibliographie betreffenden Litteratur des In- und Auslandes. Leipzig, Engelmann, 1866. 939p. **A20**

A basic list, classified, with author index.

Vereeniging ter Bevordering van de Belangen des Boekhandels, Amsterdam. Bibliotheek. Catalogus. 'sGravenhage, Nijhoff, 1920–49. v.1-6. G 65.25 **A21**

v.1-2, a classified catalog; v.3, Supplement-catalogus, 1920–1926, with index to v.1-3; v.4, Lists of bookdealers', publishers', and auction catalogs, etc.; v.5, Supplement-catalogus, 1927–1939; v.6, Supplement-catalogus, 1940–1949.

Except for v.4, each supplement follows the general classification of the basic work under the main headings: (1) Inleiding; (2) De Techniek van het Boek; (3) De Geschiedenis van het Boek; (4) De Kennis van het Boek. Bibliographie (Algemene, Nationale, Speciale); (5) De Verspreiding van het Boek. Boekhandel; (6) De Bewaring van het Boek. Bibliotheekwezen; (7) De Bescherming van het Boek, Wetten, Rechten, enz.; (8) De Couranten en Periodieken.

UNIVERSAL

Brunet, Jacques Charles. Manuel du libraire et de l'amateur de livres. 5. éd. originale entièrement refondue et augm. d'un tiers. Paris, Didot, 1860–80. 9v. il. o.p. **A22**

Facsimile reprint: Berlin, Altmann, 1921–22. 6v.; Paris, Dorbon-Aîné, 1928. 6v.

v.1-5, Author and title list, A-Z; v.6, Subject index; v.7-8, Supplement, by P. Deschamps and G. Brunet, Author and title list, with subject index in v.8; v.9, Dictionnaire de géographie ancienne et moderne à l'usage du libraire et de l'amateur de livres, par P. Deschamps. 1870.

Brunet's *Manuel* is a general bibliography of rare, important, or noteworthy books not limited to those of any one period or language but especially strong for French and Latin titles and for publications before the nineteenth century. For each book listed it gives author, full title, place, publisher, date, size, number of volumes, but not generally paging, and, in the case of rare books bibliographical and critical notes with mention of copies and prices at famous sales and occasional facsimiles of title pages, printers' marks, etc. The arrangement of the main work (volumes 1-5) is alphabetical by authors and titles and there are two subject indexes, one in volume 6 to the main work and one in volume 8 to the supplement. Footnotes throughout volumes 1-5 refer to titles omitted from the main author list but included in the subject volume (volume 6).

Covers much the same ground as Grässe's *Trésor de livres* (A25) but is generally said to contain a larger proportion of French books while Grässe lists more German titles. The two books must often be used together as each lists titles not given in the other.

Ebert, Friedrich Adolf. Allgemeines bibliographisches Lexikon. Leipzig, Brockhaus, 1821–30. 2v. **A23**

Eng. tr.: General bibliographical dictionary, tr. by Arthur Browne. Ox., Univ. Pr., 1837. 4v.

Georgi, Gottlieb. Allgemeines europäisches Bücher-Lexicon. Vor dem Anfange des XVI. seculi bis [1757]. Leipzig, Georgi, 1742–58. 5 pts. and 3 suppl. in 2v. **A24**

pt.1-4, A-Z; pt.5, French works, A-Z; Suppl. 1-3, 1739–47, 1747–54, 1753–57.

Arranged alphabetically by authors, giving, for each work, author, short title, place, publisher, date, price.

Grässe, Johann Georg Theodor. Trésor de livres rares et précieux. Dresden, Kuntze, 1859–69. 7v. **A25**

v.1-6, A-Z; v.7, Supplement.

Facsimile reprints: Paris, Welter, 1900–01. 8v.; Berlin, Altmann, 1922. 7v.

"Covers much the same ground as Brunet, but includes also a large number of books that are intrinsically valuable without being rare, and for this reason is preferable if a choice must be made between them."—Growoll in his *Bookseller's library.*

Based on Brunet, but contains more entries of German books. Sales prices of books are given.

Index translationum. Répertoire international des traductions. International bibliography of translations. Paris, International Inst. of Intellectual Cooperation, 1932–40. nos. 1-31; n.s. v.1, 1948- . Paris, UNESCO, 1949- . **A26**

The first series was quarterly, the new series is annual. Entries are arranged by country and under these by broad subjects. Complete bibliographical information including the original language and title are given when available. Both series include indexes of authors, publishers, and translators. The last issue of the first series, published in January 1940, covered twelve countries including the U.S.S.R. The new series begins with a coverage of twenty-six countries, with a note of four others in which no translations appeared during the year. The U.S.S.R. is not covered.

Peddie, Robert Alexander. Subject index of books published before 1880. Lond., Grafton, 1933- . **A27**

1st ser., 1933, 745p.; 2d ser., 1935, 857p.; 3d ser., 1939, 945p.; new ser., 1948, 872p.

Each series furnishes an alphabetical subject list of some 50,000 books in various languages published before 1880 (1881) the date from which the British Museum subject indexes (A34) continue the subject record. Includes many small and specific subject entries, e.g., place names, excluding, however, personal names.

The third series includes in its alphabetical arrangement every subject heading used in the three series with cross references to the first and second series. This record is not continued in the "new series."

Watt, Robert. Bibliotheca Britannica; or, A general index to British and foreign literature. Edinburgh, Constable, 1824. 4v. **A28**

For full description *see* A284.

Library catalogs

❦ Printed catalogs of libraries are useful reference aids both to catalogers and to reference workers, because they supply verification of titles; information about authorship; description of books; editions, contents or occasional notes which throw light on a reference search; and they often contain analytical or other added entries not given in the library's own catalog. They indicate, of course, the location of at least one copy of each title listed. Dictionary and subject catalogs are also useful as subject bibliographies.

The catalogs of the great national libraries such as the Library of Congress, the British Museum, and the Bibliothèque Nationale are of particular importance because these libraries are entitled by law to receive copies of all books copyrighted in their respective countries. These catalogs, therefore, are the most comprehensive single records of publications in these countries. National libraries also contain material in many other languages and their catalogs are often extremely usable records of foreign language materials.

There are many printed catalogs of smaller libraries only a few of which are listed here. While most of these are old they may still be useful for bibliographical information and even for locational purposes. A somewhat longer list of American library catalogs is given in Winchell, *Locating books for interlibrary loan,* p.49-55 (B76).

National libraries

U. S. Library of Congress. A catalog of books represented by Library of Congress printed cards, issued to July 31, 1942. Ann Arbor, Mich., Edwards Bros., 1942–46. 167v. $750 per set. **A29**

At head of title: Association of Research Libraries.

———— Supplement: cards issued August 1, 1942–December 31, 1947. Ann Arbor, Mich., Edwards Bros., 1948. 42v. $231.

For many years the Library of Congress placed in various large libraries situated in different parts of the country "depository sets" of Library of Congress printed cards which were kept to date by the addition of new cards as printed. As these catalogs were available only in large centers, in 1942 the Association of Research Libraries sponsored the project of reproducing a depository catalog by photographical process and issuing it in book form. The cards were photographed and printed in reduced size, 18 to a page. The main catalog includes all cards issued to July 31, 1942, the supplement those issued August 1, 1942–December 31, 1947. As cards have not been printed for all books in the Library of Congress, this is not a complete catalog of its holdings, although the cards do represent all but a small percentage.

Because of the immensity of the collections, the excellence of the cataloging and the full bibliographical descriptions, the catalog is an invaluable work in any library and indispensable in those where research is done; of first importance in cataloging, acquisition and reference work, and for the bibliographer and research worker; important for author bibliography, verification of titles, bibliographical information, historical notes, location of copies, etc.

It is an author and main entry catalog of books for which Library of Congress cards have been printed, in (1) the Library of Congress, (2) many government department libraries, (3) various libraries throughout the country, as a result of the cooperative cataloging program. (Libraries supply information for certain types of material and the Library of Congress prints the cards.) Information given is detailed and represents a high degree of accuracy; usually includes: full name of author, dates of birth and death; full title; place, publisher, and date; collation (giving paging, illustrations, size); series; edition; notes on contents, history, etc.; tracing for subject headings and added entries, Library of Congress classification number, sometimes the Dewey decimal classification number; and Library of Congress card number. Frequently there is included a considerable amount of analysis for composite books, sets, periodicals, etc.

It should be noted that the *Supplement* contains cards issued during the period covered, regardless of the imprint date of the book recorded, and treats revised cards in the same manner as new ones. The *Supplement* also includes about 26,000 title entries for anonymous and pseudonymous works for which the Library of Congress has supplied the author. This has been done by crossing out the author's name and filing the card under title. For cards printed before August 1942 the author card will be in the main set, for cards printed August 1942–1947, in the *Supplement*. This listing takes the place of the "bracketed authors" file on cards which was in many libraries (see *Guide to reference books,* 6th ed., p.417).

—— The Library of Congress author catalog; a cumulative list of works represented by Library of Congress printed cards, 1948- . Wash., Library of Congress, 1948- . (1949, $65) **A30**

Title varies: 1948, *Cumulative catalog of Library of Congress printed cards* (also used on monthly and quarterly issues of 1949, although the 1949 annual volumes carry the new title).

Printed in nine monthly issues, January, February, April, May, July, August, October, November, and December; three quarterly cumulations, January–March, April–June, July–September, and an annual cumulation (1948–49, 3v. ea.). It is expected that five-year and perhaps larger cumulations will be issued. The monthly issues contain the cards prepared for works published during the current and past two years; the quarterly and annual cumulations contain all cards printed during the period regardless of imprint date. Although the *Cumulative catalog* started in January 1947 (eight monthly and four quarterly cumulations were issued), it was decided that this record should be included in the *Supplement* published by Edwards and that future cumulations of the *Author catalog* should start with 1948. This decision was made because some of the principles and rules of cataloging were changed during 1947 and these are incorporated in the *Catalog* beginning in 1948.

The *Author catalog* contains not only main entries, but also essential added entries and cross references. The main entries are reproduced from the type set for the catalog cards and give full information including the tracing, Library of Congress call number, Dewey classification number, and Library of Congress card number. Added entries are made for names associated with the works and for titles of anonymous works and periodicals which are likely to be cited under title.

For 1948, author entries for the Army Medical Library were included as a supplement in the 1948 annual cumulation. Beginning with 1949 the Army Medical Library *Author catalog* (P287a) will be issued as a separate supplementary volume to the Library of Congress *Author catalog.*

Suggestions for using the
Library of Congress Author Catalog

❧ When checking for a particular item, it is necessary to look in (1) the main catalog (except for books published later than July 1942); (2) the *Supplement;* (3) the annual volumes of the *Author catalog;* (4) the quarterly supplements; (5) the monthly supplements (for recent books only). While the monthly supplements list only works published in the current and past two years, all the other parts include cards, both new and revised cataloging, printed during the period covered, regardless of imprint date. Therefore, even though a work is listed in the main catalog, one must also search through all of the supplements to see if a revised card has been printed that corrects or adds information. The necessity for searching through an ever-increasing number of alphabets is one of the great disadvantages of the book catalog as contrasted with the single alphabet of the card catalog.

—— The Library of Congress subject catalog, 1950- . Wash., Library of Congress, 1950- . **A31**

Issued as a complement to the Library of Congress *Author catalog* (A30) and "designed to serve as a continuing and cumulative subject bibliography of works currently received and cataloged by the Library of Congress and other American libraries participating in its cooperative cataloging program. . . . " To be issued quarterly with annual and probably larger cumulations. "The issues contain, within the governing limitations of scope, the entries included in corresponding issues of the *Author catalog* which can appropriately and usefully be listed under subject or form headings. The quarterly issues contain the cards prepared for publications issued in the current year and the past two years, excluding those for belles-lettres; the annual cumulation contains the cards prepared for publications issued in or since 1945, including belles-lettres."—*Introd.*

British Museum. Dept. of Printed Books. Catalogue of printed books. Lond., Clowes, 1881–1900. 393 pts. in 95v. (Photographic repr. Ann Arbor, Mich., Edwards, 1946. 58v. $500) **A32**

—— —— Supplement. Lond., Clowes, 1900–05. 13v. (Repr. 1950. 10v. $130)

The British Museum library, one of the largest libraries in the world, is important both because of the extent and richness of its collections as a whole, and also because its possession of the copyright privilege makes it the most comprehensive collection of English publications in existence, although not, of course, complete in this field. This printed catalog, recording accessions to about 1899, is an indispensable bibliographical source for either the cataloger or the reference worker in a large library. This catalog, in the main, is an author catalog only, with title entries (catchword titles) or cross references for anonymous books, etc., but subject entries are included also to a limited extent, principally for the following: (1) under names of authors, books about them as well as by them are entered; (2) under countries, e.g., England, France, etc., are entered official publications, some works about the country, and many titles in which the name of the country occurs; (3) under names of sacred books, e.g., Bible, Kur'an, etc., are entered both texts and works about. Two important reference features, very useful in the verification of titles, etc., are: (1) the large amount of analytical material included (analysis of sets, etc.); and (2) the many cross references from names of editors, translators, or other personal names connected with a title. The cataloging is less modern than that of the Library of Congress and Bibliothèque Nationale and the information given is briefer, including generally only author, title, editor, etc., place and date, but not publisher, size, or paging; for older works somewhat fuller information is given. Throughout the work, the letters I and J are treated as one letter, as are U and V.

For new edition see the following:

—— General catalogue of printed books. Lond. and Beccles, Clowes, 1931–48. v.1-42. (In progress) **A33**

v.1-42, A-Corb.

A new edition of the above, revised and reset throughout, which adds to the original work the accessions of more than 30 years. Uses more modern cataloging and differs from the earlier edition in certain points of detail, e.g., (1) separates the letters I and J, (U and V) instead of arranging them as one letter, (2) gives paging for one-volume works, and size, (3) often gives fuller imprint information, i.e., gives place, publisher and date in many cases.

—— —— Supplement to v.1-3. Lond., Clowes, 1932. 38p. Pr. on one side of leaf only.

"This Supplement to the first three volumes of the new edition of the General Catalogue of Printed Books contains in one alphabetical order the titles of the books, English and Foreign, added to the Museum collections during the printing of those volumes, together with a number of altered and supplementary titles."

—— Subject index of the modern works added to the Library, 1881–1900; ed. by G. K. Fortescue. Lond., 1902–03. 3v. **A34**

Includes the subject indexes published by the Trustees in 1886, 1891 and 1897, adding the works published 1896–1900, as well as the Slavonic, Hungarian and Finnish books, published between 1881 and 1900 which were not included in the former indexes.

Alphabetically arranged. No personal names are used as headings. Includes 155,000 entries. Continued by the following 5-year supplements.

—— —— 1901–05, 1906–10, 1911–15, 1916–20, 1921–25, 1926–30, 1931–35, 1936–40. Lond., 1906–44. v.1-8. (1936–40. 2v. £15 15s.)

Paris. Bibliothèque Nationale. Catalogue général des livres imprimés: Auteurs. Paris, Impr. Nat., 1900–49. v.1-175. (In progress) **A35**

v.1–175, A-Soustov.

An important modern catalog, the value of which, to either the cataloger or reference worker in the large library, cannot be overestimated. An alphabetical author catalog, including only entries under names of personal authors, with the necessary cross references; does not include title entries for anonymous books or entries for anonymous classics, periodicals or society transactions or government or corporate authors. The cataloging is excellent; the information given includes author's full name whenever possible, title, place, publisher, date, edition, paging or volumes, format, and occasional notes of con-

tents, original publication in case of reprints from periodicals, etc. An important reference feature in the case of authors whose works are voluminous or often reprinted is the detailed alphabetical title index under the author's name, which indicates in what volumes or editions a given work may be found; as these indexes include also alternative and changed titles, they are often very useful.

Each volume includes titles acquired up to the date of publication of the particular volume so that there is a wide spread in the coverage between the first volumes published in 1900 and those issued almost half a century later.

Deutscher Gesamtkatalog, hrsg. von der Preussischen Staatsbibliothek. . . . Berlin, Preussische Druckerei- u. Verlags Aktiengesellschaft, 1931– 39. v.1-14. **A36**

v.1-14, A-Beethordnung.

Volumes 1-8 had title *Gesamtkatalog der Preussischen Bibliotheken* and listed books contained in about 18 important libraries. With volume 9, 1936, beginning the letter B, the scope was changed to include the contents of some one hundred German and Austrian libraries. An ambitious undertaking, unfortunately suspended because of the war. The few volumes already published show that for the letters covered it is (1) an indispensable work for catalogers, reference workers, and bibliographical investigation generally, in the matter of German publications and (2) that it is useful for non-German subjects, also, as it contains much foreign material in many languages, including English works not listed in the British Museum catalog and French works not listed in the catalog of the Bibliothèque Nationale.

Deutscher Gesamtkatalog. Neue titel. Berlin, Staatsbibliothek, 1893- . v.1- . **A37**

Issued weekly (frequency varies slightly) with quarterly and annual cumulations which supplement the *Deutscher Gesamtkatalog* (A36).

Title varies. 1910–37 had title *Berliner Titeldrucke*.

Berlin. Preussische Staatsbibliothek. Berliner Titeldrucke; fünfjahrs Katalog, 1930–34- . Berlin, Staatsbibliothek, 1935- . **A38**

1930–34 issued in 8v. A-Z, paged continuously.

Libraries, not national

UNITED STATES

Astor Library, New York. Catalogue. N.Y., Craighead Pr., 1857–66; Camb., Mass., Riverside Pr., 1886–88. 9v. **A39**

1st catalog, known as the Cogswell catalog, from its compiler, J. G. Cogswell, 1857–66. 5v.: v.1-4, A-Z; v.5, Supplementary author list, A-Z; Subject index. 2d catalog, comp. by C. A. Nelson and known as the Nelson catalog, 1886–88. 4v. Authors: A-Z.

The books listed in these two catalogs are now part of the New York Public Library.

Boston Athenaeum. Catalogue, 1807–71. Bost., 1874–82. 5v. **A40**

Dictionary catalog, including some analysis; comp. by C. A. Cutter.

Peabody Institute, Baltimore. Catalogue of the library. Balt., 1883–1905. 13v. **A41**

1st catalog, 1882–92. 5v.; 2d catalog, including additions since 1882, 1896–1905. 8v.

A well-made dictionary catalog, with the following special features: (1) full contents of voluminous sets, arranged alphabetically; and (2) full author and subject analysis of composite books and some periodicals; this analysis makes the work almost as much an index as a catalog.

Princeton. University. Library. Alphabetical finding list. Princeton, Univ. Library, 1921. 5v. **A42**

—— Classed list. 1920. 6v.

A title-a-line catalog.

GREAT BRITAIN

[Crawford, James Ludovic Lindsay, *26th earl of*] Bibliotheca Lindesiana . . . Catalogue of the printed books preserved at Haigh Hall, Wigan co. pal. Lancast. . . . Aberdeen, Univ. Pr., 1910. 4v. **A43**

Edinburgh. University. Library. Catalogue of the printed books. Edinburgh, Univ. Pr., 1918–23. 3v. **A44**

Faculty of Advocates. Library. Catalogue of the printed books. Edinburgh, Blackwood, 1857–79. 7v. **A45**

John Rylands Library, Manchester. Catalogue of the printed books and manuscripts. Manchester, Cornish, 1899. 3v. **A46**

London Library. Catalogue, by C. T. Hagberg Wright and C. J. Purnell. Lond., 1913–14. 2v. **A47**

An author catalog of a library of more than 250,000 volumes. This edition incorporates the material of the first edition, 1903, and the eight annual supplements to that edition.

—— —— Supplement, 1913–20, 1920–28. Lond., 1920–29. 2v.

—— Subject index of the London library . . . by C. T. Hagberg Wright. Lond., 1909–38. v.1-3.

v.1, published by Williams & Norgate; v.2, printed by Neill & Co., Ltd., Edinburgh.
v.1, Main subject list; v.2, Additions, 1909–22, by C. T. Hagberg Wright and C. J. Purnell; v.3, Additions, 1923–38.

Oxford. University. Bodleian Library. Catalogus librorum impressorum bibliothecae Bodleianae in Academia oxoniensi. . . . Ox., e Typographeo Academico, 1843–51. 4v. **A48**

Reproductions

American Documentation Institute. Catalog of auxiliary publications in microfilms and photoprints. Wash., 1946. 51p. **A49**

A listing of scientific papers available on microfilm or photoprint.

Modern Language Association of America. Reproductions of manuscripts and rare printed books. Short title list. (In Modern Language Assoc. of Amer. Publications 65:289-338, April 1950) **A50**

"Complete to January 1, 1950."
"Rotographs or microfilms of the . . . materials listed . . . are now on deposit in the Library of Congress."
These are available for interlibrary loan or microfilm copies may usually be purchased.

Philadelphia Bibliographical Center and Union Library Catalogue. Committee on Microphotography. Union list of microfilms; a basic list of holdings in the United States and Canada. Phila., 1942. 379p. $3. **A51**

—— —— Supplement nos. 1-5, 1942–46. Phila., 1943–47.

Basic list includes 5221 items in some 125 libraries. The supplements are intended to keep the record to date.
Uses: "1) as an aid to libraries and possibly individuals in building up collections of specialized material; 2) as a tool to locate films and as a guide for interlibrary loan; 3) as a preventive of duplicate reproduction activities on the part of libraries wishing to secure copies of out of the way materials; 4) as an aid in the shaping of a planned policy for further filming."
Includes materials of all kinds, the fullness of information depending on what was furnished by the individual library. Usually indicates whether film is positive or negative and in many cases tells where the original work is.
Does not include the titles of the microfilms of books in the *Short title catalog* project (A292), as printed lists of these are available from University Microfilms in Ann Arbor, but a geographically representative list of institutions subscribing to these films is given under no.4472.

Incunabula and early printed books

❧ The books listed below are the principal general bibliographies and catalogs of incunabula that should be known by beginners. There are also various important bibliographies of the incunabula of special countries and catalogs of incunabula in individual libraries which will be needed for special work. For lists of these *see* Stillwell, *Incunabula and Americana*, p.251-329 (A53), the list of sources in the *Gesamtkatalog der Wiegendrucke* (A63) and Stillwell, *Incunabula in American libraries* (A62).

Guides

Haebler, Konrad. Handbuch der Inkunabelkunde. Leipzig, Hiersemann, 1925. 187p. **A52**

A handbook on the literature, history, physical makeup and printing of incunabula.

Stillwell, Margaret Bingham. Incunabula and Americana, 1450–1800. A key to bibliographical study. N.Y., Columbia Univ. Pr., 1931. 483p. $12.50. **A53**

Contents: INCUNABULA: ch.1, Printed books of the 15th century; ch.2, Identification and collation; ch.3, Bibliographical reference material; AMERICANA: ch.1, Preliminary survey of sources and methods; ch.2, Century of maritime discovery; ch.3, Two centuries of colonial growth, 1500–1700; ch.4, Later Americana and the Revolutionary periods; ch.5, Early printing in America; REFERENCE SECTIONS: 1, Notes and definitions; 2, Foreign bibliographical terms, French, German, Italian and Spanish; 3, Latin contractions and abbreviations; 4, Place names of 15th century printing towns; Bibliography: (nearly 1300 items).

An indispensable reference work for the collector or for the cataloger in a library which has collections of incunabula or Americana. Important both for the text and the extensive bibliographies.

Bibliography

Hain, Ludwig Friedrich Theodor. Repertorium bibliographicum ad annum MD. Stuttgart, Cotta, 1826–38. 2v. in 4. **A54**

1925 repr. (Berlin, Altmann).

A basic list arranged alphabetically, the items numbered serially throughout. The "Hain number" is referred to in many later bibliographies.

Copinger, W. A. Supplement to Hain's Repertorium bibliographicum; or, Collection toward a new edition of that work. Lond., Sotheran, 1895–1902. 2v. in 3. **A55**

1926 repr. (Leipzig, Lorentz).

pt.1, nearly 7000 corrections of and additions to the collation of works described in Hain; pt.2, list of nearly 6000 volumes not in Hain; v.1, A-O, v.2, P-Z; v.2 also includes "The printers and publishers of the XV century with lists of their works" by Konrad Burger (p.319-670), which is an index to the *Supplement*, to Hain's *Repertorium*, and to the works of Campbell, Pellechet, and Proctor.

Reichling, Dietrich. Appendices ad Hainii-Copingeri Repertorivm bibliographicvm; additiones et emendationes. Monachii, Rosenthal, 1905–11. 7v. **A56**

pts. 1-6 in 2 sections each: I., Additions; II., Emendations; pt.[7], Indices fascicvlorvm I-VI.

——— ——— Svpplementvm (maximam partem e bibliothecis Helvetiae collectvm) cvm indice vrbivm et typographorvm. Accedit index avctorum generalis totivs operis. Monasterii Gvestphalorvm, Theissingianis, 1914. 109, cxxxv p.

Burger, Konrad. Supplement zu Hain und Panzer. Beiträge zur Inkunabelbibliographie, Nummern-concordanz von Panzers lateinischen u. deutschen Annalen u. Ludwig Hain's Repertorium bibliographicum. Leipzig, Hiersemann, 1908. 440p. **A57**

——— Ludwig Hain's Repertorium bibliographicum. Register. Die Drucker des XV. Jahrhunderts. Leipzig, Harrassowitz, 1891. 428p. (Centralblatt für Bibliothekswesen. Beihefte, Bd.2, Hft.8) **A57a**

Panzer, Georg Wolfgang Franz. Annales typographici ab artis inventae origine ad annum 1536. Norimbergae, Zeh, 1793–1803. 11v. **A58**

Arranged by places and under each chronologically.

Maittaire, Michael. Annales typographici ab artis inventae origine ad annum 1664. Hagae-Comitum, 1719–89. 5v. and suppl., 2v. **A59**

Proctor, Robert. Index to the early printed books in the British Museum; with notes of those in the Bodleian Library. Lond., K. Paul, 1898–1938. pts. 1-2 in 6v. **A60**

pt.1, To 1500: v.1, Germany; v.2, Italy; v.3, Switzerland to Montenegro, including France, Netherlands, Spain, England, Scandinavia; v.4, Register. 1898–99. 4v.

A chronological list under each country by names of presses. The index volume contains an alphabetical list of towns, printers and publishers, a list of books mentioned in Hain and of those not in Hain, authors of books printed in the Low Countries, books printed in England.

pt.2, 1501–1520: sec. 1, Germany, 1903, 273p.; sec. 2, Italy; sec. 3, Switzerland and Eastern Europe, by Frank Isaac. Lond., Quaritch, 1938. 286p.

——— ——— Supplements 1898–1902. Lond., 1900–03. 5 pts.

pts. 1-4, supplements; pt.5, register.

British Museum. Library. Catalogue of books printed in the 15th century now in the British Museum. Lond., 1912–49. pts. 1-8. **A61**

Work supervised by A. W. Pollard.

pts. 1-2, Germany; pt.3, Germany, German-speaking Switzerland and Austria-Hungary; pts. 4-7, Italy; pt.8, France, French-speaking Switzerland.

Arranged under places by printers' names. Gives historical notes about printers, and full title, description, collation and date of purchase of each book. Part 3 contains also an introduction by A. W. Pollard, a typographical map, facsimiles, and indexes to parts 1-3 by (1) Hain's numbers, (2) concordance of Proctor's numbers, (3) printers and towns. Covers the same ground as the first part of Proctor's *Index to early printed books* (A60) but with much fuller descriptions.

Union lists

Stillwell, Margaret Bingham. Incunabula in American libraries; a second census of fifteenth-century books owned in the United States, Mexico, and Canada. N.Y., Bibl. Soc. of Amer., 1940. 619p. (Bibl. Soc. of Amer. Monograph ser. no.1) $20. **A62**

The second census to supersede the Society's *Census of fifteenth century books owned in America*, 1919. In the first census "an estimate of 13,200 copies is recorded under 6,292 titles, owned by 173 public and 255 private collections. This second census lists 35,232 copies of 11,132 titles, owned by 332 public and 390 private collections. And of these 35,232 copies, 28,491 are owned by institutions, and 6,741 are in private hands."—*Introd.*

Authors are listed alphabetically. In the main, author entries conform to Hain, or, if unknown to Hain, to the form used in the *Catalogue of books printed in the* xv*th century* (A61) or in the *Gesamtkatalog der Wiegendrucke* (A63). There is a table at the back giving variant author forms and entries, as well as concordances to the numbers used in the *Gesamtkatalog*, Hain (A54), and Proctor's *Index* (A60). A useful list of printed bibliographies of incunabula is given, p.xxvii-xliii.

Information under each entry usually includes author (with variant spellings if it differs from Hain), Hain number, short title, place, printer, date, size, references to descriptions in printed catalogs and location of copies.

Gesamtkatalog der Wiegendrucke, hrsg. von der Kommission für den Gesamtkatalog der Wiegendrucke. Leipzig, Hiersemann, 1925–40. v.1-8[1]. **A63**

v.1-8[1], A-Fredericis.

The most comprehensive record of incunabula yet made, based on information collected during more than twenty years' work by the Kommission. The sections so far issued record nearly half again as many editions as Hain (A54), and the information given for each is much fuller, including: (1) author entry, title, date, etc.; (2) collation, types, capitals and illustrations; (3) transcripts of title, colophon and other extracts; (4) references to descriptions in Hain and other bibliographies; and (5) location of copies which include a complete record of all copies if not more than ten are known and for commoner books a selection of copies in representative libraries in different countries, both European and American. Indispensable in both cataloging and reference work in the scholarly library.

Accurti, Thomas. Aliae editiones saeculi XV pleraeque nondum descriptae. Annotationes ad opus cui titulus "Gesamtkatalog der Wiegendrucke," voll.i-vi. Florentiae, Ex "Tipografia Giuntina," 1936. 130p. **A64**

Editiones saeculi XV pleraeque bibliographis ignotae. Annotationes ad opus quod inscribitur Gesamtkatalog der Wiegendrucke voll.i-iv. Florentiae, 1930. 170p. **A65**

Pellechet, Marie Léontine Catherine. Catalogue général des incunables des bibliothèques publiques de France. Paris, Picard, 1897–1909. v.1-3. **A66**

v.1-3, A-Gregorius Magnus.

Les trésors des bibliothèques de France. Manuscrits, incunables, livres rares, reliures, dessins,

estampes, objets d'art, curiosités bibliographiques. Paris, Les Ed. d'Art et d'Histoire, 1926–46. fasc. 1-26. (In progress) **A67**

Pub. varies.

Polain, Louis. Catalogue des livres imprimés au quinzième siècle des bibliothèques de Belgique. Bruxelles, Soc. des Bibliophiles, 1932. 4v. facsim. **A68**

v.1-3, A-S; v.4, T-Z; Supplément (nos. 4070-4109). Additions. Tables: A. Facsimilés; B. Concordance des numéros avec ceux de Campbell, *Gesamtkatalog*, Hain, Pellechet, Voulliéme; C. Imprimeurs; E. Gravures; F. Table générale alphabétique des matières; (D. Table des bibliothèques, announced in the introduction, p.xxi, was not published).

Book collecting
United States and Great Britain

Bennett, Whitman. A practical guide to American book collecting (1663–1940); with all items arranged in sequence as a chronological panorama of American authorship and with each subject considered from bibliographical, biographical and analytical aspects. N.Y., Bennett Book Studios, 1941. 254p. $7.50. **A69**

Lists about 1000 outstanding American books with annotations giving bibliographical information about first printing.

Brussel, Isidore Rosenbaum. Anglo-American first editions. . . . Lond., Constable; N.Y., Bowker, 1935–36. 2v. (Half title: Bibliographia, studies in book history . . . nos. 9-10) **A70**

pt.1: East to West, 1826–1900 . . . English authors whose books were published in America before their publication in England. 1935. 170p. pt.2: West to East, 1786–1930 . . . American authors whose books were published in England before their publication in America. 1936. 131p.

De Ricci, Seymour. The book collector's guide; a practical handbook of British and American bibliography. Phila., Rosenbach Co., 1921. 649p. **A71**

A guide for the collector and book buyer, covering the period from Chaucer to Swinburne and listing the 2000 or 3000 books which because of rarity, market value, etc., are most sought after by collectors, including first editions, illustrated books, seventeenth and eighteenth century drama and standard works. Arranged alphabetically by authors, giving dates of birth and death, and references to printed bibliographies of the author and, for each book listed, its title, place, publisher, date, size, and prices at sales, with occasional notes as to collation, variations in issues or editions, location of copies of rare books, etc.

Foley, Patrick Kevin. American authors, 1795–1895. A bibliography of first and notable editions chronologically arranged with notes. With an introduction by W. L. Sawyer. Bost., pr. for subscribers [Publishers' Pr. Co.], 1897. 350p. **A72**

Johnson, Merle De Vore. American first editions. 4th ed., rev. and enl. by Jacob Blanck. N.Y., Bowker, 1942. 553p. $10. **A73**

> 1st ed. 1929, planned as a continuation of Foley.
> This edition lists the first editions of over 200 American authors having "collector interest."

Private book collectors in the United States and Canada. 9th rev. ed. N.Y., Bowker, 1948. 389p. $20. **A74**

> A directory in three sections: private book collectors arranged alphabetically; arranged geographically; arranged by specialties.

France

Carteret, Léopold. Le trésor du bibliophile romantique et moderne, 1801–75. Paris, Carteret, 1924–28. 3v. and index. il. **A75**

> v.1-2, Éditions originales, A-Z; v.3, Livres illustrés du XIXᵉ siècle; Index v., Tables générales, ouvrages cités, illustrateurs et graveurs. 207p.

—— Le trésor du bibliophile; livres illustrés modernes 1875 à 1945, et Souvenirs d'un demi-siècle de bibliophile de 1887 à 1945. Paris, Carteret, 1946–48. 5v. **A76**

> Title varies.

Le Petit, Jules. Bibliographie des principales éditions originales d'écrivains français du XVᵉ aux XVIIIᵉ siècle. Paris, Quantin, 1888. 583p. il. **A77**

> Photographic repr. (Paris, Jeanne et Brulon, 1927).

Mahé, Raymond. Bibliographie des livres de luxe de 1900 à 1928 inclus. Paris, Kieffer, 1931–39. 3v. **A78**

> Includes prices.

—— Les artistes illustrateurs. Répertoire des éditions de luxe de 1900 à 1928 inclus. Complément de la Bibliographie des livres de luxe, et Addenda. Paris, Kieffer, 1943. 256p., 68 col. **A79**

Historical children's books

Darton, Frederick Joseph Harvey. Children's books in England; five centuries of social life. Camb., Univ. Pr., 1932. 359p. il. **A79a**

> A literary history, not a bibliography, by the author of the chapter on children's books in the *Cambridge history of English literature,* v.11, ch.15 (R288). Contains bibliographical footnotes throughout and "Brief book lists" at ends of chapters.

Gumuchian et Cie., booksellers, Paris. Les livres de l'enfance du XVᵉ au XIXᵉ siècle, préface de Paul Gavault. Paris, Gumuchian [1931?]. 2v. **A79b**

v.1, Text, i.e., Bibliography of 6251 items, with full bibliographical description of each; v.2, 338 plates, containing a total of 1080 facsimiles of illustrations from books described in v.1, beautifully reproduced, many of them hand colored.

> Important both for the careful description of rare books and for the wealth of illustration. May be supplemented by two simpler lists issued by the same firm: Catalogues 15 and 18, *100 noteworthy firsts in juvenile literature and 500 early juveniles* (1933. 39p.). Both free.

Rosenbach, Abraham S. Wolf. Early American children's books. With bibliographical descriptions of the books in his private collection. Portland, Maine, Southworth Pr., 1933. lix, 354p. il. $25. **A79c**

> Foreword by A. Edward Newton; Introduction; Early American children's books, p.3-287; Index of authors and titles; Index of printers and publishers; List of printers, publishers and booksellers; Bibliography.

Printers' marks

Briquet, Charles Moïse. Les filigranes. Dictionnaire historique des marques du papier des leur apparition vers 1282 jusqu'en 1600, avec 39 figures dans le texte et 16,112 facsimilés. Paris, Picard, 1907. 4v. facsim. **A80**

> 2. ed. Leipzig, Hiersemann, 1923. 4v.

Delalain, Paul Adolphe. Inventaire des marques d'imprimeurs et de libraires de la collection du Cercle de la Librairie. 2. éd. rev. et augm. Paris, Cercle de la Libr., 1892. 355p. il. (Bibliothèque technique de la Cercle de la Libr.) **A81**

McKerrow, Ronald B. Printers' and publishers' devices in England and Scotland, 1485–1640. Lond., Bibl. Soc., 1913. 216p. 65 double pl. **A82**

> Sold only to members of the society.
> Contains description and facsimiles of 428 devices, a dictionary of certain printers' names with information about transfers of devices, and five indexes of devices and compartments by: (1) sizes, (2) printers and booksellers, (3) mottoes, (4) initials of designers and engravers, (5) subjects.

Polain, Louis. Marques des imprimeurs et libraires en France au XVᵉ siècle. Paris, Droz, 1926. 207p. il. (Documents typographiques du XVᵉ siècle, t.1) **A83**

Renouard, Philippe. Marques typographiques parisiennes des XVᵉ et XVIᵉ siècles. Paris, Champion, 1926–28. 381p. il. (Revue des bibliothèques, suppl. 14-15) **A84**

Silvestre, Louis Catherine. Marques typographiques. . . . Paris, Jannet, successeur de L. C. Silvestre, 1853; Impr. Renou, 1867. 2v. facsim. **A85**

> Subtitle: Recueil des monogrammes, chiffres, enseignes, emblèmes, devises, rébus et fleurons des libraires et

imprimeurs qui ont exercé en France, depuis l'introduction de l'imprimerie, en 1470, jusqu'à la fin du seizième siècle: à ces marques sont jointes celles des libraires et imprimeurs qui pendant la même période ont publié, hors de France, des livres en langue française.

Auctions
United States

McKay, George Leslie. American book auction catalogues, 1713–1934; a union list . . . with introd. by Clarence S. Brigham. N.Y., Pub. Lib., 1937. 540p. $3.50. **A86**

A "list of some 10,000 auction catalogues . . . issued in what is now the United States, that list books, pamphlets, broadsides, newspapers, manuscripts, autographs and bookplates."—*Pref.*

—— —— Supplement nos. 1-2. 1946–48. (Repr. from New York Public Library Bull. 50:177-84, 1946; 52:401-412, 1948)

American book-prices current, a record of books, manuscripts and autographs sold at auction in New York and elsewhere 1894/95- . N.Y., 1895- v.1- . Price varies. Annual. 1949, $12.50. **A87**

Publisher varies: v.1-14, Dodd, Mead & Co.; v.15-19, Dodd and Livingston; v.20-23, R. H. Dodd; v.24-34, Dutton; v.35- , R. R. Bowker.

v.1 arranged chronologically by date of sales, v.2- , alphabetically by authors and some titles, in two lists, (1) printed books, periodicals, etc., (2) manuscripts and autographs. Later volumes add (3) broadsides; (4) maps and charts; v.1-10 have subject indexes.

Arrangement and information given varies somewhat, but volumes 11 on include author, title, edition, place, date, size, binding, condition, sale, date of sale, lot number in original auction catalog, price. Includes books of all periods and languages and is of importance in reference work both as a record of market prices of second-hand books and as a supplement to general and national bibliographies, as it not infrequently includes titles or editions not listed in such bibliographies. In case of rare books location of the copies sold can sometimes be traced by applying to the auctioneer, and the giving of the lot number in the sales catalog furnishes a clue to a fuller and sometimes important description.

—— Indexes. 1916–22. N.Y., Dutton, 1925. 1397p.; 1923–32. N.Y., Bowker, 1936. 1007p.; 1933–40. N.Y., Bowker, 1940. 765p.; 1941–45, N.Y., Bowker, 1946. 1126p. $35.

Livingston, Luther Samuel. Auction prices of books. . . . N.Y., Dodd, 1905. 4v. **A88**

Subtitle: A representative record arranged in alphabetical order from the commencement of the English *Book-prices current* in 1886 and the *American Book-prices current* in 1894, to 1904, and including some thousands of important auction quotations of earlier date.

United States cumulative book auction records, 1940- , ed. by S. R. Shapiro. N.Y., Want list—the book trade weekly, 1941- . **A89**

v.1-3, annual, superseded by v.4, cumulating 1940–45; v.5, 1945–47; v.6, 1947–48. $12.

Reports books, pamphlets, manuscripts, periodicals, autographs, and other literary property selling in American auction rooms for $3 or more.

France

Annuaire des ventes de livres. année 1-12, oct. 1918—juillet 1931. Paris, Catin, 1920–34. v.1-12. **A90**

Le guide du bibliophile et du libraire; bibliographie générale des livres passés en ventes publiques en 1942/43- (France et Belgique) avec une bibliographie complète des publications des sociétés de bibliophiles et des grandes collections de bibliophile. Paris, Rombaldi, 1945- . v.1- . Annual. **A91**

Germany

Jahrbuch der Bücherpreise, 1906–38. Leipzig, Harrassowitz, 1907–39. v.1-33. **A91a**

Subtitle varies. Annual except that issues of 1911–12, 1914–19, and 1922–23 are biennial.

Issues before 1914 covered European sales generally, exclusive of England; 1920- cover sales in Germany, German Austria, Holland, Switzerland, the Scandinavian countries, Czecho-Slovakia and Hungary, though all of these countries are not included in every issue.

Great Britain

Book-auction records, a priced and annotated record of London [and other] book-auctions, June 1902- . Lond., Karslake, 1903–1919; Henry Stevens, 1920- . v.1- . (1947, £2 18s. 6d.) Quarterly 1920–40; annual 1941/42- . **A92**

Subtitle varies. From v.12, Edinburgh, Glasgow and Dublin, sometimes included. From 1939/40, also includes principal New York auctions.

When issued quarterly each number was arranged alphabetically by authors, with an index in each volume. Annual volumes arranged alphabetically.

—— General index, 1902–12, 1912–23, 1924–33, 1934–43. Lond., Stevens, 1924–48. 4v. (v.4, £12 12s.)

Subtitle: Giving instant clues to the contents . . . and, incidentally to anonymous authors, autographs, bibliophiles, binders, bindings, distinguished owners, fore-edge paintings, holograph manuscripts, illustrations, notable presses, pseudonyms, etc. . . .

Book-prices current, Dec. 1886- . Lond., Stock, 1888–1930; Witherby, 1931- . v.1- . Annual. (v.61, 40s.) **A93**

v.1-27, 1886–1913, arranged by dates of sales; v.28- , 1914- , arranged alphabetically by authors and some titles. Useful both as a record of market prices of second-hand books, and as a supplement to the various general and national bibliographies for titles and editions not noted in such bibliographies.

—— Index, 1887–96, 1897–1906, 1907–16. Lond., Stock, 1901–20. 3v.

1887–96, v.1-10. 1901. 472p.; 1897–1906, v.11-20, by William Jaggard. 1909. 1056p.; 1907–16, v.21-30, by J. H. Slater. 1920. 1220p.

Anonyms and pseudonyms

❦ There are many reference books on the authorship of anonymous and pseudonymous works. They differ considerably in use and authority, their value depending upon their comprehensiveness within their given field, the quality of research that has gone into their making, and particularly upon whether or not they give the authority for their attribution of authorship. The last point is of special importance, as the question of authorship is often a matter of dispute and difficult to establish; hence it is frequently important to be able to check as many sources as possible in order to come to a decision. For a discussion of a selected list of such reference books *see* "Anonyms and pseudonyms, an annotated list," by Adah V. Morris, *Library quarterly*, 3:354-72, Oct. 1933.

Cushing, William. Anonyms; a dictionary of revealed authorship. Camb. [Mass.], Cushing, 1889. 829p. o.p. **A94**

Includes both English and American works. In two alphabets: (1) anonymous titles followed by name of author; (2) index of authors found only in the *Anonyms*. Does not give authorities.

—— Initials and pseudonyms; a dictionary of literary disguises. N.Y., Crowell [c1885–88]. 2v. o.p. **A95**

Includes about 18,500 initials and pseudonyms, principally English and American, with a few well-known continental names. Each series in two parts: (1) initials followed by real name; (2) real name followed by pseudonym or initials, with short biographical notices. Does not give authorities.

Halkett, Samuel and **Laing, John.** Dictionary of anonymous and pseudonymous English literature. New and enl. ed. by James Kennedy, W. A. Smith and A. F. Johnson. Edinburgh, Oliver and Boyd, 1926–34. 7v. **A96**

1st ed., Edinburgh, Paterson, 1882–88. 4v.
v.1-6, A-Z; Supplement, v.6, p.273-449; v.7, Index and 2d suppl.
A comprehensive list, arranged alphabetically by first word of title not an article, giving for each item listed: title (sometimes shortened), size, paging, place, date, author's name and (in some cases) the authority for attribution of authorship. The best list for English works, always to be used as a first aid. As most of the authorities

cited are general in character the work is not final authority in cases of disputed authorship which must be looked up in more special works, individual biographies and bibliographies, etc. The new edition differs from the first by: (1) inclusion of half again as many titles; (2) use of somewhat briefer titles; (3) minor differences in arrangement; (4) more liberal inclusion of authorities for attribution of authorship.

Stonehill, Charles A., Jr., Block, Andrew and **Stonehill, H. W.** Anonyma and pseudonyma. Lond., Stonehill, 1926–27. 4v. **A97**

Much briefer and less accurate than Halkett and Laing (A96). Gives briefer information, does not cite authorities, and contains errors.

Belgium

See Netherlands and Belgium.

Brazil

Barros Paiva, Tancredo de Barros. Achêgas a um diccionario de pseudonymos, iniciaes, abreviaturas e obras anonymas de auctores brasileiros e de estrangeiros, sobre o Brasil ou no mesmo impressas. Rio de Janeiro, J. Leite, 1929. 248p. **A98**

Simões dos Reis, Antonio. Pseudônimos brasileiros, pequenos verbetes para um dicionario. 1- . Rio de Janeiro, Z. Valverde, 1941- . (In progress) **A99**

Canada

Audet, François Joseph. Pseudonymes canadiens. Montreal, G. Ducharme, 1936. 189p. **A100**

Cuba

Figarola-Caneda, Domingo. Diccionario cubano de seudónimos. Habana, Impr. "El siglo xx," 1922. 182p. **A101**

Czechoslovakia

Dolenský, Antonín. Slovník pseudonymů a kryptonymů v československé literatuře. . . . 3. přepracované vydání. Praha [Tiskem M. Knappa v Karlíně], 1934. 155p. **A102**

France

[Manne, Louis Charles Joseph de]. Nouveau dictionnaire des ouvrages anonymes et pseudonymes avec les noms des auteurs ou éditeurs, accompagné de notes historiques et critiques. 3. éd. rev., cor. et très augm. Lyon, Scheuring, 1868. 607p. **A104**

Quérard, Joseph Marie. Les supercheries littéraires dévoilées. . . . 2. éd. Paris, Daffis, 1869-[79]. 7v. o.p.   **A105**

Subtitle: Galerie des écrivains français de toute l'Europe qui se sont déguisés sous des anagrammes, des astéronymes, des cryptonymes, des initialismes, des noms littéraires, des pseudonymes facétieux ou bizarres, etc. 2. éd., considérablement augm., pub. par Gustave Brunet et Pierre Jannet. Suivie 1°, Du Dictionnaire des ouvrages anonymes, par Ant.-Alex. Barbier. 3. éd., rev. et augm. par Olivier Barbier. . . . 2°, D'une table générale des noms réels des écrivains anonymes et pseudonymes cités dans les deux ouvrages.

v.1-3, Quérard, J. M. Les supercheries littéraires dévoilées, 2. éd., A-Z; v.4-7, Barbier, A. A. Dictionnaire des ouvrages anonymes. 3. éd., A-Z. Anonymes Latins. A-Z.

The same edition of Barbier was also issued separately (Paris, Féchoz, 4v.). The Table générale des noms réels was never issued.

Gives notes about the books and editions listed but in general does not give authority for identification of authors. Supplemented by the following:

Brunet, Gustave. Dictionnaire des ouvrages anonymes [de Barbier], suivi des Supercheries littéraires dévoilées [de Quérard]: supplément à la dernière édition de ces deux ouvrages (Édition Daffis). Paris, Féchoz, 1889. 310 col., cixp. 122 col., xivp.   **A106**

Contents: Dictionnaires des ouvrages anonymes (Supplément); Essai sur les bibliothèques imaginaires; Les devises des vieux poètes; étude littéraire et bibliographique, par M. Gustave Mouravit; Appel aux bibliophiles, aux érudits et aux curieux ["Desiderata," i.e. une liste d'anonymes et de pseudonymes dont le mystère n'a pas été découvert]; Les supercheries littéraires dévoilées (Supplément); Varia: Pseudonymes étrangers. Traductions supposées. Supercheries typographiques.

Germany

Berlin. Preussische Staatsbibliothek. Namenschlüssel die Verweisungen der Berliner Titeldrucke zu Pseudonymen, Doppelnamen und Namensabwandlungen, 1892–1935. [2d ed.] Berlin, Staatsbibliothek, 1936. 780p.   **A107**

The *Berliner Titeldrucke* (*Deutscher Gesamtkatalog, Neue Titel, see* A37) is the accessions list of books added during 1892–1935 to the Staatsbibliothek and to the libraries of the Prussian universities and "Hochschule." This *Namenschlüssel* is an alphabetical index to forms of authors' names which differ from the author entry chosen for the *Titeldrucke* and includes pseudonyms, parts of compound names not used as entries, varying spellings of transliterated names, early and medieval names for which the correct entry is not obvious, etc. For each of such unused forms is given a reference to a volume of the *Titeldrucke* where the full entry for the book may be found under the author entry chosen by the Staatsbibliothek.

Margreiter, Hans. Tiroler Anonymen- und Pseudonymen-Lexikon, mit Register der Autoren und Monogramme. 2. verm. u. verb. Aufl. Linz a Donau, Winkler, 1930. Lfg. 1-2. (Archiv für Bibliographie, Buch- u. Bibliothekswesen, Beiheft 4)   **A108**

1st ed., 1912, had title: Beiträge zu einem tirolischen Anonymen- u. Pseudonymen-Lexikon.

Holzmann, Michael and Bohatta, Hans. Deutsches Anonymen-Lexikon, 1501–1910. Weimar, Gesellschaft der Bibliophilen, 1902–28. 7v. **A109**

v.1-4, 1501–1850; v.5, supplement, 1851–1908; v.6, 1501–1910, additions and corrections; v.7, 1501–1926, additions and corrections.

Includes, in the four lists, some 83,000 entries. Arranged alphabetically by title, with author's name supplied for each, and the authority for the information indicated.

—— Deutsches Pseudonymen-Lexikon. Wien, Akad. Verlag, 1906. 323p.   **A110**

Gives pseudonym, followed by real name, and indicates the authority for the information.

Italy

Melzi, Gaetano, *conte.* Dizionario di opere anonime e pseudonime di scrittori italiani, o come che sia aventi relazione all' Italia. Milano, Coi Torchi di L. di Giacomo Priola, 1848–59. 3v.   **A111**

—— —— Supplemento comp. da Giambattista Passano. Ancona, Morelli, 1887. 517p.

—— Anonimi e pseudonimi italiani. Supplemento al Melzi e al Passano di Emmanuele Rocco. Napoli, Chiurazzi, 1888. 16p.   **A112**

Mexico

Manrique de Lara, Juana and Monroy, Guadalupe. Seudónimos, anagramas, iniciales, etc., de autores mexicanos y extranjeros. México, Secretaría de Educación Pública, 1943. 78p.   **A113**

Netherlands and Belgium

Doorninck, Jan Izaac van. Vermomde en naamlooze schrijvers opgespoord op het gebied der Nederlandsche en Vlaamsche letteren. 2. uitg. der "Bibliotheek van anonymen en pseudonymen." Leiden, Brill, 1883–85. 2 pts. in 1v. **A114**

v.1, Pseudonyms and initials; v.2, Anonyms.

Kempenaer, A. de. Vermomde Nederlandsche en Vlaamsche schrijvers, vervolg op Mr. J. I. van Doorninck's Vermomde en naamlooze schrijvers, opgespoord op het gevied der Nederlandsche en Vlaamsche letteren. Leiden, Sijthoff [1928]. 690 col.   **A115**

Poland

Bar, Adam. Słownik pseudonimów i kryptonimów pisarzy polskich oraz Polski dotyczęcych, opracował Adam Bar . . . i Tad. Godłowskiego . . . Kraków [Nakł. Krakowskiego koła Zwięzku Bibljotekarzy Polskich], 1936–38. 3v. (Prace bibljoteczne Krakowskiego koła Zwięzku bibljotekarzy polskich. VII-IX) **A116**

Contents: t.1-2, Pseudonimy i kryptonimy od A-Z; t.3, Wykaz nazwisk pisarzy.

Portugal

Fonseca, Martinho Augusto Ferreira da. Subsidios para um diccionario de pseudonymos, iniciaes e obras anonymas de escriptores portuguezes, contribuição para o estudo da litteratura portugueza. Lisboa, Acad. Real das Sciencias, 1896. 298p. **A117**

Russia

Masanov, Ivan Filippovich. Slovar' psevdonimov russkikh pisateleĭ. Moskva, Vsesoĭuznaĭa Knizhanaĭa Palata, 1941- . v.1. **A118**

v.1, A-Lĭashko, N.

Scandinavia

Bygdén, Anders Leonard. Svenskt anonym- och pseudonym-lexikon. Bibliografisk förteckning öfver uppdagade anonymer och pseudonymer i den svenska litteraturen. Upsala, Berling, 1898–1915. 2v. **A119**

Collin, Edvard. Anonymer og pseudonymer i den danske, norske og islandske literatur samt i fremmede Literaturer, forsaavidt disse omhandle nordiske Forhold, fra de aeldste tider indtil Aaret 1860. Kiøbenhavn, Lund, 1869. 209p. **A120**

Ehrencron-Müller, Holger. Anonym- og Pseudonym-Lexikon for Danmark og Island til 1920 og Norge til 1814. København, Hagerup, 1940. 391p. Kr. 30. **A120a**

Pettersen, Hjalmar Marius. Norsk anonym- og pseudonym-lexikon. Kristiana, Steenske, 1924. 690 col., [34]p. **A121**

1st ed., 1890, has title: *Anonymer og pseudonymer i den norske literatur 1678–1890.*

Slovakia

Ormis, Ján Vladimir. Slovník slovenských pseudonymov. [Turč. Sv. Martine] Slovenská národná knižnica. 1944. 366p. (Knihy slovenskej národ-

nej knižnice v Turčianskom Svätom Martine. Sväzok I) **A122**

Spain

Ponce de León Freyre, Eduardo and **Zamora Lucas, Florentino.** 1500 seudónimos modernos de la literatura española (1900–1942). Madrid, Instituto Nacional del Libro Español, 1942. 126p. **A123**

Spanish America

Medina, José Toribio. Diccionario de anónimos y seudónimos hispanoamericanos. Buenos Aires, Impr. de la Univ., 1925. 2v. in 1. (Buenos Aires. Univ. Nacional. Inst. de Investigaciones Hist. Pub. 26-27) **A124**

Victorica, Ricardo. Errores y omisiones del Diccionario de anónimos y seudónimos hispanoamericanos de José Toribio Medina. Buenos Aires, Viau & Zona, 1928. 338p. **A125**

——— Verdades que levantan roncha. Belitres enfurecidos. Gaceta del foro, ano 15, 11 abril 1930, p.273-78.

Has about 16 columns of "Nuevas adiciones al 'Diccionario' de Medina," p.274-78, in alphabetical order.

——— Nueva epanortosis al Diccionario de anónimos y seudónimos de J. T. Medina. Buenos Aires, Rosso, 1929. 207p.

Feliú Cruz, Guillermo. Advertencias saludables a un criticastro de mala ley. Buenos Aires, Impr. de la Univ., 1929. 56p. **A126**

Repr. from *Boletin del Inst. de Investigaciones Hist.* 8:254-59; 9:237-80, abril–junio, oct.–dic. 1929.

"A criticism of Ricardo Victorica's 'Errores y omisiones del Diccionario de anónimos y seudónimos hispanoamericanos de José Toribio Medina.'"

Uruguay

Scarone, Arturo. Diccionario de seudónimos del Uruguay . . . Prólogo de Ariosto D. González. Montevideo, Garcia & Cía., 1942. 632p. **A127**

"Segunda ed. con un Apéndice" of the 3d ed. which was first published under this title in 1941. The first two editions have title *Apuntes para un diccionario de seudónimos y de publicaciones anónimas.*

Miscellany
Indexes

American Library Association. Junior Members Round Table. Local indexes in American libraries; a union list of unpublished indexes, ed.

by Norma Olin Ireland. Bost., Faxon, 1947. 221p. (Useful reference ser., no.73) **A128**

Ireland, Norma Olin. An index to indexes, a subject bibliography of published indexes. . . . Bost., Faxon, 1942. 107p. (Useful reference ser., no.67) $1.75. **A129**

A brief guide incorporating special indexes, indexes to sets of books, periodicals, government documents, and cumulative indexes to individual periodicals. American only, except for a few English special indexes. Arranged by subject with author-title index.

Fictitious imprints

Brunet, Gustave. Imprimeurs imaginaires et libraires supposés, étude bibliographique suivie de recherches sur quelques ouvrages imprimés avec des indications fictives de lieux ou avec des dates singulières. Paris, Tross, 1866. 290p. **A130**

Weller, Emil. Die falschen und fingirten Druckorte. Repertorium der seit erfindung der Buchdruckerkunst unter falscher Firma erschienenen deutschen, lateinischen und französischen Schriften. 2. verm. und verb. Aufl. Leipzig, W. Engelmann, 1864. 2v. **A131**

v.1, German and Latin works; v.2, French works.

NATIONAL AND TRADE
Bibliography

Current national bibliographies. (In Library of Congress, Quarterly journal of current acquisitions. Aug. 1949- . pt.1- . In progress) **A132**

Contents: pt.1, Aug. 1949, Australia, Canada, Great Britain, and the Republic of Ireland; pt.2, Nov. 1949, Austria, Belgium, Denmark, Finland, France, Germany, Iceland, Italy, Netherlands, Norway, Sweden, Switzerland.

Published in preliminary form in the *Quarterly journal*, it is hoped that these lists will eventually appear in a definitive edition.

Includes general lists, general selective lists, government publications, and newspapers and periodicals, etc., with useful annotations.

Heyl, Lawrence. Current national bibliographies; a list of sources of information concerning current books of all countries. rev. ed. Chic., Amer. Library Assoc., 1942. 20p. 75c. o.p. **A133**

Peddie, Robert Alexander. National bibliographies; a descriptive catalogue of the works which register the books published in each country. Lond., Grafton, 1912. 34p. **A134**

An annotated list, still useful for bibliographies published before 1912.

Pinto, Olga. Le bibliografie nazionali. Veilano, Monadori, 1935. 115p. **A135**

An annotated bibliography arranged alphabetically by country.

Schneider, Georg. Allgemeine nationale Bibliographien. (In his Handbuch der Bibliographie, 4. Aufl. p.159-368 [A5]) **A136**

United States
Bibliography

Growoll, Adolf. Book-trade bibliography in the United States in the 19th century, to which is added a Catalogue of all the books printed in the United States, with the prices and places where published annexed, published by the booksellers in Boston, January, 1804. N.Y., Dibdin Club, 1898. lxxvii, 79p. **A137**

Contents: The beginnings of book-trade bibliography; Booksellers' associations, 1801–1892; Sidelights on the early conditions of the book-trade; The first book-trade catalogue; Book-trade helps, 1801–1897; Chronological list of catalogues, book-trade and literary journals; Sketches of some American bookseller-bibliographers; Catalogue . . . 1804.

Stillwell, Margaret Bingham. Americana: Selected bibliographies and bibliographical monographs. (In her Incunabula and Americana, p.341-440 [A53]) **A138**

An important list of about 550 bibliographies of Americana before 1800. For full description *see* A53.

Early

Bradford, Thomas Lindsley. Bibliographer's manual of American history, containing an account of all state, territory, town and county histories relating to the United States of North America, with verbatim copies of their titles and useful bibliographical notes, together with the prices at which they have been sold for the last forty years, and with an exhaustive index by titles, and an index by states, ed. and rev. by S. V. Henkels. Phila., Henkels, 1907–10. 5v. **A139**

Brown University. John Carter Brown Library. Bibliotheca americana. Catalogue of the John Carter Brown Library in Brown University. Providence, The Library, 1919–1931. v.1-3. **A140**

v.1, pt.1, to 1569; v.1, pt.2, 1570–99; v.2, pt.1, 1600–34; v.2, pt.2, 1634–58; v.3, 1659–74.

Church, Elihu Dwight. Catalogue of books relating to the discovery and early history of North and South America, forming a part of the library of E. D. Church, comp. and annotated by George Watson Cole. N.Y., Dodd, 1907. 5v. il. o.p. **A141**

A monumental work, the finest catalog of Americana yet published although less frequently useful than either Sabin or Evans because of the limited number of titles included. Includes 1385 entries of books about America, arranged chronologically, from the earliest period to 1884, by date of publication with author and title index. Gives for each book listed full title and collation, and important historical and bibliographical annotations, with notes of differences in copies and location of copies in other libraries, referring in all to some 50 public and private libraries. Gives many facsimile reproductions of title pages, colophons, etc. For extended review by W. N. C. Carlton *see* Bibliographical Society of America, *Papers* 7:41-46.

Evans, Charles. American bibliography; a chronological dictionary of all books, pamphlets and periodical publications printed in the United States of America from the genesis of printing in 1639 down to and including the year 1820; with bibliographical and biographical notes. Chic., priv. pr. for the author by the Columbia Pr., 1903–34. v.1-12. **A142**

No more published.

v.1, 1639–1729; v.2, 1730–1750; v.3, 1751–1764; v.4, 1765–73; v.5, 1774–78; v.6, 1779–85; v.7, 1786–89; v.8, 1790–92; v.9, 1793–94; v.10, 1795–96; v.11, 1796–97; v.12, 1798–99.

The most important general list of early American publications, indispensable in the large reference or special library. Includes books, pamphlets, and periodicals, arranged chronologically by dates of publication; gives for each book listed author's full name with dates of birth and death, full title, place, date, publisher or printer, paging, size, and in many cases, names of libraries possessing copies. Each volume has three indexes: (1) authors; (2) classified subjects; (3) printers and publishers. The location of copies is an especially important feature.

Harrisse, Henry. Bibliotheca Americana vetustissima. A description of works relating to America published between the years 1492 and 1551. N.Y., Philes, 1866. 519p. **A143**

—— —— Additions. Paris, Lib. Tross, 1872. 199p.

Anastatic reprint of both parts: Paris, Maisonneuve, 1922.

Henry E. Huntington Library and Art Gallery, San Marino, Calif. American imprints, 1648–1797, in the Huntington Library, supplementing Evans' American bibliography; comp. by Willard O. Waters. (In Huntington Library Bull. no.3, Feb. 1933. p.[1]-95) $2.50. **A144**

Arranged chronologically, with author index. Lists 736 "titles of books, pamphlets, broadsides, maps, etc., supplementary to the Evans' bibliography. It comprises, besides items apparently not listed in that work, a number appearing there but with titles or imprints varying from the copies here described."

Sabin, Joseph. Dictionary of books relating to America, from its discovery to the present time. N.Y., Sabin, 1868–92; Bibl. Soc. of Amer., 1928–36. 29v. **A145**

Half title: *Bibliotheca Americana,* by which title it is generally known.

An important bibliography of Americana, including books, pamphlets, and periodicals printed in America, and works about America printed elsewhere. Comprises 106,413 numbered entries, but the actual number of titles recorded is much greater, as that total does not count the added editions and titles mentioned in the various notes. The arrangement is by authors, with some title entries for anonymous works and other entries under names of places. Information given includes full title, place, publisher, date, format, paging, often contents and bibliographical notes with reference to a description or review in some other work and, in many cases, names of libraries possessing copies. This last feature is important for interlibrary loans.

A list of "Library Location Symbols" is given in volume 29, p.299-305, which is more extensive than the partial list given in volume 1.

19th century

Roorbach, Orville Augustus. Bibliotheca Americana, 1820–61. N.Y., Roorbach, 1852–61. 4v. **A146**

v.1, 1820–52, with a list of periodicals published in the United States; v.2, Supplement, Oct. 1852—May 1855; v.3, Addenda, May 1855—Mar. 1858; v.4, Mar. 1858—Jan. 1861.

A catalog of American publications, including reprints, arranged alphabetically by authors and titles, giving publisher, date, size, price.

Kelly, James. American catalogue of books published in the United States from Jan. 1861 to Jan. 1871. N.Y., Wiley, 1866–71. 2v. (Repr. N.Y., Peter Smith, 1938. 2v. $7.50 ea.) **A147**

Continues the record of American bibliography from Roorbach's last volume, giving about the same kind of information. Each volume contains a list of societies and their publications. Volume 1 also contains a list of pamphlets, sermons, and addresses on the Civil War, 1861–66.

Both Roorbach and Kelly are unsatisfactory as they are far from complete and often inaccurate, but they must be used as they are the most general lists for the period 1820–70.

Stevens, Henry. Catalogue of the American books in the library of the British Museum at Christmas MDCCCLVI. Lond., H. Stevens, 1866. 4 pts. in 1v. **A148**

Contents: (1) American books printed in the United States, 628p.; (2) Catalogue of the Canadian and other British North American books, 14p.; (3) Catalogue of the Mexican and other Spanish American and West Indian books, 62p.; (4) Catalogue of the American maps, 17p.

Includes some works not included in Roorbach and gives fuller titles for others that are included there.

Trübner, Nikolaus. Trübner's Bibliographical guide to American literature. A classed list of books published in the United States of America during the last forty years. Lond., Trübner, 1859. cxlix, 554p. **A149**

Contents: Bibliographies of Americana, etc., p.iii-xxxvi; Classed list of books, p.1-496; Addenda, p.496-521; Alphabetical index, p.522-54.

Blackwell, Henry. A bibliography of Welsh Americana. Liverpool, pr. for the National Library of Wales, Aberystwyth, by Hugh Evans and Sons, 1942. 92p. (National Library of Wales Journal, supplement, ser. 3, no.1) **A150**

Edited by William Williams, keeper of printed books in the National Library.

American catalogue of books, 1876–1910. N.Y., Pub. Weekly, 1876–1910. 9v. in 13. (Repr. N.Y., Peter Smith, 1941. Price varies, $12.50 to $17.50 per v.) **A151**

1876: Author and title entries of books in print, July 1, 1876; Subject entries, 2v.; July 1, 1876—June 30, 1884: Author and title alphabet; Subject alphabet, 2v.; July 1, 1884—June 30, 1890: Author and title alphabet; Subject alphabet, 2v.; July 1, 1890—June 30, 1895: Author and title alphabet; Subject alphabet, 2v.; July 1, 1895—Jan. 1, 1900: Author and title alphabet; Subject alphabet, 2v. in 1; Jan. 1, 1900—Jan. 1, 1905: Authors, titles, subjects and series in one alphabet; Jan. 1, 1905—Dec. 1907: Authors, titles, subjects and series in one alphabet; Jan. 1, 1908—Dec. 1910: Authors, titles, subjects, and series in one alphabet.

The standard American list for the period covered; comprehensive and generally reliable though information given is based upon reports from publishers and not, in most cases, on actual examination of books themselves. 1876–1910 are periodical volumes supplementary to 1876 which is a basic volume with about 70,000 entries listing the publications of over 900 publishing houses.

"The Catalogue aims to include all books (with certain exceptions) published in the United States which were in print, and for sale to the general public, July 1, 1876. The exceptions were local directories, periodicals, sheet music, books chiefly blank, unbound maps, tracts, and other low-priced pamphlets, the reasons for the exclusion of which were obvious. It embraces reprints, such importations also as are kept in stock, publications of learned societies (when for sale), the works of general importance issued by various departments of the national government (without price), and the full law reports of the courts of the different States (all of which are generally for sale, though some have no fixed price)."—*Pref.* to 1876 volume.

Annual American catalogue, 1886–1910. N.Y., Pub. Weekly, 1887–1911. 25v. **A152**

No more published. For most points superseded by the cumulated volumes of the *American catalogue,* but occasionally useful for something omitted in that work.

20th century

United States catalog; books in print, 1899, ed. by G. F. Danforth, M. E. Potter. Minneapolis, Wilson, 1900. 2v. in 1. **A153**

v.1, Author list; v.2, Title index.

—— 2d ed.; books in print, 1902. Entries for author, subject and title in one alphabet, ed. by M. E. Potter. Minneapolis, Wilson, 1903. 2150p.

—— —— Supplement. Books published 1902–05, ed. by M. E. Potter. Minneapolis, Wilson, 1906. 2034p.

—— —— [Annual supplements] Cumulative book index, 1906–10. Minneapolis, Wilson, 1907–11.

—— 3d ed.; books in print, Jan. 1, 1912 . . . ed. by M. E. Potter. N.Y., Wilson, 1912. 2837p.

—— —— Supplements, 1912–17, 1918–June 1921, July 1921—June 1924, ed. (1912–17) by M. E. Potter, (1918–24) by E. E. Hawkins. N.Y., Wilson, 1918–24. 3v.

—— —— [Annual supplements] Cumulative book index, July 1924—Dec. 1927. N.Y., Wilson, 1925–28. 3v.

—— 4th ed.; books in print, Jan. 1, 1928, ed. by Mary Burnham. N.Y., Wilson, 1928. 3164p.

—— —— [Supplements] Cumulative book index, a world list of books in the English language, 1928–32- , ed. by Mary Burnham. N.Y., Wilson, 1933- . **A153a**

Contents: 1928–32 (pub. 1933), 2298p.; 1933–37 (pub. 1938), 2680p.; 1938–42 (pub. 1945), 2722p.

Continued by the biennial, annual, and monthly cumulations listed below (A154).

Service basis; apply to publisher for price.

The four editions and their respective supplements constitute a comprehensive record of American publications from 1898 on that is indispensable for reference work in its field, and the *whole series* is necessary for full work in this period. The most frequently used parts will be the fourth edition (1928) and its supplements, but the earlier volumes must be used for: (1) books out-of-print by 1928, (2) fuller information, e.g., paging, date, etc., on some titles still in print.

Each volume is a dictionary catalog with entries under author, title, and subject.

The fourth edition includes publications in the regular book trade, privately printed books, regular importations of American publishers, Canadian books (in English) not also published in the United States, publications of universities, societies, scientific institutions e.g., Smithsonian, National Museum, and a selected list of publications of the national and state governments. For each book, gives: author, short title, edition, publisher, price, and, generally but not always, date, paging and illustration; gives also Library of Congress card numbers, and, for a book entered in the *Book review digest,* its Dewey decimal classification number and a tracing of the subject headings used for it in the *U. S. catalog.*

The supplements (1928–32-) have a wider scope and include a comprehensive listing of books and pamphlets, in English, issued by Canadian publishers, and a listing of publications from other parts of the English-speaking world, Australia, Great Britain, New Zealand, South Africa, etc. In proportion to the size of the catalog there are very few inaccuracies, although, as some of the entries have had to be made without examination of the books and are based on publishers' descriptions and lists, the work is not a final authority on bibliographical detail for such books. As a first aid it is indispensable: (1) in order department work; (2) as an adjunct to the library's own catalog; (3) as a reference tool for many subjects: verification of titles, authors' names and dates, authorship when only the title or subject of a book is known, lists of books on a given subject, etc. Subject lists of fiction, e.g., ghost stories, sea stories, etc., and the use of the subhead fiction under many subjects makes it useful for certain types of questions about fiction.

Each volume includes a list of publishers with addresses.

Continued currently by the *Cumulative book index* described below.

Current

Cumulative book index. N.Y., Wilson, 1898- . Service basis. **A154**

Subtitle, 1930- : A world list of books in the English language.

Published periodically with cumulations to form supplements to the *United States catalog*. Frequency varies. Now published monthly except August cumulating at intervals. Semiannual, annual and biennial volumes are eventually superseded by the permanent 5-year cumulation.

Compiled on the same principles as the cumulated supplements listed above including in dictionary catalog form a record of books published not only in the United States but also books published in the English language in other parts of the world.

A comprehensive and reasonably accurate record indispensable in any library.

Publishers' weekly, the American book trade journal, 1872- . N.Y., Pub. Weekly, 1872- . v.1- . $6. **A155**

The standard American book trade journal, containing lists of new publications of the week, lists of books announced for publication, news notes, editorials and articles, advertisements of books wanted, etc. The principal bibliographical list is the weekly list of new publications, which is an author list with full title, imprint, collation and descriptive notes. The last issue of each month includes a title index for the month. A monthly list by authors and subjects was formerly given in the first issue of each month, but this was discontinued after January 1919. Special numbers issued during the year vary but usually include: Spring announcement number in January, Summer number in May, Fall children's book number in July, Fall announcement number in September.

Publishers' trade list annual, 1873- . N.Y., Pub. Weekly, 1873- . Annual. $5 per yr. **A156**

A collection of publishers' catalogs, arranged alphabetically by publishers' names, and bound up in one or two large volumes. As the catalogs are not compiled on any uniform system, the amount of information given about books varies greatly, ranging from full information and occasional notes in some lists to only short title and price in others; in general dates of publication are omitted. Lists only books in print, and so is primarily useful for finding quickly the price of a book and whether or not it is in print. Corresponds in general to the English *Reference catalogue* (A310). Only two indexes were issued, an author, title and catchword subject index to the 1902 edition and a supplementary index for 1903–04, until 1948 when the following work began publication:

Books in print: an author-title-series index to the

Publishers' trade list annual, 1948- . N.Y., Bowker, 1948- . Annual. $17.50. **A157**

Each volume includes an author index and a title index in each case giving publisher and price. Fuller information may then be found by referring to the pertinent publisher's catalog in the *Publishers' trade list annual*.

A very valuable addition for both acquisition and reference work in a library.

Useful for: (1) finding the publisher and price of a book; (2) finding the author's name if only the title is known; (3) indexing the vast amount of material in the *Publishers' trade list annual*.

Orton, Robert Merritt. Catalog of reprints in series, 1940- . N.Y., Wilson, 1940- . Annual (slightly irregular). **A158**

In 2 pts.: (1) An author and title list giving the reprint edition or editions in which a work has appeared with date and price of reprint. In some cases, but not in all, gives date of original publication; (2) List of reprint publishers and series.

U. S. Copyright Office. Catalog of copyright entries, 1891–1946. Wash., Govt. Prt. Off., 1891–1947. **A159**

Title varies. Before 1906 issued by the Treasury Dept.; 1906–1946, issued by Copyright Office as *New series*.

Contents: Arrangement differs slightly, pt.1, *Books*, 1909–27 issued in 2 groups; 1928–46 in 3 groups as follows: group 1, v.25-43, *Books* proper, frequency varies, annual index; group 2, v.25-43, *Pamphlets*, etc., includes lectures, sermons, maps, etc., monthly with annual index; group 3, v.1-19, *Dramatic compositions*, motion pictures (before 1920 motion pictures were included in pt.4), monthly, with annual index; pt.2, v.1-41, *Periodicals and newspapers,* quarterly with annual index; pt.3, v.1-41, *Musical compositions,* monthly with annual index (for full information *see* Q239); pt.4, v.1-41, *Works of art,* photographs, etc., quarterly with annual index.

For 1946 each part was issued as an annual.

———— —— Ser. 3- . Wash., Govt. Prt. Off., 1947- . $20 per yr.

With the third series the arrangement and the format have been changed to make the contents of the set more easily available. The *Catalog* is now subdivided into separate parts following the classification as given in the Copyright Act: pt.1A, *Books* and selected pamphlets, $1.50; pt.1B, *Pamphlets,* serials, and contributions to periodicals, $1.50; pt.2, *Periodicals,* $1; pt.3 and 4, *Dramas* and works prepared for oral delivery, $1; pt.5A, *Published music,* $1.50; pt.5B, *Unpublished music,* $1.50; pt.6, *Maps,* 50c; pt.7-11B, *Works of art,* reproductions, prints, etc., $1; pt.12 and 13, *Motion pictures,* 50c; pt.14A, *Renewal registrations, literature, art, film,* 50c; pt.14B, *Renewal registrations, music,* $1. Subscriptions may be placed for separate parts.

Each part is published semiannually and lists the works copyrighted during the period. The *Books* section includes books published in the United States, books in foreign languages published abroad, and books in the English language first published abroad when they are copyrighted in this country.

Vertical file service catalog; an annotated subject catalog of pamphlets, 1932–34. N.Y., Wilson, 1935. 640p. Service basis. **A160**

"An annotated subject list of pamphlets, booklets, brochures, leaflets, circulars, folders, maps, posters, charts, mimeographed bulletins and other inexpensive material which falls outside the classification of books, but still has a place in the library. . . . Some of the pamphlets are frankly propaganda or advertising, often biased in viewpoint but, like the other titles in the catalogue, they are listed in the belief that they may prove to be of some reference value."—*Pref.*

For material listed gives title, author, paging, publisher and price. The 1932–34 volume is a cumulation of annual volumes 1-3 of the index, and is continued by the following:

—— Annual volumes 4- . 1935- . N.Y., Wilson, 1936- . v.4- .

The service is issued monthly (except August) with an annual cumulation in December.

Regional

❧ The various general works listed above (A151 through A160) are reasonably comprehensive for works issued at the main publishing centers, but are less complete for material printed by local presses, especially before 1875. For local publications regional bibliographies must often be consulted. A good list of such works is given in Stillwell, *Incunabula and Americana*, p.382-408 (A53).

A more recent listing is:

McMurtrie, Douglas Crawford. Locating the printed source materials for United States history; with a bibliography of lists of regional imprints. (In Mississippi Valley historical review 31:369-406, Dec. 1944) **A161**

Lists of regional imprints, arranged alphabetically by state, p.379-403; American imprints check list, p.403-6.

Historical Records Survey. Bibliography of research projects reports; check-list of Historical Records Survey publications. Rev. Apr. 1943. Wash., Federal Works Agency, W.P.A., 1943. 110p. (W.P.A. Technical ser. Research and records bibliography, no.7) **A162**

A final record of publications superseding all earlier listings.

Lists: inventories of federal archives in the states; inventories of county archives; inventories of municipal and town archives; transcriptions of public archives; vital statistics; church archives publications; manuscript publications; American imprints inventory; American portrait inventory; guides to civilian organizations; miscellaneous publications; microfilm records; depositories of unpublished material, etc.

Because of this record, the volumes published in these various series are not listed here, with the exception of the American imprints inventory which is listed below.

—— American imprints inventory, prepared by the Historical Records Survey, Division of Women's and Professional Projects. Works Progress Administration. Wash., Hist. Rec. Survey,

1937–42. nos. 1-20, 23-26, 31-32, 36, 38-42, 44-45, 52. **A163**

Nos. 21, 22, 27-30, 33-35, 37, 43, 46-51 had not been published when the work of the *American imprints inventory* ceased.

No. 1, A preliminary check list of Missouri imprints, 1808–1850. 1937. 225p.; no.2, M. R. Martin, Check list of Minnesota imprints, 1849–1865. 1938. 219p.; no.3, A check list of Arizona imprints, 1860–1890. 1938. 81p.; no.4, Check list of Chicago ante-fire imprints, 1851–1871. 1938. 727p.; no.5, D. C. McMurtrie, Check list of Kentucky imprints, 1787–1810. 1939. 205p.; no.6, D. C. McMurtrie and A. H. Allen, Check list of Kentucky imprints, 1811–1820, with notes in supplement to the Check list of 1787–1810 imprints. 1939. 235p.; no.7, A check list of Nevada imprints, 1859–1890. 1939. 127 numb.l.;no.8, Check list of Alabama imprints, 1807–1840. 1939. 159p.; no.9, Lucile M. Morsch, Check list of New Jersey imprints, 1784–1800. 1939. 189p.; no.10, Check list of Kansas imprints, 1854–1876. 1939. 773p.; no.11, Chicago Historical Society Library, A check list of the Kellogg collection of "patent inside" newspapers of 1876. 1939. 99p.; no. 12, D. C. McMurtrie, A check list of the imprints of Sag Harbor, L. I., 1791–1820. 1939. 61p.; no.13, A check list of Idaho imprints, 1839–1890. 1940. 74p.; no.14, A check list of West Virginia imprints, 1791–1830. 1940. 62p.; no.15, A check list of Iowa imprints, 1838–1860, in supplement to those recorded by Alexander Moffit in the *Iowa journal of history and politics* for Jan. 1938. 1940. 84(i.e., 85)p.; no.16, List of Tennessee imprints, 1793–1840, in Tennessee libraries. 1941. 97p.; no.17, A check list of Ohio imprints 1796–1820. 1941. 202p.; no.18, A check list of Wyoming imprints, 1866–1890. 1941. 69(i.e., 70) p.; no.19, Lucy B. Foote, Bibliography of the official publications of Louisiana, 1803–1934. 1942. 579p.; no.20, Check list of Tennessee imprints, 1841–1850. 1941. 138p.; nos. 23-24, 41-42, A check list of Wisconsin imprints, 1833–1849, 1850–1854, 1855–1858, 1859–1863. 1942. 4v.; no.25, Check list of New Mexico imprints and publications, 1784–1876, imprints, 1834–1876, publications, 1784–1876. 1942. 115p.; no.26, A check list of Nebraska non-documentary imprints, 1847–1876. 1942. 132p.; no.31, A check list of California non-documentary imprints, 1833–1855. 1942. 109p.; no.32, A check list of Tennessee imprints, 1793–1840. 1942. 285p.; no.36, A check list of Utica, N. Y., imprints, 1799–1830. 1942. 179p.; no.38 (misnumbered 25), Supplemental check list of Kentucky imprints, 1788–1820, including the original printing of the original Kentucky copyright ledger, 1800–1854, and the first account of the run of Baptist minutes in the collection of Mr. Henry S. Robinson, ed. by John Wilson Townsend. 1942. 241p.; no.39, A check list of Arkansas imprints, 1821–1876. 1942. 139p.; nos.40 and 45, A check list of Massachusetts imprints, 1801–1802. 1942. 2v.; nos. 41-42, *see* nos. 23-24; no.44, A check list of Washington imprints, 1853–1876. 1942. 89p.; no.45, *see* no.40; no.52, Preliminary check list of Michigan imprints, 1796–1850. 1942. 224p.

Albania

Legrand, Émile. Bibliographie albanaise; description raisonnée des ouvrages pub. en albanais ou relatifs à l'Albanie du 15. siècle à l'année 1900. Oeuvre posthume, compl. et pub. par Henri Gûys. Paris, Welter, 1912. 228p. **A164**

Argentina

Gutiérrez, Juan Maria. Bibliografia de la primera imprenta de Buenos Aires desde su fundación hasta el año 1810 inclusive. . . . Buenos Aires, Impr. de Mayo, 1866. 43, 34, 246p. **A165**

pt.1, Celebridades argentinas del siglo xviii; pt.2, Orijenes del arte de imprimir en la America española; pt.3, Bibliografia de la primera imprenta de Buenos Aires [215 imprints].

pts. 2-3, repr. from the *Revista de Buenos Aires,* June 1865–Aug. 1866.

Bibliografia general argentina, por Manuel Selva, Fortunato Mendílaharzu y Lorenzo J. Rosso; inventario analítico-crítico de todas las publicaciones argentinas desde el orígen de la primera imprenta en el Rio de la Plata hasta el presente. Buenos Aires, Rosso, 1931–33. v.1-2 (incompl.). (Suplemento de "La literatura argentina") **A166**

v.1-2 (incompl.), A-C.
A revision of the provisional edition of 1929.

Buenos Aires. Biblioteca Nacional. Catálogo metódico de la Biblioteca Nacional, seguido de una tabla alfabética de autores y de otra auxiliar de seudónimos y nombres. Buenos Aires, Impr. de P. E. Coni é Hijos, 1893–1931. v.1–7. **A167**

v.1, Ciencias y artes, 1893; v.2, Historia y geografía, 1900; v.3, Literatura, 1911; v.4, Derecho, 1915; v.5, Ciencias y artes, t.2, 1919; v.6, Historia y geografía, t.2, 1925; v.7, Literatura, t.2, 1931.

Anuario bibliográfico de la República Arjentina. año [1]-9. 1879–1887. Buenos Aires, 1880-88. 9v. **A168**

Edited by Alberto Navarro Viola.
A selected, critical annual list, classified by subject with author index.

Current

Boletin bibliográfico argentino . . . 1937- . no.1- . Publicación oficial. Buenos Aires, 1937- . Annual. **A169**

Published by the Comision Nacional de Cooperacion Intelectual.
Lists books in the original and translation, translations of foreign books published in Argentina and foreign books that deal with Argentina. Classified with author index.

Polibiblon; bibliografia acumulativa Argentina e Hispanoamericana. v.1, Abril 1947- . Buenos Aires, Polibiblon, 1947- . v.1- . Semimonthly. $25 Arg; $7 extranjero. **A170**

Australia

Foxcroft, A. B. Australian catalogue; a reference index to the books and periodicals published and still current in the Commonwealth of Australia. . . . Melbourne, Whitecombe and Tombs, 1911. 118p., 72p. **A171**

Australia. Commonwealth National Library, Canberra. Annual catalogue of Australian publications, no.1- . 1936- . Canberra, 1937- . **A172**

Number 1 does not include official publications; numbers 2 on generally include books published in Australia with supplement to previous issues, books of Australian interest published overseas, official publications of the commonwealth and territories, selected list of Australian periodicals, annuals and serial publications and a directory of Australian publishers.
Official publications omitted 1941–44.
Supplemented by the monthly *Books published in Australia; list of books supplied to the National Library, Canberra, under the provisions of the Copyright Act.*

Austria

Oesterreichische Bibliographie; Verzeichnis der Österreichischer Neuerscheinungen. Bearb. von der Österreichischen Nationalbibliothek. Wien, 1946- . v.2- . Quarterly. **A173**

A listing of trade publications which also includes university and official publications, newspapers, periodicals, and music scores. Classified with author and subject index. Volume 1 announced for later publication.
Frequency varies: 1946, quarterly; 1947–48, monthly; 1949- , semimonthly, with quarterly indexes, and annual cumulated indexes.

Belgium

Bibliographie nationale. Dictionnaire des écrivains belges et catalogue de leurs publications 1830–80. Bruxelles, Weissenbruch, 1886–1910. 4v. **A174**

Aims to furnish a comprehensive record, for the period 1830–80, of works by Belgian authors (either citizens or residents of the country) published either in Belgium or abroad, with record also of earlier works by the same authors and of periodicals with which they were associated as either editors or regular contributors. Includes books, pamphlets, official publications, many reprints from periodicals and newspapers, theses. Information given for each work includes author's name (frequently with brief biographical data) title, place, publisher, date, size, paging, illustrations, price. Contents and other notes are frequently included, especially notes of reprints from periodicals.

Bibliotheca belgica. Bibliographie générale des Pays-Bas, fondée par Ferd. van der Haeghen et publiée sous sa direction. 1-3. ser. Gand, Vanderpoorten; La Haye, Nijhoff, 1880–1939. 54v. (1st–2d ser.) compl.; other v. (3d ser.) in progress. il. **A175**

1st ser., v.1-26, A-Z; v.27, Indexes. 2d ser., v.1-17, A-Man; v.18-19, Marques typographiques (A-Z); v.20-

26, Martial-Z; v.27, Indexes. 3d ser., livr. 201-216, in progress, scattered parts of alphabet.

Covers early works (with some inclusion of later editions) printed in Belgium and Holland and books by Belgian and Dutch authors printed elsewhere, giving for each work listed: full title, imprint and collation, location of copies, and often full bibliographical and historical notes with biographical data about authors and references to sources. Each index volume contains three indexes: (1) alphabetical by authors, titles, etc.; (2) chronological by date of publication; (3) typographical, by place and printer.

Coopman, Theophiel and **Broeckaert, Jan.** Bibliographie van den Vlaamschen taalstrijd. Gent, Siffer, 1904–14. 10 v. (K. Vlaamsche Academie voor Taal-en Letterkunde)   **A176**

> v.1-10, 1787–1886.

Foppens, Jean François. Bibliotheca belgica, sive Virorum in Belgio vitâ, scriptisque illustrium catalogus, librorumque nomenclatura; continens scriptores à clariss. viris Valerio Andrea, Auberto Miraeo, Francisco Sweertio, aliisque, recensitos, usque ad annum MDCLXXX. Bruxellis, P. Foppens, 1738. 2v.   **A177**

Vlaamsche bibliographie. Lijst der boeken, vlugen tijdschriften, muziekwerken, kaarten, platen en tabellen, in België van 1830 tot 1890 verschenen. Uitg. op last der Koninklijke Vlaamsche Academie voor Taal- en Letterkunde, door Fr. de Potter. Gent, Siffer, 1893-[1902]. 894p.   **A178**

> Classified, with author index.
> Incorporates all the material included in the various editions of the *Vlaamsche bibliographie,* 1851 (Snellaert) to 1888.

Current

Bibliographie de Belgique, 1. partie: Liste mensuelle des publications belges ou relatives à la Belgique, acquises par la Bibliothèque Royale, 1.- . année, 1875- . Bruxelles, Bibliothèque Royale, 1875- . v.1- . Monthly. Belgium, 100fr. per yr.; Étranger, 125fr.   **A179**

> This bibliography has undergone many changes in title, scope, plan, editor and publisher. For history of these, and for a collation by volumes of the set, *see* "Histoire des transformations de la Bibliographie de Belgique" by Fernand Remy, in *Bibliographie de Belgique* 57: 356-98, 1931. As at present organized, aims to cover books, pamphlets, etc., issued in Belgium, books by Belgian authors published abroad and books by foreigners relating to Belgium. A classified list with two alphabetical indexes, (1) subjects, (2) authors, in each number, and general subject and author indexes for each volume. Information given for each entry is in full catalog form and includes author's name, full title, place, publisher, date, size, illustrations, and usually price.

Catalogue général de la librairie belge d'expression française. Sept. 1944/1945- . Bruxelles,

Consortium d' Editions, [1946-]. v.1- . Annual.   **A180**

> List by authors with title index, followed by arrangement under classes. List of periodicals.

Bolivia

Gutiérrez, José Rosendo. Datos para la bibliografia boliviana. 1. sección. La Paz, Arzadum, 1875. 255p.   **A181**

> Lists 2203 items.

—— —— 2. suplemento; últimas adiciones y correcciones a la primera sección. La Paz, Impr. de la Union Americana, 1880. 24, 126p.

> nos. 2204-3089.
> No more published.

René-Moreno, Gabriel. Biblioteca boliviana; catalogo de la sección de libros i folletos. Santiago de Chile, Impr. Gutenberg, 1879. 880p.   **A182**

> Arranged alphabetically by title with index of authors, translators, etc. 3529 entries.

—— —— 1. suplemento . . . Epítome de un Catálogo de libros y folletos. 1879–99. Santiago de Chile, Impr. Barcelona, 1900. 349p.

> nos. 3530-5176.

—— —— 2. suplemento, 1900–1908. Santiago de Chile, Impr. Univ., 1908. 349p.

> nos. 5177-6815.
> The most important Bolivian bibliography.

Abecía, Valentín. Adiciones á la Biblioteca boliviana de Gabriel René-Moreno, con un apéndice del editor, 1602–1879. Santiago de Chile, Impr. Barcelona, 1899. 440p.   **A183**

Brazil

Simões dos Reis, Antonio. Bibliografia das bibliografias brasileiras. Rio de Janeiro, 1942. 186p. il. (Ministério da Educação e Saude. Instituto Nacional do Livro. Coleção B. I. Bibliografia I.) 8$.   **A184**

Sacramento Blake, Augusto Victorino Alves do. Diccionario bibliographico brazileiro. Rio de Janeiro, Typ. Nac., 1883–1902. 7v.   **A185**

> Arranged alphabetically by *first* names.

—— —— Indice alphabetico, comp. pelo Jango Fischer. Rio de Janeiro, Imp. Nac., 1937. 127p.

Rio de Janeiro. Instituto Nacional do livro. Bibliografia brasileira, 1938/39. Rio de Janeiro, 1941. 313p.   **A186**

> A dictionary catalog of books printed in Brazil during 1938 and 1939.

Current

Anuario brasileiro de literatura, 1937- . Rio de Janeiro, Pongetti, 1937- . v.1- . Annual. **A187**

Includes besides literary articles, etc., the "Movimento bibliográfico" of the year preceding.

Bulgaria

Téodorov-Balan, A. B'lgarski knigopis za sto godini, 1806–1905. Sofia, Drzhavna Pechatnitsa, 1909. 1667p. **A188**

A century of Bulgarian bibliography.

Current

Bulgarski knigopis. t.1, Knigi. Bulletin bibliographique des livres déposés à la Bibliothèque Nationale de Bulgarie à Sofia. Sofia, Narodna Biblioteka, 1897- . Irregular, 1897- , quarterly 1945- . **A189**

Classified, with author index.

Canada

McGill University. Montreal. Library School. Bibliography of Canadian bibliographies; comp. by the 1929 and 1930 classes in bibliography . . . under the direction of M. V. Higgins. Montreal, 1930. 45p. (McGill Univ. Pub., ser. 7, no.20) **A190**

Includes general, regional, local and subject bibliographies.

Canada. Archives. Catalogue of pamphlets in the Public Archives of Canada, with index, prepared by Magdalen Casey. Ottawa, Acland, 1931–32. 2v. (Pub. of the Public Archives of Canada, no.13) $1 per v. **A191**

v.1, 1493–1877; v.2, 1878–1931.

1st ed., 1903; 2d ed., covering period 1611–1867, prepared by Norman Fee, 1911. The new edition lists a total of 10,072 items, arranged chronologically, with author and subject indexes in each volume. Includes material published in Canada and pamphlets about Canada published elsewhere.

Dionne, Narcisse Eutrope. Inventaire chronologique. . . . Québec, 1905–12. 4v. and suppl. (76p.) **A192**

Published by the Royal Soc. of Canada. Also issued in its *Proceedings and transactions,* 2d ser., v.10-12, 14, 1904–06, 1908; 3d ser., v.5, 1911.

[v.1, pt.1] Inventaire chronologique des livres, brochures, journaux et revues publiés en langue française dans la province de Québec, depuis l'établissement de l'imprimerie au Canada jusqu'à nos jours, 1764–1905; [v.1, pt.2] Tables des noms et des matières; Inventaire chronologique des livres . . . etc., pub. en langue française dans la province de Québec . . . 1764–1906; v.2, Québec et Nouvelle France, bibliographie; Inventaire chronologique des ouvrages publiés à l'étranger en diverses langues . . . 1534–1906; v.3, Inventaire chronologique des livres, brochures, journaux et revues publiés en langue anglaise dans la province de Québec . . . 1764–1906; v.4, Inventaire chronologique des cartes, plans, atlas, relatifs à la Nouvelle-France et à la province de Québec, 1508–1908; suppl. 1904–12.

Haight, Willet Ricketson. Canadian catalogue of books, 1791–1897. Toronto, Haight, 1896–1904. 3v. **A193**

Basic volume, 1791–1895, pt.1 of a projected list for that period, 1896, 130p.; Supplements 1-2, 1896–97, Annual Canadian catalogue, 2v. 1898, 48p.; 1904, 57p. No more published.

Morgan, Henry James. Bibliotheca canadensis: or, A manual of Canadian literature. Ottawa, G. E. Desbarats, 1867. 411p. **A194**

"An alphabetical list of the authors of works, pamphlets and contributions to the periodical press, written in, or by natives of, or relating to the several provinces, now constituting the Dominion of Canada, their history, affairs and resources; to which are prefixed brief biographical notices of the several authors, followed by a catalogue of their productions, the place and year of publication, the number of pages and the size of each work or pamphlet, the title and year of publication of the magazine, periodical, or journal in which the papers or contributions mentioned have appeared, with succinct notices of the press, or criticisms thereon from competent authorities."—*Pref.*

The biographical sketches are occasionally of some length and include, in addition to authors whose books are listed, sketches of Canadian journalists for whom no separate publications are listed.

Current

Canadian catalogue of books published in Canada, about Canada, as well as those written by Canadians, 1921/22- . comp. by the Public Libraries, Toronto. [Toronto] Pub. as a suppl. to the Ontario library review, 1923- . v.1- . 50c ea. Annual. **A195**

From 1921/22 to 1943 includes books, pamphlets and selected government publications; 1944- , government publications omitted. Arrangement varies. Usually each annual number is in two main sections: (1) books in English; (2) books in French. Information given in the English section includes author, title, place, publisher, date, price.

Cumulative book index (A153) now includes books in English published by Canadian publishers.

Société des Écrivains Canadiens. Bulletin bibliographique. v.1- . Montreal, Société, 1937- . Annual. **A196**

In two sections: (1) Canadian works published in French; (2) French or foreign works published or reprinted in Canada.

Chile

Briseño, Ramón. Estadística bibliográfica de la literatura chilena. Obra compuesta, en virtud de encargo especial del consejo de la Universidad de Chile. Santiago de Chile, Impr. Chilena, 1862–79. 2v.   **A197**

t.1. 1812–1859. Impresos chilenos. Obras sobre Chile. Escritores chilenos; t.2. 1860–1876. Prólogo. Prensa chilena por órden alfabético. Prensa chilena por órden cronolójico. Prensa periodistica chilena. Bibliografía chilena en el país, desde 1812 hasta 1859. Bibliografía chilena en el extranjero, desde 1860 hasta 1876. Curiosidades bibliográfico-chilenas.

Laval, Ramón Arminio. Bibliografía de bibliografías chilenas. (In Santiago de Chile. Bibliografía general de Chile. 1915. v.1, p.i-lxix) **A198**

—— ——Suplemento y adiciones, por Hermina Elgueta de Ochsenius. Santiago de Chile, Imp. Cervantes, 1930. 71p.

Medina, José Toribio. Bibliografía de la imprenta en Santiago de Chile desde sus origenes hasta febrero de 1817. Santiago de Chile, Autor, 1891. 179p.   **A199**

—— —— Adiciones y amplicaciones. Santiago de Chile, Universidad de Chile, 1939. 140p. il.

—— Biblioteca hispano-chilena. (1523–1817). Santiago de Chile, Autor, 1897–99. 3v.   **A200**

Includes no books printed in Chile, only books printed in Europe or America by Chileans or by Spaniards who wrote in Chile.

Montt, Luis. Bibliografía chilena. Santiago de Chile, Impr. Univ., 1904–21. 3v.   **A201**

v.1, 1780–1811 (1918); v.2, 1812–1817 (1904); v.3, 1817–1818 (1921).

Of volume 1, 264p. were printed which the author intended to revise; of volume 3, 160p. were printed; sheets of both of these were destroyed, but in 1918 and 1921 reprints of the pages as originally printed were issued.

Revista de bibliografía chilena. Publicada por la Biblioteca Nacional, enero 1913—oct. 1918, 1927–1929. Santiago de Chile, Impr. Univ., 1913–29. 9v.   **A202**

Quarterly, 1927–29 (1913–18, monthly); 1913–18 have title: *Revista de bibliografía chilena y extranjera.* None issued, Nov. 1918–26.

No more published.

A valuable contemporary bibliography, which included special bibliographies in addition to the current record.

Santiago de Chile. Biblioteca Nacional. Bibliografía general de Chile. Por Emilio Vaïsse. Santiago de Chile, Impr. Univ., 1915–[18]. v.1-2.   **A203**

Repr. from *Revista de bibliografía chilena y extranjera.*

1.pt. Diccionario de autores y obras (bio-bibliografía y bibliografía): t.1, Bibliografía de bibliografías chilenas, por R. A. Laval. Diccionario: A-Barros Arana; t.2, Barros B-Bustos.

—— —— Suplemento y adiciones a la Bibliografía de bibliografías, por H. Elgueta de Ochsenius. Santiago de Chile, Imp. Cervantes, 1930. 71p.

—— Anuario de la prensa chilena, pub. por la Biblioteca Nacional. 1886-1916. Santiago de Chile, 1887–1927. 31v.   **A204**

Catalog of books deposited in the library under the law of 1872; and from 1891- , books by Chilean authors, or relating to Chile, published in other countries.

From 1892- , each volume, except 1895, contained an appendix of "publicaciones omitidas" from previous volumes. Musical compositions are entered in volumes for 1896–1900.

Current

Servicio bibliográfico chileno, 1940- . Santiago de Chile, Zamorano y Caperan, 1940- . Monthly.   **A205**

A monthly record of publications which includes prices in both Chilean and United States currency.

China

See also China—Bibliography, p. 494.

Cordier, Henri. L'imprimerie sino-européenne en Chine. Bibliographie des ouvrages publiés en Chine par les Européens au xviiᵉ et au xviiiᵉ siècle. Paris, Leroux, 1901. 73p. il. (Pub. de l'École des langues orientales vivantes, 5. sér. t.3)   **A206**

Lists mainly works written in the Chinese language or translated into Chinese by missionaries.

First published in 1883 as "Essai d'une bibliographie des ouvrages publiés en Chine par les Européens au xviiᵉ et au xviiiᵉ siècles" in *Mélanges orientaux* (Pub. de l'École des langues orientales vivantes. 2 sér., t.9).

Current

Quarterly bulletin of Chinese bibliography, v.1-4, 1934–37; n.s. v.1, 1940- . Peiping, Nat. Library of Peiping, 1934- . v.1- . Irregular.   **A207**

Includes general articles, book reviews, notes and news, an annotated selected list of new books published in China, divided into three sections: (1) Books in Chinese; (2) Books in foreign languages; (3) Government publications. Scope of contents varies.

Philobiblon; a quarterly review of Chinese publications. Director, Chiang Fu-Tsung; ed., C. S. Ch'ien. Nanking, Nat. Central Library, 1946- . v.1- . Quarterly.   **A208**

Colombia

Laverde Amaya, Isidoro. Bibliografia colombiana. Bogotá, M. Rivas, 1895. v.1. 296p.   **A209**

v.1, A-0; no more published.
Bio-bibliography; includes mainly nineteenth century publications, with a few of earlier date.

Medina, José Toribio. La imprenta en Bogotá (1739–1821). Notas bibliográficas. Santiago de Chile, Impr. Elzeviriana, 1904. 101p.   **A210**

—— La imprenta en Cartagena de las Indias (1809–1820). Notas bibliográficas. Santiago de Chile, Impr. Elzeviriana, 1904. 70p.   **A211**

Posada, Eduardo. Bibliografia bogotana. Bogotá, Colombia, Impr. Nacional, 1917–25. 2v. facsim. (Biblioteca de historia nacional, v.16, 36)   **A212**

Arranged chronologically, 1738–1831, with author and subject indexes both alphabetical and by date.

Costa Rica

Dobles Segreda, Luis. Indice bibliográfico de Costa Rica. San José, Lehmann, 1927–36. v.1-9.   **A213**

t.1, sec. 1, Agricultura y veterinaria; sec. 2, Ciencias físicas y naturales; t.2, sec. 3, Filologiá y gramática; sec. 4, Geografía y geología; t.3, sec. 5, Matemáticas, ingeniería y finanzas; sec. 6, Psicología, filosofía y religión; t.4, sec. 7, Novela, cuento y artículo literario; sec. 8, Teatro; t.5, sec. 9, Historia hasta 1900; t.6, sec. 10, Historia desde 1900 hasta 1933; t.7, sec. 11, and t.8, sec. 11, (cont) Política y derecho desde 1831 hasta 1921; t.8, sec. 12, Milicia; t.9, sec. 13, Hígiene y Medicina.

Other volumes were projected to cover educación, sociología y demografía, poesía, Indice alfabetico de autores, (biográfico y bibliográfico).

Lines, Jorge A. Libros y folletos publicados en Costa Rica durante los años 1830–1849. San José, Univ. de Costa Rica, Facultad de Letras y Filosofía, 1944. 151p.   **A214**

Current

San José, Costa Rica. Biblioteca Nacional. Boletin bibliográfico; publicaciones nacionales correspondientes al año 1935–38- . San José, Impr. Nac., 1939- . Annual.   **A215**

Cuba

Bachiller y Morales, Antonio. Catálogo de libros y folletos publicados en Cuba desde la introduccion de la imprenta hasta 1840. (In his Apuntes para la historia de las letras y de la instruccion publica de la Isla de Cuba. Habana, P. Massana. 3(1861): 121-241. Reprinted in his Apuntes . . . Habana, Cultural, 1936–37. v.3, p. 243-457)   **A216**

Arranged chronologically. No index.

—— —— Suplementos y adiciones. (Revista de Cuba 7:354-64, 491-98; 8:71-78, 124-35, abril, mayo, julio, agosto 1880)

Medina, José Toribio. La imprenta en La Habana (1707–1810): notas bibliográficas. Santiago de Chile, Impr. Elzeviriana, 1904. 199p.   **A217**

Peraza Sarausa, Fermin. Bibliografías cubanas. Wash., [Govt. Prt. Off.] 1945. 58p. (U.S. Library of Congress [Latin Amer. ser. no.7]) 20c. **A218**

At head of title: The Library of Congress. Hispanic Foundation.
Introduction in Spanish and English. Annotations in Spanish.

Trelles y Govín, Carlos Manuel. Ensayo de bibliografía cubana de los siglos XVII y XVIII. Seguido de unos apuntes para la bibliografía dominicana y portorriqueña. Matanzas, "El Escritorio," 1907–08. 228p., and suppl., 76p.   **A219**

—— Bibliografía cubana del siglo XIX. Matanzas, Quirós y Estrada, 1911–15. 8v.   **A220**

t.1, 1800–1825; t.2, 1826–1840. Seguido de una Relación de periódicos publicados en Cuba en el siglo XX, por F. Llaca, y unas Noticias curiosas referentes á escritores de los siglos XVII y XVIII, por M. Perez Beato; t.3-8, 1841–1899; Ensayo de biblioteca cubana del siglo XIX; Indice.

—— Bibliografía cubana del siglo XX (1900–1916). Matanzas, Quirós y Estrada, 1916–17. 2v.   **A221**

—— Biblioteca científica cubana. Matanzas, J. F. Oliver, 1918–20. v.1-2. il.   **A222**

Lists 9500 titles of books and periodical articles.

—— Biblioteca geográfica cubana. Matanzas, J. F. Oliver, 1920–25. 340p., and suppl., 64p.   **A223**

Main work and supplement list 3900 titles of books and periodical articles.

—— Biblioteca histórica cubana. Matanzas, J. F. Oliver, 1922–26. 3v.   **A224**

Lists 17,000 titles of books and periodical articles.

Current

Anuario bibliográfico cubana: 1937- . La Habana, Anuario Bibliográfico Cubano, 1938- . v.1- . Annual. (1948, $3)   **A225**

Editor, Fermin Peraza Sarausa.
Arrangement varies from year to year but each issue gives an excellent coverage.

Czechoslovakia

Knihopis českých a slovenských tisků od doby nejstarší až do konce XVIII. století. Vydala Komise pro Knihopisný Soupis Českých a Slovenských Tisků až do konce XVIII. století. Praze, Statní Tiskarna, 1925–48. v.1-2, pts. 1-4. (In progress) Price per pt. varies.   **A226**

v.1, (to 1500) A-Z, and atlas of facsim.; v.2, Tisky z Let, 1501–1800, pts. 1-4, A-L.

Title varies: v.1-v.2, sešit 18, *Knihopis československých tisků.*

Nosovský, Karel and Pražák, Vilém. Soupis československé literatury za léta 1901–1925. . . . V Praze, Nákladem Svazu Knihkupců a Nakladatelů, 1929–38. 2v. in 3.   **A227**

v.1-2, author list, A-Z; v.3, classified subject index.

Current

Bibliografický katalog Československé Republiky; literárnatvorba z roku, 1929- . V Praze, Nákladem Ministerstva Školství a Národní Osvěty, 1930- . v.1- . Annual.   **A228**

Denmark
Early

Nielsen, Lauritz Martin. Dansk bibliografi, 1482–1550, 1551-1600, med saerligt hensyn til dansk bogtrykkerkunsts historie. København, Gyldendal, 1919–35. 2v. (xlvii, 247p.; xliii, 677p.) and registre (126p.) il. Kr. 61.   **A229**

1482–1550: Authors and titles list, A-Z, nos. 1-298, 1919, 247p.; 1551–1600: Author and title list, A-AE, nos. 299-1672, 1931–33, 677p.; Registre: alphabetical author index, alphabetical title index, chronological index, subject index.

Two companion works listing together 1672 items and giving for each item, title, detailed collation, bibliographical references and location of copies. Indexes of places and of printers and publishers in each work.

Bruun, Christian Walther. Bibliotheca danica. Systematisk Fortegnelse over den danske Literatur fra 1482 til 1830, efter Samlingerne i det Store Kongelige Bibliothek i Kjøbenhavn. Kjøbenhavn, Gyldendal, 1877–1931. v.1-4, suppl., and index.   **A230**

Bd. 1: Theologi, Retsvidenskab, Lægevidenskab, Philosophi, Pædagogik, Statsvidenskaberne, de skjønne Videnskaber og Kunster, 1877; Bd. 2: De exakte, økonomiske og tekniske Videnskaber, Geographi og Rejser, Historie I: Almindelig Historie, Historie II: De tre nordiske Riger, Danmarks Topographi, Statistik, Stats-og Kulturforhold, 1886; Bd. 3: Historie II, Fortsættelse: Danmarks Historie: Færøerne, Island og Grønland, De danske Besiddelser i Vestindien, Slesvig og Holsten, Norge, Personalhistorie, 1896; Bd. 4: Sprogvidenskab, Literatur, Tidsskrifter af blandet Indhold og Aviser, 1902; Supplement, ved Lauritz Nielsen, 1914. Registerbd. ved Lauritz Nielsen, 1927–31. 353p. (An index of: (1) Authors; (2) Anonymous works; (3) Subjects.)

—— Supplement 1831–1840 til Bibliotheca danica og Dansk Bogfortegnelse, udarbejdet af H.

Ehrencron-Müller. Hft. 1-4. København, Gads, 1943–48. Hft. 1-4. Kr. 12 per Hft.   **A231**

Hft. 1, Alfabetisk Fortegnelse, 1943, 422 col.; Hft. 2, Systematisk Fortegnelse, 1944, col. 425-860; Hft. 3-4, Supplement til Bibliotheca danica . . . Bibliotheca Slesvico-Holsatica til 1840; alfabetisk Fortegnelse, 1945, col. 863-1184; systematisk Fortegnelse, 1948, col. 1187-1564.

Hft. 1-2 are designed to fill the gap in Danish bibliography between the Bruun *Bibliotheca danica* (A230) which covers the period to 1830 and the *Dansk Bogfortegnelse* (A232) which starts with 1841. Hft. 3-4 form a catalog of Schleswig-Holstein literature from the earliest times to 1840.

19th and 20th centuries

Dansk Bogfortegnelse, 1841–58- . København, Gads, 1861- . Quinquennial since 1915.   **A232**

1841–58, Samlet af F. Fabricius, 252p.; 1859–68, 229p.; 1869–80, 308p.; 1881–92, 398p.; 1893–1900, 379p.; 1901–08, 498p.; 1909–14, 597p.; 1915–19, 598p. (includes Islandsk Bogfortegnelse, 1915–1919); 1920–24, 632p. (includes Islandsk Bogfortegnelse, 1920–24); 1925–29, 656p. (includes Islandsk Bogfortegnelse, 1925–29); 1930–34, 724p. (includes Islandsk Bogfortegnelse, 1930–34); 1935–39, 704p. Kr. 70; 1940–44, Hft. 1- , A- . (In progress) (Kr. 6. 40 per Hft.)

1859–92, Udarb. af J. Vahl; 1893–1934, Udarb. af H. Ehrencron-Müller; 1935- , Udarb. af H. Topsøe Jensen and E. A. Jensen.

Ehrencron-Müller, Holger. Stikordsregister til den danske Skønlitteratur indtil 1840. . . . København, Gads, 1941. 29p.   **A233**

—— —— 1841–1908. København, Gads, 1918. 81p.

—— —— 1909–1940. København, Gads, 1941. 128p.

Dania Polyglotta; répertoire bibliographique des ouvrages, études, articles, etc., en langues étrangères parus en Danemark de 1901 à 1944. I: Ouvrages. Copenhague, Bibliothèque Royale, 1947. 299p.   **A234**

Publié par l'Institut Danois des Échanges Internationaux de Publications Scientifiques et Littéraires sous la rédaction de son directeur K. Schmidt-Phiseldeck avec la collaboration de Henning Einersen.

Includes books and articles published in Denmark in foreign languages by native and foreign scholars. Does not include Danish works published abroad; nor material in the Scandinavian languages, which are not considered foreign; nor the writings of scholars of Iceland, Greenland and the Faroe Islands. These are to be found listed in *Dansk Bogfortegnelse* (A232).

Works are grouped under language: French (34p.); English (129p.); German (75p.); Latin (4p.); Italian, Spanish, Portuguese, Dutch, Russian (3p.); various languages (7p.). Within each language group, material covers description, early history and civilization; general history and politics; language, literature, philosophy and music; medicine; natural science, mathematics and technology. A final section lists language dictionaries. Author index.

Continued by the annual *Dania Polyglotta*, 1. année, 1945- . Copenhague, Bibl. Royale, 1946- .

Current

Dansk Bogfortegnelse, 1851- . København, Gads, 1851- . Annual. **A235**

Annual cumulation of the current list of the same title forming an annual supplement to the 5-year *Dansk Bogfortegnelse* (A232).

The current list is published irregularly, (18-20 times) throughout the year cumulating at intervals. Since volume 82, 1932, the annual cumulation forms the permanent volume for the year. An author and title list followed by a classified index.

A separately paged supplement "Islandsk Bogfortegnelse" was included irregularly, 1899–1920, *see* A378. 1851–55, called *Maanedlig dansk Bogfortegnelse*.

Dominican Republic

Floren Lozano, Luis. Bibliografia de la bibliografia dominicana. Trujillo, Roques Roman, 1948. 66p. **A236**

Current

Anuario bibliografico dominicano. 1946- . Ciudad Trujillo, 1947- . Annual. **A237**

At head of title: Oficina de Canje y Difusion Cultural. Supersedes the *Boletin bibliografico dominicano* of which only two numbers were published, number 1, July–Aug. 1945, which covered 1944 and number 2, Sept.–Dec. 1945 which covered 1945.

Ecuador

Espinosa Cordero, Nicolás. Bibliografía ecuatoriana. 1534–1809. Cuenca, Imp. del Colegio Nacional "Benigno Malo," 1934. 171p. (pt.4 of his Estudios literarios y bibliográficos, p.93-256) **A238**

Includes brief biographical notes.

Medina, José Toribio. La imprenta en el Quito (1760–1818): notas bibliográficas. Santiago de Chile, Impr. Elzeviriana, 1904. 86p. **A239**

Finland

Katalog öfver den svenska literaturen i Finland samt arbeten på främmande språk. 1886–[1900]. Helsingfors, 1892–1924. 6v. (Skrifter utgifna af Svenska Literatursällskapet i Finland. 21, 53, 54, 166: 1 and 2) **A240**

Title varies slightly.
Editors: 1886–1890, 1896–1900, H. Bergroth; 1891–95, Y. Hiru.; 1901–05, Emil Hasselblatt; 1906–15, Holger Nohrström.

Suomalainen kirjallisuus 1544- . Aakkosellinen ja aineenmukainen luettelo. La littérature finnoise 1544- . Catalogue alphabétique et sys-tématique. Helsingissä, 1878–1905; Helsinki, 1912- . (Added t.p.: Suomalaisen kirjallisuuden seuran. Toimituksia. 57osa; 1- lisävihko) **A241**

The set consists of (1) a basic volume, 1544–1877, by Valfrid Vasenius; (2) five supplements to this, covering 1878–79, 1880–85, 1886–91, 1892–95, 1896–1900; and (3) continuation volumes by S. Pakarinen, covering 1901–05, 1906–10, 1911–15, 1916–20, 1921–23, 1924–26, 1927–29, 1930–32, 1933–35, 1936–38.

Current

Suomessa Ilmestyneen Kirjallisuuden Luettelo. Katalog över i Finland utkommen Litteratur. Helsinki, Suomalaisen Kirjallisuuden Seuran Kirjapainon Oy, [19-?]. Quarterly. MK 60 **A242**

France

Paris. Bibliothèque Nationale. Catalogue général des livres imprimés. Auteurs. Paris, Impr. Nat., 1900- . v.1- . **A243**

v.1- , A- .
The Bibliothèque Nationale has received copies of all books published in France since the establishment, by law, of the *dépôt légal* in the reign of Henri II. It has the largest collection of French books in existence and its printed *Catalogue* is the most important general bibliography of French publications. For full description *see* A35.

Répertoire de bibliographie française; contenant tous les ouvrages imprimés en France et aux colonies et les ouvrages français publiés à l'étranger, 1501–1930. . . . Paris, Letouzey, 1937–41. fasc. 1-10. (In progress) 100fr. per fasc. **A244**

v.1 (fasc. 1-6), A-Angélique; v.2 (fasc. 7-10), Angelis-Arthaud.
A comprehensive record of French bibliography, 1501–1930, including, in general, books published in France and books in French published in French colonies and abroad. Omits certain types of publications, e.g., periodicals issued more frequently than once a year, certain types of public documents and administrative publications, music without text or illustrations, books in oriental languages which have title pages only in oriental characters, reprints of primary and secondary school textbooks, geographic maps, etc. (For full list of omitted classes *see* v.1, p.xiii.) An alphabetical list, including in one alphabet authors' names, anonymous titles, pseudonyms, society names; information given for each entry includes, in general: title of work, place, publisher or printer, date and size, sometimes paging, with occasional contents and other notes, e.g., periodical or other work from which a book or pamphlet was reprinted and brief biographical data about some authors.

Early

British Museum. Dept. of Printed Books. Short-title catalogue of books printed in France and or French books printed in other countries from 1470 to 1600 now in the British Museum. Lond. pr. by order of the Trustees, 1924. 491p. **A245**

Prepared by Dr. Henry Thomas assisted by A. F. Johnson and A. G. Macfarlane.

Books printed in France, p.1-450; Books in French printed elsewhere, p.451-91.

An important record of about 12,000 editions including many items not found in the printed catalog of the Bibliothèque Nationale. Information given includes: author, brief title, editor, translator, etc., place, publisher, date, size.

Brunet, Gustave. La France littéraire au xv siècle, ou, Catalogue raisonné des ouvrages en tout genre imprimés en langue française jusqu'à l'an 1500. Paris, Franck, 1865. 256p.　　**A246**

Brunet, Jacques Charles. Manuel du libraire et de l'amateur de livres. 5. éd. augm. Paris, Didot, 1860-80. 9v.　　**A247**

For full description *see* A22.

La Croix du Maine, François Grudé and **Du Verdier, Antoine.** Les bibliothèques françoises de La Croix du Maine et de Du Verdier. nouv. ed. rev. cor., and augm. . . . par Rigoley de Juvigny. Paris, Saillant & Nyon, 1772-73. 6v.　　**A248**

The original edition of La Croix du Maine published Paris, 1584; of Du Verdier, Lyons, 1585. The two works complement each other and form a bio-bibliographical catalog of French publications to about the end of the sixteenth century. A valuable record although it includes many inaccuracies.

Rothschild, James, *baron de.* Catalogue des livres composant la bibliothèque de feu M. le baron James de Rothschild. Paris, Morgand, 1884-1920. 5v. il.　　**A249**

Catalog of a fine private collection, listing many rare books with full descriptions.

v.1-3, Main list and 1st supplement; v.4, 2d supplement; appendix: Table des personnages qui figurent dans les ballets portés au present catalogue; v.5, 3d supplement; detailed general index.

Tchemerzine, Avenir. Bibliographie d'éditions originales et rares d'auteurs français des xve, xvie, xviie et xviiie siècles contenant environ 6000 fac-similés de titres et de gravures. Paris, Plée, 1927-34. v.1-10. il　　**A250**

v.1-10, A-Voiture.

18th century

Quérard, Joseph Marie. La France littéraire, ou Dictionnaire bibliographique des savants, historiens et gens de lettres de la France, ainsi que des littérateurs étrangers qui ont écrit en francais, plus particulièrement pendant les xviiie et xixe siècles. Paris, Didot, 1827-64. 12v.　　**A251**

v.1-10, A-Z; v.11-12, supplements containing: Corrections, additions; Auteurs, pseudonymes et anonymes; v.11, A-Razy; v.12, Re-Roguet.

An author list, giving brief biographical notes and titles of books with place and date of publication, publisher, size, number of volumes and original price. Some bibliographical and historical notes. Covers eighteenth century and early nineteenth century to 1826.

Volumes 11 and 12 (published 1854-64) list by real name the authors of pseudonymous and anonymous works, giving the pseudonyms, under which each has written, with brief biographical information, titles of works, etc. They serve as a kind of index to Quérard's *Supercheries littéraires dévoilées* (A105).

19th and 20th centuries

Quérard, Joseph Marie [and others]. La littérature française contemporaine, 1827-49. Le tout accompagné de notes biographiques et littéraires. Paris, Daguin, 1842-57. 6v.　　**A252**

A continuation of Quérard's *La France littéraire* (A251), on the same general plan.

Catalogue général de la librairie française, 1840-1925. Paris, Lorenz, 1867-1945. v.1-34.　　**A253**

Publisher varies.

Usually cited as *Lorenz.*

v.1-11, edited by Otto Lorenz; v.12-28, pt.2, by D. Jordell; v.28, pt.3-v.32, by Henri Stein; v.33-34, by the Service Bibliographique Hachette.

The standard French list for the nineteenth and twentieth centuries and one of the most important of modern national bibliographies. Covers French publications by periods ranging from three years to 25 years, the volumes for each period consisting of: (1) a main author and title list containing full information, i.e., author's full name, full title of book, edition, place (if other than Paris), date, publisher, paging, size, price, and occasional brief notes; and (2) a subject list arranged by broad subjects, with briefer information, i.e., title, author, size, date and price only. Includes books, pamphlets, some theses and annuals but not periodicals, and lists some Belgian and Swiss publications, i.e., books in French published in Belgium or Switzerland but handled regularly also by some French firm. Special features are: (1) the inclusion of brief biographical notes about the authors whose works are listed; (2) the linking together of all entries for the same author by cross references from the later to the earlier volumes; (3) occasional brief notes which tell whether a book has been crowned by the French Academy and which refer, in case of reissues or later editions, to date of first edition and, in case of books or pamphlets reprinted from periodicals, give reference to volume or date of the periodical, etc. The information about original publication in periodicals is often very useful.

Vicaire, Georges. Manuel de l'amateur de livres du xixe siècle, 1801-1893. Paris, Rouquette, 1894-1920. 8v.　　**A254**

v.1-7, A-Z, 1801-1893; v.8, Table des ouvrages cités. Crowned by the French Academy.

An attempt to do for nineteenth century French literature what Brunet's *Manuel* (A22) does for general literature of an earlier period. Covers in large part the same period as Lorenz (A253), but with a selection of material, listing fewer titles than Lorenz but giving fuller information and annotations for those listed. Gives full titles and bibliographical notes, original price, and, often, prices realized at various auction sales.

Le Soudier, Henri. Bibliographie française; recueil de catalogues des éditeurs français. 2. éd., augm. Paris, Le Soudier, 1900. 10v.   **A255**

Collection of about 174 publishers' catalogs, arranged alphabetically by firms, with author and subject indexes in volume 10. Lists about 125,000 titles.

—— 2. sér., paraissant par périodes quinquennales, comprenant les ouvrages parus depuis le 1er jan. 1900. . . . Paris, Le Soudier, 1908–11. 2v. in 3.

v.1, 1900–04; v.2 (in 2 pts.), 1905–09.

A dictionary catalog, authors, titles and subjects in one alphabet, with full information given under the authors' names and cross references from subject and titles. Includes books and annuals, but not periodicals. Continued by the annual indexes of the *Mémorial de la librairie française*, 1910–15, which are annual volumes on the same plan as the 5-year lists.

Chéron, Paul. Catalogue général de la librairie française au xixe siècle, indiquant, par ordre alphabétique de noms d'auteurs les ouvrages publiés en France 1800–1855. Paris, Courrier de la Libr., 1856–59. 3v.   **A256**

Gives brief biographical data.

Issued as premium (forming one volume per year) to subscribers of the *Courrier de la librairie*, which was discontinued in 1859, the work extending to Dubuisson only.

A full list, as far as issued, including books not given in Quérard (A251-A252) or Lorenz (A253). Unfortunately discontinued after the letter D.

Federn, Robert. Répertoire bibliographique de la littérature française des origines à 1911. Leipzig-Berlin, Volckmar, 1913. 612p.   **A257**

A general list of French publications in print in 1911, selective rather than complete, for books in philosophy, theology, literature and art, geography, archeology, biography and social, economic and political history. Author's name and dates, title of book, volumes, number of editions, size, date of original and of latest edition, gross and net price, publisher, series and code word for ordering by telegraph are given for each book listed. Subject and title indexes. Contains also a title list of French series, a directory of publishers, and a list of booksellers arranged by their specialties.

Current

"Biblio," catalogue des ouvrages parus en langue française dans le monde entier, Oct. 1933- . Paris, Service Bibliographique des Messageries Hachette, 1933- . v.1- . Monthly (10 issues per yr. with annual cumulations).   **A258**

Subtitle varies.

The most easily used trade bibliography covering books published in France and French books published in Belgium, Switzerland, Canada, etc. A dictionary catalog, published monthly with annual cumulation, entering each book under author, subject, and title, with many cross

references. Full information, given under author entry, includes author's name, full title, date, place (if other than Paris), publisher, paging, size, illustrations, series, price.

Bibliographie de la France; ou, Journal général de l'imprimerie et de la librairie. Paris, Cercle de la Libr., 1811- . v.1- . Weekly.   **A259**

Arrangement and parts issued vary.

The standard weekly list, recording material received through the *dépôt légal*, including books, pamphlets, official publications, music, prints and, in addition, a monthly record of gifts to the Bibliothèque Nationale. At present each number consists of three main parts: Bibliographie officielle, Chronique, Annonces.

1. pt.: The *Bibliographie* contains Livres, a classed list of books, pamphlets, etc., recorded with full cataloging information which includes author, full title, place, publisher, date, size, paging, price (if information about price is supplied by publisher), and press mark of the book in the Bibliothèque Nationale; (the cataloging for this list is done by the Bibliothèque Nationale). The following supplements are published at irregular intervals: Suppl. A, Périodiques; Suppl. B, Gravures, estampes et photographies; Suppl. C, Musique; Suppl. D, Thèses (for a previous year, e.g., 1943 is appearing in 1949); Suppl. E, Atlas, cartes et plans. At the end of the year there is a general author and title index to the record of books and gifts and an alphabetical list of periodicals.

2. pt.: The *Chronique* contains publishing news, postal and copyright information, legal and government notes, occasional historical articles, obituaries, etc.

3. pt.: The *Annonces* section consists of advertising pages with weekly and monthly classified indexes, called *Les livres de la semaine*, and *Les livres du mois*.

Librairie française, catalogue général des ouvrages en vente. 1. jan. 1930. Paris, Cercle de la Libr., 1930–34. 4v.   **A260**

1. pt.: v.1-2, Répertoire par auteurs; 2. pt.: Répertoire par titres; Supplement, to 1933.

Gives for each book listed: author, title, paging, date, publisher, binding, illustration, format, price.

—— 1933–1946, Répertoire par auteurs, 2v.; Répertoire par titres. 1204p. 1947–49.

Regional

❧ There are many regional bibliographies, for provinces, departments, towns, etc., which must often be used for local publications not included in the general bibliographies listed above. Local bibliographies are listed freely in the *Répertoire bibliographique de l'histoire de France* (V236). For lists of older publications *see* Stein's *Manuel*, p.501-07 (A6), and article "Bibliographie" in *La Grande encyclopédie* 6:637-38 (D26).

Germany
Early

Borchling, Conrad and **Claussen, Bruno.** Niederdeutsche Bibliographie; Gesamtverzeichnis der niederdeutschen Drucke bis zum Jahre 1800. . . . Neumünster, Karl Wachholst, 1931–36. 2v. **A261**

v.1, 1473–1600; v.2, 1601–1800; Nachträge, col. 1801–70; Ergänzungen u. Verbesserungen, col. 1871–91; Indexes (of places, printers, names, first lines, catchwords, etc.), col. 1893–2018; Letzte Nachträge u. Verbesserungen, col. 2019–20.

Lists more than 4700 items, described in detail and with some location of copies.

Panzer, Georg Wolfgang Franz. Annalen der ältern deutschen Litteratur. . . . Nürnberg, Grattenauer, 1788–1805. 2v. **A262**

v.1, to 1520; v.2, 1521–26.
Zusatze. . . . Leipzig, Hempel, 1802. 198p. suppl. to v.1.
Supplemented by Joseph Heller in *Serapeum*, 4. Jahrg. (1843), p.299–303, 6. Jahrg. (1845), p. 312–320, 327–333; and by E. O. Weller's *Repertorium typographicum. Die deutsche Literatur in ersten Viertel des sechzehnten Jahrhunderts*. . . . Nördlingen, 1864 (added t.-p.: Georg Wolfgang Panzers, Annalen der älteren deutschen Literatur (MD-MDXXVI. 3. Th.)

18th–20th centuries

Heinsius, Wilhelm. Allgemeines Bücher-Lexikon, 1700–1892. Leipzig, Brockhaus, 1812–94. 19v. **A263**

No more published.
Through 1867 prices are given in thalers and neugroschen, after 1867 in marks and pfennigs.
Supplementary lists: 1700–1827, Romane, Schauspiele, 1868–92, Karten und Pläne.

Hinrichs, J. C. Fünfjahrs-Katalog der im deutschen Buchhandel erschienenen Bücher, Zeitschriften, Landkarten, etc.; titel Verzeichnis und Sachregister, 1851–1912. Leipzig, Hinrichs, 1857–1913. 13v. **A264**

Five-year cumulations of *Hinrichs' Halbjahrs-Katalog*, with additions and corrections. No more published.

Kayser, Christian Gottlob. Vollständiges Bücher-Lexikon, 1750–1910. Leipzig, Tauchnitz, 1834–1911. 36v. **A265**

Publisher varies.
An author list with some title entries, giving, for each book listed, author, title, place, publisher, date, volumes, paging, series, prices of different editions, etc. Entry is generally under the author's name, but works having such titles as Wörterbuch, Lexikon, Jahresverzeichnis, etc., are generally entered under title rather than compiler, and under that entry are alphabeted by main subject word in title, the alphabetizing word being indicated by a different type or spacing. Before 1870 prices were given in thalers and neugroschen, after that date in marks and pfennigs. Includes some Austrian and Swiss publications, as well as German.

—— —— Sachregister. Leipzig, Schumann, 1838. 511p.

Indexes v.1–6, 1750–1832.

—— —— Sach-und-Schlagwortregister, 1891–1910. Leipzig, Tauchnitz, 1896–1912. 5v.

Each index covers two volumes of the main work, as follows: v.27–28, 1891–94; v.29–30, 1895–98; v.31–32, 1899–1902; v.33–34, 1903–06; v.35–36, 1907–10.

Thelert, Gustav. Supplement zu Heinsius, Hinrichs und Kayser's Bücher-Lexikon. . . . Grossenhain, Baumert, 1893. 405p. **A266**

Subtitle: Verzeichniss einer Anzahl Schriften, welche seit der Mitte des neunzehnten Jahrhunderts in Deutschland erschienen, in den genannten Katalogen aber garnicht oder fehlerhaft aufgeführt sind; mit bibliographischen Bemerkungen.

Deutsches Bücherverzeichnis der Jahre 1911–40, eine Zusammenstellung der im deutschen Buchhandel erschienenen Bücher, Zeitschriften und Landkarten, mit einem Stich-und Schlagwortregister. Leipzig, Börsenverein der Deutschen Buchhändler, 1915–43. v.1–22. **A267**

Five-year cumulations (except 1911–14 and 1915–20) usually consisting of two author volumes and two subject index volumes for each period.
A continuation of Heinsius (A263), Hinrichs (A264), and Kayser (A265) on the same general plan as Kayser but with some changes and developments, as follows: (1) the scope is enlarged to include works in German published elsewhere in Europe; (2) the subject index is much enlarged and extended.

Georg, Karl. Schlagwort-Katalog; Verzeichnis der Bücher und Landkarten sachlicher Anordnung, 1883–1912. Hannover, Lemmermann, 1889–1913. 7v. **A268**

Publisher varies.
v.1, 1883–87; v.2, 1888–92; v.3, 1893–97; v.4, 1898–1902; v.5, 1903–07; v.6, 1908–10; v.7, 1910–12.

Gesammt-Verlags-Katalog des deutschen Buchhandels. Münster in Westfalen, Russell, 1881–94. 17v. **A269**

v.0, Vorwort, General-Firmenverzeichniss, Nachzügler; v.1–11, Deutsches Reich; v.12–13, Österreich-Ungarn; v.14, Schweiz; v.15, Ausland; v.16, Ergänzungs-Band.
Arranged by place and under place by publishers' lists. Now out of date and no longer useful as an in-print list but represents a comprehensive gathering by publishers' names.

Deutscher Literatur-Katalog, 1904/05- . Leipzig, Koehler und Volckmar, 1904- . (Irregular, not issued, 1916–19, 1921–23, 1925) **A270**

Publisher, title and coverage vary.
Since 1929 in 2v. covering: [v.1] Alphabetisches Verzeichnis der Bücher, Atlanten, Kalender, Mappenwerke, Sammlungen; Alphabetisches Verzeichnis über gebundene Musikalien; [v.2] Schlagwort- und Stichwortregister und Literaturnachweise nebst Titel-Register und Verfassernachweisen.

Current

Halbjahrsverzeichnis der Neuerscheinungen des deutschen Buchhandels mit Voranzeigen, Verlags-

und Preisänderungen, Stich-und Schlagwortregister, 1797–1944. Leipzig, Börsenverein der Deutschen Buchhändler, 1798–1944. v.1-292. 1. Hlbjh. **A271**

Title varies. Until 1915 was *Hinrichs' Halbjahrs-Katalog.*

Jahresverzeichnis des deutschen Schriftums, 1945/46- . bearb. und hrsg. von der Deutschen Bücherei und dem Börsenverein der Deutschen Buchhändler zu Leipzig. Leipzig, Börsenvereins, 1948- . v.1- . **A272**

Cumulates Reihe A and B of the *Deutsche National-bibliographie* (A273) and is intended to supersede the *Halbjahrsverzeichnis* (A271) which was discontinued in 1944.

Deutsche Nationalbibliographie, bearb. von der Deutschen Bücherei, hrsg. u. verlegt vom Börsenverein der deutschen Buchhändler zu Leipzig. Allgemeine Ausg. Reihe A, Reihe B. Leipzig, 1931- . **A273**

Continues with changed title and scope, the *Wöchentliches Verzeichnis,* 1842–1930. Now includes publications outside the regular book trade.

Contents: Reihe A, Neuerscheinungen des Buchhandels; Reihe B, Neuerscheinungen ausserhalb des Buchhandels.

Reihe A suspended after no. 1/2 of 1945 until Aug. 1946. From Sept. 1946- covers Russian zone only. Continued for the western zone by *Bibliographie der deutschen Bibliothek, Reihe A* (A274). Reihe B suspended 1945–Aug. 1946. Sept. 1946- covers the Russian zone only.

Bibliographie der deutschen Bibliothek. Frankfurt am Main, Deutsche Bibliothek, 1947- . v.1- . Monthly. DM. 4 **A274**

Reihe A, Neuerscheinungen des Buchhandels. 1947 issued in 10 nos. with 2 suppl. and annual index; 1948 issued in 30 nos. with author and title indexes, published semiannually.

Berliner Verleger-und Buchhändler-Vereinigung. Das neue Buch: Katalog der Neuerscheinungen, 1945–1947. Berlin, Mann, 1947. 192p. **A275**

Börsenblatt für den deutschen Buchhandel (Leipzig, published since 1834) **A276**

Was a daily trade publication. Since 1946 it has been published in two editions, one in Leipzig (weekly), the other in Frankfurt (twice weekly).

Festschriften

Corsten, Hermann. Hundert Jahre deutscher Wirtschaft in Fest-und Denkschriften; eine Bibliographie. Köln, Schroeder, 1937. 428p. (Kölner Bibliographische Arbeiten, Bd.2) **A277**

Classified with author and subject indexes.

Harrassowitz, Otto. Festschriften, 1911–1927, in Deutschland veröffentlicht aus Anlass von Ju-

biläen in der gelehrten Welt nebst einigen Werken der Jubilare. Leipzig, Harrassowitz, [1928?]. 27p. **A278**

690 entries, classified.

Great Britain

Growoll, Adolf. Three centuries of English booktrade bibliography. . . . N.Y., Dibdin Club, 1903. 195p. **A279**

Contents: The beginnings of booktrade bibliography; Maunsell's Catalogue; Forty years of bibliographical endeavours, 1618–1658; London's Catalogues, and the Company of Stationers' list; Clavel's bibliographic work and the Term catalogues; Early English booktrade journals; Booktrade bibliography in the eighteenth century; Booktrade bibliography in the nineteenth century; A list of catalogues, etc., published for the English booktrade, 1595–1902, compiled and annotated by Wiberforce Eames.

Church, Elihu Dwight. A catalogue of books, consisting of English literature and miscellanea, including many original editions of Shakespeare, forming a part of the library of E. D. Church, comp. and annotated by George Watson Cole. . . . N.Y., Dodd, 1909. 2v. il. **A280**

An admirably made catalog of rare books, especially important for its very fine bibliographical notes, and location of copies of the books described.

Collier, John Payne. Bibliographical and critical account of the rarest books in the English language. N.Y., Scribner, 1866. 4v. **A281**

Corns, Albert Reginald and **Sparke, Archibald.** Bibliography of unfinished books in the English language, with annotations. Lond., Quaritch, 1915. 255p. **A282**

Lowndes, William Thomas. Bibliographer's manual of English literature. New ed. rev., cor., and enl. by H. G. Bohn. Lond., Bell, 1858–64. 6v. in 11. **A283**

Contents: v.1-5 (in 10 pts.), A-Z; v.6, Appendix containing lists of publications of societies and printing clubs, books issued by private presses, lists of series, etc.

Lists about 50,000 works, giving for each, author, title, place, date, size, with occasional notes as to rarity, value, editions, reprints, etc., and often records of prices at various nineteenth century sales. Now much out of date for prices, but still useful for other information.

Watt, Robert. Bibliotheca Britannica; or, A general index to British and foreign literature. Edinburgh, Constable, 1824. 4v. **A284**

v.1-2, Author list, arranged alphabetically, with author's full name and dates, very brief biographical data, and for each book brief information which generally includes title, date, size, number of volumes; v.3-4, An alphabetical subject list, serving as an index to the author volumes, giving for each book its date and brief title, and referring to the section of the author list (indicated by number and letter) where somewhat fuller information can be found.

Often useful for material not given in more modern catalogs, but sometimes inaccurate, and so must be used with some caution.

Before 1640

British Museum. Dept. of Printed Books. Catalogue of books in the library of the British Museum printed in England, Scotland, and Ireland, and of books in English printed abroad to the year 1640. Lond., British Museum, 1884. 3v. **A285**

California. State Library, Sacramento. Sutro Branch, San Francisco. Catalogue of English pamphlets in the Sutro Library. Prepared by the personnel of the Work Projects Administration. . . . A. Yedidia, supervisor; A. I. Gans, ed. Sponsored by the California State Library. San Francisco, 1941. pt.1, fasc. 1-3, pt.2. **A286**

pt.1, fasc. 1-3, 1562–1642, arranged chronologically. pt.2, Seventeenth century periodicals, comp. by Helen M. Bruner.

Cambridge University. Library. Early English printed books in the University Library, 1475–1640. Camb., Univ. Pr., 1900–07. 4v. **A287**

v.1, Caxton to F. Kingston; v.2, E. Mattes to R. Marriot and English provincial presses; v.3, Scottish, Irish and foreign presses, with addenda; v.4, Indexes.

Includes 7750 titles, arranged by presses, with full indexes of authors and titles, printers and stationers, engravers and painters, towns, portraits, music.

Collins, Douglas Cecil. A handlist of news pamphlets, 1590–1610. Lond., South-West Essex Technical College, 1943. 129p. 10s. 6d. **A288**

Arranged chronologically. Full transcripts of the title pages of 270 news pamphlets with, in many cases, annotations and extracts describing contents. Indexes of printers and publishers, persons, and subjects.

De Ricci, Seymour. Census of Caxtons. Ox., pr. for the Bibl. Soc. at the Ox. Univ. Pr., 1909. 196p. facsim. (Bibl. Soc. Illustrated monographs, 15) **A289**

Sold only to members of the society.

Hand-lists of books printed by London printers, 1501–1556, by E. G. Duff, W. W. Greg, R. B. McKerrow, H. R. Plomer, A. W. Pollard, R. Proctor. Lond., Bibl. Soc., 1913. 4 pts. in 1v. il. **A290**

Sold only to members of the society.

Lists of the books printed by 89 printers up to the grant of a charter to the Stationers' Company in 1557. Publication in parts began in 1895 and sections have no continuous paging, thus allowing the complete work to be bound either alphabetically by printers' names or chronologically by their dates. Prepared as a basis for further work in the English bibliography of the period.

London. Stationers' Company. Transcript of the registers of the Company of Stationers of London, 1554–1640, ed. by Edward Arber. Lond., priv. pr., 1875–77; Birmingham, 1894. 5v. **A291**

Pollard, Alfred William and **Redgrave, G. R.** Short-title catalogue of books printed in England, Scotland and Ireland, and of English books printed abroad, 1475–1640; comp. . . . with the help of G. F. Barwick . . . and others. Lond., Bibl. Soc., 1926. 609p. **A292**

Frequently cited as S.T.C.

The most comprehensive record of English books for this period including about 26,500 editions (26,143 numbers, with several hundred items inserted with subnumbers). Arranged alphabetically by authors and other main entries; gives, for each item, author, brief title, size, printer, date, reference to entry of the book in the Stationers' registers, and indication of libraries possessing copies. This last important feature aims to record all known copies of very rare items and in the case of commoner books a selection in representative British and American libraries and collections. The total number of libraries referred to is 148 (133 British, 15 American).

Bishop, William Warner. A checklist of American copies of "Short-title Catalogue" books. 2d ed. Ann Arbor, Univ. of Michigan Pr., 1950. 203p. $2.50; paper $2. **A293**

Compiled as a convenient guide to the location of S.T.C. titles in American libraries, this is a record of S.T.C. numbers indicating holdings in some 110 libraries and collections. The second edition includes corrections and additions to the list in the first edition published 1944 and records the holdings of about ten more libraries.

Morrison, Paul G. Index of printers, publishers, and booksellers in A. W. Pollard and G. R. Redgrave, *A Short-title Catalogue.* . . . Charlottesville, Bibl. Soc. of the Univ. of Virginia, 1950. 82p. **A293a**

Henry E. Huntington Library and Art Gallery, San Marino, Calif. Huntington library supplement to the Short Title Catalogue . . . comp. by C. K. Edmonds. Camb., Harv. Univ. Pr., 1933. 152p. (Huntington Library Bull., Oct. 1933. p.1-152) **A294**

Contains two lists: (1) short title list of books included in the S.T.C. of which the Huntington copies are either unrecorded or recorded incorrectly, and (2) list, with full cataloging information, of books or editions within the period not recorded at all in the S.T.C.

Newberry Library, Chicago. English books and books printed in England before 1641 in the Newberry Library; a supplement to the record in the Short Title Catalogue, comp. by Gertrude L. Woodward. Chic., 1939. 118p. **A295**

17th and 18th centuries

Arber, Edward. Term catalogues, 1668–1709 A.D. with a number for Easter term, 1711 A.D.

Lond., Arber; N.Y., Dodd, 1903–06. 3v. o.p. **A296**

Subtitle: A contemporary bibliography of English literature in the reigns of Charles II, James II, William and Mary, and Anne; edited from the very rare quarterly lists of new books . . . issued by the booksellers of London.

British Museum. Library. Catalogue of the pamphlets, books, newspapers, and manuscripts relating to the civil war, the commonwealth, and restoration, collected by George Thomason, 1640–1661. Lond., Trustees, 1908. 2v. **A297**

Running title: The Thomason tracts.
A very rich collection for this period.

[London, William] Catalogue of the most vendible books in England, orderly and alphabetically digested . . . with Hebrew, Greek, and Latin books, for schools and scholars. . . . Lond., 1658–60. 3v. i.e.[236]p. and 2 suppl. **A298**

London. Stationers' Company. Transcript of the registers of the Worshipful Company of Stationers; from 1640–1708 A.D. Lond., priv. pr., 1913–14. 3v. **A299**

Edited by G. E. Briscoe Eyre. Entries transcribed by H. R. Plomer.

London catalogue of books. . . . **A300**

Bibliographies with this title published first by Bent and later by Hodgson were issued covering, with considerable duplication of years, books published in Great Britain from 1700 to 1855. The nineteenth century volumes formed one of the sources from which the 1801–36 and 1835–63 volumes of the *English catalogue* (A303) were compiled and for ordinary purposes are therefore not often needed, but a library having the eighteenth century volumes will still use them for material not included in Watt (A284) or Lowndes (A283).

For record of editions published *see* Growoll, *Three centuries of English booktrade bibliography* (A279).

Morgan, William Thomas. Bibliography of British history (1700–1715) with special reference to the reign of Queen Anne. Bloomington, Ind., 1934–42. 5v. **A301**

For complete description *see* V278.

Wing, Donald Goddard. Short-title catalogue of books printed in England, Scotland, Ireland, Wales, and British America and of English books printed in other countries, 1641–1700. N.Y., pr. for the Index Soc. by the Columbia Univ. Pr., 1945–48. v.1-2. $15 ea. (In progress) **A302**

v.1-2, A-0.

Published as a continuation of Pollard and Redgrave's *Short-title catalogue . . . 1475–1640* (A292). Items are located in more than 200 libraries; relatively common books are given five locations in Great Britain and five in the United States in as varied geographical areas as possible in order to provide convenient locations for scholars in various parts of the country. It is not a census of copies and "it is only when less than five copies are located in either British or American libraries that any deduction can be drawn that copies mentioned are all that

the editor has found." Location symbols are not those used by the S.T.C. nor the Union Catalog, but follow a system devised by Mr. Wing.

The scope and method of selection and entry are described in the preface which should be carefully read before the book is used in order not to misinterpret or misunderstand the information given. There are admittedly errors and omissions but if used with the caution that Mr. Wing himself advises the work should prove an invaluable addition to the bibliographical apparatus of English publications, as it covers a period for which there has been no adequate bibliography.

19th and 20th centuries

English catalogue of books . . . issued . . . in Great Britain and Ireland . . . 1801- . Lond., S. Low, 1864–1901; Pub. Circular, 1906- . **A303**

Volume covering 1801–36, published in 1914 and unnumbered, includes authors and subjects in one alphabet. [v.1,] covers 1835–63. Later nineteenth century volumes were published at irregular intervals; 1901–1935 volumes cover 5-year periods; 1936–1941, six years.

The standard English list, reasonably comprehensive for books and pamphlets issued at the main publishing centers but less complete for the provincial presses. Includes books, pamphlets, annuals, some official publications, but not periodicals or privately printed books; books in series and publications of societies are usually listed in appendices. Arrangement is alphabetical by author with some title and catchword subject entries, except that from 1837–1889 the subject entries are in separate index volumes (*see* below). Information given includes author, brief title, publisher, date, size, and price in [v.1]-v.5; in v.6- , fuller titles are given and the *total* paging (i.e., the sum of preface paging and main paging) is added.

—— Index to the English catalogue of books, 1837–1889. Lond., S. Low, 1858–93. 4v.

Forms a subject index to v.1-4 of the author catalog. No more published, as from v.5 on the *English catalogue* includes authors and catchword subjects in one alphabet.

Whitaker's Cumulative book list, 1939–1943, 1944–1947; the complete list of all books published in the United Kingdom, giving details as to author, title, sub-title, size, number of pages, price, date, classification and publisher of every book. Lond., Whitaker, 1945–49. v.1-2. (In progress) v.2, £5; $25. **A304**

1939–43, author and title in one alphabet; 1944–47, in two sections, author list and title list.

Current

English catalogue of books . . . issued in the United Kingdom, being a continuation of the "London" and "British" catalogues . . . 1835- . Lond., Pub. Circular, 1837- . v.1- . Annual. 25s. **A305**

On the same plan as the permanent *English catalogue* (A303). Some of the later volumes contain, in addition to the main list of publications, an appendix giving learned societies, printing clubs, etc., with lists of their publications for the year, and a directory of English publishers.

Publishers' circular and the Publisher and bookseller, the official organ of the Publishers' Association of Great Britain and Ireland, the Associated Booksellers of Great Britain and Ireland. Lond., Pub. Circular, 1837- . v.1- . 21s. 8d. per year. **A306**

A weekly trade journal, including a list of publications of the week, announcements, some book reviews, general trade news, etc. Includes also a combined monthly list of new publications, given generally in the last number for the month. Follows the same plan and gives the same kind of information as the *English catalogue* (A303), for the annual volumes of which it forms the basis.

Whitaker's Cumulative book list, a classified list of publications . . . 1924- . Lond., Whitaker, 1924- . v.1- . 40s. per yr. **A307**

Issued quarterly, cumulating throughout the year, i.e., April, 3 months (5s.); July, 6 months (8s. 6d); October, 9 months (12s. 6d); January, 12 months (22s. 6d.); (forming the permanent volume); since 1939 cumulating into larger volumes as listed above (A304).

Each issue consists of a classified list of recent publications, cumulated from the weekly lists in *The Bookseller* (A308), with a detailed author and title index.

The bookseller: The organ of the booktrade, 1858- . Lond., Whitaker. 25s. per yr. **A308**

Monthly, 1858–1908; weekly, 1909- .

Includes weekly alphabetical lists with monthly cumulations in last issue of month, which cumulate into *Whitaker's Cumulative book list.*

Current literature, the monthly gazette of current literature. Lond., Whitaker, 1858- . Monthly. 4d. **A309**

Title varies.

Includes a classified "Publications of the Month" which cumulates to form the classified section of *Whitaker's Cumulative book list.*

Reference catalogue of current literature . . . 1874- . Lond., Whitaker, 1874- . Irregular. **A310**

v.1, Author index; v.2, Title index.

Subtitle; 1940, A national inclusive book-reference index of books in print and on sale in the British Empire, with details as to author, title, editor, translator, reviser, year of publication or year of latest edition, number of edition, size, number of pages, illustrations and illustrator, series, binding—where not cloth—price, whether net or non-net, and publisher's name, containing 600,000 entries and giving over 3,000,000 details concerning books published and for sale.

1874–1932, a collection of publishers' catalogs bound together alphabetically by name of firm, with a detailed alphabetical index in a separate volume. Published about every fourth year. 1936, 1938, 1940, consolidated into two lists, author and title, including information as given in subtitle.

British national bibliography, no.1, Jan. 4, 1950- . Lond., Council of the British National

Bibliography, British Museum, 1950- . Weekly. £12 per yr. **A311**

A weekly bibliography of books published in Great Britain, cataloged according to the Anglo-American cataloging code and arranged by the Dewey decimal classification. There is a monthly author index and the whole is to be cumulated annually. The list is compiled from the books deposited in the Copyright Office of the British Museum and hopes to be complete except for the exclusion of (1) cheap novelettes, (2) periodicals (except for the first issue of a new periodical and the first issue under a new title), (3) publications of the Government of Eire, (4) music, (5) maps, and (6) most publications of the British Government.

Cataloging is complete and includes full name of author, title, publisher, price, date (including month), paging, illustrations, cm.size, binding, series, occasional annotations. Pseudonymous works are cataloged under the form of name appearing on the title page as is the practice of the British Museum.

The monthly author index includes authors' names with cross references from variant forms, titles of fiction and some, but not all, titles of nonfiction.

Privately printed

Dobell, Bertram. Catalogue of books printed for private circulation, collected by Bertram Dobell and now described and annotated by him. Lond., Dobell, 1906. 238p. **A312**

An author list, with full descriptions, including author's name, title, size, paging, date, price, size of edition when known, and bibliographical and historical notes with occasional quotations from the books themselves. Includes some, but not all, of the books listed by Martin (A313).

Some 939 titles from this list are now in the Library of Congress, having been acquired in the Dobell collection of privately printed books purchased in 1914.

Martin, John. Bibliographical catalogue of privately printed books. 2d ed. Lond., pub. for the author by J. Van Voort, 1854. 593p. il. **A313**

The first edition, 1834, was in two parts; (1) List of books, omitting pamphlets, arranged chronologically 1672–1833, giving author's name, title, place and printer when known, date, size and paging, with many bibliographical and historical notes and occasional references to authorities and copies; (2) List of books printed at private presses and for distribution among members of literary clubs, arranged by presses. General index of authors and titles. The list by presses contains some material not found in the appendix volume of Lowndes (A283). The second edition is a revision of the first part only, correcting some errors, adding previously omitted titles and extending the list to 1853, but omitting the section of private presses.

Regional

The general works listed above are reasonably comprehensive for books issued at the main publishing centers but are less inclusive for material of local interest issued by provincial printers. For works of this latter type local bibliographies of towns and counties must frequently be consulted. The following local bibliographies vary greatly in character but, taken as a whole, they serve three main purposes: (1) as lists of local imprints; (2) as bibliographies of local history; (3) as regional biographical dictionaries, since some of them include biographical sketches about local writers, etc. As they sometimes include considerable analysis of material in periodicals, and even newspapers, they supplement, to that extent, the indexes to periodicals.

Aberdeen, Banff, and Kincardine: JOHNSTONE, J. F. K. and ROBERTSON, A. W. Bibliographia aberdonensis, being an account of books relating to or printed in the shires of Aberdeen, Banff, Kincardine, or written by natives or residents or by officers, graduates or alumni of the universities of Aberdeen. Aberdeen, pr. for the Third Spalding Club, 1929–30. 2v. **A314; Bolton:** SPARKE, ARCHIBALD. Bibliographia Boltoniensis: being a bibliography, with biographical details of Bolton authors, and the books written by them from 1550 to 1912; books about Bolton; and those printed and published in the town from 1785 to date. Manchester, Univ. Pr., 1913. 211p. **A315; Bradford:** [DICKONS, J. N.] Catalogue of books, pamphlets, etc., published at Bradford, in the county of York. Bradford, priv. pr., 1895. 241p. **A316; Bristol:** BRISTOL, ENG. MUNICIPAL PUBLIC LIBRARIES. Bristol bibliography. . . . A catalogue of the books, pamphlets, collectanea, etc., relating to Bristol, contained in the Central Reference Library. Ed. by E. R. N. Mathews. Bristol, Libraries Committee, 1916. 404p. **A317; Buckingham:** GOUGH, H. Bibliotheca Buckinghamiensis: a list of books relating to the county of Buckingham. Aylesbury, DeFraine, 1890. 96p. **A318; Cambridge:** BOWES, ROBERT. Catalogue of books printed at or relating to the university, town and county of Cambridge, from 1521 to 1893, with bibliographical and biographical notes. Cambridge, Macmillan and Bowes, 1894. 516p. **A319; Chester:** COOKE, J. H. Bibliotheca Cestriensis, or a biographical account of books, maps, plates, and other printed matter relating to, printed or published in, or written by authors resident in the county of Chester. . . . Warrington, Mackie, 1904. 218p. **A320; Cornwall:** BOASE, G. C. and COURTNEY, W. P. Bibliotheca Cornubiensis. A catalogue of the writings, both manuscript and printed, of Cornishmen, and of works relating to the county of Cornwall. Lond., Longmans, 1874–82. 3v. **A321; Derbyshire:** DERBY, ENG. FREE PUBLIC LIBRARY and MUSEUM. Derbyshire; a select catalogue of books about the county, by James Ormerod. Derby, Public Libraries, 1930.

127p. **A322; Devon:** DREDGE, J. I. A few sheaves of Devon bibliography. . . . Plymouth, Brendon, 1889. 250p. **A323;** DAVIDSON, JAMES. Bibliotheca Devoniensis; a catalogue of the printed books relating to the county of Devon. Exeter, W. Roberts, 1852. 226p. **A324; Dorset:** MAYO, C. H. Bibliotheca Dorsetiensis . . . account of printed books and pamphlets relating to the history and topography of the county of Dorset. Lond., Whittingham, 1885. 296p. **A325; Essex:** CUNNINGTON, AUGUSTUS. Catalogue of books, maps, and manuscripts, relating to or connected with the county of Essex. . . . Braintree, Joscelyne, 1902. 90p. **A326; Gloucester:** HYETT, F. A. and BAZELEY, WILLIAM. Bibliographer's manual of Gloucestershire literature, being a classified catalogue of books, pamphlets, broadsides, and other printed matter relating to the county of Gloucester or to the city of Bristol. . . . Gloucester, J. Bellows, 1895–97. 3v. Biographical supplement. 1915–16. 2v. **A327;** GLOUCESTER, ENG. PUBLIC LIBRARY. Catalogue of the Gloucestershire collection; books, pamphlets, and documents in the Gloucester Public Library relating to the county, cities, towns, and villages of Gloucestershire, comp. by Roland Austin. [Gloucester, H. Osborne] 1928. 1236p. **A328; Hampshire:** GILBERT, H. M. and GODWIN, G. N. Bibliotheca Hantoniensis; a list of books relating to Hampshire including magazine references; with an additional list of Hampshire newspapers, by F. E. Edwards. Southampton, 1891. 80, lxiiip. **A329; Kent:** MARGATE PUBLIC LIBRARY. Catalogue of books, pamphlets and excerpts dealing with Margate, the Isle of Thanet and the County of Kent in the local collection, comp. by A. J. Gritten. Margate, 1934. 166p. **A330;** SMITH, JOHN RUSSELL. Bibliotheca Cantiana: a bibliographical account of what has been published on the history, topography, antiquities, customs, and family history of the County of Kent. Lond., Smith, 1837. 360p. **A331; Lancashire:** FISHWICK, HENRY. Lancashire Library, a bibliographical account of books on topography, biography, history, science, and miscellaneous literature relating to the county Palatine, including an account of Lancashire tracts, pamphlets, and sermons printed before the year 1720. . . . Lond., Routledge, 1875. 443p. **A332;** WIGAN, ENG. PUBLIC LIBRARIES COMMITTEE. Lancashire printed books; a bibliography of all the books printed in Lancashire down to the year 1800 . . . compiled . . . by A. J. Hawkes. . . . Wigan, 1925. 155p. **A333;** SUTTON, C. W. List of Lancashire authors. . . . Manchester, Heywood, 1876. 164p. (Publications of the Manchester Literary Club) **A334; Lincoln:** LINCOLN PUBLIC

LIBRARY. Bibliotheca Lincolniensis; a catalogue of the books, pamphlets, etc., relating to the city and county of Lincoln, comp. by A. R. Corns. Lincoln, Morton, 1904. 274p. **A335; Isle of Man:** CUBBON, WILLIAM. Bibliographical account of works relating to the Isle of Man, with biographical notes and copious literary references. Ox., Univ. Pr., 1933–39. 2v. **A336; Newcastle and Northumberland:** NEWCASTLE UPON TYNE. CENTRAL PUBLIC LIBRARY. Local catalogue of material concerning Newcastle and Northumberland as represented in the . . . library. Newcastle upon Tyne, A. Reid, 1932. 626p. **A337;** WELFORD, RICHARD. Early Newcastle typography, 1639–1800. In *Archaeologia aeliana*, 3d ser., v.3, p.1-134. **A338; Norfolk:** COLMAN, J. J. Bibliotheca Norfolciensis; a catalogue of the writings of Norfolk men and of the works relating to the county of Norfolk, in the library of Mr. J. J. Colman, at Carrow Abbey, Norwich. Norwich, 1896. 591p. **A339; Nottinghamshire:** WARD, JAMES. Descriptive catalogue of books relating to Nottinghamshire. Nottingham, priv. pr., 1892. 40p. **A340;** Supplementary catalogue. 1898. 41p.; **Oxford:** MADAN, FALCONER. Oxford books; a bibliography of printed works relating to the university and city of Oxford, or printed or published there. Ox., Clarendon Pr., 1895–1931. 3v. **A341; Sheffield:** FREEMANTLE, W. T. Bibliography of Sheffield and vicinity. Sheffield, Pawson and Brailsford, 1911. v.1 (to the end of 1700), 285p. **A342; Somerset:** GREEN, EMANUEL. Bibliotheca Somersetensis; a catalogue of books, pamphlets, single sheets, and broadsides in some way connected with the county of Somerset. Taunton, Barnicott and Pearce, 1902. 3v. **A343; Staffordshire:** SIMMS, RUPERT. Bibliotheca Staffordiensis; or, a bibliographical account of books and other printed matter relating to, printed or published in, or written by a native, resident, or person deriving a title from any portion of the county of Stafford. . . . Lichfield, priv. pr., 1894. 546p. **A344; Surrey:** MINET. PUBLIC LIBRARY. Catalogue of the collection of works relating to the County of Surrey, comp. by W. Minet and C. J. Courtney. Aberdeen, Univ. Pr., 1901. 148p. **A345;** Supplement. 1923. 127p.; **Whitby:** SMALES, GIDEON. Whitby authors and their publications, with the titles of all books printed in Whitby, A.D. 670 to A.D. 1867. Whitby, Horne, 1867. 248p. **A346; Wiltshire:** GODDARD, ED. H. Wiltshire bibliography; a catalogue of printed books, pamphlets and articles bearing on the history, topography and natural history of the county. Frome and Lond., Wilts Education Committee, 1929. 276p. **A347; Worcestershire:** BURTON,

J. R. and PEARSON, F. S. Bibliography of Worcestershire; acts of Parliament relating to the county, ed. for the Worcestershire Historical Society. Ox., Parker, 1898–1903. 2v. **A348; Yorkshire:** BOYNE, WILLIAM. Yorkshire Library; a bibliographical account of books on topography, tracts of the seventeenth century, biography, spaws, geology, botany, maps, views, portraits, and miscellaneous literature, relating to the county of York. . . . Lond., Taylor, 1869. 304p. **A349;** YORKSHIRE ARCHAEOLOGICAL SOCIETY. Catalogue of the printed books and pamphlets in the library, comp. by G. E. Kirk. Wakefield, West Yorkshire Pr. Co., 1933–36. 2v. **A350.**

Greece

Gkines, Dēmētrios and **Balerios, G.** Hellēnikē bibliographia, 1800–1863. Anagraphē tōn kata tēn chronikēn tautēn periodon hopou dēpote Hellēnisti ekdothentōn bibliōn kai entypōn en genei. . . . Brabeutheisa hypo tēs Akadēmias Athēnōn. Tomos 1. En Athēnais, Grapheion dēmosieumatōn Akadēmias Athēnōn, 1939. v.1. (Pragmateiai tēs Akadēmias Athēnōn, Tomos II) **A351**

Contents: T.1, 1800–1839.

Legrand, Émile. Bibliographie hellénique, ou, Description raisonée des ouvrages publiés en grec par des Grecs aux xvᵉ et xviᵉ siècles. Paris, Leroux, 1885–1906. 4v. il. **A352**

Publisher varies. Title varies.
v.1-4, 1476–1600.
v.3-4 include works published in Greek and other languages.

—— Bibliographie hellénique, ou Description raisonnée des ouvrages publiés par des Grecs au dix-septième siècle. Paris, Picard, 1894–96; Maisonneuve, 1903. 5v. **A353**

v.1-3, 1601–1700; v.3-5, include Notices biographiques.
Broader in scope than his volumes for the fifteenth and sixteenth centuries, including "tout ouvrage ayant un Grec pour auteur or editeur, tout ouvrage auquel le nom d'un Grec est attaché d'un façon quelconque."

—— Bibliographie hellénique, ou, Description raisonnée des ouvrages publiés par des Grecs au dix-huitième siècle, oeuvre posthume, complétée et publ. par Louis Petit et Hubert Pernot. Paris, Garnier, 1918–28. 2v. **A354**

v.1-2, 1701–1790.

—— Bibliographie ionienne; description raisonnée des ouvrages pub. par les Grecs des Sept-Iles ou concernant ces îles du 15. siècle à l'année 1900. Oeuvre posthume complétée et publ. par Hubert Pernot. Paris, Leroux, 1910. 2v. **A355**

v.1, 1494–1854; v.2, 1855–1900.

Politēs, N. G. Hellēnikē bibliographia: katalogos tōn en Helladi ē upo Hellēnōn allachou ekdothentōn bibliōn apo tou etous. v.p. 1909-32. 3v.   **A356**

Imprint varies: v.1-2, Athens, P. D. Sakellarios; v.3, pt.1, Athens, Spendone, pt.2, Thessalonika, M. Triantspullos.

v.1-2 repr. from *Athens, Ethnikon kai kapodistriakon panepistemon. Epistemonike epeterus* 3: 393–540, 1906–07 (pub. 1909); 6: 139-612, 1909–10 (pub. 1911); v.3, issued in 2 pts., 1927–32.

v.1-2 cover years 1907–10; v.3, 1911–20. Includes books published in Greece and books by Greeks published elsewhere.

Current

Bulletin analytique de bibliographie hellénique. 1946. fasc. 1-3. Athènes, Institut français d'Athènes, 1947- . Quarterly. 500fr. par an; $8; £2.   **A357**

fasc. 1-3, cover 1946. Other fasc. to be published will cover 1940–1945 and continue from 1947. 1946 called v.7.

An annotated classed bibliography attempting to list all books published in Greece.

Guatemala

Medina, José Toribio. La imprenta en Guatemala (1660–1821). Santiago de Chile, Imp. en Casa del Autor, 1910. 696p.   **A358**

A basic work for the colonial period.

Guatemala. Tipografía Nacional. Catálogo general de libros, folletos y revistas editados en la Tipografía Nacional de Guatemala desde 1892 hasta 1943. Guatemala, Tipografía Nacional, 1944. 352p.   **A359**

Alphabetical by year, no index. Full bibliographical information.

Valenzuela, Gilberto. Bibliografía guatemalteca, catálogo de obras, folletos, etc., publicados en Guatemala desde la independencia hasta el año de 1850. Guatemala, [n.p.] 1933- . v.1- . (Folletín del "Diaro de Centro América")   **A360**

v.1, (459p.) arranged chronologically 1821–1830, annotated. Issued and bound with:

—— La imprenta en Guatemala. Guatemala, 1933. 72p. (Folletín del "Diario de Centro América")   **A361**

Additions to the work by Medina.

Villacorta Calderon, José Antonio. Bibliografía guatemalteca; Exposiciones abiertas en el Salón de historia y bellas artes del Museo Nacional, en los meses de noviembre de 1939, 40, 41 y 42. Guatemala, Tipografía Nacional, 1944. 638p. il. $5.   **A362**

Based on the exhibit on the history of printing in Guatemala held at the Museo Nacional. Covers the period from the introduction of printing in 1660 to 1942, with extensive bibliographies, location of copies, facsimiles of title pages, etc.

Current

Guatemala (City). Biblioteca Nacional. Boletin. Director: Rafael Arévalo Martínez. Guatemala City, 1932- . v.1- . Quarterly.   **A363**

Haiti

Duvivier, Ulrick. Bibliographie générale et méthodique d'Haïti. . . . Port-au-Prince, Haïti, Imp. de l'État, 1941. 2v.   **A364**

Covers material published in Haiti from the earliest period to date of publication. Classed arrangement, no index.

Honduras

Duron, Jorge Fidel. Indice de la bibliografia hondureña. Tegucigalpa, Imp. Calderon, 1946. 211p.   **A365**

Attempts to list all works published in Honduras (alphabetized by first letter only). For these it largely supersedes the *Repertorio* listed below. However, the *Repertorio* includes some lists not included in the *Indice*.

Instituto Hondureño de Cultura Interamericana. Repertorio bibliografico hondureño, por Jorge Fidel Duron. Tegucigalpa, 1943. 68p.   **A366**

First tentative edition of a national bibliography covering all periods. First three sections are books exhibited at the "Primera exposición y feria del libro hondureño y americano." (1) Repertorio bibliografico hondureño; (2) Libros de autores norteamericanos; (3) Libros de autores chilenos.

Section 4 is a list of books published in Honduras and section 5 an "Indice de nombres." All sections and index alphabetized by first letter only. Index is list of names only, does not give page references.

Hungary

Kertbeny, Károly Mária. Bibliografie der ungarischen nationalen und internationalen Literatur. Erster Band. Ungarn betreffende deutsche Erstlingsdrucke. 1454–1600. Budapest, Kön. Ung. Univ.-Buchdr., 1880. clxxxiv, 760, 14p.   **A367**

No more published.

—— Ungarns deutsche Bibliographie 1801–1860. Verzeichniss der in Ungarn und Ungarn betreffend im Auslande erschienenen deutschen Drucke. Im Auftrage des K. Ung. Ministerium für Cultus und Unterricht. Fortgesetzt und mit einer wissenschaftlichen Uebersicht versehen von

Géza Petrik. Budapest, Kön. Ung. Univ.-Buchdr., 1886. 2v. **A368**

v.1, 1801–30; v.2, 1831–60.
Added t.p. in Hungarian.

Szabó, Károly. Régi magyar könyvtár. Budapest, A. M. Tud. Akadémia Könyvkiadó Hivatala, 1879–98. 3v. in 4. **A369**

v.1, Books in Hungarian, 1531–1711; v.2, Non-Hungarian books published in Hungary, 1473–1711; v.3, Hungarian authors, non-Hungarian books published outside Hungary, pt.1, 1480–1670, pt.2, 1671–1711.
Continued by:

Petrik, Géza. Bibliographia hungarica. Magyar könyvészet [1712–1910]. Budapest, Magyar Könyvkereskedök Egyesülete, 1885–1928. 10v. **A370**

Title varies.
v.[6], 1876–1885, by Sándor Kiszlingstein.
[ser. 1] 1712–1860. 4v.; [ser. 2] 1860–75. 1v.; [ser. 3] 1876–85. 556p.; [ser. 4] 1886–1900, 2v.; [ser. 5] 1901–10. 2v.

Magyar Könyvészet, 1921–23, az 1921–23 években megjelent magyar könyvek betürendes jegyzéke és targymutatója. Budapest, Magyar Könyvkiadók és Könyvkereskedök, Zenemükiadók és Zenemükereskedök Egyesülete, 1924–26. 491p. **A371**

Published in 6 pts., A-Z.
No more published.

Lantos, firm, booksellers, Budapest. List of all Hungarian books in trade, arranged by Blanche Pikler and Robert Braun. Budapest, Lantos Co., 1925. 252p. **A372**

Iceland

British museum. Dept. of Printed Books. Catalogue of the books printed in Iceland, from A.D. 1578 to 1880. In the library of the British Museum. Lond., Clowes, 1885. 30, lvi, [i.e., 86] col. **A373**

Compiled by Thomas W. Lidderdale.
Four supplements, based upon his own collections, were issued by Willard Fiske (in his *Bibliographical notices* 1, 1886; 4, 1890; 5, 1890; 6, 1907). The fourth supplement contains a general index.

Cornell University. Library. Catalogue of the Icelandic collection bequeathed by Willard Fiske. Comp. by Halldór Hermannsson. Ithaca, N.Y., 1914. 755p. **A374**

"When this catalogue went to press the collection numbered about 10,200 volumes. . . . The catalogue, however, does not comprise all of these, since the Runic portion, containing some 500 volumes, and a few other books, have not been recorded . . . some few titles are included which are to be found in the University library outside of the collection."–*Pref.*
Contents: Author catalog; Supplement, Subject-index.

—— —— Additions, 1913–26, comp. by Halldór Hermannsson. Ithaca, N.Y.; Lond., Milford, 1927. 284p.

—— —— Additions, 1927–42, comp. by Halldór Hermannsson. Ithaca, N. Y., Cornell Univ. Pr., 1943. 295p.

Some 5000 items are included in this supplement making a total in the collection of 21,830. This supplement also includes various titles to be found in the library outside the collection.

—— Catalogue of Runic literature, forming a part of the Icelandic collection bequeathed by Willard Fiske. Comp. by Halldór Hermannsson. Lond. and N.Y., Ox. Univ. Pr., 1918. 105p. **A375**

Islandica; an annual relating to Iceland and the Fiske Icelandic collection in Cornell University Library. Ithaca, N.Y., Cornell Univ. Lib., 1908- . **A376**

The bibliographical volumes of this set by Halldór Hermannsson include: v.1, Bibliography of the Icelandic sagas and minor tales. 1908. 126p.; v.2, The Northmen in America. 1909. 94p.; v.3. Bibliography of the sagas of the kings of Norway and related sagas and tales. 1910. 75p.; v.4, The ancient laws of Norway and Iceland. 1911. 83p.; v.5, Bibliography of the mythical-heroic sagas. 1912. 73p.; v.6, Icelandic authors of today, with an appendix giving a list of works dealing with modern Icelandic literature. 1913. 63p.; v.9, Icelandic books of the 16th century (1534–1600). 1916. 72p.; v.11, The periodical literature of Iceland down to the year 1874; an historic sketch. 1918. 100p.; v.13, Bibliography of the Eddas. 1920. 95p.; v.14, Icelandic books of the 17th century (1601–1700). 1922. 121p.; v.19, Icelandic manuscripts. 1929. 80p.; v.23, Old Icelandic literature; a bibliographical essay. 1933. 50p.; v.24, The sagas of Icelanders; a supplement [to v.1]. 1935. 113p.; v.26, The sagas of the kings and the mythical-heroic sagas; two bibliographical supplements [to v.3 and v.5]. 1937. 84p.; v.29, Bibliographical notes [including] Additions to the bibliographies of Icelandic books of the 16th and 17th centuries [v.9 and v.14] 1942. 91p.

Islandsk Bogfortegnelse 1915–19—1930–34. [In Dansk Bogfortegnelse, 1915–19—1930–34 (A232)] **A377**

5-year cumulations.

Islandsk Bogfortegnelse, 1899–1910, 1912–1920. af Bogi T. J. Melsted. København, 1899–22. Annual (irregular). **A378**

Supplement to Dansk Bogfortegnelse (A235) and bound with it, as follows: 1899–1910 with v. for 1899–1910; 1912 with 1914; 1913–14 with 1915; 1915 with 1917; 1916–18 with 1918; 1919 with 1921; 1920 with 1922.

Kiel. Universität. Bibliothek. Islandkatalog der Universitätsbibliothek Kiel und der Universitäts- und Stadtbibliothek Köln, bearb. von Olaf Klose. Kiel, Universitätsbib., 1931. 423p. (Kataloge der Universitätsbibliothek Kiel, hrsg. von Christoph Weber, 1) **A379**

Ireland

Book Association of Ireland. Catalogue of books published in Ireland since 1938 and still in print. [Dublin, 1943?] 14p.　　　　　　　　**A380**

Caption title.
Classified and priced.

Dix, Ernest Reginald McClintock. Catalogue of early Dublin-printed books, 1601 to 1700, with an historical introduction and bibliographical notes by C. Winston Dugan. Dublin [O'Donoghue; Lond., Dobell], 1898–1905. 4v. in 2 and suppl., all paged continuously, 386p.　　　　**A381**

Dublin. National Library of Ireland. List of publications deposited under the terms of the Industrial and commercial property (protection) act, 1927. nos. 1-5, Aug. 1927–Dec. 1929–1935/36. Dublin, Stat. Off. [1930-37]. 1s. ea.　　**A382**

Italy
Bibliography

Ottino, Giuseppe and **Fumagalli, Giuseppe.** Bibliotheca bibliographica italica. Catalogo degli scritti di bibliologia, bibliografia e biblioteconomia pub. in Italia e di quelli risguardanti l'Italia pub. all' Estero. Roma, Pasqualucci, 1889; Torino, Clausen, 1895–1902. 2v. and 4 suppl.　　　　　　　　　　　　　**A383**

Basic volumes, 6450 entries; supplements, for 1895, 1896, 1896–99, 1900, entry nos. 6451-8259.
Supplements 1 and 2 by Ottino; supplements 3 and 4 by Emilio Calvi.
The basic bibliography of Italian bibliographies. Continued by:

Fumagalli, Giuseppe. La bibliografia. Roma, Fondazione Leonardo, 1923. lxxxix, 169p. (Guide bibliografiche)　　　　　　　　**A384**

p.1-lxxxix contain a survey of Italian bibliography and bibliographers. The rest of the work is a classified bibliography of bibliographies in all fields with an author index. It includes a selection of titles from the Ottino *Bibliotheca* (A383) and additional works published from 1901 to 1923.

Istituto Nazionale per le Relazioni Culturali con l'Estero. La bibliografia italiana, a cura di Giannetto Avanzi. 2. ed. interamente rifatta, con tre appendice e una aggiunta. Roma, 1946. 570p. (On cover: Bibliografie italiane) L400.　　**A385**

Half title: Guida sistematica e analitica degli scritti principali di bibliologia, bibliografia, biblioteconomia pubblicati in Italia dal 1921 al 1946.
App. 1, Indici e cataloghi d'incunabuli pubblicati in Italia, 1901–1942; App. 2, Esposizioni, Mostre, Fiere bibliografiche italiane. Cataloghi e notizie, 1921–1942; App. 3, Stampa periodica di bibliologia e di bibliografia.
Indici: autori; scritti anonimi; soggetti.

The second edition of one of the volumes listed in (A386) the series having changed its title. The new series announces much the same list of subjects to be covered.
A work of the first importance for the record of Italian bibliography. Includes local and individual bibliography. Continues the work of Fumagalli listed above.

——— Bibliografie del ventennio. Roma, 1941. 14v.　　　　　　　　　　　　　　　　**A386**

A series of separately published bibliographies listing works published in Italy, 1922–1941. Volumes cover Archeologia, arti figurative, musica. 498p.; La bibliografia italiana. 248p. (*see* A385 for revised edition) Filologia classica e romanza. 152p.; Geografia e viaggi. 194p.; Letteratura italiana. 238p.; Letterature straniere. 455p.; Medicina. 165p.; Mussolini e il fascismo. 81p.; Scienze economiche e sociali. 167p.; Scienzi fisiche, matematiche ed agrarie. 211p.; Scienze naturali. 101p.; Scienzi religiose, filosofia, pedagogia. 173p.; Studi storici militari, etnografia popolare. 214p.; Il pensiero giuridico italiano. 5v.

General

Associazione Italiana Editori. Catalogo collettivo della libreria italiano, con indice alfabetico per autori e per case editrici. Milano, Società Anonima per Pubblicazioni Bibliografico-Editorali, 1948. 1784p.　　　　　　　　　　**A387**

A collection of 180 publishers' catalogs with an alphabetical index of about 25,000 titles.
Earlier lists of a similar nature were the *Catalogo collettivo della libreria italiana* (1891, 2v.) and the *Catalogo dei cataloghi del libro italiano* (1922, 1923 and 1926 with supplements 1928, 1930 and 1932).

Gamba, Bartolommeo. Serie dei testi di lingua e di altre opere importanti nella italiana letteratura, scritte dal secolo XIV al XIX. 4. ed., riv., emend. e notabilmente accresciuta. Venezia, Co'tipi del Gondoliere, 1839. 794p. o.p.　　**A388**

Haym, Nicola Francesco. Biblioteca italiana, ossia Notizia de' libri rari italiani divisa in quattro parti cioè istoria, poesia, prose, arti e scienze. ed. cor., ampl. e di giudizi intorno alle migliori opere arrichita. Milano, G. Silvestri, 1803. 4v. in 2. o.p.　　　　　　　　　　　　　**A389**

Pagliaini, Attilio. Catalogo generale della libreria italiana, 1847–99. Milano, Assoc. Tip.-Libr. Ital., 1901–22. 6v.　　　　　　　　　　**A390**

Author and title list, 3v., 1901–05; Subject index, 3v., 1910–22.

——— ——— 1-3. supplemento, 1900–10, 1911–20, 1921–30. Milano, Assoc. Tip.-Libr. Ital., 1912–40. 9v. (In progress)

1st suppl., 1900–10, Authors and titles, 2v. 1912–14; 2d suppl., 1911–20, Authors and titles, 2v. 1925–28; 3d suppl., 1921–30, Authors and titles, v.1-2, 1932–38. Subject index to 1st-2d suppl., 1900–20; v.1-4, fasc. 9, A-Tossicita. 1933–40.

The standard Italian list, covering a period of 53 years in its basic volume and continued by decennial supplements which make the total period 84 years. The 1847-99 volumes include more than 200,000 titles, comprising the principal books and pamphlets of the period but omitting minor pamphlets, periodicals, separates and government and society publications. Consists of: (1) Main author and title list, giving fairly full information, i.e., author's name, title (somewhat abridged), place, publisher, date, paging, size, illustrations, original price when this was obtainable; (2) Subject index to the author list. Based upon the catalogs of the large Italian libraries, catalogs of book dealers and publishers and on about 200 Italian bibliographies.

Parenti, Marino. Prime edizioni italiane; manuale di bibliografia pratica ad uso dei bibliofili e dei librai. 2. ed. riv. e ampl. Milano, Libri d'Arte e di Filologia, 1948. 526p. **A391**

1st ed., 1935.
An alphabetical list of Italian authors from the sixteenth to the nineteenth centuries, with dates of their first editions.

La scheda cumulativa italiana, diretta e redatta da T. W. Huntington; indicatore bibliografico per autore, titolo, soggetto delle nuove pubblicazioni italiane. Anno 1-5, 1932–36. Anacapri, Scheda Cumulativa Italiana, 1932–37. v.1-5 **A392**

A "Cumulative book index" for Italy, appeared quarterly, with half-year and annual cumulations. Arranged alphabetically by author, title and subject.

Vatican. Biblioteca Vaticana. The books published by the Vatican library, 1885–1947; an illustrated analytic catalogue. Vatican City, Apostolic Vatican Library, 1947. 183p. il. **A393**

Current

Florence. Biblioteca Nazionale Centrale. Bollettino delle pubblicazioni italiane ricevute per diretto di stampa, 1866- . Firenze, Biblioteca, 1886- . v.1- . Monthly. **A394**

Classified with annual indexes. The most complete current record of Italian publications.

Giornale della libreria; pubblicazione settimanale, 1888- . Milano, Associazione Italiana Editori, 1888- . v.1- . Semimonthly with quarterly cumulations. **A395**

Publisher and frequency vary.
Superseded the "Cronaca" and "Avvisi," pub. until 1887 as pts. 2 and 3 of the *Bibliografia italiana.*
Contains classified lists of recent publications and announcements of forthcoming publications.

Il Libro italiano; rassegna bibliografica generale, pubblicazione mensile a cura del Ministro dell' educazione nazionale e del Ministro della cultura popolare, v.1, giugno 1937- . Roma, Libr. Ulpiano Editrice, 1937- . v.1- . Monthly. **A396**

A classified list, with author index.

Latin America

The bibliographies listed below cover more than one of the Latin American countries. For the national bibliography of any one country *see* name of that country.

Jones, Cecil Knight. A bibliography of Latin American bibliographies. 2d ed., rev. and enl. by the author with the assistance of James A. Granier. . . . Wash., Govt. Prt. Off., 1942. 311p. (U.S. Library of Congress. Latin American ser., no.2) **A398**

At head of title: The Library of Congress, Hispanic Foundation.
First edition published in 1922 under title *Hispanic American bibliographies.*
Includes bibliographies, collective biographies, histories of literature, some general and miscellaneous works useful for reference purposes, encyclopedias, *anuarios, almanaques,* etc.

Inter-American Book Exchange. Bibliographical series. Nos.1-7. Wash., 1938–40. nos.1-7. 50c ea. **A399**

no.1, General bibliography of Ecuadorian publications for 1936 and 1937; no.2, General bibliography of Uruguayan publications for 1938; no.3, General bibliography of Guatemalan publications for 1938; no.4, General bibliography of Ecuadorian publications for 1938; no.5, General bibliography of Honduran and Costa Rican publications for 1938; no.6, Partial bibliography of Puerto Rican publications for 1938; no.7, General bibliography of Colombian publications for 1938.

Medina, José Toribio. Biblioteca hispano-americana (1493–1810). Santiago de Chile, Impreso y Grabado en Casa del Autor, 1898–1907. 7v. il. **A400**

Treats of "Primero: Libros publicados por americanos ó españoles que vivieron en América y que no tratan de una manera directa de las cosas de nuestro continente . . . Segundo: Libros escritos en castellano ó en latin é impresos en España ó fuera de ella por españolas ó americanos, ó publicados en la Península por individuos de cualquier nacionalidad, en alguno de aquellos idiomas." —*Prologo.*
8481 titles, transcribed line for line; with bio-bibliographical notes, and frequent references to authorities and to libraries containing copies of the works described.
t.1-5, 1493–1810; t.6, Prólogo. Sin fecha determinada, siglo xvii–xix. Adiciones. Ampliaciones. Dudosos. Manuscritos; t.7, Algo más de Léon Pinelo. Nuevas adiciones. Sin fecha determinada. Ultimas adiciones. Ampliaciones. Notas biográficas.

—— Historia y bibliografía de la imprenta en al antiguo vireinato del Río de la Plata. La Plata, Taller de Publicaciones del Museo, 1892. 4 pts. in 1v. il. (Historia y bibliografía de la imprenta en la América española . . . [pt.2]) **A401**

Added half title: Anales del Museo de la Plata. Materiales para la historia física y moral del continente sudamericano. Publicados bajo la dirección de Francisco P. Moreno . . . Sección de historia americana. III.

Issued in parts, each with special t.p. and pagination (xvi, xiv, 36, xiii, 12, xliii, 452, xii, 15, xviiip).

Contents: pt.1, Historia y bibliografía de la imprenta en el Paraguay (1705–1727); pt.2, En Córdoba del Tucumán (1766); pt.3, En Buenos-Aires (1780–1810); pt.4, En Montevideo (1807–1810); Indice alfabético.

—— Notas bibliográficas referentes á las primeras producciones de la imprenta en algunas ciudades de la América española (Ambato, Angostura, Curazao, Quayaquil, Maracaibo, Nueva Orleans, Nueva Valencia, Panamá, Popayán, Puerto España, Puerto Rico, Querétaro, Santa Marta, Santiago de Cuba, Santo Domingo, Tunja y otros lugares). (1754–1823) Santiago de Chile, Impr. Elzeviriana, 1904. 116p. **A402**

Pan American bookshelf. Wash., Pan American Union, Columbus Memorial Library, 1938–1948. 11v. Monthly. **A403**

A very useful monthly bibliography with annual author index. Listed books currently received in the Columbus Memorial Library, usually but not always recent material.

Ceased publication with the Dec. 1948 issue.

Succeeded by:

Current

L E A: Librarians, editors, authors; livros, editores, autores. . . . Wash., Union Panamericana, 1949- . v.1- . Monthly. **A404**

Includes notices of new magazines, abstracts of articles in the social sciences, etc., and an Inter-American index to periodicals.

Latvia

Miššinšch, J. Latweeschu rakštneezibas rahditajs (1585–1925). . . . Rigã, Išdewuše latweeschu grahmatu tirgotaju un išdewejn beedriba, 1924–37. v.1-2. **A405**

An extensive bibliography of Latvian materials. Classified arrangement. Each volume has author and title indexes.

Mexico

Millares Carlo, Augustin and **Mantecón, José Ignacio.** Ensayo de una bibliografía de bibliografías Mexicanas. (La imprenta, el libro, las bibliotecas, etc.) Mexico, Biblioteca de la II Feria del Libro y Exposición Nacional del Periodismo, 1943. 224p. **A406**

At head of title: Departamento del Distrito Federal. Dirección de Acción Social. Oficina de Bibliotecas.

Arranged by class. 1777 entries.

Includes general bibliographies relating to America that have references to Mexico, and bibliographies relating to Mexico, including general, individual, regional, subject, periodicals, etc.

Beristain de Souza, José Mariano. Biblioteca hispano americana setentrional. 2. ed. pub. el presbítero Br. Fortino Hipolito Vera. Amecameca, Colegio Católico, 1883. 3v. **A407**

1st ed., 1816–21.

—— —— Tomo [4]; comprende los anónimos que dejó escritos el autor, las adiciones del Dr. Osores y otras añadidas posteriormente por las personas que se expresan. José Toribio Medina, publicalo ahora con una introducción bio-bibliográfica. Santiago de Chile, Impr. Elzeviriana, 1897. 198p.

—— —— Adiciones y correcciones que á su fallecimiento dejó manuscritas el José Fernando Ramírez, y son las que cita con el nombre de "Suplemento"; ó, "Adición" en las apostillas que pasó á su ejemplar de la Biblioteca hispanoamericana. México, "El Tiempo," 1898. 662p.

Gonzalez de Cossio, Francisco. La imprenta en Mexico, 1594–1820. Cien adiciones a la obra de Don José Toribio Medina. Mexico, Antiguo Libreria Robredo, 1947. 205p. il. **A408**

Medina, José Toribio. La imprenta en México (1539–1821). Santiago de Chile, Autor, 1908–1912. [v.1, 1912] 8v. il. **A409**

—— La imprenta en Guadalajara de México (1793–1821): notas bibliográficas. Santiago de Chile, Impr. Elzeviriana, 1904. 104p. **A410**

—— La imprenta en la Puebla de Los Angeles (1640–1821). Santiago de Chile, Cervantes, 1908. 823p. **A411**

—— La imprenta en Oaxaca (1720–1820): notas bibliográficas. Santiago de Chile, Impr. Elzeviriana, 1904. 29p. **A412**

—— La imprenta en Veracruz (1794–1821): notas bibliográficas. Santiago de Chile, Impr. Elzeviriana, 1904. 34p. **A413**

Garcia Icazbalceta, Joaquin. Bibliografía mexicana del siglo XVI. 1. pt. Catálogo razonado de libros impresos en México de 1539 á 1600. Con biografías de autores y otras ilustraciones. México, Andrade y Morales, 1886. 419p. il. **A414**

The second part (intended to cover sixteenth century writers whose works were either published after 1600, or remained in manuscript) was never published.

Lists 116 titles, transcribed line for line. Includes many quotations, bibliographical and historical notes, references to authorities, and location of copies.

—— —— Indice alfabetico, formado por Catarina A. Janvier, trad. y arreglo de Manuel Toussaint y Justino Fernández. Mexico, Porrúa, 1938. 19p. Mex. $6

The index was originally printed in English in New York in 1889. This is a Spanish translation.

Andrade, Vicente de Paula. Ensayo bibliográfico mexicano del siglo XVII. 2. ed. México, Impr. del Museo Nacional, 1899 [1900]. 803p. **A415**

Repr., in part, from the *Memorias de la Sociedad científica "Antonio Alzate."* 1894.

Some material left by Agustin Fischer is incorporated in the work.

Lists 1228 titles, transcribed line for line. Arranged chronologically and followed by alphabetical indexes of (1) authors, (2) anonymous works.

León, Nicholás. Bibliografía mexicana del siglo XVIII. México, Francisco Diaz de Leon, 1902–1908. v.1^{1-6a}. **A416**

Publication first begun in *Anales del Museo Michoacano,* 1890.

Planned to be issued in two parallel sections, one purely bibliographical (including reprints in whole or in part of the rarer works), the other biographical, historical and critical.

v.1$^{2, 4-5}$ are numbered 4, 8, 10 of *Boletin del Instituto Bibliografico Mexicano.*

—— —— Indice[s] . . . arreglado por Roberto Valles. Mexico, Ed. Vargas Rea, 1945–46. 3v. (Biblioteca Aportación Histórica)

Indice de nombres, 1945, 61p.; Indice de impresos, 1946, 29p.; Indice de anonimos, 1946, 44p.

Mexico. Biblioteca Nacional, Mexico. Catálogos de la Biblioteca Nacional de México, formados por el director José M. Vigil. México, Oficina Tip. de la Secretaria de Fomento, 1889–1908. v.1, 3-9. **A417**

Contents: 1. div., Introd. a los conocimientos humanos, 1894; 3. div., Filosofía y pedagogía, 1889; 4. div., Jurisprudencia, 1908; 5. div., Ciencias matemáticas, físicas y naturales, 1890; 6. div., Ciencias médicas, 1889; 7. div., Artes y oficios, 1890; 8. div. Filología y bellas letras, 1891; 9. div., Historia y ciencias auxiliares, 1893.

—— —— Primeros suplementos de las divisiones 3ª., 5ª., 6ª., 7ª., y 8ª. 1895. [122]p.

—— —— Segundo de suplementos, divisiones 1ª., 3ª., 5ª., 6ª., 7ª., 8ª., y 9ª. 1903. 396p.

Current

Anuario bibliográfico mexicano, 1931–33. Compilación de Felipe Teixidor. México, Secretaría de la Relaciones Exteriores, 1932–34. v.1-3. **A418**

Based upon the copyright accessions of the National library.

1934–39 not published:

Continued by:

Anuario bibliográfico mexicano de 1940- ; comp. por Julian Amo. Mexico, Secretaría de Relaciones Exteriores, Departamento de Información para el Extranjero, 1942- . v.1- . Annual. (Serie bibliografías mexicanas) **A419**

A classed list. There is a combined author index for 1941–42.

Bibliografía mexicana . . . Obras editadas en México, libros de autores mexicanos editados en el extranjero libros editados en el extranjero relativos a México, Canje. v.1, 1942- . México, Depto. de Publicidad y Propaganda, 1944- . **A420**

At head of title: Comisión Mexicana de Cooperación Intelectual.

Boletín bibliográfico mexicano; reseña mensual de libros y folletos, editados en México. Oct. 1939- . Mexico, D. F., 1939- . Monthly to 1947; bimonthly 1947- . $2. per yr. **A421**

Published by the Instituto Panamericano de Bibliografía y Documentación. Subtitle varies.

Classified with author indexes.

Netherlands

Hague. Koninklijke Bibliotheek. Catalogus van de pampfletten-verzameling berustende in de Koninklijke Bibliotheek. Bewerkt, met aanteekeningen en een register der schrijvers voorzien, door W. P. C. Knuttel. 'sGravenhage, Algemeene Landsdrukkerij, 1889–1920. 9v. **A422**

v.1-7, Chronological, 1486–1853; v.8, Supplement; v.9, Alphabetical subject index, 1486–1795.

Nijhoff, Wouter and **Kronenberg, M. E.** Nederlandsche bibliographie van 1500 tot 1540. 'sGravenhage, Nijhoff, 1923- . 1002p. **A423**

Gives full titles and collation, with bibliographical references and location of copies.

—— —— 1.-4. aanvulling. 1925–34. 328p.

—— —— 2. deel, door M. E. Kronenberg. 1936–40. 1158p.

Titles numbered in continuation of basic work.

—— —— Inleiding tot een derde deel. Winst en verlies. 1942. 175p.

Abkoude, Johannes van. Naamregister van de bekendste en meest in gebruik zynde Nederduitsche boeken, welke sedert het jaar 1600 tot het jaar 1761 zyn uitgekomen. . . . Nu overzien, verbeterd en tot het jaar 1787 vermeerderd door Reinier Arrenberg. 2. druk. Rotterdam, Arrenberg, 1788. 598p. **A424**

—— Alphabetische naamlijst van boeken, welke
. . . 1790–1832, in Noord-Nederland zijn uitgekomen. 'sGravenhage, van Cleef, 1835. 755p.
159p. **A425**

—— Alphabetische naamlijst van fondsartikelen,
voorkomende in het naamregister van Nederlandsche boeken, alsmede in de Alphabetische
naamlijst van boeken, achtervolgens uitg bij R.
Arrenberg en de Gebroeders van Cleef, en waar-
van het regt van eigendom aan anderen is over-
gegaan. 'sGravenhage, van Cleef, 1839. 122p.
A426

Brinkman, C. L. Alphabetische naamlijst van
boeken, plaat-en kaartwerken die 1833–1849 in
Nederland uitg. of herdrukt zijn. Amsterdam,
Brinkman, 1858. 792p. **A427**

—— —— Wetenschappelijk register . . . 1850–
1875. Met alphabetische opgave der onderwerpen.
Bewerkt door R. van der Meulen. Amsterdam,
Brinkman, 1878. 464p.

Brinkman's Catalogus van boeken, plaat-en kaartwerken die gedurende de jaren 1850- in Nederland sijn uitg. of herdrukt. . . . Amsterdam,
Brinkman, 1883–93; Leiden, Sijthoff, 1903- .
A428

    1850–82, 1437p.; 1882–91, 2v.; 1892–1900, 2v.; 1901–
10, 2v.; 1911–15- pub. in 5-yr. cumulations, each in
several divisions with separate title pages.
    Each issue, except that for 1850–82 which has only the
Catalogus, is in two main parts, separately paged: (1)
Catalogus, or main author and title list, giving full information including author, title, editor or translator, if any,
illustration, size, paging, publisher, date, price; (2)
Repertorium, or subject index to the *Catalogus*, giving
brief information only and referring to the word under
which full information is found in the *Catalogus*. From
1891–1900 on, each *Repertorium* contains a Titel-catalogus, supplementary to *Brinkman's Titel-catalogus* (A429).
In the issue for 1926–30, the scope of the work was enlarged to include (1) separate lists of periodicals and
(2) Dutch works published in Belgium. (In this volume
this is a separate list; in later volumes these titles are
incorporated in the main alphabet.)

Brinkman's Titel-catalogus van . de sedert het
begin dezer eeuw tot 1888 in Nederland verschenen werken op het gebied der nieuwe
letterkunde (romans, novellen, gedichten, toon-
eelstukken en kinder-boeken) . . . Bewerkt onder
toezicht en met voorbericht van R. van der
Meulen. . . . Amsterdam, Brinkman [1888–89].
232p. **A429**

    A title index, for works of fiction, poetry, drama, music,
juvenile literature, etc., to *Brinkman's Catalogus* (A428).
Gives brief title, date, and author's name, the latter supplying the cross reference to the fuller description in
Brinkman's Catalogus. Continued by supplements included in *Brinkman's Catalogus*.

Current

Brinkman's Cumulatieve catalogus van boeken,
. . . in Nederland en Vlaanderen zijn utig. of
herdrukt, benevens aanvullingen over vooraf-
gaande jaren in één alfabet gerangschikt volgens
auteur, titel en onderwerp. Leiden, Sijthoff,
1846- . v.1- . Monthly with annual cumulations. 1948, Fl. 52 **A430**

    Publisher varies: before 1881, Amsterdam, Brinkman.
Title varies: before 1930 had title, *Brinkman's Alphabetische lijst*.
    Before 1930 an annual list on the same plan as the
main author list in *Brinkman's Catalogus* (*see* A428) with
brief subject index to the author list. 1930 on published
at varying intervals with cumulations, the last number of
the year covering twelve months and forming an annual
volume.

Nieuwe uitgaven in Nederland. Systematisch
gerangschikt. s'Gravenhage, Nijhoff, 1937- .
v.1- . Monthly. **A431**

    Selective list classified by subjects.

Netherlands East Indies

Ockeloen, G. Catalogus van boeken en tijdschriften uitg. in Ned. Oost-Indië van 1870–1937.
Batavia, Kolff, 1940. 2v. **A432**

    Contents: [v.1] Nederlandsche taal; [v.2] Inheemsche
talen.

—— Catalogus van in Ned.-Indië verschenen
boeken in die jaren 1938–1941 en enkele aanvullingen op de gestencilde catalogus verschenen in
1939. Batavia, Kolff, 1942- . v.1- . **A433**

    Contents: v.1, Nederlandsche uitgaven.

Nicaragua

Managua. Biblioteca Americana de Nicaragua.
Bibliografía de libros y folletos publicados en
Nicaragua (en 1942, o antes según fecha de
publicación), que se encuentran en algunas
bibliotecas particulares de Nicaragua; a bibliography of books and pamphlets published in
Nicaragua (with 1942 or earlier as date of publication) to be found in certain private libraries
of Nicaragua. Managua, Editorial Nuevos Horizontes [1945]. 157p. (Its Serie bibliográfica,
no.4, pt.1, Enero 1945) **A434**

    Continued by:

—— Bibliografía de trabajos publicados en
Nicaragua . . . A bibliography of works published
in Nicaragua. 1943- . [Managua, Editorial
Nuevos Horizontes,] 1944- . v.1- . (Its Serie
bibliográfica, no. 1, 6, 7-9, Julio 1944, Mayo 1945,
Mayo 1948) **A435**

    Editor: 1943–44, Graciela González.

Norway

Sommerfeldt, Wilhelm Preuss. Norsk bibliografisk-litteratur, 1919–1944. Oslo, Damm, 1944. 42p. (Norsk bibliografisk Bibliotek, bd.3, hft.1) **A436**

A classified list of Norwegian bibliographies that appeared in books and periodicals published 1919–1944.

Pettersen, Hjalmar. Bibliotheca norvegica. Christiania, Cammeyer, 1899–1924. 4v. in 5.   **A437**

Each volume has added title page in English.
Contents: v.1, Norsk boglexikon, 1643–1813 (English t.p.: Descriptive catalogue of books printed in Norway, 1643–1813). 1899–1908. 621p.; v.2. Norge og nordmaend i udlandets literatur (Norway and the Norwegians in foreign literature; descriptive catalogue of books and papers relating to Norway). 1908–10. 2v., 566p.; v.3, Norske forfattere før 1814 (Norwegian authors before 1814: descriptive catalogue of their works). 1911–18. 595p.; v.4, Norske forfattere efter 1814. 1. samling med suppl. til Bibliotheca norvegica I-III (Norwegian authors: descriptive catalogue of their works printed in foreign countries). 1913–24. 798p.

Norsk bokfortegnelse, 1814–47–1936–40. Kristiania, 1848–1924; Oslo, Norske Bokhandlerforening, 1928–1943. (In progress)   **A438**

Title varies.
1814–47, utg. af Mart. Nissen. 215p.; 1848–65, utg. af P. Botten-Hansen og Siegwart Petersen. 302p.; 1866–72, redig. af Thorvald Boeck. 212p.; Register 1848–65 og 1866–72, utarb. af Thorvald Boeck og. O. A. Øverland. 1xvip.; 1873–82, redig. af M. W. Feilberg. 458p.; Register, 1873–82. xlviiip.; Katalog over norsk musikforlag, og norske komponisters vaerker udkomme i udlandet. 64p.; 1883–90, med tillaeg musikalier, redig. af M. W. Feilberg. 515p.; 1891–1900, utarb. af H. J. Haffner. 599p.; 1901–10, utarb. af H. J. Haffner, 599p.; 1911–20, utarb. af H. J. Haffner. 738p.; 1921–25–1936–40. 4v. utg. av Universitetsbiblioteket.

Aure, Anton. Nynorsk boklista; skrifter i bokform paa Norsk-bygdemaal og landsmaal. Kristiania, Norlis, 1916; Det norske samlaget, 1921–26. 3v.   **A439**

v.1, 1646–1915; v.2, 1916–20, and suppl. to v.1; v.3, 1921–25.

Botten-Hansen, Paul. La Norvège littéraire. Catalogue systématique et raisonné de tous les ouvrages de quelque valeur imprimés en Norvège, ou composés par des auteurs norvégiens au xixᵉ siècle, accompagné de renvois, notes, et explications littéraires . . . notices biographiques sur les auteurs, etc. Christiania, Gundersen, 1868. 271p.   **A440**

Hauff, Nils Selmer. Stikords-katalog over norsk literatur, 1883–1907. Kristiania, Cappelen, [1908–09]. 93p.   **A441**

Current

Aarskatalog over norsk litteratur, 1893-   . . . Utgitt av den Norske Boghandlerforening. . . .

Oslo, Cammermeyer, 1893-   . v.1-   . Annual.   **A442**

1893–1902 had title: Kvartalskatalog over norsk litteratur.

Norsk Bokhandlertidende. v.1-   . Oslo, Grøndahl, 1880-   . Weekly.   **A443**

Paraguay

Paraguay. Biblioteca Nacional. Bibliografía paraguaya: catálogo de la Biblioteca Paraguaya "Solano López." Asunción, Talleres Nacionales de H. Kraus, 1906. 984p.   **A444**

Rich in the early history of Paraguay.

Peru

Biblioteca peruana. Apuntes para un catálogo de impresos. Santiago de Chile, Bibl. del Inst. Nacional, 1896. 2v.   **A445**

Edited by Gabriel René-Moreno.
A fully annotated work. Basic.
Contents: v.1, pts. 1-2, Libros y folletos peruanos de la Biblioteca del Instituto Nacional; v.2, pts. 1-2, Libros y folletos de la Biblioteca Nacional y Notas bibliográficas.

Medina, José Toribio. La imprenta en Lima (1584–1824). Santiago de Chile, Autor, 1904–07. 4v.   **A446**

—— La imprenta en Arequipa, el Cuzco, Trujillo y otros pueblos del Perú durante las campañas de la independencia (1820–1825); notas bibliográficas. Santiago de Chile, Imp. Elzeviriana, 1904. 71p.   **A446a**

Current

Anuario bibliográfico peruano. 1943-   . Lima, Talleres Gráficos de la Editorial Lumen, 1945-   . v.1-   . Annual. (Ediciones de la Biblioteca Nacional, 1-   .)   **A447**

Editor: 1943-   , Alberto Tauro.
An annual bibliography which attempts to record books, pamphlets, and all other publications printed in Peru; and works of Peruvian authors and works relating to Peru printed abroad.

Lima. Universidad Mayor de San Marcos. Biblioteca. Boletín bibliográfico. v.1, 1923-   . Lima, 1923-   . Quarterly.   **A448**

Suspended 1930–Oct. 1934.

Schwab, Federico. Bibliografía de libros y folletos peruanos, 1940/1941-   . Lima, Compañía de Impresiones y Publicidad, 1942-   . v.1-   . Biennial.   **A449**

Classed list with author index.

Philippines

Medina, José Toribio. Bibliografía española de las islas Filipinas (1523–1810). Santiago de Chile, Impr. Cervantes, 1897–98. 556p. **A450**

Repr. from *Anales* de la Universidad de Chile, 1897–98. A list of 667 titles arranged chronologically, with author index.

—— La imprenta en Manila desde sus origenes hasta 1810. Santiago de Chile, Autor, 1896. 280p. facsim. **A451**

—— —— Adiciones y ampliaciones. Santiago de Chile, Autor, 1904. 203p.

Pardo de Tavera, Trinidad Hermenegildo. Biblioteca filipina. . . . Wash., Govt. Prt. Off., 1903. 439p. (pt.2 of U.S. Library of Congress. Bibliography of the Philippine Islands. Wash., Govt. Prt. Off., 1903. 57th Cong., 2d sess., Senate doc. no.74) **A452**

Subtitle: Ó sea catálogo razonado de todos los impresos, tanto insulares como extranjeros, relativos á la historia, la etnografía, la lingüística, la botánica, la fauna, la flora, la geología, la hidrografía, la geografía, la legislación, etc., de las islas Filipinas, de Joló y Marianas, pub. under the direction of the Library of Congress and the Bureau of Insular Affairs, War Department.

Pérez, Ángel and **Güemes, Cecilio.** Adiciones y continuación de "La imprenta en Manila" de D. J. T. Medina; ó rarezas y curiosidades bibliográficas filipinas de las bibliotecas de esta capital. Manila, Santos y Bernal, 1904. 620p. **A453**

Retana y Gamboa, Wenceslao Emilio. La imprenta en Filipinas; adiciones y observaciones à la Imprenta en Manila de D. J. T. Medina. Madrid, Minuesa de los Rios, 1897. 276 cols. **A454**

—— Aparato bibliaffíco de la historia general de Filipinas. Madrid, Minuesa de los Rios, 1906. 3v. **A455**

v.1, 1524–1800; v.2, 1801–86; v.3, 1887–1905.
Includes: (1) Philippine imprints regardless of subject; (2) Books about the Philippines regardless of what language written in or where published; (3) Publications of Filipinos wherever printed.
Arranged by years with the following indexes in v.1: (1) Anónimos y principales materias, refundidos; (2) Publicaciones periódicas; (3) Biblioteca idiomática oriental; (4) Lugares geográficos; (5) Nombres propíos de personas.

—— Tablas cronológica y alfabética de imprentas é impresores de Filipinas (1593–1898). Madrid, Victoriano Suárez, 1908. 114p. **A456**

Poland

Wierzbowski, Teodor. Bibliographia polonica xv ac xvi ss. . . . Varsoviae, Kowalewski, 1889–94. 3v. **A457**

v.1, contains titles of works in the Warsaw University Library; v.2-3, works found in 111 other libraries, Polish and foreign, with indication of location. Arranged chronologically with indexes of author, subjects, persons and places.

Estreicher, Karol. Bibliografia polska. Kraków, Czionkami Drukarni Uniwersytetu Jagiellońskiego, 1870–1939. v.1-33. (In progress) **A458**

In three series: (1) an alphabetical list for the 19th century (1800–1870); (2) chronological lists, 1455–1889; (3) alphabetical list, 15th-18th century.
Contents: ser. 1, 7v.: v.1-5, A-Z, v.6-7, Supplement, A-Z; ser. 2, 4v.: chronological lists, v.8-9, 1455–1799, v.10, 1800–1870, v.11, 1871–89; ser. 3, 15th-18th centuries, v.1-22 (whole no. v.12-33), A-Y.

—— Bibliografia polska 19. stulecia, lata 1881–1900. Kraków, Spólka Księgarzy Polsk., 1906–16. 4v. **A459**

20th century

Dabrowska, Wanda, Czarnecka, J. and **Słomczewska, J.** 555 ksiażek wydanych w okresie powojennym. Warszawa, Ludówy Instytut Oświaty i Kultury Wydzial Ksiaźki i Czytelnictwa, 1946. 80p. **A460**

Lists 555 books published in Poland, July 1944–May 1, 1946. Classified with author and title, and subject indexes.

Przewodnik bibliograficzny. v.1-37, no.6, 1878–June 1914; ser. 2, v.1-9, 1920–28; ser. 3, v.1-5, 1929–33. Krakow, Základ narodowy imienia Ossolinskich, 1878–1933. **A461**

1914–19 replaced by *Bibliografia polska*, v.1-6.

Rocznik bibliograficzny; druków w jezyku polskim oraz w jezykach obcych o Polsce wydanych poza terytorium Rzeczypospolitej Polskiej. Sept. 1, 1939–1943; opracował Tadeusz Sawicki. Edinburgh and Lond., Oliver and Boyd, 1942–44. v.1-3. **A462**

Added title page in English: Bibliographical yearbook; works in Polish and works relating to Poland published outside of Poland.
Items numbered consecutively, v.1-3, no. 1-1820.
Arranged by class with author and title indexes.

Portugal

Anselmo, António Joaquim. Bibliografia das bibliografias portuguesas. Lisboa, Biblioteca Nacional, 1923. 158p. (Publicações da Biblioteca Nacional. Biblioteca do bibliotecário e do arquivista 3) **A463**

Contents: (1) Bibliografias gerais; (2) Bibliografias especiais e monografias; (3) Publicações periodicas de bibliografia.

Early

Academia das Sciencias de Lisboa. Bibliografia geral portuguesa. Lisboa, Imp. Nacional, 1941–42. v.1-2. il. **A464**

Date on cover of v.2, 1944.
Contents: v.1-2, Seculo xv.
Detailed bibliographical descriptions with introduction and notes, facsimiles; and the following indexes in each volume: Matérias, Gravuras, Impressores, Bibliotecas e arquivos, Toponímico, and Geral.

Anselmo, António Joaquim. Bibliografia das obras impressas em Portugal no século xvi. Lisboa, Oficinas Gráficas da Biblioteca Nacional, 1926. 367p. il. (Publicações da Biblioteca Nacional) **A465**

Reprinted from *Anais das bibliotecas e arquivos*, sér. 2, v.2-6, 1921–25.

British Museum. Dept. of Printed Books. Short-title catalogues of Portuguese books and of Spanish-American books printed before 1601, now in the British Museum, by H. Thomas. Lond., Quaritch, 1926. 55p. **A466**

—— Short-title catalogue of Portuguese books printed before 1601, now in the British Museum, by Henry Thomas. Lond., Trustees, 1940. 43p. **A467**

Barbosa Machado, Diogo. Bibliotheca lusitana historica, critica, e cronologica. Na qual se comprehende a noticia dos authores portuguezes, e das obras, que compuseraõ desde o tempo da promulgaçaõ da ley da graça até o tempo prezente. Lisboa, 1741–59. 4v. **A468**

An abridgement by B. J. de Sousa-Farinha entitled *Summario da Bibliotheca lusitana* was published in Lisbon, 1786–87. 3v.

Manuel II, King of Portugal. Livros antigos portuguezes, 1489–1600, da bibliotheca de Sua Majestade Fidelissima, descriptos por S. M. el-rei D. Manuel. . . . Camb., Univ. Pr., 1929–32. v.1-2. il. To be in 3v.; set of 3v., 125s. **A469**

v.1, 1489–1539; v.2, 1540–1569.

Pinto de Mattos, Ricardo. Manual bibliographico portuguez de livros raros, classicos e curiosos; revisto e prefaciado pelo Camillo Castello Branco. Porto, Livr. Portuense, 1878. 582p. **A470**

Usually includes brief biographical notes on the authors.

General

Coimbra, Carlos. Dicionario de bibliografia portuguesa . . . Edição de A. de Gusmão Navarro. Lisboa, Torres, 1933–37. v.1- . **A471**

Loose-leaf. Issued in parts.
A-Barros (with a few sheets giving entries for various

other parts of the alphabet). A new attempt to list Portuguese books of all periods.

Silva, Innocencio Francisco da. Diccionario bibliographico portuguez. Estudos applicaveis a Portugal e ao Brasil. Lisboa, Imp. Nacional, 1858–1923. v.1-22. il. **A472**

v.10-21 continuados e ampliados por Brito Aranha. v.1-7, A-Z; v.8-22 (supplement v.1-15), A-Z, A-Au.
Arranged alphabetically by *first* names of authors. Includes books published from the fifteenth to the nineteenth century.

—— —— Indice alfabético [por] José Soares de Souza. [São Paulo?] Dept. de Cultura, Div. de Bibliotécas, 1938. 264p.

Current

Anais das bibliotecas e arquivos de Portugal. v.1-3; ser. 2, v.1- . Coimbra, Imp. de Universidade, 1914–17; 1920- . Quarterly. **A473**

Includes lists of Portuguese books added to the Biblioteca Nacional.

Puerto Rico

Pedreira, Antonia S. Bibliografía puertorriqueña (1493–1930). Madrid, Impr. de la Librería y Casa Editorial Hernando, 1932. 707p. (Monografías de la Universidad de Puerto Rico. Serie A. Estudios hispánicos, núm. 1) bound, $2; paper, $1.50. **A474**

Includes works by natives and foreigners about Puerto Rico, the artistic literary works of Puerto Ricans, and a selected list of works by Puerto Ricans on various subjects. —Cf. *Introd.*, p.xvii.
Classified, with author and subject indexes.

Current

Anuario bibliografico puertorriqueño; indice alfabético de libros, folletos, revistas y periódicos publicados en Puerto Rico durante 1948- , comp. por Gonzalo Velazquez. Rió Piedras, Biblioteca de la Universidad, 1950- . v.1- . **A474a**

Rumania

Bianu, Ioan and **Hodos, Nerva.** Bibliografia românească veche 1508–1830. Ed. Academiei Române. Bucureşti, Atelierele Socec & Co., 1903–36. 3v. il. **A475**

Issued in parts, 1898–1936. v.1, 1508–1716; v.2, 1716–1808; v.3, 1809–1830.

Cardas, Gh. Tratat de bibliografie. [Bucureşti] Tip. "Bucovina," 1931. 389p. **A476**

Veress, Endre. Bibliografia română-ungară. București, Cartea Românească, 1931–35. v.1-3. il.
A477

v.1, Românii in literatura ungară și Unguarii in literatura română (1473–1780); v.2, (1781–1838); v.3, (1839–1878).

Volumes 1-3 record some 2377 titles with full description and location of copies. Each volume has added title page and preface in French.

Russia
Bibliography

Mez'er, Augusta Vladimirovna. Slovarن̦yĭ ukazatel' po knigovedeniĭū. Moskva, Gosudarst. Soṭsial'no-ekon. Izdat., 1931–34. 3v. **A478**

1st ed. 1924.

A bibliographical manual covering such subjects as bibliographies, dictionaries, reference books, library science, etc.

Sokurova, M. V. Obshchie bibliografii knig grazhdanskoĭ pechati, 1708–1937. Leningrad, 1944. [192p.] (Bibliografĭă russkoĭ bibliografii; pod red. ĪŪ. A. Mezhenko, v.1) **A479**

Volume 1 of a projected 4-volume bibliography of Russian bibliographies. This is an annotated guide to 73 general bibliographies, with full descriptions, notes on authors and editors, and citations to pertinent literature and critical reviews. Includes indexes to authors, titles, personal names, and subjects; chronological lists and tables; an historical introduction; and a list of sources consulted. Other volumes will cover bibliographical periodicals, bibliography of bibliographies of bibliography, and historical bibliography.

18th and 19th centuries

Bazunov, A. F. *firm, booksellers.* Sistematicheskiĭ katalog' russkim' knigam', 1825–1869. Sostavil' V. I. Mezhov. St. Petersburg, Bazunov, 1869. 995p. **A480**

—— —— Pervoe [-shestoe] pribavlenie, 1-6, 1869–1874. St. Petersburg, 1870–75. 4v. in 2.

—— —— 7-8, 1875–76. St. Petersburg, Isakov, 1877.

Bezgin, Il'la Grigor'evich. Opisanie vsiekh russkikh knig i povremennykh izdaniĭ. St. Petersburg, Pozharov, 1905–06. 12v. **A481**

Series I treats 1708–1799; series II-XII treat by decade the period from 1800–1909.

Sopikov, Vasiliĭ Stephanovich. Opyt rossïiskoi bibliografiĭ. [Izd. 2] Red . . . V. N. Rogozhin. St. Petersburg, 1904–06. 5v. **A482**

Originally published 1813–21. 5v. v.1 is a classed arrangement of books in Church Slavic; v.2-5 list books in Russian to 1813.

Subject index in Morozov, P. O. Alfabetnyĭ ukazatel'

imen. 1876. 47p.; and Rogozhin, V. N. Ukazatel. . . . 1908. 253p.

19th and 20th centuries

U. S. Library of Congress. Reference Department. Russia: a check list preliminary to a basic bibliography of materials in the Russian language. Wash., 1944–46. pts. 1-10. **A483**

Contents: pt.1, Belles lettres. 1944. 99p.; pt.2, Economic conditions and social history prior to 1918. 1944. 74p.; pt.3, Fine arts. 1944. 38p.; pt. 4, Law and institutions prior to 1918. 1944. 62p.; pt.5, Folklore, linguistics and literary forms. 1944. 21p.; pt.6, Church and education prior to 1918. 1944. 33p.; pt.7, History, including auxiliary sciences, prior to 1918. 1945. 123p.; pt.8, Theatre and music prior to 1918. 1945. 23p.; pt.9, Soviet Union. 1945. 86p.; pt.10, Reference books. 1946. 227p.

Each section is arranged alphabetically. Titles are given in transliteration according to Library of Congress rules.

Part 10 includes in Addenda a list of reference books in languages other than Russian, and a list of bibliographical and bibliothecal periodicals.

Current

U. S. Library of Congress. Monthly list of Russian accessions. v.1, Apr. 1948- . Wash., Govt Prt. Off., 1948- . Monthly. $3 per yr.; $4 foreign **A48**

A classified list in two parts: (1) monographic literature published since 1945; and (2) periodical material printed since 1947. Both parts include titles published in Russian in and outside the Soviet Union.

Scotland

Aldis, Harry Gidney. List of books printed in Scotland before 1700, including those printed furth of the realm for Scottish booksellers, with brief notes on the printers and stationers. Edinburgh, Edinburgh Bibl. Soc., 1904. 153p. **A48**

Sold only to members of the society.

A preliminary hand-list of 3919 titles.

Maclean, Donald. Typographia scotogadelica or, Books printed in the Gaelic of Scotland from the year 1567 to the year 1914, with bibliographical and biographical notes. Edinburgh, Gran 1915. 372p. **A48**

Slovakia

Rizner, Ludovit Vladimir. Bibliografia písomníctva slovenského na spósob slovníka od najstaršíc čias do konca r. 1900- . S pripojenou bibliografiou archeologickou, historickou . . . vydáv matičná sprava. V Turcianskom sv. Martin Nákladom Matice Slovenskej, Tlacou novej kníhlaciarne, 1929–34. 6v. **A48**

South Africa

Nienaber, Petrus Johannes. Bibliografie van afrikaanse boeke. Johannesburg, Voortiekkerpers Bpk., 1943–48. v.1-2. **A488**

Contents: Deel 1, 6 April 1861–6 April 1943. 841p.; Deel 2, April 1943–Oktober 1948. 352p.
A comprehensive bibliography. Deel 2 is a cumulation of annual supplements.

South African catalogue of books; 3d complete ed. 1900–1947, with list of publishers and booksellers in South Africa. Johannesburg, 1948. 2v. **A489**

Continued by supplements, issued monthly, cumulating annually.

Spain
Bibliography

Foulché-Delbosc, Raymond and **Barrau-Dihigo, Louis.** Manuel de l'hispanisant. N.Y., Putnam, 1920; Hispanic Soc. of Amer., 1925. v.1-2. **A490**

v.1, Répertoires; v.2, Collections.
A useful manual of Spanish bibliography including material on Portugal as well as Spain. Volume 1 lists bibliographies, national, regional, special; biographical works; bibliographies of special subjects; descriptions of public and private archives, libraries and museums. Volume 2 gives contents of printed collections and series, published 1579–1923.

General

Beltrán, Francisco. Biblioteca bio-bibliográfica. Catálogo de una importante colección de libros y folletos españoles y extranjeros referentes a bibliografía, biografía, bibliologia, bibliofilia, la imprenta y sus artes auxiliares. Madrid, Libreria Española y Extranjera, 1927. 498p. il. **A491**

Boston. Public Library. Ticknor Collection. Catalogue of the Spanish library and of the Portuguese books bequeathed by George Ticknor. Bost., 1879. 476p. **A492**

California. University. Library. Spain and Spanish America in the libraries of the University of California; a catalog of books. Berkeley, Calif., 1928–30. 2v. **A493**

v.1, General and departmental libraries; v.2, The Banroft Library.

Heredia y Livermore, Ricardo, *conde de Benavis.* Catalogue de la bibliothèque de M. Ricardo Heredia. Paris, É. Paul, 1891–94. 4v. il. **A494**

Hidalgo, Dionisio. Diccionario general de bibliografía española. Madrid, Impr. de las Escuelas Pias, 1862–81. 7v. **A495**

A general list of works published in Spain, with author and classed indexes.

Molina Navarro, Gabriel. Indice para facilitar el manejo y consulta de los catálogos de Salva y Heredia. Madrid, Molina, 1913. 162p. **A496**

Palau y Dulcet, Antonio. Manual del librero hispano-americano; inventario bibliográfico de la producción científica y literaria de España y de la América latina desde la invención de la imprenta hasta nuestros dias, con el valor comercial de todos los artículos descritos. Barcelona, Librería Anticuaria, 1923–27. 7v. **A497**

A comprehensive alphabetical record, listing material under author or title for anonymous works. A very useful compilation, which will gradually be superseded by the new edition now in progress, as follows:

—— Manual del librero hispano-americano; bibliografía general española e hispano-americana desde la invención de la imprenta hasta nuestros tiempos con el valor comercial de los impresos descritos. 2. ed. corr. y aum. por el autor. Barcelona, Librería Palau, 1948- . v.1- . (In progress) £7. 7s.

v.1, A (no.1-21526).
A revised and much enlarged edition, the letter A covering four times as many pages as in the first edition. To be completed in 10v.

Ribelles Comín, José. Bibliografía de la lengua valenciana. . . . Madrid, "Rev. de arch., bibl. y museos," 1915–31. v.1-3. facsim. **A498**

Subtitle: O sea catálogo razonada por orden alfabético de autores de los libros, folletos, obras dramáticas, periódicos, coloquios, coplas, chistes, discursos, romances, alocuciones, cantares, gozos, etc., que escritos en lengua valenciana y bilingüe, han visto la luz pública desde el establecimiento de la imprenta en España hasta nuestros días.
v.1, siglo xv (i.e., descriptions and notes of printed editions to 1918 of works in the Valencian dialect composed before the end of the 15th century); v.2, siglo xvi; v.3, siglo xvii.
No more published.

Salvá y Pérez, Vicente. Catálogo de la biblioteca de Salvá, escrito por Pedro Salvá y Mallen, y enriquecido con la descripción de otras muchas obras, de sus ediciones, etc. Valencia, Impr. de Ferrer de Orga, 1872. 2v. il. **A499**

Early

Antonio, Nicolás. Bibliotheca hispana vetus; sive, Hispani scriptores qui ab Octaviani Augusti aevo ad annum Christi MD. floruerunt. Matriti, J. Ibarra, 1788. 2v. **A500**

—— Bibliotheca hispana nova; sive, Hispanorum scriptorum qui ab anno MD. ad MDCLXXXIV,

floruere notitia. Matriti, J. de Ibarra, 1783–88. 2v.
A501

The date 1783 on the t.p. of v.1 is a misprint for 1788.
The 2d ed., edited by T. A. Sánchez, J. A. Pellicer and
R. Casalbón; the 1st ed. was pub. in 1672 as *Bibliotheca
hispana*.

An excellent and indispensable work, dealing with the
writings of persons born in the Spanish peninsula regardless of the language in which they wrote. Volume 1 covering to 1500 is in narrative form, volume 2, 1500–1684,
is a bibliographical dictionary.

British Museum. Dept. of Printed Books. Short-
title catalogue of books printed in Spain and of
Spanish books printed elsewhere in Europe before 1601 now in the British Museum, by Henry
Thomas. Lond., 1921. 101p. **A502**

Haebler, Konrad. Bibliografía ibérica del siglo
xv. Enumeración de todos los libros impresos en
España y Portugal hasta el año de 1500 con notas
críticas. La Haya, Nijhoff; Leipzig, Hiersemann,
1903–17. 2v. **A503**

Hispanic Society of America. Library. List of
books printed before 1601 in the Library, comp.
by C. L. Penney. N.Y., The Trustees, 1929. 274p.
(Hispanic notes and monographs. Catalogue
ser.) **A504**

—— List of books printed 1601–1700, in the
Library, by C. L. Penney. N.Y., The Trustees,
1938. 972p. (Hispanic notes and monographs.
Catalogue ser.) **A505**

With appendices: (1) 15th-16th century books not included in *List of books printed before 1601*; (2) Check
list of printing sites and printers of Hispanic books
1468?–1700.

Vindel, Francisco. Manual gráfico-descriptivo
del bibliófilo hispano—americano (1475–1850),
con un prólogo de Pedro Sáinz Rodríguez.
Madrid [Impr. Góngora], 1930–34. 12v. in 13.
il. (incl. facsim.) **A506**

v.1-10, A-Z; v.11, Tasación e indices; v.12, Suplemento,
siglo xv.
An author list of 3442 books, mainly early. Information given for each includes: author's name, title, place,
publisher or printer, date, size, generally paging. A
special feature is that for each item there is a reproduction of some page of the work, generally title page or
colophon.

19th century

See General, p.51-52.

20th century

**Catálogo general de la librería española e his-
panoamericana,** 1901–30. Autores. Madrid, Inst.
Nac. del Libro Español, 1932–44. v.1-4. (In
progress) **A507**

v.1-4, A-Q.
Publisher varies.
A comprehensive list giving full name of author, title,
edition, place, publisher, date, paging, size, price.

Current

Bibliografía española; revista general de la imprenta, de la librería y de las industrias que
concurren à la fabricación del libro. Madrid,
Asociación de la Librería, 1901–22. 22v. **A508**

Continued by:

**Bibliografía general española e hispano-ameri-
cana,** 1923–marzo/abril 1942. Madrid-Barcelona,
1923–42. 16v. **A509**

Monthly, 1923–36; bimonthly, 1941–42. Publication
suspended July 1936–Jan. 1941. 1923–36 in three parts:
(1) *Bibliografía*, a list of new publications, giving for
each item author's name, title, place, date, publisher,
paging, size and price; (2) *Crónica;* (3) *Anuncios.*
v.1-9 have a general author index to the books listed in
the monthly *Bibliográfia;* v.10 has, instead, a cumulated
author list of the entries in v.9-10.

Continued by:

Bibliografía Hispanica, año 1- . mayo/junio
1942- . Madrid, Instituto Nacional de Libro
Español, 1942- . Monthly. **A510**

Each monthly issue in two sections: (1) articles on
the book trade, bibliographies, book reviews, etc.; (2)
Repertorio bibliográfico, which is a classed list of books
published, with an annual index of authors and titles.
This section is usually paged separately and continuously
with a special title page so that it may be bound separately. Variations are: v.1, 1942, *Repertorio* paged separately in each issue but not continuously; v.2-3, 1943,
Repertorio not separately paged; v.8, 1948, *Bibliografía*
published three times per year, *Repertorio* published
separately monthly; v.9, 1949- , monthly issues containing both sections, paged separately.

Sweden
Early

Sveriges bibliografi intill ar 1600, av Isak Collijn.
Uppsala, Svenska Litteratursällskapet, 1927–38.
3v. il. (Svenska litteratursällskapet. Skrifter)
A511

bd.1, 1478–1530 (pub. 1934–38); bd.2, 1530–82
(pub. 1927–31); bd.3, 1583–99 (pub. 1932–33); Alfabetisk register til bd.1; bd. 2-3; Typografiska tabeller,
1483–1525; 1526–99.
Volume 1 is a revision of *Sveriges bibliografi, 1481–
1600*, by G. E. Klemming and Aksel Anderson (Uppsala,
1927. 216p.).
Arranged chronologically, with alphabetical indexes.
Gives full descriptions, with bibliographical references
and location of copies. Continued by:

Sveriges bibliografi, 1600-talet. Bidrag till en
bibliografisk förteckning, av Isak Collijn. Uppsala,
Almquist, 1942–46. 2v. (Skrifter utgivna av
Svenska Literatursällskapet) **A512**

Arranged alphabetically with no chronological approach. Gives brief biographical facts, full description, and location of copies.

19th and 20th centuries

Linnström, Hjalmår. Svensk boklexikon, 1830–65. Stockholm, Linnström, 1883–84. 2v.   **A513**

Alphabetical arrangement.

Svensk bok-katalog, 1866–75—1936–40. Stockholm, Svenska Bokförläggareföreningen, 1878–1947. [v.1-12.] 1936–40. Kr. 300   **A514**

1866–75, 1876–85, 1886–95 published as 10-year volumes. Thereafter volumes have been published as 5-year cumulations.

Includes books, pamphlets, periodicals, government publications, theses. Each volume is in two parts: (1) alphabetical author and title list; (2) classed subject list.

Current

Arskatalog för svenska bokhandeln, 1.- . 1861- . Stockholm, Svenska Bokförläggareföreningen, 1862- . v.1- . Annual. Kr. 8   **A515**

Preceded by the *Förteckning öfver svenska bokhandelns,* 1855–59.

Each annual volume is in three parts: (1) alphabetical author and title list; (2) classed subject list; (3) music.

Nordisk bok kalender. 1947- . Stockholm, Förlaget Biblioteksböcker, 1947- .   **A516**

Supersedes *Svensk bokkalender.* 1943–1946. Ed. by Bengt Ahlen.

Each volume includes survey articles on the literary output of the year followed by a list of books published. Covers Denmark, Finland, Norway and Sweden.

Svensk bokforteckning, 1913- . 1.-arg. Stockholm, Svenska Bokhandlareföreningen, 1913- .   **A517**

Monthly. Classified list.

Svensk bokhandels-tidning. v.1- . 1863- . Stockholm, 1863- . v.1- .   **A518**

Weekly. Alphabetical list.

Switzerland

Bern. Schweizerische Landesbibliothek. Katalog . . . Alphabetisches Verzeichnis der bis 1900 erschienenen Druckschriften. Bern, Francke, 1910.   **A519**

Added title page in French.

Contents: Abt. A: Geschichte, Geographie und Landeskunde. 2v. No more published.

—— Katalog . . . Systematisches Verzeichnis der schweizerischen oder die Schweiz betreffenden Veröffentlichungen, 1901–20, 1921–30, 1931–40- . Bern, Huber, [1927]–49. (In progress)   **A520**

Contents and preface in German and French. Added title page: Catalogue de la Bibliothèque Nationale Suisse. Répertoire méthodique des publications suisse ou relatives à la Suisse.

Issued in parts, each under cover-title, German on front, and French on back cover.

Catalog for 1901–20 in two volumes: v.1, Classed list, arranged by the decimal classification, 1006p.; v.2, Biographical and topographical catalog: (1) Biography, p.1-128, (2) Topography, p.131-419, each arranged alphabetically.

Catalog for 1921–30, Classed list, 799p.; Personenkatalog, 93p.; Ortskatalog, 306p.; 1931–40- (incompl.).

A subject list which serves both as a short-title catalog of the works listed and as an index to the fuller descriptions in the *Bibliographisches Bulletin* (A527) for the same years. Gives author, brief title, date of publication, and also the year of the *Bulletin,* if that differs from publication date, in which full description is given. In case of periodicals reference is given to the *Catalogue des périodiques suisses,* published by the Bibliothèque Nationale.

Bibliographie nationale suisse. Répertoire méthodique de ce qui a été publié sur la Suisse et ses habitants. Publiée par la Commission Centrale pour la Bibliographie Suisse. Berne, Wyss, 1892–1927. pts. 1-5 in 48 fasc.   **A521**

Each fascicule is on a different subject, prepared by a specialist in the field.

fasc. Ia, Travaux bibliographiques préliminaires. Catalogues des bibliothèques de la Suisse, par J. H. Graf. 1894. 67p.; Ib, Bibliographie des revues, gazettes et almanachs suisses . . . par J. L. Brandstetter. 1896. 302p.; II, Littérature de la géodésíe suisse . . . pub. par le Bureau Topographique Fédéral. [1892]–96. 4 pts. in 1v.; III, Descriptions géographiques et récits de voyages et excursions en Suisse . . . par A. Wæber. 1899–1909. 2v.; IV 3a, Les lacs, pub. par H. Walser . . . et Léon W. Collet. 1913. 71p.; IV 3, Balnéologie et climatothérapie . . . par B. Reber. 1900. 111p.; IV 4, Klimatologie, von R. Billwiller . . . Erdmagnetismus, von J. Maurer. 1927. 9p.; IV 5, Flora helvetica. 1530–1900, par E. Fischer. 1901. 241p. Suppl. 1922. 40p.; IV 6, cahier 1. D, 2, 3a, 4, 5γ, 5δ, 6, 7a, 8, 9. Fauna Helvetica . . . rédigé par T. Studer, 1894–1926. 9 pts.; V 2, Anthropologie et préhistoire . . . par J. Heierli. 1901. 138p.; V 3, Histoire cantonale et locale . . . par J. L. Brandstetter. 1906. 330p.; V 4, dernier cahier. Héraldique et généalogie . . . par J. Grellet et M. Tripet. 1895. 60p.; V 5 [1, 2, 3, 4, 5] Histoire de la civilisation et des us et coutumes (folklore) de la Suisse, par F. Heinemann. 1907–13. 5 pts. in 6v.; V 6a-c, Architecture sculpture et peinture . . . par B. Haendcke. 1892. 100p.; V 6d, Bibliographie de la musique et du chant populaire, par K. Nef. 1908. 151p.; V 6e, Exercices corporels . . . par A. Landtwing. 1899. 153p.; V 8, Hygiène publique . . . par F. Schmid. 1898–1906. 2v.; V 9a-b, Agriculture. La littérature agricole depuis ses origines, au xv siècle, jusqu'à fin 1892 . . . par F. Anderegg, E. Anderegg. [1894]–1895. 6 pts. in 1v.; V 9c, Forêts, chasse et pêche . . . Compilé par la Division Forêts, Chasse et Pêche du Département Fédéral de l'Industrie et de l'Agriculture. Forêts. 231p., Pêche 57p., Chasse, 71p.; 1894–1907. 3v.; V 9c2, Forêts, chasse et pêche. Pêche. Suppl. 1916. 35p., Chasse. Suppl. 1916. 31p.; V 9d, Travaux de défense (corrections de torrents, corrections fluviales, etc.). Compilé par la Division Forêts, Chasse et Pêche (Inspection Fédérale des Forêts) du Département Fédéral de l'Industrie et de l'Agriculture. 1895. 128p.; V 9f, Industrie et métiers . . . par E. Boos-Jegher. 1904–20. cahier 1-7.; V 9gβ, Poids et mesures; monnaies. 1894. v.1; V9gγ, Service des postes et télégraphes. Postes, rédigé par la Direction Générale des Postes Suisses. Télégraphe, par E. Abrezol. 1895. 105p. Postes (Supplément) 1903. 74p. Télégraphes et téléphones (Supplément) 1906. 19p.; V 9gδ, Hôtels et cafés; commerce de boissons alcooliques. Pub. par le bureau de la Commission Centrale pour la Bibliographie Suisse. 1907. 166p.; V 9gε, Banques, statistique commerciale, assurances . . . par W. Speiser, T. Geering, J. J. Kummer. 1893. 207p.; Emigration . . . par J. Dreifuss. 1905. 68p.; V 9hβ, cahier 3. Littérature des chemins de fer suisses (1830–1901) . . . par Albert Sichler. 1902. 390p., 130p.; V 9j, Alcool et alcoolisme . . . par O. Lauterburg, E. W. Milliet, et Antony Rochat. 1895. 172p.; V 9k, Protection des animaux, par H. Fischer-Sigwart. 1906. 101p.; V 10a, Culture intellectuelle de la Suisse en general . . . par R. Luginbühl. 1903. 154p.; V 10c, Education et instruction . . . par Albert Sichler. 1906–19. v.1¹⁻², 2¹⁻², 3; V 10 ea, Bibliographie de l'Église évangélique réformée da la Suisse, 1896–1918. Cahier 1-3; V 10eβ, Bibliographie catholique du diocèse de Bâle de l'année 1750 à l'année 1893 . . . par L. R. Schmidlin. 1894–95. 2 pts. in 1v.; V 10eγ, Bibliographie catholique-chrétienne en Suisse . . . par F. Lauchert. 1893. 30p.; V 10eδ, cahier 1. Confession israélite et la question des Juifs . . . rédigé par le bureau de la Commission Centrale. 1907. 105p.; V 10f, Assistance et bienfaisance . . . par E. Anderegg. 1912. 2300p.

Lonchamp, Frédéric Charles. Bibliographie générale des ouvrages publiés ou illustrés en Suisse et à l'étranger de 1475 à 1914 par des écrivains et des artistes suisses. . . . Paris et Lausanne, Librairie des Bibliophiles, 1922. 500p. il. **A522**

A list of 3376 items giving for each: author, title, date, printer or publisher, size, paging and note of illustrations. Indexes of (1) titles, (2) artists.

Das schweizerische Buch: Le livre en Suisse. 1896–1914. Bern, Kollektivausstellung Schweizer, 1914. 287p. **A523**

Continued by:

Schweizerischer Buchhändlerverein. Das schweizerischer Buch, 1914–1930. Zürich, Orell Füssli, 1931. 282p. **A524**

—— Livres suisses; Das Buch der Schweiz, 1931–1938. Zürich, Schweizerische Landesausstellung, 1939. 232p. **A525**

Société des Libraires et Éditeurs de la Suisse Romande, Geneva. Catalogue des éditions de la Suisse romande, rédigé par Alex. Jullien. . . . Genève, Jullien, 1902–12; la Société, 1929. 4v. **A526**

Basic volume, listing books in print in 1900. 1902. 280p.; Suppléments, 1901–1909. 1912. 181p.; 1910–1927. 1929. 404p.; Supplément, corrections . . . comprenant en particulier les éditions Edwin Frankfurter à Lausanne. 1929. 16p.

—— Catalogue des ouvrages de langue française publiés en Suisse, 1928–1945, red. par Alexandre Jullien. Neuchatel, Imp. Delachaux et Niestle, 1948. 377p. **A526a**

Current

Das Schweizer Buch; Bibliographisches Bulletin der Schweizerischen Landesbibliothek. Le livre suisse . . . Il libro svizzero. 1.- ; 11 märz 1901- . Bern-Bümpliz, Benteli, 1901- . v.1- . **A527**

Frequency varies. Title varies, 1901–1942, *Bibliographisches Bulletin der Schweiz.*

Beginning with v.43, 1943, issued in two series; Ser. A (halbmonatlich), enthält die Erscheinungen des Buchhandels; Ser. B (6 nummern jährlich), die Erscheinungen ausserhalb des Buchhandels.

Der Schweizer Buchhandel; La librairie suisse; La libreria svizzera. Jrg. 1, Hft. 1- , 15 Jan. 1943- , Offizielles Organ. . . . Bern, Verlag des Schweizerischen Buchhändlervereins, 1943- . **A528**

Includes supplement, Das Schweizer Buch, Ser. A, which is also issued separately. Both have same volume numbering.

Tous les livres; catalogue général des livres de langue française publiés en Suisse. année 1- . Lausanne, 1945- . Quarterly. **A529**

Turkey

Türkiye bibliyoğrafyasi, 1928–1938. Istanbul, Devlet Basimevi, 1939. 2v. (Türkiye cümhuriyeti maarif vekilliği. Basma yazi ve resimleri derleme md.) **A530**

Contents: v.1, Resmĭ neşriyat; v.2, Hususî neşriyat. Classed with author index.

Current

Türkiye bibliyoğrafyasi . . . 1934- . Istanbul, Devlet Basimevi, 1935- . **A531**

Annual, 1934; semiannual, 1935–38; quarterly, 1939–43; monthly, 1944- .

A classified catalog with author and title indexes in each issue 1934–43; annual indexes 1944-

Uruguay

Estrada, Dardo. Historia y bibliografia de la imprenta en Montevideo, 1810–1865. Montevideo, Lib. Cervantes, 1912. 318p. **A532**

Chronological. Supplemented by:

Arredondo, Horacio. Bibliografía uruguaya. (In Revista del Instituto Histórico y Geográfico del Uruguay, Montevideo, 6:433-610, 1929) **A533**

Current

Anuario bibliográfico uruguayo, 1946- . Montevideo, Bibl. Nac., 1947- . v.1- . Annual. **A534**

The 1946 issue includes a *Bibliografía de bibliografías uruguayas.*

Venezuela

Sanchez, Manuel Segundo. Bibliografía de obras didacticas publicadas en Venezuela o por autores Venezolanos en el extranjero. Caracas, Tipografía Americana, 1946. 111p. **A535**

At head of title: Estados Unidos de Venezuela. Biblioteca Nacional. Caracas.

Includes in the "Proemio" a chronological bibliography of Venezuelan bibliographies.

Medina, José Toribio. La imprenta en Caracas (1808–1821); notas bibliográficas. Santiago de Chile, Imp. Elzeviriana, 1904. 29p. **A536**

Sánchez, Manuel Segundo. Bibliografía venezolanista: contribucion al conocimiento de los libros extranjeros relativos a Venezuela y sus grandes hombres, publicados o reimpresos desde el siglo xix. Caracas, Empresa el Cojo, 1914. 494p. **A537**

Current

Anuario bibliográfico venezolano. 1942- . Caracas, Tipografía Americana, 1944- . v.1- . Annual. **A538**

At head of title, Estados Unidos de Venezuela. Biblioteca Nacional, Caracas.

A well-arranged, classed, annual list with author, subject and title index.

Wales

Bibliotheca celtica, a register of publications relating to Wales and the Celtic peoples and languages for the years 1909–1927/28. Aberystwyth, Nat. Lib. of Wales, 1910–34. 9v. **A539**

—— n.s. v.1- . 1939- .

Volume 1 of the new series covers 1929–33 and includes only works written in one of the Celtic languages or relating to any of the Celtic people. Omits works written in English on non-Celtic subjects by Welshmen. These are included in previous volumes.

Cardiff, Wales. Free Libraries. Catalogue of printed literature in the Welsh department, by John Ballinger and J. I. Jones. Cardiff, Free Lib. Committee; Lond., Sotheran, 1898. 559p. **A540**

Rowlands, William. Cambrian bibliography: containing an account of the books printed in the Welsh language, or relating to Wales, from the year 1546 to the end of the eighteenth century; with biographical notices. Ed. and enl. by D. Silvan Evans. Llanidloes, J. Pryse, 1869. 762p. **A541**

Yucatan

Bibliografia general yucatanense. (v.8 of Enciclopedia yucatanense, 1944) 1022p. **A542**

An extensive alphabetical record of works published in and about Yucatan. Includes works published as late as 1946.

For the *Enciclopedia yucatanense see* V469.

Medina, José Toribio. La imprenta en Mérida de Yucatán (1813–21): Notas bibliográficas. Santiago de Chile, Impr. Elzeviriana, 1904. 32p. **A542a**

Current

Boletín de bibliografía Yucateca. no.1- , Oct. 1938- . Mérida, Yucatan, 1938- . Monthly and bimonthly. **A542b**

Published by the Museo Arqueológico e Histórico de Yucatan.

Contains special bibliographies, e.g., Anuario bibliográfico de Yucatan, 1939, in 15 mayo 1940; Bibliografía de los ferrocarriles de Yucatan, 1861–1927, in 1 agosto 1940.

Yugoslavia

Novaković, Stojan. Srpska biblijografija za noviju književnost. Beogradu, Drzhavnoj Shtampariji, 1869. 644p. **A543**

Covers period 1741–1867.

Current

Bibliografija jugoslavije: Knjige, brošure i muzikalije, Jan. 1950- . Beograd, Bibliografski Institut FNRJ, 1950- . Monthly. **A543a**

Slovenska bibliografija, 1945–1947- , izdala narodna in univerzitetna knjižnica. Ljubljana, Državna Založba Slovenije, 1948- . **A543b**

A classed list with author and editor indexes.

SELECTION OF BOOKS

Book selection in a library must be geared to the interests and needs of the community it serves whether it be a small town, a rural area, industrial center, a school, college, university, or business concern. Demands are as varied as are the interests of people and many types of book selection aids are needed.

In special fields, many of the cyclopedias, histories, bibliographies, and manuals contain material of first importance for the right choice of books, either for purchase or special use. *Living with books,* by Helen E. Haines (2d ed., N.Y., Columbia Univ.

Pr., 1950), discusses principles and practices of book selection by libraries and comments on many guides to selection.

The following list is a selection of general guides which, either in purpose of selection, annotation, technical excellence in cataloging and classification, or special indexing, have reference as well as advisory value.

A. L. A. catalog, 1926; an annotated basic list of 10,000 books; ed. by Isabella M. Cooper. Chic., Amer. Lib. Assoc., 1926. 1295p. o.p. **A544**

History: 1st *A.L.A. catalog,* 1893; 2d, 1904; Supplements, 1904–11, ed. by Elva L. Bascom, and 1912–21, ed. by May Massee.

The 1926 catalog is a classed list, arranged in the main by Dewey decimal classification, giving for each book, author, title, date, paging and illustration, publisher, price, Library of Congress card number, and an annotation to indicate its scope and value. There are separate lists for biography and fiction and a list of children's books, arranged in the main by Dewey decimal classification. Each item is numbered serially and the general index of authors, titles, and subjects refers to this serial number. Annotations are often quotations from other comment but without indication of source.

—— 1926–1931; 1932–1936; 1937–1941, ed. by Marion Horton. Chic., Amer. Lib. Assoc., 1933–43. 3v. $4.50; $5; $6.

Supplements to the basic list, the first listing approximately 3000 titles, the second and third, 4000 titles each.

American Library Association. International Relations Board. Committee on Aid to Libraries in War Areas. Books published in the United States, 1939–1943; a selection for reference libraries. Chic., Amer. Lib. Assoc., 1945. 85p. $1.25. **A545**

Classified and priced.

Prepared by Charles F. McCombs, with the assistance of Randall French.—Cf. *Introd.*

—— 1944; a selection for reference libraries [comp. by Foster M. Palmer]. Chic., Amer. Lib. Assoc., 1946. [41]p. 50c. **A545a**

The basic list comprises 1406 numbered items (the supplement, 468) recommended to reference libraries in war areas "of books generally considered significant contributions to knowledge in their respective fields, or books embodying the results of recent research."—*Introd.* Arranged by class with author and subject index.

Graham, Bessie. Bookman's manual; a guide to literature. 6th ed. rev. and enl. by Hester R. Hoffman. N.Y., Bowker, 1948. 785p. $10. **A546**

A guide to books and their editions designed primarily for the bookseller and for the librarian. Covers general works and the humanities with useful annotations. Limited generally to works in English, including English translations of the classics and some foreign fiction.

Hackett, Alice Payne. Fifty years of best sellers, 1895–1945. N.Y., Bowker, 1945. 140p. $3. **A547**

Lists the best sellers of each year, 10 fiction titles from 1895–1911; 10 fiction and 10 nonfiction from 1912–1944 with some variation from 1914–1921. General comment and notes are given for each year. Followed by a chapter on best seller subjects; American best sellers, 1880–1945, in order of sales; Alphabetical list of American best sellers to 1945 (includes estimated sales of representative American classics now in the public domain).

Shaw, Charles Bunsen. A list of books for college libraries; approximately 14,000 titles selected on the recommendation of 200 college teachers, librarians and other advisers . . . 2d preliminary ed. Chic., Amer. Lib. Assoc., 1931. 810p. o.p. **A548**

Prepared as a basic list of books for college libraries for the Carnegie Corporation of New York Advisory Group on College Libraries.

Grouped in 24 general classes with the appropriate subdivisions, and with an author index.

—— A list of books for college libraries, 1931–38. Chic., Amer. Lib. Assoc., 1940. 284p. $6.

Omits titles published within this period definitely known to be out of print. Gives references to book reviews when possible.

Grace, Sister Melania and **Peterson, Gilbert C.** Books for Catholic colleges; a supplement to Shaw's List of books for college libraries; comp. under the auspices of the Catholic Library Association. Chic., Amer. Lib. Assoc., 1948. 134p. $3.75. **A549**

—— —— Supplement 1948–1949. Chic., Amer. Lib. Assoc., 1950. 64p. $1.25.

Ambrose Burke assisted in the preparation of this supplement.

Sonnenschein, William Swan. Best books; a readers' guide and literary reference book, being a contribution towards systematic bibliography. 3d ed. (entirely rewritten) Lond., Routledge, 1910–35. 6v. paged continuously, 3760p. **A550**

1st ed., 1887; 2d ed., 1891; supplement to 2d ed., entitled *Reader's guide,* 1895.

A very comprehensive list, no longer current.

pt.1: classes A, Theology; B, Mythology and folklore; C, Philosophy; pt.2: classes D, Society; E, Geography; pt.3: classes F, History and historical biography; G, Archaeology and historical collaterals; pt.4: classes H, Natural science, H*, Medicine and surgery; I, Arts and trades; pt.5: class K, Literature and philology; pt.6: Authors, titles, and subjects index; a synopsis of classification; list of British publishers, learned societies, etc.

Standard catalog for public libraries, 1949 ed.; an annotated list of 12,300 titles with a full analytical index, comp. by Dorothy E. Cook and Dorothy Herbert West. N.Y., Wilson, 1950. 2057p. Service basis. **A551**

The first edition of the full *Standard catalog* was edited by Minnie Earl Sears and published in 1934. The 1949 edition is a revision of the 1940 edition and of the annual supplements 1941–47. The main part of the work is a carefully selected catalog of books suitable for small or medium-sized public libraries. Arranged by the Dewey decimal classification, each title is annotated and especially recommended titles are starred for first purchase. Besides the 12,300 titles in the main alphabet some 3555 additional titles are listed in the notes including expensive, specialized, and out-of-print books for libraries needing additional material. The second part of the work is an author, title, subject, and analytical index, which in addition to indexing all titles in the main part includes analytical entries to parts of some 2000 books.

This is the most generally useful guide to selection for the small and medium-sized library, useful also to the readers' adviser in larger libraries, for certain purposes in college and university libraries, and as an aid in cataloging, classification, and reference work. Strong points are: selection of titles was made with the advice of representative librarians and subject experts; annotations are given for all titles and many editions; books for first purchase are starred; each fully-listed book is correctly cataloged, and Dewey decimal class numbers, subject headings, and Library of Congress card numbers are included; the large amount of analysis makes it a useful reference aid for many purposes.

Kept up to date by supplements issued annually cumulating at intervals.

Yakobson, Sergius. Five hundred Russian works for college libraries. Russian reprint program. Wash., Amer. Council of Learned Societies, 1948. 38p. **A552**

An unannotated classed list, listing works in language and literature, art and music, history of culture and ideas, social and political history, economics and law.

Current

The Booklist, a guide to current books, 1905- . Chic., Amer. Lib. Assoc., 1905- . v.1- . $5 per yr. Semimonthly (monthly in August). **A553**

The Booklist is an annotated buying guide for libraries, compiled especially for small and medium-sized public libraries. Issued semimonthly September through July; the single August issue is the volume index. Semimonthly issues contain carefully selected listings of recent publications arranged by general class, fiction, books for young people, children's books, new editions and series, United States government publications, and pamphlets. Some books are listed in advance of publication. The entry for each book contains the author's full name, title, date, paging, publisher, price, Dewey decimal classification number, subject headings, Library of Congress card number, and an annotation. The annotations describe content of a book, estimate its value, compare it with other works, and indicate the kind of library for which it is recommended.

Subscription books bulletin, v.1- . Chic., Amer. Lib. Assoc., 1930- . Quarterly. $2.50 per yr. **A554**

Gives unbiased, critical reviews of encyclopedias, dictionaries, biographical works, atlases, collections, etc. prepared by a voluntary committee of librarians to help librarians and others in the selection of reference works. The reviews are based on careful examination of the books and indication is given as to whether or not the work is recommended. A valuable aid in any library.

United States quarterly book list. v.1- , A selection from books published during . . . 1945- prepared by the Library of Congress. New Brunswick, N.J., Rutgers Univ. Pr., 1945- . $3.50 per yr. ($5 foreign) **A555**

Publisher varies.

Issued in Mar., June, Sept., and Dec. Information concerning each book includes a bibliographical description in Library of Congress form with "an annotation primarily descriptive of the contents of the book, and, where information is available, a biographical sketch of the author."

"The Book list is broad in scope, is highly selective, and conversely is neither comprehensive nor exhaustive. It is intended to be useful to persons wishing to keep abreast of current contributions of the United States in the fields of the fine arts, literature, philosophy and religion, biography, the social sciences, the biological sciences, the physical sciences, technology, and reference."

Books for children and young people

Children's catalog; a dictionary catalog of 4200 books with analytical entries for 637 books and a classified list indicating subject headings, comp. by Ruth Giles, Dorothy E. Cook [and] Dorothy H. West. 7th ed., rev. N.Y., Wilson, 1946. 1104p. (Standard catalog ser.) Service basis. **A556**

Part 1, a dictionary catalog with author, title and subject entries in one alphabet. Full bibliographical information is given under the author entry, including author, title, publisher, date, paging, illustrations, price, approximate grades and Dewey decimal classification number. Annotations have usually been taken from library lists and current book reviews, source is indicated but without exact reference. Part 2, a classified list, arranged by Dewey decimal classification with separate sections for fiction and easy books. These are followed by a list by grades, an out-of-print list and a directory of publishers.

A revised edition of the most important bibliography in this field, which, because of the large amount of subject analysis, is useful (1) for reference work with young people, or with adults on subjects connected with juvenile literature, as well as (2) an aid to selection of books for either children's departments or school libraries, and (3) an aid to the cataloging (especially subject headings) and classification of children's books.

Kept to date by annual cumulative supplements.

Joint Committee of the American Library Association, National Education Association, and National Council of Teachers of English. By way of introduction; a book list for young people. rev. ed. Chic., Amer. Lib. Assoc., 1947. 142p. $1.25. **A557**

Recreational reading for high school age. Annotates over 1000 titles.

—— A basic book collection for elementary grades. 5th ed. Chic., Amer. Lib. Assoc., 1951. 130p. $2. **A558**

A classified and annotated list of 1060 titles. Each title graded, kindergarten through eighth grade, and priced.

—— A basic book collection for junior high schools, comp. by Elsa R. Berner and Mabel Sacra. Chic., Amer. Lib. Assoc., 1950. 80p. $1.75.
A559

A suggested minimum collection for junior high schools.

—— A basic book collection for high schools. 5th ed. Chic., Amer. Lib. Assoc., 1950. 195p. $2.75.
A560

Classified and annotated list of almost 1550 titles with index of authors, titles and subjects, chosen primarily for the small or medium-sized high school. Priced.

National Council of Teachers of English. We build together; a reader's guide to negro life and literature for elementary and high school use, prepared by Charlemae Rollins. rev. ed. Chic., Council, 1948. 71p. **A561**

Classed and annotated.

—— Books for you. Chic., Council, 1945. 154p. 30c. **A562**

A graded high school reading list, arranged by books and types.

—— Your reading for grades seven, eight, and nine. Chic., Council, 1946. 126p. 30c. **A563**

Annotated.

Standard catalog for high school libraries, a selected catalog of 4555 books ... 5th ed., comp. by Dorothy E. Cook, Anne T. Eaton, Dorothy Herbert West. N.Y., Wilson, 1947. 1341p. (Standard catalog ser.) Service basis. **A564**

Contents: pt.1, Dictionary catalog, giving author, title, date, and Dewey decimal classification number, the latter serving as an index to the fuller information in the classified catalog; pt.2, Classified catalog arranged by Dewey decimal number. Lists 4555 books fully cataloged and 842 books entered more briefly in notes, also 773 pamphlets. Gives author, title, imprint, collation, price, Dewey decimal classification number, suggested subject headings, annotation, Library of Congress card number and indication of titles for which Wilson printed cards are available. Titles are starred for first purchase.

Planned especially for school libraries but useful also as a guide to selection of books for smaller public libraries, and as a help in the correct cataloging and classification of the books listed. The large amount of analysis makes it useful also as an index.

Kept to date by semiannual and cumulative annual supplements.

Strang, Ruth; Checkovitz, Alice; Gilbert, Christine; Scoggin, Margaret. Gateways to readable books; an annotated graded list of books in many fields for adolescents who find reading difficult. N.Y., Wilson, 1944. 110p. **A565**

Reference books

❧ The present edition of this *Guide to reference books* should give aid on many points in the selection of reference books for different types of libraries. Earlier editions, particularly the sixth, should be consulted for works omitted here. Other lists, especially the following, prepared in other countries or from different points of view, all contain some titles not included in this book and will help in selection where additional titles are wanted.

Cundiff, Ruby Ethel. Recommended reference books for the high school library. 3d ed. rev. and enl. Chic., Wilcox and Follett, 1949. 22p
A566

Harris, John. Guide to New Zealand reference material and other sources of information [Dunedin] New Zealand Library Assoc., 1947 101p. **A567**

A classified list of New Zealand materials in all fields

Hirshberg, Herbert Simon. Subject guide to reference books. Chic., Amer. Lib. Assoc., 1942 259p. $4. **A568**

Under 246 subjects arranged alphabetically, reference is given to bibliographies, dictionaries, encyclopedias handbooks, etc., where materials may be found. Primarily for the use of the beginner in the popular field rather than for scholarly collections or for the experienced reference librarian.

Minto, John. Reference books; a classified and annotated guide to the principal works of reference. Lond., Lib. Assoc., 1929–31. 2v., i.e., 356p and suppl., 140p. **A569**

A useful list from the English point of view.

Pinto, Olga. Guida bibliografica, per lo student di lettere e di magistero. Roma, Bardi, 194 134p. L300. **A570**

Roberts, Arthur Denis. Introduction to reference books. Lond., Lib. Assoc., 1948. 181p. 12s. **A57**

Schneider, Georg. Handbuch der Bibliographi 4. Aufl. Leipzig, Hiersemann, 1930. 674p. **A57**

For full description *see* A5.

Shores, Louis. Basic reference books; an introduction to the evaluation, study, and use of reference materials with special emphasis on some 300 titles. 2d ed. Chic., Amer. Lib. Assoc., 193 472p. il. $4.25. **A5**

Subscription books bulletin, v.1- . Chic., Amer Lib. Assoc., 1930- . Quarterly. **A5**

For full description *see* A554.

Têng, Ssŭ-yü and Biggerstaff, Knight. An annotated bibliography of selected Chinese referen

works. Peiping, Harvard-Yenching Institute,
Yenching Univ., 1936. 271p. (Yenching Journal
of Chinese studies. Monograph, no.12) **A575**

Describes in English general and subject bibliographies,
encyclopedias, dictionaries, geographical works, biographical works, tables and yearbooks.

Book review indexes

Bibliographie der Rezensionen, 1900- . Gautzsch
b. Leipzig, Dietrich, 1901- . v.1- . (Internationale Bibliographie der Zeitschriftenliteratur,
Abt. C) **A576**

1901–10 inclusive, one volume per year, indexing
reviews of books printed in some 3000 German periodicals; 1911–1914, two volumes per year, the first volume
of each year indexing reviews in German periodicals, the
second volume indexing reviews in about 2000 periodicals
in other languages than German; 1915 has two volumes
for German reviews and one for non-German; 1916–24
volumes index only German reviews except that volume
3 covers non-German for 1917–19; 1925- are annual
volumes alternating German and foreign. A very comprehensive list, including more books of the university
grade than the *Book review digest* (A577) and many
references to special journals, and therefore often more
useful than the *Book review digest* in the university
library, when only references to reviews are wanted. This
particularly true of the volumes indexing foreign periodicals as many English and American sets are indexed
as well as those in other languages. Does not give digests
or quotations from the reviews listed. The volumes which
index reviews in German periodicals cover the same list
as the *Bibliographie der deutschen Zeitschriftenliteratur*
(see E87) and supplement that work; the volumes indexing non-German periodicals do the same thing for the
Bibliographie der fremdsprachigen Zeitschriftenliteratur
(see E67).

Book review digest, 1905- . N.Y., Wilson,
1905- . v.1- . **A577**

A digest and index of selected book reviews in over
75 English and American periodicals, principally general
in character. Arranged alphabetically by author of book
reviewed, with subject and title index. For each book
entered gives author, title, paging, publisher, price, a
brief descriptive note, quotations from selected reviews
with exact reference to periodical in which review appeared, and references only, without quotation, to other
reviews. Indicates length of review in number of words
and whether favorable or unfavorable. From the public
library point of view and primarily useful in the selection
of books for such a library; less useful in the university
library partly because of the type of book listed and
partly because the reviews indexed are taken principally
from the general and not to any great extent from the
special journals. Monthly, with a semiannual cumulation
in August, and an annual cumulation of the main list in
February which forms an annual volume; the subject,
title and pseudonym index cumulates monthly, the index
in a current number referring to all previous issues of
the current volume since the last cumulation.

Cumulated subject and title indexes for the previous
5 year period are included in the annual volumes for
1921, 1926, 1931, 1936, 1941 and 1946.

Review index; a quarterly guide to professional
reviews. Editors: Louis Kaplan and Clarence S.
Paine. Chic., Follett Book Co., 1940–44. v.1-5,
pt.1. **A578**

Ceased publication.
Indexed the reviews in some 70 scholarly or professional periodicals.

SELECTION OF PERIODICALS

❧ Periodicals form an important part of the reference collections of a library. Current periodicals in
many fields are needed to provide up-to-date articles
on subjects of contemporary interest, and back files,
especially those which are indexed in one or another
of the general periodical indexes, are extremely valuable for reference work. However, the acquisition,
maintenance, and binding of periodicals becomes an
ever-expanding item in the library budget, and careful consideration must be given to the selection of
titles to be acquired and preserved. The few guides
listed here are intended for small and medium-sized
libraries. Other lists will be found in the periodical
indexes; e.g., the list in the *Abridged readers' guide*
(E72) which indexes some 25 periodicals would be
useful in the small public or school library, whereas
the list of periodicals indexed in the *Readers' Guide*
(E71) would be a valuable aid to selection in a larger
library. It is well to remember that an indexed
periodical has far more reference value than one that
is not indexed. For other lists of periodicals *see*
Periodicals, p.88-93.

American Library Association. Periodicals for
small and medium-sized libraries, prepared by a
Subcommittee of the Editorial Committee. Chic.,
Assoc., 1948. 106p. $1.75. **A579**

An annotated alphabetical list with classified index,
with an introduction dealing with the problems of selecting, handling, binding and using periodicals in small and
medium-sized libraries.

Lyle, Guy R. and Trumper, Virginia M. Classified list of periodicals for the college library. 3d
ed., rev. and enl. to June 1948. Bost., Faxon,
1948. 99p. (Useful reference ser., no.75) **A580**

An annotated classified list with alphabetical title index. Information given usually includes, title, date of
volume 1, frequency, place of publication, price, Library
of Congress card number, sponsoring body if there is
one, indexes in which it is indexed and annotation giving
brief description. Titles recommended for first purchase
are starred.

Martin, Laura Katherine. Magazines for school
libraries . . . rev. ed. N.Y., Wilson, 1950. 196p.
$2.75. **A581**

1941 edition had title: *Magazines for high schools.*
A selected list of periodicals with brief annotations.

Madison. Public Schools. Magazine Committee.
Magazines for elementary grades. rev. ed. Madison, Wis., 1949. 46p.   **A582**

PRINTING AND PUBLISHING
General works
Bibliography

Benzing, Joseph. Der Buchdruck des 16. Jahrhunderts im deutschen Sprachgebiet; eine Literaturübersicht. Leipzig, Harrassowitz, 1936. 136p. (Zentralblatt für Bibliothekswesen, Beiheft 68)
A583

A bibliography of printers and printing; the general works followed by special, arranged by place, including works on individual printers.

Bigmore, Edward Clements and **Wyman, Charles William Henry.** A bibliography of printing, with notes and illustrations. Lond., Quaritch, 1880–86. 3v. il. (Repr. photo-offset. N.Y., Philip C. Duschnes, 1945. 2v.)   **A584**

Lehmann-Haupt, Hellmut. One hundred books about bookmaking; a guide to the study and appreciation of printing. N.Y., Columbia Univ. Pr., 1949. [n.p.] $1.75.   **A585**

Revised and enlarged edition of his *Fifty books about bookmaking* and *Seventy books about bookmaking.*
Classified and annotated.

McMurtrie, Douglas Crawford. The invention of printing; a bibliography. Prepared as an activity of the Work Projects Administration (Illinois). Chicago Public Library Omnibus Project . . . section on printing bibliography, co-sponsored by the Chicago Club of Printing House Craftsmen. Chic., Chic. Club of Printing House Craftsmen, 1942. 413p.   **A586**

Lists 3228 titles, of which 2026 are of separate publications, books or pamphlets. Copies located in American and European libraries (514 not located, 434 located only in European libraries).
Includes a section of commemorative writings of over a thousand items.

Printing and Allied Trades Research Association. Library. Classified lists of text books, reference books and periodicals, March 1937. Lond., Patra House, 1937. 66p.   **A587**
Annotated.

Ulrich, Carolyn Farquhar and **Küp, Karl.** Books and printing; a selected list of periodicals, 1800–1942. Woodstock, Vt., Wm. E. Rudge, 1943. 244p.
A588

An annotated and selected bibliography of periodicals classed under such headings as history of printing, printing types, design, layout and typography, illustration, paper, binding, publishing, book trade, collecting, bibliography, libraries, directories, societies, etc.

Handbooks

Melcher, Daniel and **Larrick, Nancy.** Printing and promotion handbook; how to plan, produce and use printing, advertising, and direct mail. N.Y., McGraw-Hill, 1949. 386p. il. $6.   **A589**

An alphabetically arranged handbook for persons, including beginners, who buy printing and direct mail services, plan advertising, etc.

Dictionaries and encyclopedias

American dictionary of printing and bookmaking, containing a history of these arts in Europe and America, with definitions of technical terms and biographical sketches. N.Y., Lockwood, 1894. 592p. il.   **A590**

Historical and technical, including biographical sketches and definitions. French, German, Italian, and Spanish terms are incorporated into the alphabet with equivalents and sometimes definitions in English.

C. H. Timperley's *Encyclopaedia of literary and typographical anecdote* (Lond., Bohn, 1842. o.p.) is an old work containing much miscellaneous information about the history of printing. It is a chronological digest, with a full alphabetical index to the names of persons mentioned as well as a general index.

Lexikon des gesamten Buchwesens, hrsg. von Karl Löffler u. Joachim Kirchner unter Mitwirkung von Wilhelm Olbrich. Leipzig, Hiersemann, 1935–37. 3v.   **A591**

v.1-2, A-Petrarcaschrift; v.3, Petreius-Z; Sachregister. Auslandsregister.

An encyclopedia of concise articles, many with bibliographical references, on a great variety of subjects connected with books and the book arts, e.g., printers and printing, publishing, illustration, places of printing, organizations and societies, manuscripts, etc. Contains many biographies.

Nordisk Leksikon for Bogvaesen, redg. af Esli Dansten, Lauritz Nielsen, og Palle Birkelund. København, Nyt Nordisk Forlag Arnold Busck; Oslo, Dreyers Forlag; Stockholm, Förlaget Biblioteksböcker, 1949- . v.1- . (In progress) **A592**

v.1, A-Kogebøger (pub. in pts., Hft. 1-6).
Signed articles, some of fair length, with bibliographies on all phases of the book industry, bookmaking, bibliography, illustration, etc., of Scandinavia. Includes many biographies.

TERMS

American Paper and Pulp Association. Dictionary of paper, including pulps, boards, pape properties and related papermaking terms. N.Y., American Paper and Pulp Assoc., 1940. 365p. $5.

A593

Definitions are given in nontechnical language, are full and definite. The bibliography lists the more important American and British works containing definitions of paper terms.

Cowles, Barbara. Bibliographers' glossary of foreign words and phrases; an alphabet of terms in bibliographical and booktrade use comp. from twenty languages. N.Y., Bowker, 1933. 81p.

A594

All words in one alphabet with English equivalent.

Dahl, Svend. Forsøg til en Ordbog for Bogsamlere. 3. forøgede Udg. under Medvirkning af Esli Dansten og Volmer Rosenkilde. København, Branner, 1944. 170p. il. **A595**

Includes Danish, English, French and German terms and abbreviations in one alphabet.

Desormes, Émile and Muller, Arnold. Dictionnaire de l'imprimerie et des arts graphiques en général. Paris, Imp. des Beaux-Arts, 1912. 311p.

A596

Fumagalli, Giuseppe. Vocabolario bibliografico, a cura di Giuseppe Boffito e di Giovanni de Bernard. Firenze, Olschki, 1940. 450p. (Biblioteca di bibliografia italiana, 16) **A597**

International Congress of Publishers. Vocabulaire technique de l'éditeur, en sept langues; français, deutsch, English, español, hollandsch, italiano, magyar. Berne, Congrès International des Éditeurs, 1913. 365p. **A598**

A dictionary of 3529 French printing terms with explanations in French, and with the German, English, Spanish, Dutch, Italian and Magyar equivalents given in parallel columns. There are separate indexes in each language. Appendixes giving the laws, practices, etc., of different countries are: Duration of rights of authors; Law of literary property; International union of Berne; Formats of volumes; Types; Formats of paper; Sample pages of corrected proof in the different languages.

Lafontaine, Gerard H. Dictionary of terms used in the paper, printing and allied industries. Toronto, Howard Smith Paper Mills, Ltd., 1949. [n.p.] **A599**

Gives English term, French equivalent, and definition in English. Index by French terms.

Orne, Jerrold. The language of the foreign book trade; abbreviations, terms and phrases. Chic., Amer. Lib. Assoc., 1949. 88p. $2.25. **A600**

Arranged by language. French, German, Italian, Portuguese, Spanish, Dano-Norwegian, Swedish and Dutch terms with English equivalents. Records current usage culled from booksellers' and publishers' catalogs of 1947-48.

Rubio, David and Sullivan, Mary Carmel. Glossary of technical library and allied terms in Spanish and English. Wash., Mimeoform Pr., 1936. 153p. $1.25. **A601**

English-Spanish, p.1-75; Spanish-English, p.76-147; Latin, English and Spanish names of the more important publishing centers, p.149-53. Each of the two dictionary parts contains about 1700 words, each word explained by an equivalent in the other language, with occasional definitions.

"The publication of the present compilation marks the completion of the first part of a glossary envisaged several years ago by the Inter-American Bibliographical and Library Association. The plan will see entire completion when Portuguese terms are added to the English and Spanish."—*Pref.*

Schlemminger, Johann. Buch Fachwörterbuch, deutsch-englisch-französisch. Naumburg, Uta Verlag, 1946. 200p. **A602**

Subtitle: Zusammenstellung der gebräuchlichen deutschen, englischen und französischen Fachausdrücke aus Buchhandel, Verlag, Buchgewerbe, Graphik und dem Gesamtgebiet des Buchwesens.

Walter, Frank Keller. Abbreviations and technical terms used in book catalogs and bibliographies. Bost., Bost. Bk. Co., 1912. 167p. (Useful ref. ser., 5) $2. **A603**

Explains the principal English abbreviations and terms and indicates the English equivalents of terms used in eight foreign languages: Dano-Norwegian, Dutch, French, German, Italian, Latin, Spanish and Swedish. Supplemented by the following:

Moth, Axel. Technical terms used in bibliographies and by the book and printing trades. . . . Bost., Bost. Bk. Co., 1915. 263p. $3. **A604**

Contains: (1) English terms with definitions in English and equivalents in Danish, Dutch, French, German, Italian, Spanish and Swedish; (2) Separate lists of Danish, Dutch, French, German, Italian, Latin, Spanish and Swedish terms with English equivalents.

Wheelwright, William Bond. Paper trade terms; a glossary for the allied trades. Bost., Callaway Associates, 1947. [46p.] il. $2. **A605**

Revised edition.
735 concise definitions with emphasis on current usage.

Directories

American booktrade directory; lists of publishers, booksellers, periodicals, trade organizations, book clubs, reading circles, etc. N.Y., Bowker, 1915- . Triennial (slightly irregular). (11th ed. 1949, $17.50) **A606**

Title varies: *American booktrade manual*, 1915, 1919, 1922; *American booktrade directory*, 1925- .

Includes directories of American and Canadian booksellers, with their specialties, arranged by state and city; lists of American, Canadian and British publishers; American representatives of British publishers; British representatives of American publishers; outlets for foreign publications; book clubs, reviewing mediums, etc.

Book buyer's handbook, 1947/48- . N.Y., Amer. Booksellers Assoc., 1947- . v.1- . **A607**

". . . not available for sale or loan to any bookseller who is not a member of the Association, and the *Handbook* remains the property of the Association."

An alphabetical list of publishers, giving address, telephone number, sales manager, special fields, address for returns, cash discount, trade discount schedule, returns policy.

British book trade directory, 1933. Lond., pub. for the Publishers' Assoc. of Gt. Brit. and Ireland and the Associated Booksellers of Gt. Brit. and Ireland by J. Whitaker [1933]. 306p. and suppl., July 1934, 5p. **A608**

Divided into three sections: (1) Alphabetical list of the book trade, p.1-252; (2) Geographical index, p.253-292; (3) Index of subjects, p.293-306.

Clegg's International directory of the world's book trade: booksellers, publishers, book collectors, etc. Lond., Fudge, 1886- . Irregular. **A609**

Title varies.
Ser. 1, 1886–1914; n.s. 1-4, 1927–1940/41. 1940/41 includes English-speaking countries only.

Adams, Scott. The O.P. market, a subject directory to the specialties of the out-of-print book trade, with 1944 supplement. N.Y., Bowker, 1944. 136p. **A610**

Adressbuch des deutschen Buchhandels 1839- . Bearb. von der Adressbücher-Redaktion der Geschäftstelle des Börsenvereins der deutschen Buchhändler zu Leipzig. Leipzig, Börsenverein, 1839- . Annual. **A611**

Title varies.

Adressbuch des schweizer Buchhandels, hrsg. vom Schweizerischen Buchhändlerverein. Zürich, Verlag des Schweizerischen Buchhändlervereins, 1947- . v.1- . **A612**

Guide de l'édition de la librairie; bibliophiliebeaux arts, 1947- . Paris, Olivier Lesourd, 1946- . **A613**

Internationales Adressbuch der Antiquare. International directory of antiquarian booksellers. Répertoire international de la librairie ancienne. 1- Ausgabe, 1926- . Unter Mitwirkung des Börsenvereins der deutschen Buchhändler zu Leipzig, hrsg. von Richard Matthias. Weimar, Straubing und Müller [1926-]. v.1- . **A614**

Title varies.

Sijthoff's Adresboek voor de Nederlandse Boekhandel en Aanverwante Vakken. Tevens bevattend een opgave van de in Nederland

verschijnende Nieuwsbladen en Tijdschriften. Leiden, Sijthoff, 1855- . v.1- . Annual. **A615**

Title and publisher vary.
Suspended 1944–46.

History

Hunter, Dard. Papermaking; the history and technique of an ancient craft, 2d ed. rev. and enl. N.Y., Knopf, 1947. 611p. **A616**

Chronology of papermaking, paper, and the use of paper. 2700 B.C.–1945, p.463-584; Bibliography, p.585-602.

McMurtrie, Douglas Crawford. The book; the story of printing and bookmaking. [3d. rev. ed.] N.Y., Oxford Univ. Pr., 1943. 676p. il. **A617**

Bibliography, p.603-46.

Wroth, Lawrence Counselman. A history of the printed book, being the third number of the Dolphin. N.Y., Limited Editions Club, 1938. 507p. il. **A618**

A richly illustrated history with references at the ends of chapters.

Biography

Bibliographical Society, London. [Dictionaries of printers and booksellers in England, Scotland and Ireland] Lond., Bibl. Soc., 1905–32. 5v. **A619**

Sold only to members of the Society.
Century of the English book trade . . . 1457–1557, by E. Gordon Duff. 1905. 200p.; *Dictionary of printers and booksellers in England, Scotland and Ireland and of foreign printers of English books, 1557–1640,* by R. B. McKerrow. 1910. 346p.; *Dictionary of the printers who were at work in England, Scotland and Ireland, 1641–1667,* by H. R. Plomer. 1907. 199p.; *Dictionary of the printers and booksellers who were at work in England, Scotland and Ireland from 1668 to 1725,* by H. R. Plomer. 1922. 342p.; *Dictionary of the printers and booksellers who were at work in England, Scotland and Ireland from 1726 to 1775: those in England by H. R. Plomer, Scotland by G. H. Bushnell, Ireland by E. R. McC. Dix.* 1932. 432p.

Good short biographies, with bibliographies. The different volumes in the series contain indexes as follows: 1457–1557, Index of Christian names, Index of London signs, Chronological index of foreign places, printers and stationers; 1557–1640, Indexes of (1) London signs (2) London addresses, (3) Places other than London; 1668–1725, Index of printers and places to the two volumes, 1641–67 and 1668–1725; 1726–75, Indexes of (1) Places in England, Wales other than London, (2) Places in Scotland other than Edinburgh, (3) Places in Ireland, (4) Places abroad; Circulating libraries in England and Scotland arranged in order of date.

Lepreux, Georges. Gallia typographica; ou Répertoire biographique et chronologique de tous les imprimeurs de France depuis les origine de l'imprimerie jusqu'à la révolution. Paris

Champion, 1909–14. 5v. (Revue des bibliothèques. Suppl.) **A620**

As originally planned, to consist of 20v. and a general index.

In two series, Série Parisienne and Série départmentale.

Contents: Sér. Parisienne, t.1, Livre d'or des imprimeurs du roi; Sér. départmentale, t.1, Flandre, Artois, Picardie; t.2, Champagne et Barrois; t.3, Normandie (in 2v.); t.4, Bretagne.

A monumental work, containing full biographies with detailed bibliographical references. Each volume is in two parts, (1) biographies, (2) documents.

Renouard, Philippe. Imprimeurs parisiens, libraires, fondeurs de caractères et correcteurs d'imprimerie, depuis l'introduction de l'imprimerie à Paris (1470) jusqu'à la fin du xvie siècle. Leurs adresses, marques, enseignes, dates d'exercice. Notes sur leurs familles, leurs alliances et leur descendance. Paris, Claudin, 1898. 480p. il. **A621**

Contents: Libraires, imprimeurs, correcteurs et fondeurs de caractères; Auteurs qui vendaient euxmêmes leurs ouvrages; Table des adresses classées par rues; Table des enseignes; Liste chronologique; Table des noms de personnes.

A new edition, with considerable additional material and new references to sources of information, was published in the *Revue des bibliothèques*, v.32-44, 1922–34.

Copy preparation

Chicago. University. Press. A manual of style containing typographical and other rules for authors, printers, and publishers, recommended by the University of Chicago Press, together with specimens of type. [11th ed.] Chic., Univ. of Chic. Pr., 1949. 497p. **A622**

A clearly written and much used manual.

Lasky, Joseph. Proofreading and copy-preparation; a textbook for the graphic arts industry. N.Y., Mentor Pr., 1941. 656p. $7.50. **A623**

A useful, detailed handbook including, besides chapters on the practical work of proofreading and preparation of copy, lists of compounds, abbreviations, proper syllabication of words, including Latin, Spanish, and French words, etc.

U. S. Government Printing Office. Style manual. rev. ed. Jan. 1945. Wash., Govt. Prt. Off., 1945. 435p. **A624**

A useful and extensive manual giving the practices of the Government Printing Office on copy preparation, with rules for capitalization, punctuation, abbreviations, etc., and on p.279-379, information on foreign languages, including alphabets, with pronunciation, special rules, lists of numbers, etc.

Words into type, based on studies by Marjorie E. Skillin, Robert M. Gay, and other authorities. N.Y., Appleton, Century, Crofts, 1948. 585p. **A625**

A guide in the preparation of manuscripts: for writers, editors, proofreaders and printers.

Includes sections on preparation of the manuscript, techniques for copy and proof, typography and illustration, printing style, grammar, and use of words.

Copyright

Nicholson, Margaret. A manual of copyright practice for writers, publishers, and agents. N.Y., Oxford Univ. Pr., 1945. 255p. $3. **A626**

A handbook for the layman on various phases of copyright practice. Includes such topics as authors' rights, duration of copyright, renewals, fees, etc.

Wittenberg, Philip. The protection and marketing of literary property. N.Y., Messner, 1937. 395p. $3.75. **A627**

Discusses copyright, infringement, agents, contracts, etc.

BOOK ILLUSTRATION

Bolton, Theodore. American book illustrators; bibliographic check lists of 123 artists. N.Y., Bowker, 1938. 290p. **A628**

Lists under the name of the illustrator the books illustrated by him, and attempts also to give the magazine appearance of the illustrations whenever possible. "Planned as a companion volume to Merle Johnson's *American first editions*" (A73).

BOOKBINDING

Cockerell, Douglas. Bookbinding for bookbinders and librarians. 4th ed. Lond., Pitman, 1948. 342p. il. **A629**

LIBRARIES

❧ Reference materials pertaining to libraries include works which will be used primarily by librarians as well as those which are needed by readers. The former concern library techniques and methodology, the latter are mainly directories of libraries, either of specific countries, special libraries or collections in particular fields. Many of these directories, both of this country and of other countries, will help scholars to locate libraries which house special collections or which are strong in specified subjects. In some cases specialties are described in some detail, in others mere listing of outstanding collections is given.

Readers may occasionally wish to consult the librarians' own manuals and codes, such as the lists of subject headings or the classification scheme, and it should be possible to make these available to those interested.

GENERAL WORKS
Bibliography

Cannons, Harry George Turner. Bibliography of library economy. A classified index to the professional periodical literature relating to library economy, printing, methods of publishing, copyright, bibliography, etc., from 1876 to 1920. Chic., Amer. Lib. Assoc., 1927. 680p. o.p. **B1**

1st ed., 1910, indexed 48 periodicals. This edition continues the indexing of most of those included in the 1st edition and adds several new titles making the total number 65.

A classified index with an alphabetical subject index to the classified lists, but no author index.

Continued by the following:

Library literature, 1921–32- . N.Y., Wilson, 1934- . **B2**

Subtitle and publisher vary.

1921–32, subtitle: a supplement to Cannons' *Bibliography of library economy*, compiled by the Junior Members Round Table of the American Library Association under the editorship of Lucile M. Morsch (Chic., Amer. Lib. Assoc., 1934. 430p.).

1933–35, 1936–39, 1940–42, edited by Marian Shaw, have subtitle: An author and subject index-digest to current books, pamphlets and periodical literature relating to the library profession.

1943–45 not published because of the war but work is proceeding for this volume.

1946–48, subtitle: an annotated index to current books, pamphlets and periodical literature relating to the library profession, edited by Dorothy Ethlyn Cole.

Continued by semiannual issues with bound annuals in December, cumulating triennially.

Year's work in librarianship, 1928–38, ed. for the Library Association by Arundell Esdaile [and others]. Lond., Lib. Assoc., 1929–39. v.1-11. **B3**

Running comment, each chapter by a special writer, on the principal publications of the year in various fields of librarianship and bibliography. Gives full bibliographical references in footnotes and includes both books and periodical articles.

Internationale Bibliographie des Buch-u. Bibliothekswesens, 1904- . Leipzig, Harrassowitz, 1905- . **B4**

Each issue contains a section giving material about libraries published during the past year in various countries and languages, including a large amount of analysis of periodicals. For full description *see* A17.

Terms

American Library Association. A.L.A. glossary of library terms, with a selection of terms in related fields, prepared under the direction of the Committee on Library Terminology of the American Library Association by Elizabeth H. Thompson. Chic., Amer. Lib. Assoc., 1943. 159p. $3.50 **B5**

This glossary "includes technical terms used in American libraries except those purely, or largely, of local significance; some terms . . . of historical interest; and

selected terms in several fields . . . related to library work
. . . archives, bibliography, printing and publishing, paper,
binding, illustration and prints."—*Introd.*

Foreign terms have usually been omitted.

Special Libraries Association, New York. Contributions toward a special library glossary, prepared for the A.L.A. Committee on Library Terminology by Linda H. Morley [and others]. N.Y., Special Libraries Assoc., 1943. 17p.   **B6**

Definitions of 84 terms that have special, additional, or changed meanings in the special library field. Collected in connection with the *A.L.A. glossary* (B5) but grouped together in this list for special library usage and given often with fuller definition than in the complete *Glossary.*

Chabot, Juliette. Vocabulaire technique des bibliothécaires, bibliophiles et bibliographes. Traduction de l'anglais au français. Montréal, Editions Fides, 1943. 145p.   **B7**

League of Nations. International Institute of Intellectual Cooperation. Vocabulaire technique du bibliothécaire. Paris, 1939. 3v.   **B8**

Mattice, Harold A. English-Chinese-Japanese lexicon of bibliographical, cataloguing and library terms. N.Y., New York Public Library, 1944. 38p. (Repr. from its Bulletin, May–June 1944)   **B9**

Rubio, David and **Sullivan, Mary Carmel.** Glossary of technical library and allied terms in Spanish and English. Wash., Mimeoform Pr., 1936. 153p.   **B10**

Directories

See also Directories—International, p.209-10, for directories which include libraries.

Minerva-Handbucher. Ergänzungen zu "Minerva," Jahrbuch der gelehrten Welt, hrsg. von Hans Praesent. Berlin, de Gruyter, 1929–34. Abt. 1, Bd.1-3.   **B11**

1. Abt., Bibliotheken: Bd.1, Deutsches Reich; Bd.2, Österreich; Bd.3, Schweiz.

United States

American Library Association. Handbook, 1949. Chic., Amer. Lib. Assoc., 1949. 138p. $3.   **B12**

Until 1948 issued annually as one number of the *A.L.A. bulletin* giving American Library Association publications, constitutions, committees, etc., list of members with their addresses, list of state library associations, state commissions, library clubs, library periodicals.

With 1949 the membership list is omitted and is published separately (*see* B12a). This *Handbook* gives the library bill of rights, code of ethics for librarians, A.L.A. endowment funds, charter, constitution and by-laws, officers, staff, council, committees, divisions, affiliated and national societies, state and provincial library agencies, associations, etc., accredited library schools, statistics, A.L.A. publications, etc.

New information on organization, committees, etc., appears in the *A.L.A. bulletin.*

—— A.L.A. membership directory . . . with lists of national, state, provincial, and local library associations, agencies, supervisors, periodicals. Chic., Amer. Lib. Assoc., 1950. 392p. $5.   **B12a**

To be published at irregular intervals.

American library directory, 1948, a classified list of 11,334 libraries with names of librarians and statistical data, comp. by Karl Brown. N.Y., Bowker, 1948. 719p. $15.   **B13**

1st ed. 1923. Published irregularly, approximately every three years.

Libraries are arranged alphabetically by state and then by city. Gives name, librarian and usually names of department heads, number of volumes, circulation, income, salary budget, book budget, special collections. For large libraries information is more detailed. Additional lists include: library organizations, library schools, state and provincial extension agencies, index to special collections, special subjects, and special libraries, index to memorial names.

Special Libraries Association. Directory of members, as of January 1, 1948. N.Y., Assoc., 1948. 138p.   **B14**

☙ There are also directories of special library associations, e.g., Music Library Association, Medical Library Association, American Association of Law Libraries, etc., and various local directories of libraries, e.g., *Directory of special libraries in Boston, vicinity and member libraries in New England* (5th ed. 1948); *Directory of libraries and informational services in Philadelphia and vicinity* (7th ed. 1947); *Special libraries directory of Greater New York* (1950).

Belgium

Hove, Julien van. Répertoire des organismes de documentation en Belgique: centres de documentation, bibliothèques, dépots d'archives, musées, etc. Bruxelles, Éd. de la Librairie Encyclopédique, 1947. 333p.   **B15**

Brazil

Rio de Janeiro. Instituto Nacional do Livro. Guia das bibliotecas brasileiras. Registadas até 31 Marco de 1942. 2. ed. Rio de Janeiro, Imp. Nacional, 1944. 475p. map. (Its Coleção B2. Biblioteconomia, 11)   **B16**

This edition includes a total of 1328 libraries, 463 being public or semipublic and 865 private. Describes organization and resources of each.

Cuba

Peraza Sarausa, Fermín. Directorio de bibliotecas de Cuba, 1943- . La Habana, Anuario Bibliográfico Cubano, 1943- . (Biblioteca del bibliotecario, 2) $1 ea. Annual. **B17**

France

Annuaire des bibliothèques et des archives. Nouv. ed. publiée sous les auspices du Ministère de l'Instruction Publique par A. Vidier. Paris, Champion, 1927. 477p. **B18**

First edition since 1912. No more published. Arranged alphabetically by cities except that the Paris libraries are listed first. Gives, for each library, address, hours, officials, statistics of books, manuscripts, and incunabula, budget, and refers to printed catalogs and articles about the libraries.

Leroy, Emile. Guide pratique des bibliothèques de Paris. Paris, Ed. des Bibliothèques Nationales, 1937. 283p. **B19**

Serrurier, Cornelia. Bibliothèques de France; description de leurs fonds et historique de leur formation. LaHaye, Nijhoff, 1946. 346p. **B20**

Describes about 70 important French libraries, mainly municipal, giving for each an historical sketch, indication of content, brief listing of important holdings, and bibliographical references.

Germany

Jahrbuch der deutschen Bibliotheken, hrsg. vom Verein deutscher Bibliothekare. Leipzig, Harrassowitz, 1902- . v.1- . Annual. **B21**

Principal contents of v.32, 1942: (1) List of libraries arranged alphabetically by towns; (2) List of librarians with brief biographical data; (3) Statistics.

Great Britain

Besterman, Theodore. British sources of reference and information; a guide to societies, works of reference and libraries. Lond., pub. by the British Council for Aslib, 1947. 56p. **B22**

Contents: National Central Library and its work; Library and book organizations; Copyright libraries; University libraries; Principal public libraries; Select list of special libraries; Select list of government libraries; General works of reference.

Libraries, museums and art galleries year book, 1948. Lond., James Clarke, 1948. 288p. 45s. **B23**

Founded 1897 by Thomas Greenwood and James Duff Brown; 1st and 2d eds. by Thomas Greenwood, 1897, 1900–01; 3d ed., 1910; 4th ed., 1914; 5th ed., 1923–24; 6th ed., 1928–29; 7th ed., 1932; 8th ed., 1933; 9th ed., 1935; 10th ed., 1937; 1948 ed., not numbered.

Partial contents: Library associations; Libraries, museums, galleries in Great Britain and Northern Ireland; Overseas, arranged by country. 1948 omits biographical section included in previous issues and refers to the Library Association *Year book* (B24).

Library Association. Year book, [189?]- . Lond., Library Assoc., [189?]- . Annual. **B24**

None published 1896–98, 1906, 1908, 1910–13.

Includes officers and council, committees, royal charter and by-laws, syllabus of examinations, facilities for study and training, suggested text and reference books, examination papers set, publications of the Association, list of members, etc.

Guatemala

Peraza Sarausa, Fermín. Directorio de bibliotecas de Guatemala. 1946. La Habana, Anuario Bibliografico Cubano, 1946. 24p. (Biblioteca del bibliotecario, 17) $1. **B25**

Italy

Annuario delle biblioteche italiane, 1933/34. Firenze, Bemporad, c1933. v.1. 347p. **B26**

A directory arranged by city, giving for each library, general description, hours of opening, specialties, etc.

Apolloni, Ettore. Guida alle biblioteche italiane. Milano, Mondadori, 1939. 209p. **B27**

Descriptions of the libraries of each province.

Latin America

Gropp, Arthur Eric. Guide to libraries and archives in Central America and the West Indies, Panama, Bermuda, and British Guiana, supplemented with information on private libraries, bookbinding, bookselling and printing. . . . New Orleans, Middle Amer. Research Inst., Tulane Univ. of La., 1941. 721p., incl. il. (Tulane Univ. Middle American Research Inst. Middle American research ser. pub. no.10) $5. **B28**

Bibliography: p.[683]-704.

Rivera, Rodolfo Osvaldo. Preliminary list of libraries in the other American republics. Wash., Govt. Prt. Off., 1942. 181p. (On cover: Studies of the A.L.A. Committee on Library Cooperation with Latin America, no.5) **B29**

A preliminary list of over 5000 libraries.

Netherlands

Nederlandsche Bibliotheekgids. Adresboek van bibliotheken in Nederland. 3. druk. bewerkt door F. Kossmann en C. Riezebos. 'sGravenhage, Uitgeversfonds der Bibliotheekvereenigingen, 1931. 334 col. **B30**

1st ed., 1913; 2d ed., 1924.

A list of Dutch libraries, arranged alphabetically by town, giving for each: address, name of librarian and principal assistants, statistics of hours of opening, size, circulation, expenditure, etc., and note of printed catalogs or other publications.

Mexico

Peraza Sarausa, Fermín. Directorio de bibliotecas de Mexico, 1946. La Habana, Anuario Bibliografico Cubano, 1946. 54p. (Biblioteca del bibliotecario, 15) $1. **B31**

Panama

Peraza Sarausa, Fermín. Directorio de bibliotecas de Panama. La Habana, Anuario Bibliografico Cubano, 1948. 34p. (Biblioteca del bibliotecario, 21) $1.50. **B32**

SPECIAL COLLECTIONS
United States

Downs, Robert Bingham. Resources of New York City libraries, a survey of facilities for advanced study and research. Sponsored by the A.L.A. Board on Resources of American Libraries. Chic., Amer. Lib. Assoc., 1942. 442p. $4.50. **B33**

Surveys the collections of some 400 libraries, general and special (excluding private libraries) in the five boroughs of greater New York. Arranged by broad subjects with subdivisions listing the collections in order of importance. Detailed index. Directory of libraries, p.299-307. Bibliography, p.309-403, includes 819 numbered items which locate copies in New York libraries.

Hilton, Ronald. Handbook of Hispanic source materials and research organizations in the United States. Toronto, Univ. of Toronto Pr., 1942. 441p. $5. **B34**

Describes the organizations engaged in Hispanic research and the collections of Hispanic source materials in the fine arts, humanities, and social sciences (and the natural sciences, in the case of some exceptional collections) in the United States. Hispanic comprises Spain, Portugal, and Hispanic America of the pre- and post-Columbian periods, Florida, Texas, the Southwest, and California until annexation by the United States.

Johnston, William Dawson and **Mudge, I. G.** Special collections in libraries in the United States. Wash., Govt. Prt. Off., 1912. 140p. (U.S. Bureau of Educ. Bull. 1912, no.23) **B35**

A classed subject list, with alphabetical index of subjects, names of libraries, collectors, donors, etc. Gives statistics and brief descriptions of collections, with references to printed catalogs or detailed descriptions. A supplement was printed in the *Library journal* 38: 331-33, June 1913.

New York. Public Library. A guide to the reference collections of the New York Public Library, comp. by Karl Brown. N.Y., Library, 1941. 416p. $4.50. **B36**

Reprinted with revisions from the *Bulletin* of the New York Public Library, May 1935–Feb. 1941.

Arranged according to the general classification scheme used by the New York Public Library. Usually includes under classes, statement of extent and character, strength or weakness, related subjects and class marks, special collections, special catalogs, indexes, files of clippings and pamphlets, lists of reference lists on the subject in *Bulletin*, etc. Useful, detailed index.

"History of the catalogues," by Wyllis E. Wright, p.261-71; "Manuscripts," p.272-81; "Municipal reference library," by Rebecca B. Rankin, p.281-82; "The Circulation department," p.282-85.

Special Libraries Association. Special library resources. N.Y., Special Libraries Assoc., 1941–47. 4v. **B37**

Contents: v.1, United States and Canada; v.2, Alabama-Montana; v.3, Nebraska-Wyoming, Canada; v.4, Indexes. v.1-2, ed. by Rose L. Vormelker; v.3-4, by Isabel L. Towner.

Covers research library collections in the special library field and in public and university libraries. Arranged alphabetically by state, city, and library. Usually gives name, address, name of librarian, total number on staff, professional workers on staff, specialists available, number of books, pamphlets, periodicals, vertical file drawers, etc. Gives information about interlibrary loan and reproducing facilities.

For the most part volumes 2 and 3 include additional libraries to those in volume 1. Volume 4 includes an organization index and a subject index.

U. S. Library of Congress. Loan Division. Library and reference facilities in the area of the District of Columbia. 3d ed. Wash., 1948. 132p. **B38**

Usually gives name of library, address, librarian, regulations, resources, etc.

Van Male, John. Resources of Pacific Northwest libraries, a survey of facilities for study and research. Seattle, Pacific Northwest Library Assoc., 1943. 404p. $4. **B39**

Surveys the resources of 108 libraries in British Columbia, Idaho, Montana, Oregon, and Washington, according to a modification of the system devised by Robert B. Downs. Classed arrangement with detailed index, including many titles for individual works.

Winchell, Constance Mabel. Locating books for interlibrary loan, with a bibliography of printed aids which show location of books in American libraries. N.Y., Wilson, 1930. 170p. **B40**

For full description *see* B76.

Great Britain

ASLIB directory; a guide to sources of specialized information in Great Britain and Ireland; ed.

by G. F. Barwick. Lond., Assoc. of Special Libraries and Information Bureaux, 1928. 425 double col. **B41**

Esdaile, Arundell. The British Museum Library, a short history and survey. Lond., Allen and Unwin, 1946. 388p. **B42**

pt.1, Historical survey; pt.2, The collections and their catalogues.

Philip, Alex. J. An index to the special collections in libraries, museums and art galleries (public, private and official) in Great Britain and Ireland. Lond., F. G. Brown, 1949. 190p. **B43**

LIBRARY ECONOMY

Buonocore, Domingo. Elementos de bibliotecología. 2. ed. corr. y aum. Santa Fe, Argentina, Ed. Castellvi, 1948. 571p. **B44**

A manual of library administration and practice with bibliographies of universal and trade bibliography, library economy, etc.

Douglas, Mary Peacock. The teacher-librarian's handbook. 2d ed. Chic., Amer. Lib. Assoc., 1949. 166p. $2.75. **B45**

Covers such topics as organization of the book collection, classification and cataloging, book selection and ordering, nonbook materials, instruction in the use of books and libraries, care of library, publicity, etc.

Flexner, Jennie M. Making books work; a guide to the use of libraries. N.Y., Simon & Schuster, 1943. 271p. **B46**

Covers such subjects as: the book, the catalog, reference books, bibliography for the general reader, special services, etc. Clear and readable.

Classification
Bibliography

Bliss, Henry Evelyn. A bibliography of classification, extended by systematic auxiliary schedules for composite specification and notation. N.Y., Wilson, 1940–47. v.1-2. **B47**

Title varies slightly: v.1, *A bibliographic classification.*
Contents: v.1, Introduction, anterior tables and systematic schedules and classes A-G; v.2, Classes H-K, The human sciences.

Special Libraries Association. Classification Committee. Classification schemes and subject headings lists. Loan collection of Special Libraries Association, comp. by Isabel L. Towner. rev. ed. April 1949. N.Y., Assoc., 1949. 40p. **B48**

Arranged by subject.

Manuals

Merrill, William Stetson. Code for classifiers; principles governing the consistent placing of books in a system of classification. 2d ed. Chic., Amer. Lib. Assoc., 1939. 177p. $2. **B49**

Schedules

Dewey, Melvil. Decimal classification and relative index. ed. 14, rev. and enl. Lake Placid Club, N.Y., Forest Pr., 1942. 1927p. **B50**

International Federation for Documentation, Brussels. Classification décimale universelle. Tables de classification pour les bibliographies, bibliothèques, archives, administrations, publications, brevets, musées et ensembles d'objets pour toutes les espèces de documentation en général et pour les collections de toute nature. Édition complète, publiée avec le concours de la Commission Internationale de la Classification Décimale et du Nederlandsch Instituut voor Documentatie en Registratuur (La Haye). . . . [Bruxelles] 1927–33. 4v. il. (Its Pub. 151) **B51**

—— 5. éd. internationale. Bruxelles, 1939–40. pts. 1-3. (Its Pub. no.201-203)

Contents: 1. Generalité; 2. Théologie, Religion; 3. Sciences sociales.

—— Universal decimal classification, complete English ed., 4th international ed. Lond., British Standards Institution, 1943- . v.1¹, v.2¹⁻³.

—— —— abridged English ed. Lond., British Standards Institution, 1947. 127p. 25s.

—— Classification décimale universelle. (C.D.U.) Tables abrégées. Bruxelles, Ed. Mundaneum, 1938. 64p. (Its Pub. no.109)

Subtitle: Principes et règles de la classification—la documentation et l'organization du travail intellectuel au service de la science et de la civilisation universelle.

U. S. Library of Congress. Subject Cataloging Division. Classification: Classes A-Z. Wash., Govt. Prt. Off., 1910–49. Price varies. **B52**

Previously published by the Classification Division.
Contents: Outline scheme of classes, 1920. 25 numb. l (reissued 1942 as Outline of the Library of Congress classification); Class A: General works, polygraphy. 3d ed. 1947. 47p.; Class B, pt.1, B-BJ: Philosophy. 1910. 109p.; Class B, pt.2, BL-BX: Religion. 1927. 337p.; Class C: Auxiliary science of history. 2d ed. 1948. 167p.; Class D: Universal and old world history. 1916. 633p.; Universal and old world history. European war. D501-725. 2d ed., 1933. 36p.; Suppl. 2, Second world war. Prel. ed. as of June 1946. 1947. 19p.; Class E-F: America. 2d ed., 1913. 298p.; Class G: Geography, anthropology, folklore, manners and customs, sports and games. 2d ed., 1928. 180p.; Class H: Social sciences, 2d ed., 1920. 597p.; Class J: Political science. 2d ed., 1924. 434p.; Class L: Education. 2d ed., 1929. 183p.; Class M: Music, 1917. 157p.; Class N: Fine arts. 3d ed., 1922. 167p.; Class P, P-PA: Philology, linguistic, classical philology, classical literature. 1928. 447p.; PA suppl.: Byzantine and modern Greek literature, medieval and

modern Latin literature. 1942. 24p.; PB-PH: Philology, modern European languages. 1933. 226p.; PG: in part, Russian literature. 1948. 256p.; PJ-PM: Languages and literature of Asia, Africa, Oceania, America, mixed languages, artificial languages. 1935. 246p.; PN: General literary history and collections; PR: English literature; PS: American literature; PT, pt.2: Dutch and Scandinavian literature. 1942. .102p.; PZ: Fiction and juvenile literature. 1915. 273p.; Class Q: Science. 4th ed., 1948. 213p.; Class R: Medicine. 2d ed., 1921. 184p.; Class S: Agriculture, plant and animal industry, fish culture and fisheries, hunting, sports. 3d ed., 1948. 101p.; Class T: Technology. 4th ed., 1948. 325p.; Class U: Military science. 2d ed., 1928. 95p.; Class V: Naval science. 1910. 106p.; Class Z: Bibliography and library science. 3d ed., 1927. 153p.

Grout, Catherine W. An explanation of the tables used in the schedules of the Library of Congress classification, accompanied by an historical and explanatory introduction. N.Y., Columbia Univ., School of Library Service, 1940. 108p.   **B53**

Subject headings

U. S. Library of Congress. Subject Cataloging Division. Subject headings used in the dictionary catalogs of the Library of Congress. 5th ed., ed. by Nella Jane Martin. Wash., 1948. 1204p.   **B54**

A very comprehensive list, though including only those headings used in the Library of Congress catalog. This edition integrates into the main list the *refer from* references which in the fourth edition (1943) appeared in a second volume.

Frick, Bertha Margaret. Sears list of subject headings, with practical suggestions for the beginner in subject heading work by Minnie Earl Sears. 6th ed. N.Y., Wilson, 1950. 558p.   **B55**

1st ed. 1923. 1st–3d editions by Minnie Earl Sears; 4th–5th, ed. by Isabel S. Monro. 1st–5th editions had title: *List of subject headings for small libraries.*
"Follows the Library of Congress form of headings, abridged and simplified to meet the needs of smaller libraries."—*Pref.*

Pettee, Julia. List of theological subject headings and corporate church names based upon the headings in the catalogue of the Library of Union Theological Seminary, New York City. 2d ed. Chic., Amer. Lib. Assoc., 1947. 653p. $10. **B56**

Incorporates the Library of Congress subject headings in theology. Appendix gives historical and descriptive information on all the church bodies in the list.

Cataloging
Manuals

Mann, Margaret. Introduction to cataloging and the classification of books. 2d ed. Chic., Amer.

Lib. Assoc., 1943. 276p. il. $3.25.   **B57**
The standard text.

Codes

A. L. A. cataloging rules for author and title entries, prepared by the Division of Cataloging and Classification of the American Library Association. 2d ed. ed. by Clara Beetle. Chic., Amer. Lib. Assoc., 1949. 265p. $5.   **B58**

An expansion and revision of the 1908 edition of *Catalog rules, author and title entry.*

Association Française de Normalisation. Direction des Bibliothèques. Code de catalogage des imprimés communs. Dictionnaire des cas. Paris, 1945. 256p. (Annexes, 125p.)   **B59**

British Museum. Dept. of Printed Books. Rules for compiling the catalogues of printed books, maps and music in the British Museum. rev. ed. Lond., The Trustees, 1936. 67p.   **B60**

Instruktionen für die alphabetischen Kataloge der preuszischen Bibliotheken vom 10. Mai 1899. 2. Ausg. in der Fassung vom 10. August 1908. Berlin, Behrend, 1909. 179p. (Repr. 1944) **B61**

—— The Prussian instructions; rules for the alphabetical catalogs of the Prussian libraries, tr. from the 2d ed., authorized August 10, 1908, with an introd. and notes, by Andrew D. Osborn. Ann Arbor, Mich., Univ. of Michigan Pr., 1938. 192p. (Univ. of Michigan general library pub. no.4)

Paris. Bibliothèque Nationale. Département des Imprimés. Usages suivis dans la rédaction du Catalogue général des livres imprimés de la Bibliothèque Nationale, recueillis et coordonnés par E. G. Ledos. Paris, Champion, 1923. 70p.   **B62**

Repr. from *Revue des bibliothèques,* 1922–23.

U. S. Library of Congress. Descriptive Cataloging Division. Rules for descriptive cataloging in the Library of Congress (adopted by the American Library Association). Wash., Govt. Prt. Off., 1949. 141p. $1.50.   **B63**

Vatican. Biblioteca Vaticana. Norme per il catalogo degli stampati. 3. ed. Città del Vaticano, Biblioteca, 1949. 396p.   **B64**
1st ed. 1931; 2d ed. 1939.

—— Rules for the Catalog of printed books, tr. from the 2d Italian edition by Thomas J. Shanahan [and others] ed. by Wyllis E. Wright. Chic., Amer. Lib. Assoc., 1948. 426p. $18.

One of the most comprehensive codes. Spanish translation published as *Normas para catalogación de impresos.*

Edición española. Ciudad del Vaticano, Biblioteca Apostólica Vaticana, 1940. 472p.

SPECIAL SUBJECTS

Bowler, Inez. An elementary manual of dental library practice. Ann Arbor, Univ. of Michigan Pr., 1932. 181p. il. (Univ. of Michigan general library pub. no.3) **B65**

The manual of library practice is followed by lists of recommended periodicals and books.

Basset, Elsie. Cataloging manual for law libraries. N.Y., Wilson, 1942. 365p. **B66**

Price, Miles Oscar. A catalog for a law library of 15,000 volumes. . . . N.Y., School of Library Service, Columbia Univ., 1942. 305p. $15. **B67**

"The catalog . . . was made under the general direction of the writer and the immediate direction of Miss Elsie Basset . . . by Jean Marie Christmas."—*Pref.*

"The aim of this catalog is to provide a complete working model of a full dictionary catalog for a well-selected law library of 15,000 volumes, so that an observant law librarian, even though untrained as a cataloger, may . . . catalog her own library in accordance with the same standards and techniques."—*Introd.*

Boggs, Samuel Whittemore and **Lewis, Dorothy Cornwell.** The classification and cataloging of maps and atlases. N.Y., Special Libraries Assoc., 1945. 175p. il. $8.75 ($4.50 to members) **B68**

A manual of practice, intended primarily for separate map collections.

Special Libraries Association. Social Science Group. Public administration libraries; a manual of practice, prepared by a Committee of the Social Science Group of the Special Libraries Association (with Book lists in Chapter II rev., 1948). Chic., Public Administration Service, 1948. 91p. ([Public Administration Service, Chicago] Pub. no.102.) $1.50 **B69**

Includes chapters on materials and their acquisition, classification and cataloging, administration, budgets, etc. Includes bibliographies of reference materials, etc., useful in public administration libraries. These latter have been revised for this edition to include material published since the 1941 edition was issued.

Filing and indexing

American Library Association. A.L.A. rules for filing catalog cards, prepared by a special committee, Sophie K. Hiss, chairman. Chic., Amer. Lib. Assoc., 1942. 109p. $2. **B70**

Wheeler, Martha Thorne. Indexing; principles, rules and examples. 4th ed. [Albany] Univ. of the State of N.Y. Pr. [1942]. 76p. (On cover: Univ. of the State of New York Bulletin no.1230 . . . February 16, 1942) **B71**

Reference work

Hutchins, Margaret. Introduction to reference work. Chic., Amer. Lib. Assoc., 1944. 214p. $3.50. **B72**

A good general introduction to reference work including sections on: (1) The scope of reference work; (2) Reference questions; (3) Selection of reference materials; (4) Organization of reference materials; (5) Organization and administration of reference service; (6) The less common functions of a reference librarian; (7) Evaluating and reporting reference work.

Chicago. University. The reference function of the library; papers presented before the Library Institute at the University of Chicago, June 29 to July 10, 1942, ed. by Pierce Butler. Chic., Univ. of Chic. Pr., 1943. 366p. **B73**

Surveys the reference field and covers the reference function in the large public library, the small and medium-sized public library, the school library, the college library, the university and research library; special problems in art and music, maps, social sciences, science and technology, rare books, etc., and administrative and personnel problems.

Each chapter by a specialist.

Enoch Pratt Free Library, Baltimore. Reference books; a brief guide for students and other users of the library, comp. by Mary Neill Barton. Balt., Library, 1947. 94p. il. **B74**

A revision of its *A guide to reference books* (1938).

A simple clear explanation of how to use reference books, with lists of general reference books and outstanding ones in the main subject fields.

Union catalogs and interlibrary loan

Downs, Robert Bingham. Union catalogs in the United States. Sponsored by the American Library Association. Board on Resources. Chic., Amer. Lib. Assoc., 1942. 409p. il. $5. **B75**

Contents: (1) The Administrative, fiscal and quantitative aspects of the regional union catalog, by Leroy C. Merritt; (2) Regional union catalogs; a study of services, actual and potential, by John P. Stone; (3) The National union catalog in the Library of Congress, by George A. Schwegmann, Jr.; (4) Manual of union catalog administration, by Arthur B. Berthold; (5) Directory of union catalogs in the United States, by Arthur B. Berthold; Selected bibliography; Index.

Winchell, Constance Mabel. Locating books for interlibrary loan, with a bibliography of printed aids which show location of books in American libraries. N.Y., Wilson, 1930. 170p. **B76**

pt.1: Locating books for interlibrary loan, a discussion of the standards to be met and the reference methods to be followed in finding books not in the home library; pt.2: Some 800 printed aids which show location of books in American libraries.

SOCIETIES

❧ The serial publications issued by learned societies serve somewhat the same kind of reference use as do the more general periodicals in that they supplement the book collections of the library by furnishing articles more up to date, or more authoritative and special, than the book literature of the subject in question. Since papers printed in academy and society transactions are usually scholarly and scientific in character and are based directly upon original research, they are more valuable for serious study than articles in the more general periodicals; but, because they appeal to a more limited public, they are less often indexed in the general periodical indexes, although many are listed or analyzed in special indexes or bibliographies. To use society publications intelligently, the same kind of aids are needed as in work with periodicals, i.e., indexes, bibliographies, and union lists or catalogs. The periodical indexes in some subject fields are particularly useful for society transactions, e.g., those described under Science, N3–N9. The union lists of periodicals include many society transactions, but for bibliographies and lists of societies a special type of publication is available. Both reference workers and catalogers frequently need to look for information about the history, organization, officers, publications, addresses, etc., of the various learned societies, and for such purposes the bibliographies, yearbooks, and handboooks in the following section are useful. Certain of these, e.g., Griffin, *Bibliography of American historical societies* (C9) and Lasteyrie, *Bibliographie générale des travaux historiques* (C11) are so arranged that they also serve as indexes to the contents of the publications covered.

The materials which follow are general in scope. For materials in special subjects, *see* the subject.

INTERNATIONAL

Anderson, Ellen E. Guide to women's organizations; a handbook about national and international groups. Wash., Public Affairs Pr., 1949. 167p. **C1**

A directory of national and international women's organizations, including political, social, fraternal, professional associations, etc. Gives name, address, executive officer, membership, purpose, principal activities, publications, etc.

Annuaire de la vie internationale: Unions, associations, instituts, commissions, bureaux, offices, conférences, congrès, expositions, publications; publié pour l'Union des Associations Internationales avec le concours de la Fondation Carnegie pour la Paix Internationale et de l'Institut International de la Paix, 1908/09–1910/11. Bruxelles, Off. Centr. des Inst. Internat. [1909–12]. 2v. **C2**

Contains a great deal of information about the history, organization, membership, purposes, meetings, etc., of all types of international organizations, governmental and private, but not so much about their publications. Each volume contains (1) Public (i.e., governmental) unions, conferences, etc., arranged by subject according to the Belgian decimal classification; (2) Private organizations, same arrangement; (3) Chronological list of international meetings, giving name, date and place; (4) Index of persons, Index of subjects. While the second volume contains the later information it does not entirely displace the first, but refers to it for earlier material.

British Museum. Library. Catalogue of printed books: Academies. Lond., Clowes, 1885. 1018 col., 100 col. **C3**

Included in alphabetical order under *Academies* in volume 1 of the Edwards reprint of the British Museum *Catalogue of Printed Books* (A32).

In two parts: (1) Catalogue of the publications of societies, arranged alphabetically by place with sub-arrangement by name of society; (2) Alphabetical index of names of societies.

For supplement to the first part *see* its *Catalogue of printed books, Supplement,* 1900–03, pt.1, col. 67-496.

Carnegie Institution of Washington. Handbook of learned societies and institutions: America. Wash., Carnegie Institution, 1908. 592p.   **C4**

"Includes North and South America and the adjacent islands. Omits societies and institutions devoted to medicine and agriculture, patriotic societies, local bar associations and teachers' organizations, and leagues for civic improvement or charitable purposes. Astronomical and meteorological observatories have been included only when forming departments of universities, colleges, etc."

Gives name, address, history, object, meetings, membership, serial and special publications, distribution of publications, research funds and prizes. A very useful list when first published but now badly out of date.

Index generalis; annuaire général des universités, grandes écoles . . . bibliothèques, instituts scientifiques . . . sociétés savantes, 1919- . Paris, Gauthier-Villars, 1919- .   **C5**

For description *see* L736.

Minerva; Jahrbuch der gelehrten Welt, 1891/92– 1913/14, 1920- . Berlin, de Gruyter, 1891- . v.1- .   **C6**

Includes concise information about learned societies, museums, etc., throughout the world. For full description *see* L738.

Minerva-Handbücher; Ergänzungen zu "Minerva," Jahrbuch der gelehrten Welt. Berlin, de Gruyter, 1927- .   **C7**

Contents: 1. Abt.: Die Bibliotheken. Bd.1, Deutsches Reich. 1929; Bd.2, Österreich. 1932; Bd.3, Schweiz. 1934.

2. Abt.: Die Archive. Bd.1, Deutsches Reich, Dänemark, Estland, Finnland, Lettland, Litauen, Luxemburg, Niederlande, Norwegen, Österreich, Schweden, Schweiz. 1932.

3. Abt.: Die deutschen Museen. Bd.1, Die Museen in Bayern. 1939.

4. Abt.: Die gelehrten Gesellschaften. Bd.1, Die deutschen Komissionen und Vereine für Geschichte und Altertumskunde. 1940.

UNITED STATES

Bowker, Richard Rogers. Publications of societies; a provisional list of the publications of American scientific, literary, and other societies from their organization. N.Y., Pub. Weekly, 1899. 181p.   **C8**

Based upon the material contained in the Appendixes to the *American catalogue of books,* 1884–95 (A151). Now much out of date but occasionally useful for items not given in Carnegie (C4) or National Research Council lists (N44).

Griffin, Appleton Prentiss Clark. Bibliography of American historical societies (the United States and the Dominion of Canada). 2d ed. rev. and enl. Wash., 1907. (In Amer. Hist. Assoc. Annual report, 1905. v.2)   **C9**

A very important list, useful both for information about the societies included and as an index to the contents of their publications.

For full description *see* V97.

FRANCE

Caron, Pierre and **Jaryc, Marc.** Répertoire des sociétés françaises de sciences philosophiques, historiques, philologiques et juridiques. Publié par la Fédération des Sociétés Françaises de Sciences Philosophiques, Historiques, Philologiques et Juridiques. Paris, Maison du Livre Français, 1938. 280p.   **C10**

Lasteyrie du Saillant, Robert Charles, *comte de.* Bibliographie générale des travaux historiques et archéologiques publiés par les sociétés savantes de la France, dressée sous les auspices du Ministère de l'Instruction Publique. Paris, Impr. Nat., 1888–1918. 6v.   **C11**

Publication of the Comité des Travaux Historiques et Scientifiques. Issued in parts, 1885–1918.

v.1-4 cover the literature published to the year 1885; v.5-6, 1886–1900.

A monumental undertaking, the most important work on French societies. Arranged alphabetically first by *départements,* then by towns and under each by societies. For each society gives: brief history, changes of name, suspensions, mergers, etc., full titles, dates, etc., of all of its publications, full contents of each volume. An index of societies (arranged by *départements*) at the end of volume 6 links together references to the same society in the main part and the supplement. Includes also societies in the French colonies and French societies abroad. Most useful at present for the historical matter about the societies and for the titles, collation and contents of the sets of their publications, but cannot be used rapidly for the analytical material. An alphabetical author and subject index was projected but never published. Continued on the same plan and scale by the following:

Bibliographie annuelle des travaux historiques et archéologiques publiés par les sociétés savantes de la France . . . 1901/04–1909/10. Paris, Impr. Nat., 1906–14. v.1-3 in 9 pts.   **C12**

Each volume consists of three annual issues.

Contents: v.1, 1901/02–1903/04; v.2, 1904/05– 1906/07; v.3, 1907/08–1909/10.

An annual continuation of the above, listing in the nine annuals 42,612 analyticals. Indexes to be noted: v.3, no.3, 1909/10, has general index of societies (but not of analyticals) in v.1-3; v.1, no.1, 1901/02, has both an author and a subject index to the analytical material in that issue.

Continued by:

Bibliographie générale des travaux historiques et archéologiques, publiés par les sociétés savantes de la France; dressée sous les auspices du Ministère de l'Education Nationale par René Gandilhon . . . Période 1910–1940. Paris, Impr. Nat., 1944- . (In progress)   **C13**

v.1, Ain-Creuse.

Follows the plan of the original work with slightly increased coverage adding to history and archeology such related materials as geography, folklore, prehistoric studies, obituaries, etc.

Union Française des Organismes de Documentation. La documentation en France; répertoire des centres de documentation existant en France. Paris, L'Union, 1935. 146p.   **C14**

GERMANY

Müller, Johannes. Die wissenschaftlichen Vereine und Gesellschaften Deutschlands im neunzehnten Jahrhundert; Bibliographie ihrer Veröffentlichungen seit ihrer Begründung bis auf die Gegenwart. Berlin, Asher, 1883–87; Behrend, 1917. v.1-2.   **C15**

v.1 issued in parts, 1883–87; v.2, in 2 pts. paged continuously.

Contents: v.1, to about 1882; v.2, 1882–1914.

Contents of each volume: (1) Short classified list of societies; (2) Main list arranged alphabetically by place and under place by society, giving for each society a list of its publications with record of what constitutes a complete set for the period covered, note of indexes, names of editors, etc., and, for the monographic sets, contents by author and title; (3) Alphabetical index of titles of periodicals, names of societies, editors, and authors.

ITALY

Maylender, Michele. Storia delle accademie d'Italia, con prefazione di Luigi Rava. Bologna, Cappelli, 1926–30. 5v.   **C16**

A dictionary of Italian academies of all periods and kinds, arranged alphabetically by the significant word in the academy's name. Fuller for historical than for bibliographical information, useful particularly for material about old or obscure organizations.

—— "Repertorio alfabetico e bibliografico" by Giuseppe Gabrieli. In Accademie e biblioteche d'Italia 10:71-99, marzo/aprile 1936.

NETHERLANDS

Nederlandsch Instituut voor Documentatie en Registratuur. N.I.D.E.R. Documentatiegids voor Nederland. s'Gravenhage, Nijhoff, 1937. 509p.   **C17**

ENCYCLOPEDIAS

❧ A good encyclopedia, or collection of encyclopedias, forms the backbone of much of the reference work in any library. Such books should be selected with care and used intelligently, with full understanding on the part of reference assistants of the relative merits and defects of the different works. The making of an authoritative encyclopedia is a very expensive undertaking, calling for heavy outlay for experienced writers, good editorial planning and oversight, and accurate printing and proofreading. Such work cannot be done cheaply, and reputable publishers recognize this fact and spend what is necessary to produce an authoritative, well-edited work. However, as the immediate profits from cheap work are large and as many buyers do not discriminate between good and poor encyclopedias, unscrupulous publishers will sometimes utilize cheap hack writers, or reprint, with only slight changes, out-of-date material. Such encyclopedias are made only to sell, and, from the point of view of any real authority, are nearly worthless though perhaps costing almost as much as the really good works.

CONTINUOUS REVISION. Most of the good, general encyclopedias, including the juvenile encyclopedias, are now following the "continuous revision" policy, which means that instead of publishing thoroughly revised numbered editions at spaced intervals, editorial staffs are kept constantly at work surveying subjects and planning revision, so that with each printing, once or sometimes twice a year, there are changes made to bring some articles up to date. Many of the encyclopedias try to revise all articles in a given subject field at the same time but in some cases topics may be changed in one part of the work and left unchanged in others. Even with careful editing this method results in inconsistencies and some unevenness as the editors themselves admit. A large portion of the material is stable and may be left untouched for several years, other parts are revised as deemed necessary, frequently in rotation over a period of years. Some subjects are changed with almost every printing, dates and sta-tistics are altered frequently, and new facts and developments added. Sometimes whole articles are entirely rewritten, either by the original contributor or by someone else, material may be cut from one part of an article to make room to insert something new in another part, and in some cases short articles may be omitted entirely. In some years a greater amount of revision may be made than in others.

PURCHASING AN ENCYCLOPEDIA. An encyclopedia should never be purchased without a full knowledge of its character and an examination of the work itself. If the librarian does not have the requisite knowledge or the opportunity to make a careful comparison, purchase should be deferred until the book has been examined and reviewed by experts. The reviews in *Subscription books bulletin* (A554) will often be helpful. For encyclopedias using continuous revision, librarians will need to develop a buying policy and to decide on how often sets need to be replaced. It is frequently better to depend on current publications and yearbooks for recent events and information and to use encyclopedias for the articles of basic and lasting importance.

If a library cannot afford the latest edition of a good expensive encyclopedia, it is better to buy a second-hand copy of a recent printing of a thoroughly good work than a cheap new encyclopedia of the hack-work or commercial type. An encyclopedia that was once good is never entirely superseded, and this fact should be taken into account if the publisher of a new work or a new edition offers a discount on the new edition for the return of the old. The small library may be justified in giving up its old edition, but the large library which does much reference work should keep one copy each of such older works. These are useful in supplying: (1) information as to the condition or view of a given subject, art, or science at the date when the book was compiled, and (2) minor biographical and other articles omitted from the later edition to make space for new material.

TESTING AN ENCYCLOPEDIA. Read the preface carefully to ascertain the purpose and scope of the encyclopedia. What do the editors intend to do? For whom is the work prepared? For advanced scholars? For popular use? For schools? For children? If designed for schools or colleges, are the contents geared to curriculum needs and to the indicated age levels? What is its scope? How were the topics to be treated chosen? How much revision is noted?

Having read the preface, check the volumes to see how well the promises have been carried out. If it is a new work, compare it with other works of the same general size and type. If it is a revised edition, compare it with the preceding edition and sometimes with even earlier editions to test the amount and kind of revision. Check certain sections in each, compare articles for changes in wording, dates, omissions, additions, etc. Is the article signed by the same writer as in previous editions or has it been written by another? Have the bibliographies been revised and new titles added? Read articles on subjects with which you are familiar and check them for accuracy, adequacy, and up-to-dateness.

In general test the work for authority, bibliographies, arrangement, and physical make-up as follows:

I. Authority
  A. Editor—is he capable and experienced and has he really edited the book himself or merely allowed the use of his name?
  B. Contributors—are the articles signed? Are the writers outstanding in their fields?
  C. Publisher—is he well-known, reputable, and experienced?
  D. Plan—is there a definite plan followed consistently throughout and showing editorial supervision?
    1. Are articles full and adequate or too brief?
    2. Do the articles show balance in selection and treatment? Longer articles for important subjects, briefer ones for less important?
    3. Does the work maintain a high standard throughout?
  E. Accuracy and up-to-dateness
    1. Is it an entirely new work?
    2. Is it based on an earlier work?
      a) Has it been completely revised and reset?
      b) Does it use the continuous revision policy?
      c) Have old plates been used with only slight alterations?
      d) Has revision been made consistently throughout?

3. Are articles dated?
  a) Is information dated for such frequently changing figures as population, statistics, election figures, crop reports, wages, etc.?
  b) Are maps dated?
  F. Viewpoint—does it show signs of national, political, religious, or other point of view which influences the slant or shows bias or prejudice?

II. Bibliographies
  A. Purpose
    1. Are they to serve as sources for the authority of the article and for additional information?
    2. Are they reading lists on given subjects?
  B. Arrangement
    1. Are they appended to the articles?
    2. Are they grouped together in a single volume?
  C. Adequacy
    1. Is the bibliographical information adequate and given in good form? (Minimum requirements: author's name, with initials, title, place, date.)
    2. Are titles of recent date included?
    3. If it is a revised work, have the bibliographies been revised and new works added?
    4. Are they arranged so as to be easily usable?
    5. Are books in foreign languages included?

III. Arrangement
  A. Alphabetical
    1. Are there long articles covering large fields or many short articles on small subjects?
    2. Is the arrangement "letter by letter" or "word by word"?
    3. Is there a comprehensive index which leads to small subjects within larger articles?
  B. Topical
    1. Are there tables of contents showing the arrangement?
    2. Is there an alphabetical index?

IV. Format and physical make-up
  A. General appearance
    1. Paper, typography
      a) Is the paper of good quality? Will it withstand heavy usage?
      b) Is the typography clear, of good size, and well spaced?
      c) Are the headings clear, simple, and easy to use?

2. Illustrations, plates, diagrams, maps, etc.
   a) Are these of good quality and well reproduced?
   b) Do they amplify and explain points in the articles they accompany or are they merely used to add to the general attractiveness of the book? Are they adjacent to the text they illustrate?
   c) Is the authority noted for the maps, giving date, scale, source, etc.?
3. Binding
   a) Is it substantial and suited for hard wear?
   b) Are the volumes numbered clearly on the spines?
   c) If arrangement is alphabetical, is there clear indication of coverage on the spines, i.e., are there sufficient letters given so that it is obvious where one volume ends and the next begins?
   d) If arrangement is topical, are contents noted on spines?
B. Special features
   1. Does it include supplementary lists or appendices?
   2. Are there errata lists?
   3. Is it loose-leaf?
   4. Does it include special lists of abbreviations used?
   5. Does it indicate pronunciation?
   6. How are cross references given?
      a) In the body of the work?
      b) In the index?
      c) Are they accurate and usable or are there "blind" references?

V. Method of keeping the work up to date
   A. Supplements
      1. How often are supplements issued?
      2. Are they arranged in the same manner as the basic set?
      3. Are articles in the basic set brought up to date in the supplement?
      4. Are there cross references to the main work?
      5. Do the new articles maintain the standard of the original?
   B. Annuals
      1. Is the standard of authority maintained? Are articles signed?
      2. Is there any connection maintained with the basic work, by means of cross references or other device?
      3. How promptly are volumes issued?
      4. Does the date given in the title refer to the year covered or the year published?

5. Is there any cumulated index to preceding volumes?
C. Loose-leaf sections for the encyclopedias issued in loose-leaf binders
   1. How often are pages supplied?
   2. Are they dated?
   3. Do they include completely rewritten articles, additions to earlier articles, or only slight changes?
   4. What proportion are new articles on new subjects?

AMERICAN AND ENGLISH

Encyclopedia Americana. N.Y. and Chic., Encyclopedia Americana, 1949. 30v. il. $185-$249. **D1**

History: 1st ed. 1903–04, 16v., unpaged; several partial revisions, especially an edition in 22 volumes, published 1912 under the title *The Americana*, which included some new articles and changes in other articles. The 1918–20 edition was a complete revision, reset throughout with much new material. This is the basis of the present work, and intervening editions.

A good modern encyclopedia which uses the "continuous revision" policy (*see* p.74) and therefore many articles are quite up to date, others have not been changed for some years, and some are still the same as in the 1918–20 edition.

Important articles are by specialists, are signed, and in general are excellent, the bibliographies are usually adequate, and dates of publications are given. Illustrations are numerous and good, maps are plentiful and references to them are included in the index. Pronunciation is frequently marked. Alphabeting is word by word. For the most part articles are short on small subjects, although there are many articles of some length. Sometimes considerable material has been brought together under a large subject, e.g., Latin America and World War II. Under Latin America, the biographical section contains sketches on prominent artists, musicians, educators, writers, political leaders, etc. There are no cross references in the main alphabet under the names included here, but there are references to them in the index.

The *Americana* is particularly strong in its information about American towns and cities and attempts to keep these articles to date with new statistics on population, industries, institutions, etc.; and in its articles on scientific and technical subjects. Other special features are the evaluations of particular books, operas, musical compositions, works of art, etc.

Since 1943 the index volume (volume 30) has been an alphabetical index arranged in dictionary form instead of the classed index of previous editions. It is kept to date with each printing and should always be consulted in order that pertinent material treated in various parts of the work will not be overlooked. Some inconsistencies in indexing have been found so that it is sometimes necessary to look under both the particular subject and the larger topic.

Encyclopaedia Britannica. 14th ed. A new survey of universal knowledge. Chic., Encyclopaedia Britannica, 1949. 24v. il. $255.50—$671.50. **D2**

v.1-23, A-Z; v.24, Atlas and index.

History: 1st ed. 1768–71, 3v.; 9th ed. 1875–89, 25v.; 10th ed., a supplement to the 9th ed., with a combined index to the main work and this supplement, 1902–03, 10v.; 11th ed. 1911. 29v.; 12th ed. 1922. 3v. and 13th ed. 1926. 3v., not revisions of the whole work but supplements to the 11th ed. (For dates of all editions *see Guide to reference books*, 6th ed., p.43.)

The most famous encyclopedia in English and for some purposes the best. Until modified in the twentieth century editions, it differed from most European and American encyclopedias in its fundamental plan which called for a collection of important monographs on large subjects, by specialists, often very scholarly and important, with good bibliographies, good illustrations, but with no separate treatment of small subjects and no biographical sketches of living persons. Small subjects were treated only as parts of larger subjects and could be found only through the index. This plan, which was seen most typically in the 9th edition, was modified somewhat in the supplementary 10th edition and still more, to meet modern demands, in the 11th edition. In the 14th edition the traditional monographic policy has been largely abandoned in favor of shorter articles under more specific headings.

Although the library fortunate enough to have sets of all editions of the *Britannica* will still make occasional use of the early editions for older subjects or points of view, biographies, etc., the 1st-8th editions are now mainly of only historical interest. The 9th, 11th and 14th editions and their supplements, however, must still be used. The 9th edition, under the able editorship of William Robertson Smith, was the high water mark of the *Britannica*, and its scholarly articles may be used profitably for subjects where recent information is not essential. The 11th edition, though more popular than the great 9th edition, is scholarly and carefully edited and should still keep its place on the shelves of the reference room.

The 14th edition, first published in 1929, was revised, reset, and reorganized to include short articles on small subjects as well as many long articles. Some of the latter have been carried over from the 9th and 11th editions, sometimes revised and abridged although still carrying the signature of the original author. Since 1929, the "continuous revision" policy (*see* p.74) has been used so that with each printing some changes are made. Printings are distinguished by letters on the last page of each volume.

A useful and generally well-made encyclopedia, with signed articles, good illustrations and maps, reasonably adequate bibliographies (dates are usually given), and clear typography. Alphabeting is letter by letter. Pronunciation is not indicated. The maps are in the index volume with a separate index.

Volume 24 includes a comprehensive, detailed index which must always be used to be sure that all pertinent material is found.

—— 10 eventful years; a record of events of the years preceding, including and following World War II, 1937 through 1946; prepared under the editorial direction of Walter Yust, ed. of Encyclopaedia Britannica. Chic., Encyclopaedia Britannica, 1947. 4v. il. **D3**

An alphabetically arranged encyclopedia covering events, personalities, and developments in science, technology, literature, etc., of ten years. Does not supersede the annual *Britannica book of the year* (D11) for the period as many articles in the annuals are not included, but it cumulates, summarizes and surveys the events of the period. Includes useful chronologies, tables and summaries. Many articles are signed, bibliographies are up to date, illustrations are good and clear as is the typography. Comprehensive index.

Chambers's Encyclopaedia. new ed. Lond., N.Y., Ox. Univ. Pr., 1950. 15v. il. $195. **D4**

1st ed. edited by Dr. Andrew Findlater, 1850–68; new ed. recast by David Patrick, 1888–92; 1923–27 rev. and reset.

A completely new edition of this well-known British encyclopedia with a new format, new selection of articles and apportionment of space. It "addresses itself to the educated layman who has some general grounding in a variety of subjects from which he can proceed to more exact and detailed information in a special field."

As in previous editions there are many short articles on small subjects. Most articles are signed with initials. Contributors include outstanding scholars, primarily British. Most articles seem to be new or rewritten, although some have been reprinted without change from the 1923–27 edition. Population figures are dated, illustrations are good but not distinguished, pronunciation is not indicated.

Not all articles have bibliographies but when they are given they usually include the standard works on the topic as well as recent publications.

Volume 15, Maps and indexes, includes: maps, p.1-144, by John Bartholomew and Sons, including a section of historical maps; an index to the maps which gives very brief gazetteer information; a list of contributors with titles of principal articles contributed by each; a classified list of articles; and a general subject index to the whole work with many cross references.

Collier's Encyclopedia. N.Y., Collier, 1949–50. v.1-17. il. $125-$149 per set. (In progress) **D5**

Editors: Frank W. Price, Editorial Director; Charles P. Barry, Ed.-in-chief; Louis Shores, Library Consultant and Advisory Editor.

A new encyclopedia aimed at the junior college level, of which seventeen of the twenty volumes had appeared by the end of 1950. Final judgment must await publication of the complete set. The following are preliminary comments based on volumes 1-17.

The style is popular, clear and concise, some articles are long and well-developed, but in general articles are short under small subjects. Articles have been contributed by specialists and are signed with initials— full names, positions and indication of articles by each are given at beginning of volume 1.

Alphabeting is letter by letter. Pronunciation is indicated by the international phonetic alphabet. Illustrations, both in color and black and white, are pertinent and well-reproduced; maps are prepared by Rand McNally. There are no bibliographies with the articles, but it is announced that volume 20 will include bibliographies and index.

The work is more advanced than the juvenile encyclopedias in its treatment and choice of subjects but its coverage is not as great and information is not usually as detailed as in the *Britannica* (D2) or *Americana* (D1). In most libraries it will not be a substitute for either of these, but will complement them and will be useful in senior high schools and colleges, as well as in the home.

New international encyclopaedia. 2d ed. [Reissue] N.Y., Dodd, 1922. 23v. il. **D6**

—— Supplement. 1925. v.24-25.

—— Supplement. 1930. 2v.

For history of this encyclopedia *see Guide to reference books,* 6th ed., p.41.

An encyclopedia of good modern type, with adequate and authoritative articles, many good illustrations, and excellent and useful bibliographies. Important articles are by specialists, minor articles by a capable office staff. Articles are all unsigned, but there is at the beginning of each volume a list of the authors of the principal articles in that volume. Many very small subjects, including even titles of famous works of literature, names of fictitious characters, etc., are given separate treatment, pronunciation is marked, and the system of cross references is good. There are many biographical articles, about 20,000 in all, including articles on persons who came into prominence during World War I and a considerable proportion of Latin-American biographies. The strongest feature of the encyclopedia is its excellent and usable bibliographies. A special bibliographical feature, often very useful, is the reference in articles on foreign authors to translations of their works as well as to the best editions in the original.

Now unfortunately out of date, the *New international* is still useful for articles for which recent information is not a prime concern.

Columbia encyclopedia in one volume. 2d ed. ed. by William Bridgwater and Elizabeth J. Sherwood. N.Y., Columbia Univ. Pr., 1950. 2203p. $25. **D7**

1st ed. 1935.

A compact work, with concise articles and no illustrations, planned especially for home and office use and for library use when exhaustive articles by specialists are not needed. Particularly well-adapted for quick reference. The second edition is thoroughly revised with many articles rewritten and new ones added. The publishers state that there are about 70,000 articles, 10,000 of them new. Scientific, technical, and economic articles have been brought up to date and new developments included. The work is strong in place names and in biography, including sketches of living persons. Marks pronunciation and indicates, by means of special type, cross references to headings where additional information can be found. Brief selected bibliographies, usually consisting of two or three titles of works in English, are appended to many articles.

Lincoln library of essential information; an up-to-date manual for daily reference, for self-instruction, and for general culture . . . 16th ed. Buffalo, N.Y., Frontier Press, 1946. 2174 (i.e., 2186)p. il. $19.50-$21.50. **D8**

A serviceable one-volume encyclopedia, frequently revised. Nonalphabetical. Material is grouped by subject field. Alphabetical index.

Encyclopedia annuals

See Subscription books bulletin (A554), v.21, no.1, Jan. 1950, for reviews of encyclopedia supplements.

Americana annual, an encyclopedia of current events, 1923- . N.Y., Encyclopedia Americana, 1923- . v.1- . il. **D9**

The date in the title is the date of publication, the record of events is for the previous year. Serves both as an annual supplement to the *Encyclopedia Americana* (D1) and as an annual record of progress and events in a given subject. Contains many biographies and has a necrology list in each issue. Articles are signed with full names and titles of contributors.

Appleton's Annual cyclopaedia and register of important events . . . v.[1]-15, 1861–75; v.16-35 (new ser., v.1-20), 1876–95; v.36-42 (3d ser., v.1-7), 1896–1902. N.Y., Appleton, 1862–1903. 42v. il. **D10**

Index for 1861–75 (v.1-15), 1876. 442p.; Index for 1876–87 (v.16-28, n.s., v.1-12), 1888. 144p. Other indexes included in the set are: Index to new series v.1-20, 1876–95, in n.s. v.20, p.769-866; Index to 3d series v.1-7, 1896–1902, in 3d ser. v.7, p.845-66.

Published as an annual supplement to the *American cyclopaedia.* Of little use now as a supplement, but still useful for: (1) record of the events of a given year, especially the political, governmental, economic and military events, which are given with greater detail in this year-by-year record than in later general accounts; volumes covering the Civil War and Reconstruction periods are useful to students of American history; (2) many minor articles, particularly obituaries and biographies, which are either omitted from later encyclopedias or given briefer treatment than in the annual volume for the year when the person was of especial interest.

Britannica book of the year, 1938- . Chic., Encyclopaedia Britannica; Lond., Encyclopaedia Britannica, 1938- . il. **D11**

Editors: 1938, F. H. Hopper and Walter Yust; 1939- , Walter Yust.

Annual volumes to serve as annual surveys and as supplements to the *Encyclopaedia Britannica* (D2). The date in the title is the date of publication, the record of events is for the previous year. Includes many short articles under specific headings, and many cross references. Articles in many cases are signed. Some biography is included. A necrology list is included under Obituaries.

A cumulated, combined, and condensed survey in one alphabet of the facts contained in the yearbooks 1937 through 1941 was published as the *Britannica book of the year omnibus* (1943. 1576p.).

Collier's Yearbook, 1939- , covering the events of 1938- . N.Y., Collier, 1939- . Annual. **D12**

Title varies: 1938–1940, was called *National yearbook.*

Designed to serve both as a supplement to *Collier's Encyclopedia* (D5) and as an annual survey. Alphabetically arranged.

New international year book, a compendium of the world's progress, 1907- . N.Y., Dodd, 1908–31; Funk, 1932- . v.1- . il. (1949, $10) **D13**

An excellent annual encyclopedia, up to date and authoritative, on the same plan as the *New international encyclopaedia* (D6) and useful both as a supplement to that work and as an annual record of the progress and events in any subject. Especially useful for biography. Contains an annual necrology list. Many articles are by specialists and are signed.

Planned as a supplement to the *New international encyclopaedia* (D6), volumes 1907–13 supplemented the first edition; volumes 1914- , the second edition. The volume for 1907 contains, in addition to the record for that year, brief summaries of the events of 1903–06. Preceded by the *International year book*, 1898–1902 (N.Y., Dodd, 1899–1903. 5v.).

Juvenile

Britannica junior; the boys' and girls' encyclopaedia, prepared under the supervision of the editors of the Encyclopaedia Britannica. . . . Chic., Encyclopaedia Britannica, 1949. 15v. il. $96.50. **D14**

"Published with the advice and consultation of the faculties of the University of Chicago and the University Laboratory School."

Planned for elementary and junior high school levels. First published in 1934 as a reissue, with some alterations, of *Weedon's Modern encyclopedia*. Has since been much revised. Articles are not signed but contributors are listed in volume 1, with the titles of articles for which they are responsible. Volume 1 is a ready reference index; volume 15 includes an atlas section. For review of the 1947 printing *see Subscription books bulletin*, April 1948. (A554)

Compton's Pictured encyclopedia and fact-index. Chic., Compton, [1949] 15v. il. Price to libraries: fabrikoid $104.50-$109.50; cloth $99.50-$104.50. **D15**

Subtitle: To inspire ambition, to stimulate the imagination, to provide the inquiring mind with accurate information told in an interesting style, and thus lead into broader fields of knowledge, such is the purpose of this work.

A good juvenile encyclopedia, one of the two leading American works in this field. Planned especially for upper elementary and high school use, it attempts to keep in close touch with school needs, but is useful also for the adult who needs a somewhat simpler article than that given in the standard encyclopedias for adults.

General policy is to use long articles on large subjects, with smaller subjects analyzed or treated in the Fact-index.

Uses a clear and direct style and pays especial attention to illustration, graphic charts, and maps. Indicates pronunciation. Alphabetizing is letter by letter. Not all articles include bibliographies but for some articles, reference outlines for organized study are given and these include brief bibliographies divided into books for younger readers and books for advanced students and teachers.

Instead of a general index volume, there is a Fact-index at the end of each volume which is a guide to all volumes for subjects beginning with the letter or letters covered in the volume. The Fact-index is not only an analytical index to all text and illustrative material in the main work but also includes dictionary-type information, brief biographical sketches, etc., on subjects not treated elsewhere.

Uses "continuous revision" (*see* p.74). For review of 1947 printing *see Subscription books bulletin*, Oct. 1947. (A554)

World book encyclopedia. . . . Chic., Quarrie, 1949. 19v. il. $102. **D17**

v.1-18, A-Z; v.19, Reading and study guide.

A good juvenile encyclopedia, one of the two leading American works in the field. Of all the juvenile encyclopedias this is the one that most nearly approximates the form and treatment of the standard works for adults and so is especially good for the older child who is nearly ready to use adult material.

Alphabetically arranged. For the most part has short articles on small topics although some long articles are also included. Articles are signed. There are many cross references to related subjects. Pronunciation is indicated for unusual names and words. Bibliographies are brief but well chosen, sometimes with short annotations. Illustrations and graphs in color, and black and white are clear and pertinent.

Volume 19 is a *Reading and study guide* serving as a classified index to the set. It is divided into 44 subject fields with many subdivisions. Exact references are given to volume and page.

Uses "continuous revision" (*see* p.74). For review of 1947 printing *see Subscription books bulletin*, Oct. 1947. (A554)

FOREIGN ENCYCLOPEDIAS

❧ While a good encyclopedia in English must always be the basis of encyclopedia reference work in a library used by English-speaking readers, foreign encyclopedias offer much that can not be found in English works—the *Enciclopedia italiana* (D46), for example, far surpasses any other encyclopedia in the quality and number of its illustrations and contains some articles superior to anything found elsewhere; *Espasa* (D64) is rich in Spanish and Spanish-American subjects, especially biography; *La Grande encyclopédie* (D26) contains articles on topics in European history and literature not available in the same quality in other encyclopedias, while even as old a work as *Larousse* (D27) has a wealth of articles on small topics—minor biography, individual works of literature, plays, theaters, and songs, not easily found in other encyclopedias.

In general, library use of such works will be for three main types of questions, (1) to find an article in a foreign language for a reader who does not use English readily, (2) to find a foreign article that is better than the corresponding article in English, or (3) to find something on topics omitted altogether in English encyclopedias—usually topics in biography, topography, history, or literature of the country of origin of the encyclopedia. It is for this third type of question that the foreign encyclopedia is most frequently used in American libraries.

Thus, the user of reference books will often need to make use of the great foreign encyclopedias, but to use them adequately requires a somewhat different technique from that required to use an encyclopedia in English. Theoretically the library assistant should know the language of the encyclopedia, but much can be done with a very slight knowledge of the language, if the user has an intelligent "dictionary habit" and will keep certain basic points in mind; often he does not need to read the article, but merely to find it for a reader who will use it. Without the correct technique, however, he may actually miss an article, even though it is in its proper alphabetical place. Two of the points which the library assistant, with a limited knowledge of foreign languages, needs to keep in mind are: (1) the alphabet of the language he is using, and (2) variations in the forms of proper names, personal, geographical, etc. The alphabet must be kept in mind because even languages using the Latin alphabet have variations in letters which *must be known*, if an article is to be found in its correct alphabetical place—in Spanish, for example, there are two letters not found in English, Ch and Ll, and a word or name beginning Ch follows Cz; in Norwegian the letter Æ comes after Z; Czech has 41 letters, and other languages show other variations.

Variations in form of proper names must also be kept in mind, especially when the initial letter is affected. The reference assistant looking for an Italian article on Hannibal, for example, will find it under Anibale; if he is looking for articles on St. Stephen he must look under Etienne in a French encyclopedia, Esteban in a Spanish, Stefano in an Italian. If he is looking for an Italian article on John Adams he must be prepared to recognize Giovanni Adams; if he is looking for a medieval personage named John he must search under John, Jean, Jehan, Johann, Johannes, Jan, Giovanni, or other variations according to the language of the reference work he uses. Surnames do not show so great a variation, but their alphabetizing must be watched—e.g., in a Swedish encyclopedia the biography of the German writer Görres will alphabetize at the end of the letter G, many pages after Gy, instead of with Go, as it does in German and English. Geographical names, of course, vary in form also—an Italian article on Florence must be looked for under the Italian Firenze; a Norwegian article on Egypt will be found under Ægypten at the end of the alphabet. Keeping in mind these points about alphabets and forms of names will help even an inexperienced reference assistant to use foreign encyclopedias intelligently.

Brazilian

See also Portuguese, p.84.

Encyclopedia e diccionario internacional, organizado e redigido com a collaboração de distinctos homens de sciencia e de lettras brasileiros e portuguezes. W. H. Jackson, ed. Lisboa [1919]. 20v. il.   **D18**

A good popular encyclopedia in Portuguese, general in scope but with special emphasis upon Brazilian names and topics. Contains a large amount of Brazilian biography.

Czech

Masarykuv slovník naučný; lidová encyklopedie všeobecných vědomostí. . . . V Praze, Nákladem "Československého Kompasu," 1925–33. 7v. il.   **D19**

Contains little bibliography but has many biographies, including those of persons still living.

Ottuv slovník naučný. Illustrovaná encyklopaedie obecných vedomastí. V Praze, Otto, 1888–1909. 28v.   **D20**

v.1-27, A-Z; v.28, Supplement.

—— Nové doby. Dodatky k velikému ottovu slovníku naučnému. Redakci vede. B. Němec. V Praze, "Novina," 1930–43. v.1-6². il. (In progress)

v.1-6², A-Užok.
Publisher varies.
The standard Czech encyclopedia. Signed articles, many biographies, some bibliography including works in many languages.

Danish

Salmonsens Konversationsleksikon. 2. Udg. København, Schultz, 1915–30. 26v. il.   **D21**

v.1-25, A-Ø; v.26, Supplement.
The standard Danish encyclopedia; a work of the best modern type, with signed articles, bibliographies and good illustrations. Marks pronunciation of proper names.
Kept to date by the *Salmonsen Leksikon Tidsskrift.* København, Schultz, 1941- . Aarg. 1- . Monthly with annual indexes.

Hagerups Illustrerede Konversations Leksikon. 4. gennemsete og forøgede udg. redigeret af P. Engelstoft. København, Hagerup, 1948–49. v.1-3. il. Dan Cr. 48.50. (In progress)   **D22**

v.1-3, A-Finker.
3. Udg., 1921–25.

Dutch

Eerste nederlandse systematisch ingerichte encyclopaedie . . . Samengesteld onder leiding van

H. J. Pos, J. M. Romem [and others]. Amsterdam, E.N.S.I.E., 1946–49. v.1-5. il. (In progress) **D23**

Contents: (1) Wijsbegeerte. Godsdienst. Psychologie. Opvoeding en onderwijs; (2) Taal en letterkunde. Beeldende kunsten. Muziek. Dans. Toneel. Film; (3) Geschiedenis. Sociologie. Volkenkunde. Volkskunde en Kunst. Sociografie. Economie. Recht, staat, politiek; (4) Wiskunde. Natuurkunde. Scheikunde. Sterrekunde; (5) Geodesie en cartografie. Meteorologie. Biosfeer. Mens, aarde en wereldhuishouding.

Each article written by a specialist.

Oosthoek's Encyclopaedie. 4. druk. Utrecht, Oosthoek, 1947- . v.1- . **D24**

Prins, Anthonij Winkler. Winkler Prins' algemeene encyclopaedie. 5. geheel nieuwe druk onder hoofdredactie van J. de Vries. . . . Amsterdam, Uit.-mij "Elsevier," 1932–38. 16v.; Supplement-deel. 1948. 454p. il. **D25**

A standard Dutch work of the Meyer-Brockhaus (*see* D36, D32) type with good concise articles and good illustrations. Very little bibliography.

—— 6. geheel nieuwe druk. Amsterdam, Elsevier, 1947–50. v.1-8. il. (In progress)

v.1-8, A-Fra.

This edition completely revised and reset, many articles rewritten, new ones added, etc. New plates and maps. Biographies include living persons.

French

La Grande encyclopédie, inventaire raisonné des sciences, des lettres et des arts, par une société de savants et de gens de lettres; sous la direction de Berthelot, Derenbourg, [etc.]. Paris, Lamirault, 1886–1902. 31v. il. **D26**

Secrétaire général: v.1-18, F. Camille Dreyfus; v.19-31, André Berthelot.

Volumes 23-31 published by Société Anonyme de La Grande Encyclopédie.

The most important French encyclopedia and one of the best encyclopedias in any language. Has authoritative signed articles, excellent bibliographies, many entries under small subjects. Out of date now for sciences, etc., in which there have been recent developments, but an excellent authority in other fields, especially for medieval and renaissance subjects, and for literature, history, biography, etc., of continental Europe. Very good for French and other continental biography. The bibliographies are especially important. Has fewer illustrations and plates than recent English or American encyclopedias.

Larousse, Pierre Athanase. Grand dictionnaire universel du xixe siècle français. Paris, Larousse, [1865–90?]. 17v. **D27**

v.1-15, A-Z; v.16, suppl. A-Z; v.17, suppl. A-Z.

A famous encyclopedia, well edited and well written, once of first importance and still useful in many cases if allowance is made for the fact that it is not up to date and must be checked on important points by reference to more recent authorities. Combines the features of dictionary and encyclopedia, and as an encyclopedia is an extreme example of entry under small subject, including many articles, some of considerable length, on individual works of literature, e.g., poems, plays, novels, romances, newspapers, periodicals, songs, etc., entered under their titles, and a very large amount of minor biography not included in other general encyclopedias. Gives words and music (air only) of about 600 songs. Good for questions of European literature, biography and history. Pink index pages referring to articles in the two supplements have been issued for insertion at the back of each of the original 15 volumes. As these were not issued until after the publication of the supplements, they were not included in earlier sets, but were sold separately and inserted.

—— Nouveau Larousse illustré, dictionnaire universel encyclopédique, pub. sous la direction de Claude Augé. Paris, Larousse, 1898–1907. 8v. il. **D28**

v.1-7, A-Z; v.8, suppl.

Not an abridgment or revision of the above, but an entirely new work of a more popular character, with briefer articles, and profusely illustrated in both black and white and colors. Preserves much of the old Larousse feature of separate treatment of very small subjects. Especially useful for certain kinds of questions about works of art, as one of its special features is the inclusion of separate articles on individual works of art, e.g., paintings, statues, etc., entered under their titles or subjects, and accompanied by small but usable illustrations. Contains a large amount of biography but comparatively little bibliography. For new edition *see* following:

—— Larousse du xxe siècle, pub. sous la direction de Paul Augé. Paris, Larousse, c1928–33. 6v. il. **D29**

—— Larousse mensuel illustré, revue encyclopédique universelle, pub. sous la direction de Claude Augé, [et] Paul Augé, 1907- . Paris, Larousse, 1907- . v.1- and index to v.1-7. il. 85fr. per no.; 950fr. per yr. (France); 1,200fr. (foreign). **D30**

v.1, 1907–10; v.2, 1911–13; v.3, 1914–16; v.4, 1917–1919; v.5, 1920–22; v.6, 1923–25; v.7, 1926–28; v.8, 1929–31; v.9, 1932–34; v.10, 1935–37; v.11, 1938—Mai 1940; publication suspended; v.12, Jan. 1948- .

An excellent monthly supplement to the *Nouveau Larousse* (D28), with the same size and style of page, but with longer articles and larger illustrations. Each monthly number is alphabetical, there are annual indexes for each year, to be used until a volume is completed, a final alphabetical index for each volume and, for volumes 1-7, a cumulated index in a separate volume. Articles are well up to date and numbers are issued promptly. Good work for contemporary French biography, obituaries, portraits, etc. Contains many reviews of new plays, novels, or other literary works. The issues for 1914–18 contained many articles on World War I, military art and science, terms, maps of battles and campaigns, etc.

Encyclopédie française. . . . Paris, Comité de l'Encyclopédie Française, c1935–39. v.1, 4-8,10, 15-18. il. loose-leaf. (In progress) 2300fr.-4100fr. according to binding. **D31**

v.1, L'outillage mental, pensée, language, mathématique; directeurs, Abel Rey, Antoine Meillet, Paul Montel; v.4, La vie, dirigé par André Mayer; v.5, Les êtres vivants; dirigé par Paul Lemoine, René Jeannel, Pierre Allorge; v.6, L'être humain, dirigé par René Leriche; v.7, L'espèce humaine, dirigé par Paul Rivet; v.8, La vie mentale, dirigé par Henri Wallon; v.10, L'état moderne. Aménagement, crise, transformations, dirigé par Anatole de Monzie, Henry Puget, Pierre Tissier; v.15, Éducation et instruction, dirigé par C. Bouglé; v.16-17, Arts et littératures, dirigé par Pierre Abraham; v.18, La civilization écrite, dirigé par Julien Cain.

A nonalphabetical encyclopedia containing monographic articles grouped by large classes and with alphabetical index to each volume to serve until the general alphabetical index to the whole set, which is projected as volume 21, appears. The announced plan of the publication calls for 19 subject volumes, a volume of bibliography and proper names index, and a subject index volume. Until the index volumes have been published, it is impossible to judge what the use or the value of the set as a practical general reference encyclopedia will be. In the volumes issued so far the illustrations, though good, are not numerous and there is comparatively little bibliography.

German

Brockhaus' Konversations-Lexikon. Der grosse Brockhaus; Handbuch des Wissens in zwanzig Bänden. 15. völlig neubearb. Aufl. Leipzig, Brockhaus, 1928–35. v.1-21. il. **D32**

v.1-20, A-Z; v.21, Ergänzungsbd., A-Z.
1st ed. 1796–1808; frequently revised, 14th ed. 1892–95.
2. völlig neubearb. Ausg. of the 15. Aufl. started publication 1939- .
The most recent edition of a standard German encyclopedia, earlier editions of which influenced encyclopedia making in many countries. The tenth edition, for example, furnished the model for *Chambers's Encyclopaedia* (1860–66) (D4)—some of the articles in *Chambers's* were even direct translations from *Brockhaus*—and through *Chambers's* influenced the *International encyclopaedia* (D6), the first edition of which was based on an American reprint of *Chambers's*. More distantly *Brockhaus* influenced the *Americana* also, as Francis Lieber's *Encyclopaedia Americana* (1829), from which the name and a few of the articles of the present *Encyclopedia Americana* (D1), descend, was based upon and in part translated from the seventh edition of *Brockhaus*.
This edition is a revision and complete resetting, the first revision since the fourteenth edition, 1892. Characterized by short articles, on small subjects, with profuse illustration including many small illustrations in text. Articles are unsigned, there are some brief bibliographies; illustrations include good maps, black-and-white and colored plates, many portraits, facsimiles of autographs, coats-of-arms of cities, etc. Includes biographies of living persons.

Brockhaus' Kleines Konversations-Lexikon. Brockhaus' Handbuch des Wissens. 6. gänzl. umgearb. u. wesentl. verm. Aufl. von Brockhaus' Kleinem Konversations-Lexikon. . . . Leipzig, Brockhaus, 1929–30. 4v. il. **D33**

—— Der neue Brockhaus. Allbuch in vier Bänden und einem Atlas. Leipzig, Brockhaus, 1936–38. 4v. and atlas. il. **D34**

Herders Konversations-Lexikon. Der grosse Herder; Nachschlagewerk für Wissen und Leben. 4. völlig neubearb. Aufl. von Herders Konversations-Lexikon. . . . Freiburg im Breisgau, Herder, 1931–35. 12v. il. **D35**

Meyers Konversations-Lexikon. Meyers Lexikon. 8. Aufl. in völlig neuer Bearbeitung und Bedilderung. Leipzig, Bibliograph. Inst., 1936–42. v.1-9 il. (In progress) **D36**

1. Aufl. 1840–55; 7. Aufl. 1924–35, includes v.16, Atlas and v.17, Orts- und Verkehrs-Lexikon des Deutschen Reiches.
The latest edition of a standard German work, characterized by short unsigned articles on very small subjects with some bibliographical references but not attempting to provide long bibliographies. Many illustrations, including good maps, plates (black-and-white and colored), plans of cities, coats-of-arms, etc. Includes no portraits and has somewhat less profuse text illustration than the corresponding work of Brockhaus. Includes biographies of living men. The 8th edition is much more concise than the 6th, the longer articles of which must still be used at times.

Meyers Kleines Lexikon. 9. gänzlich neu bearb. Aufl. Leipzig, Bibliograph. Inst., 1933. 4v. il. **D37**

v.1-3, A-Z; v.4, Atlas.

The following older works are frequently useful for topics not treated in the smaller modern encyclopedias:

Allgemeine Encyclopädie der Wissenschaften und Künste von genannten Schriftstellern bearb. und hrsg. von J. S. Ersch und J. G. Gruber. Leipzig, Brockhaus, 1818–50. 167v. il. o.p. **D38**

Contents: 1st sect., A-G, 99v.; 2d sect., H-Lig, 43v.; 3d sect., O-Phyx, 25v.
Unfinished. Editors vary but it is usually referred to as *Ersch und Gruber Encyclopädie.*

Zedler, Johann Heinrich. Grosses vollständiges universal Lexikon aller Wissenschaften und Künste. . . . Halle, Zedler, 1732–50. 64v. ports. **D39**

—— —— Nöthige Supplemente. . . . Leipzig, 1751–54. v.1-4.

v.1-4, A-Caq.
No more published.
One of the great encyclopedias. Particularly useful for biography and bibliography of the sixteenth and seventeenth centuries.

Greek

Eleutheroudakē enkyklopaidikon leksikon. En Athenais, "Eleutheroudakis," 1926–32. 12v. il. **D40**

v.1-12, A-Ω; Supplement, v.12, p.1079-1152, A-Ω.

On the plan of the *New international encyclopaedia* (D6), i.e., short articles on small subjects. Some articles signed with initials. Contains a large amount of biography and is useful for some other Greek subjects also, for which information in reference books in other languages is not easily found.

Megalē hellenikē enkyklopaideia. . . . Athēnai, "Pyrsos," 1926–1934. 24v. il.   **D41**

Contains articles of some length with brief bibliographies. Biographies of living persons included.

Hebrew

Encyclopaedia Hebraica. Tel-Aviv, Encyclopaedia Pub., 1948- . v.1- . il. (In progress)   **D42**

Text in Hebrew. Bibliographies include titles in many languages. A general encyclopedia with articles contributed by some 500 outstanding Jewish and non-Jewish scholars.

Hungarian

A Pallas nagy lexikona az összizes ismeretek enciklopédiája. . . . Budapesten, Pallas Irodalmi es Nyomdai Részvénytársaság, 1893–1904. 18v. il.   **D43**

v.1-16, A-Z; v.17-18, Suppl. A-Z.

Révai kétkötetes lexikona; föszerkesztö Juhász Vilmos. Budapest, Révai Irodalmi Intézet, 1947–48. 2v. il.   **D44**

A small Hungarian encyclopedia, international in scope. Very brief articles, little illustration. Numerous biographical entries are included but information is very brief. Serves chiefly for identification of Hungarian places, names, abbreviations, etc.

Révai nagy lexikona az ismeretek enciklopédiája. Kötet 1-20. Budapest, Révai Testvérek Irodalmi Intézet Részvénytársaság, 1911–27. 20v. il. **D45**

Unsigned articles, the longer ones with bibliographies of some length. Includes biography of living persons.

—— Kiegészítes: A-Z, v.21. 1935.

Italian

Enciclopedia italiana di scienze, lettere ed arti. Roma, Istit. della Encic. Ital., fondata da Giovanni Treccani, 1929–37. 35v. il.   **D46**

An important encyclopedia with excellent long articles, many bibliographies and a wealth of illustrations of all types, i.e., excellent maps and colored plates, dark sepia plates of unusual beauty, and innumerable text illustrations some of which are almost equal to plates. All articles, even very short ones, are signed. Many biographical articles, genealogical articles which contain additional biographies, and biographies of living persons are included. While all subjects are illustrated, the illustrations for travel and particularly for art subjects are most notable. Many portraits.

—— v.36, Indici. 1939.

A detailed index to the set, including Appendice I.

—— Appendice I. 1938. 1147p.

Includes new articles and additions and corrections to the main set. Four parts of an Appendice were published from 1934–36, covering the letters A-Pavia. Material in these is not entirely taken over in *Appendice I* and therefore the earlier parts should be preserved by libraries that received them.

—— Appendice II, 1938–1948. 1948–49. 2v. L20,000; $35 per v.

Treats the events and developments of ten years on the same basic plan as the main work, i.e., an alphabetical arrangement of articles signed by authorities, with bibliographies. Well illustrated, though the illustrations are not as plentiful nor as beautifully reproduced as in the main work. Cross references are used liberally when additions and corrections are made to articles in previous volumes. The second volume includes an analytical index to both volumes.

Garollo, Gottardo. Piccola enciclopedia Hoepli, 2. ed. compl. rinnovata. Milan, Hoepli, 1913–30. 4v.   **D47**

v.1-3, A-Z; v.4, Supplement, A-Z.

An excellent small encyclopedia for the public library with an Italian clientele or for the college library used by students beginning the study of Italian. Includes biographies of living men.

Grande enciclopedia popolare Sonzogno; pubbl. sotto la direzione di Palmiro Premoli. . . . Milano, Soc. Ed. Sonzogno, 1913–32. 22v. and suppl., v.1-2. il.   **D48**

v.1-22, A-Z; suppl., v.1-2, A-Z.

Popular work, with short unsigned articles and no bibliographies. A combination of dictionary and encyclopedia, with many definitions of words and their equivalents in various foreign languages. Has many short biographies, especially of Italians, not included in the other general encyclopedias.

Japanese

Dai-hyakka jiten. [Great encyclopedia] Tokyo, Heibon-sha, 1931–35, 1939. 28v. and suppl.   **D49**

Entirely in Japanese.

Lettish

Latviešu konversācijas vārdnīcā, galvenie redaktori: A. Švābe . . . A. Būmanis . . . K. Dišlērs. . . . Rīgā, A. Gulbja Apgādībā, 1928–38. v.1-17 compl., v.18 incompl. il.   **D50**

v.1-17, A-Raganas; v.18, (Burt. 137-38) Raganinas-Relativ.

Latvju mazā enciklopedija, Alfreda Bīlmana virsredakcijā, redaktors: Sigurds Melnalksnis. . . . Rīgā, "Grāmatu Draugs," 1932–36. 3v. il.   **D51**

A small encyclopedia issued in 20 parts forming three volumes paged continuously.

Norwegian

Aschehougs Konversations-Leksikon, ny utg. general-sekretaer: Trygve Aalheim. Oslo, Aschehoug, 1939–48. v.1-10. il. (In progress)   **D52**

v.1-10, A-Larsen.

1st ed. pub. as *Illustreret norsk konversationsleksikon,* 1907–13, 6v.

Short popular articles, good illustrations, little bibliography, many biographies, including persons still living. Good for contemporary Norwegian biography.

Polish

Encyklopedja powszechna Ultima Thule, pod redakcją dr. Stanislawa Fr. Michalskiego. Warszawa, Wydawnictwo Ultima Thule, 1930–37. v.1-8. il.   **D53**

v.1-8, A-Quous.

Articles unsigned, with little bibliography. Biographies include living persons.

Lam, Stanislaw. Illustrowana encyklopedja Trzaski, Everta i Michalskiego. Warszawa, Trzaska, Evert i Michalski, 1927–28. 5v. il.   **D54**

Very brief articles, unsigned, very little bibliography. Biographies include living persons.

Orgelbrand, Samuel. S. Orgelbranda Encyklopedja powszechna z ilustracjami i mapami. Warszawa, Orgelbrand, 1898–1912. 18v. il.   **D55**

v.1-16, A-Z, (supplement in v.16); v.17-18, Supplement.

Short popular articles, many biographies.

Portuguese

Grande enciclopédia portuguesa e brasileira. Lisboa, Rio de Janeiro, Editorial Enciclopédia [1935–45]. v.1-19. il. (In progress)   **D56**

v.1-19, A-Pais.

A dictionary-encyclopedia treating in one alphabet Portuguese words, including technical terms and modern slang; biographies; and encyclopedic articles on the history and culture of Portugal, national institutions, flora, fauna, geography, etc. The supplements, which have not yet appeared, will be devoted to Brazil. Articles are not signed, and bibliographies are inconsistently furnished.

Lemos, Maximiano Augusto d'Oliveira. Encyclopedia portugueza illustrada; diccionario universal. Porto, Lemos, [19-?] 11v. il.   **D57**

Rumanian

Enciclopedia României. [Bucarest? Asociatia Stiintifica Pentru Enciclopedia României] 1938–43. v.1-4. il. (In progress)   **D58**

Planned to be in six volumes. A. Organizarea politică-administrativă: v.1, Statul; v.2, Tara romanească. B. Economia: v.3, Economia natională: Cadre şi productie; v.4, Economia natională: Circulatie, distributie şi consum. Announced: C. Cultura: v.5, Cultura natională; v.6, Institutii si personalităti culturale.

Scholarly monographic articles arranged by large classes, with detailed tables of contents and indexes in each volume. Articles are signed by authorities and include up-to-date bibliographies.

Russian

Bol'shaîa sovetskaîa entŝiklopediîa; redaktŝiei N. I. Bukharina, V. V. Kuibysheva [and others]. Moskva, "Sovetskaîa Entŝiklopediîa," 1927–47. 65v.   **D59**

The most extensive of the Russian encyclopedias, soviet in treatment, international in scope. Volumes published irregularly, volumes 52 and 55 (published in 1947) complete the set. Signed articles. Extensive bibliographies.

—— Soîuz sovetskikh sotŝialisticheskikh respublik. 1947. 1946p., lxxxp.

An historical supplement on the U.S.S.R. Classed arrangement, with no index and therefore very difficult to use. Does not include government and politics. Chronology, p.i-xl; bibliography, p.xli-lxxx.

Brockhaus' Konversations-Lexikon. Novyĭ entŝiklopedicheskiĭ slovar'. Izdateli F. A. Brokgauz (Leĭptsig), I. A. Efron (S.-Petersburg). S.-Petersburg, Brokgauz-Efron [1912–17?] v.1-29. il.   **D60**

v.1-29, A-Otto. No more published.

A revised edition, showing considerable change, of the great Russian *Brockhaus* (published 1890–1907 in 41 volumes and two supplements).

Valuable for historical subjects.

Entŝiklopedicheskiĭ slovar' t-va "Br. A.i.I. Granat i Ko." Moskva, [1911?–1934?] v.1-33, 35, 37-40, 41²⁻⁸, 43-45¹⁻³, 46, 48, 50. il.   **D61**

v.1-33, A-P; v.35, Rab-Rast; v.37-40, Rîut-Sots; v.41²-41⁸, Soîus-Tors; v.43-46, Faler-chet; v.48, Chet-chulkov; v.50, Shkol-Ёvol.

Uneven in treatment but occasionally useful for material not included in the other encyclopedias.

Serbo-Croatian

Stanojević, Stanoje. Narodna enciklopedija srpsko-hrvatsko-slovenačka. Zagreb, Bibliografski Zavod., 1925–29. 4v.   **D62**

Signed articles, many with bibliographies. Biographies include some living persons.

Slovakian

Slovenský náucný slovnik; príručná encyklopedia vedomostí v troch dieloch, redakčné práce viedol. Pavel Bujnák . . . Bratislava, "Litevna," 1932. 3v. il.   **D63**

Very brief articles, unsigned and with no bibliography. Biographies include living persons.

Spanish

Enciclopedia universal ilustrada Europeo-Americana. Barcelona, Espasa, 1905–33. 80v. in 81. il.
D64

v.1-70 in 71, A-Z; apéndice, v.1-10, A-Z.
Often cited as *Espasa*.
A useful encyclopedia for the large reference or special library. It has long articles, bibliographies, good illustrations and maps, and includes short articles on small subjects. Special features are the many maps, geographical, geological, historical and statistical, the numerous plans of even small cities, colored plates of uniforms, flags, coins, etc., of each country, and the reproductions of paintings and other works of art given usually under title and sometimes under the artist's name. Useful for its large amount of Spanish and Spanish-American biography.
Etymologies are included and equivalents of words are given in French, Italian, English, German, Portuguese, Catalan and Esperanto.

—— **Suplemento anual, 1934- .** Barcelona, Espasa-Calpe, 1935- .

Arrangement of supplementary volumes is different from that of the basic work, i.e., instead of a straight alphabetical arrangement of all material they are arranged alphabetically by large classes, e.g., Agricultura, Biografía, Geografía, Química, etc., with small topics in an alphabetical arrangement under some of these large classes, and a general alphabetical index to all classes and topics at the end of the volume.
Volumes cover 1934, 1935, 1936–39, 2v. 1940–41, 1942–44 (pub. 1935–1950).

Diccionario enciclopédico abreviado; versiones de la mayoría de las voces, en Francés, Inglés, Italiano y Alemán y sus etimologías. . . . 2. ed. Buenos Aires, Espasa Calpe Argentina, 1945. 6v. il.
D65

Subtitle: Este diccionario contiene 200,000 artículos, 15,000 Americanismos, 15,000 fotograbados en negro y 120 láminas y mapas en color.

Diccionario enciclopédico hispano-americano de literatura, ciencias y artes. Barcelona, Montaner y Simón, 1887–1910. 28v. in 29. il.
D66

v.1-23, A-Z; v.24-25, 1st suppl. A-Z; v.26-28, 2d suppl. A-Z.
This is the Spanish encyclopedia which is found in many American libraries and is much used in spite of the fact that it is sometimes unsatisfactory and inaccurate. Inferior to the *Enciclopedia universal ilustrada* noted above.

Diccionario enciclopédico Salvat. 2. ed. Barcelona, Salvat Editores, 1934–46. 12v. il.
D67

1st ed. published under title: *Diccionario Salvat.*
Very brief articles, many biographies.

Enciclopedia ilustrada Segui; diccionario universal con todas las voces y locuciones usadas en España y en la América latina. Barcelona, Seguí [1907–28]. v.1-12. il.
D68

v.1-12, A-LL. Gives equivalents in French, English and Italian.

—— **Suplemento.** Gran diccionario francés-español por Enrique Diaz-Retg. Barcelona, Segui, [191–?]. 693p.

Enciclopedia Sopena; Nuevo diccionario ilustrado de la lengua española. . . . 6. ed. rev. . . . Barcelona, R. Sopena, 1935. 2v. il.
D69

6. ed. revisada, notablemente ampliada, y seguida de un suplemento que, registrando los hechos más notables y recientes, completa la obra hasta el dia.
A popular encyclopedic dictionary of the *Petit Larousse* (M172) type, but larger than that work. Not a substitute for a large Spanish encyclopedia but useful for readers needing brief Spanish articles, college students learning the language, etc. Contains many brief biographical articles, place names, etc.

Universitas; enciclopedia de iniciacion cultural. Barcelona, Salvat Editores, 1944–46. 20v. il. **D70**

A classed encyclopedia with alphabetical index at the end of volume 20.

Swedish

Nordisk familjebok; konversationslexikon och realencyklopedi. Ny, revid. och rikt illustrerad uppl. Stockholm, Nordisk Familjeboks Förlags Aktiebolag, 1904–26. 38v. il.
D71

v.1-34, pt.1, A-Ø; v.34, pt.2—v.38, supplement A-Ø.

Nordisk familjebok; encyklopedi och konversationslexikon. 3. väsentligt omarb. och koncentrerade uppl. Huvudredaktör: Erik Thyselius. Stockholm, Aktiebolaget Familjebokens Förlag, 1923–37. 23v. il.
D72

v.1-20, A-Ö; v.21-23, Suppl. A-Ö.
Contains many short articles and some longer ones, these usually signed. Illustrations and maps are plentiful. Many biographies, some bibliography.

Bonniers konversationslexikon. Nationaluppl. Stockholm, Bonnier, 1931–32. 12v. in 24, and 1 suppl. v. in 2. il.
D73

Svensk uppslagsbok. 2. omarbetade och utvidgade upplagen. Malmö, Förlagshuset Norden, 1947–49. v.1-12. il. (In progress)
D74

v.1-12, A-Hedebosöm.
This is an excellent modern encyclopedia edited by a board of specialists. Many articles are signed and include bibliographies. It is profusely illustrated with pertinent maps, city plans, portraits and many fine photographs. Contains numerous biographical sketches including living persons.

Swiss

Schweizer Lexikon. Zurich, Encyclios-Verlag, 1945–48. 7v. il.
D75

A new general encyclopedia. Articles are short, illustrations, though frequently small, are clear and well chosen. Colored plates are attractive. Includes some bibliography, often including recent works to 1944–48, depending on date of publication of volume. Population figures are dated.

Turkish

Inönü ansiklopedsisi. Ankara, Milli egitim basimevi, 1946–49. Cilt 1-2, (fasikul 1-16); cilt 3

(fasikul 17-21). il. (In progress) D76

Fasikul 1-21, A-Aristo.

Published under the auspices of the Turkish government, this encyclopedia is international and general in scope with emphasis on Turkish and Islamic materials. Contains a large amount of biography including living persons. Articles are usually short, unsigned and without much bibliography. Illustrations and maps are plentiful.

PERIODICALS

AND NEWSPAPERS

PERIODICALS

❦ Periodicals form a very important element in reference work in any library, supplementing the book collections in several important ways. They are specially useful for:

1. Subjects where it is of first importance to have the latest information available in print. (This is particularly important in the sciences, in technology, and for political, economic, and industrial questions of current interest.)
2. Subjects about which the library has no book or about which no books are written. (This is especially true in the case of very new and of small or obscure subjects, or subjects of purely local or temporary interest.)
3. Contemporary opinion on a given subject, person, book, etc. (Periodicals, newspapers, and contemporary memoirs are the three main sources for such information, and, of these three, periodical files are the most easily used and the most serviceable in the average library.)
4. Current bibliographies. (Particularly annual or periodic bibliographies in a given subject field.)

To make the best use of periodical literature and to answer the ordinary questions about periodicals, the reference worker needs, in addition to the catalog of his own library, three types of reference aids. These are:

1. The *index* to periodicals, which furnishes a guide to the contents of files of periodicals, serving the same purpose for articles in periodicals that the library catalog does for the books in the library.
2. The *bibliography* or *catalog* of periodicals, which is a list of the periodicals themselves, not an index to the contents, and which furnishes information about the periodicals listed, their correct titles, history, character, editors, prices, publishers, etc.
3. The *union list* of periodicals, which supplies information as to where sets of the periodicals

included in the list may be found. Such lists are usually national, regional, or local. They may be general, e.g., the *Union list of serials in the United States and Canada* (E62), or by subject field, e.g., *Union list of technical periodicals in two hundred libraries of the science-technology group* of the Special Libraries Association (N24).

Indexes

See Science, p.253, for comment on abstract journals.

❦ The cardinal points which determine the value of an index to periodicals are:

I. Scope of index
II. Length of period covered
III. Frequency and promptness of publication
IV. Completeness of the indexing of the material covered
V. Quality of indexing

To test an index on these points, note the following:

I. Scope of index
  A. Number and kind of periodicals indexed
    1. Are they substantial, established, likely to be of permanent interest?
    2. Are foreign periodicals included?
    3. Is other material indexed, e.g., pamphlets, documents, books, etc.
  B. When the index is general in scope
    1. Is there a balanced representation of periodicals in many fields?
    2. How does the selection compare with other indexes covering the same period?
      a) Is there much overlapping?
      b) Does it emphasize particular types of periodicals?
  C. When the index is devoted to a particular subject or specialized field
    1. How broad or how narrow is the field covered?

87

2. How comprehensive for the periodicals in the field?

3. Does it overlap other special indexes?

II. Length of period covered
   A. By the whole index. (For anything except current work, an index which covers fifty years is more than twice as useful as a similar one covering only twenty-five years.)
   B. By a single volume. (A cumulative volume for five years is easier to use than five annual volumes.)
   C. Is the index still in progress, or has it been discontinued?

III. Frequency and promptness of publication
   A. How often is the index published?
   B. How often does it cumulate?
      1. Monthly, quarterly, or semiannually?
      2. Annually?
      3. Larger cumulations?
   C. Are issues of periodicals indexed promptly upon appearance or is there a considerable lag?

IV. Completeness of the indexing of the material covered
   A. Are all articles in the periodicals included?
   B. What is the basis of selection if only selected articles are indexed? (As the emphasis on articles and subjects changes with the passage of time the selective index is much less useful than the complete index. Even the nominally complete index may omit short items, notices, etc.)

V. Quality of indexing
   A. Method of arrangement
      1. By author, title, and subject?
      2. By author and subject?
      3. By author only?
      4. By subject only?
      5. By class?
   B. Convenience of arrangement
      1. Alphabetical
         a) In dictionary form, i.e., authors, titles, and subjects in one alphabet?
         b) In one list or several?
      2. Subject
         a) What types of subjects are used? Is it real subject cataloging with a consistent system of subject headings and cross references or is it by "catchword" subjects?
         b) Is there an author index?
      3. Classed
         a) Is there a table of contents showing arrangement?
         b) Is there an alphabetical index?

4. Are there adequate cross references?
5. Is there a list of periodicals indexed?
   a) Does it show abbreviations used?
   b) Does it show volumes indexed?
6. Typography
   a) Is the type face clear and legible?
   b) Do headings stand out clearly?
   c) Is differentiation shown in types of headings?
7. Is the general scheme clear, simple, and easy to use?

C. Fullness of information for each entry. Does it include:
   1. Author's name in full or with initials?
   2. Full title of article?
   3. Title of periodical (or intelligible abbreviation)?
   4. Volume and inclusive paging?
   5. Date?
   6. Other items of information, e.g., illustrations, portraits, bibliographies, etc.?

D. Accuracy of entry

Bibliography

British Museum. Dept. of Printed Books. Catalogue of printed books; periodical publications. 2d ed. Lond., British Museum, 1899–1900. 2v. 1716p., 508p. **E1**

Repr. as v.41 of the Edwards reprint of the British Museum *Catalogue of printed books* (A32).

Arranged alphabetically by place of publication with an index of titles. Gives brief information about each title, i.e., title, dates, place, note of changed titles. For the verification of titles this is one of the most important of the general lists because of (1) the great number of periodicals included and (2) the convenient double arrangement.

Royal Society of London. Catalogue of the periodical publications in the library. Ox., Univ. Pr., 1912. 455p. **E2**

A title list of 1811 serial publications, arranged alphabetically by first word of title not an article. Gives place and dates of publication, statement of the society's files, changes in titles, series, and, in case of proceedings of meetings and congresses, a list of places at which the various meetings were held. Society index, p.285-455. Useful for verifying titles, especially titles of foreign publications, for tracing changes in title and for ascertaining what constitutes a complete set.

Rust, Werner. Verzeichnis von unklaren Titelkürzungen deutscher und ausländischer Zeitschriften. Leipzig, Harrassowitz, 1927. 142p. **E3**

Arranged alphabetically by abbreviations.

U. S. Library of Congress. European Affairs Division. The European press today. Wash., 1949. 152p. **E4**

An expansion of its *Reference notes on the press in*

European countries, 1948. Lists newspapers and outstanding periodicals dealing with current affairs, with annotations giving frequency, scope, point of view, etc. Arranged by country.

Microfilms, Inc. List of foreign periodicals available on microfilm. List no.7, June 1, 1946. Ann Arbor, Mich., Microfilms, 1946. 35p.　　**E5**

A cumulation of Lists no.1-6 including nearly 800 titles of foreign periodicals and indicating the volumes for the war years that are available on microfilm.

New York. Public Library. A check list of cumulative indexes to individual periodicals in the New York Public Library, comp. by Daniel C. Haskell. N.Y., Library, 1942. 370p. $6.　　**E6**

An alphabetical list of thousands of cumulative indexes available in the New York Public Library with the addition of a few, not available in the library, to periodicals that are in the library.

"A cumulative index is to be understood as one which indexes at least 3 volumes ... and makes at least a slight attempt at the classification of the periodical's contents, either an arrangement by authors or by subjects."

Births and deaths; a record of new titles, changed titles and deaths in the periodical world. (In Bulletin of bibliography, April, 1900-)　　**E7**

United States

BIBLIOGRAPHY AND HISTORY

Hoffman, Frederick J., Allen, Charles and Ulrich, Caroline F. The Little magazine; a history and a bibliography. Princeton, Princeton Univ. Pr., 1946. 440p. il. $3.75.　　**E8**

"A little magazine is a magazine designed to print artistic work which for reasons of commercial expediency is not acceptable to the money-minded periodicals or presses."—*Introd.*

In two sections: History, p.1-230; Bibliography, p.233-398, followed by a detailed index to titles, change of titles, editors, contributors, etc. The history gives a general survey of little magazines from about 1910, with discussion of the more important ones, many of which included the first works of writers who later achieved prominence, and thus have a definite place in the literary history of the period. The annotated bibliography gives in chronological order detailed information about a long, selected list of these little magazines which will be of particular use to libraries in determining titles, number of issues published, outstanding contributors, etc.

Mott, Frank Luther. A history of American magazines. . . . Camb., Harvard Univ. Pr., 1930–38. 3v. il. $5 ea.　　**E9**

v.1, 1741–1850, 848p.; v.2, 1850–1865, 608p.; v.3, 1865–1885, 649p.

Each volume has many bibliographical footnotes throughout and a chronological list of magazines at the end of the volume.

U. S. Bureau of the Census. History and present condition of the newspaper and periodical press of the United States, with a catalogue of the publications of the census year, by S. N. D. North. Wash., Govt. Prt. Off., 1884. 446p. maps.　　**E10**

A history of the newspaper and periodical press 1639–1880, with maps, and statistical tables; a catalog of periodical publications issued during the census year June 1, 1879—May 31, 1880, arranged by state and then alphabetically by place of publication, giving name of periodical, frequency, character, date of founding, price per year; and a chronological history.

CURRENT

Ayer, firm, Philadelphia. N. W. Ayer and Son's Directory of newspapers and periodicals. . . . Phila., Ayer, 1880- . v.1- . maps. (v.81, 1949, $25)　　**E11**

Subtitle, 1949: A guide to publications printed in the United States and its possessions, the Dominion of Canada, Bermuda, Cuba and Republic of the Philippines; descriptions of the states, provinces, cities and towns in which they are published; classified lists; 70 maps.

Title varies.

Absorbed Rowell's *American newspaper directory* (1869–1908. 40v.) in 1910.

Partial contents, 1949: (1) Statistical tables; (2) Population of cities of 2500 and over; (3) Catalog of American newspapers, dailies, weeklies and monthlies, as follows: (a) United States, arranged by states and cities, (b) Canada, arranged by provinces and cities, (c) Bermuda, (d) Cuba, (e) Republic of the Philippines; (4) List of daily newspapers with indication of whether morning or evening, and special Sunday, weekly, semiweekly editions and circulation; (5) Agricultural publications; (6) College publications; (7) Publications in foreign languages arranged by language; (8) Fraternal publications; (9) Magazines of general circulation, classified; (10) Negro publications; (11) Religious publications arranged by states with indication of denomination; (12) Trade, technical and class publications, by subject; (13) Alphabetical index (omitting daily and weekly papers).

The standard American list: comprehensive, listing newspapers and periodicals, but not claiming completeness, as it intentionally omits certain classes of papers, e.g., publications of schools and smaller colleges, local church papers and most house organs issued merely to exploit goods of their firms. The main list, number 3, covers more than 1100 pages and gives (1) some descriptive and statistical matter about each state, a list of its counties, marking those which have no newspapers, and considerable gazetteer information about each city, i.e., its distance and direction from some important place, its railroads, leading manufactures, products and institutions and (2) detailed information about each paper or periodical listed including its name, frequency, character or politics, date of foundation, size of column and page, subscription price, circulation figures, names of editors and publishers. Has many good maps, at least one for each state, and a standard time map.

Editor and publisher: International yearbook number for 1920- . N.Y., Editor and Publisher, 1920- . $5 per yr.　　**E12**

Issued annually as part of the last number for January of the weekly *Editor and publisher*. Contains a large amount of useful statistical and directory information in the field of American and foreign journalism. Not sold separately.

Printers' ink directory of house organs; internal, external, and combination. N.Y., Printers' Ink Pub., 1947. 132p. $5. **E13**

1st ed. 1944.

Lists more than 5100 items in three sections including the same titles in different arrangements: (1) by title; (2) by sponsors; (3) arranged geographically by state and city, including street address.

Ulrich's Periodicals directory; a classified guide to a selected list of current periodicals, foreign and domestic. 5th ed. (Post-war) ed. by Carolyn F. Ulrich. Including a list of clandestine periodicals of World War II by Adrienne Florence Muzzy. N.Y., Bowker, 1947. 399p. $15. **E14**

1st ed., 1932; 2d ed., 1935; 3d ed., 1938; 4th ed., 1943.

A very useful classed list of about 7500 periodicals with the emphasis on the publications of North and South America and the British empire. Also includes some magazines from other foreign countries if issues have been received of 1944 or later.

The fourth edition was an Inter-American edition covering North, Central, and South America, the West Indies and Hawaii.

Entries usually include title, subtitle, supplements, date of origin, frequency, price, size, publisher, place of publication, annual index and cumulative indexes if they exist. Gives information as to the particular characteristics of a periodical, e.g., bibliographies, book reviews, film reviews, illustrations, maps, markets and prices, patents, statistics, etc. Indicates in which general periodical index each is indexed or abstracted.

The bibliographies which followed each subject group in previous editions have been omitted. Current bibliographies on a specific subject are put in the regular listing under subject; general bibliographies are listed under heading General bibliographies.

The useful and interesting list of clandestine periodicals of World War II is on p.329-47, but the titles are not included in the general index.

The Working press of the nation. Ed. and publisher Tom Farrell. N.Y., Farrell Pub., 1947- . v.1- . Annual. (1950, $15) **E15**

First issue was entitled: *Working press of New York City.*

Subtitle on cover of 1950 edition: Directory and guide to newspapers, news services, news magazines, feature syndicates, newsreels, photo services, radio and television. Lists personnel.

Australia

Press directory of Australia and New Zealand, 1914- . Sydney, N.S.W., Country Pr., 1914- . v.1- . Irregular (11th ed. 1947, 7s. 6d.) **E16**

Canada

McKim's Directory of Canadian publications, 1892- . Irregular (v.35, 1942, $3) **E17**

Subtitle: A complete list of the newspapers and periodicals published in the Dominion of Canada and Newfoundland, with full particulars.

Title varies.

Colombia

Bogotá. Biblioteca Nacional. Catálogo de todos los periódicos que existen desde su fundación hasta el año de 1935, inclusive. Ed. oficial. Bogotá, El Gráfico, 1936. 2v. **E18**

Contents: t.1, Periódicos nacionales, A-P; t.2, Periódicos nacionales, R-Z. Periódicos extranjeros, A-Z.

Cuba

Directorio de revistas y periódicos de Cuba. 1942- . La Habana, Anuario Bibliográfico Cubano, 1942- . v.1- . Annual. (Biblioteca del bibliotecaria) $1 per yr. **E19**

Editor: 1942–1944, Fermin Peraza y Sarausa.

Czechoslovakia

Adresář československého tisku. roč. 1- . 1948- . Praha, Orbis, 1948- . **E20**

Bibliografický katalog časopisectva. Republiky československé za rok 1920. Vydal Československý ústav bibliografický (při Veřejné a universitní knihovně) v Praze. Praha, Nákladem Vlastním. —V kom. J. Springer, 1921. 243p. **E21**

Alphabetical, with indexes to places of publication, subjects, and authors.

France

Annuaire de la presse française et étrangère et du monde politique, 1880- . Paris, Administration et Rédaction, 1880- . v.1- . il. Annual. **E22**

Title varies. Continues E. Mermet's *La publicité en France,* 1878–80.

An important and useful bibliography and annual, containing not only full information about French journals and the French press but also a considerable amount of the statistical, gazetteer, political and governmental information needed by French journalists. Contains many portraits. Scope and contents of volumes before 1914 differ somewhat from the volumes issued since 1914.

Principal contents, 1948: Names and portraits of French officials, Lists of members of the Senate and Chamber of deputies, Press associations with names of officers and members, Critics, Pseudonyms, Advertising agencies, Lists of papers and periodicals published in (1) Paris, arranged alphabetically by classes, (2) Départements, arranged alphabetically by départements and towns, (3) Colonies, (4) Abroad.

nnuaire des journaux, revues et publications
ériodiques publiés à Paris, 1880–1913, 1921–29.
aris, Le Soudier, 1881–1914, 1922–30. v.1-43.
E23

Issued annually but revised only every other year,
the odd years; in the even years the previous issue
lus a supplement of new titles was printed. Publica-
on suspended, 1914–20. Ceased publication 1930.

Includes only Paris publications; for provincial period-
als the *Annuaire de la presse française* (E22) must be
sed.

rgus. Nomenclature des journaux et revues en
ngue française du monde entier, 1936/37. Paris,
rgus, [1936?]. 758p. **E24**

1st ed. 1917. Gives brief information, title, address,
equency of publication, date of founding, sometimes
ames of editors.

aron, Pierre and Jaryc, Marc. Répertoire des
ériodiques de langue française, philosophiques,
istoriques, philologiques et juridiques. Publié
ar la Fédération des Sociétés Françaises de
ciences, Philosophiques, Historiques, Philolo-
iques et Juridiques. Paris, Maison du Livre
rançais, 1935. 351p. **E25**

Alphabetical list, p.1-278, nos. 1-1421; Supplément,
279-292, nos. 1421 bis-1476. II°. supplément, nos.
477-1496.

—— 1. supplément, nos. 1477-1686. 1937. 68p.

Incorporates in regular alphabetical order and number-
g the titles (nos. 1477–1496) of the original II°. supplé-
ent.

—— 2. supplément, nos. 1687-1900. 1939. 62p.

latin, Louis Eugène. Bibliographie historique
t critique de la presse périodique française. . . .
aris, Firmin-Didot, 1866. cxvii, 660p. **E26**

Subtitle: Catalogue systématique et raisonné de tous
s écrits périodiques de quelque valeur publiés ou
yant circulés en France depuis l'origine du journal
squ'à nos jours, avec extraits, notes historiques, critiques,
t morales, indication des prix que les principaux jour-
aux ont atteints dans les ventes publiques, etc.

A bibliography of the retrospective, not the current
ype, with detailed bibliographical and historical notes
bout each periodical listed. Useful, though never com-
lete and now very far from up to date.

Germany

erlin. Deutsches Institut für Zeitungskunde.
tandortskatalog wichtiger Zeitungsbestände in
eutschen Bibliotheken. Leipzig, Hiersemann,
933. 254p. **E27**

In two parts: Deutsches Reich und abgetrennte Ge-
iete; Ausland. Indexes of titles and of places of publi-
ation.

erlin. Institut für Zeitungswissenschaft. Hand-
uch der deutschen Tagespresse. 7. Aufl. Leip-
ig, Armanen-Verlag, 1944. 478p. **E28**

Surveys German daily and weekly newspapers, press
agencies, organizations, and institutions in wartime. For
each paper usually gives title, beginning date, publisher,
editions, title changes, personnel and often brief characterization.

Deutscher Zeitschriften-Katalog für 1865–1922,
Zusammenstellung von über 3200 Titeln deutscher
Zeitschriften. Leipzig, Schulze, 1865–1922. v.1-58.
E29

Title, before 1916, *Deutscher Journal-Katalog.* Discontinued after 1922.

An annual trade bibliography, listing only the periodicals and transactions regularly handled by the German
dealers.

Diesch, Carl. Bibliographie der germanistischen
Zeitschriften. Leipzig, Hiersemann, 1927. 441p.
(Modern Language Assoc. of America. Germanic
Sect. Bibliographical pub. v.1.) **E30**

A chronological, classed arrangement with title and
name indexes.

Kirchner, Joachim. Die Grundlagen des deutschen
Zeitschriftenwesens mit einer Gesamtbibliographie der deutschen Zeitschriften bis zum Jahre
1790. Leipzig, Hiersemann, 1928–31. 2v. **E31**

Contents: T.1, Bibliographische und Buchhandelsge-
schichtliche Untersuchungen; T.2, Die Bibliographie der
deutschen Zeitschriften bis zur französischen Revolution.
Statistische Ergebnisse. Register der Zeitschriften.
Namenregister.

Der Leitfaden. 1947-   . Essen-Stadtwald, Rhein-
isch-Westfälisches Verlags-Kontor, 1947-   . **E32**

1947: T.1, Deutsche Tageszeitungen; T.2, Deutsche
Zeitschriften; T.3, Hilfsmittel der Werbung.

Lists the newspapers and periodicals published in the
four zones of Germany.

Sperlings Zeitschriften-und Zeitungs-Adressbuch;
Handbuch der deutschen Presse. 1858-   . Leipzig, Börsenverein der Deutschen Buchhändler,
1858-   . v.1-   . **E33**

Title varies; place and publisher vary. Suspended
1940–46.

Alphabetical list of newspapers and periodicals; classed
list. Indexes. Useful for identifying title, for finding what
German periodicals there are on a given subject and for
securing the information needed before placing a subscription, but of little value for information about history,
editorship, etc., of the periodicals listed, or for collation
of complete sets.

Great Britain

Times, London. Tercentenary handlist of English
& Welsh newspapers, magazines and reviews.
Lond., The Times, 1920. 324p. **E34**

Contents: Sect. I: London and suburban press, arranged
chronologically, 1620–1919; separate list, periodicals in
Armenian, Hebrew, Yiddish, Russian and Turkish; title
index to section I; Sect. II: The provincial press, arranged
chronologically by date of first known issue, 1701–1919;
alphabetical index to section II.

A chronological bibliography of English periodicals from 1620 to 1919, which attempts to include all types of periodicals except (1) official periodicals issued during the war, (2) annuals and yearbooks, (3) publications of societies classed as academies in the British Museum, and (4) local church periodicals, and, while avowedly incomplete for the difficult period of the eighteenth century, claims to be nearly exhaustive for the seventeenth and nineteenth centuries. Is based upon the collections of the British Museum, including the two special Thomason and Burney collections, with some reference to copies and numbers in other libraries not found in the British Museum. Each title is listed under the date of the earliest copy which has been found for examination, and the information given for it includes number and date of the earliest issue, date of discontinuance, if known, and in some cases name of printer, editor, distributor, and a reference to the library or collection if it is other than the British Museum's general collection.

Useful as a means of identifying titles, and as showing, by its chronological arrangement, what periodicals are available for a given date.

BEFORE 1800

Crane, R. S. and **Kaye, F. B.** Census of British newspapers and periodicals, 1620–1800. Chapel Hill, Univ. of North Carolina Pr., 1927. 205p. **E35**

Lists 970 papers and periodicals, with indication of the holdings in 62 American libraries.

Henry E. Huntington Library and Art Gallery, San Marino, Calif. Check list of English newspapers and periodicals before 1801 in the Huntington library; comp. by Anthony J. Gabler. (In Huntington Library Bulletin. Camb., Mass., 1931. no. 2, p.1-66) **E36**

Arranged alphabetically with chronological index.

Oxford University. Bodleian Library. Catalogue of English newspapers and periodicals in the Bodleian Library, 1622–1800. By R. T. Milford and D. M. Sutherland. Ox., Society, 1936. p.167-346. (Oxford Bibl. Soc. Proceedings and papers, v.4, pt.2) **E37**

Alphabetical title catalog, p.171-344; index to editors, authors and contributors, p.345-46.

Weed, Katherine Kirtley and **Bond, Richmond Pugh.** Studies of British newspapers and periodicals from their beginning to 1800; a bibliography. Chapel Hill, Univ. of North Carolina Pr., 1946. 233p. (Studies in philology, extra ser., no.2) **E38**

Contents: Bibliographies and bibliographical studies; Beginnings of the newspaper; General studies; Individual newspapers and periodicals; Editors, authors and publishers; Towns and counties; Special subjects; Newspapers and periodicals in Europe and in America.

Lists some 2100 books and periodical articles printed mainly 1800–1940, under subject with author index.

Couper, William James. Edinburgh periodica press; being a bibliographical account of th newspapers, journals, and magazines issued i Edinburgh from the earliest times to 180 Stirling, Mackay, 1908. 2v. facsim. **E3**

v.1, 1642–1711; v.2, 1711–1800.

19TH AND 20TH CENTURIES

Newspaper press directory; and advertiser guide. . . . Lond., Mitchell, 1846- . v.1- . Annual. (1949, 30s.) **E4**

Subtitle, 1949: Containing particulars of newspaper magazines, reviews and periodicals published in Gre: Britain and Northern Ireland, and Eire, the Britis dominions and colonies, the continent of Europe, Ame ica, the Far East, etc.

Publication suspended 1941–1944.

Sell's World press; the handbook of the fourt estate. . . . Lond., Sell, 1884–1921. v.1-36. il. **E4**

Title varies. Discontinued after 1921.

Not only a bibliography of English newspapers ar periodicals but also an annual of information abo journalists and journalism in England and the colonies.

Willing's Press guide, 1874- . Lond., Willin; 1874- . v.1- . Annual. (1948, 15s.) **E4**

A useful inexpensive list.

Principal contents, 1948: Alphabetical list of newsp pers, and periodicals issued in the United Kingdom, wi year of establishment, when published, price, publisher name and address; Classified list; London suburban p pers; London addresses of provincial publications; Pr vincial publications arranged under counties; Provinci publications arranged under towns; Titular changes ar amalgamations; Dominion, colonial and foreign public tions; Reporting and news agencies.

Italy

Annuario della stampa italiana, a cura del Sind; cato Nazionale Fascista dei Giornalisti, 191(1937/38. Bologna, Zanichelli [1916–37]. v. 15/16. **E4**

No volume issued for 1918, 1920, 1922–23, 1935–3

A useful list while published, listing newspapers ar periodicals and also giving brief notes about Italian jou nalists, associations, etc.

Italy. Consiglio Nazionale delle Ricerche. Peri dici italiani scientifici, tecnici e di cultu: generale. 5. ed. interamente rinnovata. 193 Roma, Arti Grafiche Trinacria, 1939. 3v. **E4**

Japan

Kyoto. Deutsches Forschungsinstitut. Bibli: graphischer Katalog ausgewählter Japanisch: Zeitschriften. Kyoto, 1942. 408p. **E4**

Latin America

La Plata. Universidad Nacional. Biblioteca. Catálogo de periódicos sudamericanos existentes en la Biblioteca pública de la Universidad (1791–1861). La Plata, 1934. 231p. **E46**

Pan American Union. Division of Intellectual Cooperation. Latin American university journals and serial publications; a tentative directory by Katherine Lenore Morgan. Wash., Pan American Union, 1944. 74p. 50c. **E47**

U. S. Library of Congress. Latin American periodicals currently received in the Library of Congress and in the Library of the Department of Agriculture. Charmion Shelby, ed. Wash., 1944. 249p. **E48**

An annotated list, giving full titles, date of founding, editor, address, price and descriptive note.

Russia

Ezhegodnik periodicheskîkh izdaniĭ SSSR. Moskva, Izdatel'stvo Vsesoiūznoĭ Knizhnoi Palat', 1933- . **E49**

Title varies: 1933, *Spisok periodicheskikh izdaniĭ RSFSR;* 1934–35, *Letopis' periodicheskikh izdaniĭ SSSR.* Volume 6, 1938, in two parts; Zhurnali; Gazeti.

Lisovskiĭ, Nikolaĭ Mikhaĭlovich. Russkaiā periodicheskaiā pechat' 1703–1900 gg., bibliografiiā i graficheskiiā tablitsy. Petrograd, Shumakhora, 1915. 267p. tables. **E50**

—— Bibliografiiā russkoi periodicheskoi pechati 1703–1900 gg. (Materialy dlia istorii russkoi zhurnalistiki) Petrograd, 1915. 1067p. **E51**

South Africa

Catalogue of union periodicals, ed. for the National Research Council and National Research Board. . . . Johannesburg, 1943- . (In progress) **E52**

v.1, Science and technology. 525p.

Spain

Givanel Mas, Juan. Bibliografía catalana: premsa. Barcelona [Imprenta Altés] 1931. v.1, 557p. **E53**

v.1, A-Barcelona.

Hartzenbusch é Hiriart, Eugenio. Apuntes para un catálogo de periódicos Madrileños desde el año 1661 al 1870. Madrid, Succesores de Riva-deneyra, 1894. 421p. **E54**

Madrid. Hemeroteca Municipal. Catálogo de las publicaciones periódicas madrileñas existentes en la Hemeroteca Municipal de Madrid, 1661–1930. Madrid, Artes Gráficas Municipales, 1933. 360p. **E55**

Sweden

Lundstedt, Bernhard Wilhelm. Sveriges periodiska litteratur. Bibliografi. Stockholm, Iduns Tryckeri, 1895–1902. 3v. in 2. **E56**

v.1, 1645–1812; v.2, Stockholm, 1813–1894; v.3, Landsorten, 1813–99.

Switzerland

Association de la Presse Suisse. Annuaire, 1909–1917/18, et chronique politique, année 1-8. Zürich, Füssli, 1911–18. v.1-8. **E57**

Title page also in German, text partly in German, partly in French. Discontinued after 1918.

Contains a regional list and a subject list. Full information, including full title, address, date of founding, price, editor, etc., given in the regional list; the classed list gives only brief title, and place of publication.

Bern. Schweizerische Landesbibliothek. Verzeichnis der laufenden schweizerischen Zeitschriften. Catalogue des périodiques suisses, revues, journaux, annuaires, almanachs, collections, etc., reçus par la Bibliothèque Nationale à Berne. 2. éd. refondue et considérablement augm., publ. par la direction de la Bibliothèque. Bern-Bümpliz, Benteli, 1925. 217p. **E58**

—— —— Nachtrag, 1926–30. Bern-Bümpliz, Benteli, 1926–31. 5v.

Katalog der in der Schweiz erscheinenden Zeitungen und Zeitschriften nach Kantonen, Ortschaften und Branchen geordnet. Basel, Schweizer-Annoncen A.-G., 1934. 62p. **E59**

In German, French and Italian.

Schweizerischer Zeitschriften- und Zeitungskatalog. Catalogue des revues et journaux suisses. Olten, Schweizerisches Vereinssortiment [1945]. 239p. **E60**

Classed with title index.

Union lists

See also Science—Periodicals, p.255-56.

❦ A union list of periodicals is a catalog, usually in alphabetical title arrangement, of the periodicals to be found in the libraries of a specific country or region, with indication of the libraries which own any given title. Such lists may be general in scope and include titles of periodicals in all fields or they may be limited to the periodicals in some particular subject or class. There are two main types of union lists: (1) lists of periodicals currently received; (2) lists of sets, with exact indication of what portion of each set is in the libraries listed. The first type is useful within the region covered for the location of current issues. Information about the periodical is usually very brief, frequently limited to title and place of publication. The second type is more useful for reference as details are usually given concerning title, changes of title, place of publication, date of founding, and of last volume if publication has ceased, volume numbers, etc., and exact indication of the portions of each set held by the libraries listed.

The principal use of such lists is for reference and interlibrary loan purposes but they are also useful to catalogers. Even when periodicals are not available for interlibrary loan, the knowledge of the location of particular volumes or sets either in this country or in another, is frequently useful because of the possibility of obtaining microfilms or photostats of the material. For this reason union lists of periodicals in foreign countries, as well as those published in this country, are needed by research libraries.

Because of the comprehensiveness of the *Union list of serials* (E62) and because it includes a *Bibliography of union lists of serials* (E61) regional union lists are not included here, although they should be acquired by libraries according to need and locale. Smaller libraries will need the union lists of their own region, large research libraries will need union lists from many parts of this country and abroad.

Bibliography of union lists of serials, comp. by D. C. Haskell and Karl Brown. (In Union list of serials in libraries of the United States and Canada. 2d ed. N.Y., 1943. p.3053-65)   **E61**

Includes union lists of periodicals and of newspapers.
For newspapers supersedes the list in *American newspapers* (E103).

Union list of serials in libraries of the United States and Canada. 2d ed., ed. by Winifred Gregory. Advisory committee: Donald B. Gilchrist, Wyllis E. Wright, Robert B. Downs, James Thayer Gerould, Harry M. Lydenberg, Nathan van Patten, Helmer L. Webb. N.Y., Wilson, 1943. 3065p. Subscription, apply to pub. for price. **E62**

1st ed. 1927 (Supplements, Jan. 1925–Dec. 1932. 2v.).
The most important and comprehensive union list, indispensable in any American library which does much reference work with periodicals. This edition follows the general pattern of the first but lists between 115,000 and 120,000 titles as against 75,000 in the first and lists holdings for more than 600 libraries as against 200 in the first. Gives catalog description of each title and a statement of what constitutes a complete set and indicates exact holdings for all periodicals including those common

periodicals that were listed in the first as "Complete sets generally found in large libraries." The scope has been enlarged by the addition of: (1) Annual publications recording or summarizing the progress of research in various fields; (2) Numbered monograph series; (3) Children's magazines; and (4) in instances where the run of volumes justified inclusion, those usually discarded magazines known as "pulps." In general, the following classes are excluded: Government publications (except periodicals and monograph series issued by governments), administrative reports of societies, universities, corporations, etc., almanacs, gift books, American newspapers, English and other foreign newspapers after 1820, law reports and digests, publications of agricultural and other experiment stations, local religious, labor and fraternal organizations, boards of trade, chambers of commerce, national and international conferences and congresses, etc., house organs (unless of technical and scientific value), alumni, undergraduate and intercollegiate fraternal publications, trench papers and in general all titles having a highly limited or ephemeral value.—Cf. *Introd.*

The closing date for new titles was Dec. 31, 1940.
In its alphabetical place under "Société," p.2579-83, there is a "Place index to French societies" giving under place name the exact names of French local societies.
"Bibliography of union lists of serials," compiled by Daniel C. Haskell and Karl Brown, p.3053-65.

—— Supplement Jan. 1941–Dec. 1943. N.Y., Wilson, 1945. 1123p. Service basis.

—— 2d Suppl. to the 2d ed., Jan. 1944–Dec. 1949, ed. by Marga Franck. Checking ed. Sect. 1-3, A-Q, June 1949-Aug. 1950. N.Y., Wilson, 1949-   . (In progress)

Consists largely of new titles but also includes some serials previously included, if they have changed title, ceased publication, or been revived after a period of suspension.

Union catalogue of the periodical publications in the university libraries of the British isles, with their respective holdings, excluding titles in the World list of scientific periodicals, 1934. Comp. on behalf of the Joint Standing Committee on Library Cooperation by Marion G. Roupell. Lond., National Central Library, 1937. 712p. **E63**

An important union list of 23,115 periodicals other than those listed in the *World list of scientific periodicals . . . 1900–1933* (N25) with indication of exact holdings in the libraries of some 113 British universities and university institutions as of December 1935. Arranged alphabetically by title with many cross references from changed or variant titles, names of societies and institutions, and places appearing in titles. Primarily useful in British libraries, but useful in American libraries also for titles not included in the *Union list of serials in libraries of the United States and Canada* (E62).

List of the serial publications of foreign governments, 1815–1931, ed. by Winifred Gregory, for the American Council of Learned Societies, American Library Association, National Research Council. N.Y., Wilson, 1932. 720p. Apply to publisher for price.   **E64**

A union list on the same general plan as the *Union st of serials* (E62) for a type of serial publication xcluded from that list, i.e., government serials. For full description *see* F25.

ontificio Istituto Biblico, Rome. Elenco alfaetico delle pubblicazioni periodiche esistenti elle biblioteche di Roma e relative a scienze 1orali, storiche, filologiche, belle arti, ecc. Roma, ontificio Istituto Biblico, 1914. 406p.　　**E65**

Alphabetical title list, with indication of files, of periicals in 45 libraries in Rome. Partial subject index.

russia. Auskunftsbureau der deutschen Biblio- 1eken. Gesamt-Zeitschriften-Verzeichnis. Ber- 1, Königliche Bibliothek, 1914. 355p.　　**E66**

——Gesamtverzeichnis der ausländischen Zeit- 1hriften (GAZ) 1914–1924. Berlin, Staatsbiblio- 1ek, 1929. 784p.

An extensive union list of periodicals in German li- 'aries. The first volume includes both German and reign periodicals, the second, only foreign.

Indexes

e name of subject for the indexes to particular 1bjects, e.g., for the *Education index see* Educa- 1n; for the *Art index see* Fine Arts, etc.

International

1bliographie der fremdsprachigen Zeitschriften- 1eratur; Répertoire bibliographique interna- 1nal des revues; International index to periodi- 1ls 1911–19, 1925/26- . Gautzsch b. Leipzig, 1etrich, 1911- . v.1-20, n.F. v.1- . (Interna- 1nale Bibliographie der Zeitschriftenliteratur, 1t. B)　　**E67**

An important index similar in general plan and arrange- 1nt to the *Bibliographie der deutschen Zeitschriften- 1ratur* (E87) which now forms Abteilung A of the 1ternationale Bibliographie. Indexes about 1400 peri- 1cals and general works in the principal non-German 1guages. The first series is a subject index only, the 1ond series gives, in addition, an author index to each 1ject list. Beginning with n.F. volume 4, some supple- 1ntary indexing of material earlier than the covering 1te of the volume is included. The volumes for 1920–24 not yet published. Because of its wide coverage it is very useful for 1ding materials in American and English periodicals, well as in French, Italian and other European publi- 1ions. Because of the lack of French periodical indexes, 1s particularly important for French articles.

1ternational index to periodicals, devoted chief- to the humanities and science, v.1- . 1907- . cumulative author and subject index to a 1ected list of the periodicals of the world. N.Y., 1lson, 1916- . v.1- . Service basis.　　**E68**

Title varies: v.1-2, *Readers' guide to periodical litera- ture supplement;* v.3, *International index to periodicals (formerly Readers' guide supplement).*

A cumulative index made up of three forms: (1) per- manent cumulated volumes now covering three years, (2) annual volumes to be used as supplements to the perma- nent volumes until a new cumulated volume is issued, and (3) current numbers issued four times a year, June, Sept., and Dec., with bound annual cumulation in March. (Frequency varies.)

An important index for the large or scholarly library. An author and subject index on the same plan as the *Readers' guide* (E71) but covering periodicals of a dif- ferent type, i.e., the more scholarly journals and some foreign titles mainly in the humanities and sciences. Only 74 periodicals were indexed in the first volume, but be- ginning with volume 2 the number was enlarged by in- cluding 45 serials, principally foreign titles, previously indexed by the analytic cards issued by the American Library Association Publishing Board.

Coverage in later volumes varies, e.g., with volume 5, 22 titles were transferred to the new *Education index* (L716) and six to the new *Art index* (Q14), and many new titles were added to the *International index.* Before World War II a number of foreign titles were included, e.g., in volume 8, 1937–1940, 221 titles were indexed, 125 American, 39 English, 3 Canadian, 25 French, 20 German, 4 Oriental, 2 Italian, 1 each Dutch, Irish and Spanish.

However, because of the difficulties of obtaining for- eign periodicals during the war, most of those in foreign languages were dropped and have not yet been reinstated. The Apr. 1947–Mar. 1948 volume indexes 189 titles: 147 American, 37 British, 4 Canadian, 1 Irish.

United States and Great Britain

Poole's Index to periodical literature, 1802–81. rev. ed. Bost., Houghton, 1891 [Pref. 1891, c.1882]. 2v.　　**E69**

——Supplements, Jan. 1882–Jan. 1, 1907. Bost., Houghton [c1887–1908]. 5v.

Repr. by photo-offset, N.Y., Peter Smith, 1938. 6v. in 7. $10 per vol.

Originally edited by William Frederick Poole, con- tinued by him and W. I. Fletcher, with the cooperation of members of the American Library Association.

v.1, 1802–81; 1st suppl. 1882–86; 2d suppl. 1887–91; 3d suppl. 1892–96; 4th suppl. 1897–1901; 5th suppl. 1902–1906.

The pioneer index and, though now discontinued, still an important index to American and English periodicals, since it covers the longest period, 105 years, and indexes the large total of about 590,000 articles in 12,241 volumes of 470 American and English periodicals. A subject index only, includes *no author entries;* authors' names appear frequently as entries, but only as subject entries for bio- graphical or critical articles about such authors. To make intelligent use of the index the student should remember the following points: (1) no author entries; (2) all articles having a distinct subject are entered under that subject; (3) articles having no subject, i.e., fiction, poems, plays, are entered under the first word of the title not an article; (4) book reviews are entered in two ways: (a) reviews of a book which has a definite subject are entered under subject of the book; (b) reviews of a book which does not have a distinct subject, i.e., a novel, poetry, a drama, are entered under the name of the author reviewed. Approximately complete for the periodicals covered, except in the following respects: (1) very brief articles, notes, etc., generally omitted; (2) minor book reviews not included; (3) some English periodicals included in volume 1 are incompletely indexed because of failure in collaboration between English and American indexers. Information given about each article includes its title, author's name in curves when it was known or could be ascertained, abbreviated title of periodical, volume and page reference. Neither inclusive paging nor date is given, but the date (year only) can be worked out from the "Chronological conspectus" in each volume. Indexes principally periodicals of a general nature but a few selected periodicals on special subjects are included. In general the work of both indexing and printing is very accurate, with comparatively few typographical errors. For list of errata *see Bulletin of bibliography* 2:24-25, 40-41, 56-58, 75-76, 133-134; 3:25; 4:11-12, 72, Jan. 1900—Oct. 1905.

Nineteenth century readers' guide to periodical literature, 1890–1899, with supplementary indexing, 1900–1922. ed. by Helen Grant Cushing and Adah V. Morris. . . . N.Y., Wilson, 1944. 2v. Service basis. **E70**

An author, subject and illustrator index to the material in 51 periodicals (1003 volumes) mainly in the period from 1890 to 1899. Some indexing has been done for volumes published after 1899 "in order to make the indexing of each title complete from the year 1890 to the time when it was added to the list of one of the Wilson indexes. Fourteen of the 51 titles included have been indexed beyond 1899, some as far as 1922."—*Pref.*

Periodicals indexed are mainly general and literary but some are included from special fields. Short stories, novels, and plays are indexed under author and title. Book reviews are listed under author entry only. Dramatic criticism may be found under the heading Dramas—criticism, plots, etc., as well as under the author entry. More than 13,000 poems are listed under Poems by title. Full entry is under author's name. Poems on particular persons, events, etc., are also under subject.

In some nineteenth century periodicals it was the editorial practice to publish articles anonymously, e.g., in the *Edinburgh review* and the *Quarterly review*. For many of these articles the authors' names have been ascertained from the publishers' records and are indicated in this index.

These two volumes were planned as part of a larger project to cover the whole nineteenth century by a modern periodical index in dictionary form. Work on other sections has been discontinued for the present but with the hope that it can be resumed at a later date.

Readers' guide to periodical literature [cumulated], 1900- . N.Y., Wilson, 1905- . v.1- . Service basis. **E71**

A cumulative index, made up of three forms or sections: (1) permanent cumulated volumes (since 1935, two years to a volume; previous volumes varied from three to five years), (2) annual volumes, to be used as supplements to the cumulated volumes until superseded by a new permanent volume, and (3) issues published semimonthly, Sept. to June, monthly, July-Aug., cumulating at intervals until the last number of each current

volume, which covers the twelve months, forms a new annual volume. A complete set to date always consists of all permanent cumulated volumes, all annuals since the last cumulated, and the subsequent numbers for the current year.

Started in 1901 as an index for the small library, covering at first only 15 of the more popular periodicals and gradually extended until in 1903 it absorbed the *Cumulative index* (1896–1903) and in 1911 took over the work of the *Annual library index* (E77). List of periodicals indexed varies from volume to volume, 1947-48 indexes about 125 titles, the coverage including general and popular magazines, as well as some scientific and scholarly publications.

A modern index of the best type. Its special features are: (1) full dictionary cataloging of all articles, i.e., their entry under author, subject, and title when necessary; (2) uniformity of entries, owing to the fact that the work is done by a few professional indexers rather than by many voluntary collaborators; (3) use of catalog subject headings instead of catchword subject; (4) full information in the references, i.e., refers not only to volume and page, but also to exact date and inclusive paging, and indicates illustrations, portraits, etc.; (5) the cumulative features which keep the index well to date without multiplying alphabets to be consulted; (6) the indexing of all book reviews, through 1904, under author reviewed; after 1905 reviews are generally omitted because included in the *Book review digest* (A577); (7) the indexing, in the second and third cumulated volumes, of some 597 composite books, thus forming an unofficial continuation of the *A.L.A. index to general literature* (R166). This book indexing was abandoned after 1914.

Abridged readers' guide to periodical literature, July 1935- . Author and subject index to selected list of periodicals. N.Y., Wilson, 1936- . v.1- . Service basis. **E7[?]**

An index to 24 to 30 periodicals, designed especially for school and small public libraries unable to afford the regular *Readers' guide* (E71). For the public library which is growing and can possibly afford the greater expense, the unabridged guide is the better investment.

Monthly, cumulating, the June number forming a new annual volume cumulating biennially.

Annual magazine subject index, 1907- ; a subject index to a selected list of American and English periodicals and society publications. Bost., Faxon, 1908- . v.1- . (1947, $17.50) **E7[?]**

v.1, had title *Magazine subject index* and is a basic volume indexing 79 periodicals (44 from their first issue to Dec. 31, 1907 and 35 for the year 1907); v.2- are annual supplements, with title *Annual magazine subject index.*

An index of subjects only, not of authors or titles, except that fiction when included is indexed under author's name. Indexes material with exact reference giving abbreviated title of periodical, volume, date, inclusive paging and indication of illustrations, portraits, maps, and plans. Intended as a supplement to other indexes and so aims to include no periodicals indexed either *Poole* (E69), the *Readers' guide* (E71), or *Annual library index* (E77). While the list of periodicals general in character about half of the titles relate to history, especially local history, and the index specializes also in travel, mountaineering, exploration, outdoor life, and fine arts. Indexes all important articles in the periodicals covered but omits short articles, poetry, and most fiction, though continued stories and short stories by notable writers are included.

In accordance with the plan of not indexing periodicals covered by other general indexes, this index varies its list from year to year, dropping periodicals which have been taken over by other indexes and adding new titles. 1947 indexes more than 140 titles. Includes many local history titles, especially transactions of local history societies indexed in Griffin, *Bibliography of American historical societies* (*see* V97), and as these are often indexed back to the date when Griffin stopped, the index constitutes an informal continuation of Griffin. The only exception to the rule not to index material included elsewhere is in the case of these history periodicals.

Catholic periodical index; a cumulative author and subject index to a selected list of Catholic periodicals, 1930–33, Jan. 1939–June 1943- . N.Y., pub. for the Catholic Library Assoc., by Wilson, 1939- . Price on application.　**E74**

1930–33 forms the first permanent volume in a series of projected 4-year cumulations, and supersedes an earlier v.1-2 for 1930–31. 1934–38, not yet published.

Jan. 1939–June 1943, second cumulation, published 1945. Continued by quarterly issues, cumulating into annual or biennial volumes.

Indexes 50 to 70 periodicals, mainly published in the United States, Canada, England and Ireland.

Subject index to periodicals, 1915- . Lond., Library Assoc., 1919- . Annual. (1946, £3 17s.)　**E75**

An English index, started in 1915 under the title *Athenaeum subject index;* title changed, 1919, to *Subject index.* Issued, 1915–16, in two forms: (1) preliminary class lists, each an alphabetical subject index with brief author index to the subject part, and (2) annual volume for each year, combining in one alphabet the material of all the class lists. The annual for 1915 covered one year only and is superseded by the 1916 annual, a cumulated volume, covering the two years 1915-16. After the 1915-16 cumulation the combined issue was abandoned and only the class lists were continued. These class lists covered six years: 1917–19, in one set, with a general author index, and from 1920 to 1922 one year each, with no author index. The class lists are: A, Theology and philosophy; B-E, Historical, political and economic sciences; F, Education and child welfare; G, Fine arts and archaeology; H, Music; I, Language and literature, pt.1: Classical, oriental and primitive; pt.2: Modern, including bibliography and library administration; K, Science and technology.

1923–25 not published.

The form was changed in 1926 when it became an alphabetical subject list (with no author index) to articles on definite subjects. Magazine fiction, poetry, and essays not on definite subjects are omitted. Until the time of World War II (approx. 1940), it indexed more than 500 periodicals, principally British and American but including a number of foreign titles. Though duplicating much of the indexing in the *Readers' guide* (E71) and the *International index* (E68), it indexed many periodicals not covered by those indexes including British local history periodicals, antiquarian society proceedings, etc.

During the war, the indexing of foreign titles was discontinued and with the 1947 volume (published 1949), the indexing of American periodicals was also dropped. This volume indexes 353 titles, entirely British.

"The *Subject Index to Periodicals* is intended principally to serve the general reader, and highly specialized periodicals whose contents are covered by sectional indexes or abstracts are not dealt with."—*Pref.* to 1947.

The 1937 and 1938 volumes include an alphabetical list of the periodicals indexed with their locations in more than 170 libraries.

Among the older indexes still sometimes useful are:

Annual literary index, 1892–1904. Including periodicals, American and English; essays, book-chapters, etc. N.Y., Pub. Weekly, 1893–1905. 13v. o.p.　**E76**

Contents of each volume: (1) Subject index to periodicals; (2) Subject index to general literature; (3) Author index to (1) and (2); (4) Bibliographies; (5) Necrology; (6) Index to dates of principal events.

A composite annual index containing among the six sections of the contents noted above four distinct indexes: (1) a subject index which was an annual continuation of *Poole* (E69) indexing the same periodicals in the same way and forming the basis for the 5-year supplements; (2) a subject index to essays, which continued the *A.L.A. index* (R166); (3) a much needed author index, never incorporated in *Poole,* and (4) an index to dates, which served practically as an index to newspapers. In large measure superseded by the *Poole* supplements and the *A.L.A. index* (2d edition and supplement) but still useful for the author indexes which furnish the only extensive author key to the sets of *Poole* periodicals before 1900. Continued by the following:

Annual library index, 1905–10. Including periodicals, American and English; essays, book-chapters, etc. N.Y., Pub. Weekly, 1906–11. 6v. o.p.　**E77**

Contents of each volume: (1) Index to periodicals, author, title and subject in one alphabet; (2) Index to general literature; (3) Bibliographies; (4) Necrology; (5) Index to dates of principal events; (6) Selected list of public libraries in the United States and Canada; (7) Selected list of private collectors of books.

Of the above contents (1) to (5) are found in all volumes, (6) in 1908–10 only, and (7) in 1910 only.

As an index the *Annual library index* differed from its predecessor, the *Annual literary index,* principally in the fact that its index to periodicals contained authors, titles and subjects in one alphabet instead of two separate subject and author lists. Now largely superseded, although it must still be used for some author entries for 1905-06; for subject entries it is now practically superseded by the *Readers' guide* (E71) and the *International index* (E68).

Review of reviews. Index to the periodicals of 1890–1902. [v.1]-13. Lond. and N.Y., Review of Reviews, 1891–1903. 13v. Annual. o.p.　**E78**

Title varies: v.1, *Annual index of periodicals and photographs for 1890;* v.2-4, *Index to the periodical literature of the world.*

Primarily a subject index, but contains a fair number of author entries also, especially in the later volumes. Indexes material under broad subjects and gives for each, brief title, author's name when known, periodical, volume, month, and page reference, and a reference to the volume, month, and page of the *Review of reviews* where a summary or other notice of the article is to be found. Indicates maps and illustrations. Indexes novels, short stories and poems under authors' names, not under title; gives under such subjects as music, architecture, fiction, etc., a list of persons connected with those subjects who are noticed elsewhere in the index. The number of periodicals indexed varies from 117 in 1890 to 195 in 1902. Principally useful because it covers many English periodicals (about 100 in the later volumes) not indexed in *Poole* (E69).

Belgium

Bibliographie de Belgique: 2ème partie, Sommaire des périodiques, 1897–1914. Bruxelles, Van Oest, 1897–1914. **E79**

Title and frequency vary. 1899–1911, is third part of *Bibliographie de Belgique* and has title *Bulletin des sommaires;* 1912–13, is second part and has title *Sommaire des périodiques;* 1899–1911, frequency varied, monthly (sometimes bimonthly or quarterly) with annual author index; 1912–14, semiannual with annual author and subject indexes. Each number is a classed subject index arranged by the universal decimal classification numbers; indexes a large number of periodicals, gives fairly full information for each article. A cumbersome but usable index supplying material not easily found in any other way.

Discontinued 1915, because of World War I. Continued by the following:

Bibliographie de Belgique: 2ème partie; Bulletin mensuel des articles de fond parus dans les revues belges. Janvier, 1921–25. Bruxelles, Service de la Bibliogr. de Belgique, 1921–25. n.s. v.47–51. Monthly. **E80**

No more published.

Canada

Canadian periodical index, 1st annual cumulation, 1931. Windsor, Ont., Public Library, 1932. 87p. $1.50. **E81**

An author and subject index to 38 Canadian periodicals, only five of which are indexed in the *Readers' guide* (E71) and the *International index* (E68); forms the first printed and cumulated number in the series of quarterly indexes issued in multigraphed form since January 1928. Continued 1932 by quarterly multigraphed numbers which index 41 periodicals.

Not published 1933–1937.

Continued by:

Canadian periodical index, 1938–1947; a cumulation of the quarterly indexes published in the Ontario library review, comp. by the Circulation Department of the University of Toronto Library, under the direction of May L. Newton. Toronto,

Public Libraries Br., Ontario Dept. of Educ., 1939–49. 10v. $1 ea. **E82**

Indexes about 30 Canadian periodicals, by author and subject.

Canadian index; a guide to Canadian periodicals and films, 1948- . v.1- . Ottawa, Canadian Library Assoc., 1949- . Monthly, Sept–June with annual cumulations. **E83**

A new index to 61 periodicals planned to continue on an enlarged scale the preceding index. Includes a listing of documentary films.

Denmark

Copenhagen. Kommunebiblioteker. Danske blandede Tidsskrifter, 1855–1912; indholdsoversigt til 27 danske Tidsskrifter, udarb. af: Ellen Bruun, Povl Rehling Fischer, [and others] red. af Svend Thomsen. København, Bianco Lunos, 1928–29. 2v. **E84**

A classified subject index, arranged by a decimal classification, with author and alphabetical subject indexes to the classified part, of articles contained in 27 general periodicals. Useful as supplying indexing of some material earlier than that covered by the more comprehensive *Dansk Tidsskrift-Index,* 1915- . Later indexing of five of the 27 periodicals covered is given in the *Dansk Tidsskrift-Index.*

Dansk Tidsskrift-Index, 1- Aarg., 1915- udgivet af Statens Bibliotekstilsyn. København, Hagerup, 1916- . v.1- . **E85**

Pub. varies.

A classified subject index with an alphabetical subject index to the main classified list. Number of periodicals indexed varies: v.1, 165; v.33 (1947), about 300, Danish and other Scandinavian.

France

Répertoire bibliographique des principales revues françaises. 1897–99. Paris, Per Lamm, 1898–1900. v.1-3. o.p. **E86**

A useful index, unfortunately discontinued because of lack of support. Each volume contains: (1) subject index giving title of article, author's name, title and volume or number of the periodical, and page reference, (2) author index giving somewhat briefer information. Volume 1 indexes 147 periodicals, volume 2, 257, and volume 3, 346.

Germany

Bibliographie der deutschen Zeitschriftenliteratur, mit Einschluss von Sammelwerken. . . . Verzeichnis von Aufsätzen, die in Zeitschriften und Sammelwerken deutscher Zunge erschienen sind, 1896- . Gautzsch b. Leipzig, 1897- . v.1- . Semiannual. (Internationale Bibliographie der Zeitschriftenliteratur, Abt. A) Price per v. varies. **E87**

A comprehensive index valuable because of the large number of important German periodicals, transactions, yearbooks and other composite works indexed, but difficult to use for quick reference partly because of the abbreviation of references and compactness of printing, and partly because the form of publication in semiannual volumes with no cumulation necessitates the consultation of many alphabets. Except in the case of volumes 34-35, volumes 40, 40a-41, and volumes 43-46, for which combined author indexes in three separate volumes have been published, each volume consists of (1) a subject index arranged alphabetically by rather large subjects, giving for each article indexed its title, author's name in curves when known, reference to periodical by key number instead of title, page, and sometimes volume; and (2) an author index to the subject index, the latter omitted in some volumes. The number of periodicals indexed is large, ranging from 275 in the first volume to some 4500 in later volumes. The retrospective indexing of the *Ergänzungsbände* carries the work back to 1868. Important in university work and in large libraries which have many German periodicals, but not generally recommended for other libraries. Often especially important for biography because it indexes many yearbooks of learned societies containing obituary notices.

——Ergänzungsband 1- . Gautzsch b. Leipzig, Dietrich, 1908- . v.1- .

Numbered in set as v.22A, 24A, 28A, 30A, 32A, 33A, 35A, 35B, 36B, 37A, 39B, 41A, 42A, 72A, 78A, 80A, 82A.
Contents: Ergbd. 1, 1896–98; 2, 1896–1908; 3, 1893–95; 4, 1891–92; 5, 1889–90; 6, 1911–13; 7, 1887–88; 8, 1913–14; 9, 1885–86; 10, 1914–15; 11, 1883–84; 12, 1881–82; 13, 1915–17; 14, 1879–81; 15, 1876–78; 16, 1873–75; 17, 1870–73; 18, 1868–70.

Italy

Italy. Parlamento. Camera dei Deputati. Biblioteca. Catalogo metodico degli scritti contenuti nelle pubblicazioni periodiche italiane e straniere. Parte 1. Scritti biografici e critici. Roma, Tip. della Camera dei Deputati, 1885- . v.1- . **E88**

Contents: v.1, to 1883; suppl. 1, 1884–87 and earlier; suppl. 2, 1887–88 and earlier; suppl. 3, 1889–94; suppl. 4, 1895–1900; suppl. 5, 1901–1906; n.s. v.1, 1907–12; n.s. v.2, 1913–1918; n.s. v.3, 1919–24; n.s. v.4, 1925–30 (1935). Indice generale, a tutto l'anno 1906. 1909. 117p.
Not a general index but a subject catalog of biographical articles in the sets of periodicals (19,785 volumes) contained in the library of the Italian Chamber of Deputies. Each volume has (1) a main subject list which gives for each article indexed its title, author, and the title and volume or year of the periodical in which it is to be found, and (2) a brief author index referring to the subject list. The supplements index the volumes added during the period covered and earlier material omitted from the first volume. The "Indice generale" refers to all names included in the subject lists of the first volume and supplements 1-5. Sets indexed include the principal Italian periodicals and society transactions and also many important English, French, German and Spanish titles. In the American library the principal use of this catalog is for the Italian and French material indexed, but it is occasionally useful even for material already indexed in

Poole (E69), because it can be used from the author as well as the subject side.

Italy. Provveditorato Generale dello Stato. Pubblicazioni edite dallo stato o col suo concorso: Spoglio dei periodici e delle opere collettive 1901- . Roma, Libr. dello Stato, 1926- . v.1- . **E89**

Basic work, 1901–25, 2v. 1926; 1926–30, 2v. 1931; 1931–35, pt.1, 1937.
A subject index to over 200 Italian periodicals and collected works which are either government publications or issued under government auspices or aid. Each volume in two parts: (1) Index to biographical and critical articles arranged alphabetically by name of person written about, and (2) Subject index, arranged by large classes, e.g., agriculture, archeology, etc., with subdivisions under each, and an alphabetical index of small topics referring to the large classes. Entries in the biographical section are repeated in the classed section. Information given about each article is full and includes author and title of article, and title, volume, page and date of the volume in which it appears.

Mexico

Mexico. Universidad Nacional. Facultad de Filosofia y Letras. Registro bibliografico. [1940-] Mexico, 1941- . (Suplemento de la revista Filosofia y letras) Annual. **E90**

An index to periodicals in the fields of philosophy, history, and literature.

Netherlands

Hague. Koninklijke Bibliotheek. Repertorium op de nederlandsche tijdschriften. Jaarg. 1-8, 1914–21. 'sGravenhage, 1914–21. 8v. **E91**

Monthly, Feb.-Dec., 11 nos. a year. The first volume indexed 440 periodicals. A monthly classified subject index arranged by a modified decimal classification with annual index of (1) authors, (2) small subjects, alphabetically. Gives for each article author, full title, periodical, volume, year, inclusive paging and decimal classification number, with occasional contents or descriptive notes. Issued in three forms: (1) on ordinary paper printed on both sides; (2) on thin paper printed on one side only; (3) on cards.

Nijhoff's Index op de nederlandsche periodieken van algemeenen inhoud. 'sGravenhage, Nijhoff, 1910- . v.1- . Subs., Fl.20 per yr. **E92**

v.1, Sept. 1909–Dec. 1910, v.2- . (Jan.–Dec.) 1911- .
The number of periodicals indexed varies from 19 in the earlier volumes to more than 60.
Monthly index to general periodicals, including a few newspapers. Each number contains authors and subjects in one alphabet with a separate list of book reviews at the end. There are no cumulations of the monthly indexes, but beginning with the volume for 1925, there is an annual author index and a catchword subject index to the entries in the 12 monthly numbers.

New Zealand

Index to New Zealand periodicals, 1940- . Wellington, New Zealand Library Assoc., 1940- .
                                                        E93

1940, prepared by the Otago Branch of the Library Association as a preliminary index to 12 periodicals: v.1-2, 1941–42, issued quarterly, cumulated annually; v.3, no. 1, Jan.–June 1943; publication suspended July 1943–Dec. 1946; 1947- called n.s. v.1- published semiannually with annual cumulation. Indexes 38 periodicals. Annual volumes are announced for the future.

Norway

Deichmanske Bibliotek. Register til Norges tidsskrifter, v.1-2. Kristiania, Cammermeyer, 1908–11. 2v. **E94**

Contents: v.1, Topografi; v.2, Norsk biografi.

Arranged by subject, each volume indexing one subject. Volume 1 (1908) indexes the topographical articles in 75 periodicals of varying dates from about the beginning of the nineteenth century to 1907; volume 2, indexes nearly 15,000 biographical articles in more than 700 periodicals of the nineteenth and the first part of the twentieth century, giving not only references to periodicals, but also dates of birth and death and very brief characterization for each name indexed. The list of periodicals included in volume 2 furnishes a nearly complete bibliography of Norwegian periodicals.

Norsk tidsskriftindex, 1918- , systematisk fortegnelse over indholdet av norske periodiske skrifter. Oslo, Steenske Forlag, 1919–35; Fabritius, 1936- . v.1- . (v.24/25, Kr. 13.44) **E95**

Subtitle varies.

A classified subject index with an alphabetical subject index to the main classed list.

Issued in annual volumes, with a general title page, list of abbreviations and periodicals indexed, and alphabetical subject index to the classed lists for v.1-3 (1918–20); v.4-8 (1921–25); v.9-13 (1926–30); v.14-18 (1931–35); v.19-23 (1936–40); v.24-25 (1941–42).

Beginning with v.18, 1935, the publisher changed from Steenske Forlag to Fabritius & Sønner, and the index became a part of the bibliographical series *Norsk bibliografisk bibliotek*, v.18 being numbered as bd.1 hft. 5 in that series, (with retrospective numbering of v.14-17 as bd.1 hft. 1-4), and v.19-23 as bd.4; the detailed indexing of articles of individual biography formerly a feature of the index under the heading Personalhistorie, is omitted there from 1931- and included instead in a separate series, the first volume of which is *Biografiske artikler i norske tidsskrifter 1931–35* which is numbered as bd.2. hft. 3 of the *Norsk bibliografisk bibliotek* (S183).

Russia

Ul'îanov, N. A. Ukazatel' zhurnal'noĭ literatury, alfabitnyĭ, predmetnyĭ, sistematicheskiĭ. Moskva, "Nauka," 1911–13. v.1-2. **E96**

Contents: v.1, 1906–10 indexing 6 periodicals; v.2, 1896–1905 indexing 9 periodicals.

An index to a selected list of general periodicals of a solid character. Each volume contains (1) an author index which gives the full entries for the articles indexed and (2) an alphabetical subject index and (3) a classed or systematic subject index; both subject indexes refer to the main author index.

South Africa

Index to South African periodicals. Johannesburg, Public Library, v.1- . Annual. **E97**

More than 125 periodicals are indexed selectively. Each issue is divided into three sections: (1) Subject index, English; (2) Subject index, Afrikaans; (3) Combined author index to both sections.

Volumes 1-3, published by the South African Library Association; volumes 4- , by the Johannesburg Public Library.

NEWSPAPERS

❦ Newspapers are important in certain lines of reference work. Current issues are helpful on questions of the day, events, policies, opinion, politics, personalities, and many others. Back volumes serve the same purpose for the contemporary history of an earlier period and often record details of a situation or information local in its application that are not found in general reference books. Bound files of newspapers have always been important additions to the reference equipment of a library which could afford them. However, they created many problems because of the difficulties and expense of binding, shelving and preserving them, particularly because of the rapid deterioration of newsprint. In recent years many files of important papers have been microfilmed and in this form are available for purchase or interlibrary loan. For a record of newspapers available on microfilm *see* the check list by George A. Schwegmann, Jr. listed below (E98).

To make intelligent use of newspapers the reference worker needs the same type of reference aids that he needs for periodicals, i.e., (1) indexes, (2) bibliographies and (3) lists of holdings of other libraries. These differ in some ways from the corresponding aids for periodicals. There is, for example, no general index to newspapers similar to the *Readers' guide* (E71). Such a work would be a practical impossibility, and is not needed in just the same way as an index to periodicals. Newspapers all publish reports of any event of general interest at approximately the same time. The date of an event is the clue needed and an index of dates, or an index to one newspaper, will furnish a workable index to all newspapers for subjects of general interest. This, of course, is not true of purely local or special articles, editorials, and many obituaries.

Bibliographies and union lists

See Union list of serials, p.3053-65 (E61) for a bibliography of union lists of newspapers.

Association of Research Libraries. Newspapers on microfilm; a union check list, comp. under the direction of George A. Schwegmann, Jr. Phila., Office of the Executive Secretary, 1948. 176p. $2.
E98

Chicago University. Libraries. Newspapers in libraries of Chicago; a joint checklist. Chic., 1936. 257p.
E99

New York. Public Library. Check-list of newspapers and official gazettes in the New York Public Library, comp. by D. C. Haskell. N.Y., Library, 1915. 579p.
E100

Reprinted from the New York Public Library, *Bulletin,* July–Dec. 1914 and July 1915.

Includes all the newspapers and official gazettes in possession of the library at the end of 1914; in three lists: (1) main list arranged alphabetically by cities in which the papers are published, with exact statement of issues in the library; (2) alphabetical title index; (3) chronological index.

Yale University. Library. List of newspapers in the . . . library. New Haven, Conn., Yale Univ. Pr., 1916. 216p.
E101

United States

See also U.S. Bureau of the Census (E10); Ayer's *Directory* (E11); *Editor and publisher* (E12); and *The Working press of the nation* (E15).

Brigham, Clarence S. History and bibliography of American newspapers, 1690–1820. Worcester, Mass., American Antiquarian Soc., 1947. 2v. **E102**

Originally published in the *Proceedings* of the American Antiquarian Society, 1913–1927. A work of the first importance, this cumulated edition includes corrections, additions, and more detailed listings. Arranged alphabetically by states and towns, it lists 2120 newspapers which were published between 1690 and 1820 with indication of location of files in all parts of the country. Historical notes for each paper give title, date of establishment, exact dates of changes of titles, names of editors and publishers, frequency, etc.

The bibliography is followed by lists of libraries, and private owners; an index of titles; and an index of printers.

With *American newspapers,* 1821–1936 (E103) there is now a comprehensive record of American newspaper files from 1690–1936.

American newspapers 1821–1936; a union list of files available in the United States and Canada, ed. by Winifred Gregory under the auspices of the Bibliographical Society of America. N.Y., Wilson, 1937. 791p. Service basis.
E103

A union list of first importance which lists the exact holdings of newspapers in nearly 5700 depositories, such as libraries, county court houses, newspaper offices and private collections. In addition to the main union list, contains (p.787-89) A bibliography of union lists of newspapers, compiled by Karl Brown and Daniel C. Haskell.

Brayer, Herbert O. Preliminary guide to indexed newspapers in the United States, 1850–1900. (Repr. from the Mississippi Valley historical review, v.33, no.2, Sept. 1946) p.237-58. $1.25.
E104

Arranged by state and then library or other depository. Indicates indexes to files of newspapers, dates covered, and physical nature of index, i.e., cards, manuscript, or printed.

Duke University. Library. Checklist of the United States newspapers (and weeklies before 1900) in the general library, comp. by Mary Wescott and Allene Ramage. Durham, N.C., Duke Univ., 1932–37. 6v.
E105

pts. 1-6, Alabama-Wyoming.

Arranged alphabetically by states, with subarrangement by cities. Gives some historical notes about the papers, e.g., dates of founding, editors' and publishers' names, changes of name, or publisher, etc., and a detailed record of the library's holdings.

U.S. Library of Congress. Check-list of American newspapers in the Library of Congress, comp. under the direction of A. B. Slauson. Wash., Govt. Prt. Off., 1901. 292 leaves.
E106

Arranged by states and towns and under each town alphabetically by catchword title. Gives for each paper exact title, frequency, often politics and date of founding, and exact statement of Library of Congress files.

—— **Periodical Division.** Check list of American 18th century newspapers in the Library of Congress, originally comp. by John Van Ness Ingram. New ed., rev. and enl. under the direction of Henry S. Parsons. Wash., Govt. Prt. Off., 1936. 401p.
E107

Arranged alphabetically by states subdivided by towns. Gives, for each newspaper, the date of establishment, changes in title, names of printers, publishers and editors and a statement of the Library of Congress file. Title index; and index to printers, publishers and editors.

Wisconsin State Historical Society. Library. Annotated catalogue of newspaper files in the library. 2d ed. Madison, Society, 1911–18. 591p. and suppl., 91p.
E108

Arranged alphabetically by states, subdivided by towns. Gives statement of library files and some information about date of establishment of newspaper, founder's name, editors' names, etc. Includes not only newspapers in the ordinary acceptation of the term but also all journals that are organs of societies, trades or special interests. The supplement records files acquired 1911–17.

ARKANSAS

Historical Records Survey. Arkansas. Union list of Arkansas newspapers, 1819–1942. A partial inventory of Arkansas newspaper files available in offices of publishers, libraries, and private collections in Arkansas. Prepared by Historical Records Survey, Division of Community Service Programs, Work Projects Administration. Little Rock, Ark., 1942. 240p.   **E109**

CALIFORNIA

California Library Association. A union list of newspapers in offices of publishers and in libraries of Southern California, comp. under the direction of the Newspaper Section of the Coordinating Committee for the Union List of Serials in the Libraries of Southern California. 1936. 200p. (Calif. Lib. Assoc. 6th District. Pub. no.2)   **E110**

COLORADO

Rex, Wallace Hayden. Colorado newspapers bibliography, 1859–1933, comp. by Wallace Hayden Rex, under the direction of Elsie Louise Baechtold. Denver, Bibl. Center for Research, Rocky Mt. Region, 1939. 69 p.l., 394, 72, 184, 34, 17 numb. l. $10.   **E111**

"Published by the Denver Public Library and the State Dept. of Education as a report on Official Project no. 665-84-3-59, Work Project no. 3787, conducted under the auspices of the Works Progress Administration, Women's and Professional Division."

Contents: Authority for information on Colorado newspapers; Colorado newspapers 1859–1933, arranged alphabetically by title; arranged alphabetically by town and title; arranged chronologically by establishment date; Colorado newspaper editors 1859–1933, arranged alphabetically. Colorado publications other than newspapers 1859–1933, arranged alphabetically by town and title; editors of Colorado publications other than newspapers, arranged alphabetically by name; location of holdings.

LOUISIANA

Historical Records Survey. Louisiana. Louisiana newspapers, 1794–1940. A union list of Louisiana newspaper files available in offices of publishers, libraries, and private collections in Louisiana. Prepared by the Louisiana Historical Records Survey, Division of Community Service Programs, Work Projects Administration. Baton Rouge, La., Louisiana State Univ., 1941. 295p.   **E112**

MASSACHUSETTS

Ayer, Mary Farwell. Check-list of Boston newspapers, 1704–1780, with bibliographical notes by Albert Matthews. [Boston, The Society, 1907. 527p. (Publications of the Colonial Society of Massachusetts, v.9. Collections)   **E113**

Contents: (1) Chronological list of titles, Alphabetical list, List by years; (2) Check-list, listing issues in 14 American libraries, p.13-400; (3) Bibliographical notes by Albert Matthews, p.401-508; (4) Index.

MISSISSIPPI

Historical Records Survey. Mississippi. Mississippi newspapers, 1805–1940. A preliminary union list of Mississippi newspaper files available in county archives, offices of publishers, libraries and private collections in Mississippi. Prepared by the Mississippi Historical Records Survey Service Division, Work Projects Administration Jackson, Miss., 1942. 323p.   **E114**

OHIO

Ohio State Archeological and Historical Society Newspaper Division. Union list of Ohio newspapers available in Ohio; comp. by Arthur D. Mink. Columbus, Ohio, The Society, 1946. 124p. $2.   **E115**

Gives data concerning all Ohio newspapers in 162 Ohio libraries.

PENNSYLVANIA

Pennsylvania Historical Survey. Checklist of Pennsylvania newspapers. v.1, Philadelphia county. Prepared by the Pennsylvania Historical Survey, Division of Community Service Programs, Work Projects Administration. Harrisburg, Pa., Historical Commission, 1944. 323p.   **E116**

". . . Covers all known newspapers which have been published in the area that is now Philadelphia since 1719 including the former villages of Germantown and Frankford. A second volume, which includes the counties constituting the western part of Pennsylvania is now in preparation. . . ."—*Pref.*

Lists some 700 newspaper titles with Pennsylvania locations when found.

TEXAS

Historical Records Survey. Texas. Texas newspapers, 1813–1939. A union list of newspaper files available in offices of publishers, libraries and a number of private collections. Prepared by Historical Records Survey Program, Division of Professional and Service projects, Work Projects Administration of Texas. Houston, San Jacinto Museum of History Assoc., 1941. 293p. (San Jacinto Museum of History Assoc. Pub., v.1)   **E117**

VIRGINIA

Cappon, Lester J. Virginia newspapers, 1821–1935; a bibliography with historical introduction and notes. N.Y., Appleton, Century, Crofts, for Inst. for Research in the Social Sciences, Univ. of Virginia, 1936. 299p. (Guide to Virginia historical materials, pt.1)   E118

Contents: Historical introduction, p.3-34; Newspapers, arranged alphabetically by towns, p.39-234; Alphabetical list of titles, p.239-57; Chronological guide, p.259-62; Index of names and subjects, p.263-95. Key to libraries on end papers.

Foreign

See also Australia, p.90; Canada, p.90; Cuba, p.90; Czechoslovakia, p.90; France, p.90; Germany, p.91; Italy, p.92; Switzerland, p.93.

U. S. Library of Congress. Check-list of foreign newspapers in the Library. . . . newly comp. under the direction of H. S. Parsons. Wash., Govt. Prt. Off., 1929. 209p.   E119

Arranged geographically by places of publication and under each place alphabetically by title of the newspaper. Gives for each paper exact statement of Library of Congress files. Includes many titles which are really periodicals rather than newspapers.

GREAT BRITAIN

See also Great Britain, p.91-92.

British Museum. Dept. of Printed Books. Catalogue of printed books: Supplement: Newspapers published in Great Britain and Ireland, 1801–1900. Lond., Clowes, 1905. 552 col. E120

Contents: (1) London papers; (2) English and Welsh provincial papers, (a) by place of publication, (b) alphabetical title list; (3) Scotch newspapers (a) by places (b) alphabetical list; (4) Irish newspapers, (a) by places (b) alphabetical list.

NEW ZEALAND

New Zealand. General Assembly. Library. A union catalogue of New Zealand newspapers preserved in public libraries, newspaper offices, etc. G. H. Scholefield, Chief Librarian. Wellington, N.Z., E. V. Paul, Govt. Pr., 1938. 38p. E121

Indexes

United States

New York Times index, v.1- . 1913- . N.Y., N.Y. Times, 1913- . v.1- . semimonthly, $35 yr.; annual cumulation, $35; semimonthly and annual, $50.   E122

Frequency varies; 1913–29, quarterly with no cumulations, the four quarterly parts constituting a volume; 1930, monthly with quarterly cumulations and an annual cumulated volume; 1931–47, monthly with annual cumulations; 1948- , semimonthly with annual cumulations.

A carefully made index giving exact reference to date, page and column, and plentiful cross references to names and related topics. The brief synopses of articles answer some questions without reference to the paper itself. Indexes the Last Edition of the *New York Times,* but also serves as an independent index to dates and even as a guide to the reporting of current happenings in other newspapers.

An earlier index originally issued in columnar form, covering 1851–58; 1860, 1863—June 1905 is now available on microfilm.

New York Daily Tribune index, 1875–1906. N.Y., Tribune Assoc., 1876–1907. 31v.   E123

Annual; no more published. A much briefer index than the *N. Y. Times index* (E122), but useful for the period covered.

Denmark

Avis-Kronik-Index, udgivet af Folkebibliotekernes bibliografiske Kontor med Støtte af Undervisningsministeriet og Pressen. Red. af E. A. Jensen og K. H. Nielsen. 1940- . Aarg. 1- . Monthly. Dan. Kr. 15   E124

A monthly index of the main contents of about 50 Danish daily newspapers. Especially valuable for biographical material and literary reviews.

Germany

Monatliches Verzeichnis von Aufsätzen aus deutschen Zeitungen in sachlichalphabetischer Anordnung, mit Jahres-Gesamt-Sach-und-Verfasser-Register, 1909- . Gautzsch bei Leipzig, Dietrich, 1909- . v.1- . (Bibliographie d. deutschen Zeitschriftenliteratur, Abt. A. Beilage Bde. pub. at irregular intervals)   E125

Weekly, 1928–29; fortnightly, 1909–22, 1930–33; monthly, 1934- ; an index to the principal articles in German and some Austrian papers, the issues for one year forming a volume, with a subject and an author index to the volume. Not published 1923–27; during that period indexing of the same papers was included in the *Bibliographie der deutschen Zeitschriftenliteratur* (E87).

Great Britain

Times, London. Official index, 1906- . Lond., Times Off., 1907- . v.1- .   E126

Monthly, 1906—June 1914, with annual cumulations for 1906–13 and semiannual cumulation Jan.—June 1914; quarterly, July 1914- .

Detailed alphabetical index referring to date, page and column. Very useful.

—— Palmer's Index to the Times newspaper, 1790- . Lond., Palmer, 1868- .   E127

Quarterly, beginning with the index covering Oct.–Dec. 1867, published in 1868. The indexes for preceding volumes have been issued in the reverse order, beginning with the one covering July–Sept. 1867, published in 1875.

Much briefer than the *Official index* noted above but useful because of the importance of the newspaper and the long period covered by the index. The indexing of obituary, death and funeral notices under the heading "Deaths" in each volume frequently supplies biographical material difficult to find elsewhere.

JOURNALISM

Guides

Nafziger, Ralph O. and **Wilkerson, Marcus M.** An introduction to journalism research. Baton Rouge, La., State Univ. Pr., 1949. 142p. (Journalism monographs, no.4) $2.50. **E128**

Bibliography

Cannon, Carl L. Journalism, a bibliography. N.Y., Public Library, 1924. 360p. (Repr. with additions from the Bull. of the New York Public Library) **E129**

Wolseley, Roland Edgar. The Journalist's bookshelf; an annotated and selected bibliography of United States journalism. 4th ed. Chic., Quill and Scroll Foundation, Northwestern Univ., 1946. 133p. paper $1.50. **E130**

1st ed. 1939.

Intended to supplement Cannon, *Journalism; a bibliography* (E129). This includes only American works of dominantly journalistic content. Classed arrangement, with author and title indexes. Brief annotations.

An annotated bibliography on journalistic subjects in American magazines, Jan. 1930– . (In Journalism quarterly, 1930–) **E131**

The *Journalism quarterly* also includes "A supplementary bibliography selected from British journals, Oct. 1935– " and from time to time lists of thesis subjects in journalism.

Swindler, William F. A bibliography of law on journalism. N.Y., Columbia Univ. Pr., 1947. 191p. **E132**

Classed with author and subject indexes.

Bömer, Karl. Internationale Bibliographie des Zeitungswesens. Leipzig, Harrassowitz, 1932.

373p. (Sammlung Bibliothekswissenschaftlicher Arbeiten. 43. Hft.) (II. Ser., 26. Hft.) **E133**

1. T. Das deutsche Zeitungswesen. p.1-163; 2. T. Das ausländische Zeitungswesen. p.167-302. Personen-, Sach- und Schlagwortregister.

Encyclopedias

Handbuch der Zeitungswissenschaft, hrsg. von Walther Heide, bearb. von Ernst Herbert Lehmann. Leipzig, Hiersemann, 1940–43. Lfg. 1-7. il. RM. 15 per Lfg. (In progress) **E134**

Lfg. 1-7, A-Kommunistische Presse.

Deals with the history and practices of the newspaper press. Long, signed articles with extensive bibliographies.

History

Bourne, Henry Richard Fox. English newspapers; chapters in the history of journalism. Lond., Chatto, 1887. 2v. **E135**

Craig, Mary Elizabeth. Scottish periodical press, 1750–1789. Edinburgh, Oliver, 1931. 113p. **E136**

A history of periodicals and newspapers of the period, considered in regional groups, i.e., Edinburgh, West of Scotland, etc., with some account of each journal and a bibliographical list, p.95-104, which locates copies in 13 British and 19 American libraries.

Grant, James. Newspaper press; its origin, progress and present position. Lond., Tinsley, 1871-[72]. 3v. **E137**

v.3 has title: *The Metropolitan weekly and provincial press*. Lond., Routledge [1872].

Madden, Richard Robert. History of Irish periodical literature from the end of the 17th to the middle of the 19th century; its origin, progress and results, with notices of remarkable persons connected with the press in Ireland during the past two centuries. Lond., Newby, 1867. 2v. **E138**

Mott, Frank Luther. American journalism; a history of newspapers in the United States through 260 years, 1690 to 1950. rev. ed. N.Y., Macmillan, 1950. 835p. il. $5. **E139**

A detailed history with bibliographical notes.

Muddiman, Joseph George. History of English journalism to the foundation of the Gazette, by J. B. Williams [pseud.]. Lond., Longmans, 1908. 293p. il. **E140**

GOVERNMENT DOCUMENTS

❧ Much important reference material is to be found in the reports, bulletins, and other publications issued by the various national, state and municipal governments. These publications, which are generally known as "government publications" or "public documents," cover topics in nearly the whole field of knowledge, but are most important for subjects in the fields of social and political science, economics, finance, labor, industry, statistics, education, history, etc., and in certain sciences such as agriculture, ethnology, geology, meteorology, etc., to the study and promotion of which certain government bureaus or commissions are devoted. No extended reference work can be done in questions of labor conditions in America, for example, without the use of some of the publications of the United States Department of Labor, or in American geology without those of the United States Geological Survey.

Public documents are popularly supposed to be difficult to use and understand, and reference workers often fail to make the best use of such material because this difficulty is overrated. Documents are published in complicated forms and sets and must be used through the printed catalogs, bibliographies and indexes provided for the purpose, but so used the documents for the periods covered by modern indexes are no harder to use than periodical literature which has to be found through periodical indexes.

For indexes and bibliographies relating to special subjects *see* those subjects. Listed below are some of the most important general guides and indexes for the United States and Great Britain and also a few bibliographies for other countries that have been published since 1942 when the third edition of the excellent bibliography by Childs (F1) was issued. This lists and describes document bibliographical work in the various countries and should always be consulted whenever more detailed information is required.

GUIDES

Childs, James Bennett. Government document bibliography in the United States and elsewhere. 3d ed. Wash., Govt. Prt. Off., 1942. 78p. 20c. **F1**

At head of title: The Library of Congress, Division of Documents.

The bibliography is divided into five sections: United States; Confederate States of America; States; Foreign Countries; League of Nations. The catalogs, indexes and guides to the documents of each country are listed, sometimes with brief annotations.

Brown, Everett S. Manual of government publications: United States and foreign. N.Y., Appleton-Century-Crofts, 1950. 121p. $2.75. **F1a**

A brief manual which discusses the government publications of the various countries of the world with emphasis on the United States, Great Britain, and international affairs, particularly the League of Nations and the United Nations.

UNITED STATES
The Serial Set

❧ The collected edition of U.S. government publications is known as the *Congressional edition* or *Serial set*. It includes Senate and House journals, Senate and House documents, and Senate and House reports. The documents include a large variety of reports from executive departments and independent bodies which are printed in the set by order of Congress.

For purposes of easy arrangement each bound volume is given a "serial number." (A volume may include from one to several individual items.) Volumes are numbered consecutively beginning with the 15th Congress (1817). In many libraries documents are arranged on the shelves by these serial numbers, and the number must be ascertained in order to find a particular document. These serial numbers are included in many of the lists and indexes noted below, sometimes in numerical lists, and sometimes under specific entries. A complete record, with some overlapping, can be found in the following:

15th-60th Congress (1817–1909) in the *Checklist* (F13); 54th-76th Congress (1895–1940) in the *Document catalog* (F14) under Congressional documents list; 73rd Congress (1933/34-) in the *Numerical lists* (F16).

The *American state papers* which contain reprints of the documents of the first fourteen congresses (1789–1817), grouped by class into 38 volumes, have been assigned special serial numbers from 01-038. These numbers can be found in the *Checklist* (F13).

Guides

American Library Association. Committee on Public Documents. Public documents . . . papers presented at the conference of the American Library Association, 1933–1942. Chic., Amer. Lib. Assoc., 1934–1942. 7v. **F2**

Not published, 1939–41.

Boyd, Anne Morris. United States government publications. 3d ed. rev. by Rae Elizabeth Rips. N.Y., Wilson, 1949. 627p. $6.50. **F3**

1st ed. 1931; 2d ed. 1940.

Following a discussion of the nature, printing and distribution, catalogs and indexes of United States government publications, the arrangement of material follows that of the organization of the government, i.e., the legislative, judicial and executive branches, each subdivided by major divisions: Congress; the courts; the ten departments; and independent agencies and institutions.

Lists and describes the important and typical publications of each, but does not attempt to be complete. Originally planned as a library school textbook, this edition has been extended to increase its usefulness in a reference department, and has been revised to include the many changes in government departments and agencies made during the war and postwar years to July 1, 1948.

Hirshberg, Herbert Simon and **Melinat, Carl Herman.** Subject guide to United States government publications. Chic., Amer. Lib. Assoc., 1947. 228p. $5. **F4**

". . . a selection of those books and pamphlets, most of them published during the past twenty years, believed to be most generally useful in libraries."—*Pref.*

Schmeckebier, Laurence Frederick. Government publications and their use. 2d rev. ed. Wash., Brookings Inst., 1939. 479p. (Institute for Government Research of the Brookings Institution. Studies in administration, no.33) **F5**

1st ed. 1936. The second edition presents government

agencies and their publications as of the beginning of 1939.

A useful guide to government publications including descriptions of catalogs and indexes, bibliographies, classification, distribution; congressional publications, constitutions (federal and state), laws (federal and state), court decisions, administrative regulations, presidential papers, foreign affairs, reports, organization and personnel, maps, etc.

Answers many questions as to what was published, when, by whom, in what form, etc.

Tompkins, Dorothy C. Materials for the study of federal government. Chic., Public Administration Service, 1948. 338p. **F6**

Treats government publications dealing with federal administration, covering: the constitution; laws and codes; publications of the legislative, executive and judicial branches, and the President; the federal budget, government statistics, the New Deal and World War II.

Wilcox, Jerome Kear. New guides and aids to public documents use, 1945–1948. (In Special libraries, Nov.–Dec. 1949) **F7**

Lists guides and aids in five groups: (1) General publications; (2) Federal; (3) State; (4) Foreign; (5) International organizations.

—— Official war publications; guide to state, federal, and Canadian publications. Berkeley, Bureau of Public Administration, Univ. of California, 1941–1945. 9v. in 3. **F8**

v.1-2 have title: Official defense publications; guide to state and federal publications.

Each volume has a subject index.

Catalogs and indexes
Early period to 1893

Greely, Adolphus Washington. Public documents of the first fourteen congresses, 1789–1817. Papers relating to early congressional documents. Wash., Govt. Prt. Off., 1900. 903p. (56th Cong., 1st sess. Senate doc. 428) **F9**

—— —— Supplement. Wash., Govt. Prt. Off., 1904.

Reprinted from the *Annual report* of the American Historical Association, 1903, v.1, p.343-406.

Poore, Benjamin Perley. A descriptive catalogue of the government publications of the United States, September 5, 1774–March 4, 1881, comp. by order of Congress. Wash., Govt. Prt. Off., 1885. 1392p. (48th Cong., 2d sess. Senate. Misc. doc. 67) **F10**

Arranged chronologically, with general index. For each document gives full title, author, date, and a brief abstract of contents. Exact reference is given to the series in which each document appears. Contains much valuable material but is difficult to use for quick reference because the index is not sufficiently complete, detailed or specific.

Ames, John Griffith. Comprehensive index to the publications of the United States government, 1881–1893. Wash., Govt. Prt. Off., 1905. 2v. (58th Cong., 2d sess. House doc. 754) **F11**

The *Comprehensive index*, 1889–93, by J. G. Ames, published in 1894, is superseded by this work.

Bridges the gap between Poore's *Descriptive catalogue* (F10), and the first volume of the *Document catalog* (F14).

Arranged in three columns. In the first is given the author of the document or the department by which it was issued; in the second, a list of the documents arranged alphabetically by the key word in the title; in the third, if the document is in the serial set, reference is made to the congress, session, the volume of the series in which each is embraced, and the number of the document. Personal name index.

A good usable index, although less minute and detailed than the *Document catalog*. Indicates the different editions in which a document was issued and gives serial numbers in a table under the heading Congressional documents.

U. S. Superintendent of Documents. Tables of and annotated index to the congressional series of United States public documents. Wash., Govt. Prt. Off., 1902. 769p. **F12**

In two parts: (1) tables of the American state papers and the documents of the 15th through the 52nd congress, arranged by serial number; (2) minute alphabetical subject index to these documents. The first part is now superseded by the third edition of the *Checklist* noted below, but the subject index is still very useful as a key to the congressional set before 1893.

—— Checklist of United States public documents, 1789–1909. 3d ed., rev. and enl. Wash., Govt. Prt. Off., 1911. v.1. 1707p. **F13**

v.1, Lists of Congressional and departmental publications; v.2 was to have been an index, but was never issued.

A check list, not a catalog, covering Congressional documents through the 60th congress, and department and bureau publications to the end of 1909. Lists: (1) American state papers, with serial numbers; (2) Congressional documents, 15th-60th congresses, with serial numbers; (3) Department publications arranged alphabetically by government author. The list of departmental publications gives, for periodical publications, a statement of the volumes and dates which constitute a complete set and the serial numbers if the publication is contained also in the serial set; for separate publications the full title and date are given and the serial number if the document appears also in the serial set. The preface contains a list and description of previous indexes and catalogs of U.S. documents. This edition replaces the second edition of the *Checklist* and the tables of the *Tables and index* (F12), but not its index.

A brief errata list is printed in the *Monthly catalogue*, May, 1912, p.720-721. (F15).

1893–1940

U. S. Superintendent of Documents. Catalog of the public documents of Congress and of all departments of the government of the United States for the period March 4, 1893—December 31, 1940. Wash., Govt. Prt. Off., 1896–1945. v.1-25. **F14**

The "comprehensive index" provided for by the act approved January 12, 1895. Publication terminated with v.25.

This index, which is generally referred to by its binder's title as the *Document catalog*, forms for the years 1893 to 1940 the permanent and complete catalog of all government publications both congressional and departmental. It is a dictionary catalog in form, listing all documents under author (governmental or personal), subject, and, when necessary, title, and giving full catalog information for each book or pamphlet included. Includes a large amount of analysis, refers to all editions in which a document has appeared, and gives serial numbers for documents in the serial set, as follows: in volumes 1-4, serial numbers are given only in the table under the entry "Congressional documents"; beginning with volume 5, serial numbers are also given throughout the list under the main (i.e., author) entry for each document, but not under the analytical entries.

Volumes 23-25 include government publications reproduced by duplicating processes other than ordinary printing, mimeographing, etc., now called "processed" by the Office of the Superintendent of Documents.

1940 to date

U. S. Superintendent of Documents. United States government publications: Monthly catalog, 1895- . Wash., Govt. Prt. Off., 1895- . Monthly. $3. **F15**

Title varies: 1895—June 1907, *Catalogue of the United States public documents;* July 1907–1939, *Monthly catalog, United States public documents.*

A current bibliography of publications issued by all branches of the government, including both the congressional and the department and bureau publications. Each issue contains general instructions for ordering documents, and a list of the documents published during the month arranged by department and bureau, with indication, for each publication, of its full title, date, paging, price, Library of Congress card number, etc. There is an annual index in each volume and beginning with July 1945 an author and subject index in each monthly issue. Since April 1947 the catalog has been made more inclusive, and it appears more promptly. An added feature is a section called "Previews," which lists important titles before they are issued, so that prepublication orders may be placed.

—— —— Supplements: 1941–1942; 1943–1944; 1945–1946. Wash., Govt. Prt. Off., 1947–48. 3v.

Include publications received by the Public Documents Division Library, which had not been listed previously in any Superintendent of Document's catalog. No further supplements will be published, as, beginning in April 1947, all documents are listed in the *Monthly catalog* as received, regardless of publication date.

—— Numerical lists and schedule of volumes of the reports and documents of the 73rd Congress, 1933/34- . Wash., Govt. Prt. Off., 1934- . **F16**

Usually a separate volume appears for each session of Congress.

Prior to 1941 it is superseded by the "Congressional documents" tables in the *Document catalog* (F14). From the 77th Congress, 1st session, Jan. 3, 1941—Jan. 2, 1942, on, it must be used to obtain serial numbers for the Congressional reports and documents now listed only in the *Monthly catalog* (F15).

—— Price lists. Wash., Govt. Prt. Off. nos. 1-79.
                                                F17

Contents (of numbers in active stock and on current topics; frequently revised): no.10, Laws; 10A, Decisions; 11, Foods and cooking; 15, Geology; 18, Engineering and surveying; 19, Army; 20, Public domain; 21, Fish and wildlife service; 25, Transportation; 28, Finance; 31, U.S. Office of Education; 33, Labor; 33A, Occupations; 35, National parks; 36, Government periodicals; 37, Tariff; 38, Animal industry; 41, Insects; 42, Irrigation, drainage, water power; 43, Forestry; 44, Plants; 45, Roads; 46, Agricultural chemistry, and soils and fertilizers; 48, Weather, astronomy and meteorology; 50, American history and biography; 51, Health; 51A, Diseases; 53, Maps; 54, Political science; 55, National Museum, Smithsonian institution, Indians; 58, Mines; 59, Interstate commerce; 60, Territories and insular possessions; 62, Commerce and manufactures; 63, Navy; 64, Standards of weight and measures; 64A, Masonry; 65, Foreign relations of U.S.; 67, Immigration; 68, Farm management; 70, Census; 71, Children's bureau; 72, Suburbanites; 75, Federal specifications; 78, Industrial workers; 79, Aviation. Current unnumbered lists: Army regulations; Field manuals and technical manuals; Posters and charts; Publications of the National Advisory Committee for Aeronautics; Radio publications.

Include no material not already listed in the more general publications noted above, but present the same material in a different arrangement and grouping which is sometimes more convenient for quick reference. Give prices, indicate material still in print, and sometimes supply useful annotations.

Congressional committee hearings

U. S. Congress. House. Library. Index of congressional committee hearings in the Library of the United States House of Representatives prior to January 3, 1943. Comp. by Elizabeth M. Shumaker, under the direction of South Trimble, clerk of the U.S. House of Representatives. Wash., Govt. Prt. Off., 1944. 399p.   **F18**

—— —— Supplemental index to congressional committee hearings, January 3, 1943, to January 3, 1947, in the Library of the United States House of Representatives. Comp. by Elizabeth M. Shumaker, under the direction of John Andrews, clerk of the House of Representatives. Wash., Govt. Prt. Off., 1947. 63p.

U. S. Congress. Senate. Library. Index of congressional committee hearings (not confidential in character) prior to January 3, 1935, in the

United States Senate Library. Wash., Govt. Prt. Off., 1935. 1056p.   **F19**

—— —— Supplement, January 3, 1935, to January 3, 1941. Wash., Govt. Prt. Off., 1941. 402p.

Legislative debates

U. S. Congress. Congressional record: Containing the proceedings and debates of the 43d Congress- . March 4, 1873- . Wash., Govt. Prt. Off., 1873- . v.1- . Price varies.   **F20**

Issued daily while Congress is in session, revised and issued in bound form at the end of the session, the issue for each session numbered as one volume and paged continuously though bound in several parts. There are frequent indexes during the session and a final index to the whole volume, this index sometimes bound separately, sometimes included in the last bound part.

Contains the presidents' messages, congressional speeches and debates in full, and record of votes. Does not include text of bills. Each index is in two parts: (1) Alphabetical index of names and subjects, giving under subjects bills and bill number, and (2) History of bills, arranged by bill number. This second index is the one to use for full information about a bill, as it gives page references to everything in the *Record* about the bill from its introduction to its final passage and signing.

For material before 1873 the following earlier compilations should be consulted: *Debates and proceedings* (generally known by its binder's title *Annals of Congress*), 1st-18th Congress, 1789–1824 (42v. 1834–56); *Register of debates*, 18th Congress, 2d sess.—25th Congress, 1st sess. 1824–37 (14v. in 29, 1825–37); *Congressional globe*, 23d-43d Congress, 1833–73 (46v. in 108, 1834–73).

State

Guides

Wilcox, Jerome Kear. Manual on the use of state publications. Chic., Amer. Lib. Assoc., 1940. 342p. $6.   **F21**

Sponsored by the American Library Association's Committee on Public Documents. Each section is written by a specialist. There are general descriptions plus bibliographies of "basic state publications."

Bibliographies

National Association of State Libraries. Collected public documents of the states: A check list, comp. by William S. Jenkins. Bost., 1947. 87p   **F2**

—— **Public Documents Clearing House Committee.** Check-list of legislative journals of the state of the United States of America; comp. by Grace E. Macdonald. Providence, R.I., Oxford Pr 1938. 274p.   **F2**

———— ————Supplement; comp. by William S. Jenkins. Bost., 1943. 107p.

U. S. Library of Congress. Processing Department. Monthly checklist of state publications, v.1, 1910- . Wash., Govt. Prt. Off., 1910- . Monthly. $1.50. **F24**

Sponsoring division of the Library of Congress varies.

A current bibliography, arranged alphabetically by states' names, of the publications of the states, territories and insular possessions of the United States. Though limited to the publications received by the Library of Congress, it is approximately complete, as the library aims to acquire all such material issued. Each title is given with full cataloging information, including contents in the case of composite reports. The annual index refers to the contents notes as well as to the main titles, so the list can be made to serve as a subject index as well as a bibliography.

FOREIGN COUNTRIES

See also Childs, *Government document bibliography* (F1).

List of the serial publications of foreign governments, 1815–1931, ed. by Winifred Gregory, for the American Council of Learned Societies, American Library Association, National Research Council. N.Y., Wilson, 1932. 720p. Apply to publisher for price. **F25**

A union list on the same general plan as the *Union list of serials* (E62) for a type of serial publication excluded from that list, i.e., government serials, including only genuine government serials and omitting publications of universities, societies, etc., subsidized by a government. Arranged alphabetically by country name (except that Russia is in a separate list at the end) with subarrangement by government departments, bureaus, etc., and with indication of holdings of the various publications in some 85 American libraries.

France

Dampierre, Jacques de. Les publications officielles des pouvoirs publics: Étude critique et administrative. Paris, Picard, 1942. 628p. **F26**

Germany

Neuburger, Otto. Official publications of present-day Germany: Government, corporate organizations, and National Socialist Party; with an outline of the governmental structure of Germany. Wash., Govt. Prt. Off., 1942. 130p. 20c. **F27**

At head of title: The Library of Congress.

". . . . originally prepared by Dr. Otto Neuburger in the Division of Documents for the Public Documents Committee meeting at the conference of the American Library Association, San Francisco, June, 1939."—*Pref. note.*

Lists and describes the governmental and quasigovernmental publications of the departments and offices of Nazi Germany.

Great Britain
Guides

Cowell, Frank Richard. Brief guide to government publications. Lond., Stat. Off., 1938. 43p. **F28**

Lees-Smith, H. B. A guide to parliamentary and official papers. Lond., Oxford Univ. Pr., 1924. 23p. **F29**

Catalogs and indexes
18TH CENTURY

Great Britain. Parliament. House of Commons. Catalogue of papers printed by order of the House of Commons for the year 1731 to 1800, in the custody of the Clerk of the Journals. [Lond.] 1807. v.p., i.e., 101p. **F30**

Consists of three chronological lists, each with its own subject index: (1) Bills; (2) Reports; (3) Accounts and Papers.

———— Catalogue of parliamentary reports and a breviate of their contents, arranged under heads according to the subjects, 1696–1834. [Lond.] 1834. 220p. **F31**

Indexes the "1st series" of parliamentary reports (15v.), the reports in the *Journals* and those in the *Sessional papers*, 1801–34.

19TH CENTURY TO DATE

Great Britain. Parliament. House of Commons. General alphabetical index to the bills, reports, estimates, accounts and papers, printed by order of the House of Commons and to the Papers presented by command, 1801–1943/4. Lond., Stat. Off., 1853–1946. 8v. (In progress) **F32**

Consists of the following unnumbered volumes: General index to the accounts and papers, reports of commissioners, estimates, etc., 1801–1852; Indexes to bills and reports, 1801–1852, in two sections: General index to the bills, and General index to the reports of select committees; General index, 1852–1899; General index, 1900–1909; General index, 1910–1919; General index, 1920–1928/29; General index, 1929–1943/44. The first of these, long out of print, was reproduced in 1938 from the original print.

An index to the documents included in the parliamentary papers of the House of Commons, not including the papers of the House of Lords except in so far as these are duplicated in the Commons papers and not including the publications of bureaus and departments. It is arranged alphabetically by rather large subjects, and does not include many analytical entries. Gives fairly full information about each paper, however, including its full title, date, and bill, document or command number, and a reference to the year and volume of the sessional papers in which it is to be found, and the paging as made up for the House of Commons set.

—— List of the bills, reports, estimates, and accounts and papers printed by order of the House of Commons and of the Papers presented by command . . . with a general alphabetical index thereto, 1801- . Lond., Stat. Off. Annual. **F33**

Issued annually as the final volume for each session of the *Sessional papers* of the House of Commons.

From 1828 contain not only an index, but also a list of bills and papers in their numerical order; in 1834 a list of command papers is added, and in 1867 a preliminary list showing the make-up of the set for each session.

The index section is superseded through 1944 by the *General alphabetical index* described above, but the numerical lists are still the only ones available, and are useful for identifying command papers which are often asked for by number only.

—— —— **House of Lords.** General index to sessional papers printed by order of the House of Lords or presented by special command. Lond., Eyre, 1860–86. 3v. **F33a**

Publisher varies. v.1 reprinted: Lond., Stat. Off., 1938. v.1, 1801–59; v.2, 1859–70; v.3, 1871–85.

From 1886–1920 annual indexes were published. Subsequently the only lists that are printed are un-numbered annual lists of titles.

Great Britain. Stationery Office. Quarterly list (with prices and postage affixed) of official publications issued by H. M. Stationery Office . . . , 1897–1921. Lond., Stat. Off., 1897–1922. **F34**

—— Consolidated list of parliamentary and stationery office publications, 1922- . Lond., Stat. Off., 1923- . Annual. ls. **F35**

—— Government publications monthly list. Lond., Stat. Off. Monthly. 2s. 6d. a year. **F36**

Superseded by the *Consolidated list* (F35). They are both intended primarily as sales catalogs.

Parliamentary debates

Gt. Brit. Parliament. Parliamentary debates, v.1-41 (1803–20), n.s. v.1-25 (1820–30), 3d ser. v.1-356 (1830–90/91), 4th ser. v.1-199 (1892–1908), 5th ser. Commons v.1- (1909-) Lords v.1- (1909-) Lond., 1804- **F37**

Generally cited as *Hansard*. Publisher varies.

There is a general index to the 66 volumes of the 1st-2d series. (Lond., Baldwin, 1834. 2v.); for series 3-5 the sessional indexes, sometimes in separate volumes, sometimes included in the last volume of debates of the session, must be used.

The 5th series is official and contains complete and verbatim reports of debates, and all division lists. The 1st-4th series were unofficial; their reports of debates are neither complete nor verbatim and not all division lists are given in full. For an interesting account of Parliamentary debates of the nineteenth to the twentieth century *see* Jordan, H. D., "Reports of parliamentary debates 1803–1908," in *Economica* 11:437-49, Nov. 1931.

The period before 1803 is covered by Cobbett's *Parliamentary history of England from the earliest period to the year 1803* (Lond., Hansard, 1806–20. 36v.), which is of course a retrospective compilation rather than a current record. For an interesting account of sources upon which it is based, or which are available for the early period, *see* "General collections of reports of Parliamentary debates for the period since 1660" (in London, University, *Bulletin of the Institute of Historical Research* 10:171-77, Feb. 1933).

Latin America

Hill, Roscoe R. The national archives of Latin America; ed. for the Joint Committee on Latin American Studies of the National Research Council, the American Council of Learned Societies, and the Social Science Research Council. Camb., Harvard Univ. Pr., 1945. 169p. il. (Joint Committee on Latin American Studies. Misc. pub. no.3) $1.50. **F38**

Survey of the history, housing, personnel and contents of the national archives of each of the 20 Latin American republics.

U. S. Library of Congress. A guide to the official publications of the other American republics. James B. Childs, general ed. Wash., Govt. Prt. Off., 1945–49. v.1-19. (Latin Amer. ser.) **F39**

Contents: v.1, Argentina. 1945. 124p.; v.2, Bolivia. 1945. 66p.; v.3, Brazil, comp. by John De Noia. 1948 (1949). 223p.; v.4, Chile, comp. by Otto Neuburger. 1947. 94p.; v.5, Colombia, [comp. by] James B. Childs. 1948. 89p.; v.6, Costa Rica, comp. by Henry V. Besso. 1947. 92p.; v.7, Cuba. 1945. 40p.; v.8, Dominican Republic, comp. by John De Noia. 1947. 40p.; v.9, Ecuador, comp. by John De Noia. 1947. 56p.; v.10, El Salvador, comp. by John De Noia. 1947. 64p.; v.11, Guatemala, comp. by Henry V. Besso. 1947. 88p.; v.12, Haiti. 1947. 25p.; v.13, Honduras. 1947. 31p.; v.14, Nicaragua, comp. by John De Noia. 1947. 33p.; v.15, Panama, comp. by John De Noia. 1947. 34p.; v.16, Paraguay, [comp. by] James B. Childs. 1947. 61p.; v.17, Peru, comp. by John De Noia. 1948 (1949). 90p.; v.18, Uruguay, comp. by John De Noia and Glenda Crevenna. 1948 (1949). 91p.; v.19, Venezuela, comp. by Otto Neuburger. 1948 (1949). 59p.

A series of guides each of which gives information about general publications, including official gazettes, session laws, codes, constitution, etc., followed by the publications of the legislative, executive, and judicial branches.

DISSERTATIONS

❦ Dissertations for the doctorate form a special class of publications, and catalogs or bibliographies of these dissertations, both American and foreign, assume definite importance in university, reference, or special libraries where much use is made of thesis material. As the doctor's degree is given only for original work and as each doctoral dissertation must deal with some aspect of a subject which has not previously been treated, the value of a dissertation to the reader interested in the subject is obvious.

While some dissertations are issued by commercial publishers, and some are privately printed, many are available only in typewritten form or on microfilm. Only those issued by commercial publishers appear in the trade bibliographies, the others are listed in special bibliographies of dissertations, of which there are various types:

I. National
  A. Completed
    1. General—covering the dissertations of all the universities of a given country
      a) Cumulative—covering a number of years
      b) Annual
    2. Subject—covering the theses of all universities in a given country in a particular subject field
  B. In progress

II. Individual university
  A. Lists
  B. Abstracts

These bibliographies are of primary importance in research libraries: (1) to show the student who is trying to select a thesis subject whether that subject has already been treated or is being worked on; (2) to show from what university a particular dissertation can be obtained either on exchange or through interlibrary loan; (3) to show the acquisitions department whether a publication not listed in the trade lists is a dissertation; (4) to show the research worker what material has been written on very special subjects; (5) to provide biographical data, about the authors of dissertations, which is included in some of the lists.

It has been the general practice to distribute printed dissertations to university libraries and to special libraries interested in particular subjects. In many cases when the dissertation is not printed a manuscript copy may be borrowed on interlibrary loan or a microfilm copy may be purchased either direct from the university library or through University Microfilms (*see* G11).

For current work, especially in university libraries where it is important to keep track of research being done, the various lists of "dissertations in progress" are very useful.

MANUALS

Campbell, William Giles. A form book for thesis writing. Bost., Houghton, 1939. 123p.   **G1**

Hurt, Peyton. Bibliography and footnotes; a style manual for college and university students, rev. and enl. by Mary L. Hurt Richmond. Berkeley and Los Angeles, Univ. of California Pr., 1949. 167p. $1.50.   **G2**

Turabian, Kate L. A manual for writers of dissertations. Chic., Univ. of Chic. Pr., 1937. 61p. **G3**

Williams, Cecil B. and **Stevenson, Allan H.** A research manual with a bibliographical guide to college studies and interests. N.Y., Harper, 1940. 264p.   **G4**

  p.1-110, manual; p.113-182, bibliographical guide.

BIBLIOGRAPHY
International

Oxford. University. Bodleian Library. Catalogus dissertationum academicarum quibus nuper aucta est bibliotheca Bodleiana MDCCCXXXII. Ox., Typ. Acad., 1834. 448, 63p. **G5**

Paris. Bibliothèque Nationale. Département des Imprimés. Catalogue des dissertations et écrits académiques provenant des échanges avec les universités étrangères et reçus par la Bibliothèque Nationale, 1882–1924. Paris, Klincksieck, 1884–1925. t.1-43. **G6**

Varnhagen, Hermann. Systematisches Verzeichnis der Programmabhandlungen, Dissertationen und Habilitationsschriften aus dem Gebiete der romanischen und englischen Philologie sowie der allgemeinen Sprach-und Litteraturwissenschaft und der Pädagogik und Methodik. 2. vollst. umgearb. Aufl. Besorgt von Johannes Martin. Leipzig, Koch, 1893. 296p. **G7**

United States
Bibliography

Palfrey, Thomas Rossman and **Coleman, Henry E., Jr.** Guide to bibliographies of theses, United States and Canada. 2d ed. Chic., Amer. Lib. Assoc., 1940. 54p. o.p. **G8**

General lists; lists in special fields; institutional lists.

Rosenberg, Ralph P. Bibliographies of theses in America. (In Bulletin of bibliography, 18:181-2, 201-3 Sept./Dec. 1945–Jan./Apr. 1946) **G9**

Additions and corrections to Palfrey and Coleman (G8).

General lists

See subject for lists of dissertations in a special subject field.

Doctoral dissertations accepted by American universities, 1933/34- . Comp. for the Assoc. of Research Libraries. N.Y., Wilson, 1934- . no.1- . Annual. (no. 17, $4.50) **G10**

Contents: Alphabetical subject index; Publication and preservation of American doctoral dissertations; List of periodic university publications abstracting dissertations; Statistical tables; List of dissertations arranged by subject and then by university, giving for each dissertation its author, title, and, in the case of those printed, bibliographical data as to separate publication or inclusion in some periodical or collection; Alphabetical author index.

The section, "Publication and preservation," gives important reference information about the practice of different universities as to requirement of printing, publication of abstracts, number of copies deposited in home library, and library regulations about interlibrary loan of dissertations.

Microfilm abstracts; a collection of abstracts of doctoral dissertations and monographs which are available in complete form on microfilm. v.1- . Ann Arbor, Mich., University Microfilms, 1938- . **G11**

A collection of abstracts of dissertations which are available in complete form on microfilm. The plan is to make doctoral dissertations available without the high cost of printing. The abstract is submitted by the author and is printed in this book of abstracts which is distributed to leading libraries and journals accompanied by printed library cards for each abstract. The dissertation is microfilmed in full and copies are available for sale through University Microfilms.

U. S. Library of Congress. Catalog Division. List of American doctoral dissertations printed in 1912–38. Wash., Govt. Prt. Off., 1913–40. 26v. **G12**

Contents of each volume: (1) Alphabetical list of theses printed during the year; (2) Classified list, arranged under the broad classes of the Library of Congress scheme; (3) Index of subjects; (4) Doctors whose theses have been printed during the year, arranged by institutions.

Lists 1 and 2 give full catalog information and, in case of reprints, indicate the periodical or other publication in which the thesis was first printed. Includes the printed theses of about 45 colleges and universities. No more published.

Austria

Vienna. Universität. Philosophische Fakultät. Verzeichnis über die seit dem Jahre 1872 an der philosophischen Fakultät der Universität in Wien eingereichten und approbierten Dissertationen. Wien, 1935–36. 3v. **G13**

Arranged by large subjects, with a catchword subject index at end of each group and an author index at end of each volume.

—— Bd.4, Nachtrag: Verzeichnis der 1934 bis 1937 an der philosophischen Fakultät der Universität in Wien u. der 1872 bis 1937 an der philosophischen Fakultät der Universität in Innsbruck eingereichten und approbierten Dissertationen . . . . Wien [c1937]. 292 p.

Volume 4 of the basic set listed above providing a 1934–37 supplement to the Vienna list and a basic list for Innsbruck.

Belgium

Louvain. Université Catholique. Bibliographie. Louvain, 1880–1936. v.1-6. **G14**

Publisher varies: v.1-5, C. Peeters; v.6, Bibliothèque de l'Université.

Contents: v.1, Bibliographie académique (1834–79). 1880. 311p.; v.2, Bibliographie (1834–1900). [3. éd.]

1900. 386p.; v.3, Bibliographie, 1. supplément (1899–1901). 1901. 74p., 2. supplément (1901–03). 1904. 92p., 3. supplément (1903–05). 1906. 88p.; v.4, Liste des professeurs (1834–1908). Travaux du corps académique 1908. Institutions universitaire et 4. supplément (1906–07). 1908. 333p.; v.5, Bibliographie, 5. supplément (1908–11). 1911. 100p., 6. supplément (1911–13). 1913. 82p.; v.6, Bibliographie académique (1914–34). 1937. 452p.

The volume numbers given above represent a new assignment of numbers made by the editors of volume 6, and do not agree with earlier voluming.

France

France. Ministère de l'Education Nationale. Catalogue des thèses et écrits académiques . . . 1884/85- . Paris [etc.], 1885- . **G15**

1884/85–1930/31 published by the Ministère de l'Instruction Publique.

Issued annually, 5 annuals forming a volume. The official French list. Each annual issue 1885–1913 is arranged alphabetically by universities, with subarrangement by *facultés;* beginning 1914, the arrangement is by *facultés.* Gives for each thesis: author's name, full title, place, publisher, 1930/31- , date, size, paging. Volumes 1–9 (1884/89–1928/29) have author and subject indexes. Issued in two editions: (1) ordinary paper printed on both sides, (2) thin paper printed on only one side, for clipping. Of great value in the university library, as the French theses are among the most important published.

The *Bibliographie de la France* (A259) contains an alphabetical list of dissertations 1930- published as supplements to the *Bibliographie*, part 1, 1932- .

Maire, Albert. Répertoire alphabétique des thèses de doctorat és lettres des universités françaises, 1810–1900. Paris, Picard, 1903. 226p. **G16**

List of 2182 theses, arranged alphabetically by author. Gives for each: author, title, place, publisher, date, paging, university, and whether published also in any other form. Marks rejected theses.

Mourier, Athénaïs and **Deltour, F.** Notice sur le doctorat és lettres, suivie du catalogue et de l'analyse des thèses françaises et latines admises par les facultés des lettres depuis 1810. 4. éd., cor. et considérablement aug. Paris, Delalain, 1880. 442p. **G17**

—— Catalogue et analyse des thèses latines et françaises. Paris, Delalain, 1882–1901. 21v. **G18**

The main list and the 21 annuals include practically the same theses as Maire's *Répertoire* (G16) but arrange them by years and universities instead of alphabetically, and give, in addition to title and paging, full contents of each thesis, and very brief biographical data. Use is for contents. Indexes: (1) subjects; (2) authors.

Germany

Berlin. Universität. Bibliothek. Verzeichnis der Berliner Universitätsschriften, 1810–85. Berlin, Weber, 1899. 848p. **G19**

Bibliographischer Monatsbericht über neu erschienenen Schul-, Universitäts- und Hochschulschriften, 1889/90- . Leipzig, Fock, 1890- . Jahr. 1- . **G20**

Classified arrangement, with annual author index, and, from volume 4 on, an annual "Sachregister."

Jahresverzeichnis der an den Deutschen Schulanstalten erschienenen Abhandlungen, 1889–1930. Berlin, de Gruyter, 1890–1931. v.1-28. **G21**

Publisher varies.

v.1-27 cover one year each, 1889–1915; v.28 covers the 15 years, 1916–30.

Jahresverzeichnis der Deutschen Hochschulschriften, 1885- . Berlin und Leipzig, Börsenverein der Deutschen Buchhändler, 1887- . Bd.1- . **G22**

Publisher varies.

Title varies: 1885/86–1923; 1924–35, *Jahresverzeichnis der an den Deutschen Universitäten und Hochschulen erschienen Schriften.*

The standard official German list including the theses of all the German universities from 1885, the theses of the Technische Hochschulen from 1913 and the theses of the Hochschulen der Länder from 1924. Arranged, Bd.1-28 and Bd.38-51, by universities, Bd.29-37, by faculties, Bd.52- by place, with an author index in each volume, a separate subject index for Bd.1-5, and a subject index in each volume, Bd.6- . Gives for each thesis: author's full name, title of thesis, date, publisher, paging, size, and whether reprinted from some scientific journal, report, etc.

Klussmann, Rudolf. Systematisches Verzeichnis der Abhandlungen welche in den Schulschriften sämtlicher an dem Programmtausche teilnehmenden Lehranstalten erschienen sind, 1876–85, 1886–90, 1891–95, 1896–1900, 1901–10. Leipzig, Teubner, 1889–1916. 5v. **G23**

Classified, with index of places and index of authors.

Milkau, Fritz. Verzeichniss der Bonner Universitätsschriften, 1818–1885. Bonn, Cohen, 1897. 440p. **G24**

Mundt, Hermann. Bio-bibliographisches Verzeichnis von Universitäts- u. Hochschuldrucken (Dissertationen) vom Ausgang des 16. bis Ende des 19. Jahrhunderts. Bd.1- . Leipzig, Carlsohn, 1936- . **G25**

Bd.1, A-Kühn (appeared as Lfg. 1-9, 1934–36). [Bd.2] Kühn-Ritter (appeared as Lfg. 10-13, 1937–42). Incomplete.

A list of theses which contains biographical data about the various persons connected with them, arranged alphabetically by respondent. Chiefly German, with some Dutch and Scandinavian dissertations of the seventeenth to nineteenth century.

Pretzsch, Karl. Verzeichnis der Breslauer Universitätsschriften, 1811–1885. Breslau, Korn, 1905. 387p. **G26**

Strassburg. Universität. Verzeichniss der an der Kaiser-Wilhelms-Universität Strassburg vom Sommer-Semester 1872 bis Ende 1884 erschienenen Schriften. Strassburg, Heitz, 1890. 74p. **G27**

Great Britain

Cambridge. University. Abstracts of dissertations approved for the Ph.D., M.Sc. and M. Litt. degrees in the University of Cambridge . . . 1925/26- . Camb., Univ. Pr., 1927- . **G28**

London. University. Subjects of dissertations, theses and published works presented by successful candidates at examinations for higher degrees 1937/44- . [Lond.] Univ. of Lond. [1944]- . **G29**

—— Institute of Historical Research. Historical research for university degrees in the United Kingdom, 1931/32- . (Bulletin . . . Theses supplement. no.1-) Lond., Longmans, 1933- . **G30**

Each number is in two parts: (1) Theses completed during the year; (2) Theses in progress. "The former follows on the lists published annually in *History* from 1920 to 1929, and in the *Bulletin* from 1930 to 1932; the latter is an innovation suggested by the Anglo-American Historical Committee."—*Pref. note to No.1.*

Continues earlier lists published in the *Bulletin* as follows: Historical research 1928/29, 1929/30, 1930/31, *Bulletin* 7:173-79, February 1930; 8:171-77, February 1931; 9:181-88, February 1932. In continuation of the following:

University research 1911/19–1927/28. (In History n.s. v.4-14) **G31**

Lists of dissertations in progress in the universities of Great Britain, 1911–28. Form an annual record for that period except that the first list (in volume 4) covers the years 1911–19, and the list in volume 14 is an author index to all preceding lists. For each thesis gives author, subject or title, and note of publication if the thesis is printed.

Oxford. University. Committee for advanced studies. Abstracts of dissertations for the degree of doctor of philosophy, v.1- , 1925/28- . Ox., Univ. Pr., 1928- . v.1- . **G32**

Netherlands

Nederlandsche Vereeniging van Bibliothecarissen. Catalogus van academische Geschriften in Nederland en Nederlandsch Indië verschenen, jaarg. 1- , 1924- . Utrecht, 1925- . **G33**

Combined author and subject index for jaargang 1-5, 1924–28, which form volume 1; jaargang 6- , 1929- , have author index only.

Scandinavia

Copenhagen. Universitet. Bibliotek. Danish theses for the doctorate and commemorative publications of the University of Copenhagen, 1836–1926, a bio-bibliography. Copenhagen, Levin, 1929. 395p. **G34**

In two parts: (1) class list, arranged by the main classes of the decimal classification; (2) alphabetical author list which gives brief biographies of the authors and references to fuller biographies elsewhere and also serves as an author index to the class list. Bibliographical detail given for each thesis includes: author's name, title, English translation of a Danish title sometimes with brief abstract in English, date, paging and illustrations, date of maintenance.

Hjelt, Otto Edvard August. Det Finska universitetets disputations-och program-litteratur under åren 1828–1908 systematiskt ordnad. Dissertationes academicae et programmata Universitatis literarum Fennorum Helsingforsiae annis 1828–1908 edita. Helsingfors, Helsingfors Centraltryckeri, 1909. 162p. **G35**

Josephson, Aksel Gustav Salomon. Avhandlingar ock program, uitg. vid svenska ock finska akademier ock skolor, 1855–1890. Uppsala [1891–1897]. 2v. **G36**

Liden, Johan Henrik. Catalogus disputationum in academiis et gymnasiis Sueciae atque etiam a Suecis extra patriam habitarum, quotquot huc usque reperiri potuerunt. Upsaliae, Typ. Edmannianis, 1778–80. 5 pts. **G37**

Marklin, Gabriel. Catalogus disputationum in academiis Scandinaviae et Finlandiae Lidenianus continuatus a Gabr. Marklin. Upsaliae, Reg. Academiae Typ., 1820. 3 pts. **G38**

Covers 1778–1819.
Contents: (1) Disputationes upsalienses; (2) Disputationes lundenses. Disputationes christianienses; (3) Disputationes aboënses.

—— —— Ad catalogum disputationum in academiis et gymnasiis Sueciae Lidenianum supplementa addidit. Gabr. Marklin. Upsaliae, Reg. Academiae Typ., 1820. 117p.

—— Catalogus disputationum in academiis Sveciae et Fenniae habitarum Lidenianus iterum continuatus a Gabr. Marklin. . . . Stockholm, 1874. 3v. in 1. **G39**

First issued Upsaliae, 1856.
Covers 1820–55.
Contents: (1) Disputationes upsalienses; (2) Disputationes lundenses; (3) Disputationes fennorum.

Melander, Samuel Erik. Förteckning öfver afhandlingar och uppsatser som ingå i eller medfölja årsredogörelserna för rikets allmänna läroverk, 1858–1909. Lund, H. Ohlssons Boktryckeri, 1909–12. 2v. **G40**

Contents: 1858–82 (pub. 1912); 1883–1909 (pub. 1909).

Tuneld, John. Akademiska avhandlingar vid sveriges universitet och högskolor, läsåren 1910/11–1939/40; bibliografi. Lund [Ohlsson], 1945. 336p. **G40a**

Nelson, Axel Herman. Akademiska afhandlingar vid Sveriges universitet och högskolor läsåren 1890/91–1909/10 jämte förteckning öfver svenskars akademiska afhandlingar vid utländska universitet under samma tid. Uppsala, Akademiska Bokhandeln [1911–12]. 149p. **G41**

In two parts, an author list and a subject list. The author list is printed also in Uppsala Universitets, Arsskrift, 1911, v.2.

South Africa

Robinson, Anthony Meredith Lewin. Catalogue of theses and dissertations accepted for degrees by the South African universities; Katalogus van proefskrifte en verhandelinge vir grade deur die suid-afrikaanse universiteite goedgekeur, 1918–1941. . . . (Pub. with the assistance of the National Research Board) . . . Cape Town, 1943. 155p. 7s. 6d. **G42**

1757 items. Classified with subject and author indexes.

Switzerland

Geneva. Université. Catalogue des ouvrages, articles et mémoires publiés par les professeurs et privat-docents de l'Université de Genève . . . et des thèses présentées . . . pour l'obtention de grades universitaires, 1873–95, 1896–1907, 1908–13, 1914–26, 1927–37, 1938–42. Genève, "Journal de Genève," 1896–1944. 6 v. (Documents pour servir à l'histoire de L'Université de Genève, IV, V [I], VI, VII, VIII, IX) . **G43**

Publisher varies.
1873–95 comp. by Charles Soret; 1896–1907 by Charles Julliard; 1908–13 by Albert Kohler; 1914–26 by Albert Roussy; 1927–37, 1938–42 by Hermann Blanc.

Jahresverzeichnis der Schweizerischen Hochschulschriften, 1897- . Basel, Verlag der Universitätsbibliothek, 1898- . Bd.1- . **G44**

Publisher varies. Title varies.
Arranged by universities. Each issue has an author index (1925, Personen-Register) and, 1926- , a catchword subject index.

—— Verfasser-register zu den Jahrgängen 1897/98–1922/23. Basel, Univ.-Bibliothek, 1927. 87p.

Zürich. Universität. Verzeichnis Zürcherischer Universitätsschriften 1833–97. Im Anhang: Programmarbeiten der Kantonsschule Zürich 1834–1903. Zürich, Verlag der Kantonsbibliothek, 1904. 218p. **G45**

Issued as volume 4 of the "Zuwachs-Catalog der Bibliothek der Cantonallehranstalten in Zürich."

PHILOSOPHY

❦ Philosophy and psychology are often classed together in libraries and many of the older reference books include both subjects, although psychology is now becoming more closely allied with the biological sciences. General histories and textbooks are especially needed to supplement the reference materials in philosophy. In the average American library the most used reference work in this class is Baldwin, *Dictionary of philosophy and psychology* (H11), volume 3 of which is Rand, *Bibliography of philosophy, psychology, and cognate subjects* (H1). This is now much out of date but is still useful for material up to the end of the nineteenth century. A bibliography to cover 1900–32 is in process. The *Journal of philosophy* published an annual bibliography from 1933–36 (H2), when the record was taken over by the *Bibliographie de la philosophie* (H3), published by the Institut International de Philosophie. Together these give a fairly comprehensive record for this period.

BIBLIOGRAPHY

Rand, Benjamin. Bibliography of philosophy, psychology and cognate subjects. N.Y., Macmillan, 1905. 2v. (Repr. by National Bibliophile Service. $10 ea.) **H1**

Forms volume 3 of Baldwin's *Dictionary of philosophy;* also sold separately. The most important bibliography of the subject. For contents *see* H11. The section on psychology is continued by the *Psychological index* (J9). For later literature on topics and names in philosophy and particularly for the foreign literature of the subject the bibliographies in the latest edition of Ueberweg's *Grundriss* (H22) should be used.

Bibliography of philosophy, 1933–36. N.Y., Journal of Philosophy, 1934–37. v.1-4. $1 ea. **H2**

Reprinted from *Journal of philosophy.*

A classified list with alphabetical name index. Intended to include all the scholarly philosophical literature published during the year in English, French, German and Italian, with some items in other languages. Excludes reviews, translations from one into another of the four languages and new editions unless they are extensive revisions or enlargements.

No more published.

Bibliographie de la philosophie . . . 1- . 1937- . Paris, Lib. Phil. J. Vrin, 1937- . v.1- . Semiannual. **H3**

At head of title: Institut International de Philosophie.

Each issue contains a bibliographical section and a systematic section. The first includes lists of publishers, periodicals, and an author catalog of publications; the second includes indexes arranged by period, country, names of philosophers, and a classification of contents according to the key words of the titles.

Includes doctoral dissertations.

Bibliographische Einführungen in das Studium der Philosophie, hrsg. von I. M. Bochenski. Bern, Francke, 1948- . no.1-11. (In progress) **H4**

A series of bibliographies on various aspects of philosophy.

Contents: (1) Bochenski, I. M. and Monteleone, F. Allgemeine philosophische Bibliographie. 42p.; (2) Winn, Ralph B. Amerikanische Philosophie. 32p.; (3) Beth, E. W. Symbolische Logik und Grundlegung der exakten Wissenschaften. 28p.; (4) Jolivet, Régis. Kierkegaard. 33p.; (5) Gigon, Olaf. Antike Philosophie. 52p.; (6) Menasce, P. J. de. Arabische Philosophie. 49p.; (7) Sciacca, M. F. Italienische Philosophie der Gegenwart. 36p.; (8) Phillippe, M. D. Aristoteles. 48p.; (9) Jolivet, Régis. Französische Existenzphilosophie. 36p.; (10) Sciacca, M. F. Augustinus. 32p.; (11) Dürr, Karl. Der logische Positivismus. 24p.

Istituto Nazionale per le Relazioni Culturali con l'Estero. Scienze religiose, filosofia, pedagogia. Roma, I.R.C.E., 1941. 173p. (Bibliografie del ventennio) **H5**

List of works published in Italy, 1920–1941.

Jessop, T. E. A bibliography of David Hume and of Scottish philosophy from Francis Hutcheson to Lord Balfour. Lond., A. Brown, 1938. 201p. **H6**

Mandonnet, Pierre and **Destrez, J.** Bibliographie thomiste. La Saulchoir, Kain (Belgique), Revue des Sciences Philosophiques et Théologiques, 1921. 116p. **H7**

Supplemented by:

Bourke, Vernon Joseph. Thomistic bibliography, 1920–1940. . . . The Modern schoolman, supplement to v.21. St. Louis, 1945. 312p. $2.50. **H8**

Poortman, Johannes Jacobus. Repertorium der Nederlandse Wijsbegeerte. Amsterdam, Antwerp, Wereldbibliotheek, 1948. 403p. **H9**

A bibliography of philosophical works printed in Dutch in the Netherlands regardless of the nationality of the author, and of works by Netherlanders wherever printed. In two parts, subjects and authors.

Répertoire bibliographique de la philosophie, t.1- , fév. 1949- . Louvain, Editions de l'Institut Supérieur de Philosophie, 1949- . Quarterly Bel.Fr.120 **H9a**

At head of title: Société philosophique de Louvain.

Publié sous les auspices de l'Institut International de Philosophie avec le patronage de l'UNESCO.

A comprehensive bibliography of books and articles on philosophy appearing in various countries. Classified lists with annual author indexes.

Schweizerische Philosophische Gesellschaft. Bibliographie der philosophischen, psychologischen und pädagogischen Literatur in der deutschsprachigen Schweiz, 1900–1940, hrsg. von E. Heuss, P. Kamm, H. Kunz, M. Landmann. Basel, Verlag für Recht und Gesellschaft, 1944. 207p. (Its Jahrbuch . . . Beihefte II) **H10**

—— [Supplement] 1941–1944, von Hans Zantop. 1945. p.218-78. (Its Jahrbuch, v.5. Separatum)

The main part of the work includes German works only, the supplement covers German, French and Italian.

DICTIONARIES AND ENCYCLOPEDIAS

Baldwin, James Mark. Dictionary of philosophy and psychology, including many of the principal conceptions of ethics, logic, aesthetics, philosophy of religion, mental pathology, anthropology, biology, neurology, physiology, economics, political and social philosophy, philology, physical science and education, and giving a terminology in English, French, German and Italian. N.Y., Macmillan, 1901–05. 3v. in 4. il. v.3 in 2 pts. (Repr. National Bibliophile Service. $10 ea.) **H11**

v.1, A-Laws; v.2, Le-Z; Indices: (1) Greek terms, (2) Latin terms, (3) German terms, (4) French terms, (5) Italian terms; v.3, Bibliography of philosophy: pt.1, History of philosophy, Bibliographies of individual philosophers; pt.2, Systematic philosophy, Logic, Aesthetics, Philosophy of religion, Ethics, Psychology.

The only encyclopedia of the subject in English, excellent and authoritative when first issued and still useful for many topics though now out of date for modern developments. Concise rather than exhaustive in treatment, with signed articles by specialists and many bibliographies. Covers the whole field but is fuller for modern than for earlier aspects of the subject and does not attempt to cover the whole of Greek and scholastic philosophy. Includes very brief biographies of men no longer living. A special feature is the inclusion of French, German and Italian equivalents of English terms.

A new edition, 1910, differed from the original only in the correction of a few typographical errors.

Blanc, Elie. Dictionnaire de philosophie ancienne, moderne et contemporaine. Paris, Lethielleux, 1906. 1248 col. **H12**

—— —— Supplément . . . années 1906, 1907, 1908. Paris, 1908. 154 col.

Brugger, Walter. Philosophisches Wörterbuch. . . . Wien, Herder, 1948. 532 p. **H13**

Explanations of philosophical terms, with bibliographies.

Eisler, Rudolph. Handwörterbuch der Philosophie. 2. Aufl. neuhrsg. von Richard Müller-Freienfels. Berlin, Mittler, 1922. 785p. **H14**

1st ed. 1913.

A condensation and popularization of his *Wörterbuch der philosophischen Begriffe* (H15), utilizing also some material from his *Philosophen-Lexikon* (H21). An excellent small work, useful where short, concise articles are wanted, but not a substitute in a college library for the two larger works.

—— Wörterbuch der philosophischen Begriffe, historisch-quellenmässig. 4. völlig neubearb. Aufl. hrsg. unter Mitwirkung der Kantgesellschaft. Berlin, Mittler, 1927–30. 3v. **H15**

1st ed. 1889, 1v.; 2d ed. 1904, 2v.; 3d ed. 1910, 3v.

Scholarly articles with bibliographies, on philosophical concepts and terms, tracing their use, meanings and treatment through the writings of the philosophers, and giving many references to sources. For the specialist, not the general reader. Of first importance in advanced work.

Literatur-Verzeichnis, v.3, p.695-906.

—— Kant-Lexikon; Nachschlagewerk zu Kants sämtlichen Schriften, Briefen und handschriftlichen Nachlass; hrsg. unter Mitwirkung der Kantgesellschaft. Berlin, Mittler, 1930. 642p. **H16**

Encyclopaedisch Handboek van het moderne Denken, on redactie van A. C. Elsbach, H. T. de Graaf, H. J. Jordan, en K. F. Proost. Arnheim, Staterus, 1931. 2v. **H17**

Signed articles with some bibliography.

Ferrater Mora, José. Diccionario de filosofía. 2d ed. corr. y aumentada. Mexico, Ed Atlante, 1944. 760p. (Diccionarios cientifícos Atlante) **H18**

A general philosophical dictionary with definitions of terms, biographies, etc. Includes living persons. Not limited by country or period.

Hoffmeister, Johannes. Wörterbuch der philosophischen Begriffe, begrundet von Friedrich Kirchner und Carl Michäelis. Vollst. neu. Bearb. Leipzig, Meiner, 1944. 776p. (Der Philosophische Bibliothek, Bd.225) **H19**

Concise articles with some bibliography.

Lalande, André. Vocabulaire technique et critique de la philosophie, revu par MM. les membres et correspondants de la Société française de Philosophie, et publié, avec leurs corrections et observations. 5. éd. augm. d'un grand nombre d'articles nouveaux. Paris, Presse Univ. de France, 1947. 1280p. 1200fr. **H20**

Defines and discusses philosophical terms, giving equivalents in various languages, references to sources, etc. This edition revised and enlarged.

Philosophen-Lexikon; Handwörterbuch der Philosophie nach Personen, unter Mitwirkung von Gertrud Jung, verfasst und hrsg. von Werner Ziegenfuss. Berlin, de Gruyter, 1949- . v.1- . **H21**

A biographical dictionary of philosophers of all periods and all countries, but with the emphasis on philosophy since Hegel. Includes living persons. Planned to take the place of the earlier *Philosophen-Lexikon* by Rudolf Eisler (Berlin, Mittler, 1912. 889p.) and on the same general plan as that work, but with longer articles, inclusion of additional names and of considerable additional material on names included by Eisler. Nearly all articles, even the short ones, have bibliographies.

The first six parts, A-Juvalta, were published in 1937

but further publication was prohibited on political grounds. The present text remains almost unaltered except for the addition of some later death dates and of bibliographical data, to 1945 for German publications, to 1939 for other countries.

HISTORY

Ueberweg, Friedrich. Grundriss der Geschichte der Philosophie. 11.-12. Aufl. Berlin, Mittler, 1923–28. 5v. **H22**

Important reference history, particularly useful for its full bibliographies and its biographical information.

Covers ancient, patristic and scholastic, and modern philosophy. Written by specialists.

BIOGRAPHY

McCabe, Joseph. Biographical dictionary of modern rationalists. Lond., Watts, 1920. 934 col. **H23**

Riedl, John O. Catalogue of Renaissance philosophers (1300–1650), comp. by Robert A. Baker [and others] under the direction of John O. Riedl. Milwaukee, Marquette Univ. Pr., 1940. 179p. $2.50. **H24**

Arranged by schools with alphabetical author index. Gives biographical notes and bibliographies of writings.

Who's who in philosophy. Dagobert D. Runes, ed.; Lester E. Denonn, Ralph B. Winn, assoc. eds. v.1. [N.Y.] Philosophical Library, 1942. 293p. $5. **H25**

Contents: v.1, Anglo-American philosophers.

PSYCHOLOGY

❧ Many of the older reference books in philosophy include psychology (*see* Philosophy, p.116), although in this century psychology has built up a literature of its own with bibliographies, indexes, and dictionaries to make it available to research workers. The *Psychological index* (J9) lists both books and periodical articles published from 1894–1935; *Psychological abstracts* (J8), which was started in 1927, not only lists material but is of importance because it gives abstracts of the items included (for discussion of abstract journals *see* Science, p.253).

GENERAL WORKS
Guides

Louttit, Chauncey McKinley. Handbook of psychological literature. Bloomington, Ind., Principia Pr., 1932. 273p. (Pub. of Indiana Univ. Psychological Clinics, ser. 2, no.4) **J1**

A manual for research workers and a guide to psychological literature. Now out of date but still useful for earlier materials.
Bibliography of journals in psychology and related subjects, p.137-239.

Bibliography

Chandler, Albert Richard and **Barnhart, E. N.** A bibliography of psychological and experimental aesthetics, 1864–1937. Berkeley, Univ. of California Pr., 1938. 190p. **J2**

Lists books and periodical articles. An enlarged and rearranged edition of Chandler's *Bibliography of experimental aesthetics* (1933) with its supplements.

Harvard University. Depts. of Psychology and Social Relations. The Harvard list of books in psychology, comp. and annotated by the psychologists in Harvard University. Camb., Harv. Univ. Pr., 1949. 77p. **J3**

612 titles chosen as "important and valuable in psychology at the present time," annotated and arranged by class with author index. Replaces *Books in psychology*, 1938, and its *Supplement*, 1944.

Hildreth, Gertrude Howell. Bibliography of mental tests and rating scales. 2d. ed. N.Y., Psychological Corp., 1939. 295p. $4. **J4**

—— 1945 supplement. N.Y., Psychological Corp., 1946. 86p. $1.75.

Louttit, Chauncey McKinley. Bibliography of bibliographies on psychology, 1900–1927. Wash., National Research Council, 1928. 108p. (Bull. of the National Research Council, no.65) **J5**

Schweizerische Philosophische Gesellschaft. Bibliographie der philosophischen, psychologischen und pädagogischen Literatur . . . 1900–1940. **J6**

For record *see* H10.

Abstracts and indexes

L'anneé psychologique. v.1, 1894- . Paris, Presses Universitaires de France, 1895- . **J7**

Includes signed abstracts with exact references to sources.

Psychological abstracts, 1927- . Lancaster, Pa., Amer. Psych. Assoc., 1927- . v.1- . $7 a yr. **J8**

An important monthly bibliography listing new books and articles grouped by subjects, with a signed abstract of each item. Author index to each number and full author and subject indexes for each volume. Includes somewhat fewer articles than the *Psychological index* (J9), but has the advantage of more frequent issue, detailed index of small subjects, and, especially, the important abstract feature.

Psychological index, 1894–1935, an annual bibliography of the literature of psychology and cognate subjects. Princeton, N.J., Psych. Rev. Co., 1895–1936. 42v. Some v. o. p.; some still available at $2 per v. **J9**

Lists original publications in all languages, both books and periodical articles, together with translations and new editions in English, French, German and Italian. A classified subject list, with an alphabetical author index but no subject index. For books, gives author, title, place, publisher and paging, and for magazine articles, author, title, periodical, date, volume and inclusive paging. Lists about 5000 titles each year, and indexes about 350 periodicals. The list of the principal periodicals indexed, with abbreviations used, is given in volume 30. Very useful for advanced work.

Discontinued after volume 42, its work to be carried on by *Psychological abstracts* (J8).

Psychological index. Abstract references. . . . Columbus, Ohio, Amer. Psych. Assoc., 1940–41 (v.1, 1941). 2v. $2 ea. **J10**

v.1, v.1-25, 1894–1918; v.2, v.26-35, 1919–1928.

Editor, H. L. Ansbacher. Prepared by the American Psychological Association in cooperation with the Work Projects Administration of the City of New York.

These abstract references have been compiled to serve as a backward extension of *Psychological abstracts* (J8), which was founded in 1927. It is a list of the numbers of those titles of the *Psychological index* (J9) for which one or more abstracts were located in the periodicals examined, with reference to volume and page of the abstract. As numbers only are given, it must be used in conjunction with the *Psychological index*. References to abstracts have been supplied for 43 per cent of the titles in the *Psychological index* (45,000 of the 107,000 titles from 1894–1928). Since more than one abstract was found for some titles, references are given to over 75,000 abstracts.

Dictionaries and encyclopedias

English, Horace Bidwell. Student's dictionary of psychological terms. 4th ed. N.Y., Harper, 1934. 131p. $1.20. **J11**

Erdélyi, Michael and **Grossman, Frank.** Dictionary of terms and expressions of industrial psychology ("Psychotechnics") in German, English, French, Hungarian. Preface by H. L. Hollingworth. N.Y., Pitman, 1939. 98p. $2.75. **J12**

". . . not for the use of beginners . . . for use of persons who have a fair knowledge of these foreign languages and desire to familiarize themselves with the special technical terms used in this particular field."—*Introd.*

Hinsie, Leland Earl and **Shatzky, Jacob.** Psychiatric dictionary with encyclopedic treatment of modern terms. Lond. and N.Y., Oxford, 1940. 559p. $10.50. **J13**

Gives pronunciations. Includes explanations, illustrative quotations and references.

Warren, Howard C. Dictionary of psychology. Bost., Houghton, c1934. 372p. $4.50. **J14**

Contents: Definitions of terms, English and foreign, p.1-299; Tables, p.303-39; Bibliography of technical dictionaries of philosophy and psychology, p.340-41; Glos-

saries of (1) French terms, p.343-58, (2) German terms, p.359-72.

Authoritative and generally reliable.

Winn, Ralph Bubrich. Encyclopedia of child guidance. N.Y., Philosophical Lib. [1943]. 456p. $7.50. **J15**

Definitions of terms and brief discussions of topics relating to the behavior of children with emphasis on the psychological aspect. Articles are signed, many by authorities in their fields, but there is lack of uniformity in treatment with frequent overlapping in articles on similar subjects by different authors.

Directories

National Committee for Mental Hygiene. Directory of psychiatric clinics in the United States, 1948. N.Y., 1948. 90p. **J16**

9th ed. Published at irregular intervals since 1920. Includes psychiatric clinics, mental hygiene societies, state institutions, state governmental departments, veterans administration and other federal mental hospitals.

Biography

American Association for Applied Psychology. Directory of applied psychologists, members of the American Association for Applied Psychology Inc. 2d ed., ed. by C. M. Louttit. Bloomington, Ind., Assoc., 1943. 111p. $1.50. **J17**

1st ed. 1941.

Includes biographical sketches, geographical, and specialties indexes.

American Psychological Association. Directory, 1916- . Wash., Assoc., 1916- . Annual (1949, $2). **J18**

1916–1947, called *Yearbook.* 1949 lists 6735 members, gives addresses, present positions, last degrees, and class of membership.

Psychological register, ed. by Carl Murchison. Worcester, Mass., Clark Univ. Pr., 1929–32. v.2-3. **J19**

Includes brief biographies with very full bibliographies of psychologists throughout the world, arranged by country; volume 2 (1929) included 1250 psychologists from 29 countries; volume 3 (1932), a revision and expansion of the 1929 volume, included 2400 from 40 countries; volume 1 was announced to include persons deceased before the initiation of the series and to extend back to the time of the early Greek psychologists, but has not been published.

OCCULTISM

Caillet, Albert Louis. Manuel bibliographique des sciences psychiques ou occultes. Paris, Dorbon, 1912–13. 3v. **J20**

Subtitle: Sciences des mages. Hermétique. Astrologie. Kabbale. Francmaçonnerie. Médecine ancienne. Mesmerisme. Sorcellerie. Singularités. Aberrations de tout ordre. Curiosités. Sources bibliographiques et documentaires sur ces sujets.

Lists 11,648 items, with full title, imprint and collation of each, and, in many cases, notes about the books and brief biographical data about the authors.

Spence, Lewis. Encyclopaedia of occultism, a compendium of information on the occult sciences, occult personalities, psychic science, magic, demonology, spiritism and mysticism. Lond., Routledge, 1920. 451p. il. **J21**

Thorndike, Lynn. History of magic and experimental science. N.Y., Macmillan, 1929; Columbia Univ. Pr., 1934–41. v.1-6. (v.3-4, History of Science Soc. Pub. n.s. 4) v.1-2, Macmillan, $10 ea.; v.3-6, Columbia Univ. Pr., $10 ea. **J22**

v.1-2, First 13 centuries; v.3-4, 14th-15th centuries; v.5-6, 16th century.

A well-documented history with separate indexes in volumes 1-4, and a combined index to volumes 5-6 in volume 6.

RELIGION

❧ In the field of religion, both Christian and non-Christian, reference materials are very extensive. They include encyclopedias, dictionaries, directories and manuals in English and in other languages, which should be acquired by libraries according to need.

A basic working collection of materials in English might include the *Encyclopaedia of religion and ethics* (K1); the *Catholic encyclopedia* (K182); the *Universal Jewish encyclopedia* (K246); an edition of the Bible (*see* p.127); Strong, *Exhaustive concordance of the Bible* (K76); Stevenson, *Home book of*

Bible quotations (K85); Hastings, *Dictionary of the Bible* (K89); Julian, *Dictionary of hymnology* (K54); the *Yearbook of American churches* (K108) and whatever denominational yearbooks are needed. For mythology and folklore: *Funk and Wagnalls Standard dictionary of folklore* (K267); Gayley, *Classic myths* (K260); and Frazer, *Golden bough* (K3).

Large libraries and libraries specializing in religious materials will need to add many of the more specialized works, including some of those in foreign languages.

GENERAL WORKS
Encyclopedias

Encyclopaedia of religion and ethics; ed. by James Hastings, with the assistance of John A. Selbie, and other scholars. Edinburgh, Clark; N.Y., Scribner, 1908–27. 12v. and index. il. **K1**

Low priced edition on thinner paper and bound in 7 volumes, $65.

The most recent and comprehensive work in this class, including articles on all religions, ethical systems and movements, religious beliefs and customs, philosophical ideas, moral practices, related subjects in anthropology, mythology, folklore, biology, psychology, economics and sociology, and names of persons and places connected with any of these subjects. Signed articles, full bibliographies.

Ferm, Vergilius. An encyclopedia of religion. N.Y., Philosophical Lib., [c1945]. 844p. $10. **K2**

A desk-size dictionary with brief signed articles on "the theologies of the major religions, denominations and cults. . . ." Religion is interpreted broadly to include besides the expected theological subjects, such fields as sociology, psychology, philosophy, art, musicology, etc., as they relate to religion. Includes many biographies. Bibliographies are included for many articles, sometimes annotated.

Frazer, Sir James George. The Golden bough; a

study in magic and religion. 3d ed. Lond., Macmillan, 1907–15. 12v. **K3**

v.1-2, The magic art and the evolution of kings; v.3, Taboo and the perils of the soul; v.4, The dying god; v.5-6, Adonis, Attis, Osiris; studies in the history of oriental religion; v.7-8, Spirits of the corn and of the wild; v.9, The scapegoat; v.10-11, Balder the Beautiful, the fire festivals of Europe and the doctrine of the external soul; v.12, Bibliography and general index.

Not a reference book in the ordinary sense of the word, but a great storehouse of information about primitive religion. The very detailed general index makes it possible to use the set for ready reference.

—— Aftermath; a supplement to the Golden bough. Lond., Macmillan, 1936. 494p. 21s.; $3 **K4**

This supplementary volume contains new matter gathered from works published since 1915, when the third edition of the *Golden bough* was completed, and from some earlier sources not utilized in the basic work.

Herzog, Johann Jakob. Realencyklopädie für protestantische Theologie und Kirche, begründet von J. J. Herzog; in 3. verb. und verm. Aufl. . . . hrsg. von Albert Hauck. Leipzig, Hinrichs, 1896–1913. 24v. **K5**

v.1-21, A-Z; v.22, Index; v.23-24, Supplement, A-Z.

Long signed articles by specialists, full bibliographies. The most extended German work, and one of the most important in any language from the Protestant point of

iew. Formed the basis for the *New Schaff-Herzog* (K8).
)f value in the theological, university or large reference
brary, but not needed in other types.

Mathews, Shailer and **Smith, G. B.** Dictionary of
eligion and ethics. N.Y., Macmillan, 1921. 513p.
K6

A dictionary of terms, not a detailed encyclopedia,
*r*hich aims to define all terms definitely connected with
*r*e subjects of religion and ethics and to discuss fully the
*r*ore important terms, especially those in primitive and
*r*hnic religions. Includes biographies of persons not
*r*ving. The longer articles are signed.

)ie Religion in Geschichte und Gegenwart;
Iandwörterbuch für Theologie und Religions-
*r*issenschaft. 2. völlig neubearb. Aufl., in Ver-
indung mit Alfred Bertholet, Hermann Faber
nd Horst Stephan, hrsg. von Hermann Gunkel
nd Leopold Zscharnack. Tübingen, Mohr, 1927–
2. 5v. and Registerbd. **K7**

1st ed. 1909-13. 5v.
The index volume to the first edition, though an-
*)*unced, was never published. The Registerband of the
*r*cond edition contains the following indexes and lists:
*r*stematische Uebersicht, col. 1-32; Verzeichnis der Mit-
beiter und ihrer Beiträge, col. 33-102; Stichwortregi-
*r*r, col. 103-890; Berichtigungen, col. 891-96.
Cited as RGG.
Signed articles written by specialists from an advanced
*)*int of view; full bibliographies. Many biographical ar-
*r*les, including articles on men still living.

:haff, Philip. New Schaff-Herzog encyclopedia
religious knowledge, embracing biblical, his-
*r*ical, doctrinal and practical theology and bibli-
*r*l, theological and ecclesiastical biography, from
*r*e earliest times; based on the 3d ed. of the Real-
*r*ncyklopädie founded by J. J. Herzog and ed. by
lbert Hauck. S. M. Jackson, ed.-in-chief. N.Y.,
rnk, 1908–12. 12v. and index. (Repr.: Grand
rpids, Mich., Baker Book House, 1949–50. 13v.)
K8

This encyclopedia is one of the most important refer-
*r*ce books on its subject in English. Based upon the
*r*rd edition of the Herzog-Hauck *Realencyklopädie*
*r*5), and so Protestant in tone, but not biased. It is
*r*t a mere translation of the German work, however, as
*r*ich of the material has been condensed, fresh material
*r*ded and the bibliographies extended and improved.
*r*t limited to the Christian religion but includes articles
other religions and religious leaders. Covers the
*r*ole field of biblical, historical and contemporary theol-
*r*y, church history and religious biography, including
*r*arate articles on all sects, denominations and churches,
*r*anizations and societies, missions, doctrines, contro-
*r*sies, etc. Biographical notices include those of men
*r*ing at the time the work was published. The strongest
*r*ture of the work, when first published, was the bib-
*r*graphical feature, in three forms: (1) an excellent gen-
*r*l bibliographical survey, with critical comment, in the
*r*face (xii-xiv), (2) the bibliographical appendix at
r beginning of each volume listing recent literature,
*r*l (3) the fine bibliographies appended to each article.

Sacred books

The Bible of the world, ed. by Robert O. Ballou,
in collaboration with Friedrich Spiegelberg, and
with the assistance and advice of Horace L.
Friess. N.Y., Viking, 1939. 1415p. $5. **K9**

Includes selections designed to give the "scriptural
essence of eight great living source religions for the use
of the modern English reader,"—Hindu, Buddhist, Con-
fucianist, Taoist, Zoroastrian, Judeo-Christian, and Mo-
hammedan.

Champion, Selwyn Gurney. The eleven religions
and their proverbial lore, a comparative study.
. . . Foreword to the American ed. by Rufus M.
Jones. . . . A reference book to the eleven surviving major religions of the world, with introductions by thirteen leading authorities. N.Y., Dutton, 1945. 340p. $4. **K10**

A reference book of quotations with subject matter
index and alternative chief word index. Bibliography,
p.336-40.

Hume, Robert Ernest. Treasure house of the living religions; selections from their scriptures.
N.Y., Scribner, 1932. 493p. **K11**

A classified anthology of 3,074 selected quotations from
the sacred books of the eleven great historical religions—
Buddhism, Christianity, Confucianism, Hinduism, Islam,
Jainism, Judaism, Shinto, Sikhism, Taoism, and Zoroas-
trianism—with exact indication of sources of each quotation, a full "Bibliography showing the canonical order
of the constituent documents of the several sacred scriptures together with the English translations of each document," p.405-43, and an alphabetical topical index. A
work of wide and precise scholarship useful to the general
reader for the interest of the selections and to the specialist for both selections and bibliographical apparatus.

CHRISTIAN RELIGION
General works
Bibliography

Allison, William Henry. History of Christianity.
(sec. 5 of A guide to historical literature, ed. by
G. M. Dutcher and others. N.Y., Macmillan,
1931. p.233-75. [V2]) **K12**

A useful annotated bibliography covering the basic
works on the history of the Christian religion and church,
including reference works and general and special histories.

Case, Shirley Jackson. Bibliographical guide to
the history of Christianity; comp. by S. J. Case,
J. T. McNeill, W. W. Sweet, W. Pauck, M. Spinka;
ed. by S. J. Case. Chic., Univ. of Chic. Pr.;
Camb., Univ. Pr., 1931. 265p. (University of
Chicago publications in religious education.
Handbooks of ethics and religion) **K13**

A selected annotated bibliography and useful handbook for the public library or for the student of church history in a college or theological seminary.

Heussi, Karl. Kompendium der Kirchengeschichte. 9. Aufl. Tübingen, Mohr, 1937. 520p. **K14**

New York (City). Union Theological Seminary. Library. Catalogue of the McAlpin collection of British history and theology; comp. and ed. by Charles Ripley Gillett. N.Y., 1927–30. 5v. **K15**

v.1-4, 1500-1700; v.5, Index.
A rich collection of material including many pamphlets on British theology and history.

Richardson, Ernest Cushing. An alphabetical subject index and index encyclopaedia of periodical articles on religion, 1890–1899. N.Y., Scribner, 1907–11. 2v. o.p. **K16**

Subject volume, 1907. 1168p.; author volume, 1911. 876p.
An index to 58,000 articles by 21,000 writers, in more than 600 periodicals and transactions in English and the principal foreign languages. The subject volume, arranged alphabetically, has a special feature not ordinarily found in indexes, i.e., each heading used is briefly defined and the definition is followed by a reference to some encyclopedia article. The author volume indexes the same articles as the subject volume, with equally full information.

Theologischer Jahresbericht, 1881–1913. Tübingen, Mohr, 1882–1916. v.1-33. **K17**

An important serial bibliography of books and periodical material; for the university, theological or large reference library. Discontinued after the outbreak of World War I.

Theologische Literaturzeitung, 1., 1876- . Leipzig, Hinrichs, 1876- . Biweekly. **K18**

—— Bibliographisches Beiblatt. Die theologische Literatur des Jahres 1922- . Leipzig, Hinrichs, 1922- . Biweekly, 1922–24; quarterly, 1925- . **K19**

A comprehensive survey of book and periodical material in many languages.

Encyclopedias

❦ For most questions asked by English-speaking readers the *Encyclopaedia of religion and ethics* (K1) and the *Schaff-Herzog* (K8) will be adequate. In the large reference library it will often be necessary to use some of the foreign works, especially for topics in foreign church history, foreign religious biography, etc. The most extended modern work of reference in the field of theology is the great French series now in course of publication under the general title *Encyclopédie des sciences religieuses,* composed of the following separate works: *Dictionnaire d'archéologie chrétienne* by Cabrol (K28); *Dictionnaire d'histoire et de géographie ecclésiastiques* by Baudril-

lart (K20); *Dictionnaire de théologie catholique* b Vacant and Mangenot (K184); *Dictionnaire de l Bible* by Vigouroux (K95); and *Dictionnaire du dro canonique* (L641a). These are listed separately un der their subjects. Parts of this series contain th finest material on the subject published in any lan guage and the work as a whole represents the highes level of French Catholic scholarship. The price the sets puts them beyond the reach of the small medium-sized library and the work is too special be of much use except in a theological library, large general reference library or a library whic specializes in medieval and ecclesiastical history an literature.

Baudrillart, Alfred. Dictionnaire d'histoire et géographie ecclésiastiques, commencé sous la d rection de Mgr. Alfred Baudrillart, continué p A. de Meyer et Et. van Cauwenbergh, avec concours d'un grand nombre de collaborateur Paris, Letouzey, 1912–38. v.1-10. il. 30fr. p fasc. (In progress) **K**

v.1-10, A-B.
Scope of the work covers all subjects in the history the Roman Catholic church, and other churches as th affect the Roman church, from the beginning of Chr tianity to the present time. The geographical mater includes separate articles on towns and other small di sions, past and present, indicating the connection of t place with ecclesiastical history, its present ecclesiastic status, a list of its religious institutions, and, in case it or has been an episcopal see, a list of the bishops, e There are biographical articles on all important a some minor names in the Roman Catholic church, me bers of other churches who have had any effect on t Roman church, all ecclesiastical and theological write saints in the Russian and other churches, ecclesiasti musicians, artists, etc. Signed articles, good biblic raphies.

Buchberger, Michael. Lexikon für Theologie u Kirche. 2. neuarb. Aufl. des Kirchlichen Han lexikons in Verbindung mit Fachgelehrten u mit Konrad Hofmann als Schriftleiter. Freibur Br., Herder, 1930–38. 10v. **K**

Short articles, signed with names in full, not init bibliographies. Many biographies. From the Ron Catholic point of view.

Christelijke encyclopaedie voor het nederla sche volk; samengesteld onder redactie van F. Grosheide, J. H. Landwehr, C. Lindeboom, J. Rullmann. Kampen, Kok [pref. 1925–31]. 6v. Fl. 11. per v. **K**

v.1-5, A-Z; v.6, Supplement, A-Z, p.1-469; Regis p.473-720.

Dictionnaire pratique des connaissances gieuses, publié sous la direction de J. Bric Paris, Letouzey, 1925–29. 6v. and suppl. 50

Contains signed articles, with some bibliography.

more compact dictionary, under different editorship, issued by the publisher of the great French religious dictionaries by Baudrillart, Cabrol, etc. (*see* p.124). Not a substitute for the larger works which are fundamental in libraries which can afford them. From the Roman Catholic point of view.

Enciclopedia ecclesiastica, pubblicata sotto la direzione dell' eccellenza Mons. Adriano Bernareggi. Milano, Vallardi; Torino, Marietti, 1942- . v.1- . il. (In progress) **K24**

An Italian Catholic encyclopedia which includes brief articles on all phases of religions, dogmas, rites, customs, philosophies, history, canon law, architecture, archaeology and art, etc., and a large amount of biography. Bibliographies at end of most articles.

Kirke-leksikon for Norden, udg. af Fredrik Nielsen [og J. O. Andersen]. København, Hagerup, 1900–29. 4v. Kr. 85. **K25**

Signed articles, little bibliography; includes many biographies.

Migne, Jacques Paul. Encyclopédie théologique. 1.-3. series. Dictionnaires sur toutes les parties de la science religieuse. Paris, Migne, 1844–66. 168v. in 171. o.p. **K26**

The various dictionaries in this set were unequal in value, some of them were uncritical even when new, and many of them are now entirely superseded by later and more scholarly works. They covered a wide field, however, included some subjects for which there are no comprehensive modern dictionaries (e.g., the *Dictionnaire des mystères*), and some of them contained a large amount of minor biography. Such dictionaries may still be useful even though they do not give the latest critical information. For complete contents *see* Paris, Bibl. Nat., *Catalogue général des livres imprimés*, v.114, col. 948-62 (A35) or Lorenz, *Catalogue général*, v.3 and 6 (A253).

Viller, Marcel. Dictionnaire de spiritualité, ascétique et mystique, doctrine et histoire, pub. sous la direction de Marcel Viller, assisté de F. Cavallera et J. de Guibert, avec le concours d'un grand nombre de collaborateurs. Paris, Beauchesne, 1932–38. fasc. 1-8. 20fr. per fasc. (In progress) **K27**

v.1, fasc. 1-6, A-B; v.2, fasc. 7-8, C-Chappuis.

Long signed articles with bibliographies and references to sources; includes many biographies.

CHRISTIAN ANTIQUITIES

Cabrol, Fernand. Dictionnaire d'archéologie chrétienne et de liturgie. Paris, Letouzey, 1907–48. v.1-14. il. 30fr. per fasc. (In progress) **K28**

v.1-14, A-Rome.

Excellent signed articles, with full bibliographies, on institutions, manners and customs of primitive Christianity, on the architecture, Christian art, inconography, symbols, epigraphy, paleography, numismatics, liturgy, rites and ceremonies of the early church to the time of Charlemagne. Covers about the same ground as Smith's *Dictionary of Christian antiquities* (K29) but with fuller and more up-to-date treatment. Excellent illustrations.

Smith, *Sir* William and **Cheetham, Samuel.** Dictionary of Christian antiquities. Lond., Murray; Bost., Little, 1876–80. 2v. il. **K29**

Treats subjects connected with the organization of the church, its officers, legislation, discipline and revenues, social life, ceremonials, church music, vestments, instruments, insignia, ecclesiastical architecture and art and their symbolism, sacred days, burial places, etc. Omits literature, sects, doctrines, heresies, etc., as such subjects are covered in the companion work *Dictionary of Christian biography* (K30). Covers period to the age of Charlemagne. Long signed articles; exact reference to many sources, bibliographies. Not abreast of modern scholarship but still useful on many points.

Smith, *Sir* William and **Wace, Henry.** Dictionary of Christian biography, literature, sects, and doctrines. Lond., Murray; Bost., Little, 1877–87. 4v. **K30**

A companion work to the *Dictionary of Christian antiquities* (K29).

Aims to supply an adequate account, based upon original authorities, of all persons connected with the church down to the age of Charlemagne about whom anything is known, of all literature connected with them, and of the controversies about doctrine and discipline in which they were engaged. Covers the whole church from the time of the Apostles to the age of Charlemagne but pays special attention to subjects and names in English, Scotch and Irish church history. Signed articles, bibliographies.

Wace, Henry and **Piercy, William C.** Dictionary of Christian biography and literature to the end of the sixth century. A.D., with an account of the principal sects and heresies. Lond., Murray; Bost., Little, 1911. 1028p. **K31**

A revised and abridged edition of Smith's *Dictionary of Christian biography* (K30). Adds later references but does not supersede Smith, which must still be used for long articles, for minor names and for subjects of the seventh and eighth centuries, as this new edition covers only the first six centuries.

Biography

Bie, J. P. de and **Loosjes, J.** Biographisch Woordenboek van protestantsche Godgeleerden in Nederland. 'sGravenhage, Nijhoff, 1896–1949. v.1-6[1] (In progress) **K32**

v.1-6, pt. 1 (Afl. 29), A-Linden.

Long biographical sketches with bibliographies of works both by and about.

Haag, Eugène and **Haag, Émile.** La France protestante; ou, Vies des protestants français qui sont fait un nom dans l'histoire. . . . Paris, Cherbuliez, 1846–59. 10v. **K33**

For description *see* S111.

Meusel, Karl. Kirchliches Handlexikon. In Verbindung mit einer Anzahl ev.-lutherischer Theologen. Leipzig, Naumann, 1887–1902. 7v. **K34**

Religious leaders of America; v.2, 1941–42, ed. by J. C. Schwarz. N.Y., Author, 1941. 1147p. $12.50. **K35**

Volume 1 had title *Who's who in the clergy*, 1935–36. This edition has been revised and enlarged. In some cases where more recent material was not obtained, reference is made to the first edition. Includes biographical sketches of Protestant, Catholic, and Jewish leaders.

Sprague, William Buell. Annals of the American pulpit; or, Commemorative notices of distinguished American clergymen of various denominations, from the early settlement of the country to the close of the year 1855. With historical introductions. N.Y., R. Carter, 1857–[69]. 9v. il. o.p. **K36**

v.1-2, Trinitarian Congregational; v.3-4, Presbyterian; v.5, Episcopalian; v.6, Baptist; v.7, Methodist; v.8, Unitarian Congregational; v.9, Lutheran. Reformed Dutch. Associate. Associate Reformed. Reformed Presbyterian.

Creeds

Schaff, Philip. Bibliotheca symbolica ecclesiae universalis. The creeds of Christendom; with a history and critical notes. 4th enl. ed. N.Y., Harper, 1890 [c77]. 3v. o.p. **K37**

v.1, History of creeds, church by church, with many bibliographical references; v.2, Creeds of the Greek and Latin churches, giving for each the full Greek or Latin text and an English translation in parallel columns, with an index of subjects; v.3, Creeds of the Evangelical Protestant churches, in language of original with parallel English translations, index of subjects.

Church history and expansion

History

American church history series, consisting of a series of denominational histories published under the auspices of the American Society of Church History; general editors: Philip Schaff, H. C. Potter, S. M. Jackson. N.Y., Christian Lit. Co. (Scribner), 1893–97. 13v. o.p. **K38**

Now much out of date but still occasionally useful. Consists of separate histories of major denominations by various authors. Includes a bibliography of American church history, 1820–1893, in volume 12.

Ekklesia; eine Sammlung von Selbstdarstellungen der christlichen Kirchen. Gotha, Klotz, 1934–39. v.1-5,10 (incompl.). (In progress) **K39**

Edited by Friedrich Siegmund-Schultze.
Contents: Bd.1, Die Britischen Länder. 1. Lfg., Die Kirche von England. 1934; Bd.2, Die skandinavischen Länder. 5. Lfg. Die Kirche in Schweden. 1935; 6. Lfg. . . . in Norwegen. 1936; 7. Lfg. . . . in Dänemark . . . in Island. 1937; 8. Lfg. . . . in Finland. 1938; Bd.3, Die mitteleuropäischen Länder. 9. Lfg. Die evangelischen Kirchen der Niederlande. 1934; 10. Lfg. Die evangelischen Kirchen der Schweiz. 1935; 11. Lfg. Die alt-

katolische Kirche. 1935; Bd.4, Deutschsprachige Länder. 14. Lfg. Die evangelische Kirche in Österreich. 1935; Bd.5, Die osteuropäischen Länder. 20. Lfg. Die Kirchen der Tschechoslowakei. 1937; 21. Lfg. Die evangelischen Kirchen in Polen. 1938; Bd.10, Die orthodoxe Kirche auf dem Balkan und in Vorderasian. 45. Lfg., Geschichte, Lehre und Verfassung der orthodoxen Kirche. 1939.

Latourette, Kenneth Scott. A history of the expansion of Christianity. N.Y., Harper, 1937–45. 7v. maps. $22.50. **K40**

Bibliography in each volume.
Covers from the earliest times to the present.

Schaff, Philip. History of the Christian church. N.Y., Scribner, 1889–1910. 7v. in 8. il. o.p. **K41**

Sweet, William Warren. Religion on the American frontier. A collection of source material. Chic., Univ. of Chic. Pr., 1931–46. v1-4. il. (In progress) **K42**

Pub. varies.
Contents: [v.1.] The Baptists, 1783–1830. 1931; v.2, The Presbyterians, 1783–1840. 1936; v.3, The Congregationalists, 1783–1850. 1939; v.4, The Methodists, 1783–1840. 1946.
Each volume includes bibliography.

Walker, Williston. A history of the Christian church. N.Y., Scribner, 1945. 624p. $4.50. **K43**

Reprint of 1918 edition. A useful one-volume history.

SOURCE BOOKS

Gee, Henry and **Hardy, William John.** Documents illustrative of English church history, comp. from original sources. Lond., Macmillan, 1896. 670p. **K44**

Covers 314 to 1700.

Kidd, Beresford James. Documents illustrative of the history of the church. Lond., Soc. for Promoting Christian Knowledge; N.Y., Macmillan, 1920–41. v.1-3. 8s. 6d. ea. **K45**

Contents: v.1, To A.D. 313; v.2, 313–461; v.3, c.500–1500.

Missions

Parker, Joseph I. Directory of world missions. Missionary boards, societies, colleges, cooperative councils, and other agencies related to the Protestant churches of the world. N.Y., Lond., International Missionary Council, 1938. 255p. $2. **K46**

—— Interpretative statistical survey of the world mission of the Christian Church. Summary and detailed statistics of churches and missionary societies, interpretative articles, and indices. N.Y., Lond., International Missionary Council, 1938. 323p. **K47**

Grubb, Kenneth, G. and **Bingle, E. J.** World Christian handbook. Lond., World Dominion Pr., 1949. 405p. 21s.; $7.50. **K48**

Limited in scope. Includes general survey articles on each country or area with statistics.

Institute of Social and Religious Research. World missionary atlas. . . . Ed. by H. P. Beach, C. H. Fahs. Maps by John Bartholomew. N.Y., Inst. of Soc. and Rel. Research, 1925. 251p. 29 col. maps. tables. 37cm. **K49**

pt.1, Directory of missionary societies; pt.2, Statistics of Protestant missions; pt.3, Maps; pt.4, General descriptive notes about mission lands, their population, races, economic and cultural conditions, etc.; Indices.

Now much out of date, but still valuable for its maps.

Streit, Robert. Bibliotheca missionum. . . . Münster i. Westfalen, Aachen, Franziskus Xaverius Missionsverein Zentrale, 1916–39. v.1-11. (Veröffentlichungen des Internationalen Instituts für Missionswissenschaftliche Forschung) **K50**

Imprint varies.

v.1, Grundlegender und allgemeiner Teil; v.2, Amerikanische Missionsliteratur, 1493–1699; v.3, Amerikanische Missionsliteratur, 1700–1909; v.4, Asiatische Missionsliteratur, 1245–1599; v.5, Asiatische Missionsliteratur, 1600–1699; v.6, Missionsliteratur Indiens, der Philippinen, Japans und Indochinas, 1700–1799; v.7, Chinesische Missionsliteratur, 1700–1799; v.8, Missionsliteratur Indiens und Indonesiens, 1800–1909; v.9, Missionsliteratur der Philippinen, 1800–1909; v.10, Missionsliteratur Japans und Koreas, 1800–1909; v.11, Missionsliteratur Indochinas, 1800–1909.

Includes voyages, relations, official documents, etc. Gives full bibliographical details, critical estimates, annotations, reference to sources, and in many cases location of copies in European libraries.

Statistics

U. S. Bureau of the Census. Religious bodies: 1936. Wash., Govt. Prt. Off., 1941. 3v. $3.50. **K51**

v.1, Summary and detailed tables; v.2-3, Separate denominations: statistics, history, doctrine, organization, and work.

Statistics given are, as nearly as possible, those for the year 1936, and cover membership, church edifices and parsonages, value of church property and debt on same, expenditures, and Sunday schools. Is limited to the continental United States and does not include the outlying territories or the American churches abroad.

Census taken every ten years, previous full reports covered 1906, 1916, and 1926.

Hymnology

Analecta hymnica medii aevi, hrsg. von Guido Maria Dreves und Clemens Blume. Leipzig, Reisland, 1888–1922. v.1-55. **K52**

A very comprehensive collection, giving texts of hymns and detailed historical and bibliographical notes.

Chevalier, Cyr Ulysse Joseph. Repertorium hymnologicum. Catalogue des chants, hymnes, proses, séquences, tropes en usage dans l'église latine depuis les origines jusqu'à nos jours. Louvain et Bruxelles, Soc. des Bollandistes, 1892–1920. 6v. **K53**

Published in parts as a separately paged supplement to the *Analecta bollandiana,* 1889–1920 (K208).

For each hymn gives *incipit,* saint or feast of the church to which the hymn belongs and its place in the office, number of strophes, author's name, date of composition if known and reference to manuscripts or printed sources in which the hymn is found.

Julian, John. Dictionary of hymnology setting forth the origin and history of Christian hymns of all ages and nations. Rev. ed. Lond., Murray; N.Y., Scribner, 1907. 1768p. o.p. **K54**

First edition, 1892; the revised edition corrects some typographical errors and adds a new supplement of 131 pages to cover later information, and new indexes.

Contents: (1) Dictionary; (2) Cross reference index to first lines in English, French, German, Greek, Latin, etc.; (3) Index of authors, translators, etc.; (4) Appendix, A-Z, late articles; (5) Appendix, A-Z, additions and corrections to articles in main part; (6) New supplement; (7) Indexes to appendixes and supplement.

Deals with Christian hymns of all ages and nations, with special reference to those in the hymn books of English-speaking countries. Articles on subjects in hymnology, hymn writers and separate hymns, all in one alphabet; important subjects treated at considerable length; signed articles, bibliographies.

Mearns, James. Early Latin hymnaries; an index of hymns in hymnaries before 1100, with an appendix from later sources. Camb., Univ. Pr., 1913. 107p. **K55**

Indexes some hymns not indexed in Chevalier (K53) or included in the *Analecta* (K52).

Bible

❧ While the Bible itself is not a reference book in the ordinary sense of the word, at least one copy or edition will be needed in even the small reference collection. Others should be acquired according to need. The first to be purchased should be a good parallel text edition of the **Authorized,** or **King James version,** and the **Revised version:** a good edition is the *Oxford parallel Bible,* (Ox., Univ. Pr.; N.Y., Nelson, 18s 6d.; $4.50) **K56;** and an edition of the **American revised** (1901) which differs on some points from the English revision printed in the parallel edition (Nelson, v.p. $1-$3.25) **K57.** A new **Revised standard version** by a group of scholars is now in preparation, the Old Testament will soon be ready, the New Testament was published by Nelson in 1946 ($.50-$15) **K58.**

To these should be added a copy of the **Douay Bible,** the authorized Catholic translation from the

Latin Vulgate, the latest version being the Confraternity edition published by the Catholic Book Publishing Co., 1949, **K59** (the Old Testament in the Douay version with modernized spelling; the New Testament in the Challoner-Rheims version edited by Catholic scholars under the patronage of the Confraternity of Christian Doctrine; and the Psalms in a new translation from the new Latin Psalter authorized by Pope Pius XII in 1945). Larger libraries will need copies of the **Latin Vulgate,** New historical edition, edited by Cardinal Gasquet, now in progress (Rome, Vatican, 1926-) **K60;** or a good practical edition edited by P. M. Hetzenauer (Oeniponte, 1906) **K61;** and of the **Greek text,** of which a good edition is edited by Alfred Rahlfs (Stuttgart, 1935. 2v.) **K62.**

A convenient collection of various English translations of the New Testament is the *English hexapla*, exhibiting the six important translations, Wiclif 1380, Tyndale 1534, Cranmer 1539, Genevan 1557, Anglo-Rhenish 1582, Authorized 1611, and the original Greek text (Lond., Bagster, o.p.) **K63.**

A good reference edition of the English translation of the Old Testament used by Jews is published by the Jewish Publication Soc. (Phila. $1.25) **K64.**

Among many good modern translations the following are particularly notable: the translation by James Moffatt (N.Y., Harper, 1926. $3.75 up) **K65;** the American translation (Univ. of Chicago Pr., 1939. $4 up) **K66** (The Old Testament translated by J. M. Powis Smith, the Apocrypha and New Testament translated by Edgar J. Goodspeed. The New Testament is also published separately.)

Bibliography

British and Foreign Bible Society. Historical catalogue of the printed editions of Holy Scripture in the library of the society. Comp. by T. H. Darlow and H. F. Moule. Lond., Bible House, 1903–11. 2v. in 4. **K67**

v.1, English; v.2, Polyglots and languages other than English: pt.1, Polyglots; Acawoio to Grebo; pt.2, Greek to Opa; pt.3, Ora to Zulu; Indexes.

Rumball-Petre, Edwin A. America's first Bibles, with a census of 555 extant Bibles. Portland, Maine, Southworth-Anthoensen Pr., 1940. 184p. $4. **K68**

New Testament literature; an annotated bibliography, v.1- ed. by William Nelson Lyons and Merrill M. Parvis. Chic., Univ. of Chic. Pr., 1948- . v.1- . $4. **K69**

Volume 1 covers 1943–45 and continues the series of annual bibliographies published by the New Testament Club of the University of Chicago under the title *New Testament literature* in 1940, 1941, 1942.

A comprehensive bibliography of books and periodical articles, with annotations and references to reviews. Prices are given for the books listed.

North, Eric McCoy. The book of a thousand tongues; being some account of the translation and publication of all or part of the Holy Scriptures into more than a thousand languages and dialects with over 1100 examples from the text. Pub. for the American Bible Soc., N.Y., Harper, 1938. 386p. il. **K70**

Descriptive notes and facsimiles of extracts from the printed Bibles in over a thousand languages. Particularly useful for identifying Bibles in varying tongues including many versions in English. Includes chronological lists of the languages in which the Bible has been published in whole or in part.

Princeton theological seminary. Library. A bibliography of Bible study for theological students. Princeton, N.J., Seminary, 1948. 85p. (Princeton Seminary pamphlets, no.1) 85c. **K71**

A useful classified list restricted to books in the English language except for original texts, dictionaries, grammars, etc. Lists editions of the Bible, dictionaries, commentaries, etc., and works on the individual books of the Bible. Also background works on the history and religion of the Hebrews, New Testament history, the early church, etc., and linguistic aids.

Concordances

Cruden, Alexander. Complete concordance to the Old and New Testament . . . with . . . a concordance to the Apocrypha. . . . Lond., Warne [pref. 1737]. 719p. 10s. 6d. (Winston, $3) **K72**

1st ed. 1737. Frequently reprinted.

Contents: (1) Common words; (2) Proper names; (3) Apocryphal books.

A well-known older concordance, issued in various editions by different publishers. Not complete, and now superseded as far as the canonical books are concerned by the later concordances noted below, but still useful for its concordance to the Apocrypha. Some modern reprints omit the Apocrypha.

Gant, William John. The Moffatt Bible concordance; a complete concordance to: The Bible, a new translation by James Moffatt. N.Y., Harper, 1950. 550p. $5. **K72a**

Also published in London by Hodder and Stoughton with title: *Concordance of the Bible in the Moffatt translation.*

Hazard, Marshall Custis. Complete concordance to the American standard version of the Holy Bible. N.Y., Nelson, 1932. 1234p. **K73**

Joy, Charles Rhind. Harper's Topical concordance. N.Y., Lond., Harper, 1940. 478p. $3.50 **K74**

Some 25,000 texts arranged under topics.

The Oxford cyclopedic concordance, containing new and selected helps to the study of the Bible, including summaries of the books of the Bible, all being arranged in one alphabetical order. . . . Lond., Oxford Univ. Pr., 1947. 370p. il. $2.50. **K75**

Strong, James. Exhaustive concordance of the Bible. Lond., Hodder; N.Y., Hunt, 1894 [c'90]. 1340 + 262 + 126 + 79p. **K76**

Frequently reprinted.
N.Y., Abingdon-Cokesbury Pr., $8.75.
The most complete concordance, giving every word of the text of the common English version and a comparative concordance of the authorized and revised versions, with brief dictionaries of the Hebrew and Greek words of the original, with references to the English texts. Forty-seven very common words are cited in the appendix by reference only and are not given in the main concordance.

Thompson, Newton Wayland and **Stock, Raymond.** Complete concordance to the Bible (Douay version). St. Louis, Lond., Herder, 1945. 1914p. $10. **K77**

First published in 1942 under title: *Concordance to the Bible (Douay version).*
This edition is much enlarged with many additional words and additional references to words included in the first edition.

Thompson, Newton Wayland. Verbal concordance to the New Testament (Rheims version). Balt., Murphy, 1928. 394p. $4. **K78**

Young, Robert. Analytical concordance to the Bible . . . about 311,000 references, subdivided under the Hebrew and Greek originals with the literal meaning and pronunciation of each . . . index lexicons to the Old and New Testaments . . . and a complete list of Scripture proper names. 7th ed. rev. throughout by W. B. Stevenson. Edinburgh, Young; N.Y., Funk [1902]. v.p. $10. **K79**

1st ed. 1879; rev. ed., rev. by W. B. Stevenson, 1902; editions of later date are reprints of this.

The following concordances to the Latin, Greek and Hebrew texts are useful in the large reference library:

Bechis, Michael. Repertorium biblicum, seu totius Sacrae Scripturae concordantiae juxta vulgatae editionis exemplar. Augustae Taurinorum, in Officina Salesiana, 1899. 2v. **K80**

Büchner, Gottfried. Hand-Konkordanz. Biblische real-und-verbal Konkordanz . . . durchgesehen und verb. von H. L. Heubner. 28 Aufl. Leipzig, Heinsius, 1922. 1148p. **K81**

Hatch, Edwin and **Redpath, H. A.** Concordance to the Septuagint and the other Greek versions of the Old Testament (including the Apocryphal books). Ox., Clarendon Pr., 1897–1906. 2v. and suppl. 200s; $65. **K82**

Mandelkern, Solomon. Veteris Testamenti concordantiae hebraicae atque chaldaicae, quibus continentur cuncta quae in prioribus concordantiis reperiuntur vocabula, lacunis omnibus expletis, emendatis cuiusquemodi vitiis, locis ubique denuo excerptis atque in meliorem forman redactis, vocalibus interdum adscriptis, particulae omnes adhuc nondum collatae, pronomina omnia hic primum congesta atque enarrata, nomina propria omnia separatim commemorata, servato textu masoretico librorumque sacrorum ordine tradito. Editio altera locupletissime aucta et emendata. Berlin, Margolin, 1937. 1532, 16p. **K83**

Hebrew and Latin.

Moulton, William Fiddian and **Geden, A. S.** Concordance to the Greek Testament, according to the texts of Westcott and Hort, Tischendorf and the English revisers. 3d ed. Edinburgh, Clark; N.Y., Scribner, 1926. 1033p. **K84**

Quotations

Stevenson, Burton. The Home book of Bible quotations. N.Y., Harper, 1949. 645p. $6. **K85**

The quotations are arranged under subject with many cross references and there is a word concordance index to the whole. Based on the King James version, with a few references to variations in the Revised version. Includes the Apocryphas of both the Old and the New Testaments. Exact citation is given to book, chapter and verse.

Dictionaries

Cheyne, Thomas Kelly and **Black, J. S.** Encyclopaedia biblica; a critical dictionary of the literary, political, and religious history, the archaeology, geography, and natural history of the Bible. N.Y., Macmillan, 1899–1903. 4v. il. **K86**

Reprinted in one volume on India paper, with rectification of some typographical errors, 1914.
Signed articles by specialists, with bibliographies. Prepared with the cooperation of many foreign scholars, primarily for the scholar and professional Bible student. Standpoint is that of the advanced higher criticism.

Davis, John D. The Westminster dictionary of the Bible . . . rev. and rewritten, by Henry Snyder Gehman. . . . Phila., Westminster Pr., 1944. 658p. il. (Westminster aids to the study of the Scriptures) $3.50. **K87**

Previously published under title: *A dictionary of the Bible.*
A scholarly one-volume dictionary of the Bible, conservative in interpretation. Good maps. Indicates pronunciation.

Hastings, James. Dictionary of the Bible, dealing with its language, literature, and contents, including biblical theology. Edinburgh, Clark; N.Y., Scribner, 1898–1904. 5v. il. **K88**

Volume 5 is an "extra" volume, containing indexes, maps and some articles not alphabetically arranged.

Signed articles, bibliographies. From a less advanced point of view than *Cheyne* (K86) and intended for use by the general reader as well as the professional Bible student.

—— Dictionary of the Bible, ed. by James Hastings, with the cooperation of J. A. Selbie, and with the assistance of J. C. Lambert and of Shailer Mathews. Edinburgh, Clark; N.Y., Scribner, 1909. 992p. 24s.; $10. **K89**

Good one-volume dictionary; an independent work, not a condensation of Hastings' larger work. Frequently reprinted.

—— Dictionary of Christ and the gospels. N.Y., Scribner; Edinburgh, Clark, 1906–08. 2v. **K90**

Complementary to Hastings' *Dictionary of the Bible* (K88). Purpose is to give an account of (1) everything relating to the person, life, work, and teaching of Christ, whether found in the Gospels or elsewhere, and (2) everything contained in the Gospels. Planned especially for preachers; most of the articles written by men who are or have been preachers. Signed articles; bibliographies.

—— Dictionary of the Apostolic church. N.Y., Scribner; Edinburgh, Clark, 1916. 2v. **K91**

A continuation of his *Dictionary of Christ and the Gospels* (K90), doing for the rest of the New Testament what that did for the Gospels.

International standard Bible encyclopedia; James Orr, general editor; J. L. Nuelsen, E. Y. Mullins, assistant editors. [rev. ed.] Chic., Howard-Severance, 1930. 5v. il. $39.50. **K92**

Represents the conservative point of view and useful, therefore, for readers for whom Hastings (K88) and Cheyne (K86) are too advanced.

Jacobus, Melancthon Williams, Lane, E. C. and **Zenos, A. C.** New standard Bible dictionary, designed as a comprehensive help to the study of the Scriptures, their languages, literary problems, history, biography, manners and customs, and their religious teachings. 3d rev. ed. N.Y. and Lond., Funk, 1936. 965p. il. (Repr. 1948. $6) **K93**

1st ed., 1909, had title *Standard Bible dictionary*.

Miller, Madeleine Sweeny and **Miller, John Lane.** Encyclopedia of Bible life. [3d ed.] N.Y., Harper, 1944. 493 (i.e., 497)p. il. $4.95. **K94**

Arranged by chapters under such headings as agriculture, archeology, arts and crafts, geography, homes, professions and trades, social structures, worship, etc., with Bible references and bibliography for each chapter. Includes maps, many illustrations, index of Biblical quotations and general index. A useful work but must be watched for small inaccuracies.

Vigouroux, Fulcram Grégoire and **Pirot, Louis.** Dictionnaire de la Bible, contenant tous les noms de personnes, de lieux, de plantes, d'animaux mentionnés dans les Saintes Écritures, les questions théologiques, archéologiques, scientifiques relatives à l'Ancien et au Nouveau Testament et des notices sur les commentateurs anciens et modernes. Paris, Letouzey, 1907–50. 5v. and supp. v.1-5[1]. il. (In progress) **K95**

v.1-5, A-Z, 1907–12; Supplement, ed. by Louis Pirot, v.1-5[1], A-Langdon, 1928–50.

The standard Bible dictionary from the French Catholic point of view, containing long signed articles by Catholic scholars, good bibliographies and excellent illustrations. Differs from Hastings' *Dictionary of the Bible* (K88) and the *Encyclopaedia biblica* (K86) in several points, notably in the inclusion of separate biographical articles, with bibliographies, on the various commentators on the Bible, ancient and modern, Catholic, Protestant and Jewish.

Commentaries

Cambridge Bible for schools and colleges. General editors: A. F. Kirkpatrick, A. Nairne, R. St. J. Parry. Camb., Univ. Pr.; N.Y., Macmillan, 1895–1922. 58v. maps. Price per v. varies, 60c-$1.90 ea. **K96**

Some volumes issued in revised editions.

Eiselen, Frederick Carl, Lewis, Edwin and **Downey, D. G.** Abingdon Bible commentary. N.Y., Abingdon Pr., 1929. 1452p. maps. $7.50. **K97**

Nicoll, *Sir* **William Robertson** (Claudius Clear, *pseud.*) Expositor's Bible; a complete exposition of the Bible, with index, with a general introduction and a brief biographical and literary introduction to each book of the Bible, by Oscar L. Joseph. Grand Rapids, Mich., Eerdmans, 1943. 6v. $25. **K98**

New edition. Originally published 1892–1905. 50v.

Gore, Charles, Goudge, H. L. and **Guillaume, Alfred.** New commentary on Holy Scripture, including the Apocrypha. Lond., S.P.C.K.; N.Y., Macmillan, 1928. 697p., 158p., 743p. 16s.; $6.50. **K99**

International critical commentary on the Holy Scriptures, under the editorship of the Rev. Samuel Rolles Driver, the Rev. Alfred Plummer and the Rev. Charles Augustus Briggs. Edinburgh, Clark; N.Y., Scribner, 1896–1937. v.1-40. 12s.-20s. per v.; $3.50-$9 per v. **K100**

Commentaries on individual books of the Bible, each by an authority.

Peake, Arthur Samuel. Commentary on the Bible, with the assistance for the New Testament of A. J. Grieve. Lond., Jack; N. Y., Nelson, 1919. 1014p. maps. 12s. 6d.; $7.50. **K101**

——— ——— Supplement, ed. by A. J. Grieve. 1936. 38p. 2s.

The supplement includes surveys of the literature published between 1919 and 1936, many of them by specialists.

Westminster commentaries, ed. by Walter Lock. Lond., Methuen, 1907–1927. 15v. maps. 6s.-21s. per v. **K102**

Atlases

Rand McNally historical atlas of the Holy Land. N.Y., Chic., Rand McNally, 1938. 32p. incl. 55 col. maps. 30cm. $1. **K103**

Smith, George Adam. Atlas of the historical geography of the Holy land. Lond., Hodder, 1915. 60p., 12p. 57 col. maps. 38cm. **K104**

Wright, George Ernest and **Filson, Floyd Vivian.** Westminster historical atlas of the Bible. Phila., Westminster Pr., 1945. 114p. il. 40cm. (Westminster aids to the study of the Scriptures) $4. **K105**

Good maps accompanied by historical discussion and illustrations.

Protestant denominations

Wright, Charles Henry Hamilton and **Neil, Charles.** Protestant dictionary containing articles on the history, doctrines and practices of the Christian church. New ed., ed. by Charles Sydney Carter and G. E. Alison Weeks. Lond., Harrison Trust, 1933. 805p. il. 31s. 6d. **K106**

1st ed. 1904.

Includes signed articles on the tenets of Protestantism in contrast to Roman Catholicism.

Annuaire protestant, 1880- , renseignements relatifs aux églises et aux oeuvres du Protestantisme de langue française. Paris, Fischbacher, 1880- . v.1- . Annual. **K107**

Directory and institutional information; no biography.

Yearbook of American churches, 1932- . Issued under the auspices of the Federal Council of the Churches of Christ in America. Lebanon, Pa., Sowers Pr. Co., 1933- . Biennial. (1947, $3.50) **K108**

Title and publisher vary.

Continues an earlier work the title of which varied: v.1-2, *Federal Council year book;* v.3-8, *Year book of the churches;* v.9 (1927), *Handbook of the churches.* This work has a somewhat wider scope, as it now covers all Protestant organizations and activities.

Usually contains biographical section.

Palmer, Gordon. A manual of church services; with a summary of state laws governing marriage. N.Y., Revell, 1947. 164p. $2.25. **K109**

Baptist

Starr, Edward Caryl. A Baptist bibliography, being a register of printed material by and about Baptists; including works written against the Baptists. Phila., Judson Pr., 1947- . [v.1-] $2.50. **K110**

Published for the Samuel Colgate Baptist Historical Collection, Colgate University, Hamilton, N.Y.

Arranged alphabetically by authors, the first volume covers the letter A and includes a title index. Locates copies.

Whitley, William Thomas. Baptist bibliography; being a register of the chief materials for Baptist history, whether in manuscript or in print, preserved in Great Britain, Ireland, and the Colonies . . . comp. for the Baptist Union of Great Britain and Ireland. Lond., Kingsgate Pr., 1916–22. 2v. 42s.; $4.50. **K111**

v.1, 1526–1776; v.2, 1777–1837; Addenda, 1613–53; Indexes: (1) Anonymous pamphlets, (2) Authors, (3) Places, (4) Subjects.

Locates copies in 31 libraries, mainly British.

Baptist handbook for 1860- . Lond., Baptist Union Pub. Dept., 1860- . il. Annual (slightly irregular). (1948, 10s. 6d) **K112**

Imprint and title vary. Preceded by: *Baptist manual* (Lond., Houlston and G. Stoneman, 1845–1859).

General directory information. Ministerial list gives brief biographies.

Baptist who's who, an authoritative reference work and guide to the careers of ministers and lay officials of the Baptist churches. . . . Lond., Shaw Pub. Co. in conjunction with Kingsgate Pr., 1933. 195p. 10s. **K113**

Contents: Historical and statistical material, p.19-27; Biographies: Ministers of the Baptist churches of Great Britain and Ireland, p.31-83; Lay officials, p.84-195.

Northern Baptist Convention. Yearbook, 1941- . Phila., Amer. Baptist Pub. Soc., 1941- . il. Annual. (1948, $1.25) **K114**

Combining its *Annual* and the *American Baptist year book.*

Includes minutes of the annual conventions, historical documents and tables; directories of councils and committees; cooperating, affiliated and associated organizations; and churches, ministers, and missionaries.

Southern Baptist handbook; prepared by Dept. of Survey, Statistics, and Information. Porter Routh, Sec'y. Nashville, Tenn., Sunday School Board of the Southern Baptist Convention, 1921- . **K115**

Statistical and directory information.

Church of England

Crockford's Clerical Directory, with which is incorporated the Clergy list, clerical guide and ecclesiastical directory, being a statistical book of reference for facts relating to the clergy and the church, 1858- . Ox., Univ. Pr., 1858- . v.1- . il. Annual. (1948, £4 4s.) **K116**

Includes biographical sketches for Church of England clergy in the British Isles and overseas, as well as statistical and directory information.

LeNeve, John. Fasti Ecclesiae anglicanae; or, A calendar of the principal ecclesiastical dignitaries in England and Wales, and of the chief officers in the Universities of Oxford and Cambridge, from the earliest time to the year MDCCXV . . . corrected and continued to the present time by T. Duffus Hardy. Ox., Univ. Pr., 1854. 3v. **K117**

Official year book of the National Assembly of the Church of England, 1883- . Lond., S.P.C.K., 1883- . Annual. (1948, 12s. 6d.) **K118**

Title varies.
General directory information. Gives brief biographies of members of the church assembly.

HISTORY

History of the English church, ed. by W. R. W. Stephens and William Hunt. Lond., Macmillan, 1899–1910. 8v. in 9. 8s. 6d. per v. **K119**

Covers from the Norman conquest to 1890.

Ollard, Sidney Leslie, Crosse, Gordon and **Bond, M. F.** Dictionary of English church history. [3d ed. rev.] Lond., Mowbray; N.Y., Morehouse, 1948. 698p. 25s. **K120**

1st ed. 1912; 2d ed. 1919.
Scope of this work is strictly that of the English Church, i.e., the provinces of Canterbury and York, and does not include discussion of the church in Ireland, Scotland or America. Good signed articles with brief bibliographies (usually undated) on history, beliefs, controversies, architecture, costume, music, etc., of the Church. Many biographies of persons deceased. A special feature is the list of bishops under the name of each see. High Church point of view.
The third edition has been quite thoroughly revised, with some new articles and rewriting of others. The diocesan histories have been brought up to date.

RITUAL

Church of England. Book of Common Prayer. The Book of common prayer and administration of the sacraments, and other rites and ceremonies of the Church according to the use of the Church of England. . . . Ox. Univ. Pr. **K121**

For editions *see* current issues of *Oxford Bible catalogue* of the Oxford University Press.

—— Annotated Book of common prayer, being an historical, ritual and theological commentary on the devotional system of the Church of England by John Henry Blunt. New impression, 1899, reissue, with additions and corrections. Lond., Longmans, 1903. [pref. 1883] 732p. **K122**

Benton, Josiah Henry. Book of common prayer and books connected with its origin and growth; catalogue of the collection of Josiah Henry Benton . . . 3d ed. prepared by William Muss-Arnolt. Bost., priv. pr., 1914. 142p. **K123**

Harford, George and **Stevenson, Morley.** The Prayer book dictionary. Lond., Pitman, 1912. 832p. **K124**

Treats principally the English prayer book, and contains slight information about the prayer book of the Protestant Episcopal church.

Morison, Stanley. English prayer books; an introduction to the literature of Christian public worship. Camb., Univ. Pr.; N.Y., Macmillan, 1943. 143p. 7s. 6d.; $1.75. **K125**

An historical and bibliographical account of English prayer books.

Muss-Arnolt, William. Book of common prayer among the nations of the world; a history of translations of the prayer book of the Church of England and of the Protestant Episcopal church of America, a study based mainly on the collection of Josiah Henry Benton. Lond., S.P.C.K., 1914. 473p. **K126**

Church of England in Canada

Year book and clergy list of the Church of England in the Dominion of Canada. Toronto, General Synod of the Church of England in Canada, [1915?-]. Irregular. $1. **K127**

Church of Ireland

Phillips, Walter Alison. History of the Church of Ireland, from the earliest times to the present day. Ox., Univ. Pr., 1933–34. 3v. 31s. 6d.; $10. **K128**

Church of Scotland

Church of Scotland year-book, 1886- . Edinburgh, pub. by the Church of Scotland Committee on Publications, 1886- . v.1- . (1948, 5s.) **K129**

Title and imprint vary.
Historical, directory and statistical information.

Macgregor, Malcolm B. The sources and literature of Scottish church history. Glasgow, Mc-Callum, 1934. 260p.   **K130**

A bibliography of sources and secondary materials. Includes biographical sketches of outstanding persons in Scottish religious history from the earliest times to the present.

Scott, Hew. Fasti ecclesiae scoticanae; the succession of ministers in the Church of Scotland from the Reformation. New ed., rev. and continued to the present time under the superintendence of a committee appointed by the General Assembly. Edinburgh, Oliver and Boyd, 1915–28. 7v.   **K131**

1st ed. 1866–71, 3v. in 6.

Gives a brief historical sketch of each parish and a concise biography of each minister with a list of his writings and bibliographical references where such are available. Each volume has a bibliography of local and parish histories. Number of biographies is more than 15,000.

Congregational

Dexter, Henry Martyn. The Congregationalism of the last 300 years, as seen in its literature . . . with a bibliographical appendix. N.Y., Harper, 1880. 716p., 326p.   **K132**

Includes: Collections toward a bibliography of Congregationalism. 326p. 7250 entries.

Peel, Albert. The Congregational two hundred, 1530–1948. Lond., Independent Pr., 1948. 288p. 10s. 6d.   **K133**

Incorporates *A hundred eminent Congregationalists,* 1927.

Biographical sketches of 200 outstanding Congregationalists in England and America.

Who's who in Congregationalism; an authoritative reference work and guide to the careers of ministers and lay officials of the Congregational churches. Lond., Shaw Pub. Co. in conjunction with Independent Pr., 1933. 217p. 10s.   **K134**

Historical and statistical material, p.17-27; Biographies: Ministers and evangelists of the Congregational churches of Great Britain and Ireland, p.31-96; Lay pastors, p.96-217.

Congregational year-book, 1846- . Lond., Congregational Union, 1847- . v.1- . il. Annual. (1948, 15s.)   **K135**

Contains the annual proceedings of the Congregational Union, statistics, list of ministers with brief biographical data, and fuller biographies of deceased ministers.

Yearbook of the Congregational Christian churches of the United States of America, 1879- . N.Y., General Council of the Congregational and Christian churches, 1879- . v.1- . Annual. (1947, $1.50)   **K136**

Imprint varies, title varies. After the union of the Congregational and Christian churches the yearbooks of the two denominations were combined and the volume numbering of both has been continued on the title page, i.e., since 1929 the *Yearbook of the Congregational Christian churches* has formed volume 52- of the *Congregational year-book* and volume 58- of the *Christian annual.*

Disciples of Christ

Disciples of Christ. Year book . . . of . . . organizations of Disciples of Christ, 1920/21- . Indianapolis, Ind., International Convention of Disciples of Christ, 1921- . Annual (1946/47, $2.50)   **K137**

Directory and statistical information.

Spencer, Claude Elbert. An author catalog of Disciples of Christ and related religious groups. Canton, Mo., Disciples of Christ Hist. Soc., 1946. 367p. $7.50.   **K138**

Evangelical and Reformed

Evangelical and Reformed Church. Yearbook and almanac, 1864- . Phila., Board of Christian Educ. of the Reformed church in the U.S., 1864- . v.1- . il.   **K139**

Title varies.

Directory and statistical information; obituary notices with portraits.

Year book of the Evangelical church, 1923- . Harrisburg, Pa., Evangelical Pub. House, 1923- . (1945, 35c)   **K140**

Directory, historical and statistical information; biographies, i.e., obituaries, portraits.

Friends

Friends, Society of. World Committee for Consultation. Handbook of the Religious Society of Friends. Lond., Phila., Friends World Committee for Consultation, 1941. 113p.   **K141**

Quaker records; being an index to The Annual monitor, 1813–92, containing over 20,000 obituary notices of members of the Society of Friends, alphabetically and chronologically arranged. Ed. by Joseph J. Green. Lond., Hicks, 1894. 458p.   **K142**

Smith, Joseph. Bibliotheca anti-Quakeriana; or, A catalogue of books adverse to the Society of Friends, alphabetically arranged, with biographical notices of the authors, together with the answers which have been given to some of them. . . . Lond., J. Smith, 1873. 474p.   **K143**

——— Bibliotheca Quakeristica, a bibliography of miscellaneous literature relating to the Friends (Quakers), chiefly written by persons not members of their society. . . . Lond., J. Smith, 1883. 32p. **K144**

——— Descriptive catalogue of Friends' books, or books written by members of the Society of Friends . . . from their first rise to the present time . . . with critical remarks and occasional biographical notices. Lond., J. Smith, 1867. 2v. **K145**

——— ——— Supplement. Lond., Hicks, 1893. 364p.

Lutheran

Concordia cyclopedia. A handbook of religious information with special reference to the history, doctrine, work and usages of the Lutheran church. L. Fuerbringer, Th. Engelder, P. E. Kretzmann, editors-in-chief. St. Louis, Concordia Pub. House, 1927. 848p. $4.50. **K146**

Concise articles, little bibliography. Includes biography.

Lutheran world almanac and encyclopedia for 1921–1934/37. N.Y., Nat. Lutheran Council, 1921–37. v.1-8. il. $1.25. **K147**

Published at irregular intervals.

First volume is a basic volume and includes some information not repeated in later ones. Annual volumes contain detailed directory lists, statistics, necrology lists, some biographies, historical articles. Fullest for Lutherans in the United States, but contains information for other countries.

Mennonite

Bender, Harold Stauffer. Two centuries of American Mennonite literature, a bibliography of Mennonitica Americana, 1727–1928. Goshen, Ind., Mennonite Hist. Soc., Goshen College, 1929. 181p. incl. facsims. (Studies in Anabaptist and Mennonite history no.1) $3. **K148**

Chronologically arranged by date of publication under the distinct groups of Mennonites, with author and title indexes.

Kauffman, Daniel. Mennonite cyclopedic dictionary; a compendium of the doctrines, history, activities, literature, and environments of the Mennonite church, especially in America. Scottdale, Pa., Mennonite Pub. House, 1937. 443p. $2. **K149**

Includes biography.

Mennonite year-book and directory, 1905- . Scottdale, Pa., Mennonite Pub. House, 1905- . Annual. (1948, 25c) **K150**

Directory and statistical information with annual survey articles.

Mennonitisches Lexikon, hrsg. von Christian Hege, und Christian Neff. Frankfort am Main, Authors, 1913- . v.1-2. **K151**

v.1-2, A-Mähren.

Signed articles with bibliographies.

Methodist

Leete, Frederick Deland. Methodist bishops, personal notes and bibliography with quotations from unpublished writings and reminiscences. Nashville, Tenn., Parthenon Pr., 1948. 457p. il. **K152**

Lists biographies of and writings by, and gives brief biographical sketches.

Methodist church, (United States). Minutes of the annual conferences. N.Y., Methodist Pub. House, 1940- . Semiannual. **K153**

Statistical and directory information.

Before 1940, published under Methodist Episcopal church.

Who's who in Pan-Methodism, v.1, 1940/41- . Nashville, Tenn., Parthenon Pr., 1940- . il. **K154**

Volume 1 published as a *Souvenir of first general conference, the Methodist church,* edited by Elam F. Dempsey. Conference notes, illustrations, and who's who.

Presbyterian

Official hand-book of the Presbyterian church of England, 1902- . Lond., Pub. Off. of the Presb. Church, 1902- . v.1- . **K155**

Directory information.

Presbyterian Church in the United States of America. Minutes of the general assembly; 137th- . Phila., General Assembly, 1925- . **K156**

Since the 137th General Assembly (1925) the *Minutes* have been published in two volumes: v.1, Journal and statistics; v.2, Reports of the Boards.

Previous series issued 1789- in varying forms.

Presbyterian Church in the United States. Minutes of the general assembly, with an appendix. Richmond, Va., Presbyterian Committee, 1865- . Annual. **K157**

Reports and statistics.

Scott, Eugene Crampton. Ministerial directory of the Presbyterian Church, U.S., 1861–1941. Austin, Texas, Von Boeckmann-Jones Co., 1942. 826p. **K158**

Published by order of the General Assembly of the "Southern Presbyterian Church."

Gives brief biographies of "all ordained ministers who have served in the Presbyterian Church in the U.S.," which is, the Presbyterian Church, South.

Protestant Episcopal

Living church annual, the yearbook of the Episcopal church, 1882- . Milwaukee, Morehouse, 1882- . v.1- . il. Annual. (1948, $3) **K159**

Title and imprint vary.
General directory and institutional information.

Stowe's Clerical directory of the Protestant Episcopal church in the United States of America. N.Y., Church Hymnal Corp., 1898- . **K160**

Previous titles: *Lloyd's Clerical directory* and *Stowe's Clerical directory of the American church.*
Contains biographical sketches of clergymen of the Protestant Episcopal church throughout the world; issued approximately every third year.
None issued between 1941 and 1947.

RITUAL

❦ The *Book of common prayer* of the Protestant Episcopal church was adopted after the Revolution and put into use in 1790. There have been two revisions, in 1892 and 1928. The 1928 revision made numerous changes in arrangement of material, the addition of new prayers and the rewriting of others. In 1934 a standardized paging was approved for the main part of the book, i.e., from Morning Prayer to the end of the Articles of Religion. In 1943, additional material was added to the prefatory paging which uses Roman numerals. The *Index* noted below (K163) is based on these latest revisions.

Jones, Joseph Courtney. Concordance to the Book of common prayer, according to the use of the Protestant Episcopal church in the United States. Phila., Jacobs, 1898. 198p. o.p. **K161**

Applies to the *Book of common prayer* in use before the 1928 revision.

Protestant Episcopal Church in the U. S. A. Book of Common Prayer. Book of common prayer and administration of the sacraments and other rites and ceremonies of the church, according to the use of the Protestant Episcopal church in the United States of America, together with the Psalter or Psalms of David. N.Y., Oxford Univ. Pr., 1944. 611p. $2. **K162**

The latest revision, adopted 1928, paged according to the Standard Prayer Book.

Pepper, George Wharton. An analytical index to the Book of common prayer; and a brief account of its evolution. Together with a revision of Gladstone's Concordance to the Psalter. Phila., Winston, 1948. 251p. $2.50. **K163**

Based on the 1928 revision, with the prefatory matter paged according to the resolution of 1943 and the remainder upon the pagination provided for by the resolution of 1934.

Includes a table showing the principal changes in the Psalter made in the Revision of 1928.

Parsons, Edward Lambe and **Jones, Bayard Hale.** The American prayer book; its origins and principles. N.Y., Scribner, 1937. 340p. $2.50. **K164**

Bibliography, p.321-27.

Reformed

Corwin, Charles E. Manual of the Reformed Church in America (formerly Reformed Protestant Dutch Church) 1628–1933. 5th ed., rev. N.Y., Board of Pub. of the Reformed Church in America, 1922–33. 782p. and suppl. 60p. il. $5. **K165**

1st-4th editions by Edward Tanjore Corwin.
Not a dictionary, but contains a large amount of useful reference information; especially useful for its biographies.
Contents: pt.1, History of the Reformed church in America; pt.2, The ministry, biographical sketches alphabetically arranged, with bibliographies, and many references to biographies in earlier editions, p.235-606; pt.3, Churches alphabetically arranged; Appendix, chronological list of ministers 1628–1922, chronological list of churches; Supplement, 1923–33.

United Church of Canada

United Church of Canada. Year book, 1925- . Toronto, United Church of Canada, 1925- . v.1- . (1945, $2) **K166**

Statistical and directory information; no biography.
"The United Church of Canada. Instituted June 10, 1925, by the Union of the Congregational churches of Canada, the Methodist church, The Presbyterian church of Canada, and the Local Union churches in Western Canada."

Unitarian

Unitarian and Free Christian Churches. Yearbook of the general assembly for 1890- . Lond., Essex Hall, 1890- . v.1- . (1939, 2s.) **K167**

Title varies.
Directory information, and brief biographies of ministers in the British Isles.

Unitarian year book, 1846- . Bost., Amer. Unit. Assoc., 1848- . v.1- . Annual. (1948, $1) **K168**

Title varies.
Directory and statistical information.

Roman Catholic
Bibliography

Cadden, John Paul. The historiography of the American Catholic church, 1785–1943. Wash., Catholic Univ. of America Pr., 1944. 122p. $1.

(Catholic Univ. of America. Studies in sacred theology, no.82) **K169**

The first part of a projected history and bibliography of American Catholic historical writing to be published in three parts. Part 1 describes its development with particular attention to the outstanding critical historians and the growth and publications of various Catholic historical institutions, such as Catholic historical societies and seminars in history. As planned, part 2 is to be entitled "The literature of American Catholic church history," and is to be "a description and evaluation of the literature in the field, including all the important bibliographical aids." Part 3 is to be "a selected catalogue of approximately 5,000 items on American Catholic church history."

Carlen, Mary Claudia, sister. A guide to the encyclicals of the Roman pontiffs from Leo XIII to the present day (1878–1937). N.Y., Wilson, 1939. 247p. $2. **K170**

Ellis, John Tracy. A select bibliography of the history of the Catholic church in the United States. N.Y., McMullen, 1947. 96p. $1.25. **K171**

Guide to Catholic literature, 1888–1940. Detroit, Romig, 1940. 1240p. $20. **K172**

Issued in 5 pts., A-Z.

Subtitle: An author-subject-title index in one straight alphabet of books and booklets, in all languages, on all subjects by Catholics or of particular Catholic interest, published or reprinted during the fifty-two years, January 1, 1888 to January 1, 1940, with more than a quarter of a million biographical, descriptive, and critical notes, each with complete reference to its authoritative source for further reference, reading and study.

Under the author entry material is entered in this order: biography of the author, books by him, books and appreciable parts of books about him and his works, magazine articles about him and his works. Critical annotations and brief extracts from reviews, with exact citations are included. Subject and title entries are cross references to the author entry.

—— v.2-3, 1940–44, 1945–48 . . . ed. by Walter Romig. Detroit, Romig, [1945–49]. v.2-3. $10 ea. (In progress)

Quadrennial supplements to be supplemented by annual volumes cumulating every four years.

On the same plan as the basic volume, the supplements list "books and pamphlets by Catholics or of particular Catholic interest, published . . . in any language and in any country" during the period covered, with biographical and critical notes.

Parsons, Wilfrid. Early Catholic Americana; a list of books and other works by Catholic authors in the United States, 1729–1830. . . . N.Y., Macmillan, 1939. 282p. $10. **K173**

Includes 1187 numbered entries. Locates copies.

Supersedes except for the notes and comment the *Bibliotheca Catholica Americana* of J. M. Finotti (1872).

—— —— Some additions and corrections . . . by Forrest B. Bowe. (Repr. from *Catholic historical review* 28:229-47, July 1942)

Ritual

❧ "The official books of the Roman Rite are seven—the Missal, Pontifical, Breviary, Ritual, Caerimoniale Episcoporum, Memoriale Rituum, and Martyrology. These contain all and only the liturgical services of this rite. Several repeat matter also found in others . . . (a) The Roman Missal *(Missale Romanum)* [contains the rites for the celebration of the Mass] . . . (b) The Pontifical *(Pontificale Romanum)* is the bishop's-book . . . (c) The Breviary *(Breviarium Romanum)* contains all the Divine Office without chant . . . (d) The Ritual *(Rituale Romanum)* contains all the services a priest needs besides those of the Missal and Breviary . . . (e) The Ceremonial of Bishops *(Caerimoniale Episcoporum)* in spite of its title contains much matter needed by other people than bishops. It is entirely a book of rubrical directions. . . . Much of it is already contained in the Missal, Pontifical and Ritual . . . (f) The Memorial of Rites *(Memoriale Rituum)* or Little Ritual *(Rituale parvum)* . . . gives directions for certain rites (the blessing of candles, ashes, palms, the Holy Week services) in small churches where there are no ministers (deacon and subdeacon) . . . (g) The Martyrology *(Martyrologium Romanum)* is an enlarged calendar giving the names and very short accounts of all saints (not only martyrs) commemorated in various places each day."—"Liturgical books," *Catholic encyclopedia* 9: 300-02.

For fuller description of these books *see* the above article in the *Catholic encyclopedia* (K182). For ordinary reference purposes complete editions of four of these books, although not covering the whole rite of the Church, are adequate for most questions. Good editions of these four are the following:

Catholic Church. Liturgy and Ritual. Breviary. Breviarium Romanum ex decreto Sacrosancti Concilii Tridentini restitutum S. Pii v Pontificis Maximi jussu editum aliorumque pontificum cura recognitum Pii Papae x, auctoritate reformatum. Editio vigesima juxta typicam. Turonibus, Typ. A. Mame, 1933. 4v. **K174**

Issued in four unnumbered volumes covering the four seasons, i.e., Pars Verna (Spring); Pars Aestiva (Summer); Pars Autumnalis (Autumn); Pars Hiemalis (Winter).

Only editions since 1908 contain the revised forms now in use. For historical questions older editions containing older forms will have to be used.

—— **Breviary.** The Roman breviary, restored by the Sacred Council of Trent . . . An English version; comp. by the Benedictine Nuns of the Abbey of Our Lady of Consolation at Stanbrook in Worcestershire; rev. and ed. by Charles Francis Brown. Lond., Oates and Washbourne, 1936 4v. **K175**

—— **Ritual.** Rituale Romanum Pauli v Pontificis Maximi jussu editum, aliorumque pontificum cura recognitum, atque auctoritate Ssmi D. N. Pii Papae xi ad norman codicis juris canonici accomodatum; cui accedit benedictionum et instructionum appendix. Editio quinta post typicam. Turonibus, Typ. A. Mame; N. Y., Benziger, 1928. 710, 29p. $2.75. **K176**

Gives the complete Latin text. A usable edition of selections only with text in Latin, English, French and German is *The Sacristy manual*, containing the portions of the Roman Ritual most frequently used in parish church functions; comp. by Rev. Paul Griffith (Balt., Murphy [c1905]. 80p. $2).

—— **Missal.** New Roman missal in Latin and English by F. X. Lasance and F. A. Walsh . . . with an illustrated study plan. . . . To which is added a supplement comprising an explanation of "The ecclesiastical year and the sacred liturgy; Short accounts of certain feasts and brief lives of the saints" contained in this missal. . . . N.Y., Benziger, 1945. 1852p. $4. **K177**

—— **Martyrology.** The Roman martyrology, pub. by order of Gregory xiii, rev. by authority of Urban viii and Clement x, aug. and corr. in 1749 by Benedict xiv. 3d Turin ed., according to the original, complete with the proper eulogies of recent saints and offices. Tr. by Raphael Collins. Westminster, Md., Newman Bookshop, 1946. 352p. **K178**

Bohatta, Hanns. Bibliographie der Breviere, 1501–1850. Leipzig, Hiersemann, 1937. 349p. **K179**

Weale, William Henry James. Bibliographia Liturgica; Catalogus Missalium, ritus Latini ab anno mcccclxxiv Impressorum, iterum edidit H. Bohatta. Lond., Quaritch, 1928. 380p. **K180**

Britt, Matthew. Dictionary of the Psalter, containing the vocabulary of the Psalms, hymns, canticles and miscellaneous prayers of the breviary Psalter. N.Y., Benziger, 1928. 299p. $4.50. **K181**

A dictionary of the Latin words, with English equivalents, and quotations given in each language. Is concerned primarily with the Vulgate text, but translations of the Hebrew text are given when they throw light on obscure terms in the Vulgate text.

Encyclopedias

Catholic encyclopedia; an international work of reference on the constitution, doctrine, discipline and history of the Catholic church. N.Y., Catholic Encyclopedia Pr. [c1907–22]. 17v. il. $6.50 ea. **K182**

v.1-15, A-Z, Errata; v.16, Additional articles, Index; v.17, Supplement.

"It differs from the general encyclopedia in omitting facts and information which have no relation to the Church. On the other hand it is not exclusively a church encyclopedia, nor is it limited to the ecclesiastical sciences and the doings of churchmen. It records all that Catholics have done, not only in behalf of charity and morals, but also for the intellectual and artistic development of mankind."—*Pref.*

Authoritative work with long signed articles by specialists, good bibliographies and illustrations. Very useful for many questions on subjects in medieval literature, history, philosophy, art, etc., as well as for questions of Catholic doctrine, history, biography. The standard work in English, but for very full information often not so complete as the great French Catholic works, and now somewhat out of date.

Need for a revision was felt and in 1936, volume 1 of a revised and enlarged edition was published by the Gilmary Society in New York, but no more volumes have appeared.

Dictionnaire apologétique de la foi catholique contenant les preuves de la vérité de la religion et les réponses aux objections tirées des sciences humaines. 4. éd., entièrement refondue, pub. sous la direction de A. d'Alés. Paris, Beauchesne, 1911–31. 4v. and index. **K183**

v.1-4, A-Z; Index volume: Supplement, col. 5-62; Subject index, col. 69-492.

Dictionnaire de théologie catholique contenant l'esposé des doctrines de théologie catholique, leurs preuves et leur histoire, commencé sous la direction de A. Vacant et E. Mangenot continué sous celle de É. Amann. . . . Paris, Letouzey, 1909–49. v.1-15. il. 30fr. per fasc., subs. 20fr. (In progress) **K184**

v.1-15 (fasc. 148-49), A-Wyclif.

Authoritative; long signed articles, excellent bibliographies. More exhaustive in treatment than the *Catholic encyclopedia* (K182). Good for topics and names in scholastic and medieval philosophy. More recent information on topics treated in the earlier volumes is frequently given under allied subjects in later volumes.

—— —— Table analytique, t.1-9, A-L (inclus.). 1929. 143p.

Enciclopedia cattolica. Citta del Vaticano, Enciclopedia Cattolica, 1948–50. v.1-5. il. $180. (In progress) **K185**

v.1-5, A-Gen.

An entirely new work to be in ten volumes which will be of major importance. Written in Italian and mainly by Italian scholars, it deals with all matters pertaining to the Catholic church, historical and contemporary. Articles vary in length from a few lines to several pages, are signed and include long bibliographies which give dates and exact references.

Koch, Ludwig. Jesuiten-Lexikon; die Gesellschaft Jesu einst und jetzt. Paderborn, Verlag Bonifacius Druckerei, 1934. 1878 col. **K186**

Contains many biographies but is not entirely biographical, i.e., has articles on subjects connected with the work and history of the order.

Wetzer, Heinrich Joseph. Wetzer und Welte's Kirchenlexikon, oder Encyklopädie der katholischen Theologie und ihrer Hülfswissenschaften. 2. Aufl., in neuer Bearb. unter Mitwirkung vieler katholischen Gelehrten begonnen von Joseph, cardinal Hergenröther, fortgesetzt von Franz Kaulen. Freiburg im Br., Herder, 1882–1903. 12v. and index. **K187**

The standard German Catholic encyclopedia.

Dictionaries

A Catholic dictionary (The Catholic encyclopaedic dictionary). General ed., Donald Attwater, with the assistance of the Rev. J. P. Arendzen . . . T. E. Flynn [and others], 2d ed. rev. N.Y., Macmillan, 1949. 552p. $5. **K188**

"This book, originally published in 1931 under the title *The Catholic encyclopaedic dictionary*, is reissued under new title because of a conflict in titles."

Definitions and meanings of terms, names and phrases in the philosophy, theology, canon law, liturgy, institutions, etc., of the Catholic church. Omits biography except for the saints in the general calendar of the Roman Church.

Catholic encyclopedia dictionary; containing 8,500 articles on the beliefs, devotions, rites, symbolism, tradition and history of the church; her laws, organizations, dioceses, missions, institutions, religious orders, saints; her part in promoting art, science, education and social welfare. Comp. and ed. under the direction of the editors of the Catholic encyclopedia. N.Y., Gilmary Soc., 1941. 1095p. il. $6.50. **K189**

A reissue with no revision of the *New Catholic dictionary*, published in 1929 by the Universal Knowledge Foundation.

Concise articles, many of them signed, on all phases of Catholic life. Includes biography.

History

Mourret, Fernand. A history of the Catholic church, tr. by Newton Thompson. St. Louis, Lond., Herder, 1931–45. v.1-6. (v.6, $4). **K190**

v.1-6, From the beginning through the eighteenth century. Each volume includes bibliography and index.

A translation of the French Catholic work: *Histoire générale de l'église* (1919–21. 9v.).

Annuals

Almanach catholique français, 1920- . Paris, Bloud, 1920- . il. Annual. (1937, 7fr.) **K191**

Directory information and brief biographies of "Les principales personnalités catholiques françaises."

American Catholic who's who, 1934/35- . *See* S41.

Annuaire pontifical catholique, 1.- année, 1898- . Paris, La Bonne Presse, 1897- . v.1- . il. Annual. (1948, 800fr.) **K192**

Contains a large amount of historical, gazetteer and biographical information about the Catholic church throughout the world, and many bibliographical references, both to earlier volumes of the *Annuaire* and to other sources. Partial contents: alphabetical list of cardinals with portraits and biographies; list of patriarchs, archbishops; Latin names of episcopal sees; list of patriarchates, Latin and oriental, with geographical, historical and statistical information and bibliographical notes; list of archbishoprics and bishoprics, with the name of the incumbent and some geographical, historical and statistical data, and bibliographical notes; religious orders, with bibliography; various biographical lists. There is a general index to the first 20 volumes, 1898–1917. Contents not the same in all volumes.

Annuario pontificio, 1716- . Roma, Tip. Poliglotta Vaticana, 1716- . il. Annual. **K193**

Contains list of popes from St. Peter on; Roman Catholic hierarchy at Rome and throughout the world, with brief biographical notes; institutions, offices, at Rome; list of religious orders with dates of founding and name of present head; Latin names of sees according to the Roman Curia, with classical Latin and vernacular names; Latin names of religious orders; index of personal names, etc.

Catholic directory, ecclesiastical register and almanack for. . . . 1838- . Lond., Burns, 1838- . v.1- . maps. Annual. (1948, 15s.) **K194**

"The official handbook of the Catholic church in England and Wales."—*Pref.*

Catholic who's who, 1908- . Lond. *See* S132.

National Catholic almanac . . . comp. by the Franciscan Clerics of the Holy Name College, Washington, D.C. Paterson, N.J., St. Anthony's Guild, 1904- . Annual. (1948, $1.50.) **K195**

Title, imprint and sponsoring body vary. Former titles: *St. Anthony's almanac* and *Franciscan almanac*.

Official Catholic directory, 1886- . N.Y., Kenedy, 1886- . il. Annual. (1947, $8.) **K196**

Title varies, imprint varies.

Useful annual, containing a large amount of detailed directory, institutional and statistical information about the organization, clergy, churches, missions, schools, religious orders, etc., of the Catholic church in the United States and its possessions, Great Britain and Ireland, Canada and other parts of British America, Cuba and Mexico.

Orbis Catholicus, ed. by Donald Attwater. Lond., Oates and Washbourne, 1938- . 7s. 6d. **K197**

Includes: Territorial divisions of the Catholic church in the various countries of the world, titular sees, religious orders and congregations, the Roman curia, Supreme Pontificate, Cardinalate and Episcopate, Index to bishops' names, etc.

Atlases

Streit, Karl. Atlas hierarchicus, descriptio geographica et statistica S. Romanae Ecclesiae tum occidentis tum orientis juxta statum praesentem accedunt non-nullae notae historicae necnon ethnographicae. . . . ed. 2. Paderborn, St. Boniface Pr.; Fribourg im Br., Herder, 1929. 68(i.e., 132)p., 47p. pl. maps, tables. 40cm.   **K198**

Contains text giving descriptive, historical, and ethnographical information, 38 large maps, and an index (9p.). Preface and text are given in German, Italian, French, and Spanish. First edition, 1913, contained English text also and a list of sources omitted in the second edition. An English issue of the revised edition appeared under the title: *Catholic world atlas containing a geographical and statistical description with maps of the Holy Roman Catholic church* . . . (Paderborn, St. Boniface Pr.; N.Y., Soc. for the Propagation of the Faith, 1929).

Saints

Baring-Gould, Sabine. Lives of the saints, with introduction and additional lives of English martyrs, Cornish, Scottish, and Welsh saints, and a full index to the entire work. New and rev. ed. illustrated by 473 engravings. Edinburgh, Grant, 1914. 16v. il.   **K199**

v.1-15, January–December (July, October and November in 2v. each); v.16, Appendix; indexes.

—— and **Fisher, John.** Lives of the British saints; the saints of Wales and Cornwall and such Irish saints as have dedications in Britain. Lond., Soc. of Cymmrodorion, 1907–13. 4v. il.   **K200**

Book of saints, a dictionary of servants of God canonized by the Catholic church, extracted from the Roman and other martyrologies, comp. by the Benedictine monks of St. Augustine's Abbey, Ramsgate. 4th ed. rev. and enl. with a calendar of saints. Lond., Black; N.Y., Macmillan, 1947. 708p. 25s; $6.   **K201**

A concise handbook which includes all saints in the Roman martyrology and some others, especially those who have given place-names to towns and villages in the British Isles.

The fourth edition is thoroughly revised and rewritten with additional material, omitting some matter included in the third edition.

Butler, Alban. Lives of the saints, new ed., rev. and copiously supplemented by Herbert Thurston. Lond., Burns, Oates; N.Y., Kenedy, 1925–38. 12v. 9s. ea.; $3.50.   **K202**

—— —— A dictionary of saints; being also an index to the rev. ed. of Butler's Lives of the saints, comp. by Donald Attwater. N.Y., Kenedy, 1938. 319p. $3.50.   **K203**

Holweck, Frederick George. Biographical dictionary of the saints, with a general introduction on hagiology. St. Louis, Herder, 1924. 1053p. $10.   **K204**

The most comprehensive one-volume dictionary of the subject in English, including all saints recognized in any Christian church. Concise biographies, with some bibliographical reference to sources of information for each biography.

O'Hanlon, John. Lives of the Irish saints, with special festivals and the commemoration of holy persons, comp. from calendars, martyrologies, and various sources relating to the ancient church history of Ireland. Dublin, Duffy; Lond., Burns; N.Y., Benziger, 1875-[19-?]. v.1-9. il.   **K205**

v.1-9, January–September. No more published.

Russo-Alesi, Anthony I. Martyrology pronouncing dictionary; it contains the proper pronunciation of over 5000 names of martyrs, confessors, virgins, emperors, cities and places occurring in the Roman martyrology with a daily calendar and a list of patron saints. N.Y., Edward O'Toole, 1939. 177p. $1.50.   **K206**

Gives pronunciation only but lists many names not easily found elsewhere.

❧ The foregoing are popular works, useful for ordinary purposes. For research purposes, however, the indispensable work is the *Acta sanctorum* of the Bollandists, described below. For a brief account of this work and its history, *see* the *Encyclopaedia Britannica*, 11th ed., 4:177-78 or the 14th ed., 3:821-22 (slightly abridged with indication of volumes published to 1931). For a much fuller account *see* the *Catholic encyclopedia* 2:630-39 (K182).

Acta sanctorum quotquot toto orbe coluntur, vel a catholicis scriptoribus celebrantur, quae ex Latinis et Graecis, aliarumque gentium antiquis monumentis collegit, digessit, notis illustravit Joannes Bollandus . . . operam et studium contulit Godefridus Henschenius. . . . Editio novissima curante Joanne Carnandet. Parisiis, Palmé, 1863–1931. Jan.–Nov. 85v. in 67.   **K207**

Contents: Jan.–Apr., 3v. ea.; May, 7v. and Propylaeum; June–July, 7v. ea.; Aug., 6v.; Sept., 8v.; Oct., 13v. in 14; Nov., v.1-4 and Propylaeum.

—— Ad Acta sanctorum . . . supplementum, volumen complectens Auctaria Octobris et Tabulas generales. Scilicet ephemerides et indicem alphabeticum decem priorum mensium . . . cura et opere L. M. Rigollot. Parisiis, 1875. 2v.

—— Supplément aux Acta sanctorum pour des vies de saints de l'époque mérovingienne par M. l'Abbé C. Narbey. . . . Paris, LeSoudier, 1899–1900. v.1-2.

Supplemented by:

Analecta bollandiana, v. 1- . Bruxelles, Soc. des Bollandistes; Paris, Picard, 1882- . Quarterly. **K208**

Gives the current bibliography of the subject, with critical reviews of new publications, and supplements the *Acta sanctorum* (K207) by printing texts, commentaries, etc., not included in the *Acta*.

—— Indices in tomos I-XX (1882–1901), XXI-XL (1902–1922), XLI-LX (1923–1942). Bruxelles, Soc. des Bollandistes, 1904–45. 3v.

Popes, bishops, etc.

Eubel, Conrad. Hierarchia catholica medii aevi; sive, Summorum pontificum S.R.E. cardinalium, ecclesiarum antistitum series e documentis tabularii praesertim Vaticani collecta, digesta. 2d ed. Monasterii, Sumptibus et Typis Librariae Regensbergianae, 1913–14. 3v. **K209**

v.1-3, 1198–1600.

Gams, Pius Bonifacius. Series episcoporum ecclesiae Catholicae, quotquot innotuerunt a Beato Petro Apostolo. Ratisbonae, G. J. Manz, 1873–86. 965p. and suppl. **K210**

(Repr. Leipzig, Hiersemann, 1931. 2v.)
Historical list of the bishops of each see from the beginning. Useful in the large or research library. Supplement covers 1870–85.

Mann, Horace Kinder. Lives of the popes in the early middle ages. . . . Lond., Kegan Paul, 1902–32. v. 1-18 in 19. 15s. per v. **K211**

Covers 590–1305.
Volumes 6-18 have title *Lives of the popes in the middle ages.*

Pastor, Ludwig, *Freiherr von.* History of the popes, from the close of the middle ages. Drawn from the secret archives of the Vatican and other original sources. From the German. Tr. and ed. by F. I. Autrobus, Ralph Kerr, Ernest Graf. Lond., Hodges, 1891–1941. v. 1-34. 15s. per v. (In progress.) **K212**

Imprint varies.
v.1-34, 1305 to Clement XII (1730–40).

Code, Joseph Bernard. Dictionary of the American hierarchy. N.Y., Longmans, 1940. 425p. $3.75. **K213**

Contains biographies of more than 500 American Catholic bishops from 1790 to date.

Patrology

For certain kinds of reference work, especially in large reference libraries, theological libraries and in college and university work in medieval history, literature and philosophy, the writings of the Fathers of the Church, either in the original Latin or Greek, or in English translation, are often wanted. The following are important collections for such needs:

Migne, Jacques Paul. Patrologiae cursus completus, seu bibliotheca universalis . . . omnium SS. patrum, doctorum, scriptorumque ecclesiasticorum. . . . Series Latina . . . a Tertulliano ad Innocentium III. Parisiis, Migne, 1844–80. 221v. o.p. **K214**

Contents: v.1-217, Texts; v.218-221, Indexes.

—— —— Series Graeca . . . a S. Barnaba ad Photium. Parisiis, Migne, 1857–66. 161v. in 166. o.p. **K215**

—— —— —— Indices digessit Ferdinandus Cavallera. Parisiis, Garnier, 1912. 218p.

—— —— —— Index locupletissimus [by] Theodurus Hopfner. Paris, Geuthner, 1928–39. v.1-2$^{1-3}$.

Monumental sets, useful both for the large amount of material included and for the indexes, especially the full subject indexes of many kinds included in volumes 218-221 of the *Series Latina*. The index to the *Series Graeca* is less detailed, though one to places is now in progress. Texts included are all reprints; those in the *Series Graeca* are given both in Latin and Greek, in parallel columns.

Altaner, Berthold. Précis de patrologie; tr. par l'Abbé Marcel Grandclaudon. Mulhouse (Haut-Rhin), Ed. Salvator, 1941. 466p. **K216**

Strong in bibliography.

Ante-Nicene Christian fathers; translations of the writings of the fathers down to A.D. 325. Alexander Roberts and James Donaldson, editors. American repr. of the Edinburgh ed. rev. and chronologically arranged with brief prefaces and occasional notes by A. C. Coxe. N.Y., Christian Lit. Co., 1896–97. 10v. **K217**

The Edinburgh edition, with title *Ante-Nicene Christian library,* was published by Clark, 24v.
Contents of American edition: v.1-8, Text; v.9, Additional volume, containing early Christian works . . . and selections from the commentaries of Origen; v.10, Bibliographical synopsis, by E. C. Richardson; General index to v.1-8, by Bernard Pick.

Select library of Nicene and post-Nicene fathers of the Christian church. 1st-2d ser. tr. into English. N.Y., Christian Lit. Co., 1886–1900. 28v. **K218**

Bardenhewer, Otto. Patrology; the lives and works of the fathers of the church. Tr. from the 2d ed. by Thomas J. Shahan. Freiburg im Br.; St. Louis, Herder, 1908. 680p. o.p. **K219**

A useful reference manual intended primarily for Catholic seminary students but useful in any library which does much reference work on the subject. Gives for each of the fathers (1) a brief biographical sketch,

(2) a general statement about his writings, their character, doctrine, etc., and (3) bibliography, indicating complete editions, selections and separate works, translations, and works about.

Cayré, Fulbert. Patrologie et histoire de la théologie. 4. ed. Paris, Soc. de S. Jean l'Évangeliste, 1944–47. 3v. **K220**

v.1-2 (Bks. 1-4) pub. 1947; v.3 (Bk. 5) pub. 1944 without edition note.

Translated from the first edition as *Manual of patrology and history of theology*, by H. Hewitt (Paris, Soc. of St. John the Evangelist, 1936–40. 2v. [Bks. 1-4]).

Religious orders

See Buchberger, *Lexikon für Theologie und Kirche*, 1930–38 (K21) under the name of the order, for bibliographies on each order.

Cottineau, L. H. Répertoire topo-bibliographique des abbayes et prieurés. Macon, Protat, 1935–38. 2v. 900fr. **K221**

Arranged by the place where the religious house is situated; gives variant forms of name, location with reference to larger places, order to which religious house belongs, sometimes brief history of the house and references to sources of information.

Kapsner, Oliver L. Catholic religious orders, listing conventional and full names in English, foreign language, and Latin, also abbreviations, date and country of origin. Collegeville, Minn., St. John's Abbey Pr., 1948. 351p. $4. **K222**

A listing of names of orders primarily for the use of library catalogers, but with its many cross references from the variant forms it may also serve as a handy guide for others. Information under the main entry includes variant forms of name, abbreviation, date and country of founding.

Hélyot, Pierre. Dictionnaire des ordres religieux; ou, Histoire des ordres monastiques, religieux et militaires, et des congrégations séculières de l'un et de l'autre sexe, qui ont été établies jusqu'à présent. . . . Mise par ordre alphabétique, corr. et augm. . . . d'un supplément où l'on trouve l'histoire des congrégations omises par Hélyot, et l'histoire des sociétés religieuses établies depuis que cet auteur a publié son ouvrage, par Marie-Léandre Badiche. Paris, Migne, 1859–63. 4v. il. (1ère encyclopédie théologique, pub. par M. l'abbé Migne, t. 20-23.) o.p. **K223**

An older work, useful in the absence of a later dictionary of the subject.

See Mudge, *Guide to reference books*, 6th ed. 1936, p. 309-11; Schneider, *Handbuch der Bibliographie*, 1930, p.417-21 (A5); and Foulché-Delbosc, *Manuel de l'hispanisant*, 1920, v.1, p.101-11 (A490) for lists of bio-bibliographies of religious orders.

Orthodox Eastern Church

Greek Church. Liturgy and Ritual. Service book of the Holy orthodox-Catholic apostolic church, comp., tr. and arranged from the old church-Slavonic service books of the Russian church, and collated with the service books of the Greek church, by Isabel Florence Hapgood. Rev. ed., with endorsement by Patriarch Tikhon. N.Y., Assoc. Pr., 1922. 615p. $3.50. **K224**

Langford-James, Richard Lloyd. A dictionary of the Eastern Orthodox Church. Lond., Faith Pr., 1923. 144p. 4s. 6d. **K225**

History

Attwater, Donald. The Christian churches of the East. [rev. ed.] Milwaukee, Bruce, 1947–48. 2v. $4 ea. **K226**

Contents: v.1, Churches in communion with Rome; v.2, Churches not in communion with Rome.
Includes bibliographies.

Fortescue, Adrian. The lesser Eastern churches. Lond., Catholic Truth Soc., 1913. 468p. il. **K227**

Treats the various churches of the Nestorians; the Copts; the Abyssinians, Jacobites, and Malabar Christians; the Armenians.
A continuation of his *Orthodox Eastern church* (K228).

—— The Orthodox Eastern church. 3d ed. Lond., Catholic Truth Soc., 1911. 451p. il. **K228**

Frequently reprinted.

—— The Uniate Eastern churches; the Byzantine rite in Italy, Sicily, Syria, and Egypt, ed. by George D. Smith. Lond., Oates and Washbourne, 1923. 244p. **K229**

"List of books," p.xi-xxi.

NON-CHRISTIAN RELIGIONS

Sacred books of the East, tr. by various oriental scholars and ed. by F. Max Müller. Ox., Clarendon Pr., 1879–1910. 50v. **K230**

v.1, 15, The Upanishads, tr. by F. Max Müller; v.2, 14, The sacred laws of the Âryas, tr. by George Bühler; v.3, 16, 27, 28, The sacred books of China, the texts of Confucianism, tr. by James Legge; v.4, 23, 31, The Zend-Avesta, tr. by James Darmsteter and L. H. Mills; v.5, 18, 24, 37, 47, Pahlavi texts, tr. by E. W. West; v.6, 9, The Qur'ân, tr. by E. Palmer; v.7, The Institutes of Vishnu, tr. by Julius Jolly; v.8, The Bhagavadgîtâ, with the Sanatsugâtîya and the Anugîtâ, tr. by Kâshinâth Trimbak Telang; v.10, The Dhammapada, tr. from Pâli by F. M. Müller, The Sutta-nipâta, tr. from Pâli by V.

Fausböll; v.11, Buddhist suttas, tr. from Pâli by T. W. Rhys Davids; v.12, 26, 41, 43, 44, The Satapathabrâhmana, tr. by Julius Eggeling; v.13, 17, 20, Vinaya texts, tr. from the Pâli by T. W. Rhys Davids and Hermann Oldenberg; v.19, The Fo-sho-hing-tsan-king by Asvaghosha, tr. by Samuel Beal; v.21, The Saddharma-pundarika, tr. by H. Kern; v.22, 45, Gaina sûtras, tr. from Prâkrit by Herman Jacobi; v.25, The laws of Manu, tr. by G. Bühler; v.29, 30, The Grihya-sûtras, tr. by Hermann Oldenberg; v.32, 46, Vedic hymns, tr. by F. M. Müller and H. Oldenberg; v.33, The minor law books, pt.1 tr. by Julius Jolly; v.34, 38, 48, The Vedânta sûtras, tr. by George Thibaut; v.35, 36, The questions of King Milinda, tr. by T. W. Rhys Davids; v.39, 40, The sacred books of China, the texts of Tâoism, tr. by James Legge; v.42, Hymns of the Atharva-veda, tr. by Maurice Bloomfield; v.49, Buddhist Mâhâyana texts, tr. by E. B. Cowell; v.50, General index, by M. Winternitz.

Includes all the most important works of the seven non-Christian religions that have influenced the civilization of Asia: the Vedic-Brahmanic system, Buddhism, Jainism, Islam, Confucianism, Taoism and the Parsi religion. Excellent and detailed general index which can be used for both large and small topics, beliefs, myths, names of deities, etc. Index also issued separately, as follows:

Winternitz, Moriz. Concise dictionary of Eastern religion, being the index volume to the Sacred books of the East. Ox., Clarendon Pr., 1910. 683p. 21s. **K231**

Lin, Yu-t'ang. The wisdom of China and India. N.Y., Random House, 1942. 1104p. **K232**

Buddhism

Bibliographie Bouddhique, 1928/29–1934/36. Paris, Librairie d'Amér. et d'Orient, 1930–37. v.1-8. **K233**

v.1, Jan. 1928—Mai 1929, Bibliographie; v.2, Mai 1929—Mai 1930, Retrospective, L'oeuvre de Léon Feer; v.3, Mai 1930—Mai 1931, Retrospective, L'oeuvre de J. Ph. Vogel; v.4-5, Mai 1931—Mai 1933, Retrospective, L'oeuvre de Paul Pelliot; v.6, Mai 1933—Mai 1934, Index général des t.1-6; v.7-8, Mai 1934—Mai 1936, Retrospective, L'oeuvre complet de Sylvain Lévi.

An important current bibliography which includes both books and the indexing of about 200 periodicals. The special author bibliographies contained in volumes 2-5 and 7 contain material of earlier date than the period 1928–35 covered by the annual issues.

Hôbôgirin; dictionnaire encyclopédique du bouddhisme d'après les sources chinoises et japonaises, publié sous le haut patronage de l'Académie Impériale du Japon et sous la direction de Sylvain Lévi et J. Takakusu. Rédacteur en chef, Paul Demiéville. Tôkyô, Maison Franco-Japonaise, 1929–37. fasc. 1-3. il. **K234**

fasc. 1-3, A-Chi.

—— Fasicule annexe. Tables du Taishô Issaikyo, nouvelle édition du Canon bouddhique chinois, publié sous la direction de J. Takakusu et K.

Watanabe. . . . Tôkyô, Maison Franco-Japonaise, 1931. 202p.

Soothill, William Edward and **Hodous, Lewis.** A dictionary of Chinese Buddhist terms, with Sanskrit and English equivalents and Sanskrit-Pali index. Lond., Kegan Paul, 1937. 510p. 84s. **K235**

Hinduism

Bloomfield, Maurice. Vedic concordance, being an alphabetic index to every line of every stanza of the published Vedic literature and to the liturgical formulas thereof, that is, an index to the Vedic mantras; together with an account of their variations in the different Vedic books. Camb., Harvard Univ. Pr., 1906. 1078p. (Harvard oriental ser. v.10.) **K236**

Dowson, John. Classical dictionary of Hindu mythology and religion, geography, history, and literature. Lond., Trübner, 1879. 411p. **K237**

Frequently reprinted.

Macdonnell, Arthur Anthony and **Keith, A. B.** Vedic index of names and subjects. Lond., Murray, pub. for the Govt. of India, 1912. 2v. **K238**

Judaism
Bibliography

Roth, Cecil. Magna bibliotheca Anglo-Judaica; a bibliographical guide to Anglo-Jewish history. New ed., rev. and enl. Lond., Jewish Hist. Soc. of England, Univ. College, 5698, 1937. 464p. 31s. 6d. **K239**

Classified.

A revised edition of *Bibliotheca Anglo-Judaica* comp. by Joseph Jacobs and Lucien Wolf (Lond. 1888). In two parts: part 1, "Histories" consisting largely of secondary works; part 2, "Historical material" listing primary sources usually up to the year 1837, though material on the reform movement is extended to 1842 and on Jewish emancipation to 1858. Includes the material on the study of Anglo-Jewish history in the Mocatta library and the allied collections housed in University College, London.

Shunami, Schlomo. Bibliography of Jewish bibliographies. Jerusalem, Univ. Pr., 1936. 399p. **K240**

Includes works in many languages. Classified, with index of names and subjects and an index of Hebrew titles.

Encyclopedias

Encyclopaedia Judaica; das Judentum in Geschichte und Gegenwart. Berlin, Verlag Eschkol [c1928-34]. v.1-10. **K241**

v.1-10, A-Lyra. (No more published.)
v.1-2 only issued also in an edition in Hebrew.

A scientific work of high scholarship, with signed articles and valuable bibliographies, covering all aspects of Jewish life, thought, literature, religion, customs, history, etc., especially full in biography, since for many centuries Jewish history has been so largely a history of individuals, not of a nation. Richly illustrated. For scholarly purposes, and for readers who can read German, it is more useful than the *Jewish encyclopedia* (K243) which is now out of date on some points. Praised by Dr. L. Blau, in the *Revue des études juives,* as a book which ought to be in every large public library. For his detailed reviews of volumes 1 and 4 of the German edition *see Revue des études juives* 86:92-107, juil./sep. 1928; 88:107-09, juil./sep. 1929; for his review of volume 1 of the Hebrew edition *see* 88:102-07.

Evreĭskaĭa entsiklopedĭa. S.-Petersburg', Brokgaus'-Efron', 1906–13. 16v. il. **K242**

Especially valuable for its treatment of Jews in eastern Europe.

Jewish encyclopedia; a descriptive record of the history, religion, literature, and customs of the Jewish people from the earliest times to the present day; prepared under the direction of Cyrus Adler [and others] . . . Isidore Singer, managing editor. N.Y., Funk, 1901–06. 12v. il. **K243**

Signed articles by specialists; bibliographies.

"On one side, it is a true encyclopaedia, and speaks, always from a Jewish standpoint, *de omni scibili;* on another, it is a cyclopaedia as the record of a single branch of knowledge—the civilization of a single race. . . . The chief value of this book . . . is to be found in its biographies, its descriptions of the present state of Jews throughout the world and in its elucidations of Talmudic law. On all these points it gives first-hand information of a kind and to an extent not accessible elsewhere."—*Nation* 73:341-42, Oct. 31, 1901.

Jüdisches Lexikon; ein enzyklopädisches Handbuch des jüdischen Wissens . . . begr. von Georg Herlitz und Bruno Kirschner. Berlin, Jüdischer Verlag [c1927-30]. 4v. in 5. il. **K244**

More popular in character than the *Encyclopaedia Judaica* (K241) with brief signed articles and some bibliography. Lavishly illustrated. For review by Dr. L. Blau *see Revue des études juives* 86:199-210, oct./dec. 1928.

Philo-Lexikon; Handbuch des judischen Wissens. . . . 4. verm. u. verb. Aufl. Berlin, Philo Verlag, 1937. [c1935] 831 col. il. **K245**

Small handbook with concise articles.

Universal Jewish encyclopedia . . . an authoritative and popular presentation of Jews and Judaism since the earliest times; ed. by Isaac Landman in collaboration with . . . Board of Editors. N.Y., Universal Jewish Encyclopedia, Inc., 1939-44. 10v. and reading guide and index (78p.). il. $100 per set. **K246**

A useful, modern encyclopedia more popular in treatment than the scholarly *Jewish encyclopedia* (K243), but accurate in facts and more up to date. Especially strong in its treatment of American subjects. Contains many biographies, including living persons. Many articles signed, some bibliography.

Vallentine's Jewish encyclopaedia, ed. by Albert M. Hyamson and A. M. Silbermann. . . . Lond., Shapiro, Vallentine and Co., 1938. 696p. il. **K247**

A useful one-volume encyclopedia including brief articles, some of them signed, on various subjects of Jewish interest, historical and modern, including biographies of living Jews. There are no bibliographies or references to sources.

Annuals

American Jewish year book, 5660- , Sept. 5, 1899- . Phila., Jewish Pub. Soc., 1899- . v.1- il. $3. **K248**

Contains important directory and statistical information, and special articles, biographies, necrologies, and bibliographies. Many of these from earlier issues continue to have reference value. Volume 40 contains a subject index to special articles in volumes 1-40. Beginning with volume 44 each volume contains an American Jewish bibliography.

Jewish year book, 5657- (1896-). Lond., "Jewish Chronicle," 1896- . v.1- . (1948, 10s.) **K249**

Contains statistical and institutional information, bibliographies, and a communal directory which contains brief biographical sketches.

Biography

✤ All of the encyclopedias and annuals listed above include biographies, in some cases of considerable reference importance. The following are limited to biography and include many names not given in the more general works:

Winiger, Salomon. Grosse jüdische National-Biographie, mit mehr als 12,000 Lebensbeschreibungen namhafter jüdischer Männer und Frauen aller Zeiten und Länder. Ein Nachschlagewerk für das jüdische Volk und dessen freunde. Cernauti, "Arta," 1928–37. v.1-7[1-7]. **K250**

v.1-5, A-St; v.6, St-Z; Nachträge, A-Geldern; v.7 (incompl.), Geiler-Z; 2. Nachträge, A-Fink.

Who's who in American Jewry, *see* S47.

Mohammedanism
Bibliography

Munro, Dana Carleton. History of Mohammedanism and of Moslem peoples. (sect. G of A guide to historical literature, ed. by G. M. Dutcher. N.Y., Macmillan, 1931. p.276-94. V2) **K251**

A useful guide to the basic works; bibliographies, reference works and histories.

Gabrieli, Giuseppe. Manuale di bibliografia Musulmana. Parte 1. Bibliografia generale. Roma, Tip. dell' Unione Editrice, 1916. 491p.
K252

A comprehensive bibliography of books and periodical material on all phases of Moslem life and culture. Includes comparative tables of Mussulman and Christian calendars.

Pfannmüller, Gustav. Handbuch der Islam-Literatur. Berlin, de Gruyter, 1923. 436p. **K253**

A comprehensive critical manual and bibliography on religious literature.

Encyclopedias and handbooks

Annuaire du monde musulman, statistique, historique, social et économique, rédigé par L. Massignon. 3. éd. 1929. Paris, Leroux, 1930. 484p. **K254**

1st-2d issues, 1923, 1925, pub. 1924, 1927. No more published.

Contains important descriptive and statistical information on the population, religion, government and economic conditions of the various peoples of the Moslem world in Europe, Africa and Asia. Bibliographies.

Encyclopaedia of Islam; a dictionary of the geography, ethnography and biography of the Muhammadan peoples; ed. by M. Th. Houtsma, A. J. Wensinck and others. Leyden, Brill; Lond., Luzac, 1911–38. 4v. and suppl. il. **K255**

The most important reference work in English on Islamic subjects.

A work of high scholarship and authority, containing signed articles, with bibliographies, on subjects in biography, history, geography, religious beliefs, institutions, manners and customs, tribes, industries, sciences, terms of different sorts, etc. Geographical material includes separate articles on towns and larger political divisions in the Ottoman Empire and on foreign countries in which Islam is of importance, e.g., China.

As the encyclopedia was published in parts over a period of almost thirty years, it is, necessarily, not equally up to date in all its volumes. Later information is supplied in some cases in the supplement, and the following contents, with dates of publication in parts, shows what volumes contain articles that may need to be supplemented by later data or bibliography.

v.1, A–D, in pts., 1908–13; v.2, E–K, in pts., 1913–28; v.3, L–R, in pts., 1928–36; v.4, S–Z, in pts., 1924–34.

Handwörterbuch des Islam, im Auftrag der K. Akademie van Wetenschappen, Amsterdam, hrsg. von A. J. Wensinck und J. K. Kramers. Leiden, Brill, 1941. 833p. il. **K256**

A scholarly one-volume work with long signed articles and bibliographies.

Koran

Koran. Holy Qur-án, containing the Arabic text with English translation and commentary, by Maulvi Muhammad Ali. 2d ed. Lahore, Punjab, India, Ahmadiyya anjuman-i-isháat-i-Islam, 1920. 1275p. **K257**

Printed in Gt. Brit. by Unwin Brothers, Ltd., Woking and Lond.

—— The Qur'án. Tr. with a critical re-arrangement of the Surahs, by Richard Bell. Edinburgh, T. Clark, 1937–39. 2v. **K258**

See also Sacred books of the East, v.6 and 9, The Qur'ân, tr. by E. Palmer (K230).

MYTHOLOGY

Edwardes, Marian. Dictionary of non-classical mythology. Lond., Dent; N.Y., Dutton, 1912. 214p. (Everyman's library) **K259**

Short articles, with some bibliographical references, on names and myths in the Assyrian, Babylonian, Celtic, Chinese, Egyptian, Hindu, Japanese, Mexican, North and South American Indian, Persian, Scandinavian and Teutonic mythologies.

Gayley, Charles Mills. Classic myths in English literature and in art, based originally on Bulfinch's Age of fable (1855) accompanied by an interpretative and illustrative commentary. . . . new ed., rev. and enl. Bost., Ginn [c1911]. 597p. il. **K260**

Mythology of all races, Louis Herbert Gray, ed. v.1, 3, 6, 9-12; John Arnott MacCulloch, ed. v.2, 4-5, 7-8, 13. Bost., Archaeol. Inst. of Amer., Marshall Jones Co., 1916–32. 13v. il. $10 per v. **K261**

v.1, Greek and Roman, by W. S. Fox; v.2, Eddic, by J. A. MacCulloch; v.3, Celtic, by J. A. MacCulloch; Slavic by Jan Machal; v.4, Finno-Ugric Siberian, by Uno Holmberg; v.5, Semitic, by S. H. Langdon; v.6, Indian, by A. Keith; Iranian, by A. J. Carnoy; v.7, Armenian by M. H. Ananikian; African, by Alice Werner; v.8, Chinese, by J. C. Ferguson; Japanese, by Masaharu Anesaki; v.9, Oceanic, by R. B. Dixon; v.10, North American, by H. B. Alexander; v.11, Latin-American, by H. B. Alexander; v.12, Egypt, by W. Max Müller; Indo-Chinese by J. G. Scott; v.13, Index.

An important set which contains valuable reference material in both text and illustrations. The general index makes it the most useful single reference work in the whole field available in English.

Roscher, Wilhelm Heinrich. Ausführliches Lexikon der griechischen und römischen Mythologie. Leipzig, Teubner, 1884–1937. 6v. and 3 suppl. il. **K262**

v.1-6, A-Z und Nachträge; Supplements: Epitheta deorum ed. by C. F. H. Bruchmann and I. B. Carter,

1893–1902. 2v.; Mythische Kosmographie der Griechen, by E. H. Berger, 1904. 2v.; Geschichte der klassischen Mythologie u. Religionsgeschichte, by Otto Gruppe, 1921. 248p.

Scholarly signed articles with bibliographies and good illustrations. The most complete work, for large reference or university libraries but not suited to other types.

Werner, Edward Theodore Chalmers. Dictionary of Chinese mythology. Shanghai, Kelly, 1932. 627p. **K263**

"This dictionary has been written with the object of furnishing, in a compact form, information concerning the entities, animate and inanimate, constituting the Chinese supernal and infernal hierarchies."—*Pref.*

Williams, Charles Alfred Speed. Outlines of Chinese symbolism and art motives; . . . an alphabetical compendium of antique legends and beliefs, as reflected in the manners and customs of the Chinese. 2d rev. ed. Shanghai, Kelly and Walsh, 1932. 468p. **K264**

See also Frazer, *The Golden bough* (K3).

POPULAR CUSTOMS AND FOLKLORE
Bibliography

Hague. Koninklijke Bibliotheek. Catalogus van Folklore in de Koninklijke Bibliotheek. Den Haag, Drukkerij "Humanitas," 1919–22. 3v. in 2. **K265**

Contents: 1. deel, Europa; 2. deel, Buiten Europa, Supplement, Registers.

A very rich collection for all countries. Continued chronologically by *Volkskundliche Bibliographie* (K266).

Volkskundliche Bibliographie, 1917–1934. Im Auftrage des Verbandes deutscher Vereine für Volkskunde mit Unterstützung, begonnen von E. Hoffmann-Krayer, weitergeführt von Paul Geiger. Berlin, de Gruyter, 1919–39. v.1-12. **K266**

A comprehensive current bibliography, listing in the 1933–34 volume some 7421 items in addition to many reviews of the items listed. Includes both books and analytical articles in periodicals, etc.; indexes articles in some 1100 periodicals. Classified arrangement with full author and subject indexes. Annual, except that volumes 5-7, 10-12 cover two years each.

❧ Useful current bibliographies of folklore are published in "Articles on American literature appearing in current periodicals" in quarterly issues of *American literature* (*see* R190); *Handbook of Latin American studies* (V367); "American bibliography" in *PMLA* (*see* R11); and the March issues of *Southern folklore quarterly.*

Handbooks and dictionaries

Funk and Wagnalls Standard dictionary of folklore, mythology and legend. Maria Leach, ed. N.Y., Funk and Wagnalls, 1949–50. 2v. $7.50 ea. **K267**

v.1-2, A-Z. A separate index is announced for publication.

A representative selection of gods, heroes, tales, motifs, customs, beliefs, songs, dances, games, proverbs, etc., of the cultures of the world. Volume 1 includes 23 "survey articles" with bibliographies on regions and on special subjects (ballad, dance, fairy tale) written by specialists.

Hone, William. Every-day book and Table book. . . . Lond., Tegg. 1838. 3v. il. **K268**

Subtitle: Everlasting calendar of popular amusements, sports, pastimes, ceremonies, manners, customs, and events, incident to each of the three hundred and sixty-five days, in past and present times; forming a complete history of the year, months, and seasons, and a perpetual key to the almanac.

Thompson, Stith. Motif-index of folk-literature; a classification of narrative elements in folk-tales, ballads, myths, fables, mediaeval romances, exempla, fabliaux, jest-books, and local legends. Bloomington, Ind., 1932–36. 6v. (Indiana Univ. studies, v.19, nos. 96-97, v.20, nos. 100-101, v.21, nos. 105-106, v.22, nos. 108-110, v.23, nos. 111-112) $3 per v. **K269**

Also issued as *FF communications* nos. 106-109, 116-117, Helsinki, 1932–36.

v.6, Detailed alphabetical index, 647p.

A sort of Dewey decimal classification scheme for cataloging motifs of folk literature. Includes references to materials about motifs for a number of them, and lists at least one instance of the appearance of each motif in the literature where no reference is known.

Walsh, William Shepard. Curiosities of popular customs and of rites, ceremonies, observances, and miscellaneous antiquities. Phila., Lippincott, 1898. 1018p. il. $6. **K270**

Frequently reprinted.

United States

Lys, Claudia de. Treasury of American superstitions. N.Y., Philosophical Library, 1948. 494p. **K271**

General account of superstitions arranged under 24 headings with index.

Argentina

Cortazar, Augusto Raúl. Guía bibliográfica del folklore argentino; primera contribución. Buenos Aires, Imp. de la Universidad, 1942. 291p. (Facultad de Filosofía y Letras de la Universidad de

Buenos Aires. Instituto de Literatura Argentina . . . [Publicaciones] Seccion de bibliografía, t.I, no.1) **K272**

Annotated.

Brazil

Gorham, Rex. The folkways of Brazil; a bibliography, comp. by Rex Gorham, ed. by Karl Brown. N.Y., New York Pub. Lib., 1944. 67p. (Repr. with additions and corrections from the New York Public Library Bulletin, Apr., July 1943 and Apr.-May 1944) $1.25. **K273**

Annotated.

France

Gennep, Arnold van. Bibliographie méthodique [de folklore français]. (In his Manuel de folklore français contemporain, t.3-4. Paris, A. Picard, 1937–38) **K274**

Very comprehensive in scope. Annotated.

Germany

Erich, Oswald Adolf and Beitl, Richard. Wörterbuch der deutschen Volkskunde. . . . Leipzig, Alfred Kröner, 1936. 864p. il. **K275**

Handwörterbuch des deutschen Aberglaubens, hrsg. unter besonderer Mitwirkung von E. Hoffmann-Krayer und mitarbeit zahlreicher Fachgenossen von Hanns Bächtold-Stäubli. Berlin, de Gruyter, 1927–1941. 9v. and Nachträge in v.9. (Handwörterbücher zur deutschen Volkskunde, hrsg. vom Verband deutscher Vereine für Volkskunde. Abt. I) **K276**

Handwörterbuch des deutschen Märchens, hrsg. unter besonderer Mitwirkung von Johannes Bolte und mitarbeit zahlreicher Fachgenossen von Lutz Mackensen. Berlin, de Gruyter, 1930–40. v.1-2. (Handwörterbücher zur deutschen Volkskunde. . . . Abt. II. Märchen) **K277**

v.1-2, A-Gyges.
Signed articles by specialists, bibliographies.

Great Britain

Brand, John. Popular antiquities of Great Britain. Faiths and folklore . . . [ed.] by W. Carew Hazlitt. Lond., Reeves, 1905. 2v. il. **K278**

Subtitle: A dictionary of national beliefs, superstitions and popular customs, past and current, with their classical and foreign analogues, described and illustrated. Forming a new edition of "The Popular Antiquities of Great Britain" by Brand and Ellis, largely extended, corrected and brought down to the present time, and now first alphabetically arranged.

Chambers, Robert. Book of days; a miscellany of popular antiquities in connection with the calendar. Phila., Lippincott, 1899. 2v. o.p. **K279**

Published originally 1862–64. Later editions show little change.

Radford, Edwin and Radford, M. A. Encyclopaedia of superstitions. Lond., Rider [1947?]. 269p. **K280**

Wright, Arthur Robinson. British calendar customs: England . . . ed. by T. E. Lones. Lond., Folk-Lore Soc., W. Glaisher, 1936–40. v.1-3. il. (Folk-Lore Soc. Pub., 97, 102, 106) **K281**

Contents: v.1, Movable festivals; v.2-3, Fixed festivals, January–December.

Iceland

Islandica; an annual. Ithaca, 1908- . **K282**
For full description see A376.

Italy

Pitrè, Giuseppe. Bibliografia delle tradizioni popolari d'Italia . . . con tre indici speciali. Torino-Palermo, Carlo Clausen, 1894. 603p. **K283**

Toschi, Paolo. Bibliografia delle tradizioni popolari d'Italia dal 1916 al 1940. Firenze, Barbera, 1946- . v.1, pt.1-2. (R. Museo di Etnografia Italiana) (In progress) **K284**

v.1, pt.1, Generalità; pt.2, Usi e costumi, credenze e pregiudizi.
To be completed in 9 parts (4v.). pt.3, Poesia, musica, danza e teatro popolare; pt.4, Novellistica popolare; pt.5, Proverbi; pt.6, Terminologia; pt.7, Arti popolari; pt.8, Scienze popolari; pt.9, Giochi e giocattoli.
Continues Pitrè's *Bibliografia* [v.1] 1894, and [v.2], as yet unpublished, which covers the period 1895–1916.—*Pref.*
Annotated.

Latin America

Boggs, Ralph Steele. Bibliography of Latin American folklore. N.Y., Wilson, 1940. 109p. (Inter-American Bibliographical and Lib. Assoc. Pub., ser. 1, v.5) $1.50. **K285**

643 numbered items published "as a partial guide to the field."—*Pref.* Classified by types of folklore and then arranged by country. Author index.

Netherlands

Laan, Kornelius ter. Folkloristisch woordenboek van Nederland en Vlaams België. 'sGravenhage, G. B. van Goor, 1949. 503p. **K286**

"Lijst von geraadpleegde werken," p.497-503.

Scotland

Banks, Mary Macleod. British calendar customs: Scotland. . . . Lond., Folk-Lore Soc., W. Glaisher, 1937–41. 3v. il. (Pub. of the Folk-Lore Soc., 100, 104, 108)   **K287**

Contents: v.1, Movable festivals, Harvest, March riding and Wapynshaws, Wells, Fairs; v.2, The Seasons, the Quarters, Hogmanay, Jan. to May; v.3, June to Dec., Christmas, the Yules.

—— ——Orkney and Shetland. Lond., Folk-Lore Soc., W. Glaisher, 1946. 110p. il. (Pub. of the Folk-Lore Soc., 112)   **K288**

HOLIDAYS

Douglas, George William. The American book of days: A compendium of information about holidays, festivals, notable anniversaries and Christian and Jewish Holy Days with notes on other American anniversaries worthy of remembrance. Rev. by Helen Douglas Compton. N.Y., Wilson, 1948. 697p. il. $6.   **K289**

Significant dates and biographical sketches of the great leaders of World War II have been added to this revised edition.

Guaranty Trust Company of New York. Bank and public holidays throughout the world [19-?]. N.Y., Guaranty Trust Co., Annual. Free.   **K290**

Hazeltine, Mary Emogene. Anniversaries and holidays; a calendar of days and how to observe them . . . 2d ed., completely rev. with the editorial assistance of Judith K. Sollenberger. Chic., Amer. Lib. Assoc., 1944. 316p. $6.   **K291**

A very useful guide originally published in 1928. pt.1, Calendar; pt.2, Books about holidays, special days, and seasons, including the origin and history of holiday customs, plays and pageants for holidays, programs and program making, entertainments, etc.; pt.3, Books about persons referred to in the calendar; pt.4, Classified index; pt.5, General index.

Schauffler, Robert Haven. Our American holiday series. N.Y., Moffat, 1907–47. 19v. Dodd, $2.50 and $2.75 ea.   **K292**

Volumes so far published are: Arbor day. 1909; Armistice day, comp. by A. P. Sanford. 1927; Christmas. 1907; Columbus day, comp. by H. C. Paulmier. 1938; Democracy days, comp. by H. C. Paulmier. 1942; Easter, comp. by S. T. Rice. 1916; Flag day. 1912; Good Will days, comp. by H. C. Paulmier. 1947; Hallowe'en. 1933; Independence day. 1912; Lincoln's birthday. 1909; Memorial day. 1911; Mother's day, comp. by S. T. Rice. 1915; Music week. 1935; Pan-American day, comp. by H. C. Paulmier. 1943; Peace days, comp. by H. C. Paulmier. 1946; Roosevelt day (October 27), comp. by H. C. Paulmier. 1932; Thanksgiving day. 1907; Washington's birthday. 1910.

—— The days we celebrate. N.Y., Dodd, 1940. 4v. $2.75 ea.   **K293**

Designed to bring to date *Our American holidays* (K292) and *Plays for our American holidays*. Most of the material is of more recent publication than the material in the corresponding volume of the earlier set.

v.1, Christmas, St. Valentine's day, St. Patrick's day, Easter; v.2, New Year's day, All Fool's day, May day, Arbor day, Harvest festival, Thanksgiving; v.3, Lincoln's birthday, Washington's birthday, Memorial day, Flag day, Independence day, Armistice day, Columbus day; v.4, Mother's day, Music week, Graduation day, Father's day, Hallowe'en, Book week.

SOCIAL SCIENCES

❧ The term "social sciences" embraces a large number of subjects which deal with the relationship of man to society. In this *Guide*, the term is used to cover the works concerned with sociology, including family life, criminology, racial groups; statistics, political science and government; economics and business; law; and education. There are only a few reference works which deal with the social sciences as a whole but among these the *Encyclopaedia of the social sciences* (L14) is outstanding. An authoritative work, comprehensive in coverage, it is basic for any reference collection. *Public affairs information service* (L9) is the most generally useful index for these subjects as it includes books, documents, pamphlets, and multigraphed material, as well as periodical articles.

GENERAL WORKS
Bibliography

Australian public affairs information service; a subject index to current literature. no.1- , July 1945- . Canberra, Commonwealth National Library, 1945- . Monthly.   **L1**

Subject index of selected articles on Australian political, economic and social affairs. New books, pamphlets, current periodical articles, and government publications from all English speaking countries are included.

Bibliographie der Staats- und Wirtschaftswissenschaften; Internationale Monatshefte der Buch- und Zeitschriftenliteratur über Volk, Wirtschaft, Kultur und Politik. Hrsg. vom Statistischen Reichsamt. 1905- . Berlin, Reimar Hobbing, 1906- . v.1- . Monthly (irregular). RM. 36 per yr.   **L2**

v.1-3 (1905–07) issued as a section of *Kritische Blätter für die gesamten Sozialwissenschaften;* v.4-8 (1908–12) as a section of the continuation of that journal, *Blätter für die gesamten Sozialwissenschaften;* v.9- , issued independently. Title varies: usually *Bibliographie der Sozialwissenschaften,* with variant subtitles, through 1936.

A classified subject list with annual author and subject indexes, listing both the book and periodical literature of the various subdivisions of the social and political sciences. A comprehensive current bibliography of the subject, containing a large amount of valuable material but difficult to use quickly because of lack of cumulations. An annual cumulation (Jahrbuch) was published in three volumes for the years 1906–08.

―――― Sonderheft: Einführung in die systematische Anordnung der Jahrgänge 1905–1936. Berlin, 1937. 58p.

Culver, Dorothy C. Methodology of social science research: A bibliography. Berkeley, Univ. of California Pr., 1936. 159p. (Pub. of the Bureau of Public Administration, Univ. of Calif.)   **L3**

Not a manual but a bibliography of materials published in English from 1920–1935, arranged by class with author and subject indexes. Includes bibliographies on: methodology of special fields; sources of material; use of libraries; collection and analysis of data, including the survey, interview, questionnaire, case study, tests and measurements, etc.; and the preparation of the manuscript. Some of the titles have brief annotations.

Fondation Nationale des Sciences Politiques. Bulletin analytique de documentation politique, économique et sociale contemporaine. 1. année- . Paris, Presses Universitaires de France, 1946- . Bimonthly. France, 1000fr.; étranger, 1200fr.   **L4**

"Rédigé avec la collaboration de la Bibliothèque de Documentation Internationale Contemporaine, de l'Institut National d'Études Démographiques et de l'Institut de Science Économique Appliquée."

Lists articles from some 675 French and foreign periodicals on political, economic, and social questions, frequently with a very brief descriptive note. Gives exact citation with inclusive paging. Arranged by class with annual subject index. No author index.

Grandin, A. Bibliographie générale des sciences

juridiques, politiques, économiques et sociales de 1800 à 1925/26. Paris, Recueil Sirey, 1926. 3v. **L5**

v.1-2, classified bibliography; v.3, indexes of authors, titles and subjects.

——— —— 1.-17. supplement, 1926–47/48. Paris, Recueil Sirey, 1928–49. v. 1-17. (In progress) (v.17, 1600fr.)

Holbrook, Franklin F. Survey of activities of American agencies in relation to materials for research in the social sciences and the humanities. Comp. for the Joint Committee on Materials for Research of the American Council of Learned Societies and the Social Science Research Council. Wash. and N.Y., Coöperating Councils, 1932. 184p. **L6**

A listing and survey of all American agencies active in collecting, recording, or disseminating materials in the wide range of the social sciences and the humanities.

London bibliography of the social sciences . . . comp. under the direction of B. M. Headicar, and C. Fuller, with an introd. by Sidney Webb (Lord Passfield). Lond., Lond. School of Econ., 1931– 37. 4v. and 2 suppl. (London School of Economics. Studies: Bibliographies no.8) **L7**

v.1-3, Subjects; v.4, Author index, p.1-915; Periodicals list, p.917-42; Table of subject headings, p.943-83; 1st suppl., June 1, 1929–May 31, 1931. 596p.; 2d suppl. June 1, 1931–May 31, 1936. 1374p.

The most extensive subject bibliography in its field recording (v.1-3) more than 600,000 items; important to all large libraries and research workers. Records material in nine London libraries and special collections—Royal Anthropological Institute, University College, Edward Fry Library of International Law, Goldsmiths' Library, Royal Institute of International Affairs, National Institute of Industrial Psychology, Reform Club, Royal Statistical Society, University Library—and marks location of copies of works listed. Arranged alphabetically by subjects, with brief but adequate information—author, title (often abbreviated), paging, date, location and information as to whether the work contains a bibliography— with many cross references.

Maunier, René. Manuel bibliographique des sciences sociales et économiques. Paris, Sirey, 1920. 228p. **L8**

A guide to bibliographies and reference books of social sciences and economics, particularly useful for historical purposes as it includes many eighteenth and nineteenth century publications. Includes works in French, English, German and Italian.

Public affairs information service. Bulletin of the Public Affairs Information Service, a cooperative clearing house of public affairs information, 1st- annual cumulations. N.Y., Pub. Aff. Inform. Service, 1915- . v. 1- . Compl. service $100 a year; cumulations only, including the annual, $50 a year; also service basis. **L9**

Usually cited as PAIS. Issued in three forms: (1) weekly bulletins; (2) cumulations published five times a year, the fifth cumulated issue forming (3) the permanent annual volume.

A subject index to the current literature in its field— books, documents, pamphlets, articles in periodicals, multigraphed material, etc. Includes selective indexing to more than 1000 periodicals.

A very useful index for political science, government, legislation, economics, sociology, etc. Indispensable in the large library.

Social science abstracts; a comprehensive abstracting and indexing journal of the world's periodical literature in the social sciences. N.Y., Soc. Sci. Abstr. Inc., Columbia Univ. 1929–33. 5v. **L10**

v.1-4, Abstracts 1929–32; v.5, Indexes: Subject, p.1-548; Authors, p.551-677; List of periodicals and serials in the social sciences; p.681-725.

An extensive bibliography with abstracts written by specialists. Covers practically the same field as the *Encyclopaedia of the social sciences* (L14), as it includes the subjects of human geography, cultural anthropology, history, economics, political science, sociology, and statistics. Each annual volume has an index of authors, and a very detailed index of subjects. Unfortunately discontinued for lack of funds.

Societies

American foundations and their fields. VI. N.Y., Raymond Rich Associates, 1948. 284p. **L11**

The first three issues covering foundation disbursements for 1930, 1931 and 1934 were published by the Twentieth Century Fund. 4th ed. 1939; 5th ed. 1942.

It was first planned to issue the sixth survey in quarterly parts and Parts I and II were published in that form, edited by W. B. Cherin. After Mr. Cherin's death, the plans were again changed and a full sixth edition was published in one volume, edited by W. S. Rich and N. R. Deardorff.

This edition gives information about 899 foundations, giving specific facts when available, such as donor, officers and trustees, purpose, year established, direct activities, total capital assets, total expenditures, total grants, method of operation, etc.

Supplemented by:

American foundation news service. v.1, June 15, 1949- . N.Y., Raymond Rich, 1949- approx. 8 times a yr. $12. **L11a**

Cumulated index to volume 1, 1949/50.

Gives information on new foundations, foundation policies, reports, etc.

SOCIOLOGY
Encyclopedias

Dictionary of sociology, ed. by Henry Pratt Fairchild. N.Y., Philosophical Library, 1944. 342p. $6. **L12**

Brief signed articles giving definitions of sociological terms.

Dictionnaire de sociologie, familiale, politique, économique, spirituelle, générale, publié sous la direction de G. Jacquemet avec le concours de nombreux collaborateurs. Paris, Letouzey, 1931–39. v.1-4 (incompl.). 30fr. per fasc.; sub. 20fr. (In progress) **L13**

v.1-3, A-Bouclier; v.4 (fasc. 19-22), Boud-Cercles.

Signed articles, with bibliographies often of some length. Contains biographies, and many short articles on tribes, clans, etc. From the Catholic point of view.

Encyclopaedia of the social sciences; ed.-in-chief, E. R. A. Seligman, associate ed., Alvin Johnson. N.Y., Macmillan, 1930–35. 15v. **L14**

v.1, Introductions: I, Development of social thought and institutions (12 articles); II, The Social sciences as disciplines by country (11 articles); Encyclopaedia articles A-All; v.2-15, All-Z; Index.

The first comprehensive encyclopedia of the whole field of the social sciences, projected and prepared under the auspices of ten learned societies: American Anthropological Assoc., American Assoc. of Social Workers, American Economic Assoc., American Historical Assoc., American Political Science Assoc., American Psychological Assoc., American Sociological Society, American Statistical Assoc., Assoc. of American Law Schools, National Education Assoc. Aims to cover all important topics in the fields of political science, economics, law, anthropology, sociology, penology, and social work, and the social aspects of ethics, education, philosophy, psychology, biology, geography, medicine, art, etc. Is international in scope and treatment but fuller for the English-speaking world and western Europe than for other regions or interests. Articles are by specialists and signed by full names, not merely initials, and there are bibliographies which in the main are adequate and in unusually good form. Includes many biographies of deceased persons; about 50 per cent of articles are biographical.

Handwörterbuch der Soziologie, in Verbindung mit G. Briefs, F. Eulenburg [u. Anderen] hrsg. von Alfred Vierkandt. Stuttgart, Enke, 1931. 690p. **L15**

Contains long signed articles on rather large subjects, with brief bibliographies, including mainly German titles. Two indexes: (1) names; (2) smaller subjects.

Social work

Elliott, Edward C. and **Chambers, M. M.** Charters of philanthropies; a study of the charters of twenty-nine American philanthropic foundations. N.Y., 1939. 744p. (The Carnegie Foundation for the Advancement of Teaching in cooperation with Purdue Univ.) **L16**

Lallemand, Léon. Histoire de la charité. Paris, Picard, 1902–12. v.1-4 in 5. **L17**

v.1, L'antiquité (les civilisations disparues), 1902; v.2, Les neuf premiers siècles de l'ère chrétienne, 1903; v.3, Le moyen âge (du xᵉ au xvɪᵉ siècle), 1906; v.4, Les temps modernes (du xvɪᵉ au xɪxᵉ siècle), 1912, 2v.

Young, Earl Fiske. Dictionary of social welfare. N.Y., Social Sciences Pub., 1948. 218p. **L18**

Includes technical, psychological and slang terms.

Directories

❦ There are many local directories of welfare agencies, by state, city or region. Libraries should acquire those for their own locality according to need.

Although now somewhat out of date, the Russell Sage Foundation Library published *A list of directories of social agencies* (rev. ed. 1941. 10p.) which lists directories of state agencies as well as others, by subject.

Harrison, Shelby Millard and **Andrews, F. E.** American foundations for social welfare. Includes a directory of 505 foundations. N.Y., Russell Sage Foundation, 1946. 249p. il. $2. **L20**

Bibliography, p.221-34.

New York Academy of Medicine. Committee on Public Health Relations. Directory of convalescent homes in the United States. 6th ed. N.Y., 1947. 112p. 50c. **L21**

Public welfare directory, 1940- . Chic., Amer. Public Welfare Assoc., 1940- . il. (1949, $3.50) **L22**

Lists federal, state, and local public assistance and welfare agencies, with directors.

Social work year book, 1929- . A description of organized activities in social work and in related fields. Ed., Russell H. Kurtz. N.Y., Russell Sage Found., 1930- . Biennial. (1949, $4.50) **L23**

A very useful handbook containing in each volume: Part I, Topical articles descriptive of functions, organized activities, and programs, written and signed by specialists, with bibliographies; Part II, Directories of national agencies giving name, date of founding, address, officers, membership, purpose and activities, periodicals, etc.; Index to Parts I and II.

Annual charities register and digest, being a classified register of charities in or available for the metropolis. Lond., Longmans, 1884- . Annual. (1948, 10s. 6d.) **L24**

Previous to 1899 published every four years.

Blind

Lende, Helga. Books about the blind; a bibliographical guide to literature relating to the blind. N.Y., Amer. Found. for the Blind, 1940. 215p. $2. **L25**

An annotated bibliography of about 2700 references to the "more important and relevant items" relating to the blind. Includes material on education, psychology, vocations and economic adjustment, social adjustment, literature and reading, the deaf-blind, etc.

American Foundation for the Blind, Inc. Directory of activities for the blind in the United States and Canada, including prevention of blindness organizations and sight-saving classes, comp. by Helga Lende 1st ed.- . N.Y., Foundation, 1926- . (1945, $1.50) **L26**

Published irregularly.

Children and youth

Menefee, Louise Arnold and **Chambers, Merritt Madison.** American youth, an annotated bibliography, prepared for the American Youth Commission. Wash., Amer. Council on Educ., 1938. 492p. $3. **L27**

Annotated and classified, with alphabetical index. Supplemented by:

Chambers, Merritt Madison and **Exton, Elaine.** Youth—key to America's future; an annotated bibliography. Wash., Amer. Council on Education, 1949. 117p. $2. **L27a**

Chambers, Merritt Madison. Youth-serving organizations; national non-governmental associations. 3d ed. Prepared for the Committee on Youth Problems. Wash., Amer. Council on Educ., 1948. 162p. diagrs. $3. **L28**

1st ed. 1937.

A comprehensive list of organizations that concern themselves directly or indirectly with youth, arranged by class or type, with an index by names of organizations. For each organization usually gives information on membership, officers, purpose, activities, publications, staff, and finances.

National Society for Crippled Children. Directory of hospitals and convalescent institutions engaged in work for crippled children in the United States of America, comp. by A. R. Shands, Jr. Elyria, Ohio, Society, 1942. 115p. $1. **L29**

First edition was published as the *Directory* of the International Society for Crippled Children, 1938. This second edition gives information in tabular form about the professional staffs and facilities of over 600 hospitals and institutions.

Tuttle, George. Youth organizations in Canada; a reference manual. Prepared for the Canadian Youth Commission. Toronto, Ryerson Pr., 1946. 110p. $1.50. **L30**

Gives name, membership, organization, purpose, activities, publications, staff, finances, etc.

U. S. Children's Bureau. Directory of state, District of Columbia, county and municipal training schools caring for delinquent children in the United States. Wash., 1943. 25p. **L31**

U. S. National Youth Administration, New York (City). Directory of youth organizations, comp.

by Mary Rodgers Lindsay . . . assisted by Simon Uhrman. . . . rev. and enl. ed. 1940. N.Y., Federal Security Agency, National Youth Administration for New York City, 1940. 293 numb. 1. **L32**

Includes complete listings for 216 organizations, and partial listings for 65, making a total of 281. It aims to include all youth organizations which are nationwide in scope as well as citywide organizations in New York City. Information was furnished by the organizations and usually includes: general character, officers, membership, purpose, history, program, activities, publications and affiliations.

Youth organizations of Great Britain. 1944/45- ed., Douglas Cooke. Lond., Jordan, 1944- . Biennial. 8s. 6d. **L33**

A directory giving organization, personnel, history, description, etc., of the various organizations devoted to youth.

Criminology

American Prison Association. State and national correctional institutions of the United States of America, Great Britain and Canada. Official [19-?]- . N.Y., Assoc., [19-?]- . Annual. (1948, $1) **L34**

Title varies slightly.

Cabot, Phillippe Sidney de Q. Juvenile delinquency; a critical annotated bibliography. N.Y., Wilson, 1946. 166p. $3.75. **L35**

972 numbered entries of books and periodical articles covering the period 1914–1944. Arranged alphabetically with subject index.

Cumming, *Sir* **John Ghest.** A contribution towards a bibliography dealing with crime and cognate subjects. 3d ed. Lond., pr. by the Receiver for the Metropolitan Police District, New Scotland Yard, 1935. 107p. 2s. 6d. **L36**

A bibliography of books, and some periodical articles covering approximately fifty years. International in scope but from the British viewpoint.

Dizionario di criminologia, per opera di numerosi autori ed a cura di Eugenio Florian, Alfredo Niceforo [e] Nicola Pende. Milano, Vallardi, 1943. 2v. il. **L37**

Long signed articles with bibliographies.

Encyclopedia of criminology ed. by Vernon C. Branham and Samuel B. Kutash. N.Y., Philosophical Lib., 1949. 527p. $12. **L38**

Includes some 100 fairly long articles signed by specialists. Bibliographies are appended. Uneven.

Greer, Sarah. Bibliography of police administration and police science. N.Y., Inst. of Public Administration, 1936. 152p. $1.50. **L39**

Social Science Research Council. Committee on Survey of Research on Crime and Criminal Jus-

tice. Guide to material on crime and criminal justice . . . prepared by Augustus Frederick Kuhlman. . . . N.Y., Wilson, 1929. 633p. Service basis. **L40**

"A descriptive, classified, union catalog of books, monographs, and pamphlets in thirteen selected libraries, and of articles listed in the leading periodical indexes relating to all phases of crime and criminal justice in the United States."—*Pref.*
Arranged by class with a subject index.

—— —— Author index, prepared by D. C. Culver. N.Y., Wilson, 1934. 32p.

Issued in form to be inserted in the back of the main volume.
Continued by:

California. University. Bureau of Public Administration. Bibliography of crime and criminal justice, 1927–1931, 1932–1937, comp. by Dorothy Campbell Culver. N.Y., Wilson, 1934–39. 2v. 413p., 391p. Service basis. **L41**
Supplemented by:

Tompkins, Dorothy Campbell. Sources for the study of the administration of criminal justice. Sacramento, Calif., Special Crime Study Commissions and California State Board of Corrections, 1949. 294p. **L41a**

Includes items published since 1938, thus supplementing the above. Emphasizes material pertinent to conditions in California.

Temperance

Standard encyclopedia of the alcohol problem; ed.-in-chief, Ernest Hurst Cherrington. . . . Westerville, Ohio, Amer. Issue Pub. Co., 1924–30. 6v. il. **L42**
Includes biography.

Racial groups

Directory of agencies in race relations; national, state and local. Chic., Julius Rosenwald Fund, 1945. 124p. $1. **L43**
Usually gives purpose, activities and personnel.

U. S. Bureau of the Census. Sixteenth census of the United States: 1940. Population. Characteristics of the nonwhite population by race. . . . Wash., Govt. Prt. Off., 1943. 112p. il. **L44**

Indians

Hargrett, Lester. A bibliography of the constitutions and laws of the American Indians. Camb., Harvard Univ. Pr., 1947. 124p. **L45**
Annotated. Locates copies in some fifty public and private libraries.

Hodge, Frederick Webb. Handbook of American Indians north of Mexico. Wash., Govt. Prt. Off., 1907–10. 2v. **L46**
For full description *see* N318.

Steward, Julian Haynes. Handbook of South American Indians. . . . Wash., Govt. Prt. Off., 1946- . v.1- . (In progress) **L47**
For full description *see* N321.

Negroes

BIBLIOGRAPHY

Hampton, Va. Normal and Agricultural Institute. Collis P. Huntington Library. A classified catalogue of the Negro collection, comp. by the Writers' Program of the Works Project Administration in the state of Virginia. Sponsored by Hampton Institute. [n.p.] 1940. 255p., [35]p. **L48**

Over 5000 titles on the Negro in Africa and America. Particularly strong in material on slavery and reconstruction.

National Urban League (for Social Service among Negroes). Dept. of Research. Selected bibliography on the Negro. 3d ed. Nov. 1940. N.Y., League, 1940. 58p. 15c. **L49**

—— —— Supplements. 1-2, June 1942—Apr. 1944. 10c-15c.

Thompson, Edgar T. and **Thompson, Alma Macy.** Race and region; a descriptive bibliography. Chapel Hill, Univ. of North Carolina Pr., 1949. 194p. $5. **L50**

A comprehensive classified bibliography on race relations compiled with special reference to the relations between Whites and Negroes in the United States. Based on collections in Duke University, the University of North Carolina and North Carolina College in Durham, with indication of location of copies in these libraries.

Work, Monroe Nathan. Bibliography of the Negro in Africa and America. N.Y., Wilson, 1928. 698p. $12, also service basis. **L51**

A comprehensive bibliography of more than 17,000 selected titles of books, pamphlets and periodical articles.

ENCYCLOPEDIAS AND HANDBOOKS

Encyclopedia of the Negro, preparatory volume with reference lists and reports, by W. E. B. DuBois . . . and Guy B. Johnson. Rev. and enl. Introd. by Anson Phelps Stokes. N.Y., Phelps-Stokes Fund, 1946. 215p. $3.25. **L52**

An introductory volume to a projected encyclopedia of the Negro including a statement of the need for such a work; originally published in 1945. Republished with some corrections and additions. Includes an alphabetical list of the major subjects to be treated with notes and bibliographical suggestions; a survey of library resources for Negro studies in the United States and abroad; and a bibliography of bibliographies dealing directly or indirectly with the Negro.

Negro handbook. 1942- . Ed. by Florence Murray. N.Y., Current Books, Inc., 1942- . Biennial. (4th ed. 1949, pub. by Macmillan, $5) **L53**

Aims "to present current factual information in a concise and handy medium, and, in so doing, to give a picture of the status of the Negro in American life."—*Introd.*

Negro year book, 1912- . Tuskegee Inst., Ala., Dept. of Records and Research, 1912- . v.1- . **L54**

Published 1912, 1913, 1914/15, 1916/17, 1918/19, 1921/22, 1925/26, 1931/32, 1937/38, 1941/46.
1st-9th ed., ed. by Monroe N. Work; 10th ed., ed. by Jessie P. Guzman.
Statistics and survey articles on the Negro in the United States, conditions and achievements.

Hellmann, Ellen and **Abrahams, Leah.** Handbook on race relations in South Africa. Pub. for the South African Institute of Race Relations. Capetown, Lond., Ox. Univ. Pr., 1949. 778p. 42s. **L55**

Survey articles by authorities on various phases of race relations in South Africa. Covers such subjects as population, government, law, labor, trade unions, agriculture, taxation, education, social welfare, politics, religion, literature, music, art, race cooperation, race attitude, etc.

BIOGRAPHY

Who's who in colored America; a biographical dictionary of notable living persons of African descent in America. Brooklyn, N.Y., Who's Who in Colored America, 1927- . $10. **L56**

For full record *see* S48.

STATISTICS

❧ Reference questions calling for statistics are frequent in any library, and books which furnish reliable and up-to-date statistics are of great importance in any reference collection, especially in libraries where original research in social, political, economic, or industrial questions, is done.

Statistical reference works fall into six main classes: (1) general dictionaries or compends, (2) almanacs or annuals of miscellaneous statistics and general information, (3) census reports and bulletins, (4) national yearbooks and statistical annuals limited to the figures of one particular country, (5) periodicals, official and nonofficial, (6) statistics of a particular subject, e.g., agriculture, foreign commerce, etc.

Of these six classes, the first and second are of easiest and most frequent use for popular questions and are useful within their limitations although they are usually neither detailed nor authoritative enough for important questions. For reliable and authoritative statistics works falling in the other classes must be used.

The third class is always official (i.e., prepared by a government) and no attempt has been made to list these here, except for guides to the U.S. census. For information about recent census reports in various other countries consult the two bibliographies published by the Census Library Project of the Library of Congress, *General censuses and vital statistics in the Americas* (1943) (L83), and *National censuses and vital statistics in Europe, 1918–1939* (1948), *Supplement, 1940–1948* (1948) (L62); and the *Bibliography of selected statistical sources of the American nations* (1947) (L77).

These bibliographies also list the national yearbooks and statistical annuals in more detail than can be given here, as well as the official current serial publications which are very important for up-to-date information. The *Population index* (L61) and the *Public affairs information service* (L9) are both useful indexes to the statistical material to be found in periodicals.

For statistics on special subjects *see* names of individual subjects. Frequently recourse must also be had to government publications of varying kinds. The bibliographies and indexes listed below will be helpful. Statistics for regions, states, and smaller subdivisions may be found in census publications, regional surveys, state and municipal handbooks, etc.

Bibliography and indexes

Buros, Oscar Krisen. Research and statistical methodology; books and reviews of 1933–1938. New Brunswick, N.J., Rutgers Univ. Pr., 1938. 100p. **L57**

—— Second yearbook of research and statistical methodology; books and reviews. Highland Park, N.J., Gryphon Pr., 1941. 383p.

Covers 1938–41 and contains 1652 excerpts from reviews from 283 periodicals on 346 books.

Institut International de Statistique. Revue, 1. année, 1933- . La Haye, 1933- . Quarterly. **L58**

"Bibliographie statistique internationale" included in each number. An important current bibliography, international in scope, unfortunately not cumulated, nor indexed.

Koren, John. History of statistics, their development and progress in many countries; in memoirs to commemorate the seventy-fifth anniversary of the American Statistical Association. N.Y., Macmillan, 1918. 773p. **L59**

Especially useful for information about the history of official statistical publications.

Kuczynski, Robert R. Colonial population. Lond., Ox. Univ. Pr., 1937. 101p. $1.75; 5s. **L60**

Populations of colonies in all parts of the world, with reference to sources.

Population index. v.1, 1935- . Princeton, N. J., School of Public Affairs, Princeton Univ., and the Population Assoc. of America, 1935- . v.1- . Quarterly. $3 per yr. **L61**

An annotated bibliography of book and periodical literature on all phases of population problems. Arranged by class with annual cumulated indexes by author and country. Includes special articles and current items.

Title varies: Jan. 1935–Oct. 1936, *Population literature.* Volume 1, number 1 (revised, May 1, 1935) "replaces 'Review of current research, 1,' including all titles from that publication as well as additional foreign and American citations for 1933. (No 1934 or 1935 titles were added.) The period covered by this number begins Jan. 1, 1933, which terminates the period covered by *Social science abstracts* (1929–1932)."—*Note*, v.1, p.1.

Volumes 1-2 published by the Population Association of America, Washington, D.C.

U. S. Library of Congress. Census Library Project. National censuses and vital statistics in Europe, 1918–1939; an annotated bibliography. Wash., Govt. Prt. Off., 1948. 215p. 40c. **L62**

A very useful guide to the national censuses and official statistical publications of the various countries of Europe, for the period between the two world wars.

—————— 1940–1948 Supplement. 1948. 48p. 15c.

Verwey, Gerlof. Economist's handbook, a manual of statistical sources . . . with assistance of D. C. Renooij. Amsterdam, H. J. Paris, 1937. 460p. and suppl., 79p. **L63**

pt.1, Subject list, arranged alphabetically by subject word with indication of sources of statistical information on each, p.15-200; pt.2, Sources classified according to country, p.201-415; Alphabetical index, p.419-60; Supplement, 79p.

Part 2 is a comprehensive listing of publications giving statistical material.

Dictionaries and compendiums

Kurtz, Albert K. and **Edgerton, Harold A.** Statistical dictionary of terms and symbols. N.Y., Wiley; Lond., Chapman and Hall, 1939. 191p. $2. **L64**

International

Annuaire général, 1919–1928. Paris, Larousse, 1919–28. v.1-9. il. **L65**

No more published.

An unofficial yearbook of the *Statesman's yearbook* type (L71), useful for the period covered. Until 1926 had title *Annuaire général de la France et de l'étranger* and were less general in character than the later volumes.

Anuario de estatistica mundial. Yearbook of world statistics. Annuaire de statistique mondiale. Anuario de estadistica mundial. 1940. Rio de Janeiro, Centro de Estudos, 1940. 223p. **L65a**

2d issue, 1st pub. 1938.

Institut International de Statistique. Office Permanent. Annuaire international de statistique. La Haye, 1916–21. v.1-8. maps. **L66**

Contents: (1) État de la population (Europe), 1916; (2) Mouvement de la population (Europe), 1917; (3) État de la population (Amérique), 1919; (4) Mouvement de la population (Amérique), 1920; (5) État de la population (Afrique, Asie, Océanie), 1921; (6) Salaires et durée du travail, conventions, collectives, chomage, placement, syndicats ouvriers et patronaux, grèves et lock-outs; (7) Enseignement primaire, agriculture, postes, télégraphie et téléphonie, sociétés anonymes, coopératives, habitations, indices des prix de gros; (8) Finances d'états, production, cours des changes.

No more published. v.1-5, continued by:

—————— Aperçu de la démographie des divers pays du monde, 1922–36. La Haye, Van Stockum, 1922–39. v.1-6. **L67**

v.6, pub. 1939, covers 1929–1936.

—————— Statistique internationale des grandes villes. 1927–34. La Haye, Van Stockum, 1927–39. v.1-3. **L68**

Mulhall, Michael George. Dictionary of statistics. 4th ed. rev. Lond., Routledge, 1899. 853p. o.p. **L69**

pt.1, Statistics from the time of Emperor Diocletian to 1890, arranged alphabetically; pt.2, 1890–98, List of books of reference; Index to pts. 1-2. Does not give authorities for statistics included.

Webb, Augustus Duncan. New dictionary of statistics. Lond., Routledge; N.Y., Dutton, 1911. 682p. o.p. **L70**

A supplement for 1899–1909, to Mulhall's *Dictionary of statistics* (L69). Arranged on the same general plan as Mulhall, but superior to that work in that authorities for all statistics are given.

Statesman's year-book; statistical and historical annual of the states of the world, 1864- . Lond. and N.Y., Macmillan, 1864- . v.1- . (v.86, 1949, 36s.; $8) **L71**

Not an almanac of miscellaneous statistics but a concise and reliable manual of descriptive and statistical information about the governments of the world. Contents vary somewhat but usually give: (1) British Commonwealth and Empire; (2) United States; (3) Other countries, arranged alphabetically. For each country, gives information about its ruler, constitution and government, area, population, religion, social welfare, instruction, justice and crime, state finance, defence, production and industry, agriculture, commerce, navigation, communications, banking and credit, money, weights and measures, diplomatic representatives, etc. A valuable feature is the selected bibliography of statistical and other books of reference given for each country. Recent volumes include information on the United Nations.

The most useful of all the general yearbooks; indispensable in any type of library.

Statistical year-book of the League of Nations, 1926–1942/44. Geneva, 1927–45. (Publications of the League of Nations. II. Economic and financial) Annual. **L72**

Ceased publication with v.17, 1942–44. For continuation *see* United Nations, *Statistical yearbook* (L75).

Title varies. Since 1935, in French and English.

Annual survey of commerce, finance and industry in the various countries of the world. Particularly useful for comparative purposes.

United Nations. Statistical Office. Demographic yearbook; Annuaire démographique, 1948- . Prepared in collaboration with the Dept. of Social Affairs. Lake Success, N.Y., 1949- . Annual. **L73**

Hopes to serve as a central source for international demographic data in such fields as: area and population; economically active population; international migration; natality; mortality; morbidity; marriage and divorce.

1948 includes a bibliography, p.549-96, of "available official publications containing census and other demographic statistics for each political area" prepared by the Census Library Project of the U.S. Bureau of the Census and the Library of Congress.

—— Monthly bulletin of statistics, no.1, Jan. 1947- . Lake Success, N.Y., 1947- . Monthly. $5 per yr. **L74**

In English and French. Aims to show by statistics the changing economic and social conditions in different countries.

—— Statistical yearbook; Annuaire statistique, 1948- . Lake Success, N.Y., 1949- . v.1- . Annual. $6. **L75**

A summary of international statistics to continue the *Statistical yearbook of the League of Nations* (L72). Covers population, agriculture, mining, manufacturing, finance, trade, social statistics, education, etc., of the various countries of the world, the tables usually covering a number of years, often 1928–1948. References are given to sources.

U. S. National Office of Vital Statistics. Summary of international vital statistics, 1937–1944 [by Nora P. Powell]. Wash., Govt. Prt. Off., 1947. 299p. **L76**

Bibliography, p.293-99.

Inter-American

Inter American Statistical Institute. Bibliography of selected statistical sources of the American nations. Bibliografía de fuentes estadísticas escogidas de las naciones Americanas. 1st ed. Wash., Inst., 1947. 689p. **L77**

Subtitle: A guide to the principal statistical materials of the 22 American nations, including data, analyses, methodology, and laws and organization of statistical agencies.

In English and Spanish.

A comprehensive classified bibliography with annotations. Detailed alphabetical index and a classified index. A very useful guide giving detailed information about the statistical publications of each country, including censuses, yearbooks, current serials and works in special subjects, e.g., economics, labor, etc.

There is also a section on general statistical works.

Anuario estadistico interamericano. Inter American statistical yearbook. Anuario estatistico interamericano. Annuaire statistique interamericain. 1942. Raul C. Migone, director. N.Y., Macmillan; Buenos Aires, El Ateneo; Rio de Janeiro, Freitas Bastos, 1942. 1066p. $10. **L78**

In Spanish, English, Portuguese, and French. Enlarged and revised version of the first edition published 1940. Sections have been enlarged on industry, social questions, and international cooperation and also on transportation, communications, population, public health, finance, and the armed forces.—Cf. *Introd.* Contains section of sources.

Pan American yearbook, 1945; an economic handbook and ready-reference directory of the western hemisphere including a special industries section, Who's who in inter-American trade. N.Y., Pan American Associates, 1945. 829p. maps. $6. **L79**

General introductory chapters are followed by descriptions of each country giving historical, geographical and cultural background. Main emphasis is on statistics and economic and trade conditions followed by a classified trade directory.

Includes bibliography.

South American handbook, 1924- ; a yearbook and guide to the countries and resources of South and Central America, Mexico and Cuba. Lond., Trade and Travel Publications, 1924- . maps. Annual. (1948, $1.25) **L80**

Continues the *Anglo-South American handbook,* 1921–22. Title and publisher vary.

A very useful handbook giving travel and gazetteer information about each country, also natural resources, government, communications and transportation, etc.

Statistical activities of the American nations, 1940; a compendium of the statistical services and activities in 22 nations of the western hemisphere, together with information concerning statistical personnel in these nations, ed. under the direction of the Temporary Organizing Committee of the Inter American Statistical Institute by Elizabeth Phelps. . . . Wash., Inter American Statistical Inst., 1941. 842p. $2. **L81**

"Presents a current account of the statistical services and activities of the American nations, with bibliographies—and a partial biographical list of the principal statistical personnel in those nations other than the U.S." An "author's article" appears for each of the 22 countries, usually in the language of the country, with a summary in English and in the language of the country.

The biographical section has been continued separately as the *Directory of statistical personnel in the American nations,* 3d ed. (Wash., Inter Amer. Stat. Inst., 1947. 156p. $2).

U. S. Bureau of the Census. Summar[ies] of biostatistics. Maps and charts, population, natality and mortality statistics. Prepared by U. S. Dept. of Commerce, Bur. of the Census, in cooperation with Off. of the Coordinator, Inter-American Affairs. Wash., 1944–45. 17v. maps. **L82**

Argentina, 1945. 152p.; Bolivia, 1945. 69p.; Brazil, 1945. 130p.; Colombia, 1944. 138p.; Costa Rica, 1944. 92p.; Cuba, 1945. 113p.; Dominican Republic, 1945. 93p.; Ecuador, 1944. 61p.; Guatemala, 1944. 98p.; Haiti, 1945. 72p.; Nicaragua, 1945. 89p.; Panama, 1945. 81p.; Paraguay, 1944. 66p.; Peru, 1944. 74p.; El Salvador, 1944. 111p.; Uruguay, 1944. 129p.; Venezuela, 1944 [loose-leaf].

U. S. Library of Congress. Census Library Project. General censuses and vital statistics in the Americas; prepared under the supervision of Irene B. Taeuber, chief, Census Library Project. Wash., Govt. Prt. Off., 1943. 151p. 65c. **L83**

Subtitle: An annotated bibliography of the historical censuses and current vital statistics of the 21 American republics, the American sections of the British Commonwealth of Nations, the American colonies of Denmark, France, and the Netherlands, and the American territories and possessions of the United States.

United States

U. S. Library of Congress. Census Library Project. Catalog of United States census publications, 1790–1945, prepared by Henry J. Dubester, chief, Census Library Project. Wash., Govt. Prt. Off., 1950. 320p. $1.50. **L84**

Designed to serve both as a "guide to census statistics and to record the historical development of publication patterns." Annotated. In two sections: pt.1, decennial census publications; pt.2, other publications, arranged by subject, e.g., agriculture, business, industry, religious bodies, etc. The index is to the subjects contained in titles and annotations.

For brief information largely supersedes earlier bibliographical surveys and indexes but these are sometimes useful for more detailed information: U.S. Bureau of Labor Statistics, *The history and growth of the United States census* (Wash., Govt. Prt. Off., 1900. 967p.) **L85**; U.S. Office of the Census, *A century of population growth from the first census . . . to the twelfth, 1790–1900* (Wash., Govt. Prt. Off., 1909. 303p.) **L86**; its *Circular of information concerning census publications, 1790–1916* (Jan. 1, 1917. 124p.) **L87**; its *Topical index of population census reports, 1900–1930* (1934. 76p.)

L88; its *Periodic and special reports on population, 1930–1939* (1939. 12p.) **L89**.

Supplemented by:

U. S. Bureau of the Census. Census publications; Catalog and subject guide, 1945- . Wash., Govt. Prt. Off., 1945- . Quarterly (cumulating into annual volumes). $2.50 per yr. **L90**

1945 appeared in three parts: pt.1, Catalog of 16th decennial census; pt.2, List of publications issued (monthly, not cumulated); pt.3, Subject guide (monthly, Jan.–Mar., quarterly, Apr.–Dec. not cumulated).

1946- , *Catalog and subject guide* (quarterly, cumulating each time, the fourth issue forming a final annual volume). Supplemented by a monthly *List of publications issued* which is superseded by the quarterly issues.

Lists all reports issued during the period covered, in two sections: by departmental division and by subject. Annotated. Some volumes include special appendices: in 1947, an *Index to the publications of the 1945 Census of agriculture;* in 1948, a listing of *Facts for industry,* Wartime series and Current series.

Two issues deserve special listing:

—— Catalog of 16th decennial census publications. (Its Census pub., v.1, pt.1, Dec. 31, 1945. 11p.) **L91**

Lists the final reports of the sixteenth census published to 1945.

—— Catalog of current census publications. (Its Census pub., v.2, pt.1, Mar. 16, 1946) **L92**

Lists the census publications issued for a few years prior to the beginning of 1946.

—— Statistical abstract of the United States 1878- . Wash., Govt. Prt. Off., 1879- . v.1- Annual. (1948, $2.75) **L93**

1st-25th no., 1878–1902, prepared by the Bureau of Statistics (Treasury Dept.); 26th-34th no., 1903–1911 by the Bureau of Statistics (Dept. of Commerce and Labor); 1912–37, by the Bureau of Foreign and Domestic Commerce.

A single volume work presenting quantitative summary statistics on the political, social, industrial and economic organization of the United States. Indispensable in any library, it serves not only as a first source for statistics of national importance but as a guide to further information, as references are given to the sources of all tables.

Statistics given in the tables cover a period of several years, usually about 15 or 20; some tables run back to 1789 or 1800.

—— —— Cities supplement . . . selected data for cities having 25,000 or more inhabitants in 1940- . 1944- . (Its Series G-1.) 15c. **L94**

—— —— County data book. A supplement 1947. 431p. $2.75. **L95**

"Presents in compact form some of the more important social and economic facts about each county in the United States."

—— —— Historical statistics of the United States, 1789–1945. 1949. 363p. $2.50. **L96**

A supplement to the *Statistical abstract* (L93) includ

ing comparative historical statistics of the same type as those in the *Abstract*. Prepared with the cooperation of the Social Science Research Council.

—— Statistical atlas of the United States. Prepared under the supervision of Charles S. Sloane, Geographer of the Census. Wash., Govt. Prt. Off., 1925. 476p. 412 pl. $2. **L97**

"Contains the maps and diagrams used for illustrating the Reports of the Fourteenth Census, as well as a number of illustrations which have been prepared and published in the special and annual reports of the Bureau of the Census."—*Letter of transmittal*, p.ii.

—— Vital statistics of the United States . . . 1937- . Wash., Govt. Prt. Off., 1939- . v.1- . pt.1, $2; pt.2, $1.25. **L98**

Each year issued in two parts: pt.1, Natality and mortality data for the United States, tabulated by place of occurrence with supplemental tables for Hawaii, Puerto Rico, and the Virgin Islands; pt.2, Natality and mortality data for the United States tabulated by place of residence.

Supersedes its *Mortality statistics* and its *Birth, still-birth and infant mortality statistics*.

—— —— Supplement, 1939/1940 Natality and mortality data for counties and cities in the United States tabulated by place of residence, 2-year totals, 1939/40. Wash., Govt. Prt. Off., 1943. 581p. **L99**

Called pt.3.
The supplement is planned "to make available for the first time detailed nation-wide data on births and deaths which are tabulated by place of residence for small geographic areas."—*Introd.*

U. S. Library of Congress. Census Library Project. State censuses; an annotated bibliography of censuses of population taken after the year 1790 by states and territories of the United States; prepared by Henry J. Dubester. Wash., Govt. Prt. Off., 1948. 73p. 20c. **L100**

American yearbook; a record of events and progress, 1910–19, 1925- . N.Y., Nelson, 1929- . v.1- . (1949, $15) **L101**

Publisher varies.
Excellent yearbook, with long signed articles by specialists. Gives good narrative accounts, including bibliographies and statistics, of the events of the year grouped by large subjects, covering politics, national and international, American government, economics and business, social conditions, science, humanities, etc. Each section concludes with a list of Periodical publications and Cognate societies and research institutions. Each volume has a chronology and a necrology, and a general index to all classes except the chronology and necrology. Each article covers its subject in all countries, but aims especially to record progress in the United States.

Information please almanac, 1947- . John Kieran, ed. Supervised by Dan Golenpaul Associates. N.Y., Farrar, Strauss, 1947- . Annual. $2. **L102**

Publisher varies.
An almanac of miscellaneous information, with a general class arrangement, and a subject index. There are special timely articles in each volume; reviews of the year in Washington, sports, theater, fiction, screen, music, etc., written by specialists; statistical and historical descriptions of the various countries of the world; sports records; and many kinds of general information.

Sources for many of the tables and special articles are noted. The who's who section groups the names of outstanding persons by class, gives place and date of birth but no other biographical information. Names in this section are not indexed individually in the general index.

Tribune almanac and political register, 1838–1914. N.Y., 1838–1914. 76v. **L103**

Title varies: 1838, *Whig almanac and politician's register;* 1839–41, *Politician's register;* 1843–55, *Whig almanac and United States register.*

A reliable and useful almanac for American statistics, especially political statistics, election returns, etc. Includes full texts of party platforms. Discontinued, but still useful for historical information.

World almanac, and book of facts, 1868- . N.Y., World-Telegram, 1868- . v.1- . Annual. (1949, $1.10, cloth, $1.85) **L104**

The most comprehensive and most frequently useful of the American almanacs of miscellaneous information. Contains statistics on social, industrial, political, financial, religious, educational and other subjects, political organizations, societies, historical lists of famous events, etc., well up to date and in general reliable; sources for many of the statistics are given. A useful handbook, and one with which the reference worker should familiarize himself thoroughly. Alphabetical index at the front of each volume. Each issue before 1915 had also a short index of notable articles in preceding volumes.

Alaska

Alaska (Ter.). Planning Council. General information regarding Alaska. Juneau, Alaska Planning Council, 1941. 176p. il. **L105**

Revision of booklet with same title issued in 1931 by the Dept. of the Interior. Gives information on geography, population, government, commerce, natural resources, education, transportation, communication, etc.

Australia

Australia. Bureau of Census and Statistics. Official year book of the Commonwealth of Australia, 1901/08- . Canberra, 1908- . v.1- . maps. (v.36, 5s.) **L106**

The various states of Australia also each publish an annual *Statistical register*. For New South Wales there is also an *Official yearbook* (annual); for Victoria, a *Victorian yearbook* (annual); and for Queensland, a *Queensland yearbook* (annual).

Moorhead, Arthur Francis. The Australian blue book; a national reference book containing information on matters Australian from authoritative sources for all members of the community. Sydney, N.S.W., Blue Star Publishers, [1942]. 118, 90, 114, 104, 56p. incl. il. 20s. **L107**

Contents: Australia—general, Business interests, Rural, Woman's interests, Hobbies.

Austria

Austria. Statistisches Landesamt. Statistisches Jahrbuch für Österreich. Wien, 1920–38. Jahrg. 1-18. **L108**

Title varies: v.1-17, *Statistisches Handbuch* was published by the Bundesamt für Statistik. v.18, 1938, *Statistisches Jahrbuch für Österreich,* was published by the Statistisches Landesamt after the annexation of Austria by Germany.

Österreichisches Jahrbuch, 1920- , hrsg. vom Bundespressedienst. Wien, Staatsdruckerei, 1920- . v.1- . Annual. **L109**

Suspended 1937–44. v.18, 1945–46.

Belgium

Belgium. Ministère de l'Interieur. Annuaire statistique de la Belgique et du Congo belge, 1870- . Gand, 1870- . v.1- . maps. Annual. (1938, v.60, 20fr.) **L110**

Belgian Congo and United States of America economic handbook. 1943- . N.Y., Moretus Pr. Inc., [c1943-]. v.1- . il. Annual. $10 per v. **L111**

Title varies: 1943, *Belgian Congo and United States of America directory;* 1944/45–46, *Belgian Congo and United States of America economic handbook.*

Brazil

Brazil. Instituto Brasileiro de Geografía e Estatística. Anuario estatístico do Brazil. Año 1- , 1935- . Rio de Janeiro, 1936- . **L112**

At head of title: Conselho Nacional de Estatística.

Brazil. Ministerio das Relações Exteriores. Brazil —resources—possibilities—development. Statistics and diagrams, 1929- . Rio de Janeiro, 1929- . v.1- . Annual. **L113**

Office of issue varies.
Also published in Portuguese.

Ribeiro Campos, Carlos Augusto. Atlas estatístico do Brasil. Statistic atlas of Brazil. Atlas statistique du Brésil. Organizado por Carlos Augusto Ribeiro Campos com a colaboração do Departamento Nacional do Café. Rio de Janeiro, 1941. 111 numb. l, 112-32p. il. 25x36cm. **L114**

Bulgaria

Bulgaria. Glavna Direktsiiā na Statistikata. Statisticheski godishnik na bulgarskoto tsarstvo.

Annuaire statistique du Royaume de Bulgarie, 1909- . Sophia, 1910- . v.1- . Annual (irregular). **L115**

Canada

Canada. Bureau of Statistics. Canada year book, 1905- . The official statistical annual of the resources, history, institutions and social and economic conditions of the Dominion. Ottawa, 1906- . v.1- . maps. Annual. (1947, $2) **L116**

Official data on the physiography, history, constitution and government, institutions, population, production, industry, trade, transportation, finance, labor, administration, and general social and economic conditions of the Dominion.

Canada overseas reference book, including the Northwest territories, the Yukon, Labrador and Newfoundland. Advisory ed., Robert Hamilton Coates. Lond., Todd Reference Bks. Ltd., 1949. 512p. $25. **L117**

A general handbook giving historical, statistical, and directory information. Includes material on the national and provincial governments, public services, industry, trade and commerce; city and town guide, directories, and classified lists, etc.

Canadian almanac and directory for the year 1847- . Toronto, Copp Clark Co., 1847- . Annual. **L118**

Title varies.
Subtitle 1949: Containing authentic, legal, commercial, statistical, astronomical, departmental, ecclesiastical, financial, educational, and general information, and railway and natural resources map of the Dominion.

Canadian annual review of public affairs, 1901- . Toronto, Canadian Rev. Co., 1903- . v.1- . il. **L119**

Very useful historical review of events year by year, particularly economic and social. Includes lists of books published in Canada during the year covered.

Chile

Chile. Dirección General de Estadística. Anuario estadística, 1848- . Santiago, 1860- . **L120**

The general statistics of Chile first appeared in 1860 the initial volumes covering 1848–58, and ran until 1887/88 (26v. in all). Next published covered 1909 (3v.) and 1910 (3v.). From 1911—(1938) the statistics have appeared in from 7 to 12 subseries, e.g., Demografía, Agricultura, Política y administracíon, etc.
Title varies, some volumes called *Estadística anual.*

Chile. Dirección General de Informaciones y Cultura. Anuario DIC 1946- , Año 1- . Santiago de Chile, 1946- . il. Annual. **L121**

A survey of life and culture in Chile: politics and government, economics, arts and sciences.

China

China annual, 1943- . Shanghai, Asia Statistics Co., 1943- . **L122**

China. Ministry of Information. China handbook, 1937–1945; a comprehensive survey of major developments in China in eight years of war, [3d ed.] rev. and enl. with 1946 supplement. N.Y., Macmillan, 1947. 862p. **L123**

1st ed. 1943.

Includes material on the Kuomintang, government, foreign relations, finance, communications, judicial system, industry and labor, education, resources, the Sino-Japanese war, relief activities, trade, agriculture, press, etc.

Chinese who's who, p.632-706.

China year book, 1912–19, 1921/22–1939. Lond., Routledge; N.Y., Dutton, 1912–19; Tientsin, Tientsin Pr., 1921–29; Shanghai, North China Daily News, 1931–39. **L124**

Unofficial but of the first importance while published for reliable detailed information about the people, government, economic condition, religion, education, products, etc., of China. Includes a "Who's who in China."

Edited by H. G. W. Woodhead and H. T. Montague Bell.

The Chinese yearbook . . . Issue 1- , 1935/36- . Prepared from official and other public sources by the Council of International Affairs, Chungking. Bombay, Lond., Thacker, 1935- . **L125**

Publisher varies.

Contains a large amount of historical, descriptive, industrial, economic and directory information, as well as statistical material. Differs from the *China year book* (L124) primarily in being compiled by Chinese authorities, and also contains considerably fuller discussions of some subjects than are given in that work. Does not contain the "Who's Who in China" which is a feature of the *China year book*.

Colombia

Colombia. Dirección Nacional de Estadística. Anuario general de estadística, 1915- . Bogota, Imp. Nac., 1915- . Annual. **L126**

—— Síntesis estadística, 1941- . Bogota, 1941- . Irregular.

Costa Rica

Costa Rica. Dirección General de Estadística. Anuario estadístico, 1883- . San José, Imp. Nac., 1884- . **L127**

Suspended between v.10, 1893, and v.11, 1907.

Czechoslovakia

Czechoslovak Republic. Státní úřad statistický. Annuaire statistique de la République Tchécoslovaque. Prague, 1934- . v.1- . **L128**

Continues *Manuel statistique de la République Tchécoslovaque (Statistisches Handbuch der Čechoslovakischen Republik),* v.1-4, 1920–32.

Published also in German.

Denmark

Denmark. Statistiske Departement. Statistisk Aarbog. Annuaire statistique, 1892- . København, Gyldendal, 1896- . v.1- . Annual. (v.53, 1948, Kr. 2) **L129**

Text in Danish and French.

Denmark, 1924- pub. by the Royal Danish Ministry for Foreign Affairs and the Danish Statistical Department. Copenhagen, Luno, 1924- . Irregular. (1947, Kr. 7.50) **L130**

Some years published in French or German.

Dominican Republic

Dominican Republic. Dirección General de Estadística. Anuario estadístico, 1936- . Trujillo, 1937- . Annual. **L131**

Ecuador

Ecuador. Dirección Nacional de Estadística. Ecuador en cifras, 1938 à 1942. Quito, Imp. del Ministerio de Hacienda, 1944. 515p. **L132**

Ecuador does not publish an *Anuario* but this work provides a basic compilation for the years covered.

Egypt

Egypt. Government Press. Almanac, 1902- . Cairo, Govt. Pr., 1902- . Annual. (1938, P.T. 5.) **L133**

Issuing office varies. 1913–26 had title: *Egyptian government almanac.*

Estonia

Estonia. Riigi Statistiska Keskbüroo. Estonia; population, cultural and economic life, ed. by Albert Pullertis. Tallinn, 1937. 207, 68p. il. **L134**

Finland

Finland. Tilastollinen Päätoimisto. Suomen tilastollinen vuosikirja, uusi sarja. Statistisk ärsbok för Finland, ny ser. Annuaire statistique de Finland, nouv. sér., 1902- . Helsinki, 1903- . v.1- . Annual. **L135**

Finland year book, 1936/37- ed., with the assistance of the Press Department of the Ministry for Foreign Affairs and specialists in different branches. Helsinki, Mercatorin Kirjapaino ja Kustannus, 1937- . il. $5 ea. **L136**

A survey in English of government, life and culture in Finland.

France

U. S. Library of Congress. Census Library Project. National censuses and vital statistics in France between two world wars, 1921–1942; a preliminary bibliography. Wash., 1945. 22p. (Free to libraries only) **L137**

Largely duplicated by its *National censuses and vital statistics in Europe, 1918–1939*, and *Supplement* (L62).

Almanach Hachette; petite encyclopédie populaire, 1894- . Paris, Hachette, 1894- . il. Annual. **L138**

France. Direction de la Statistique Générale. Annuaire statistique de la France, 1877- . Paris, Impr. Nat., 1878- . v.1- . Annual. **L139**

v.55, 1941; v.56, 1940–45.

France. Statistique Générale. Annuaire statistique abrégé. v.1- . Paris, Imp. Nat., 1943- . **L140**

At head of title: Ministère de l'Économie Nationale et des Finances. Service National des Statistiques.

An abridged compendium of statistics, frequently giving comparative figures for several years.

Germany

U. S. Library of Congress. Census Library Project. National censuses and vital statistics in Germany after the first world war, 1919–1944. Wash., 1946. 37p. (Free to libraries only) **L141**

Largely duplicated in its *National censuses and vital statistics in Europe, 1918–1939*, and *Supplement* (L62).

Germany. Statistisches Reichsamt. Statistisches Jahrbuch für das Deutsche Reich, 1880–1938. Berlin, Hobbing, 1880–1938. v.1-57. **L142**

Statistisches Jahrbuch deutscher Gemeinden. Amtlichen Veröffentlichung des deutschen Gemeindetages. Bearb. von der Arbeitsgemeinschaft für gemeindliche Statistik. 1890- . Jena, Fischer, 1890- . Annual. **L143**

v.1-28 had title: *Statistisches Jahrbuch deutscher Städte*, begründet von M. Neefe; hrsg. vom Verbande der deutschen Städtestatistiker.

Latest received 1939.

Gold Coast

Gold Coast handbook, 1937. Produced in England by the authority of the Gold Coast government. Lond. and Accra, West Africa Publicity, 1937. 442p. il. 7s. 6d. **L144**

1st ed., Accra, 1923; 3d ed., London, 1928.

Great Britain

Gt. Brit. Central Statistical Office. Annual abstract of statistics, v.1, 1840- . Lond., Stat. Off., 1854- . v.1- . Annual. (v.85, 10s.) **L145**

v.1-83, issued by the Board of Trade, as *Statistical abstract of the United Kingdom*. Each of these volumes contained statistics for the preceding fifteen years.

Volume 83, covering 1924 to 1938 was published in 1940. No volumes were published during the war but volume 84 with a new title and under a new issuing body appeared in 1948, and covers 1935–1946; volume 85, published 1948, covers 1937–1947.

Gt. Brit. Permanent Consultative Committee on Official Statistics. Guide to current official statistics, being a systematic survey of the statistics appearing in all official publications, 1922–38. Lond., Stat. Off., 1923–39. v.1-17. Annual. 1s. ea. **L146**

Gt. Brit. Board of Trade. Statistical abstract for the British Empire, 1850- . Lond., 1865- . v.1- . (v.68, 1938, 3s. 6d.) **L147**

Title varies.

Each number contains the statistics for a period varying from six to fifteen preceding years.

Whitaker, Joseph. Almanack; 1869- . Lond., Whitaker, 1869- . v.1- . Annual. 6s. per v. (1949, 12s. 6d.) **L148**

Especially full for statistics of the British Empire, with brief statistics for foreign countries.

Greece

Greece. Genikē Statistikē Hypēresia. Statistikē eletēris tēs Hellados. Annuaire statistique de la Grèce, 1930- . Athènes, Imp. Nat., 1931- . Annual. **L149**

v.10, 1939.

Title and text in Greek and French.

Hawaii

Thrum's Hawaiian annual and standard guide, combined with All about Hawaii, 1st, 1875- . Honolulu, Honolulu Star-Bulletin, 1875- . il. Annual. (1948/49, $1) **L150**

Title varies: 1940/41- , combined with *All about Hawaii*.

—— Index; v.1-58, 1875–1932.

Hungary

Hungary. Statisztikai Hivatal. Annuaire statistique hongrois. Nouv. cours, 1901- . Budapest, 1903- . v.9- . (v.40, p.6) **L151**

v.9, 1901, first issue in French. Published in Hungarian from 1893- , and in German until 1918.

India

India. Office of the Economic Adviser. Guide to current official statistics. . . . Prepared under instructions from the Economic Adviser by S. Subramanian, statistician. Delhi, Manager of Publications, 1943–45. v.1-2. v.1, Rs. 4 or 6s. 6d.; v.2, Rs. 1 or 2s. 6d.   **L152**

Contents: v.1, Production and prices, (2d ed.); v.2, Trade, transport and communications, and finance (excluding public finance).

It is announced that volume 3 will cover public finance and social welfare.

India. Commercial Intelligence Dept. Statistical abstract for British India, with statistics, where available, relating to certain Indian States, 1911/12-1939/40. Lond., 1924–43. n. s. v.1-18.   **L153**

Continuation of *Statistics of British India* and the *Statistical abstract relating to British India*, published respectively by the Commercial Intelligence Department, India, and the India Office, Great Britain.

Continued by:

India. Office of the Economic Adviser. Statistical abstract for 1946/47- . New Delhi, Manager of Publications, 1949- .   **L153a**

Called the "last issue of the *Abstract* for pre-partition India."—*Cf.* Pref.

Supplemented by its *Monthly abstract of statistics,* 1948- .

Indian year book, 1914- . A statistical and historical annual of the Indian Empire. Bombay, Bennett, 1914- . v.1- . Annual. (v.33, 1947, Rs. 10)   **L154**

Unofficial; very useful. Contains a large amount of descriptive and statistical information and, 1918- , a "Who's who in India."

Ireland

Ireland (Eire). Dept. of Industry and Commerce. Statistical abstract, 1931- . Dublin, Stat. Off., 1931- . v.1- . Annual. (1949, 4s.)   **L155**

Italy

U. S. Library of Congress. Census Library Project. National censuses and official statistics in Italy since the first world war, 1921–1944; a preliminary bibliography. Wash., 1945. 58p. (Free to libraries only)   **L156**

Material before 1939 is largely duplicated in the general *National censuses and vital statistics in Europe, 1918–1939,* and *Supplement* (L62).

Italy. Istituto Centrale di Statistica. Annuario statistico italiano. 1878- . Roma, Istituto Poligrafico dello Stato, 1878- . Annual (irregular).   **L157**

In five series: ser. 1, 1878–1907; ser. 2, 1911–1925; ser. 3, 1927–1933; ser. 4, 1934–1943; ser. 5, 1944/48- .

Series 1-2 issued by the Direzione Generale della Statistica.

—— Compendio statistico italiano, 1927- . Roma, Istituto Poligrafico dello Stato, 1927- . Annual.   **L158**

Publication suspended 1943–45.

1946, called ser. 2, v.1, serves as an abridged edition of the *Annuario* (L157).

Jamaica

Handbook of Jamaica, 1881- , comprising historical, statistical and general information . . . comp. from official and other reliable records. Lond., Crown Agents; Jamaica, Govt. Prt. Off., 1881- . v.1- . maps. (1939, 8s.)   **L159**

Japan

Taeuber, Irene B. and **Beal, Edwin G., Jr.** Guide to the official demographic statistics of Japan. Pt.1, Japan proper, 1868–1945. 36p. (Population index, Oct. 1946. Supplement)   **L160**

Japan. Bureau of General Statistics. Résumé statistique de l'empire du Japon, 1884- . Tokio, 1887- . v.1- . (v. 54, 1940)   **L161**

Japanese and French.

A resumé of the Japanese statistical annual which is published in Japanese.

Japan. Dept. of Finance. Financial and economical annual of Japan. Tokyo, Govt. Prt. Off., 1901- . v.1- . maps. Annual.   **L162**

Japan year book, 1933- . v.1- . [Tokyo] For. Affairs Assoc. of Japan [1933-]. v.1- . Annual.   **L163**

"This year book has no connection with that published by the late Prof. Takenobu under the same title, which is now defunct," but was published 1906–31, by the Japan Yr. Bk. Off.

1943/44, republished by the Interdepartmental Committee for the Acquisition of Foreign Publications (Wash., Govt. Prt. Off., 1945. 1099p.).

1946–48 includes an appendix giving texts of the constitution, laws, documents, etc.

Manchoukuo yearbook, 1931- . Hsinking, Manchoukuo, Manchoukuo Yearbook Co., 1931- . Annual.   **L164**

Pub. varies.

1931–32 had title *Manchuria year book.*

1942, republished by the Interdepartmental Committee for the Acquisition of Foreign Publications.

Includes who's who section.

Orient yearbook, 1942. Republished by the Interdepartmental Committee for the Acquisition of Foreign Publications. Tokyo, Japan, Asia Statistics Co., 1942. 1364p. il. **L165**

Successor to the *Japan-Manchoukuo year book, 1934–41.*

A general and statistical handbook on Japan, Manchoukuo, China, Thailand, Malaya, the Philippines, French Indo-China, and the East Indies.

Includes a who's who section and a business directory.

Latvia

Latvia. Valsts Statistikā Pārvalde. Latvijas statistikā gada grāmata, 1920- . Annuaire statistique de la Lettonie. Riga, 1921- . **L166**

In Lettish and French.

Lithuania

Lithuania. Centralinis Statistikos Biuras. Lietuvos statistikos metraštis. . . . Annuaire statistique de la Lithuanie, 1924/26- . Kaunas, 1927- . v.1- . Annual. **L167**

—— Valstybes statistikos kalendorius, 1937. The Lithuanian government statistical almanac. [Kaunas], 1937. 515p. **L168**

p.1-266 in Lithuanian; p.271-515 in English.

Luxemburg

Luxemburg. Office de Statistique. Aperçu statistique. Annexe à l'Annuaire officiel. Luxembourg, 1931- . **L169**

Statistics were previously included in the *Annuaire officiel.*

Manchoukuo

See Japan.

Mexico

Mexico. Dirección General de Estadística. Bibliografía Mexicana de estadística. Mexico, Talleres Gráficos de la Nacion, 1942. 2v. **L170**

Contents: t.1, Generalidades, Teoria y aplicaciones metodologicas, Demografia, Estadistica social, economica, administrativa Geografia; t.2, Historia, Lingüistica, Publicaciones periodicas, Cartografia, Titulos complementarios. Indice general geografico. Indice onomastico de autores.

Mexico. Dirección General de Estadística. Anuario estadístico, 1914- . Mexico, Talleres Gráficos de la Nacion, 1916- . v.1- . **L171**

Covers population, education, labor, agriculture, industry, communication, commerce, finance, etc.

—— Compendio estadístico. Mexico, D.F., Sec. de la Econ. Nac., Dir. Gen. de Estadística, 1941. 117p. **L172**

A small, compact compendium including statistics of population, education, public assistance, delinquency, labor, cost of living, agriculture and fisheries, industry, commerce, communications, transportation and finance, with index.

The dates of the different tables vary, some come to 1940 and some are earlier.

Morocco

Spain. Dirección General de Estadística (1938-). Zona de protectorado y de los territorios de soberanía de España en el norte de Africa. Anuario estadístico, 1941- . Madrid, 1942- . il. Annual. **L173**

Netherlands

Netherlands. Centraal Bureau voor de Statistiek. Jaarcijfers voor Nederland. 1881- . s'Gravenhage, Centraal Bureau voor de Statistiek [1882]- . **L174**

Text in Dutch and French; 1941/42 in Dutch and German; 1943–46 in Dutch and English.

From 1887 to 1921 each volume consisted of two parts: (1) Rijk in Europa, (2) Kolonien; after 1921 the Kolonien section was continued as a separate publication by the following:

Netherlands East Indies. Departement van Landbouw, Nijverheid en Handel. Statistisch Kantoor. Statistisch jaaroverzicht van Nederlandsch-Indie. Statistical abstract for the Netherlands East Indies; new series of the Statistical annual of the Netherlands (part Colonies) 1922/23- . Batavia, 1924- . v.1- . **L175**

Title page and text in both Dutch and English.

1930–37 are part 2 of *Indisch Verlag, 1931–40.*

New Zealand

Neale, Edward Percy. Guide to New Zealand official statistics. . . . . Auckland, N.Z., London Whitcombe and Tombs, 1938. 94p. (Auckland University College texts, no.2) 3s. 6d. **L176**

New Zealand. Census and Statistics Dept. New Zealand official year-book, 1892- . Wellington 1892- . v.1- . Annual. (v. 54, 1946, 7s. 6d.) **L177**

v.54, p.898-914, includes a general bibliography, compiled by C. R. H. Taylor, of some of the principal works dealing with New Zealand, Samoa and the Cook Islands published since 1912. Earlier works are listed in the 1930 issue of the *Year-book.*

Nicaragua

Nicaragua. Dirección General de Estadística. Anuario estadístico. 1938- . Managua, Tall Nac., 1939- . **L178**

Northern Ireland

Northern Ireland. Ministry of Finance. Registrar-General's Division. Ulster year book, 1926- . Belfast, 1926- . Triennial. **L179**
None published 1938–1946.

Norway

Norway. Statistiske Sentralbyrå. Statistisk årbok för Norge, 1880- . Annuaire statistique de la Norvège. Oslo, Aschehoug, 1881- . v.1- . **L180**

1886- , in Norwegian and French.
v.62-64, 1943–45, pub. in 1 v. 1946.

Norway year book, 1924, 1931, 1938. 1st-3d year of issue. Oslo, Sverre Mortensen, [c1923]–38. v.1-3. il. **L181**
A survey in English of the life and culture of Norway.

Palestine

Palestine. Dept. of Statistics. Statistical abstract of Palestine, 1936- . Palestine, Govt. Printer, 1937- . Annual (slightly irregular). (1944/45, 800 mils; 16s.) **L182**
"To be purchased from the Government Printer, Jerusalem, or from the Crown Agents for the Colonies, London."

Palestine year book. v.1, 5706- ; review of events July 1944- , ed. by Sophie A. Udin. N.Y., Zionist Organization of Amer., 1945- . Annual. $3.50. **L183**
Survey of political, economic and social progress in Palestine including chapters on the Zionist movement and Zionism in the United States. Lists newspapers, periodicals, and books published in Palestine, Zionist organizations, and contains a chronology and necrology, etc.

Statistical handbook of Jewish Palestine, 1947- , comp. under the supervision of D. Gurevich, ed. by A. Gertz. Jerusalem, Jewish Agency for Palestine, Dept. of Statistics, 1947- . **L184**
1947 (438p.) gives statistical data on the development of Jewish Palestine during the past 30 years.

Statistical handbook of Middle Eastern countries: Palestine, Cyprus, Egypt, Iraq, the Lebanon, Syria, Transjordan, Turkey. 2d ed. Jerusalem, Jewish Agency for Palestine, Economic Research Institute, 1945. 183p. **L185**
1st ed. 1944. Reprinted with the correction of a few misprints and the addition of a Supplement containing new figures.

Panama

Almanaque Panameño, 1941- . Panama, Ed. Balboa, 1940- . **L186**

Panama (Republic). Dirección General de Estadística. Anuario de estadística, año 1934. Panamá, Imp., Nac., 1936. 418p. **L187**
Previously published very irregularly under varying titles.

Paraguay

Paraguay. Dirección General de Estadística. Anuario estadístico, 1886- . Asunción, Imp. Nac., 1888- . Irregular. **L188**
1943/44, pub. 1946.

Peru

Peru. Dirección Nacional de Estadística. Anuario estadístico del Peru, 1944/45- . Lima, 1947- . Annual. **L189**
Continues its *Extracto estadístico del Peru.*

Philippines

Philippines (Republic). Bureau of the Census and Statistics. Yearbook of Philippine statistics, 1941, 1946- . Manila, Bureau of Printing, 1941- . **L190**
1941 was the first *Yearbook*, covering general statistics for 1939/40. 1946, the second issue (pub. 1947), covers the war years and the first two postliberation years.

Poland

Statistical year book of Poland. Warsaw, Central Statistical Office, 1930- . Annual. (1948, zl 200) **L191**
Title varies: 1930–39, *Concise statistical yearbook.* Publication suspended 1940–46.
Some years published in four editions, Polish, English, French, and German. Postwar issues in Polish and English editions.
The *Annuaire statistique de la République Polonaise,* 1920/21–1930 was published 1921–31.

Szturm de Sztrem, Edward. Statistical atlas of Poland. Lond., Polish Ministry of Information [1945?]. 120p. **L192**
Gives maps and diagrams surveying conditions in Poland in the period between the two wars, 1919–1939, and showing latent possibilities of development. Includes material on climate, population, nationality problems, professions, vital statistics, education, agriculture, industry, labor, transport, finances, etc.

Portugal

Portugal. Direcção Geral da Estatística. Anuário estatístico de Portugal (1875-). Lisboa, Impr. Nac., 1877- . **L193**

Rhodesia

Rhodesia, Southern. Dept. of Statistics. Statistical year book of Southern Rhodesia, official annual of the social and economic conditions of the colony, 1924- . Salisbury, S. Rhodesia, 1924- . 5s. **L194**

v.1, 1924; v.2, 1930; v.3, 1932; v.4, 1938- .
Title varies: v.1-3, *Official yearbook.*

Year book and guide of the Rhodesias and Nyasaland, with biographies. Salisbury, S. Rhodesia, Rhodesian Pub., 1937- . il. Annual. (1948/49, 7s. 6d.) **L195**

Rumania

Rumania. Direcţiunea Statisticei Generale. Anuarul statistic al României. Annuaire statistique de la Roumanie, 1902–15/16, 1922- . Bucureşti, 1904- . **L196**

Text and tables in Rumanian and French.
First issue, 1902; second, 1909; third, 1912.

Rumania. Institut Central de Statistique. Bréviaire statistique de la Roumanie, 1940- . Bucarest, Inst. Cent. de Stat., 1940- . v.1- . **L197**

The first volume of a new series in a "language of international circulation." 1938–39 were published in Rumanian only, *Breviarul statistic al României.*

Russia

Malevskii-Malevich, Petr Nikolaevich. Russia, U.S.S.R.; a complete handbook. N.Y., W. F. Payson [c1933]. 712p. maps. $10. **L198**

—— Soviet Union today, being a supplement . . . and containing an index to both volumes. . . . 1936. 102p. $1. **L199**

Issued both in separate form and bound in with the basic work.
A comprehensive survey of all phases of life in Russia, now quite out of date but useful as a record of the early years of Soviet Russia.

U. S. S. R. handbook. Lond., V. Gollancz, 1936. 643p. 15s. **L200**

Includes descriptive and statistical material on political, economic, industrial and cultural conditions, with the following appendices: (1) Diary of events since 1917; (2) Social and cooperative organizations; (3) Who's who (very brief biographies of about 500 persons); (4) Principal newspapers and periodicals.

U. S. S. R. Tsentralnoe Upravlenie Narodno-Khoziaistvennogo Ucheta. Sotsialisticheskoe stroitelstvo SSR. Statisticheskii ezhegodnik. Moscow, 1934- . **L201**

An English edition containing data based on the 1935 and 1936 yearbooks was published as: *Socialist construc-*

tion in the U.S.S.R. *Statistical abstract* (Moscow, 1936. 538p.).
Supplemented by:

—— —— Statisticheskii sbornik, 1933–38. Moscow-Leningrad, Gosplanizdat, 1939. 208p. **L202**

Salvador

Salvador. Dirección General de Estadística. Anuario estadístico, 1911–23, 1927- . San Salvador, Imp. Nac., 1912- . **L203**

(1944- , in 3v.)

Siam

Siam. Central Service of Statistics. Statistical year book, no.1- . Bangkok, 1916- . **L204**

no. 19, 1935/36 and 1936/37.
In Siamese and English.
Publisher varies.

South Africa

Mockford, Julian. Overseas reference book of the Union of South Africa, including South-west Africa, Basutoland, Bechuanaland Protectorate and Swaziland. Lond. and N.Y., Todd Pub. Co., [1945]. 567p. il. $25; £5 5s. **L205**

A general handbook on South Africa giving historical and statistical information on various phases of life in South Africa, including industry, production, trade and commerce, population, etc., and lists of organizations, libraries, newspapers and periodicals, books, etc. Gazetteer and groups of maps.

South Africa. Office of Census and Statistics. Official year book of the Union of South Africa and of Basutoland, Bechuanaland Protectorate and Swaziland, 1917- . Pretoria, Govt. Printer, 1918- . v.1- . maps. Annual. 5s. per v. **L206**

An important year book, giving detailed statistical, descriptive and historical information. Bibliographies and lists of government publications.
1946 being published in parts, 1947- .

South and East African year book and guide, with atlas, town plans and diagrams, ed. annually for the Union-Castle Mail Steamship Co., 1st ed., 1901- . Lond., Sampson, Low, 1901- . maps. Annual. (1949, 8s. 6d.) **L207**

Atlas at back.
A useful and inexpensive yearbook, containing a large amount of descriptive, statistical and gazetteer information.

Spain

Spain. Dirección General de Estadística (1938-). Anuario estadístico de España,

1912- . Madrid, 1913- . v.1- . Annual (slightly irregular). **L208**

Suspended publication 1935–1942.

Previously published by varying departments and from 1930–34 by the Instituto Geográfico, Catastral y de Estadística. v.20, 1943- by the Dirección General de Estadística.

—— —— Edicion manual, 1941- .

Sweden

Sweden. Statistika Centralbyrån. Statistisk årsbok för Sverige, 1914- . Annuaire statistique de la Suède. Stockholm, Norstedt, 1914- . v.1- . Annual. (v.35, 1948) **L209**

Swedish and French.

Andersson, Ingvar. Introduction to Sweden. Stockholm, Swedish Institute, 1949. 311p. il. **L210**

A survey in English of life and culture in Sweden replacing the *Sweden yearbook* which was published irregularly 1921–38.

Switzerland

Schweizerische Bibliographie für Statistik und Volkswirtschaft. Bibliographie suisse de statistique et d'économie politique, bearb. vom Eidgenössischen Statistischen Amt, Bern. 1.-7. Jahrg.; 1937–1943/44. Bern, Schweizerische Gesellschaft für Statistik und Volkswirtschaft, 1938–44. v. 1-7. **L211**

Classified. Volume 7 has author index; previous volumes do not.

Switzerland. Statistisches Bureau. Statistisches Jahrbuch der Schweiz. Annuaire statistique de la Suisse, 1891- . Bern, 1891- . v.1- . Annual. (v. 45, 1945) **L212**

In place of the yearbook for 1897, there was issued the *Graphischstatistischer Atlas der Schweiz*, 1897.

Trinidad

Trinidad and Tobago year book, 1865- , containing information obtained from official records and reliable sources. Trinidad, Yuille, 1865- . Annual. **L213**

Turkey

Turkey. Istatistik Umum Müdürlügü. Istatistik villigi. Annuaire statistique, 1928- . Ankara, 1928- . v.1- . Annual. **L214**

Uruguay

Uruguay. Dirección General de Estadística. Anuario estadístico, 1884- . Montevideo, Imp. Nac., 1885- . Annual. **L215**

—— Síntesis estadística, 1918- . Annual. **L216**

Venezuela

Venezuela. Dirección General de Estadística. Anuario estadístico de Venezuela, 1877–1912, 1938- . Caracas, Ed. Grafolit, 1878- . **L217**

None published, 1913–37.

West Indies

West Indies year book, 1926/27- . Lond., Skinner, 1927- . il. Annual. (1948, £1; $5) **L218**

Title varies.

Covers Bermuda, Bahamas, Jamaica, Trinidad and Tobago, Barbados, Leeward Islands, Windward Islands, British Guiana, British Honduras, Puerto Rico, Virgin Islands of U.S.A., Dominican Republic, Haiti, Cuba, Netherlands West Indies, Dutch Guiana (Suriname), French West Indies, French Guiana.

Statistical information and trade directories.

Yugoslavia

Yugoslavia. Direktsīja Drzhavne Statīstīke. Statistički godišnjak. Annuaire statistique. Knjiga 1., 1929- . Beograd, 1932- . **L219**

v.9, 1938–39.

POLITICAL SCIENCE
General works
Guides

See also Guides, p.106.

Burchfield, Laverne. Student's guide to materials in political science. N.Y., Holt, 1935. 426p. $3. **L220**

"Designed to introduce the student interested in political science to the more important source materials, finding devices, bibliographies, and general reference works which will be of major assistance to him in prosecuting research."—*Foreword*.

Each section is introduced by an outline and a "general statement." Covers such fields as: national, state and local government, political parties, administration, public finance, law, international relations, allied fields and general works. Many titles annotated.

Special Libraries Association. Social Science Group. Public administration libraries; a manual of practice, with book lists in Ch. II. rev. 1948. Chic., Public Admin. Service, 1948. 91p. $2.50 (Public Admin. Serv. Pub. no.102) **L221**

A handbook with bibliographies.

—— Source materials in public administration. 1948. 30p. (Public Admin. Serv. Pub. no. 102A) $1.   **L221a**

Reprint of the bibliographical sections of the above.

Bibliography

Current research projects in public administration, reported to Public Administration Service. Chic., Pub. Admin. Serv., 1938–43, 1947- . Annual. $1 ea.   **L222**

Title varies: 1938–43, *Check list of current research in public administration.* None published 1942, 1944–46.

Includes work in progress for masters' and doctors' degrees and faculty and staff research.

Foreign affairs bibliography; a selected and annotated list of books on international relations. 1919–32, 1932–42. N.Y. and Lond., pub. by Harper for Council on Foreign Relations, 1933–45. 2v. (Pub. of the Council on Foreign Relations) $6 ea.   **L223**

1919–32 edited by William L. Langer and Hamilton Fish Armstrong; 1932–42 edited by Robert Gale Woolbert.

Very useful bibliographies with critical annotations, based on bibliographies appearing quarterly in *Foreign affairs,* revised and enlarged, with some titles dropped, many added and many annotations rewritten. Include books in various languages, including the Asiatic, these last transliterated into the Latin alphabet.

Greer, Sarah. Bibliography of public administration. N.Y., Nat. Inst. of Pub. Admin., 1926. 238p.   **L223a**

A second enlarged edition was started in 1933 but only part 1, General literature, was published.

Mattei, Rodolfo de. La storia delle dottrine politiche. Firenze, Sansoni, 1938. 173p. (Guide bibliografiche dell' Istituto Nazionale di Cultura Fascista)   **L224**

Pinson, Koppel S. A bibliographical introduction to nationalism. N.Y., Columbia Univ. Pr., 1935. 70p. 75c.   **L225**

Dictionaries and encyclopedias

Aleksandrov, G., Gal'ïanov, V. and **Rubinshteĭn, N.** Politicheskiĭ slovar'. Moskva, Gosudarstvennoe izdatel'stvo politicheskoĭ literaturi, 1940. 671p. (Repr. Ann Arbor, Mich., Edwards, 1948. $5.50)   **L226**

Diplomaticheskiĭ slovar'. Moskva, OGIZ. [Gosudarstvennoe izdatel'stvo politicheskoĭ literaturi] 1948- . v.1- . (In progress)   **L227**

v.1, A-K.

An historical dictionary of diplomacy and international affairs covering materials from the sixteenth century to May 1947. International in scope with a natural emphasis on Russia. Includes definitions of diplomatic terms and a considerable amount of biography. Especially strong in its articles on international conferences, treaties, diplomatic proceedings, and on the foreign policies of many countries and statesmen. Some articles are signed, and a few have bibliographies. Volume 1 contains an index of subjects arranged by country. A general subject index is planned for the second volume.

Dizionario di politica, a cura del Partito Nazionale Fascista. Roma, Istituto della Enciclopedia Italiana, 1940. 4v. maps.   **L228**

Long signed articles with bibliographies. International in scope and covering all periods. Includes biography.

Handwörterbuch der Staatswissenschaften, hrsg. von Ludwig Elster, Adolf Weber, Fr. Wieser. 4. gänz. umgearb. Aufl. Jena, Fischer, 1923–29. 8v. and suppl.   **L229**

1st ed. 1890–94, 6v.; 2d ed. 1898–1901, 7v.; 3d ed. 1909–11, 8v. 1st-3d eds., ed. by J. Conrad, L. Elster, W. Lexis and E. Loening, often cited as *Conrad's Handwörterbuch.*

The most comprehensive German work, and in some respects the finest encyclopedia of political science in any language. Long signed articles by specialists, bibliographies. Many biographies, excluding those of living men.

Staatslexikon; im Auftrag der Görres-Gesellschaft unter Mitwirkung zahlreicher Fachleute hrsg. von Hermann Sacher. 5. von Grund aus neubearb. Aufl. Freiburg i. Br., Herder, 1926–32. 5v.   **L230**

A standard German work, though not equal to *Conrad's Handwörterbuch* (L229). Signed articles, bibliographies. From the Catholic standpoint.

White, Wilber W. White's Political dictionary. N.Y., World Publishing Co., 1947. 378p. $3.50.   **L231**

A popular dictionary, international in scope, including many names and terms of recent origin, especially the names of government organizations, conferences, treaties, and political events. Many cross references from abbreviations. The appendices give the constitutions of the League of Nations and the United Nations.

UNITED STATES

❦ For current information about government machinery, committees, work of various bureaus, personnel of the government, etc., consult the *Congressional directory* (L249) and the *United States government organization manual* (L252).

Cyclopedia of American government, ed. by A. C. McLaughlin and A. B. Hart. N.Y., Appleton, 1914. 3v. il. (Repr. N.Y., Peter Smith, 1949. 3v. $27)   **L232**

A useful work now much out of date. Covers topics in theory or philosophy of political society, forms of political organization and government, international and constitutional law, history of political parties and other American political topics. Many biographies. Arranged alphabetically by small subjects, with an analytical index. Signed articles by specialists, bibliographies.

For the earlier political history of the United States, J. J. Lalor's *Cyclopaedia of political science* (N.Y., Merrill, 1888–90. 3v.) is still occasionally useful.

Mitchell, Edwin Valentine. An encyclopedia of American politics. Garden City, N.Y., Doubleday, 1946. 338p. $3.75. **L233**

Includes brief articles on the presidents, states, parties, political terms and slogans, texts of important documents, e.g., the Constitution, the Declaration of Independence, the United Nations charter, etc.

Articles are popular in style and usually without definite reference or citation. There are many fewer headings than in Smith and Zurcher (L234).

Smith, Edward Conrad and **Zurcher, Arnold John.** New dictionary of American politics. N.Y., Barnes and Noble, 1949. 437p. maps. $3.25. **L234**

Earlier editions had title *Dictionary of American politics*. 1st ed., 1888, by Everit Brown and Albert Strauss; 2d ed., 1924, was almost completely rewritten by Edward C. Smith; 3d ed., 1944 (and 1946), was revised by the present editors.

This edition has been completely revised and reset with the addition of some 500 new terms bringing the total to over 3500. Some deletions have been made particularly in the case of temporary wartime agencies. Aims "to incorporate all leading ideas and institutions in each of the special areas . . . of American government and politics." Also includes slogans, political slang, nicknames, etc. There are many more articles than in Mitchell's *Encyclopedia of American politics* (L233), usually briefer and more concise. Gives summaries of documents and charters, not full texts, except for the Constitution and the Declaration of Independence.

Gallup political almanac for 1946- . comp. by American Institute of Public Opinion. Princeton, N.J., 1946- . v.1- . $4.50. **L235**

Compiled to aid in analyzing national political trends of recent years. Gives election information for federal elections by state; for state governors; special election information; voting turnout; tables of city, state, and national vote percentages, etc.

Annuals

United Nations. Secretariat. Dept. of Social Affairs. Yearbook on human rights for 1946- . Lake Success, N.Y., United Nations, 1947- . v.1- . **L236**

The first issue, 1946, is a survey of the constitutional and legal provisions of the various countries of the world in regard to the rights of the citizen, his status before the law, right of petition, property rights, rights of the press, assembly, education, religion, culture, status of women, etc.

Directories

Europa: The encyclopaedia of Europe; a survey of world economic and social conditions, a directory of international administration, and of European political, industrial, financial, cultural and scientific organizations. Lond., Europa Publications, 1946- . loose-leaf. **L237**

Started in 1930 as a successor to the *Europa year book*, this loose-leaf service continues to send periodical revisions. A new title page was issued in 1946.

In two sections: pt.1, International; pt.2, European countries.

Part 1 covers the United Nations and its specialized agencies, international organizations, and world politics which includes the texts of various international documents.

Part 2 gives information on each European country, including such material as: Administration, Constitution, Statistical survey, Publishers, press, and broadcasting, Financial, trade and industrial associations, Learned societies and educational institutions, libraries, museums, etc.

Material from this last section is now cumulated and issued as a separate yearbook, the *World of learning (see* L740).

The Who's who section formerly included is now replaced by the *International who's who* (see S28).

Middle East, 1948- . Lond., Europa Publications, 1948- . il. 50s. **L238**

1st issue (1948. 377p.) covers Aden, Afghanistan, Anglo-Egyptian Sudan, Cyprus, Egypt, Iran, Iraq, Syria and Lebanon, Palestine, Saudi Arabia, Transjordan, Turkey, with a section on the League of Arab states.

Organization similar to part 2 of *Europa* (L237). Information for each country includes an outline map, geography, peoples and religions, history, government, (with names of officials), communications, economic life, education, places of interest, press, bibliography, etc.

Orbis; encyclopaedia of extra-European countries; a survey and directory of political, industrial, financial, cultural and scientific organizations in the countries of Africa, America, Asia and Australasia. Lond., Europa Publications [1938-]. **L239**

Loose-leaf. A companion volume to *Europa* (L237), using the same format and general arrangement.

Political handbook of the world; parliaments, parties and press . . . January 1, 1927- . N.Y., Council on Foreign Relations [c1927-]. v.1- . Annual. (1949, $3.50) **L240**

1st issue, 1927, had title: *Political handbook of Europe*.

Usually gives chief government officials, party programs and leaders, political events, and the press (names of newspapers with political affiliation, and proprietor or editor, in some cases the circulation).

United Nations who's who in government and industry. [Ed. by Joel Cang and Ruth Howe] Lond., United Nations Pub., 1941- . **L241**

Title varies: 1941–44, *Who's who in allied governments.*

Arranged by country, giving under each, government officials, diplomatic representatives, biographical notes and brief information about trade and industrial organizations and statistics.

UNITED STATES

American Political Science Association. Directory. 2d ed., 1948, ed. by Franklin L. Burdette. Indianapolis, Nat'l. Foundation for Educ. in Amer. Citizenship [1949]. 374p. $4; to members, $3. **L242**

Serves as a "Who's who in political science." Detailed biographical information of members of the association.

Public administration organizations; a directory of unofficial organizations in the field of public administration in the United States and Canada. Chic., Pub. Admin. Clearing House, 1932- . v.1- . Biennial. **L243**

Title varies: 1932, *Organizations in the field of public administration;* 1934–36, *A directory of organizations in the field of public administration.*

The term "public administration" is interpreted very broadly.

The 1948 edition lists 2381 organizations, usually giving information about membership, finances, secretariat, organization, activities, affiliations and publications.

Arranged alphabetically, followed by classified and geographical lists.

Read, Charles Rodes and **Marble, Samuel.** Guide to public affairs organizations, with notes on public affairs informational materials. Wash., Public Affairs Pr., Amer. Council on Public Affairs, 1946. 135p. $2. **L244**

Identifies and describes some 400 organizations which are "endeavoring to improve the society in which they live." Includes only those organizations with national or international activities or memberships and which invite public participation, thus excluding regional societies and many technical and learned societies. A brief bibliography of "informational materials" is given for each chapter.

Rosow, Jerome M. American men in government; a biographical dictionary and directory of federal officials. Wash., Public Affairs Pr., 1949. 472p. **L245**

A biographical dictionary of 1570 of the men and women who hold the top administrative, diplomatic, military, professional, scientific and technical positions in the federal government.

National governments
Official registers

For certain kinds of current information about the governments of the world the *Statesman's yearbook* (L71) is the most reliable and useful handbook

in English. A very useful work of the same sort in French was the *Annuaire général* (L65). Such publications as the official registers, legislative directories, office lists, etc., of the various governments are useful for many questions about government organization, machinery, duties and personnel. While books of this sort vary in character, they usually contain information about the departments, bureaus, and other offices of a government, the scope, activities and histories of these, sometimes references to the laws creating them, lists of officials, sometimes with biographical data, institutions and societies which have some kind of government relation, etc. The biographical material is often important for names not included in the more general biographical dictionaries.

Jameson, John Franklin. Provisional list of printed lists of ambassadors and other diplomatic representatives. . . . Paris, Les Presses Universitaires de France [1928]. 16p. **L246**

Extract from the *Bulletin* of the International Committee of Historical Sciences (no.4, March 1928).

A convenient record of printed lists of diplomats arranged by country. In some cases the record goes back to the Middle Ages.

Almanach de Gotha, annuaire généalogique, diplomatique et statistique, 1763- . Gotha, Perthes, 1763- . Annual. **L247**

A standard handbook in two main sections: (1) Annuaire généalogique, which gives genealogies of the royal and princely houses of Europe, and (2) Annuaire diplomatique et statistique, which gives some statistical and descriptive information about the various countries of the world, with lists of the principal executive, legislative and diplomatic officials of each.

World diplomatic directory and world diplomatic biography, 1950- . Lond., Diplomatic Publishers, 1950- . Annual. $15. **L247a**

The first edition of this directory (964p.) is divided into two parts, each arranged alphabetically by country. Part 1 gives the principal missions and consular offices abroad of each country including the United Nations. Part 2 gives brief biographical information for officials included in the first part. Supplements are to be issued at irregular intervals.

UNITED STATES

U. S. Congress. Biographical directory of the American Congress, 1774–1927. Wash., Govt. Prt. Off., 1928. 1740p. (69th Cong. 2d sess. House doc. 783) $4.50. **L248**

Contents: (1) Lists: Executive officers 1789–1929; The Continental Congress; Representatives under each apportionment; Members of each congress arranged by states; (2) Biographies, arranged alphabetically.

—— Official congressional directory for the use of the U.S. Congress, 1809- . Wash., Govt. Prt.

Off., 1809- . il. Irregular. (1948, $1.50) **L249**

From 1865 printed at the Government Printing Office; before that by private firms.

Contents, approximately the same in recent volumes though sometimes varying the order: (1) Biographical sketches of members of Congress, arranged by states; alphabetical list of names; (2) State delegations; (3) Terms of service; (4) Committees, membership and days of meetings; (5) Congressional commissions and joint committees; (6) Sessions of Congress, 1789–1928; (7) Votes cast for senators and representatives; number of representatives under each apportionment; (8) Governors of states and territories, present list; (9) Presidents and vice-presidents, 1789–1945; (10) The Capitol: officers of the Senate, officers of the House, members' rooms, etc.; (11) Miscellaneous officers; (12) Executive departments, biographical sketches of each member of the cabinet and lists of principal officials in each department; (13) Independent offices and establishments; (14) Judiciary, biographies of members of Supreme court, lists of the courts; (15) District of Columbia government; (16) Diplomatic and consular service, (a) Foreign diplomatic representatives in the United States, (b) Foreign consular officers in the United States, (c) Foreign service of the United States; (17) Official duties of executive departments and subdivisions, independent commissions; (18) Press galleries: representatives of newspapers and periodicals, photographers, radio correspondents, members, rules, etc.; (19) Maps of Congressional districts; (20) Home addresses of members of Congress; (21) Individual index.

U. S. Civil Service Commission. Official register of the United States; 1933- , persons occupying administrative and supervisory positions in the legislative, executive and judicial branches of the Federal Government, and in District of Columbia Government. Wash., Govt. Prt. Off., 1933- . (1949, $2.25) **L250**

Biennial until 1921; not issued 1922–24; annual, 1925- .

Before 1861, published by the Dept. of State; 1861–1905, by the Dept. of the Interior; 1907–32, by the Bureau of the Census; 1933- , by the Civil Service Commission.

1907, 1909, 1911, issued in two volumes, respectively: v.1, Directory; v.2, Postal Service. 1913–21 issued in one volume, Directory.

The official register, formerly known as the *Blue book*, is the official list of government employees. In two main parts: (1) a classified list, arranged by departments, bureaus, offices, etc., in Washington, and in the territorial possessions, giving names of the principal officials and assistants, showing, for each, official title, salary, legal residence and place of employment; (2) alphabetical index of names included in the classified list.

Until 1911 the *Official register* included the names of all government employees, including the postal service; from 1913 to 1921 it was complete except for the postal service. The issues from 1925 on are much reduced in size and include only principal officials.

U. S. Dept. of State. Register, 1869- . Wash., Govt. Prt. Off., 1869- . Annual (some years not pub.). (1949, $1.50) **L251**

Title varies: 1869–1942, *Register of the Department of State*; 1944- , some years called *Biographic register*. (Not published 1943)

Contents vary. The *Register* usually contains sections on departmental organization, information about the foreign service of the United States, historical lists, lists of the clerical, administrative, and fiscal service, and a biographical section for administrative and professional employees. The *Biographic register* published since 1944 includes only the biographical section.

United States Government organization manual . . . 1935- . Wash., 1935- . Irregular. (1949, $1) **L252**

Title varies: 1935–48, *United States government manual*.

Loose-leaf, 1935–1937.

1935–1937 issued by the National Emergency Council; Oct. 1939–July 1940, by the Office of Government Reports; fall, 1940– spring, 1942, by the Information Service; fall, 1942–1945, 1st ed., by the Division of Public Inquiries of the Office of War Information; 1945, 2d ed.–1947, 1st ed., by the Bureau of the Budget, Government Information Service, Division of Public Inquiries; 1947, 2d ed., by the Office of Government Reports; 1948, by the Division of the Federal Register of the National Archives; 1949, by the Division of the Federal Register of the National Archives Establishment; 1950/51- , by Federal Register Division, National Archives and Records Service.

A manual of information on the organization, activities, and current officials of the various departments, bureaus, offices, commissions, etc., of the government.

U. S. Office of War Information. American handbook. Wash., Public Affairs Pr., 1945. 508p. il. $3.75. **L253**

A revised edition of the *Handbook of the United States* published by the Office of War Information in 1944, the foreword of which states: "This handbook . . . has been especially prepared for use overseas. All the material in it has been selected on that basis."

The 1945 edition has been rearranged somewhat but the material differs little. Describes the organization and work of the government, its branches, bureaus, and wartime agencies; surveys the economics, resources and cultural life of the country.

❧ The above are official lists. Earlier unofficial publications which are occasionally useful are: Lanman, Charles, *Biographical annals of the civil government of the United States* (2d ed., 1887), Mosher, R. B., *Executive register of the United States*, 1789–1902, (1903) and Poore, B. P., *Political register* (1878). For officials and organization of the state governments, the various state manuals and state legislative handbooks must be consulted. Record of such manuals will be found in the *Book of the states* (L286), which also lists current officers.

AUSTRALIA

Australia. Parliament. Joint Library Committee. Parliamentary handbook and record of elections. 1, 1915- . Canberra, Govt. Printer, 1915- . Irregular. **L254**

10th issue (1945) covers 1938–1945.
Title varies: v.1-7, *Biographical handbook and record of elections.*

AUSTRIA

Österreichischer Amtskalender, 1. Jahrgang, 1922-
. Wien, Staatsdrückerei, 1922- . Annual. **L255**

A new series combining the *Niederösterreichische Amtskalender* and the *Hof- und Staatshandbuch.* Title pages of each issue carry the volume numbering of each of the earlier series as well as the new series.

Suspended publication 1938–1948. Resumed with v.17, 1949.

BELGIUM

Almanach royal officiel, publié depuis 1840. Bruxelles, Guyot, 1840- . Annual. (1915–19 not published) **L256**

CANADA

Canadian parliamentary guide. (Published with the Patronage of the Parliament of Canada and of the Legislatures of the various Provinces) ed. by G. Pierre Normandin. Ottawa, Syndicat des Oeuvres Sociales Limitée, 1912- . $4. **L257**

DENMARK

Kongelig dansk Hof-og Statskalender, Statshaandbog for kongeriget Danmark for Aaret 1734- . . . . København, Schultz, 1734- . Annual. (1950, Kr. 45) **L258**

FINLAND

Finlands Statskalender för året 1811- utg. av Helsingfors Universitet. Helsingfors, Osakeyhitö Weilin & Göös Aktiebolag, 1811- . Annual. **L259**

FRANCE

Robert, Adolphe. Dictionnaire des parlementaires français, comprenant tous les membres des assemblées françaises et tous les ministres français depuis le 1er mai 1789 jusqu'au 1er mai 1889. Publié sous la direction de Adolphe Robert, Edgar Bourloton et Gaston Cougny. Paris, Bourloton, 1891. 5v. il. **L260**

Fairly long biographical sketches.

Samuel, René Claude Louis. Les parlementaires français, II. 1900–1914. Dictionnaire biographique et bibliographique des sénateurs, députés, ministres ayant siégé dans les assemblées législatives. Paris, Roustan, 1914. 479p. **L261**

Started as a continuation of the preceding work by Robert, but the volume covering 1889–1900 was never published. This volume called volume 2.

Almanach national; annuaire officiel de la République française, 1872–1919. Paris, Berger-Levrault, 1872–1919. v.173-217/221. **L262**

Published since 1700. Earlier volumes had title, *Almanach royal, Almanach impérial,* etc.

Volume for 1919 is 217th-221st années. No more published.

Of first importance for information about the organization and personnel of the government of France. Gives many official lists, e.g., Cabinet, Senate and Chamber, principal officers of the various government offices and bureaus, outline of duties and functions of these bureaus. Includes also lists of Legion of Honor, and other orders, courts, departmental prefectures, universities, academies, societies, museums, etc., chambers of commerce, etc.

Annuaire diplomatique et consulaire de la République française. Paris, Impr. Nat., 1858- . Annual. **L263**

Title varies.

❦ Fuller biographical information, etc., is sometimes given in the *annuaires* of the various ministries e.g., Ministère de l'Instruction Publique et des Beaux Arts; Ministère des Finances; Ministère des Colonies etc.

GERMANY

Deutsche Reich von 1918 bis Heute hrsg. vor Cano Horkenbach [1918/30–33] Berlin, Verlag für Presse, Wirtschaft und Politik [c1930]–35. 4v **L264**

Contents: (1) History; (2) Politics and government (3) Statistics; (4) Who's who of leading persons in Ger man political life.

Deutschland-Jahrbuch, 1949- , hrsg. von Klau Mehnert und Heinrich Schulte. Essen, West Verlag, 1949- . **L265**

This first volume is a comprehensive handbook cover ing May 7, 1945 to the autumn of 1948. Material is di vided under five broad headings: (1) Government, law politics; (2) Economics; (3) Social life; (4) Church education, science; (5) Art and culture.

Germany. Reichsministerium des Innern. Hand buch für das deutsche Reich, 1874- . Berlin Heymann, 1874- . Annual (irregular). **L266**

GREAT BRITAIN

British imperial calendar and civil service lis Lond., Stat. Off., 1809- . Irregular. (1949 10s. 6d.) **L267**

Title varies.
Contents: Royal households; Public departments, Eng land and Wales, Scotland, Northern Ireland; Alphabetic list of officers; Index to departments and subdepartment

Gives names, official positions, degrees and honors, salaries.

Colonial office list, 1862- , comprising historical and statistical information respecting the colonial empire, lists of officers serving in the colonies, etc., and other information. Lond., Stat. Off., 1862- . Annual to 1940; biennial from 1946- . (1948, 15s.) **L268**

Title varies: 1862–1925, *Colonial office list;* 1926–1940, *Dominions office and Colonial office list;* 1946- , *Colonial office list.* Subtitle varies.

Scope of contents varies but usually includes extensive historical and statistical information on each colony or dominion, with biographical sections and maps. The maps are omitted from the 1948 volume and published in a separate map supplement (£1 1s.).

Dod's Parliamentary companion for 1832- . Lond., Business Dictionaries, Ltd., 1832- . Annual. (1949, 15s.) **L269**

Publisher varies.

Includes Biographies of peers and members of the House of Commons; Procedure; Ministries and government departments, etc.

Foreign office list and diplomatic and consular year book; ed. for Godfrey E. P. Hertslet by members of the staff of the Foreign Office. 1806- . Lond., Harrison, 1806- . Annual. (1949, 42s.) **L270**

Gives organization of the office, various diplomatic and consular lists, "Statement of services" with biographical notices of some length, obituaries, references to biographical notices in earlier volumes, various chronological lists, etc.

Foster, Joseph. Members of Parliament, Scotland, including the minor barons, the commissioners for the shires, and the commissioners for the burghs, 1357–1882. On the basis of the parliamentary return 1880, with genealogical and biographical notices. 2d ed. rev. and cor. Lond., priv. pr. by Hazell, Watson and Viney, 1882. 360p. **L271**

Gt. Brit. Parliament. House of Commons. Members of Parliament . . . [Return of the name of every member of the Lower House of Parliament of England, Scotland and Ireland, with name of constituency represented and date of return, from 1213 to 1874]. Lond., Stat. Off., 1878–01. 2 pts. in 4. (House of Commons. Reports and papers, 1878. no.69, 69I, 69II; 1892, no.169; also numbered 69III) **L272**

pt.1, Parliaments of England 1213–1702, arranged chronologically; Index to pt. 1, with appendix and corrigenda; pt.2, Parliaments of Great Britain, 1705–96, Parliaments of the United Kingdom, 1801–74, Parliaments and Conventions of the Estates of Scotland, 1357–1707, Parliaments of Ireland, 1559–1800; Index to pt.2, with appendix, i.e., names and members, 1880–85, and corrigenda.

A very important record.

India office and Burma office list. Lond., Harrison, 1886- . Annual. (v.54, 1940, £1 10s.) **L273**

Contains some descriptive and statistical information and many biographies.

Title varies from 1803- . In its present series, *India office list,* 1887–95; *India list and India office list,* 1896–1906; *India office list,* 1907–37; *India office and Burma office list,* 1938- .

Wedgwood, Josiah Clement. History of Parliament, 1439–1509. Lond., Stat. Off., 1936–38. v.1-2. col. coats of arms, facsim. **L274**

v.1, Biographies of members of the Commons House; v.2, Register of the ministers and of the members of both houses, 1439–1509.

The first two of a series of three volumes dealing with the history of Parliament from 1439–1509. It is announced that this first series is to be followed by other series tracing the growth of parliamentary representation and government in Great Britain from the thirteenth century to 1918.—Cf. *Pref.*

For note on volume 1 *see* S129.

Volume 2, *Register,* contains: introductory chapters on treatment, sources and analyses; time analysis and lists of Parliaments, arranged chronologically; notes on each constituency with alphabetical lists of members; tables and appendixes. '

ITALY

Italy. Parlamento. Camera dei Deputati. Annuario parlamentare, 1948/49- . Rome, Tip. della Camera dei Deputati, 1948- . **L275**

JAPAN

Political handbook of Japan, 1949- ; with data on the press. Tokyo, Tokyo News Service; S. Pasadena, Calif., P. D. and Ione Perkins, 1949- . $5. **L276**

Political organization, statistics, texts of some official documents, lists of book and newspaper publishers, who's who in politics and the press.

NETHERLANDS

Parlement en Kiezer, jaarboekje, 1911/12- . s'Gravenhage, Nijhoff, 1911- . Annual. **L277**

Staatsalmanak voor het Koninkrijk der Nederlanden, 1808, 1815- . s'Gravenhage Nijhoff, 1808- . Annual. **L278**

NORWAY

Norges statskalender for året 1815- . Oslo, Aschehoug, 1815- . Annual (irregular). **L279**

SWEDEN

Sveriges statskalender för året 1877- . Utg. efter Kungl.Maj:ts nådigste förordnande av dess

Vetenskapsakademi. Uppsala och Stockholm, Almquist, 1877- . Annual. **L280**

Continues *Sveriges och Norges statskalender,* 1764–1876.

SWITZERLAND

Staatskalender der Schweizerischen Eidgenossenschaft. Annuaire de la Confédération suisse. Hrsg. von der Bundeskanzlei. Bern, 1849- . Annual. **L281**

Local government
Bibliography

Greer, Sarah. Bibliography of civil service and personnel administration. N.Y. and Lond., McGraw-Hill, 1935. 143p. (Commission of Inquiry on Public Service Personnel. Monograph 1) **L282**

Gross, Charles. Bibliography of British municipal history. N.Y., Lond., Longmans, 1897. 461p. **L284**

For full entry *see* V269.

Munro, William Bennett. Bibliography of municipal government in the United States. Camb., Harvard Univ. Pr., 1915. 472p. (Harvard University. Pub. of the Bureau for Research in Municipal Government. 2.) **L285**

A selected annotated list of about 5000 titles, arranged in classified order, with an alphabetical author and subject index. Planned for both the general reader and the special student of municipal affairs. Includes books, public documents and articles in periodicals and society publications.

Encyclopedias and handbooks

UNITED STATES

Book of the states, 1935- , v.1- . Chic., Council of State Governments, 1935- . il. Biennial. (1948/49, $7.50; $10 with 2 suppl.) **L286**

A comprehensive manual on state activities. Contents 1948–49: sec. 1, Intergovernmental relations; sec. 2, Constitutions and elections; sec. 3, Legislatures and legislation; sec. 4, Administrative organization and finance; sec. 5, Major state services; sec. 6, The Judiciary; sec. 7, Directory of the states and territories (giving officers, statistics and general information); sec. 8, Bibliography and index.

"Beginning with the 7th ed. will be issued biennially in January of the even-numbered years. . . . Two supplements will be issued in the odd-numbered years, one on Jan. 1, listing all legislators and elective officials, and one on July 1, including appointed administrative officials."— *Foreword* to 7th ed. (1948/49).

Municipal index, 1924- . A yearbook for city, town and county officials, highway engineers and for all others interested in public improvement activities. N.Y., Amer. City Magazine, 1924- . v.1- . il. Annual. (1949, $5) **L287**

Contains articles on municipal subjects, directories of organizations, statistics, illustrations of machinery, bibliographies.

Municipal year book, 1934- ; an authoritative résumé of activities and statistical data of American cities. Chic., International City Managers' Assoc., 1934- . Annual. (1949, $10) **L288**

Contents vary. 1949 includes: pt.1, Governmental units; pt. 2, Municipal personnel; pt. 3, Municipal finance; pt.4, Municipal activities; pt.5, Directories of officials.

Parts 1-4 include two types of information, signed annual surveys by various writers and statistical tables. Bibliographies appended.

U. S. Bureau of the Census. City finances, 1942- . Wash., Govt. Prt. Off., 1944- . Annual. **L289**

1909–1941, *Financial statistics of cities.*

Since 1937 issued in parts covering: cities having a population over 250,000; cities having a population over 25,000, with a final volume called *Statistical compendium.* Form and volume numbering vary.

—— County finances, 1940- . Wash., Govt. Prt. Off., 1942- . **L290**

1940 has title: *Financial statistics of counties.*

—— State finances, 1942- . Wash., Govt. Prt. Off., 1944- . Annual. **L291**

1915–1941, *Financial statistics of states.*

Since 1938, published annually in parts; form and volume numbering vary, but usually covers: individual state reports; topical reports, e.g., budgets, expenditure, debt, tax collections, etc.; statistical compendiums (preliminary and final).

FRANCE

Seine. Service du Travail et de la Statistique Municipale. Annuaire statistique de la ville de Paris, 1.- année, 1880- . Paris, 1881- . v.1- **L292**

GERMANY

Handwörterbuch der Kommunalwissenschaften, hrsg. von J. Brix, H. Lindemann [u.a.]. Jena, Fischer, 1914–24. 4v. **L293**

—— Ergänzungsbd. 1927. 2v.

v.1-4, A-Z; Suppl. 2v., A-Z, Nachtrag; classed index to whole work.

Long signed articles, bibliographies. Principally German municipal subjects.

"The best of all local government encyclopedias."—
Munro, *Bibliography of municipal government* (p.18).

Handwörterbuch der preussischen Verwaltung.
3. vollständig umgearb. Aufl. . . . Berlin, de Gruyter, 1928. 2v. **L294**

Articles by specialists; bibliographies.

GREAT BRITAIN

**London. County Council. Local Government
and Statistical Dept.** London statistics, 1890- .
Lond., 1893- . v.1- . 15s. ea. **L295**

—— Statistical abstract for London, 1897- .
Lond., 1897- . v.1- . (v.29, 1937, 2s. 9d.)
L296

Municipal year book, an encyclopaedia of local
government administration. Lond., Municipal
Journal, 1897- . v.1- . (1949, 52s. 6d.) **L297**

Includes articles on all phases of English local government, finance, fuel and power, roads, education, parks, public health, etc.; list of associations and societies concerned with local government; information about municipal corporations with lists of offices, county and district councils, with officers, etc.

NEW ZEALAND

New Zealand. Census and Statistics Dept. Local
authorities handbook of New Zealand, 1926- .
1st- . Wellington, 1926- . v.1- . Annual.
7s. 6d. ea. **L298**

Takes the place of the *Annual statistical report on local
government,* issued annually since 1875, biennial 1903–24, and the *Municipal handbook.*

SOUTH AFRICA

Official South African municipal year book
1909- . Cape Town, Juta (Lond., E. G. Allen),
1910- . v.1- . il. (1946/47, 25s.) **L298a**

Legislative procedure

U. S. Congress. Senate. Senate manual, containing the standing rules, orders, laws, and resolutions affecting the business of the United States
Senate; Jefferson's Manual; Declaration of Independence; Articles of Confederation; Constitution of the United States, etc. Wash., Govt. Prt.
Off., 1820- . **L298b**

Title varies. Issued for each session of Congress.

—— **House.** Constitution, Jefferson's Manual and
Rules of the House of Representatives. Wash.,
Govt. Prt. Off., 1824- . **L298c**

The *House manual.* Title varies. Issued for each session of Congress.

Political parties

The standard histories of political parties and the campaign textbooks issued by the principal parties are the main sources of information in this field. Contents of the campaign textbooks vary but usually contain party platforms, statements of the party's stand on principal issues, acceptance speeches of candidates, committee members, etc. Political and election statistics, accounts of national conventions, texts of party platforms, were given in the *Tribune almanac* (L103) to 1914. Statistics and chief points of party platforms are given in the *World almanac* (L104). Summary election statistics on federal offices are given in *Historical statistics of the United States, 1789–1945* (L96) and in the *Statistical abstract* (L93). State manuals and legislative handbooks often give statistics of state and local elections.

Sait, Edward McChesney. Sait's American
parties and elections. 4th ed. by Howard R.
Penniman. N.Y., Appleton-Century, 1948. 668p.
il. **L299**

Cousens, Theodore Wells. Politics and political
organizations in America. N.Y., Macmillan, 1942.
617p. il. **L299a**

Bibliography, p.541-62.

McKenzie, Charles Wallace. Party government
in the United States. N.Y., Ronald Pr., 1938.
597p. il. **L299b**

Bibliography, p.565-81.

Merriam, Charles Edward and **Gosnell, Harold
Foote.** The American party system; an introduction to the study of political parties in the United
States; 4th ed. N.Y., Macmillan, 1949. 530p.
$4.65. **L299c**

Porter, Kirk H. National party platforms. N.Y.,
Macmillan, 1924. 522p. $3.75. **L299d**

A useful compilation. Gives text of 104 platforms in
the 22 presidential campaigns 1840–1924.

U. S. Congress. House. Platforms of the two
great political parties, 1856–1928, comp. by Leroy
D. Brandon. rev. ed. Wash., Govt. Prt. Off., 1936.
334p. **L299e**

—— —— 1932–44. 1945. p.335-458.

—— —— 1948. 1948. 21p.

McKee, Thomas Hudson. National conventions
and platforms of all political parties, 1789–1905;
convention, popular and electoral vote. Also the
political complexion of both houses of Congress
at each biennial period. 6th ed. rev. and enl.
Baltimore, Friedenwald Co., 1906. 418p. 33p.
L299f

Yearbooks

Constitutional year book; a treasury of political information; 1855- . 1st- issue. Lond., Harrison, [1885]- . Annual. 5s. **L299g**

Labour party year book, 1946/47- ed. by the Research Dept. of the Labour Party. Lond., 1947- . Annual. 6s. 8d. **L299h**

A new series of yearbooks covering approximately the period since 1945 when the Labour party was elected to the Government. A previous series of *Labour year books* was published from 1916–1932.

Public opinion

Childs, Harwood L. A reference guide to the study of public opinion. Princeton, Princeton Univ. Pr., 1934. 105p. $2. **L300**

Smith, Bruce Lannes, Lasswell, Harold D. and **Casey, Ralph D.** Propaganda, communication, and public opinion; a comprehensive reference guide. Princeton, Princeton Univ. Pr., 1946. 435p. $6. **L301**

An expansion of *Propaganda and promotional activities; an annotated list,* published in 1935.

This new edition includes four essays on *The science of mass communication* followed by an annotated, selective bibliography of almost 3000 titles arranged by class. Includes books, periodicals and articles which appeared between the middle of 1934 and early 1943 with a few titles of earlier dates. 150 titles have been starred as "outstanding" and given somewhat fuller annotations than most of the others. Some annotations are very brief. Well indexed.

International directory of opinion and attitude research, ed. by Laszlo Radvanyi. Mexico, La Ciencias Sociales, 1948. 292p. $7. **L302**

Includes lists of research organizations and educational institutions and biographical information about individuals in the field.

Army and Navy
Bibliography

Copenhagen. Marinens Bibliothek. Katalog . . . udarbejdet . . . af H. A. Ø. Bistrup. København, Levin, 1933–36. 2v. and annual suppl. **L303**

Contents: v.1, Catalog of literature concerning the discoveries and the explorations of the polar environs and the oceans, whale and seal fisheries; biography; periodicals, annuals and other periodical papers; v.2, Naval, nautical, and technical literature.

An extensive collection containing books in many languages.

—— —— Aarligt tillaeg (Yearly supplement). 1933- . København, 1934- .

Favitski de Probobysz, A. de. Répertoire bibliographique de la littérature militaire et coloniale française depuis cent ans. Paris, G. Thone, 1935. 363p. **L304**

Arranged alphabetically with a subject index.

Gt. Brit. War Office. Library. Catalogue of the War Office Library. Lond., Stat. Off., 1906–16. 3v. and suppl. pts. 1-3. **L305**

pt.1, Author catalogue, 1906; pt.2, Official publications (not including parliamentary papers), annuals and periodicals, 1910; pt. 3, Subject index.

Pohler, Johann. Bibliotheca historico-militaris. Systematische Uebersicht der Erscheinungen aller Sprachen auf dem Gebiete der Geschichte der Krieg und Kriegswissenschaft seit Erfindung der Buchdruckerkunst bis zum Schluss des Jahres 1880. Leipzig, Lang, 1887–99. 4v. **L306**

U. S. Adjutant General's Office. List of unofficial unit histories and unit associations, comp. in Departmental Records Branch, Administrative Services Division. [Wash.] 1947. 91p. **L307**

Lists the histories of the various divisions, regiments, etc.

U. S. Military Academy, West Point. The centennial of the U. S. Military Academy at West Point, N.Y., 1802–1902. v.2, Statistics and bibliographies. Wash., Govt. Prt. Off., 1904. 433p. **L308**

Includes: Bibliographies of West Point, 1694–1902; Bibliography of the U.S. Military Academy, 1776–1902; Bibliography of the writings of graduates, 1802–1902.

U. S. Naval Academy, Annapolis. Library. Bibliography of naval literature in the United States Naval Academy Library, comp. by L. H. Bolander. [Annapolis, 1929] 3v. in 1. **L309**

"Works dealing with naval strategy, tactics, ordnance, and gunnery, seamanship, and navigation have not been included."

pt.1, American naval biography; pt.2, Foreign naval biography; pt.3, Naval history.

Manuals

Ageton, Arthur Ainsley. The Naval officer's guide. [3d ed.] N.Y., Whittlesey House (McGraw-Hill), [1946] 588p. il. $3.50. **L310**

Accurate and authoritative.

Air officer's guide. A ready-reference encyclopedia of all military information pertinent to commissioned officers of the United States Air Force 2d ed. Harrisburg, Pa., Military Serv. Pub. Co. 1949. 582p. il. $3.50. **L311**

The officers' guide; a ready reference on customs and correct procedures which pertain to commissioned officers of the Army of the United States. 1st ed., June 1930- . Harrisburg, Pa.

Military Serv. Pub. Co., 1930- . Irregular. (1948, $3.50) **L312**

The first edition produced for the *Infantry journal* by the National Service Publishing Company, Washington.

U. S. Army Air Forces. The Official guide to the Army Air Forces, AAF; a directory, almanac and chronicle of achievement. N.Y., Simon & Schuster, 1944. 380p. il. $2.50. (Also pub. by Pocket Books, Inc., N.Y., 25c) **L313**

On cover: AAF; the official guide to the Army Air Forces.
Selected bibliography of aviation, p.358-65.

National Geographic Society. Insignia and decorations of the United States armed forces. rev. ed., Dec. 1, 1944. Wash., National Geographic Soc., 1945. 208p. il. $1. **L314**

Descriptions and illustrations, many in color, of decorations, medals, service ribbons, badges, and other insignia of the U.S. armed forces.

Naval annuals

Brassey's Naval annual, 1886- . Lond., Clowes, 1886- . v.1- . il. 25s. per v. **L315**

Title varies, publisher varies.
An annual chronicle with statistics of British and foreign fleets. The volume for 1948 differs from earlier years in that it is almost entirely devoted to one subject, Fuehrer Conferences on Naval Affairs (translations of records of conferences between Hitler and his naval officers), followed by a brief reference section giving changes in the fleets in 1947, etc.

Jane's Fighting ships. v.1- , 1898- . Lond., S. Low, 1898- . il. Annual. **L316**

Title varies.
Detailed information on the warships of the world.

Navy yearbook, ed. by Phillip Andrews and Leonard Engel. N.Y., Duell, Sloan & Pearce, 1944- . il. **L317**

Statistics and information about the large navies of the world, arranged by country, with many photographs. Includes a naval chronology of World War II and a war loss section.

Biography

Cullum, George Washington. Biographical register of the officers and graduates of the U.S. Military Academy at West Point, N.Y., since its establishment in 1802. 3d ed., rev. and extended. Bost., etc., 1891-1940. 8v. **L318**

Place and publisher vary: v.1-3, Bost., Houghton, 1891; v.4, Camb., Mass., Riverside Pr., 1901; v.5-6, Saginaw, Mich., Seeman & Peters, 1910-20. 2v. in 3; v.7-8, Chic., Donnelley, 1932-40.
v.1-3, 1802-90; v.4, 1890-1900, ed. by E. S. Holden; v.5, 1900-10, ed. by Lieut. Charles Braden; v.6, A&B, 1910-20, ed. by Col. Wirt Robinson; v.7, 1920-30, ed.

by Capt. W. H. Donaldson; v.8, 1930-40, ed. by Lt. Col. E. E. Farman.
v.4-8 called supplements.

Heitman, Francis Bernard. Historical register of officers of the continental army . . . April 1775 to December 1783. New, rev., and enl. ed. Wash., Rare Bk. Shop Pub. Co., 1914. 685p. $10. **L319**

—— Historical register and dictionary of the United States army . . . September 29, 1789, to March 2, 1903. Pub. under act of Congress approved March 2, 1903. Wash., Govt. Prt. Off., 1903. 2v. (57th Cong., 2d sess. House, Doc. no.446) **L320**

Powell, William Henry. List of officers of the army of the United States from 1779-1900 . . . register of all appointments in the volunteer service during the civil war and of volunteer officers in the service of the United States June 1, 1900, comp. from the official records. N.Y., Hamersly, 1900. 863p. **L321**

A list of officers, 1779-1815, is arranged by years, followed by the army list, 1815 to 1900, which is arranged alphabetically by name, a list of officers of volunteers, general officers of the Revolution, etc., also dates of certain wars, campaigns, etc. Known also as the *United States army list.*

—— Officers of the army and navy (volunteer) who served in the civil war. Phila., Hamersly, 1893. 419p. il. **L322**

—— and **Shippen, Edward.** Officers of the army and navy (regular) who served in the civil war. Phila., Hamersly, 1892. 487p. il. **L323**

❧ The Adjutant-general issues an annual *Official army register* (1950, $3.25).

Callahan, Edward W. List of officers of the navy of the United States and of the marine corps, from 1775 to 1900; comp. from the official records. N.Y., Hamersly, 1901. 749p. **L324**

❧ The Navy department issues an annual *Register of commissioned and warrant officers of the United States Navy and Marine corps* (1949, $5).

ECONOMICS
General works
Bibliography

❧ Documents issued by the federal government are particularly useful in the field of economics. Only a few of the many valuable publications of various departments and bureaus can be listed here. The Bureau of Labor Statistics, Bureau of the Census, Bureau of Foreign and Domestic Commerce and many others are prolific publishers. For further information consult the *United States government pub-*

lications: *Monthly catalog* (F15), Hirshberg, H. S. and Melinat, C. H., *Subject guide to United States government publications* (F4), etc.

Batson, Harold Edward. A select bibliography of modern economic theory, 1870–1929. Lond., Routledge, 1930. 224p. **L325**

An annotated bibliography of books and periodical articles: pt.1, by subject; pt.2, by author.

Harvard University. Bureau for Economic Research in Latin America. Economic literature of Latin America, a tentative bibliography. Camb., Harvard Univ. Pr., 1935–36. 2v. $4; 17s. ea. **L326**

An extensive bibliography of books, pamphlets and periodical articles listing, in the two volumes, a total of 12,520 numbered items. Arranged geographically by countries or regions, with a subject arrangement under each and a general index of authors for each volume. Special features are the introductory notes at the heads of important sections, the appendixes on the statistical sources of South America, Mexico and the Caribbean, and notes on collections of Latin American economic literature in leading libraries.

Hasse, Adelaide Rosalie. Index of economic material in documents of the states of the United States. Prepared for the Department of Economics and Sociology of the Carnegie Institution of Washington. Wash., Carnegie Inst., 1907–22. 13v. in 16. **L327**

Volumes issued are:
California, 1849–1904. 1908. 316p.
Delaware, 1789–1904. 1910. 137p.
Illinois, 1809–1904. 1909. 393p.
Kentucky, 1792–1904. 1910. 452p.
Maine, 1820–1904. 1907. 95p.
Massachusetts, 1789–1904. 1908. 310p.
New Hampshire, 1789–1904. 1907. 66p.
New Jersey, 1789–1904. 1914. 705p.
New York, 1789–1904. 1907. 553p.
Ohio, 1787–1904. 1912. 2v.
Pennsylvania, 1790–1904. 1919–22. 3v.
Rhode Island, 1789–1904. 1908. 95p.
Vermont, 1789–1904. 1907. 71p.
No more published.

Includes a comprehensive history of all economic material (with definite reference to volume and page) to be found in the printed reports of administrative officers, legislative committees, and special commissions of the states, and in the governors' messages, for the period covered.

The word economic has been interpreted very liberally to include almost any aspect of American history. Indexing is by rather general headings and broad subjects.

Omits reports of bureaus of labor before 1902 as these are covered in the *Index to all reports issued by bureaus of labor statistics . . . to March 1902,* issued by U.S. Bureau of Labor (L479).

Hollander, Jacob Harry. The economic library of Jacob H. Hollander, comp. by Elsie A. G. Marsh. Balt., priv. pr., 1937. 324p. **L328**

3860 titles, chronologically arranged, 1574–1935. Particularly rich in eighteenth century English tracts.

Istituto Nazionale per le Relazioni Culturali con l'Estero. Scienze economiche e sociali. Roma, I.R.C.E., 1941. 167p. (Bibliografie del ventennio) **L329**

Works published in Italy in the period between World Wars I and II.

McCulloch, John Ramsay. Literature of political economy; a classified catalogue of select publications in the different departments of that science, with historical, critical, and biographical notices. Lond., Longmans, 1845. 407p. (Repr. by the London School of Economics and Political Science. Ser. of reprints of scarce works on political economy, no.5, 1938. 12s. 6d.) **L330**

Schwartz, Harry. The Soviet economy; a selected bibliography of materials in English. Syracuse, N.Y., Syracuse Univ. Pr., 1949. 93p. **L331**

A classified, annotated bibliography of book, pamphlet, and periodical material.

Abstract journals

Bollettino emerografico di economia internazionale, redatto dall'Istituto di Economia Internazionale. v.1, no.1, gennaio 1948- . Genova, Camera di Commercio, Industria e Agricoltura, 1948- . Quarterly. Italia, L600; Estero, L1000. **L332**

Abstracts of outstanding articles from the periodicals of the principal countries of the world. (438 publications from 45 countries and 8 international organizations; these numbers vary slightly.) Classified. Gives citation to month of periodical but not to volume or page.

Documentation économique; revue bibliographique trimestrielle, publie les analyses classées par sujets des articles parus dans les principales revues économiques. v.1, 1934- . Paris, Press Universitaires de France, 1934- . Quarterly. France, 750fr.; Étranger, 900fr. par an. **L333**

Subtitle and publisher vary. Suspended Dec. 1938 through Dec. 1946.

At head of title: Institut National de la Statistique et des Etudes Économiques, Association de Documentation Économique et Sociale.

Abstracts articles in American, Dutch, English, French, German, Greek, Italian, Portuguese, Spanish, Swedish, and Russian economic periodicals. Classified by subject with author index.

Dictionaries and encyclopedias

Bedrijfseconomische encyclopedie onder algemeene leiding van J. G. Stridiron. Utrecht, W. de Haan, 1947–49. v.1-3. il. (In progress) **L334**

Contents: Deel 1, Economie, 518p.; Deel 2, Algemeene bedrijfseconomie, 355p.; Deel 3, Bedrijfseconomie, 398p.

Signed articles with bibliographies. Each volume, A-Z. The first volume treats general economic problems, the second business economy in its general aspects, and the third business economy in its special aspects. The fourth will deal with management, and the fifth with statistics and accounting.—Cf. *Voorwoord,* v.1.

Horton, Byrne Joseph, Ripley, Julien and **Schnapper, M. B.** Dictionary of modern economics. Wash., Public Affairs Pr. [1948]. 365p. $5. **L335**

A popular dictionary of short articles, designed for the layman or college student, defining current terms used in economic theory and practice. Includes biographies of 120 leading economists of various periods and nationalities.

Palgrave, *Sir* **Robert Harry Inglis.** Palgrave's Dictionary of political economy, ed. by Henry Higgs. Lond. and N.Y., Macmillan, 1923–26. 3v. 108s.; $25, $8.50 ea. **L336**

First edition, 1894–96; reprinted 1910 without change in the text, but with a supplement of new articles in volume 3, p.693-803; a reprint of the 1910 edition, issued 1915–18, contains the same supplement but with cross references to the supplement incorporated in the main alphabet. The 1923–26 edition is printed from the stereotyped plates of the first edition, with some changes in the plates and with a supplement which uses some of the material from the earlier supplement and adds some new articles.

The standard English work, including some general and foreign aspects of the subject but largely limited to developments of economic study in the English-speaking world. Signed articles by specialists, bibliographies. Useful and authoritative, but unfortunately not up to date.

Schweizerische Gesellschaft für Statistik und Volkswirtschaft. Handbuch der schweizerischen Volkswirtschaft. Bern, Benteli, 1939. 2v. **L337**

Alphabetical arrangement. Long signed articles with bibliographies.

Sloan, Harold S. and **Zurcher, Arnold J.** Dictionary of economics. N.Y., Barnes and Noble, 1949. 268p. $3. **L338**

Definitions and explanations of economic terms covering the fields of economics, international trade, money, banking, business, insurance, etc., with "brief digests and descriptions of the more important relevant American statutes and judicial decisions and American and international regulatory agencies."—Cf. *Pref.* Many cross references.

Wörterbuch der Volkswirtschaft, hrsg. von Ludwig Elster. 4. völlig umgearb. Aufl. Jena, Fischer, 1931–33. 3v. **L339**

The standard German encyclopedia of economics, supplementary to the *Handwörterbuch der Staatswissenschaften* (L229) which covers political science. Signed articles, bibliographies, biographies of deceased persons.

TERMS

Price, Hereward T. Economic dictionary: English-German, German-English. Berlin, Springer, 1926–29. 2v. **L340**

Added title page in German: Volkswirtschaftliches Wörterbuch.

A very useful dictionary of the language used by economists, including economics, philosophy, jurisprudence, etc., with references to the use of the terms in the literature of the subject.

Annuals

Economic almanac for 1940- ; a handbook of useful facts about business, labor and government in the United States and other areas. N.Y., National Industrial Conf. Bd., 1940- . Annual. $5. **L341**

An annual statistical compendium covering such subjects as: prices, banking, finance, national income, resources, manufacturing, communication and transportation, industries, agriculture, labor, foreign trade, international economic statistics, etc.

Commerce
Commercial products

See also Directories, p.300.

Commodity year book. v.1, 1939- . N.Y., Commodity Research Bureau, Inc., 1939- . v.1- . il. Annual. (suspended 1943–47) (1948, $10) **L342**

——— ——— Master edition . . . 1942. 413p. $7.50; with statistics $10.

Designed to serve as a permanent reference volume covering "virtually all the important raw and semi-finished products that serve to make up our national economy."—*Introd.* Arranged alphabetically by commodity.

U. S. National Bureau of Standards. National directory of commodity specifications; classified and alphabetical lists and brief descriptions of specifications of national recognition. Wash., Govt. Prt. Off., 1945. 1311p. (Its Misc. pub. M178) $4. **L343**

3d ed. Previous eds. 1925 and 1932. Supersedes its Misc. pub. M130.

——— ——— Supplement. 1947. 322p. $2.25.

U. S. Technical Committee on Standard Commodity Classification. Standard commodity classification. Wash., Govt. Prt. Off., 1943–44. 2v. (U. S. Bur. of the Budget. Technical paper, no.26-27) $1.25 ea. **L344**

(1) Standard classified list of commodities; (2) Alphabetical index.

—— ——Supplement to v.2. 1945. 1222p. $2.

The supplement contains about 50,000 additional commodity items, not listed in volumes 1-2.

Vanstone, J. Henry. Dictionary of the world's commercial products, with French, German, and Spanish equivalents for the names of the . . . products. 3d ed. Lond. and N.Y., Pitman, 1930. 164p. **L345**

Descriptions of the products.

❧ Guides to the purchasing of all types of products from the consumer point of view are given in various publications reporting the results of tests of the items with indication of recommended and nonrecommended brands. Two of the most used of these periodicals are:

Consumers' research bulletin, Sept. 1931- . Washington, N.J., Consumers' Research, 1931- . il. Monthly. $3 per yr. **L346**

Frequency varies.

Each monthly issue includes an abridged cumulative index to the preceding issues of the current year.

Consumers Union of the United States. Consumer reports, May 1936- . N.Y., Consumers Union, 1936- . il. Monthly (with annual Buying guide). $5 per yr. **L347**

December issue is its *Buying guide.*

Each monthly issue includes cumulated index to preceding issues for the current year.

Foreign trade

BIBLIOGRAPHY

Pellett, Mirl Edison. Water transportation; a bibliography, guide and union catalogue . . . with the cooperation of thirty-four North American libraries. v.1, Harbors, ports, and port terminals. N.Y., Wilson, 1931. 685p. v.1, $4.50. **L348**

No more published.

5700 entries. Classified arrangement with author and subject indexes. Includes material published from 1900 to 1930 readily accessible in American libraries, with an indication of the principal foreign sources. Locates copies.

U. S. Dept. of Commerce. Office of Information. Inquiry and Reference Section. Foreign trade; basic information sources. Wash., 1945. 26p. **L349**

Comprehensive list of governmental and nongovernmental publications.

DIRECTORIES, HANDBOOKS, ETC.

Carmel, John Philip. International traders' manual, a publication for exporters and importers.

N.Y., Int. Traders' Manual, Inc., 1946. 151p. $3. **L350**

Includes sections on: Quotations, bids, offers and contracts, English-Spanish; Definition of foreign trade quotations, English-Spanish; Glossary of foreign words; Packing; Units of weight and measure with conversion tables; Distances—ship, airline, Great Lakes, etc.; Trade directory, steamship and airline, etc.

Exporters' encyclopaedia. 1st, 1904- . Containing full and authentic information relative to shipments for every country in the world. N.Y., T. Ashwell, 1904- . $25, including supplementary bulletins which keep the Encyclopaedia up to date throughout the subscription year. **L351**

Contents: (1) Alphabetical index of ports and trade centers; (2) Countries, arranged alphabetically, consular regulations, ports and trade centers, shipping routes, mail, radio and cable, telephone, exchange restrictions, money, weights, holidays, etc.; (3) General export information; (4) Ports of the United States, etc.

Foreign commerce handbook, 1922/23- . Wash., Foreign Commerce Dept., Chamber of Commerce of the U.S., 1922- . Biennial (irregular). (1950, $1) **L352**

A guide to the sources of export and import services and information.

Foreign trade handbook; a guide to exporting, by Edward Ewing Pratt. 1st ed. Chic., Dartnell, 1948. 1463p. $10. **L353**

Covers the organization, management, financing, of foreign trade and its technical and legal aspects.

Henius, Frank. Dictionary of foreign trade. 2d ed., completely rev. and greatly expanded. N.Y., Prentice-Hall, 1947. 959p. il. $10; text ed. $7.50. **L354**

Includes foreign trade terms, usages, practices, and procedures.

Lloyd's Calendar, 1898- . Lond., Lloyd's, 1898- . il. Annual. 5s. **L355**

A useful yearbook containing much miscellaneous commercial shipping and navigation information; laws affecting commerce and navigation, lists of British chambers of commerce, weights and measures of various nations, legal holidays of the world, etc.

Ports of the world, ed. by Sir Archibald Hurd. 2d ed. Lond., Shipping World, Ltd., 1948. 1138p. 30s. **L356**

1st ed. 1946.

Part 1 lists the ports of the United Kingdom and Eire in one alphabet; part 2, Dominion, colonial and foreign ports, usually gives: location, population, accommodations, charges, pilotage, imports and exports.

Formerly a section of the *Shipping world year book* (L357).

Shipping world year book; ed. by Sir Archibald Hurd, 1883- . Lond., Shipping World Off., 1883- . Annual. (1948, 20s.) **L357**

Subtitle varies: 1948, General maritime information, statutory rules and regulations, statistical tables, classified world directories of shipowners, ship builders, ship-repairers, towing services, marine engine builders, etc., training for the merchant navy, shipping and shipbuilding organizations, "Who's who" in the shipping world.

U. S. Bureau of Foreign and Domestic Commerce. Commerce yearbook, 1922–1932. Wash., Govt. Prt. Off., 1923–33. 10v. in 16. il. **L358**

Gave detailed information on business conditions in the United States and foreign countries, summarizing statistical information originally collected by government bureaus, trade associations and trade journals, with references to sources of information.

Part 1, United States, was discontinued in 1932; part 2, Foreign countries, was continued by the following:

—— Foreign commerce yearbook, 1933–39. Wash., Govt. Prt. Off., 1934–42. **L359**

Publication suspended.

U. S. Bureau of the Census. Foreign commerce and navigation of the United States, 1821- . Wash., Govt. Prt. Off., [18-?]. Annual. **L360**

Publishing body varies. Before 1865 published by the Register of Treasury.

Current figures given in its *Monthly summary of foreign commerce and navigation* (cumulated quarterly; $1.25 per yr. including monthly and quarterly issues).

United States

American register of exporters and importers, 1945/46- . N.Y., Amer. Register of Exporters and Importers, Inc., 1946- . Annual. $10. **L361**

Lists some 5000 active American export and import concerns, and allied lines.

Custom house guide. N.Y., Import Publications, Inc., 1862- . Annual (with monthly supplements). (1949, $25 incl. suppl.) **L362**

United States customs tariff, customs ports, internal revenue code, customs, shipping and commerce regulations, reciprocal trade agreements.

Monthly supplements called *American import and export bulletin.*

Alaska

Tewkesbury's Who's who in Alaska and Alaska business index, v.1, 1947- . Juneau, Tewkesbury, 1947- . (v.1, $4.50) **L363**

The Business index section to be issued annually ($2.50). For full record *see* S45.

Canada

Heaton's Commercial handbook of Canada (Heaton's Annual), 1905- . Toronto, Heaton, 1905- . v.1- . Annual. (v.36, 1948, $6.50) **L364**

Title varies.
Trade directories and commercial information.

Far East

Directory and chronicle of China, Japan, Straits Settlements, Malaya, Siam, Korea, Indo-China, Netherlands Indies, Borneo, the Philippines with which are incorporated The China directory, The Hongkong directory, and Hong list for the Far East. Hongkong, Hongkong Daily Pr., [18-?]- . Annual. (1941, 79th yr.) **L365**

Title varies.
Contains texts of treaties, tariffs, much useful gazetteer and descriptive material, directories of residents, officials, merchants, etc. A very useful annual.

Great Britain

Kelly's Directory of merchants, manufacturers and shippers for Great Britain, and the British Empire with supplement for other countries. Lond., Kelly's Direct., 1880- . Annual. $22.50; £5. **L366**

Very useful for its directory and descriptive material. Alphabetical and classified lists.

Ireland

O'Neill's Commercial who's who and industrial directory of Ireland. Dublin, Parkside Pr., 1935- . Annual. (8th ed., 1946/47, 21s.) **L367**

Title varies.

Latin America

U. S. Bureau of Foreign and Domestic Commerce. Commercial travelers' guide to Latin America. Wash., Govt. Prt. Off., 1938–40. 3v. (Trade promotion ser., no.179, 187, 208) **L368**

pts. 1-3: pt.1, West coast of South America, 1938. 116p. 20c; pt.2, East coast of South America, 1938. 97p. 20c; pt.3, Mexico, Central America and Caribbean countries, 1940. 238p. 40c.

Succeeds Trade Promotion Series no.122, *Commercial travelers' guide to Latin America,* 4th ed., 1931.

See also Pan American yearbook (L79) **and** *South American handbook* (L80).

Middle East

Comprehensive economic directory of the Middle East; Middle East directory. 1946/47- . Palestine, Economic Office for the Middle East, 1947- . **L369**

Subtitle: Contains complete lists of names and addresses of manufacturing, trading and financial concerns as well as of institutions and other professional lines in Palestine, Trans Jordan, Egypt, Cyprus, Lebanon, Syria, Iraq, Iran, Turkey.

Palestine directory; the register of commerce and industry in Palestine. 1935- . Tel-Aviv, Register of Commerce and Industry, 1935- . Annual. (v.14, 1948)   **L370**

In English and Hebrew.

Title varies: 1935–38, *Register of commerce and industry in Palestine; the Palestine directory;* 1939 on, *the Palestine directory.*

TABLES OF DISTANCES

Reed's Tables of distances between ports and places in all parts of the world. Comprising over 31,000 distances with a table of contents and complete alphabetical index, comp. by H. Whittingham and C. T. King. 11th ed. Repr., 1947. Sunderland, Eng., Reed, 1947. 192p. 5s.   **L371**

U. S. Coast and Geodetic Survey. Distances between United States ports. rev. (1938) ed. Wash., Govt. Prt. Off., 1938. 51p. (United States coast pilot ser. no.444) 10c.   **L372**

U. S. Hydrographic Office. Table of distances between ports via the shortest navigable routes as determined by the Hydrographic Office, U.S. Navy Dept. Wash., Govt. Prt. Off., 1943. 485p. (Its pub. no.117) $1.50.   **L373**

"This publication, the 1943 edition . . . supersedes all previous editions."–*Pref.*

SOCIETIES

Judkins, Calvert Jay. United States associations in world trade and affairs. Wash., Govt. Prt. Off., 1947. 125p. il. ([U.S.] Bur. of Foreign and Domestic Commerce. Industrial ser. no.70) **L374**

Enlarged edition of a preliminary report, issued in 1945, entitled *Foreign trade associations in the U.S.* Includes bibliographies.

Tariff

U. S. Tariff Commission. Dictionary of tariff information. Wash., Govt. Prt. Off., 1924. 1036p. $2.25.   **L375**

Includes articles on tariff systems, methods, practices, history, biographical articles on men connected with American tariff history, and descriptive and statistical articles on all commodities mentioned in the tariff act of 1922. Contains some bibliography.

—— List of publications . . . 1920- . Wash., Govt. Prt. Off., 1920- . Irregular.   **L376**

—— The tariff; a bibliography. A select list of references. Wash., Govt. Prt. Off., 1934. 980p. (Miscellaneous ser.) $1.   **L377**

Classified and annotated list of almost 6500 items, with author index and subject and title index.

—— **Library.** Reciprocal trade: a current bibliography; selected list of references comp. as a W.P.A. project under the supervision of Cornelia Notz, with the assistance of Sadie Jarvinen and others of the library staff. 3d ed. Wash., 1937. 282, 129p.   **L378**

The third edition consists of the second edition and its index enlarged by the addition of an indexed supplement. The indexes also include references to the *Congressional record* (F20) and to hearings on reciprocal trade agreements.

—— —— Supplement to the 3d ed. Wash., 1940. 232p.

Includes material issued 1937–1939.

Money, weights and measures

Doursther, Horace. Dictionnaire universel des poids et mesures, anciens et modernes, contenant des tables des monaies de tous les pays. Bruxelles, Hayez, 1840. 604p. o.p.   **L379**

Out of date, but useful for questions involving historical information because of the many older and unusual terms included.

International traders' handbook, 1931, incorporating Foreign and domestic weights, measures and moneys (previously issued separately). Phila., Commercial Museum, 1931. 152p. $1.
                                                      L380

Subtitle: A handy guide and reference work for exporters, importers, bankers, shippers, journalists, students and others interested in international trade. Conversion tables and price comparisons, trade terms and abbreviations, commercial languages of all countries, definitions of United States terms used in export quotations, a gazeteer [*sic*], regulations for exportation of merchandise by freight and parcel post, etc.

Incorporates the material formerly included in Macfarlane, J. J. *Conversion tables of foreign and domestic weights,* 10th ed., (Phila., Commercial Museum, 1929. 109p.).

Tate, William. Tate's Modern cambist. Centenary ed. A manual of the world's monetary systems, the foreign exchanges, the stamp duties on bills of exchange in foreign countries, the principal rules governing bills of exchange and promissory notes, foreign weights and measures, bullion and exchange operations. 28th ed., by W. F. Spalding. Lond., Wilson; N.Y., Bankers Pub. Co., 1929. 734p. $12.   **L381**

—— Tate's Money manual, being the 1st-2d annual editions of additions, alterations and amendments to the centenary edition of Tate's Modern cambist, by W. F. Spalding. Lond., Wilson; N.Y., Bankers Pub. Co. [1931–33]. v.1-2. **L382**

U. S. Bureau of Foreign and Domestic Commerce. Handbook of foreign currencies. Prepared in Finance Division. Wash., Govt. Prt. Off., 1936. 232p. (Trade promotion ser. no.164) 20c. **L383**

Supersedes the *Handbook of foreign currency and exchange* (1930) (Trade promotion ser. no.102) and the circulars on *Metal and paper currencies* (1930–1931).

U. S. Bureau of Standards. Units of weight and measure (United States customary and metric). Definitions and tables of equivalents. Issued January 1936. . . . Wash., Govt. Prt. Off., 1936. 68p. (National Bureau of Standards misc. pub. M121) 15c. **L384**

"Superseding Bureau of Standards Circular C47."

Postal guides

Canada. Post Office Dept. Canada official postal guide, chief regulations of the Post Office, rates of postage and other information and alphabetical list of post offices in Canada. Ottawa, Cloutier, 1875- . Annual. $1 per yr.; monthly supplements 25c per year. **L385**

Kept to date by monthly supplements.
Title and frequency vary.

Gt. Brit. Post Office Dept. Post office guide. Lond., Stat. Off., 1856- . 1s. **L386**

From 1856–79, called *British postal guide*, published quarterly. Frequency thereafter varies, usually annual with supplements and since 1937, associated volumes; *Post offices in the United Kingdom*, 1s. 6d. (pub. irregularly); *London post offices and streets*, 9d. (pub. irregularly).

U. S. Post Office Dept. United States official postal guide, 1874- . Wash., Govt. Prt. Off., 1874- . **L387**

Beginning with July 1937 issued in two parts; pt.1, Domestic postal service, $1.50; pt.2, International postal service, 70c.
Supplemented by quarterly supplements to pts. 1-2, $1 per yr.
The authoritative manual for American postal information, postal rulings and regulations, postal savings banks, foreign mails, etc.; state, county, and alphabetical lists of post offices; classified list with salaries; discontinued offices.

Transportation and communication

RAILROADS

Bureau of Railway Economics. Railway economics, a collective catalogue of books in fourteen American libraries. Chic., Univ. of Chic. Pr., 1912. 446p. $3. **L388**

Canada. Bureau of Statistics. Library. Bibliographical list of references to Canadian railways, 1829–1938. Ottawa, 1938. 99p. $1. **L389**

Thomson, Thomas Richard. Check list of publications on American railroads before 1841; a union list of printed books and pamphlets, including state and federal documents, dealing with charters, by-laws, legislative acts, speeches, debates, land grants, officers' and engineers' reports, travel guides, maps, etc. N.Y., Public Library, 1942. 250p. $2. **L390**

"Reprinted with additions from the *Bulletin* of the New York Public Library of January–July–October 1941."
Includes 2671 numbered entries, arranged chronologically, of works which are predominantly related to railroads, or which have the words "railroad" or "railway" on the title page. Includes books, pamphlets, broadsides (except stock or contract certificates or bonds), and maps. Locates copies in 36 libraries that cooperated in checking the list.

Röll, Victor von. Enzyklopädie des Eisenbahnwesens. 2. völlst, neubearb. Aufl. Berlin, Urban, 1912–23. 10v. il. **L391**

Signed articles by experts, bibliographies, good illustrations and maps. General in scope, but treats most fully German and Austrian railroads and other railroads in which Germans have been especially interested. Includes articles on individual railroads and biographies. For many terms equivalents are given in English, French and Italian.

Universal directory of railway officials and railway year book, comp. from official sources. Lond., Directory Pub. Co., 1895- . Annual. (1949/50, 30s.) **L392**

Includes brief notes about the railways in the various countries of the world with lists of officials. Includes a name index.

U. S. Interstate Commerce Commission. Annual report on the statistics of railways in the United States, 1887/88- . Wash., Govt. Prt. Off., 1889- . v.1- . Annual. **L393**

—— Railway statistical terms; a collection of definitions of words and phrases, frequently used in the discussions of railway statistics. Wash., 1941. 58p. (Its statement, no.4119) **L394**

Who's who in railroading in North America. 11th ed. N.Y., Simmons Boardman, 1946. 780p. $8.50. **L395**

Prior to 1930 known as the *Biographical directory of railway officials of America*.
This edition includes some 5700 entries.

Who's who in transportation and communication; a biographical dictionary of important living people in the transportation and communication industries. v.1, 1942–43. Bost., Larkin, Roosevelt, 1942. 778p. $14. **L396**

Includes almost 8000 names of persons outstanding in the fields of railroads, motor cars, airplanes, telephone, telegraph, cinema, radio and newspaper.

SHIPS

Howe, Octavius Thorndike and **Matthews, F. C.** American clipper ships, 1833–1858. Salem, Mass., Marine Research Soc., 1926–27. 2v. il. (Marine Research Society, Salem, Mass. Pub. 13) $15. **L397**

Arranged alphabetically by names of ships, giving description and history of each and often a picture. Index includes names of captains, owners, etc., and of ships not described separately.

Matthews, Frederick C. American merchant ships, 1850–1900. Salem, Mass., Marine Research Soc., 1930. 399p. il. (Marine Research Society, Salem, Mass. Pub. 21) $7.50. **L398**

A companion work to the above, on the same general plan.

Smith, Eugene Waldo. Trans-Atlantic passenger ships, past and present. [1st ed.] Bost., Dean, 1947. 350p. il. $3.50. **L399**

Deals with the principal passenger ships operating in the North Atlantic 1840–1940. Lists alphabetically some 1000 ships giving date of construction, name of builder and owner, tonnage, dimensions, activities, changes of name, and final disposition.

Wallace, Frederick William. Record of Canadian shipping. A list of square-rigged vessels, mainly 500 tons and over, built in the eastern provinces of North America . . . 1786 to 1920. Illustrated with photographs, paintings and drawings. Toronto, Musson [c1929]. 302p. il. $10. **L400**

Arranged alphabetically by names of ships.

Annuals

American Bureau of Shipping. Record of the American Bureau of Shipping, "American Lloyds," established 1867 to provide a standard American classification of vessels. N.Y., 1867- . Annual. **L401**

Lloyd's Register of shipping. Founded 1760, reconstituted 1834, united with the Underwriters' registry for iron vessels in 1885. Lond., Lloyd's, 1834- . Annual. 2v. (1941, £12 12s.) **L401a**

Sample contents: v.1, Steamers and motorships of 300 tons gross and over, steamers and motorships under 300 tons, trawlers, tugs, dredgers, etc., sailing vessels and list of ship owners; v.2, List of shipbuilders in Great Britain and Ireland and abroad and vessels built by them; List of marine insurance companies; Particulars of dry docks, etc.; Particulars of wet docks, etc.; List of telegraphic addresses; List of steamers and motorships (10,000 tons and above) arranged according to nationality and gross tonnage; Statistical tables; Alphabetical list of cargo steamers and motorships of 500 tons deadweight capacity and above.

Merchant ships, 1936- . ed. by Eric Talbot-Booth. . . . N.Y., Macmillan, 1936- . il. Annual. $19 ea. **L402**

Pictures and line drawings of the merchant ships of the various countries of the world, with pertinent information on tonnage, distinguishing features, history, etc. A continuation and extension of *British merchant ships*, edited by Talbot-Booth (Lond., Rich and Cowan, 1934. 220p.).

U. S. Bureau of Customs. Merchant vessels of the United States (including yachts and government vessels) 1866/67- . Wash., Govt. Prt. Off., 1869- . v.1- . il. (1947, $5) **L403**

Title varies; issuing office varies.

Includes an alphabetical list of vessels, giving name, tonnage, size, where built, name of owner, home port, etc.; former names of merchant vessels; owners of vessels, etc.

RADIO AND TELEVISION

Rose, Oscar. Radio broadcasting and television; an annotated bibliography. N.Y., Wilson, 1947. 120p. $1.50. **L404**

An annotated bibliography listing the nontechnical books and pamphlets published in the United States in the English language in the fields of radio broadcasting and television, primarily programming and program content. Does not include technological works.

Radio alphabet; a glossary of radio terms. N.Y., Hastings House, 1946. 85p. il. $1.50. **L405**

Popular. Includes illustrations of radio sign language. Issued by the Columbia Broadcasting System.

Kempner, Stanley. Television encyclopedia. N.Y., Fairchild Pub. Co., 1948. 415p. il. $6.50. **L406**

Contents: pt.1, Milestones to present day television; pt.2, Pioneers and contemporaries in television; pt.3, Television's technical vocabulary. Appendix; the urban market for television. Bibliography.

A handbook, rather than an encyclopedia, giving a chronological record of the history of television, biographical sketches of outstanding personalities and vocabulary of technical and production terms.

Business
Bibliography

Coman, Edwin T. Jr. Sources of business information. N.Y., Prentice-Hall, 1949. 415p. $6; text ed. $4.50. **L407**

A comprehensive manual and guide, arranged by field, covering statistics, finance, real estate and insurance, accounting, management, marketing, sales management, and advertising, industrial relations, basic industries, transportation, etc. Lists bibliographies, manuals, services, texts, periodicals, etc., with comment. Detailed index. Limited to American (with a few English) publications.

Handbook of commercial, financial and information services, comp. by Walter Hausdorfer. N.Y.,

Special Libraries Assoc., 1944. 207p. $3. **L408**

Earlier editions under slightly different titles were published in 1924, 1931, and 1939. This is a revised edition containing descriptions of 577 current services and listing 311 services which have been discontinued in recent years. Arrangement is by company or publisher, with subject index.

Harvard University. Graduate School of Business Administration. Baker Library. The Kress Library of business and economics. Catalogue, covering material published through 1776, with data upon cognate items in other Harvard libraries. Bost., Baker Lib., Harvard Grad. School of Bus. Admin. [c1940]. 414p. $5. **L409**

Arranged chronologically, with alphabetical index of authors and anonymous titles.

Newark, N. J. Free Public Library. Business information and its sources, comp. by Marian C. Manley. Newark, N. J., Public Library, 1931. 32p. **L410**

———— Supplement. 1939. 37p. $1.00

—— **Business Branch.** The business bookshelf; a list based on use, comp. by Marian C. Manley and Mary E. Hunt, under the direction of Beatrice Winser. Newark, N.J., Public Library, 1935. 75p. $2. **L411**

A selected bibliography with well-written concise annotations.

Current record may be found in its monthly *Business literature*.

—— Business magazines, classified by subject, comp. by Marian C. Manley. [3d ed.] Newark, N.J., Public Library, 1933. 31p. $1. **L412**

Supplemented by lists in *Business literature*.

—— 2400 business books and guide to business literature, by L. H. Morley and A. C. Kight. N.Y., Wilson, 1920. 456p. **L413**

1st ed. 1916, entitled *1600 business books*. A useful dictionary catalog, containing many analytics.

—— Business books: 1920–26. An analytical catalog of 2600 titles. . . . Supplement to 2400 business books and guide to business literature. Comp. by L. H. Morley and A. C. Kight. N.Y., Wilson, 1927. 592p. **L414**

Special Libraries Association. Business and trade dictionaries; a classified guide to the sources of business terminology and definitions. . . . N.Y., Assoc., 1934. 39p. **L415**

—— **Commercial Technical Group.** Guides to business facts and figures; an indexed and descriptive list emphasizing the less known business reference sources; comp. by Special Libraries Assoc., with the cooperation of the staff of the Business Branch of the Newark Public Library,

Branch Librarian, Marian C. Manley. N.Y., Special Libraries Assoc., 1937. 59p. $1.50. **L416**

Trade-names index, with definitions and sources from a card file in the Technology Dept. of the Carnegie Library of Pittsburgh and a bibliography of sources of trade-names and trade-marks. N.Y., Special Libraries Assoc., 1941. 178p. $4. **L417**

Gives definitions of materials, processes, and equipment by trade name, usually with reference to a source. Bibliography of sources of trade-names and trade-marks, p.161-78.

U. S. Dept. of Commerce. List of publications of the Department of Commerce available for distribution . . . Jan. 1944. . . . Wash., Govt. Prt. Off., 1944. 202p. **L418**

BUSINESS SERVICES

❦ Business is a field which changes so rapidly that reference works soon become out of date, and many types of questions can be answered only by the use of current material. Fundamental for this purpose are the different business and financial "services," most of which are now issued in loose-leaf form. In general, each service is devoted to one specialized subject and consists of basic material kept up to date by revisions, supplied periodically, covering new laws, regulations, rulings, decisions, etc. Some services are completely factual, others include editorial explanations.

A listing of these services is given in the *Handbook of commercial, financial, and information services*, compiled by Walter Hausdorfer (L408), and a discussion of their use with a record of some of the most important services is given in E. T. Coman's *Sources of business information* (L407). Although these listings deal primarily with American services, similar enterprises exist in various other countries.

Since these services are quite expensive, they will be out of reach of the smaller library, but any large library which does much work in business will have to have at least some of them. Information about price, form and frequency may be secured by writing directly to the company concerned.

Dictionaries and encyclopedias

❦ There are no really comprehensive and satisfactory dictionaries for the whole large subject of business and commerce. Older works in the field are out of date for modern terms and practice, and modern works neither comprehensive enough in the terms and topics covered nor entirely adequate in definition. They must often be supplemented by smaller glossaries of special industries, etc., as well as by the book and periodical literature of special business subjects. Many of these smaller glossaries of special branches and trades are listed in the Newark Public Library's *2400 business books* (L413) and *Business books: 1920–26* (L414), continued in its *Business literature.*

Bogardus, Emory Stephen. Dictionary of cooperation (including encyclopedic materials). [3d ed.] N.Y., Cooperative League of the U.S.A., 1948. 94p. 75c. **L419**

Includes terms used in the cooperative movement, names of organizations in this country and abroad, and brief biographical sketches of past leaders.

Crowell's Dictionary of business and finance. N.Y., Crowell, 1930. 601p. $3.50. **L420**

Now out of date but still useful for many definitions.

Haller, Max and **Hotzel, Werner.** Kaufmännisches Handwörterbuch; Nachschlagewerk für das gesamte Wirtschaftsleben und Wirtschaftsrecht in ABC Ordnung. Berlin-Schöneberg, Langenscheidt, 1938. 2v. (Langenscheidts Wörterbücher) **L421**

Handwörterbuch der Betriebswirtschaft, hrsg. von H. Nicklisch in Verbindung mit zahlreichen Betriebswirtschaften an in- und ausländischen Hochschulen und aus der Praxis. Stuttgart, Poeschel, 1926–28. 5v. il. **L422**

Signed articles, with bibliographies of some length. Not limited to material on Germany.

—— 2. Aufl. Stuttgart, Poeschel, 1938–39. 2v.

This edition has been completely reorganized and rewritten in accordance with the ideas and philosophies of National Socialism.

FOREIGN TERMS

Polyglot

Gaynor, Frank. International business dictionary in five languages: English, German, French, Spanish, Italian. N.Y., Philosophical Lib., 1946. 452p. $6. **L423**

International Chamber of Commerce. International Distribution Commission and Committee on Advertising. Terms commonly used in distribution and advertising. Basel, Verlag für Recht und Gesellschaft, 1940–48. v.1-4. 10fr. (Swiss) (Sold in N.Y., J. Phiebig. v.1-2, $3.60 ea.; v.3, $4.20; v.4, $4.50) (In progress) **L424**

v.1, English, French, German; v.2, German, Italian, Spanish; v.3, English, Spanish, Portuguese; v.4, French, Swedish, English.

Zestalig handels Woordenboek. Groningen, Wolters, 1931. 871p. **L425**

Nederlandsch, H. G. de Maar; Engelsch, H. G. de Maar; Fransch, S. E. van Praag; Duitsch, N. C. Stalling; Zweedsch, N. C. Stalling en A. Zethraeus; Spaansch, J. A. van Praag.

French

Kettridge, Julius Orman. French-English and English-French dictionary of commercial and financial terms, phrases and practice. . . . Lond., Routledge, 1931. 647p. 25s. Dutton, $8.50. **L426**

Subtitle: Comprising mercantile business, exporting and importing, produce exchange transactions, transport and travel by water, land and air, customs, marine insurance, finance, banking, currency, foreign exchange and stock exchange transactions, company work, accountancy, income tax, secretarial and office work, postal, telegraphic and telephonic services, and allied subjects, also abbreviations in common use, conventional signs, weights and measures.

Includes the author's *Dictionary of financial and business terms, phrases, and practice,* revised and brought up to date.

German

Eitzen, Friedrich Wilhelm. Wörterbuch der Handelssprache. Neu bearb. u. ergänzt von Wilhelm Eitzen. Leipzig, Haessel, 1922–23. 2v. **L427**

v.1, German-English; v.2, English-German. 2d-3d ed. 1902–06.

Italian

Carnaroli, Sergio. Dizionario industriale e commerciale italiano-inglese, inglese-italiano. Milano, Hoepli, 1945. 285p. **L428**

Subtitle: mano d'opera, materiali, organizzazione aziendale, contabilità, costi, commercio, banca, finanza, trasporti, assicurazioni, statistica, matematica, technologia.

Macdonald, George Robert. Italian-English and English-Italian commercial dictionary. Lond and N.Y., Pitman, 1930. 1166p. **L42**

Spinelli, Nicola. Dizionario commerciale, italiano-inglese e inglese-italiano. Torino-Genova, Lattes [1925?–27]. 2v. **L43**

v.1, Italian-English; v.2, English-Italian.

Japanese

Kenkyusha English-Japanese dictionary, commercial and technical terms, by Nintaro Fujita. South Pasadena, Calif., P. D. and Ione Perkin 1944. 1220p. il. $7. **L43**

"The Japanese edition was published by Messrs. Kenkyusha on August 1st [1941]."—*3d prelim. leaf.*

Portuguese

Sousa Gomes, Luiz. Dicionário econômico comercial e financeiro. (Terminologia do comé cio, econômica, finanças e contabilidade) 3. ed. rev. Rio de Janeiro, Pongetti, 1945. 310p. 50$. **L432**

Subtitle: Com . . . um apendice bio-bibliográfico sobre os principais economistas brasileiros e estrangeiros, e ligeiras referências às suas diretrizes econômicas.

Spanish

Frias-Sucre Giraud, Alejandro. Novísimo diccionario comercial "El secretario." Madrid-Barcelona, Ed. Juventud, 1940. 150, 129p. **L433**

1. ed.
Española-inglesa, inglesa-española.

Macdonald, George Robert. Spanish-English and English-Spanish commercial dictionary of the words and terms used in commercial correspondence. 3d. ed. rev. and enl. Lond. and N.Y., Pitman [1920]. 820p. **L434**

Directories

Davis, Marjorie Veith. American business directories, 2d ed., Apr. 1947. Wash., Govt. Prt. Off., 1947. 198p. (U.S. Bureau of For. and Dom. Com. Industrial ser. no.67) 65c. **L435**

Arranged in two sections: (1) Classed list arranged alphabetically; (2) Names of "general" directories arranged geographically.
Substantially the same material in slightly different arrangement is given in her *Guide to American business directories* (Wash., Public Affairs Pr., 1948. 242p. $3.75).

U. S. Dept. of Commerce. Office of Domestic Commerce. National associations of the United States, by Jay Judkins. Wash., Dept. of Commerce, 1949. 634p. il. $3.50. **L436**

Earlier ed. 1942 had title: *Trade and professional associations of the United States.*
"Consists of a directory and review of the services and accomplishments of trade associations, professional societies, labor unions, farm cooperatives, chambers of commerce, better business bureaus, and other organizations which play a prominent part in American life."— *Foreword.*

National Research Council. Industrial research laboratories of the United States. 8th ed. Wash., 1946. **L437**

For full description *see* N51.

Sales Research Associates. A guide to membership lists and directories (business and professional). N.Y., Sales Research Associates, 1944. 54p. $5.95. **L438**

Special Libraries Association. Business Group. Directories for the business man, comp. by Laura A. Eales. N.Y., Special Libraries Assoc., 1938. 66p. $1. **L439**

Lists 975 directories grouped by subject.

U. S. Bureau of Foreign and Domestic Commerce. State-local businessmen's organizations. Wash., 1943–44. **L440**

A series of lists each dealing with a separate state.

—— Foreign directories, comp. in the Commercial Intelligence Division. Wash., Govt. Prt. Off., 1939. 59p. (Trade information bulletin no.841) 10c. **L441**

U. S. National Bureau of Standards. Directory of commercial and college laboratories. Wash., 1947. **L442**

For full description *see* N52.

Zimmerman, Oswald Theodore and **Levine, Irvin.** Industrial research service's Handbook of material trade names. Dover, N.H., Industrial Research Service, 1946. 503p. $7.50. **L443**

Cover title: Handbook of material trade names.
Lists about 5000 trade names under which products are sold with manufacturers' names and addresses. Physical and chemical properties of many of the products are given in summary form.

❦ Many individual states or regions have industrial directories, e.g., *New York State industrial directory, Directory of New England manufacturers,* which should be consulted for local information.

Statistics

Blackett, O. W. The literature of business statistics, a bibliography. Ann Arbor, Mich., Univ. of Mich., School of Business Admin., Bur. of Business Research, 1936. 67p. (Mich. business studies, v.8. no.1) **L444**

Croxton, Frederick Emory and **Cowden, Dudley Johnstone.** Practical business statistics, 2d. ed. N.Y., Prentice-Hall, 1948. 568p. $6.35; text ed. $4.75. **L445**

Davenport, Donald Hills and **Scott, Frances V.** An index to business indices. Chic., Business Publications, 1937. 187p. **L446**

A guide to sources for business statistics, in two parts: pt.1, a finding index covering index numbers of commodity prices, securities, and other general activities; pt.2, includes descriptions of the indexes, giving title, compiler, frequency of publication, current data, and a brief description.

Handbook of basic economic statistics, 1947-   . Wash., Government Statistics Bureau, 1947-   . Annual (with monthly supplements) $12; monthly and quarterly services available; for subscription rates apply to publisher. **L447**

Subtitle: A manual of basic economic data on industry, commerce, labor, and agriculture in the United States.
Includes more than 1000 statistical series assembled from governmental and private sources.

Hauser, Philip M. and **Leonard, William R.** Government statistics for business use. N.Y., Wiley, 1946. 432p. il. $5.   **L448**

A guide to the "major types of data available in the Federal government for management, production, and marketing needs." Each chapter by a specialist in the field.

Survey of current business. U.S. Bureau of Foreign and Domestic Commerce. v.1, Aug. 1921- . Wash., Govt. Prt. Off., 1921- . Monthly. $3 per year.   **L449**

Basic source for statistical surveys of current business. Covers prices, foreign trade, commodities, industries, etc.

—— Statistical supplement. 1932–42; 1947- . Biennial. (1949, $1.25)

1932–42, called *Supplement.*
Published biennially, each volume consolidates for a 4-year period the statistics appearing in the *Survey of current business.* 1949 covers 1945–48.

U. S. Bureau of Foreign and Domestic Commerce. Sources of current trade statistics, comp. by Jettie Turner. Wash., 1937. 47p. (Market research ser. no.13)   **L450**

—— Sources of regional and local current business statistics by Elma S. Moulton. Wash., Govt. Prt. Off., 1940. 57p. (Domestic commerce series, no.115) 30c.   **L451**

History

Hall, Hubert. Select bibliography for the study, sources, and literature of English mediaeval economic history. Lond., King, 1914. 350p.   **L452**

Larson, Henrietta Melia. Guide to business history; materials for the study of American business history and suggestions for their use. Camb., Harvard Univ. Pr., 1948. 1181p. (Harvard studies in business history, v.12) $12.   **L453**

Contents: (1) Introduction; (2) Historical background and setting of American business; (3) Business administrators: Biographical and autobiographical books, pamphlets and articles; (4) The history of individual business units; (5) History of industries; (6) General topics in business history; (7) Research and reference materials. Index.
4904 entries, annotated. A highly useful compilation and guide to historical study.

Biography

Business executives of America. 2d ed. N.Y., Inst. for Research in Biography, 1950. 754p.   **L454**

A biographical dictionary of some 10,000 living executives of the largest American and Canadian corporations. The first edition, 1944, included a second section listing American corporations with their officers. This is omitted in the second edition.

Directory of directors in the city of New York. N.Y., Directory of Directors Co., 1898- . Annual. (1950, $40)   **L454a**

For each director, gives his name and address and the companies of which he is a director. The second section is a list of corporations and firms with lists of directors.
Similar publications are issued for various other large cities.

Poor's Register of directors and executives, United States and Canada. N.Y., Standard and Poor's Corp., 1928- . Annual (monthly supplements). (1948, $85; to subscribers $60)   **L455**

Lists corporations with officers and directors followed by an alphabetical list of directors and executives with brief biographical data and companies of which they are directors. Also contains an obituary and a new name section.
Geographical section in separate volume.

Who's who in commerce and industry; the international business who's who. 6th international ed. Chic., Marquis, 1948. 1552p.   **L456**

1st ed. 1936.
Gives international coverage of business men.

Who's who in the public utilities industry. . . . 1st ed. Phila., L. Stotz, 1942. 205p. il. $3.   **L457**

Editor: 1942, Louis Stotz.
Includes biographical sketches of about 200 men in the gas and electric field.

Business management
Bibliography

American Management Association. Progress in seven fields of management; a complete catalogue to publications of the American Management Association, February 1932—November 1949. N.Y., Assoc. [1949]. 31p.   **L458**

The 1945 edition had title *The Management index* and included a subject index which is omitted in the 1949 issue.

Berg, Rose Monica. Bibliography of management literature (up to January 1931); comp. . . . under the direction of the A.S.M.E. Management Division. N.Y., Amer. Soc. of Mechanical Engineers [1931]. 142p. $2.   **L459**

An alphabetical list, under subject, with author index. Includes books and periodicals.

—— —— Supplement (covering 1931–35). 1937. 88p. $1.50.

The two issues together list some 7000 items.

Hopf, Harry Arthur. Soundings in the literature of management; fifty books the educated practitioner should know. Ossining, N.Y., Hopf Inst. of Management, 1945. 28p. (Hopf Inst. of Management. Pub. no.6)   **L460**

An annotated list of basic works on the techniques of management. Reprinted in Coman, E. T. *Sources of business information,* p.156-77, (L407).

Handbooks

American Management Association. Handbook of business administration; W. J. Donald, ed.-in-chief. N.Y. and Lond., McGraw-Hill, 1931. 1753p. il. $10; text ed. $7.50. **L461**

Brown, Stanley M. Business executive's handbook, rev. by Lillian Doris. 3d ed., rev. and enl. N.Y., Prentice-Hall, 1947. 1600p. il. $7.50; to schools $5.60. **L462**

1st ed. 1936. A useful, clearly written handbook covering such subjects as: business mathematics, business letters, direct-mail selling, advertising, credits and collections, financial statements, corporate meetings, etc.

Maze, Coleman Lloyd. Office management; a handbook. N.Y., Ronald Pr., 1947. 870p. il. $6. **L463**

Published under the auspices of the National Office Management Association.

Occupations

See also Guidance, p.214.

Dictionary of occupational titles, prepared by the Job Analysis and Information Section, Division of Standards and Research, U.S. Employment Service. Wash., Govt. Prt. Off., 1939–44. 4v. **L464**

pt.1, Definitions of titles. 1939. 1287p. $2; pt.2, Group arrangement of occupational titles and codes. 1939. 330p. $1; pt.3, Conversion tables. 1939. 259p. $1; pt.4, Entry-occupational classification. rev. ed. 1944. 242p. 35c.

—— Supplement [to pts. 1-2]. Ed. 3. 1945. 747p. (Manpower Utilization Bur.) $1.25.

"Each release of the supplement is a new edition containing not only all the data released since publication of pts. 1-2 of the Dictionary but also new additional data."

Occupational index. v.1, 1936- . N.Y., N.Y. Univ. [c1936-] v.1- . Quarterly. $7.50 per yr. **L465**

Pub. varies.
Bibliography with abstracts of current publications on occupational information. Each volume has cumulated author, title, and subject indexes to the abstracts listed during the year.
Monthly through 1940; Jan. 1941 on, quarterly.

U. S. Bureau of Labor Statistics. Occupational outlook handbook; employment information on major occupations for use in guidance. Wash., Govt. Prt. Off., 1949. 453p. il. (Its Bull. no.940) $1.75. **L466**

The first edition of a new handbook superseding V. A. Manual M7-1 issued in 1946 as *Occupational outlook information.*

Information is given on 288 occupations, covering such topics as: outlook summary, nature of work, qualifications, earnings and working conditions, how to enter, where to go for more information, etc.

U. S. Bureau of the Census. Alphabetical index of occupations and industries. Wash., Govt. Prt. Off., 1950. 374p. $1.75. **L467**

1950 census of population.
Prepared for each decennial census, with occasional editions in between. This edition is revised and expanded and supersedes the 1948 edition which followed the 1940 edition.

—— Classified index of occupations and industries. 1950 census of population. Wash., Govt. Prt. Off., 1950. 228p. $1.50. **L468**

Labor and industrial relations

❧ For many questions on various kinds of labor topics the best information will often be found in publications of the national government, especially in the bulletins and reports of the United States Bureau of Labor Statistics and the National Labor Relations Board, and in the publications of state labor boards, factory inspection bureaus, and labor unions. While the publications of the Bureau of Labor Statistics deal primarily with American topics, they contain also some information on foreign aspects of the subject. The *Monthly labor review* (L476) is especially useful for current information and statistics. The British *Ministry of labour gazette* and the Canadian *Labour gazette* (issued monthly in both French and English editions, by the Canadian Department of Labour) serve much the same purpose for current topics in the field of British and Canadian labor.

Bibliography and indexes

The American labor press; an annotated directory. Introduction by John R. Commons. Wash., Amer. Council on Public Affairs [1940]. 120p. $2. **L473**

"Compiled by the University of Wisconsin, Work Projects Administration, Official Work Project no.9422."
Includes information about 646 American and 30 Canadian current labor publications. Material arranged under the following heads: American Federation of Labor and its branches, Congress of Industrial Organizations and its affiliates, Independent trade unions, Cooperative organizations, Communist party, Socialist party, Farmer-labor groups, Other "left-wing" organizations, General labor publications, Canadian labor publications. There is no index.

Gt. Brit. Interdepartmental Committee on Social and Economic Research. Guides to official sources. no.1, Labour statistics. Lond., Stat. Off., 1948. 32p. 9d. **L474**

Index to labor articles, v.1- , Dec. 1926- . N.Y., Rand School of Social Science, 1926- . Monthly; bimonthly. $1.50 per yr. **L475**

Classified arrangement with no cumulations and no author index. Indexes labor articles in general periodicals and in some labor papers not indexed elsewhere. From the labor point of view.

Monthly labor review. v.1, July 1915- . Wash., Bur. of Labor Statistics, 1915- . Monthly. $4.50 per yr. **L476**

Contains special articles and summaries of special reports in the field of labor. Statistics cover employment, labor turnover, earnings and hours, work stoppages, prices and cost of living, etc. Each issue also contains a bibliography of recent labor literature.

—— Subject index. Wash., Govt. Prt. Off., 1941. 2v. (Its Bull. no.695-96)

Covers v.1-11, July 1915—Dec. 1920; v.12-51, Jan. 1921—Dec. 1940.

Princeton University. Industrial Relations Section. A trade union library, 1949, prepared by Hazel C. Benjamin. 5th ed. Princeton, N.J., 1949. 53p. **L477**

Special Libraries Association. Social Science Group. A source list of selected labor statistics. rev. ed. N.Y., Special Libraries Assoc., 1950. 79p. $1.75. **L478**

U. S. Bureau of Labor. Index to all reports issued by bureaus of labor statistics in the United States prior to March 1902, prepared by Carroll D. Wright. Wash., Govt. Prt. Off., 1902. 287p. **L479**

Indexes the reports of the federal and various state bureaus, whatever their designation, which published labor statistics.

Encyclopedias and handbooks

American Federation of Labor. American federation of labor; history, encyclopedia, reference book . . . pub. by authority of the 1916 and 1917 conventions. Wash., 1919–24. 2v. il. **L480**

Main list in volume 1 is an alphabetical arrangement of about 800 subjects considered at conventions of the A.F.L. during 38 years, with abstract of the action taken or opinion expressed, and reference to sources; volume 2 is supplementary.

Contains also a section on the war record of the A.F.L. and various lists and tables, e.g., affiliated unions, tables of voting strength of unions, etc. General index.

Dartnell Corporation, Chicago. The handbook of industrial relations. 3d ed., ed. by John Cameron Aspley and Eugene Whitmore. Chic. and Lond., Dartnell Corp., 1948. 1254p. il. $10. **L481**

On spine: Industrial relations handbook.
1st ed., 1943.
Bibliography: current books and publications on industrial relations and related subjects, p.1206-1218.

Giese, Fritz. Handwörterbuch der Arbeitswissenschaft. Halle a. S., Marhold, 1930. 2v. **L482**

Horton, Byrne. Dictionary of labor economics. Wash., Public Affairs Pr., 1948. 32p. $1. **L483**

This includes the definitions of labor terms from his *Dictionary of modern economics* (L335), often in slightly abbreviated form. Would not be needed in any library which has the larger work unless duplication was desirable.

International Labour Office, Geneva. Occupation and health; encyclopaedia of hygiene, pathology and social welfare. Geneva, 1930–34. 2v. il. **L484**

A dictionary of occupations, materials, products, etc., that are sources of danger to health, arranged alphabetically by the English word, with equivalents given in French, German, Italian and Spanish terms. For each occupation gives some account of the industry, its sources of danger, statistics of pathology, account of hygiene needed, and summary of existing legislation. Signed articles with bibliography.

Issued in two editions, the volume edition, listed above, and a preliminary brochure edition which may be rearranged alphabetically and bound.

—— —— Special supplement. Industrial health in wartime. Montreal, 1944. 39p.

Lees-Smith, Hastings Bertrand. Encyclopaedia of the labour movement. Lond., Caxton, 1928. 3v. il. **L485**

Now out of date, but useful historically.

U. S. Bureau of Labor Statistics. Handbook of labor statistics, 1924/26–1947. Wash., Govt. Prt. Off., 1927–48. v.1-6. (Its Bulletin, 439, 491, 541, 616, 694, 916) (1947, loose-leaf, 75c) **L486**

Summarizes material and statistics from the various publications of the Bureau and from some other government publications on related subjects.

—— History of wages in the United States from colonial times to 1928. Revision of bulletin no. 499 with supplement, 1929–1933. Wash., Govt. Prt. Off., 1934. 574p. tables (Its Bulletin, 604) 50c. **L487**

Annuals

American labor year book, 1916–32. N.Y., Rand School Pr., 1916–32. v.1-13. **L488**

Prepared by the Labor Research Department of the Rand School of Social Science.

An annual survey of labor conditions here and abroad, statistics, directory, bibliography, etc. No more published.

Indian labour year book, 1946- . Delhi, 1948- . v.1- . Rs3/10/10 or 5s. 9d. **L489**

At head of title: Government of India. Ministry of Labour: Labour Bureau.

International Federation of Trade Unions. Jahrbuch des Internationalen Gewerkschaftsbundes. Annuaire de la Fédération Syndicale Internationale. Yearbook, 1st-8th, 1922–38. Amsterdam 1922–30]; Paris [1934–38]. v.1-8. Irregular. **L490**

Title and text in German, French and English.

Contains information on the International Federation; names, addresses, memberships and official organs of the national trade union centers and organizations, arranged by countries; names, addresses and memberships of the international trade secretariats and organizations arranged by trades.

International Labour Office. Yearbook of labour statistics. 1st year, 1930- . Montreal, Int. Labour Off., 1931- . Biennial. 10s. 6d.; $3. **L491**

Title varies: v.1, *Annual review;* v.2-5, *I.L.O. yearbook.* Text in French, Spanish, and English.

Summarizes labor statistics for some 60 countries. Many of the tables are kept up to date in the monthly *international labour review.*

Labour party year book, 1946/47- . Lond., 1947- . **L492**

For full description *see* L299h.

Labor Research Association. Labor fact book. N.Y., International Pub., 1931- . il. Biennial. no.9, 1949, $2.50) **L493**

no.6 has title: Labor and the war.

The Management almanac, 1944- . N.Y., Natl. Industrial Conference Bd., 1944- . Annual. **L494**

"A handbook of facts for executives and labor officials: personnel policies, labor relations, business practices." Includes glossary and bibliography.

Trade unions

Gt. Brit. Ministry of Labour and National Service. Directory of employers' associations, trade unions, joint organizations, etc., 1947. Lond., Stat. Off. 1947. 190p. 3s. 6d. **L495**

Lists 1943 employers' associations; 814 trade unions and other employees' associations; 340 joint industrial councils, conciliation and arbitration boards; 69 wages councils.

Gives name of organization, officer and address.

Peterson, Florence. American labor unions; what they are and how they work. [3d ed.] N.Y., Harper, 1945. 338p. $3. **L496**

Discusses the history, structure and internal government of unions, educational and beneficial activities, union and employer relationships, etc. Includes a glossary of labor terms, p.248-75; a list of unions in each industry; texts of the constitutions of the American Federation of Labor and the Congress of Industrial Organizations; and a Directory of international unions with addresses and 1944 membership.

—— Handbook of labor unions. Wash., Amer. Council on Public Affairs [1944]. 415p. $5. **L497**

Contains "Factual information about each of the international and national unions which comprise the American labor movement at the present time."—*Introd.*

For each union gives name, address, affiliation, membership, locals, coverage, publications, trade jurisdiction, membership qualifications and regulations, fees and finances, benefits, strikes and lockouts, etc.

Reynolds, Lloyd George and **Killingsworth, Charles C.** Trade union publications: the official journals, convention proceedings, and constitutions of international unions and federations, 1850–1941. Balt., Johns Hopkins Pr., 1944–45. 3v. $25. **L498**

Contents: 1, Description and bibliography; 2-3, Subject index, A-Z.

U. S. Bureau of Labor Statistics. Directory of labor unions, Apr. 1943- . Wash., Govt. Prt. Off., 1943- . Semiannual. (June 1948, 20c) **L499**

Supersedes its *Directory of AFL unions,* 1939–1942, and its *Directory of CIO unions,* 1939–1942.

Lists national and international unions and state labor organizations, with address, officers and, for the unions, information about conventions, publications, membership, etc.

—— Handbook of American trade-unions, 1936 ed. Wash., Govt. Prt. Off., 1936. 340p. (Its Bulletin, 618) 30c. **L500**

Fairly detailed information about each union.

History

Dulles, Foster Rhea. Labor in America, a history. N.Y., Crowell, 1949. 402p. (Growth of America ser.) **L500a**

A one-volume history giving a straight chronological account of labor in the United States.

History of labor in the United States. N.Y., Macmillan, 1918–35. 4v. **L500b**

A comprehensive history of the labor movement, with introductions by John R. Commons, each part by a specialist. Includes extensive bibliographies.

Biography

Who's who in labor; the authorized biographies of the men and women who lead labor in the United States and Canada and of those who deal with labor [ed. by Marion Dickerman and Ruth Taylor] . . . authorized ed. N.Y., Dryden Pr., 1946. 480p. $12. **L501**

Contents: Men and women who lead labor, p.1-390; Men and women who deal with labor, p.391-443; List of international labor unions, p.445-51; Directory of the labor press, p.453-56; List of educational and research directors, p.457-65; Chronology of labor legislation, p.465-66; Glossary of labor terminology, ed. by J. R. Steelman, p.467-72; The constitution of the American Federation of Labor, p.473-78; The constitution of the Congress of Industrial Organizations, p.479-80.

Manufactures

Alford, Leon Pratt. Management's handbook for manufacturing industries, by a staff of specialists. N.Y., Ronald Pr. [c1924]. 1607p. il. $7.50. **L502**

Now out of date in many respects but still includes useful material not brought together in other handbooks.

—— and **Bangs, John R.** Production handbook. Staff ed., George E. Hagemann. N.Y., Ronald Pr., 1944. 1676p. il. $7.50. **L503**

"Covers . . . the problems of directing the men, materials, and machines of a manufacturing establishment." —*Pref.*

Clark, Victor Selden. History of manufactures in the United States . . . 1929 ed. N.Y., pub. for the Carnegie Institution of Washington by McGraw, 1929. 3v. il. $15. **L504**

"The volumes comprise a revision of . . . *History of manufactures in the United States 1607-1860*, published . . . in 1916 . . . a continuation of this history down to 1914 . . . and additional chapters reviewing the principal facts of our manufacturing development from the beginning of the World War to the present time."—*Pref.*

Heyel, Carl. The foreman's handbook. 1st ed. N.Y., McGraw-Hill, 1943. 410p. il. $3.50. **L505**

U. S. Bureau of the Census. Census of business; 1939. Wash., Govt. Prt. Off., 1941–43. 5v. (16th Census of the U.S.; 1940) **L506**

Contents: v.1, Retail trade, pt.1-3; v.2, Wholesale trade; v.3, Service businesses; v.4, Construction; v.5, Distribution of manufacturers' sales.
Figures are as of 1939.

—— Biennial census of manufactures, 1921–37. Wash., Govt. Prt. Off., 1924–39. **L507**
v.1-9.
No volumes issued for 1929 or 1939, the volumes on manufactures issued as part of the fifteenth and sixteenth censuses taking their places.

—— Sixteenth census of the United States. Manufactures, 1939. . . . Wash., Govt. Prt. Off., 1942. 4v. il. **L508**

v.1, General report. Statistics by subjects; v.2, Reports by industries. 2v.; v.3, Reports for states and outlying areas.

U. S. Technical Commitee on Industrial Classification. Standard industrial classification manual. Wash., Govt. Prt. Off., 1946–49. 2v. **L508a**

Revision of the manual published in 1941–42 (2v.) as *Technical paper* no. 2 of the Bureau of the Budget.
Contents: v.1, Manufacturing industries: pt.1, Titles and descriptions of industries, pt.2, Alphabetic index; v.2, Nonmanufacturing industries.

Lace

Jackson, [Emily]. History of hand-made lace. Dealing with the origin of lace, the growth of the great lace centres, the mode of manufacture, the methods of distinguishing and the care of various kinds of lace, by Mrs. F. Nevill Jackson; with suppl. information by Ernesto Jesurum. Lond., Gill; N.Y., Scribner, 1900. 245p. il. 20s. **L509**

Bibliography: p.98-105.
"Dictionary of lace": p.[107]-206.

Whiting, Gertrude. Lace guide for makers and collectors; with bibliography and five-language nomenclature, profusely illustrated with halftone plates and key designs. N.Y., Dutton [c1920]. 415p. il. $15. **L510**

Nomenclature in English, French, Italian, Spanish and German, p.38-68.
Bibliography, p.243-401.

Leather

Hide and leather and shoes' encyclopedia of the shoe and leather industry; a complete reference work covering leather, shoes, technology and terminology of the shoe, leather and associated industries, Ralph B. Bryan, ed.-in-chief. Chic., Hide and Leather Pub. Co., 1941. 491p. il. $7.50. **L511**

Includes in alphabetical arrangement, brief definitions and descriptions and long articles on various important phases.

Perfume

Parry, Ernest John. Parry's Cyclopaedia of perfumery; a handbook on the raw materials used by the perfumer, their origin, properties, characters and analysis. Lond., Churchill; Phila., Blakiston, 1925. 2v. **L512**

Poucher, William Arthur. Perfumes, cosmetics and soaps with especial reference to synthetics. 5th-6th ed. Lond., Chapman & Hall; N.Y., Van Nostrand, 1941–42. 3v. il. **L513**

v.1, 5th ed.: Dictionary of raw materials together with an account of the nomenclature of synthetics. 1941. 30s., $8; v.2, 6th ed.: Treatise on the production, manufacture and application of perfumes of all types. 1941. 30s., $7; v.3, 6th ed.: Treatise on modern cosmetics. 1942. 25s., $7.

Spices

Parry, J. W. The Spice handbook; spices, aromatic seeds and herbs. Brooklyn, N.Y., Chemical Pub. Co., 1945. 254p. il. $6.50. **L514**

Under name of each commodity usually gives information about plant, family, nativity and cultivation, description, properties, uses, adulteration, grinding, packing, government standards, etc. Also includes extracts from the Pure Food Laws, glossary and index.

Textiles

Bendure, Zelma and **Pfeiffer, Gladys.** America's fabrics; origin and history, manufacture, characteristics and uses; photographic layout by Crystal Stephen, fabric photographs by Nat Messik. N.Y., Macmillan, 1946. 688p. il.   **L515**

Bibliography, p.xi-xii.
Lavishly illustrated, some plates in color. Text is in nontechnical language. Full index.

Merrill, Gilbert R., Macormac, A. R. and **Mauersberger, H. R.** American cotton handbook, a practical reference book for the entire cotton industry. Over 600 illustrations, tables and charts. 1st ed. N.Y., Amer. Cotton Hdbk. Co., 1941. 1024p. il. $4.80.   **L516**

Covers the history, growing, processing, marketing, weaving, dyeing, etc., of cotton. "English cotton literature," p.907-24; "Cotton glossary," p.925-70.

Von Bergen, Werner and **Mauersberger, Herbert R.** American wool handbook; a practical text and reference book for the entire wool industry. 2d enl. ed. N.Y., Textile Book Pubs. Inc., 1948. 1055p. il. $8.   **L517**

A useful handbook including chapters on all phases of the wool industry.
Bibliography. Glossary.

Wingate, Isabel Barnum. Textile fabrics and their selection. 3d ed. N.Y., Prentice-Hall, 1949. 640p. $6; text ed. $4.50.   **L518**

Bibliography, p.617-24.

TERMS

Carmichael, W. L., Linton, George E. and **Price, Isaac.** Callaway textile dictionary. 1st ed. La Grange, Ga., Callaway Mills, 1947. 392p. il. $4.   **L519**

Defines some 6000 terms used in the textile trade, including fabrics and yarns, fibers, dyes, processes, colors, etc.

Marter, Marcel. Dictionnaire à l'usage des industries textiles et du vêtement; anglais-français et français-anglais. Paris et Liége, Béranger, 1931. 219p.   **L520**

Textile mercury. Dictionary of textile terms. (Appeared weekly in *Textile mercury and argus,* Jan. 1936–March 17, 1939)   **L521**

A comprehensive list alphabetically arranged with definitions and descriptions.

Marketing

Aspley, John Cameron. Sales manager's handbook. 5th ed. Chic., Dartnell, 1947. 1101p. il. $10.   **L522**

A very useful handbook emphasizing sales organization, training, methods of selling and marketing research.

Bradford, Ernest S. Survey and directory, marketing research agencies in the United States. N.Y., Bureau of Business Research, College of the City of New York, 1945- . Annual. (1947, $3.50)   **L523**

Lists agencies and individuals engaged in marketing and economic research, etc.

Editor and publisher. Market guide, v.1, 1924- . N.Y., 1924- . Annual. (1948, $5)   **L524**

1948 surveys 1465 daily newspaper markets. Arranged by state and city, gives for each city such information as: population, location, trade area, banks, principal industries, colleges and universities, largest department stores, chain stores, retail outlets and sales, newspapers, etc.

Market data book, 1921- . Chic., Advertising Publications, 1920- . Annual.   **L525**

1939- , issued as a regular number of *Industrial marketing.*
An annual survey supplying "primary information on industrial and trade markets and the business publications serving those markets to trade and industrial advertisers and their advertising agencies."
Gives the salient facts on format, rates and specifications of 2000 business papers.

Nystrom, Paul Henry. Marketing handbook. 1st ed. N.Y., Ronald Pr., 1948. 1321p. $7.50.   **L526**

Covers principles and techniques of selling, advertising, promotion, research and management.

Standard rate and data service. Chic., Standard Rate and Data Service, Inc., 1919- . Monthly. $80.   **L527**

Excellent source for information on rates and advertising facilities. Published in five sections: (1) Newspaper section; (2) Radio and television section, issued on the first of the month; (3) Business paper section; (4) Consumer magazines, farm publications and transportation advertising section, issued on the fifteenth of the month; (5) ABC weekly newspaper section issued Jan. 15 and July 15.

See also Ayer's *Directory of newspapers and periodicals* (E11) for advertising media, etc.

Accounting
Bibliography

See also Coman, *Sources of business information,* p.148-50 (L407) for a list of works on accounting for specialized subjects and interests.

Accountants digest, v.1, Sept. 1935- . Burlington, Vt., L. L. Briggs, Univ. of Vermont, 1935- . Quarterly. $2 per yr. **L528**

"A quarterly presenting in compact form the substance of outstanding articles selected from leading accounting journals of the English-speaking world."

American Institute of Accountants. Accountants' index; a bibliography of accounting literature. N.Y., Institute, 1921–48. (In progress) $10 per v. **L529**

Basic volume, 1912–20; Supplements: (1) 1921–23; (2) 1923–27; (3) 1928–31; (4) 1932–35; (5) 1936–1939; (6) 1940–43; (7) 1944–47.

A detailed author and subject bibliography of the book, pamphlet and periodical literature of the subject. Includes a large amount of indexing of periodicals, and references to parts of books dealing with specific subjects.

Bently, Harry C. and **Leonard, Ruth S.** Bibliography of works on accounting by American authors, 1796–1934. Bost., Author, 1934–35. 2v. $7.50. **L530**

v.1, Books published 1796–1900; v.2, 1901–1934.

Columbia University. Library. Montgomery library of accountancy; a check list of books, printed before 1850, in the Montgomery Library of Accountancy at Columbia University, N.Y., Columbia Univ. Pr., 1927–30. 2v. **L531**

v.1, Basic list, 45p.; v.2, Accessions, June 1927–Sept. 1930, 32p.

Institute of Chartered Accountants in England and Wales, *London.* **Library.** Library catalogue. Lond., Council of the Inst., 1937. 2v. 2s. 6d. ea. **L532**

v.1, Subjects, p.1-148; Authors, p.149-256; v.2, Bibliography of bookkeeping, 259p.

—— —— First supplement. 1939. 36p.

Dictionaries and handbooks

Bienvenu, Emile. Accounting and business dictionary. 2d ed. rev. and enl. An encyclopedia of accounting, financial and miscellaneous business terms. New Orleans, Poynton Pr. Co., 1940. 273p. **L533**

Lang, Theodore. Cost accountants' handbook. N.Y., Ronald Pr., 1944. 1482p. $7.50. **L534**

Lasser, Jacob Jay. Handbook of accounting methods. N.Y., Van Nostrand, 1943. 1349 (i.e., 1357)p. $10. **L535**

Contents: sec. 1, How to design an accounting system, by B. V. Tornborgh; sec. 2, Records required for tax and other legislation; sec. 3, Systems used in specific industries; sec. 4, Comprehensive bibliography, p.1215-1331, (arranged by specific industries).

Paton, William Andrew. Accountants' handbook. 3d ed. N.Y., Ronald Pr., 1943. 1505p. $7.50. **L536**

The standard handbook, various sections having been handled by leading authorities. Treats all the major divisions of accounting.

Pixley, Francis W. Accountant's dictionary, a comprehensive encyclopaedia and direction on all matters connected with the work of an accountant. 3d ed. Lond. and N.Y., Pitman, 1930. 2v. **L537**

Gives the English practice, which differs from the American in many ways.

Commercial correspondence

Aurner, Robert Ray. Effective English in business. 2d ed. Cincinnati, Ohio, South-western Pub. Co., 1940. 848p. il. **L538**

Butterfield, William H. The business letter in modern form. Enl. ed. N.Y., Prentice-Hall, 1941. 302p. $4. **L539**

Williams, Cecil B. Effective business writing. N.Y., Ronald Pr., 1947. 427p. $4. **L540**

Finance and banking
Bibliography

Humpert, Magdalene. Bibliographie der Kameralwissenschaften. Köln, Schroeder, 1937. 1184p. (Kölner Bibliogr. Arbeiten, 1) **L541**

Originally planned to include works published 1727–1835, but starting on p.105, the sixteenth and seventeenth centuries are also included so that the greater part of the work covers 1520–1850.

Masui, Mitsuzo. A bibliography of finance. Kobe, International Finance Seminar in the Kobe Univ. of Commerce, 1935. 1614p., 116p. **L542**

Contents: British books and articles; Ouvrages françaises; Deutsche Literatur; American books and articles; Author index.

Dictionaries, encyclopedias and handbooks

Bogen, Jules I. [and others]. Financial handbook. 3d ed. N.Y., Ronald Pr., 1948. 1289p $7.50. **L543**

Earlier eds. by Robert Hiester Montgomery.

An indispensable handbook for detailed informatior on the financial management of a business.

Brooks, William Collin. Concise dictionary of finance . . . specialized terms and expressions employed in the business of the stock exchange, the money market, and the commodity markets, and in banking, insurance, shipping, and other financial transactions. Lond., Pitman, 1934. 406p. **L544**

Dillen, Johannes Gerardus van. History of the principal public banks, accompanied by extensive bibliographies of the history of banking and credit in eleven European countries, collected by J. G. van Dillen in his quality of Secretary to the International Committee for the Study of the History of Banking and Credit. The Hague, Nijhoff, 1934. 480p. **L545**

Covers banking history from end of the fifteenth century to 1815 in Spain, Italy, Holland, Germany, Sweden, England, France, Poland, Russia, Belgium, Denmark; chapters written variously in French, German, English or Italian, are by different authors.
Extensive bibliographies.

Monetti, Ugo. Enciclopedia di amministrazione, ragioneria, commercio, banca, borsa. Milano, Vallardi [1924–38]. v.1-4. **L546**

v.1-4, A-G.
Signed articles, some with bibliographies.

Munn, Glenn Gaywaine. Encyclopedia of banking and finance. 5th ed. by F. L. Garcia. Camb., Mass., Bankers Pub. Co., 1949. 727p. $12. **L547**

1st ed., 1924.
Definitions of terms and encyclopedic articles with bibliographies on money; credit; banking practice, history, law, accounting and organization; trusts, finance; foreign exchange; investments; securities; speculation; business organization; insurance; commodities; markets; brokerage.

Palyi, Melchior and **Quittner, P.** Handwörterbuch des Bankwesens, unter Mitwirkung von in- und ausländischen Mitarbeitern aus Wissenschaft und Praxis. Berlin, Springer, 1933. 614p. **L548**

Thomson, William. Thomson's Dictionary of banking; a concise encyclopaedia of banking law and practice. 9th ed. by R. W. Jones. Scottish banking by C. J. Shimmins; Irish land laws in their relation to banking by Ernest F. Leet. Lond., Pitman, 1939. 709p. 40s.; $14. **L549**

Contains concise articles on the English law and practice, from the business rather than the historical point of view. Omits American terms and American practice.

FOREIGN TERMS

Polyglot

Herendi, L. Complete dictionary of banking terms in three languages (English-German-French) with alphabetic system in each of these languages. Lond. and N.Y., Pitman, 1928. 3v. in 1. **L550**

Scott, Herbert. English, French and German banking terms, phrases and correspondence, arranged in parallel dictionary form, including an appendix of the lesser-known French and German financial terms and their English equivalents, together with an index from French and German into English. 3d rev. and enl. ed. Lond., E. Wilson, 1931. 200p. **L551**

3d ed. contains additions and corrections, p.vi-xxviii.

French

Kettridge, Julius Orman. French-English and English-French dictionary of commercial and financial terms. . . . Lond., Routledge, 1931. 647p. **L552**

For full description *see* L426.

German

Steneberg, Wilhelm. Handwörterbuch des Finanzwesens in deutscher und englisher Sprache; wörterbuch des Geld-, Bank- und Börsenwesens sowie verwandter Fachgruppen, unter gleichzeitiger Berücksichtigung amerikanischer und englischer Verhältnisse. 2. durchgesehene Aufl. Berlin, Siemens, 1947. 2v. (Siemens' Wissenschaftliche Fachwörterbücher, Bd.1) **L553**

T.1, Englisch-Deutsch; T.2, Deutsch-Englisch.
Added title page in English.
A second edition with only slight changes of the work with the same title by Karl T. Langguth (1933).

Statistics

U. S. Board of Governors of the Federal Reserve System. Banking and monetary statistics. Wash., National Capital Pr., 1943. 979p. $1.50. **L554**

A compilation of statistics covering, for the most part, 1914–1941 inclusive. Similar statistics after 1941 can be found in the *Federal reserve bulletin.*

Federal reserve bulletin. v.1, 1915- . Wash., Bd. of Governors of the Federal Reserve System, 1915- . Monthly. $2 per yr. **L555**

The most complete current information on financial conditions in the United States. Also includes financial developments in foreign countries.

Annuals

Bankers' almanac and year book . . . full particulars of the principal banks of the world. The standard international banking work of reference. A bankers' guide to the principal insurance offices. Lond., Skinner, 1844- . Annual. (1948/49, 70s.) **L556**

Polk's Bankers encyclopedia; the bank directory. 1895- . N.Y., Polk's Bankers Encyclopedia Co.,

1895- . v.1- . $27.50 per v.; 5-yr. contract, $20 per v. **L557**

Title and imprint vary.
Issued semiannually in March and September with monthly supplements.

Rand-McNally bankers directory; the bankers blue book, 1872- . Chic., Rand, 1872- . v.1- . $25 per v. (incl. monthly suppl.) **L558**

Issued semiannually in January and July.

Security dealers of North America. 1922- . N.Y., Herbert D. Seibert, 1922- . Semiannual. $6. **L559**

Stock exchange official year-book, 1934- , comp. and ed. by the Secretary of the Share and Loan Department of the Stock Exchange. Lond., Skinner, 1934- . Semiannual. (1949, £6) **L560**

Annual through 1948.
Kept up to date by the *Stock exchange gazette* which is not officially a part of the service, but is issued by the same publisher.
Supersedes the *Stock exchange year book* and the *Stock exchange official intelligence.*

Tax Foundation, Inc., New York. Facts and figures on government finance, 1941- . N.Y., Foundation, 1941- . Gratis. **L561**

Title varies.

Tax systems; a year book of legislative and statistical information including all the states of the United States and certain foreign data. 1st ed. 1930- . Chic., Commerce Clearing House, 1930- . **L562**

Title varies.
Collects in tabular form the tax systems in the various states.

Real Estate

Holmes, Lawrence G. and **Jones, Carrie M.** The Real estate handbook. N.Y., Prentice-Hall, 1948. 783p. il. $10; to schools $7.60. **L563**

Insurance
Bibliography

Institute of Actuaries, London. Library. Catalogue. London [Cambridge, pr. by W. Lewis at the Univ. Pr.], 1935. 202p. **L564**

Insurance book reviews. Special Libraries Assoc., Insurance Group. Bull. no.1- . Phila., Assoc., 1933- . 10 issues per yr. $2. **L565**

Classified lists of current books and pamphlets. Frequency varies.

Insurance Society of New York. Newsletter, 1914- . N.Y., The Society, 1914- . no.1- . Irregular. Free to libraries. **L566**

Each number, 1914 on, contains a list of "Additions to the library" which, as the accessions list of a library purchasing widely and discriminatingly in this special field, forms a useful check list of worthwhile material.

Encyclopedias and handbooks

Chamber of Commerce of the United States of America. Insurance Dept. Dictionary of insurance terms [ed. by Ralph H. Blanchard]. Wash., 1949. 74p. **L567**

Crobaugh, Clyde J. Handbook of insurance. N.Y., Prentice-Hall, 1949- . v.1- . $7.50; text ed. $5.65. **L567a**

A useful practical dictionary of insurance subjects and terms, first published 1931. Arranged in alphabetical order. Volume 1 of this new revised edition covers: Life insurance and annuities; Accident and health insurance.

Cyclopedia of insurance in the United States, 1891- . N.Y., Index Pub. Co., 1891- . Annual. (1948/49, $5) **L568**

Contents of volumes similar but vary somewhat. 1948/ 49 includes lists of insurance companies and organizations, important court decisions, definitions of insurance terms, biographical sketches, p.715-1069, and a list of biographical sketches appearing in earlier volumes.

Dominge, Charles Carrol and **Lincoln, W. O.** Fire insurance inspection and underwriting; nontechnical encyclopedic handbook. 6th ed. rev. and enl. N.Y., Spectator Co., 1948. 1257p. il. $10.50. **L569**

Defines terms and gives brief encyclopedic information. Especially useful for fire hazards.

Manes, Alfred. Versicherungslexikon, ein Nachschlagewerk für alle Wissensgebiete der gesamten Individual- und Sozial-Versicherung, hrsg. von Alfred Manes. 3. wesentlich erweiterte u. umgearb. Aufl. Berlin, Mittler, 1930. 1934 col. **L570**

1st ed. Tübingen, Mohr, 1909; Ergänzungsband, 1913; 2d ed. Berlin, Mittler, 1924.
The best encyclopedia of the whole subject, with signed articles by specialists and bibliographies. Includes biographies of deceased persons.

Social security almanac; a handbook of facts about voluntary and compulsory provision for social security in the United States and other countries. N.Y., National Industrial Conference Board, 1949. 112p. (Studies in individual and collective security, no.7) $4. **L571**

FOREIGN TERMS

Schloemer, Heinrich and **Thomsen, Alfred.** Deutsch-englisch-französisch-spanisch-italienisch-dänisches assekuranz Wörterbuch. Berlin, Verband öffentl. Feuerversicherungs-Anstalten, 1926. 79p. **L572**

Shimomura, S. New English, French and German-Japanese insurance dictionary. Tokyo, Taiyodo, 1930. 538p. **L573**

Annuals and directories

See also Coman, *Sources of business information,* p.127-31 (L407) for yearbooks and other works on special forms of insurance.

Insurance almanac; who, what, where and when in insurance, an annual of insurance facts. N.Y., Underwriter Pr. and Pub. Co., 1912- . (1948, $5) **L574**

Title varies.
Includes directory material (companies, organizations, state departments, etc.), recent laws, a list of historical conflagrations, a death roll of the past year, and a "Who's who in insurance."

Insurance directory and year book (Post magazine almanack) containing statistics and facts of ordinary life, industrial life, fire, accident and marine insurance, 1931- . Lond., Buckley Pr., 1931- . Annual. (1947/48, 10s.) **L575**

Title varies. *Post magazine almanack* established 1840.

Spectator insurance year book, 1874- . Phila., Spectator Co., 1874- . v.1- . Annual. **L576**

Title varies: formerly *Insurance year book.*
Number of parts in each annual issue has varied from two to five parts per year; 1948/49 in three volumes: (1) Life; (2) Fire and marine; (3) Casualty and surety.
Useful and important compilation containing a large amount of directory and statistical information with some historical lists.

Stone and Cox accident, fire and marine insurance year book. Lond., Stone and Cox, 1908- . Annual. (1948, 30s.) **L577**

U. S. Social Security Board. Social security yearbook, 1939- . Wash., Board, 1940- . (Annual supplement to the Social security bulletin) Price varies, 25c–75c. **L578**

Who's who in insurance; a section of the Insurance almanac. N.Y., Underwriter Pr. and Pub. Co., 1948- . v.1- . Annual. $4. **L579**

A continuation of the biographical section formerly appearing in the *Insurance almanac* (L574), which will be omitted in the future issues.

LAW

❦ Because law is such a highly specialized subject most legal research is done in special law libraries. These may be independent or they may be connected with some institution, such as state, legislative

research, or university libraries. Few general libraries can buy many law books, both because they are so expensive and because they are so technical that they can be used satisfactorily only by those trained in the law. Therefore, the smaller general library should buy only those books which are needed for supplying the less technical legal information and should refer all other legal questions to a nearby law library.

The larger general library, however, will need at least a small collection of law reference books, as they are needed to answer questions in the fields of history, economics, political and social science, as well as the more general law questions. The minimum equipment should include: (1) a law dictionary; (2) a set of the *Revised statutes of the United States* (L629) and either the *United States code* (L631) or the *United States code annotated* (L632); (3) the latest revision or compilation of the laws of the home state, with subsequent session laws; (4) the charter and ordinances of the home city; (5) the latest compilation of the United States *Treaties in force* (L660) and Moore's *Digest of international law* (L646). To this minimum the library would add, as public demand and library funds justified, one of the large law encyclopedias and, if the library contains many legal periodicals, the indexes of legal periodicals.

General works
Guides

Beardsley, Arthur Sydney and **Orman, Oscar C.** Legal bibliography and the use of law books. 2d ed. Brooklyn, N. Y., Foundation Pr., 1947. 653p. $6. **L580**

A useful manual covering such topics as: Teaching and use of law books; Classes of law books—constitutional and statutory, judicial and quasi-judicial; Books of reference; Search for authorities; Brief making, etc.

Hicks, Frederick Charles. Materials and methods of legal research. 3d rev. ed. Rochester, N.Y., Lawyers Co-operative Pub. Co., 1942. 659p. $6. **L581**

A standard work for the specialist, not for the beginner.

Morgan, Edmund M. and **Dwyer, Francis X.** Introduction to the study of law. 2d ed. Chic., Callaghan, 1948. 357p. $5.50. (National textbook ser.) **L582**

Notz, Rebecca Laurens Love. Legal bibliography and legal research; detailed descriptions of law books and specific instructions, with short cuts, for locating statutory law and cases in point. 2d ed. Wash., National Law Bk. Co., 1947. 234p. $5. **L583**

Small but very useful for quick reference.

—— —— 1948 supplement. 1948. p.237-288.

Includes corrections, additions, etc.

Putnam, Carlton B. How to find the law; a comprehensive treatment of the problems of legal research with illustrations from various publications, together with a legal bibliography for each state and the federal government. A legal reference handbook. 4th ed. St. Paul, West Pub. Co., 1949. 740p. maps. $5. **L584**

1st ed. by Fred A. Eldean. Supersedes to a large extent *Brief making and the use of lawbooks* by R. W. Cooley (1926) which for many years was a standard guide.

Bibliography

Beale, Joseph Henry. Bibliography of early English law books. Camb., Harvard Univ. Pr., 1926. 304p. $7.50. **L585**

—— —— Supplement comp. for the Ames Foundation, by R. B. Anderson. Camb., Harvard Univ. Pr., 1943. 50p. $2.50.

Grandin, A. Bibliographie générale des sciences juridiques, politiques, économiques et sociales de 1880 à 1925–26. Paris, Recueil Sirey, 1926. 3v. **L586**

v.1-2, classified bibliography; v.3, indexes of authors, titles and subjects.

—— —— 1- . supplément, 1926– . Paris, Recueil Sirey, 1928– . v.1– . (In progress)

For full description *see* L5.

Hazard, John Newbold and **Stern, William B.** Bibliography of the principal materials on Soviet law. N.Y., Foreign and International Book Co., 1945. 46p. (Amer. Foreign Law Assoc. Bibliographies of foreign law ser. no.12) $2.25. **L587**

Bibliography of the principal materials on Soviet law published in the English, French, German, and Russian languages to Dec. 31, 1943.

Macdonald, Grace Elizabeth. Check list of session laws, comp. . . . for the Public Document Clearing House of the National Association of State Libraries. N.Y., Wilson, 1936. 266p. **L588**

—— —— Supplement with bibliographical notes, emendations and additions, comp. by Ervin H. Pollock. . . . prel. ed. Bost., National Assoc. of State Libraries, 1941. 48p.

Sweet and Maxwell's Legal bibliography. Lond., Sweet and Maxwell, 1925–38. v.1-6. **L589**

Title varies: v.1-4, *Sweet and Maxwell's Complete law book catalogue.*

v.1, English law to 1650, by W. Harold Maxwell. 1925. 44p.; v.2, Bibliography of English law, 1651–1800, by Leslie F. Maxwell. 1931. 270p. 10s.; v.3, Bibliography of English law, 1801–June 1932, by Leslie F. Maxwell.

1933. 334p. 12s. 6d.; v.4, Bibliography of Irish law from earliest times to Dec. 1935, by Leslie F. Maxwell. 1936. 88p. 5s.; v.5, Bibliography of Scottish law from earliest times to Nov. 1936, together with a list of Roman law books in the English language, by Leslie F. Maxwell. 1937. 147p. 7s. 6d., $2.25; v.6, A bibliography of the laws of Australia, New Zealand, Fiji and the western Pacific from earliest times to June 1938 with lists of reports of cases, digests, and collections of statutes and rules. 1938. 144p.

—— Cumulative supplements, 1-2. Lond., Sweet and Maxwell, 1936–38.

Contents: 1, to end of 1935. 1936. 64p. 5s.; 2, to end of 1938. 1939. 92p.

U. S. Library of Congress. Law Library. Anglo-American legal bibliographies; an annotated guide by William L. Friend. Wash., Govt. Prt. Off., 1944. 166p. facsim. $1.50. **L590**

An historical survey of Anglo-American legal bibliography is followed by an alphabetical list of all types of legal bibliographical publications except "works devoted exclusively to American statutory materials, and library and publishers' catalogues."

—— Guides to the law and legal literature of foreign countries, prepared under the direction of Edwin M. Borchard. Wash., Govt. Prt. Off., 1912–31. 5v. **L591**

Contents: Guide to the law and legal literature of Argentina, Brazil and Chile, by E. M. Borchard. 1917. 523p.; Guide to the law and legal literature of France, by G. W. Stumberg. 1931. 242p. $1.25; Guide to the law and legal literature of Germany, by E. M. Borchard. 1912. 226p. 65c; Bibliography of international and continental law, by E. M. Borchard. 1913. 93p. 15c; Guide to the law and legal literature of Spain, by T. W. Palmer. 1915. 174p. 50c.

—— Guide[s] to the law and legal literature of [Latin American countries]. Wash., Library of Congress, 1943–48. (In progress) **L592**

Published as numbers of its "Latin American series" as follows; no.3, Cuba, the Dominican Republic, and Haiti. 1944. 276p. $1.75; no.4, Colombia. 1943. 222p. $1.50; no.6, Mexico. 1945. 269p. $2; no.12, Bolivia. 1947. 110p. 55c; no.13, Mexican states. 1947. 180p. 60c; no.14, Paraguay. 1947. 59p. 25c; no.16, Venezuela. 1947. 128p. $1.50; no.18, Ecuador. 1947. 100p. 40c; no.20, Peru. 1947. 188p. $1; no.26, Uruguay. 1947. 123p. 50c; no.28, Chile. 1917–1946. 1947. 103p. 40c; no.32, Argentina, 1917–1946. 1948. 180p. 60c.

—— Legal codes of the Latin American republics. Wash., Library of Congress, 1942. 95p. (Latin Amer. ser. no.1) 75c. **L592a**

Dictionaries

Ballentine, James Arthur. Law dictionary with pronunciations, 1948 ed. Rochester, N.Y., Lawyers Co-operative Pub. Co., 1948. 1494p. $15 **L593**

Excellent one-volume dictionary.

—— The College law dictionary. Abridged from "Law dictionary with pronunciations." Rochester, Lawyers Coop. Pub. Co., 1948. 978p. $6. **L594**

2d students ed.

Subtitle: Contains over 23,000 English and Latin words, terms and phrases. . . . Also a very complete list of abbreviations of legal literature.

Bouvier, John. Bouvier's Law dictionary and concise encyclopedia, 3d revision (being the 8th ed.), by Francis Rawle. Kansas City, Mo., Vernon; St. Paul, West, 1914. 3v. o.p. **L595**

A standard American law dictionary that has gone through many printings.

Black, Henry Campbell. Black's Law dictionary, containing definitions of the terms and phrases of American and English jurisprudence, ancient and modern, and including the principal terms of international, constitutional, ecclesiastical and commercial law, and medical jurisprudence, with a collection of legal maxims, numerous select titles from the Roman, modern, civil, Scotch, French, Spanish and Mexican law, and other foreign systems, and a table of abbreviations. 3d ed. St. Paul, West, 1933. 1944p. $6.50. **L596**

1st ed. 1891; 2d ed. 1910.

Shumaker, Walter Adams and **Longsdorf, George Foster.** The Cyclopedic law dictionary. 3d ed., by Frank D. Moore. Chic., Callaghan [1940]. 1188p. $6.50. **L597**

Subtitle: Defining terms and phrases of American jurisprudence, of ancient and modern common law, the French and Spanish law, and other juridical systems, with an exhaustive collection of legal maxims.

Table of abbreviations: p.xi-lv.

Wharton, John Jane Smith. Wharton's Law-lexicon; forming an epitome of the laws of England under statute and case law, and containing explanations of technical terms and phrases, ancient, modern and commercial, with selected titles relating to the civil, Scots, and Indian law. 14th ed., by A. S. Oppé. Lond., Stevens, 1938. 1081p. 63s. **L598**

FOREIGN TERMS

❧ For many purposes the large general bilingual dictionaries are more satisfactory than these books of legal terminology which frequently give synonyms only without explanatory usage. However, the following are sometimes useful.

French

Aglion, Raoul. Dictionnaire juridique, anglais-français. Paris, Librairie Générale de Droit et de Jurisprudence. N.Y., Brentano, 1947. 256p. $7. **L599**

English-French only.

Capitant, Henri. Vocabulaire juridique, rédigé par des professeurs de droit, des magistrats et des juriconsultes. Paris, Presses Univ., 1930–36. 530p. 165fr. **L600**

Dalrymple, A. W. French-English dictionary of legal words and phrases. 2d ed. Lond., Stevens, 1948. 130p. **L601**

German

Beseler, Dora von. Englisch-deutsches und deutsch-englisches Wörterbuch der Rechts-und Geschäftssprache. Berlin, de Gruyter, 1929. 223p. **L602**

Schlegelberger, Franz. Rechtsvergleichendes Handwörterbuch für das Zivil-und Handelsrecht des In- und Auslandes. Berlin, Vahlen, 1927–1938. v.1-6. **L603**

v.1-6, A-Unsittliche.

Italian

Scalfati Fusco, Giovanni. Dizionario giuridico inglese-italiano. Napoli, Ed. "La Toga," 1936. 163p. **L604**

English-Italian only.

Latin

Latin for lawyers. 2d ed. Lond., Sweet and Maxwell, 1937. 300p. **L605**

Containing: (1) A course in Latin, with legal maxims and phrases as a basis of instruction; (2) A collection of over 1000 Latin maxims, with English translations, explanatory notes, and cross-references; (3) Vocabulary of Latin words.

Spanish

Bean, Mary Elizabeth. Manual español-inglés e inglés-español de palabras y términos legales; un libro de fácil referencia para el uso de traductores de documentos y obras en español o inglés. N.Y., Appleton, 1933. 257p. $2.50. **L606**

Tejada y Sainz, Juan de Dios. Spanish and English legal and commercial dictionary. A revision and enlargement of the Law translator's reference glossary. Santa Maria del Rosario, Cuba, Editorial Var-I-tek, 1945. 158p. **L607**

Subtitle: Contains over 10,000 terms . . . pertinent to: canon, civil, commercial, international, municipal and penal law; transportation, accounting, banking and finance; insurance, metrology; and numerous abbreviations.

Encyclopedias

American jurisprudence. A comprehensive text statement of American case law, as developed in the cases and annotations in the annotated reports system; being a rewriting of Ruling case law to reflect the modern developments of the law. San Francisco, Bancroft-Whitney; Rochester, N.Y., Lawyers Co-op. Pub. Co., c1936–48. 58v. $10 ea. **L608**

> v.1-58, A-Zoning. A new ed. of *Ruling case law*, 1914–31, 28v.
> Cited as *Am. Jur.*

Corpus juris; being a complete and systematic statement of the whole body of the law as embodied in and developed by all reported decisions; ed. by William Mack . . . and W. B. Hale. N.Y., Amer. Law Bk. Co., 1914–37. 72v. $8 per v. **L609**

> Cited as *C.J.*
> v.72, Descriptive word index and concordance; a complete alphabetical index descriptive of the legal holdings and facts contained in v.1-71.
> *Corpus juris* is a new edition of the *Cyclopedia of law and procedure.*

—— Permanent volumes of annotations to Corpus juris. N.Y., Amer. Law Bk. Co., 1921–31. 3v.

> Supplemented by annual volumes of *Annotations* covering cases reported during the year.

—— Quick search manual, being a complete collection of the analyses and cross references in the Corpus juris-Cyc system. N.Y., Amer. Law Bk. Co., 1928. 2450p.

Corpus juris secundum; a complete restatement of the entire American law as developed by all reported cases, by William Mack and Donald J. Kiser, assisted by the combined editorial staffs of the American Law Book Co. and the West Publishing Co. Brooklyn, N.Y., Amer. Law Bk. Co., 1937–48. v.1-58. $7.50 ea. (In progress) **L610**

> v.1-58. A-Mortgage.
> Cited as *C.J.S.*
> A new edition of *Corpus juris (C.J.).* Although when completed *C.J.S.* will largely supersede *C.J.*, it is necessary to use *C.J.* now for the part of the alphabet not yet covered in the *C.J.S.* and for footnote references not carried over.

Laws of England, being a complete statement of the whole law of England, by the Rt. Hon. the Earl of Halsbury and other lawyers. 2d ed. under the general editorship of the Rt. Hon. the Viscount Hailsham. Lond., Butterworth, 1931–42. 37v. Price on application. **L611**

> 1st ed. 1907–17.
> Kept up to date by annual supplements.

Indexes

Legal periodical digest, 1928- . N.Y., Commerce Clearing House, Inc., 1928- . v.1- . **L612**

> Title varies.
> Loose-leaf abstracting service, consisting of monthly issues of digests of the leading articles appearing in American, British and Canadian legal periodicals. Digests are on sheets for insertion in a loose-leaf binder according to subject. There are four indexes, (1) topical, (2) case comments by case names, (3) author, (4) table of articles, issued semiannually and annually, the annual index being cumulated for the year.

Index to legal periodical literature. Bost., Boston Book Co., 1888–1919; Chipman, 1924; Indianapolis, Bobbs-Merrill, 1933; Los Angeles, Parker and Baird, 1939. v.1-6. **L613**

> v.1-2, ed. by Leonard A. Jones; v.3-6, by Frank E. Chipman.
> v.1, to 1886; v.2, 1887–98; v.3, 1898–1908; v.4, 1908-22; v.5, 1923–32; v.6, 1932–37.
> Each volume consists of a main subject index with brief author index to the subject part. Indexes material on technical and historical law subjects, legal biography and a considerable number of articles on political, economic and sociological subjects. The first volume indexes practically all articles in 158 legal periodicals (1373v.), all articles on law subjects in 113 general periodicals (including a few sets published in the eighteenth century) and the proceedings of various bar associations. The fourth volume indexes 91 periodicals and is practically a consolidation of volumes 1-14 of the annual *Index to legal periodicals* noted below but does not entirely supersede these as it omits some articles of temporary interest included in the annuals; the number of periodicals indexed in other volumes varies from 60 to 110. Useful in the general library as well as in the law library.

Index to legal periodicals, 1908- . published for the American Association of Law Libraries. N.Y., Wilson, 1909- . Service basis. **L614**

> Monthly lists (frequency varies), with annual cumulations and, from 1926, 3-year cumulations which supersede the annual. The cumulated volumes consist of an author index and a subject index, and include a table of cases, and since 1940 a book review index. Number of periodicals indexed varies from 39 in the 1908 annual to 152 legal periodicals, 46 bar association reports, and 12 judicial council reports in the 1943–46 cumulation. A complete working set of this index consists of the annuals for 1908–25, and the 3-year cumulations with supplementary issues since then.

Commerce Clearing House. Congressional index service. 75th Congress, 1937/38- . Chic., Commerce Clearing House, Inc., Loose Leaf Service Division of the Corporation Trust Co., 1937- . **L615**

> Loose-leaf.
> "Indexes all congressional bills and resolutions of general interest and lists their current status. It is designed to lay open to the user a complete record of federal legislation and its progress from initial introduction to final disposition."
> Now includes treaties.

U. S. Library of Congress. Legislative reference service. Digest of public general bills with index, 74th Congress-   , 1936-   . Wash., Govt. Prt. Off., 1936-   . 10c-15c ea. no.   **L616**

Shepard, The Frank Co. A table of cases which have been cited by popular name; federal and state to January 1, 1941. Shepard's Citations. N.Y., Shepard, 1940. 63p.   **L617**

—— A table of federal acts by popular names or short titles to Jan. 1, 1947. Shepard's Citations. N.Y., Shepard, 1946. 121p.   **L618**

U. S. Library of Congress. Legislative reference service. State law index; an index to the legislation of the states of the United States enacted . . . 1925/26-   . no.1-   . Wash., Govt. Prt. Off., 1929-   . v.1-   . Biennial. $1.50-$2.50 per v.
                                              L619

Title varies.

Directories

American bar; a biographical directory of the leading lawyers of the United States and Canada. Minneapolis, Fifield, 1918-   . v.1-   . Annual. $30.   **L620**

Arranged by firm name under state and place. Includes brief statement of character of firm and type of practice with brief biographies of members of the firm. No index.

Lawyers directory. Cincinnati, Ohio, Lawyers Directory, 1883-   . Annual.   **L621**

Semiannual, 1888–1925; annual, 1926-   .
Includes digests of laws and a selection of leading lawyers with biographical data. Less inclusive for lawyers directory but more inclusive for law digest than the *Martindale-Hubbell* (L622).
Title varies: Until 1925 was called *Sharp & Alleman Co.'s Lawyers and bankers directory*.

Martindale-Hubbell law directory (annual) . . . 1931-   . [63d-   ] N.Y., Martindale-Hubbell [c1931-   ].   **L622**

Consolidation of *Martindale's American law directory*, 1868–1930, and *Hubbell's Legal directory*, 1870–1930; published annually in two volumes, continuing the edition numbering of *Martindale's American law directory*.
v.1, List of lawyers of the United States, Canada and Newfoundland; Selected list of foreign lawyers; Roster of registered patent attorneys; Biographical section; v.2, Digests of the laws of the states, territories and possessions of the United States, Canada and its provinces, Newfoundland and foreign countries, also United States patent, tax and trademark laws; Court calendars and uniform acts.

American Association of Law Libraries. Law libraries in the United States and Canada, 1948. [4th ed] Balt., Baltimore Bar Library, 1948. 70p. $2 to nonmembers; free to members.   **L623**

Geographical arrangement of libraries, giving name, librarian and number of volumes, followed by personnel index.

Biography

See also Martindale-Hubbell law directory (L622) for biographical data about American lawyers of the present time.

American Bar Association. Directory. Chic., Assoc. Annual.   **L624**

Lists officers, committees, etc.

Foss, Edward. Biographia juridica; a biographical dictionary of the judges of England . . . 1066–1870. Lond., Murray, 1870. 792p.   **L625**

Association of American law schools. Teachers' directory, 1922-   . St. Paul, West Pub. Co., 1923-   . Annual. Free.   **L626**

Alphabetical list of teachers with biographies.
Suspended 1943–45.
Resumed 1946/47. 233p.

Who's who in law; v.1, 1937, ed. by J. C. Schwarz. N.Y., Schwarz, c1937. 1086p. $15.   **L627**

Gives biographies of about 12,000 lawyers, more than half of whom are not included in *Who's who in America* (S29).

Statutes
United States

U. S. Laws, statutes, etc. Index to the federal statutes [1789–1873, 1874–1931] general and permanent law. . . . Wash., Govt. Prt. Off., 1911–33. 2v. v.1, o.p.; v.2, $3.50.   **L628**

The volume for 1789–1873 indexes v.1-17 of the *Statutes at large* (L630); the volume for 1874–1931 indexes the *Revised statutes of 1874* (L629) and the *Statutes at large*, v.18-46; this latter volume is a revision by W. H. McClenon and W. C. Gilbert of the Scott and Beaman *Index analysis of the federal Statutes 1874–1907*.

—— Revised statutes of the United States, passed at the first session of the Forty-third Congress, 1873–74; embracing the statutes of the United States, general and permanent in their nature, in force Dec. 1, 1873. 2d ed. Wash., Govt. Prt. Off., 1878. 1394p.   **L629**

In 1867 a commission was appointed to compile all the general and permanent laws by subject. The first revision, accepted and published as the *Revised statutes of 1873*, contained certain liberties in the texts taken by the revisers. The *Revised statutes*, 2d ed., 1878, restored the original text, and is the edition usually cited. Supplements were made and published in 1891 and 1901, but these are now largely superseded by the *Code* (L631).

—— The statutes at large of the United States, concurrent resolutions, recent treaties, conventions and executive proclamations. Bost., Little, 1845–1873; Wash., Govt. Prt. Off., 1875–1948. v.1-61. (In progress) (v.61, $6.75.) **L630**

Price per volume varies. *See Price list no.10* (F17), issued by Superintendent of Documents.

Each volume contains the acts and joint resolutions, public and private, permanent and temporary, and the concurrent resolutions, treaties, conventions, and presidential proclamations published during the congressional term. Arrangement is chronological by the date of the passage of the act under the divisions: Public laws, Private laws, Treaties, etc.

Through 1936 each volume of the *Statutes at large* covered the laws of one congress, i.e., two years. Beginning with the 75th Congress, 1937, each volume covers one session. The "session" or "pamphlet" laws were preliminary compilations of "slip" laws, each volume covering one session of a congress. These were discontinued at the end of the 74th Congress. For description *see Price list no.10*.

—— United States code. 1946 ed. Wash., Govt. Prt. Off., 1947–48. 5v. (with annual supplements) **L631**

Supersedes previous editions published 1926, 1934, 1940.

Arranged under 50 titles with general index, this code consolidates all general and permanent laws of the United States in force on Jan. 2, 1947.

—— United States code annotated. The code of the laws of the United States in force December 7, 1925, as enacted by Congress June 28 and approved June 30, 1926. Annotated from all cases construing the laws. St. Paul, West Pub. Co., 1927–1949. v.1-76. **L632**

Cited as *U.S.C.A.*
Each volume covers one title in the *U.S. code* (1926) (L631), and arrangement is identical with that *Code*.
Supplemented by pocket parts containing amendments and additions. Later replacement volumes are issued in revised editions from time to time.

—— Federal code annotated; all federal laws of a general and permanent nature . . . fully annotated to the decisions of federal and state tribunals, together with annotations of uncodified laws and treaties. . . . Indianapolis, Bobbs-Merrill, 1937- . 13v. in 16. Yearly service $20. **L633**

Cited *F.C.A.*
Volumes replaced at intervals by perpetual revision plan. Groups related material into volumes, e.g., Federal taxation, Transportation and Communication, Bankruptcy, etc.

—— —— Ten-year cumulative supplement for v.1-13. Titles 1-50, 1947- . v.1-5. (In progress)

Code of federal regulations. 1949 ed., containing a codification of documents of general applicability and future effect as of Dec. 31, 1948, with ancillaries and index. Pub. by the Division of the Federal Register, National Archives. Wash., Govt. Prt. Off., 1949- . (In progress) **L634**

Cited as *C.F.R.*
Kept up to date by pocket supplements, cumulating annually.
This is the second edition of the *Code* (first edition, 1938) and contains a "codification of the Federal Administrative rules and regulations, general and permanent . . . duly promulgated on or before Dec. 31, 1948, and effective as to facts arising on and after Jan. 1, 1949."
These form basic volumes for the type of material published currently in the *Federal register* (L635).

United States. Federal register, Mar. 12, 1936- . Wash., Govt. Prt. Off., 1936- . Daily, except Sun., Mon., and day following a legal holiday. $15 per year. **L635**

Contains all presidential proclamations and executive orders, rules and regulations of the various bureaus and departments of the government, and decisions of fact-finding bodies. Has monthly, quarterly, and annual indexes.

U. S. Laws, statutes, etc. United States code congressional service. Acts of 76th Congress, Jan. 3, 1939- . St. Paul, West Pub. Co.; Brooklyn, N.Y., Edward Thompson Co., 1942- . **L636**

Published monthly (slightly irregular) with annual bound cumulations. Coverage varies somewhat, recent volumes include all public laws (full text), congressional comments, executive orders, presidential proclamations, administrative regulations, messages of the president, legislative history, popular names of laws, etc. Current issues include index-digest of bills introduced.

Great Britain

Gt. Brit. Laws, statutes, etc. Statutes of the realm, printed by command of His Majesty King George the Third from original records and authentic manuscripts. [Lond., Record Commission] 1810–28. 11v. **L637**

v.1-9, Statutes, 1235–1713; [v.10] Alphabetical index; [v.11] Chronological index.

—— Statutes revised, 1236–1920. 2d ed. Lond., Stat. Off., 1928–29. 4v.

Kept up to date by the annual volumes of *Public general statutes*.

Complete statutes of England, classified and annotated; in continuation of Halsbury's Laws of England, and for ready reference entitled "Halsbury's Statutes of England." Lond., Butterworth, 1923–31. 22v. **L638**

Kept up to date by annual continuation and supplementary volumes.
v.21, Consolidated table of cases; v.22, General index; v.23-40, Continuation volumes, 1930–47; Supplements 1-17, 1932–48. (Supplements are cumulative)

—— Halsbury's Statutes of England. 2d ed. Ed.-in-chief, Roland Burrows. Lond., Butterworth, 1948- . v.1- . (In progress) **L639**

v.1-6, A-Easements.

Chitty, Joseph. Chitty's Statutes of practical utility. Arranged in alphabetical and chronological order, with notes and indexes. 6th ed. by W. H. Aggs. Lond., Sweet, 1911–13. 16v. 42s. per v. **L640**

A compilation of selected statutes of general interest. Annotated.

Volume 16 contains: addenda, corrigenda and delenda; tables of short and popular titles, regnal years and chapters, statutory rules and orders; general index.

Kept up to date by annual supplements. (Price varies; 1946, 60s.)

Gt. Brit. Laws, statutes, etc. Acts and ordinances of the Interregnum, 1642–1660, ed. by C. H. Firth and R. S. Rait. Lond., Stat. Off., 1911. 3v. **L641**

Covers the period of the Commonwealth.

Canon law

Dictionnaire de droit canonique, contenant tous les termes du droit canonique, avec un sommaire de l'histoire et des institutions et de l'état actuel de la discipline. Commencé sous la direction de A. Villien et E. Magnin; continué sous la direction de A. Amanieu, avec le concours d'un grand nombre de collaborateurs. Paris, Letouzey, 1935–49. v.1-4. (In progress) **L641a**

Published in fascicules. fasc. 1-23, 1924–49, form v.1-4, and cover A-Disparité.

Signed articles by specialists, with bibliographies. Contains many biographies. Forms part of the *Encyclopédie des sciences religieuses* (*see* p.124).

International law

Déak, Francis and Jessup, Philip C. Collection of neutrality laws, regulations and treaties of various countries. Wash., Carnegie Endowment for International Peace, 1939. 2v. $10. **L642**

Includes laws, regulations and treaties from 1800 to Oct. 1, 1938.

Flournoy, Richard Wilson and Hudson, Manley O. Collection of nationality laws of various countries, as contained in constitutions, statutes and treaties. N.Y., Oxford Univ. Pr., 1929. 776p. $4. (Pub. of the Carnegie Endowment for International Peace. Div. of International Law) **L643**

Hasse, Adelaide Rosalie. Index to United States documents relating to foreign affairs, 1828–1861. Wash., Carnegie Inst., 1914–21. 3v. (Carnegie Inst. Pub. 185) $22. **L644**

Indexes the reports of Congress, the Senate executive journal for diplomatic and consular appointments and treaty ratifications, the opinions of the attorney-general for decisions of questions of international controversy, the statutes-at-large, and the *Congressional globe*.

Holborn, Louise Wilhelmine. War and peace aims of the United Nations. Bost., World Peace Foundation, 1943–48. 2v. v.1, $2.50; v.2, $6. **L645**

v.1, Sept. 1, 1939–Dec. 31, 1942; v.2, Jan. 1, 1943–Sept. 1, 1945.

A collection of documents designed to show the war and peace aims of the various countries of the United Nations, consisting chiefly of statements and speeches by statesmen, agreements, treaties, etc. References are given to sources.

Moore, John Bassett. Digest of international law. Wash., Govt. Prt. Off., 1906. 8v. (U.S. 56th Cong., 2d sess. House doc. 551) $15 **L646**

Full title: A digest of international law as embodied in diplomatic discussions, treaties and other international agreements, international awards, the decisions of municipal courts, and writings of jurists, and especially in documents, published and unpublished, issued by presidents and secretaries of state of the United States, the opinions of the attorneys-general, and the decisions of courts, federal and state.

v.1-7, Digest; v.8, Index, Table of cases, List of documents.

Hackworth, Green Haywood. Digest of international law. Wash., Govt. Prt. Off., 1940–44. 8v. $15.50. (U.S. Dept. of State. Pub. 1506 and 1521) **L647**

Includes the documents and files accumulated in the Dept. of State since 1906. Supplements and does not duplicate Moore's *Digest* (L646).

Volume 8, General index and list of cases.

Treaties

GENERAL

International Intermediary Institute, The Hague. Répertoire général des traités et autres actes diplomatiques conclus 1895–1920, publié avec le concours financier du Legatum Visserianum de Leyde. La Haye, Nijhoff, 1926. 516p. **L648**

Indexes 4414 items and refers to text in 144 printed collections and other sources.

Continues, Ribier, Gabriel de, *Répertoire des traités de paix . . . entres toutes les puissances du globe, depuis 1867 jusqu'à nos jours* (Paris, 1895–99. 2v.).

Continued in its *Bulletin*.

League of Nations. Treaty series; publication of treaties and international engagements registered with the Secretariat of the League. v.1-205. (Treaty no.1-4834) Sept. 1920–1944/46. Lond., Harrison, 1920–46. 205v. Price per v. varies. **L649**

—— —— General index, 1920–1946. no.1-9. (v.1-205) Geneva, 1927–46. 9v.

Issued at end of every 500 treaties.

Myers, Denys Peter. Manual of collections of treaties and of collections relating to treaties.

Camb., Harvard Univ. Pr., 1922. 685p. (Harvard bibliographies. Library ser. v.2) $7.50.　　**L650**

United Nations. Systematic survey of treaties for the pacific settlement of international disputes, 1928–1948. Lake Success, N.Y., 1948. 1202p.　　**L651**

pt.1, Analyses of treaties; pt.2, Texts of treaties; pt.3, Tables of treaties: chronological, alphabetical, multipartite.

—— Treaty series; treaties and international agreements registered or filed and recorded with the Secretariat of the United Nations. v.1- , 1946/47- . Lake Success, N.Y., 1947- . (Columbia Univ. Pr. $3.75 ea.)　　**L652**

U. S. Dept. of State. Catalogue of treaties, 1814–1918. Wash., Govt. Prt. Off., 1919. 716p.　**L653**

A general chronological catalog of treaties with an index by countries. Gives information as to place and date signed and ratified, with references to printed text and indication of the languages involved.

UNITED STATES

Davenport, Frances Gardiner. European treaties bearing on the history of the United States and its dependencies. Wash., Carnegie Inst., 1917–37. v.1-4. (Carn. Inst. Pub. 254) $11.25.　　**L654**

v.1-4, to 1815.
v.4, ed. by Charles Oscar Paullin.

Documents on American foreign relations, [v.1]- , Jan. 1938/39- . Bost., World Peace Foundation, 1939- . Annual.　　**L655**

v.8, covers July 1, 1945 to Dec. 31, 1946 ($6) instead of the 12-month period July-June of previous volumes.

U. S. Dept. of State. List of treaties submitted to the Senate, 1789–1934. Wash., Govt. Prt. Off., 1935. 138p. (Its Pub. 765) 20c.　　**L656**

Contents: List of treaties submitted, p.15-61; Notes on treaties listed, p.62-93; Treaties pending in Senate, Treaties awaiting further proceedings, p.94-96; Numerical list of the Treaty series, including all numbers to May 31, 1935, p.97-131.

The "List of treaties submitted" gives for each treaty its date, subject and status, e.g., whether accepted without change, accepted with amendment, withdrawn, etc.; the "Numerical list of the Treaty series" gives for each treaty its date, country with which negotiated, subject, and a reference to the volume of the *Statutes at large* (L630) containing the text.

—— Treaties submitted to the Senate, 1935–1944. Wash., 1945. 28p. (Its Pub. no.2311) 10c.

Supersedes annual supplements.

—— United States treaty developments. Wash., Govt. Prt. Off., 1947- . loose-leaf. $4. (Its Pub. 2851)　　**L657**

Designed to serve as a guide to factual information on the status of agreements and on subsequent developments affecting them. "It is a combination and extension of *Treaties submitted to the Senate* and *A list of treaties and other international acts,* and it will eventually replace them."

—— Papers relating to the foreign relations of the United States, with the annual message of the President, 1861- . Wash., Govt. Prt. Off., 1862- . Price varies, about $2.25 per v.　　**L658**

Usually cited by binder's title, *Foreign relations.*

Annual volumes of diplomatic correspondence between the United States and foreign countries. Includes correspondence, text of treaties, the President's annual message to Congress (in volumes after 1865), and special messages on foreign subjects, etc. One or more volumes published each year, the date of publication being much later than the year covered, e.g., volumes on 1930, published 1945.

In this series have also been issued World War Supplements 1914–18 as follows: The Lansing papers, 1914–20. (1939–40) 2v. $2.75; Russia, 1918. (1931–32) 3v. $4.25; 1919. (1937) 807p. $1.75; Paris Peace Conference. (1942–47) v.1-13. Pr. varies, $1.25–$3.25 per v.; Japan, 1931–41. (1943) 2v. $4.

—— —— General index, 1861–99, 1900–1918. Wash., Govt. Prt. Off., 1902–41. 2v. v.1, o.p.; v.2, $1.25.

U. S. Treaties. Treaties, conventions, international acts, protocols and agreements between the United States of America and other powers, 1776–1937. Wash., Govt. Prt. Off., 1910–38. 4v. v.1-2, $1.25 ea.; v.3, o.p.; v.4, $2.25.　**L659**

v.1-2, comp. by William M. Malloy, 1910; v.3, comp. by C. F. Redmond, 1923; v.4, comp. by Edward J. Trenwith, 1938.

"Contains treaties, conventions, international acts, important protocols and agreements by exchange of notes whether in force or not, to which the United States has been a party from 1776 . . . together with other material pertaining to treaties, a chronological list of treaties by countries, etc."—*Pref.*

Contents: v.1-4, Treaties 1776–1937.
v.4, includes index to v.1-4.

—— Treaties in force: A list of treaties and other international acts of the United States in force on Dec. 31, 1941. Wash., Govt. Prt. Off., 1944. 275p. (U.S. Dept. of State. Pub. 2103) 40c.　**L660**

A revision of Publication 436, "A list of treaties and other international acts . . . in force, Dec. 31, 1932."

—— Treaties and other international acts of the United States of America; ed. by Hunter Miller. Wash., Govt. Prt. Off., 1931–48. v.1-8. (Dept. of State. Pub. no.175, 237, 453, 645, 1017, 1719, 1791, 3141) v.1-7, $4–$5 per v.; v.8, $4.75. (In progress)　　**L661**

v.1, Plan of the work, Lists, Tables; v.2-8, 1776–1863.
A new and revised collection, to take the place, when completed, of the collection by W. M. Malloy (L659).

Arranged chronologically, with the text of each treaty given in English and also in the foreign language in which it was concluded. Volume 1 is issued in a preliminary edition to be used while the rest of the work is in progress and to be replaced eventually by a definitive edition.

—— Treaties and other international acts, no. 1501- . Wash., Govt. Prt. Off., 1946- . Price varies, 5c-10c. **L662**

Continues the "Treaty" series, and the "Executive agreement" series. The combined numbers in these two series having reached 1500, the new series begins with 1501.

Contains authentic texts of treaties, declarations, constitutions and charters of international organizations, etc.

—— —— Subject index to the Treaty series and the Executive Agreement series, July 1, 1931. Wash., Govt. Prt. Off., 1932. 214p. 60c.

Treaties to which the United States is a party are published in the *Statutes at large* (L630).

GREAT BRITAIN

Gt. Brit. Foreign Office. Treaty series, 1892- . Lond., Stat. Off., 1892- . **L663**

Issued as command papers but numbered and indexed so that they can be bound as a separate set. General indexes are issued every few years as one of the numbers in the middle of a volume.

—— British and foreign state papers, with which is incorporated Hertslet's Commercial treaties. Lond., Stat. Off., 1841- . v.1- . **L664**

v.116- , incorporated *Hertslet's Commercial treaties*. Contains treaties, correspondence about foreign affairs, and many documents of historical interest and importance, especially texts of the constitutions of foreign countries and similar organic laws. Each volume has a good index, and there are three general indexes, which together cover nearly the whole set: v.64 indexes v.1-63; v.93 indexes v.65-92; v.115 indexes v.94-114; v.138 indexes v.116-137. Material included is mainly that of the nineteenth and twentieth centuries, but there are some papers of an earlier date.

Hertslet's Commercial treaties; a collection of treaties and conventions between Great Britain and foreign powers, and of the laws, decrees, orders in council, etc., concerning the same, so far as they relate to commerce and navigation, slavery, extradition, nationality, copyright, postal matters, etc. Lond., Stat. Off., 1827–1925. 31v. **L665**

v.22 is general index to v.1-21; v.31 is index to v.23-30. Title varies.

Gt. Brit. Treaties, etc. Handbook of commercial treaties, etc., with foreign powers . . . 4th ed. Lond., Stat. Off., 1931. 1171p. 21s. **L666**

LATIN AMERICA

U. S. Tariff Commission. Reference manual of Latin American commercial treaties. Wash., Govt. Prt. Off., 1940. 281p. **L667**

Attempts to list all commercial treaties and agreements negotiated by the twenty Latin-American countries during the entire period of their history. Also lists noncommercial treaties and agreements which contain commercial provisions.—Cf. *Foreword.*

Arranged alphabetically by country and chronologically under country. Usually gives date signed, date ratified, date effective, duration, termination, remarks as to provisions and references to sources where texts in various languages may be found.

Pan American Union. Dept. of International Law and Organization. Division of Legal Affairs. Bilateral treaties, conventions and agreements in force between the United States of America and other American republics, as of March 1, 1948. Wash., Pan American Union, 1948. 42p. **L668**

Constitutions

BIBLIOGRAPHY

Spencer, Richard Carleton and **Spencer, Pearl C.** Topical index to national constitutions. Phila., American Acad. of Pol. and Soc. Science, 1942. 84p. ([Amer. Academy of Political and Social Science, Phila.] James-Patten-Rowe pamphlet ser., no.12) $1. **L669**

Includes a bibliography of collections of constitutions and a list of the texts of constitutions by country, both those separately published and in collections.

COLLECTIONS

Dareste de la Chavanne, François Rodolphe. Les constitutions modernes . . . traductions accompagnées de notices historiques et de notes explicatives par F. R. Dareste et P. Dareste. 4. éd., entièrement refondue par Joseph Delpech et Julien Laferrière. Paris, Recueil Sirey, 1928–34. 6v. in 8. maps. **L670**

v.1, Europe: Albanie-Grèce; v.2, Europe: Hongrie-Yougoslavie; v.3, Europe, additions aux tomes 1 et 2, et Appendice; Index alphabétique des textes reproduits ou analysés aux tomes 1 et 2, au supplément et à l'Appendice, p.i-civ; v.4, Amérique latine; v.5, Empire britannique, Afrique, Asie, Territoires sous mandat A; v.6, États-Unis d'Amérique du Nord. Les États de l'Union de l'Amérique du Nord; Extra volume, unnumbered, Espagne: Constitution du 9 déc. 1931. 59p.

A comprehensive standard collection; for each country gives (1) Historical notes, (2) Bibliographical references, (3) Text, in French, of the constitutions in force, with explanatory notes.

Gt. Brit. Foreign Office. Constitutions of all countries. v.1, The British Empire. Lond., Stat. Off., 1938. 678p. 10s. 6d. **L671**

Includes the constitutions of the various, separate parts of the British Empire.

Hawgood, John Arkas. Modern constitutions since 1787. Lond., Macmillan, 1939. 539p. **L672**

Bibliography, p.467-525.

A textbook with a useful annotated bibliography which includes collections, texts, commentaries, histories, etc.

International Labor Office. Constitutional provisions concerning social and economic policy; an international collection of texts covering 450 countries and other governmental units. Montreal, 1944. 755p. $5. **L673**

"List of international declarations and constitutional instruments," p.xxx-lix.

Bibliography, p.711-35, gives General collections of documents; Collections of constitutions; Collections of treaties; Official gazettes (by country); Collected editions of laws and regulations; Other reference works.

McBain, Howard Lee and **Rogers, Lindsay.** New constitutions of Europe. Garden City, N.Y., Doubleday, 1922. 612p. **L674**

Gives English text of the constitutions of Germany, Prussia, Württemberg, Baden, Austria, Czechoslovakia, Jugoslavia, Russia, Poland, Danzig, Esthonia, Finland, Belgium and France, with historical note about each and a bibliography.

Mirkine-Guetzévitch, Boris. Les constitutions de l'Europe nouvelle, avec les textes constitutionnels. 10. éd. entièrement refondue et augm. Paris, Delagrave, 1938. 2v. (638p.) Bibliothèque d'hist. et de politique) **L675**

United States

✤ The text of the constitution of the United States is given in many general reference books, e.g., *World almanac* (L104), etc., and is included also in the *U.S. code* (L631), the House and Senate *Manuals* (L298c, L298b) and the various state or legislative manuals. A good edition to keep on hand for reference purposes is that of the *House manual* which is indexed and contains full notes of all ratifications. State constitutions are given in the various state manuals.

U. S. Constitution. Constitution of the United States of America (annotated), annotations of cases decided by Supreme Court of U.S. to Jan. 1, 1938. Wash., Govt. Prt. Off., 1938. 1246p. (74th Cong., 2d sess. Sen. doc. 232) $4.25. **L676**

Thorpe, Francis Newton. Federal and state constitutions, colonial charters, and other organic laws of the states, territories, and colonies now or heretofore forming the United States of America. Wash., Govt. Prt. Off., 1909. 7v. (59th Cong., 2d sess. House doc. 357) **L677**

Arranged: (1) United States, (2) States, alphabetically. Supersedes the earlier collection by Poore, correcting Poore's more obvious errors and adding the new material since 1876. The work is useful as a comprehensive collection, but enough errors and omissions have been pointed out to show that it should be used with caution.

Chicago. Univ. Libraries. Official publications relating to American state constitutional conventions. N.Y., Wilson, 1936. 91p. **L678**

The Americas

Fitzgibbon, Russell Humke. The constitutions of the Americas, as of January 1, 1948. Chic., Univ. of Chic. Pr., 1948. 847p. $10. **L679**

Bibliography, p.819-24.

Texts in English of the constitutions of the 20 Latin American republics, the United States and Canada.

Lazcano y Mazón, Andrés María. Constituciones políticas de América. La Habana, Cuba, Cultural, 1942. 2v. **L680**

Near and Middle East

Davis, Helen Miller. Constitutions, electoral laws, treaties of states in the Near and Middle East. Durham, N.C., Duke Univ. Pr., 1947. 446p. $5. **L681**

A documentary source book for the Near East covering Afghanistan, Egypt, Iran, Iraq, Lebanon, Palestine, Saudi Arabia, Syria, Transjordan, and Turkey. Includes constitutions, electoral laws and international treaties and conventions. A few of the documents are in French but most have been translated into English.

International organizations

Documents of international organizations; a selected bibliography. v. 1–3, Nov. 1947–Sept. 1950. Bost., World Peace Foundation, 1947–50. Quarterly. $2.50 per year. (75c per copy) **L682**

Lists a selection of the more important publications of the various major international organizations.

Harley, John Eugene. Documentary textbook on the United Nations. . . . Los Angeles, Center for International Understanding, 1947. 952p. $7 **L683**

Part 1 lists very briefly the most important documents in the history of international cooperation up to the League of Nations—from ancient China's League of Fourteen States (545 B.C.) to the London Naval Conference (1909). Part 2 covers the period from the League of Nations to the United Nations, including discussion and texts of documents.

Selected bibliography, p.835-912, includes periodical articles. Chronological outline of world peace proposals from 600 B.C. to 1946 A.D., p.913-925.

International organization, v.1- . Bost., World Peace Foundation, 1947- . $3.50 per year. Quarterly. **L684**

Includes summaries of activities, documents on international organizations and bibliographies of current materials.

United Nations Association yearbook, 1946- ed. by H. R. Madol. Lond., Hutchinson, 1945- . Annual. 25s. **L685**

1st v., 1946, had title *United Nations yearbook*.

Contains texts of the more important international and regional agreements, and information on the individual governments of the allied nations, with names of the members of the government and bibliography of books about the country.

Year book of world affairs, 1947- . pub. under the auspices of the London Institute of World Affairs. Lond., Stevens and Sons, 1947- . (1949, 20s.) **L686**

Survey articles, book reviews, etc.

DIRECTORIES

International congresses and conferences, 1840–1937; a union list of their publications available in libraries of the United States and Canada, ed. by Winifred Gregory under the auspices of the Bibliographical Society of America. . . . N.Y., Wilson, 1938. 229p. Service basis. **L687**

Running title: Union list of international congresses. "Committee: James Thayer Gerould, Chairman, Harry Miller Lydenberg, Milton Edward Lord."

Excludes diplomatic congresses and conferences and those held under the auspices of the League of Nations. Lists holdings in over 100 libraries.

Annuaire des organisations internationales. Yearbook of international organizations. 1948- . 1ere ed.- . Geneva, Société de l'Annuaire des Organisations Internationales, 1948- . (3. ed. 1950, $7) **L688**

In French and English.

Gives a general survey and detailed information about international organizations and associations, currently active. Alphabetical, analytical, geographical indexes are in both French and English, and there is also an index of officers.

League of Nations. Handbook of international organizations (associations, bureaux, committees, etc.). Geneva, 1938. 491p. $3. **L689**

Classed arrangement with subject, alphabetical and geographical indexes.

Fairly detailed information giving when possible name in English and French, seat, date of founding, object, members, governing body, officers, finance, activities, historical survey, committees and conferences, official publications.

Savord, Ruth. American agencies interested in international affairs, ccmp. by Ruth Savord. Rev.

ed. N.Y., Council on Foreign Relations, 1948. 195p. $2.50. **L690**

First edition, 1931, dealt with approximately 100 organizations in its main list. This third edition treats over 300, usually giving name, address, director, definition, date founded, organization, finance, staff, activities, conditions of membership, publications, etc. Arranged alphabetically with subject and personnel indexes.

Includes a list of organizations that have changed their names, amalgamated with others, are dormant, or have discontinued their activities.

American Council of Learned Societies. Directory of organizations in America concerned with China, by Wilma Fairbank. Wash., Council, 1942. 116p. $1. **L691**

Gives information on the founding, activities, membership, income, publications, etc., of over 100 organizations.

Carnegie Endowment for International Peace. Division of International Law. Handbook of international organizations in the Americas, prepared by Ruth D. Masters and others. Wash., Endowment, 1945. 453p. (Its Pub.) $5. **L692**

Description of 109 international organizations which have their headquarters in the Western hemisphere. For each organization usually gives history, purpose and functions, membership, administration, meetings, publications and a brief bibliographical note.

LEAGUE OF NATIONS

Breycha-Vauthier, Arthur Carl von. Sources of information: A handbook on the publications of the League of Nations. Lond., Allen and Unwin; N.Y., Columbia Univ. Pr. [1939]. 118p. **L693**

Covers publications through December 1, 1938. Gives descriptions of a selection of publications of the League of Nations proper, as an introduction to all its publications.

Carroll, Marie Juliette. Key to League of Nations documents placed on public sale, 1920–1929. Bost., World Peace Foundation, 1930. 340p. **L694**

—— —— First supplement, 1930. Bost., 1931. 111p.

—— —— Second supplement, 1931. Bost., 1933. 127p.

—— —— Third supplement, 1932–1933. Bost., 1934. 107p.

—— —— Fourth supplement, 1934–1936. N.Y., Columbia Univ. Pr., 1936. 188p.

UNITED NATIONS

Arne, Sigrid. The United Nations primer. Rev. ed. N.Y., Farrar and Rinehart, 1948. 266p. $2.50; to colleges $1.85. **L695**

Discussions and texts of documents of the international conferences that preceded and led up to the organization of the United Nations.

The revised edition adds the Potsdam conference and the meeting of the Council of Foreign Ministers.

Goodrich, Leland Matthew and **Hambro, Edvard.** Charter of the United Nations; commentary and documents. 2d and rev. ed. Bost., World Peace Foundation, 1949. 710p. $4.75.   **L696**

Select bibliography, p.659-81.

United Nations. United Nations publications: Catalogue no.1- . Lake Success, N.Y., 1947- .
L697

Intended primarily as a sales catalog, listing publications with prices.

—— Yearbook of the United Nations, 1946/47- . Lake Success, N.Y., Dept. of Public Information, U.N., 1947- . $12.50; £4.   **L698**

Summarizes the activities and achievements of the United Nations. The first volume 1946/47 covers the origin and evolution of the United Nations, the first General Assembly; and the organization and work of subsidiary and allied organizations. Includes texts of documents, a selected bibliography and a "Who's who."

—— **Secretariat. Dept. of Public Information. Library Services.** Checklist of United Nations documents. Lake Success, N.Y., 1949- . **L699**

To be "a complete list of the documents issued by the organs of the United Nations," printed and mimeographed.

To be issued in parts, each one devoted to the documents of a particular organ, as follows: (1) General Assembly (and subsidiary organs); (2) Security Council (and subsidiary organs); (3) Atomic Energy Commission; (4) Trusteeship Council; (5) Economic and Social Council; (6) Functional Commissions of the Economic and Social Council; (7) Regional Economic Commissions of the Economic and Social Council; (8) Other bodies; (9) Conferences; (10) Narcotic Drugs Reports; (11) International Court of Justice; (12) Secretariat.

Every part will be issued in consecutive numbers, the initial numbers covering 1946-1949.

A very detailed indexing with information as to original publication and where documents were republished if they were. Detailed subject index.

To be continued by:

—— **Library. Documents Index Unit.** United Nations documents index, January 1950- : United Nations and specialized agencies documents and publications. Lake Success, N.Y., 1950- . v.1- . Monthly. $7.50 per yr. **L699a**

A checklist and an index, the index to be cumulated annually.

—— **Secretariat. Dept. of Public Information.** Everyman's United Nations. Introd. by Trygve Lie. N.Y., Funk & Wagnalls, in assoc. with United Nations World, 1948. 201p. pa. $1; lib. ed. $2.; pa. 7s. 6d.; lib. ed. 10s. 6d.   **L700**

A handbook in four parts: pt.1, discusses the organization of the United Nations; pt.2, its work, covering, political and security questions, economic and social questions, trusteeship questions, legal questions, administrative and budgetary questions, headquarters; pt.3, the specialized agencies, e.g., International Labor Organization (I.L.O.), Food and Agriculture Organization (F.A.O.), United Nations Educational, Scientific, and Cultural Organization (UNESCO), and many others; pt.4, Appendices, Roster of the United Nations, Selected bibliography, Addresses of U.N. Information Centers.

United Nations documents, 1941-1945. Lond. and N.Y., Royal Inst. of International Affairs, 1946. 271p. $3; 10s. 6d.   **L701**

Includes the texts of various documents "concerning the origin of the United Nations, its character and other international organizations formed in association with it down to the end of 1945," (*Pref.*) for example, the Declaration of solidarity of the United Nations, the Atlantic charter, the lend-lease agreements, the communiqués or reports of the Teheran, Cairo, Yalta, Berlin, and Moscow conferences, constitutions of international organizations, etc.

EDUCATION
General works
Guides

Alexander, Carter and **Burke, Arvid J.** How to locate educational information and data; an aid to quick utilization of the literature of education. 3d ed., rev. and enl. N.Y., Bureau of Publications, Teachers College, Columbia Univ., 1950. 441p. $4.50.   **L702**

1st ed. 1935; 2d ed. 1941.

This is a much revised and reorganized edition, arranged to be used as a textbook for individual or class study. In two main sections: pt.1, Basic techniques of library utilization; pt.2, Special applications of library utilization techniques. The first covers such subjects as procedures for library searching, the card catalog, locating books and periodicals, using the *Education index* (L716), making a bibliography, note-taking, etc.; the second takes up reference books, evaluation of books, government documents, biographical information, quotations, statistics and statistical methodology, etc.

The "Library experiences" consisting of questions appended to each chapter were originally published in a separate volume but are now incorporated with the pertinent material.

Brickman, William W. Guide to research in educational history. N.Y., New York Univ., Bookstore, 1949. 220p. $2.75.   **L703**

A manual dealing with methods and procedures, including the search for source materials, aids in the writing of history, applying the historical method to research in education, note-taking and documentation, presentation evaluation, etc.

Bibliography

Monroe, Walter Scott and **Shores, Louis.** Bibliographies and summaries in education to July 1935; a catalog of more than 4000 annotated bibliographies and summaries listed under author and subject in one alphabet. N.Y., Wilson, 1936. 470p. $4.75. **L704**

Die erziehungswissenschaftliche Forschung; pädagogische Gesamtbibliographie . . . hrsg. von Arthur Hoffmann. Erfurt, Stenger, 1926–43. Hft. 1-36. Irregular. **L705**

A quarterly bibliography, arranged by classes. Includes analytics to periodicals, Festschriften, etc., and books. Has full classification tables at beginning of each issue but is not indexed.

Smith, Henry Lester and **Painter, William Isaac.** Bibliography of literature on education in countries other than the United States of America. Bloomington, Ind., Bureau of Cooperative Research, Indiana University, 1937. 341p. (Bull. of the School of Education, Indiana Univ. v. 13, no.2) **L706**

An annotated bibliography of book and periodical material on foreign education, published Jan. 1, 1925–Dec. 31, 1936.

U. S. Office of Education. Index to the Reports of the Commissioner of Education: 1867–1907. Wash., Govt. Prt. Off., 1909. 103p. (Bull., 1909, no.7.) 10c. **L707**

—— List of publications, 1867–1910. Wash., Govt. Prt. Off., 1910. 55p. (Bull., 1910, no.3) Repr. 1940. 10c. **L708**

—— List of publications, 1910–1936; including those of the former Federal Board for Vocational Education for 1917–1933, with author and subject indexes. Wash., Govt. Prt. Off., 1937. 158p. (Bull., 1937, no.22) **L708a**

Buros, Oscar Krisen. Mental measurements yearbook, v.3, 1940–47. New Brunswick, N.J., Rutgers Univ. Pr., 1949. 1047p. $12.50. **L709**

v.1, 1938; v.2, 1940. Title varies.
Includes sections "Tests and reviews" and "Books and reviews." The first lists all commercially available tests with reviews written by authorities representing different viewpoints. Covers educational, psychological, and vocational tests.

Educational Press Association of America. America's educational press: A classified list of educational publications issued in the U.S. with a listing of foreign journals. Wash., Assoc., 1926- . Annual. (1948, 75c) **L710**

Reprint of the list published each year in its *Yearbook*.

Elementary teachers guide to free curriculum materials, ed. by John Guy Fowlkes and Donald A. Morgan. 1st ed. 1944- . Randolph, Wis., Educators Progress Service, 1944- . $4.50. Annual. **L711**

Arranged by curricular field with source index.

Schweizerische Philosophische Gesellschaft. Bibliographie der philosophischen, psychologischen und pädagogischen Literatur . . . 1900–1940, 1941–44. Basel, 1944–45. **L711a**

For full record *see* H10.

DISSERTATIONS

Gray, Ruth A. Doctors' theses in education; a list of 797 theses deposited with the Office of Education and available for loan. Wash., Govt. Prt. Off., 1935. 69p. (U.S. Office of Educ. Pamphlet no.60) 10c. **L712**

Monroe, Walter S. Ten years of educational research, 1918–27. Urbana, Ill., Univ. of Illinois, 1928. 367p. (Univ. of Ill. Bureau of Educ. Research. Bull. no.42, Aug. 1928) **L713**

U. S. Office of Education. Library. Bibliography of research studies in education, 1926/27–1939/40. Prepared in the Library Division, Office of Education. Wash., Govt. Prt. Off., 1929–42. v.1-14. Annual. (U.S. Bureau of Education. Bulletin) Price varies, 35c-50c. **L714**

Discontinued during World War II.
Lists doctors' dissertations, masters' essays and other research studies. A classed list with institution, author and subject indexes.

In preparation

Doctors' dissertations under way in education, comp. by Carter V. Good, in *Journal of educational research,* 1931–1946 (January issue); in *The Phi Delta Kappan,* 1947- . **L715**

Indexes and abstracts

Education index, Jan. 1929- ; a cumulative author and subject index to a selected list of educational periodicals, books and pamphlets. N.Y., Wilson, 1932- . Service basis. **L716**

Published monthly cumulating periodically throughout the year with annual and triennial cumulations (v.1-6 of the 3-yr. cumulations cover 1929–June 1947).

Indexes more than 150 periodicals varying somewhat from volume to volume, and adds many references to pamphlets, books and analytics in books and society transactions. Articles in general are indexed under both author and subject or subjects, except that (1) book reviews are indexed only under that heading and (2) poems are listed only under word *poems* unless the author is very well known.

National Research Council. Committee on Child Development. Child development abstracts and bibliography. 1927- . Wash., Council, 1927- . Bimonthly. **L717**

Subject arrangement. Each issue has an author index. Cumulates annually with author and general subject indexes.

See also Nutrition abstracts (P359).

Encyclopedias, dictionaries, and handbooks

Münster. Deutsches Institut für Wissenschaftliche Pädagogik. Lexikon der Pädagogik der Gegenwart. Freiburg im Br., Herder, 1930–32. 2v. **L718**

Long signed articles with bibliographies.

Dizionario delle scienze pedagogiche; opera di consultazione pratica con un indice sistemático. Direttore: Marchesini Giovanni. Milano, Soc. Ed. Libreria, 1929. 2v. **L719**

Signed articles, some biography but no bibliography.

Monroe, Walter Scott. Encyclopedia of educational research. Rev. ed. N.Y., Macmillan, 1950. 1520p. **L720**

Not an encyclopedia in the usual sense but a critical and evaluative synthesis of the literature of educational research arranged alphabetically by subject. Particularly useful for its fairly long selective bibliographies. Articles are signed by specialists. This edition has been revised and enlarged. For most topics needed research is indicated. A 29-page subject-index on green paper has been inserted in the middle of the volume.

Supplemented informally by the current record in the *Review of educational research.*

Encyclopedia of modern education; ed., Harry N. Rivlin . . . associate ed., Herbert Schueler. . . . N.Y., Philosophical Library, 1943. 902p. $10. **L721**

Includes signed articles on educational trends, policies, and activities.

Useful as a first aid although information given frequently needs to be checked. The brief bibliographies are almost entirely to publications in the English language, often to secondary rather than primary sources.

Encyclopédie française. v.15, Éducation et instruction. Paris, Société de Gestion de l'Encyclopédie Française, 1939- . il. loose-leaf. **L722**

Survey articles on education in France and other countries, signed by specialists. Bio-bibliographical list of collaborators; Bibliographies; Indexes.

For description of full set *see* D31.

Good, Carter Victor. Dictionary of education, prepared under the auspices of Phi Delta Kappa. 1st ed. N.Y. and Lond., McGraw-Hill, 1945. 495p. (McGraw-Hill ser. in education) $4. **L723**

A much-needed, scholarly dictionary defining some 16,000 educational terms and words that have special meaning in the educational field. Has omitted items of an encyclopedic nature such as persons, institutions, school systems, organizations, publications and standard tests. Over 100 specialists who served as "coordinators" selected and wrote definitions for the terms included, which were then evaluated by some 100 reviewing committees in order to get as standardized practice as possible. The list of coordinators, associates and reviewers with their official connections is given on p.xiii-xxxii.

Pronunciation is given for difficult words. Educational terms used in foreign countries are grouped at the end of the book: Canada, p.458-64; England, p.465-73; France, p.474-78; Germany, p.479-84; Italy, p.485-95.

Handbook of adult education in the United States, comp. under the auspices of the Institute of Adult Education, Teachers College, Columbia University, with the cooperation of the American Association for Adult Education. Mary L. Ely, ed. 3d ed. N.Y., Inst. of Adult Educ., 1948. 555p. $5. **L724**

Survey articles by specialists on various aspects and areas of adult education, p.1-302; Notes on representative organizational programs, p.303-514; Suggested supplementary reading p.515-28.

The directory information of organizational agencies is particularly helpful.

International Federation of University Women. Lexique international des termes universitaires. [Paris] Fédération Internationale des Femmes Diplômées des Universités, 1939. 755p. **L725**

Title on cover: International glossary of academic terms.

"Avant-propos" signed: M. O. Monod, présidente de la Commission du Lexique des Termes Universitaires de la Fédération Internationale des Femmes Diplômées des Universités.

Explains in French and English, but does not translate, the official titles and technical terms used by the various universities of the world. Arranged by country with an alphabetical index to terms. South America and the Far East are not included. Also omits, because lists were not received, Greece, Portugal and Spain.

Kalashnikov, A. G. and **Epstein, M. S.** Pedagogicheskaĭa entsiklopediĭa. Moskva, Rabotnik Prosveshcheniĭa, 1927–29. 3v. **L726**

Monroe, Paul. Cyclopedia of education, ed. by Paul Monroe, with the assistance of departmental editors and more than 1000 individual contributors. N.Y., Macmillan, 1911–13. 5v. il. o.p. **L727**

Excellent when issued, now somewhat out of date. Has signed articles by specialists, good bibliographies and excellent illustrations, some in color. The scope of the work is general, including education in all countries and all periods, but American subjects receive somewhat fuller treatment than foreign topics. Analytical index in volume 5 groups articles by larger subjects than those used in main alphabet.

Psykologisk pedagogisk uppslagsbok. Stockholm, Natur och Kultur, 1943–46. 3v. and Suppl.-och Registerbd. **L728**

Long signed articles with bibliographies. Contains biography including living persons. The supplement volume includes a Svensk-Engelsk-Fransk-Tysk Ordlista.

Schwartz, Hermann. Pädagogisches Lexikon; in Verbindung mit der Gesellschaft für evangelische Pädagogik und unter Mitwirkung zahlreicher Fachmänner. . . . Bielefeld und Leipzig, Velhagen, 1928–31. 4v. **L729**

v.1-4, A-Z; Nachträge, A-Z, v.4, col. 1259-1504.

Watson, Foster. Encyclopaedia and dictionary of education . . . principles and practice . . . types of teaching institutions and educational systems throughout the world. Lond., Pitman, 1921–22. 4v. il. **L730**

General in scope, but most useful for British subjects, as they are treated with much greater fullness. Rather popular in treatment, longer articles are signed, brief bibliographies often given without any dates of publication; includes considerable biography and many illustrations.

Annuals

Annuaire international de l'éducation et de l'enseignement, 1933- . Genève, Bur. International d'Éducation, 1933- . Annual. (Publications du Bureau International d'Éducation) (1948, 15fr.) **L731**

Publication suspended, 1940–45.
The 1948 issue surveys current educational conditions in 43 countries, preceded by a general survey of the principal events in education in the school year 1947/48. Issued jointly by UNESCO and the International Bureau of Education and published also in English as *International yearbook of education.*

Teachers College. International Institute. Educational yearbook of the International Institute of Teachers College, Columbia University, 1924–44. Ed. by I. L. Kandel. N.Y., Macmillan, 1925–27; Teachers College, 1928–44. 20v. **L732**

Contains articles on the various national systems, activities, organizations, problems, developments, etc., arranged by countries. Each volume includes some special articles also. Beginning with 1930 most volumes are devoted to some particular aspect of education.

U. S. Office of Education. Biennial survey of education, 1916/18- . Wash., Govt. Prt. Off., 1919- . (Pub. biennially in its Bull.) **L733**

Woellner, Robert Carlton and **Wood, M. Aurilla.** Requirements for certification of teachers and administrators for elementary schools, secondary schools, junior colleges. v.1, 1935- . Chic., Univ. of Chic. Pr., 1935- . Annual. (1949/50, $3.50) **L733a**

Yearbook of education, 1932- . Lond., Evans Bros., 1931- . Annual. (1949, 63s.) **L734**

Suspended 1940–47.
Contains surveys of education in English-speaking countries and in the major European countries.

Directories

BIBLIOGRAPHY

Anderson, Ruth E. A bibliography of school and college information. (Repr. from Bull. of the National Assoc. of Secondary School Principals. Nov. 1948. p.90-115) 50c. **L735**

Lists educational directories in three groups: general; special — institutions which train for specific occupations (including correspondence schools); geographical — institutions within a specific area.

INTERNATIONAL

Index generalis; annuaire général des universités, grandes écoles, académies, archives, bibliothèques, instituts scientifiques, jardins botaniques et zoologiques, musées, observatoires, sociétés savantes, 1919–39. Paris, "Editions Spes," 1920–39. Annual. **L736**

Title varies; publisher varies. Publication suspended after 1939.
(1) Universities and schools of science and technology grouped by countries, giving for each institution name and address, brief general and statistical information, list of principal professors, etc.; (2) Observatories; (3) Libraries and archives; (4) Scientific institutes arranged by place; (5) Learned societies and academies arranged by subject; (6) Alphabetical index of personal names; (7) Index of countries; (8) Index of places.

League of Nations. International Institute of Intellectual Co-operation. Handbook of national centres of educational information. 2d ed. rev. and enl. Paris, 1938. 107p. **L737**

Also in French.

Minerva; Jahrbuch der gelehrten Welt, 1.-33. Jahrg., 1891/92–1913/14, 1920–38. Strassburg, Trübner, 1891–1914; Berlin, de Gruyter, 1920–38. v.1-33. Annual. **L738**

Suspended during World War I, and after 1938. A convenient and reliable list, arranged by names of towns giving under each town the names of the universities, colleges, technical schools, libraries, museums, and learned societies located there with information as to their income, size, names of principal officials, publications, etc. Index of personal names. Issues for 1927–30 are in three volumes each, volumes 1-2, main part, volume three, Index of names. Volumes 31-33, 1936–38, appear in two sections: 1. Abt.: Forschungsinstitute, Observatorien, Bibliotheken, Archive, Museen, Kommissionen, Gesellschaften (volume 33, Abt. 1, not published); 2. Abt.: Universitäten und Fachhochschulen.

Universities of the world outside U. S. A. ed. by M. M. Chambers. 1st ed. 1950. Wash., Amer. Council on Education, 1950. 924p. **L739**

On the same plan as *American universities and colleges* (L742). Treats more than 2000 institutions of higher education in more than 70 countries outside the United States.

Arranged by country. Each national section is headed by a brief introduction on the educational system of the country, "with especial attention to the duration and content of the secondary school courses." A bibliography is appended to each introduction usually including postwar titles, which for the most part are in the English language.

The descriptions of the individual institutions generally include: name, location, history, administration, calendar, housing, admission requirements, language of instruction, organization and staff, enrollment, degrees and diplomas, degrees conferred, grading system, student aid, foreign students, and faculty members, library, research facilities, buildings and grounds, finances, chief administrative officers.

There is an index by name of institutions but no personnel or subject indexes.

World of learning, 1947- . Lond., Europa Publications, 1947- . Annual. £3. **L740**

Continues the section on institutions of learning formerly published in *Europa* (L237) and *Orbis* (L239). Arranged alphabetically by country. Lists learned societies and research institutions, libraries, museums, universities, and other institutions of higher education. For most institutions gives date of founding, administrative officers, faculties, etc. Fullness of information varies.

Similar in many respects to *Minerva* (L738) but lacks the useful personnel index.

UNITED STATES

American Council on Education. American junior colleges, ed. by Jesse P. Bogue. 2d ed. Wash., Amer. Council on Educ., 1948. 537p. $6.50. **L741**

The first edition (1940) of this excellent handbook was compiled by W. C. Eells. This second edition is revised and expanded and published as a companion volume to *American universities and colleges,* 5th ed., (L742).

Contents: types of junior colleges; development; present status; accreditation and accreditation agencies. Lists 564 junior colleges giving for each the same type of information as given in *American universities and colleges.* Appendixes include American association of junior colleges; classified lists of junior colleges; list of junior colleges omitted from main part of work because of change of status, etc.

—— American universities and colleges; ed. by A. J. Brumbaugh. 5th ed. Wash., Amer. Council on Educ., 1948. 1054p. $8. **L742**

Previous editions published 1928, 1932, 1936, 1940.

The most generally useful educational directory for higher education presenting a summary of the present resources of American colleges and universities, in three main sections: (1) Survey articles on higher education in the United States, the college, university, professional school, graduate school, and the foreign student; (2) Alphabetical list of 820 colleges and universities of the accredited list of the American Council on Education, giving for each definite information about its history, organization, resources and equipment, requirements, staff, enrollment, degrees, fees, scholarships and fellowships, sessions, etc.; (3) Appendices, giving various lists of accredited colleges, educational associations, degree abbreviations, a general index and an institutional index.

American Association of Junior Colleges. Junior college directory. 1927- . Wash., Assoc., 1927- . Annual. (1949, $1) **L743**

Earlier issues were compiled by Walter C. Eells, later ones by Winifred R. Long.

A directory of all junior colleges, accredited and non-accredited, with very brief information as to name, location, administrative head, accreditation, type, enrollment, number on staff. Includes lists of junior college societies, organizations, etc.

College Entrance Examination Board. Annual handbook, 1941- . Terms of admission to member colleges. N.Y., Board, 1941- . Annual. $1.50. **L744**

For the member colleges, gives programs of study, admission requirements, expenses, financial aid, housing, etc.

Good, Carter Victor. A guide to colleges, universities, and professional schools in the United States. Wash., Amer. Council on Educ., 1945. 681p. $5. **L745**

Planned primarily to present essential information for the use of veterans of World War II. In tabular form it gives comprehensive information about 3389 institutions: 417 junior colleges, 719 liberal arts colleges, 318 teachers colleges and normal schools, and 431 extension divisions. Gives information on curricula offered, areas of specialization, admission of veterans, credit granted for work taken in armed services, special instruction for veterans, etc.; costs, health services, housing arrangements, student aid, physical education; special regulations as to smoking, drinking, dancing, etc.

Handbook of private schools for American boys and girls by Porter Sargent, 1915- . Bost., Sargent, 1915- . v.1- . il. $8. Annual. **L746**

Partial contents, 1948: (1) Special articles (these vary from year to year) Educational year in review; (2) Schools arranged by states and towns, giving name, address, and information about type, tuition, staff, enrollment, specialties, etc.; (3) Schools classified by type; (4) Supplementary lists, e.g., tutoring schools, professional and vocational schools, etc.; (5) Educational associations; (6) Directories of associations, agencies, bureaus, lecturers, advertising mediums, etc.; (7) Index of schools.

Institute of Women's Professional Relations. Director[ies] of colleges, universities and professional schools offering training in occupations concerned with. . . . New London, Conn., Inst., 1940- . **L747**

An unnumbered series of monographs published in various editions, including volumes on: . . . health. 1945. 346p. $1.50; . . . professions other than those concerned with health and the arts. 1945. 246p. $2; . . . business and industry. 1947. 645p. $2.50; . . . art in industry. 1940. 390p. $1.50.

A very useful series, usually giving for each institution such information as: name and location, administrative officer, entrance requirements, length of course and degrees granted, curricula, estimated expenses, placement of graduates, summer sessions, etc.

Lovejoy, Clarence Earle. Lovejoy's Complete guide to American colleges and universities. N.Y., Simon & Schuster, 1948. 158p. $1.49.   **L748**

First published, 1940, under title: *So you're going to college.*

Arranged alphabetically under states. Gives concise information on accreditation, type, enrollment, equipment, expenses, scholarships, degrees, etc.

Emphasizes how to choose a college; how to get scholarships, loans, etc.; how to work your way; cost of college education.

National Council of Business Schools. Directory of private business schools in the United States; a handbook for vocational advisors and guidance officers. 1st-3d ed. Wash., Council, 1943–48. Gratis.   **L749**

Includes proposed minimum standards of practice for private business schools, and a directory of private business schools arranged by state, giving in tabular form name and location of school, administrative head, date of founding, attendance, faculty, courses, and equipment.

National Council of Technical Schools. Approved technical institutes, comp. by J. S. Noffsinger. Wash., Council, 1945- . il. Annual. 25c.   **L750**

"A handbook of information for vocational counsellors to veterans, vocational guidance instructors in secondary schools, and all others interested in better technical institute type of instruction."

National Education Association of the U. S. NEA handbook and manual for local, state, and national associations, 1945/46- . Wash., Assoc., 1945- . v.1- . Annual. $1.   **L751**

Title and contents vary.

Includes lists and personnel of N.E.A. committees, commissions, and councils; N.E.A. departments and divisions; lists of publications; affiliated state and local associations, etc.

Patterson's American educational directory. Chic., Amer. Educ. Co., 1904- . v.1- . Annual. (1949, $7.50)   **L752**

(1) Educational systems of states, including schools and colleges, arranged first by states and then by towns; (2) Classified directory of schools; (3) Library directory; (4) College and university colors; (5) Alphabetical index of schools; (6) Educational associations; (7) Educational business directory.

A comprehensive list including in its geographical arrangement public and private schools, colleges, universities and other special schools. Includes officers of state, county and city educational systems, etc. Not always adequately revised and information is sometimes out of date.

U. S. Office of Education. Accredited higher institutions. Wash., Govt. Prt. Off., 1917- . (Its Bull., 1917, no.17; 1922, no.30; 1926, no.10; 1927, no.41; 1929, no.7; 1930, no.19; 1934, no.16; 1938, no.16; 1944, no.3-)   **L753**

—— Accredited secondary schools in the United States. Wash., Govt. Prt. Off., 1913- . (Its Bull., 1913, no.29; 1915, no.7; 1916, no.20; 1922, no.11; 1925, no.11; 1928, no.26; 1930, no.24; 1934, no.17, Suppl. 1937; 1939, no.2; 1942, no.3 [Suppl. to 1939, no.2]; 1944, no.4, 30c)   **L754**

—— Directory of secondary schools in the United States. Wash., Govt. Prt. Off., 1949- . v.1- . (Its Circular, no.250) $1.50.   **L755**

The first comprehensive list of secondary schools that the Office has published. In two parts: public schools, private schools. Each arranged alphabetically by state and under state by city. Shows accredited status, enrollment, staff, and other data. 496p.

—— Educational directory, 1912- . Wash., Govt. Prt. Off., 1912- . v.1- . Annual.   **L756**

A continuation of the directory published as a chapter of the annual report of the Commissioner of Education, 1895–1911, and as a *Bulletin* of the Office of Education, 1912–41.

A useful annual varying in format and contents. Since 1934 has been issued in four parts: (1) Federal and state education officers. 10c; (2) County and city school officers. 20c; (3) Higher education. 30c; (4) Educational associations and directories. 15c.

CANADA

Canada. Bureau of Statistics. Educational institutions of Canada. Ottawa, 1944. 93p. il.   **L757**

"Handbook of Canadian universities, colleges, and private schools for use in other countries."

pt.1, General information; pt.2, Courses of study in institutions of higher education, including liberal arts colleges and professional schools; pt.3, Directory of institutions.

Yearbook of Canadian universities. Annuaire des universités canadiennes, 1948- . Lond. Ont., 1948- . v.1- .   **L758**

Issued under the auspices of the National Conference of Canadian Universities.

Includes information on each university; e.g., administrative officers, degrees authorized, diplomas offered, admission requirements, registration, fees, scholarships and fellowships, etc.

CHINA

China Institute in America. Chinese colleges and universities. N.Y., Inst., 1941. 14p.   **L759**

List of 121 colleges and universities in China as of Dec. 1940.

FRANCE

Annuaire général de l'Université et de l'enseignement français . . . France, Tunisie, Maroc, avec les établissements d'enseignement des beaux-arts et la liste des établissements aux Colonies et à l'étranger. 1929/30–1939/40. Paris, L'Information Universitaire, 1930–40. v.1-11. Annual. **L760**

GERMANY

Handbuch der deutschen Wissenschaft. Berlin, Koetschau-Verlag, 1949. 2v. **L760a**

Volume 1 lists under place, universities, technical schools, schools of engineering, agriculture, government, theology and medicine with lists of faculties; learned societies, museums, libraries, etc., with titles of publications; over 300 serial publications with editors and addresses arranged by subject.

Volume 2 gives brief biographical information for some 6000 German scholars.

GREAT BRITAIN

Education authorities directory and annual, 1909- . Lond., School Govt. Pub. Co., 1909- . Annual. (v.47, 1949, 21s.) **L761**

Includes a large amount of official, institutional and personal directory material.

Girls' school year book (public schools). The official book of reference of the Association of Headmistresses. 1st- year, 1906- . Lond., Black, 1906- . v.1- . Annual. (v.43, 1949, 12s. 6d.) **L762**

Counterpart to the *Public and preparatory schools yearbook* (L763).

Public and preparatory schools year book. The official book of reference of the Headmasters' Conference and of the Association of Preparatory Schools. 1st- , 1889- . Lond., Black, 1889- . v.1- . Annual. (v.60, 1949, 15s.) **L763**

Title varies.

Gives descriptive information, teaching staffs, etc., of public and preparatory schools for boys.

Schools; the most complete directory of the schools in Great Britain, arranged in order of their counties and towns, including statistical information regarding recognized public schools for boys and a supplementary list of schools on the continent. v.1- . Lond., Truman and Knightley, 1924- . il. Annual. (v.26, 1949, 5s.) **L764**

Brief directory information for schools for boys and girls.

Yearbook of the universities of the Commonwealth. 1914- . Lond., Bell, 1914- . v.1- . Annual. **L765**

Publication suspended 1941–46.

Binder's title: Universities yearbook.

Through 1947, title was *Yearbook of the Universities of the Empire.* Title changed with 1948.

Gives fairly detailed information about the universities of the British Commonwealth including names of administrative officers and faculties, general information as to history, library, museums, requirements for admission and degrees, scholarships, etc. Index of names.

LATIN AMERICA

Pan American Union. Division of Intellectual Cooperation. Latin American universities; a directory. 1947. Wash., Union, 1947. 55p. 15c. **L766**

Brief listing only.

For more detailed information about each university see its series *Higher education in Latin America* which treats universities in: (1) Argentina. 1943; (2) Chile. 1944; (3) Colombia. 1945; (4) Cuba, Dominican Republic, Haiti. 1946. 50c; (5) Mexico. 1946; (6) Costa Rica, El Salvador, Guatemala, Honduras, Nicaragua, Panama. 1947. 50c; (7) Paraguay and Uruguay. 1947.

Biography

Cattell, Jaques. Directory of American scholars, a biographical directory. Lancaster, Pa., Science Pr., 1942. 928p. $10. **L767**

A companion volume to *American men of science* (N63) and *Leaders in education* (L768). This volume is devoted to scholars in the humanities and social sciences and follows the same plan as the others, giving concise sketches of some 12,000 scholars.

—— and **Ross, E. E.** Leaders in education, a biographical directory; 3d ed. Lancaster, Pa., Science Pr., 1948. 1208p. $15. **L768**

Contains short biographies of nearly 17,000 American educators, giving for each: name; title and address; place and date of birth; education and degrees; positions held; honors and society membership; activities; fields of specialization. This edition is thoroughly revised with many new biographies. Planned as a companion volume to *American men of science* (N63) and the *Directory of American scholars* (L767), some names previously included in *Leaders in education* have been transferred to one of these.

Who's who in American education; an illustrated biographical dictionary of eminent living educators of the United States, ed. by Robert C. Cook and Mary Alice Smith. v.1, 1928- . Nashville, Tenn., Who's Who in Amer. Educ., 1928- . il. Biennial. $10 ea. **L769**

The thirteenth edition, 1947–48, includes some 6000 biographies. Who's who type of information, including titles of published works. Many illustrations. While sometimes useful, is not always accurate and should be used with caution.

COLLEGE GRADUATES

United States

A library doing much reference work in American biography will do well to build up as comprehensive a collection as possible of biographical registers of American schools and colleges. While many alumni directories include only names and addresses, the biographical and historical registers frequently include more detailed information than can readily be found elsewhere. Two outstanding examples of these registers are listed below. (A list of such works to 1915, prepared by E. A. Cole, appeared in the *N.Y. genealogical and biographical record*, 46:51-57, Jan. 1915.)

Sibley, John Langdon. Biographical sketches of those who attended Harvard college with bibliographical and other notes. Bost., Mass. Historical Soc., 1873–1945. v.1-7. il. (In progress) **L770**

v.1-3 have title: *Biographical sketches of graduates of Harvard University.*
v.4-7 ed. by C. K. Shipton.
v.1-7, 1642–1725.

Dexter, Franklin Bowditch. Biographical sketches of the graduates of Yale college. N.Y., Holt, 1885–1912. 6v. **L771**

v.6 pub. by Yale University Press, and whole set now sold by that press.
v.1, 1701–45; v.2, 1745–63; v.3, 1763–78; v.4, 1778–92; v.5, 1792–1805; v.6, 1805–15.
Good biographies with full bibliographies of works by authors and references to authorities.

—— Biographical notices of graduates of Yale college, including those graduated in classes later than 1815, who are not commemorated in the annual obituary records. Issued as a supplement to the Obituary Record. New Haven, Conn., 1913. 411p. **L771a**

Covers the years 1815–84. Kept up to date by the following:

Yale University. Obituary record of graduates . . . 1859- . New Haven, Conn., 1860- . no.1- . Annual. **L771b**

Great Britain

Johnston, Marjorie and **Raven-Hart, H.** Bibliography of the registers (printed) of the universities, inns of court, colleges and schools of Great Britain and Ireland. (In London. University. Inst. of Historical Research. Bull. 9:19-30, 65-83, 154-70, June, Nov. 1931, Feb. 1932; 10:109-13, Nov. 1932) **L772**

A bibliography of registers, most of which include some biographical material. pt.1, Universities, Inns of Court, colleges, and other similar institutions; pt.2, Schools; Addenda and Corrigenda.

Only a few of the most comprehensive biographical records are listed below.

Aberdeen. University. Roll of the graduates of the University of Aberdeen, 1901–1925, with supplement, 1860–1900, comp. by Theodore Watt. Aberdeen, Univ. Pr., 1935. 952p. **L773**

Continues and supplements the *Roll of graduates of the University of Aberdeen, 1860–1900*, comp. by Col. William Johnston (Aberdeen, 1906. 687p.). Taken together, the two volumes furnish biographical data for about 8900 persons.

Cambridge. University. Alumni Cantabrigienses: A biographical list of all known students, graduates and holders of office at the University of Cambridge from the earliest times to 1900, comp. by John Venn and J. A. Venn. Camb., Univ. Pr., 1922–47. pt.1, v.1-4; pt.2, v.1-3. (In progress) **L774**

pt.1, From the earliest times to 1751. v.1-4, A-Z; pt.2, 1752–1900, v.1-3, A-Justamond.

Cooper, Charles Henry. Athenae Cantabrigienses, 1500–1611, by C. H. Cooper and Thompson Cooper. Camb., Deighton, 1858–61; Bowes, 1913. 3v. **L775**

v.1, 1500–85; v.2, 1586–1609; v.3, 1609–11; index to whole work by G. J. Gray.
A standard work containing many biographies, of which about 700 are on names not included in the *Dictionary of national biography* (S32).

Dublin. University. Trinity College. Alumni Dublinenses; a register of the students, graduates, professors and provosts of Trinity college . . . 1593–1860, ed. by the late George Dames Burtchaell and Thomas Ulick Sadleir. New ed. (with supplement). Dublin, Thom, 1935. 905p., 148p. **L776**

Eton College. The Eton college register, 1441–1698; alphabetically arranged and ed. with biographical notes by Sir Wasey Sterry. . . . Eton, Spottiswoode, Ballantyne, 1943. 414p. **L777**

—— —— 1698–1752, by Richard Arthur Austen-Leigh. 1927. 412p.

—— —— 1753–1790. 1921. 622p.

Glasgow. University. A roll of the graduates . . . from 31st December 1727 to 31st December 1897. With short biographical notes, comp. by W. Innes Addison. Glasgow, MacLehose, 1898. 695p. **L778**

Foster, Joseph. Alumni Oxonienses: The members of the University of Oxford, 1500–1714, their

parentage, birthplace and year of birth, with a record of their degrees. Ox., Parker, 1891–92. 4v.
L779

———— 1715–1886. Ox., Parker, 1887–88. 4v.

Wood, Anthony à. Athenae Oxonienses. An exact history of all the writers and bishops who have had their education in the University of Oxford. New ed. with additions and a continuation by Philip Bliss. Lond., Rivington, 1813–20. 5v.
L780

Audio-visual materials

See Recorded Music, p.356, for guides to records.

Blue book of 16mm. films. . . . Chic., Educational Screen, 1920- . v.1- . Annual. $1.50.
L781

Title varies: 1920–48, *1000 and one, the blue book of non-theatrical films.*
A useful, comprehensive list, classified under subject.

Educational film guide; formerly Educational film catalog. N.Y., Wilson, 1936- . Annual. (Standard catalog ser.) $4.
L782

Changed title with the 1945 annual edition.
Kept up to date by monthly supplements.
Lists films for use in classrooms, libraries, clubs, etc. In two parts: pt.1, alphabetical title and subject list; pt.2, classified and annotated list.

Educators guide to free films. 1st ed. 1941- . Randolph, Wis., Educators Progress Service, 1941- . Annual. $5.
L783

A guide to sources for free films, primarily for classroom use. Arranged by broad curricular area with subject and title indexes. The index to sources gives addresses, terms and conditions, and probable availability of loan.

Educators guide to free slidefilms. 1st ed.- . Randolph, Wis., Educators Progress Service, 1949- . Annual. $3.
L784

Arranged by broad curricular areas with subject and title indexes. The index to sources gives address and terms of loan.

Falconer, Vera M. Filmstrips; a descriptive index and users' guide. N.Y., McGraw-Hill, 1948. 572p. il.
L785

Lists filmstrips prior to 1947. For current record *see:*

Filmstrip guide, Sept. 1948- . N.Y., Wilson, 1948- . Annual. $3 per yr.
L786

Published monthly except July, August and September. Cumulates annually. Lists latest releases of filmstrips, stripfilms, slidefilms, and filmslides.

Guidance

❦ There are many books and pamphlets published on the choice of an occupation or vocation and there have been various bibliographies listing such material. The following are typical bibliographies in this field:

Forrester, Gertrude. Occupational pamphlets, an annotated bibliography. N.Y., Wilson, 1948. 354p. $2.50.
L787

A revised and enlarged edition of *Occupations, a selected list of pamphlets* (1946).
An annotated, priced list arranged by occupation.

Greenleaf, Walter James. Guide to occupational choice and training; suggestions, books, and materials for guidance programs. [Wash., 1947] 150p. (U.S. Office of Education. Vocational Division. Bull. no.236. Occupational information and guidance ser. no.15) 35c.
L788

National Association of Deans of Women. Guide to guidance; [v.1]- , a selected bibliography of [1938]- publications of interest to deans, counselors, advisers, teachers, and administrators. . . . Syracuse, N.Y., Syracuse Univ. Pr., 1939- . v.1- Annual. $1 ea.
L789

Subtitle and publisher vary.
Annotated classed list, with author and title index.

Laws

Huston, Wendell. School laws of the forty-eight states: Loose leaf services, state and federal supplements. Seattle, Wash., Huston, 1947. **L790**

Incomplete and sometimes inaccurate but a useful compilation.

Yearbook of school law, ed. by M. M. Chambers [and others]. Wash., Amer. Council on Educ., 1933–42. v.1-10. Annual.
L791

Includes digests of court decisions affecting schools, as well as feature articles. Indexed in the *Education index* (L716) and the *Index to legal periodicals* (L614).

Fellowships and scholarships

Feingold, S. Norman. Scholarships, fellowships and loans. 1st ed. Bost., Bellman Pub. Co., 1949. 254p. $6.
L792

Lists nearly 300 administering agencies giving name and address, qualifications for scholarships, fellowships and loans, funds available, special fields of interest and information, where to apply for information and to send application. Alphabetical index of administering agencies and names of scholarships, fellowships, and loans; index by vocational goals or fields of interest.
Scholarships made available by individual colleges and universities are not included.

Institute of Women's Professional Relations Fellowships and other aid for advanced work New London, Conn., 1940. 351p.
L793

Lists "all fellowships, scholarships, assistantships, and

special grants for professional or advanced work having a value of $250 or more for the academic year."

United Nations Educational, Scientific and Cultural Organization. Study abroad; International handbook: fellowships, scholarships and educational exchange. v.1, 1948- . Paris, UNESCO, 1948- . Annual. (Distributed by Columbia Univ. Pr., $1) **L794**

Gives details of available fellowships and scholarships for international study. Arranged by originating country and alphabetically by donor or administering agency. In tabular form gives name, field of study, where tenable, conditions and purpose, value, duration, number available, where to send application and date limit. Index by fields of study.

Academic costume

Baty, T. Academic colours. Tokio, Kenkyusha Pr., 1934. 172p. **L795**

Descriptions of the academic costumes worn in British universities with additional chapters on other countries. Includes a section on "Hoods classified according to degree and colour."

Stringer, E. W. Scobie. The degrees and hoods of the world's universities and colleges. Originally comp. by Frank W. Haycraft [4th ed.], completely rev. and enl. Cheshunt, Herts., Cheshunt Pr., 1948. 159p. il. 35s. **L796**

1st ed. 1923.

A useful guide to academic costume primarily for the British Empire. A list of the colors used by American universities is given but these are not included in the index by colors.

College colors

Snyder, Henry L. Our college colors. Kutztown, Pa., Kutztown Pub. Co., 1949. 260p. $3. **L797**

Gives the colors for each American college and university with date of adoption and brief history of the reason for the choice where ascertainable.

Fraternities

Baird, William Raimond. Baird's Manual of American college fraternities. 15th ed. Harold J. Baily, ed. Menasha, Wis., George Banta, 1949. 966p. il. $6.75. **L798**

A new edition of the standard manual of American college fraternities. First published, 1879. Gives a descriptive analysis with a detailed account of each fraternity. Includes men's and women's social and professional fraternities, honor societies and recognition societies.

LANGUAGE DICTIONARIES

❦ For a general survey of the whole field of language dictionaries consult the article "Dictionary" in the *Encyclopaedia Britannica*, 11th edition. This is valuable for its historical information and includes an extensive bibliography of dictionaries in many languages, which is now, of course, considerably out of date.

Dictionaries are the main sources for information about words, their spelling, pronunciation, meaning, derivation, etc. Theoretically the dictionary is concerned only with the word, not with the thing represented by the word, differing in this respect from the encyclopedia which gives information primarily about the thing. Practically, however, the large modern dictionary is very often encyclopedic and gives information about the thing as well as the word, thus combining the features of the two types of reference books. As the large English dictionary is the most familiar "family reference book," this encyclopedic feature has been continually strengthened by the addition of many special lists and excellent illustrations, until the best modern works of this sort can now be used for many more purposes than information about words. Dictionaries which contain many illustrative quotations can often be used to find or identify a quotation, thus supplementing the special dictionaries of quotations. The student of reference books should familiarize himself with the special features and supplementary lists of each of the great dictionaries if he is to make each of these books serve all the purposes that it can be made to serve.

Dictionaries should be purchased cautiously. Because they are expensive undertakings, unscrupulous publishers sometimes employ incompetent editors or insufficient help or offer a reprint of an old work with little or no revision. Furthermore, devious means are employed to hide such practices. The prospective purchaser, therefore, should use the same care in examining a dictionary before purchase as is recommended in the case of encyclopedias.

In studying a dictionary the student should follow the general directions for examining reference books, and should also note carefully the following points:

1. Period of the language covered
2. Vocabulary
   a) Extent and how counted—is the count by main words only or does it include all derived and compound forms, etc.?
   b) Special elements included, e.g., slang, dialect, obsolete forms, scientific or technical terms, etc.
3. Treatment of each word, with reference to:
   a) Spelling, including plurals, verb tenses, participles
   b) Syllabication and hyphenization
   c) Pronunciation—how marked; is the system accurate and intelligible?
   d) Etymology
   e) History—are changes in meaning, usage, etc., marked and *dated*?
   f) Definition—is it clear, correct, adequate?
   g) Illustrative quotations—are they given freely, with exact reference, and in chronological order and dated so that the history can be traced?
   h) Standard and usage—is a word indicated as obsolete, colloquial, etc.?
   i) Encyclopedic information
   j) Synonyms and antonyms
4. Illustrations
5. Abbreviations—to what extent included, and how, i.e., in separate list or in main alphabet?
6. Special types of words included in addition to the ordinary vocabulary, i.e., Christian names, foreign phrases, biographical lists, geographical names, etc. To what extent are these included, and where—in main alphabet or in appended lists?
7. Special features

216

ENGLISH LANGUAGE

❧ Dictionaries of the English language have been divided rather arbitrarily, according to their place of compilation and publication, into American and English dictionaries. Of course both types cover the same field, the English language as a whole, and conform, in the main, to the same standards, but there are certain minor differences. In cases where there are known differences in spelling, pronunciation, meaning, etc., each dictionary will generally give both usages, but the English work will prefer the English usage or form, while the American work will prefer the American. An American dictionary generally includes more Americanisms, an English dictionary, more local English terms, colonial words, etc.

Murray, *Sir* **James A. H.** Evolution of English lexicography. Ox., Univ. Pr., 1901. 51p. **M1**

An interesting and authoritative survey of the history and development of the English dictionary.

Starnes, DeWitt Talmage and **Noyes, Gertrude Elizabeth.** The English dictionary from Cawdrey to Johnson, 1604–1755. Chapel Hill, Univ. of North Carolina Pr., 1946. 299p. il. $3.50. **M2**

Includes a bibliography and census of copies in American libraries of all known editions, p.228-41.

Mathews, Mitford McLeod. A survey of English dictionaries. Ox., Univ. Pr.; Lond., Milford, 1933. 123p. il. 5s. **M3**

American

Century dictionary and cyclopedia with a new atlas of the world. N.Y., Century [c1911]. 12v. il. o.p. **M4**

1st ed. 1889–91, 6v., with two supplementary volumes, Cyclopedia of names, 1894, and Atlas, 1897; partially revised from time to time and plates altered; but never entirely revised and reset. Revisions to note especially are: (1) edition of 1901, 10v., v.1-8, Dictionary, v.9, Names, v.10, Atlas; (2) two supplementary volumes published 1909, numbered v.11-12 to continue the 1901 edition and containing about 100,000 new words, senses, and phrases and a 92-page supplement to the Cyclopedia of names; (3) the 1911 edition, 12v.

v.1-10, Dictionary; v.11, Cyclopedia of names; v.12, Atlas.

Printed from the same plates as the earlier editions but with alterations in the plates to include a considerable amount of new material. In addition there is bound at the end of each volume the corresponding portion of the alphabet from the two supplementary volumes published 1909, making two alphabets in each volume linked together by cross references.

The most comprehensive and detailed American dictionary and the best example of the encyclopedic type. Its special features were its free inclusion and careful treatment of the technical terms of the various sciences, arts, trades and professions, its excellent illustrations and plates, and, particularly, the large amount of encyclopedic material included. Now out of date for current usage but still useful for many types of questions.

New century dictionary of the English language, based on matter selected from the original Century dictionary and entirely rewritten, with the addition of a great amount of new material. . . . ed. by H. G. Emery and K. G. Brewster. N. Y., Appleton-Century, 1948. 2v. 2798p. il. $25. **M5**

Supplements: Synonyms and antonyms, Abbreviations, Business terms, Foreign words and phrases, Proper names exclusive of biography and geography, Biographical names, Geographical names.

Not a revision of the *Century dictionary*, but a much smaller work including a smaller vocabulary selected from the *Century* with new definitions and a different selection of illustrative quotations. Over 160,000 entries with over 12,000 illustrative quotations.

Funk and Wagnalls New standard dictionary of the English language, prepared by more than 380 specialists and other scholars under the supervision of I. K. Funk, Calvin Thomas, F. H. Vizetelly. N.Y., Funk & Wagnalls, 1947. 2814p. il. $25. **M6**

1st ed. 1893 had title *Standard dictionary*; a new ed., 1901, had 85 pages of addenda containing 13,000 new words but was otherwise printed from the same plates as the first ed.; the *New standard*, first published in 1913, is a thorough revision of the 1893 edition, reset and printed from new plates throughout. Later issues or reprints of this edition show changes in the plates, insertion of new words, etc.; e.g., the issues published since World War II include some new words inserted in their proper alphabetical place by cutting out or compressing old material. Essentially, however, there has been no thorough revision since 1913.

Contents: (1) Dictionary, including in one alphabet all ordinary dictionary words and also the various proper names, i.e., biographical, geographical, mythological, Biblical, etc.; (2) Appendix: Disputed pronunciations, Rules for simplified spelling, Foreign words and phrases, Statistics of population.

A serviceable one-volume work. Its special feature is emphasis upon current information, i.e., present-day meaning, pronunciation, spelling, and the subordination of the historical to the current information. Full vocabulary, about 450,000 words including 65,000 proper names, aims to include all live words of the language in standard speech and literature of the day and terms commonly used dialectically by large numbers of people in different parts of the English-speaking world. Prefers simpler spelling and when several forms are used by authorities indicates those used by American Philological Association, American Spelling Reform Association, and Simplified Spelling Board. Marks syllabication and hyphenated words plainly, using single hyphen for the first and double hyphen for the second; indicates pronunciation by two respellings (1) by the revised scientific alphabet, N.E.A., and (2) by the ordinary respelling used in textbooks. Gives antonyms as well as synonyms. Contains considerable encyclopedic information and many illustrations and good colored plates.

Webster's New international dictionary of the English language. 2d ed., unabridged . . . a Merriam-Webster. William Allan Neilson, ed.-in-chief; Thomas A. Knott, general ed.; Paul W. Carhart, managing ed. Springfield, Mass., Merriam, 1950. cxxxii, 3214p. il. $30.   **M7**

1st ed. of *Webster's Dictionary*, 1828; the *New international*, 1909; 2d ed. of *New international*, 1934, revised throughout and reset. Later printings show some changes and corrections in plates, mainly in spelling, punctuation, or pronunciation, but in some cases adding new information or revising the treatment. In 1939 a "New words" section was added at the front of the book, p.xcvii-civ; in 1945, this section was revised and expanded, p.xcvii-cxii; in 1950, this section is called "Addenda section" and is expanded by 20 pages, p.xcvii-cxxxii. It includes several thousand new words or words used with new or different meanings, including scientific and technical terms, slang, abbreviations, etc. The biographical section has also been revised and enlarged, adding four pages and about 1500 names, so that the section now totals about 15,000 names.

Contents: (1) Dictionary, including in the same list both the usual dictionary words and also foreign phrases, abbreviations, proverbs, noted names of fiction and all proper names except those in the biographical and geographical lists; (2) Appendix: (a) Abbreviations, (b) Arbitrary signs and symbols, (c) Forms of address, (d) Pronouncing gazetteer, (e) Pronouncing biographical dictionary. In addition to the foregoing the "Reference history" edition contains a separately paged supplement "Reference history of the world" by A. B. Hart, c1934.

The oldest and most famous American dictionary, well-rounded, with no marked specialization or bias, ably edited, reliable, and noted particularly for the clearness of its definitions. The most used, and for general purposes the most useful, of the one-volume dictionaries. A special feature introduced in the 1909 edition and continued in the second edition (1934) is the divided page, containing in the upper part the main words of the language and in the lower part in finer print various minor words, e.g., different kinds of cross references, reformed spellings, such Biblical proper names as are entered only to show pronunciation, a few rare obsolete words and a few extremely rare words, and foreign language quotations, proverbs and longer phrases. Other special points to remember in using the work are: definitions given in historical sequence, pronunciation indicated by Webster phonetic alphabet (not by the International phonetic), hyphenization indicated by single hyphen, division of syllables by either accent or centered period; vocabulary claimed is "600,000 vocabulary entries."

Desk dictionaries

❧ Good desk dictionaries are needed both in libraries and in homes, and librarians should know the main features and merits of the various works available. The three listed below are planned for much the same kind of use and include comparable vocabularies. All have been issued in postwar editions and include new words and meanings developed during the war. The Webster *New Collegiate*

(M10) and the Funk and Wagnalls *New college standard* (M9) are both based on unabridged dictionaries; the *American college* (M8) is a completely new work. All are authoritative, all give clear, concise definitions, etymologies, synonyms, antonyms, etc., and all have small line drawings.

General arrangement in each differs, as does the arrangement under individual entry, and systems of indicating pronunciation vary. Some of the particular features and special points of each are noted below. Fuller discussion will be found in *Subscription books bulletin* (A554).

Several smaller abridgements are published by Funk and Wagnalls in its Standard Dictionary Series and Random House has issued two abridgements of the *American college dictionary*.

American college dictionary, ed. by Clarence L. Barnhart, with the assistance of 355 authorities and specialists. N.Y., Random House, 1947. 1432p. il. $5; thumb indexed $6.   **M8**

A completely new desk-size dictionary designed to provide an accurate guide to current usage. All entries are in one alphabet including proper names of persons and places, abbreviations, inflected forms of words in which the stem is changed, etc. Pronunciation is indicated by the "traditional textbook key." Definitions are given in reverse chronological order, modern usage first. Etymologies follow.

The typography is particularly good.

Funk and Wagnalls New college standard dictionary of the English language. Em′·pha·type ed. Charles Earle Funk, ed. N.Y., Funk & Wagnalls, 1947. 1404p. il. $5.50; thumb indexed $6.   **M9**

1st ed. 1922. Based on the *New standard dictionary* (M6), the particular feature of this edition is its new method of indicating pronunciation by underlining stressed syllables. Contains some 145,000 entries. Proper names are included in the main alphabet. Appendixes give populations of places in the United States and Canada, and foreign places; in many cases places are listed both in the main alphabet for description and location and in the appendix for population, with no cross references between.

Abbreviations are given in an appendix.

Definitions show current usage. Etymologies are given after the definitions.

Webster's New collegiate dictionary: a Merriam-Webster based on Webster's New international dictionary. 2d ed. Springfield, Mass., Merriam, 1949. 1209p. il. $5; thumb indexed $6.   **M10**

1st ed. 1898, 5th ed. 1936. This new edition including more than 125,000 entries has been thoroughly revised and reset, new words, particularly in the scientific and technical fields added, definitions rewritten when necessary, the biographical and gazetteer sections expanded etc.

Pronunciation is indicated by a Merriam-Webster phonetic alphabet. Etymologies and definitions follow the order used in the *New international* (M7), i.e., etymologies first, definitions in chronological order. Foreign words and phrases are included in the main alphabet.

Appendixes include: Abbreviations; Arbitrary signs and symbols; Biographical names (over 5000 names with pronunciation, dates, and identifying phrase); Pronouncing gazetteer containing more than 10,000 names of places; Colleges and universities in the United States and Canada; Pronouncing vocabulary of common English given names; Vocabulary of rhymes; Orthography, Punctuation.

English

Murray, *Sir* **James Augustus Henry.** New English dictionary on historical principles; founded mainly on materials collected by the Philological Society. Ox., Clarendon Pr., 1888–1933. 10v. and suppl. **M11**

v.1-10, A-Z; Supplementary volume: Historical introduction, p.vii-xxvi; Supplement A-K, 542p., L-Z, 325p.; List of spurious words, p.327-30; Bibliography, i.e., list of books most commonly quoted in the Dictionary, 91p.

Known variously as *Murray's Dictionary,* the *New English dictionary,* and the *Oxford dictionary.* Often cited as *N.E.D.,* or *O.E.D.* For history of the work *see* Suppl. p.vii-xxvi.

For "corrected reissue" of the *New English dictionary* see *Oxford English dictionary* (M12).

The great dictionary of the language, compiled on a different plan from any of the other standard English dictionaries and serving a different purpose. It is based upon the application of the historical method to the life and use of words and its purpose is to show the history of every word included from the date of its introduction into the language, showing differences in meaning, spelling, pronunciation, usage, etc., at different periods of the last 800 years, and supporting such information by numerous quotations from the works of more than 5000 authors of all periods, including all writers whatever before the sixteenth century and as many as possible of the important writers since then. The vocabulary is very full, and is intended to include all words now in use or known to have been in use since 1150, excluding only words which had become obsolete by 1150. Within these chronological limits, aims to include: (1) all common words of speech and literature, and all words that approach these in character, the limits being extended further into science and philosophy than into slang and cant; (2) in scientific and technical terminology, all words English in form except those of which an explanation would be intelligible only to a specialist, and such words not English in form as are in general use or belong to the more familiar language of science; (3) dialectal words before 1500, omitting dialectal words after that date except when they continue the history of a word once in general use, illustrate the history of a literary word or have a literary currency. Words included are classified as (1) main words, (2) subordinate words, (3) combinations; information for all main words is entered under the current modern or most usual spelling, or if obsolete under most typical later spelling, with cross references from all other forms. Information given about each main word is very full and includes: (1) identification, with (a) usual or typical spelling, (b) pronunciation indicated by respelling in an amplified alphabet or in

case of obsolete words by marking of stress only, (c) grammatical designation, (d) specifications, e.g., musical term, etc., (e) status, if peculiar, e.g., obsolete, archaic, etc., (f) earlier spelling, (g) inflexions; (2) morphology, including derivation, subsequent form history, etc.; (3) signification, arranged in groups and historically, with marking of obsolete senses, erroneous uses, etc.; (4) quotations, arranged chronologically to illustrate each sense of a word, about one quotation for each century, given with exact reference. The complete work has a total vocabulary of 414,825 words and includes 1,827,306 quotations.

The most important use of this dictionary is for historical information about a word but it has many other secondary uses; e.g., while not intentionally encyclopedic it has a good deal of encyclopedic information including some not given in other dictionaries, and while not specializing in slang it does include many colloquial and slang words, Americanisms, etc., and where such words are included the information is often better than in the special slang dictionaries.

The supplementary volume is a partial, not a complete, supplement, in that it does not comprise all supplementary material collected since the publication of the first parts of the original work but is limited in the main to new words and senses of the past 50 years with inclusion also of (1) other items of modern origin and currency omitted in the main work, (2) earlier evidence of American uses, (3) some correction or amplification of previous definitions to bring the work into line with recent research. Recent words added include scientific and technical terms, colloquialisms and slang—American, British and colonial—and a larger proportion of proper names than in the original work.

The *New English dictionary,* large and comprehensive though it is, is necessarily selective, and could not include all words for the whole period covered or even all material that was collected during the compilation of the work. Since the completion of that dictionary in 1928, four period and regional dictionaries, on the same large plan, have either been published or are in course of publication, to supplement the *New English dictionary* by including words, uses, illustrations, etc., which could not be included in that dictionary. These are:

Dictionary of middle English, started under the editorship of Professor Clark S. Northup at Cornell University, continued under Professor Samuel Moore and Dr. Thomas A. Knott at the University of Michigan and now being edited there by Prof. Hans Kurath.

Dictionary of American English, under the editorship of Sir William Alexander Craigie (Univ. of Chic. Pr., 1936–44. 4v.) (M60).

Dictionary of the older Scottish tongue, edited by Sir William Alexander Craigie (M67).

Scottish national dictionary under the editorship of William Grant (M71).

—— **Oxford English dictionary,** being a corrected re-issue, with an introduction, supplement and bibliography, of A New English dictionary on historical principles, founded mainly on the materials collected by the Philological Society and ed. by James A. H. Murray, Henry Bradley, W. A. Craigie, C. T. Onions. Ox., Clarendon Pr., 1933. 12v. and suppl. $175 per set. **M12**

A reprint, on thinner paper and with somewhat smaller margins, from the plates of the original edition with the correction of such typographical errors as have been discovered.

In 1895 "a new name for the Dictionary was introduced, though no change was made on the title-page. On the cover of the section containing *Deceit to Deject* . . . above the title, appeared for the first time the designation 'The Oxford English Dictionary,' which was repeated on every section and part issued after 1 July of that year. The new name being more distinctive than the old has steadily come more and more into use, and the abbreviation O.E.D. tends to supplant N.E.D., although the latter is still frequently employed. A third abbreviation, H.E.D. (with H for Historical), though employed for a number of years in *Notes and Queries,* never attained general currency. Popularly the work is often referred to as Murray's, and the Philological Society, by a natural tradition, has continued to call it 'the Society's Dictionary.' "—*Historical Introd.,* p.xx.

—— **Shorter Oxford English dictionary** on historical principles; prepared by W. Little, H. W. Fowler, J. Coulson . . . rev. and ed. by C. T. Onions. 2d ed. Ox., Clarendon Pr., 1936. 2v. $35. **M13**

First published February 1933; this revised reprint shows a number of small corrections, changes and additions.

An authorized abridgment of the *New English dictionary,* which, while in the main an abridgment, also includes some additional material, especially new words too recent to have been included in the original work or older words omitted there, and also some later illustrative quotations. Important therefore in the library which already has the larger work, as well as in the small library which has not been able to afford the complete *Oxford dictionary.*

"The aim of this Dictionary is to present in miniature all the features of the principal work. It is designed to embrace not only the literary and colloquial English of the present day together with such technical and scientific terms as are most frequently met with . . . but also a considerable proportion of obsolete, archaic and dialectal words and uses."—*Pref.*

Fowler, Henry Watson and **Fowler, F. G.** Concise Oxford dictionary of current English, adapted from the Oxford dictionary. 3d ed., rev. by H. W. Fowler and H. G. LeMesurier. Ox., Clarendon Pr., 1934. 1524p. $4.50. **M14**

Often cited as *C.O.D.*

Includes words in current use or preserved in much used quotations or proverbs, scientific and technical terms that are current in general speech but are not purely learned terms, and many colloquial, facetious, slang and vulgar expressions. An excellent small desk dictionary, based upon the work done for the *New English dictionary.*

Pocket Oxford dictionaries are also issued in both English and American editions.

Abbreviations

🍃 Lists of abbreviations are important in most libraries. Some of the separately compiled lists follow. Abbreviations are also included freely in the *Century dictionary* (M4) and the *New standard* (M6) in their alphabetical places and in the *Webster's New international* (M7) in one list under the heading Abbreviations. The lists in *Who's who* (S131) and *Who's who in America* (S40) are useful for the abbreviations of societies, academies, degrees, etc.

Allen, Edward Frank. Allen's Dictionary of abbreviations and symbols; over 6000 abbreviations and symbols commonly used in literature, science, art, education, business, politics, religion, engineering, industry, war. N.Y., Coward-McCann, 1946. 189p. $3.50. **M15**

Particularly strong in the business field. Includes more symbols than the following works.

Matthews, Cecily C. A dictionary of abbreviations, comprising all standard forms in commercial, social, legal, political, naval and military, and general use. Lond., Routledge, 1947. 232p. **M16**

In one alphabetical list with appendixes of scientific symbols. From the British point of view.

Partridge, Eric. A dictionary of abbreviations [3d ed. further rev. and enl.] Lond., Allen and Unwin [1949]. 114p. 7s. 6d. **M17**

First published in 1942.

A straight alphabetical arrangement. Includes both English and American abbreviations but is from the English point of view.

Shankle, George Earlie. Current abbreviations. N.Y., Wilson, 1945. 207p. $3. **M18**

The most comprehensive compilation, all in one alphabetical arrangement except that Greek letter fraternities are alphabetized at the end of the appropriate English letter according to the English spelling of the Greek initial.

Stephenson, Herbert John. Abbrevs. (A dictionary of abbreviations) N.Y., Macmillan, 1943. 126p. $2. **M19**

A general alphabetical list of abbreviations with special lists for the Books of the Bible, Shakespeare's works, Legal literature, Christian names, Geography, Months (in various languages), Principal American railroad companies, Symbols for chemical elements, Foreign monetary units, Federal agencies, etc.

Basic English

Ogden, Charles Kay. The general Basic English dictionary, giving more than 40,000 senses of over 20,000 words, in Basic English. . . . N.Y., Norton, 1942. 441p. il. $2.50. **M20**

Originally published in London, Evans Bros., 1940. The American edition adds, p.439-41, lists of Basic English words by form, such as Operations, 100; Things, 400 General, 200 Pictorial; Qualities, 100 General, 50 Opposites.

"For the use of learners of English. . . . Using only the 850 words of Basic . . . and fifty international words, which go with them, it gives a knowledge of over 20,000 English words, covering at least 40,000 separate senses and special word-groups. . . . Great care has been given to idioms."—*Note.*

Etymology

❧ For the etymology of the English language the best authority is Murray's *New English dictionary* (M11). Smaller works include:

Skeat, Walter William. Etymological dictionary of the English language. New ed., rev. and enl. [4th ed.] Ox., Clarendon Pr., 1910. 780p. $17.50. **M21**

Contents: (1) Dictionary; (2) Appendix: Lists of Prefixes, Suffixes, Homonyms, Doublets, Indogermanic roots, Distribution of words according to languages from which they are derived.

—— Concise etymological dictionary of the English language. New and cor. imp. Ox., Clarendon Pr., 1911. 663p. $4.25. **M22**

Schröer, Michael Martin Arnold. Englisches Handwörterbuch in genetischer Darstellung auf Grund der Etymologien und Bedeutungsentwicklungen, mit phonetischer Aussprachebezeichnung und Berücksichtigung des Amerikanischen und der Eigennamen, mitbearbeitet und hrsg. von P. L. Jaeger. Heidelberg, Carl Winter, 1937–41. Lfg. 1-6. RM. 2.25 per Lfg. (In progress) **M23**

Lfg. 1-6, A-edit.

Weekley, Ernest. Etymological dictionary of modern English. Lond., Murray; N.Y., Dutton, 1921. 1659 col. **M24**

Popular work, for the general reader rather than the specialist.

Idioms, usage, etc.

Fowler, Henry Watson. Dictionary of modern English usage. . . . Ox., Clarendon Pr., 1926. 742p. $4.50. **M25**

Horwill, Herbert William. Dictionary of modern American usage. 2d ed. Ox., Clarendon Pr., 1944. 360p. $4; 8s. 6d. **M26**

1st ed. 1935.
Not a dictionary of standard American usage, but a handbook, by an English writer, intended primarily to assist English visitors in America or English readers of American books and magazines by explaining words or phrases which have a meaning or use in the United States different from that in England. Includes about 300 main words.

Vizetelly, Francis Horace and **DeBekker, L. J.** Desk-book of idioms and idiomatic phrases in English speech and literature. N.Y., Funk, 1923. 498p. (Standard desk-book series) **M27**

Obsolete

❧ Smaller dictionaries of unusual, obsolete and provincial words are often useful for additional instances and quotations and for incidental information about local customs, observances, etc., even though most or all of the words in such dictionaries are now included in the large works of Murray (M11) and Wright (M66). The following are the best known dictionaries of this type:

Halliwell-Phillips, James Orchard. Dictionary of archaic and provincial words, obsolete phrases, proverbs, and ancient customs from the 14th century. 13th ed. Lond., Routledge, 1889. 2v. **M28**

1st ed. 1847. Frequently reprinted without change.

—— —— Supplementary English glossary by T. Lewis O. Davies. Lond., Bell, 1881. 736p.

Nares, Robert. Glossary of words, phrases, names, and allusions in the works of English authors, particularly of Shakespeare and his contemporaries. New ed., with considerable additions both of words and examples, by J. O. Halliwell and Thomas Wright. Lond., Routledge, 1905. 981p. **M29**

1st ed. 1822; 1st Halliwell and Wright ed. 1857. Frequently reprinted.

Skeat, Walter William. Glossary of Tudor and Stuart words, especially from the dramatists. Ed., with additions, by A. L. Mayhew. Ox., Clarendon Pr., 1914. 461p. **M30**

Wright, Thomas. Dictionary of obsolete and provincial English. Lond., Bell, 1886. 2v. o.p. **M31**

1st ed. 1852. Frequently reprinted without change.
Subtitle: Containing words from the English writers previous to the 19th century which are no longer in use, or are not used in the same sense, and words which are now used only in the provincial dialects.

Pronunciation

Greet, William Cabell. World words, recommended pronunciations. 2d ed. rev. and enl. N.Y., Columbia Univ. Pr., 1948. 608p. $6.75; Ox., 37s. 6d. **M32**

A revised and much enlarged revision of *War words* published in 1943, and of *World words* published 1944. Gives pronunciation of some 25,000 names and words including battlefields, places made familiar by the war, names of persons in the news and difficult words. Pronunciation is given "by a simplified Websterian alphabet . . . and by a phonetic respelling." Compiled especially for radio broadcasters of the Columbia Broadcasting System. Includes the pronunciation of many names not easily found elsewhere.

Jones, Daniel. English pronouncing dictionary containing 56,280 words in international phonetic transcription. 7th ed. (rev. with supplement.) N.Y., Dutton, 1947. 490p. $3.75.　　**M33**

1st ed. 1917.

Kenyon, John Samuel and **Knott, Thomas Albert.** A pronouncing dictionary of American English. [2d ed.] Springfield, Mass., Merriam, 1949. 484p. il. $3.　　**M34**

A dictionary giving the pronunciation by the phonetic alphabet of the colloquial speech of cultivated Americans, recording the variant pronunciations in different parts of the country, as East, South, North. Includes besides the common words, proper names, especially for America, some British personal and place names and a few foreign names of general interest; also names in literature and history that are likely to be encountered by college students in their reading.

Larsen, Thorleif and **Walker, Francis Cox.** Pronunciation, a practical guide to American standards. Ox., Univ. Pr., 1930. 198p. $3.　　**M35**

National Broadcasting Company, Inc. NBC handbook of pronunciation, comp. by James F. Bender under the supervision of the National Broadcasting Company. Foreword by James Rowland Angell. N.Y., Crowell, 1943. 289p. $2.75.　　**M36**

A guide to the pronunciation of over 12,000 words currently in use, including many war terms, proper names, place names, etc. The pronunciation is given in two ways for each word, "respelling" and phonetically. The pronunciation as given reflects "general American" usage, and is intended to be that spoken by the professional broadcaster and commentator.

Punctuation

Summey, George. American punctuation. N.Y., Ronald Pr., 1949. 182p. $2.50.　　**M37**

Rhymes

Johnson, Burges. New rhyming dictionary and poets' handbook. N.Y. and Lond., Harper, 1931. 455p. $3.50; 12s. 6d.　　**M38**

Contents: Forms of English versification with examples; Rhyming dictionary, in three parts: (1) one-syllable rhymes, (2) two-syllable rhymes, (3) three-syllable rhymes.

[Lathrop, Lorin Andrews.] Rhymers' lexicon, comp. and ed. by Andrew Loring [pseud.] . . . introd. by George Saintsbury. 2d ed. rev. Lond., Routledge; N.Y., Dutton, 1905. 879p.　　**M39**

pt.1, monosyllables and words accented on the last syllable; pt.2, words accented on the penult; pt.3, words accented on the antepenult.

Walker, John. Rhyming dictionary of the English language, rev. and enl. by L. H. Dawson. Lond., Routledge; N.Y., Dutton, 1924. 549p. 12s. 6d.; $2.50.　　**M40**

1st ed. 1775; rev. and enl. by J. Longmuir, 1865. Frequently reprinted.

Wood, Clement. Wood's Unabridged rhyming dictionary, introd. by Ted Robinson. . . . Cleveland and N.Y., World Pub. Co. [1943]. 1040p. $2.95.　　**M41**

Gives rhyming sounds for single rhymes, double rhymes, and triple rhymes grouped according to consonantal opening. Rhymes are based on sound, not spelling, and pronunciation is given.

Also includes sections on: the vocabulary of poetry, complete formbook for poets, fixed forms, mechanics of rhyme, versification self-taught, and advanced versification.

Slang

Burke, William Jeremiah. The literature of slang . . . with an introductory note by Eric Partridge. N.Y., Public Library, 1939. 180p. $1.50. (Reprinted from the N.Y.P.L. Bulletin, 1936–38) **M42**

An annotated, classified list with author index.

Adams, Ramon F. Western words; a dictionary of the range, cow camp and trail. Norman, Univ. of Oklahoma Pr., 1944. 182p. $3.　　**M43**

Barrère, Albert and **Leland, C. G.** Dictionary of slang, jargon and cant, embracing English, American and Anglo-Indian slang, pidgin English, gypsies' jargon and other irregular phraseology. Lond., Bell, 1897. 2v. o.p.　　**M44**

Berrey, Lester V. and **Van den Bark, Melvin.** American thesaurus of slang, with supplement; a complete reference book of colloquial speech. N.Y., Crowell, 1947. 1174p., 57p. $7.50.　　**M45**

Arranged in two parts: general slang and colloquialisms subdivided into categories arranged according to dominant idea; and special slang of particular classes and occupations including such sections as underworld, trades and occupations, art, entertainment, sports, military, western, etc. Includes an alphabetical word index.

1st ed. 1942. This edition includes a 57-page supplement, covering "Teen talk and jive jargon" and military slang.

Farmer, John Stephen and **Henley, W. E.** Slang and its analogues, past and present; a dictionary, historical and comparative, of the heterodox speech of all classes of society for more than three hundred years, with synonyms in English, French, German, Italian, etc. Lond., Routledge, 1890–1904. 7v. o.p.　　**M46**

The most comprehensive and important slang dictionary, listing about 100,000 words. Gives explanation derivation, kind of usage, illustrative quotations with references to sources, and synonyms in French, German, Italian and Spanish.

—— Dictionary of slang and colloquial English; abridged from Slang and its analogues. Lond., Routledge; N.Y., Dutton, 1905. 533p. **M47**

Partridge, Eric. Dictionary of slang and unconventional English. 3d ed. rev. and much enl. Lond., Routledge; N.Y., Macmillan, 1949. 1230p. 63s.; $11.50. **M48**

Subtitle: Colloquialisms and catch-phrases, solecisms and catachreses, nicknames, vulgarisms and such Americanisms as have been naturalized.

—— Dictionary of the underworld, British and American. Lond., Routledge; N.Y., Macmillan, 1949 [i.e., 1950]. 804p. 50s.; $9. **M48a**

Subtitle: Being the vocabularies of crooks, criminals, racketeers, beggars and tramps, convicts, the commercial underworld, the drug traffic, the white slave traffic, spivs.

—— A dictionary of forces' slang, 1939–1945. Lond., Secker and Warburg; N.Y., Saunders, 1948. 212p. 12s. 6d.; $3.50. **M49**

Naval slang by Wilfred Granville; Army slang by Frank Roberts; Air Force slang by Eric Partridge.
All in one alphabet.

—— Slang, today and yesterday, with a short historical sketch and vocabularies of English, American and Australian slang. Lond., Routledge, 1933. 476p. 10s. 6d. **M50**

A history and discussion with glossaries of words.

Taylor, Anna Marjorie. The language of World War II; abbreviations, captions, quotations, slogans, titles and other terms and phrases. Rev. and enl. ed. N.Y., Wilson, 1948. 265p. $3. **M51**

Sources cited. Includes words, phrases, etc., used during World War II, a list of war songs, a bibliography of books cited and an index.

Synonyms and antonyms

Allen, Frederic Sturges. Allen's Synonyms and antonyms. Rev. and enl. ed., ed. by T. H. Vail Motter. N.Y. and Lond., Harper, 1938. 427p. $3.50. **M52**

First published in 1921.
Alphabetical arrangement giving for each word a list of its synonyms and antonyms, but no definitions. This edition, largely rewritten, adds "(1) additional main entry words, synonyms and antonyms; (2) sense discriminations. Among the words added . . . are numerous examples of cant, slang and colloquialisms . . . and many British equivalents of American terms."—*Pref.* These last are usually listed only under the American word.

Crabb, George. Crabb's English synonyms. Rev. and enl. by the addition of modern terms and

definitions arranged alphabetically, with complete cross references throughout, with introd. by John H. Finley. N.Y., Harper, 1945. 717p. $2.50; Grosset, $2. **M53**

1st ed. 1817; several times revised or reprinted. A spot check of the 1945 printing shows no change from the 1917 centennial edition.
An alphabetical list, arranged by the first word of a group of synonymous words, with explanation and differentiation of the use and meaning of the words in the group; cross references from each of the words.

Fernald, James Champlin. Funk and Wagnalls Standard handbook of synonyms, antonyms, and prepositions. Completely rev. ed. by Funk and Wagnalls editorial staff. N.Y., Funk & Wagnalls, 1947. 515p. **M54**

Previously published in 1914 under title: *English synonyms and antonyms.* This edition is revised and reset. Arranged by "key-words," listing synonyms and antonyms and giving a discussion on the discrimination among the words. Alphabetical index.

Laird, Charlton. Laird's Promptory; a dictionary of synonyms and antonyms and specific equivalents. N.Y., Holt, 1948. 957p. **M55**

March, Francis Andrew and **March, F. A., Jr.** March's Thesaurus dictionary; a treasure house of words and knowledge. Phila., Historical Pub. Co., 1925. 1189p., 251p. il. **M56**

A standard work first published in 1902. The 1925 edition includes "An amplified appendix, completely indexed."

Roget's International thesaurus. New ed. rev. and reset. The complete book of synonyms and antonyms in American and British usage. N.Y., Crowell, 1946. 1194p. $5. **M57**

A new edition of a standard work, first published 1852. Arranged by category according to the idea or signification of a word. Alphabetical index.

Soule, Richard. A dictionary of English synonyms and synonymous expressions, designed as a guide to apt and varied diction. New ed., rev. and enl. by Alfred Dwight Sheffield. Bost., Little, 1938. 614p. $3.50. **M58**

Alphabetical listing followed by synonyms. No definitions or discussion.

Webster's Dictionary of synonyms. 1st ed. A Merriam-Webster. A dictionary of discriminated synonyms, with antonyms and analogous and contrasted words. Springfield, Mass., Merriam, 1942. 907p. $3.50; thumb indexed $5. **M59**

"The writing of the articles was done chiefly by Miss Rose F. Egan, assistant editor on the permanent editorial staff, who also prepared the essays that form the larger part of the introductory matter."—*Pref.*
A comprehensive dictionary of synonyms including also antonyms and lists of analogous words and their oppo-

sites. Words of like meaning are distinguished from each other by careful discrimination and illustrations from classical and contemporary writers. Includes an introduction on the history of English synonymy.

For many purposes the most useful of the dictionaries of synonyms.

Regional and dialect
American

❦ There are now two important dictionaries of American usage, Craigie's *Dictionary of American English on historical principles* (M60) and Thornton's *American glossary* (M62) which together give a fairly comprehensive coverage. Mencken's *American language* (M61), while not technically a dictionary, is useful for its historical treatment and the large number of words included. Additional lists and articles on special, historical, and current usage may be found in *American speech,* 1925- , and *Dialect notes* published by the American Dialect Society, 1890–1939.

While the above are the most generally useful dictionaries, some older works are still occasionally helpful, e.g., Bartlett, J. R., *Dictionary of Americanisms* (1877); Clapin, Sylva, *New dictionary of Americanisms* (1902); Maitland, James, *American slang dictionary* (1891).

Craigie, *Sir* William Alexander and **Hulbert, James R.** Dictionary of American English on historical principles. Chic., Univ. of Chic. Pr., 1936–44. 4v. $100; Ox., Univ. Pr., 17s. ea. **M60**

Volume 4, p.2529-52, Bibliography, giving "a record of the bulk of the reading done for the Dictionary . . . and expanding into completeness the short-title references used in citations."

Compiled on historical principles, with explanations of meaning or use dated when period is clearly determined, and with illustrative quotations dated and arranged chronologically; symbols indicate: a word or sense found in English before 1600; a word or sense originating within the present limits of the United States; a term or sense known only from the passage cited.

Does not attempt to present a complete historical dictionary of every word which has been current since the settlement of the first English colonists but, instead, to show "those features by which the English of the American colonies and the United States is distinguished from that of England and the rest of the English-speaking world," including for that purpose "not only words or phrases which are clearly or apparently of American origin, or have greater currency here than elsewhere, but also every word denoting something which has a real connection with the development of the country and the history of its people."–Cf. *Pref.*, p.v.

The period covered is to the end of the nineteenth century, with later information in the case of some words established before that date. Types of words included are: names of plants, trees and animals, and of natural or artificial products, special terms, e.g., topographical,

medical, legal, military, naval, business, educational, etc Colloquialisms are included but slang and dialect word are restricted to those of early date or special prominence

Mencken, Henry Louis. The American language an introduction into the development of English in the United States. 4th ed., cor., enl. and re written. N.Y., Knopf, 1936. 769p., xxixp. $6. **M6**

———— Supplements, 1-2. N.Y., Knopf, 1945 48. 2v. v.1, $6; v.2, $7.50.

An historical treatment of the development of th English language in the United States covering such sub jects as: the two streams of English; the beginning an growth of the American language; pronunciation an spelling; the common speech; proper names in America American slang, etc. Appendix: Non-English dialect in America. List of words and phrases. Index.

The supplements follow the same plan as the origina work, the first containing supplemental material to chap ters 1-6 and the second to chapters 7-13 and the appen dix, with cross references to the main volume.

Each volume includes copious footnotes, reference to sources, a list of words and phrases with reference the text, and an index.

Thornton, Richard H. An American glossary being an attempt to illustrate certain American isms upon historical principles. Lond., Franci Phila., Lippincott, 1912; New Haven, Conn Amer. Dialect Soc., 1931–39. 3v. v.1-2, o.p.; v.3 in Dialect notes, 1931–39. **M6**

v.1-2, A-Z; v.3, Supplement A-Z.

Includes forms of speech now obsolete or provinci in England which survive in the United States, words an phrases of American origin, nouns which indicate quae rupeds, birds, trees, etc., that are distinctly America names of persons, of classes of people and of place words that have assumed a new meaning, words an phrases of which there are earlier examples in America than in English writers.

The list of words is largely historical and includes litt modern slang. For each word there is given a definitic and explanation and illustrative quotations with refe ences to sources.

The supplement is based on material collected t Thornton after the publication of his *Glossary* and lat turned over by him to the American Dialect Society. E amples and illustrative quotations are from a wide gener reading, but especially full for the *Congressional glo* and *Congressional record,* 1860–1900, with indication the case of words taken from this source of both th name of the speaker and the part of the country fro which he came. This third volume though published *Dialect notes,* is separately paged and has its own tit page, so that it can be bound to stand with volumes 1-

Wentworth, Harold. American dialect dictio ary. N.Y., Crowell, 1944. 747p. $6. **M(**

"American printed sources quoted": p.737-47.

Includes over 10,000 terms ,with 60,000 quotatio showing usage. "Deals mainly with dialect in the sen of localisms, regionalisms, and provincialisms; folk speec urban as well as rustic New England and Southern Unit States dialects viewed in their deviations from Gene Northern or Western. . . ."–*Pref.*

ATLASES

Kurath, Hans. Linguistic atlas of New England . . . Hans Kurath, director and ed., Miles L. Hanley, assoc. director, Bernard Bloch, asst. ed., Guy S. Lowman, Jr., principal field investigator, Marcus L. Hansen, historian. Sponsored by the American Council of Learned Societies and assisted by universities and colleges in New England. Providence, R.I., Brown Univ., 1929–43. v.1-3 in 6v. 56 cm. double maps. (Linguistic atlas of the U.S. and Canada) $60 per pt. **M64**

Each volume in two parts. Maps numbered consecutively, 1-734.

—————— Handbook of the linguistic geography of New England. Providence, R.I., Brown Univ., 1939. 240p. maps. $5. **M65**

Bibliography of linguistic geography, p.54-61; Bibliography of New England history, p.105-121.

British

Wright, Joseph. English dialect dictionary; being the complete vocabulary of all dialect words still in use, or known to have been in use during the last 200 years; founded on the publications of the English Dialect Society. Lond., Frowde, 1898–1905. 6v. **M66**

Contents: v.1-6, A-Z; Supplement, Bibliography, Grammar.

Aims to cover the complete vocabulary of all English dialect words still in use, or known to have been in use from 1700 on, in England, Ireland, Scotland and Wales, including words occurring in both the literary language and spoken dialect. Gives for each word: (1) exact geographical area over which it extends, (2) pronunciation, (3) etymology. Includes American and colonial words still in use in Great Britain or contained in early books and glossaries. Gives many illustrative quotations and incidentally considerable information about popular games, customs and superstitions, with bibliographical references to sources of fuller information.

Scottish

Craigie, *Sir* **William Alexander.** Dictionary of the older Scottish tongue from the 12th century to the end of the 17th. Chic., Univ. of Chic. Pr.; Ox., Univ. Pr., 1931–49. pts. 1-12. (In progress) $5; 21s. per pt. $200 per set. **M67**

pts. 1-12, A-Futher.

"Intended to exhibit the whole range of the Older Scottish vocabulary, as preserved in literature and documentary records, and to continue the history of the language to 1700, so far as it does not coincide with the ordinary English usage of that century."—*Pref. note.*

Jamieson, John. Etymological dictionary of the Scottish language . . . to which is prefixed a dissertation on the origin of the Scottish language.

New ed., carefully rev. and collated, with the entire supplement incorporated, by John Longmuir and David Donaldson. Paisley, Gardner, 1879–82. 4v. and suppl. v. 1887. o.p. **M68**

1st ed., 2v. 1808; supplement by Jamieson, 2v. 1827; an ed. incorporating the words of the suppl. but omitting its quotations, ed. by J. Johnstone, 1840–41; the rev. ed. by Longmuir and Donaldson, as above.

A comprehensive work, now out of date for etymologies, but still useful for the number of words included, the definitions, and the large amount of incidental information on local usages, customs, etc.

Jamieson's Dictionary of the Scottish language, abridged by J. Johnstone and rev. and enl. by Dr. Longmuir, with supplement . . . by W. M. Metcalfe. Paisley, Gardner, 1910. 2v. in 1. **M69**

1st ed. of the Johnstone abridgment of Jamieson, 1840; ed. rev. by Longmuir, 2v. 1867.

v.1, The Johnstone-Longmuir abridgement, 635p.; v.2, Supplementary dictionary, by W. M. Metcalfe, 263p.

Jarvie, James Nicol. Lallans; a selection of Scots words arranged as an English-Scottish dictionary, with pronunciation and examples. Lond., Wren Books, 1947. 159p. 15s. **M70**

English-Scottish. Includes Scots proverbs and quotations.

Scottish national dictionary, designed partly on regional lines and partly on historical principles, and containing all the Scottish words known to be in use or to have been in use since *c.*1700; ed. by William Grant and David Murison. Edinburgh, Scottish Nat. Dict. Assoc., 1931–48. v.1-3, pt.2. In progress, to be completed in about 10v. Subscription £20. **M71**

v.1-3[2], A-dayligaun.

Scope: "*The Scottish National Dictionary* deals with (1) Scottish words in existence since *c.*1700: (a) in Scottish literature, (b) in public records, (c) in glossaries and in dictionaries, (d) in private collections, (e) in special dialect treatises, and (2) Scottish words gathered from the mouth of dialect speakers by competent observers. The general vocabulary will include (1) Scottish words that do not occur in Standard English except as acknowledged loan words; (2) Scottish words the cognates of which occur in St. Eng.; (3) words which have the same form in Scots and St. Eng. but have a different meaning in Sc., *i.e.*, so-called Scotticisms; (4) legal, theological or ecclesiastical terms which within our period have been current in Scottish speech . . . (5) words borrowed since *c.*1700 (from other dialects or languages) which have become current in General Scots, or in any of its dialects, especially Gaelic words in counties on or near the Sc. Western limit and Gypsy words in the Border counties."—*Introd.*, p.xlv.

Treatment: For each word gives variant spellings, grammatical function, status (e.g., obsolete, colloquial etc.), pronunciation, illustrative quotations, with exact references to sources, and origin of word, if known.

Warrack, Alexander. Scots dialect dictionary, comprising the words in use from the latter part of the seventeenth century to the present day with an introduction and a dialect map by William Grant. Lond., Chambers; Phila., Lippincott, 1911. 717p. map. **M72**

Includes modern dialect words, words which have survived the transition period between middle and modern Scottish, and "literary words" which have a dialect meaning in Scotland.

Colonial

Baker, Sidney J. New Zealand slang; a dictionary of colloquialisms, the first comprehensive survey yet made of indigenous English speech in this country—from the argot of whaling days to children's slang in the twentieth century. Christchurch, Whitcombe and Tombs [1941]. 114p. 2s. 9d. **M73**

Morris, Edward Ellis. Austral English; a dictionary of Australasian words, phrases, and usages, with those aboriginal-Australian and Maori words which have become incorporated in the language, and the commoner scientific words that have had their origin in Australasia. Lond., Macmillan, 1898. 525p. o.p. **M74**

Pettman, Charles. Africanderisms; a glossary of South African colloquial words and phrases, and of place and other names. Lond. and N.Y., Longmans, 1913. 579p. o.p. **M75**

Good definitions. Illustrative quotations are given with date and exact page reference.

Yule, *Sir* **Henry** and **Burnell, A. C.** Hobson-Jobson; a glossary of colloquial Anglo-Indian words and phrases, and of kindred terms, etymological, historical, geographical and discursive. New ed., by William Crooke. Lond., Murray, 1903. 1021p. **M76**

Anglo-Saxon

Bosworth, Joseph. Anglo-Saxon dictionary; ed. and enl. by T. N. Toller. Ox., Clarendon Pr., 1882–98. 1302p. $22.50. **M77**

—— —— Supplement, by T. N. Toller. Ox., Clarendon Pr., 1908–21. 768p. $16.75.

Hall, John Richard Clark. Concise Anglo-Saxon dictionary. 3d ed., rev. and enl. Camb., Univ. Pr.; N.Y., Macmillan, 1931. 437p. **M78**

1st ed. 1894; 2d ed. rev. and enl., 1916. The third edition is still further enlarged, e.g., a considerable number of words from twelfth-century texts, not recorded in *Bosworth-Toller* (M77), have been added.

As in the second edition the work refers to the headings in the *New English dictionary* (M11) under which quotations from the Anglo-Saxon texts are given, thus serving as an index to the large amount of valuable information on Old English words included in the *New English dictionary* but often overlooked because it is found under the head of words now obsolete.

Sweet, Henry. Student's dictionary of Anglo-Saxon. N.Y., Ox., Univ. Pr., 1911. 217p. **M79**

Middle English

Stratmann, Francis Henry. Middle-English dictionary, containing words used by English writers from the 12th to the 15th century; new ed., rearranged, rev. and enl. by Henry Bradley. Ox., Clarendon Pr., 1891. 708p. **M80**

FOREIGN LANGUAGES

Foreign language dictionaries are important in any library, though their use will vary greatly according to the size and type of the library and the character of the library clientele. The needs of the small library used by English-speaking readers may be met by a modest equipment of French, German and Latin dictionaries, while the small or branch library in a locality which has a considerable foreign population will need also the dictionaries of the languages represented. Large public libraries and especially university libraries need the best dictionaries of all principal languages and many minor languages.

Two main types of dictionaries are represented in the following list: (1) the standard dictionary of a language in that language only, such as Littré's French dictionary (M173), and (2) the bilingual dictionary, such as the various French-English and German-English dictionaries. The first type is the more complete and must be consulted when the fullest vocabulary or detailed and historical information is needed, but it can be used only by someone fairly familiar with the language, and is not generally needed in the smaller library. The second type, which is the kind most used in the average library, is planned for people who are learning a language, is much less complete in vocabulary and usually contains no historical information, as its main purpose is not detailed definition but the explanation of a foreign word by its English equivalent.

The ordinary bilingual dictionary is generally satisfactory for most words of the "literary" language but is often weak in scientific terms and popular expressions. Bilingual dictionaries also differ according to the users for whom they are compiled. In a French-English dictionary, prepared for the use of English-speaking students who are learning French, the French-English half of the book is the more important and this will be worked out carefully, while the English-French half may be given briefer or less careful treatment. The reverse is true of a dictionary prepared for French students learning English. A library which can afford to have several dictionaries of a language should take this difference into account and represent both points of view.

As so large a proportion of the use of foreign dictionaries in an American library is for the purpose of finding the English meaning of a foreign word, the many other possible uses of such books are sometimes overlooked. The larger dictionaries frequently contain some encyclopedic information, those that include many quotations may often be used to supplement the dictionaries of foreign quotations, and the larger historical or dialectal dictionaries which include obsolete words, local usages, etc., may be used for information on small points of local history, manners and customs, folklore, etc.

See name of subject for scientific, technical and other special dictionaries, e.g., Science — Dictionaries; Chemistry — Dictionaries, etc.

Bibliography

U. S. Library of Congress. Division of Bibliography. Foreign language-English dictionaries. A selected list; comp. by Grace Hadley Fuller under the direction of Florence S. Hellman. . . . Wash., Library, 1942. 132p. **M81**

1133 items arranged alphabetically by language, with many cross references from dialects, variant forms, etc.

—— —— Supplementary list. 1944. 42p.

362 items.

Synonyms

Buck, Carl Darling. A dictionary of selected synonyms in the principal Indo-European languages; a contribution to the history of ideas. Chic., Univ. of Chic. Pr., 1949. 1515p. $40. **M82**

Arranged according to the meaning of words by semantic grouping. Under each meaning the equivalent word is given in about 30 of the major Indo-European languages, followed by a description of its etymology and semantic history.

Afrikaans

Boshoff, Stephanus Petrus Erasmus. Etimologiese woordeboek van afrikaans. Kaapstad, Nasionale Pers, Beperk, 1936. 121p. **M83**

Bosman, Daniel Brink and **Merwe, I. W. v. d.** Tweetalige woordeboek. Kaapstad, Nasionale Pers, Beperk, 1931–36. 2v. **M84**

v.1, Engels-Afrikaans, 1931, 625p.; v.2, Afrikaans-Engels, 1936, 865p.

Albanian

Drizari, Nelo. Fjalór Shqip-Inglisht dhe Inglisht-Shqip; Albanian-English and English-Albanian dictionary. N.Y., N. Nassy, 1934. 313p. $2.50. **M85**

Leotti, Angelo. Dizionario albanese-italiano. Roma, Istituto per l'Europa Orientale, 1937. 1710p. (Istituto per l'Europa Orientale. Pubblicazioni. Ser. 5: Grammatiche e dizionari, 3) **M86**

Mann, Stuart Edward. An historical Albanian-English dictionary. Lond., Longmans, 1948. 601p. $20. **M87**

Amharic

Ambruster, Carl Hubert. Initia amharica; an introduction to spoken Amharic. Camb., Univ. Pr., 1908–20. v.1-3[1]. **M88**

No more published.

Baeteman, Joseph. Dictionnaire amarigna-français, suivi d'un vocabulaire français-amarigna. Dire-Daoua (Ethiopie), Impr. Saint Lazare, 1929. 1262, 426 col. **M89**

Annamese

Emeneau, Murray Barnson and **Steinen, Diether von den.** Annamese-English dictionary, with an English-Annamese index based on work by John Sherry. Berkeley, Calif., Army Specialized Training Program, Univ. of California, 1945. 279 numb. l. **M90**

"Prepared . . . for . . . special use . . . in the Army specialized training program."—*1st prelim. leaf.*

Arabic

Badger, George Percy. English-Arabic lexicon, in which the equivalents for English words and idiomatic sentences are rendered into literary and colloquial Arabic. Lond., Paul, 1881. 1244p. **M91**

Catafago, Joseph. An English and Arabic dictionary . . . in two parts, Arabic and English, and English and Arabic in which the Arabic words are represented in their oriental character, as well as their correct pronunciation and accentuation shown in English letters. 2d ed., carefully cor., improved and enl.; also containing a number of extracts and illustrations from the best Arabic writers, especially the "Arabian nights" and the "Hariri." London, Quaritch, 1873. 1096p. **M92**

Elias, Elias A. Elias' Modern dictionary, English-

Arabic. 5th ed. entirely recast and enl. Cairo, Elias, 1946. 806p. il. **M93**

Elias, Edward E. Elias' Practical dictionary of the colloquial Arabic; English-Arabic. Cairo, Elias, 1942. 252p. **M94**

Hava, J. G. Arabic-English dictionary for the use of students. New ed. Beirut, Catholic Pr., 1921. [pref. 1915] 916p. **M95**

Excellent medium-sized dictionary.

Hindie, Alfred. The student's dictionary, English-Arabic and Arabic-English, of the classical Arabic, for the use of students of the English language, rev. by Socrates Spiro Bey. Cairo, Hindie Pr., 1927. 480, 476p. **M96**

Khalil Saad, *bey.* Centennial English-Arabic dictionary . . . Paul Erdmann, managing ed.; Asa'ad Kheirallah, Arabic ed. Beirut, Amer. Mission Pr. [pref. 1926] 1058p. **M97**

Lane, Edward William. Arabic-English lexicon, derived from the best and the most copious eastern sources. In two books: the first containing all the classical words and significations commonly known to the learned among the Arabs; the second, those that are of rare occurrence and not commonly known. Book I. Lond., Williams and Norgate, 1863–93. 1v. in 8 pts., paged continuously. **M98**

Bk. II never published.

Salmoné, Habib Anthony. Arabic-English dictionary on a new system. Lond., Trübner, 1890. 2v. **M99**

v.1, Arabic-English; v.2, English index.

Spiro, Socrates, *bey.* Arabic-English and English-Arabic vocabulary of the modern and colloquial Arabic of Egypt. 2d-3d ed. rev. Cairo, Elias, 1923–29. 2v. **M100**

Arabic-English. 2d ed. 1923. 516p.; English-Arabic. 3d ed. 1929. 325p.

Armenian

Aukerian, Haroutiun and **Brand, John.** Dictionary, English and Armenian. Venice, Armenian Acad. of St. Lazarus, 1821–25. 2v. **M101**

Bedrosian, Madatia. New dictionary Armenian-English. Venice, S. Lazarus Armenian Acad., 1875–79. 786p. **M102**

Chakmakjian, Haroutioun Hovanes. Comprehensive dictionary, English-Armenian. Bost., E. A. Yeran, 1922. 1424p. **M103**

Yacoubian, Adour H. English-Armenian and Armenian-English concise dictionary. (Armenian

words are spelled in Latin letters) Map, pictures of mosaic and bas-reliefs of Armenians. . . . Los Angeles, Calif., Armenian Archives Pr., 1944. 176p. il. $3. **M104**

Assyro-Babylonian

Bezold, Carl. Babylonisch-assyrisches Glossar; nach dem Tode des Verfassers unter Mitwirkung von Adele Bezold zum Druck gebracht von Albrecht Götze. Heidelberg, Winter, 1926. 343p. **M105**

Delitzsch, Friedrich. Assyrisches Handwörterbuch. Leipzig, Hinrichs; Balt., Johns Hopkins Pr., 1896. 730p. **M106**

Muss-Arnolt, William. Concise dictionary of the Assyrian languages. Berlin, Reuther; N.Y., Lemcke, 1905. 1202p. **M107**

Assyrian, English and German.

Basque

Lhande, Pierre. Dictionnaire basque-français et français-basque (dialectes labourdin, bas-navarrais et souletin) d'après le Dictionnaire basque-espagnol-français de l'abbé R. M. de Askué [i.e., Azkué] et les dictionnaires manuscrits des abbés M. Harriet, M. Hiribarren et Pierre Foix. Paris, G. Beauchesne, 1926–38. v.1- . **M108**

v.1, Basque-français. 1117p. (pub. in 9 pts.)

Bengali

Mitra, Subal Chandra. Student's Bengali-English dictionary. 2d ed. Calcutta, New Bengal Pr., 1923. 1393p. **M109**

—— Student's concise Anglo-Bengali dictionary. 8th ed. Calcutta, New Bengal Pr., [193–?] 1591p. **M109a**

Bohemian

See Czech.

Breton

Du Rusquec, H. Dictionnaire français-breton. Morlaix, Chevalier, 1886. 492p. **M110**

—— Nouveau dictionnaire pratique et étymologique du dialecte de Léon, avec les variantes diverses, dans les dialectes de Vannes, Tréguier et Cornouailles. Paris, Leroux, 1895. 320p. **M111**

Ernault, Émile. Dictionnaire étymologique du breton moyen. (In his Le mystère de Sainte Barbe. Nantes, Soc. des Bibliophiles Bretons 1885–87. p.189-400) **M112**

—— Glossaire moyen breton. 2. éd. corr. et augm. Paris, Bouillon, 1895–96. 833p. **M113**

Supplement to the above.

Forms volume 2 of Arbois de Jubainville, Henry d' and Ernault, Émile, *Études grammaticales sur les langues celtiques* (Paris, 1881–96).

Henry, Victor. Lexique étymologique des termes les plus usuels du breton moderne. Rennes, Plihon, 1900. 350p. (Bibliothèque bretonne armoricaine, pub. par la Faculté des Lettres de Rennes. fasc. 3) **M114**

Issued in installments with the "Annales de Bretagne, pub. par la Faculté des Lettres de Rennes," v.15, no. 3–v.18, no.3, 1900–03.

Bulgarian

Chakalov, G. Anglo-Bŭlgarski rechnik. English-Bulgarian dictionary. Sophia, IUni, 1948. 1229p. **M115**

Bogorov, I. A. Bulgarsko-Frenski rĭechnik. Viena, Sommerov, 1871. 506p. **M116**

Miladinov, Ivan An. Deutsch-bulgarisches [bulgarisch-deutsches] Wörterbuch. 2. umgearb. u. verm. Aufl. Sofia, Selbstverlag des Autors, 1912–15. 2v. **M117**

v.1, German-Bulgarian; v.2, Bulgarian-German.

Stephanove, Constantine. Complete Bulgarian-English [and English-Bulgarian] dictionary (including a lexicon of geographical, historical, proper, etc., names, a list of the English irregular verbs, weights and measures, etc.) Sofia, Nickoloff, 1914; Haemus, 1929. 2v. **M118**

Bulgarian-English. Nickoloff, 1914. 902p.; English-Bulgarian, 2d ed. rev. and enl. Haemus, 1929. 1063p.

Burmese

Judson, Adoniram. The Judson Burmese-English dictionary. Rev. and enl. by Robert C. Stevenson; ed. by F. H. Eveleth. Rangoon, Amer. Baptist Mission Pr., 1921. 1123p. **M119**

—— English and Burmese dictionary. 8th ed. Rangoon, Amer. Baptist Mission Pr., 1922. 928p. **M120**

Also published in London by Kegan Paul.

Catalan

Aguiló y Fúster, Mariano. "Diccionari Aguiló"; materials lexicogràfics aplegats. Barcelona, Inst. d'Estudis Catalans, 1914–34. 8v. (Biblioteca filològica de l'Inst. de la Llengua Catalana, III, VIII) **M121**

Alcover Sureda, Antonio Maria. Diccionari català-valencià-balear; inventari lexical y etimologich de la llengua que parlen Catalunya espanyola y Catalunya francesa, el regne de València, les illes Balears y la ciutat d'Alguer de Sardenya, en totes ses formes literàries y dialectals, antigues y modernes. Palma de Mallorca, Alcover, 1930–50. v.1-3. il. (In progress) **M122**

v.1-3, A-Cuy.

Diccionari enciclopèdic de la llengua catalana, amb la correspondència castellana. Nova ed., redactada segons les normes de l' "Institut d'Estudis Catalans," la qual conté tots els vocables, modismes i aforismes, mots tècnics de ciències, arts i indústries, biografies de personatges cèlebres, antics i moderns, nom i descripció de poblacions, rius i muntanyes de les comarques on és parlat et català en qualsevol de les seves variants. Barcelona, Salvat, 1930–35. 4v. il. **M123**

Previously published under title: *Diccionari de la llengua catalana ab la correspondencia castellana.*

Celtic

Holder, Alfred. Alt-celtischer Sprachschatz. Leipzig, Teubner, 1896–1913. 3v. **M124**

Chinese

Shu, Hsin-ch'êng [and others]. Tz'ŭ hai. [Chinese encyclopedic dictionary] Shanghai, Commercial Pr., 1915. 2v. **M125**

—— —— Supplement. Shanghai, Commercial Pr., 1931. unpaged.

Comes in five editions, edition A, B, C, D and E, all having the same text but differing in size of page, kind of paper, etc.

Bilingual

Fenn, Courtenay Hughes. The Five thousand dictionary, a Chinese-English pocket dictionary and index to the character cards of the College of Chinese Studies, California College in China, originally comp. by Courtenay H. Fenn . . . with the assistance of Mr. Chin Hsien Tseng. 5th ed., with add. and rev. by George D. Wilder . . . and Mr. Chin Hsien Tseng. . . . Peking, 1940. 697p. **M126**

"Numerical list of radicals" attached to lining-paper.

Reprinted as: rev. American ed. Camb., Harv. Univ. Pr., 1942. 694p. $1.50.

Giles, Herbert Allen. Chinese-English dictionary. 2d ed., rev. and enl. Shanghai, Kelly; Lond., Quaritch [1909]-12. 3v. **M127**

Mathews, Robert Henry. Mathews' Chinese-English dictionary. Rev. American ed., pub. for the Harvard-Yenching Institute. Camb., Harv. Univ. Pr., 1943. 1226p. **M128**

Originally published in 1931.

"Within the necessary limitations of a photographic edition, and as far as interstices of the original edition allow, errors have been corrected, pronunciations and definitions revised, and new entries inserted—in all amounting to some 15,000 items. A whole introduction on pronunciation has been added, and a list of the syllabic headings is included for quick reference. . . . An additional feature of the new edition is that all cases of the neutral, i.e., unstressed, tone are indicated."—*Foreword* to American edition.

—— A Chinese-English dictionary, comp. for the China Inland Mission. Rev. English index. Pub. for the Harvard-Yenching Institute. Camb., Harv. Univ. Pr., 1944. 186p. $3.50.

Williams, Samuel Wells. A syllabic dictionary of the Chinese language; arranged according to the Wu-Fang Yuen Yin, with the pronunciation of the characters as heard in Peking, Canton, Amoy and Shanghai. Shanghai, Amer. Presbyterian Mission Pr., 1903. 1254p. **M129**

A reprint of the 1874 edition, with four pages of "Errata and corrections."

[Yen, Hui-ch'ing] An English and Chinese standard dictionary, comprising 120,000 words and phrases, with translations, pronunciations, definitions, illustrations, etc., with a copious appendix. 4th ed. Shanghai, Commercial Pr., 1916. 1377p. il. **M130**

Coptic

Crum, Walter Ewing. Coptic dictionary. Ox., Clarendon Pr., 1929–39. pts. 1-6. 42s. ($14) per pt.; whole work 147s. ($50) **M131**

Coptic-English.

Cornish

Jago, Frederick William Pearce. English-Cornish dictionary, comp. from the best sources. Lond., Simpkin; Plymouth, Luke, 1887. 211p. **M132**

Nance, R. Morton. A new Cornish-English dictionary. St. Ives, pr. for the Federation of Old Cornwall Societies, by James Lanham, 1938. 209p. 7s. 6d. **M133**

—— and **Smith, A. S. D.** English-Cornish dictionary. St. Ives, pr. for the Federation of Old Cornwall Societies, by James Lanham, 1934. 137p. 4s. **M134**

Williams, Robert. Lexicon Cornu-Britannicum; a dictionary of the ancient Celtic language of Cornwall, in which the words are elucidated by copious examples from the Cornish works now remaining; with translations in English. Llandovery, Roderic, 1865. 400p. **M135**

—— **Loth, Joseph.** Remarques et corrections au Lexicon Cornu-Britannicum de Williams. Paris, Bouillon, 1902. 70p. **M135a**

Croatian

See Serbian and Croatian.

Czech

Procházka, Jindřich and **Hokes, Jaroslav.** Dictionary of the English and Czech languages. Prague, Kvasnička & Hampl, 1949. 1000p. Kč.180. **M136**

Vása, Pavel and **Trávníček, František.** Slovnik jazyka českého. 3. přepr. a dopl. vyd. V Praze, Borový, 1946. 1765p. **M137**

Bilingual

Česko-anglický slovník . . . Czech-English dictionary . . . comp. by H. T. Cheshire, V. Jung, L. Klozner [and others]. V Praze, Otto, 1933–35. 2v. (Ottovy velké slovníky) **M138**

Jonáš, Karel. A complete pronouncing dictionary of the English and Bohemian languages for general use. Uplný slovník anglicko-český pro obecnou potřebu. S dokonalou anglickou výslovností. [Chic., Pancner, 1941] 723p. $2. **M139**

"Third edition."

Practically a reprint of the 1892 edition. Checking of various samplings of the alphabet showed no changes.

—— Slovnik česko-anglicky s úplnou anglickou výslovností. A Bohemian and English dictionary. Vydáni se všeobecným doplňkem. 4th ed. Chic., Pancner, 1942. 621p. $2. **M140**

Jung, Václav Alois. Slovnik anglicko-český. Dictionary of the English and Bohemian languages. 2d ed. V Praze, Otto [1923?]. 1564p. **M141**

English-Bohemian only.

Danish and Norwegian

Norsk riksmålordbok, utarb. av Trygve Knudsen og Alf Sommerfelt. Oslo, Aschehoug, 1930–[50?]. v.1-2[10]. Kr. 1 per heft. (In progress) **M142**

bd.1, A-L; bd.2, hft. 1-10, M-Strekke.

Ordbog over det danske Sprog, grundlagt af Verner Dahlerup; med Understøttelse af Undervisningsministeriet og Carlsbergfondet udg. af det Danske Sprog-og Litteraturselskab. København, Gyldendal, 1919–1948. v.1-24. (In progress) **M143**

bd.1-24, A-Taeve.

—— Liste over Forkortelser i Bind I-XII, med en Lydskrifttavle. København, 1931. 69p.

Bilingual

Brynildsen, John. Dictionary of the English and Dano-Norwegian languages. Danisms supervised by Johannes Magnussen, English pronunciation by Otto Jespersen. Copenhagen, Gyldendal, 1902–07. 2v. **M144**

Added title page: Engelsk-dansk-norsk Ordbog.

—— Norsk-engelsk ordbog. 3. omarb. utg. Oslo, Aschehoug, 1927. 1228p. **M145**

Jorgenson, Theodore. Norwegian-English school dictionary. [Northfield, Minn.] St. Olaf College Pr., 1943. 460p. $3. **M146**

Uses the new orthography made obligatory by the language reform of 1938 but also gives many parallel forms and may be used in reading older literature. Shows articles, plural endings, principal parts, forms of the adjectives, etc.

Larsen, Anton Laurentius. Dictionary of the Dano-Norwegian and English languages, rev. by Johannes Magnussen. 4th ed. Copenhagen, Gyldendal, 1910. 687p. **M147**

Raknes, Ola. Engelsk-norsk ordbok, med grunnlag i engelsk-norsk ordbok af Th. Gleditsch. Oslo, Aschehoug, 1927. 1049p. **M148**

Etymology

Falk, Hjalmar Sejersted and **Torp, Alf.** Norwegisch-dänisches etymologisches Wörterbuch. Auf Grund der Übersetzung von H. Davidsen neu bearb. deutsche Ausg., mit Literaturnachweisen strittiger Etymologien sowie deutschen und altnordischem Wörterverzeichnis. Heidelberg, Winter, 1910–11. 2v. **M149**

Synonyms

Albeck, Ulla. Dansk synonym-ordbog. 3. udg. København, J. H. Schultz, 1948. 307p. Kr. 14. **M150**

Dialects

Christie, Wilhelm F. K. Norsk dialect-lexicon og nokre folkeminne og brev. Gustav Indrebø

gav ut. Bergen, Grieg, 1937. 261p., 374p. (Bergens Museums aarbog. 1937. Historisk-antiqvarisk rekke, nr.1) **M151**

Dutch

Dale, Johan Hendrik van. Van Dale's Groot woordenboek der Nederlandsche taal. 6. geheel opnieuw bewerkte uitgave. 'sGravenhage, Nijhoff, 1924. 2155p. **M152**

—— Van Dale's Nieuw groot woordenboek der Nederlandse taal. 'sGravenhage, Nijhoff, 1947–50. 2379p. **M153**

Appeared in 15 Afl. Includes a supplement containing: proper names in Greek and Roman mythology; foreign phrases; Biblical names; errata.

—— Van Dale's Handwoordenboek der Nederlandse taal. 5. geheel nieuwe uitgave. 'sGravenhage, Nijhoff, 1948. 1034p. **M154**

Elzinga, Johannes Jacobus Becker and **Jong, A. J. de.** Nieuw Nederlands woordenboek, berattende tevens verklaring van de meest gebruikelijke woorden van vreemde oorsprong. 2. druk volgens de spelling 1947 herzien door A. C. de Jong en A. J. de Jong. Amsterdam, "Kosmos," 1947. 510p. **M155**

Verdam, Jacob. Middelnederlandsch handwoordenboek. 2. uitg. 'sGravenhage, Nijhoff, 1932. 812p. **M156**

Enlarged by 112 pages from the first edition 1911, with revision of section Sterne-Z by C. H. Ebbinge Wubben.

Verwijs, Eelco and **Verdam, Jacob.** Middelnederlandsch woordenboek. 'sGravenhage, Nijhoff, 1885–1943. deel 1-10$^{1-2}$, 11. **M157**

Contents: deel 1-9, A-Z; deel 10^1, Tekstcritiek van J. Verdam, en Bouwstoffen, eerste gedeelte (A-F) door Willem de Vreese. Fl. 28; deel 10^2 (incompl.), Bouwstoffen, tweede gedeelte (G-Nijh) door G. I. Lieftinck; deel 11, afl. 1-5, Aanvullingen en verbeteringen op het gebied van dijk-en waterschapsrecht, bodem en water, aardrijkskunde, enz. door A. A. Beekman (A-Z). Fl. 3 per afl.

Woordenboek der Nederlandsche taal. 'sGravenhage, Nijhoff, 1882–1949. v.1-18. (In progress) **M158**

Edited by M. de Vries and others.
v.1-11, 13-16 compl.; v.12, pt.1 (fasc. 1-20), P-Plets; pt.2 (fasc. 21-39), Pletten-Quar; pt.3 (fasc. 1-4), R-Recht; v.17 (fasc. 1-7), Tiend-Toew; v.18 (fasc. 1-4), V-Varen.

—— Supplement, 1942-49. v.1, fasc. 1-8, A-ambach.

—— Bronnenlijst, bewerkt door C. H. A. Kruyskamp. 1943. 144p. Fl. 14.

Bilingual

Bruggencate, Karel ten. Engels woordenboek. 13. verb. en verm. uitg., door A. Broers. Groningen, Wolters, 1933–39. 2v. Fl. 7.50. **M159**

v.1, English-Dutch, 1939; v.2, Dutch-English, 1933.

Callisch, Isaac Marcus. New complete dictionary of the English and Dutch languages. 2d ed. rev. by N. S. Calisch. Tiel, Campagne, 1890–92. 2v. **M160**

Kramers, Jacob. Kramers' Engels woordenboek; engels-nederlands en nederlands-engels, bewerkt door F. P. H. Prick van Wely. 17. druk. Den Haag, van Goor, 1946. 1236p. Fl. 7.90. **M161**

Added title page in English with imprint: Lond., Bailey Bros. and Swinfen.

Prick van Wely, F. P. H. Engels handwoordenboek. 5. verbeterde druk, bewerkt door F. Prick van Wely. Den Haag, van Goor, 1948. 2v. Fl. 7.50. **M162**

Contents: 1. deel, Engels-nederlands; 2. deel, Nederlands-engels.
Uses the new spelling.

Etymology

Franck, Johannes. Franck's Etymologisch woordenboek der Nederlandsche taal. 2. druk door Dr. N. van Wijk. Met registers der Nieuwhoogduitsche woorden, enz. 'sGravenhage, Nijhoff, 1912. 897p. **M163**

—— Supplement door C. B. van Haeringen. 'sGravenhage, Nijhoff, 1936. 235p. Fl. 17.50.

Egyptian

Erman, Adolf and **Grapow, Hermann.** Wörterbuch der aegyptischen Sprache; im Auftrage der deutschen Akademien. Leipzig, Hinrichs, 1926–36. v.1-5, 6, pt.1. **M164**

—— Die Belegstellen, bearb. von H. Grapow u. W. Erichsen. Leipzig, Hinrichs, 1937–40. v.2. 767p.

Finnish

Alanne, Severi. Suomalais-englantilainen sanakirja. Finnish-English dictionary. Superior, Wis., Työmies Kustannusyhtiön Kustannuksella, 1919. 957p. **M165**

Nuorteva, Santeri. Englantilais-suomalainen sanakirja. English-Finnish dictionary. Fitchburg, Mass., Finnish Socialistic Pub. Co., 1915. 587p. **M166**

Swan, Carl Gustaf and **Granström, Hanna.** English and Finnish dictionary. [Helsingissä, Suomal. Kirjallis. Seuran Kirjapainon Osakeyhtiö, 1904] 1218p. **M167**

English-Finnish only.

Tuomikoski, Aune and **Slöör, Anna.** Englantilais-Suomalainen sanakirja. Helsinki, Suomalaisen Kirjallisuuden Seura, 1939. 1068p. (Suomalaisen Kirjallisuuden Seuran Toimituksia 212. osa) **M168**

French

Académie Française, Paris. Dictionnaire de l'Académie Française. 8. éd. Paris, Hachette, 1931–35. 2v. **M169**

Bescherelle, Louis Nicholas. Dictionnaire usuel de tous les verbes français, tant réguliers qu'irréguliers, entièrement conjugués, contenant par ordre alphabétique les 7000 verbes de la langue française avec leur conjugaison complète. Nouv. éd. Paris, Garnier [186-?]. 2v. **M170**

Hatzfeld, Adolphe and **Darmesteter, Arsène.** Dictionnaire général de la langue française du commencement du XVIIe siècle jusqu'à nos jours. 8. éd. Paris, Delagrave, 1926. 2v. **M171**

1. éd. 1895–1900.

Larousse, Pierre. Nouveau petit Larousse illustré; dictionnaire encyclopédique publié sous la direction de Claude Augé et Paul Augé. Nouv. éd., entièrement refondue. Paris, Larousse, 1948. 1767p. il. **M172**

Contents: Dictionnaire, A-Z; Locutions latines e étrangères; Histoire et géographie.
A compact desk dictionary which is very useful fo students. The first part gives definitions of words witl examples of usage. This is followed by a brief section of foreign phrases, and then by an alphabetical dictionar of proper names, biographical, geographical, and his torical, with brief information. Illustrated with small lin drawings.
Frequently reprinted.

Littré, Émile. Dictionnaire de la langue française contenant la nomenclature, la grammaire la signification des mots, la partie historique l'étymologie. Paris, Hachette, 1873–78. 4v. an suppl. **M17**

v.1-4, A-Z, 1873; Supplément, renfermant un gran nombre de termes d'art, de sciences, d'agriculture . . suivi d'un dictionnaire étymologique de tous les mot d'origine orientale, par Marcel Devic, 1878. 375p., 84p.

—— Dictionnaire de la langue française. Abrég du dictionnaire de É. Littré par A. Beaujea 12. éd. conforme pour l'orthographe a la dernièr éd. du Dictionnaire de l'Académie Française. Paris, Hachette, 1914. 1295p., 123p. **M174**

Bilingual

Cassell's French-English, English-French dictionary, ed. by Ernest A. Baker. Lond., Cassell, 1941. 582p., 437p. $3.50. **M175**

Frequently reprinted.

Also published as *Heath's New French and English dictionary*.

Chevalley, Abel [and others]. Concise Oxford French dictionary. Ox., Clarendon Pr., 1934–40. 2v. **M176**

French-English. 1934. 895p.; English-French. 1940. 295p.

"In accordance with our wish to emulate in the French-English field the work of the brothers Fowler on current English, the principles governing the selection of vocabulary in the *Concise Oxford Dictionary* [M14] have been adopted."—*Pref.*, volume 1.

Clifton, C. Ebenezer and **Grimaux, A.** Nouveau dictionnaire anglais-français et français-anglais, composé sur un plan nouveau . . . entièrement refondu et considerablement augm. par J. McLaughlin. Paris, Garnier [1923]. 2v. **M177**

Elwall, Alfred. Dictionnaire anglais-français [et français-anglais] à l'usage des établissements d'instruction publique et des gens du monde. Paris, Delalain, 1929. 2v. **M178**

Français-anglais, 880p.; Anglais-français, 1076p.

Guiraud, Jules. Dictionnaire anglais-français [et français-anglais] a l'usage des professeurs, des littérateurs, des traducteurs, des commerçants, des industriels, des élèves, des facultés, des grandes écoles et des classes supérieures des lycées et collèges. Paris, Berlin, 1932–37. 2v. **M179**

Anglais-français, 2. éd. 1937. 2187p.; Français-anglais, 1932. 1127p.

Harrap's Standard French and English dictionary, ed. by J. E. Mansion. Lond., Harrap, 1947–48. 2v. v.1, 42s.; v.2, 63s. **M180**

pt.1, French-English, repr. with corrections. 1948. 912p.; pt.2, English-French, repr. with corrections. 1947. 488p.

1st ed. 1934–39.

American edition has title: *Heath's Standard French and English dictionary* (N.Y., Heath. 2v. $28).

—— Shorter French and English dictionary. Lond., Harrap, 1940–44. 2v. **M181**

Abridgment of the above (M180).

pt.1, French-English. 1940. 8s. 6d.; pt.2, English-French. 1944. 12s. 6d.

Spiers, Alexander. Nouveau dictionnaire général anglais-français et français-anglais. Nouv. éd.

Supplément renfermant un grand nombre de termes usuels et littéraires nouveaux, des termes scientifiques et techniques . . . par Victor Spiers. Paris, Mesnil-Dramard [1905–11]. 2v. **M182**

Sachs, Karl and **Villatte, Césaire.** Encyklopädisches französisch-deutsches und deutsch-französisches Wörterbuch. 17.-19. Aufl. Berlin, Langenscheidt, 1906–07. 2v. **M183**

v.1, French-German; v.2, German-French.

Etymology

Bloch, Oscar and **Wartburg, W. von.** Dictionnaire étymologique de la langue française. 2. éd. refondue par W. von Wartburg. Paris, Presses Universitaires de France, 1950. 651p. **M184**

Dauzat, Albert. Dictionnaire étymologique de la langue française. 4. éd. rev. Paris, Larousse, 1946. 799p. 200 fr. **M185**

Gamillscheg, Ernst. Etymologisches Wörterbuch der französischen Sprache . . . mit einem Wort- und Sachverzeichnis von Heinrich Kuen. Heidelberg, Winter, 1928. 1136p. (Sammlung romanischer Elementar- und Handbücher hrsg. von Wilhelm Meyer-Lübke, 3. Reihe, Wörterbücher) **M186**

Wartburg, Walther von. Französisches etymologisches Wörterbuch; eine Darstellung des galloromanischen Sprachschatzes. Bonn, Klopp; Basel, Helbing und Lichtenhahn, 1928–48. v.1-5. (In progress) **M187**

Bd.1, A-B, 1928; Bd.2 (Lfg. 29-38), C K Q, 1936–46; Bd.3, D-F, 1934; Bd.4, (Lfg. 39-40, 42), g-hors, 1946–48; Bd.5 (Lfg. 41), jacere-Langobardus, 1948.

Slang

France, Hector. Dictionnaire de la langue verte; archaismes, néologismes, locutions étrangères, patois. Paris, Librairie du Progrès, 1907. 497p. il. **M188**

Leroy, Olivier. A dictionary of French slang. Lond., Harrap, 1935. 237p. **M189**

Synonyms

Lafaye, Pierre Benjamin. Dictionnaire des synonymes de la langue française. 8. éd. suivie d'un supplément. Paris, Hachette, 1903. 1106p., 336p. **M190**

1st ed., 1858; 3d ed., 1865–69, was the first edition to include the supplement.

Maquet, Charles. Dictionnaire analogique. Répertoire moderne. Des mots par les idées. Des idées par les mots, d'après les principes de P. Boissière. Rédigé sur un plan nouveau. Paris, Larousse, 1936. 591p. **M191**

Rouaix, Paul. Dictionnaire-manuel-illustré des idées suggérées par les mots; contenant tous les mots de la langue française groupés d'après le sens. 18. éd. Paris, Colin, 1939. 538p. il. **M192**

Old and 16th century

Levy, Raphael. Répertoire des lexiques du vieux français. N.Y., Modern Language Assoc. of America, 1937. 64p. **M193**

Godefroy, Frédéric Eugène. Dictionnaire de l'ancienne langue française et de tous ses dialectes, du IXe au XVe siècle, composé d'après le dépouillement de tous les plus importants documents, manuscrits ou imprimés, qui se trouvent dans les grandes bibliothèques de la France et de l'Europe, et dans les principales archives départementales, municipales, hospitalières ou privées. Pub. sous les auspices du Ministère de l'Instruction Publique. Paris, Bouillon, 1891–1902. 10v. **M194**

v.1-7, A-Traioir; v.8, Traire-Z; Complément, A-Carrefour; v.9-10, Complément, Carrel-Z.
The standard dictionary of old French.

—— Lexique de l'ancien français, pub. par les soins de J. Bonnard et Am. Salmon. Paris, Welter, 1901. 544p. **M195**

An abridgment of the larger work, omitting the quotations and many of the words.

Grandsaignes d'Hauterive, R. Dictionnaire d'ancien français. Moyen Age et Renaissance. Paris, Larousse, 1947. 592p. 450 fr. **M196**

Gives spelling variations, meaning, modern approximation, etymology, time when current, etc.

Huguet, Edmond. Dictionnaire de la langue française du seizième siècle. Paris, Champion; Didier, 1925-49. v.1-3, 4 (incompl.). (In progress) **M197**

v.1-3, A-Fabrique; v.4 (fasc. 31/32–35/36), Fabriqueur-Heure.

Tobler, Adolf. Tobler-Lommatzsch, Alt-französisches Wörterbuch; Adolf Toblers nachgelassene Materialien bearbeitet und mit Unterstützung der Preussischen Akademie der Wissenschaften hrsg. von Erhard Lommatzsch. Berlin, Weidmann, 1925-43. v.1-3⁶. (In progress) **M198**

v.1-2, A-D; v.3 (Lfg. 1-6), E-eslee.

Vandaele, Hilaire. Petit dictionnaire de l'ancien français. Paris, Garnier [1940]. 536p. **M199**

Compiled to furnish students with a compact, convenient dictionary to Old French. Not a substitute for *Godefroy* (M194) but useful as a small dictionary.

Regional and dialect

BIBLIOGRAPHY

Wartburg, Walther von. Bibliographie des dictionnaires patois. Paris, Droz, 1934. 146p. map. (Société de Publications Romanes et Françaises, v.8) **M200**

A comprehensive listing of regional and dialect dictionaries from all parts of France, and other French-speaking countries. A review with some additions and corrections by Raphael Levy, appeared in *Modern language notes* 50:128, 1935.

Location of copies of the dictionaries listed is indicated in George S. C. Adams' *Census of French and Provençal dialect dictionaries in American libraries* (Lancaster, Pa., Lancaster Pr., 1937. Linguistic Soc. of America special pub., 50c) which also indicates some additional titles.

ATLASES

Gilliéron, Jules and **Edmont, E.** Atlas linguistique de la France. Paris, Champion, 1902–10. 1920 (i.e., 2048) maps in 17 portfolios. **M201**

—— —— Table. 1912. 519p.

—— —— Supplements. v.1. 1920. 308p.

—— Atlas linguistique de la France. Corse. Paris, Champion, 1914–15. pt.1-4, 799 maps.

An appendix to the preceding work.

DICTIONARIES

VERRIER, A. J., and **ONILLON, R.** Glossaire étymologique et historique des patois et des parlers de l'**Anjou.** Angers, Germain, 1908. 2v. **M202**—
THIBAULT, ADRIEN. Glossaire du pays **blaisois.** Blois, 1892. 355p. **M203**—**HAIGNERÉ, DANIEL.** Le patois **boulonnais** comparé avec les patois du nord de la France; vocabulaire. Boulogne-sur-Mer, Deligny, 1903. 638p. (Mémoires de la Société Acad. de l'Arrondissement de Boulogne-sur-Mer) **M204**—**SOCIÉTÉ DU PARLER FRANÇAIS AU CANADA.** Glossaire du parler français au **Canada.** Québec, L'Action Sociale, 1930. 709p. **M205**—**JAUBERT, HIPPOLYTE FRANÇOIS.** Glossaire du **centre** de la France. 2. éd. Paris, Chaix, 1864–69. 732p. and suppl. 159p. **M206**—**VAUTHERIN, AUGUSTE.** Glossaire du patois de **Châtenois** avec vocables des autres localités du territoire de Belfort. Belfort, Devillers, 1896–1901. 543p. and suppl. 8p. **M207**—**DEVAUX, ANDRÉ.** Les patois du **Dauphiné.** Lyon, Bibliothèque de la Faculté Catholique des Lettres, 1935. 2v. (t.1, Dictionnaire des patois des Terres froides; t.2, Atlas lin-

guistique) **M208**—PALAY, SIMIN. Dictionnaire du béarnais et du **gascon** modernes (Bassin de l'Adour), embrassant les dialectes du Béarn, de la Bigorre, du Gers, des Landes, et de la Gascogne maritime. Pau, Marrimpouey, 1932. 2v. 576p., 670p. **M209**—DITCHY, JAY K. Les Acadiens **louisianais** et leur parler. Paris, Droz; Balt., Johns Hopkins, 1932. 272p. **M210**—PHILLIPS, HOSEA. Étude du parler de le paroisse Évangéline (**Louisiane**). Paris, Droz, 1931. 133p. (Soc. de Publications Romanes et Françaises. XVII) **M211**—MCDERMOTT, JOHN FRANCIS. A glossary of Mississippi Valley French, 1673–1850. St. Louis, 1941. 161p. (Washington Univ. studies: n.s. Language and literature, no.12) **M212**—READ, WILLIAM A. **Louisiana**-French. Baton-Rouge, Louisiana State Univ. Pr., 1931. 253p. (Louisiana State Univ. studies, 5) **M213**—DOTTIN, GEORGES. Glossaire des parlers du Bas-**Maine** (département de la Mayenne). Paris, Welter, 1899. 682p. **M214**—MONTESSON, CHARLES R., comte de. Vocabulaire du Haute-**Maine**. Nouv. éd. augm. Le Mans, Dehallais, 1859. 498p. Suppl. 1921. 201p. **M215**—CHAMBURE, EUGÈNE DE. Glossaire de **Morvan**: étude sur la langage de cette contrée comparé avec les principaux dialectes ou patois de la France, de la Belgique wallone et de la Suisse romande. Paris, Chambion, 1878. 966p. **M216**—ZÉLIQZON, LÉON. Dictionnaire des patois romans de la **Moselle**. Savergne, Fuchs, 1922–24. 718p. Suppl. 1 and 2. 1929–32. **M217**—MÉTIVIER, GEORGES. Dictionnaire franco-**normand**; ou, Recueil des mots particuliers au dialecte de Guernesey. Lond., Williams, 1870. 499p. **M218**—MOISY, HENRI. Dictionnaire de patois **normand**, indiquant particulièrement tous les termes de ce patois en usage dans la région centrale de la Normandie. Caen, Delesques, 1887. 716p. **M219**—ROBIN, EUGÈNE. Dictionnaire du patois **normand**, en usage dans le département de l'Eure. Pub. sous les auspices du Conseil Général par le Société Libre d'Agriculture, Sciences, Arts, et Belles-lettres de l'Eure. Évreux, Hérissey, 1879–82. 458p. **M220**—SOCIÉTÉ JERSIAISE. Glossaire du patois jersiais, recueil de mots particuliers au dialecte de Jersey. Jersey, Beresford Library, 1924. 182p. **M221**—DANIEL, JEAN. Dictionnaire **périgourdin**, 1. pte. Dictionnaire français—périgourdin, avec supplement. Périgueux, Imp. Ribes, 1914. 378p. **M222**—[**Picardie**] COCHET, E. Le patois de Gondecourt (Nord); grammaire et lexique. Paris, Droz, 1933. 216p. (Soc. de Publications Romanes et Franaises. IX) **M223**—FAVRE, LÉOPOLD. Glossaire du Poitou, de la **Saintonge** et de l'Aunis. . . . Niort, Favre, 1867. 356p. **M224**—ÉVEILLÉ, A. Glossaire

saintongeais, étude sur la signification, l'origine et l'historique des mots et des noms usités dans les deux Charentes. Paris, Champion, 1887. 408p. **M225**—MUSSET, GEORGES. Glossaire des patois et des parlers de l'Aunis et de la **Saintonge.** La Rochelle, Masson, 1929–32. v.1-3. A-M. **M226**—CONSTANTIN, AIMÉ and DÉSORMAUX, J. Dictionnaire **savoyard**. Paris, Bouillon, 1902. 443p. (Études philologiques savoisiennes. I) **M227**—Glossaire des patois de la **Suisse** romande par L. Gauchat [and others]. Ouvrage pub. sous les auspices de la Confédération Suisse et des Cantons Romands. Neuchâtel, Attinger, 1924–49. fasc. 1-23 (A-brɔz). (In progress) (Mémoires et documents pub. par la Soc. d'Histoire de la Suisse Romande, v.B) **M228**—PIERREHUMBERT, WILLIAM. Dictionnaire historique du parler neuchâtelois et **suisse** romand. Neuchâtel, Attinger, 1926. 763p. (Pub. de la Soc. d'Histoire et d'Archéologie du Canton de Neuchâtel, nouv. sér. t.2.) **M229**—ROBERT-JURET, M. A. Les patois de la région de **Tournus.** Paris, Droz, 1931. 156p. (Soc. de Publications Romanes et Françaises. V) **M230**—MARTELLIÈRE, PAUL. Glossaire du **vendômois.** Pub. sous les auspices de la Soc. Archéologique du Vendômois. Orléans, Herluison, 1893. 366p. **M231**—FORIR, HENRI J. Dictionnaire liégeois-français [**wallon**]. Liége, Severeyns, 1866–74. 2v. **M232**—GRANDGAGNAGE, CHARLES. Dictionnaire étymologique de la langue **wallonne.** Liége, Oudart, 1845–80. 2v. **M233**—REMACLE, LAURENT. Dictionnaire **wallon**-français dans lequel on trouve la correction de nos idiotismes vicieux et de nos wallonismes par le traduction, en français, des phrases wallones. 2. éd. corr., et augm. de plus de 10,000 mots. Liége, Gnusé [1857?]. 2v. **M234**

Friesian

Dijkstra, Waling. Friesch woordenboek (Lexicon frisicum), met medewerking van anderen, benevens lijst van Friesche eigennamen, bewerkt door Johan Winkler. Uitg. ingevolge besluit der Staten van Friesland, onder toezicht van de door Gedeputeerde staten benoemde commissie. Leeuwarden, Meijer [1896–1911]. 4v.   **M235**

Gaelic

Dieckhoff, Henry Cyril. Pronouncing dictionary of Scottish Gaelic; based on the Glengarry dialect according to oral information obtained from natives born before the middle of the last century. Edinburgh, Johnston, 1932. 185p.   **M236**

Appendix, p.173-86: (1) Personal names, (2) Names of places and their inhabitants.

Dwelly, Edward. The Illustrated Gaelic-English dictionary, containing every Gaelic word and meaning given in all previously published dictionaries, and a great number never in print before. To which is prefixed a concise Gaelic grammar. Glasgow, MacLaren [1941]. 1034p. 675 il. 25s. **M237**

> Half title: Faclair gàidhlig agus beurla le dealbhan.
> "First published, 1901–1911 . . . fourth edition . . . 1941."
> "The first edition . . . appeared in parts under the title of Faclair gàidhlig le dealbahn, and the nom-de-plume of 'Ewen MacDonald.' "—*Pref.*
> Appendix: Proper names.—A short account of the principal persons and places mentioned in old Gaelic folktales and poetry from Armstrong's *Gaelic dictionary.*

Macbain, Alexander. Etymological dictionary of the Gaelic language. Stirling, Mackay, 1911. 412p. **M238**

> 1st ed. 1896.

Maclennan, Malcolm. Pronouncing and etymological dictionary of the Gaelic language: Gaelic-English, English-Gaelic. Edinburgh, Grant, 1925. 613p. **M239**

MacLeod, Norman and **Dewar, Daniel.** Dictionary of the Gaelic language: Gaelic and English, English and Gaelic. Edinburgh, Grant, 1909. 1005p. **M240**

German

Grimm, Jacob and **Grimm, Wilhelm.** Deutsches Wörterbuch. Im Auftrage des Deutschen Reiches und Preussens mit Unterstützung des Reichsministeriums des Innern, des Preussischen Ministeriums für Wissenschaft, Kunst und Volksbildung, und der Notgemeinschaft der deutschen Wissenschaft hrsg. von der Preussischen Akademie der Wissenschaften. Leipzig, Hirzel, 1854–1940. v.1-16. (Some volumes still incomplete, issued in Lieferungen) **M241**

> Letters still incomplete are G, S, T, V-Z, though some portions of each have appeared.
> "In the Deutsches Wörterbuch of Jacob and Wilhelm Grimm the scientific spirit . . . first found expression in general lexicography. . . . Their design, in brief, was to give an exhaustive account of the words of the literary language (New High German) from about the end of the 15th century, including their earlier etymological and later history, with references to important dialectal words and forms; and to illustrate their use and history abundantly by quotations. . . . The scope and methods of this dictionary have been broadened somewhat as the work advanced. In general it may be said that it differs from the New English dictionary chiefly in its omission of pronunciations and other pedagogic matter; its irregular treatment of dates; its much less systematic and less lucid statement of etymologies; its less systematic and less fruitful use of quotations; and its less convenient and less

intelligible arrangement of material and typography." —*Encyclopaedia Britannica,* 11th ed. 8:189.
> As Grimm's dictionary throughout uses small letters instead of capitals for common nouns, it is the main German authority for the noncapitalization of nouns in German.

Heyne, Moriz. Deutsches Wörterbuch. 2. Aufl. (nach der neuesten amtlichen Rechtschreibung) Leipzig, Hirzel, 1905–06. 3v. **M242**

Lexer, Matthias von. Mittelhochdeutsches Taschenwörterbuch. 24. überarbeitete Aufl. Leipzig, Hirzel, 1944. 343p. **M243**

> Revised by Erich Henschel and Richard Kienast.

Paul, Hermann. Deutsches Wörterbuch. 4. Aufl. von Karl Euling. Halle, Niemeyer, 1933–34. Lfg. 1-6 (p.1-480). **M244**

> Lfg. 1-6, A-Seele.
> 1st ed. 1897; 2d ed. 1908; 3d ed. 1921.

Schulz, Hans. Deutsches Fremdwörterbuch. Strassburg, Trübner; Berlin, de Gruyter, 1913–42. 2v. **M245**

> Volume 2, in the series "Wörterbücher der deutschen Academie."

Trübners Deutsches Wörterbuch; im Auftrage der Arbeitsgemeinschaft für deutsche Wortforschung hrsg. von Alfred Goetze. Berlin, de Gruyter 1936–43. v.1-5[1]. RM. 3 per Lfg. (In progress) **M246**

> After the publication of the early parts of this work, the volume numbering was completely changed. Some parts were published for various parts of the alphabet, some of which have been superseded by newly published volumes. New volume numbers have not yet been assigned to the Lfg. in the latter part of the alphabet.
> According to the new numbering the following volumes have appeared: Bd.1, A-B; Bd.2, C-F; Bd.3, G-H; Bd.4 I-N; Bd. 5[1], O-Quit. (S-schicklich, T-Topf)

Ziesemer, Walther. Preussisches Wörterbuch. Sprache und Volkstum Nordostdeutschlands. In Auftrag und mit Unterstützung der Preussischen Akademie der Wissenschaften, der Deutschen Forschungsgemeinschaft und der Provinz Ostpreussen. Königsberg, Gräfe und Unzer, 1935-44. v.1- . (In progress) **M247**

> Bd.1, A-C; Bd.2, Lfg. 1-8, D-Fingern.

Bilingual

Breul, Karl H. Cassell's New German and English dictionary with a phonetic key to pronunciation. Rev. and enl. by J. H. Lepper and Rudolf Kottenhahn. N.Y., Funk & Wagnalls, 1939. 813p. 687p. **M248**

> First published 1909. This edition revised and reset.
> Also published as *Heath's New German and English dictionary.*

Flügel, Johann Gottfried. Allgemeines englisch-deutsches und deutsch-englisches Wörterbuch, von Felix Flügel. 3. verb. u. verm. Abdruck der 4 gänzlich umgearb. Aufl. von J. G. Flügel's Vollständigem Wörterbuch. . . . Braunschweig, Westermann, 1908–12. 2v. in 3. **M249**

Th.1, Bd.1-2, Englisch-Deutsch; Th.2, Deutsch-Englisch.

Grieb, Christoph Friedrich. Englisch-deutsches und deutsch-englisches Wörterbuch, mit besonderer Rücksicht auf Aussprache und Etymologie neubearb. und verm. von Arnold Schröer. 11. Aufl. Berlin-Schöneberg, Langenscheidtsche Verlagsbuchhandlung [c1911]. 2v. **M250**

Muret, Eduard and **Sanders, Daniel.** Muret-Sanders Enzyklopädisches englisch-deutsches und deutsch-englisches Wörterbuch. Parallelwerk zu Sachs-Villattes Französisch-deutschem und deutsch-französischem Wörterbuche. Mit Angabe der Aussprache nach dem phonetischen System der Methode Toussaint-Langenscheidt. Grosse Ausg. Berlin-Schöneberg, Langenscheidt, 1908. 2v. in 4. **M251**

Two parts, each in two volumes, paged continuously. Frequently reprinted.
Prefixed to volume 4: German, Austrian, and Swiss measures, weights, coins, bearb. von Hubert Jansen (xlviii p.).

—— —— Hand-und-Schulausg. (Auszug aus der groszen Ausg.) Berlin, Langenscheidt, c1910. 2v.

—— —— —— Nachtrag. . . . Berlin-Schöneberg, Langenscheidt [1931]. 2 pts.

Paechter, Heinz [and others]. Nazi-Deutsch; a glossary of contemporary German usage, with appendices on government, military and economic institutions. N.Y., Frederick Ungar [1944]. 128p. diagrs. $2.50. **M252**

Explanations of new terms coined by the Nazis and of old terms used by them in senses different from the original meanings.

Pfeffer, Jay Alan. Dictionary of everyday usage German-English, English-German. New ed. N.Y., Holt, 1947. 369p., 504p. $4. **M253**

Originally prepared for the Office of the Provost Marshal General, as a guide to current usage. Entries have been limited to words of "highest importance and frequency" and illustrations are given to show use in phrases and sentences.

Schmidt, Immanuel and **Tanger, G.** Flügel-Schmidt-Tanger, a dictionary of the English and German languages for home and school. . . . With special reference to Dr. Felix Flügel's Universal English-German and German-English dictionary. N.Y., Lemcke, 1901–[1917?]. 2v. **M254**

Etymology

Kluge, Friedrich. Etymologisches Wörterbuch der deutschen Sprache; 12. und 13. unveränderte Aufl. mit Unterstützung durch Wolfgang Krause, bearb. von Alfred Götze. Berlin, de Gruyter, 1943. 740p. **M255**

This edition has same paging as 11th edition and revision is very slight.

Orthography and usage

Duden, Konrad. Der grosse Duden; Rechtschreibung der deutschen Sprache und der Fremdwörter. 12. Aufl. Leipzig, Bibliog. Inst., 1941. 692p. **M256**

Swiss ed.: Zurich, Fretz und Wasmuth, 1948. 690p.
Early editions had title *Orthographisches Wörterbuch der deutschen Sprache.*
A companion work, sometimes bound with this is:

—— Der grosse Duden: Stilwörterbuch der deutschen Sprache; eine Sammlung der Richtigen und der gebräuchlichen Ausdrücke und Redewendungen, mit einer Einleitung von Ewald Geissler. 3. verb. Aufl. Leipzig, Bibliog. Inst., 1938. 694p. **M257**

Deals with correct use of words.

Synonyms

Dornseiff, Franz. Deutsche Wortschatz, nach Sachgruppen. Berlin, de Gruyter, 1940. 509p. **M258**

Eberhard, Johann August. Synonymisches Handwörterbuch der deutschen Sprache. 17. Aufl. durchgängig umgearb., verm. und verb. von Otto Lyon. Mit Übersetzung der Wörter in die englische, französische, italienische, und russische Sprache. Leipzig, Grieben, 1910. 1201p. **M259**

Schlessing, Anton. Deutscher Wortschatz, ein Wegweiser zum treffenden Ausdruck. 9. Aufl. nach A. Schlessing; "Der passende Ausdruck," von Hugo Wehrle. Stuttgart, Klett, 1942. 516p. **M260**

Dialect

Martin, Ernst and Lienhart, Hans. Wörterbuch der elsässischen Mundarten. Strassburg, Trübner, 1899–1907. 2v. M261—Ochs, Ernst. Badisches Wörterbuch. Lahr, M. Schauenburg, 1925–40. (In progress) v.1 covers A, B P, D T,

E. **M262**—WOSSIDLO, RICHARD and TEUCHERT, HERMANN. **Mecklenburgisches** Wörterbuch. Neumünster, Wacholtz, 1937- . (In progress) Bd.1, A-Brot; Bd.2, pt.1, Brotät-Bulloss. **M263** —LAMBERT, MARCUS BACHMAN. Dictionary of the non-English words of the **Pennsylvania**-German dialect. [Lancaster] Pa., Lancaster Pr., 1924. 193p. **M264**—Rheinisches Wörterbuch, im Auftrag der Preussischen Akademie der Wissenschaften [and others] bearb. u. hrsg. von Josef Müller. Bonn, Klopp, 1928–50. (In progress) Bd.1-6, A-Q; Bd.7, Lfg. 1-6, R-riemen. **M265**— MÜLLER-FRAUREUTH, KARL. Wörterbuch der **obersächsischen** und erzgebirgischen Mundarten. Dresden, Baensch, 1914. 2v. **M266**—MENSING, OTTO. **Schleswig-holsteinisches** Wörterbuch (Volksausgabe). Neumünster, Wachholtz, 1927– 35. 5v. **M267**—FISCHER, HERMANN VON. **Schwäbisches** Wörterbuch. Tübingen, H. Laupp, 1904– 36. v.1-6 in 7. **M268**—Schweizerisches Idiotikon. Wörterbuch der schweizerdeutschen Sprache. Gesammelt auf Veranstaltung der Antiquarischen Gesellschaft in Zurich. . . . Begonnen von Friedrich Staub u. Ludwig Tobler. Frauenfeld, Huber, 1881–1950. Bd.1-10, A-Stack; Bd.11, Bogen, 1-140. Stal-str. **M269**—Siebenbürgisch-sächsisches Wörterbuch. Mit Benützung der Sammlungen Johann Wolffs. Berlin, de Gruyter, 1924–31. v.1-2, A-F; v.5 (incompl.) R-Salarist. **M270**

Greek
Bilingual

Edwards, Gerald Maclean. English-Greek lexicon. 2d ed. Camb., Univ. Pr., 1915. 338p. **M271**

An excellent small dictionary frequently reprinted. This work and the somewhat larger dictionary by Woodhouse (M274) practically supersede Yonge's *English-Greek lexicon* (M275).

Liddell, Henry George and **Scott, Robert.** Greek-English lexicon. . . . A new ed. rev. and augm. throughout by Henry Stuart Jones . . . with the assistance of Roderick McKenzie . . . and with the cooperation of many scholars. . . . Ox., Clarendon Pr., 1925–40. 2111p. £5 5s. **M272**

1st ed. 1843. This new edition is revised throughout and enlarged by the addition of many words including scientific and technical terms.

Issued in ten parts. With each of parts 2-9 there were issued Aids to the reader and Addenda and corrigenda. These have all been consolidated in the new Addenda and corrigenda (p.2043-2111) and in the new Preliminary leaves issued with part 10. These include: List of authors and works, p.xvi-xli; Epigraphical publications, p.xli-xliii; Papyrological publications, xliii-xlv; Periodicals, xlv-xlvi; General list of abbreviations, xlvi-xlviii.

The standard Greek and English lexicon, covering the language to about 600 A.D., omitting Patristic and Byzantine Greek. Omits place names for which Passow's dictionary (*see* M273) must be used.

—— Abridged. 26th ed. rev. and enl. Chic., Follett, 1941. 835p. $2.85.

Passow, Franz. Handwörterbuch der griechischen Sprache. Neu bearb. und zeitgemäss umgestaltet von Val. Chr. Fr. Rost und Friedrich Palm. Des ursprünglichen Werkes 5. Aufl. Leipzig, Vogel, 1841–57. 2v. in 4. **M273**

The standard Greek and German lexicon, useful to the English reader also because it includes geographical names omitted in Liddell and Scott (M272). A new, much enlarged edition, by Wilhelm Crönert, was started but only parts 1-3 were issued (Göttingen, Vanderhoeck, 1912–13).

Woodhouse, Sidney Chawner. English-Greek dictionary; a vocabulary of the Attic language. Lond., Routledge, 1910. 1029p. **M274**

Yonge, Charles Duke. English-Greek lexicon; ed. by Henry Drisler. N.Y., Amer. Book Co., 1890 [c'70]. 663p., cxvp. **M275**

Includes Greek synonyms from the French of Alex. Pillou, edited with notes by T. K. Arnold (cxvp.).

Moulton, James Hope and **Milligan, George.** Vocabulary of the Greek New Testament, illustrated from the papyri and other non-literary sources. Lond., Hodder, 1914–29. [pref. 1929] 705p. **M276**

Preisigke, Friedrich. Wörterbuch der griechischen Papyrusurkunden mit Einschluss der griechischen Inschriften, Aufschriften, Ostraka, Mumienschilder usw. aus Ägypten hrsg. von Emil Kiessling. Heidelberg, Selbstverlag des Erben, 1924–44. v.1-4, pt.1. **M277**

Contents: Bd.1-2, A-Ω; Bd.3, Besondere Wörterliste; Bd.4, Lfg. 1, A-ärtos.

Etymology

Boisacq, Émile. Dictionnaire étymologique de la langue grecque, étudiée dans ses rapports avec les autres langues indo-européennes. 3. éd., augm. par un index. Heidelberg, Winter; Paris, Klincksieck, 1938. 1155p. **M278**

Juret, Étienne Abel. Dictionnaire étymologique, grec et latin. Mâcon, Protat Frères, 1942. 463p. (Publ. de la Faculté des Lettres de l'Université de Strasbourg. fasc. 98) **M279**

Modern Greek

Kykkōtēs, Hierotheos. English-Greek and Greek-English dictionary. . . . Lond., Humphries [1942]. 704p. $5. **M280**

Modern Greek.

Subtitle: Including English and Greek grammar, geographical and proper names and abbreviations.

Kyriakidēs, A. Modern Greek-English dictionary with a Cypriote vocabulary. 2d ed. (rev. throughout) Athens, Constantinides, 1909. 908p. **M281**

Hawaiian

Andrews, Lorrin. Dictionary of the Hawaiian language. Rev. by Henry H. Parker. Prepared under the direction of the Board of Commissioners of Public Archives of the Territory of Hawaii. Honolulu, pub. by the Board, 1922. 674p. **M282**

Judd, Henry, Pukui, Mary Kawena and **Stokes, John F. G.** Introduction to the Hawaiian language (an English-Hawaiian vocabulary) . . . with a complementary Hawaiian-English vocabulary. Honolulu, Hawaii, Tongg Pub. Co., 1945. 314p. **M283**

Subtitle: Comprising five thousand of the commonest and most useful English words and their equivalents, in modern Hawaiian speech, correctly pronounced.

Hebrew

Ben-Yehudah, Eliezer. Thesaurus totius hebraitatis et veteris et recentioris auctore Elieser Ben Iehuda. Berlin-Schöneberg, Langenscheidt; Jerusalem, Ben-Yehudah Hozaa-la'Or, [1908]–46. v.1-12. (In progress) **M284**

Added title pages in Hebrew, German, French, and English. Equivalents given in these languages but all explanations are in Hebrew. Volumes 8-12 edited by Morris Hirsch Segal.

Grasovsky, Yehudah. Milon ivri. 2d ed. [Tel Aviv] [1947] 1113p. **M285**

Includes both Biblical and modern Hebrew.

Bilingual

Arnold-Kellner, P., and **Gross, M. D.** Complete Hebrew-English dictionary containing a list of Hebrew abbreviations. Lond., Shapiro, Vallentine, n.d. 467p., 20p. **M286**

Good small dictionary of Biblical, Talmudic and modern Hebrew.

Gesenius, Wilhelm. Hebräisches und aramäisches Handwörterbuch über das Alte Testament . . . 17th ed. 1921. Leipzig, Vogel. 1921. 1013p. **M287**

Hebrew-German.

—— Hebrew and English lexicon of the Old Testament, with an appendix containing the Biblical Aramaic. . . . Bost., Houghton, 1906. 1127p. **M288**

Subtitle: Based on the lexicon of William Gesenius as translated by Edward Robinson. Edited, with constant reference to the Thesaurus of Gesenius as completed by E. Rödiger, and with authorized use of the latest German editions of Gesenius' Handwörterbuch über das Alte Testament, by Francis Brown with the coöperation of S. R. Driver and Charles A. Briggs.

The best Hebrew-English dictionary of Biblical Hebrew.

Harkavy, Alexander. Student's Hebrew and Chaldee dictionary to the Old Testament with suppl.: Neo-Hebrew vocabulary. 2d ed. rev. N.Y., Hebrew Pub. Co., 1918. 786p., 102p. **M289**

Jastrow, Marcus. Dictionary of the Targumim, the Talmud Babli and Yerushalmi, and the Midrashic literature. With an index of Scriptural quotations. Lond., Luzac; N.Y., Putnam, 1903. 2v. **M290**

A photographic reprint, less expensive, is issued by Shapiro, Vallentine, London, 1926.

The best English dictionary of Talmudic Hebrew.

Kaufman, Judah. English-Hebrew dictionary by Israel Efros, Judah Ibn-Shmuel Kaufman, Benjamin Silk, ed. by Judah Kaufman. Tel Aviv, Dvir [1929]. 751p. **M291**

Levy, Jacob. Wörterbuch über die Talmudim und Midraschim. Nebst beiträgen von Heinrich Leberecht Fleischer. 2. Aufl. mit Nachträgen u. Berichtigungen von Lazarus Goldschmidt. Berlin, Harz, 1924. 4v. **M292**

1st ed. 1876–89.

Lexicon in veteris testamenti libros. Wörterbuch zum Hebräischen alten Testament in deutscher und englischer Sprache. A dictionary of the Hebrew Old Testament in English and German, ed. by Ludwig Koehler; Wörterbuch zum Aramäischen Teil des alten Testaments in deutscher und englischer Sprache. A dictionary of the aramaic parts of the Old Testament in English and German, ed. Walter Baumgartner. Leiden, Brill, 1948–49. Lfg. 1-4. (In progress) **M293**

Segal, Morris Hirsch. A concise Hebrew-English dictionary comprising the Hebrew of all ages. Tel Aviv, Dvir, 1946. 260p. **M294**

Bound with: *A concise English-Hebrew dictionary with the English pronunciation in Hebrew transliteration.* 4th ed. by H. Danby and M. H. Segal. Tel Aviv, 1947. 461p.

Waldstein, Abraham Solomon. Hebrew-English dictionary. 6th ed. rev. and enl. Tel Aviv, "Mizpah" Pub. Co., 1939. 468p. **M295**

—— English-Hebrew dictionary. 8th ed. 1939. 610p. **M295a**

Hindustani

Craven, Thomas. New royal dictionary; English into Hindustani and Hindustani into English, comp. originally by Rev. Thomas Craven . . . and in subsequent editions rev. and enl.; 1932 ed. rev. by Bishop J. R. Chitambar. Lucknow, Methodist Pub. House, 1932. 328p., 372p. **M296**

pt.1, English-Hindustani; pt.2, Hindustani-English.

Fallon, S. W. New Hindustani-English dictionary, with illustrations from Hindustani literature and folk-lore. Banāras, Medical Hall Pr.; Lond., Trübner, 1879. 1216p. **M297**

—— New English-Hindustani dictionary, with illustrations from English literature and colloquial English, tr. into Hindustani, by S. W. Fallon. . . . Lahore, Rai Sahib M. Gulab Singh [1905?]. 703p. il. **M298**

Platts, John Thompson. Dictionary of Urdu, classical Hindi and English. 4th impr. Lond., Lockwood, 1911. 1259p. **M299**

Hungarian

Szarvas, Gábor and **Simonyi, Zsigmond.** Lexicon linguae Hungaricae aevi antiquioris, auspiciis Academiae Scienciarum Hungaricae. Budapestini, Sumptibus et typis Victoris Hornyánszky, 1890–93. 3v. **M300**

Bizonfy, Ferencz. English-Hungarian and Hungarian-English dictionary. 6th ed. Budapest, Franklin-Társulat, 1938. 2v. **M301**

Yolland, Arthur Battishill. Dictionary of the Hungarian and English languages. Budapest, Franklin-Társulat, 1908–24. 2 pts. in 3v. **M302**

pt.1, English-Hungarian, 1908. 836p.; pt.2, Hungarian-English, 1924. 2v.

Frequently reprinted. Still the best Hungarian-English, English-Hungarian dictionary though now much out of date and not abreast of orthographical changes.

Icelandic

Blöndal, Sigfús. Islandsk-dansk ordbog. Hovedmedarbejdere: Björg Thorláksson Blöndal, Jón Ófeigsson, Holger Wiehe. Reykjavík, Thorlaksson, 1920–24. 1052p. **M303**

Old Icelandic.

Zoëga, Geir Tómasson. Concise dictionary of old Icelandic. Ox., Clarendon Pr., 1910. 551p. **M304**

Based on Cleasby, Richard, *Icelandic-English dictionary,* enlarged by G. Vigfusson (Ox., Clarendon Pr., 1874. 779p.).

—— Icelandic-English and English-Icelandic dictionary. 2d-3d ed. Reykjavík, Kristjánsson, 1922–32. 2v. **M305**

Icelandic-English, 1922. 631p.; English-Icelandic, 1932. 712p.

The best dictionaries of modern Icelandic and English. Frequently reprinted.

Irish

Royal Irish Academy, Dublin. Dictionary of the Irish language based mainly on old and middle Irish materials: General ed., Osborn Bergin. Dublin, Royal Irish Acad., 1913–32. fasc. 1-2. **M306**

fasc. 1, D-Degóir, ed. by Carl J. S. Marstrander; fasc. 2, E-Extais, ed. by Maud Joynt and Eleanor Knott.

The authoritative dictionary of the Irish language based on materials collected for many years by the Academy from printed books, manuscripts and the spoken language. Arranged on historical principles with many quotations illustrating the development both of meanings of words and their grammatical inflexions. Begins with the letter D, leaving A-C to be published last, because the letters A-Dn were covered in Kuno Meyer's *Contributions to Irish lexicography* (Halle, Niemeyer; Lond., Nutt, 1906. 670p.) of which the Academy's dictionary is a continuation.

—— Contributions to a Dictionary of the Irish language. . . . Dublin, Royal Irish Acad., [1939–48]. **M307**

M [1939?], 208 col. 5s.; N-O-P [1940?], 212 col. 5s.; R, 1944. 124 col. 4s.; T-tnut, 1943. 198 col. 5s.; to-tu, 1948. 394 col. 5s.; U, 1942. 98 col. 3s.

M, N-O-P, R, arr. by Maud Joynt; T, arr. by David Greene and E. G. Quin; U, arr. by Teresa Condon.

"The object of the present publication is to make immediately available . . . the mass of collected material . . . in the Royal Irish Academy pending publication of the . . . Dictionary as planned. This and the following fasciculi are then to be regarded merely as 'Contributions' towards a dictionary, not as installments of the final work."—*Note in fasc. M.*

Bilingual

Dineen, Patrick Stephen. Irish-English dictionary; being a thesaurus of the words, phrases and idioms of the modern Irish language. New ed. rev. and greatly enl. Dublin, Educ. Co. of Ireland, 1927. 1340p. **M308**

1st ed. 1904.

—— A smaller Irish-English dictionary for the use of schools. Pub. for the Irish Texts Society. Dublin, Gill, 1945. 240p. **M309**

Lane, Timothy O'Neill. Larger English-Irish dictionary. New ed. thoroughly rev. and greatly enl. Dublin, Educ. Co. of Ireland, 1916. 1748p. **M310**

McKenna, Lambert A. J. English-Irish dictionary. Dublin, Govt. Publications, 1935. 1546p.
M311

O'Reilly, Edward. Irish-English dictionary, with copious quotations from the most esteemed ancient and modern writers . . . and numerous comparisons of Irish words with those of similar orthography, sense, or sound in the Welsh and Hebrew languages. A new edition, carefully rev. and cor. With a supplement, by John O'Donovan. Dublin, Duffy, 1864. 724p.
M312

Italian

Accademia d'Italia. Vocabolario della lingua italiana. Milano, Soc. Anonima per la pubblicazione del Vocabolario, 1941- . v.1- . (In progress)
M313
v.1, A-C.

Accademia della Crusca, Florence. Vocabolario degli Accademici della Crusca. 5. impressione. Firenze, Tip. Galileiana di M. Cellini ec., 1863–1923. v.1-11.
M314
v.1-11, A-O.

Melzi, Gian Battista. Il novissimo Melzi. Dizionario italiano. 32. ed., ampl., riv. e agg. Milano, Vallardi, 1947. 2v. il.
M315
pte. 1, Linguistica. 1230p.; pte. 2, Scientifica. 1288p.
A useful small dictionary and encyclopedia of the *Petit Larousse* (M172) type.

Mestica, Enrico. Dizionario della lingua italiana. 4. ristampo. Torino, Lattes, 1938. 2098p. **M316**

Panzini, Alfredo. . . . Dizionario moderno delle parole che non si trovano negli altri dizionari. 7. ed. interamente rinnovata. . . . Milano, Hoepli, 1935. 773p.
M317
Subtitle: Conversazione, politica, guerra, fascismo, filosofia, medicina, moda, aeronautica, sport, voci straniere, dialetto, gergo, giornalismo, banca, legge, scienze, burocrazia, bizarrie, amenità, motti, motteggi, ecc., nuove accezioni, modi latini e greci, etimologia, storia del costume nel sorgere e tramontare delle parole.

Tommaseo, Niccolò and **Bellini, Bernardo.** Dizionario della lingua italiana, nuovamente compilato; con oltre 100,000 giunte ai precedenti dizionarii raccolte da Niccolò Tommaseo, Gius. Campi, Gius. Meini, Pietro Fanfani e da molti altri distinti filologi e scienziati, corredato di un discorso preliminare dello stesso Niccolò Tommaseo. . . . Torino, Unione Tip.-ed. [1861–79]. 4v. in 8.
M318
Half title: Nuovo dizionario della lingua italiana.
Reprinted, without revision, 1924. 7v.

Bilingual

Baretti, Giuseppe. New dictionary of the Italian and English languages, based upon that of Baretti. Comp. by John Davenport and Guglielmo Comelati. Lond., Whittaker [18-?]. 2v.   **M319**
v.1, Italian-English; v.2, English-Italian.

Hoare, Alfred. Italian dictionary. 2d ed. Camb., Univ. Pr., 1925. 906p.
M320
1st ed. 1915.
The best Italian-English dictionary.

—— Short Italian dictionary, abridged from the author's larger dictionary. Camb., Univ. Pr., 1923–26. 2v.
M321
v.1, Italian-English, 2d ed.; v.2, English-Italian, new and enl. ed.
Frequently reprinted.

Lysle, A. de R. The latest modern Italian-English and English-Italian dictionary. Turin, Casanova, 1938. 644p., 755p. $4.
M322
Repr. N.Y., Hafner Pub. Co., $4.
Includes words in common use, historical, geographical, commercial, modern scientific terms, also colloquial and slang expressions, with pronunciation.

Millhouse, John. English and Italian pronouncing and explanatory dictionary, new phototypic ed. rev., cor. and enriched with an appendix containing all the words and technical terms in general use during the last twenty years in science, industry, arts, crafts, sport, etc., ed. by Francesco Bracciforti. Milan, Nicola, 1925. 2v.
M323

Etymology

Pianigiani, Ottorino. Vocabolario etimologico della lingua italiana. Milano, Sonzogno, 1936–37. 2v. (Repr. 1942)
M324

Synonyms

Tommaseo, Niccolò. Dizionario dei sinonimi della lingua italiana. Completamente riveduta e aumentato da Giuseppe Rigutini. Milano, Vallardi, 1944. 1000p.
M325

Japanese

Dai-jiten [Great dictionary]. Comp. by Heibonsha. Tokyo, Heibonsha, 1934–36. 26v. **M326**

Daniels, Otome. Dictionary of Japanese (sōsho) writing forms. Lond., Lund Humphries, 1944. 309p., 48p.
M327

Ming, Lou Yet. Sōsho dictionary, by Technical Sergeant L. Y. Ming, U.S. Marine Corps. South

Pasadena, Calif., P. D. and Ione Perkins, 1944. 145p. $2.50. **M328**

Added title page and text in Chinese.
"The 2400 characters chosen from Professor [Basil Hall] Chamberlain's book, which he considered essential, and a Hentai Gana chart are . . . included."—*Foreword*.
Handwritten Chinese characters as used in Japanese.

Otsuki, Fumihiko. Dai-genkai. Tokyo, Fuzambo, 1932–35. 4v. and index. **M329**

Entirely in Japanese.
Compiled along western lines by an author educated in western countries. Said by a Japanese authority to be especially important for inclusion of the etymology of words, something not done by other Japanese lexicographers.

Ueda, Mannen. Ueda's Daijiten; a Japanese dictionary of Chinese characters and compounds. American ed. Camb., Harv. Univ. Pr., 1942. [2918]p. il. $6. **M330**

Entirely in Japanese.
Various pagings.
Table on lining papers.
"Published under the sponsorship of the Department of Far Eastern Languages of Harvard University, with the financial aid of the Rockefeller Institute."—*Foreword*.

—— and **Matsui, K.** Dai-nihon kokugo jiten. Tokyo, Fuzambo, 1928–29. 4v. and index. **M331**

1st ed. 1921.

Bilingual

Kenkyusha's New English-Japanese dictionary on bilingual principles; Y. Okakura, general ed. Berkeley and Los Angeles, Univ. of Calif. Pr., 1942. 2514p. **M332**

First printing, 1936; sixtieth printing, 1940. Cf. p.[2515].
"Photographically reproduced and printed by offset in the United States of America."
A standard dictionary.

Kenkyusha's New Japanese-English dictionary . . . Takenobu Yoshitaro, general ed., American ed. Camb., Harv. Univ. Pr., 1942. 2280p. **M333**

"Reproduced by a photolithographic process from the eighty-second printing of 1939."—*2d prelim. leaf.*

Rose-Innes, Arthur. Beginners' dictionary of Chinese-Japanese characters, with common abbreviations, variants and numerous compounds, American ed. Camb., Harv. Univ. Pr., 1942. 507p., 25p. **M334**

Tables on lining papers.
"Reproduced by a photolithographic process from the second enlarged edition of 1927."—*2d prelim. leaf.*

Saito, H. Saito's Japanese-English dictionary. Tokyo, The Nichieisha, 1931. 1160p. **M335**

Satow, *Sir* Ernest Mason and **Ishibashi, Masakata.** An English-Japanese dictionary of the spoken language. Rev. by E. M. Hobart-Hampden and Harold G. Parlett. American ed. South Pasadena, Calif., P. D. and Ione Perkins, 1942. 1530p. **M336**

A reproduction of the fourth edition of 1919, and therefore somewhat out of date. Useful for American students, however, because the Japanese equivalents of English words are given both in romanization and in characters.

Korean

Gale, James Scarth. Unabridged Korean-English dictionary. 3d ed., ed. by Alexander A. Pieters. Seoul, Christian Lit. Soc., 1931. 1781p. **M337**

Lew, Hyungki J. New life English-Korean dictionary. Seoul, New Life Pr., 1946. 1139p. il. **M338**

Lappish

Nielsen, Konrad. Lappisk ordbok, grunnet på dialektene i Polmak, Karasjok og Kautikeino. Oslo, Aschehoug; Camb., Harv. Univ. Pr.; Lond., Williams, 1932–38. 3v. (Inst. for Sammenlignende Kulturforskning. [Publikasjoner] ser. B: Skrifter. 17) $10. **M339**

Lappish, English, and Norwegian; preliminary matter in Norwegian and English in parallel columns.

Latin

Thesaurus linguae latinae, editus auctoritate et consilio academiarum quinque Germanicarum Berolinensis, Gottingensis, Lipsiensis, Monacensis, Vindobonensis. Lipsiae, Teubner, 1900–50. price varies. **M340**

v.1-5[1], A-D, and v.6[1-3], F-H, compl.; v.5[2], fasc. 1-12, E-Exstinguo; v.7[1], fasc. 1-7, I-Inde; v.8, fasc. 1-5, M-Mercor.
The great dictionary of the language, in Latin; indispensable in the university or large reference library. Plans to record, with representative quotations from each author, every word in the text of each Latin author down to the Antonines, with a selection of important passages from the works of all writers to the seventh century. In the section A-B proper names are included in the main alphabet, but from C on they are given in the following supplement:

—— Supplementum: Nomina propria [Onomasticon]. Lipsiae, Teubner, 1909- . v.1-2.

v.1-2, A-H.

—— Index librorum scriptorum inscriptionum ex quibus exempla adferunter. Lipsiae, Teubner, 1904. 109p.

Olcott, George N. Thesaurus linguae latinae epigraphicae; a dictionary of the Latin inscriptions. Rome, Loescher, 1904–12; N.Y., Columbia Univ. Pr., 1935–36. v.1 (compl.); v.2$^{1-4}$.   **M341**

v.1, A-Astv, 520p.; v.2, fasc. 1-4, Astvuica-Avillinlanvs, by Leslie F. Smith, John H. McLean and Clinton W. Keyes.

Bilingual

Benoist, Eugène and **Goelzer, Henri.** Nouveau dictionnaire latin-français . . . 10. ed. rev. corr. Paris, Garnier [192-?]. 1713p.   **M342**

Cassell's Latin dictionary. (Latin-English and English-Latin) rev. by J. R. V. Marchant and Joseph F. Charles. N.Y., and Lond., Funk & Wagnalls, 1938. 927p. $3.25.   **M343**

Harpers' Latin dictionary. A new Latin dictionary founded on the translation of Freund's Latin-German lexicon, ed. by E. A. Andrews. Rev., enl., and in great part rewritten by Charlton T. Lewis and Charles Short. N.Y., Cincinnati, Amer. Bk. Co., 1907. 2019p.   **M344**

Frequently reprinted. The most generally useful of Latin-English dictionaries.

Lewis, Charlton T. Latin dictionary for schools. N.Y., Cincinnati, Amer. Bk. Co., 1916. 1191p.   **M345**

Miguel y Navas, Raimundo de and **Morante, Joachim.** Nuevo diccionario latino-español etimológico . . . seguido de un tratado de sinónimos y de un vocabulario español-latino. 23. ed. Madrid, Suárez, 1943. 997p., 76p., 256p.   **M346**

Smith, *Sir* **William** and **Hall, T. D.** Copious and critical English-Latin dictionary. N.Y., Amer. Bk. Co., 1871. 754p.   **M347**

Includes a dictionary of proper names.

Smith, *Sir* **William.** Smaller Latin-English dictionary. [3d ed.] rev. by J. F. Lockwood. Lond., Murray, 1933. 823p.   **M348**

Frequently reprinted.

Medieval Latin

Arnaldi, Francisco. Latinitatis italicae medii aevi inde ab a. CDLXXVI usque ad a. MXXII lexicon imperfectum cura et studio. . . . Bruxelles, 1936–37. fasc. 1-2. (Union Académique Internat. Bulletin Du Cange Archivum Latinitatis medii aevi. v.10, 12)   **M349**

fasc. 1-2, A-Medicamen.

Du Cange, Charles Du Fresne, *sieur.* Glossarium mediæ et infimæ latinitatis conditum a Carolo Du Fresne, domino Du Cange, auctum a monachis ordinis S. Benedicti, cum supplementis integris D. P. Carpentarii, Adelungii, aliorum, suisque digessit G. A. L. Henschel; sequuntur Glossarium gallicum, Tabulae, Indices auctorum et rerum, Dissertationes. Ed. nova, aucta pluribus verbis aliorum scriptorum a Léopold Favre. Niort, L. Favre, 1883–87. 10v. il. (Repr. Paris, Lib. des Sciences et des Arts, 1937–38)   **M350**

v.1-8, A-Z; v.9, Glossaire français; v.10, Indices.

The great dictionary of medieval Latin, originally published 1678 and several times revised. This is the latest edition but is very little changed from the edition of 1840–57, eight volumes, which is still usable and as good for general purposes as the later edition.

——— ——— Petit supplément au Dictionnaire de Du Cange par Charles Schmidt. Strasbourg, Heitz, 1906. 71p.

Baxter, James Houston and **Johnson, Charles.** Medieval Latin word-list from British and Irish sources prepared . . . with the assistance of Phyllis Abrahams under the direction of a committee appointed by the British Academy. Ox., Univ. Pr., 1934. 466p.   **M351**

A word-list rather than a formal dictionary, forming a first step in the task of making a comprehensive dictionary of medieval British Latin on which committees of the British Academy have been working since 1924. Gives brief information, i.e., Latin word, date and equivalent English word or phrase.

Brinckmeier, Eduard. Glossarium diplomaticum zur Erläuterung schwieriger, einer diplomatischen, historischen, sachlichen oder Worterklärung bedürftiger lateinischer, hoch-und besonders niederdeutscher Wörter und Formeln . . . des gesammten deutschen Mittelalters finden. Gotha, Perthes, 1855–56. 2v.   **M352**

Castro, Américo. Glosarios latino-españoles de la edad media. Madrid, 1936. lxxxviip., 378p. (Revista de filología española, anejo 22)   **M353**

Vocabulario general (Latin) A-Z, p.1-314; Voces españolas, p.315-48.

Maigne d'Arnis, W. H. Lexicon manuale ad scriptores mediae et infimae latinitatis, ex glossariis Caroli Dufresne D. Ducangii, D. P. Carpentarii, Adelungii et aliorum, in compendium accuratissime redactum; ou, Recueil de mots de la basse latinité. Paris, Migne, 1866. 2336 col.   **M354**

Sleumer, Albert. Kirchenlateinisches Wörterbuch . . . 2. sehr verm. Aufl. des "Liturgischen Lexikons" unter umfassendster Mitarbeit von . . . Joseph Schmid, hrsg. von . . . Albert Sleumer. . . . Limburg a. d. Lahn, Steffen, 1926. 840p.   **M355**

Subtitle: Ausführliches Wörterverzeichnis zum Römischen Missale, Breviarium, Rituale, Graduale, Pontificale, Caeremoniale, Martyrologium, sowie zur Vulgata und zum Codex juris canonici; desgleichen zu den Proprien der Bistümer Deutschlands, Österreichs, Ungarns, Luxemburgs, der Schweiz und zahlreicher kirchlicher Orden und Kongregationen.

Abbreviations

Cappelli, Adriano. Lexicon abbreviaturarum . . . 4. ed. (anastatica) cor. con 9 tavole fuori testo. Milano, Hoepli, 1949. 531p. **M356**

Subtitle: Dizionario di abbreviature latine ed italiane usate nelle carte e codici, specialmente del medio-evo, riprodotte con oltre 14,000 segni incisi, con l'aggiunta di uno studio sulla brachigrafia medioevale, un prontuario di Sigle Epigrafiche, l'antica numeraz, romana ed arabica ed i segni indicanti monete, pesi, misure, etc.

Main part of the dictionary consists of an alphabetical list of abbreviations, given both in manuscript facsimile and in printed letters, followed by the words in full for which they stand. Supplementary lists are: (1) Conventional signs, (2) Epigraphical abbreviations, (3) Bibliography of works on abbreviations.

An anastatic reprint of the third edition published 1929.

Martin, Charles Trice. The Record interpreter: A collection of abbreviations, Latin words and names used in English historical manuscripts and records. 2d ed. Lond., Stevens, 1910. 464p. **M357**

Contents: (1) Abbreviations of Latin words used in English records; (2) Abbreviations of French words used in English records; (3) Glossary of Latin words found in records and other English manuscripts, but not occurring in classical authors; (4) Latin names of places in Great Britain and Ireland; (5) Latin names of bishoprics in England; (6) Latin names of bishoprics in Scotland; (7) Latin names of bishoprics in Ireland; (8) Latin forms of English surnames; (9) Latin Christian names with their English equivalents.

Compiler was Assistant keeper of the public records. The first edition published in 1892 was an amplification of his appendix to Wright's *Court hand restored* (9th ed. 1879).

Etymology

Ernout, Alfred and **Meillet, A.** Dictionnaire étymologique de la langue latine; histoire des mots. Paris, Klincksieck, 1932. 1108p. **M358**

Juret, Etienne A. Dictionnaire étymologique, grec et latin. Mâcon, 1942. 463p. **M359**

For full record *see* M279.

Walde, Alois. Lateinisches etymologisches Wörterbuch. 3. neu bearb. Aufl. von J. B. Holman. Heidelberg, Winter, 1930–49. (In progress) **M360**

Bd.1, A-L, Nachträge und Berichtigungen; Bd.2, (Lfg. 12-14) M-parō.

Lettish

Brants, Kārlis and **Matthews, William K.** Latvian-English dictionary, ed. by P. Schmidt. Riga, Gulbis, 1930. 420p. **M361**

Dravnieks, Jēkabs. Anglu latviesu vārdnīca. 3. iespiedums. Rīgā, Valtera un Rapas Akciju Sabiedrības Izdevums, 1933. 606p. **M362**

Mühlenbach, K. Mülenbacha Latviešu valodas vārdnīca. Redigējis, papildinājis, turpinājis J. Endzelīns . . . Mühlenbachs Lettisch-deutsches Wörterbuch. Redigiert, ergänzt und fortgesetzt von J. Endzelin. Riga, 1923–32. 4v. **M363**

Lettish-German.

Lithuanian

Lalis, Anthony. Dictionary of the Lithuanian and English languages. 3d rev. and enl. ed. Chic., "Lietuvos," 1910–15. 2 pts. **M364**

pt.1, Lithuanian-English, 1910. 439p.; pt.2, English-Lithuanian, 1915. 835p.

Niedermann, Max, Senn, Alfred and **Brender, Franz.** Wörterbuch der litauischen Schriftsprache: litauisch-deutsch. Heidelberg, Winter, 1932–39. v.1-2. (v.2 incompl.) (Indogermanische Bibliothek, hrsg. von H. Hirt und W. Streitberg. 5. Abt. Baltische Bibliothek; 3) **M365**

Contents: Bd.1, A-K; Bd.2, (Lfg. 9-13) L-nuziurëti.

Malay

Hendershot, Vernon Edwards and **Shellabear, William G.** A dictionary of standard Malay (Malay-English). . . . Mountain View, Calif., Omaha, Nebr. [etc.] Pacific Press Pub. Assoc., 1945. 235p. $3.75. **M366**

Wilkinson, Richard James. Malay-English dictionary (romanised). Mitylene, Greece, Salavopoulos and Kinderlis; Singapore, Kelly and Walsh, 1932. 2v. **M367**

——— An abridged Malay-English dictionary: 7th ed. (romanised), rev. by A. E. Coope. N.Y., Macmillan, 1948. 269p. $2.25. **M368**

Winstedt, Sir Richard Olof. Dictionary of colloquial Malay (Malay-English and English-Malay). . . . Lond., Paul, Trench, Trubner, 1943 [i.e., 1944]; Forest Hills, N.Y., Transatlantic Arts. 1944. 175p. **M369**

Manx

Cregeen, Archibald. Cregeen's Manx dictionary Repr. for the Manx Language Society. Douglas Brown, 1910. 247p. **M370**

Gill, W. Walter. Manx dialect, words and phrases. Lond., Arrowsmith, 1934. 192p. (Manx scrapbooks, no.4) **M371**

Intended to be supplementary to Moore (M372).

Moore, Arthur William. Vocabulary of the Anglo-Manx dialect. Ox., Univ. Pr., 1924. 206p. **M372**

Persian

Hayyīm, Sulaimān. New Persian-English dictionary, complete and modern . . . English meanings of over 50,000 words, terms, idioms, and proverbs in the Persian language as well as the transliteration of the words in English characters. Teheran, Bēroukhim, 1934–36. 2v. **M373**

—— The Larger English-Persian dictionary . . . Persian meanings of 80,000 words, idioms, phrases and proverbs in the English language. Tehēran, Bēroukhim, 1941–43. 2v. **M374**

Palmer, Edward H. Concise dictionary, English-Persian; Persian-English. Lond., K. Paul, 1924–26. 2v. **M375**

English-Persian, 1926. 546p.; Persian-English, 1924. 726p.

Steingass, F. Comprehensive Persian-English dictionary including the Arabic words and phrases to be met with in Persian literature, being Johnson's and Richardson's Persian, Arabic and English dictionary rev., enl. and entirely reconstructed. Lond., K. Paul, 1892. 1539p. 2d impr., 1930. **M376**

Wollaston, *Sir* Arthur Naylor. Complete English-Persian dictionary, comp. from original sources. Lond., Murray, 1904. 1491p. **M377**

First impression: Lond., Low, 1894.

—— English-Persian dictionary, comp. from original sources. 2d ed. Lond., Murray, 1904. 462p. 21s. **M378**

Polish

Karlowicz, Jan, Krynski, Adam [and others]. Słownik języka polskiego. Warszawa, Wydawnictwo kasy im. Mianowskiego, Instytutu Popierania Nauka, 1900–35. 8v. **M379**

Imprint varies.

Bilingual

Kierst, W. Słownik angielsko-polski i polsko-angielski. Warszawa, Trzaska, Evert i Michalski, 1926–28. 2v. **M380**

v.1, English-Polish; v.2, Polish-English.
The best Polish-English dictionary.
Frequently reprinted. (Lond., Orbis, 1947. 25s.)

Lilien, Ernest. Lilien's Dictionary . . . pt.1, English-Polish. Buffalo, N.Y., Wydawnictwa Slownika Liliena, 1944–50. pts. 1-17. $1 per fasc. (In progress) **M381**

fasc. 1-17, A-Gametogen.

Poland. Ministerstwo Spraw Wojskowych. Centralna Komisja Regulaminowa. Angielsko-polski i polsko-angielski słownik wojskowy. English-Polish and Polish-English military dictionary. [Edinburgh, Riverside Pr., 1943] 143p., 195p. **M382**

Booch-Arkossy, Friedrich Wilhelm. Neues vollständiges polnisch-deutsches und deutsch-polnisches Wörterbuch. Leipzig, Haessel, 1913. 2v. **M383**

Polyglot

The Duden pictorial encyclopedia, in five languages: English, French, German, Italian, Spanish. Containing 30,000 words explained by pictures. . . . N.Y., pub. by the Murray Print. Co. for Frederick Ungar Pub. Co., [c1943]. [2588]p. il. $20. **M384**

"Based on the widely used Duden picture vocabularies, which originally were produced in Germany, in the late 1930's."—*Pref.*

Covers science and arts, state and community, man, family and home, trades and vocations, trade and transport, physical culture and recreation, etc.

Eaton, Helen Slocomb. Semantic frequency list for English, French, German, and Spanish. A correlation of the first 6000 words in four single-language frequency lists. Issued by the Committee on Modern Languages of the American Council on Education. Chic., Univ. of Chic. Pr., 1940. 441p. **M385**

Portuguese

Freire, Laudelino de Oliveira. Grande e novíssimo dicionário da língua portuguesa . . . com a colaboração técnica do J. L. de Campos. Rio de Janeiro, Noite, 1939–44. 5v. **M386**

Lima, Hildebrando and **Barroso, Gustavo.** Pequeno dicionário brasileiro da língua portuguesa, revisto . . . por Manuel Bandeira e José Baptista da Luz. 6. ed. inteiramente revista e consideràvelmente aumentada—sobretudo na parte de brasileirismos—por Aurelio Buarque de Hollanda Ferreira. . . . Rio de Janeiro, Civilização Brasileira, 1946. 1316p. Cr. $55. **M387**

Sixth edition has been revised and reset, and additions and corrections are made throughout. Includes proper names with especial emphasis on South America.

Moreno, Augusto. Dicionário complementar da língua portuguesa (ortoépico, ortográfico e etimológico) com um glossário de arcaísmos e uma lista das principais locuções estrangeiras, aplicáveis em português. 2. ed. melhorada. Porto, Livraria Ed. Educação Nacional, 1938. 1430p. **M388**

Bilingual

Franco, Alvaro. Dicionário: Inglês-Português, Português-Inglês. 3. ed. Porto Alegre, Livraria do Globo, 1941. 671p., 396p. **M389**

Michaelis, Henriette. Novo diccionario da lingua portugueza e ingleza, enriquecido com os termos technicos do commercio e da industria, das sciencias e das artes e da linguagem familiar. 8. ed. Leipzig, Brockhaus, 1932. 2v. **M390**
Reprint of 7th ed. 1923.
v.1, Portuguese-English; v.2, English-Portuguese.

Richardson, Elbert L., Sá Pereira, Maria de L. and Sá Pereira, Milton. Modern Portuguese-English, English-Portuguese dictionary. Phila., McKay [1943]. 347p. $3. **M391**
Uses reformed spelling. Conforms to Brazilian usage.

Etymology

Silva Bastos, J. T. da. Diccionário etymológico, prosódico e orthográphico da lingua Portugueza. 2. ed. Lisboa, Parceria António Maria Pereira, 1928. 1434p. **M392**

Provençal

Hombres, Maximin d' and Charvet, Gratien. Dictionnaire languedocien-français; contenant les définitions, radicaux et étymologiques des mots, les idiotismes, dictions, maximes et proverbes. Alais, Brugueirolle, 1884. 655p. **M393**

Mistral, Frédéric. Lou trésor dóu Felibrige; ou, Dictionnaire provençal-français, embrassant les divers dialectes de la langue d'oc moderne. Aix-en-Provence, Remondet-Aubin [1879–87]. 2v. 1196p., 1165p. **M394**
Reprinted 1932.
Largely supersedes earlier works though for certain aspects and etymologies they still need to be consulted.

Romansh

Dicziunari rumantsch Grischun, publichà de la Società Retorumantscha cul agüd da la confe-

raziun; dal chantun grischun e da la lia rumantscha. Fundà da Robert de Planta e Florian Melcher. Redacziun: Chasper Pult ed Andrea Schorta. Cuoira, Bischofberger, 1938–46. fasc. 1-13. il. (In progress) **M395**
fasc. 1-13, A-Azur.

Velleman, Antoine. Dicziunari scurznieu de la lingua ladina . . . Ladinisches Notwörterbuch mit deutscher, französischer und englischer Übersetzung. . . . Abridged dictionary of the Ladin (or Romansh) language, with German, French and English translation and numerous indications referring to topography and population. Samaden, Engadin Pr., 1929. 928p. **M396**

Rumanian

Academia Română, Bukharest. Dicţionarul limbii române, intocmit şi publicat după indemnul si cu cheltuiala Maiestăţii Sale Regelui Carol I. Bucureşti, Impr. Naţională, 1913–40. v.1, pt.1, pt.2, fasc. 1-8; v.2, pt.1, pt.2, fasc.1-2. **M397**
v.1, pt.1, A-B; pt.2, fasc.1-8, C-Cojoáică; v.2, pt.1, F-I; pt.2, fasc.1-2, J-Lepăda.
Definitions and explanations are in Rumanian, but an equivalent word in French is also given.

Axelrad, Philip. Complete Roumanian-English dictionary. N.Y., Biblioteca Română, 1918. 532p. (Repr. Phila., McKay, 1942. $3) **M398**

Damé, Frédéric. Nouveau dictionnaire roumain-français. Bucarest, Impr. de l'État, 1893–95. 4v. **M399**

Lolliot, Henry L. Dictionar englez-romăn. Operă tipărită cu cheltuiala statului. Bucureşcti, Impr. Statului [190-?]. 2v. **M400**
English-Rumanian only.

Russian

U. S. Library of Congress. Preliminary check list of Russian dictionaries, published in the U.S.S.R. 1917–1942, comp. by George A. Novossiltzeff . . . in consultation with and with a preface by Sergius Yakobson. Wash., 1944. 143p **M401**
Approximately 840 items. Includes dictionaries, in the Russian language and Russian bilingual and polyglot dictionaries, arranged by language and by subject.

Akademiía Nauk, S S S R. Vtoroe otdelenie Slovar' russkago íazyka sostavlemnnií Vtoryn otdieleniyem Imperatorskoí Akademiĭ Nauk Petrograd, 1895–1930. v.1-9 (incompl.). **M402**
No more published of this edition.
v.1, A-D; v.2, E-Zíã; v.3, pt.1-2, I-Izba; v.4, pt. 1-10 K-Krol; v.5, pt.1-3, L-Lis; v.6, pt.1-2, M-Mas; v.8, pt.1-2 N-Nedov; v.9, pt.1-2, O-Obkat.

Akademiı̈a Nauk. Institut Ī̃azyka i myshlenı̈a imeni N. Īa. Marra. Slovar' russkogo ı̈azyka. Novoe pererabotannoe i dopolnennoe, izdanie. Leningrad, Akad. Nauk, 1932–36. v.1- . (In progress) **M402a**

v.1, pt.1-4; v.8, pt.2; v.9, pt.1; v.11, pt.3-4; v.12, pt.2-3; v.13, pt.3-4; v.14, pt.3-5.

Dal', Vladimir Ivanovich. Tolkovyĭ slovar zhivogo velikorusskago ı̈azyka . . . pod redakt̃sieı̈ I. A. Borduena-de-Kurtene. St. Petersburg, Wolf, 1913. 4v. (Repr. Tokio, Tachibana Tsioten, 1934) **M403**

Tolkovyi slovar' russkogo ı̈azyka. Pod. red. D. N. Ushakova. Moskva, Gosud. izd-vo inostrannykh i nat̃sional'nykh slovareĭ, 1935–40. 4v. **M404**

American Council of Learned Societies. Reprints: Russian Series. no.1. Ann Arbor, Mich., Edwards Bros. 4v. $29.

Bilingual

Aleksandrov, A. Complete Russian-English dictionary. 6th ed. rev. and enl. N.Y., Maisel, 1919. 765p. $6.50. **M405**

—— Complete English-Russian dictionary. 7th ed. rev. and enl. Petrograd, 1916. 918p. **M406**

N.Y., Hebrew Pub. Co., n.d. 904p.

Makarov, Nikolaĭ Petrovich. Dictionnaire français-russe complet. 12. éd., nouv. rev. et considérablement augm. Saint-Pétersbourg, Trenké, 1906. 1149p. **M407**

Mūller, Vladimir Karlovich. English-Russian [Russian-English] dictionary. 60,000 words used in the Russian spoken language, science, politics, literature and mechanics (technology) with the addition of short grammatical rules. New 1944 ed. N.Y., Dutton, 1944. 2v. **M408**

Added title page in Russian.
"First published in the United States, 1944."
English-Russian. 776p. $3; Russian-English. 3d ed. rev. and enl. 822p. $3.50.
A useful modern dictionary.

O'Brien, M. A. New English-Russian and Russian-English dictionary (new orthography). . . . N.Y., Dover Publications, 1944. 344p., 366p. $1.98. **M409**

A small convenient dictionary for modern usage. Photo-offset from 1930 edition (Leipzig, Tauchnitz).

Pavlovskiĭ, Ivan Ī̃Akovlevich. Deutsch-russisches Wörterbuch. 4. gänzl. umgearb. u. sehr verm. Aufl. Riga, Kymmel, 1911. 2v. **M410**

Segal, Louis. New complete Russian-English dictionary (new orthography). N.Y., Stechert, 1942. 965p. $10. **M411**

—— New complete English-Russian dictionary. 1st ed. Lond., Humphries, 1948. 1111p. **M412**

Added title page in Russian.

A new standard dictionary using the new orthography and embodying the changes made in the Russian language after the revolution. Attempts to list as many new words as possible relating to aviation, moving pictures, art and science as well as new political, economic and technical terms. Also contains words and expressions that occur in the works of the Russian classical authors.—Cf. *Pref.*

Appendixes to volume 1 include: Additional list of abbreviations; List of the more usual Christian names—male and female; Principal geographical names; Historical and mythological dictionaries.

Abbreviations

Bahder, Egon von. Russkie sokrashchenı̈a. Russische Abkürzungen und ihre Auflösung aus dem Gebiet von Staat, Verwaltung, Wirtschaft, Wissenschaft, Wehrwesen und Sprachgebrauch. Leipzig, Birnbach, 1942. 140p. (Arbeitshefte für den Sprachmittler, Hft. 34) **M413**

Patrick, George Z. A list of abbreviations commonly used in the U.S.S.R. Berkeley, Calif., Univ. of Calif., 1937. 124p. **M414**

Sanskrit

Apte, Vaman Shivaram. The practical Sanskrit-English dictionary; containing appendices of Sanskrit prosody and important literary and geographical names in the ancient history of India. (For the use of schools and colleges) 3d ed. rev. and enl. Bombay, Gopal Narayen, 1924. 1048p. **M415**

Böhtlingk, Otto von and **Roth, Rudolph.** Sanskrit-Wörterbuch hrsg. von der Akademie der Wissenschaften. St. Petersburg, Akad. der Wissenschaften, 1855–75. 7v. **M417**

"Verbesserungen und Nachträge zu Theil 1-5," Bd.5, col. 941-1678; "Verbesserungen und Nachträge zum ganzen Werke," Bd.7, col. 1685-1822.

—— Sanskrit-Wörterbuch in kürzerer Fassung. St. Petersburg, Akad. der Wissenschaften, 1878–89. 7v. in 4.

Repr. 1923–25 (Leipzig, Markert und Petters).

Macdonell, Arthur Anthony. Practical Sanskrit dictionary; with transliteration. . . . Lond., Milford, 1924. 382p. **M418**

A reissue, with new preface and rearranged addenda but no change in text, of his Sanskrit-English dictionary (Lond., Longmans, 1893).

Monier-Williams, *Sir* Monier. Sanskrit-English dictionary etymologically and philologically arranged with special reference to cognate Indo-European languages. New ed., greatly enl. and improved, with the collaboration of E. Leumann, C. Cappeller, and other scholars. Ox., Clarendon Pr., 1899. 1333p. **M419**

Shchupak, N., Nitti, L. and Renou, L. Dictionnaire sanskrit-français. Paris, Maisonneuve, 1931–32. 897p. (Pub. de l'Inst. de Civilisation Indienne) **M420**

Serbian and Croatian

Rječnik hrvatskoga ili srpskoga jezika, na svijet izdaje Jugoslavenska akademija znanosti i umjetnosti. Obraduje D. Daničić. U. Zagrebu, U Kńižarnici L. Hartmana na Prodaju, 1880–1931. v.1-10. **M421**

v.1-10, A-Posmrtnica. Issued in 46 pts.

Bilingual

Bogadek, Francis A. New English-Croatian and Croatian-English dictionary. 2d ed. enl. and cor. N.Y., Stechert, 1944. 1082p. **M422**

Lochmer, Šandor. Englesko-hrvatski rječnik . . . Senj, Croatia, Ivo Pl. Hreljanovic, 1906. 1112p. **M423**

English-Croatian only.

Petrović, Ilija M. A practical dictionary of the English and Serbian languages. Belgrad, Kona, 1933. 770p. **M424**

Popovič, Georg. Wörterbuch der serbischen und deutschen Sprache . . . 2. durchgesehene und verm. Aufl. Pančova, Verlag der Brüder Jovanovićschen Buchhandlung, 1886–95. 2v. **M425**

v.1, Deutsch-serbischer Theil; v.2, Serbisch-deutscher Theil.

Ristić, Svetomir and Kangrga, Jovan. Wörterbuch der serbokroatischen und deutschen Sprache. Belgrad, Rajković und Čuković, 1928. v.2. **M426**

T.2, Serbokroatisch-Deutsch. 1263p.

Slovenian

Kern, Frank Jauh. A pronouncing English-Slovene dictionary for general use. Angleško-slovenski besednjak z angleško izgovarjavo. [Cleveland, Amer. Home Pub. Co., 1944] 273p. $5. **M427**

Cover title: English-Slovene dictionary . . . 2d ed.
First published 1919 under title: *A complete pronouncing dictionary of the English and Slovene languages.*

Spanish

Academia Española, Madrid. Diccionario de la lengua española. 16. ed. Madrid, Espasa-Calpe, 1939. 1334p. **M429**

1st ed. 1726–39. 6v.

—— Diccionario histórico de la lengua española. Madrid, Hernando, 1933–36. v.1-2. **M430**

v.1-2, A-Cevilla.

Caballero, Ramón. Diccionario de modismos de la lengua castellana. Ed. Argentina presentada por A. Herrero Mayor. Buenos Aires, El Ateneo, 1942. 1179p. **M431**

Larousse, Pierre. Pequeño Larousse ilustrado; nuevo diccionario enciclopédico pub. bajo la dirección de Claude Augé; adaptación española de Miguel de Toro y Gisbert. Paris, Larousse, 1947 [c1912]. 1528p. il. **M432**

Diccionario, A-Z, p.1-970; Locuciones latinas y extranjeras, p.971-1002; Historia y geografia, p.1003-1528.
Frequently reprinted.

Vox; diccionario general ilustrado de la lengua española. Prólogo de Ramon Menéndez Pidal; révision de Samuel Gili Gaya. Barcelona, Spes, 1945. 1557p. il. **M433**

Bilingual

Castillo, Carlos and Bond, Otto F. The University of Chicago Spanish dictionary; a new concise Spanish-English and English-Spanish dictionary of words and phrases basic to the written and spoken languages of today. Chic., Univ. of Chic. Pr., 1948. 226p., 252p. $6. **M434**

"Compiled for the general use of the American learner of Spanish and the Spanish learner of English, with special reference in either case to New World usages as found in the United States and in Latin America."—*Foreword.*

Includes about 30,000 words most commonly used. Introductory material to each section deals with pronunciation, parts of speech, suffixes, lists of irregular verbs, etc.

Cuyas, Arturo. Appleton's New English-Spanish and Spanish-English dictionary, containing more than six thousand modern words and twenty-five thousand acceptations, idioms and technical terms not found in any other similar work: with a pronouncing key and the fundamental tenses of irregular verbs; rev. and enl. by Antonio Llano. 3d ed. with supplements. N.Y., Lond., Appleton-Century, 1940. 2v. in 1. $5. **M435**

Martinez Amador, Emilio M. Diccionario ingles-español y español-ingles. Barcelona, Sopena, 1946. 946p., 985p. **M436**

Subtitle: "Each part contains over 50,000 articles, thousands of modern colloquialisms, idioms, Americanisms and technical terms; the fundamental tenses of irregular verbs; full list of geographical and personal names; the abbreviations most commonly used in both languages, etc."

Velázquez de la Cadena, Mariano. A new pronouncing dictionary of the Spanish and English languages . . . rev. and enl. by Edward Gray . . . Juan L. Iribas . . . with supplement of new words by Carlos Toral. . . . Chic., Wilcox and Follett, 1942. 2v. in 1. $3.95. **M437**

Contents: pt.1, Spanish-English; pt.2, English-Spanish. For general purposes the most useful of the Spanish-English dictionaries. First published 1852, revised 1900 and frequently reprinted. The revision in this edition consists of two sections of "new words": volume 1, Spanish-English, 14 pages; volume 2, English-Spanish, 15 pages.

U. S. War Dept. Military Dictionary Project. Dictionary of spoken Spanish; Spanish-English, English-Spanish. Wash., Govt. Prt. Off., 1945. 513p. (War Dept. Technical manual, TM30-900) **M438**

Grammatical introduction, p.1-25.

Synonyms

Benot y Rodriguez, Eduardo. Diccionario de ideas afines y elementos de tecnología. Buenos Aires, Ed. Anaconda, 1940. 1515p. **M439**

Diccionario de sinónimos. (22,000 artículos) Barcelona, Seix, 1944. 800p. **M440**

Regional

While there is, as yet, no one comprehensive authoritative dictionary of the "Americanisms" of the Spanish language, there are various regional compilations which give the different meanings, words, pronunciations, etc., in use in the various Spanish-speaking countries of the New World.

For a comprehensive bibliography of materials in American Spanish consult:

Nichols, Madaline W. A bibliographical guide to materials on American Spanish, ed. for the Committee on Latin American Studies of the American Council of Learned Societies. Camb., Harv. Univ. Pr., 1941. 114p. **M441**

Includes an analysis of the work of national philological organizations, followed by bibliographies of works on American Spanish in general and in each separate country. Each subdivided into General works, Dictionaries and vocabularies, Individual words, Influence of other languages, Toponimia, Flora and Fauna. Useful annotations.

General. MALARET, AUGUSTO. Diccionario de Americanismos. 2. ed. extensamente corr. San Juan, Puerto Rico, Impr. "Venezuela," 1931. 520p.; Supplemento. Buenos Aires, Acad. Argentina de Letras. 1942–44. 2v. (Bibliog. p.10-35) **M442**—RUBIO, DARIO. La anarquia del lenguage en la America española. México, Confed. Reg. Obrera Mex., 1925. 2v. **M443**—SANTA-MARIA, FRANCISCO JAVIER. Diccionario general de americanismos . . . 1. ed. . . . Méjico, D.F., Ed. P. Robredo, 1942 [i.e., 1943]. 3v. **M444**

Special countries. ZAYAS Y ALFONSO, ALFREDO. Lexicografia antillana; diccionario de voces usadas por los aborigenes de las **Antillas** Mayores y de algunas de las menores y consideraciones acerca de su significado y de su formación. 2. ed. Habana, Molina, 1931. 2v. **M445**—[Argentina] Diccionario manual Espasa-Calpe. 1. ed. Buenos Aires, Espasa-Calpe Argentina, 1947. 1379p. il. **M446**—GARZÓN, TOBIAS. Diccionario **argentino,** ilustrado con numerosos textes . . . pub. bajo los auspicios de la Comisión Nacional del Centenario de la Revolución de Mayo y de la Universidad Nacional de Córdoba (República Argentina). Barcelona, Borrás y Mestres, 1910. 519p. **M447**—SEGOVIA, LISANDRO. Diccionario de **argentinismos,** neologismos y barbarismos con un apéndice sobre voces extranjeras interesantes. . . . Obra pub. bajo los auspicios de la Comisión Nacional del Centenario. Buenos Aires, Coni Hermanos, 1911. 1095p. **M448**—SALAZAR GARCÍA, SALOMÓN. Diccionario de provincialismos y barbarismos **centro-americanos,** y ejercicios de ortología clásica. (Vicios y correcciones de idioma español, etc.) 2. ed. corr. y mejorada. San Salvador, "La Unión," 1910. 312p. **M449**—LENZ, RODOLFO. Diccionario etimológico de las voces **chilenas** derivadas de lenguas indijenas americanas. . . . Santiago de Chile, Impr. Cervantes, 1904–10. 938p. **M450**—MEDINA, JOSÉ TORIBIO. **Chilenismos** apuntes lexicográficos. . . . Santiago de Chile, Soc. Impr. y Lit. Universo, 1928. 383p. **M451**—ROMÁN, MANUEL ANTONIO. Diccionario de **chilenismos,** y de otras voces y locuciones viciosas. Santiago de Chile, "Revista Católica," 1901–18. 5v. **M452**—VALENZUELA, PEDRO ARMENGOL. Glosario etimológico de nombres de hombres, animales, plantas, ríos y lugares, y de vocablos incorporados en el lenguaje vulgar, aborígenes de **Chile,** y de algún otro país americano. Santiago de Chile, Impr. Univ., 1918. 2v. **M453**—SUNDHEIM, ADOLFO. Vocabulario costeño; o Lexicografía de la región septentrional de la República de **Colombia.** Paris, Cervantes, 1922. 656p. **M454**—GACINI, CARLOS. Diccionario de **costarriqueñismos.** 2. ed. San José de Costa Rica,

Impr. Nac., 1919. 275p. **M455**–DIHIGO, JUAN MIGUEL. Léxico **cubano**; contribución al estudio de las voces que lo forman. Habana, Ed. "Selecta," 1928–46. v.1-2, A-B. **M456**–PICHARDO, ESTÉBAN. Diccionario provincial casi razonado de vozes y frases **cubanas**. 4. ed. Habana, L. F. Dediot, 1875. 393p. **M457**–SUÁREZ, CONSTANTINO. Vocabulario **cubano**, suplemento a la 14ª ed. del Diccionario de la R. A. de la Lengua. Habana, Ricardo Veloso, 1921. 576p. **M458**– LEMOS RAMÍREZ, GUSTAVO. Semántica; o, Ensayo de lexicografía **ecuatoriana**, con un apéndice sobre nombres nacionales compuestos de raíces quichuas. Guayaquil, Ecuador, J. F. Molestina, 1920. 222p. **M459**–LEMOS RAMÍREZ, GUSTAVO. Barbarismos fonéticos del **Ecuador**; suplemento a Semántica ecuatoriana. Guayaquil, Uzcátegui, 1922. 166p. **M460**–MATEUS, ALEJANDRO. Riqueza de la lengua castellana y provincialismos **ecuatorianos**. 2. ed. Quito, Ecuador, "Ed. Ecuatoriana," 1933. 499p. **M461**–TOBAR, CARLOS R. Consultas al diccionario de la lengua (algo que falta en el vocabulario académico y de lo que sobra en el de los **ecuatorianos**, etc.) 3. ed. Barcelona, Martin, 1911. 516p. **M462**–SANDOVAL, LISANDRO. Semántica **guatemalense**; o, Diccionario de guatemaltequismos. 1. ed. Guatemala, Tip. Nac., 1941–42. 2v. **M463**–MEMBREÑO, ALBERTO. **Hondureñismos.** 3. ed., notablemente corr. y aum. Méjico, Müller, 1912. 172p. **M464**– GARCÍA ICAZBALCETA, JOAQUÍN. Vocabulario de **mexicanismos**, comprobado con ejemplos y comparado con los de otros paises hispano-americanos. México, Tip. y Lit. "La Europea," 1899. v.1, 241p. (A-G) (No more published.) **M465**– RAMOS Y DUARTE, FÉLIX. Diccionario de **mejicanismos**; colección de locuciones i frases viciosas con sus correspondientes críticas i correcciones fundadas en autoridades de la lengua; máximas, refranes, provincialismos i remoques populares de todos los estados de la República Mejicana. 2. ed. Méjico, Herrero Hermanos, 1898. 584p. **M466**–[PAZ SOLDÁN Y UNÁNUE, PEDRO] Diccionario de **peruanismos**; ensayo filológica, por Juan de Arona [pseud.]. Lima, J. Galland [1882]. 529p. (3. ed. Paris, Desclée de Brouwer, 1938. 399p. Biblioteca de cultura Peruana. 1. ser. no.10) **M467**–MALARET, AUGUSTO. Vocabulario de **Puerto Rico.** San Juan, P.R., Imp. Venezuela, 1937. 293p. **M468**–ALVARADO, LISANDRO. Glosarios del bajo español en **Venezuela.** Caracas, Litotip. Mercantil, 1929. 703p. **M469**

Sumerian

Deimel, Anton. Šumerisches Lexikon. Roma, Pontificii Inst. Biblici, 1927–37. 3v. in 7. **M470**

v.3¹, Šumerisch-Akkadisches Glossar; v.3², Akkadisch-Šumerisches Glossar.

Delitzsch, Friedrich. Šumerisches Glossar. . . Leipzig, Hinrichs, 1914. 295p. **M471**

Swedish

Ordbok öfver svenska språket, utg. af Svenska Akademien. Lund, Lindstedt, 1898–1935. v.1-13 **M472**

v.1-13, A-Kazik.

Östergren, Olof. Nusvensk ordbok. Stockholm, Wahlström, 1918–48. v.1-7. (In progress) Kr 1 per hft. **M473**

bd.1-6, A-Sp; bd.7 (hft. 85-89), St-Stut.

Söderwall, Knut Fredrik. Ordbok öfver svenska medeltids-språket. Lund, Berlingska Boktryckeri, 1884–1918. 2v. in 3. (Samlingar utgifna af Svenska Fornskrift-Sällskapet) **M474**

Issued in 24 parts.

—— —— Supplement. 1925–45. hft. 1-10, A-härra. (In progress)

Bilingual

Björkman, C. G. Svensk-engelsk ordbok. Stockholm, Norstedt, 1889. 1360p. **M475**

Wenström, Oscar Edmund. Engelsk-svensk ordbok. Fullständigt omarbetad av Ruben Nöjd och Anna C. Petterson. Stockholm, Norstedt, 1941. 648p. **M476**

Harlock, Walter Ernest. Svensk-engelsk ordbok skolupplaga, under medverkan av Arvid Gabrielson, John Holmberg och Margareta Angström. 2 översedda uppl. Stockholm, Svenska Bokförlaget 1947. 1048p. **M477**

1st ed. 1944. Earlier editions by Oscar E. Wenström and Walter E. Harlock.

Wessely, Ignaz E. Wessely's Swedish-English dictionary. In two parts, Swedish-English, English-Swedish. New ed. rev. and enl. Phila., McKay, 1941. 300p., 435p. **M478**

Etymology

Hellquist, Elof. Svensk etymologisk ordbok. Ny omarb. ach utv. uppl. Lund, Gleerup, 1935–39 2v. **M479**

Synonyms

Afzelius, J. A. Swedish-English dictionary of synonyms. Lond., Bailey, 1925. 740p. **M480**

Dalin, Anders Fredrik. Svenska språkets syno-
nymer. 4. (rev.) uppl. granskad och redigerad
av N. G. Bergman. Stockholm, Beckman, 1941.
407p. **M481**

Syriac

Brockelmann, Carl. Lexicon Syriacum. Editio 2,
aucta et emendata. Halis Saxonum, Niemeyer,
1928. 930p. **M482**

Oraham, Alexander Joseph. Oraham's Dictionary
of the stabilized and enriched Assyrian language
and English. Chic., Consolidated Pr., (Assyrian
Pr. of Amer.), 1943. 576p. $12.50. **M483**
This is not a dictionary of classical Assyrian but of that
language which is sometimes called by scholars "Nes-
torian Syriac."

Payne Smith, Robert. Thesaurus syriacus, col-
legerunt Stephanus M. Quatremere, Georgius
Henricus Bernstein [et alii]. Ox., e Typ. Claren-
oniano, 1879–1901. 2v. **M484**

—— —— Supplement . . . collected and arranged
by his daughter, J. P. Margoliouth. Ox., Claren-
on Pr., 1927. 345p.

—— Compendious Syriac dictionary, founded
upon the Thesaurus syriacus of R. Payne Smith,
ed. by J. Payne Smith (Mrs. Margoliouth). Ox.,
Clarendon Pr., 1903. 626p. **M485**

Thai

McFarland, George Bradley. Thai-English dictionary. . . . Stanford Univ., Calif., Stanford
Univ. Pr.; Lond., Milford, Ox. Univ. Pr., 1944.
1019p., 39p. $9. **M486**
"A photolithographic reprint of the first edition" origi-
ally published in Bangkok in 1941.
Bibliography, p.xx-xxi.

Tibetan

Bell, C. A. English-Tibetan colloquial dictionary.
2 ed. Calcutta, Bengal Secretariat Bk. Depot,
1920. 562p. **M487**
English-Tibetan only.

Gould, Sir Basil John and Richardson, Hugh
Edward. Tibetan word book. . . . Lond., N.Y.,
and Bombay, Milford, Ox. Univ. Pr., 1943. 447p.
$0. **M488**
First published May 1943.

Jaschke, Heinrich August. Tibetan-English dictionary, with special reference to the prevailing
dialects, to which is added an English-Tibetan

vocabulary. Prepared and published at the charge
of the Secretary of State for India in Council.
Lond., Kegan Paul, 1934. 671p. **M489**

Sarachchandra Dāsa. Tibetan-English dictionary
with Sanskrit synonyms, by Sarat Chandra Das.
Rev. and ed. under the orders of the government
of Bengal, by Graham Sandberg and A. William
Heyde. Calcutta, Bengal Secretariat Bk. Depot,
1902. 1353p. **M490**

Turkish

Redhouse, *Sir* James William. Turkish and English lexicon, showing in English the significations
of the Turkish terms. Constantinople, pr. for the
Amer. Mission by A. H. Boyajian, 1890. 2224p.
M491

—— English and Turkish lexicon, showing in
Turkish the literal, incidental, figurative and colloquial and technical significations of the English
terms. Lond., Ox. Univ. Pr., 1884. 828p. **M492**

—— Turkish dictionary in two parts, English and
Turkish and Turkish and English, in which the
Turkish words are represented in the Oriental
character as well as their correct pronunciation
and accentuation shown in English letters. 2d ed.
enl. by Charles Wells. Lond., Quaritch, 1880.
884p. **M493**

❧ The above are in the Turkish characters. The
following are in the new Latin alphabet adopted
1928.

Hony, H. C. Turkish-English dictionary. Ox.,
Clarendon Pr.; N.Y., Ox. Univ. Pr., 1947. 397p.
$7.50. **M494**
In Latin alphabet.

Okçugil, Vâsif. Ingilizce-türkçe büyük lûgat. A
complete dictionary, English-Turkish. İstanbul,
Kanaat Kitabevi, 1941–43. 2v. **M495**
Turkish words transcribed in Latin alphabet.

Thomson, H. M. Türkçe ingilizce yeni lûgat.
New Turkish-English dictionary. İstanbul, Kanaat Kütüphanesi, 1932. 560p. N.Y., Ungar,
[1944?] $4. **M496**

Vahid Moran, A. Türkçe-ingilizce sözluk. A
Turkish-English dictionary. İstanbul, Sirketi,
1945. 1462p. **M497**
Attempts to include new words and technical terms as
well as those used in the older Turkish literature. Includes
Turkish proverbs and sayings with English translation,
and when possible the corresponding English phrases. An
appendix lists new words used in the new Turkish constitution.

251

Welsh

Evans, Daniel Silvan. Dictionary of the Welsh language. Carmarthen, Spurrell, 1887–1906. pts. 1-5.   **M498**

  pts. 1-5, A-Eiddig.

Lloyd-Jones, J. Geirfa barddoniaeth gynnar Gymraeg. Caerdydd, Gwasg Prifysgol Cymru; Ox., Univ. Pr., 1931–46. pt.1-5. 12s. 6d. per pt.; subs. 10s. per pt.   **M499**

  pt.1-5, A-Enryded.

Spurrell, William. Spurrell's Welsh-English [and English-Welsh] dictionary; ed. by J. B. Anwyl. 10th-12th eds. Carmarthen, Spurrell, 1932–34. 2v.   **M50**

  Welsh-English, 12th ed. 1934. 415p.; English-Welsh 10th ed. 1932. 390p.

Yiddish

Abelson, Paul. English-Yiddish encyclopedic dictionary; a complete lexicon and work of reference in all departments of knowledge. N.Y., Jewish Pr. Pub. Co., 1915. 1749p. il.   **M50**

Harkavy, Alexander. Yiddish-English [and English-Jewish] dictionary. 6th ed. rev. and en N.Y., Hebrew Pub. Co. [1910]. 2v.   **M50**

SCIENCE

In both science and technology, subjects change and develop so rapidly and the importance of having the most up-to-date information is so great that reference work has to be done largely through the periodical literature of the subject, and thus the relative importance of encyclopedic reference books is less than in other fields. The supply of such reference books, too, is limited. A scientific encyclopedia is out of date for some subjects as soon as it is printed and needs to be revised so frequently, if it is to be of real service, that publishers hesitate to undertake many such books. In scientific subjects for which there is no reliable encyclopedia, recent treatises, college textbooks, etc., if well indexed, often furnish good substitutes and these should be used freely.

As much scientific literature is in foreign languages, dictionaries of foreign scientific and technical terms usually omitted in the general language dictionaries, are much used. Yearbooks and directories are needed for summaries of recent progress, addresses of individuals and organizations; and histories and biographical dictionaries should be provided for the historical side of the subject. Handbooks of tables, formulas, statistics, etc., are an important group for ready reference.

In view of the extent and character of the periodical literature in science and technology, the most important reference books in the field are those which furnish the key to this literature, that is, the bibliographies, both current and retrospective, the indexes to periodicals, and the abstract journals which, in addition to listing the new literature of a subject, give brief abstracts of the books and periodical articles listed. The mass of literature produced in the scientific field makes an abstracting service of prime importance, and many of the branches of science now have their own abstracting journals, whose purpose is to provide concise summaries of articles appearing in periodicals and society publications, in doctoral dissertations, patents, etc., and thus enable the searcher to find readily and promptly references to the literature available on a needed topic.

The important features in an abstract journal are: authority, completeness of coverage, promptness, and the kind and comprehensiveness of the indexes.

I. Authority
   A. Is it sponsored by a recognized society or group?
   B. Is the abstracting done by a competent office force with the help and advice of experts? By scholars who are specialists in their fields?

II. Completeness of coverage and adequacy of abstracting and listing
   A. Is the coverage comprehensive including all articles in the field published in the periodicals of all countries?
   B. Are the abstracts adequate including precise and detailed data, formulas, measurements, etc.?
   C. Are the titles of articles given in the original language or in translation?
   D. Is there a complete and up-to-date list of abbreviations for the periodicals abstracted?

III. Comprehensiveness and kind of indexes
   A. Are there author, subject, formula, and patent indexes?
   B. Are they detailed and well organized?
   C. How frequently are they published? Do they cumulate?

For more detailed descriptions of abstract journals *see* the guides listed under Chemistry, N165, N166, N167. For a survey and listing of current abstracting services *see* the following publications of the International Federation for Documentation:

Varossieau, W. W. A survey of scientific abstracting and indexing services, prepared on behalf of the Committee for the Coordination of Abstracting Services of the International Federation for Documentation for the International Conference on Science Abstracting, Unesco House, 20-25 June 1949. The Hague, 1949. 22p. (F.I.D. Pub. no.236) **N1**

International Federation for Documentation. List of current abstracting and indexing services. 1st ed. prepared for the International Conference on Scientific Abstracting, Unesco House, Paris 20-25 June 1949. The Hague, 1949. 23p. (F.I.D. Pub. no.235) **N1a**

The first of what it is hoped will be a biennial publication listing the abstracting services of the world. Arranged by the Universal Decimal classification, it contains title, place of publication, frequency, subscription price, and approximate number of abstracts included.

GENERAL WORKS
Bibliography

Association of Special Libraries and Information Bureaux. Select list of standard British scientific and technical books, comp. at the request of the British Council. 3d ed. rev. and enl. Lond., Aslib, 1946. 63p. 3s. 6d. to members; 5s to non-members. **N2**

A select list designed to help in the establishment of a representative library of the best books in science and technology. Classed arrangement with subject index.

British Museum (Nat. Hist.) Library. Catalogue of the books, manuscripts, maps and drawings in the British Museum (Natural History). Lond., Trustees, 1903–40. 8v. **N2a**

v.1-5, A-Z; v.6-8, Supplement, A-Z.
An author catalog of one of the world's finest collections on natural history. Includes many analytics.

Reuss, Jeremias David. Repertorium commentationum a societatibus litterariis editarum. Secundum disciplinarum ordinem digessit I. D. Reuss. . . . Gottingae, apud Henricum Dieterich, 1801–21. 16v. **N3**

Contents: (1) Historia naturalis, generalis et zoologia; (2) Botanica et mineralogia; (3) Chemia et res metallica; (4) Physica; (5) Astronomia; (6) Oeconomia; (7) Mathesis; mechanica; hydrostatica; hydraulica; hydrotechnia; aerostatica; pnevmatica technologia; architectura civilis; scientia navalis; scientia militaris; (8) Historia; (9) Philologia; linguae; scriptores graeci; scriptores latini; litterae elegantiores; poesis; rhetorica; ars antiqua; pictura; musica; (10-16) Scientia et ars medica et chirurgica.

A very valuable index to the publications of the learned societies of various countries from the time of the founding of each society to 1800, thus preceding the Royal Society *Catalogue of scientific papers* (N4).

Royal Society of London. Catalogue of scientific papers, 1800–1900. Lond., Clay, 1867–1902; Camb., Univ. Pr., 1914–25. 19v. **N4**

v.1-6, 1st ser., 1800–63; v.7-8, 2d ser., 1864–73; v.9-11, 3d ser., 1874–83; v.12, Supplementary volume, 1800–83; v.13-19, 4th ser., 1884–1900.

A monumental index of the first importance in scientific or large reference libraries. An author index for the whole of the nineteenth century to 1555 periodicals in various languages including the transactions of the European academies and other learned societies. Gives, for each article entered: author's name in full when it can be found, full title, title of periodical, volume, date, and inclusive paging. For Russian articles the original title is given followed by French, German or English translation in brackets.

—— Subject index. Camb., Univ. Pr., 1908–14. v.1-3 in 4.

v.1, Pure mathematics; v.2, Mechanics; v.3, Physics: pt.1, Generalities, heat, light, sound; pt.2, Electricity and magnetism.

A subject index to the same material as the above author catalog, classified according to the schedules of the *International catalogue of scientific literature* (N6) It was originally planned to publish separate index volumes for each of the seventeen sciences of the schedules of the *International catalogue*, but only the first three were issued. These index 116,687 articles from 155? periodicals divided as follows: Mathematics, 38,74? articles from 700 serials; Mechanics, 21,295 articles from 959 serials; Physics, 56,644 articles from 1261 serials The subject index gives sufficiently full information to b used independently of the author volumes, i.e., author' name, brief title, periodical, volume date and paging—though for full title, reference must be made to the autho index.

Continued for material after 1900 by the *Internationc catalogue of scientific literature.*

Deniker, Joseph and **Descharmes, René.** Bibliog raphie des travaux scientifiques (Sciences mathe matiques, physiques et naturelles) pub. par le sociétés savantes de la France depuis l'origin jusqu'en 1888; dressée sous les auspices du Minis tère de l'Instruction Publique. Paris, Impr. Nat 1922. v.1-2. **N**

Pub. in parts, 1895–1922; v.1 ed. by Joseph Denike v.2, by René Descharmes.

Contents: v.1-2, pt.1, Ain-Sarthe.
A companion work to Lasteyrie's *Bibliographie géné rale des travaux historiques* . . . on the same scale ar intended to do for scientific societies what Lasteyrie h done for historical. Unfortunately not finished.

Arranged by *départements* and then by city. Comple contents are given for each volume of the publicatio of the societies included. For plan and general arrang ment *see* Lasteyrie (C11).

International catalogue of scientific literatur 1st-14th annual issues. Pub. for the Internation Council by the Royal Society of London. Lond Harrison, 1902–19. 14v. **N**

An annual bibliography covering books and articles a large number of important scientific journals.

Each annual issue consists of 17 volumes: A, Mathematics; B, Mechanics; C, Physics; D, Chemistry; E, Astronomy; F, Meteorology; G, Mineralogy; H, Geology; J, Geography, mathematical and physical; K, Paleontology; L, General biology; M, Botany; N, Zoology; O, Human anatomy; P, Anthropology; Q, Physiology; R, Bacteriology.

Each part includes: (1) schedules and indexes in four languages, (2) an author catalog, (3) a subject catalog. "The purpose is to record the titles of all original contributions since Jan. 1, 1901, in certain branches of science."

While issued, this was the most important current bibliography covering all the sciences. Publication was suspended after the issue of the volumes for 1914.

—— List of journals with abbreviations used in the catalogue as references. Lond., 1903. 312p. Suppl., 1904. 68p.

Bibliographie der deutschen naturwissenschaftlichen Literatur, hrsg. im Auftrage des Reichsamtes des Innern vom Deutschen Bureau der Internationalen Bibliographie in Berlin. Jena, Fischer; Berlin, Heymanns, 1902–14. 18v.   **N7**

The German titles as furnished to the *International catalogue of scientific literature* (N6).

Bibliographie scientifique française; recueil mensuel publié sous les auspices du Ministère de l'Éducation Nationale par la Commission du Répertoire de Bibliographie Scientifique. t.1- , 1902- . Paris, Gauthier-Villars, 1902- . t.1- . 6 nos. par an.   **N8**

Beginning with volume 2, 1903, each issue is in two parts: Section 1, Sciences mathématiques et physiques; Section 2, Sciences naturelles et biologiques.

Volumes 1-18, 1902–21, published by the Bureau Français du Catalogue International du Littérature Scientifique, and included the French titles submitted to the *International catalogue* (N6). Arranged by the same classification.

Some volumes with author indexes.

—— Table générale des tomes 1-13. Paris, Gauthier-Villars, 1919–36. (In progress)

Being published in fascicles: Astronomie, Paleontologie, Biologie, Zoologie, Botanique.

Bibliographie der schweizerischen naturwissenschaftlichen und geographischen Literatur, hrsg. von der Schweizer. Landesbibliothek. v.1, 1925- . Bern, 1927- . Annual. (Hft. 21, 1945, 6.50 fr.)   **N9**

Added title page in French.

Records books and articles in the exact, geological and biological sciences.

Hawkins, Reginald Robert. Scientific, medical, and technical books published in the United States of America, 1930–1944; a selected list of titles in print, with annotations. Prepared under the direction of the National Research Council's Committee on Bibliography of American Scien-

tific and Technical Books. Wash. (R. R. Bowker, N.Y., distributors for the U.S.), 1946. 1114p. $20.   **N10**

A carefully chosen list of some 6000 titles with tables of contents and descriptive and evaluative annotations. A compilation which is very useful as an aid in the selection of scientific and technical works or for information about particular titles. Includes college textbooks but usually omits secondary school textbooks; omits publications of state governments.

Classed arrangement, with author and subject indexes. Priced.

—— —— Supplement of books published 1945–1948. Wash., 1950. 514p. $10.

Lists over 2550 titles selected and described in the same manner as in the main work.

Bonn. Universität. Neuerscheinungen der deutschen wissenschaftlichen Literatur von 1939–1945. Bonn, Dümmlers, 1946- . T.1- . (In progress)   **N11**

T.1, Auswahl von wichtigen Lehrbüchern und Monographien aus den Gebieten der Naturwissenschaften und Medizin.

Nature; a weekly illustrated journal of science. v.1- . Lond., Macmillan, 1870- . il. Weekly. £4 10s. yearly.   **N12**

Subtitle varies slightly.

Abstracts, reviews, articles and reports of work in progress. Covers all sciences.

Periodicals
Bibliography

Académie des Sciences, Paris. Inventaire des périodiques scientifiques des bibliothèques de Paris, dressé sous la direction de Alfred Lacroix par Léon Bultingaire avec la collaboration des bibliothécaires de Paris et le concours de Ad. Richard. Paris, Masson, 1924–29. 1102p. and suppl. 283p.   **N13**

An alphabetical title list of more than 19,000 periodicals, with indication of their location in 132 Paris libraries. Gives cataloging information about each title, indicates exact holdings and has two indexes, one by place of publication and one by subject.

Bolton, Henry Carrington. Catalogue of scientific and technical periodicals, 1665–1895 . . . together with chronological tables and a library check-list. 2d ed. Wash., Smithsonian Inst., 1897. 1247p. (Smithsonian misc. coll. v.40)   **N14**

8603 titles. Part I, 4954 titles, is a reprint of the first edition, 1885, with changes to date; part II includes additions to titles in part I, and titles 5001 to 8477; addenda, 8478 to 8603.

"Intended to contain the principal independent periodicals of every branch of pure and applied science, published in all countries from the rise of this literature to the present time."—*Pref.* Excludes medicine but includes anatomy, physiology and veterinary science. Usually omits publications of learned societies. Gives full titles, names of editors, changes of titles, dates, etc.

The chronological tables permit the finding of the volume numbers for specific years. The library check list giving locations in over 100 American libraries is now largely superseded by the *Union list of serials* (E62).

Catalogue of union periodicals. v.1, Science and technology. Ed. for the National Research Council and National Research Board by Percy Freer. . . . Johannesburg, 1943–49. 525p. and suppl. 522p. **N15**

The first volume of a union list of periodicals in South African libraries. Arranged by subject "catchword" with subarrangement by language and by country.

Comité Argentino de Bibliotecarios de Instituciones Científicas y Técnicas, Buenos Aires. . . . Catálogo de publicaciones periódicas científicas y técnicas, recibidas en las bibliotecas de las instituciones adheridas al comité. Buenos Aires, La Comisión Nacional de Cultura, 1942. 342p. **N16**

7387 numbered entries, arranged alphabetically with locations in 64 libraries, most of them in Buenos Aires.

Dublin. National Library of Ireland. List of scientific and technical periodicals in the Dublin libraries. Dublin, Stat. Off., 1929. 147p. **N17**

A union list of holdings in 18 Dublin libraries.

Italy. Consiglio Nazionale delle Ricerche. Periodici italiani scientifici, tecnici e di cultura generale. 4. ed. interamente rif. Roma, Tip. delle Terme, 1934. 478p. **N18**

Full details of format, editors, address, frequency, etc.

Ker, Annita Melville. A survey of Mexican scientific periodicals, to which are appended some notes on Mexican historical periodicals. Balt., Waverly Pr., 1931. 105p. (Pub. of the Harvey Bassler Foundation) **N19**

Lomer, Gerhard Richard and **Mackay, Margaret S.** Catalogue of scientific periodicals in Canadian libraries. Pub. by McGill University, in cooperation with the Honorary Advisory Council for Scientific and Industrial Research. Montreal, McGill Univ., 1924. 255p. **N20**

Nederlandsch Instituut voor Documentatie en Registratuur, 'sGravenhage. Inventaris van natuurwetenschappelijke, medische en technische periodieken in Nederlandsche bibliotheken. 'sGravenhage, 1941. 469p. (Its Pub. no.197) **N21**

Pan American Union. Division of Intellectual Cooperation. Journals dealing with the natural, physical and mathematical sciences published in Latin America; a tentative directory. Wash., Pan American Union, 1944. 62p. **N22**

Scudder, Samuel Hubbard. Catalogue of scientific serials of all countries, including the transactions of learned societies in the natural, physical, and mathematical sciences, 1633–1876. Camb., Harv. Univ., 1879. 358p. (Library of Harvard Univ. Special pub., 1) **N23**

Classified by countries, with indexes of towns, titles and subjects.

Special Libraries Association. Science-Technology Group. Union list of technical periodicals in two hundred libraries of the Science-Technology Group. 3d ed. comp. by Elizabeth Gilbert Bowerman. N.Y., Special Libraries Assoc., 1947. 285p. $6. **N24**

Gives holdings of some 5000 serials in pure and applied sciences in 200 special libraries only 13 of which are represented in the *Union list of serials* (E62). The object has been to select, within the scope of the contributing libraries, the most complete sets in various geographical areas and to indicate location of at least one copy of all reported issues.

A valuable supplement to the *Union list of serials.*

World list of scientific periodicals published in the years 1900–1933. 2d ed. Ox., Univ. Pr., 1934. 779p. 63s. **N25**

An alphabetical list of over 36,000 periodicals showing location in 187 libraries in Great Britain. Each entry includes the full name of the periodical, place of publication, recommended abbreviation, and library symbols with holdings. Arrangement differs from many American lists in that entries are alphabetized by title of publication rather than by the name of the society or institution.

The first edition (published 1925–27) covering periodicals published 1900–21, was issued in two volumes: v.1, List of periodicals; v.2, Abbreviated titles and location of sets. The second volume is therefore still useful as a list of abbreviations.

Abbreviations

Davidsson, Åke. Periodica technica abbreviata: A list of initial abbreviations of technical and scientific periodicals. Stockholm, Victor Petterson's Bokindustrieaktiebolag, 1946. 52p. (Handbook no.1 of the Tekniska Litteratursällskapet) **N26**

Title page and preface in Swedish and English.

Lists some 2100 initial abbreviations of serial publications.

❧ Two of the most useful lists of scientific periodical abbreviations are the *List of periodicals abstracted by Chemical abstracts* (N176) and *Journals abstracted in Biological abstracts* (N330).

Encyclopedias and handbooks

Darmstaedter, Ludwig. Handbuch zur Geschichte der Naturwissenschaften und der Technik . . . 2. umgearb. und verm. Aufl. unter Mitwirkung von R. du Bois-Reymond und C. Schaefer, hrsg. von L. Darmstaedter. Berlin, Springer, 1908. 1262p.   **N27**

Chronological list of about 12,000 important scientific discoveries and inventions, giving for each its date, name of discoverer or inventor and other brief data. Alphabetical indexes of (1) names, (2) subjects.

Enciclopedia storica delle scienze e delle loro applicazioni, opera compilata con la collaborazione di eminenti specialisti. . . . Milano, Hoepli [1941–43]. v.1-2. il.   **N28**

Editor, Arturo Uccelli.
Contents: v.1, Le scienze fisiche e matematiche; v.2, 1-2. Le scienze applicate e la tecnica.
Nonalphabetical. A survey of pure and applied science from ancient to modern times. Includes biographies and some bibliographies. Embodies much of the same material, text and illustrations appearing in the French work *La Science, ses progrès, ses applications* (Paris, Larousse, 1933. 2v.).

Handwörterbuch der Naturwissenschaften. 2. Aufl. hrsg. von R. Dittler, G. Joos, E. Korschelt, G. Linck, F. Oltmanns, K. Schaum. Jena, Fischer, 1931–35. 10v. il.   **N29**

—— Sachregister und systematische Inhaltsübersicht. Jena, Fischer, 1935. 242p., 16p.

An authoritative work for scholars and specialists, covering all the natural sciences, botany, zoology, physiology, mineralogy and geology, physics and chemistry. Long signed articles on large subjects, good illustrations, bibliographies, biographies of men not living. Does not give separate articles on species or other small subjects and does not include definitions or derivations of terms.

Van Nostrand's Scientific encyclopedia; aeronautics, astronomy, botany, chemical engineering, chemistry, civil engineering, electrical engineering, electronics and radio, geology, mathematics, mechanical engineering, medicine, metallurgy, meteorology, mineralogy, navigation, photography, physics, statistics, zoology. 2d ed. N.Y., Van Nostrand, 1947. 1600p. il. $15.   **N30**

A single alphabetical arrangement of terms used in science and technology. Articles vary in length from a few lines to two or three columns. All are signed. No bibliography. Originally published in 1938, this edition is much enlarged and revised. New material has been added on such subjects as the atomic bomb, radar, plastics, electronics, etc. Illustrations and tables are well-adapted. Extensive cross references aid in finding related materials. A useful work for both the scientist and the layman.

Zimmerman, Oswald Theodore and **Lavine, Irwin.** Scientific and technical abbreviations, signs and symbols. 2d ed. Dover, N.H., Industrial Research Service, 1949. 541p. il. $8.   **N31**

1st ed. 1948. This edition has some rearrangement of material and expansion of tables. Arranged by groups including: General list of abbreviations and symbols, Chemistry, Mechanics, Shop terms, Electricity, Mapping, Railways, Aeronautics, Communications, Meteorology, Military, Medicine, Botany and Zoology, Commerce, Astronomy, Technical Journals, etc.
Brief subject index but no general index to abbreviations. In some sections arrangement is by abbreviation or symbol, in most it is by the word followed by the abbreviation. The chief purpose is to answer the question "What is the standard abbreviation for . . .?" rather than "What does this abbreviation stand for?" It attempts to list the standard abbreviations adopted by the American Standards Association as well as others frequently used.

Dictionaries

See also Dictionaries under name of special science, e.g., Physics—Dictionaries and Chemistry—Dictionaries.

Beadnell, Charles Marsh. Dictionary of scientific terms as used in the various sciences. Lond., Watts, 1942. 232p., 13p. (The thinker's library, no.65) 2s.   **N32**

A reprint of the 1938 edition with a supplementary section of 13 pages.

De Vries, Louis. French-English science dictionary for students in agricultural, biological and physical sciences. N.Y., McGraw-Hill, 1940. 546p. $4.50.   **N33**

43,000 entries.

—— German-English science dictionary for students in chemistry, physics, biology, agriculture, and related sciences. 2d ed., rev. and enl. N.Y., McGraw-Hill, 1946. 558p. $4.50.   **N34**

1st ed. 1940.
Contains some 48,000 entries. This edition has been revised and much enlarged to include more chemical terms as well as more terms in other fields. The number of idioms and abbreviations has also been increased.

Tables

National Research Council. International critical tables of numerical data, physics, chemistry and technology, prepared under the auspices of the International Research Council and the National Academy of Sciences by the National Research Council of the United States of America; ed.-in-chief: Edward W. Washburn; assoc. eds.: C. J. West, N. E. Dorsey. . . . N.Y., pub. for Nat. Research Council by McGraw-Hill, 1926–33. 7v. and index. diagrs. $110; index $10.   **N35**

Selected data based on the material in the *Tables annuelles* (N37) listed below. Covers to 1924.

—— **American Committee on Annual Tables.** Annual tables of physical constants and numerical data. 1941- . Princeton, N.J., 1942- . **N36**

Loose-leaf.

"To constitute a permanent continuation of *International critical tables* and a current tabulation of critically edited numerical data."

Tables annuelles de constantes et données numériques de chimie, de physique et de technologie, pub. sous le patronage de l'Association Internationale des Académies, par le Comité International nommé par le V11ᵉ Congrès de Chimie Appliquée (Londres, 2 juin 1909). . . . v.1-11[1], année 1910–34. Paris, Gauthier-Villars; Chic., Univ. of Chic. Pr., 1912–37. (In progress) **N37**

Publisher varies.

—— Table des matières des v.1-10, années 1910–30. Paris, Hermann, 1930–37. 2v.

v.7- , text in both French and English.

v.1-7, 1910–26 contain the original experimental values upon which the selected data of the *International critical tables* (N35) are based; v.8-10, cover numerical data determined 1927–30.

Societies and congresses

See also Societies, p.71-73, Museums, p.259-60, and Societies, p.300.

Annuario degli istituti scientifici italiani, diretto dal Silvio Pivano. Bologna, Zanicelli, 1918–20. 2v. **N38**

v.1, 1918; v.2, 1920.

Covers scientific institutions in general, including academies, societies, universities, libraries, museums and art galleries, archives, etc. Arranged in regional groups, by *compartimenti* with subarrangement by provinces and towns. For each institution gives name, brief facts of organization and history, statement of its publications and bibliographical references to books or articles where fuller description can be found.

Bates, Ralph S. Scientific societies in the United States. N.Y., Wiley, 1945. 246p. $3.50. **N39**

A history of the growth of American scientific societies from 1727 to date including the main national societies and the specialized and technical societies of the various states.

Bibliography, p.193-220.

Brauer, Ludolph, Bartholdy, A. M. and **Meyer, A.** Forschungsinstitute; ihre Geschichte, Organisation und Ziele, unter Mitwirkung zahlreicher Gelehrter, unter redaktioneller Mitarbeit von Johannes Lemcke. Hamburg, P. Hartung, 1930. 2v. il. **N40**

Historical and descriptive material about research institutes primarily in Germany but also about some in America and other countries, written by authorities. Many autographed portraits.

Eijkman, P. H. L'internationalisme médical. Publication du Bureau Préliminaire de la Fondation pour L'internationalisme. La Haye, Amsterdam, F. van Rossen, 1910. 44p., 51 l. **N41**

"Notes" (list of international congresses, conferences and associations), 51 leaves at end.

—— L'internationalisme scientifique (sciences pures et lettres), avec un avantpropos du Paul S. Reinsch. La Haye, van Stockum, 1911. 108p., 162 l. **N42**

Contents: Introduction contenant un supplément à *L'internationalisme médical;* L'internationalisme scientifique (sciences et lettres, sciences, lettres, conclusion). Notes (List of international congresses, conferences, associations).

Though no longer up to date, the two volumes contain a good deal of historical information not easily found elsewhere. Difficult to use quickly because of the lack of a subject index.

Italy. Consiglio Nazionale delle Ricerche. Istituti e laboratori scientifici italiani. 3. ed. Roma, Consiglio Nazionale delle Ricerche, 1939–41. 4v. L60 per v. **N43**

Grouped by subject field with indexes by city of location. Usually gives name, address, purpose, regulations, library, chief personnel, activities, bibliography, etc.

National Research Council. Handbook of scientific and technical societies and institutions of the United States and Canada. 5th ed. United States section, comp. by Callie Hull; Canadian section comp. by S. J. Cook and J. R. Kohr. Wash., Nat Research Council, 1948. 371p. (Bull. of the Nat Research Council, no.115, Apr. 1948) $5. **N4**

"A directory to those societies, associations and simila organizations in the natural sciences and related fields tha contribute to the advancement of knowledge throug their meetings, publications, and other resources."—*Pref*

Lists 1468 societies (1302 American, 166 Canadian) giving for each: address, officers, history, purpose, mem bership, library, research funds, serial publications, etc.

The indexes (United States and Canada) include subject classification of activities, purposes, and researc funds; a list of all current periodicals mentioned; name of research funds, prizes, medals, etc.; and changes c name in societies and institutions after 1940.

Official year-book of the scientific and learned societies of Great Britain and Ireland. . . . Lond Griffin, 1884- . v.1- . Annual. **N4**

Contents usually include: (1) General societies; (2 Subject groups, e.g., Astronomy, Chemistry, Geography Literature, etc.; (3) Index of society names.

A very useful list, giving for each society: its corpora name, address, date of founding, object, officers, mee ings, membership, titles of publications with prices, an in some cases contents of publications for the year cov ered. The first volume, 1884, was a basic volume, cor taining considerable historical information not reprinte in later issues.

Title on title page, 1884–1929, *Year-book of the scie tific and learned societies of Great Britain and Ireland.*

Pan American Sanitary Bureau. Sociedades e instituciones científicas de la América Latina. Latin American scientific societies and institutions. . . . Primera revisión. Wash., Bureau, 1942. 146p. (Pan American Sanitary Bureau, pub. no. 141) Free. **N46**

Arranged by subject with alphabetical arrangement by country, first of societies and then of institutions. Gives address and usually name of president and secretary and titles of serial publications. No name index.

Sparn, Enrique. Las sociedades científicas, literarias y técnicas del mundo con más de 1,000 miembros. Cordoba, 1931. 76p. (Argentina. Academia Nacional de Ciencias. Miscelánea no.18) **N47**

Stümke, Hans. Bibliographie der internationalen Kongresse und Verbände. . . . Leipzig, Harrassowitz, 1939- . v.1- . **N48**

Bd.1, Bibliographie der internationalen medizinischen Kongresse und Verbände.

The first volume of a projected set on the bibliography of international congresses. The other subjects announced for treatment were: Naturwissenschaften; Sprachwissenschaften, Philosophie, Geschichte; Religionswissenschaft; Künste; Pädagogik und Jugendpflege; Rechts- und Staatswissenschaften; Sozialwissenschaft; Wirtschaftswissenschaft; Technik; Landwirtschaft; Sport.

U. S. Army Medical Library. Congresses; tentative chronological and bibliographical reference list of national and international meetings of physicians, scientists and experts. Wash., Govt. Prt. Off., 1938. 288p. **N49**

Reprinted from U.S. Army Medical Library, *Index-catalogue* (4th ser., v.3, p.1-288, 1938. [P287]).

Arranged by field, with subject, word and title index.

———— First additions. . . . Wash., Govt. Prt. Off., 1939.

Reprinted from its *Index-catalogue* (4th ser., v.4, p.29-51. [P287]).

Werkgemeenschap van Wetenschappelijke Organisaties in Nederland. Natuurwetenschappelijk onderzoek in Nederland, een overzicht van hetgeen in de laatste vijf jaren in Nederland verricht is op het gebied der natuurwetenschappen, der medische en der technische wetenschappen. . . . Amsterdam, Noord-Hollandsche Uitgevers Maatschappij, 1942. 261p. **N50**

Lists the institutions and laboratories of the Netherlands in the various fields of science. Gives name, address, date of founding and brief record of work.

Laboratories

National Research Council. Industrial research laboratories of the United States, including consulting research laboratories. 8th ed., 1946, comp. by Callie Hull [and others]. Wash., Nat. Research Council, 1946. 415p. (Bull. of the Nat. Research Council, no.113, July 1946) $5. **N51**

24,343 numbered entries. Appendix lists universities and colleges offering research service to industry. Indexes: geographical location; personnel; subject index to research activities.

U. S. National Bureau of Standards. Directory of commercial and college laboratories . . . issued August 30, 1947. . . . Wash., Govt. Prt. Off., 1947. 65p. (Misc. pub. M187) 30c. **N52**

Frequently revised; this edition supersedes "Misc. pub. M171," 1942.

A list of 220 commercial and 189 college laboratories with facilities for testing commodities, with indication of specialties.

Museums

American Association of Museums. Bibliography of museums and museum work, by Ralph Clifton Smith. Wash., Assoc., 1928. 302p. $5. **N53**

Murray, David. Museums, their history and their use, with a bibliography and list of museums in the United Kingdom. Glasgow, MacLehose, 1904. 3v. **N54**

v.1, History. List of museums in the United Kingdom; v.2-3, Bibliography.

International in scope. Still valuable for its extensive bibliography which lists works about museums and museum work, and catalogs and other works relating to particular museums.

Handbook of American museums; with an appended list of museums in Canada and Newfoundland. Wash., Amer. Assoc. of Museums, 1932. 779p. $4. **N55**

Compiled by Lewis Barrington and special aides, and edited by L. C. Everard.

A list of 1400 American museums arranged alphabetically by state and town, covering principally "museums that are open to the public, and collections of universities, colleges, and schools that are formally on exhibition . . . also medical collections, herbariums, and a few other important collections of teaching institutions that are not accessible to visitors." Information given about each museum varies considerably but aims to include address, brief history, control and president, special field and collections, library, building and finances, membership, affiliated societies, publications, admission and attendance.

Directory of museums and art galleries in the British Isles; comp. by S. F. Markham. South Kensington, Museums Assoc., 1948. 392p. il. £1 2s. **N56**

Directory of museums and art galleries in Canada, Newfoundland, Bermuda, the British West Indies, British Guiana, and the Falkland Islands; comp. by Sir Henry A. Miers and S. F. Markham. Lond., Museums Assoc. [1932]. 92p. **N57**

Forms a complementary volume to their *Report on the museums of Canada*, 1932.

❦ Other directories published by the Museums Association, London, include *Directory of museums and art galleries in British Africa and in Malta, Cyprus, and Gibraltar*, 1933; *Directory of museums and art galleries in Australia and New Zealand*, 1934; *Directory of museums in Ceylon, British Malaya, Hong Kong, Sarawak, British North Borneo, Fiji, the West Indies, British Guiana*, 1934; *The museums of India*, 1936.

History
Bibliography

Forbes, Robert James. Bibliographia antiqua. Philosophia naturalis. . . . Leiden, Nederlandsch Instituut van het Nabije Osten, 1940–49. v.1-8. (In progress)   **N58**

Contents: (1) Mijnbouw en geologie; (2) Metallurgie; (3) Bouwmaterialen; (4) Aardewerk, faience, glas, glazuur, siersteenen; (5) Verven, kleurstoffen, vernissen, inkten en hunne toepassing; (6) Leder, bereiding en toepassing; (7) Vezelstoffen, grondstoffen en industrie; (8) Papier, papyrus en ander schrijftmateriaal.

A listing of books and periodical articles in various languages published through 1939 on science and its applications in ancient times in various countries.

John Crerar Library. A list of books on the history of science. January 1911. Prepared by A. G. S. Josephson. Chic., 1911. 297p.   **N59**

"Includes the social, physical, natural and medical sciences, but omits the applied sciences. . . . Publications on the history of learned institutions have not been included . . . and only such biographies as have a direct bearing on the position of their subjects in the history of science."—*Pref.*

Classed arrangement with author index.

———— Supplement, Dec. 1916. Chic., 1917. 139p.

———— 2d supplement, prepared by R. B. Gordon. Chic., 1942–46. pts. 1-6. (In progress)

pt.1, General science; pt.2, Mathematics; pt.3, Astronomy; pt.4, Physics; pt.5, Chemistry, crystallography and mineralogy; pt.6, Geology, paleontology.

Sarton, George. Critical bibliography of the history and philosophy of science and of the history of civilization. (In Isis, v.1, 1913- . Quarterly)   **N60**

A valuable annotated bibliography, classed arrangement with author index.

Histories

Sarton, George. Introduction to the history of science. Balt., pub. for Carnegie Inst. by Wil-

liams & Wilkins, 1927–48. v.1-3 in 4. (Carnegie Inst. Pub. 376) v.1-2, o.p.; v.3, pts. 1-2, $20.   **N61**

v.1, Homer to Omar Khayyam, 839p., 52p.; v.2, Rabbi Ben Ezra to Roger Bacon, 1251p.; v.3, Science and learning in the 14th century, 2155p.

An important reference history, covering European and Asiatic countries, rich in biography and bibliography. There is a general index in volume 3 which is relatively complete for volume 3 but for volumes 1 and 2 it lists only the main personalities treated, giving the page of the main article and the page of the index in volume 1 or 2 where other references may be found.

Addenda and errata are included in the *Critical bibliography of the history and philosophy of science . . .* appearing in *Isis* (N60).

———— The study of the history of science. Camb., Harv. Univ. Pr., 1936. 75p.   **N62**

Includes bibliography of the literature.

Biography

Cattell, Jaques. American men of science, a biographical directory. 8th ed. N.Y., Science Pr., 1949. 2836p.   **N63**

Gives brief biographical data, i.e., full name, date of birth, address, marital status and number of children, education and positions, and special fields of research of about 50,000 American scientists. 30,000 of the 34,000 in the seventh edition are included in the eighth, plus about 20,000 not entered before. Contains a necrology of scientists who have died since the seventh edition.

First edition, 1906. Revised at irregular intervals. In the first to seventh editions the names of outstanding persons in each field were starred. These persons are sometimes referred to as "starred men of science." The eighth edition omits the starring.

Mieli, Aldo. Gli scienziati italiani dall'inizio del medio evo al nostri giorni. Repertorio biobibliografico: dei filosofi—matematici—astronomi—fisici—chimici—naturalisti—biologi—medici—geografi italiani. Roma, Nardecchia, 1921–23. v.1. il. **N64**

v.1, pt.1-2, p.1-464, contains 58 biographies of scientists of all periods. Not alphabetically arranged but has alphabetical, chronological and regional indexes.

An ambitious work of which only the first volume was published. Has long, signed biographies, detailed bibliographies giving lists of editions and translations of each scientist's writings, notes of manuscripts and the libraries in which they may be found, lists of books about the person, and portraits.

Poggendorff, Johann Christian. Poggendorff's Biographisch-literarisches Handwörterbuch zur Geschichte der exacten Wissenschaften. Leipzig, Barth, 1863–1904; Verlag Chemie, 1925–40. Bd. 1-6 in 11. (In progress) (Facsimile reprint pub. Ann Arbor, Mich., Edwards, 1945. 10v.)   **N65**

Title varies.

Bd.1-2, to 1857; Bd.3, 1858–83; Bd.4, 1883–1904; Bd.5, 1904–22; Bd.6, 1923–31.

The standard and indispensable work for information about the life and works of mathematicians, astronomers, physicists, chemists, mineralogists, geologists, and other scientists of all countries. For each scientist gives brief biographical sketch followed by a detailed bibliography of his writings including periodical articles.

Royal Society of London. Obituary notices of fellows of the Royal Society, v.1, 1932/35- . Lond., Society, 1932- . il. Annual. **N66**

Issued annually, three years forming a volume with alphabetical table of contents. (Volume 1 covers four years.)

Long biographical articles with excellent autographed portraits of deceased fellows of the Royal Society, including foreign members. Usually includes bibliographies, some quite extensive.

Previous obituary notices were published in the *Proceedings*. In 1905, volume 75 of the *Proceedings* was published "containing obituaries of deceased fellows chiefly for the period 1898–1904 with a general index to previous obituary notices." This general index covers 1860–1899.

❧ Most scientific societies and associations publish lists of members from time to time either in their official proceedings or elsewhere. As many of these include biographical information, pertinent ones should be acquired as needed.

MATHEMATICS
General works
Guides

Parke, Nathan Grier. Guide to the literature of mathematics and physics including related works on engineering science. N.Y., McGraw-Hill, 1947. 205p. $5. **N67**

A useful handbook comprising chapters on principles of reading and study, searching the literature, types of materials, library usage, etc., and an annotated bibliography of some 2300 titles arranged by subject with author and subject indexes. Its primary interest is mathematics and physics but it is also useful for some engineering subjects, particularly aeronautical, electrical, radio, and mechanical engineering.

Loria, Gino. Guida allo studio delle storia delle matematiche generalità, didattica, bibliografia. Appendice: Questioni storiche concernenti le scienze esatte. 2. ed. rif. e aum. Milano, Hoepli, 1946. 385p. **N68**

A comprehensive guide to the literature of the history of mathematics covering all periods and all countries. Includes material on the history, manuscripts, biographical sources, reviews, periodicals, etc. Many typographical errors.

Miller, G. A. Historical introduction to mathematical literature. N.Y., Macmillan, 1916. 302p. **N69**

A useful handbook for the reference librarian, especially chapter 2, which covers mathematical societies, congresses, periodicals, bibliographies, encyclopedias, tables, etc.; chapter 8, which gives biographies of promi-

nent deceased mathematicians; and the appendix which gives a brief selected bibliography with critical annotations.

Now much out of date but still useful for early information.

Sarton, George. The study of the history of mathematics. Camb., Harv. Univ. Pr., 1936. 112p. **N70**

Includes an interesting annotated bibliography of works dealing with the history of mathematics and biographies of modern mathematicians.

Bibliography

International catalogue of scientific literature: A, Mathematics. 1st-14th annual issues, 1901–14. Lond., Harrison, 1902–17. v.1-14. **N71**

For full description *see* N6.

Karpinski, Louis Charles. Bibliography of mathematical works printed in America through 1850 ... with the cooperation for Washington libraries of Walter F. Shenton. Ann Arbor, Univ. of Michigan Pr.; Lond., Milford, Ox. Univ. Pr., 1940. 697p. il. (incl. facsim.) $6. **N72**

A chronological record of mathematical works in various languages printed in America. Later editions and issues of each title are listed under the first edition. Includes over a thousand titles and some three thousand editions. Locates copies in over one hundred libraries.

Indexes: General index of authors' names and anonymous titles; Topical indexes; Index of non-English and Canadian works; Index of printers and publishers.

—— —— Supplements, 1-2. (In Scripta mathematica, 8:233-36, Dec. 1941; 11:173-77, June 1945)

Müller, Felix. Führer durch die mathematische Literatur mit besonderer Berücksichtigung der historisch wichtigen Schriften. Leipzig, Teubner, 1909. 252p. (Abhandlungen zur Geschichte der mathematischen Wissenschaften . . . 27. Hft.) **N73**

A selected annotated list with emphasis on the history of the subjects.

t.1, Geschichte der Mathematik, Enzyklopädisch-historisches; t.2, Philosophie, Pädagogik, Algebra, Arithmetik, Analysis; t.3, Geometrie.

Royal Society of London. Catalogue of scientific papers, 1800–1900; Subject index, v.1, Pure mathematics. Camb., Univ. Pr., 1908. 666p. **N74**

For full description *see* N4.

Smith, David Eugene. Rara arithmetica; a catalogue of the arithmetics written before the year MDCI, with a description of those in the library of George Arthur Plimpton, of New York. Bost. and Lond., Ginn, 1908. 507p. il. $10. **N75**

—— —— Addenda. . . . Bost. and Lond., Ginn, 1939. 52p. il. $4.

This collection was presented to the Columbia University Libraries in 1936.

Wölffing, Ernst. Mathematischer Bücherschatz; systematisches Verzeichnis der wichtigsten deutschen und ausländischen Lehrbücher und Monographien des 19. Jahrhunderts auf dem Gebiete der mathematischen Wissenschaften. Leipzig, Teubner, 1903. 416p. (Abhandlungen zur Geschichte der mathematischen Wissenschaften mit Einschluss ihrer Anwendungen. v.16, pt.1) **N76**

Abstracts

Jahrbuch über die Fortschritte der Mathematik, begr. von Carl Ohrtmann, Bd.1- , 1868- . Berlin, de Gruyter, 1871- . Bd.1- . **N77**

Editor and publisher vary.

Brief signed abstracts. Classed arrangement with author index.

Bd.59, 1933, has title: Jahrbuch über die Fortschritte der Mathematik vereinigt mit Revue semestrielle des publications mathématiques, hrsg. von der Preussischen Akademie der Wissenschaften unter besonderer Mitwirkung der Wiskundig Genootschap te Amsterdam. . . .

The *Revue semestrielle des publications mathématiques,* t.1-39, 1893–1934, was a bibliography of material in various languages, with a very few abstracts. With its volume 37, joined with the *Jahrbuch* and ceased separate publication after volume 39.

Zentralblatt für Mathematik und ihre Grenzgebiete (reine und angewandte Mathematik, theoretische Physik, Astrophysik, Geophysik . . .) Bd.1- , 1931- . Berlin, Springer, 1931- . Bd.1- . **N78**

Gives signed abstracts of material in various languages. Classed arrangement with author and subject indexes.

Mathematical reviews, v.1, 1940- . Lancaster, Pa., Amer. Math. Soc., 1940- . v.1- . Monthly except Aug. $13 per yr. ($6.50 to members of sponsoring societies) **N79**

Signed abstracts of articles in many languages. The abstract is sometimes in English and sometimes in a foreign language, not necessarily the language of the original article. Reviewers are from various countries.

Sponsored by the American Mathematical Society, Mathematical Association of America, Institute of Mathematical Statistics, Edinburgh Mathematical Society, l'Intermédiaire des Recherches Mathématiques, Matematisk Forening i København, het Wiskundig Genootschap te Amsterdam, the London Mathematical Society, Polish Mathematical Society, Union Matemática Argentina, and the Indian Mathematical Society.

Sponsoring societies vary.

Dictionaries and encyclopedias

Encyklopädie der mathematischen Wissenschaften mit Einschluss ihrer Anwendungen.

Hrsg. im Auftrage der Akademien der Wissenschaften zu Göttingen, Leipzig, München und Wien, sowie unter Mitwirkung zahlreicher Fachgenossen. Leipzig, Teubner, 1898/1904—1935. 6v. in 23. **N80**

Contents: (1) Arithmetik; (2) Analysis; (3) Geometrie; (4) Mechanik; (5) Physik; (6¹) Geodäsie und Geophysik; (6²) Astronomie.

—— 2. völlig neubearb. Aufl. hrsg. von H. Hasse und E. Hecke. Leipzig, Teubner, 1939- . (In progress)

Contents: Bd.1, Algebra und Zahlentheorie; 1. Teil: A, Grundlagen; B, Algebra.

The most important encyclopedia of the subject, containing long articles by specialists, with full bibliographic notes, though in some cases articles are now out of date. For the special student and teacher, not for the untrained reader. Originally issued also in a French edition, never completed but including some revision, the *Encyclopédie des sciences mathématiques pures et appliquées* (Paris, Gautier-Villars, 1904–16. v.1-7).

James, Glenn and **James, Robert C.** Mathematics dictionary. N.Y., Van Nostrand, 1949. 432p. il. $7.50. **N81**

A much enlarged edition of James' *Mathematics dictionary* (1942. rev. ed. 1946). Gives definitions of mathematical words and phrases, including both popular and technical terms, as well as formulas, tables, mathematical symbols, etc.

Moritz, Robert Édouard. Memorabilia mathematica; or, The philomath's quotation-book. Lond. and N.Y., Macmillan, 1914. 410p. $5.50. **N82**

A book of over 2100 quotations about mathematics, its nature, value, philosophy, application, etc., grouped by class with an extensive index. Quotations from foreign authors are given only in English but references to original sources are cited.

Handbooks

Clements, Guy Roger and **Wilson, Levi Thomas.** Manual of mathematics and mechanics. N.Y. and Lond., McGraw-Hill, 1947. 2d ed. 349p. $3.75. **N83**

Jansson, Martin E. and **Harper, Herbert Druery.** Handbook of applied mathematics. 2d ed. rev. and enl. With a section on business mathematics, by Peter L. Agnew. N.Y., Van Nostrand, 1936. 1010p. il. $6. **N84**

Tables

BIBLIOGRAPHY

Fletcher, Alan, Miller, J. C. P. and **Rosenhead, L.** An index of mathematical tables. N.Y., McGraw-Hill; Lond., Scientific Computing Service, 1946. 450p. il. $16. **N85**

An important index to well-known tables of functions nd to other less-known tables in books and periodicals.

Part 1 is an index according to functions; part 2 is an lphabetical bibliography by author listing date of pub-ication, title, publisher and edition. There is a subject ndex to part 1.

Lehmer, Derrick Henry. Guide to tables in the heory of numbers. Wash., Nat. Research Coun-il, Nat. Academy of Sciences, 1941. 177p. incl. ables. (Bull. of the Nat. Research Council, no. 05. Feb. 1941.) $2.50. **N86**

"Division of Physical Sciences, Committee on Mathe-matical Tables and Aids to Computation. . . . Report 1."

"Report of the Subcommittee on Section F: Theory f numbers."

Bibliography with location of copies in libraries of the United States and Canada, p.85-125.

Contents: pt.1, Descriptive account of existing tables; t.2, Bibliography arranged alphabetically by authors ;iving exact reference to the source of the tables referred o in pt.1; pt.3, Lists of errata in the tables.

Mathematical tables and aids to computation; a quarterly journal ed. on behalf of the Committee n Mathematical Tables and other Aids to Com-putation by Raymond Clare Archibald and Derrick Henry Lehmer. Wash., Nat. Research Council, 1943- . v.1- . Quarterly. $3. per yr. **N87**

A quarterly abstract journal to serve as a clearing-ouse for information concerning mathematical tables nd other aids to computation. Gives references to tables ublished in books or periodicals with reviews, bibliog-aphies, etc.

COMPENDIUMS

Barlow, Peter. Barlow's Tables of squares, cubes, quare roots, cube roots and reciprocals of all nteger numbers up to 12,500, ed. by L. J. Comrie . . 4th ed. Lond., Spon; N.Y., Chem. Pub. Co., 941. 258p. **N88**

Bierens de Haan, David. Nouvelles tables l'intégrales définies . . . ed. of 1867- corrected; vith an English translation of the introduction >y J. F. Ritt. N.Y., Stechert, 1939. 716p. **N89**

British Association for the Advancement of cience. Committee for the Calculation of Mathematical Tables. Mathematical tables. . . . Lond., British Assoc., 1931–40. v.1-6¹, 7-9. (v.1, 'nd ed. 1946) (In progress) **N90**

v.1, 2d ed., Circular and hyperbolic functions, exponen-ial and sine and cosine integrals, factorial function and llied functions, hermitian probability functions, 1946; .2, Emden functions, being solutions of Emden's equa-ion together with certain associated functions; v.3, Mini-num decompositions into fifth powers, prepared by L. E. Dickson; v.4, Cycles of reduced ideals in quadratic fields repared by E. L. Ince; v.5, Factor table, giving the com-lete decomposition of all numbers less than 100,000,

prepared by J. Peters, A. Lodge, E. J. Ternouth, E. Gif-ford; v.6, Bessel functions: pt.1, Functions of orders zero and unity; v.7, The probability integral by W. F. Shep-pard; v.8, Number-divisor tables, designed and in part prepared by J. W. L. Glaisher; v.9, Table of powers, giv-ing integral powers of integers, initiated by J. W. L. Glaisher.

Burington, Richard Stevens. Handbook of math-ematical tables and formulas. 3d ed. 1949. Sandusky, Ohio, Handbook Pub., 1949. 296p. $1.60. **N91**

Davis, Harold Thayer. Tables of the higher mathematical functions, computed and comp. under the direction of Harold T. Davis with the cooperation of Muriel E. Adams, Catherine Ben-nett [and others]. Bloomington, Ind., Principia Pr., 1933–35. 2v. $6.50 ea. **N92**

Mathematical Tables Project. [Mathematical tables] prepared by the Mathematical Tables Project, Work Projects Administration of the Federal Works Agency. Conducted under the sponsorship of the National Bureau of Standards. . . . N.Y., Columbia Univ. Pr., 1939–44. 40v. **N93**

Originally published by the Work Projects Administra-tion for the City of New York under the sponsorship of the National Bureau of Standards. After 1942 when the W.P.A. was discontinued the work was taken over by the sponsoring agency and the later volumes were pub-lished by the Columbia University Press.

For complete contents *see* Parke, *Guide to the literature of mathematics*, p.135-37 (N67).

Thompson, Alexander John. Logarithmetica Britannica, being a standard table of logarithms to 20 decimal places. Camb., Univ. Pr., 1924–37. pts. 1, 3-9. (Tracts for computers, no.11, 14, 16-21) (In progress) 15s. ea. **N94**

Contents: pt.1, nos. 10,000-20,000. 1934; pt. 3, nos. 30,000-40,000. 1937; pt. 4, nos. 40,000-50,000. 1928; pt.5, nos. 50,000-60,000. 1931; pt.6, nos. 60,000-70,000. 1933; pt.7, nos. 70,000-80,000. 1935; pt.8, nos. 80,000-90,000. 1927; pt.9, nos. 90,000-100,000. 1924.

PHYSICS
General works
Guides

Parke, Nathan Grier. Guide to the literature of mathematics and physics including related works on engineering science. N.Y., McGraw-Hill, 1947. 205p. $5. **N95**

For full description *see* N67.

Bibliography

Darrow, Karl Kelchner. Classified list of pub-lished bibliographies in physics, 1910–1922, comp. for the Research Information Service. Wash., Nat. Research Council, 1924. 102p. (Bull. of the Nat. Research Council, no.47. v.8, pt.5, July 1924) **N96**

International catalogue of scientific literature: C, Physics. 1st-14th annual issues, 1901–1914. Lond., 1902–17. 14v. **N97**

⁓ For full description *see* N6.

Royal Society of London. Catalogue of scientific papers, 1800–1900: Subject index, v.3, Physics. Camb., Univ. Pr., 1912–14. 2v. **N98**

pt.1, Generalities, heat, light, sound; pt.2, Electricity and magnetism.
For full description *see* N4.

Reuss, Jeremias David. Repertorium commentationum a societatibus litterariis editarum . . . t.4, Physica. Gottingae, Dieterich, 1805. 416p. **N99**

A valuable index to the publications of learned societies up to 1800. Classed arrangement with author index.
For full description *see* N3.

Abstracts and reviews

Physikalische Berichte . . . Jahrg. 1- . Braunschweig, Vieweg, 1920- . Semimonthly. **N100**

A comprehensive abstract journal. Titles are given in the original language, abstracts in German. Continues the abstracting service of the *Fortschritte der Physik,* 1845–1918 (Braunschweig, 1847–1919. 74v. in 141).

Science abstracts . . . Sect. A, Physics abstracts. Lond., Institution of Electrical Engineers, 1898- . v.1- . Monthly. A, 35s.; A and B, 60s. **N101**

Publisher varies.
1898–1902 title reads: Science abstracts, physics and electrical engineering; 1903- , issued in two sections: A, Physics; B, Electrical engineering. Beginning with 1941 titles changed to A, Physics abstracts and B, Electrical engineering abstracts.
Arranged by subject according to Universal Decimal classification. The January issue includes tables of the U.D.C. and the December issue, author, brief subject indexes and list of journals. Abstracts are frequently some months or even years late in appearing. Titles are not given in the original language but are translated into English. 1947 lists more than 350 journals.

Reviews of modern physics . . . published for the American Physical Society, v.1- . Lancaster, Pa., American Inst. of Physics, 1929- . Quarterly. $4.40. **N102**

―― Cumulative index, v.1-10, July 1929―October 1938. Issued with v.10.

Includes articles on the latest developments.

American journal of physics. v.1- . N.Y., American Inst. of Physics, 1933- . il. Quarterly, 1933–36; bimonthly, 1937- . **N103**

Title varies: 1933–39, *The American physics teacher.* Includes section "Digest of periodical literature."

Physical Society of London. Reports on progress in physics, 1934- . Lond., Physical Soc., 1934- . v.1- . il. **N104**

Encyclopedias

Glazebrook, *Sir* **Richard.** Dictionary of applied physics. Lond. and N.Y., Macmillan, 1922–23. 5v. il. **N105**

v.1, Mechanics, engineering, heat; v.2, Electricity; v.3, Meteorology, metrology and measuring apparatus; v.4, Light, sound, radiology; v.5, Aeronautics, metallurgy. General index.
An authoritative work, with signed articles by experts and bibliographies. Not one alphabetical encyclopedia but made up of five encyclopedias of special subjects, each alphabetically arranged and with its own detailed index. General index to the whole work is less detailed.
Now somewhat out of date but still useful.

Handbuch der experimental Physik hrsg. von W. Wien und F. Harms. Bd.1-26. Leipzig, Akademische Verlagsgesellschaft M.B.H., 1926–37. 26v. in 40. il. (In progress) **N106**

Not all volumes complete.

―― Ergänzungswerk. Bd.1-2. Leipzig, 1931–35. (In progress)

Handbuch der Physik, unter redaktioneller Mitwirkung von R. Grammel, hrsg. von H. Geiger und Karl Scheel. Berlin, Springer, 1926–29. 24v. and index, 26p. il. (Repr. Ann Arbor, Mich., Edwards, 1944) **N107**

v.1, Geschichte der physik Vorlesungstechnik, von E. Hoppe; v.2, Elementare Einheiten und ihre Messung, von A. Berroth; v.3, Mathematische Hilfsmittel in der Physik von A. Duschek; v.4, Allgemeine Grundlagen der Physik von G. Beck; v.5, Grundlagen der Mechanik; Mechanik der Punkte und starren Körper, von H. Alt; v.6, Mechanik der elastischen Körper, von R. Grammel; v.7, Mechanik der flüssigen und gasförmigen Körper, von J. Ackeret; v.8, Akustik, von H. Backhaus; v.9, Theorien der Wärme, von K. Bennewitz; v.10, Thermische Eigenschaften der Stoffe, von C. Drucker; v.11, Anwendung der Thermodynamik, von E. Freundlich; v.12, Theorien der Elektrizität, Elektrostatik, von A. Güntherschulze; v.13, Elektrizitätsbewegung in festen und flüssigen Körpern, von E. Baars; v.14, Elektrizitätsbewegung in Gasen, von G. Angenheister; v.15, Magnetismus elektromagnetische Feld, von E. Alberti; v.16, Apparate und Messmethoden für Elektrizität und Magnetismus, von E. Alberti; v.17, Elektrotechnik, von H. Behnken; v.18, Geometrische Optik, optische Konstante, optische Instrumente, von H. Boegehold; v.19, Herstellung und Messung des Lichts, von H. Behnken; v.20, Licht als Wellenbewegung, von L. Grebe; v.21, Licht und Materie, von Th. Dreisch; v.22, Elektronen, Atome, Moleküle, von W. Bothe; v.23, Quanten, von W. Bothe; v.24, Negative und positive Strahlen zusammenhängende Materie, von H. Baerwald.
Of the above, some volumes are now available in the second edition, 1933- .

See also Encyklopädie der mathematischen Wissenschaften, t.5, Physik (N80).

Dictionaries

Auerbach, Felix. Wörterbuch der Physik. Berlin, de Gruyter, 1920. 466p. il. **N108**

Berliner, Arnold and **Scheel, Karl.** Physikalisches Handwörterbuch . . . 2. Aufl. mit 1114 Textfiguren. Berlin, Springer, 1932. 1428p. il. **N109**

Articles are signed and vary in length from a few lines to several columns. Bibliography.

Weld, LeRoy Dougherty. Glossary of physics, comp. and ed. with the collaboration of a large group of consultant physicists. N.Y., McGraw-Hill, 1937. 255p. $2.50; 15s. **N110**

A dictionary of about 3250 terms with definition of each and in many cases bibliographical references to sources of supplementary information.

"The references do not necessarily represent the original source of the term or the authority for the definition. Nor is it intimated that they are the best possible references."—*Pref.*, p.vi.

Tables

See also Tables, p.257-58 and p.262-63.

Kaye, George William Clarkson and **Laby, Thomas Howell.** Tables of physical and chemical constants and some mathematical functions. 10th ed., completed by Jean Laby. Lond. and N.Y., Longmans, 1948. 194p. $5.50. **N111**

Landolt, Hans Heinrich. Landolt-Börnstein Physikalisch-chemische Tabellen. 5. umgearb. und verm. Aufl. hrsg. von Walther A. Roth und Karl Scheel. Berlin, Springer, 1923–36. 2v. and suppl. 1-3. il. (Repr. Ann Arbor, Mich., Edwards Bros., 1944) **N112**

—————— 6. Aufl. Berlin, 1949- . v.1- . (In progress)

v.1, Atom-und molekular Physik, pt.1, Atome und Ionen. $31.

Madelung, E. Die mathematischen Hilfsmittel des Physikers. 3. verm. und verb. Aufl. Berlin, Springer, 1936. 384p. (Die Grundlehren der mathematischen Wissenschaften. Bd.4) (Repr. N.Y., Dover, 1943) **N113**

"Practical and comprehensive collection of formulae used in mathematical physics."—*Pref.*

Mattauch, Josef. Nuclear physics tables and An introduction to nuclear physics by S. Fluegge. tr. from the German by Eugene P. Gross and S. Bargmann. N.Y., Interscience Publishers, 1946 [i.e. 1947]. 173p. il. $12. **N114**

Smithsonian Institution. Smithsonian physical tables. 8th rev. ed., prepared by Frederick E. Fowle. Wash., Smithsonian Institution, 1933. 682p. (Smithsonian misc. coll., v.88) $3. **N115**

Colors

See also Dyes, p.274-75.

Maerz, Aloys John and **Paul, Morris Rea.** Dictionary of color. 1st ed. N.Y., McGraw-Hill, 1930. 207p. 56 col. pl. $14. **N116**

Partial contents: Introduction; Table of terms found in literature; Table of principal color names; Polyglot table of principal color names; Bibliography; Color plates; Brief history of color standardization; Notes on color names; Index of color names.

"Intended . . . to relate colors with the names by which they are commonly identified."—*Pref.*

Ridgway, Robert. Color standards and color nomenclature . . . with 53 colored plates and [a dictionary of] 1115 named colors. Wash., Author, 1912. 43p. 53 col. pl. **N117**

A revised and much enlarged edition of the author's *Nomenclature of color*, 1886, including: (1) a dictionary list of 1115 named colors, and (2) mounted colored samples of 1431 different shades. The best color dictionary, including somewhat fewer colors than the *Répertoire de couleurs* by René Oberthür (Rennes, 1905) but showing more even gradations between colors. Prepared especially for the ornithologist but useful also to botanists, florists, merchants, chemists, dyers, artists, etc. Author was curator of Division of Birds, U.S. National Museum.

ASTRONOMY
General works
Bibliography

Brown, Basil. Astronomical atlases, maps and charts; an historical and general guide. Lond., Search Pub. Co., 1932. 200p. il. **N118**

Half title: An historical and general guide relating to the atlases, maps and charts of astronomy and certain associated sciences.

Brussels. Observatoire Royal de Belgique. Bibliothèque. Catalogue alphabétique des livres, brochures et cartes par A. Collard. Bruxelles, Hayez, 1910–12. 2v. **N119**

A well-made catalog of a very rich collection, containing more than 13,000 entries. Includes many reprints or extracts from periodicals and society publications.

Collard, Auguste. L'astronomie et les astronomes. Bruxelles, Van Oest, 1921. 119p. (Répertoire des ouvrages à consulter) **N120**

A classed catalog with author index, including works published after 1880, to supplement Houzeau and Lancaster (N121).

Houzeau, Jean Charles and **Lancaster, Albert.** Bibliographie générale de l'astronomie, ou catalogue méthodique des ouvrages, des mémoires et des observations astronomiques publiés dépuis l'origine de l'imprimerie jusqu'en 1880. Bruxelles, Havermans, 1882; Hayez, 1887–89. 2v. in 3. **N121**

Volume 1 (published 1887–89) is a classed bibliography of manuscripts and separately published works, with no author index; volume 2, is a classed index to material in periodicals and society publications with author index.

International catalogue of scientific literature: E, Astronomy. 1st-14th annual issues. Lond., 1902–18. 14v. **N122**

For full description *see* N6.

Müller, Gustav and **Hartwig, Ernst.** Geschichte und Literatur des Lichtwechsels, der bis Ende 1915 als sicher veränderlich anerkannten Sterne. Leipzig, Poeschel, 1918–22. 3v. **N123**

Continued by:

Prager, Richard. Geschichte und Literatur des Lichtwesels der veränderlichen Sterne. 2. Ausg. enthaltend die Literatur der Jahre 1916- . Berlin, Dümmler, 1934–41. v.1-2, 4. (In progress) **N124**

Contents: v.1-2, Andromeda-Ophiuchus. 1934–36; [v.4] was pub. as History and bibliography of the light variations of variable stars. 2d ed. Suppl. v., containing the stars recognized to be variable during the years 1931–1938. Camb., Mass., Observatory, 1941. 251p. (Annals of the Astron. Observ. of Harvard College. v.3.)

Reuss, Jeremias David. Repertorium commentationum a societatibus litterariis editarum, t.5, Astronomia. Gottingae, Dieterich, 1804. 548p. **N125**

A valuable index to the publications of learned societies up to 1800. For description of complete set *see* N3.

Shapley, Harlow. Star clusters. N.Y., McGraw-Hill, 1930. 276p. il. (Harv. Observatory monographs. no.2) **N126**

General bibliography (p.235-67) of over 800 references and a bibliography of bibliographies on star clusters.

U. S. Coast and Geodetic Survey. Catalog of U.S. Coast and Geodetic Survey nautical and aeronautical charts, coast pilots, tide tables, current tables, tidal current charts; Atlantic and Gulf coasts, Puerto Rico, Virgin Islands, and Canal Zone, Pacific Coast, Alaska, Hawaiian Islands and Guam, and the Philippine Islands. ed. Oct. 1941. Wash., Govt. Prt. Off., 1941. 62p. (Serial no.641) **N127**

—— Library. List and catalogue of the publications issued by the Survey, 1816–1902, by E. L. Burchard. Repr. with supplement 1903–08.

Wash., Govt. Prt. Off., 1908. 237p., 44p. **N128**

U. S. Hydrographic Office. General catalogue of mariners' and aviators' charts and books, corrected to Jan. 1941. Wash., Govt. Prt. Off., 1941. 185p. maps. **N129**

—— —— Corrections, Jan. 1941–Nov. 22, 1941.

Zinner, Ernst. Geschichte und Bibliographie der astronomischen Literatur in Deutschland zur Zeit der Renaissance. Leipzig, Hiersemann, 1941. 452p. **N130**

Includes astronomical works and works in related fields if they affected the development of astronomy.
Covers 1448–1630, arranged chronologically with author index.

Abstracts

Astronomischer Jahresbericht, Bd.1- . 1899- . Berlin, de Gruyter, 1900- . Bd.1- . Annual. **N131**

A comprehensive classed bibliography covering the literature of a year from all countries, in some cases including abstracts.

Bibliographie mensuelle de l'astronomie, t.1- . Publications reçues en 1933- . Paris, Société Astronomique de France, 1933- . Monthly. **N132**

Classified bibliography and abstract journal with annual subject and author indexes.

Encyclopedias

Handbuch der Astrophysik, hrsg. von G. Eberhard, A. Kohlschütter, H. Ludendorff. Berlin, Springer, 1928–36. 7v. in 10. **N133**

Contents: v.1-3, Bernheimer, W. E. [and others]. Grundlagen der Astrophysik; v.4, Abetti, Georgio. Das Sonnensystem; v.5-6, Becker, Friedrich [and others]. Das Sternsystem; v.7, Ergänzungsband, Berücksichtigend die Literatur bis ende 1934. Generalregister.

See also Encyklopädie der mathematischen Wissenschaften, t.6¹, Geodäsie und Geophysik; t.6², Astronomie (N80).

Directories

Brussels. Observatoire Royal de Belgique. Service Astronomique. Les observatoires astronomiques et les astronomes, par P. Stroobant, J. Delvosal, E. Delporte, F. Moreau, H. L. Vanderlinden. Ouvrage publié sous les auspices de l'Union Astronomique Internationale. Tournai, Casterman, 1931. 314p. **N134**

Contents: (1) Observatoires astronomiques et astronomes (alphabetically by place—gives publications, staff, historical note, instruments, and travaux astronomiques);

(2) Sociétés astronomiques; (3) Comités nationaux d'astronomie; (4) Revues astronomiques; (5) Liste alphabétique des noms.

——— ——— Supplément. . . . Gembloux, Duculot, 1936. 106p.

Sterns, Mabel. Directory of astronomical observatories in the United States. Ann Arbor, Mich., J. W. Edwards, 1947. 162p. $2.85. **N135**

Gives address, description of building, telescopes, equipment, activities, etc.

Yearbooks and nautical almanacs

Berliner astronomisches Jahrbuch . . . 1776- hrsg. von dem Astronomischen Rechen-Institut. Berlin, Dümmler, 1774- . Annual. **N136**

Title and issuing body varies.

France. Bureau des Longitudes. Annuaire pour l'an 1796/97- , avec des notices scientifiques. Paris, Gauthier-Villars, 1796- . il. Annual. **N137**

Gt. Brit. Nautical Almanac Office. Nautical almanac and astronomical ephemeris for the year 1767- for the meridian of the Royal Observatory at Greenwich. Pub. by order of the Lords Commissioners of the Admiralty. . . . Lond., Stat. Off., 1766- . Annual. (1950, pub. 1949. 15s.) **N138**

Sponsoring body varies.

U. S. Nautical Almanac Office. American ephemeris and nautical almanac 1855- . Wash., Govt. Prt. Off., 1852- . Annual. (1950, pub. 1948. $3.50.) **N139**

——— American air almanac. 1933, 1941- . Wash., Govt. Prt. Off., 1932- . 3 issues per yr. $1. **N140**

Loose-leaf.

1933 had title *The Air almanac*. None issued 1934–1940.

Astronomical data required for aerial navigation.

Navigation

Bowditch, Nathaniel. American practical navigator: An epitome of navigation and nautical astronomy . . . (rev. ed. 1938) pub. by the United States Hydrographic Office under the authority of the Secretary of the Navy. Wash., Govt. Prt. Off., 1939. 391p., 386p. (U.S. Hydrographic Office no.9) $2.25. **N141**

First published in 1802 under title: *The New American practical navigator*. Since 1866 revised and published at intervals by the Hydrographic Office.

Dreisonstok, Joseph Young. Navigation tables for mariners and aviators. 6th ed. Wash., Govt. Prt. Off., 1942. 109p. il. $1.20. (U.S. Hydrographic Office no.208) **N142**

Gt. Brit. Admiralty. Admiralty manual of navigation, 1928. Lond., Stat. Off., 1928. 2v. il. 10s. **N143**

Harbord, John Bradley. Glossary of navigation; a vade mecum for practical navigators. 4th ed. rev. and enl. by C. W. T. Layton. Glasgow, Brown and Ferguson, 1938. 451p. il. 12s. 6d. **N144**

A modern revision of a standard handbook first published in 1862.

U. S. Hydrographic Office. Altitude, azimuth and line of position comprising tables for working sight of heavenly body for line of position by the Cosine-Haversine formula, Marcq Saint Hilaire method and also Aquino's altitude and azimuth tables for line of position, Marcq Saint Hilaire method. (5th repr.) Wash., Govt. Prt. Off., 1928. 327p. il. (Its Pub. no.200) 90c. **N145**

——— Radio navigational aids; marine direction-finding stations, radio beacons, time signals, navigational warnings, distress signals, medical advice, and quarantine, loran, weather, and radio regulations for territorial waters. 1925- . Wash., Govt. Prt. Off., 1925- . (Its Pub. no.205) Annual. (1947, $1.25) **N146**

Title varies.

Statistics for 1926, 1934, 1936 and 1940 were not published separately.

——— Radio weather aids to navigation. Radio weather broadcasts, 1941- . Wash., Govt. Prt. Off., 1940- . tables. (Its Pub. no.206) **N147**

Statistics for 1938–39 were published in 1938 and 1939 as volume 2 of the *Radio navigational aids* (N146).

——— Sumner line of position furnished ready to lay down upon the chart by means of tables of simultaneous hour angle and azimuth of celestial bodies. Between 27° and 63° of declination, latitude 60°N to 60°S. [2d ed.] Wash., Govt. Prt. Off., 1933. [892]p. il. (Its Pub. no.204) $2.25. **N148**

——— Star identification tables giving simultaneous values of declination and hour angle for values of latitude, altitude and azimuth, ranging from 0° to 88° in latitude and altitude and 0° to 180° in azimuth. Wash., Govt. Prt. Off., 1939. 364p. (Its Pub. no.127) 90c. **N149**

——— Star tables for air navigation, computed altitude and true azimuth for all latitudes. Prelim. ed. Wash., Govt. Prt. Off., 1947. 321p. (Its Pub. no.249) $2. **N150**

——— Tables of computed altitude and azimuth. . . . Wash., Govt. Prt. Off., 1939- . v.1- . (Its Pub. no.214) (v.9, 1946, $2.25) **N151**

Arranged by latitudes, v.1-9 covering Lat. 0°–89° incl.

U. S. Laws, Statutes. Navigation laws of the United States, 1931. Wash., Govt. Prt. Off., 1932. 468p. tables. $1.   **N152**

Stars

There are many useful guides to the stars for the amateur. The following are representative:

Barton, Samuel Goodwin and **Barton, William H.** Guide to the constellations. 3d ed. N.Y., McGraw-Hill, 1943. 80p. il. $4.   **N153**

"Written for the beginner but should prove to be a valuable reference book for all who are interested in constellations."—*Pref.*

New handbook of the heavens; by Hubert J. Bernhard, Dorothy A. Bennett, and Hugh S. Rice. Rev. ed. N.Y., Whittlesey House, McGraw-Hill, 1948. 360p. il. $3.   **N154**

Phillips, Theodore E. R. and **Steavenson, W. H.** Splendour of the heavens; a popular authoritative astronomy, containing 1104 black and white illustrations with 25 coloured plates. N.Y., McBride, 1931. 976p. il. $8.50.   **N155**

Originally published as *Hutchinson's Splendour of the heavens* (Lond., Hutchinson, 1923. 2v.).

Monthly evening sky map; a journal for the amateur—northern and southern hemisphere—also a star, constellation, and planet finder map, arranged for the current month—morning and evening—and practical anywhere in the world. Brooklyn, N.Y., Celestial Map Pub. Co., 1906-   . Quarterly. $2.   **N156**

Founded by Leon Barritt, now edited by Mrs. Leon Barritt.

Gives morning and evening sky maps for each month.

Norton, Arthur Philip. Star atlas and reference handbook (epoch 1950) for students and amateurs. 10th ed. Lond., Gall, 1946. 55p., 35p. il. 35s.   **N157**

Subtitle: Covering the whole star sphere, and showing over 9000 stars, nebulae and clusters; with descriptive lists of objects mostly suitable for small telescopes; notes on planets, star nomenclature, etc.

Chronology

See Dictionaries, Outlines, Tables, etc., p.478-79, for historical chronology and dictionaries of dates.

Bibliography

Frick, Bertha Margaret and **Connolly, Alice B.** Calendar revision bibliography. N.Y., World Calendar Association, 1947. 100p.   **N158**

A chronological listing of writings in various languages about calendar reform from 1682–1947.

♤ For a brief account of systems *see* Stamp, Alfred Edward, *Methods of chronology* (Lond., Bell, 1933. 16p. Hist. Assoc. leaflet 92). The following contain longer treatments and detailed tables and calendars:

Bond, John James. Handy-book of rules and tables for verifying dates with the Christian era; giving an account of the chief eras, and systems used by various nations, with easy methods for determining the corresponding dates; with regnal years of English sovereigns from the Norman Conquest to the present time, 1066–1874. 4th ed. Lond., Bell, 1889. 465p. (Bohn's Reference lib.)   **N160**

Cappelli, Adriano. Cronologia, cronografia e calendario perpetuo. Dal principio dell' êra Cristiana ai giorni nostri. Tavole cronologico-sincrone e quadri sinottici per verificare le date storiche. 2. ed. interamente rif. ed ampl. Milano, Hoepli, 1930. 566p. (Manuali Hoepli)   **N161**

Ginzel, Friedrich Karl. Handbuch der mathematischen und technischen Chronologie, das Zeitrechnungswesen der Völker. Leipzig, Hinrichs, 1906–14. 3v. il.   **N162**

v.1, Zeitrechnung der Babylonier, Ägypter, Mohammedaner, Perser, Inder, Südostasiaten, Chinesen, Japaner u. Zentralamerikaner; v.2, Zeitrechnung der Juden, der Naturvölker, der Römer u. Griechen; Nachträge; v.3, Zeitrechnung der Makedonier, Kleinasier u. Syrer, der Germanen u. Kelten, des Mittelalters, der Byzantiner (und Russen), Armenier, Kopten, Abessinier, Zeitrechnung der neueren Zeit; Nachträge, v.1-3.

Discussion, bibliography and tables.

Master Reporting Company. A 200-year series of calendars, 1828–2028. N.Y., Master Report. Co. [1932]. [16]p.   **N163**

A convenient, small handbook to keep at an information desk.

Schram, Robert Gustav. Kalendariographische und chronologische Tafeln. Leipzig, Hinrichs, 1908. 368p.   **N164**

CHEMISTRY

See also Chemical Engineering, p.304-05.

General works

Guides

♤ The first three handbooks listed below are essential for anyone needing guides to the literature of chemistry. While to a certain extent they all deal with the same types of material, they complement each other in their varying treatment. They would be useful not only in a chemistry library but also in a general library where for purposes of book selection or interlibrary loan one needs to know what materials exist. They should be consulted for additions to the standard works listed here.

Crane, Evan Jay and **Patterson, Austin M.** Guide to the literature of chemistry. N.Y., Wiley; Lond., Chapman, 1927. 438p. $5. **N165**

Although now somewhat out of date, this work is still useful for its general discussions and its descriptions of standard works. A second fully revised edition is in preparation.

Mellon, Melvin Guy. Chemical publications, their nature and use. 2d ed. N.Y., McGraw-Hill, 1940. 284p. il. (International chemical ser.) $3. **N166**

A comprehensive survey of all types of chemical publications with descriptions and comment.

Soule, Byron Avery. Library guide for the chemist . . . 1st ed. N.Y., McGraw-Hill, 1938. 302p. (International chemical ser.) $3. **N167**

A convenient guide, covering the use of a chemistry library and how to find materials. Includes bibliographies and descriptions of outstanding works.

Serrallach, Maria. Bibliografía química; documentación científico-industrial. . . . Barcelona, José Bosch, 1946. 358p. Ps.130. **N168**

A Spanish guide to the literature of chemistry including books and periodicals in all languages but particularly strong in Spanish. Includes English-Spanish and German-Spanish terminologies, lists of abbreviations, etc.

See also such bibliographies as Hawkins, *Scientific, medical and technical books* (N10); *New technical books,* published by the New York Public Library (P13); and the *Technical book review index* (P16).

Bibliography

Bolton, Henry Carrington. Select bibliography of chemistry 1492–[1902]. Wash., Smithsonian Inst., 1893–1904. 4v. **N169**

Basic list, 1492–1892. 1212p.; 1st suppl., 1492–1897. 1899. 489p.; 2d suppl., 1492–1902. 1904. 462p.; Academic dissertations. 1901. 534p.
Eight sections: (1) Bibliography; (2) Dictionaries; (3) History; (4) Biography; (5) Chemistry, pure and applied; (6) Alchemy; (7) Periodicals; (8) Academic dissertations.
Includes some 18,000 independent works but does not list analytics. Section 8, Academic dissertations (published 1901, with additions in the second supplement) is particularly strong in dissertations from the universities of France, Germany, Russia and the United States.

Duveen, Denis I. Bibliotheca alchemica et chemica; an annotated catalogue of printed books on alchemy, chemistry and cognate subjects in the library of Denis I. Duveen. Lond., Weil, 1949. 669p. il. £9 9s. **N170**

Includes works from the sixteenth to the nineteenth centuries.

Ferguson, John. Bibliotheca chemica: A catalogue of the alchemical, chemical and pharmaceutical books in the collection of the late James Young of Kelly and Durris. Glasgow, Maclehose, 1906. 2v. **N171**

Collection bequeathed to the chair of technical chemistry of Anderson's College now incorporated in the Royal Technical College, Glasgow.

A rich collection of early works useful for the history of chemistry, particularly in alchemy.

International catalogue of scientific literature: D, Chemistry. 1st-14th annual issues, 1901–14. Lond., Harrison, 1902–19. **N172**

For full description *see* N6.

National Research Council. Research Information Service. Bibliography of bibliographies on chemistry and chemical technology, 1920–1924; comp. by Clarence J. West and D. D. Berolzheimer. Wash., Council, 1925. 308p. (Bull. of the Council, no.50) $2.50. **N173**

———— 1st-2d suppl., 1924/28–1929/31. Wash., Council, 1929–32. 2v. (Bull. of the Council, nos. 71, 86)

Main volume includes: General bibliographies, Abstract journals and yearbooks, General indexes of serials, Bibliographies on special subjects, Personal bibliographies.
The supplements continue the last two sections.

Reuss, Jeremias David. Repertorium commentationum a societatibus litterariis editarum . . . t.3, Chemia et res metallica. Gottingae, Dieterich, 1803. 221p. **N174**

A valuable index to the publications of learned societies up to 1800. Classed arrangement with author index. For description of complete set *see* N3.

Sohon, Julian Arell and **Schaaf, William L.** Reference list of bibliographies: Chemistry, chemical technology, and chemical engineering since 1900. N.Y., Wilson, 1924. 100p. $1.50. **N175**

Arranged by subject, includes bibliographies in books and periodicals published from 1900–23.

Periodical abbreviations

Chemical abstracts. List of periodicals abstracted. Dec. 20, 1946. ccixp. (v.40, no.24, pt.2 of Chemical abstracts) $2. **N176**

An important and useful list furnished from time to time by *Chemical abstracts,* listing over 4000 current publications, not only chemical journals but also other scientific periodicals carrying articles of chemical interest. For each periodical gives full title, authorized abbreviation, frequency, 1946 volume number, number of volumes per year, price, publisher and address, and numbers showing location in 280 libraries in the United States, Canada, Hawaii, and Puerto Rico. Includes many cross references from names of societies, academies, etc.

Useful not only for determining full titles from the abbreviations, but also for obtaining information on the publications of many scientific organizations in many parts of the world; information on recently discontinued and suspended periodicals; and location of files, frequently including designations indicating lending service, microfilming or photoprinting facilities, and translating services.

Pflücke, Maximilian. Periodica chimica; Verzeichnis der im Chemischen Zentralblatt referierten Zeitschriften mit den entsprechenden genormten Titelabkürzungen sowie Angaben über den Besitz in Bibliotheken Grossdeutschlands. . . . Berlin, Verlag Chemie, 1940. 208p. RM. 15.
N177

Abstracts

Chemical abstracts, published by the American Chemical Society, 1907- . Easton, Pa., 1907- . v.1- . Semimonthly. $15 per yr. to nonmembers; $7 to members. **N178**

—— Decennial indexes: v.1-10, 1907–16, Authors, 2v., Subjects, 2v.; v.11-20, 1917–26, Authors, 2v., Subjects, 3v.; v.21-30, 1927–36, Authors, 3v., Subjects, 5v.; v.31-40, 1937–46, Authors, 4v., Subjects, v.1-5, A-P. (In progress)

Now the most comprehensive of the abstract journals. Author index in each issue. Annual author, subject, and formula indexes from 1920- ; Patent no. index, 1935- .

—— List of periodicals abstracted. Dec. 20, 1946. ccixp. (v.40, no.24, pt.2 of Chemical abstracts) $2.

For full description *see* N176.

—— Patent index to Chemical abstracts, 1907–1936, comp. by the Science-Technology Group of Special Libraries Association. . . . Ann Arbor, Mich., Edwards, 1944. 479p. $12.50. **N179**

Numerical lists by countries of all patents reviewed in the first 30 volumes of *Chemical abstracts* (N178).

—— Collective numerical patent index to Chemical abstracts, v.31-40, 1937–1946. Wash., Amer. Chem. Soc., 1949. 182p. **N179a**

See also Mellon, *Chemical publications* (N166), and Soule, *Library guide for the chemist* (N167), for lists of other abstract journals and for review journals, yearbooks, and annual surveys.

British abstracts, issued by the Bureau of Abstracts. A, Pure chemistry; B, Applied chemistry; C, Analysis and apparatus. Lond., Bureau of

Abstracts, 1926- . A and B, monthly; C, quarterly. **N180**

Title varies: 1926–37, *British chemical abstracts;* 1938–44, *British chemical and physiological abstracts.* Continues the abstract volumes previously published in the *Journal* of the Chemical Society and the *Journal* of the Society of Chemical Industry.

The list of periodicals abstracted duplicates to a considerable extent the list of *Chemical abstracts* (N178 but does include some not covered there. There are joint annual indexes to parts A and B by author, subject, and patent number.

Since 1937, part A has been in three sections: (1 General physical and inorganic chemistry and geochemistry. £2 15s.; (2) Organic. £2 15s.; (3) Physiology biochemistry and anatomy. £4; 1, 2, and 3 together £8. Since 1945, part B has been in three sections: (1 Chemical engineering and industrial inorganic chemistr including metallurgy. £2 15s.; (2) Industrial organi chemistry. £2 15s.; (3) Agriculture, foods, sanitatio £1 15s.; part C, Analysis and apparatus, was added i 1945. 15s. All above prices per year, annual index in cluded.

—— Collective index of British chemical al stracts (A) Pure chemistry and (B) Applie chemistry, 1923–32, 1933–37. Lond., Bureau c Chemical and Physiological Abstracts, [1934? 40?]. 4v. **N180**

Author and subject indexes. The index for 1923–£ includes the abstracts published with the *Journal* of th Chemical Society and the *Journal* of the Society Chemical Industry during 1923–25.

Chemisches Zentralblatt. Vollständiges Repe torium für alle Zweige der reinen und ang wandten Chemie . . . Jahrg. 1- . Berlin, Verl Chemie, 1830- . v.1- . il. Biweekly (fr quency varies). **N18**

Title and imprint vary. Since 1897 published by t Deutsche Chemische Gesellschaft. v.112-116, pt.1, printed by J. W. Edwards, Ann Arbor, Mich.

Author index in each issue; semiannual author a patent indexes, 1897- , subject, 1889–1924; annual dexes, subject, organic formula, 1925- . Cumulati author and subject, 1870–81; 5-year cumulations authors, subjects, patents, 1897–1921; author, subje patent, organic formula, 1922–24, 1925–29, 1930–1935–39. (1922–34, reprinted by Edwards, Ann Arb Mich.)

This journal is particularly valuable because of length of the period covered. Many of the abstracts more detailed than those in *Chemical abstracts* (N17 Before 1919 it did not include abstracts on applied che istry as these appeared in *Angewandte Chemie.*

Société Chimique de France. Bulletin . . .: Doc mentation, fasc. 1- , oct. 1933- . Paris, M son, 1933- . Monthly. **N1**

From 1858–1932 abstracts were included in the *B letin;* from 1892, in the even numbered volumes. Fr 1933–45 the *Memoires* and *Documentation* appeared separate volumes; from 1946, in one volume.

Includes signed abstracts of material in various guages in the field of pure chemistry. Since 1918 app chemistry has been abstracted in *Chimie et industrie* which is particularly strong for French patents.

Annual reports on the progress of applied chemistry. Lond., Soc. of Chemical Industry, 1915- . v.1- .   **N183**

Annual reports on the progress of chemistry. Lond., Chemical Soc., 1904- . v.1- .   **N184**

These two annual reviews have world-wide coverage and include all fields of pure and applied chemistry. Written by authorities; extensive bibliographies.

Encyclopedias

Encyclopedia of chemical technology; ed. by Raymond E. Kirk, Donald F. Othmer [and others]. N.Y., Interscience Encyclopedias, Inc., 1947–50. v.1-5. il. (In progress) $20 per v. **N185**

v.1-5, A-Explosions.
A new encyclopedia of high standard to be completed in 10 volumes. Arranged by broad subjects with many cross references. Articles are written by specialists, are signed and include selected bibliographies. United States patents are noted.

Kingzett, Charles Thomas. Kingzett's Chemical encyclopaedia; a digest of chemistry and its industrial applications; rev. and ed. by Ralph K. Strong. 7th ed. N.Y., Van Nostrand, 1946. 1092p. $16.   **N186**

Malisoff, William Marias. Dictionary of biochemistry and related subjects. N.Y., Philosophical Library [1943]. 579p. $7.50.   **N187**

A dictionary giving many short definitions but also including longer encyclopedic articles, many of them signed and with bibliographies. Present-day terms are included as well as those occurring in the literature of the last decade but no longer in current use. Not always accurate.

Merck index. 5th ed. An encyclopedia for the chemist, pharmacist, physician, dentist and veterinarian. Rahway, N.J., Merck & Co., 1940. 1060p. il. $3.   **N188**

Subtitle: Containing useful scientific data and other information on the physical, chemical and medicinal properties, as well as the various uses, of chemicals and drugs; also more than 4500 chemical, clinicochemical reactions, tests and reagents; formulas for preparation of culture media, fixatives and staining solutions; useful tables; antidotes for poisons; literature references.

Neues Handwörterbuch der Chemie, auf Grundlage des von Liebig, Poggendorff und Wöhler, Kolbe und Fehling herausgegebenen Handwörterbuchs der reinen und angewandten Chemie und unter Mitwirkung von mehren Gelehrten bearbeitet und redigirt von Hermann v. Fehling. Braunschweig, Vieweg, 1871–1930. 10v. il.   **N189**

Schoengold, Morris D. Encyclopedia of substitutes and synthetics. N.Y., Philosophical Library [1943]. 328p. $10.   **N190**

Lists and describes substances and products of current interest as substitutes. Information given for the different products varies widely in fullness but usually tries to give name, brief description, properties, uses, and substitutes. Includes many products known chiefly by trade name.

Thorpe, Jocelyn Field and **Whiteley, M. A.** Thorpe's Dictionary of applied chemistry . . . 4th ed. rev. and enl. N.Y. and London., Longmans, 1937–49. v.1-9. (In progress) $30 ea.   **N191**

v.1-9, A-Pituitary.
The standard encyclopedia in English for applied chemistry. Volume 6 includes index to volumes 1-6 compiled by J. N. Goldsmith.

Ullmann, Fritz. Enzyklopädie der technischen Chemie. 2. völlig neubearb. Aufl. Berlin, Urban, 1928–32. 10v. and index (200p.). il.   **N192**

Important encyclopedia with long, signed articles, bibliographies and good illustrations. 1st ed. 1914–23.
A Spanish translation of the above is being issued under the title *Enciclopedia de química industrial* (Barcelona, Gili, 1931-).

Dictionaries

Bailey, Dorothy and **Bailey, Kenneth C.** An etymological dictionary of chemistry and mineralogy. Lond., Arnold; N.Y., Longmans, 1929. 307p. $9.   **N193**

Includes references to book or journal in which derivation is given.

Bennett, Harry. Concise chemical and technical dictionary. Brooklyn, N.Y., Chemical Pub. Co., 1947. 1055p. $10.   **N194**

Chemical terms predominate but there are also terms from engineering, mathematics, biology, etc. Definitions are brief and written for the scientist rather than the layman.

"Chemical age" chemical dictionary; chemical terms. Lond., Benn; N.Y., Van Nostrand, 1924. 158p. diagrs.   **N195**

Condensed chemical dictionary; a reference volume for all requiring quick access to a large amount of essential data regarding chemicals, and other substances used in manufacturing and laboratory work, comp. and ed. by the staff of the Chemical Engineering Catalog, Francis M. Turner, ed.-in-chief. 4th ed. completely rev. and enl. by Arthur and Elizabeth Rose. N.Y., Reinhold, 1950. 721p. diagrs. $10.   **N196**

Lists about 18,000 chemicals and chemical products, giving synonyms, properties, solubilities, grades, uses, etc. Includes many brand names and trade-marks.

Gardner, William. Chemical synonyms and trade names; a dictionary and commercial handbook. 5th ed. rev. and enl. by Edward I. Cooke. Lond., Technical Pr.; N.Y., Van Nostrand, 1948. 558p. 50s. **N197**

Hackh, Ingo Waldemar Dagobert. Hackh's Chemical dictionary (American and British usage). Containing the words generally used in chemistry, and many of the terms used in the related sciences of physics, astrophysics, mineralogy, pharmacy, agriculture, biology, medicine, engineering, etc.; based on recent chemical literature. . . . 3d ed., completely rev. and ed. by Julius Grant. Phila., Blakiston [1944]. 925p. il. $8.50. **N198**

This edition contains concise definitions for some 57,000 terms, including such new words as plutonium, penicillic acid and the various sulpha compounds. Other definitions have been revised and modernized, but pronunciation given in former editions is omitted. Includes names of outstanding chemists (some with portraits) dates and brief characterizations.

Miall, Stephen and **Miall, L. Mackenzie.** New dictionary of chemistry. 2d ed. Lond. and N.Y., Longmans, 1949. 589p. $12; £3. **N199**

FOREIGN TERMS

Chinese

Zee, Zai-Zang and **Cheng, Lan-Hua.** A modern English-Chinese chemical lexicon. Shanghai, China Science Corp. [1946]. 1265p. **N200**

French

Patterson, Austin McDowell. French-English dictionary for chemists. N.Y., Wiley, 1921. 384p. $3.50. **N201**

German

Patterson, Austin McDowell. German-English dictionary for chemists. 3d ed. N.Y., Wiley, 1950. 541p. $5. **N202**

59,000 entries primarily in chemistry but also including terms used in physics, biology, geology, etc.

Thurow, Willy H. Englisch-deutsches und deutsch-englisches Wörterbuch der Chemie. Berlin-Schöneberg, Tetzlaff, 1929–32. 2v. **N203**

v.1, Englisch-Deutsch; v.2, Deutsch-Englisch.

Japanese

Ishihara, Jun, Inoue, Toshi and **Tamamushi, Bunichi.** Japanese dictionary of physics and chemistry. Rev. and enl. ed. Rikagaku jiten zoho-

kaitei han. American ed. Ann Arbor, Mich., G. Wahr, 1942. [1966p.] il. $5. **N204**

Various pagings.
"The first edition . . . appeared in 1935; the second revised and enlarged edition, which is here reproduced, in 1939."

Polyglot

Cornubert, R. Dictionnaire anglais-français-allemand de mots et locutions intéressant la physique et la chimie. Paris, Dunod, 1922. 297p. **N205**

In columns, English, French, German, with the key words in all three languages integrated into one alphabet.

Mayer, Albert Willy. Chemisches Fachwörterbuch, deutsch-englisch-französisch, für Wissenschaft, Technik, Industrie und Handel. Leipzig, Spamer, 1929–31. v.1-2. **N206**

v.1, Deutsch-Englisch-Französisch; v.2, Englisch-Deutsch-Französisch.

An English translation of volume 1 was published as:

—— Chemical-technical dictionary (German-English-French-Russian) v.1, translation under the direction of B. N. Menshutkin and M. A. Bloch. 1st Amer. ed. Brooklyn, N.Y., Chemical Pub. Co., 1942. 870p. $8. **N207**

Russian

Callaham, Ludmilla Ignatiev. Russian-English technical and chemical dictionary. N.Y., Wiley, 1947. 794p. $10. **N208**

Besides chemical and engineering terms also includes some terms for mathematics, medicine, biology, agriculture, etc.

Handbooks

Chemical Rubber Co., Cleveland. Handbook of chemistry and physics; a ready-reference book of chemical and physical data. 31st ed. Ed.-in-chief, Charles D. Hodgman. . . . Cleveland, Chemical Rubber Pub. Co., 1949. il. 2737p. $6. **N209**

A useful handbook usually revised annually giving the constants and formulae used in chemistry and physics, including mathematical and conversion tables.

Lange, Norbert Adolph and **Forker, Gordon M.** Handbook of chemistry; a reference volume for all requiring ready access to chemical and physical data used in laboratory work and manufacturing . . . with an appendix of mathematical tables and formulas by Richard Stevens Burington . . . 6th ed. rev. and enl. Sandusky, Ohio, Handbook Publishers, 1946. 1767p., 271p., 28p. $7. **N210**

Frequently revised.

Seidell, Atherton. Solubilities of inorganic and metal organic compounds: A compilation of quantitative solubility data from the periodical literature. 3d ed. N.Y., Van Nostrand, 1940–41. 2v. v.1, $12, v.2, $10. **N211**

Volume 2 has title: *Solubilities of organic compounds.*

Welcher, Frank. Chemical solutions; reagents useful to the chemist, biologist, and bacteriologist. N.Y., Van Nostrand, 1942. 404p. $4.75. **N212**

"The purpose . . . is to collect in one place for convenient reference the methods for preparing those solutions most frequently required by the chemist."—*Pref.* Usually gives for each solution, the use, procedure of use, preparation, remarks, and reference.

Tables

See chemistry tables in the handbooks listed above and Tables, p.257-58, p.262, and p.265.

History

Moore, Forris Jewett and Hall, William T. History of chemistry. 3d ed. N.Y., McGraw-Hill, 1939. 447p. il. **N213**

Biography

Chemical who's who, v.2, 1937. Ed. by William Haynes. New Haven, Conn., Haynes and George Co., 1937. 543p. $6. **N214**

First issue (1928) had title: *Who's who in the chemical and drug industry.* The 1937 issue contains about 4800 biographies, including many names not found in *Who's who in America* (S40).

Smith, Henry Monmouth. Torchbearers of chemistry; portraits and brief biographies of scientists who have contributed to the making of modern chemistry. N.Y., Academic Pr., 1949. 270p. il. $6. **N215**

A remarkable collection of portraits of 223 chemists who have been influential in the history of chemistry, including some contemporary chemists. A short biographical sketch accompanies each portrait. The "Bibliography of biographies" by Ralph E. Oesper, p.263-70 gives further references for each person.

Organic

Beilstein, Friedrich. Handbuch der organischen Chemie. 4. Aufl. Die Literatur bis 1. Januar 1910 umfassend, hrsg. von der Deutschen Chemischen Gesellschaft, bearb. von Bernhard Prager und Paul Jacobson, unter ständiger Mitwirkung von Paul Schmidt und Dora Stern. . . . Berlin, Springer, 1918- . v.1- . tables. **N216**

v.28, General-Sachregister für die Bände 1-27 des Hauptwerks und ersten Ergänzungswerks. 1938. 2 pts.

v.29, General-Formelregister für die Bände 1-27 des Hauptwerks und ersten Ergänzungswerks. 1939–40. 2 pts.

—— —— I. Ergänzungswerk, die Literatur von 1910–1919 umfassend, hrsg. von der Deutschen Chemischen Gesellschaft, bearb. von Friedrich Richter. Berlin, Springer, 1928- . v.1- .

—— —— II. Ergänzungswerk, die Literatur von 1920–1929 umfassend. . . . Berlin, Springer, 1941- . v.1- . (In progress)

This monumental compilation, the most important reference work in organic chemistry, provides a complete summary of published data on organic compounds to January 1, 1910. The first supplement covers 1910–19 and the second supplement, 1920–29.

The third edition of this work is frequently referred to in Richter's *Lexikon* (N220). The fourth edition has been much enlarged and its arrangement modified. Each volume contains a detailed table of contents and an index. The plan of arrangement is given in the *System der organischen Verbindungen* (N217) and in Huntress (N219) noted below. Another brief description and explanation of this indispensable work may be found in Soule, *Library guide for the chemist,* p.127-53 (N167).

Deutsche Chemische Gesellschaft. System der organischen Verbindungen; ein Leitfaden für die Benutzung von Beilsteins Handbuch der organischen Chemie. . . . Berlin, Springer, 1929. 246p. **N217**

—— Kurze Anleitung zur Orientierung in Beilsteins Handbuch der organischen Chemie, bearb. von Friedrich Richter. . . . Berlin, Springer, 1936. 23p. **N218**

Huntress, Ernest Hamlin. A brief introduction to the use of Beilstein's Handbuch der organischen Chemie. 2d ed. rev. N.Y., Wiley, 1938. 44p. $1. **N219**

A simple explanation in English of the method of classification used in the fourth edition of Beilstein.

Richter, Max Moritz. Lexikon der Kohlenstoff-Verbindungen. 3. Aufl. Leipzig, Voss, 1910–12. 4v. diagr. **N220**

A formula index to all compounds known to December 31, 1909. Includes more than 144,000 compounds with references to the literature which describes preparation and properties, but not to purely theoretical papers. References to Beilstein refer to the third edition of the *Handbuch* rather than to the fourth edition listed above (N216).

Deutsche Chemische Gesellschaft. Literatur Register der organischen Chemie, geordnet nach M. M. Richters Formelsystem, redigiert von Robert Stelzner. Bd.1-5, 1910/11–1919/21. Leipzig, Verlag Chemie, 1913–26. 5v. (Repr. Ann Arbor, Mich., Edwards, 1948. $350) **N221**

Cited as *Stelzner*. Publisher varies.

Arranged by formulas in continuation of Richter (N220). Each volume covers the literature of from two to three years.

Merged with *Chemisches Zentralblatt, Generalregister* (N181).

Heilbron, Isidor Morris and **Bunbury, H. M.** Dictionary of organic compounds: The constitution and physical and chemical properties of the principal carbon compounds and their derivatives, together with the relevant literature references. Lond., Eyre, 1943. 3v. $75 ($30 per v.) **N222**

v.1, new rev. and enl. ed.; v.2-3 are reprints of the 1st ed. including material on the new compounds in the form of a supplement at the end of each volume. Supplements to v.2-3 also issued separately in one volume.

Elsevier's Encyclopaedia of organic chemistry, ed. by E. Josephy and F. Radt. N.Y., Elsevier Pub. Co., 1940- . il. (In progress) v.12A, 1948, $104; v.12B, 1949, $32; v.14, 1947, $60. **N223**

A new work in English which, like Beilstein (N216), attempts to present all known facts on the chemical, physical and physiological properties of organic compounds. It covers the literature up to and including 1936 and in certain cases the literature up to the date a particular volume went to press. Each volume includes a subject and a formula index. Expected to be in 20 volumes with general subject and formula indexes. The first volumes to be issued include fields not covered or only partially covered by the fourth edition of Beilstein and its supplements.

Inorganic

Gmelin, Leopold. Gmelins Handbuch der anorganischen Chemie. 8. völlig neubearb. Aufl. hrsg. von der Deutschen Chemischen Gesellschaft, bearb. von R. J. Meyer. . . . Berlin, Verlag Chemie, 1924- . v.1- . (In progress) **N224**

A monumental work which attempts to include all inorganic compounds ever described with references to the original articles. Volumes not published in regular numerical sequence.

Mellor, Joseph William. A comprehensive treatise on inorganic and theoretical chemistry. Lond., N.Y., Longmans, 1922–37. 16v. il. $30 ea. **N225**

Contains bibliographies.
Volume 16 includes index.

Abegg, Richard, Auerbach, Friedrich and **Koppel, Ivan.** Handbuch der anorganischen Chemie. Leipzig, Hirzel, 1905–39. v.2-4. (In progress) **N226**

A valuable compilation, still incomplete. The reviews were prepared by specialists and include extensive bibliographies.

Hoffmann, Max Konrad. Lexikon der anorganischen Verbindungen. Dictionary of inorganic

compounds. Hrsg. mit Unterstützung des König Sächsischen Ministeriums des Kultus und Öffen lichen Unterrichts, der Königl. Preussische Akademie der Wissenschaften und der König Sächsischen Gesellschaft der Wissenschaften. M einer Rechentafel von A. Thiel. Leipzig, Bart 1910–19. v.1-3 in 4v. **N22**

A complete listing of all analytical and synthetic organic compounds known up to April 1909, with fo mula, and references to articles in periodicals, etc.

Jacobson, Carl Alfred. Encyclopedia of chem ical reactions. N.Y., Reinhold, 1946–49. v.1- (In progress) v. 1, $10; v.2-3, $12 ea. **N2**

Patents

See also Patents, p.300.

See Mellon, *Chemical publications*, p.52- (N166), and Soule, *Library guide for the chemi* p. 207-49 (N167) for description of patent lite ature for the chemist.

Worden, Edward Chauncey. Chemical pater index. . . . N.Y., Book Dept., Chemical Catal Co., 1927–34. 5v. $100. **N2**

Subtitle: A comprehensive and detailed index of t subject matter of specification and claims of Unit States patents and patent reissues granted during decennial period of 1915–1924, inclusive, covering entire field of chemical technology; comprising the ra fications of patented inorganic and organic chemical pr esses and products as applied to biology, microsco botany, mineralogy, pharmacy, medicine, photograp and dyestuffs in both the warlike and peaceful arts.

v.1, Index of names, A-Z; Index of subjects, A-B; v.2 Index of subjects, C-Z.

Dyes

Schultz, Gustav. Farbstofftabellen. 7. Au neubearb. und erweitert von Ludwig Lehmar . . . Leipzig, Akademische Verlagsgesellscha 1931–32. 2v. **N2**

Published in parts, 1928–32.

—— —— Ergänzungsband I, umfassend die teratur bis 31. Dezember 1933. Leipzig, Akac mische Verlagsgesellschaft, 1934. 182p. diag

—— —— Ergänzungsband II, umfassend die teratur bis 31. Dezember 1937. Leipzig, Akac mische Verlagsgesellschaft, 1939. 352p. (Lit printed by Edwards Bros., Ann Arbor, Mic 1945)

Society of Dyers and Colourists. Colour ind ed. by F. M. Rowe. Bradford, Yorkshire, S 1924–28. 371p., 370p. and suppl., 55p. **N**

Includes commercial name index.

teressengemeinschaft Farbenindustrie Aktien-
esellschaft. Fachwörterbuch für die Farbstoffe
nd Textilhilfsmittel verbrauchenden Industrien.
erman-English. Comp. by I. G. Farbenindustrie
.G. N.Y., Dictionaries, Inc., 1947. 489p. **N232**

Meanings only. No definitions or discriminations.

GEOLOGY
General works
Bibliography

argerie, Emmanuel de. Catalogue des bibliog-
phies géologiques, rédigé avec le concours des
embres de la Commission Bibliographique du
ongrès. Paris, Gauthier-Villars, 1896. 733p.
Congrès Géologique International. 5ᵉ session,
ash., 1891; 6ᵉ session, Zürich, 1894) **N233**

Covers approximately 1726–1895. Arranged by coun-
 or region with author but not complete subject in-
xes. The table of contents should be consulted for
rangement. Especially useful for sections on biography
d bibliography of individual geologists.

athews, Edward B. Catalogue of published
bliographies in geology, 1896–1920. . . . Wash.,
at. Research Council, 1923. 228p. (Bull. of
e Council, no.36) $2.50. **N234**

Continues in a somewhat simplified form the bibliog-
phy by Margerie (N233). Arranged by subject with
thor index. Separate section for personal bibliographies.

arton, Nelson Horatio. Catalogue and index of
ntributions to North American geology, 1732–
91. Wash., Govt. Prt. Off., 1896. 1045p. (U.S.
eological Survey. Bull. no.127) **N235**

An author, subject index in one alphabet. Includes
th book and periodical material.

ickles, John Milton. Geologic literature of North
merica, 1785–1918. Wash., Govt. Prt. Off., 1923–
. 2v. (U.S. Geological Survey. Bull. nos. 746,
7) $3.15. **N236**

An author list with subject index, covering the geology
 the continent of North America and the adjoining
ands, Panama, and the Hawaiian Islands. Lists both
oks and periodical articles; indexes all articles on
nerican geology in about 140 periodicals, including
ne foreign journals. A cumulation of the annual bib-
graphies issued by the Geological Survey.

Continued by:

bliography of North American geology, 1919–
28, 1929–1939. Wash., Govt. Prt. Off., 1931–
. v.1-2. (U.S. Geological Survey. Bull. nos.
3, 937) $2.50. **N237**

1919–1928, comp. by John M. Nickles; 1929–1939,
mp. by Emma M. Thom.

A cumulation of and continued by biennial supple-
nts published with the same title in the *Bulletin* series.

Nickles, John Milton and Miller, Robert B. Bibliography and index of geology exclusive of North
America. v.1, 1933- . Wash., Geological Soc. of
America, 1934- . (Geological Society of America. Bibl. contributions) (1948, $3.25) **N238**

v.1-8 annual; v.9- biennial; v.7-10, comp. by J. M.
Nickles, Marie Siegrist and Eleanor Tatge; v.11- by
Marie Siegriest and Eleanor Tatge.

A comprehensive bibliography of articles from the
periodicals of many countries dealing with the geology of
all parts of the world except North America, thus com-
plementing the *Bibliography of North American geology*
(N237).

Annotated bibliography of economic geology,
1928- . [Urbana, Ill.] Econ. Geol. Pub. Co.,
1929- . v.1- . Semiannual. **N239**

v.1-8 prepared under the auspices of the National Research Council; v.9- , the Society of Economic Geologists and the Geologic Society of America. A bibliography with signed annotations of both book and periodical material in various languages. Covers about 100
periodicals.

—— General index, v.1-10, 1928–1938. Urbana,
Ill., Econ. Geol. Pub. Co., 1939. 496p. $5.

A 10-year index to this important bibliography, containing 23,100 references. Covers material through 1937.

Geological Society of London. Library. Geological literature added to the Geological Society's
library [no.1]-37, July, 1894–1934. . . . Lond.,
Geological Society, 1895–1935. Annual. **N240**

Not published, 1913–19. Ceased publication with
1934.

Bibliographie des sciences géologiques, publiée
par la Société Géologique de France avec le concours de la Société Française de Minéralogie.
1.-7. année, juil. 1923–29; 2. sér. t.1- , 1930- .
Paris, Société Géologique de France, 1923- .
v.1- . **N241**

A classed bibliography with author index covering
materials in various languages.

**Deutsche Geologische Gesellschaft, Berlin. Bib-
liothek.** Katalog der Bibliothek, im Auftrage der
Gesellschaft bearb. von P. Dienst. Stuttgart, Enke
[1930]. 1161p. **N242**

The classified subject catalog with author index of an
outstanding collection.

Bibliography of hydrology, United States of
America. . . . 1935/36- . Wash., American Geo-
physical Union, Section of Hydrology, 1937- .
 N243

"The United States cahier . . . of the International
Bibliography of Hydrology established by the International Association of Scientific Hydrology."

U. S. Geological Survey. Publications of the Geological Survey, May 1948. Wash., Govt. Prt. Off.,
1948. 322p. **N244**

A useful list formerly revised annually. Now to be revised quinquennially with annual supplements. Each issue contains a complete list to date of (1) Book publications of the survey, including annual reports, monographs, professional papers, bulletins, water-supply papers, mineral resources of the United States, folios of the *Geologic atlas of the United States*, the *World atlas of commercial geology*, and miscellaneous reports, and (2) Maps and charts including geological maps, mineral resources maps, topographic maps and miscellaneous maps. A detailed index by states, areas, and subjects and a finding list of authors are useful for reference questions. Earlier issues did not include topographic maps, which were, however, listed in the monthly list of new publications.

Warman, Philip Creveling. Catalogue and index of the publications of the United States Geological Survey, 1880–1901. Wash., Govt. Prt. Off., 1901. 858p. (U.S. Geological Survey. Bull. no. 177)   **N245**

—— —— 1901 to 1903. Wash., Govt. Prt. Off., 1903. 234p. (U.S. Geological Survey. Bull. no.215)

Canada. Geological Survey. Annotated catalogue of and guide to the publications of the Geological Survey, Canada, 1845–1917, by W. F. Ferrier, assisted by Dorothy J. Ferrier. Ottawa, Taché, 1920. 544p.   **N246**

—— General index to Reports of progress, 1863–1884, comp. by D. B. Dowling. Ottawa, Dawson, 1900. 475p.   **N246a**

—— General index to Reports, 1885–1906, comp. by F. J. Nicolas. Ottawa, Govt. Prt. Bur., 1908. 1014p.   **N246b**

—— Index to separate reports, 1906–10, and Summary reports, 1905–1916, comp. by F. J. Nicolas. Ottawa, Acland, 1923. 305p.   **N246c**

—— Index to Memoirs, 1910–1926; Bulletins, 1913–1926; Summary reports, 1917–1926; Sessional papers (administrative), 1921–1926, comp. by Frank Nicolas. Ottawa, Acland, 1932. 666p. (Misc. ser. 3)   **N246d**

—— Index to paleontology (Geological publications), comp. by Frank Nicolas. Ottawa, Acland, 1925–30. 2v.   **N246e**

v.1, 1847–1916; v.2, 1917–26.

Faessler, Carl. Cross-index to the maps and illustrations of the Geological Survey and the Mines Branch (Bureau of Mines) of Canada, 1843–1946 (incl.) Quebec, Université Laval, 1947. 525p. (Université Laval. [Faculté des Sciences] Géologie et Minéralogie. Contribution no.75) v.1, pts. 1-4.   **N247**

A guide to the geological illustrations to be found in the various series of publications of the Geological Survey

and the Bureau of Mines of Canada. pt.1, Introduction pt.2, Numerical listings of the various series; pt.3, Autho index; pt.4, Subject index.

Hall, Arthur Lewis. A bibliography of Sout African geology to the end of 1920: Author index. . . . Pretoria, Govt. Pr. and Stat. Off., 192: 376p. (South Africa. Geological Survey. Memo: no.18)   **N24**

—— A subject index to the literature on th geology and mineral resources of South Afric: Pretoria, Govt. Pr. and Stat. Off., 1924. 384 (South Africa. Geological Survey. Memoir no.22

A companion volume and supplement to Memoir no.1 (N248).

—— A bibliography of South African geology fc the years 1921 to 1935 (inclusive). Authors' ii dex. Pretoria, Govt. Pr. and Stat. Off., 1927–3 3v. (South Africa. Geological Survey. Memo nos. 25, 27, 30) 5s. ea.

[v.1] 1921–25; [v.2] 1926–30; [v.3] 1931–35.

—— Subject index to the literature of Sout African geology and mineral resources for th years 1921 to 1935 (inclusive). A companio volume to Memoirs 25, 27, and 30 (Bibliogr: phies 1921–1935, Authors' index). . . . Pretori: Govt. Pr., 1939. 288p. (South Africa. [Geolog cal Survey] Memoir no.37)

Singewald, Joseph Theophilus. Bibliography (economic geology of South America. . . . [N.Y Geol. Soc. of Amer., 1943. 159p. (Geological So of Amer. Special papers no.50)   **N24**

Contains the bibliographies, brought up to date, whic were published, 1919, in *The Mineral deposits of Sout America*, by B. L. Miller and J. T. Singewald, Jr. Lis 2912 titles, largely periodical articles in various lar guages. Alphabetical by author under each country.

Jeannet, Alphonse. Bibliographie géologique d la Suisse pour les années 1910 à 1920. . . . Bern A. Francke, 1927. 2v. (Beiträge zur geologische Karte der Schweiz; hrsg. von der Geologische Kommission der Schweiz. Naturforschenden G sellschaft, subventionert von der Eidgenosser schaft, n.F., 56. Lfg. des ganzen Werkes 86. Lfg.   **N25**

Paged continuously.
Supplementing two earlier bibliographies: (1) *Ge logische Bibliographie der Schweiz . . . 1770–1900*, vc L. Rollier, pub. 1907–08, in 2 v. as Bd.29 of the serie (2) *Geologische Bibliographie . . . 1900–1910*, von I Gogarten und W. Hauswirth, pub. 1913, as Bd.70 (n. I 40) of the series.

Abstracts and review journals

Geologisches Zentralblatt. Anzeiger für Geolc gie, Petrographie, Palaeontologie und verwandt

Wissenschaften . . . Bd.1- , 1901- . Leipzig, Borntraeger, 1901- . v.1- . Semi-monthly. **N251**

1932- , in 2 pts.: Abt. A, Geologie; Abt. B, Palaeontologisches Zentralblatt.

Signed abstracts of book and periodical material in various languages.

―――――― Generalregister zu Bd.1-30. Leipzig, Borntraeger, 1927. 2v. [1.] 1-15. 472p.; [2.] 16-30. 398p.

―――――― Sachlich geordnetes Inhaltsverzeichnis zu Bd.31-50. Leipzig, 1935. 493p.

Neues Jahrbuch für Mineralogie, Geologie und Paläontologie . . . Referate, 1925- . Stuttgart, E. Schweigerbart'sche Verlagsbuchhandlung, 1925- . **N252**

1925–27, each v. in 2 Abt.: (A) Mineralogie und Petrographie; (B) Geologie und Paläontologie; 1928- , each v. in 3 Abt.: (1) Kristallographie, Mineralogie; (2) Allgemeine Geologie, Petrographie, Geochemie, Lagerstättenlehre; (3) Historische und regionale Geologie, Paläontologie.

Signed abstracts of book and periodical material in various languages.

Repertorium der mineralogischen und krystallographischen Literatur, 1876–1902; und Generalregister der Zeitschrift für Krystallographie und Mineralogie . . . Bd. 1-40. Leipzig, Engelmann, 1886–1910. 4v. **N253**

Each volume is in two parts, the first being a bibliography of material published during the period covered, the second an index to the *Zeitschrift.* The *Repertorium* covers 1876–85, 1885–91, 1891–97, 1897–1902.

Revue de géologie et des sciences connexes . . . année 1- , 1920- . Liége, Vaillant-Carmanne, 1920- . v.1- . **N254**

Subtitle: Organe publié mensuellement avec le concours de la Fondation Universitaire de Belgique sous le patronage de la Société Géologique de Belgique avec la collaboration de la revue *The American mineralogist,* de la Société Géologique de France, du Service Géologique de Pologne, du Comitato della Rassegna di Geologia, des *Australian science abstracts,* du Bureau d'Histoire Naturelle de Prague, de divers services géologiques et de nombreux géologues.

Signed abstracts of book and periodical material in various languages. Abstracts are not all in French, some being in English, Italian or German.

U. S. Geological Survey. Geophysical abstracts. no.1, 1929- . [Wash., 1929]- . **N255**

Abstracts 1-86 were issued in mimeographed form by the Bureau of Mines. On July 1, 1936, the geophysical section was transferred to the Geological Survey, which issued abstracts 87-111. By Departmental Order of Oct. 5, 1942, the geophysical work was again placed with the Bureau of Mines, and abstracts 112-127 were issued by that bureau. Beginning July 1, 1947, it was transferred again to the Geological Survey.

Dictionaries

Beringer, Carl Christoph. Geologisches Wörterbuch; Erklärung der geologischen Fachausdrücke für Geologen, Paläontologen, Mineralogen, Bergingenieure, Geographen, Bodenkundler, Studierende und alle Freunde der Geologie. 2. verb. u. erweit. Aufl. Stuttgart, Enke, 1943. 154p. il. **N256**

Meunier, Stanislas. Dictionnaire de géologie. Paris, Dunod, 1926. 716p. il. **N257**

Brief articles. No bibliography.

Rice, Clara Mabel. Dictionary of geological terms (exclusive of stratigraphic formations and paleontologic genera and species) [Ann Arbor, Mich., Lithoprinted by Edwards Bros., Inc.] 1945. 464p. $6. **N258**

Reprint of the 1940 edition with addenda, p.463-64.

Aims to include the definitions of terms used in general geology, structural geology, economic geology, physiography, glacial geology, petrology, mineralogy, evolution, invertebrate and vertebrate paleontology, and stratigraphy.

Wilmarth, Mary Grace. Lexicon of geologic names of the United States (including Alaska). (Also includes the names and ages, but not the definitions, of the named geologic units of Canada, Mexico, the West Indies, Central America and Hawaii) Wash., Govt. Prt. Off., 1938. 2v. (U.S. Geological Survey. Bull. 896) $2.50. **N259**

Name is followed by a definition usually giving lithology, thickness, age, underlying and overlying formations and type locality, with bibliographical references.

FOREIGN TERMS

Davies, George MacDonald. French-English vocabulary in geology and physical geography. Lond., Murby; N.Y., Van Nostrand [1932]. 140p. **N260**

Geologisch-mijnbouwkundig genootschap voor Nederland en koloniën. Geologische Nomenclator; Geologische Nomenklatur; Geological nomenclator; Nomenclateur géologique, onder redactie van . . . L. Rutten. s'Gravenhage, G. Naeff, 1929. 338p. **N261**

Dutch, German, English and French in parallel columns with indexes in each language.

Huebner, Walther. Geology and allied sciences, a thesaurus and a coordination of English and German specific and general terms. pt. 1, German-English. N.Y., Veritas Pr., 1939. 405p. $7.50. **N262**

Includes some 25,000 general and specific terms used not only in geology but in the various allied sciences, e.g., biology, chemistry, geography, paleontology, physics, seismology, etc.

Jones, William R. and **Cissarz, Arnold.** Englisch-deutsche geologisch-mineralogische Terminologie; eine Einführung in die im deutschen und englischen in Geologie, Mineralogie, Gesteinskunde und Lagerstättenkunde gebräuchlichen Ausdrücke. Lond., Murby, 1931. 250p. 12s. 6d. **N263**

Windhausen, Heriberto. Diccionario y nomenclatura geológica en castellano, alemán, inglés. La Plata, 1945. 200p. il. (Publicaciones didácticas y de divulgación científica del Museo de La Plata, no.3) **N264**

In columns, arranged alphabetically by Spanish form with explanations of meaning in Spanish and German. German and English indexes.

Directories

Howell, Jesse V. and **Levorsen, A. I.** Directory of geological material in North America. (In Amer. Assoc. of Petroleum Geologists, Bulletin 30:1321-1432, Aug. 1946) **N265**

Includes information on maps, wells, aerial photography, geological publications, microfilming and other specialized services of interest to geologists with a record of the firms, libraries, museums, book dealers, etc., from which the material may be obtained. In two parts, a general section applying to the whole country or to large areas, and a local section arranged by state or province.

Tables

Handbook of physical constants, ed. by Francis Birch [and others]. N.Y., Soc., 1942. 325p. tables. (Geol. Soc. of Amer. Special papers. no.36) $1.40 **N266**

A collection of tables of interest primarily to geologists. Introductory notes and bibliographies.

History

Adams, Frank Dawson. Birth and development of the geological sciences. Balt., Williams, 1938. 506p. il. **N267**

Merrill, George Perkins. Contributions to a history of American state geological and natural history surveys. Wash., Govt. Prt. Off., 1920. 549p. il. (U.S. National Museum. Bull. 109) **N268**

—— First 100 years of American geology. New Haven, Conn., Yale Univ. Pr.; Lond., Milford, 1924. 773p. il. **N268a**

A survey history including biographies of geologists but no bibliographical references. A revised version of his *Contributions to the history of American geology* (1904).

National Research Council. Committee on State Geological Surveys. Summary information on the state geological surveys and the United States geological survey. . . . Wash., Council, 1932. 136p. (Bull. of the Council, no.88, Nov. 1932) $1. **N269**

For each survey gives date of founding, location, scope of activities, organization, appropriations, publications, principal accomplishments since 1911, present main lines of work, previous survey organizations.

Seismology

Montessus de Ballore, Fernand de. Bibliografía general de temblores y terremotos. Publicada por la Sociedad Chilena de Historia y Geografía. Chile, Imp. Universitaria, 1915-19. 7 pts. (1515p.) **N270**

Contents: 1. pt., Teorías sismológicas. Efectos geológicos de los terremotos. Catálogos sísmicos mundiales; 2. pt., Europa septentrional y central; 3. pt., Países circunmediterráneos; 4. pt., Asia, África, y Oceanía; 5. pt., América, Tierras antárticas y océanos; 6. pt., Fenómenos accesorios. El movimiento sísmico . . . Literatura sísmica. Historia de la sismología. Misceláneas; 7. pt., Prólogo. Suplemento e Índices. (Indexes not pub?)

Also published in *Revista Chilena de historia y geografía,* 1915-1919.

U. S. Coast and Geodetic Survey. Earthquake history of the United States. Wash., Govt. Prt. Off., 1947- . v.1- . (Its Serial no.609. Rev. 1947 ed.) **N271**

Contents: v.1, Continental United States (exclusive of California and western Nevada) and Alaska, by N. H. Heck.

—— United States earthquakes, 1928- . Wash., Govt. Prt. Off., 1930- . Annual. (1947, pub. 1950. 35c.) **N272**

An annual report of earthquakes felt in the United States.

Meteorology
Bibliography

International catalogue of scientific literature: F, Meteorology, 1st-14th annual issues. Lond., Harrison, 1902-19. v.1-14. **N273**

For full description *see* N6.

Royal Meteorological Society, London. Bibliography of meteorological literature, prepared . . with the collaboration of the Meteorological Office, v.1- . Lond., Royal Meteorological Society [1922-]. v.1- . (v.6, no.5, Jan.-June 1948 pub. 1949. 5s.) **N274**

In continuation of the *Bibliography of meteorological literature received in the Library of the Society or in the Library of the Meteorological Office* published in the Society's *Quarterly journal* from January 1917 to October 1920.

A semiannual bibliography except that the first number covers the period October 1920–June 1921.

Up to 1935, arrangement was a modification of that used in the *International catalogue of scientific literature* (N6); since 1936 arrangement follows the Universal Decimal Classification.

J. S. Signal Office. Bibliography of meteorology. . . Wash., Signal Off., 1889–91. 4v. **N275**

Subtitle: A classed catalogue of the printed literature of meteorology from the origin of printing to the close of 1881; with a supplement to the close of 1887, and an author index. Prepared under the direction of Brigadier General A. W. Greely . . . ed. by Oliver L. Fassig.

Only title page and introduction are printed; the body of the work is lithographed.

v.1, Temperature; v.2, Moisture; v.3, Winds; v.4, storms.

Volumes 3-4 include literature to 1889.

Includes some 60,000 titles by 13,000 authors.

American Meteorological Society. Meteorological abstracts and bibliography. Malcolm Rigby, ed. v.1, no.1, Jan. 1950- . Bost., Soc., 1950- . Monthly. $3 per yr. **N276**

Includes: "(1) Current abstracts in English on important meteorological literature in every language; (2) bibliographic references to other items of interest to the profession; (3) Cumulative, annotated bibliographies on subjects of immediate and special interest to meteorologists."

Handbooks

Berry, Frederic Aroyce, Bollay, E. and Beers, Norman R. Handbook of meteorology. N.Y., McGraw-Hill, 1945. 1068p. il. $7.50. **N277**

Aims to include practical meteorological information with emphasis on the scientific and engineering aspects. Includes bibliographies.

Shaw, *Sir* William Napier. Manual of meteorology. Camb., Univ. Pr., 1926–31. 4v. **N278**

v.1, Meteorology in history, 1926; v.2, Comparative meteorology, 1928; v.3, Physical processes of weather, 1930; v.4, Meteorological calculus; pressure and wind. Rev. ed. 1931.

Contains much historical, biographical and bibliographical material.

Dictionaries

Thiessen, Alfred Henry. Weather glossary. Wash., Govt. Prt. Off., 1946. 299p. (U.S. Weather Bur. W.B. no.1445) 65c. **N279**

Defines terms as used in relation to meteorology, with, in many cases, references to sources of quotation or to fuller discussions. More comprehensive than *The Meteorological glossary* published by the Meteorological Office of Great Britain (3rd ed., 1939, 251p.), though that included diagrams and charts, and lists of equivalents in English, Danish, Dutch, French, German, Italian, Norwegian, Portuguese, Spanish, Swedish.

U. S. Weather Bureau. Statistics Division. Russian-English dictionary of meteorological and related terms. April 1943 . . . in cooperation with Weather Information Service, Headquarters Army Air Forces. Wash., Govt. Prt. Off., 1943. 65p. 25c. **N280**

Atlases

Bartholomew, J. G. and **Herbertson, A. J.** Atlas of meteorology, a series of over 400 maps, ed. by Alex. Buchan. Under the patronage of the Royal Geographical Society. Westminster, Constable, 1899. 40p. maps. **N281**

(1) Maps and descriptive text; (2) Appendices: Meteorological services and their publications, Bibliography, Glossary of meteorological terms, Meteorological tables.

Grant, Hugh Duncan. Cloud and weather atlas. N.Y., Coward-McCann, 1944. 294p. il. $7.50. **N282**

Author was the former Superintendent of the Meteorological Service of the Royal Navy and fellow of the Royal Meteorological Society.

The atlas includes chapters on cloud formation, classification, air movements, air-mass and frontal analysis, fog and visibility, etc.; excellent photographs showing cloud formations; international meteorological symbols, etc.

Weather records

Clayton, Henry Helm. World weather records, collected from official sources by Dr. Felix Exner and others. Assembled and arranged for publication by H. Helm Clayton. Pub. under grant from John A. Roebling. Wash., Smithsonian Inst., 1927. 1199p. (Smithsonian misc. coll. v.79) 1st repr. 1944. $3. **N283**

—— —— Errata. Wash., Smithsonian Inst., 1929. 28p.

Covers records to about 1920.

—— World weather records . . . 1921–1930, 1931–1940. Wash., Smithsonian Inst., 1934–47. 2v. (Smithsonian misc. coll., v.90, v.105)

Continued from volume 79.

U. S. Weather Bureau. Climatological data for the United States by sections, v.1, Jan. 1914- . Wash., Weather Bureau, 1914- . il. Monthly (with annual summaries). $6 per year; foreign $8. **N284**

Contains weather statistics from 42 separate sections in continental United States, each section, as a rule, corresponding to a state. Climatological data are also issued monthly, with an annual summary, for Hawaii, Alaska, West Indies and the Caribbean. Printed in the various section centers and assembled and bound in Washington. Subscriptions may be placed for the separate sections with the Government Printing Office at the rate of 25c a year for each section (5c a copy).

—— Daily synoptic series. Historical weather maps, northern hemisphere, sea level. Jan. 1899–June 1939. Wash. [1946?] 486v. Maps. Monthly. 50c per month. **N285**

Maps prepared cooperatively by the Army Air Forces and the Weather Bureau with the assistance of university meteorological staffs. This valuable series consists of synoptic maps showing the day-by-day weather of the northern hemisphere from Jan. 1, 1899–June 1, 1939, compiled from such sources as the national meteorological services or observatories, the meteorological offices of various governments, etc.

Distribution is restricted to an approved list of official agencies.

—— Daily weather map, forecasts and general weather information [of United States published at Wash., D.C. showing weather conditions for U.S. and forecasts belonging to Washington forecast district]. Daily, including Sundays and holidays. 30c per month. $3.60 per yr.; foreign $9.10. **N286**

Prepared from observations taken daily at hundreds of stations throughout North America. "A complete explanation of these maps (including all symbols and tables) is printed frequently on the reverse side. Periodically during each month, climatological charts and graphs appear in place of the Explanation; and occasionally illustrated articles of special meteorological interest are published."

An interesting and informative service. The maps are excellent for daily display on bulletin boards.

—— Monthly weather review. v.1- , July 1872- . Wash., Govt. Prt. Off., 1872- . v.1- . il. $2 per yr.; foreign $2.75. **N287**

Presents meteorological and climatological data for the United States and adjacent regions, and brief articles on special subjects.

Volumes 1-19 published by the Signal Service of the War Department.

—— United States meteorological yearbook, 1935- . Wash., Govt. Prt. Off., 1937- . v.1- . maps. **N288**

Before 1935 the annual summaries of weather conditions in the United States were published as the statistical sections of the *Annual report* of the Chief of the Weather Bureau.

Petrology

Holmes, Arthur. Nomenclature of petrology, with references to selected literature. Lond., Murby [1928]. 284p. **N289**

First edition, 1920; the 1928 edition incorporates a few corrections and modifications.

Johannsen, Albert. A descriptive petrography of the igneous rocks. Chic., Univ. of Chic. Pr.,

1931–38. 4v. il. (v.1, 2d ed. 1939) $4.50 per v **N290**

Contents: v.1, Introduction, textures, classifications and glossary; v.2, The Quartz-bearing rocks; v.3, The Intermediate rocks; v.4, pt.1, The Feldspathoid rocks, pt.2 The peridotites and perknites. Index of authors, of localities, of rock names.

A standard, basic work, with bibliographical footnotes Volume 1 includes appendixes: Miscellaneous definitions Definitions of textural and structural terms, Definition of rocks.

Handbooks

See also Natural History, p.294.

Fenton, Carroll Lane and **Fenton, Mildred Adams.** Rock book. N.Y., Doubleday, 1940 357p. il. **N29**

Paleontology

Camp, Charles Lewis [and others]. Bibliography of fossil vertebrates. 1928–1933, 1934–1938, 1939-1943. N.Y., Geological Soc. of Amer., 1940–49 3v. (Special papers, nos. 27, 42, Memoir 37 $3.50; $4.75; $4.50. **N29:**

1928–1933. 503p.; 1934–1938. 663p.; 1939–1943 371p.

Comprehensive author bibliographies with subject and systematic indexes. Published in continuation of Hay Oliver Perry, *Bibliography and catalogue of the foss vertebrata of North America.* ([v.1] published as Bul no.179 of the U.S. Geological Survey, 1902; [v.2] pub lished by the Carnegie Institution of Washington, Pub no.390, v.1-2, 1929–30.

Ellis, Brooks Fleming and **Messina, Angelina R** Catalogue of foraminifera…. Special publication N.Y., Amer. Museum of Natural History, 1940-46. 30v. $275 per set. **N29:**

Conducted under the auspices of the Work Project Administration.

Volume 30, Index to taxonomic changes and Bibliography.

—— —— Partial supplement. [v.1-5] [N.Y., 1940 5v.

—— —— Supplement for 1943–45. N.Y., Amer Museum of Natural History, 1944–46. 3v. il.

International catalogue of scientific literature K, Paleontology. Lond., 1902–19. 14v. **N29**

For full description *see* N6.

McGuire, I. General bibliographies for paleon tology. (In Geol. Soc. of Amer. Bull. 41:188-93 1930) **N294**

Shimer, Hervey Woodburn and **Shrock, Rober R.** Index fossils of North America. A publication of the Technology Pr., Massachusetts Institute of Technology. N.Y., Wiley, 1944. 837p. il. **N295**

"Based on the complete revision and reillustration of Grabau and Shimer's *North American index fossils.*"

Mineralogy
Abstracts and indexes

International catalogue of scientific literature: G, Mineralogy. 1st-14th annual issues, 1901-14. Lond., 1902-17. 14v. **N296**

For full description *see* N6.

Mineralogical abstracts, issued by the Mineralogical Society, v.1- , 1920- . Lond., Simpkin, Marshall, 1922- . v.1- . **N297**

A classified list of signed abstracts of current literature, books, pamphlets, reports, periodical articles, etc. Twelve quarterly numbers constitute a volume, and each volume has a topographical index and a detailed author and subject index which cover both the *Abstracts* and the *Magazine.*

Issued as quarterly supplements to the *Mineralogical magazine* (subscription, 40s. per year).

Has attempted to supplement the record in the *International catalogue of scientific literature* (N6) by summarizing the mineralogical literature from 1915.

Reuss, Jeremias David. Repertorium commenationum a societatibus litterariis editarum . . . v.2, Botanica et mineralogia. Gottingae, Dieterich, 1802. 604p. **N298**

A valuable index to the publications of learned societies up to 1800. Classed arrangement with author index. For description of complete set *see* N3.

Strukturbericht 1913/1928- . Leipzig, Akademische Verlagsgesellschaft, 1931- . v.1- . (Zeitschrift für Kristallographie, Kristallgeometrie, Kristallphysik, Kristallchemie . . . Ergänzungsband, 1-) **N299**

Bd.1, 1913–28; Bd.2, 1928–32; Bd.3, 1933–35; Bd.4- . Annual. An important abstract journal for crystallography.

Handbooks and statistics

Dana, James Dwight and **Dana, Edward S.** The system of mineralogy. 7th ed. entirely rewritten and greatly enl. by Charles Palache, Harry Berman and Clifford Froudel. N.Y., Wiley, 1944- . v.1- . **N300**

The latest edition of a standard work. J. D. Dana's *Manual of mineralogy* revised by C. S. Hurlbut (15th ed. N.Y., Wiley, 1941. 480p. il.) is also a basic work.

Mineral industry, its statistics, technology, and trade, 1892–1941. N.Y., McGraw-Hill, 1893–1942. v.1-50. Annual. il. **N301**

Publisher varies. Ceased publication.

U. S. Bureau of Mines. Minerals yearbook, 1932/33- . Wash., Govt. Prt. Off., 1933- . **N302**

Supersedes its *Mineral resources of the United States,* 1882–1931, as well as various interim summaries.

The volumes dated 1932/33 through 1940 contain reviews of 1932 through 1939. In 1941 designation was changed to use the date of period covered. Therefore there are two volumes bearing the date 1940: (1) 1940 (review of 1939) and (2) the actual review of 1940.

——— ——Statistical appendix. 1932/33–1935. Wash., Govt. Prt. Off., 1934–36. 3v. il.

No more published. Later figures included in *Yearbook.*

U. S. Bureau of Mines and **U. S. Geological Survey.** Mineral resources of the United States . . . foreword by J. A. Krug. Wash., Public Affairs Pr., 1948. 212p. il. $5. **N303**

A report of the results of an appraisal begun in 1944 of the United States mineral position. Discusses the production and reserves of the various mineral resources of the country.

Dictionaries

Chambers's Mineralogical dictionary, with 40 plates of coloured illustrations. Lond., Chambers; Brooklyn, N.Y., Chemical Pub. Co., 1948. 47p. il. $4.75. **N304**

Concise definitions of mineralogical terms with brief descriptions of the more important minerals.

Chester, Albert Huntington. Dictionary of the names of minerals, including their history and etymology. 1st ed. N.Y., Wiley; Lond., Chapman and Hall, 1896. 320p. **N305**

Under each name is given the name of its author, a reference to its first publication, original spelling, derivation, reason for choosing the name and a brief description.

ETHNOLOGY
Bibliography

American anthropologist, 1888- . Menasha, Wis., George Banta. Quarterly. $6 per yr. **N306**

Bibliography of recent articles in each issue.

——General index. American anthropologist, Current anthropological literature and Memoirs of the American Anthropological Association. 1888–1928, 1929–1938. Menasha, Wis., 1930–40. 2v.

International catalogue of scientific literature: P, Anthropology. 1st-14th annual issues, 1903–19. Lond., 1903–20. 14v. **N307**

For full description *see* N6.

Kennedy, Raymond. Bibliography of Indonesian people and cultures. New Haven, Conn., Yale

Univ. Pr., 1945. 212p. (Yale anthropological studies, v.4) $2.50.   **N308**

Krogman, Wilton Marion. A bibliography of human morphology, 1914–1939. Chic., Univ. of Chic. Pr., 1941. 385p. $3.   **N309**

Classed index to materials in over 900 periodicals under such headings as Osteology, Races of man, Pre-history of man, Craniology, Human heredity, Nervous system, etc. Author index.

Martin, Rudolf. Lehrbuch der Anthropologie in systematischer Darstellung mit besonderer Berücksichtigung der anthropologischen Methoden für Studierende, Ärzte und Forschungsreisende. 2. verm. Aufl. Jena, Fischer, 1928. 3v. il. **N310**

Bd.3, Bibliographie, Literaturverzeichnis, Sachregister, Autorenregister.

A comprehensive bibliography of books and periodical articles of all periods in many languages.

Miller, Mamie Ruth Tanquist. ... An author, title, and subject check list of Smithsonian Institution publications relating to anthropology. Pub. in coöperation with the School of American Research. ... Albuquerque, N.M., Univ. of New Mexico Pr., 1946. 218p. $1.50. (Univ. of New Mexico. Bull. Bibliographical ser., v.1, no.2; whole no.405)   **N311**

Murdock, George Peter. Ethnographic bibliography of North America. New Haven, Conn., Yale Univ. Pr.; Lond., Milford, 1941. 168p. (Yale anthropological studies, v.1) $2.   **N312**

Ripley, William Zebina. Selected bibliography of the anthropology and ethnology of Europe. Bost., Public Library, 1899. 160p.   **N313**

Also published as supplement to his *Races of Europe* (N.Y., Appleton, 1899).

Rouse, Irving and **Goggin, John M.** An anthropological bibliography of the eastern seaboard, comp. under the auspices of the Federation. New Haven, Conn., pub. by the Federation at the Yale Peabody Museum, 1947. 174p. (Eastern States Archeological Federation. Research pub. no.1) $2.50.   **N314**

U. S. Bureau of American Ethnology. List of publications of the Bureau of American Ethnology, with index to authors and titles, rev. to June 30, 1944. Wash., Govt. Prt. Off., 1944. 68p.   **N315**

—— General index: Annual reports of the Bureau, v.1-48 (1879–1931) ... comp. by Biren Bonnerjea. Wash., Govt. Prt. Off., 1933. p.25-1220. (In its 48th Annual report, 1930/31) $2.

pt.1, Subject index; pt.2, List of annual reports ... with an index to authors and titles.

Wieschhoff, Heinrich Albert. Anthropological bibliography of Negro Africa. New Haven, Conn., American Oriental Soc., 1948. 461p. $7. (American oriental ser. v.23)   **N316**

Arranged by names of tribes and geographical areas in alphabetical order.

Dictionaries and handbooks

Coon, Carleton Stevens. The races of Europe. N.Y., Macmillan, 1939. 739p. il. $8.50. (Repr. 1948)   **N317**

A well-documented text. Includes: Glossary p.666-83; Bibliography: Serials, p.684-91; Books, p.692-700.

Hodge, Frederick Webb. Handbook of American Indians north of Mexico. Wash., Govt. Prt. Off., 1907–10. [Reissued 1912] 2v. il. (U.S. Bureau of Amer. Ethnology. Bull. 30) $3.   **N318**

"Contains a descriptive list of the stocks, confederacies, tribes, tribal divisions and settlements north of Mexico, accompanied with the various names by which these have been known, together with biographies of Indians of note, sketches of their history, archeology, manners, arts, customs and institutions, and the aboriginal words incorporated in the English language. ... Accompanying each synonym (the earliest known date always being given) a reference to the authority is noted, and these references form practically a bibliography of the tribe for those who wish to pursue the subject further."—*Pref.*

—— Handbook of Indians of Canada. Published as an appendix to the Tenth report of the Geographic Board of Canada. Ottawa, Parmelee, 1913. 632p. maps.   **N319**

A reprint, with some additional material, of the articles in his *Handbook of American Indians north of Mexico* (N318), which relate to Canada.

Peoples of all nations, their life today and the story of their past, by our foremost writers of travel, anthropology and history ... with upwards of 5000 photographs, numerous color plates and 150 maps. Ed. by J. A. Hammerton. Lond., Fleetway House, 1922–24. 7v. il.   **N320**

Paged continuously. Articles on countries, arranged alphabetically, p.1-5325; Dictionary of races, by N. W. Thomas, p.5327-72; Index, p.5389-5436.

Steward, Julian Haynes. Handbook of South American Indians. ... Prepared in cooperation with the United States Department of State as a project of the Interdepartmental Committee on Cultural and Scientific Cooperation. Wash., Govt. Prt. Off., 1946–50. v.1-6. il. ([U.S.] Bur. of Amer. Ethnology. Bull. 143) v.1, $2.75; v.2, $4.25; v.3, $4.50; v.4, $3.50; v.5, $3; v.6, $5. (In progress)   **N321**

At head of title: Smithsonian Institution. Bureau of American Ethnology. ...

To be in six volumes with separate index: v.1, The Marginal tribes; v.2, The Andean civilizations; v.3, The trop-cal forest tribes; v.4, The circum-Caribbean tribes; v.5, The comparative ethnology of South American Indians; v.6, Physical anthropology, linguistics, and cultural geography of South American Indians.

Anthropological descriptions by American scientists of all phases of life of the tribes considered, with especial attention to the time of a tribe's first contact with Europeans. Well illustrated. Good ethnographical maps. Extensive bibliographies.

U. S. Immigration Commission, 1907. Dictionary of races or peoples. Wash., Govt. Prt. Off., 1911. 150p. maps. (Its Reports, v.5) **N322**

"While this dictionary treats of more than 600 subjects covering all the important and many of the obscure branches of the human family, it is intended primarily as a discussion of the various races and the peoples indigenous to the countries furnishing the present immigration movement to the United States or which may become sources of future immigration."—*Pref.*

Popular rather than scientific; has short articles, general bibliography, p.8-12, but no bibliographies in the text; maps, good cross references.

History

Penniman, Thomas Kenneth. A hundred years of anthropology. Lond., Duckworth, 1935. 400p. **N323**

"A chronological list of men and events in the history of anthropology," p.355-60.
"Some principal congresses, anthropological museums, societies, and periodicals in various countries of the world," p.361-69.
Bibliography, p.371-92.

Biography

National Research Council. Division of Anthropology and Psychology. International directory of anthropologists. [2d ed.] Wash., 1940. 2v. Paged continuously. $2. **N324**

Section 1, Western hemisphere; Section 2, Eastern hemisphere. Information is usually as of 1939.
1st ed. 1938.
A biographical directory which usually includes name, address, date of birth, education, positions, areas of interest and field trips.

BIOLOGY
General works
Bibliography

Bourliére, F. Éléments d'un guide bibliographique du naturaliste. Mâcon, Protat, 1940. 302p. **N325**

—— —— Suppléments, 1-2. Paris, Lechevalier, 1941. p.303-368.

A comprehensive classified guide (no index) to the literature of the natural sciences. Unannotated. General

sections are followed by regional sections covering all parts of the world.

International catalogue of scientific literature: L, General biology. 1st-14th annual issues, 1901–14. Lond., 1901–19. 14v. **N326**
For full description *see* N6.

British Museum. Dept. of Printed Books. A catalogue of the works of Linnaeus (and publications more immediately relating thereto) preserved in the libraries of the British Museum (Bloomsbury) and the British Museum (Natural History) (South Kensington). 2d ed. Lond., British Museum, 1933. 246p., 68p. il. **N327**

—— An index to the authors (other than Linnaeus) mentioned in the Catalogue. . . . Lond., British Museum, 1936. 59p.

Meisel, Max. Bibliography of American natural history; the pioneer century, 1769–1865. . . . Brooklyn, N.Y., Premier Pub. Co., 1924–29. 3v. $20. **N328**

Subtitle: The role played by the scientific societies; scientific journals; natural history museums and botanic gardens; state geological and natural history surveys; federal exploring expeditions in the rise and progress of American botany, geology, mineralogy, paleontology and zoology.
v.1, Annotated bibliography of the publications relating to the history, biography and bibliography of American natural history and its institutions during colonial times and the pioneer century, which have been published up to 1924; with a classified subject and geographical index and a bibliography of biographies; v.2, Institutions which have contributed to the rise and progress of American natural history which were founded or organized between 1769 and 1844; v.3, The institutions founded or organized between 1845 and 1865. Bibliography of books, articles, etc., . . . not published in the proceedings and transactions of scientific societies. . . . Chronological tables. Index of authors and institutions. Addenda to volume 1.

Abstracts

L'année biologique, comptes rendus des travaux de biologie générale, v.1, 1895- . Paris, Masson, 1897- . **N329**
Abstracts, bibliographical reviews and critical reports.

Biological abstracts; a comprehensive abstracting and indexing journal of the world's literature in theoretical and applied biology, exclusive of clinical medicine.... Published (beginning with the literature of 1926) under the auspices of the Union of American Biological Societies. Phila., Univ. of Pennsylvania, 1926- . v.1- . $30 per annual v. **N330**

"In its departments dealing with theoretical and applied bacteriology and botany the journal represents a continuation of *Abstracts of bacteriology* and *Botanical abstracts.*"

Ten issues per year plus index.

A very full abstract bibliography with subject, systematic, geographical, geological and author indexes.

In 1939 the form was changed and it is now issued in sections. Subscriptions may be placed to the complete edition or to any of the individual sections as follows:

Sec. A, Abstracts of general biology, 1939- , $4.50.

Sec. B, Abstracts of basic medical sciences (title varies), 1939- , $8.50.

Sec. C, Abstracts of microbiology, immunology and parasitology, 1939- , $5.50.

Sec. D, Abstracts of plant sciences, 1939- , $6.50.

Sec. E, Abstracts of animal sciences, 1939- , $5.50.

Sec. F, Abstracts of animal production and veterinary science, 1942- , $5.50.

Sec. G, Abstracts of food and nutrition research, 1943- , $6.50.

Sec. H, Abstracts of human biology, 1946- , $6.50.

Sec. J, Abstracts of cereals and cereal products, 1947- , $6.

—— Journals abstracted in Biological abstracts. (Repr. from v.10, no.5, May 1945) xviiip.

A comprehensive list of biological periodicals and of other journals from which biological articles are abstracted.

Berichte über die wissenschaftliche Biologie. Berlin, Springer, 1926- . Bd.1- . Semimonthly. (Berichte über die gesamte Biologie, Abt. A) **N331**

Includes abstracts and also lengthy reviews of books and periodical articles. Author and subject indexes in each volume.

Jahresbericht wissenschaftliche Biologie; bibliographisches Jahresregister der Berichte über die wissenschaftliche Biologie . . . Bd.1- , 1926- . Berlin, Julius Springer, 1928- . v.1- . **N332**

A classified annual bibliography containing the authors and titles of the reviews and abstracts appearing in the *Berichte über die wissenschaftliche Biologie* (N331) with a key number to show location of abstract.

Dictionaries

Artschwager, Ernst Friedrich. Dictionary of biological equivalents, German-English. Balt., Williams and Wilkins, 1930. 239p. 20s. **N333**

Henderson, Isabella Ferguson and **Henderson, W. D.** Dictionary of scientific terms; pronunciation, derivation and definition of terms in biology, botany, zoology, anatomy, cytology, embryology, physiology. 4th ed., rev. by J. H. Kenneth. N.Y., Van Nostrand, 1949. 480p. $10. **N334**

For the biological sciences, "omits specific, generic, ordinal and other systematic names of plants and animals."

Jaeger, Edmund Carroll. A source-book of biological names and terms. . . . Illustrations by

Merle Gish and the author. 2d ed. Springfield, Ill., C. C. Thomas, 1950. 287p. il. $4.50. **N335**

1st ed. 1944.

"Lists fully 12,000 elements from which scientific biological names and terms are made. With them are given their Greek, Latin, or other origins and their concise meanings, together with numerous examples of their use in scientific nomenclature."—*Pref.*

Woods, Robert S. The naturalist's lexicon, a list of classical Greek and Latin words used, or suitable for use, in biological nomenclature, with abridged English-classical supplement. Pasadena, Calif., Abbey Garden Pr., 1944. 282p. $2.75. **N336**

Includes over 15,000 words designed to facilitate the use by naturalists of Latin and Greek terms in naming species. An excellent guide.

—— —— Addenda . . . Comprehensive classified English-classical key to descriptive terms. Additions and emendations to the classical-English lexicon. Pasadena, Calif., Abbey Garden Pr., 1947. 47p. 25c.

Directories

Directory of biological laboratories, Dec. 1946. 3d ed. Chic., Burns Comp. and Research Org., 1947. 117p. $3. **N337**

Includes buyers guide.
Earlier editions in 1941 and 1943.

Everard, L. C. Zoological parks, aquariums and botanical gardens. Wash., Amer. Assoc. of Museums, 1932. 72p. (Pub. of the Amer. Assoc. of Museums, n.s. no.12) $1. **N338**

Supplementary to the *Handbook of American museums* (N55) and gives same type of information.

Hirsch, Gottwalt Christian. Index biologorum, investigatores, laboratoria, periodica. 1. ed. Berlin, Springer, 1928. 545p. **N339**

International in scope.

(1) List of biologists, giving brief biographical information and field of study of each; (2) Laboratories; (3) Periodicals.

Jack, Homer Alexander. Biological field stations of the world. Waltham, Mass., Chronica Botanica Co., 1945. 73p. il. (Chronica botanica, v.9, no.1) $2.50. **N340**

A study of the biological field stations of the world under such headings as purpose, history, location, administration, equipment, living facilities, instruction offered, and research. Followed by a directory of biological stations arranged by country.

Lehmann, Ernst and **Martin, Otto.** Deutsches Biologen-Handbuch; eine Übersicht über die deutschen Biologen, die biologischen Institute nd Organisationen. 2. Aufl. München-Berlin, ehmann, 1938. 261p. **N341**

A directory of German biological institutes and organi-tions with personal name index.

aw, **H. K. Airy.** Directory of natural history cieties. Lond., Amateur Entomologists' Soc.,)48. 155p. (Pamphlet no.7) 7s. 6d. **N342**

erborn, **Charles Davies.** Where is the —— llection? An account of the various natural story collections which have come under the tice of the compiler . . . between 1880 and 39. Camb., Univ. Pr., 1940. 149p. 3s. 6d.; 90c. **N343**

Statistical handbooks

sher, **Ronald Aylmer.** Statistical methods for search workers. 10th ed. rev. and enl. Edin-rgh, Oliver and Boyd, 1946. 354p. il. (Bio-gical monographs and manuals, no.9) $5.50. **N344**

—— and **Yates, Frank.** Statistical tables for bio-gical, agricultural and medical research. 2d ed. 7. and enl. Lond., Oliver and Boyd, 1943. 98p. bles. $5. **N345**

penheimer, **Karl** and **Pincussen, L.** Tabulae ologicae, ed. W. Junk; unter Mitwirkung von Fachgelehrten. Berlin, W. Junk, 1925- . Bd. . **N346**

—— —— General-Register zu Bd.1-10, 1925– 35. Den Haag, W. Junk, 1935. 584p.

edecor, **George W.** Statistical methods applied experiments in agriculture and botany. 4th ed. es, Iowa, Iowa State College Pr., 1946. 485p. les. $5. **N347**

BOTANY
General works
Bibliography

, **Jens Christian.** Bibliographies of botany; a tribution toward a bibliotheca bibliographica. Progressus rei botanica, v.3, pt.2, p.331-456. a, Fischer, 1909) **N348**

valuable annotated bibliography of bibliographies ding detailed records of periodicals, general, local subject bibliographies, library catalogs, auction and catalogs, etc.

EARLY

ss, **Jeremias David.** Repertorium commenta-um a societatibus litterariis editarum . . . t.2,

Botanica et mineralogia; t.6, Oeconomia. Got-tingae, Dieterich, 1802–06. 604p.; 476p. **N349**

A valuable index to the publications of learned socie-ties up to 1800. Classed arrangement with author index. For description of complete set *see* N3.

Pritzel, Georg August. Thesaurus literaturae botanicae omnium gentium, inde a rerum botani-carum initiis ad nostra usque tempora, quindecim millia operum recensens. Ed. novam reformatam. Lipsiae, Brockhaus, 1872–[77]. 576p. (Repr. Milan, Görlizh, 1950. L7500) **N350**

Arranged alphabetically with a systematic index. In-cludes only separately published books. Comprehensive and accurate.

Jackson, Benjamin Daydon. Guide to the litera-ture of botany. Being a classified selection of botanical works, including nearly 6000 titles not given in Pritzel's "Thesaurus." Lond., pub. for the Index Society, by Longmans, 1881. 626p. (Index Society. Pub. VIII) **N351**

A short-title catalog, selective not exhaustive, listing some 9000 works.

The early literature of botany is well covered by the bibliographies listed above. For other early bibliog-raphies consult Bay (N348).

MODERN

Blake, Sidney Fay. Geographical guide to floras of the world, an annotated list with special refer-ence to useful plants and common plant names. pt.1. . . . Wash., Govt. Prt. Off., 1942. 336p. (U.S. Dept. of Agriculture. Misc. pub., no.401) 75c. **N352**

Joint contribution from U.S. Bureau of Plant Industry and U.S. Dept. of Agriculture Library.

pt.1, Africa, Australia, North America, South America, and Islands of the Atlantic, Pacific and Indian Oceans.

An annotated list of floras and floristic works, including those in periodical literature, relating to vascular plants, including bibliographies and publications dealing with useful and medicinal plants, vernacular names and botan-ical bibliography. Includes about 2597 primary titles and 428 subsidiary titles (supplements, reviews, etc.). Ar-ranged alphabetically by continent and then by country. Author index includes birth and death dates.

Christensen, Carl Frederik Albert. Den danske botaniske Litteratur. Bibliographia botanica danica, 1880–1911, 1912–1939. København, Munksgaard, 1913–40. 2v. il. **N353**

Brief biographical sketches followed by lists of works, both books and periodical articles.

Harvard Univ. Arnold Arboretum. Library. Cat-alogue . . . by Ethelyn Maria Tucker. . . . Camb., Mass., Cosmos Pr., 1914–33. 3v. **N354**

v.1, Serial publications—Authors and titles; v.2, Sub-ject catalogue with supplement to v.1; v.3, Serial publi-cations—Authors and titles supplement, 1917–1933.

A very rich collection specializing in "dendrology, general descriptive botany, the cultivation of trees, the works of travellers in which appear descriptions of trees and of general features of vegetation." Is now adding pathology, cytology and genetics.

International catalogue of scientific literature: M, Botany. 1st-14th annual issues, 1901–14. Lond., Harrison, 1902–19. 14v. **N355**

For full description *see* N6.

Merrill, Elmer Drew and **Walker, Egbert Hamilton.** A bibliography of eastern Asiatic botany. . . . Sponsored by the Smithsonian Institution, Arnold Arboretum of Harvard University, New York Botanical Garden, Harvard-Yenching Institute. Jamaica Plain, Mass., Arnold Arboretum of Harvard Univ., 1938. 719p. $12.50. **N356**

A comprehensive annotated bibliography of books and material appearing in periodicals. Arranged by authors, with three subject indexes; general, geographical and systematic. Covers material through 1936.

Abstract journals and indexes

Botanical abstracts; a monthly serial furnishing abstracts and citations of publications in the international field of botany in its broadest sense. v.1-15; Sept. 1918—Nov. 1926. Balt., Williams and Wilkins, 1918–26. 15v. and index to v.1-10, Sept. 1918—Feb. 1922. 418p. **N357**

Classified abstracts, with detailed author and subject indexes in each volume, volumes 1-11, and a cumulated author and subject index to the first 10 volumes. Volumes 12-15 have no indexes. Last volumes give nearly 10,000 abstracts a year.

After Nov. 1926, merged in *Biological abstracts* (N330).

Botanisches Centralblatt; referierendes Organ für das Gesamtgebiet der Botanik. Im Auftrage der Deutschen Botanischen Gesellschaft . . . 1.-40. Jahrg. (Bd.1-142) 1880–1919; Bd.143- . (Neue Folge, Bd.1-) 1922- . Cassell, T. Fischer, etc., 1880–1905; Jena, G. Fischer, 1906- . il. **N358**

Weekly, 1880–1919; publication suspended, 1920–21; irregular, 1922- . Title varies.

Includes the section "Neue Litteratur," forming a separate volume from 1902 to 1919 (v.91, 94, 97, 100, etc.). Beginning with the new series, each volume is in two parts (Referate and Litteratur), each part having separate title page and paging. Gives signed abstracts of material in various languages.

—— Generalregister zu den Bänden 1 bis 30 [Neue Folge], (Bd.143-172) bearb. von Wilhelm Dörries. . . . Jena, Fischer, 1927–38. 3v.

Just's Botanischer Jahresbericht. Systematisch geordnetes Repertorium der botanischen Literatur aller Länder. 1. Jahrg., 1873- . Berlin and Leipzig, Borntraeger, 1874- . v.1- . **N359**

Review journal especially useful for the early period. Volumes late in appearing. Title varies.

Review of applied mycology. v.1- . Kew, Surrey, Imperial Mycological Institute, 1922- . **N36[**

Publisher varies.
Abstract journal with author and subject indexes in each volume.

Torrey Botanical Club. Index to American botanical literature. . . . (In Torrey Botanical Club Bulletin, v.15- , 1888-) **N36[**

Beginning with volume 21, 1894, the index has also been reprinted on cards for which annual subscription may be placed. Cards are issued monthly.

Aims to list "all current botanical literature written by Americans, published in America, or based upon American material, the word America being used to include the entire Western Hemisphere."

Dictionaries

American Joint Committee on Horticultural Nomenclature. Standardized plant names. [ed. A revised and enlarged listing of approved scientific and common names of plants and plant products in American commerce or use, prepared by Harlan P. Kelsey and William A. Dayton. Harrisburg, Pa., J. Horace McFarland Co., 194[675p. $10.50. **N3[**

"Plant patents" through July 1, 1941, p.455-67.

Britten, James and **Holland, Robert.** Dictionary of English plant-names. Lond., for the English Dialect Society, Trübner, 1886. 618p. **N3[**

Originally issued in three parts, 1878–84, as numbers 22, 26, 45 (forming volume 10) of *Publications* of the English Dialect Society.

Arranged by common name followed by scientific name, with explanation of origin and references to use in literature, frequently with quotations.

Camp, W. H., Rickett, H. W. and **Weatherby, C. A.** International rules of botanical nomenclature. . . . Waltham, Mass., Chronica Botanica, 1948. 120p. $3.50. **N8[**

Originally issued in a special edition as a service to members of the American Society of Plant Taxonomists, 1947 (*Brittonia*, v.6, no. 1, Apr. 9, 1947).

Formulated by the International Botanical Congress of Vienna, 1905, Brussels, 1910, and Cambridge, 19[adopted and revised by the International Botanical Congress of Amsterdam, 1935. Compiled from various sources.

Carpenter, John Richard. An ecological glossary. Norman, Univ. of Oklahoma Pr., 1938. 306p. $4. **N[**

Defines nearly 3000 terms with references to the work in which term is used or discussed.

Index kewensis plantarum phanerogamarum nomina et synonyma omnium generum et specierum a Linnaeo usque ad annum MDCCCLXXXV complectens nomine recepto auctore patria unicuique plantae subjectis. Sumptibus beati Caroli Roberti Darwin ductu et consilio Josephi D. Hooker confecit B. Daydon Jackson. . . . Ox., Clarendon Pr., 1893–95. 2v. $85. **N366**

Added title page in English: Index Kewensis, an enumeration of the genera and species of flowering plants from the time of Linnaeus to the year 1885 inclusive together with their authors' names, the works in which they were first published, their native countries and their synonyms.

—— Supplementum . . . nomina et synonyma omnium generum et specierum ab initio anni MDCCCLXXXVI usque ad finem anni MDCCCCXXX nonnulla etiam antea edita complectens. . . . Ox., Clarendon Pr., 1901–47. v.1–10. (In progress)

(1) 1886–95. 1901–06. $25; (2) 1896–1900. 1904. $10.50; (3) 1901–05. 1908. $10.50; (4) 1906–10. 1913. $10.50; (5) 1911–15. 1921. $10.50; (6) 1916–20. 1926. n.p.; (7) 1921–25. 1929. $21; (8) 1926–30. 1933. $25; (9) 1931–35. 1938. $28; (10) 1936–40. 1947. $30.

Index londinensis to illustrations of flowering plants, ferns and fern allies, being an emended and enlarged edition continued up to the end of the year 1920 of Pritzel's Alphabetical register of representations of flowering plants and ferns comp. from botanical and horticultural publications of the XVIIIth and XIXth centuries; prepared under the auspices of the Royal Horticultural Society of London at the Royal Botanic Gardens, Kew, by O. Stapf. Ox., Clarendon Pr., 1929–31. 6v. $185. **N367**

Added title page: Iconum botanicarum index Londinensis.

—— Supplement for the years 1921–35 . . . Prepared under the auspices of the Royal Horticultural Society of London at the Royal Botanic Gardens, Kew, by W. C. Worsdell under the direction of Arthur W. Hill. Ox., Clarendon Pr., 1941. 2v. $65.

"This supplement to the six volumes of the *Index londinensis* . . . now concludes that work. . . . Although no further supplements are to be issued, it has been arranged that references to new illustrations shall be given in the entries of new names included in future supplements of the *Index kewensis* from 1936 onwards. Such entries will be prefixed by an asterisk."—*Pref.*, v.1.

Includes references to illustrations from periodicals and independent works published during the years 1921–35 inclusive and also some references from books prior to 1921 not included in the main work.

Jackson, **Benjamin Daydon**. Glossary of botanic terms with their derivation and accent. 4th ed. rev. and enl. Phila., Lippincott, 1928. 481p. **N368**

Lemée, **Albert Marie Victor**. Dictionnaire descriptif et synonymique des genres de plantes phanérogames. Brest, Impr. Commerciale et Admin., 1929–43. 8v. in 9. **N369**

Marshall, **William Taylor** and **Woods, Robert S.** Glossary of succulent plant terms; a glossary of botanical terms and pronouncing vocabulary of generic and specific names used in connection with xerophytic plants. [Pasadena, Calif., Abbey Garden Pr.] 1945. 112p. il. $3. **N370**

1st printing 1938.

Marzell, **Heinrich**. Wörterbuch der deutschen Pflanzennamen, mit Unterstützung der Preussischen Akademie der Wissenschaften. . . . Leipzig, Hirzel, 1937–43. v.1– . il. (In progress) RM. 5. per Lfg. **N371**

Appeared in parts. Lfg. 1–9, covering A–C, complete the first volume.

Schneider, **Camillo Carl**. Illustriertes Handwörterbuch der Botanik. 2. völlig umgearb. Aufl. hrsg. von Karl Linsbauer. Leipzig, Engelmann, 1917. 824p. il. **N372**

FOREIGN TERMS

Artschwager, **Ernst Friedrich** and **Smiley, Edwina M.** . . . Dictionary of botanical equivalents. German-English, Dutch-English, Italian-English by Ernst Artschwager. . . . French-English by Edwina M. Smiley. Balt., Williams and Wilkins, 1925. 124p. $3.25. **N373**

Bedevian, **Armenag K.** Illustrated polyglottic dictionary of plant names in Latin, Arabic, Armenian, English, French, German, Italian and Turkish languages; including economic, medicinal, poisonous and ornamental plants and common weeds. . . . Cairo, Argus and Papazian Presses, 1936. 2 pts. in 1v. (644p. and 450p.) 23s. 6d; $9. **N374**

Gerth van Wijk, **H. L.** Dictionary of plant names. Pub. by the Dutch Society of Sciences at Haarlem. The Hague, Nijhoff, 1911–16. 2v. **N375**

Contents: v.1, Latin names, A–Z; v.2, Index of English, French, Dutch, and German names.

A dictionary of names and terms only; arranged alphabetically by the Latin names and giving under each Latin name the equivalent popular and literary names in the English, Dutch, French, and German languages. Aims to include names of all wild and cultivated plants, flowers and fruits, varieties and subvarieties and parts of plants now or formerly used in medicine or industry. The only work of its kind; accurate.

Directories

Wyman, **Donald**. The arboretums and botanical gardens of North America. Waltham, Mass.,

Chronica Botanica Co., 1947. p.395-482. il. (Repr. from Chronica botanica v.10, no.5/6) $1.50. **N376**

Lists active and discontinued arboretums and botanical gardens of United States, Canada and Cuba. Includes a bibliography.

History

Sachs, Julius von. History of botany (1530–1860), authorized tr. by H. E. F. Garnsey, rev. by Isaac Bayley Balfour. Ox., Clarendon Pr., 1890. 568p. **N377**

Original German ed., 1875.
Continued by:

Green, Joseph Reynolds. History of botany 1860–1900. Ox., Clarendon Pr., 1909. 543p. **N378**

Biography

Britten, James and **Boulger, George S.** Biographical index of deceased British and Irish botanists. 2d ed., rev. and completed by A. B. Rendle. Lond., Taylor and Francis, 1931. 342p. **N379**

Brief biographical facts followed by references to further information. Includes names of "all who have in any way contributed to the literature of botany, who have made scientific collections of plants, or have otherwise assisted directly in the progress of botany, exclusive of pure horticulture."—*Pref.*

International address book of botanists; being a directory of individuals and scientific institutions, universities, societies, etc., in all parts of the world interested in the study of botany, prepared in accordance with a resolution passed at the Fifth International Botanical Congress, Cambridge, 1930. Lond., pub. for the Bentham Trustees by Baillière, Tindall and Cox, 1931. 605p. **N380**

Arranged alphabetically by countries with index of persons.
Preface and index of countries in English, French and German.

Naturalists' directory, containing names, addresses and special subjects of study of professional and amateur naturalists of North and South America, etc.; and a list of periodicals dealing with the subjects of natural history, also a list of natural history museums. 1st ed.- . Salem, Mass., Cassino Pr., 1878- . $3. **N381**

Title varies. Published at frequent but irregular intervals.

Handbooks

See also Natural History, p.294.

Ferns

Clute, Willard Nelson. Our ferns; their haunts, habits, and folklore . . . 2d ed. N.Y., Stokes, 1938.

388p. il. $4.50. **N382**

A guide to the ferns east of the Rockies and north of the Gulf states with some references to the varieties of the western and southern states.
Includes glossary. Index to common names. Index to scientific names.

Flora

Bailey, L. H. Manual of cultivated plants. . . . N.Y., Macmillan, 1938. 851p. il. $5. **N383**

Subtitle: A flora for the identification of the most common or significant species of plants grown in the continental United States and Canada for food, ornament, utility, and general interest, both in the open and under glass.
Arranged by scientific name with indexes to scientific and common names. Includes glossary and key to families.

Britton, Nathaniel Lord and **Brown, Addison.** An illustrated flora of the northern United States, Canada and the British possessions, from Newfoundland to the parallel of the southern boundary of Virginia, and from the Atlantic Ocean westward to the 102d meridian. 2d ed., rev. and enl. . . . N.Y., Scribner, 1913. 3v. il. $13.50. **N384**

The first edition, 1896–98, illustrated 4162 species. This second edition illustrates 4666 species and adds about 300 pages of text to that of the first edition.
"The present work is the first complete illustrated flora published in this country. Its aim is to illustrate and describe every species, from the ferns upward, recognized as distinct by botanists and growing wild within the area adopted."—*Pref.*
For each species gives description, variant name with references to sources, habitat, illustration. Includes many popular names. Two general indexes: (1) Latin names (2) English names, including popular names.

Matthews, Ferdinand Schuyler. Field book of American wild flowers . . . new ed. rev. and enl. N.Y., Putnam, 1929. 558p. il. $3.75. **N385**

Subtitle: Being a short description of their character and habits, a concise definition of their colors, and incidental references to the insects which assist in their fertilization.

Small, John Kunkel. Manual of the southeastern flora; being descriptions of the seed plants growing naturally in Florida, Alabama, Mississippi, eastern Louisiana, Tennessee, North Carolina, South Carolina and Georgia. N.Y., Author, 1933. 1554p. il. $10.50. **N386**

"This manual supplements, in part, the *Flora of the Southeastern United States* published by the author in 1903 (Second edition 1913)."—*Introd.*
"Species are grouped in genera, families, and orders."

Willis, J. C. Dictionary of the flowering plants and ferns. 6th ed. rev. Camb., Univ. Pr., 1931. 752p. (Cambridge biological ser.) 20s. **N387**

In one main alphabet including Latin and popular names, technical terms, etc.

Fruits

Hedrick, Ulysses Prentiss. Cyclopedia of hardy fruits. 2d enl. ed. N.Y., Macmillan, 1938. 402p. il. $6. **N388**

Designed for fruit-growers, nurserymen, students, etc. Descriptions aid in the identification of varieties, giving synonyms, description of tree or plant and fruit, date of its introduction in the United States, regions to which it is best adapted, etc.

Fungi

Ainsworth, Geoffrey Clough and **Bisby, Guy Richard.** A dictionary of the fungi. 2d ed. Kew, Surrey, Imperial Mycological Inst., 1945. 431p. il. 20s. **N389**

Lists the generic names of the fungi, giving for each genus its systematic position, its distribution and number of species; gives common and scientific names of important fungi, etc.

Wolf, Frederick A. and **Wolf, Frederick T.** The fungi. N.Y., Wiley, 1947. 2v. il. v.1, $6; v.2, $6.50. **N390**

A scientific text and reference book including much bibliography with author and subject indexes. Emphasis is on habitat and behavior.

Mosses

Dunham, Elizabeth Marie. How to know the mosses. . . . Bost., Houghton, 1916. 287p. il. $2.50. **N391**

Subtitle: A popular guide to the mosses of the northeastern United States, containing keys to eighty genera and short descriptions of over 150 species with special reference to the distinguishing characteristics that are apparent without the aid of a lens.

Trees

Collingwood, George Harris. Knowing your trees. With 529 photographs showing typical trees and their leaves, bark, flowers, and fruits. 5th and rev. printing. Wash., Amer. Forestry Assoc., 1941. 213p. il. $2.50. **N392**

Contains 101 tree descriptions.

Hough, Romeyn Beck. Handbook of the trees of the northern states and Canada east of the Rocky Mountains. Photo-descriptive. N.Y., Macmillan, 1947. 470p. il. $5.50. **N393**

Good illustrations show trunk, branchlet, leaves, fruit, pods, seeds, etc. Maps show distribution.
First published 1907.

Rehder, Alfred. Manual of cultivated trees and shrubs hardy in North America, exclusive of the subtropical and warmer temperate regions. 2d ed. rev. and enl. N.Y., Macmillan, 1940. 996p. $10.50. **N394**

Descriptions arranged by scientific name, with index to scientific and common names. Not illustrated.

Sargent, Charles Sprague. The silva of North America; a description of the trees which grow naturally in North America exclusive of Mexico . . . il. with figures and analyses drawn from nature by Charles Edward Faxon. Bost., Houghton, 1891–1902. 14v. 740 pl. (Repr. 1947. 14v. in 7. $200) **N395**

ZOOLOGY
General works
Guides

Smith, Roger C. Guide to the literature of the zoological sciences. [rev. ed.] Minneapolis, Burgess Pub. Co., 1945. 114p. $2. **N396**

A useful handbook providing an annotated bibliography to the important reference materials in the zoological sciences, with notes on library usage and the preparation of bibliographies and research papers.

Wood, Casey Albert. An introduction to the literature of vertebrate zoology; based chiefly on the titles in the Blacker Library of Zoology, the Emma Shearer Wood Library of Ornithology, the Bibliotheca Osleriana and other libraries of McGill University, Montreal. Lond., Ox. Univ. Pr., 1931. 643p. 63s. **N397**

Issued also as McGill University publications, series XI (Zoology), no.24.
Introduction to the literature of vertebrate zoology, p.1-146; Students' and librarians' ready index to short author-titles on vertebrate zoology arranged geographically and in chronological order, p.147-72; A partially annotated catalog of the titles on vertebrate zoology in the libraries of McGill University, p.173-643.

Bibliography

See also Bibliography, p.254-55.

Agassiz, Louis. Bibliographia zoologiae et geologiae. A general catalogue of all books, tracts, and memoirs on zoology and geology. Cor., enl. and ed. by H. E. Strickland. Lond., Ray Soc., 1848–54. 4v. **N398**

A comprehensive bibliography not entirely satisfactory, but attempting to cover all works published up to 1840.

Reuss, Jeremias David. Repertorium commentationum a societatibus litterariis editarum . . . t.1, Historia naturalis, generalis et zoologia. Gottingae, Dieterich, 1801. 574p. **N399**

A valuable index to the publications of learned societies up to 1800. Classed arrangement with author index. Index to volume 1 is combined with that for volume 2. For record of complete set *see* N3.

Engelmann, Wilhelm. Bibliotheca historico-naturalis. Verzeichniss der Bücher über Naturgeschichte, welche in Deutschland, Scandinavien, Holland, England, Frankreich, Italien und Spanien 1700–1846 erscheinen sind. . . . Mit einem Namen-und Sach-Register. Leipzig, Engelmann, 1846. 786p. **N400**

Contents: Bücherkunde. Hülfsmittel. Allgemeine Schriften. Vergleichende Anatomie und Physiologie. Zoologie. Palaeontologie.

For zoology continued by:

Bibliotheca zoologica [I]. Verzeichnis der Schriften über Zoologie welche in den periodischen Werken enthalten und vom Jahre 1846–1860 selbständig erscheinen sind. Mit Einschluss der allgemein-naturgeschichtlichen periodischen und paleontologischen Schriften. Bearb. von J. Victor Carus und Wilhelm Engelmann. Leipzig, Engelmann, 1861. 2v. (Bibliotheca historico-naturalis. hrsg. von Wilhelm Engelmann. Supplement Band) **N401**

Autoren-und Sach-Register.

Continued by:

Bibliotheca zoologica II. Verzeichnis der Schriften über Zoologie welche in den periodischen Werken enthalten und vom Jahre 1861–1880 selbständig erscheinen sind. . . . Bearb. von O. Taschenberg. Leipzig, Engelmann, 1887–1923. 8v. **N402**

No indexes.

International catalogue of scientific literature: N, Zoology. 1st-14th annual issues, 1901–14. Lond., 1902–16. 14v. **N403**

For full description *see* N6.

Of this section, v.6-14, 1906–14 were issued jointly with the *Zoological record*, v.43-51.

Ruch, Theodore Cedric. Bibliographia primatologica; a classified bibliography of primates other than man . . . v.1. Springfield, Ill., Balt., C. C. Thomas, 1941. 241p. (Yale Univ. School of Medicine. Yale Medical Library. Historical Library. Pub. no.4) $8.50. **N404**

Contents: pt.1, Anatomy, embryology and quantitative morphology; physiology, pharmacology and psychobiology; primate phylogeny and miscellanea.

Covers material published through 1938. Classed arrangement, author index. 4630 entries.

U. S. Bureau of Animal Industry. Index-catalogue of medical and veterinary zoology . . . Authors, by Albert Hassall and Margie Potter. Wash., Govt. Prt. Off., 1932–50. pt.1-11. (In progress) **N405**

pt.1-11, A-O.

This catalog is a revision and continuation of the *Index catalogue of medical and veterinary zoology: Authors*, by C. W. Stiles and Albert Hassall, published in 1902–12 as Bureau of Animal Industry *Bull*. 39.

Each part contains a very useful list of periodical abbreviations.

Abstract journals, indexes and surveys

See also Abstracts, p.283-84.

Archiv für Naturgeschichte. Jahrg. 1-77, 1835–1911. Berlin, Nicolai, 1835–1911. il. **N406**

—— —— Register, 1.-25.; 26.-60.; 57.-74.

Volume 2 of each year contains annual reviews of the various departments of natural history.

Continued in two sections: Abt. A, Original-Arbeiten, v.78-92, 1912–1926; Abt. B, Jahresberichte, v.78-89, 1912–1926. The *Jahresberichte* includes annual surveys with bibliographies, limited to the fields of zoology.

Zoological record . . . being records of zoological literature. v.1, 1864- . Lond., Zoological Soc. of Lond., 1865- . v.1- . Annual. **N407**

Publisher varies.

Volumes 1-6 have title *Record of zoological literature*.

A comprehensive annual index to the zoological literature published in all parts of the world. Particularly useful for systematic zoology. Volumes 43-52, 1906–15, issued also as Sec. N of the *International catalogue* (N6), with bindings to match either set.

Zoologischer Jahresbericht. Hrsg. von der Zoologischen Station zu Neapel. Leipzig, 1879–1913. v.1-35. Annual. **N408**

—— Autoren-und Sach Register, 1886–90, 1891–1900, 1901–10.

A bibliographical and review journal covering the whole field of zoology through 1885. After 1886 systematic zoology was omitted as that was covered by the *Zoological record* (N407).

Concilium bibliographicum. Zurich, 1896–1940. **N409**

A bibliography published on cards covering current publications (primarily periodical articles, with some books and pamphlets) in zoology, paleontology, general biology, microscopy, anatomy, physiology, and kindred sciences, from all countries. Arranged by a decimal system based on Dewey.

The zoology references were also published annually in book form in the *Bibliographia zoologica* (N410); and the physiology references, in *Bibliographia physiologica*, 1893–96; n.s. v.1-2, 1897–98; ser. 3, v.1-9, 1905–14; ser. 4, v.1-2, 1922–26 (Zurich, Concilium bibliographicum, 1894–1927).

Bibliographia zoologica . . . v.1-43, 1896–1934. Zurich, Sumptibus Concilii Bibliographici, 1896–1934. 43v. **N410**

Volumes 1-22 published as volumes 19-35 of *Zoologischer Anzeiger*, continuing "Literatur" published in that periodical, volumes 1-18.

The individual volumes have no indexes but the *Bibliographia zoologica* is indexed in the *Register* of the *Zoologischer Anzeiger* (Jahrg. 16-40. 1899–1922. 5v.). Publisher varies.

Zentralblatt für Zoologie, allgemeine und experimentelle Biologie. Bd.1-6. Leipzig, Teubner, 1912–18. 6v.   **N411**

Formed by the union of the *Zoologisches Zentralblatt* 1894–1911 and the *Zentralblatt für allgemeine und experimentelle Biologie.* Includes surveys of the literature with abstracts for the most important papers.

Zoologischer Bericht; im Auftrage der Deutschen Zoologischen Gesellschaft . . . Bd.1- . Jena, G. Fischer, 1922- . v.1- .   **N412**

——— General-Autoren Register. Bd.1-25, 1922–31; Bd.26-50, 1931–40.

Contains abstracts of books and periodical material in various languages.

Periodical abbreviations

Apstein, Carl and **Wasikowski, Kasimir.** Periodica zoologica; Abkürzungs-Verzeichnis der wichtigsten Zeitschriften-Titel aus dem gebiet der Zoologie und ihrer Grenzgebiete. . . . Leipzig, Akademische Verlagsgesellschaft, 1938. 82p.   **N413**

Generic indexes

See Smith, *Guide to the literature of the zoological sciences,* p.91-93 (N396), for earlier generic indexes.

Neave, Sheffield Airey. Nomenclator zoologicus; a list of the names of genera and subgenera in zoology from the tenth edition of Linnaeus 1758 to the end of 1945. Lond., Zoological Soc. of Lond., 1939–50. v.1-5. £8 8s. 5d. per set. **N414**

This comprehensive list supersedes to a large extent earlier generic indexes, and with *Biological abstracts,* Sec. E (N330) or the *Zoological record* (N407) from 1945 to date, forms a complete record from 1758 to date.

Atlases

Bartholomew, J. G. Atlas of zoögeography. . . . Edinburgh, Bartholomew, 1911. 67p. 36 double maps.   **N415**

Subtitle: A series of maps illustrating the distribution of over 700 families, genera and species of existing animals, prepared by J. G. Bartholomew, W. E. Clarke and P. H. Grimshaw. Under the patronage of the Royal Geographical Society.
Forms volume 5 of Bartholomew's *Physical atlas.*
Includes all families of mammals, birds, reptiles and amphibians together with several of the more important

genera and species, most of the families of fishes and a selection of families and genera of molluscs and insects. Text furnishes concise information about the groups whose distribution is shown on the plates. About 200 maps all together, as most of the 36 plates contain 6 maps each. Contains also a bibliography of about 1000 titles arranged by regions subdivided by animals.

Animals
Bibliography

Phillips, John Charles. American game mammals and birds; a catalogue of books, 1582–1925, sport, natural history and conservation. Bost., Houghton, 1930. 638p. $10.   **N416**

Most of the titles are from the Charles Sheldon Library which now belongs to Yale University.
Contents: Introduction; pt.1, General catalog; pt.2, Conservation, general, federal, state, Canadian; pt.3, Periodical publications, pamphlets, etc.

Handbooks

Hegner, Robert. Parade of the animal kingdom. N.Y., Macmillan, 1935. 675p. il. $4.95.   **N417**

Covers all types of animals including the protozoa and sponges, fish, insects, snakes, birds, mammals, etc.

Birds
Bibliography

Field Museum of Natural History. Chicago. Edward E. Ayer Ornithological Library. Catalogue, by John Todd Zimmer. Chic., 1926. 2v. il. (Its Pub. 239, 240. Zoological ser. v.16) **N418**

Mullens, William Herbert and **Swann, H. Kirke.** Bibliography of British ornithology, from the earliest times to the end of 1912, including biographical accounts of the principal writers and bibliographies of their published works. Lond., Macmillan, 1917. 673p., 675-91 numb. l. **N419**

Particularly useful for its biographical sketches.

——— ——— Supplement: A chronological list of British birds. Lond., Wheldon and Wesley, 1923. 42p.

Strong, Reuben Myron. A bibliography of birds; with special reference to anatomy, behavior, biochemistry, embryology, pathology, physiology, genetics, ecology, aviculture, economic ornithology, poultry culture, evolution, and related subjects. Chic., Natural History Museum, 1939–46. 3v. (Museum. Pub. 442, 457, 581. Zoological ser. v.25, pts. 1-3) $11 per set.   **N420**

20,000 titles from earliest times to 1926 with some additional titles to 1938.

Author catalog with subject index.

Handbooks

Chapman, Frank M. Handbook of birds of eastern North America; with introductory chapters on the study of birds in nature. . . . 2d rev. ed. N.Y., Appleton-Century, 1934. 581p. il. **N421**

Forbush, Edward Howe. Birds of Massachusetts and other New England states, il. with colored plates and drawings by Louis Agassiz Fuertes and figures and cuts from drawings and photographs by the author and others. Bost., Mass. Dept. of Agriculture, 1925–29. 3v. il. **N422**

v.1, Waterbirds, marsh birds and shore birds; v.2, Land birds from bob-whites to grackles; v.3, Land birds from sparrows to thrushes.

Issued also in a revised and abridged edition entitled *Natural history of the birds of eastern and central North America* by E. H. Forbush (rev. and abridged with the addition of more than 100 species. Bost., Houghton, 1939. 551p. il. $3.75).

Hickey, Joseph J. A guide to bird watching. With illustrations by Francis L. Jacques and bird tracks by Charles A. Urner. Lond., N.Y., Ox. Univ. Pr., 1943. 262p. il. $3.50; 16s. **N423**

Includes an annotated list of bird books, p.208-39.

National Geographic Society, Washington, D. C. The book of birds; the first work presenting in full color all the major species of the United States and Canada . . . ed. by Gilbert Grosvenor and Alexander Wetmore . . . with 950 color portraits by Major Allan Brooks. . . . Wash., National Geographic Soc., 1937. 2v. il. $5. **N424**

A collection of articles from the *National geographic magazine.* Excellent color plates and many photographs. Index.

Peterson, Roger Tory. A field guide to the birds, giving field marks of all species found east of the Rockies. 2d rev. and enl. ed. sponsored by the National Audubon Society. Bost., Houghton, 1947. 290p. il. $3.50. **N425**

Ridgway, Robert. The birds of North and Middle America. . . . Wash., Govt. Prt. Off., 1901–46. v.1-10. il. (U.S. National Museum. Bull. 50) (In progress) **N426**

Subtitle: A descriptive catalogue of the higher groups, genera, species, and subspecies of birds known to occur in North America, from the Arctic lands to the Isthmus of Panama, the West Indies and other islands of the Caribbean Sea and the Galapagos Archipelago.

Exhaustive treatment with full descriptions and synonymies.

Fish

Bibliography

Dean, Bashford. Bibliography of fishes, enl. and ed. by C. R. Eastman. N.Y., Amer. Museum of Natural History, 1916–23. 3v. **N427**

v.1-2, Author list; v.3, Subject index, list of general bibliographies, voyages, periodicals, etc.

Volume 3 extended and enlarged by Eugene Willis Gudger, with the cooperation of Arthur Wilbur Henn.

U. S. Bureau of Fisheries. An analytical subject bibliography of the publications of the Bureau of Fisheries, 1871–1920, by Rose M. E. MacDonald . . . Appendix V to the Report of the U.S. Commissioner of Fisheries for 1920. . . . Wash., Govt. Prt. Off., 1921. 306p. (U.S. Bureau of Fisheries. Doc. 899) **N428**

Handbooks

Schrenkeisen, Raymond Martin. Field book of fresh-water fishes of North America north of Mexico. Ed. by J. T. Nichols and F. R. LaMonte. . . . N.Y., Putnam, 1938. 312p. il. $3.50. **N429**

Gives scientific name, common name, description, habits, distribution and related forms for each fish. Short glossary and bibliography.

Shells

Morris, Percy A. A field guide to the shells of our Atlantic coast. Bost., Houghton, 1947. 190p. il. (Field guide ser.) $3.50. **N430**

Snakes

Ditmars, Raymond Lee. Field book of North American snakes. N.Y., Doubleday, 1939. 305p. il. $3.50. **N431**

Turtles

Pope, Clifford Hillhouse. Turtles of the United States and Canada, il. with 99 photographs. N.Y., Knopf, 1939. 343p. il. $3.75. **N432**

Bibliography, p.325-37.

BACTERIOLOGY
General works
Bibliography

Abstracts of bacteriology. v.1-9, Feb. 1917–Dec. 1925. Balt., Williams and Wilkins, 1917–26. 9v. il. **N433**

Bimonthly, 1917–20; monthly, 1921–25.

No more published; united with *Botanical abstracts* to form *Biological abstracts* (N330). Signed abstracts of material in various languages.

International catalogue of scientific literature: R, Bacteriology. 1st-14 annual issues. Lond., 1901–20. 14v.   **N434**

For full description *see* N6.

Paris. Institut Pasteur. Bulletin de l'Institut Pasteur; revues et analyses des travaux de bactériologie et de médecine, biologie générale, physiologie, chimie biologique dans leurs rapports avec la microbiologie. t.1- . Paris, Masson, 1903- .   **N435**

Zentralblatt für Bakteriologie, Parasitenkunde und Infektions-Krankheiten. Abt. 1, Medizinisch-hygienische Bakteriologie, Virusforschung und tierische Parasitologie. Referate. Jena, 1902- . v.31- .   **N436**

Earlier volumes, 1887–1901, included *Originale* and *Referate* in same volume but beginning with 1902 they are issued separately. Extensive coverage especially for European material.

McCoy, Elizabeth and McClung, Leland Swift. The anaerobic bacteria and their activities in nature and disease; a subject bibliography. Berkeley, Calif., Univ. of Calif. Pr., 1939. 2v. $10.   **N437**

v.1, Chronological author index; v.2, Subject index.

—— —— Supplement one. Literature for 1938 and 1939. Berkeley and Los Angeles, Univ. of Calif. Pr., 1941. 244p. $3.50.

Authors' names reversed on title page of supplement.

Dictionaries

Partridge, William. Dictionary of bacteriological equivalents; French-English, German-English, Italian-English, Spanish-English. Lond., Baillière; Balt., Williams and Wilkins, 1927. 140p. $2.50.   **N438**

In four sections arranged by language. Particularly useful for medical translation.

Manuals

Bergey, David Hendricks, Breed, R. S. [and others]. Bergey's Manual of determinative bacteriology. 6th ed. Balt., Williams and Wilkins, 1948. 1529p.   **N439**

Arranged by a committee of the Society of American Bacteriologists.

Medical Research Council. (Gt. Brit.) A system of bacteriology in relation to medicine. Lond., Stat. Off., 1929–31. 9v.   **N440**

GENETICS

Bibliographia genetica. deel 1- . 'sGravenhage, Nijhoff, 1925- .   **N441**

Monographic articles on the literature of genetics.

Resumptio genetica. deel 1- , 1924- . 'sGravenhage, Nijhoff, 1926- . il. Bimonthly (irregular).   **N442**

Abstract journal, international in scope. Abstracts are given in English, French or German.

Knight, Robert L. Dictionary of genetics, including terms used in cytology, animal breeding and evolution [1st ed.] Waltham, Mass., Chronica Botanica, 1948. 183p. il. (Lotsya, a biological miscellany. v.2) $4.50.   **N443**

Contains some 2500 definitions.

ENTOMOLOGY
General works
Bibliography

Carpenter, Matilde M. Bibliography of biographies of entomologists. (In American midland naturalist 33:1-116, 1945) 75c.   **N444**

A second edition of the bibliography by J. S. Wade that appeared in the *Annals* of the Entomological Society of America, 21:489-520, 1928.

Chamberlin, Willard Joseph. Entomological nomenclature and literature. 2d ed. Ann Arbor, Mich., Edwards Bros., 1946. 135p. $3.25.   **N445**

Horn, Walther and Schenkling, Sigmund. Index litteraturae entomologicae. ser.I, Die Welt-Literatur über die gesamte Entomologie bis inklusive 1863. Berlin, Dahlem, 1928–29. 4v.   **N446**

A revision of H. A. Hagen, *Bibliotheca entomologica* (Leipzig, 1862–63. 2v.) with the addition of some 8000 titles, covering the field up to the beginning of the *Zoological record* (N407). Arranged alphabetically by author, this edition has no index although Hagen included an author-subject index which may be used for either work for the material covered.

Index to the literature of American economic entomology. 1905/14—1935/39. Melrose Highlands, Mass., Amer. Assoc. of Economic Entomologists, 1917–38. v.1-6. (In progress)   **N447**

Continues *Bibliography of the more important contributions to American economic entomology,* issued by the U.S. Dept. of Agriculture, Bureau of Entomology.

An important index, the first volume covered a 10-year period, succeeding volumes each cover 5 years.

Volume 1 compiled by Nathan Banks; volumes 2-6 compiled by Mabel Colcord and edited by E. P. Felt.

U. S. Bureau of Entomology. Library. Checklist of publications on entomology issued by the U.S.

Dept. of Agriculture through 1927, with subject index, by Mabel Colcord, Ina L. Hawes, and Angelina J. Carabelli. Wash., 1930. 261p. (U.S. Dept. of Agriculture Lib. Bibl. contrib., no.20) **N448**

Handbooks

Comstock, John Henry. An introduction to entomology. 9th ed. rev. Ithaca, N.Y., Comstock Pub. Co., 1947. 1064p. il. $6. **N449**

De La Torre-Bueno, José Rollin. A glossary of entomology; Smith's "An explanation of terms used in entomology," completely rev. and rewritten. Lancaster, Pa., Science Pr., 1937. 336p. il. $5. **N450**

Published by Brooklyn Entomological Society, Brooklyn, N.Y.

Swain, Ralph B. Insect guide; orders and major families of North American insects. N.Y., Doubleday, 1948. 261p. il. $3. **N451**

A nontechnical but well-arranged guide to the major groups of insects. 450 illustrations of which 330 are in color. Bibliography, p.227-35.

NATURAL HISTORY

Altsheler, Brent. Natural history index-guide. An index to 3,365 books and periodicals in libraries; a guide to things natural in the field. . . . N.Y., Wilson, 1940. 583p. Service basis. **N452**

Comstock, Anna Botsford. Handbook of nature-study; 24th ed. Ithaca, N.Y., Comstock Pub. Co. 1939. 937p. il. $6; text ed. $5. **N453**

Contents: pt.1, Teaching of nature-study; pt.2, Animals; pt.3, Plants; pt.4, Earth and sky; Bibliography.

Palmer, Ephraim Laurence. Fieldbook of natural history. N.Y., Whittlesey, 1949. 664p. il. $7; text ed. $5. **N454**

A guide to birds, animals, fish, plants, minerals, etc.

There are various publishers' series of nature handbooks the individual volumes of which are frequently useful. Some of these series are:

Handbooks of American natural history, v.1- . Ithaca, N.Y., Comstock Pub. Co., 1942- . il. (In progress) **N455**

Contents: v.1, Handbook of frogs and toads, by A. A. Wright and A. H. Wright. 3d ed. 1949. 652p. $6.50; v.2, Mammals of the eastern United States, by W. J. Hamilton. 1943. 432p. $4; v.3, Handbook of salamanders, by S. C. Bishop. 1943. 555p. $5; v.4, Aquatic plants of the United States, by W. C. Muenscher. 1944. 374p. $5; v.5, Handbook of the mosquitoes of North America, by Robert Matheson. 2d ed. 1944. 314p. $4; v.6, Handbook of lizards, by Hobart Smith. 1946. 557p. $5.75.

Nature library. N.Y., Doubleday, 1905–12. 17v. il. **N456**

Includes separate volumes on animals, fishes, birds, butterflies, frogs, grasses, insects, mosses, moths, mushrooms, reptiles, shells, spiders, trees.

Six volumes reissued 1947. $19.50 (not sold separately) including Birds, by Neltje Blanchau; Animals, by Ernest Thompson Seton; Wild flowers, by Neltje Blanchau; Butterflies, by Clarence M. Weed; Garden flowers, by Robert M. McCurdy; Trees, by Julia Ellen Rogers.

Putnam's Nature field books. N.Y., Putnam, 1928- . il. Price varies. **N457**

Includes separate volumes on wild flowers, trees and shrubs, ferns, insects, rocks and minerals, birds, mammals, mushrooms, fishes, stars, etc.

See also Meisel, *Bibliography of American natural history* (N328).

APPLIED SCIENCE

❦ This section includes a selected list of reference works in general technology, the various branches of engineering, agriculture, forestry, home economics, and medicine. For libraries specializing in these fields, much more material will be needed and the various guides to the literature of the subjects should be consulted. As in the pure sciences, current literature is of prime importance and the indexes and abstract journals are essential as guides to this material.

(For a discussion of abstract journals *see* Science, p.253). Many of the branches of engineering have handbooks and manuals which include data, charts, statistics, etc., useful to the practicing engineer. These handbooks are usually revised frequently to include new developments and practices. Dictionaries of technical terms, bilingual as well as those giving definitions in English, are much used in many libraries.

GENERAL TECHNOLOGY
General works
Guides

Dalton, Blanche H. Sources of engineering information. Berkeley and Los Angeles, Univ. of Calif. Pr., 1948. 109p. **P1**

A handbook and bibliography designed to aid in the finding of material in all branches of engineering. Classified. Little annotation. No index.

Holmstrom, J. E. Records and research in engineering and industrial science. 2d ed. rev. and enl. Lond., Chapman and Hall, 1947. 366p. 21s. **P2**

Subtitle: A guide to the sources, processing and storekeeping of technical knowledge with a chapter on translating.
A useful guide particularly to English works. First edition, 1940.

Parke, Nathan Grier. Guide to the literature of mathematics and physics including related works on engineering science. N.Y., McGraw-Hill, 1947. 205p. $5. **P3**

For description *see* N67.

Roberts, Arthur Denis. Guide to technical literature; introductory chapters and engineering. Lond., Grafton, 1939. 279p. **P4**

Useful bibliography of engineering literature. Includes material published through 1938.

Bibliography

See Periodicals—Bibliography, p.255-56, for lists of technical periodicals.

Association of Special Libraries and Information Bureaux. Select list of standard British scientific and technical books, comp. at the request of the British Council. 3d ed. rev. and enl. Lond., Aslib, 1946. 63p. 5s. to nonmembers; 3s. 6d. to members. **P5**

For description *see* N2.

Grombach, Hannah. Bibliographie des publications des principaux organismes et congrès internationaux dans le domaines des sciences appliquées. Zurich, École Polytechnique Fédérale, 1945. 66p. **P6**

Arranged by the Universal Decimal Classification, this is a list of international congresses in the field of applied sciences, with a record of their publications and in many cases location of copies in Swiss libraries. Includes names of the congresses in the various languages concerned, cities and dates of meetings, full titles and dates of publications, and when found the library location. Subject index.

Hawkins, Reginald Robert. Scientific, medical, and technical books published in the United

States of America, 1930–1944; a selected list. Wash., 1946. 1114p. $20. **P7**

For full description *see* N10.

International catalogue of scientific literature: B, Mechanics. 1st–14th annual issues, 1901–1914. Lond., 1902–15. 14v. **P8**

For full description *see* N6.

John Crerar Library. List of books on the history of industry and the industrial arts. Prepared by Aksel G. S. Josephson. Chic., Library, 1915. 486p. **P9**

Lovell, Eleanor Cook and **Hall, Ruth Mason.** Index to handicrafts, model-making, and workshop projects. Bost., Faxon, 1936. 476p. (Useful reference ser. no.57) $4. **P10**

————— Supplement. . . . Bost., Faxon, 1943. 527p. (Useful reference ser. no.70) $6.

Royal Society of London. Catalogue of scientific papers, 1800–1900: Subject index, v.2, Mechanics. Camb., Univ. Pr., 1909. 355p. **P11**

For full description *see* N4.

CURRENT

Association of Special Libraries and Information Bureaux. Aslib book list: Quarterly recommendations of recently published scientific and technical books. v.1, Oct. 1935- . Lond., Aslib, 1935- . 17s. 6d. per yr. to nonmembers. **P12**

Classed arrangement. Cumulated annual indexes. Priced.

New York Public Library. New technical books; a bi-monthly list of additions to the New York Public Library. 1915- . N.Y., Library, 1915- . v.1- . Bimonthly. $1.50 per yr. **P13**

A very useful current bibliography, with good annotations. Published quarterly through volume 32, 1947. Subtitle varies. Arranged by subject with annual author indexes. Helpful for book selection. Changed form with volume 33, number 1, to conform to the style of Hawkins, *Scientific, medical, and technical books* (N10) and includes table of contents for each book.

Repertorium technicum. Nederlandsch Instituut voor Documentatie en Registratur. v.1, 1931- . 'sGravenhage, Nijhoff, 1931- . Bimonthly. **P14**

An international bimonthly bibliography, listing some 25,000 to 30,000 titles annually, of books and articles appearing in periodicals on technical and allied subjects. Arranged by the Universal Decimal Classification. Besides the citation to the location of the article, reference is also given when possible to a journal in which an abstract may be found.

Technical book review index, issued by the Technology Dept. of the Carnegie Library of Pittsburgh, 1917–28. Pittsburgh, Carnegie Library, 1917–29. 12v. Quarterly. **P15**

A quarterly index important as listing much material not given in the *Book review digest* (A577) and as a useful aid to book selection in a special field. Gives title of book and bibliographical data, references to periodicals, and brief quotations.

Continued informally, though with a gap of seven years, by:

Technical book review index. Comp. and ed. in the Technology Dept., Carnegie Library of Pittsburgh. N.Y., Special Libraries Assoc., 1935- . v.1- . Monthly (except July and August). $7.50. **P16**

A very useful guide to reviews in scientific, technical, and trade journals, with in many cases brief quotations from the reviews.

U. S. Dept. of Commerce. Office of Technical Services. Bibliography of scientific and industrial reports. v.1, 1946- . Wash., 1946- . (Weekly until v.9, no.13, June 25, 1948) Monthly v.10, no.1, July 1948- . $10 per yr. **P17**

"The reports listed have been received from civil and military agencies of the U.S. Government and from cooperating foreign governments. Many of the reports cover information captured in enemy countries. Secrecy restrictions on all reports listed have been lifted."

————— Numerical index, v.1-10, 1946–48. N.Y., Special Libraries Assoc., 1949. 532p. $10.

Indexes and abstracts

Engineering index, 1884–1905. N.Y., Engineering Magazine, 1892–1906. 4v. o.p. **P18**

v.1, 1884–1891, published under the title *Descriptive index of current engineering literature;* v.1, 1884–1891, and v.2, 1892–1895, ed. by J. B. Johnson; v.3, 1896–1900, and v.4, 1901–1905, ed. by H. H. Suplee and J. H. Cuntz.

An alphabetical subject index, with no author index, to about 250 technical and engineering periodicals in English, French, German, Italian, Spanish and Dutch; about three quarters of the periodicals indexed are in English. Gives fairly full information, i.e., title, author, brief digest or description of the article, length in number of words, periodical and exact date. Does not give volume or page. Continued after 1905 by the following:

Engineering index, 1906- . N.Y., Engineering Magazine, 1907–19; Amer. Soc. of Mechanical Engineers, 1920–34; Engineering Index, Inc., 1934- . Annual. **P19**

Title varies.

Continues the *Engineering index,* 1884–1905, covering the same field in the same detail, but, for the years 1906–18, with a different arrangement, i.e., a classed subject index, not an alphabetical subject index, grouped in eight large classes, Civil engineering, Electrical engineering, Industrial economy, Marine and naval engineering, Mechanical engineering, Mining and metallurgy, Railway engineering, Street and electric railways.

Beginning 1919, the form changed to an alphabetical subject index, giving for each article exact reference to title, date, volume and page of the periodical, number of illustrations and a brief digest. From 1928 on, an author index is included. International in scope. Indexes an extensive list of engineering and industrial periodicals, publications of scientific and technical societies, government bureaus, engineering experiment stations, universities, and other research organizations.

For current work the annual index may be kept up to date by a weekly card service which supplies printed cards with brief abstracts for articles in periodicals, transactions, reports, etc., in various languages. This service can be subscribed for either in part or as a whole; annual subscriptions vary according to divisional subject. For information apply to Engineering Index, Inc. 29 West 39th St., New York 18.

Industrial arts index, 1913- , subject index to a selected list of engineering, trade and business periodicals, books and pamphlets. N.Y., Wilson, 1913- . Service basis. **P20**

Monthly index, cumulating throughout the year, with the December number forming an annual cumulation. From volume 7 to volume 19, a 2-year cumulation was issued every other year. Beginning with volume 20 (1932), the 2-year cumulation was discontinued. Indexes many of the same periodicals as the *Engineering index* (P19) but differs from that index in having (1) a wider range of subjects, including commercial and business, as well as technological, subjects, (2) less foreign material. More useful than the *Engineering index* in the general library. In general follows the same plan of indexing as the *Readers' guide* except that articles are indexed only under subjects and not under authors also. Indexes principally material in English.

Institution of Civil Engineers, London. Engineering abstracts prepared from the current periodical literature of engineering and applied science, published outside the kingdom . . . n.s. no.1-76, Oct. 1919—Oct. 1937. Lond., Institution, 1919–37. 76 nos. diagrs. **P21**

Quarterly. Title varies.
1875–1916 printed in the *Minutes of proceedings* of the Institution. The new series is issued as a supplement to the *Minutes.*
Beginning with 1938, issued monthly in four sections; Sec. 1, Engineering construction, v.1, Jan. 1938- ; Sec. 2, Mechanical engineering, v.1, Jan. 1938- ; Sec. 3, Shipbuilding and marine engineering, v.1, Feb. 1938- ; Sec. 4, Mining engineering, v.1, Jan. 1938- .
Sections 1, 2, and 4 were suspended with v.2, no.9, Sept. 1939; Section 3 has been continued by the Institute of Marine Engineers, in cooperation with the Institute of Naval Architects.

Repertorium der technischen Journal-Literatur, 1823–1908. Berlin, Heymann, 1856–1909. 40v. **P22**

Title varies; publisher varies.
Contents: 1823–53, pub. 1856. 1049p.; 1854–68, pub. 1871–73. 2v.; 1869–73, pub. 1876–78. 2v.; 1874–1908, pub. 1875–1909. 35v.
1823–76, hrsg. im Auftrage des Königlich preussischen Ministeriums für Handel, Gewerbe und öffentliche Ar-

beiten; 1877–1908, hrsg. im Auftrage des Kaiserlichen Patentamts.
A subject index to more than 400 periodicals in various languages, arranged alphabetically by the German subject word followed, in volumes from 1892 on, by the French and English equivalents. Each volume has a detailed subject index to this subject list which, in volumes before 1892, is an index of German words only, but from 1892 includes French and English words in the same alphabet; volumes from 1897 on have an author index also. Not now up to date, but still useful for older and foreign material.
Continued by the *Fortschritte der Technik* (1.-2. Jahrg., 1909–11. Berlin, Bibliog. Zentralverlag, 1910–11. 9v.).

Reuss, Jeremias David. Repertorium commentationum a societatibus litterariis editarum . . . t.7. Gottingae, Dieterich, 1808. 514p. **P23**

Contents: Mathesis; Mechanica; Hydrostatica; Hydraulica; Hydrotechnica; Aerostatica; Pnevmatica; Technologia; Architectura civilis; Scientia navalis; Scientia militaris.
For description of complete set *see* N3.

Applied mechanics reviews; a critical review of the world literature in applied mechanics. v.1, Jan. 1948- . Easton, Pa., American Soc. of Mechanical Engineers, 1948- . Monthly. **P24**

An abstract journal, international in scope, covering much the same field as the *Zentralblatt für Mechanik* (Apr. 1933- . Berlin, Springer, 1933-).

Encyclopedias and handbooks

Engineer's year-book of formulae, rules, tables, data and memoranda for 1894- . A compendium of the modern practice of civil, mechanical, electrical, marine, gas, aero, mine, and metallurgical engineering, originally comp. by H. R. Kempe and W. Hanneford Smith . . . rev. under the direction of L. St. L. Pendred. Lond., Morgan, 1894- . Annual. **P25**

Subtitle varies.

Eshbach, Ovid Wallace. Handbook of engineering fundamentals, prepared by a staff of specialists. . . . N.Y., Wiley; Lond., Chapman, 1936. 1098p. il. (Wiley engineering handbook ser. v.1) $6; college ed. $5. **P26**

Hutchinson's Technical and scientific encyclopaedia; terms, processes, data in pure and applied science. Construction and engineering. The principal manufacturing industries. The skilled trades, with a working bibliography, naming three thousand books and other sources of information, under subjects; ed. by C. F. Tweney and I. P. Shirshov. Lond., Hutchinson; N.Y., Macmillan [1935–36]. 4v. il. £5; $25. **P27**

Jones, Franklin Day. Engineering encyclopedia; a condensed encyclopedia and mechanical dictionary for engineers, mechanics, technical schools, industrial plants, and public libraries, giving the most essential facts about 4500 important engineering subjects. 2d ed. N.Y., Industrial Pr.; Brighton, Eng., Machinery Pub. Co. [1943]. 2v. il. $8. **P28**

Paged continuously.
1st ed. 1941.
Definitions of engineering terms and brief articles are in one alphabetical arrangement. Includes some historical and background material.

O'Rourke, Charles Edward. General engineering handbook; ed.-in-chief, Charles Edward O'Rourke . . . 2d ed. N.Y. and Lond., McGraw-Hill, 1940. 1120p. il. $6.50. **P29**

The purpose of this general handbook is to cover the essentials of all branches of engineering in a compact survey, but not to take the place of the specialized handbooks of the various branches of engineering.

See also Encyklopädie der mathematischen Wissenschaften, t.4, Mechanik (N80); Van Nostrand's Scientific encyclopedia (N30).

Dictionaries

See also Dictionaries, p.257.

Brown, Victor Jacob and **Runner, Delmar G.** Engineering terminology; definitions of technical words and phrases. 2d ed. Chic., Gillette Pub. Co., 1939. 439p. **P30**

A classified list of some 5500 terms grouped according to the branch of engineering in which they are used, with an alphabetical index. Covers electrical, chemical, geological, mechanical, architectural and civil engineering. Appendixes include lists of English-Spanish, Spanish-English and German-English terms, abbreviations, symbols, conversion tables, etc.

Chambers's Technical dictionary, ed. by C. F. Tweney and L. E. C. Hughes. Rev. ed. with supplement. N.Y., Macmillan, 1948. 976p. $6.50. **P31**

Supplement, p.952-76 (including Addenda, p.975-76).
Subtitle: Comprising terms used in pure and applied science; medicine; the chief manufacturing industries; engineering construction; the mechanic trades; with definitions by recognized authorities.

Crispin, Frederic Swing. Dictionary of technical terms, containing definitions of commonly used expressions in aeronautics, architecture, woodworking and building trades, electrical and metal-working trades, printing, chemistry, etc. (rev. ed.) Milwaukee, Bruce Pub. Co., 1948. 440p. il. $3.25. **P32**

Newmark, Maxim. Illustrated technical dictionary containing standard technical definitions of current terms in the applied sciences, graphic and industrial arts and mechanized trades; incl. air navigation, meteorology, shipbuilding; synthetics and plastics. . . . N.Y., Philosophical Library, 1944. 352p. il. $5. **P33**

POLYGLOT

Newmark, Maxim. Dictionary of science and technology in English-French-German-Spanish, containing 10,000 current terms in the English language most frequently used in the physical sciences and their applied fields, together with separate indices in French, German, and Spanish, conversion tables, and technical abbreviations. N.Y., Philosophical Library [1943]. 386p. $6. **P34**

Somewhat limited in scope and usefulness. Gives foreign equivalents of English words but no definitions or explanations. Separate indexes in French, German, and Spanish are cross-indexed to each of the other languages.
Spanish edition published in Buenos Aires, Glem, 1944.

Schlomann, Alfred. Illustrated technical dictionary in six languages, English, German, French, Russian, Italian, Spanish. N.Y., McGraw-Hill, 1906–32. v.1-17. Price per v. varies. **P35**

Editor varies: v.1-3 ed. by K. Deinhardt and Alf. Schlomann; v.4-17 by A. Schlomann. Series title varies: v.7-11, Deinhardt-Schlomann series; v.12-16, Schlomann-Oldenbourg series. Also published, Munich, Oldenbourg, Lond., Constable.
v.1, Elements of machinery; v.2, Electrical engineering and electrochemistry [2d ed.]; v.3, Steam boilers, steam engines, steam turbines; v.4, Internal combustion engines; v.5, Railway construction and operation; v.6, Railway rolling stock; v.7, Hoisting and conveying machinery; v.8, Reinforced concrete; v.9, Machine tools; v.10, Motor vehicles; v.11, Metallurgy of iron; v.12, Hydraulics, pneumatics, refrigeration; v.13, Building construction, civil engineering; v.14, Textile raw materials; v.15, Spinning processes and products; v.16, Weaving and woven fabrics; v.17, Aeronautics.
An excellent dictionary, much used by translators.
Many volumes now out of date. New edition was started in 1938 as:

Illustrierte technische Wörterbücher; deutsch, englisch, französisch, italienisch, spanisch, russisch. Bearb. im Auftrage der Gesellschaft zur Herausgabe der illustrierten technischen Wörterbücher von Walter Eppner . . . unter Mitwirkung des Vereines deutscher Ingenieure, des deutschen Normenausschusses, mehrerer Normenauschüsse des Auslandes und zahlreicher Industriefirmen und Fachleute des In- und Auslandes. Berlin, VDI-Verlag, 1938. v.1. 438p il. **P36**

v.1, Maschinenelemente . . . verbesserte und vervollständige 3. Aufl. mit 1632 Abbildungen.
Classified with alphabetical indexes.

Technologisches Wörterbuch . . . 6. vollkommen neubearb. Aufl., hrsg. von Alfred Schlomann. Berlin, Springer, 1932. 3v. **P37**

Subtitle: Gewerbe, Industrie, Technik und ihre wissenschaftlichen Grundlagen, Berg- und Hüttenwesen, Aufbereitungsindustrie, Rohstoffe, Werkstoffe, Materialprüfung, Halb- und Fertigerzeugnisse, Elektrotechnik, Fernmeldetechnik, Messtechnik, Filmtechnik, optische Industrie, Waffentechnik, Artz- und Gesundheitstechnik, Unfallverhütung, Bauwesen, chemische Technologie, Landwirtschaft und Forstwesen, Nahrungsmittelindustrie, Textilindustrie, Bekleidungsindustrie, Handel, Messewesen, Bankwesen, Verkehr, Kraftfahrwesen, Schiffbau, und Schiffahrt Patentwesen, Zollwesen, Rechtskunde und zahlreiche andere Fachgebiete.

At head of title: Hoyer-Kreuter.

v.1, German-English-French; v.2, English-German-French; v.3, French-German-English.

Tekniikan sanasto, saksa-englanti-suomi-ruotsi. Teknisk ordbok, tysk-engelsk-finsk-svensk. Technisches Wörterbuch, deutsch-englisch-finnisch-schwedisch. Technical vocabulary, German-English-Finnish-Swedish. Toimituskunta: Väinö Airas . . . Väinö Valkola . . . Lauri Hendell-Auterinen . . . [etc.] Helsinki, Kustannusosakeyhtiö Otava [1940]. 1232 col. **P38**

FRENCH

Cusset, Francis. English-French and French-English technical dictionary; metallurgy, mining, electricity, chemistry, mechanics, sciences. Brooklyn, N.Y., Chemical Pub. Co., 1946. 590p. $5. **P39**

Kettridge, Julius Orman. French-English and English-French dictionary of technical terms and phrases used in civil, mechanical, electrical and mining engineering, and allied sciences and industries, including geology, physical geography, petrology, mineralogy, crystallography, metallurgy, chemistry, physics, geometry, abbreviations and symbols, weights and measures, compound conversion factors, etc., and a method of telegraphic coding by which any entry in the dictionary can be expressed by a 10 letter cipher word with indicator and check . . . containing the translations of 100,000 words, terms and phrases. N.Y., Wilson; Lond., Routledge [1925]. 2v. **P40**

Contents: v.1, French-English; v.2, English-French.

GERMAN

Webel, A. German-English technical and scientific dictionary. 2d ed. Lond., Routledge, 1937. 887p. **P41**

1st ed. 1930. Corrected and reprinted, 1937.

HUNGARIAN

Cserepy, Istvan. English and Hungarian glossary of technical terms, rev. and enl. by Tibor Gyengö. 2d ed. Budapest, Fövarosi Könyvkiado Kft., 1947. 244p. **P42**

English-Hungarian, Hungarian-English. Added title page in Hungarian.

Includes terms in architecture, town planning, road making, bridge building, water engineering; and conversion data for the metric system.

ITALIAN

Denti, Renzo. Dizionario tècnico, Italiano-Inglese, Inglese-Italiano; elementi generali; con perticolare riguardo alla chímica, meccanica, motore a scoppio, macchine utensili, all'ingegneria civile ed all'elettrotecnica. Milano, Hoepli, 1946. 509p. $4. **P43**

Marolli, Giorgio. Dizionario tecnico, inglese–italiano, italiano–inglese. 2d ed. Firenze, Le-Monnier, 1949. 630p. il. $10. **P44**

RUSSIAN

Bray, Alexander. Russian-English scientific-technical dictionary. N.Y., International Univ. Pr., 1945. 551p. $10. **P45**

Added title page in Russian.

Includes some 25,000 Russian scientific words and phrases, both the new terms and the older basic ones, with their English meanings.

Callaham, Ludmilla I. Russian-English technical and chemical dictionary. N.Y., Wiley; Lond., Chapman and Hall, 1947. 794p. **P46**

SPANISH

Sánchez, José and **Baig, Samuel.** Scientific and technical dictionaries of the Spanish and English languages . . . N.Y., Public Library, 1944. (Repr. from its Bull. July 1944) 22p. **P47**

A classed list with author index. Unannotated.

Guinle, R. L. A modern Spanish-English and English-Spanish technical and engineering dictionary, containing all the words used in civil, mechanical and electrical engineering; also many on aviation, wireless, architecture, railways, automobiles, shipbuilding, marine, chemistry, physics, mathematics, geology, mining, metallurgy, geography, surveying, commerce, agriculture, textile machinery, machine-tools, etc. Suitable for Spain and all the Spanish-speaking countries of Central America and South America. Lond., Routledge; N.Y., Chemical Pub. Co., 1938. 311p. $7. **P48**

Perol Guerrero, Antonio. Nuevo diccionario técnico-comercial. Brooklyn, N.Y., Editorial Técnica Unida, 1942. 600p. $10. **P49**

Subtitle: Contiene más de 50,000 vocablos indispensables en ingeniería, eléctrica, mécanica, química y naval, radio, minería, industria textil, etc. Así como las más modernas palabras referentes a guerra mecanizada y motorizada, aviación, meterología, etc. Palabras de uso constante en el comercio y tablas de conversión de pesos y medidas del sistema métrico al inglés.

Added title page in English.

pt.1, Spanish-English; pt.2, English-Spanish; pt.3, Conversion tables of weights, measures and monetary units.

Robb, Louis Adams. Engineers' dictionary, Spanish-English and English-Spanish. 2d ed. N.Y., Wiley; Lond., Chapman and Hall [1949]. 664p. $15. **P50**

Includes over 44,000 current terms as used in the 18 American republics.

Directories

Davis, Marjorie Veith. American business directories, 2d ed., April 1947. Wash., Govt. Prt. Off., 1947. 198p. **P51**

A classified and annotated list of business and industrial directories, including many on technical and engineering subjects.

For full description *see* L435.

MacRae's Blue book, America's greatest buying guide and Hendricks' Commercial register. Chic., MacRae's Blue Book Co. [1895?]- . Annual. $15; foreign $20. **P52**

Title varies.

Sweet's Catalog Service. Sweet's Catalog file. N.Y., Sweet's Catalog Division of F. W. Dodge Corp., 1914- . Annual. **P53**

Consists of six separately bound files of manufacturers' catalogs: for architecture, engineering, process industries, mechanical industries, power plants, product designers.

Thomas' Register of American manufacturers. N.Y., Thomas Pub. Co., [190-?]- . Annual. $15. **P54**

Title varies.

1948 in four volumes: v.1-2, Product classifications, A-Z; v.3, A-Z Alphabetical list; Trade names, brands, etc.; International trade section, Boards of trade, and other commercial organizations, leading trade papers; v.4, Index, Product finding guide to contents, v.1-3.

There is also a small, abridged edition known as *Thomas' Register, jr.*

Societies

See also Societies and Congresses, p.258.

Engineering societies yearbook for 1948- , the periodical reference book on engineering socie-ties, clubs and councils in the United States and Canada; joint, national, regional, state, local. N.Y., Amer. Soc. of Mechanical Engineers, 1948- . v.1- . $3. **P55**

National Research Council. Handbook of scientific and technical societies and institutions of the United States and Canada. 5th ed. Wash., 1948. 371p. **P56**

For full description *see* N44.

Yearbooks

International industry yearbook, the encyclopedia of industrial progress, 1948- . ed. by Lloyd J. Hughlett. N.Y., Kristen-Browne Pub. Co., 1948- . il. $10; $7.50 to libraries. **P57**

A new yearbook which hopes to present annual surveys of "the technological progress achieved in the various fields of engineering and industry." The first volume summarizes the developments of about the last five years. Separate chapters are devoted to each of the major industries, e.g., chemicals, communications, electronics, food-packing, mining, paper and pulp industry, paint, varnish and lacquer industries, and many more. Each chapter is written by a specialist and includes a bibliography of pertinent literature, to which statements in the text are keyed. Subject index.

Biography

Who's who in engineering; a biographical dictionary of the engineering profession, 1922/23- . N.Y., Lewis Hist. Pub. Co., 1922- . v.1- . $10. **P58**

Subtitle varies. Editions issued for 1922/23, 1925, 1931, 1937, 1941, 1948.

The sixth edition, 1948, contains approximately 16,000 names.

Patents

See also Patents, p.274.

Hohendorff, Elsa von. Bibliography of journals, books, and compilations (American and foreign) which list and abstract patents. Balt., Special Libraries Assoc., 1936. 70p. $1. **P59**

Reprinted from *Journal* of the Patent Office Society Oct. 1935–Feb. 1936.

Annotated.

Severance, Belknap. Manual of foreign patents. Wash., Patent Office Soc., 1935. 161p. **P60**

Arranged by country, describing the patent publications; periodicals, specifications, abridgments, indexes, etc., as they apply to each.

See also Roberts, *Guide to technical literature* p.28-34 (P4).

U. S. Patent Office. Official gazette, 1872- . Wash., Govt. Prt. Off., 1872- . v.1- . il. $16 per yr.; annual index $19.50. **P61**

Weekly; contains brief advance descriptions and simple drawings of the patents, trade-marks, designs and labels, issued each week; and decisions of the Commissioner of Patents and of United States courts in patent cases.

———— General index, 1872–75. Wash., Govt. Prt. Off., 1872–76. 4v.

Continued by the following:

———— Annual report of the Commissioner of Patents, 1876–1925. Wash., Govt. Prt. Off., 1873–1927. il. $2 per yr. **P62**

Forms an annual index to the *Official gazette* (P61) and to the *Specifications and drawings of patents* (1871–1912).

Contents, 1925: (1) alphabetical list of patentees; (2) alphabetical list of registrants of trade-marks; (3) alphabetical list of trade-mark applicants published for opposition; (4) alphabetical list of registrants of labels; (5) alphabetical list of registrants of prints; (6) alphabetical list of disclaimers; (7) alphabetical list of inventions; (8) classified list of trade-marks registered; (9) classified list of trade-mark titles published for opposition; (10) alphabetical list of labels registered; alphabetical list of prints registered; (11) list of disclaimers arranged by inventions.

Continued by the following:

———— Index of patents issued from the United States Patent Office, 1920- . Wash., Govt. Prt. Off., 1921- . v.1- . Annual. **P63**

The indexes for 1920–25 are included also in the *Annual report of the Commissioner of Patents;* 1926 on issued only in this separate form.

Contents vary somewhat but include alphabetical list of patentees and one of inventions.

———— Index of trade-marks issued from the United States Patent Office, 1927- . Wash., Govt. Prt. Off., 1928- . v.1- . Annual. (1947, $1.50 pa.; $3 cloth) **P64**

Standards

American Society for Testing Materials. Book of A.S.T.M. standards, including tentative standards (a triennial publication). 1939- . Phila., Society, 1939- . il. **P65**

1942–46 "issued with only a two-year interval."

Number of parts varies. 1946 in five parts: pt.IA, Ferrous metals; pt.IB, Nonferrous metals; pt.II, Nonmetallic materials—constructional; pt.IIIA, Nonmetallic materials—fuels, petroleum, aromatic hydrocarbons, soaps, water, textiles; pt.IIIB, Nonmetallic materials—electrical insulation, plastics, rubber, shipping containers, paper, adhesives.

Supersedes *A.S.T.M. standards* and *A.S.T.M. tentative standards.*

Now kept up to date by annual supplements to each of the five parts.

———— A.S.T.M. methods of chemical analysis of metals. Recommended practices for apparatus and reagents, analytical procedures for ferrous and non-ferrous metals, spectrochemical analysis methods. Phila., Society, 1946. 402p. diagrs. $4.50. **P66**

British Standards Institution. Yearbook, 1937- . Lond., Institution, 1937- . **P67**

Title varies: 1937—July 1941, *Handbook of information.* The *Yearbook* contains lists of British standards in numerical order, and a subject index. Kept up to date by *Monthly information sheets.*

U. S. Bureau of Standards. Standards and specifications for metals and metal products, nationally recognized standards and specifications for ores, metals, and manufactures, except machinery, vehicles and electrical supplies. . . . Prepared by George A. Wardlaw, under the direction of A. S. McAllister, chief of the Division of Specifications. Wash., Govt. Prt. Off., 1933. 1359p. il. (Misc. pub. no.120) $3. **P68**

———— Standards and specifications for non-metallic minerals and their products. Prepared by John Q. Cannon, Jr., under the direction of A. S. McAllister. . . . Wash., Govt. Prt. Off., 1930. 680p. il. (Misc. pub., no.110) $2.75. **P69**

U. S. National Bureau of Standards. Publications of the Bureau of Standards complete from the establishment of Bureau (1901) to June 30, 1947. Wash., Govt. Prt. Off., 1948. 375p. (Its Circular 460) 75c. **P70**

Includes brief abstracts.

———— National directory of commodity specifications.

For record *see* L343.

Recipes

Bennett, Harry. Chemical formulary; a collection of valuable, timely, practical commercial formulae and recipes for making thousands of products in many fields of industry. v.1-8. Brooklyn, N.Y., Chemical Pub. Co., 1933–48. (In progress) (v.8, $7) **P71**

———— Cumulative index for v.1-6. 1944. 164p. $4.

The index gives names and addresses of firms that handle the materials.

Hiscox, Gardner Dexter. Henley's Twentieth century book of formulas, processes and trade secrets . . . containing 10,000 selected household, workshop and scientific formulas, trade secrets, chemical recipes, processes and money saving ideas for both the amateur and professional worker. 1945. Rev. and enl. ed. by Prof. T. O'Conor Sloane. . . . N.Y., Henley, 1945. 867p. (i.e., 871p.) **P72**

Frequently issued with slight changes. Title varies.

Hopkins, Albert Allis. Scientific American cyclopedia of formulas, partly based upon the 28th ed. of Scientific American cyclopedia of receipts, notes and queries. 15,000 formulas. N.Y., Munn, 1911. 1077p. **P73**

1932 repr. N.Y., Scientific Am. Pub.

AERONAUTICAL ENGINEERING

General works

Bibliography

Boffito, Giuseppe. Biblioteca aeronautica italiana illustrata. Precede uno studio sull' aeronautica nella letteratura, nell' arte e nel folklore. Firenze, Olschki, 1929. cxvp., 544p. il. **P74**

—— —— Primo supplemento decennale (1927–1936) con aggiunte all' intera "Biblioteca" e appendice sui manifesti aeronautici del Museo Caproni in Milano descritti da Paolo Arrigoni. Firenze, Olschki, 1937. 678p. il.

A comprehensive bibliography on the history of aeronautics. Arranged alphabetically with analytical indexes to names and subjects. Contents are given for many periodicals. The *Supplement* gives biographical notes about many of the authors.

Brockett, Paul. Bibliography of aeronautics. Wash., Smithsonian Inst., 1910. 940p. (Smithsonian misc. coll., v.55) **P75**

An important bibliography of almost 13,500 titles, arranged alphabetically by author or title, including books and pamphlets and indexing the articles in nearly 200 periodicals. Covers the period up to July 1909.

Continued by: U.S. National Advisory Committee for Aeronautics, *Bibliography of aeronautics. See* below (P79).

Dennis, Willard Kelso. An aeronautical reference library; a selected list of technical books essential to aeronautical library. N.Y., Special Libraries Assoc., 1943. 31p. $1. **P76**

A basic list giving prices of approximately 800 titles selected for an aeronautical reference library at an initial cost of about $2600. Selected with the help of 18 cooperating librarians.

—— —— Supplement. . . . East St. Louis, Ill., W. K. Dennis, 1944. 30 l.

New York. Public Library. History of aeronautics; a selected list of references to material in the New York Public Library, comp. by William B. Gamble. N.Y., Public Library, 1938. 325p. (Repr. from the Bulletin of the N.Y. Public Library Jan. 1936–Sept. 1937) **P77**

A classed list of over 5500 entries to books and periodical articles in many languages, with indexes of authors and subjects.

U. S. Library of Congress. Division of Aeronautics. Checklist of aeronautical periodicals and serials in the Library of Congress, prepared by Arthur G. Renstrom. Wash., 1948. 129p. **P78**

Includes 1585 separate titles and represents 52 countries. An expansion of an earlier list of which two sections appeared: *Aeronautical periodicals—Serials in the Library of Congress:* (1) United States (1936); (2) British Empire (1938).

U. S. National Advisory Committee for Aeronautics. Bibliography of aeronautics, 1909–1932. Wash., Govt. Prt. Off., 1921–36. v.1-14. $6.75. **P79**

v.1, 1909–16, 1493p. $2; v.2, 1917–19, 494p. 75c; v.3, 1920-21, 448p. 35c; v.4-14 (annual volumes), 1922–32.

A continuation, on the same plan, of the basic bibliography by Brockett noted above (P75).

U. S. Works Progress Administration. Bibliography of aeronautics . . . comp. from the Index of aeronautics of the Institute of the Aeronautical Sciences. N.Y., 1936–41. [pt.1, 1938] pts. 1-50 and suppl. to pts. 1- . **P80**

Published under the sponsorship of the N.Y. City Dept. of Docks with the cooperation of the Institute of Aeronautical Sciences. Prepared by workers under the supervision of the U.S. Works Progress Administration and the Federal Works Agency, Work Projects Administration for the City of New York.

Contents: (1) Air transportation; (2) Meteorology; (3) Insurance; (4) Dynamics of the airplane; (5) Seaplanes; (6) Flying boats; (7) Amphibians; (8) Autogiros; (9) Helicopters; (10) Cyclogiros, Gyroplanes; (11) Medicine; (12) Landing gears; (13) Refueling in flight; (14) Tailless airplanes; (15) Airplane catapults; (16) Airplane carriers; (17) Diesel aircraft engines; (18) Laws and regulations; (19) Control surfaces; (20) Slots and flaps; (21) Blind flight, automatic pilot, ice formation; (22) Radio; (23) Airships; (24) Air mail; (25) Air navigation; (26) Flight instruments; (27) Aircraft propellers; (28) Fuels; (29) Lubricants; (30) Aerial photography; (31) Metal construction of aircraft; (32-33) Engines, 2v.; (34) Engines—by manufacturer; (35) Engine parts and accessories; (36) Engine instruments; (37) Airports; (38) Skin friction and boundary flow; (39) Stress analysis; (40) Helium; (41) Comfort in aircraft; (42) Plastic materials; (43) Metals and light alloys; (44) Airways; (45) Wind, tunnels and laboratories; (46) Gliding and soaring; (47) Women in aeronautics; (48) Parachutes; (49) Rocket propulsion; (50) Stratospheric flight.

—— —— Supplements to pts. 1-17, 21, 24, 28, 29, 37, 48-50. N.Y., 1938–41.

—— —— Alphabetical list of aeronautical bibliographies with subject contents, pts. 1-50. Issued
in cooperation with the Institute of Aeronautical
Sciences. N.Y., 1941. 50 numb. l.

CURRENT

Aeronautical engineering index. 1947- . N.Y.,
Inst. of the Aeronautical Sciences, 1947- . $3.
P81

Index to literature reviewed in *Aeronautical engineering review* (P82).

Aeronautical engineering review. v.1- . Easton,
Pa., Inst. of Aeronautical Sciences, 1942- . v.1-
. Monthly. il. $3 per yr. **P82**

Includes annotated bibliographies of books, abstracts,
of periodical articles, special bibliographies, articles, etc.
Continues the aeronautical review section of the *Jour-
al of the aeronautical sciences,* which from Nov. 1940
to March 1942 issued bibliographies on special subjects
revised and brought up-to-date from the fifty volume
bibliography of Aeronautics." (P80)

Technical data digest. Dayton, Ohio. Semimonthly to 1942; monthly, 1943- . **P83**

More than 50 scientific periodicals supply abstracts of
articles in advance of publication.

Yearbooks

American aviation directory: Aviation officials
and companies, United States, Canada, Latin
America, Africa, Europe, and Australasia. Wash.,
Amer. Aviation Publications, 1940- . v.1- .
semiannual. $5 per v. **P84**

Subtitle varies.
Lists carriers, companies, manufacturers, equipment
sources, publications, organizations, government agencies,
etc. Index of personnel.

Aviation annual of 1944- , ed. by Reginald M.
Cleveland and Frederick P. Graham. N.Y.,
Doubleday, 1943- . v.1- . il. Annual. $5 per v.
P85

Includes survey articles on American civil and mili-
ary aviation; directory of aviation organizations and
associations; aviation books of the year.

Jane's All the world's aircraft, 1909- Lond., S.
ow, 1909- . v.1- . il. Annual. (1949/50,
6.50) **P86**

Title varies: [v.1-2] *All the world's airships;* [v.3]-19,
l the world's aircraft; v.20- , *Jane's All the world's
rcraft.*

World aviation annual, 1948- . J. Parker Van
andt, ed.-in-chief. N.Y., Aviation Research Inst.,
48- . v.1- . $17.50. **P87**

Comprehensive data on aviation for all countries of
the world, including air transport operations and com-

panies, registered aircraft, manufacturing plants, United
States aircraft with popular names, etc.

Dictionaries

Baughman, Harold Eugene. Baughman's Aviation dictionary and reference guide; aero-
thesaurus. 2d ed. Glendale, Calif., Aero Publishers, Inc. [1942]. 906p. il. $6.50. **P88**

Half title: Baughman's Aero-thesaurus; aviation dictionary and reference guide.
Dictionary of terms and abbreviations; reference sections on flying aircraft design and production; directory
information; tables.

British Standards Institution, London. British
standard glossary of aeronautical terms. (Rev.
Aug. 1940) Lond., Institution, 1940. 165p. il.
P89

At head of title: No.185—1940. Provisional ed. for
war-time use.

Jordanoff, Assen. Jordanoff's Illustrated aviation
dictionary. N.Y., Harper, 1942. 415p. il. $3.50.
P90

Defines more than 2000 aeronautical terms, each one
illustrated with a small but clear line drawing. Should
be useful particularly to the student and layman. Includes
an appendix of aviation slang, also illustrated.

Williams, Henry Lionel. Casey Jones cyclopedia
of aviation terms; comp. and arr. in cooperation
with the staff of the Acad. of Aeronautics,
LaGuardia Field, N.Y., under the supervision of
Aviation Research Associates. N.Y., McGraw-
Hill, 1946. 246p. il. $5. **P91**

Zweng, Charles Alfonso. Zweng aviation dictionary. . . . Los Angeles, pr. by Wolfer Printing
Co. [1944] 366p. il. $6. **P92**

Cover title: Encyclopedic aviation dictionary.
"Published by Pan American navigation service . . .
N. Hollywood, California."
A general dictionary of aeronautical terms, descrip-
tions of planes, short biographical sketches of a few
prominent American aviators, etc.

POLYGLOT

Ahrens, Lothar. Dictionary of aeronautics: English, French, German, Italian, Spanish. N.Y.,
Frederick Ungar [1943]. 562p. $5. **P93**

A reissue of the author's *Taschenwörterbuch Flug-
wesen fünfsprachig* (Berlin, 1939) with an English title,
published and distributed by the authority of the Alien
Property Custodian.
Classified arrangement in parallel columns with alphabetical index in each language.

Lanz, John E. Lanz aviation dictionary in nine
languages: English, Spanish, Portuguese, French,
Italian, German, Russian, Chinese [and] Japa-

nese; contributing ed., H. N. von Koerber. . . .
South Pasadena, Calif., P. D. and Ione Perkins,
1944. 430p. il. $6.50. **P94**

A useful dictionary giving definitions in simple, nontechnical language and then the translation into the other
languages. Includes charts for meteorologists, tables of
weights and measures with conversion methods, etc.

Schlomann, Alfred. Illustrierte technische Wörterbücher . . . Bd. 17, Luftfahrt, aeronautics. . . .
Berlin, Technische Wörterbücherverlag [c1932].
292p., 108p., 337p. **P95**

Bearb. unter Mitwirkung und Förderung des Reich-
verkehrsministeriums, des Deutschen Luftrates, der Wissenschaftlichen Gesellschaft für Luftfahrt, des Deutschen
Verbandes technisch-wissenschaftlicher Vereine, des Vereines deutscher Ingenieure, des Germanischen Lloyd, des
R. Ministero dell'aeronautica italiana, des Registro italiano
navale ed aeronautica, des Ministère de l'air de la République française und der Fédération aéronautique internationale.

A full dictionary of technical terms, prepared with considerable international cooperation, as American and
British authors in addition to the organizations and officers
listed above have cooperated. Includes airmen's slang as
well as technical terms. In three main parts: (1) Dictionary list arranged by the German word, followed by
the equivalent in English, French and Italian; (2) Illustrations; (3) Indexes of (a) German, (b) English, (c)
French, (d) Italian. Unlike earlier dictionaries in the
series, it does not include Spanish and Russian terms.

For description of complete set *see* P35.

FRENCH

**France Combattante. Forces Aériennes Fran-
çaises Libres.** An aeronautical dictionary in
French and English, comp. by technicians of the
Free French Air Force. Lond., Harrap, 1943.
[406]p. **P96**

Compiled for the use of the Free French Air Force
in England. Arranged by group, e.g., organization, drill,
tools and machinery, aerodynamics, flying, navigation,
radio, etc. Each group has French-English and English-
French section. French and English indexes.

JAPANESE

Gerr, Stanley. Japanese-Chinese-English dictionary of aeronautical and meteorological terms, including aero- and hydrodynamics, airplane
construction and stress analysis, propeller theory,
internal combustion engines, airports and ground
installations [and] meteorology, with a section in
kana. N.Y., Stechert [1945]. 439p. $8. **P97**

Comprises "more than 11,000 [Japanese] terms . . .
Arranged in the regular Sino-Japanese character dictionary order based on radical and stroke. This arrangement, and the fact that a good percentage . . . of all Chinese and Japanese technical terms are identical, makes it
perfectly feasible to use this book as a Chinese-English
aeronautical dictionary as well."—*Pref.*

PORTUGUESE

Nayfeld, Carlos. Dicionário aerotécnico inglês
português. [Rio de Janeiro] Ed. Leitura, 1945
331p. **P9**

Includes list of abbreviations, p.323-31.

SPANISH

Serrales, Juan K. English-Spanish and Spanish
English dictionary of aviation terms. N.Y.
McGraw-Hill, 1944. 131p. $2.75. **P9**

Intended primarily for use in the United States an
Latin America. Covers aerodynamics, electricity, h
draulics, propellers, meteorology, engines, navigatio
radio, flight, military terminology, etc.

SWEDISH

Sundström, Lennart. Flyglexikon, svensk
engelskt, engelskt-svenskt. Stockholm, Lindquis
1946. 216p. S. Kr. 4.75. **P10**

Biography

The "Aeroplane" directory of British aviatio
1949- (incorporating Who's who in British av
ation) ed. by W. C. M. Whittle. Lond., Temp
Pr., 1949- . 10s. 6d. **P1**

Guide to aviation throughout the British Empire, wi
a biographical section of over 1250 entries.

Who's who in aviation; a directory of living me
and women who have contributed to the growt
of aviation in the United States, 1942–43. Com
by the Writers' program of the W.P.A. . . . c
sponsored by the Illinois Aeronautics Commi
sion and the Chicago Aero Commission. Chi
and N.Y., Ziff-Davis, 1942. 486p. $5. **P1**

Aims to cover both civil and military aviation. Includ
officials and key employes of aircraft and instrume
manufacturing companies and airlines, officers in the
service of high rank or distinguished service, membe
and employes of the Civil Aeronautics Board and A
ministration, U.S. Weather Service, Air Mail Division
the Post Office Department, distinguished members
Early Birds and Quiet Birdmen, members of aeronaut
and meteorological faculties of universities, colleges, tec
nical schools, etc.

CHEMICAL ENGINEERING

See also Chemistry, p.268-75.

American Gas Association. Gas chemists' han
book, Jan. 1, 1929. Rev. by the Committee
Analysis, Tests and Editing, Gas Chemists' Han
book. 3d ed. N.Y., Amer. Gas Assoc. [192
795p. **P1**

Being revised by a series of handbooks of which three have been published: [v.1] Altieri, V. J. *Gas chemists' book of standards for light oils and light oil products.* 1943; [v.2] Seil, G. E. *Gas chemists' manual of dry box purification of gas.* 1943; [v.3] Altieri, V. J. *Gas analysis and testing of gaseous materials.* 1945. v.1-2, $5 ea., to members $3.50; v.3, $7.50, to members $5.

Keyes, Donald Babcock and **Deem, Arden Garrell.** Chemical engineer's manual. N.Y., Wiley, 1942. 221p. il. $2.75; college ed. $2.25. **P104**

Pacific Coast Gas Association. Gas Engineers' Handbook Committee. Gas engineers' handbook . . . reviewed by a special committee of the American Gas Association endorsed by the directors of the American Gas Association. 1st ed. N.Y., McGraw, 1934. 1017p. il. $9. **P105**

Perry, John Howard. Chemical engineers' handbook, prepared by a staff of specialists. 3d ed. rev. and enl. N.Y., McGraw-Hill, 1950. 1942p. il. (Chemical engineering ser.) $15. **P106**

Plastics

Dickinson, Thomas A. Plastics dictionary; illustrations by Joseph W. Dickinson. N.Y., Pitman, 1948. 312p. il. $5. **P107**

3500 terms defined. Includes many trade names.

Modern plastics encyclopedia, 1941- . N.Y., Plastic Catalogue Corp., 1940- . il. **P108**

Title varies: 1941, *Modern plastics catalog;* 1942–45, *Plastics catalog;* 1946- , *Modern plastics encyclopedia.*

Resins, rubbers, plastics. The science of plastics, a comprehensive source book based on the original literature for 1942–1946, ed. by H. Mark and E. S. Proskauer. . . . v.1- . N.Y., Interscience Publishers, 1948- . il. **P109**

A collection of abstracts which appeared originally in the monthly abstracting service *Resins, rubbers, plastics,* 1942- .

v.1, Physical and chemical properties of plastics. 632p. $9; v.2, to cover specific kinds of plastics.

Simonds, Herbert R., Weith, Archie J. and **Bigelow, M. H.** Handbook of plastics. 2d ed. N.Y., Van Nostrand, 1949. 1511p. il. $25. **P110**

1st ed. 1943. 2d ed. much enlarged and brought up to date.

A comprehensive work giving the chemical and physical properties of plastics, their manufacturing processes, production, and equipment. Includes a chapter on trademarks and trade-names, glossaries, conversion tables and bibliography, p.1453-63.

Society of the Plastics Industry, Inc. S P I handbook. N.Y., Soc., 1947. 451p. il. $7.50. (Members gratis) **P111**

Chapters written by specialists. Discusses and appraises various plastic materials.

CIVIL ENGINEERING
General works

American civil engineers' handbook; ed.-in-chief, Thaddeus Merriman; associate ed.-in-chief, Thos. H. Wiggin. 5th ed., thoroughly rev. and enl. N.Y., Wiley; Lond., Chapman, 1930. 2263p. il. $9; 40s. **P112**

Follows closely the plan of the first four editions, edited by Mansfield Merriman, but is revised throughout and reset, with considerable new material.

Urquhart, Leonard Church. Civil engineering handbook. 3d ed. N.Y., McGraw-Hill, 1950. 1002p. il. $8.50. **P113**

Dictionaries

Bodson, Fernand. Dictionnaire des termes récents, symboles et abbréviations; architecture, art de construire, génie civil. Bruxelles, Editec S.P.R.L., 1948. 244p. 300 fr. **P114**

For terms gives etymology, definition and description, and, in many cases, references to source or usage.

Mosqueira Roldán, Salvador. Diccionario ingles-español de ingeniería civil, contiene más de nueve mil vocables de ingeniería civil incluyendo términos compuestos, ordenados en la forma más fácil para consulta rápida. Mexico, Ed. M. C. Huerta, 1942. 328p. **P115**

Highways

Road abstracts, v.1, 1934/35- . Lond., 1935- . Monthly. 15s. per yr. **P116**

Comp. by the Dept. of Scientific and Industrial Research and the Ministry of War Transport; issued by the Institution of Municipal and County Engineers (in cooperation with the Institution of Civil Engineers, v.4-).

Issued as a supplement to the *Journal* of the Institution of Municipal and County Engineers.

Blanchard, Arthur H. American highway engineers' handbook. N.Y., Wiley, 1919. 165p. o.p. **P117**

Harger, Wilson Gardner and **Bonney, Edmund A.** Handbook for highway engineers, containing information ordinarily used in the design and construction of rural highways. 4th ed., rev. and enl. N.Y., McGraw, 1927. 1721p. il. $8. **P118**

Railroads

See also Transportation and Communication, p.181-82.

Association of American Railroads. Mechanical Division. Car builders' cyclopedia of American

practice. 17th ed. 1946. N.Y., Simmons-Boardman, 1946. 1444p. il. $6. **P119**

Subtitle: Definitions and typical illustrations of railroad and industrial cars, their parts and equipment; cars
built in America for export to foreign countries; descriptions and illustrations of shops and equipment employed
in car construction and repair.

1st ed., *Car builders' dictionary*, 1879.

—— Locomotive cyclopedia of American practice. 13th ed. 1947. N.Y., Simmons-Boardman,
1947. 1418p. il. **P120**

Subtitle: Definitions and typical illustrations of steam,
turbine, electric and Diesel locomotives for railroad and
industrial service; their parts and equipment; also locomotives built in America for operation in foreign countries—including a section on locomotive shops and engine
terminals.

1st ed. 1906.

**Railway engineering and maintenance cyclo-
pedia;** an authoritative manual of engineering,
maintenance and signaling, including definitions,
descriptions, illustrations and methods of use of
the materials, equipment and devices employed
in the construction and maintenance of tracks,
bridges, buildings, water-service, signals and
other fixed railway properties and facilities. 6th
ed. 1945. Ed., C. Miles Burpee [and others],
comp. and ed. in cooperation with the American
Railway Engineering Association and the Signal
Section, Association of American Railroads. Chic.,
Simmons-Boardman, 1945. 1294p. il. $7. **P121**

Röll, Victor von. Enzyklopädie des Eisenbahnwesens. 2. Aufl. Berlin, Urban und Schwarzen-
burg, 1912–23. 10v. il. **P122**

Includes many technical articles. For full description
see L391.

Biography

Who's who in railroading in North America.
1946 (11th) ed. N.Y., Simmons-Boardman, 1946.
780p. $8.50. **P123**

Prior to 1930, known as the *Biographical directory of
railway officials of America.* 9th ed., 1930; 10th ed.,
1940. The eleventh edition includes some 5700 sketches.

Structural

Dingman, Charles Francis. Estimating building
costs. 3d ed. N.Y., McGraw-Hill, 1944. 401p.
$3.50. **P124**

Hool, George Albert and **Johnson, N. C.** Handbook of building construction; data for architects,
designing and constructing engineers, and contractors. Comp. by a staff of fifty specialists. 2d
ed. N.Y., McGraw-Hill, 1929. 2v. il. $11. **P125**

Kidder, Frank Eugene and **Parker, Harry.** Kid-
der-Parker architects' and builders' handbook;
data for architects, structural engineers, contractors, and draughtsmen . . . comp. by a staff of
specialists and Harry Parker, ed.-in-chief. 18th
ed., enl. N.Y., Wiley; Lond., Chapman, 1931.
2315p. il. $8.50; 48s. **P126**

American Institute of Steel Construction. Steel
construction; a manual for architects, engineers
and fabricators of buildings and other steel structures. 5th ed. N.Y., Institute, 1947. 432p. il.
P127

Wood

Hansen, Howard James. Timber engineers' handbook. N.Y., Wiley; Lond., Chapman and Hall,
1948. 882p. il. $10. **P128**

"An attempt to bring under one cover the latest information necessary to the design of wood structures."—
Pref.

**U. S. Forest Service. Forest Products Laboratory,
Madison.** Wood handbook, basic information on
wood as a material of construction with data for
its use in design and specification. (Slightly rev.,
June 1940) Wash., Govt. Prt. Off., 1940. 326p.
il. 35c. **P129**

Glossary, p.3–9; Standard lumber abbreviations, p.95–
97. Includes bibliographies.

ELECTRICAL ENGINEERING
General works
Bibliography

**American Institute of Electrical Engineers. Li-
brary.** Catalogue of the Wheeler gift of books,
pamphlets and periodicals in the Library of the
American Institute of Electrical Engineers, ed.
by W. D. Weaver. N.Y., Inst., 1909. 2v. **P130**

Now consolidated into the Engineering Societies' Library, New York.

Mottelay, Paul Fleury. Bibliographical history
of electricity and magnetism chronologically arranged. Lond., Griffin, 1922. 673p. il. **P131**

Subtitle: Researches into the domain of the early sciences, especially from the period of the revival of scholas-
ticism, with biographical and other accounts of the most
distinguished natural philosophers throughout the Middle
Ages.

**Special Libraries Association. Electrical Engi-
neering Committee.** A bibliography of electrical
literature, current sources and reference books
comp. by the Electrical Engineering Committee

of the Commercial-Technical Group, Special Libraries Association. . . . Providence, R.I., Special Lib. Assoc., 1928. 62p. (Contribution from the Department of Electrical Engineering. Serial no.62. June, 1928) 50c. **P132**

On cover: Vol. 63, no.90. Pub. serial 563. Publications from the Massachusetts Institute of Technology.

—— Bibliography of bibliographies in electrical engineering, 1918–1929; ed. by Katharine Maynard. Providence, R.I., Special Lib. Assoc., 1931. 156p. (Special Lib. Assoc. Information bull. 11) $1.50. **P133**

The present list is in the nature of a somewhat expansive supplement to the *Bibliography of electrical literature: current sources and reference books,* published by the Committee in 1928.—Cf. *Pref.*

Abstracts

Elektrotechnische Berichte, unter Mitwirkung des Verbandes deutscher Elektrotechniker E. V. Berlin, Springer, 1937- . 1. Bd.- . Semimonthly. **P134**

Signed abstracts in German covering more than 300 German and foreign publications. Titles are given in original language with translation into German. Subject and author indexes to each volume.

Science abstracts: Section B, Electrical engineering abstracts. v.1- , 1898- . Ed. and issued by the Institution of Electrical Engineers, in association with the Physical Society, the American Physical Society, the American Institute of Electrical Engineers. Lond., Spon; N.Y., Spon and Chamberlain, 1898- . v.1- . Monthly. 35s. a yr. **P135**

1898–1902 title reads: *Science abstracts. Physics and electrical engineering.* 1903- issued in two sections: A, Physics; B, Electrical engineering. Beginning with 1941, titles of sections changed to *Physics abstracts* and *Electrical engineering abstracts.* Sponsoring societies vary.
Signed abstracts. Titles of foreign articles translated into English.

Handbooks

Abbott, Arthur L. National electrical code handbook. 6th ed. N.Y., McGraw-Hill, 1947. 633p. $4. **P136**

Based on the 1946 edition of the National Electrical Code (adopted as 1947 code).

Pender, Harold and **Del Mar, William Arthur.** Electrical engineers' handbook. Prepared by a staff of specialists. 4th ed. N.Y., Wiley, 1949–50. 2v. il. (Wiley engineering handbook ser.) $8.50 per v. **P137**

3d ed. 1936.

Contents: v.1, Electric power; v.2, Electric communication and electronics, Harold Pender and Knox McIlwain, eds. Each volume complete in itself.

Standard handbook for electrical engineers, prepared by a staff of specialists; Archer E. Knowlton, ed.-in-chief. 8th ed. rev. and enl. N.Y., McGraw-Hill, 1949. 2311p. il. $12. **P138**

A standard, authoritative handbook with good bibliographies.

Creager, William Pitcher and **Justin, J. D.** Hydroelectric handbook. 2d ed. N.Y., Wiley, 1950. 1151p. il. $12.50. **P139**

1st ed. 1927.
This edition thoroughly revised and new sections added.

Croft, Terrell Williams. American electricians' handbook; a reference book for practical electrical workers. 6th ed., rev. by C. C. Carr. N.Y., McGraw-Hill, 1948. 1788p. il. $6. **P140**

Checked and revised in accordance with the National Electrical Code, 1947 ed.
New section added on use of electron tubes and circuits in industry—new material on control generators, electronic control of motors, automatic electric drive control, etc.

Illuminating Engineering Society. I.E.S. lighting handbook; the standard lighting guide. 1st ed. N.Y., Soc., 1947. v.p. il. **P141**

Includes: Reference Division, Fundamentals of illuminating engineering; Application Division, Current practice in lighting; Manufacturers' data, Information on lighting equipment, supplied by the makers; and a complete alphabetical index to all sections.

Dictionaries

American Institute of Electrical Engineers. American standard definitions of electrical terms. Approved American Standards Association, August 12, 1941, Canadian Engineering Standards Association, March 2, 1942. N.Y., Institute, 1942. 311p. $1. **P142**

Stubbings, George Wilfred. Dictionary of heavy electrical engineering, containing definitions and concise explanations of the most important technical terms relating to the theory and practice of heavy electrical engineering. 2d ed. Lond., Spon, 1948. 225p. il. 10s. 6d. **P143**

1st ed. 1945 had title: *Dictionary of electrical engineering.*

Thali, Hans. Technical dictionary of terms used in electrical engineering, radio, television, electrical communication including the most usual terms of acoustics, illumination, mathematics, materials, mechanics, optics, thermodynamics,

etc. Hitzkirch (Lucerne), Thali, 1947–48. v.1-2.
P144

v.1, 2d ed.; v.2, 1st ed.
v.1, English-German-French, 277p.; v.2, Deutsch-Englisch-Französisch, 311p.
Added title page in German and French. Title varies slightly.

Radio
Bibliography

Electronic engineering master index; a subject index to electronic engineering periodicals, Jan. 1925 to June 1945, ed. by Frank A. Petraglia. 1st annual ed., 1945. N.Y., Electronics Research Pub. Co., 1945. 318p. $17.50. **P145**
pt.1, Jan. 1925–Dec. 1934; pt.2, Jan. 1935–June 1945. Contains approximately 15,000 entries arranged by subject.

—— July 1945–Dec. 1946. 1947. 202p.
Contains some 7500 new entries from more than 85 periodicals (including foreign) in the electronics and allied engineering fields. The subject index is to both volumes.

Electronic engineering patent index. A compilation of electronic engineering patents issued during 1946- by the U.S. Patent Office. N.Y., Electronics Research Pub. Co., 1946- . Annual. $14.50. **P146**
The first volume records over 2000 patents as given in the *Official gazette* of the U.S. Patent Office.

Handbooks

Henney, Keith. The Radio engineering handbook. 4th ed. N.Y., McGraw-Hill, 1950. 1197p. il. $10. **P147**

Federal Telephone and Radio Corporation. Reference data for radio engineers. 2d ed. N.Y., Corporation, 1946. 322p. il. **P148**

Terman, Frederick Emmons. Radio engineers' handbook. 1st ed. N.Y., McGraw-Hill, 1943. 1019p. il. $7. **P149**
Thorough and comprehensive. Extensive footnotes serve as bibliography.

Rider, John Francis. Perpetual trouble shooter's manual. v.1- . N.Y., Rider, 1933- . il. **P150**
Loose-leaf. Continuously revised.
Each volume arranged alphabetically by manufacturers giving descriptions of all radios, current diagrams and parts lists for all radio sets.

—— —— Master index, v.1-15.

Strichartz, M. H. Marine radio manual. N.Y., Cornell Maritime Pr., 1944. 518p. il. $4. **P151**

Manly, Harold Phillips and **Gorder, L. O.** Drake's Cyclopedia of radio and electronics; a reference and instruction book; 12th ed. Chic., Drake, 1946. [764]p. il. $6. **P152**
Subtitle: Radio, sound systems, television, photo-electricity, electronic tubes, electronics in industry.

Westinghouse Electric Corporation. Industrial electronics reference book, by electronics engineers. . . . N.Y., Wiley, 1948. 680p. il. $7.50. **P153**
A comprehensive manual.

Rider, John Francis. Television manual. v.1- . N.Y., Rider, 1948- . **P154**
Loose-leaf.
A new service compiled on the same principles as the radio manual listed above (P150).

Radio amateur's handbook. 1st ed.- . West Hartford, Conn., Amer. Radio Relay League, 1926- . il. Annual. $2 per v. **P155**
Good handbook for the layman, revised annually.

Dictionaries

Cooke, Nelson Major and **Markus, John.** Electronics dictionary; an illustrated glossary of over 6,000 terms used in radio, television, industrial electronics, communications, facsimile, sound recording, etc. 1st ed. N.Y., McGraw-Hill, 1945. 433p. il. $5. **P156**
Well-selected terms with clear, accurate definitions suitable for the student and engineer. Includes abbreviations. Good illustrations.

Heimbürger, Boris. Radio vocabulary; German, English, Russian, Swedish, Finnish. N.Y., Stechert-Hafner, 1948. 458p. $14.50. **P157**

Regen, Bernard R. and **Regen, Richard R.** German-English dictionary for electronics engineers and physicists with a patent-practice vocabulary. 1st ed. Ann Arbor, Mich., Edwards, 1946. 358p. $6. **P158**
"Contains nearly 21,000 entries, representing most of the terminology current in 1939 and an appreciable number of terms introduced during the war years."—*Pref.*

MARINE ENGINEERING
General works
Handbooks

Hughes, Charles H. Handbook of ship calculations, construction and operation; a reference book for naval architects, marine engineers, ship and engine draftsmen, deck officers, and others engaged in the building and operating of ships.

d ed. N.Y., McGraw-Hill, 1942. 558p. il. $5.50. **P159**

ane's Fighting ships, 1898- . Lond., S. Low, 898- . v.1- . Annual. **P160**

Title varies: 1898–1904, *All the world's fighting ships;* 905–15, *Fighting ships;* 1916- , *Jane's Fighting ships.* Pictures, descriptions, plans of naval ships of all coun-ries.

abberton, **John Madison** and Marks, **Lionel S.** Marine engineers' handbook; prepared by a staff f specialists . . . with the general engineering undamentals reproduced from *Mechanical engi-eers' handbook.* 1st ed. N.Y., McGraw-Hill, 945. 2013p. il. $8. **P161**

)sbourne, **Alan.** Modern marine engineer's man-ial. N.Y., Cornell Maritime Pr., 1941–43. 2v. il. .1, $6; v.2, $4. **P162**

Dictionaries

American Association of Port Authorities. Com-mittee on Standardization and Special Research. A port dictionary of technical terms. New Or-eans, Amer. Assoc. of Port Authorities, 1940. 208p. $1.50. **P163**

Based on the *Port glossary,* compiled by Dr. R. S. Mc-Clwee for the Association's Committee on Technical Language, 1927.—Cf. *Foreword.*
Contains over 1000 definitions.

Eddington, **Walter J.** Glossary of shipbuilding and outfitting terms. N.Y., Cornell Maritime Pr., 943. 435p. il. $3.50. **P164**

A comprehensive dictionary of practical maritime terms y a member of the U.S. Maritime Commission. Includes ppendixes giving lists of deck department, engine room nd machine tools, tables and other data.

Kerchove, **Rene de.** International maritime dic-ionary; an encyclopedic dictionary of useful mar-time terms and phrases, together with equiva-ents in French and German. N.Y., Van Nostrand, 948. 946p. il. $10. **P165**

A comprehensive dictionary including terms with clear, oncise definitions relating to seamanship, commercial hipping, maritime law, ship construction, insurance, avigation, meteorology, commercial fisheries, nautical in-truments, etc. Describes characteristics of native or local raft from all parts of the world. French and German quivalents are given for most terms and there are French nd German indexes at the back. Occasional biblio-raphical references.

Accademia d'Italia. Dizionario di marina, medie-ale e moderno. Roma, Accad. d'Italia, 1937. 366p. il. (Its Dizionari di arti e mesteri, 1) **P166**

A very full dictionary of Italian terms with definitions, ften of some length, in Italian, some bibliographical eferences and many illustrative plates.

An appendix (p.1237-1360) includes additional terms, additional meanings, and cross references.

MECHANICAL ENGINEERING
General works
Handbooks

Camm, **Frederick James.** Newnes Engineer's reference book. 4th ed. Lond., Newnes, 1949. 1608p. il. 45s. **P167**

A standard handbook from the English point of view.

Colvin, **Fred Herbert** and Stanley, **Frank A.** American machinists' handbook and dictionary of shop terms; a reference book of machine-shop and drawing-room data, methods and definitions. 8th ed. rev. and enl. N.Y., McGraw-Hill, 1945. 1546p. il. $6. **P168**

Kent, **William.** Mechanical engineer's handbook, prepared by a staff of specialists. 12th ed. N.Y., Wiley, 1950. 2v. il. (Wiley engineering hand-book ser.) $8.50 per v. **P169**

Contents: v.1, Design and production, ed. by Colin Carmichael; v.2, Power, ed. by J. Kenneth Salisbury.

Machinery's Handbook for machine shop and drafting-room; a reference book on machine de-sign and shop practice for the mechanical engi-neer, draftsman, toolmaker and machinist by Erik Oberg and F. D. Jones. 1st ed.- . N.Y., Industrial Pr.; Lond., Machinery Pub. Co., 1914- . il. (14th ed. 1949, $7) **P170**

A frequently revised standard handbook.

Marks, **Lionel Simeon.** Mechanical engineers' handbook; 4th ed. N.Y., McGraw-Hill, 1941. 2274p. il. $10. **P171**

A standard handbook in its field.

Tool engineers handbook; a reference book on all phases of planning, control, design, tooling and operations in the mechanical manufacturing in-dustries. Frank W. Wilson, ed.-in-chief. N.Y., McGraw-Hill, 1949. 2070p. il. $15. **P172**

Automotive

Dierfeld, **Benno Reinhold.** Autodictionaer, drei-sprachen Wörterbuch des Kraftfahrwesens. 2. erw. Aufl. Zürich, Scientia Ag., 1938–40. v.1-4. **P173**

Volume 2 has imprint: Lond., Massie, 1938.
Contents: (1) Autodictionaer. Deutsch-Französisch-Englisch; (2) Motor dictionary. English-French-German; (3) Auto-dictionnaire. Français-Anglais-Allemand; (4) Motor dictionary. English-Spanish-Portuguese.

Dyke, Andrew Lee. Dyke's Automobile and gasoline engine encyclopedia. 20th ed. Chic., Goodheart, Wilcox, 1943. 1244p., 111p. il. $6. **P174**

Subtitle: The elementary principles, construction, operation and repair of automobiles, gasoline engines and automobile electric systems; including trucks, tractors, motorcoaches, automotive Diesel engines, aircraft engines and motorcycles; simple, thorough, and practical.

SAE handbook, 1926- . N.Y., Society of Automotive Engineers, 1926- . Annual (slightly irregular). **P175**

A standard handbook.

Heating and Ventilating

Heating, ventilating, air conditioning guide, v.1- , 1922- . N.Y., Amer. Soc. of Heating and Ventilating Engineers, 1922- . il. Annual. (1948, $7.50) **P176**

Includes a technical data section of reference material on designs and specifications, a manufacturers' catalog data section, the roll of membership of the society, and complete indexes to technical and catalog data sections.

Heating and Ventilating's Engineering databook; selected tables and charts for supplying engineers and contractors with essential data on the design, operation and maintenance of equipment and systems for air conditioning, refrigeration, piping, heating, air sanitation and ventilation in buildings; by Clifford Strock. 1st ed. N.Y., Industrial Pr., 1948. [570p.] il. $7. **P177**

Refrigeration

American Society of Refrigerating Engineers. The Refrigerating data book and catalog. 1st ed.- . 1932/33- . N.Y., Soc., 1932- . il. (6th ed. 1949, $7) **P178**

6th ed. 1949 published in two volumes: v.1, (basic volume) The Refrigerating data book (treating of theory and equipment); v.2, Refrigeration applications (called 2d ed.; 1st ed. was published 1940, with the 4th ed. of the data book).

A comprehensive handbook with up-to-date material on new developments and practices in refrigeration and air-conditioning. Chapters are written by specialists. Includes glossary and index.

Welding

American Welding Society. Welding handbook, prepared under the direction of the Welding Handbook Committee. 3d ed. N.Y., Society, 1950. 1651p. il. $12. **P179**

This edition reset, much revised and with new material added. Includes bibliographies.

The Welding encyclopedia completely rev. and re-ed. by T. B. Jefferson (originally comp. and

ed. by L. B. Mackenzie) . . . 12th ed. N.Y. Welding Engineer Pub. Co., 1947. 1024p. il. $6 **P18**

Frequently revised. The encyclopedic section is a alphabetical listing of welding terms with definitions an descriptions of equipment, methods, etc. Also include dictionary of some 2000 trade-names with names an addresses of manufacturers.

MILITARY AND NAVAL ENGINEERING
General works

Alten, Georg von. Handbuch für Heer un Flotte, Enzyklopädie der Kriegswissenschafte und verwandter Gebiete, unter Mitwirkung vo zahlreichen Offizieren Sanitätsoffizieren, Beamten, Gelehrten, Technikern, Künstlern, usw. Berlin, Bong, 1909–14. v.1-6, 9, 9a. il. **P18**

v.1-6, A-Österreich; v.9, Kriege vom Altertum bis zu Gegenwart; v.9a, Kriege (Karten zu Bd.9).

Contains definitions, French and English equivalent and encyclopedic articles, some with bibliographie Many biographical articles, including sketches of me still living when the work was published.

Armaments year-book, general and statistical in formation, 1st-15th. 1924–1939/40. Geneva 1924–40. 15v. il. **P18**

Published by the League of Nations. Also in Frenc under title *Annuaire militaire.* No more published.

Franke, Herman. Handbuch der neuzeitliche Wehrwissenschaften. Berlin, de Gruyter, 1936 39. v.1-3 in 4. il. **P18**

Contents: Bd.1, Wehrpolitik und Kriegführung; Bd. Das Heer; Bd.3, 1. T., Die Kriegsmarine, 2. T., Die Luf waffe.

Each volume arranged alphabetically, with signe articles, bibliography, maps, and illustrations, some co ored.

U. S. Engineer Dept. Index to the reports of th chief of engineers, U.S. Army (including the re ports of the Isthmian Canal commissions, 1899 1917) 1866–1917. . . . Wash., Govt. Prt. Off., 1915 21. 3v. maps. (63d Cong., 2d sess. House do 740; 66th Cong., 2d sess. House doc. 724) **P18**

Contents: v.1, 1866–1912, Rivers and harbors; v. 1866–1912, Fortifications, bridges, Panama canal, etc v.3, 1913–1917, Supplement.

Foreign terms

Azevedo Lima, Alexandre de. Nautical term termos nauticos; in English and Portuguese, en inglez e portuguez . . . 2d ed., rev., extended an improved throughout. Rio de Janeiro, Imp. Nava 1939. 2v. **P18**

v.1, English-Portuguese; v.2, Portuguese-English.

Creswell, Harry Innes Thornton, Hiraoka, Junzo and Namba, Ryozo. A dictionary of military terms, English-Japanese, Japanese-English. American ed. Chic., Univ. of Chic. Pr. [1942]. 1226 col., 175 col. $7. **P186**

American edition published 1942.

Planographed reproduction of the original edition, published in Tokyo in 1937.—Cf. *Pref. notice.*

Gives English definition, romanization of Japanese words and Japanese characters. Appendixes include: English military abbreviations; Japanese military abbreviations; Grades of military officers and men, Japanese, British and American; List of orders and medals, Japanese, British and American; Tables of money, weights and measures.

Czechoslovak Republic. Ministerstvo Národní Obrany. Studijní Skupina. Army and air force technical dictionary. English-Czech. Cesko-anglický. Vojensko-technický slovník. Lond., pub. by the Research Dept. of the Czechoslovak Ministry of National Defence by Evans Bros., 1942. 206p. il. **P187**

trom, Hans. Wörterbuch für die Waffen-, Munitions- und Sprengstoff-Industrie, unter Einschluss des Kriegsbedarfes, von Hans Strom; unter Mitarbeit der Herren A. F. Stoeger, Jr. . . . Jules Michaux, U. W. Baldi, W. Boehm. Deutsch-nglisch-französisch-italienisch-spanisch. 2. Aufl. uhl, Hans Strom [1939]. 440p. **P188**

Reissued with English title, *Dictionary of ordnance terms* (N.Y., Ungar, 1944).

U. S. War Dept. Military Dictionary Project. Military dictionary. Wash., Govt. Prt. Off., 1941–4. 7v. (U.S. War Dept. Technical manuals, TM 30-250, 30-253, 30-254, 30-255, 30-257, 30-541, 30-533) **P189**

Contents: English-Spanish, Spanish-English, 1941, 33p., 199p. 50c; English-French, French-English, 1943, 43p. o.p.; English-Russian, Russian-English, 1941. 10p. 65c; English-German, German-English, 1941. 99p. 75c; English-Portuguese, Portuguese-English, 1941. 33p., 190p. 45c; Japanese-English, English-Japanese, 044. 615p. $1; Chinese-English, English-Chinese, 044. 415p. 55c.

Portuguese section also published with title *Diccionario militar* (Brooklyn, N.Y., Ed. Tecnica Unida, 1942).

The first five volumes called "Advance installments."

MINING AND METALLURGY
General works
Guides

mbach, Richard. How to find metallurgical formation. Pittsburgh, Author, 1936. 32p. $1. **P190**

A handbook and bibliography.

Bibliography

American Society for Metals. A.S.M. review of metal literature; an annotated survey of articles and technical papers appearing in the engineering, scientific and industrial journals and books here and abroad, received in the Library of the Batelle Memorial Institute, Columbus, Ohio. v.1, 1944- . Cleveland, Soc., 1945- . Annual. $15. **P191**

Classified with author and subject indexes. Titles of articles are given in the original language, followed by translation into English. The reviews were originally published monthly in the *Metals review.*

Crane, Walter Richard. Index of mining engineering literature, comprising an index of mining, metallurgical, civil, mechanical, electrical and chemical engineering subjects as related to mining engineering. N.Y., Wiley, 1909–12. 2v. **P192**

Covers American and English material with some Australian and Canadian works, including periodicals, society transactions and some government reports. Volume 1 indexes 18 publications covering 30 years to the end of 1907; volume 2 brings up to date the periodicals indexed in that volume and indexes several additional titles, giving complete indexing for 26 periodicals and incomplete indexing for 20 other serials and 20 books. Classified arrangement with alphabetical index by subjects. No author indexes. A special feature is the section of references on cost.

Materials and methods; the metalworking industries' engineering magazine, v.1, July 1929- . N.Y., Reinhold Pub. Co., 1929- . **P193**

Title varies: 1929—Sept. 1945, *Metals and alloys.*

Includes section *Materials and methods digest* (title varies: 1929–39, called *Metallurgical abstracts;* 1940–45, called *Metallurgical engineering digest*). Since Oct. 1945, has had title *Materials and methods digest* and is much reduced in size.

—— Cumulative index of metallurgical abstracts published in Metals and alloys, v.1-2, July 1929—Dec. 1931, v.3-5, 1932–34. 1931–35. 2v.

Continued by annual indexes.

Metallurgical abstracts (general and non-ferrous) n.s. v.1- . Lond., Inst. of Metals, 1934- . Annual. **P194**

Issued monthly as a supplement to the *Journal* of the Institute of Metals (1931–33). A classified abstracting service of material in all languages. Titles of foreign articles are translated into English.

U. S. Bureau of Mines. List of publications . . . complete from establishment of the bureau 1910 to June 30, 1937, with subject and author index. Wash., Govt. Prt. Off., 1938. 356p. **P195**

—— —— Supplement, July 1, 1937 to December 31, 1942, with subject and author index. Wash., Govt. Prt. Off., 1943. 157p.

Kept up to date by annual and monthly supplements.

Handbooks

American Foundrymen's Association. Cast metals handbook. 1944 ed. Chic., Assoc., 1944. 745p. il. $6.   **P196**

Covers cast steel, malleable iron, cast iron and nonferrous alloys. Includes bibliographies.

Hoyt, Samuel L. Metals and alloys data book. N.Y., Reinhold, 1943. 334p. il. $4.75.   **P197**

Contains 340 tables of properties and data on wrought and cast steels, stainless steel, cast irons, heat- and corrosion-resistant casting alloys and nonferrous alloys. Designed especially for metallurgists, industrial designers and others working with metals.

Liddell, Donald Macy. Handbook of non-ferrous metallurgy prepared by a staff of specialists. 2d ed. N.Y., McGraw-Hill, 1945. 2v. il. v.1, $6.50; v.2, $7.   **P198**

v.1, Principles and processes; v.2, Recovery of the metals.

—— Metallurgists' and chemists' handbook; a reference book of tables and data for the student and metallurgist. 3d ed., rev. and enl. N.Y., McGraw-Hill, 1930. 847p. il. $6.   **P199**

Lippert, T. W. 10,000 trade names. 1st ed. N.Y., Iron Age, 1947. 112p.   **P200**

Subtitle: All American and foreign ferrous and nonferrous metals and alloys, plastics, non-metals, refractories, cements, lubricants, chemicals, plywoods, machine tools, small tools, rolling mills, cranes, bearings, joining devices and other equipment made and used by the metals industry. Also processes, proprietary and otherwise, in the production, shaping, treating and finishing of metals.

Metals handbook. 1948 ed. Prepared under the direction of the Metals Handbook Committee, ed. by Taylor Lyman. Cleveland, Amer. Soc. for Metals, 1948. 1444p. il. $15.   **P201**

Comprehensive and reliable. This edition thoroughly revised.

Peele, Robert and **Church, John A.** Mining engineers' handbook, written by a staff of forty-six specialists ... 3d ed. N.Y., Wiley, 1941. 2v. il. (Wiley engineering handbook ser.) $16.   **P202**

The standard handbook for mining engineers. This edition has been thoroughly revised and several sections completely rewritten, noting new methods and equipment. Includes bibliographies.

Taggart, Arthur F. Handbook of mineral dressing; ores and industrial minerals. N.Y., Wiley, 1945. [1926p.] il. $15.   **P203**

Supersedes his *Handbook of ore dressing* (1927).

Uhlig, Herbert H. The Corrosion handbook; ... sponsored by the Electrochemical Society, Inc. N.Y., Wiley, 1948. 1188p. il. $12.   **P204**

Woldman, Norman Emme and **Metzler, Roger J.** Engineering alloys; names, properties, uses. [2d ed.] [Cleveland, Amer. Soc. for Metals, 1945] 801p. tables. $10.   **P205**

Dictionaries

Fay, Albert Hill. Glossary of the mining and mineral industry. Wash., Govt. Prt. Off., 1920. 754p. (U.S. Bureau of Mines. Bull. 95) Repr. without change, 1947. $1.75.   **P206**

Contains about 20,000 terms, including technical and purely local terms relating to metal mining, coal mining, quarrying, petroleum, and natural gas, and metallurgical works, names of minerals and rocks and geological terms, many terms relating to ceramics and the clay industry, glass making, foundry practice, railway and building construction, etc., and chemical terms relating to metallurgical practice. Definitions are given with sufficient fullness, with reference to authorities, and in case of local terms indication of the place where used.

Merlub-Sobel, Menahem. Metals and alloys dictionary. ... Brooklyn, N.Y., Chemical Pub. Co., 1944. 238p. $4.50.   **P207**

Brief definitions of metallurgical terms mainly relating to American practice. Includes composition, properties and uses of commercial alloys. Intended for the layman as well as the technologist.

Rolfe, Robert Thatcher. Dictionary of metallography. Lond., Chapman and Hall, 1945. 242p. 15s.   **P208**

Fewer terms and longer definitions than the Merlub-Sobel (P207). From the English point of view.

Tieman, Hugh Philip. Iron and steel (a pocket encyclopedia) including allied industries and sciences. 3d ed. N.Y., McGraw-Hill, 1933. 590p. il.   **P209**

Still standard in its field. An alphabetically arranged glossary with definitions and encyclopedic articles.

FOREIGN TERMS

Freeman, Henry. Fachwörterbuch der Metallurgie (Eisen-und Metallhütten Kunde). Leipzig, Spamer, 1933–34. 2v.   **P210**

T.1, Deutsch-Englisch; T.2, English-German.

Halse, Edward. Dictionary of Spanish, Spanish-American, Portuguese and Portuguese-American mining, metallurgical and allied terms. 3d ed. containing an enlarged English-Spanish-Portuguese suppl. Lond., Griffin; Phila., Lippincott, 1926. 447p. il. 15s.; $7.50.   **P211**

Seebach, Hans Jobst von. Fachwörterbuch f. Bergbautechnik und Bergbauwirtschaft. Dictiory for mining engineering and economics. Essen, Glückauf, 1947. 311p. **P212**

pt.1, German-English; pt.2, English-German.

Singer, Tibor Eric Robert. German-English dictionary of metallurgy, with related material on ores, mining and minerals, crystallography, welding, metal-working, tools, metal products, and metal chemistry. 1st ed. N.Y. and Lond., McGraw-Hill, 1945. 298p. $4.50. **P213**

Directories

Mines register; successor to the Mines handbook and the Copper handbook, describing the non-ferrous metal mining companies in the western hemisphere. N.Y., Mines Register, 1900- . v.1- . **P214**

Title varies. A directory of mines in North, South, and Central America, foreign mines, mining company officials, etc.

Mining year book, with which is incorporated the Mining manual. v.1- . Lond., Skinner, 1887- . **P215**

62nd year, 1948. 2v. 30s.
Title varies.
Records mining and mining finance companies throughout the world. Includes a list of mining engineers, mangers, etc., and a buyers' guide.

Standard metal directory. 11th ed. 1948/49. N.Y., Standard Metal Directory, 1949. 999p. $15. **P216**

Lists iron and steel plants, foundries, metal rolling mills, metal smelters and refiners, steel rolling mills, scrap iron and metal dealers, etc. Frequently revised.

PETROLEUM ENGINEERING

General works

Bibliography

DeGolyer, Everette Lee and **Vance, Harold.** Bibliography on the petroleum industry. College Station, Texas. 1944. 730p. il. (Bulletin no.83. School of Engineering, Texas Engineering Experiment Station) **P217**

A bibliography combining one of some 12,000 items comp. by Dr. DeGolyer, with the bibliography of the Petroleum Engineering Dept. at the A. and M. College of Texas, and a bibliography on the Air-Gas Lift prepared by S. F. Shaw. Arranged by a decimal system of classification devised by Prof. L. C. Uren of the University of California with an alphabetical subject index.

Hardwicke, Robert Etter. Petroleum and natural gas bibliography. Austin, Univ. of Texas, 1937. 37p. $2. **P218**

A classified listing of some 14,000 items including books, pamphlets, etc., and also "references to all articles, notes and comments relating to petroleum and natural gas appearing in legal periodicals published in the United States." Author index.

U. S. Bureau of Mines. Bibliography of petroleum and allied substances in 1915–22/23. Wash., Govt. Prt. Off., 1918–29. 7v. (Bull. 149, 165, 180, 189, 216, 220, 290) **P219**

Supplemented until 1933 by a monthly mimeographed list, "Recent articles on petroleum and allied substances."

Dictionaries and handbooks

American Petroleum Institute. Petroleum facts and figures. 8th ed. N.Y., Inst., 1947. 236p. il. $2. **P220**

Revised at irregular intervals.

Giddens, Paul H. The beginnings of the petroleum industry: Sources and bibliography. Harrisburg, Pa., Pa. Hist. Commission, 1941. 195p. il. **P221**

"Bibliography on the beginnings of the petroleum industry to 1871," p.87-172.

Leven, David D. Petroleum encyclopedia, "Done in oil"; ed. and rev. by Sylvain J. Pirson. N.Y., Ranger Pr., 1942. 1084p. il. $10. **P222**

Subtitle: The cavalcade of the petroleum industry from a practical economic and financial standpoint; history, past and present, sciences, drilling operations, production, transportation, refining, marketing, finance, investments, oil royalties, regulation of securities and securities markets, taxation, glossary.

1st ed. 1941, published under title, *Done in oil.*

A comprehensive manual and treatise, primarily from the economic point of view. Glossary, p.961-1002.

Petroleum almanac; a statistical record of the petroleum industry in the United States and foreign countries. N.Y., National Industrial Conference Board, 1946- . **P223**

Production, transportation, refining, marketing, finances, taxation, regulation, labor, history.

Petroleum data book. 1st ed.- . Official sourcebook of information for the world's oil and gas industry. H. J. Struth, ed.; J. P. Love, asst. ed. Dallas, Texas, Petroleum Engineer Pub. Co., 1947- . il. Annual. $15. **P224**

Porter, Hollis Paine. Petroleum dictionary for office, field and factory. 4th ed. Houston, Texas, Gulf Pub. Co., 1948. 326p. $6. **P225**

An enlarged edition of a standard work now including some 4600 terms dealing with the prospecting, producing, and refining of petroleum.

Zaba, Joseph and **Doherty, W. T.** Practical petroleum engineers' handbook. 3d ed. rev. and

enl. Houston, Texas, Gulf Pub. Co., 1949. 654p.
il. $10. **P226**

Atlases

World oil atlas. . . . Houston, Texas, World oil,
1946- . Annual. **P227**

Published as a section of *World oil*.
1946–47 published by *The Oil weekly;* title changed in
1948 to *World oil*.
"Up-to-date maps and statistical data dealing with the
oil industry's activities in every part of the world."—
Foreword to 1948.

AGRICULTURE
General works
Bibliography and indexes

International Institute of Agriculture. Library.
Catalogue systématique: Classified catalogue.
Rome, European Regional Office, 1948. 2747p.
P228

The catalog of a large and comprehensive collection
arranged by the Universal Decimal Classification. Subjects
are given in French. There is an alphabetical index of
subjects and one of authors (including main entries).

International Institute of Agriculture. Decennial
index of publications issued by the International
Institute of Agriculture (1930–1939). Rome, 1942.
55p. **P229**

Includes a classed list of all monographs, yearbooks
and periodicals published during 1930–39; an author and
title index to the articles published in the *International
review of agriculture* (English ed.); and a subject index
to both sections.

Niklas, Hans and **Hock, A.** [and others]. Litera-
tursammlung aus dem Gesamtgebiet der Agrikul-
turchemie. . . . Leipzig, Helingsche Verlagsanstalt, 1931–39. 5v. **P230**

Publisher varies.
Added title page, v.1-3, A bibliographical list of the
entire domain of agricultural chemistry.
Contents: (1) Bodenkunde; (2) Bodenuntersuchung;
(3) Pflanzenernährung; (4) Düngung und Düngemittel;
(5) Ergänzungsband zu Bd.4.

Agricultural index, subject index to a selected list
of agricultural periodicals and bulletins, 1916- .
N.Y., Wilson, 1919- . v.1- . (In progress)
Service basis. **P231**

Issued monthly, cumulating at intervals, the September number being the annual cumulation for the year,
except that every third year the annual volume is omitted
and a 3-year cumulation, constituting a new volume in
the permanent set, is issued instead. Until 1939 the cumulations covered the calendar year.
Detailed alphabetical subject index to agricultural and
related periodicals and to many reports, bulletins and
circulars of agricultural departments, experiment stations,

etc. Most of the periodicals are in English, includin
American, British and colonial publications, but there ar
also a few journals in foreign languages. A record c
new books and book reviews is included and the whol
forms a useful index for subjects in agriculture, horti
culture and rural life.

U. S. Office of Experiment Stations. Experimen
station record. Sept. 1889–1946. Wash., Gov
Prt. Off., 1890–1948. 95v. Monthly. $1.25 per v.
foreign $2. **P23**

Discontinued.

——— ——— General index, v.1-70, 1889–1934
Wash., Govt. Prt. Off., 1903–37. 6v.

1889–1901, v.1-12, 671p. o.p.; 1901–11, v.13-25
1159p. o.p.; 1912–19, v.26-40, 640p. 75c; 1919–24, v.41
50, 709p. $1.25; 1924–29, v.51-60, 677p. 60c; 1929–34
v.61-70, 752p. 75c.
A record and digest of current agricultural literatur
not planned as an index of the subject but covering th
field so fully that it serves practically as an index to th
periodical, bulletin, and report material on this subjec
in English and the principal foreign languages. Eac
monthly number contains a digest of recent importar
articles and reports with exact reference to the fu
article. There are no cumulations of the digests, bu
there is an author and subject index to each volume refe
ring to the monthly issues and the general indexes liste
above. Less easy to use for quick reference than th
Agricultural index (P231), but fuller for scientific us
as it indexes more scientific material and includes foreig
language material as well as English.

U. S. Dept. of Agriculture. Library. Bibliograph
of agriculture. v.1- , July 1942- . Wash
1942- . Monthly, 6-month cumulated autho
and subject indexes. $6 per yr; $8 per yr. foreig
P23

A classified bibliography designed to list all currer
publications, domestic and foreign, in the field of agr
culture. Now includes some 80,000 titles annually.
Volumes 1-2 issued monthly in six sections, coverin
Agricultural economics and rural sociology, Agricultur
engineering, Entomology, Plant science, Forestry, an
Food processing and distribution. Beginning with th
issue for July 1943, volume 3, number 1, Sections A-
were combined and issued as a single monthly publicatio
with cumulated author and subject indexes. The scop
was broadened to include human nutrition, animal indu
try, soils and fertilizers, and other agricultural subjects.
Supersedes: *Agricultural economics literature; Currer
literature in agricultural engineering; Entomology curre
literature; Plant science literature; Forestry current liter
ture; List of agricultural experiment station publication*

U.S. DEPT. OF AGRICULTURE
LISTS AND INDEXES

❦ The U.S. Department of Agriculture has been
prolific publisher of material on all phases of agricu
ture and much valuable information may be foun
in its various publications. Some of the lists and i
dexes which help to make this material available ar

U. S. Dept. of Agriculture. List by titles of publications of the U.S. Department of Agriculture from 1840 to June, 1901, inclusive. Comp. and compared with the originals by R. B. Handy and Minna A. Cannon. Wash., Govt. Prt. Off., 1902. 16p. (Div. of Pub. Bull. no.6) **P234**

—— List of publications of the U. S. Department of Agriculture from January, 1901, to December, 1925, inclusive; comp. by comparison with the originals by Mabel G. Hunt . . . supplementary to Bull. no.6, Division of Publications, issued in 1902 but duplicating that list for months of January—June, 1901. Wash., Govt. Prt. Off., 1927. 182p. (Misc. pub. 9) **P235**

Continued by 5-year supplements as follows: 1926–30. 1932; 1931–35. 1936; 1936-40. 1941. (Misc. pub. 63, 252, 443)

—— Index to authors with titles of their publications appearing in the documents of the U.S. Department of Agriculture, 1841–1897, by George F. Thompson. Wash., Govt. Prt. Off., 1898. 303p. (Div. of Pub. Bull. no.4) **P236**

—— Index to publications of the U. S. Dept. of Agriculture, 1901–40, ed. by Mary A. Bradley. Wash., Govt. Prt. Off., 1932–43. 4v. **P237**

1901–25. 2689p. $3.25; 1926–30. 694p. $1.50; 1931–35. 518p. $1.25; 1936–40. 763p. $1.50.

Zimmerman, Fred Lyon and Read, Phyllis Rogers. Numerical list of current publications of the U.S. Dept. of Agriculture, comp. by comparison with the originals. . . . Wash., Govt. Prt. Off., 1941. 929p. (U.S. Dept. of Agriculture. Misc. pub. 450) $1.75. **P238**

U. S. Superintendent of Documents. List of publications of the agricultural department, 1862–1902, with analytical index. Wash., Govt. Prt. Off., 1904. 623p. (Bibliography of United States public documents. Dept. list no.1) **P239**

Annual reports

U. S. Dept. of Agriculture. Index to the annual reports of the U.S. Department of Agriculture for the years 1837 to 1893 inclusive. Wash., Govt. Prt. Off., 1896. 252p. (Div. of Pub. Bull. no.1) **P240**

Bulletins

U. S. Dept. of Agriculture. Index to department bulletins, nos. 1-1500; by Mabel G. Hunt. Wash., Govt. Prt. Off., 1936. 384p. **P241**

Department bulletins ceased publication, continued by technical bulletins. For index see P242.

—— Index to technical bulletins, nos. 1-750; by Mabel G. Hunt. Wash., Govt. Prt. Off., 1937–41. 2v. **P242**

No.1-500. 1937. 249p.; no.501-750. 1941. 169p.

—— Index to farmers' bulletins, nos. 1-1750. . . . Wash., Govt. Prt. Off., 1920–41. 3v. **P243**

[v.1], Index to bulletins, nos. 1-1000, prepared by C. H. Greathouse; [v.2], Index to bulletins nos. 1001-1500, comp. by M. G. Hunt; [v.3], Index to bulletins nos. 1501-1750, comp. by M. H. Doyle.

Reports of the statistician

U. S. Dept. of Agriculture. Synoptical index of the reports of the statistician, 1863 to 1894, by George F. Thompson. Wash., Govt. Prt. Off., 1897. 258p. (Div. of Pub. Bull. no.2) **P244**

Agricultural experiment stations

U. S. Dept. of Agriculture. List of bulletins of the agricultural experiment stations from their establishment to the end of 1920. Wash., Govt. Prt. Off., 1924. 186p. (Its Bull. 1199) **P245**

"A list of approximately 12,500 of the 17,500 or more publications of the State experiment stations (including those of Alaska and the insular possessions) from 1875 to 1920, inclusive."

Continued by biennial supplements: Bull. 1199, suppl. 1, 2, 3; Misc. pub. 65, 128, 181, 232, 294, 362, 459; Bibliographical bull. no.4, covers 1941/42 (pub. 1944).

Other bureaus

U. S. Bureau of Plant Industry. Library. Check list of publications issued by the Bureau . . . 1901–20, and by the divisions and offices which combined to form this Bureau, 1862–1901. Wash., Govt. Prt. Off., 1921. 127p. (Dept. of Agriculture. Library. Bibliog. contrib. no.3) **P246**

—— Contents of and index to bulletins of Bureau . . . nos. 1-100, by J. E. Rockwell. 1907. 102p. (Its Bulletin 101)

U. S. Bureau of Chemistry and Soils. Index of publications of the Bureau of Chemistry and Soils, originally the Bureau of Chemistry and the Bureau of Soils. 75 years, 1862–1937. Wash., 1939. v.1. **P247**

v.1, Chronological lists of titles grouped by divisions with general author index, prep. by H. P. Holman, V. A. Pease and others.

PERIODICALS

Pan American Union. Division of Agricultural Cooperation. Tentative directory of agricultural periodicals, societies, experiment stations, and schools in Latin America. Wash., Union, 1945. 90p. **P248**

Stuntz, Stephen Conrad. List of the agricultural periodicals of the United States and Canada published during the century July 1810 to July 1910, ed. by Emma B. Hawks. Wash., Govt. Prt. Off., 1941. 190p. (U.S. Dept. of Agriculture. Misc. pub. no.398) 20c. **P249**

Gives title, place of publication, frequency, volumes and inclusive dates, change of name, consolidations, etc. Lists 3375 journals, not counting changes of title.

Abbreviations

U. S. Dept. of Agriculture. Abbreviations used in the Department of Agriculture for titles of publications, by Carolyn Whitlock. Wash., Govt. Prt. Off., 1939. 278p. (Misc. pub. no.337) 30c. **P250**

Supersedes Department Bulletin 1330, *Abbreviations employed in Experiment station record for titles of periodicals,* by F. A. Bartholow.

Dictionaries and encyclopedias

Bailey, Liberty Hyde. Cyclopedia of American agriculture; a popular survey of agricultural conditions, practices, and ideals in the United States and Canada. N.Y., Macmillan, 1907–09. 4v. il. **P251**

v.1, Farms; v.2, Crops; v.3, Animals; v.4, Farm and community, Biographies.

Contains signed articles by specialists, with bibliographies. Not alphabetically arranged. Excellent when first issued but not now up to date.

A "new edition" issued 1917 was a reprint with no change in text. In 1922, volume 2, Crops, and volume 3, Animals, were reissued, with no change in text, but with new title pages and prefaces, as separate books, under the titles *Cyclopedia of farm crops* and *Cyclopedia of farm animals.*

—— Standard cyclopedia of horticulture. N.Y., Macmillan, 1914–17. 6v. il. (reissue, 1947, in 3v. $35) **P252**

Subtitle: A discussion, for the amateur, and the professional and commercial grower, of the kinds, characteristics and methods of cultivation of the species of plants grown in the regions of the United States and Canada, for ornament, for fancy, for fruit and for vegetables; with keys to the natural families and genera, descriptions of the horticultural capabilities of the states and provinces and dependent islands, and sketches of eminent horticulturists.

Founded upon his *Cyclopedia of American horticulture* (4v., 1902–04), but so revised and enlarged as to be practically a new work. Aims to cover completely the horticultural floras of the continental United States and Canada and to include the more outstanding species grown in a horticultural way in Puerto Rico, Hawaii, and the other islands. The last volume includes also supple-

mentary articles, a finding list of binomials, and a general index. Includes biographies. Signed articles by specialists, bibliographies.

Special features to be noted are: (1) the very comprehensive inclusion of American native plants, trees and shrubs, which makes the work useful for questions in botany; (2) the full indexing of illustrations, both black-and-white and colored, included in many other works, e.g., periodicals, collections, etc.

—— and **Bailey, Ethel Zoe.** Hortus second; concise dictionary of gardening, general horticulture and cultivated plants in North America. N.Y., Macmillan, 1941. 778p. $6. **P25**

"New ed., rev. and reset, April 1941." First edition entitled *Hortus* published 1930. "Designed to account for all the species and botanical varieties of plants in cultivation in the continental United States and Canada in the decade ending midyear 1940, together with brief directions on uses, propagation and cultivation." Includes common names, descriptive terms and definitions, inventories of families of plants, etc.—Cf. *Pref.*

Bezemer, Tammo Jacob. Dictionary of terms relating to agriculture, horticulture, forestry, cattle breeding, dairy industry and apiculture, in English, French, German and Dutch. Balt., William and Wilkins, 1935. 267p., 248p., 250p., 294p. **P25**

Black's Gardening dictionary, ed. by E. T. Ell … with contributions by the leading gardening experts and specialists of our time. 2d ed. Lond., Black, 1928. 1237p. 7s. 6d. **P25**

Popular work; gives English information and practice.

Taylor's Encyclopedia of gardening, horticulture and landscape design. Ed. by Norman Taylor. 2d ed. rev. and enl. of the Garden dictionary first published in 1936. Bost., Amer. Garden Guild and Houghton Mifflin, 1948. 1225p. il. $ **P25**

Authoritative articles written by specialists, but in language for the layman. Alphabetical arrangement, including scientific names (with pronunciation), cross references from popular names of plants and species, methods of propagation, types and methods of gardening, gardening conditions of various states and geographical locations, etc.

Hunter, Herbert. Baillière's Encyclopaedia of scientific agriculture. Lond., Baillière, Tindall and Cox, 1931. 2v. il. **P25**

"Although the subject-matter is largely concerned with British agriculture, it is applicable in its broad outline to Canada, New Zealand, Australia, and large areas of the United States of America and other countries characterized by a temperate climate."—*Pref.*

Seymour, Edward Loomis Davenport. The New garden encyclopedia; a complete practical and convenient guide to every detail of gardening incl. special supplement on Gardening for the small home; il. with 250 halftones and more than 500 line drawings made expressly for this work, written by a group of horticultural experts. . . . rev. ed.] N.Y., Wise, 1946. 1380p. il. $5.　**P258**

Published in 1936 with the title *The Garden encyclopedia*. Revised editions include corrections and additions. A useful, popular work.

White, John M. The farmer's handbook. Norman, Univ. of Oklahoma Pr., 1948. 440p. il.　**P259**

A useful handbook of ready reference on crops, farm animals, farm engineering, and other major phases of farming.

Directories

International Institute of Agriculture. Bibliothèques agricoles dans le monde et bibliothèques spécialisées dans les sujets se rapportant à l'agriculture. International directory of agricultural libraries and of libraries specialized in subjects related to agriculture. Rome, Imp. C. Colombo, 1939. 311p. $1.50; L25.　**P260**

Descriptions are given in French and English; usually include date of founding, size and subjects of collections, type of catalog, hours of opening, publications, etc.

Yearbooks

Farming and mechanised agriculture, 1945- . Lond., Todd Reference Books, Ltd., 1945- . Annual. 21s.　**P261**

A British yearbook of agriculture, giving surveys of the current situation, legislation, education, etc. Lists of organizations with descriptive statements, government departments with personnel, statistics, bibliography, and brief "Who's who."

International yearbook of agricultural statistics, 1910- . Rome, International Institute of Agriculture, 1912- . v.1- .　**P262**

Some volumes have title in French: *Annuaire international de statistique agricole.*

A statistical compilation of the first importance for figures of distribution, acreage, yield, importation and exportation, prices, census of farm animals, etc.

The *Yearbook* published in 1947 covered the war years 1941/42–1945/46 in three volumes: v.1, Agricultural production and numbers of livestock; v.2, International trade; v.3, Apportionment of areas, agricultural production and numbers of livestock in various countries.

In French and English, countries are listed in the French alphabetical order.

U. S. Dept. of Agriculture. Agricultural statistics, 1936- . Wash., Govt. Prt. Off., 1936- . Annual. Price varies. (1949, $1.75)　**P263**

Includes the statistics previously published in the *Yearbook* (P264). Covers production, foreign trade, farm capital and income, conservation, etc.

—— Yearbook of agriculture, 1894- . Wash., Govt. Prt. Off., 1895- . Annual. (1949, $2) **P264**

Title varies.

Beginning with 1936, statistics are published in a separate volume entitled *Agricultural statistics* (P263), and the *Yearbook* instead of containing brief summaries of miscellaneous developments devotes itself to particular subjects, as follows: 1936, Better plants and animals, I; 1937, Better plants and animals, II; 1938, Soils and men; 1939, Food and life; 1940, Farmers in a changing world; 1941, Climate and man; 1942, Keeping livestock healthy; 1943–47, Science in farming; 1948, Grass; 1949, Trees.

—— —— Indexes, 1894–1900, 1901–1905, 1906–1910, 1911–1915.

Census

International Institute of Agriculture. The first world agricultural census (1930). Rome, 1939. 5v. L50 per v.　**P265**

Combines the edition previously published in Bulletins 1-41. Issued also in French. v.1, Standard form; methodological study; notes on tabulation of the census results. 267p.; v.2, Austria, Belgium, Czechoslovakia, Denmark, Estonia, Finland, France. 493p.; v.3, Germany, Greece, Irish Free State, Italy, Latvia, Lithuania, Netherlands, Norway, Spain, Sweden, Switzerland, United Kingdom, England and Wales, Scotland, Northern Ireland. 590p.; v.4, Canada, United States, outlying territories and possessions of the United States, Mexico, Argentina, Chile, Peru, Uruguay. 505p.; v.5, India, Japan, Algeria, Egypt, French West Africa, Kenya, Mauritius, Mozambique, Union of South Africa, Commonwealth of Australia, New Zealand. 479p.

The census of each country was carried out by its government and reported according to the standard form issued by the Institute.

Atlases

U. S. Dept. of Agriculture. Atlas of American agriculture. Physical basis including land relief, climate, soils, and natural vegetation of the United States. Prepared under the supervision of O. E. Baker, Bureau of Agricultural Economics. Contributions from the Weather Bureau, Bureau of Chemistry and Soils, Bureau of Plant Industry, Forest Service, Bureau of Agricultural Economics. Wash., Govt. Prt. Off., 1936. 6v. in 1. il. 47cm. $17.　**P266**

Contents: Land relief, by F. J. Marschner, 1936; Climate, temperature, sunshine and wind, by Joseph B. Kincer, 1928; Climate, frost and the growing season, by William Gardner Reed, 1922; Climate, precipitation and humidity, by J. B. Kincer, 1922; Soils of the United States, by C. F. Marbut, 1935; Physical basis of agriculture, Natural vegetation, Grassland and desert shrub, by H. L. Shantz, 1924; Forests, by Raphael Zon, 1934.

History

BIBLIOGRAPHY

Edwards, Everett Eugene. Bibliography of the history of agriculture in the United States. Wash.,

Govt. Prt. Off., 1930. 307p. (U.S. Dept. of Agriculture. Misc. pub. 84) 45c.　　　　**P267**

"This bibliography is an amplification of a brief list of references prepared in the fall of 1927 for use in a course on the history of agriculture in the United States, taught in the Graduate School of the United States Department of Agriculture."—*Foreword.*

Perkins, Walter Frank. British and Irish writers on agriculture. Lymington, King, 1932. 142p.　　　　**P268**

"A bibliography of some 1300 British and Irish writers on the agriculture of the United Kingdom from the earliest printed books until, and including 1900. . . . Included are books on Agricultural Chemistry, Botany, Grasses, Weeds, Drainage, Improvements, Weights and Measures."—*Introd.*

Rothamsted Experimental Station. Library. Library catalogue of printed books and pamphlets on agriculture published between 1471 and 1840, 2d. ed. comp. by Mary S. Aslin. Aberdeen, Univ. Pr., 1940. 293p. 15s.　　　　**P269**

UNITED STATES

Bidwell, Percy Wells and **Falconer, John I.** History of agriculture in the northern United States, 1620–1860. Wash., Carnegie Inst., 1925. 512p. il. (Carnegie Inst. of Washington. Pub. no.358) (Repr. N.Y., Peter Smith, 1941. $7.50)　　**P270**

A scholarly, well-documented work covering the field of agriculture and agricultural economics in the northern states to the time of the Civil War. Includes a classified and critical bibliography with discussions of source materials, public and private records, books, periodicals, society publications, etc.

Gray, Lewis Cecil. History of agriculture in the southern United States to 1860 by Lewis Cecil Gray, assisted by Esther Katherine Thompson. Wash., Carnegie Inst., 1933. 2v. il. (Carnegie Inst. of Washington. Pub. no.430) (Repr. N.Y., Peter Smith, 1941. 2v. $7.50 ea.)　　**P271**

A companion work to the above covering all phases of agriculture and its economics in the southern states up to the time of the Civil War. Well documented. Extensive bibliography, including references to books, periodicals, newspapers and manuscripts.

FORESTRY
General works
Bibliography

Munns, Edward Norfolk. A selected bibliography of North American forestry. Wash., Govt. Prt. Off., 1940. 2v. (U.S. Dept. of Agriculture. Misc. pub. 364) 75c per v.　　　　**P272**

Classified list with author index.

Includes references to material in books, periodicals, government bulletins, etc., published in the United States, Canada and Mexico prior to 1930.

Dictionaries

Corkhill, Thomas. Glossary of wood. Lond., Nema Pr., 1948. 656p. £1 1s.　　　　**P27**

Classifies and describes all kinds of timber grown in all countries. Qualities, weights and uses are given.

Society of American Foresters, Washington, D. C. Committee on Forestry Terminology. Forestry terminology, a glossary of technical terms used in forestry, comp. and ed. by Committee on Forestry Terminology, Ralph C. Hawley, chairman. Wash., Soc. of Amer. Foresters, 1944. 84p. $2.　　　　**P27**

List of glossaries in allied sciences, p.2.

Suomalais - Ruotsalais - Saksalais - Englantilainen Metsäsanakirja . . . Finnish-Swedish-German-English forest dictionary. Toimituskunta Paavo Aro, Yrjö Ilvessalo, Erkki Laitakari, Jarl Lindfors. Helsinki, Kustannusosakeyhtiö Otava, 1944. 37p., 343 col., 51p., 65p., 76p., 6p.　　**P27**

U. S. Forest Service. Southern Forest Experiment Station. German-English dictionary for foresters, comp. by Oran Raber. Wash., Forest Service, 1939. 346p.　　　　**P27**

Yearbooks

The Forestry directory. Wash., Amer. Tree Assoc., 1924- . (1949, $3)　　　　**P27**

Title varies: 1924–33, *Forestry almanac.* Not published 1934–1942. 1943 compiled by Tom Gill and E. C. Dowling.

A comprehensive reference book on forestry activities, includes material on the U.S. Forest Service, national forests, conservation, national, regional, trade and state organizations, forestry schools, Canadian forestry, tropical forestry, industrial forestry, etc.

International yearbook of forestry statistics, 1932–1936/39. Rome, International Inst. of Agriculture, 1933–42. (In progress)　　　　**P27**

1932. 225p. L25; 1933–35, v.1, Europe and U.R.S.S. 327p. L25; v.2, America. 201p. L30; 1936–39, Africa (actually covers 1930–39). 1942. Suppl., 1943.

HOME ECONOMICS

See also Nutrition, p.326-27.

U. S. Bureau of Human Nutrition and Home Economics. Completed theses in home economics and related fields in colleges and universities of the United States, 1942/46- . Wash., 1946- . v.1- .　　　　**P27**

"The compilation is intended to supplement the list *Research in foods, human nutrition and home economics at the land-grant institutions* compiled annually by the Office of Experiment Stations . . . and the *Notes on research in home economics education* compiled by the Office of Education."

U. S. Office of Experiment Stations. Research in foods, human nutrition, and home economics at the land-grant institutions, 1935/36- . Wash., 1936- . v.1- . Annual. **P280**

Caption title. Title varies: 1935/36—1941/42, *Research in home economics at the land-grant institutions.*

1935/36–1945/46 include published works and research in progress; 1946/47- include publications only.

U. S. Office of Education. Notes on graduate studies and research in home economics and home economics education. no.1, 1934/36- . Wash., 1936- . **P281**

Compiled under the auspices of the Research Committee of the Home Economics Section of the Association of Land-grant Colleges and Universities and the Research Department of the American Home Economics Association. Title and issuing body varies.

Woman's home companion household book, ed. by Henry Humphrey. N.Y., Collier, 1948. 929p. il. $5.70. **P282**

A useful manual dealing with the various phases of home care, e.g., equipping a home, room arrangement and decoration, upholstering, housekeeping, maintenance and repair, safety, etc. Well-arranged with an alphabetical index.

MEDICINE

❧ Medical reference books often present a difficult problem in the general library because (1) they are expensive, (2) they are often so technical that they can be used intelligently only by the physician or medical student, and (3) when placed in a general collection they are sometimes misused by certain types of readers. It is therefore important to buy only the books which are actually needed, and unless the library is maintaining a special medical reference collection it is usually best not to place such books upon the open shelves. This latter restriction applies especially to the large medical encyclopedias, not to the biographical, bibliographical or historical reference books on this subject.

The titles listed here have been chosen with the general research rather than the medical library in mind. For other titles consult the *Handbook of medical library practice* (P283).

General works
Guides

Medical Library Association. A handbook of medical library practice, including annotated bibliographical guides to the literature and history of the medical and allied sciences; based on a preliminary manuscript by M. Irene Jones, comp. by a committee of the Medical Library Assoc., Janet Doe, ed. Chic., Amer. Library Assoc., 1943. 609p. il. $5. **P283**

An indispensable handbook. Chapters are by medical librarian specialists and discuss the various phases of work in medical libraries especially as they differ from other libraries. They cover the development, distribution and administration of medical libraries; periodical and book selection, and ordering; cataloging; subject headings; classification; pamphlets, pictures, maps, and microfilms; reference work, including an annotated list of reference books. This list includes about 625 items of importance in medical library work carefully described from this point of view. Items of first importance are starred. Appendixes include lists of medical libraries in the United States and abroad, expansions of medical classification schemes, and a guide to bibliographies, biographical collections and histories.

Bibliography

Callisen, Adolph Carl Peter. Medicinisches Schriftsteller-Lexikon der jetzt lebenden Aerzte, Wundärzte, Geburtshelfer, Apotheker, und Naturforscher aller gebildeten Völker. Copenhagen, [Author], 1830–45. 33v. **P284**

Contents: v.1-21, A-Z; v.22, anonymous and miscellaneous works; v.23-25, periodicals and society publications; v.26-33, Nachtrag, A-Z.

An author catalog of the works of men of all nationalities living at the time of publication, and therefore covers early nineteenth and some late eighteenth century works (including the contents of periodicals). Usually gives brief biographical notes. The catalog of periodicals covers 1780–1833 and includes medical periodicals and others containing articles of medical interest.

Hawkins, Reginald Robert. Scientific, medical and technical books published in the United States of America, 1930–1944; a selected list. Wash., 1946. 1114p. $20. **P285**

For full description *see* N10.

Reuss, Jeremias David. Repertorium commentationum a societatibus litterariis editarum. Secundum disciplinarum ordinem . . . t.10-16, Scientia et ars medica et chirurgica. Gottingae, Dieterich, 1813–21. **P286**

Contents: t.10, Propaedeutica, anatomia et physiologia, hygiene, pathologia seu nosologia generalis, semeiotica; t.11, Materia medica, pharmacia; t.12-15, Therapia generalis et specialis, A-Z; Operationes chirurgicae, Medicina forensis, legalis et politica; t.16, Ars obstetricia, Ars veterinaria.

A very valuable index to the contents of the publications of the learned societies of various countries before 1800. Classed arrangement with author indexes for each section.

For description of complete set *see* N3.

U. S. Army Medical Library. Index-catalogue of the library of the Surgeon General's Office, United States Army (Army Medical Library) authors and subjects. ser. 1-4, v.1-10. Wash., Govt. Prt. Off., 1880–1948. ser. 1-3 compl. ser. 4 in progress. **P287**

ser. 1, A-Z. 1880–95. 16v.; ser. 2, A-Z. 1896–1915. 21v.; ser. 3, A-Z. 1918–32. 10v.; ser. 4, v.1-10, A-Mez. 1936- .

A dictionary catalog, including not only books and pamphlets but also a large number of references to periodical articles and other analytics. The Army Medical Library (formerly the Surgeon General's Library) is one of the largest medical libraries of the world and this monumental catalog is therefore a very important bibliography of all aspects of the subject. Especially useful for medical biography, as it indexes a large number of biographical and obituary articles.

Announcement was made in the spring of 1950 that publication would be discontinued after the appearance of the volume then in preparation. Coverage for medical literature will be maintained for *books* by the *Army Medical Library author catalog* (P287a) and for *periodicals* by the *Current list of medical literature* (P295) and the *Quarterly cumulative index medicus* (P294).

—— Army Medical Library author catalog, 1949- . Wash., Library of Congress, 1950- . Annual. $12.50 per yr. **P287a**

For 1948, author entries for the Army Medical Library were included as a supplement in the 1948 Library of Congress *Cumulative catalog* (A30). Beginning with 1949 issued as a separate supplementary volume to the Library of Congress *Author catalog* (A30).

INCUNABULA

Boston Medical Library. A catalogue of the medieval and renaissance manuscripts and incunabula in the Boston Medical Library, comp. by James F. Ballard. Bost., priv. pr., 1944. 246p. il. $7.50. **P288**

Lists with brief bibliographical descriptions and annotations the 52 manuscripts and 674 incunabula in the library.

Klebs, Arnold Clark. Incunabula scientifica et medica; short title list. Bruges, St. Catherine Pr., 1938. [i.e., 1937] 359p. (History of medicine ser. issued under the auspices of the Library of the New York Academy of Medicine) **P289**
Reprinted from *Osiris*, v.4.

PERIODICAL ABBREVIATIONS

Kuntze, Max. Periodica medica; Verzeichnis und Titelabkürzungen der wichtigsten Zeitschriften der Medizin und ihre Grenzgebiete. 3. verm. und vollst. neu bearb. Aufl. hrsg. von Kurt Klare-Scheidegg. Leipzig, Geo. Thieme, 1937. 84p. **P290**

U. S. Army Medical Library. Alphabetical list of abbreviations of titles of medical periodicals employed in the Index-catalogue of the library of the Surgeon General's Office. . . . Wash., Govt. Prt. Off., 1895–1916. 2v. (Repr. from 1st ser. v.16; 2d ser. v.21) **P291**

Abbreviations used in the third series were published in the various volumes of the third series as additions to the list for the second series.

—— —— 4th series. (In Index-catalogue. . . . 4th ser. v.10, p.1-138, 1948 [P287])

Indexes

Index medicus, a . . . classified index of the current medical literature of the world. v.1-21, Jan. 1879—Apr. 1899; 2d ser. v.1-18, 1903–20; 3d ser. v.1-12, 1921–26. N.Y., Bost. and Wash., 1879–1927. **P292**

Editor: Jan. 1879—Apr. 1899, J. S. Billings, Robert Fletcher; 1903–11, Robert Fletcher, F. H. Garrison; 1912–22, F. H. Garrison [and others]; 1922–26, A. N. Tasker, Albert Allemann.

Publication suspended, May–Dec. 1895. The index for that period is included in the succeeding volume after that of Apr. 1896.

Ceased publication with Apr. 1899; was revived by the Carnegie Institution of Washington in Jan. 1903. During the interval a similar index, *Bibliographia medica (Index Medicus)* was published by the Institut de Bibliographie of Paris.

From 1879 to 1926 this was a standard current bibliography of medicine; a classified list with annual author and subject index. Covers publications in all principal languages and includes periodical articles and other analytical material as well as books, pamphlets and theses. Series 1-2 published monthly, series 3, quarterly.

Discontinued after 1926 and merged in the new *Quarterly cumulative index medicus* (P294).

Quarterly cumulative index to current medical literature, 1916–26. Chic., Amer. Med. Assoc., 1917–27. 12v. **P293**

An important author and subject index to nearly 300 medical periodicals and society transactions including a large amount of foreign material. Published quarterly cumulating throughout the year, the January number formed a permanent bound index to the material of the year. Each annual volume includes, in addition to the index to periodicals, a bibliography of the important new medical books of the year, exclusive of new editions, and a list of government documents on medical subjects.

In 1926 two semiannual volumes were issued instead of one annual.

Discontinued after 1926 and succeeded by the *Quarterly cumulative index medicus* (P294).

Quarterly cumulative index medicus. v.1, 1927- Chic., Amer. Med. Assoc., 1927- . v.1- . $12 per yr.; foreign $14. **P294**

Preceded by the *Quarterly cumulative index to current medical literature* (P293) and the *Index medicus* (P292).

An author and subject index to cover 1200 periodicals in many languages, forming a practically complete index to the journal literature of an important subject. Issued four times a year, the months of the issue being approximately May, August, November and February. The August issue (covering January-June) and the February issue (covering July-December) form the permanent semiannual volumes. Includes medical biography.

Includes lists of new books published during the period.

Current list of medical literature, v.1- . Wash., Army Medical Library, 1941- . v.1- . Weekly. $3 per yr. (including suppl.) **P295**

A weekly listing by subject of the contents of current medical journals. Monthly subject index since 1945. Publisher varies.

The new publication program of the Army Medical Library announced in April 1950 new plans for the *Current list.* It is to be expanded and improved so as to fill the place, for periodical analyzation, of the *Index-catalogue* of the Army Medical Library (P287) which is to be discontinued. The *List* will be issued monthly with cumulated annual indexes and will cover more than 1200 journals.

Abstract journals

See Handbook of medical library practice (P283) for lists of the many abstracting journals in medical fields published in various countries.

Excerpta medica; a complete monthly abstracting service of every article from every medical journal in the world comprising 15 sections and covering the whole field of clinical and experimental medicine. Amsterdam, Excerpta Medica, 1947- . Monthly. **P296**

sec. 1, Anatomy, anthropology, embryology and histology, v.1, Oct. 1947- ; sec. 2, Physiology, biochemistry and pharmacology, v.1, Jan. 1948- ; sec. 3, Endocrinology, v.1, Aug. 1947- ; sec. 4, Medical microbiology and hygiene, v.1, Jan. 1948- ; sec. 5, General pathology and pathological anatomy, v.1, July 1948- ; sec. 6, Internal medicine, v.1, Oct. 1947- ; sec. 7, Pediatrics, v.1, Oct. 1947- ; sec. 8, Neurology and psychiatry, v.1, Jan. 1948- ; sec. 9, Surgery, v.1, Sept. 1947- ; sec. 10, Obstetrics and gynaecology, v.1, Jan. 1948- ; sec. 11, Oto-, rhino-, laryngology, v.1, Jan. 1948- ; sec. 12, Ophthalmology, v.1, Nov. 1947- ; sec. 13, Dermatology and venereology, v.1, Apr. 1947- ; ser. 14, Radiology, v.1, June 1947- ; sec. 15, Tuberculosis, v.1, Jan. 1948- .

Encyclopedias

Nelson loose-leaf medicine; a perpetual system of living medicine, prepared under the direction of an international advisory board. N.Y., Edinburgh, Nelson, 1920- . 8v. and index. il. loose-leaf. **P297**

A loose-leaf service issuing revised pages to keep the work up to date. Replacement pages are not dated and it is advisable for libraries to date them as received. Subject index.

Oxford medicine, by various authors, ed. by Henry A. Christian and Sir James Mackenzie. N.Y. and Lond., Ox. Univ. Pr., 1920- . 7v. in 17 and index. il. **P298**

Loose-leaf; frequent revisions.

Articles written by American and English specialists, frequently revised, pages dated so that one can tell at a glance when revision was made. Good bibliographies. Index volume includes authors' names.

British encyclopaedia of medical practice, including medicine, surgery, obstetrics, gynaecology and other special subjects; under the general editorship of Sir Humphrey Rolleston. Lond., Butterworth, 1936–39. 12v. and index. **P299**

Cumulative suppl. 1939- . (Annual)
Survey and abstracts. 1939- .
The supplementary volumes survey current work and make additions to articles in main work.

Fishbein, Morris. Modern home medical adviser; your health and how to preserve it. Completely rev. and re-ed. 1942. Unabridged. Garden City, N.Y., Doubleday, 1942. 907p. il. **P300**

Dictionaries

Dorland, William Alexander Newman. American illustrated medical dictionary . . . 21st ed., rev. and enl. Phila. and Lond., Saunders, 1947. 1660p. il. $8. **P301**

Subtitle: A complete dictionary of the terms used in medicine, surgery, dentistry, pharmacy, chemistry, nursing, veterinary science, biology, medical biography, etc., with the pronunciation, derivation, and definition . . . 21st ed., with 880 illustrations, including 233 portraits. With the collaboration of E. C. L. Miller.

A standard dictionary of terms, with an approximate triennial revision.

Blakiston's New Gould medical dictionary, ed. by Harold Wellington Jones, Normand L. Hoerr, and Arthur Osol. 1st ed. Phila., Blakiston, 1949. 1294p. il. $8.50. **P302**

A newly organized dictionary based on *Gould's Medical dictionary* (5 editions, 1926–41) and its predecessors published with varying titles, 1890, 1894, and 1904.

Subtitle: A modern comprehensive dictionary of the terms used in all branches of medicine and allied sciences.

Stedman, Thomas Lathrop and **Garber, Stanley Thomas.** Stedman's Practical medical dictionary. 16th rev. ed. with etymologic and orthographic rules, ed. by Norman Burke Taylor. Balt., Williams and Wilkins, 1946. 1291p. il. $7.50. **P303**

Revised at approximately 3-year intervals.

Comrie, John Dixon. Black's Medical dictionary, rev. by William A. R. Thomson. 19th ed. Lond., Black, 1948. 995p. 25s. **P304**

The standard British dictionary, not as comprehensive as the standard American dictionaries listed above. Useful for British terminology.

FOREIGN TERMS

See also Dictionaries, p.257. In many cases the bilingual medical dictionaries are not adequate and the large general dictionaries must be consulted. *See* p.227-52.

See Handbook of medical library practice (P283) for more specialized titles.

French

Garnier, Marcel and **Delamare, V.** Dictionnaire des termes techniques de médecine, contenant: les étymologies grecques et latines, les noms des maladies, des opérations chirurgicales et obstétricales, des symptômes cliniques, des lésions anatomiques, les termes de laboratoire, etc. 14. éd. rev. et augm. par V. Delamare et J. Delamare. . . . Paris, Maloine, 1945. 909p. **P305**

Gordon, Alfred. French-English medical dictionary. Phila., Blakiston, 1921. 161p. $3.50. **P306**

German

Abderhalden, Rudolf. Medizinische Terminologie; Wörterbuch der gesamten Medizin und der verwandten Wissenschaften. Basel, Schwabe, 1948. 1214 col. **P307**

Dornblüth, Otto. Klinisches Wörterbuch, von Willibald Pschyrembel. Gegründet von Otto Dornblüth. 61. bis 84. Aufl. Berlin, de Gruyter, 1944. 805p. il. **P308**

Lang, Hugo. Lang's German-English dictionary of terms used in medicine and the allied sciences with their pronunciation; rev. and ed. by M. K. Meyers. 4th ed., enl. Phila., Blakiston [c1932]. 926p. $10. **P309**

The best of the German-English dictionaries of medical terms, including some 56,000 definitions.

Italian

Arcieri, Giovanni P. Italian-English medical dictionary. Roma, Consorzio Nazionale, 1931. 194p. **P310**

Ferrio, Luigi. Terminologia medica. 3. ed. rev. e molto ampl. Torino, Unione Tip-Ed. Toreniese, 1946. 789p. **P311**

Portuguese

Fortes, Hugo. Dicionário médico, inglês-português: contem cêrca de 18,000 palavras de uso corrente na linguagem médica inglesa. Rio de Janeiro, Gráfica olímpica, 1945. 329p. **P312**

Spanish

Cardenal Pujals, Leon. Diccionario terminológico de ciencias médicas. 3. ed. por E. Capdevila Casas. Barcelona, Salvat, 1945. 1324p. il. **P313**

1st ed. 1918; 2d ed. 1926.
Includes proper names.

Goldberg, Morris. English-Spanish chemical and medical dictionary. . . . N.Y., McGraw-Hill, 1947. 692p. $10. **P314**

Subtitle: Comprising terms employed in medicine, surgery, dentistry, veterinary, biochemistry, biology, pharmacy, allied sciences and related scientific equipment.

A very good dictionary including brief definitions in Spanish as well as Spanish equivalent.

McElligott, Maurice. Spanish-English medical dictionary. Lond., Lewis, 1946. 250p. **P315**

Directories

American and Canadian hospitals . . . 2d ed. Chic., Physicians' Record Co., c1937. 1464p. il. **P316**

Subtitle: A reference book of historical, statistical and other information regarding the hospitals and related institutions of the United States and possessions and the Dominion of Canada. Published under the supervision of American Hospital Association, Catholic Hospital Association of the United States and Canada, American Protestant Hospital Association, Canadian Hospital Council.

1st ed. 1933, ed. by J. C. Fifield.

American hospital directory, 1945- . [Chic.] Amer. Hospital Assoc., 1945- . Annual. $10. **P317**

1949 published as part 2 of the June 1949 issue of *Hospitals.*

A geographical listing of civilian hospitals, allied schools and organizations. Omits military hospitals. Includes general information about the American Hospital Association such as officers, committees, membership lists, related groups and associations, etc.

American medical directory. Chic., Amer. Med. Assoc., 1906- . v.1- . Biennial. **P318**

Subtitle: A register of legally qualified physicians of the United States, Alaska, Canal Zone, Hawaii, Philippines, Puerto Rico, Guam, Samoa, Virgin Islands, Midway Islands and Wake Island, Canada, Newfoundland, Labrador, Yukon, and Northwest Territories.

In three parts: pt.1, General information about the American Medical Association, Lists of medical schools, examining boards, hospitals approved for training interns, approved residences and fellowships, medical libraries, medical journals, medical officers of government service, medical societies, members of special societies; pt.2, Directory of physicians and hospitals arranged geographically; pt.3, Index of physicians.

Hospitals year-book, 1931- ; an annual record of the hospitals of Great Britain and Ireland incorporating "Burdett's Hospitals and charities" founded 1889. Lond., British Hospital Assoc., 1931- . v.1- . Annual. **P319**

Publisher varies.

Medical directory, 1845- . Lond., Churchill, 1845- . Annual. **P320**

Title varies.

Subtitle: London, provinces, Wales, Scotland, Ireland, abroad, navy, army and air force, temporarily registered practitioners.

Gives brief biographical sketches; includes lists of hospitals with staffs, etc.

Medical register, printed and published under the direction of the General Council of Medical Education of the United Kingdom . . . comprising the names and addresses of medical practitioners. . . . Lond., pub. for the General Medical Council by Constable, 1859- . Annual. **P321**

Subtitle varies.

Brief directory information only, consisting of address, date and place of registration, qualifications. Includes names from the Commonwealth and foreign lists.

See Strieby, "Check list of foreign directories of the medical and some allied professions, 1930–40," in Medical Library Association, *Bulletin* n.s. 28:205-18, 1940, for titles of foreign directories.

Congresses

See also Societies, p.71-73, and Societies and Congresses, p.258-59.

Stümke, Hans. Bibliographie der internationalen medizinischen Kongresse und Verbände. Leipzig, Harrassowitz, 1939. 281p. (Bibliographie der internationalen Kongresse und Verbände, Bd.1) **P322**

A very useful detailed listing of international medical congresses with record of meetings, publications, etc. For record of other projected volumes in the series *see* N48.

History

BIBLIOGRAPHY

Bibliography of the history of medicine in the United States and Canada. 1939- . (Repr. from the Bulletin of the history of medicine) Annual. **P323**

1939, prepared by the Committee on Research in the History of American Medicine of the American Association of the History of Medicine. 1940- , edited by Genevieve Miller.

Incomplete but useful for what it includes. No index.

Garrison, Fielding Hudson. A medical bibliography; a check-list of texts illustrating the history of the medical sciences, originally comp. by the late Fielding H. Garrison, and now rev. with additions and annotations, by Leslie T. Morton. . . . Lond., Grafton, 1943. 412p. 50s. **P324**

Based upon the author's "A revised students' check-list of texts illustrating the history of medicine," published in the *Bulletin* of the Institute of the History of Medicine (Balt., v.1, p.333-434, 1933).—Cf. *Introd.*

A classified list with author index of over 5500 books and periodical articles.

Kelly, Emerson Crosby. Encyclopedia of medical sources. Balt., Williams and Wilkins, 1948. 476p. $7.50. **P325**

A list of the "earliest or best" articles or books on medical discoveries and practices arranged alphabetically by the name of the author with a subject index. Information given includes full name of author, dates and identifying phrase, statement of subject, and references in full to source of article.

Mayer, Claudius F. Bio-bibliography of XVI century medical authors. Wash., Govt. Prt. Off., 1941. p.1-52. il. (In Index catalogue. . . . 4th ser. v.6. [P287]) **P326**

fasc. 1, Abarbanel-Alberti, S.

The first fascicule of a detailed bibliography of sixteenth century writers of medical works or writings by medical men, giving variant forms of authors' names, pseudonyms, etc., biographical sketch with references, list of works with descriptions and listing of all editions and translations, manuscript works and spurious works, with location of copies.

Osler, *Sir* **William.** Bibliotheca Osleriana; a catalogue of books illustrating the history of medicine and science, collected, arranged and annotated by Sir William Osler . . . bequeathed to McGill University. Ox., Clarendon Pr., 1929. 785p. 63s. **P327**

Particularly valuable for its annotations.

HISTORICAL SURVEYS

Castiglioni, Arturo. A history of medicine, tr. from the Italian and ed. by E. B. Krumbhaar. 2d ed. rev. and enl. N.Y., Knopf, 1947. 1192p. il. **P328**

Bibliography, p.1147-92.

Does not supersede Garrison (P329) but serves to supplement it and bring it up to date. Comprehensive and readable. Includes useful bibliography arranged by subject.

Garrison, Fielding Hudson. Introduction to the history of medicine, with medical chronology, suggestions for study and bibliographic data. 4th ed., rev. and enl. Phila., Saunders, 1929. 996p. il. **P329**

The most valuable reference history in English, covering the whole history of medicine from the earliest times to the 1920's. Much biography and bibliography is included for every period. Appendixes contain: chronology of medicine, bibliographies of medical biography, general medical histories and histories of special subjects in medicine.

Mettler, Cecilia Charlotte. History of medicine; a correlative text, arranged according to subjects. Phila., Blakiston, 1947. 1215p. il.　　**P330**

Arranged by subject, with "selected readings" for each chapter. Indexes of personal names and subjects.

Packard, Francis Randolph. History of medicine in the United States. 103 illustrations. N.Y., Hoeber, 1931. 2v. il.　　**P331**

Paged continuously, 1323p.

An enlargement of the author's earlier work (1901). Contains much useful reference material, in both text and illustrations, on American medical history, biography and bibliography; gives a bibliography of pre-Revolutionary medical publications, p.489-512, and a general bibliography, p.1241-66.

Biography

Biographisches Lexikon der hervorragenden Ärzte aller Zeiten und Völker, unter Mitwirkung [von] E. Albert . . . A. Anagnostakis [u.A.] und unter Spezial-Redaktion von E. Gurlt und A. Wernich, hrsg. von August Hirsch. 2. Aufl. durchgesehen und ergänzt von F. Hübotter und H. Vierordt. Berlin, Urban, 1929–35. 5v. und Ergänzungsband. ports.　　**P332**

A very valuable medical biographical dictionary, international in scope, covering physicians who had reached maturity before 1880.

Includes biographical facts, bibliography of works by, and sometimes bibliographical references for further information.

The *Ergänzungsband* includes corrections and additions to the main set.

To a large extent replaces its own first edition published 1884–88, and the *Biographisches Lexikon hervorragender Ärzte des neunzehnten Jahrhunderts* by Julius Leopold Pagel (Berlin, 1901), though occasionally these are useful for material omitted in the second edition.

Continued by:

Biographisches Lexikon der hervorragenden Ärzte der letzten 50 Jahre, hrsg. u. bearb. von I. Fischer . . . Zugleich Fortsetzung des Biographischen Lexikons der hervorragenden Ärzte aller Zeiten u. Völker. Berlin, Urban, 1932–33. 2v.　　**P333**

Serves as a continuation of the preceding set, covering the period from 1880–1930. Similar in scope, the articles are somewhat briefer.

International who's who in world medicine, 1947-　. N.Y., Amer. Universities Medical Research Publications, Inc., 1947-　. (1947, 745p., $18.50)　　**P334**

Preponderantly American. Sketches are very brief and especially for foreign entries lacking in dates. Much of the information for foreign names is almost identical with that given in *Who's who in world medicine* (1939) though dates and titles of publications given in the 1939 work are frequently omitted. Rarely includes more recent information or change of address for these names though information for American entries is more up to date.

See also the list of biographical directories in *Handbook of medical library practice,* p.491-509 (P283).

AMERICAN

American Psychiatric Association. Biographical directory of fellows and members. N.Y., Assoc., 1941. 489p. $4.　　**P335**

Contains 2405 biographical sketches, giving date and place of birth, address, professional data, languages spoken, and bibliographies.

Geographical index.

Directory of medical specialists, holding certification by American Boards, v.4. Chic., pub. for the Advisory Board for Medical Specialists, Marquis, 1949. 1182p. $14.50.　　**P336**

1st ed. 1939; 2d ed. 1942; 3d ed. 1946. Arrangement varies.

Lists nearly 29,000 specialists certified prior to July 1948 by the sixteen American boards certifying in the medical specialties. Includes brief biographical sketches arranged alphabetically, followed by statements concerning each board with their qualifications for certification and a geographical listing of their diplomates.

Kelly, Howard Atwood and **Burrage, Walter L.** Dictionary of American medical biography. N.Y., Appleton, 1928. 1364p.　　**P337**

Published in 1912 under the title *Cyclopedia of American medical biography,* and in 1920 as *American medical biographies.*

Good biographies, with bibliographies, of 2049 deceased American physicians and surgeons from Colonial days to 1927.

Although each edition includes new biographical sketches, some material is dropped from each, and therefore the earlier editions are not entirely superseded and may still need to be used.

Who's important in medicine. 1st ed., 1945-　. N.Y., Inst. for Research in Biography, 1945-　. il. $15.　　**P338**

A biographical encyclopedia of physicians, surgeons, medical educators and hospital administrators, including some 10,000 sketches. Includes the United States and Canada with some representation from Latin American republics. Nonalphabetical but with alphabetical index.

Who's who among physicians and surgeons, v.1, 1938, ed. by J. C. Schwarz. N.Y., 1938. 1336p. $15.　　**P339**

Includes biographies of who's who type for more than 12,000 medical workers in the United States and Canada. Edited by the same editor as *Religious leaders of America* (K35) and *Who's who in law* (L627). Includes many names not in *Who's who in America*.

Who's who in industrial medicine, 1948- . Chic., Industrial Medicine Pub. Co., 1948- . Biennial. $10. **P340**

Called 2d ed.

Half title: A biographical dictionary of the notable physicians and surgeons, hygienists and dentists active in industrial medical and related services.

✣ An early work which is still useful is James Thacher's *American medical biography* (1828), supplemented by *American medical biography* by Stephen Williams (1845). There are various other nineteenth century biographical dictionaries in this field, notably those by W. B. Atkinson, S. D. Gross and R. F. Stone. Full description for each in the Medical Library Assoc., *Handbook of medical library practice,* p.504-07 (P283).

BRITISH

Munk, William. Roll of the Royal College of Physicians of London; comprising biographical sketches of all the eminent physicians, whose names are recorded in the annals from the foundation of the College in 1518 to its removal in 1825 from Warwick Lane to Pall Mall east. 2d ed. rev. and enl. Lond., pub. by the College, 1878. 3v. **P341**

Plarr, Victor Gustave. Lives of the fellows of the Royal College of Surgeons of England, rev. by Sir D'Arcy Power. Bristol, Royal College; Lond., Simpkin, Marshall, 1930. 2v. **P342**

FRENCH

Wickersheimer, Ernest. Dictionnaire biographique des médecins en France au moyen âge. Paris, Droz, 1936. 2v. **P343**

Biographical notices are usually brief with bibliographical references to other material.

ITALIAN

Capparoni, Pietro. Profili bio-bibliografici di medici e naturalisti celebri italiani dal sec. xv al sec. XVIII. Roma, Ist. Naz. Medico Farmacologico "Serono," 1928-32. 2v. il. **P344**

v.1, 1932, "con correzioni ed eggiuntie." First published separately in 1925.

Biographical sketches with bibliographies and portraits.

Dentistry
Bibliography

Black, Arthur Davenport. Index of the periodical dental literature published in the English language, 1839-1936/8. Buffalo, Dental Index Bureau; Chic., Amer. Dental Assoc., 1921-39. 15v. **P345**

Volumes unnumbered and not issued in regular chronological sequence.

Contents: 1839-75, 1923; 1876-85, 1925; 1886-90, 1926; 1891-95, 1927; 1896-1900, 1930; 1901-05, 1931; 1906-10, 1934; 1911-15, 1921; 1916-20, 1922; 1921-23, 1928; 1924-26, 1929; 1927-29, 1932; 1930-32, 1936; 1933-35, 1938; 1936-38, 1939.

Each volume is in two parts: (1) a classified subject index arranged by an extension of the Dewey decimal classification, and (2) an author index.

Index to dental literature in the English language . . . from Australia, Canada, England, India, South Africa, and the United States. 1939-1941; 1942-1944. An alphabetical subject and author index; a list of dental books. Chic., Amer. Dental Assoc., 1943-46. v.1-2. (In progress) **P346**

A continuation of Black's *Index of the periodical dental literature published in the English language,* covering 1839-1936/38 (P345).

Prepared by a committee of the American Dental Association; this is an author and subject index in one alphabet. Each volume covers three years. Kept up to date by printed cards, which can be obtained by subscription.

New York Academy of Medicine. Library. Dental bibliography; index to the literature of dental science and art as found in the libraries of the New York Academy of Medicine, and Bernard Wolf Weinberger, comp. by B. W. Weinberger. 2d ed. [N.Y.] First District Dental Society, State of N.Y. [c1929-32]. 2v. **P347**

Contents: [pt.1] A reference index; pt.2, A subject index, with additional reference index.

Dental abstracts, v.1- , Jan. 1945- . N.Y., Columbia Univ., School of Dental and Oral Surgery, Dental Abstracts Soc., 1945- . **P348**

A few numbers of an earlier series were issued Dec. 1941-March 1943.

Dictionaries

Dunning, William Bailey and **Davenport, S. E., Jr.** A dictionary of dental science and art, comprising the words and phrases proper to dental literature, with their pronunciation and derivation. Phila., Blakiston [1936]. 635p. il. **P349**

An excellent dictionary giving pronunciation, derivation and definition of dental terms.

Holzapfel, Attalus. Dental lexicon, Wörter-Verzeichnis, dictionary, dictionnaire, diccionario. . . .

Dental products and related matters in German, English, French and Spanish. . . . Mainz, Medizinische Verlagsanstalt, 1939. 640p. **P350**

Marie, Joseph S. F. Dental vocabulary, including many medical terms. Lancaster, Pa., Cattell, 1943. 159p. il. $4. **P351**

English-Spanish and Spanish-English. Includes names of instruments, equipment, diseases, medicaments, dental supplies, and many anatomical and medical terms. Gives equivalent terms only, no definitions or explanations.

Directories

American dental directory. [Chic.] American Dental Assoc., 1947- . v.1- . **P352**

Arranged by state and city with an alphabetical index. Gives address, specialization and dental school with year of graduation.

Nursing
Bibliography

National League of Nursing Education. Committee on the Nursing School Library. Books suggested for libraries in schools of nursing. [4th ed. rev.] N.Y., League, 1948. 197p. **P353**

A classed list of suggested titles for libraries in schools of nursing. Author index. Indicates titles recommended for first purchase. A revision and amplification of the *Basic book list* issued in 1937.

Handbooks

Young, Helen [and others]. Lippincott's Quick reference book for nurses . . . 5th ed. compl. rev. Phila., Lippincott, 1943. [602p.] il. $2. **P354**

A brief handbook of outlines and tables. Material is arranged alphabetically under the following categories: Abbreviations, Calculations, Solutions, Tables, Materia medica, Nursing technics, Dietotherapy, Medical and surgical nursing, Obstetrical nursing. No index, but many cross references.

Dictionaries

Price, Alice Louise. The American nurses dictionary; the definition and pronunciation of terms in the nursing vocabulary. Phila., Saunders, 1949. 656p. $3.75. **P355**

History

Goodnow, Minnie. Nursing history. 8th ed. Phila. and Lond., Saunders, 1948. 404p. il. **P356**

A frequently revised textbook.

Nutting, Mary Adelaide and **Dock, Lavinia L.** A history of nursing; the evolution of nursing systems from the earliest times to the foundation of the first English and American training schools for nurses. N.Y. and Lond., Putnam, 1907–12. 4v. il. **P357**

Volumes 3-4 have title: A history of nursing from the earliest times to the present day, with special reference to the work of the past thirty years, ed. and in part written by Lavinia L. Dock.

A standard comprehensive history.

Seymer, Lucy R. B. A general history of nursing. . . . Lond., Faber and Faber; N.Y., Macmillan, 1933. 307p. il. $3.25. **P358**

Especially useful for the years since Nutting and Dock (P357). Includes a bibliography, nursing magazines of a national character; and summary of registration requirements in England, France, New York, New Zealand and Prussia.

Nutrition
Bibliography

Nutrition abstracts and reviews, v.1, 1931/32- , issued under the direction of the Imperial Agricultural Bureaux Council, the Medical Research Council and the Reid Library. Aberdeen, Univ. Pr., 1931- . Quarterly. £2 2s.; $10 per year. **P359**

—— Author and subject index, v.1-5. £3 3s.; $15.

A comprehensive abstract journal with broad subject arrangement. Cumulates annually with author and subject indexes.

Food science abstracts, Mar. 1929- . Lond., Stat. Off., 1929- . v.1- . **P360**

Published by the Food Investigation Board of the Dept. of Scientific and Industrial Research.

Title varies: 1929–48, *Index to the literature of food investigation;* 1949- , *Food science abstracts.*

American Medical Association. The vitamins; a symposium arranged under the auspices of the Council on Pharmacy and Chemistry and the Council on Foods of the American Medical Association. Chic., Assoc., 1939. 637p. il. **P361**

Summaries and bibliographies.

Stechow, M. Register der Weltliteratur über Vitamine und der von ihnen beeinflussten Gebiete soweit aus deutschen Zentralblättern erfassbar. Leipzig, Helingsche Verlagsanstalt, 1943- . v.1- . **P362**

Contents: Bd.1, 1890–1929.

Bitting, Katherine Golden. Gastronomic bibliography. San Francisco, priv. pr., 1939. 718p. il. $8. **P363**

Handbooks

American Medical Association. Council on Foods and Nutrition. Accepted foods and their nutritional significance; containing descriptions of the products which stand accepted by the Council. Chic., Assoc., 1939. 492p. **P364**

Covers commercial brands.

McLester, James Somerville. Nutrition and diet in health and disease. 4th ed. thoroughly rev. Phila. and Lond., Saunders, 1943. 849p. $9.50. **P365**

Winton, Andrew Lincoln and **Winton, Kate Barber.** Structure and composition of foods. N.Y., Wiley, 1932–39. 4v. il. **P366**

A fundamental work arranged by type of food, giving description, structure, composition and adulterations.

Contents: v.1, Cereals, starch, oil seeds, nuts, oils, forage plants. $11; v.2, Vegetables, legumes, fruits. $15.50; v.3, Milk, butter, cheese, ice-cream, eggs, meat, meat extracts, gelatin, animal fats, poultry, fish, shellfish. $8.50; v.4, Sugar, sirup, honey, tea, coffee, cocoa, spices, extracts, yeast, baking powder. $9.50.

Public health

Bulletin of hygiene, v.1, Jan. 1926- . Lond., Bureau of Hygiene and Tropical Diseases, 1926- **P367**

Abstracting journal for public health.

U. S. Public Health Service. Public health engineering abstracts. v.1, 1928- . Wash., Govt. Prt. Off., 1928- . v.1- . Monthly. **P368**

Frequency varies.

International Labour Office. Occupation and health; encyclopaedia of hygiene, pathology and social welfare. Geneva, 1930- . **P369**

For full description *see* L484.

Paterson, Robert Gildersleeve. Historical directory of state health departments in the United States of America. Columbus, Ohio, Ohio Public Health Assoc., 1939. 68p. **P370**

Arranged by state, giving official name, names and terms of executive officers since founding, publications, reports, etc.

Cavins, Harold M. National health agencies; a survey with especial reference to voluntary associations. . . . including a detailed directory of major health organizations. Wash., Public Affairs Pr., 1945. 251p. $3. **P371**

Detailed surveys of 14 associations, followed by a directory of over 80 other agencies, giving name, address, secretary or other official, and brief description of organization and activities.

Tobey, James Alner. Public health law. 2d ed. N.Y., Commonwealth Fund, 1939. 414p. $3.50. **P372**

Pharmacy

Abstracts

Pharmaceutical abstracts, v.1-12, pub. by the American Pharmaceutical Association. Wash., 1935–47. 12v. Monthly. **P373**

Ceased publication. Material now largely covered in *Chemical abstracts* (N178).

Dispensatories and pharmacopoeias

AMERICAN

American Medical Association. Council on Pharmacy and Chemistry. New and non-official remedies, containing descriptions of the articles which stand accepted by the Council on Pharmacy and Chemistry of the American Medical Assoc. Chic., Assoc., 1909- . Annual. **P374**

Kept up to date by reports of the Council in the A.M.A. *Journal.*

American Pharmaceutical Association. The national formulary. 8th ed. National formulary. VIII. N.F. VIII, prepared by the Committee on National Formulary under the supervision of the Council by authority of the American Pharmaceutical Association; official from Apr. 1, 1947. Wash., Assoc., 1946. 850p. $5. **P375**

Gutman, Alexander Benjamin. Modern drug encyclopedia and therapeutic index. 3d ed. N.Y., Yorke Pub. Co., 1946. 1157p. $10. **P376**

A new edition of Jacob Gutman's *Modern drug encyclopedia,* 1941. This edition has been completely rewritten and reset. Descriptions of newly introduced drugs and biologicals have been added . . . and obsolete preparations have been deleted. The arrangement of the subject matter has been greatly simplified."—*Foreword.*

Kept up to date by *Modern drugs,* a quarterly supplementary service. 1941–48, called *New modern drugs.*

Pharmacopoeia of the United States of America. (The United States pharmacopoeia) 13th rev. (U. S. P. XIII) By authority of the United States Pharmacopoeial Convention meeting at Washington, D.C., May 14 and 15, 1940, prepared by the Committee of Revision and published by the Board of Trustees. Official from Nov. 1, 1947. Easton, Pa., Mack Print. Co., 1947. 957p. **P377**

——Epitome of the Pharmacopoeia of the United States and the National formulary with comments. Issued under the direction and supervision of the Council on Pharmacy and Chemistry of the American Medical Association. 8th ed. Phila., Lippincott, 1947. 238p.   **P378**

[Wood, George Bacon]. The dispensatory of the United States of America. 24th ed. by Arthur Osol and George E. Farrar. . . . Based on the 13th revision of the United States pharmacopoeia, the National formulary 8th edition, and the British pharmacopoeia, 1932 and its addenda. Phila., Lippincott, 1947. 1928p. il. $15.   **P379**

BRITISH

Ct. Brit. General Council of Medical Education and Registration. British pharmacopoeia 1948, published under the direction of the General Council of Medical Education and Registration of the United Kingdom. Lond., Gen. Med. Council, Constable, 1948. 914p. 18s. 6d.   **P380**
7th ed.

Martindale, William. Extra pharmacopoeia. 22d ed. Lond., Pharmaceutical Pr., 1941–43. 2v. 27s. 6d. ea.   **P381**
"Published by direction of the Council of the Pharmaceutical Society of Great Britain."

FINE ARTS

❧ Reference materials in art—painting, sculpture, engraving and architecture—include bibliographies, dictionaries, and indexes, but textbooks, histories, collections of plates, and other works not definitely classed as reference are particularly useful in this field. Many art books containing large numbers of plates are too expensive for the small and medium-sized library. For these, such inexpensive reproductions as those listed here, Q74-Q77, will sometimes be useful.

This section also includes various applications of art, e.g., metal arts, coins, and postage stamps, as well as works on costume, dancing and the theater. Music has a large body of reference material and is particularly rich in encyclopedias, dictionaries and biographical works.

GENERAL WORKS

Bibliography

Amsterdam. Rijksmuseum. Kunsthistorische Bibliotheek. Catalogus. Amsterdam, Dept. van Onderwijs, Kunsten en Wetenschappen, 1934–36. 4v. **Q1**

Classified with indexes in volume 4.

Hall, H. van. Repertorium voor de geschiedenis der Nederlandsche schilder- en graveerkunst, sedert het begin der 12de eeuw tot het eind van 1932. 'sGravenhage, Nijhoff, 1935. 716p. **Q2**

A classed bibliography of books and periodical articles with author and subject index. A second volume to cover 1933–43 has been announced. Continued by Q10.

Hammond, William A. A bibliography of aesthetics and of the philosophy of the fine arts, 1900–1932. Rev. and enl. ed. N.Y., Longmans, 1934. 205p. $3. **Q3**

Classified and annotated, with author index.

Internationale Bibliographie der Kunstwissenschaft, 1902–17/18. Berlin, Behr, 1902–20. 15v. **Q4**

Useful bibliography for the large or special library. Includes books and periodical articles in various languages. Discontinued.

Lopez Serrano, Matilde. Bibliografía de arte español y americano, 1936–1940. Madrid [Gráficas Uguina], 1942. 243p. **Q5**

At head of title: Consejo Superior de Investigaciones Científicas. Instituto Diego Velásquez.

A comprehensive bibliography of books, pamphlets and periodical articles on the art and archaeology of Spain, Spanish America, and the Philippines, published 1936–1940. It was hoped to continue the survey with annual volumes.

Lucas, Edna Louise. Books on art; a foundation list. Camb., Mass., Fogg Museum of Art, Harvard Univ., 1938. 84p. (Harvard-Radcliffe fine arts ser.) $2. **Q6**

Classified list of English and foreign titles, with author index. In general the closing date has been 1935, though a few later books are included.

First edition published as *Art bull.,* v.11, no.3, Sept. 1929, of the College Art Association of America.

Schlosser, Julius, *ritter von.* Die Kunstliteratur; ein Handbuch zur Quellenkunde der neueren Kunstgeschichte. Wien, Schroll, 1924. 640p. **Q7**

A very useful bibliographical manual to the literature of the history of art.

Italian translation: *La letteratura artistica, manuale delle fonti della storia dell' arte moderna.* Ed. emend. ed accres. dall' autore. Tr. italiana di Filippo Rossi. Firenze, "La Nuova Italia," 1935. 647p.

——— ——— Appendice di Otto Kurz. Firenze, "La Nuova Italia," 1937. 37p.

South Kensington Museum, London. National Art Library. First proofs of the Universal catalogue of books on art, comp. for the use of the National Art Library and the schools of art in the

United Kingdom. Lond., Chapman and Hall, 1870–77. 2v. and suppl. **Q8**

"Not only the books in the library, but all books printed and published, at the date of the issue of the Catalogue, that could be required to make the library perfect."—p.iv.

Sturgis, Russell. Annotated bibliography of fine art: Painting, sculpture, architecture, arts of decoration and illustration; music, by Henry E. Krehbiel. Boston, pub. for the Amer. Lib. Assoc. by the Library Bureau, 1897. 89p. **Q9**

Current

Netherlands. Rijksbureau voor Runsthistorische Documentatie. Bibliography of the Netherlands Institute for Art History. Hague, Rijksbureau, 1943- . **Q10**

London. University. Courtauld Institute of Art. Annual bibliography of the history of British art. v.1-4. 1934–37. Camb., Univ. Pr., 1936–39. 7s. 6d. ea. **Q11**

"Includes both books and articles on the history of British art excluding Roman but including Celtic and Viking art, and covering architecture, painting, sculpture, the graphic arts and the applied arts. Writings on British private collections and museums have been noted though the arts discussed may not be British; also writings on foreign artists working in Great Britain. Although the bibliography is primarily concerned with the history of art, writings on modern art and on living artists are included, also contemporary criticism."—*Pref.*

The 161 periodicals indexed are principally in English but include some 25 foreign journals.

In volume 4, certain sections have been omitted or curtailed when they are covered by other bibliographical publications; e.g., heraldry, costume, etc., which are included in *Writings on British history* (V281).

Répertoire d'art et d'archéologie, dépouillement des périodiques et des catalogues de ventes, bibliographie des ouvrages d'art français et étrangers, 1910- , fasc. 1- . Paris, Morancé, 1910- . v.1- . (v.46/48, 1942–44 (1950), 1800fr.) **Q12**

Publisher varies.

Issued annually except that there is a combined volume for 1914–19. From 1910 to 1925 inclusive each volume is in three parts: (1) List of periodical articles; (2) Record of art sales; (3) Art bibliography of the year, arranged by subjects. The list of periodical articles covers a large number of important periodicals, but these are given in the form of detailed contents of each periodical, not in a subject or classified list. From 1926 on, the arrangement is changed to that of a classified list by large subjects (e.g., periods and countries). From 1910 to 1919 and 1925 on, each volume has a general index of authors, subjects and places. The volumes for 1920–1924 inclusive contain no indexes but a combined index for these five years was issued as fascicule 29.

Indexes

A. L. A. portrait index; index to portraits contained in printed books and periodicals; ed. by W. C. Lane and N. E. Browne. Wash., Lib. of Congress, 1906. 1600p. $3. **Q13**

An index to portraits contained in 1181 sets (6216 volumes) including both books and periodicals through the year 1904. Indexes 120,000 portraits of about 35,000 or 45,000 persons. Information given includes dates of birth and death and brief characterization of the person, artist, engraver, etc., of the portrait, and volume and page of the work where the portrait may be found. Does not index portraits in local histories, genealogical works, or collections of engravings as such, or portraits of writers included in sets of their collected works.

Art index, Jan. 1929- , a cumulative author and subject index to a selected list of fine arts periodicals and museum bulletins. N.Y., Wilson, 1933- . Service basis. **Q14**

3-yr. cumulations, annual cumulations in Sept., and quarterly numbers issued Dec., March and June.

Indexes American and foreign periodicals, museum bulletins, annuals, etc., in the fields of archaeology, architecture, arts and crafts, ceramics, decoration and ornament, graphic arts, industrial design, interior decoration, landscape architecture, painting and sculpture. Method of indexing, which differs somewhat from that followed in the other special indexes issued by the same publisher, is as follows: (1) ordinary articles are indexed under author and subject or subjects; (2) book reviews are indexed under the author *reviewed* and under subject or subjects; (3) exhibitions are indexed under the artist; (4) illustrations accompanying an article are listed in the entry for that article but not indexed individually; illustrations without text are indexed under the artist's name.

Ellis, Jessie Croft. Nature and its applications; over 200,000 selected references to nature forms and illustrations of nature as used in every way. Bost., Faxon, 1949. 861p. **Q15**

A revised and very much enlarged edition of her *Nature index* (1930), broader in scope and in coverage. Indexes illustrations of nature forms in some 130 books and periodicals, including some encyclopedias. Indexed works are mainly in English but a few foreign are included.

—— Travel through pictures: References to pictures, in books and periodicals, of interesting sites all over the world. Bost., Faxon, 1935. 699p. $6. **Q16**

Index of 20th century artists. v.1-4, no.7. Oct. 1933—Apr. 1937. N.Y., College Art Assoc., 1933–37. v.1-4, no.7. **Q17**

Each monthly number contains detailed information about one or more artists which includes for each artist: biographical data, awards and honors, membership in associations, museums containing his work, exhibitions in which he was represented and bibliographical references including books, periodical articles and reproductions of his work. Cumulated index to volumes 1-3 is given in volume 3 and the total number of artists included in the three volumes is 101.

Publication suspended after April 1937.

Dictionaries and encyclopedias

Adeline, Jules. Art dictionary; tr. from the French and enlarged. Lond., Virtue; N.Y., Appleton, 1891. 422p. il. $3.50; 15s. **Q18**

Frequently reprinted.

Aims to include terms used in art, archaeology, architecture, heraldry, painting, sculpture, engraving, etching, and technical terms used in describing articles in museums, e.g., costume, armor, pottery, etc. Incorporates all the material in the original French work and also considerable information from Fairholt, F. W., *Dictionary of terms in art* (Lond., Virtue, 1854. 474p.).

Harper's Encyclopedia of art; architecture, sculpture, painting, decorative arts, based on the work of Louis Hourticq . . . and translated under the supervision of Tancred Borenius . . . fully rev. under the supervision of J. Leroy Davidson and Philippa Gerry, with the assistance of the staff of the Index of Twentieth-Century Artists, College Art Association, New York City . . . N.Y. and Lond., Harper, 1937. 2v. il. $30. **Q19**

Based on the following French work by Louis Hourticq (Q20).

Short articles, brief bibliographies. Many small illustrations. Contains biography including living persons. Reprinted as *New standard encyclopedia of art* (N.Y., Garden City Pub. Co., 1937. 2v. in 1. $3.95). Review in *Subscription books bulletin*, Apr. 1939, p.28-29. (A554).

Hourticq, Louis. Encyclopédie des beaux-arts; architecture, sculpture, peinture, arts décoratifs. [Paris] Hachette [c1925]. 2v. il. **Q20**

Includes definitions of terms, general history of the arts and encyclopedic articles. Includes biography.

Réau, Louis. Dictionnaire illustré d'art et d'archéologie. Paris, Larousse [c1930]. 488p. il. **Q21**

An alphabetical dictionary of terms.

—— Lexique polyglotte des termes d'art et d'archéologie. Paris, Laurens, 1928. 175p. **Q22**

Langues Latines: Latin, Italien, Espagnol, Portugais; Langues Germaniques: Anglais, Allemand, Hollandais, Danois, Suédois; Langues Slaves: Tchèque, Polonais, Russe.

Arranged by language with synonyms given in French.

Runes, Dagobert David and **Schrickel, Harry G.** Encyclopedia of the arts. N.Y., Philosophical Lib., 1946. 1064p. $10. **Q23**

Contains definitions of terms and longer articles on schools of art, forms, phases, etc., including music with the other arts. Many articles signed. Coverage and treatment uneven. Does not include biography.

Schmitt, Otto. Reallexikon zur deutschen Kunstgeschichte. Stuttgart, Metzler, 1937–46. Lfg. 1-23. il. (In progress) **Q24**

Bd.1, Lfg. 1-12, A-Baubetrieb; Bd.2, Lfg. 13-23, Bauer-Buchillustration.

Long, signed articles, with bibliographies and good illustrations, on subjects in art history and on works of art.

Directories

See also Museums, p.259-60.

American art annual, 1898- . N.Y., Amer. Federation of Arts, 1899- . v.1- . (v.37, 1948, $12) **Q26**

A very useful annual for current directory and institutional information.

Principal contents: museums, associations and other organizations, giving for the museums, address, officers, hours, scope of collection, work, exhibitions, and for the associations, address, officers, date of founding, meetings, dues, memberships, exhibitions; art schools; art magazines; newspapers carrying art notes; paintings sold at auction, etc.

Volume 37 includes Canada and Latin America.

Until 1935 included "Who's who in art" every other year, in the odd years; in the volumes for the even years other biographical lists, e.g., craftsmen, museum workers, college art instructors, etc., were given instead, but not each list every even year.

Biographical section continued by *Who's who in American art*, 1936/37- (Q59).

Arts, musées et curiosité en France. 1. ed. 1946- . Paris, Ed. Artistiques et Documentaires, 1946- . il. Annual. 750fr. **Q27**

A directory listing government bureaus, museums, schools, libraries, prizes, societies, artists, art galleries, the press, etc.

International Museum Office. Répertoire international des musées. [2d ed.] Paris, Société des Nations, Institut de Coopération Intellectuelle, 1933–35. v.1-3. **Q28**

Contents: (1) Pays-Bas et Indes néerlandaises. 1933. 64p.; (2) Pologne. 1935. 48p.; (3) France. 1933. 169p. No more published.

Covers collections of art, history, archaeology, ethnography and folk art.

Mastai, Boleslaw. Mastai's Classified directory of American art and antique dealers. Including Canada, Mexico, and South America. v.1, 1943- . N.Y., Boleslaw Mastai, 1942- . (v.3, 1947, $6) **Q29**

Geographically arranged, subdivided by specialties of dealer: antiques, interior decorators, china, silver, rugs, gift shops, etc.

Year's art, 1880- , a concise epitome of all matters relating to the arts of painting, sculpture, engraving and architecture, and to schools of design, which have occurred during the year together with information respecting the events of the year. Lond., Hutchinson, 1880- . v.1- . il. Annual. (v.64, 63s.) **Q30**

Compiled 1880–93 by M. B. Huish and 1894- by A. C. R. Carter.

Volume 63 covers 1942–44; volume 64, 1945–47.

Sales

Lancour, Adlore Harold. American art auction catalogues, 1785–1942; a union list. N.Y., N.Y. Public Library, 1944. 377p. $4.50.   **Q31**

"Reprinted with revisions and additions from the *Bulletin* of the New York Public Library, Jan. 1943–Feb. 1944."

A union check list of over 7000 catalogs of art objects including paintings, drawings, statuary, furniture, rugs, jewelry, textiles, musical instruments, curios, etc. Excludes books, maps, bookplates, stamps, and coins. Locates copies in 21 libraries. Includes list of auction houses.

Lugt, Frits. Répertoire des catalogues de ventes publiques intéressant l'art ou la curiosité. La Haye, Nijhoff, 1938- . v.1- . (Publications du Rijksbureau voor Kunsthistorische en Ikonografische Documentatie) (In progress)   **Q32**

v.1, Vers 1600–1825, tableaux, dessins, estampes, miniatures, sculptures, bronzes, émaux, vitraux, tapisseries, céramiques, objets d'art, meubles, antiquités, monnaies, medailles, camées, intailles, armes, etc.

Monod, Lucien. Aide-mémoire de l'amateur et du professionnel. Le prix des estampes, anciennes et modernes, prix atteints dans les ventes, suites et états, biographies et bibliographies. Paris, Albert Morancé, 1920–[31] 9v.   **Q33**

v.1-9, A–Z; v.9 contains also: Graveurs identifiés par leurs monogrammes ou par des désignations particulières (xvᵉ et xv1ᵉ siècles), p.61-73; Bibliographie générale, p.77-109; Nomenclature des estampes par catégories et par sujets (indication des planches typiques, bibliographies, planches anonymes), p.113-281.

A dictionary of artists and their works with very brief biographical data, bibliography, and record of prices realized at various sales.

Current

Annuaire général des ventes publiques en France. Année 1- , 1941/42- . Paris, Ed. Art et Technique, 1942- .   **Q34**

2. année, 1942/43 in 2v.: v.1, Tableaux. 95fr.; v.2, Livres, autographes, gravures, monnaies, sculptures, céramiques, arts d'Extrême-Orient, tapisseries, meubles, timbres-poste, etc. 125fr.

Art prices current. 1907–15/16, v.1-9; 1921/22- , n.s. 1- , a record of sale prices at the principal London and other auction rooms. Lond., Art Trade Pr., 1908- . v.1-9; n.s. v.1- . (v.23, 1944/45, £7 7s.)   **Q35**

Cote des tableaux, ou, Annuaire des ventes de tableaux, dessins, aquarelles, pastels, gouaches, miniatures; guide du marchand, de l'amateur, publié par L. Maurice Lang. t.1-11, Tous les prix des ventes de l'année, Oct. 1918–fin Juillet 1929. Paris, L. Maurice [1919-31]. v.1-11. **Q36**

Title varies. Earlier issues called *Annuaire des ventes de tableaux;* 1923–29, *Cote des tableaux.*

Print prices current; being a complete alphabetical record of all engravings, etchings and Baxter prints sold by auction in Great Britain and America, each item annotated with the date of sale, price realized and the quality and condition of the prints. v.1-21. Oct. 1918–Aug. 1939. Lond., F. L. Wilder, 1919–40. 21v.   **Q38**

American prices included for the first time in volume 13, 1930/31.

History

Cossío, Manuel Bartolomé and **Pijoán y Soteras, José.** Summa artis, historia general del arte . . . 1. ed. Bilbao, Madrid, Espasa-Calpe, 1931–47. v.1-11. il. (In progress)   **Q39**

v.1, Arte de los pueblos aborígenes; v.2, Arte del Asia occidental; v.3, El arte egipcio hasta la conquista romana; v.4, El arte griego hasta la toma de Corinto por los Romanos (146 a. J.C.); v.5, El arte romano hasta la muerte de Diocleciano; Arte etrusco y arte helenístico después de la toma de Corinto; v.6, El arte prehistórico europeo; v.7, Arte Cristiano primitivo; Arte bizantino; v.8, Arte Bárbaro y Prerrománico, desde el siglo ıv hasta el año 1000; v.9, El arte Románico, siglos xı y xıı; v.10, Arte precolombiano, mexicano y maya; v.11, Arte gótico de la Europa Occidental. Siglos xııı, xıv, y xv.

Excellent illustrations. Includes bibliographies.

Faure, Élie. Histoire de l'art. Paris, Plon, 1939–40. 5v. il.   **Q40**

—— History of art. tr. from the French by Walter Pach. N.Y., Harper, 1921–30. 5v. il. (Repr. N.Y., Dover Publications, 1948. 2v. $12.50)   **Q41**

Contents: Ancient art, mediaeval art, renaissance art, modern art, the spirit of the forms.

Gardner, Helen. Art through the ages. 3d ed. N.Y., Harcourt, 1948. 851p. il. $6; text ed. $4.50.   **Q42**

A survey history of art in all parts of the world from ancient to modern times. Bibliographies given at end of chapters. The index indicates pronunciation of many foreign names and terms.

Michel, André. Histoire de l'art depuis les premiers temps chrétiens jusqu'à nos jours. . . . Paris, Colin [c1905–29]. 8v. in 17. il.   **Q43**

—— —— Index d'ensemble. Noms d'artistes, noms de lieux, sujets et table générale par Louise Lefrançois-Pillion. Paris, Colin [c1929]. 279p.

A fundamental history of the first importance and authority, with good bibliographies and index.

Pijoán y Soteras, José. History of art, foreword by R. B. Harshe, tr. by R. L. Roys. 2d ed. Lond., Batsford, 1933. 3v. il. $35.   **Q44**

Also published in a cheaper edition with title *An outline history of art* (Chic., Univ. of Knowledge, 1938. 3v. $9).

Good reference history, with bibliography at end of each chapter, many illustrations, some colored. Indexes: alphabetical list of artists, archaeologists, etc.; list of illustrations; alphabetical index of all works of art reproduced or mentioned in the text.

Reinach, Salomon. Apollo; an illustrated manual of the history of art throughout the ages, from the French, by Florence Simmonds; with 600 illustrations. Completely rev. and new chapter by the author. N.Y., Scribner, 1935. 378p. il. $3. **Q45**

An excellent manual, profusely illustrated.

Robb, David M. and **Garrison, J. J.** Art in the western world. Rev. and enl. ed. N.Y., Harper, 1942. 1045p. il. $7.50; text ed. $5. **Q46**

A useful one-volume history with "Selected critical bibliography," p.978-1000; Glossary, p.1001-14; Chronological table, p.1015-35. Index.

Springer, Anton. Handbuch der Kunstgeschichte. . . . Leipzig, Kröner, 1918–29. 6v. il. **Q47**

v.1, Die Kunst des Altertums. 11. Aufl. nach Adolf Michaelis bearb. von Paul Wolters. 1920; v.2, Frühchristliche Kunst und Mittelalter. 10. umgearb. Aufl., bearb. von Joseph Neuwirth. 1919; v.3, Die Kunst der Renaissance in Italien. 10. erweiterte Aufl., bearb. von Adolf Philippi. 1918; v.4, Die Kunst der Renaissance im Norden: Barock und Rokoko. 10. verb. und erweiterte Aufl., bearb. von Paul Schubring. 1920; v.5, Die Kunst von 1800 bis zur Gegenwart. 7. verb. und erweiterte Aufl., bearb. von Max Osborn. 1920; v.6, Die aussereuropäische Kunst . . . von Curt Glaser, Stella Kramrisch, Ernst Kuhnel. . . . 1929.

Upjohn, Everard Miller, Wingert, Paul Stover and **Mahler, Jane Gaston.** History of world art. N.Y., Ox., 1949. 560p. il. (654 il.) $6; college ed. $4.50. **Q48**

A survey history designed for introductory college courses, concentrating "on the painting, sculpture, and architecture of civilized peoples in Europe, North America, and Asia from the birth of history in Egypt and Mesopotamia to the present time." The illustrations are grouped together at the beginning serving as a graphic history of the arts. The text is followed by a glossary, p.503-11; suggested reading, p.513-23; chronological charts, p.556-60; and index.

Biography

Bénézit, Emmanuel. Dictionnaire critique et documentaire des peintres, sculpteurs, dessinateurs et graveurs de tous les temps et de tous les pays, par un groupe d'écrivains spécialistes français et étrangers. Nouv. ed. entièrement refondu, rev. et cor. sous la direction des héritiers de E. Bénézit. Paris, Gründ, 1948–50. v.1-3. il. (In progress) **Q49**

v.1-3, A-Forain.

1st ed., 1911-13. 3v.

A very comprehensive list, including many minor names. Information is usually very brief, but usually includes list of chief works, museums where displayed and in some instances prices paid for works. In many cases these lists have been brought up to 1945 or later.

The new edition has been revised to include twentieth century names. Symbols and signatures are reproduced in facsimile, and at the end of each letter there is a list of the signatures used by anonymous artists.

Brun, Carl. Schweizerisches Künstler Lexikon. Dictionnaire des artistes suisses. Hrsg. vom Schweizerischen Kunstverein. Frauenfeld, Huber, 1905–17. 4v. **Q50**

v.1-3, A-Z; v.4, Supplement, A-Z.

Du Peloux de Saint Romain, Charles, *vicomte.* Répertoire biographique et bibliographique des artistes du xviiie siècle français. Accompagné de notices sur l'art du xviiie siècle, les expositions, les académies et manufactures royales, les amateurs d'art, les ventes publiques et d'une importante bibliographie. Paris, Champion, 1930–41. 2v. **Q51**

Contents: v.1, Répertoire biographique: Peintres, dessinateurs, graveurs, p.1-160; Sculpteurs, ciseleurs, orfèvres, fondeurs, ferronniers, p.161-212; Architectes, p.213-46; Ébénistes, doreurs, décorateurs du bois, p.247-72; [Sociétés, amateurs, ventes publiques] p.288-328; Bibliographie, p.329-449; v.2, Notices historiques sur l'art français dans les pays scandinaves, les manufactures particulières de faïence, de porcelaine et de tapisseries . . .; Bibliographie, p.38-97; Errata et addenda au 1. volume.

Edouard-Joseph, René. Dictionnaire biographique des artistes contemporains, 1910–1930, avec nombreux portraits, signatures et reproductions. Paris, Librairie Grund, 1930–34. 3v. il. 600fr. **Q52**

Publisher varies.

Intended to include primarily artists living or exhibited in France from 1910–30.

—— —— Supplément. Paris, 1936. 162p. il. 75fr.

Fielding, Mantle. Dictionary of American painters, sculptors and engravers. N.Y., Paul A. Struck, 1945. 433p. il. $20. **Q53**

"The present edition is identical to the one published in 1926. . . . The revisions and additional factual material, covering the years from 1926 to 1945, will be incorporated in a supplementary volume, which is now in preparation."—*Pref.*

Brief biographical sketches of nearly 8000 American artists.

Kaltenbach, Gustave Émile. Dictionary of pronunciation of artists' names, with their schools and dates, for American readers and students. 2d ed. Chic., Art. Inst., 1938. 74p. 50c. **Q54**

Mallett, Daniel Trowbridge. Mallett's Index of artists; international — biographical. Including painters, sculptors, illustrators, engravers and etchers of the past and the present. N.Y., Bowker, 1935. 493p. **Q55**

———— Supplement. 1940. 319p.

Both volumes reprinted: N.Y., Peter Smith, 1948. $12 and $8.50.

An index to biographical material about artists of all countries and periods in general reference works and in many specialized books as well. The entry gives full name, pseudonym, premarriage name (for women), nationality, place and year of birth and death, active years and place of residence. In the *Supplement,* in the case of an artist where no reference has been found in the sources used, reference is given to the art gallery, museum, library, publisher, etc., from which data may be obtained, or where his work may be seen.

While this is a useful index it should be used with some caution as it contains various inaccuracies in names, dates, places, etc. As some of the books listed are only selectively indexed, they may contain needed material not indexed here.

Müller, Hermann Alexander and **Singer, H. W.** Allgemeines Künstler-Lexicon. Leben und Werke der berühmtesten Bildenden Künstler. 3. umgearb. u. bis auf die neueste Zeit ergänzte Aufl. Frankfurt am Main, Rütten, 1895–1922. 6v. **Q56**

Smith, Ralph Clifton. A biographical index of American artists. . . . Balt., Williams and Wilkins, 1930. 102p. $4. **Q57**

An index to biographical material on some 4700 American artists to be found in 42 reference works. The index gives for each artist place and date of birth and death, medium in which he worked, and references to biographical information.

Thieme, Ulrich and **Becker, Felix.** Allgemeines Lexikon der bildenden Künstler von der Antike bis zur Gegenwart, unter Mitwirkung von etwa 400 Fachgelehrten des In-und Auslandes. Leipzig, Seemann, 1911–47. v.1-36. M. 60 per v. **Q58**

The most complete and authoritative dictionary of artists, covering painters and sculptors, engravers, etchers and architects. Includes living persons. There are good bibliographies and the longer articles are signed.

Who's who in American art; a biographical directory of contemporary artists, editors, critics, executives, etc. v.1- , 1936/37- . Wash., Amer. Fed. of Arts, c1935- . v.1- . (v.4, $12) **Q59**

Subtitle varies. v.1, 1936/37; v.2, 1938/39; v.3, 1940/41; v.4, 1940/47.

An important dictionary of contemporary biography which continues, in separate, enlarged form, various biographical lists previously included at intervals in the *American art annual* (Q26). The obituary and necrology lists (not included in every volume), used in connection with the necrology given in volume 25 of the *Annual,* give a comprehensive listing of data about artists deceased since 1897.

Volume 4 includes a selected bibliography on American art, p.611-57.

Who's who in art. Biographies of leading men and women in the world of art today. 4th ed. Lond., Art Trade Pr., 1948. 283p. 22s. **Q60**

1st ed., 1927; 2d ed., 1929; 3d ed., 1934.

Includes artists, designers, craftsmen, critics, writers, teachers, collectors, and curators, with an appendix of signatures.

Wurzbach, Alfred, *Ritter von Tannenberg.* Niederländisches Künstler-Lexikon. Leipzig und Wien, Halm, 1904–11. 3v. **Q61**

An important biographical dictionary, with bibliographies, lists of works, location of pictures, etc. Gives facsimiles of signatures in many cases.

SYMBOLISM IN ART

Bailey, Henry Turner and **Pool, Ethel.** Symbolism for artists, creative and appreciative. Worcester, Mass., Davis Pr., 1925. 247p. il. $4.50. **Q62**

Alphabetical list of elements and their meanings, with illustrations. Includes a list of College and university colors, p.222-35; Bibliography p.236-38; Plate and figure references p.239-47.

Bles, Arthur de. How to distinguish the saints in art by their costumes, symbols and attributes. N.Y., Art Culture Publications, 1925. 168p. $7.50. **Q63**

Contents: (1) Chapters 1-12, symbolism in general and for different groups, e.g., Virgin Mary, Evangelists, monastic orders, etc., with illustrations and explanations of pictures showing symbols; (2) Appendixes: Alphabetical table of martyrdoms; Tables of saints classified by habitual costume; Saints classified by categories; Alphabetical table of symbols and attributes with names of those who bear them; Chronological tables of bishops and popes of Rome; List of illustrations; General index.

Drake, Maurice and **Drake, Wilfred.** Saints and their emblems. Lond., Laurie; Phila., Lippincott, 1916. 235p. il. o.p. **Q64**

(1) Dictionary of saints; (2) Dictionary of emblems; (3) Appendixes: Patriarchs and prophets, Sibyls, Patron saints of arts, trades and professions, Other patron saints.

Künstle, Karl. Ikonographie der Christlichen Kunst. Freiburg im Br., Herder, 1926–28. 2v. il. **Q65**

Contents: v.1, Prinzipienlehre, Hilfsmotive, Offenbarungstatsachen. 1928; v.2, Ikonographie der Heiligen. 1926.

The second volume is a dictionary of saints, with brief biographical data, indication of their emblems, information about how and where depicted in mosaics, paintings, etc., and bibliographical references to printed descriptions of these representations. Important for either the art, theological, or large reference library.

Marle, Raimond von. Iconographie de l'art profane au Moyen-Âge et à la Renaissance et la décoration des demeures. La Haye, Nijhoff, 1931/32. 2v. il. **Q66**

[v.1] La vie quotidienne. 539p.; [v.2] Allégories et symboles. 506p.

Includes bibliographies.

Webber, Frederick Roth. Church symbolism; an explanation of the more important symbols of the Old and New Testament, the primitive, the mediaeval and the modern church . . . introd. by Ralph Adams Cram. 2d ed. rev. Cleveland, J. H. Jansen, 1938. 413p. il. $7.50. **Q67**

Glossary of the more important symbols, p.357-88; Bibliography, p.389-94.

The following older works, though not up to date, are often useful for popular work. They have been published in many editions.

Jameson, Anna Brownell Murphy. The history of Our Lord as exemplified in works of art; with that of His types; St. John the Baptist; and other persons of the Old and New Testament. Lond., Longmans, 1865. 2v. il. **Q68**

—— Legends of the Madonna, ed. with additional notes by E. M. Hurll. Bost., Houghton, 1896. 372p. il. o.p. **Q69**

—— Legends of the monastic orders, ed. with additional notes by E. M. Hurll. Bost., Houghton, 1896. 467p. il. o.p. **Q70**

—— Sacred and legendary art, ed. with additional notes by E. M. Hurll. Bost., Houghton, 1896. 2v. il. o.p. **Q71**

Waters, Clara Erskine Clement. Handbook of Christian symbols and stories of the saints as illustrated in art. 2d ed. Bost., Ticknor [c1871–86]. 349p. il. o.p. **Q72**

—— Handbook of legendary and mythological art. 22d ed. Bost., Houghton, 1890. [c1871–86] 575p. il. o.p. **Q73**

ART REPRODUCTIONS

Catalogue of selected color reproductions, prepared for the Carnegie Corporation of New York. N.Y., Raymond and Raymond, 1936. 2v. il. loose-leaf. $7.50. **Q74**

A catalog of reproductions primarily of the masters arranged alphabetically by name of artist, except that all Near Eastern, Chinese, Japanese, and Indian art are grouped under Oriental. Gives name of artist with nationality and dates, title of picture, date, medium, size and location of the original; publisher, process, size and American price of reproduction. Price is as of 1936.

Monro, Isabel Stevenson and **Monro, Kate M.** Index to reproductions of American paintings; a guide to pictures occurring in more than eight hundred books. N.Y., Wilson, 1948. 731p. $8.50. **Q75**

"This index to reproductions of paintings lists the work of artists of the United States occurring in 520 books and in more than 300 catalogues of annual exhibitions held by art museums. The paintings are entered (1) under name of the artist, followed by his dates when obtainable, by title of the picture and by an abbreviated entry for the book in which the reproduction may be found; (2) under titles; and (3) in some cases under subjects. Locations of pictures in permanent collections have also been included whenever this information was available."—*Pref.*

New York Graphic Society, Inc. Fine art reproductions, old and modern masters. N.Y., Soc., 1946. 232p. il. **Q76**

—— —— Supplement. 1948. 236-312p. pa.$2.

A catalog of reproductions available for sale in color and in black and white, with description, size and price and in many cases the location of the original.

University Prints, Boston. University prints. Art reproductions for students. Series A-H, K-P. Newton, Mass., Univ. Prints, 19-?. 14 ser. il. bound, $5 ea.; loose-leaf, price per v. varies; special price on sets. **Q77**

Contents: Ser. A, Greek and Roman sculpture; Ser. B, Early Italian art; Ser. C, Later Italian art; Ser. D, Art of the Netherlands and Germany; Ser. E, French and Spanish art; Ser. F, British painting; Ser. G, European architecture; Ser. GM, Modern architecture; Ser. H, American art; Ser. K, Mediaeval art; Ser. L, Woodcuts and engravers; Ser. M, Pre-Greek art; Ser. O, Oriental art; Ser. P, Art in American collections.

All series are issued in loose-leaf form, and in addition, bound volumes are obtainable for Ser. A, B, C, D, G and GM, each of which contains 500 prints, except GM with only 265. Additional prints have been published for most of the volumes. The remaining series contain from 120 to 250 prints each and are issued in loose-leaf form only.

These are inexpensive reproductions issued for student use. All prints (except 107 in original colors arranged as a history of painting) are in black-and-white half tone. All are 5½ by 8 inches. A printed catalog gives the full record.

PAINTING

Champlin, John Denison and **Perkins, C. C.** Cyclopedia of painters and paintings. N.Y., Scribner, 1892. [1885–87] 4v. il. **Q78**

Gives in one alphabet biographical articles on painters and descriptive articles on famous paintings. The biographies give main facts of the artist's life, list of his paintings, with reference to the museums or collections where they are located, and some bibliography. Articles on paintings give brief description, some facts of history, museum, a statement of whether engraved and by whom, and some bibliographical references. Illustrated by outline drawings.

McColvin, Eric Raymond. Painting: A guide to the best books with special reference to the requirements of public libraries. Lond., Grafton, 1934. 216p. 10s. 6d. **Q79**

Titles of most general value have been starred.

❦ The history of painting is usually well covered in the general histories of art. For more detailed histories consult the bibliographies in Robb and Garrison (Q46) and in Upjohn, Wingert, and Mahler (Q48). A few of the most generally useful histories are:

Isham, Samuel. The history of American painting. New ed. with supplementary chapters by Royal Cortissoz. N.Y., Macmillan, 1927. 608p. il. Reissue 1942. $4.95; 20s. **Q80**

Bibliography, compiled by Henry Meier, p.593-600.

Mather, Frank Jewett. A history of Italian painting. [rev. ed.] N.Y., Holt, 1938. 497p. il. $5. **Q81**

A standard, systematic treatment.

—— Western European painting of the Renaissance. N.Y., Holt, 1939. 873p. il. (Repr. N.Y., Tudor Pub. Co., 1948. $3.98) **Q82**

A comprehensive survey.

Muther, Richard. History of painting from the ɪᴠth to the early xɪxth century. Authorized English ed., tr. from the German and ed. with annotations by George Kriehn. N.Y., Putnam, 1907. 2v. il. $10. **Q83**

An older standard work.

—— History of modern painting. Rev. ed. . . . to the end of the xɪx century. N.Y., Dutton, 1907. 4v. il. $50. **Q84**

Covers the nineteenth century.

❦ The Museum of Modern Art, New York, publishes many monographs and brochures on various phases of modern painting. These include publications on particular movements, e.g., Cubism and Fantastic art, Dada, Surrealism, etc.; and on special artists, e.g., Salvador Dali, Picasso, etc.

Biography

Ancona, Paola d' and **Aeschlimann, Erardo.** Dictionnaire des miniaturistes du moyen âge et de la renaissance dans les différentes contrées de l'Europe, avec clv planches dont vii en couleurs. 2d ed. rev. et augm. contenant un index ordonné par époques, régions, écoles. Milan, Hoepli, 1949. 239p. L12,500. **Q85**

Brief biographical notes with bibliographical references. The second edition has been revised, with some new names and additional references.

Thirteen new plates have been added but the plates in the first edition seem definitely superior to those in the second. An index arranged by epochs subdivided by country is new in the second edition.

The first edition was published in 1940 under the name of Aeschlimann, "Le nom de M. Paolo D'Ancona ne pouvait figurer en raison des lois raciales qui étaient en rigueur en Italie à cette époque."—*Pref.* 2d ed.

Bessone-Aurelj, Antonietta Maria. Dizionario dei pittori italiani. 2. ed. ampl. Milano, Albrighi, 1928. 678p. **Q86**

Bradley, John William. Dictionary of miniaturists, illuminators, calligraphers, and copyists, with reference to their works, and notices of their patrons, from the establishment of Christianity to the 18th century. Lond., Quaritch, 1887–89. 3v. o.p. **Q87**

Bryan, Michael. Bryan's Dictionary of painters and engravers. New ed., rev. and enl. under the supervision of G. C. Williamson. Lond., Bell; N.Y., Macmillan, 1903–05. 5v. il. **Q88**

A standard biographical dictionary which usually lists works and frequently indicates location.

Foster, Joshua James. Dictionary of painters of miniatures, 1525–1850, with some account of exhibitions, collections, sales, etc., pertaining to them; ed. by Ethel M. Foster. Lond., Philip Allan; N.Y., Macmillan, 1926. 330p. 21s.; $6. **Q89**

Long, Basil S. British miniaturists. Lond., Geoffrey Bles, 1929. 475p. 32 pl. (containing 153 figures) £5 5s. **Q90**

A biographical dictionary of miniaturists, chiefly painters who lived in Great Britain and Ireland, 1520–1860, including also foreigners who worked in England and miniaturists born in Great Britain who worked elsewhere, for same period.

ENGRAVING

Delteil, Loys. Manuel de l'amateur d'estampes du xvɪɪɪᵉ siècle. Paris, Dorbon-Aîné [1910]. 447p. il. **Q91**

Manuel, p.1-364; Table alphabétique des vents publiques, avec noms des propriétaires, mentionnées au cours du Manuel, p.365-68; Table des noms d'artistes et des estampes cités, p.369-442.

—— Manuel de l'amateur d'estampes de xɪxᵉ et xxᵉ siècles (1801–1924). Paris, Dorbon-Aîné [c1925]. 4v. il. **Q92**

v.1-2, Manuel; Table alphabétique des vents avec noms des propriétaires mentionnées dans le présent manuel; Table des noms d'artistes et des titres d'estampes cités; v.3-4, 700 reproductions d'estampes des xɪxᵉ et xxᵉ siècles pour servir de complément au *Manuel*.

Hind, Arthur Mayger. History of engraving and etching, from the 15th century to the year 1914;

being the 3d and fully rev. ed. of "A short history of engraving and etching." Bost., Houghton [1923]. 487p. il. $12. **Q93**

Appendixes: (1) Classified list of engravers; (2) General bibliography; (3) Index of engravers and individual bibliographies.

Perhaps the best history of engraving.

Fine prints of the year; an annual review of contemporary etching, engraving, and lithography. ed. by Malcolm C. Salaman . . . v.1-16, 1923–Oct. 1938. Lond., Halton; N.Y., Minton, Balch, 1924–38. v.1-16. il. $10 ea. **Q94**

Subtitle and editor vary.

No more published. Each volume includes "Directory of etchers and engravers."

Biography

Beraldi, Henri. Les graveurs du xixe siècle; guide de l'amateur d'estampes modernes. Paris, Conquet, 1885–92. 12v. **Q95**

Fielding, Mantle. American engravers upon copper and steel; biographical sketches and check lists of engravings, a supplement to David McNeely Stauffer's American engravers. Phila., priv. pr., 1917. 365p. il. **Q96**

Good biographies containing many facts not found in Stauffer (Q97). Includes a special list of engravings (unknown and unsigned), p.296-316; Index by subject of engraving, p.321-65.

Stauffer, David McNeely. American engravers upon copper and steel. N.Y., Grolier Club, 1907. 2v. il. **Q97**

v.1, Biographical sketches; Index to engravings described with check-list numbers and names of engravers and artists; v.2, Check-list of the works of the earlier engravers, alphabetical by names of engravers.

—————— An artist index to Stauffer's "American engravers," by Thomas Hovey Gage. Worcester, Mass., Amer. Antiquarian Soc., 1921. 49p. (Repr. from Proceedings of the Amer. Antiquarian Soc., Oct. 1920)

Waller, François Gerard. . . . Biographisch woordenboek van noord nederlandsche graveurs, uitgegeven door beheerders van het Wallerfonds en bewerkt door W. R. Juynboll; met 61 portretten in lichtdruk. s'Gravenhage, Nijhoff, 1938. 551p. il. **Q98**

Includes references to printed sources.

SCULPTURE

Chase, George Henry and **Post, Chandler Rathfon.** History of sculpture. N.Y., Harper [c1925]. 582p. il. $5. **Q99**

The standard one-volume history.

Post, Chandler Rathfon. History of European and American sculpture from the early Christian period to the present day. Camb., Harv. Univ. Pr., 1921. 2v. il. **Q100**

Biography

Bessone-Aurelj, Antonietta Maria. Dizionario degli scultori ed architetti italiani. Genova, Roma, Soc. Anonima Ed. Dante Alighieri, 1947. 523p. **Q101**

Lami, Stanislas. Dictionnaire des sculpteurs de l'école française. Paris, Champion, 1898–1921. 8v. **Q102**

Contents (not volumed as a set): Du Moyen âge au regne de Louis xiv. 1898. 581p.; Sous le regne de Louis xiv. 1896. 504p.; Au 18e siècle. 1910–11. 2v.; Au 19e siècle. 1914–21. 4v.

Each period arranged alphabetically by artist giving biographical sketch, list of works and bibliography.

ARCHITECTURE
Bibliography

Columbia University. Library. Catalogue of the Avery Architectural Library: A memorial library of architecture, archeology, and decorative art. N.Y., Columbia Univ., 1895. 1139p. **Q103**

Author list.

Hitchcock, Henry Russell. American architectural books; a list of books, portfolios and pamphlets on architecture and related subjects published in America before 1895. 3d rev. ed. Minneapolis, Univ. of Minnesota Pr.; Lond., Ox. Univ. Pr., 1946. 130p. **Q104**

Lists 1461 editions of American architectural works, distinguishing editions and locating copies in over 130 public and private libraries.

Roos, Frank J. Writings on early American architecture; an annotated list of books and articles on architecture constructed before 1860 in the eastern half of the United States. Columbus, Ohio State Univ. Pr., 1943. 271p. $2.75. **Q105**

Royal Institute of British Architects. London. Library. Catalogue of the . . . library. Lond., Inst., 1937–38. 2v. 70s. **Q106**

v.1, Authors; v.2, Classified index and alphabetical subject index of books and manuscripts.

The catalog of an important library which has trebled in size since its last preceding general catalog was published 1889–99.

Dictionaries and encyclopedias

Architectural Publication Society. Dictionary of architecture. Lond., Richards, 1852–92. 6v. il. o.p. **Q107**

Includes terms, architectural forms and subjects, places with some account of their architectural features, biographies of architects. Gives bibliographical references and is still of great importance.

Handbuch der Architektur, unter Mitwirkung von Fachgenossen hrsg. von Josef Durm, Hermann Ende, Eduard Schmitt und Heinrich Wagner. Darmstadt, Diehl, 1883–1943. il. (In progress) **Q108**

1st-4th ed. Publisher varies.
1. Teil, Allgemeine Hochbaukunde, Bd.1-5; 2. Teil, Die Baustile, Bd.1-7; 3. Teil, Die Hochbauconstructionen, Bd.1-6; 4. Teil, Entwerfen, Anlage und Einrichtung der Gebäude, Hlbbd. 1-10.

Longfellow, William Pitt Preble. Cyclopaedia of works of architecture in Italy, Greece, and the Levant. N.Y., Scribner, 1903. 546p. il. **Q109**

Arranged alphabetically by names of places with an account of the chief architectural monuments in each. Has good illustrations, a glossary, and a selected bibliography, but no bibliographical references in the text.

Planat, Paul. Encyclopédie de l'architecture et de la construction. Paris, Dujardin [1888–92]. 6v. in 12. il. **Q110**

Sartoris, Alberto. Encyclopédie de l'architecture nouvelle. Milan, Hoepli, 1948- . il. v.1, L5000. **Q111**

Contents: v.1, Ordre et climat méditerranéens. Introd. de Edmond Humeau. Préface de Le Corbusier.

Sturgis, Russell. Dictionary of architecture and building, biographical, and descriptive. N.Y., Macmillan, 1901. 3v. il. o.p. **Q112**

The standard dictionary in English, though now almost fifty years old.

Viollet-Le-Duc, Eugène Emmanuel. Dictionnaire raisonné de l'architecture française du XIᵉ au XVIᵉ siècle. Paris, Morel, 1854–68. 10v. il. **Q113**

——— ——— Table analytique et synthétique, avec table alphabétique des noms de lieux par départements, pour la France et par contrées, pour l'étranger, [par] Henri Sabine. Paris, Imprimeries Réunies, 1889. 387p.

Wasmuths Lexikon der Baukunst. Berlin, Wasmuth [c1929–37]. 5v. **Q114**

Covers both the practical and art sides of subjects, including terms, encyclopedic articles, many biographies, excellent illustrations. No exhaustive bibliographies, but many short bibliographical references, often consisting of only one or two titles.

Terms

Bodson, Fernand. Dictionnaire des termes récents, symboles et abbréviations; architecture,

art de construire, génie civil. Bruxelles, Editec S.P.R.L., 1948. 244p. 300fr. **Q115**

For description *see* P114.

Corkhill, Thomas. A concise building encyclopaedia; an explanation of words, terms, and abbreviations used in building and constructional work, and a work of reference for architects, surveyors, civil and structural engineers, and the various craftsmen engaged in building. 2d ed. Lond., Pitman, 1945. 287p. il. 7s. 6d.; $3. **Q116**

Defines over 7000 terms used in building and construction trades in Great Britain. Terminology differs from that used in this country and therefore its main use here is for those reading works published in England.

Ware, Dora and **Beatty, Betty.** A short dictionary of architecture, including some common building terms. With an introd. on The study of architecture by John Gloag. Lond., Allen and Unwin; N.Y., Philosophical Lib., 1946. 109p. il. 6s.; $2.75. **Q117**

First pub. 1944; 2d ed. rev. 1946.
An excellent small dictionary of architectural terms with simple, graphic line drawings.

Handbooks

American Institute of Architects. Handbook of architectural practice. Wash., Institute, 1943. 204p. $5. **Q118**

Includes chapters on registration of architects, organization of office, surveys, letting of contracts, legal aspects, etc.

Dirlam, Clyde Nixon, Huls, H. P. and others. Modern building inspection; "The Building inspector's handbook" . . . 1st ed. Los Angeles, R. C. Colling and Associates, 1942. 404p. il. $5. **Q119**

A practical handbook covering technical problems and the business routine. Includes an annotated bibliography of some 450 titles.

Voss, Walter Charles, Henry, Ralph Coolidge and **Varney, Edward A.** Architectural construction. N.Y., Wiley, 1925–27. v.1-2 in 3v. il. $36.50. **Q120**

Annuals

Architects' year book, v.1- . Lond., Elek, 1945- . (v.2, 1948, 35s.) **Q121**

Editor, Jane B. Drew.

Planning and construction. 1st ed., 1942- . Lond., Todd Ref. Bks., [1942-]. il. Annual. (1948, 25s.; $7) **Q122**

Advisory ed., F. J. Osborn.

Title varies: 1942–1943, *Planning and reconstruction year book;* 1944/45–1946, *Planning and construction.* Not published 1947. Contents vary but usually include such information as: technical aspects and replanning of cities, legislation, reconstruction policies; official directories, organizations interested in planning, statistics, bibliography, regional planning authorities, who's who in planning, etc.

History

Hamlin, Talbot Faulkner. The American spirit in architecture. New Haven, Conn., Yale Univ. Pr., 1926. 353p. il. (Pageant of America. v.13) **Q123**

—— Architecture through the ages. Rev. ed. N.Y., Putnam, 1944. 680p. il. $7.50; students' ed. $6. **Q124**

An excellent survey history from the social point of view.

Kimball, Sidney Fiske. American architecture. Indianapolis, Bobbs-Merrill, 1928. 262p. il. $2.50. **Q125**

A brief survey with a useful bibliography, p.231-43.

—— and **Edgell, George Harold.** History of architecture. N.Y., Harper [c1918]. 621p. il. (Harper's Fine arts series) $4.50. **Q126**

Bibliographies at the ends of chapters. Glossary of terms, p.589-602.

Tallmadge, Thomas E. The story of architecture in America. New, enl. and rev. ed. N.Y., Norton, 1936. 332p. il. $4.75. **Q127**

CERAMICS

American Ceramic Society. Ceramic abstracts. . . . v.1, 1922- . Easton, Pa., Amer. Ceramic Soc., 1922- . v.1- . Monthly. **Q128**

Abstracts were included in the *Journal* of the society without separate paging in v.2, no.6–v.4, June 1919–Dec. 1921. Since Jan. 1922 they have been issued in the monthly numbers of the *Journal* with separate paging and independent title page and volume numbering.

McClelland, Ellwood Hunter. Enamel bibliography and abstracts, 1928 to 1939, inclusive, with subject and co-author indexes. Columbus, Ohio, Amer. Ceramic Soc., 1944. 352p. $5. **Q129**

An abstract bibliography of approximately 5000 items.

Solon, Louis Marc Emmanuel. Ceramic literature; an analytical index to the works published in all languages on the history and technology of the ceramic art; also to the catalogues of public museums, private collections and of auction sales . . . and to the most important price-lists of the ancient and modern manufactories. . . . Lond., Griffin, 1910. 660p. **Q130**

pt.1, Author list; pt.2, Classified list.

Barber, Edwin Atlee. Ceramic collector's glossary. N.Y., Walpole Soc., 1914. 119p. il. **Q131**

A dictionary of terms only, frequently with small line drawings.

Chaffers, William. Marks and monograms on European and oriental pottery and porcelain, with historical notices of each manufactory; over 5,000 potters' marks and illustrations, ed. by Frederick Litchfield . . . 14th ed. . . . Lond., Reeves, 1932. 1095p. il. (Los Angeles, Borden Pub. Co., $17.50) **Q132**

The standard work in English.

—— Collector's handbook of marks and monograms on pottery and porcelain of the renaissance and modern periods, with upwards of 5,000 marks, chiefly selected from his larger work entitled "Marks and monograms on pottery and porcelain." New ed., rev. and considerably aug. by Frederick Litchfield, ass'ted by R. L. Hobson and Justus Brinkman. Los Angeles, Borden Pub. Co., 1947. 367p. il. $4. **Q133**

Selected from the thirteenth edition of his *Marks and monograms* . . . 1912 (Q132).

—— New keramic gallery, containing 700 illustrations of rare, curious and choice examples of pottery and porcelain from early times to the beginning of the twentieth century . . . 3d ed., enlarged by over 100 additional illustrations, with descriptions . . . rev. and enl. by H. M. Cundall. Lond., Reeves, 1926. 2v. il. **Q134**

Garnier, Édouard. Dictionnaire de la céramique; faïences-grès-poteries . . . Aquarelles, marques et monogrammes d'après les dessins de l'auteur. Paris, Librairie de l'Art [1893]. 258p. il., col. pl. (Bibliothèque internat. de l'art. Guides du collectionneur) **Q135**

Includes biography.

Searle, Alfred Broadhead. Encyclopaedia of the ceramic industries. Lond., Benn, 1929–30. 3v. il. **Q136**

Subtitle: Being a guide to the materials, methods of manufacture, means of recognition, and testing the various articles produced in the clayworking and allied industries. Bibliographical references.

CLOCKS AND WATCHES

Baillie, G. H. Watchmakers and clockmakers of the world. 2d ed. Lond., N.A.G. Press, 1947. 388p. maps. **Q137**

1st ed. 1929.

An alphabetical directory giving name, place, date, type of clock or watch and sometimes other brief information. Lists makers to 1825 with a few outstanding later names. The second edition includes some 35,000 names, 10,000 more than the first edition.

Britten, Frederick James. Old clocks and watches and their makers; being an historical and descriptive account of the different styles of clocks and watches of the past, in England and abroad, to which is added a list of nearly 12,000 makers. 6th ed., much enl. Lond., Spon [pref. 1932]. 891p. il. 32s.; $12.75. **Q138**

—— The watch and clock maker's handbook, dictionary and guide. 14th ed., rev. by J. W. Player. Lond., Spon; N.Y., Chemical Pub. Co., 1938. 547p. il. 34s.; $6. **Q139**

In this edition the section on "History of horological instruments and the men who designed and constructed them" has been omitted as it is treated in his *Old clocks and watches and their makers* (Q138).

FURNITURE

Grand Rapids, Mich. Public Library. List of books on furniture, with descriptive notes. Issued in connection with the 100th furniture market in Grand Rapids, January, 1928. Grand Rapids, 1927. 143p. $1.50. **Q140**

Aronson, Joseph. The encyclopedia of furniture. N.Y., Crown, 1938. 202p. il. $4. **Q141**

Alphabetical arrangement of short articles, illustrated with 1115 photographs and many line cuts.
Bibliography, p.201-02.

Bajot, Édouard. Encyclopédie du meuble du xvᵉ siècle jusqu'à nos jours. Recueil de planches contenant des meubles de style de toutes les époques et de tous les pays, depuis le xvᵉ siècle . . . classées par ordre alphabétique . . . 2000 meubles de style reproduits à grande échelle. Paris, C. Schmid [1901–09]. 20 pts. in 19v. 600 pl. **Q142**

Johnson, Axel Petrus and **Sironen, M. K.** Manual of the furniture arts and crafts, ed. by W. J. Etten. Grand Rapids, Mich., A. P. Johnson, 1928. 899p. il. $5.50. **Q143**

A handbook of brief information on furniture history, period styles, woods and veneers, manufacturing and merchandising, museum collections in the United States, etc. Gives bibliographical references throughout and contains a general bibliography based on the collection of the Grand Rapids Public Library and a glossary of furniture terms based, with additions, on the Penderel-Brodhurst Glossary (Q147).

Lockwood, Luke Vincent. Furniture collectors' glossary. N.Y., Walpole Soc., 1913. 55p. il. **Q144**

"Compiled with the idea of bringing together in convenient form the words used in the cabinet-maker's art."—*Pref.*

Macquoid, Percy and **Edwards, Ralph.** Dictionary of English furniture, from the middle ages to the late Georgian period. Lond., "Country Life"; N.Y., Scribner, 1924–27. 3v. il. £15 15s.; $120. **Q145**

Alphabetically arranged. Excellent illustrations, some in color. Of first importance.

Nutting, Wallace. Furniture treasury (mostly of American origin). All periods of American furniture with some foreign examples in America also American hardware and household utensils. Framingham, Mass., Old American Co., 1928–33. 3v. il. (v.1-2 reissued: N.Y., Macmillan, 1948. $20) **Q146**

Volumes 1-2 include 5000 plates numbered consecutively, with an index in volume 2. Volume 3 (1933) has subtitle: Being a record of designers, details of designs and structure, with lists of clock makers in America, and a glossary of furniture terms, richly illustrated,—and designed to supplement the first two volumes by supplying fuller details.

Penderel-Brodhurst, James George Joseph. Glossary of English furniture of the historic periods. Lond., Murray, 1925. 196p. **Q147**

Viollet-Le-Duc, Eugène Emmanuel. Dictionnaire raisonné du mobilier français de l'époque Carlovingienne à la Renaissance. Paris, Morel, 1874–75. 6v. il. **Q148**

v.1, pt.1, Meubles; v.2, pt.2, Ustensiles; pt.3, Orfévrerie; pt.4, Instruments de musique; pt.5, Jeux, passetemps; pt.6, Outils, outillages; v.3-4, pt.7, Vêtements bijoux de corps, objets de toilette; v.5-6, pt.8, Armes de guerre offensives et défensives.

❧ There are many types of books dealing with interior decoration. A useful series of popular works is published by J. B. Lippincott as "Lippincott's Practical books for the enrichment of home life" including separate volumes on wall-treatments, tapestries, chinaware, oriental rugs, period furniture, furnishing the small house and apartment, etc.

METAL ARTS
Gold and silver

Chaffers, William. Hall marks on gold and silver plate, illus. with revised tables of annual date letters employed in the Assay Offices of England Scotland and Ireland. 10th ed. extended and enl and with the addition of new date letters and marks, and a bibliography. C. A. Markham. Lond., Reeves, 1922. 395p. il. **Q149**

Jackson, Charles James. English goldsmiths and their marks: A history of the goldsmiths and plateworkers of England, Scotland and Ireland; with over thirteen thousand marks, reproduced in facsimile from authentic examples of plate, and tables of date-letters and other hallmarks used in the Assay Offices of the United Kingdom. 2d ed., rev. and enl. Lond., Macmillan, 1921. 747p. **Q150**

"The term 'Goldsmith' is used, as it formerly was, not only with reference to the worker in gold, but as comprising the Silversmith and the worker in both gold and silver."—*Introd.*

Nocq, Henry. Le poinçon de Paris; répertoire des maîtres-orfèvres de la juridiction de Paris depuis le moyen-âge jusqu'à la fin du xviiie siècle. Paris, H. Floury, 1926–31. 4v., and Errata and add. list, 96p. il. **Q151**

Arranged alphabetically by name of the gold- or silversmith, giving brief information and mark.

Okie, Howard Pitcher. Old silver and old Sheffield plate. . . . Garden City, N.Y., Doubleday, 1928. 420p. il. $5. **Q152**

Subtitle: History of the silversmith's art in Great Britain and Ireland, with reproductions in facsimile of about thirteen thousand marks; tables of date letters and other marks; American silversmiths and their marks; Paris marks and Paris date letters with a description of the methods of marking employed by the Paris Guild of Silversmiths; hallmarks, and date letters when used, of nearly all the countries of Continental Europe, reproduced in facsimile; a history of Old Sheffield Plate and a description of the method of its production, with the names and marks in facsimile of every known maker.

Rosenberg, Marc. Der Goldschmiede Merkzeichen. 3. erweit. u. illustrierte Aufl. Frankfurt am Main, Frankfurter Verlagsanstalt, 1922–28. 4v. il. **Q153**

v.1-3, Deutsches Reich; v.4, Das europäische Ausland.

Pewter

Denman, Carolyn. A bibliography of pewter. Bost., Pewter Collectors' Club of America, 1945. 21p. (Its Bull. no.15) $1. **Q154**

Cotterell, Howard Herschel. Old pewter; its makers and marks in England, Scotland and Ireland. An account of the old pewterer and his craft, illustrating all known marks and secondary marks of the old pewterers with a series of plates showing the chief types of their wares. Lond., Batsford; N.Y., Scribner, 1929. 432p. il. $35; £5 5s. **Q155**

Alphabetical list of pewterers with illustrations of their marks where known, p.145-344; Initialled marks, alphabetical list of those marks which, with the device, bear the initial letters only of their owners' names, p.345-83; Il-

lustrations of those marks which bear neither their owner's names nor initials, p.384-89; Index to the devices, p.390-415; Index to the "Hallmarks," p.416-21; General index, p.425-32.

Laughlin, Ledlie Irwin. Pewter in America, its makers and their marks. Bost., Houghton, 1940. 2v. il. $25. **Q156**

Bibliography: v.2, p.[161]-[192].
78 plates, including portraits.

NUMISMATICS

Bowker, Howard Franklin. A numismatic bibliography of the Far East; a check list of titles in European languages. N.Y., Amer. Numismatic Soc., 1943. 144p. (Numismatic notes and monographs, no.101) $1.50. **Q157**

910 bibliographical items plus 71 dealers' catalogs dealing with the currency of China, Annam, Korea, Tibet, and Japan and the coinages of Nepal, Siam and Mexico.

Bullowa, David M. The Commemorative coinage of the United States, 1892–1938. . . . N.Y., Amer. Numismatic Soc., 1938. 192p. il. (Numismatic notes and monographs, no.83) $2.50. **Q158**

Continues and amends the *Commemorative coinage of the United States* by Howland Wood (N.Y., 1922). "From . . . 1892 to . . . 1922, the present text is still substantially as it originally appeared. . . ."—*Pref.*

Frey, Albert Romer. Dictionary of numismatic names, their official and popular designations. N.Y., 1917. 311p. (Amer. journal of numismatics. v.50) $5. **Q159**

A dictionary of names of coins and paper money, numismatic terms, materials, etc. Gives definitions, brief encyclopedic and historical information, and some bibliographical references. Does not tell the rarity or present values of old coins. Has a Geographical index and a Paper money index.

Reprinted as part 1 of *Dictionary of numismatic names* (N.Y., Barnes and Noble, 1947. $5); part 2 being *Glossary of numismatic terms in English, French, German, Italian, Swedish,* by Mark M. Salton (94p.).

Raymond, Wayte. Coins of the world; 19th century issues. 1st ed. N.Y., Raymond, 1947. 252p. il. **Q160**

Subtitle: Containing an extensive list of the silver and minor coins issued by the countries of the whole world, their colonies or dependencies, with illustrations of the principal or most interesting types and giving the average valuation among collectors and dealers.

—— Coins of the world; 20th century issues. 3d ed. N.Y., Raymond, 1948. 253p. il. **Q161**

Subtitle: Containing a complete list of all the coins issued by the countries of the whole world, their colonies or dependencies, with illustrations of most of the types and the average valuation among collectors and dealers.

—— Standard catalogue of United States coins and tokens from 1652 to present day, 1935- . N.Y., Raymond, 1934- . il. Annual. (1949, $3.50) **Q162**

Title varies. 1935–38 published by the Scott Stamp and Coin Co.

—— Standard paper money catalogue; early colonial notes, state issues, continental currency; bills of the Confederacy and southern states; notes of cities and towns. Giving the average valuations among collectors and dealers for the notes usually obtainable, with many illustrations. Comp. and pub. by Wayte Raymond, Inc. N.Y., 1940. 106p. il. (facsim.) $2. **Q163**

—— —— pt.2, 1946. U.S. notes and fractional currency. New ed. 48p. $1.

Schrötter, Friedrich, *Freiherr von.* Wörterbuch der Münzkunde, in Verbindung mit N. Bauer, K. Regling [u.A.]. Berlin, de Gruyter, 1930. 777p. il. **Q164**

An encyclopedia of numismatics from ancient to modern times.

Stockvis, Albert. Standard coin and medal catalogue of the world . . . from the earliest times (1000 B.C.) to the present day . . . [1st] ed., 1940- . Cleveland, c1939- . il. **Q165**

Title varies: 1940, *Standard coin catalogue of the world, from the earliest times (700 B.C.) to the present time.*
1945- , *Standard coin and medal catalogue of the world.*

Biography

Forrer, Leonard. Biographical dictionary of medallists: Coin, gem, and seal-engravers, mint-masters, etc., ancient and modern, with references to their works B.C. 500—A.D. 1900. Lond., Spink, 1902–30. 8v. **Q166**

v.1-6, A-Z; v.7-8, Supplement, A-Z.

POSTAGE STAMPS

[**Crawford, J. L. L.**] Bibliotheca Lindesiana. v.7, A bibliography of the writings, general, special, and periodical forming the literature of philately. Aberdeen, Univ. Pr., 1911. 924 col. **Q167**

—— —— Supplement . . . by E. D. Bacon. Lond., Philatelic Literature Soc., 1926. 136 col.

For record of catalog *see* A43.

Brookman, Lester G. The 19th century postage stamps of the U.S. [1st ed.] N.Y., Lindquist, 1947. 2v. il. **Q168**

Konwiser, Harry Myron. American philatelic dictionary and Colonial and Revolutionary posts N.Y., Minkus, 1947. 152p., 56p. il. $2.75. **Q169**

Colonial and Revolutionary posts, a history of the American postal systems (56p. at end) is a partial reprint of a work with the same title published in 1931 (Richmond, Dietz Pub. Co.).

Scott Publications, Inc. N.Y. Standard postage stamp catalogue (the encyclopedia of philately) N.Y., Scott, 1867- . (1949, 2v. $3.50 ea.; combined ed., $7) Annual. **Q170**

Gives illustration, description, denomination, and value used and unused, of all the principal stamps of all countries.
Publisher varies: Scott and Co.; Scott Stamp and Coin Co., Ltd., etc. For complete record of editions to 1908 *see* Crawford, *Bibliotheca Lindesiana,* v.7 (Q167).
1949, v.1, The American and the British Commonwealth of Nations; v.2, European countries and colonies and the independent nations of Africa and Asia.

Standard catalogue of postage stamps of the world, 1899- . Ipswich, Whitfield King, 1899- **Q171**

v.47, 1948, in 2 pts.; pt.1, The British Empire. 1947 7s. 6d.; pt.2, Foreign countries. 1948. 15s.

Stanley Gibbons, Ltd., London. Stanley Gibbons Simplified stamp catalogue . . . a priced catalogue of the postage stamps of the whole world, excluding varieties of paper, perforation, shade and watermark. 1st ed., 1934- . Lond., Gibbons, 1934- . il. Irregular. (1948, v.14, 15s.) **Q172**

U. S. Post Office Dept. Division of Stamps. A description of United States postage stamps, issued by the Post Office Dept. from July 1, 1847 to May 31, 1947. Wash., Govt. Prt. Off., 1947. 163p. il. 30c. **Q173**

Frequently revised.

COSTUME
Bibliography

Hiler, Hilaire and **Hiler, Meyer.** Bibliography of costume, a dictionary catalog of about eight thousand books and periodicals . . . ed. by Helen Grant Cushing, assisted by Adah V. Morris. N.Y., Wilson, 1939. 911p. $10.50. **Q174**

A dictionary catalog, with author, title, subject, editor, illustrator, engraver, and other entries in one alphabet. Lists "approximately eighty-four hundred works on costume and adornment, including books in all languages." —*Pref.*

Munro, Isabel Stevenson and **Cook, Dorothy E.** Costume index; a subject index to plates and illustrated text. N.Y., Wilson, 1937. 338p. Service basis. **Q175**

An important index to more than 600 works either wholly on costume or containing much material on the subject. Indexing is specific and detailed, under countries and localities, under classes of persons having special types of costume and under details of costume, e.g., shoes, hats, etc., with chronological subdivisions under important or large classes. The list of books indexed marks location of copies in some 33 libraries. The index as a whole serves three important uses: (1) primarily as a guide to the finding of some wanted costume or costume detail; (2) a guide to the building up of a collection of books on costume, and (3) the location of copies of such books not in the home library.

Colas, René. Bibliographie générale du costume et de la mode. Description des suites, recueils, séries, revues et livres français et étrangers relatifs au costume civil, militaire et religieux, aux modes, aux coiffures et aux divers accessoires de l'habillement. Avec une table méthodique et un index alphabétique. Paris, Colas, 1932. 2v. 200fr. **Q176**

Lipperheide, Franz Joseph, *Freiherr von.* Katalog der Freiherrlich von Lipperheide'schen Kostümbibliothek. Berlin, Lipperheide, 1896–1905. 2v. il. o.p. **Q177**

Classed catalog of an important collection which became the property of the Staatliche Kunstbibliothek, Berlin.

History and illustration

Davenport, Millia. The book of costume. N.Y., Crown, 1949. 2v. il. $15. **Q178**

3000 illustrations, a useful work.

Lester, Katherine Morris and **Oerke, Bess Viola.** Illustrated history of those frills and furbelows of fashion which have come to be known as: Accessories of dress; drawings by Helen Westerman. Peoria, Ill., Manual Arts, 1940. 587p. il. $10. **Q179**

Treats in groups the accessories worn or carried in connection with the costume; hats, veils, earrings, combs, fans, bracelets, walking-sticks, muffs, buttons, buckles, etc.

McClellan, Elizabeth. History of American costume, 1607–1870; with an introductory chapter on dress in the Spanish and French settlements in Florida and Louisiana. N.Y., Tudor, 1942. 661p. $3.48. **Q180**

Previous editions published under title: *Historic dress in America.*

Norris, Herbert. Costume and fashion. Lond., Dent, 1931–40. v.1-3 (in 4v.). $40. **Q181**

Contents: [v.1] Evolution of European dress through the earlier ages; v.2, Senlac to Bosworth, 1066–1485; v.3, The Tudors, Bk.1, 1485–1547; Bk.2, 1547–1603. 2v.

Planché, James Robinson. Cyclopaedia of costume; or, Dictionary of dress. Lond., Chatto, 1876–79. 2v. il. **Q182**

v.1, Dictionary of terms, materials, fabrics, etc.; v.2, History of costume in Europe to 1760. Many illustrations, some in color.

Racinet, Auguste. Le costume historique. Paris, Firmin-Didot, 1886. 6v. **Q183**

500 planches, 300 en couleurs, or et argent, 200 en camaïeu.

A comprehensive collection covering clothing of all periods and countries, furniture, arms, etc.

Truman, Nevil. Historic costuming. Lond., Pitman, 1937. 152p. il. $3.50. **Q184**

Planned for the theatrical costumer, describes details of costumes by country and period. Useful also for anyone interested in accurate details of historical costume.

Terminology

Picken, Mary Brooks. The language of fashion; dictionary and digest of fabric, sewing and dress by Mary Brooks Picken and the editorial and research staff of the Mary Brooks Picken School. N.Y., Funk & Wagnalls, 1939. 175p. il. $5. **Q185**

Gives in alphabetical arrangement the definitions of more than 8000 words associated with wearing apparel. Indicates pronunciation. Many line drawings.

DANCING

Bibliography

Magriel, Paul David. A bibliography of dancing; a list of books and articles on the dance and related subjects. N.Y., Wilson, 1936. 229p. il. **Q186**

—— —— Fourth cumulated supplement, 1936–40. 1941. 104p.

Guide to dance periodicals. . . . Asheville, N.C., Stephen Pr., 1948- . **Q187**

Compiled by S. Y. Belknap.

Volume 3, Jan. 1941–Dec. 1945, issued 1948, indexed by author and subject the articles in seven periodicals devoted to the dance.

Volume 1, 1931–35, volume 2, 1936–40, volume 4, 1946–50, are in preparation.

Minneapolis Public Library. Music Dept. Index to folk dances and singing games. Chic., Amer. Lib. Assoc., 1936. 216p. $1. **Q188**

Includes folk dances, singing games, classic dances, tap and clog, and some earlier square and contra dances.

—— —— Supplement. 1949. 98p. $1.25.

Indexes 60 collections published 1936–48.

Encyclopedias and handbooks

Beaumont, Cyril William. Complete book of ballets; a guide to the principal ballets of the 19th and 20th centuries. N.Y., Putnam, 1938. 900p. il. (Repr. N.Y., Garden City Pub. Co., 1941. $1.98) **Q189**

Gives synopses of the ballets.

———— Supplement. 1942. 208p. il.

Chujoy, Anatole. The Dance encyclopedia. N.Y., Barnes, 1949. 546p. $7.50. **Q190**

Includes long encyclopedic articles on various forms of the dance written by specialists, in the same alphabet with briefer articles covering biography, special ballets, types of dances, terms used in dancing, ballet, etc. Appendixes include a bibliography of books in English on the dance and a discography of theater dance music.

THEATER

See also Drama, p.370-72.

Handbooks

Sobel, Bernard. Theatre handbook and digest of plays. N.Y., Crown Pub., 1948. 897p. $4. **Q191**
1st ed. 1940.
Includes in one alphabetical arrangement theatrical terms, biographical notices, digests of plays, and short essays, many of them signed by specialists, on particular phases of the theater or drama. Covers all periods and all countries. Bibliography compiled by George Freedley, p.867-90. List of plays arranged by subject under heading "Drama, Subjects," p.277-95.
The 1948 edition shows very little change from the 1940 edition. There are almost no new entries, in a few cases titles of new plays have been added to an actor's repertoire but this has not been done consistently. A very few titles have been added to the bibliography. No new plays 1940-48 seem to be treated. Would not be needed in most libraries having the first edition.

History

Mantzius, Karl. History of theatrical art in ancient and modern times, with an introduction by William Archer; authorized translation by Louise von Cossel. Lond., Duckworth; Phila., Lippincott, 1903–21. 6v. il. (Repr. N.Y., Peter Smith, 1937. $6 ea.) **Q192**
v.1, Earliest times; v.2, Middle ages and renaissance; v.3, Shakespearean period in England; v.4, Molière and his times; the theatre in France in the 17th century; v.5, The Great actors of the eighteenth century; v.6, Classicism and romanticism, tr. by C. Archer.

Annuals

The Theatre book of the year, 1942/43- ; a record and an interpretation, by George Jean Nathan. N.Y., Knopf, 1943- . v.1- . Annual. **Q193**
The plays are arranged in chronological order by opening date. Gives cast and personal, critical review by

George Jean Nathan of each play. Index of plays, index of authors and composers.

Theatre world, ed. by Daniel Blum, 1944/45- . N.Y., Theatre World, 1945- . v.1- . il. **Q194**
Annual survey of the theater, with many illustrations, listing plays that appeared on Broadway, with casts, dates of opening and closing, etc., but with no critical comment. Brief biographical sketches of outstanding players, producers, designers, etc. Obituaries.

Dobson's Theatre yearbook, 1948/49- . ed. by John Andrews and Ossia Trilling. Lond., Dobson, 1948- . **Q195**
A survey of the theater in London and England, followed by a list of theater organizations, bibliographies, directories of theaters in the United Kingdom, etc.

Amateur production and dramatic technique

Bibliography

British Drama League. Library. Player's library and bibliography of the theatre, comp. by Violet Kent, with introd. by Geoffrey Whitworth and F. S. Boas. Lond., Drama League, 1930–34. 2v. **Q196**
v.1, Basic volume, 401p.; v.2, Accessions since 1930.
The basic volume is a catalog of over 12,000 plays, giving for each play listed brief descriptive information, i.e., kind of play, number of acts, changes of scenery, number of characters, period, etc. Title index of plays. Plays listed are largely modern.

Perry, Clarence Arthur. Work of the little theatres; the groups they include, the plays they produce, their tournaments, and the handbooks they use. N.Y., Russell Sage Foundation, 1933. 228p. $1.50. **Q197**

Smith, Milton Myers. Guide to play selection; a descriptive index of full-length and short plays for production by schools, colleges and little theaters. N.Y., Appleton-Century, 1934. 174p. il. **Q198**
A publication of the National Council of Teachers of English.

Handbooks

Dean, Alexander. Fundamentals of play directing. N.Y., Farrar and Rinehart, 1941. 428p. il. $3.50. **Q199**
A practical manual for both the professional and the amateur.

Gassner, John. Producing the play, with the New scene technician's handbook, by Philip Barber. N.Y., Dryden, 1941. 744p. il. $4.50. **Q200**

A useful handbook on all phases of play production combining the esthetic and practical aspects. Some chapters have been contributed by specialists. The last section is a technical handbook on scenery construction, making of costumes, lighting, acoustics, etc.

Biography

Eisenberg, Ludwig Julius. Grosses biographisches Lexikon der deutschen Bühne im XIX. Jahrhundert. Leipzig, List, 1903. 1180p. **Q201**

Fairly long sketches but no references to sources.

Lyonnet, Henry. Dictionnaire des comédiens français (ceux d'hier): Biographie, bibliographie, iconographie. Genève, Bibliothèque de la Revue Universelle Internationale Illustrée, 1911–12. 2v. il. **Q202**

Issued in 80 parts, 1902–12.
Does not include living persons. Biographies are of some length with many bibliographical references. Some portraits and facsimiles of autographs included.

Nungezer, Edwin. Dictionary of actors and of other persons associated with the public representation of plays in England before 1642. New Haven, Conn., Yale Univ. Pr.; Lond., Milford, 1929. 438p. (Cornell studies in English, 13) **Q203**

Fuchs, Max. Lexique des troupes de comédiens au XVIIIe siècle. Paris, Droz, 1944. 231p. (Bibliothèque de la Société des Historiens du Théâtre, IX) **Q204**

Brief biographical and identifying information with indications of source.

Parker, John. Who's who in the theatre; a biographical record of the contemporary stage. 10th ed. rev. Lond., Pitman, 1947. 2014p. **Q205**

1st ed. 1912; 2d ed. 1914; 3d ed. 1916; 4th ed. 1922; 5th ed. 1925; 6th ed. 1930; 7th ed. 1933; 8th ed. 1936; 9th ed. 1939.
Fairly detailed biographies of persons connected with the modern theater, including actors, actresses, dramatists, composers, critics, managers, scenic artists, historians, and biographers.
Contents: Theatrical calendar, arranged by months; London play bills, 1939–1946; Biographies, critics; Index names of living persons in previous editions; Miscellaneous lists, e.g., genealogies of theatrical families, title list of notable productions of the London stage, title list of long runs, in London and New York, theatrical and musical obituary, theatrical wills, etc.

Rasi, Luigi. I comici italiani, biografia, bibliografia, iconografia. Firenze, Bocca, 1897–1905. 3v. il. **Q206**

Sundström, Einer. Svenska konstnärer inom teaterns, musikens och filmens värld . . . för teateravdelningen, Arne Lindenbaum; för musik-avdelningen, Ake Vretblad. . . . Stockholm, Mimer [1943]. 531p. il. **Q207**

An historical section including a sketch of the Swedish theater from 1500 to 1900 and sketches of Swedish music, opera, films, ballet, etc., is followed by a biographical section, p.209-527, giving biographical sketches with portraits of the outstanding persons in these fields, primarily of the twentieth century.

PHOTOGRAPHY
Bibliography

Columbia University. Library. Epstean Collection. A catalogue of the Epstean collection on the history and science of photography and its applications especially to the graphic arts. N.Y., Columbia Univ. Pr., 1937. 109p. il. **Q208**

—— Authors and short title index. Corrected, with additions, to May 1, 1938. N.Y., 1938. 31p.

—— Accessions, May 1938–Dec. 1941 with addenda 1942. N.Y., 1942. 29p.

Eastman Kodak Co. Research Laboratories. Monthly abstract bulletin, 1915- . Rochester, Company, 1915- . v.1- . Monthly. **Q209**

Signed abstracts with annual index of authors but not topics.

Photographic abstracts, v.1, 1921- . Lond., Royal Photographic Soc. of Gt. Brit., 1921- . Quarterly. 30s. per yr. **Q210**

Signed abstracts of British and foreign periodical material. Annual author index.

Dictionaries and encyclopedias

Fenner, Frank, Jr. A glossary for photography defining over 3000 words having a photographic significance. Chic., Ziff-Davis, 1939. 147p. (Little technical library) 95c. **Q211**

Lester, Henry M. Photo-lab-index; the cumulative formulary of standard recommended photographic procedures. [10th ed.] N.Y., Morgan and Lester, 1939- . loose-leaf annual with quarterly supplements. $9. **Q212**

A basic manual.
Includes *A guide to the literature of photography and related subjects,* compiled by Albert Boni.

Modern encyclopedia of photography; a standard work of reference for amateur and professional photographers. General ed., S. G. Blaxland Stubbs, assoc. eds., F. J. Mortimer and Gordon S. Malthouse. . . . Bost., Amer. Photographic Pub. Co. [1938?]. 2v. il. $12. **Q213**

Paged continuously.

Contents: v.1, Aberration-Epidiascope; v.2, Exakta-Zoo. Bibliography, p.1330-33. General index, p.1334-50.

An English work, printed in England, distributed in America under an American imprint, therefore the differences between English and American terminology must be borne in mind. Contributors are largely British authorities in various fields of photography. Some 60 per cent of the articles are signed. The style is generally popular though some of the articles would be useful to the professional. Illustrations are good, some in color. The arrangement is usually alphabetical under broad headings but there are also many short articles on small subjects.

Wall, Edward John. Wall's Dictionary of photography and reference book for amateur and professional photographers, ed. by F. J. Mortimer. 17th ed. rev. and largely rewritten by A. L. M. Sowerby. Lond., pub. for Amateur Photographer by Fountain Pr., 1948. 705p. il. 15s. **Q214**

Frequently reprinted, with some corrections and additions.

Annuals

American annual of photography, v.1, 1887- . Bost., Amer. Photographic Pub. Co., 1887- . v.1- . il. (v.63, 1949, $3) **Q215**

British journal photographic almanac and photographer's daily companion, with which is incorporated the Year book of photography and amateurs' guide and the Photographic annual, 1861- . Lond., Greenwood, 1861- . il. Annual. (v.90, 1949, 7s. 6d.) **Q216**

Microfilms

Special Libraries Association. Committee on Microfilming and Documentation. Directory of microfilm services in the United States and Canada. Rev. ed. N.Y., Assoc., 1947. 30p. $1.50. **Q217**

A list of libraries and commercial firms equipped to make microfilms; gives prices and services available at each.

Moving pictures

Reinert, Charles. Kleines Filmlexikon; Kunst, Technik, Geschichte, Biographie, Schrifttum. Einsiedeln-Zürich, Benziger, 1946. 424p. il. **Q218**
2. Aufl.

International. Biographical sketches include both authors and film stars with lists of works or films acted in.

Winchester's Screen encyclopedia, ed. by Maud M. Miller. Lond., Winchester Publications, 1948. 385p. il. 21s.; $6.25. **Q219**

Biographical and directory information with sections on history of the film, film music, documentaries, foreign

language films, etc. From the British viewpoint but includes American stars, companies, pictures, etc.

Annuals

Informational film year book, v.1, 1947- . Edinburgh, Albyn Pr., 1947- . il. Annual. (1948, 12s. 6d.; $3.75) **Q220**

Includes information on documentary and educational films, etc. Gives lists of societies, producers, services, etc.

International motion picture almanac, 1929- N.Y., Quigley Pub. Co., 1929- . il. Annual. **Q221**

1949/50 includes sections on who's who in motion pictures; corporations; theater circuits; pictures; services; theater equipment and materials; organizations; codes and censorship; world market; the industry in Great Britain; the press; nontheatrical motion pictures; television and radio.

MUSIC
General works
Guides

Haydon, Glen. Introduction to musicology; a survey of the fields, systematic and historical of musical knowledge and research. N.Y., Prentice Hall, 1941. 329p. **Q222**

Bibliographies at end of each chapter and a general bibliography, p.301-13.

Bibliography

Bobillier, Marie. Bibliographie des bibliographies musicales, par Michel Brenet [pseud.]. (In L'Année musicale 3:1-152, 1913) **Q223**

An extensive listing of musical bibliographies in five sections: (1) General works, arranged alphabetically by author (or by title for anonymous works); (2) Individual bibliographies, by name of musician; (3) Catalogs of public libraries, by name of city; (4) Catalogs of private libraries by names of owners; (5) Catalogs of publishers and booksellers.

Fischer, Wilhelm. Verzeichnis von bibliographischen Hilfswerken für musikhistorische Arbeiten. (In Adler, Guido. Methode der Musikgeschichte. Leipzig, 1919. p.200-22) **Q224**

Krohn, Ernst C. The bibliography of music. (In Musical quarterly 5:231-54, 1919) **Q225**
A survey article.

King, A. Hyatt. Recent work in music bibliography. (In The library, 4th ser., v.26, p.122-48, Sept.–Dec. 1945) **Q226**

A survey of important reference works in music from 1935–1944.

BOOKS

American Council of Learned Societies Devoted to Humanistic Studies. Committee on Musicology. A bibliography of periodical literature in musicology and allied fields. Wash., Council, 1940–43. 2v. $1. **Q227**

no.1, Oct. 1, 1938–Sept. 30, 1939, by D. H. Daugherty, includes a *Record of graduate theses accepted;* no.2, Oct. , 1939–Sept. 30, 1940, by D. H. Daugherty, L. Ellinwood, and R. S. Hill.
No more published.

—— Report on publication and research in musicology and allied fields in the United States, 1932–1938. Wash., 1938. 84p. **Q228**

p.41-47, Libraries (Suppl. to Strunk [Q238]).
p.57-74, Graduate theses related directly or indirectly , musicology accepted in the United States, 1932–1938.
p.75-84, General bibliography, 1932–37.
Indexing of articles relating to music in general periodicals.

Boston. Public library. Catalogue of the Allen . Brown collection of music in the Public Library of the City of Boston. Bost., Library, 1908– 5. 4v. **Q229**

v.1-3, A-Z; v.4, suppl.
A dictionary catalog of an important collection.
Includes many analytics.

Chase, Gilbert. Guide to Latin American music. Wash., Library of Congress, Music Division 1945]. 274p. (U.S. Library of Congress. Latin Amer. ser. no.5) 45c. **Q230**

An annotated bibliography with introductory comments for each country. Subheadings for each country vary somewhat but usually include: Introduction; General and miscellaneous; Biography and criticism; National them; Folk and primitive music.

Eitner, Robert. Biographisch-bibliographisches Quellen-Lexikon der Musiker und Musikgelehrten der christlichen Zeitrechnung bis zur Mitte es neunzehnten Jahrhunderts. Leipzig, Breitkopf, 1900–04. 10v. **Q231**

Gives brief biographies and full bibliographies; the most important work for bibliographies of manuscripts, early editions, etc., of authors and composers. In many ses indicates location of the items in European libraries. criticism by Michel Brenet (Marie Bobillier) in *La vue musicale,* 1905, p. 480-89, contains various corrctions. Corrections and additions are also included in *Miscellanea musicae bio-bibliographica: Musikgeschichtliche Quellennachweis,* by Hermann Springer ublished quarterly, 1912–16).
There is an anastatic reprint, undated, which embodies ne corrections but which has no outward indication t it differs from the first printing. The whole work, luding the *Miscellanea* was reproduced from the first nting by Musurgia Publishers in 1947, at $117.35.

Handbuch der musikalischen Literatur; oder, lgemeines systematisch-geordnetes Verzeichnis der in Deutschland und in den angrenzenden Ländern gedruckten Musikalien auch musikalischen Schriften und Abbildungen, mit Anzeige der Verleger und Preise. 3., bis zum Anfang des Jahres 1844 ergänzte Aufl. Bearb. und hrsg. von Adolf Hofmeister. Leipzig, Hofmeister, 1844–45. 3v. **Q232**

First published in Leipzig by Anton Meysel, 1817, covering music and music literature to 1815 with nine supplements to 1825.
Karl Friedrich Whistling issued a revised second edition in 1828 with three supplements, 1829, 1834 and 1839.
Adolf Hofmeister edited this third edition called C. F. Whistling's *Handbuch* with supplementary volumes, as follows: Handbuch der musikalischen Literatur; oder, Verzeichnis der im Deutschen Reiche, in den Ländern deutschen Sprachgebietes, sowie der für den Vertrieb im Deutschen Reiche wichtigen, im Auslande erschienenen Musikalien auch musikalischen Schriften, Abbildungen und plastischen Darstellungen, mit Anzeige der Verleger und Preise. [4.]-18.Bd. oder 1.-[15.]Ergänzungsbd. 1844– 1933. . . . Leipzig, Hofmeister, 1852–1934. v.1-15.
Ergänzungsbd. 1 covers 1844–51; 2, 1852–59; 3, 1860– 67; thereafter each Ergänzungsbd. covers 6 years through 1903. 1904–08- . Quinquennial.

Hofmeisters Jahresverzeichnis; Verzeichnis sämtlicher Musikalien, Musikbücher, Zeitschriften, Abbildungen und plastischen Darstellungen, die in Deutschland und in den deutschsprachigen Ländern erschienen sind. . . . Leipzig, Hofmeister, 1852- . v.1- . Annual. **Q233**

Title varies.
Cumulated in *Handbuch der musikalischen Literatur* (Q232). Supplemented by:

Hofmeisters musikalisch-literarischer Monatsbericht neuer Musikalien, musikalischen Schriften und Abbildungen. . . . Leipzig, Hofmeister, 1829- . Monthly. **Q234**

Heyer, Anna Harriet. A check-list of publications of music. Ann Arbor, Univ. of Michigan, School of Music, 1944. 49p. **Q235**

A union list of holdings for important musical periodicals, historical collections of music, and the collected editions of individual composers, in 113 libraries. Prepared as a supplementary section to the author's masters essay at the University of Michigan on the "State and Resources of Musicology in the U.S. 1942."

McColvin, Lionel Roy and **Reeves, Harold.** Music libraries: Their organization and contents, with a bibliography of music and musical literature. Lond., Grafton, 1937–38. 2v. 10s. 6d. ea. **Q236**

Includes chapters on organization, cataloging, classification, binding, storage, etc. Bibliographies: v.1, p.55-214, Musical literature; v.2, p.6-209, Music. Directory of libraries and collections of music and musical literature, v.2, p.213-92.

National Association of Schools of Music. List of books on music 1935; supplements 1-5, 1936–1946. Memphis, Tenn., Assoc., 1935–46. 6v. (Its Bulletin, nos. 3, 6, 11, 15, 18, 24) 1935, 25c; suppl. 1, 3, 4, 10c ea.; suppl. 2, 5, 15c ea.   **Q237**

Strunk, William Oliver. State and resources of musicology in the United States; a survey made for the American Council of Learned Societies. Wash., Council, 1932. 76p. 25c.   **Q238**

p.63-68, Musicological publications in American libraries. A union list of the holdings of 57 libraries for 44 of the most important musicological publications. Partially amplified and brought up to date by Heyer (Q235).

p.43-51, Theses bearing directly or indirectly on music, accepted at American universities since 1919 (includes Masters and Doctors). Supplemented by American Council of Learned Societies, *Report* (Q228).

U. S. Copyright Office. Catalog of copyright entries. 3d ser. v.1, 1947- . Wash., Govt. Prt. Off., 1947- .   **Q239**

pt.5A, Published music, $3 per yr.; pt.5B, Unpublished music, $3 per yr.; pt.14A, Renewal registrations—Music, $2 per yr.

Each part is published in two numbers per year, January—June and July—December. Part 5A, Published music, lists all music published in the United States and foreign countries deposited for copyright registration during the period covered. Arranged alphabetically under main headings (composer, editor, arranger, or in some cases title) with cross references from other names. There is a title index. Beginning with the second number of the 1948 volume there is a classified index listing each publication under its medium of performance, form or subject. Part 5A forms the most comprehensive bibliography of recently published music available.

Part 5B contains all current registrations of unpublished music, listed alphabetically by title.

Part 14B lists alphabetically by title all music on which copyright has been renewed during the period covered.

This latest series which has been much improved in organization and format was preceded by:

—— Catalog of copyright entries . . . pt.3, Musical compositions, n.s. v.1-41, 1906–46. Monthly, 1906–45; annually, 1946.

Through 1945 all musical compositions published and unpublished were entered by title in one alphabet in each monthly issue followed by the list of renewals, with an annual index.

In 1946 the catalog was divided into four groups: (1) Unpublished music; (2) Published music; (3) Renewals; (4) Title index to groups 1 and 2.

For full description of the *Catalog of copyright entries* see A159.

❧ Useful current listings of new materials are to be found in *Acta musicologica*; Music Library Association, *Notes: A magazine devoted to music and its literature with bibliographies and reviews of books, records, music; Music and letters;* and the *Musical quarterly.*

Many of the encyclopedias and bibliographies of music include lists and descriptions of libraries and collections with indication of printed catalog Among the more useful are (1) *Grove's Dictiona of music and musicians* (Q254) under "Librari and collections of music" (main work and Supp ment); (2) McColvin and Reeves, *Music librari* (v.2, p.213-92. [Q236]); (this list is planned supplement that in Grove); (3) "Bibliothèques p bliques et bibliothèques privées" in Bobillier, *Bi liographie des bibliographies musicales* (Q223).

DISSERTATIONS

❧ The record of graduate theses (Masters and Do tors), bearing directly or indirectly on music, a cepted in the United States may be found as follow 1919–31, in Strunk, *State and resources of mu cology in the United States* (Q238); 1932–38, American Council of Learned Societies, *Report*, 19 (Q228); 1938–39, in American Council of Learne Societies, *Bibliography*, no.1 (Q227).

MANUSCRIPT AND
PUBLISHED MUSIC

British Museum. Dept. of Manuscripts. Cat logue of manuscript music in the British Museu by Augustus Hughes-Hughes. Lond., printed order of the Trustees, 1906–09. 3v.   **Q2**

Classified list, with author, subject and title inde in each volume.

Contents: v.1, Sacred vocal music; v.2, Secular vo music; v.3, Instrumental music, treatises, etc.

—— **Dept. of Printed Books.** Catalogue printed music published between 1487 and 18 now in the British Museum, by W. Barcl Squire. Lond., printed by order of the Truste 1912. 2v.   **Q2**

Volume 2 includes first supplement.

—— —— 2d supplement, by William C. Smi Camb., Univ. Pr., 1940. 85p. 6s.

Dichter, Harry and **Shapiro, Elliott.** Early Am ican sheet music, its lure and its lore, 1768–18 including a directory of early American mu publishers. . . . N.Y., Bowker, 1941. 287p. facsim. (incl. music) $7.50.   **Q2**

"Famous American musical firsts," p.xxv-xxvii.

Part 3, "Lithographers and artists working on Americ sheet music before 1870, by Edith A. Wright and Jo phine A. McDevitt," p.249-57.

Arranged by class in chronological periods. Each pi is described with bibliographical details, illustrations, ∈

Sonneck, Oscar George Theodore. Bibliograp of early secular American music (18th centur Rev. and enl. by William Treat Upton. Was

Library of Congress, Music Division, 1945. 616p. $1.75. **Q243**

The original edition was published in 1905. Revised edition follows the same general principles but adds much new material. Locates copies.

Indexes and reviews

Music index; the key to current music periodical literature. Detroit, Mich., Information Service, 1949- . Monthly (cumulating annually). $125 per yr. **Q244**

Starting in January 1949, this new project indexes more than 40 American and English periodicals representing various aspects of the music field, ranging from musicology to the retailing of music. Gives complete indexing for musical periodicals, and indexes articles pertinent to music in some more general ones. All first performances and all obituaries are indexed. All music reviews are listed both under composer and medium. There is detailed subject indexing but authors of articles are not indexed individually. Foreign periodicals may be added at a later date.

Music reporter. N.Y., City Center of Music and Drama, Sept. 1947- . Monthly. Loose-leaf. $24 per yr. **Q245**

A reprinting of reviews of serious music as they actually appeared in the *N.Y. Times, N.Y. Herald Tribune, N.Y. Sun, N.Y. World Telegram* and the *N.Y. Journal American.* Reviews are reprinted in their entirety without editing or selection. Cumulated indexes are furnished monthly, cumulating finally into 6-month issues from September through February, March through August. The index includes a listing of first performances of new works.

Encyclopedias and biographical dictionaries

ASCAP biographical dictionary of composers, authors and publishers, ed. by Daniel I. McNamara. N.Y., Crowell, 1948. 483p. $5. **Q246**

Biographical data about past and present members of the American Society of Composers, Authors and Publishers, both standard and popular. Includes for each writer a list of his best known works.

Baker, Theodore. Baker's Biographical dictionary of musicians. 4th ed. rev. and enl. N.Y., Schirmer, 1940. 1240p. $6. **Q247**

1st ed. 1900; 2d ed. 1905; 3d ed. 1919. A useful and reliable dictionary, giving compact biographies, varying from a few lines to ten pages, of musicians of all ages and nations, with bibliographies of the musician's own works and titles about him. Indicates pronunciation of foreign names.

—— Supplement, 1949, by Nicolas Slonimsky. N.Y., Schirmer, 1949. p.1224-98. 75c.

Barlow, Harold and **Morgenstern, Sam.** A dictionary of musical themes; introd. by John Erskine. N.Y., Crown, 1948. 656p. $5. **Q248**

The "Bartlett" for musical themes, this work contains some 10,000 themes of instrumental music arranged by composers, with a notation index arranged alphabetically by the first notes of the themes. There is also an index of titles.

Cobbett, Walter Wilson. Cobbett's Cyclopedic survey of chamber music. Lond., Milford, 1929-30. 2v. $42. **Q249**

Signed articles, of some length, on all subjects connected in any way with chamber music—topics, persons, instruments, organizations, national developments, etc. Includes a large amount of biography. Contains full lists of composers' works, but otherwise little bibliography.

Dictionary of modern music and musicians. General ed., A. Eaglefield-Hull. Lond., Dent; N.Y., Dutton, 1924. 543p. 35s.; $5. **Q250**

Covers the modern music of all countries. Published also in a German translation (with some additional material) by Alfred Einstein entitled *Neue Musiklexikon* (Berlin, Hesse, 1926. 729p.).

Ewen, David. American composers today; a biographical and critical guide. N.Y., Wilson, 1949. 265p. il. $4. **Q251**

Includes biographies of contemporary composers of the United States, the major Latin American composers, and European composers who live in the Americas. Includes bibliographies.

—— Living musicians. N.Y., Wilson, 1940. 390p. il. $5. **Q252**

Biographies of 500 living musicians including singers, instrumentalists and conductors. Primarily those who would be of interest to the American public. Includes articles on such musical organizations as quartets, chamber music ensembles, etc.

Fétis, François Joseph. Biographie universelle des musiciens et bibliographie générale de la musique. 2. éd. entièrement refondu et augm. de plus de moitié. Paris, Didot, 1867-70. 8v. **Q253**

—— —— Supplément et complément publiés sous la direction de Arthur Pougin. Paris, Didot, 1878-80. 2v.

Grove, *Sir* George. Grove's Dictionary of music and musicians. 3d ed., ed. by H. C. Colles. Lond. and N.Y., Macmillan, 1927-28. 5v. il. $25. **Q254**

1st ed. 4v., 1879-89; 2d ed., ed. by J. A. Fuller-Maitland, 5v., 1904-08; American supplement to 2d ed., N.Y., 1920. 412p. The third edition (reprinted at various times without change) is extensively revised with considerable additional material and is reset throughout but not entirely rewritten.

The standard encyclopedia in English covering the whole field from 1450, with special emphasis, however, on English subjects.

Includes musical history, theory and practice, instruments, terms, etc., biographies of musicians, and articles on individual compositions, songs, operas, all in one alphabet. Does not give opera plots. Signed articles by specialists. The bibliographies are not always adequate, because of brevity, failure to include periodical articles, and dates and place of publication. Lists of composers' works are inadequately and inconsistently treated. In some cases these were better handled in the first edition of 1889. The full record of the work of important composers is usually more complete in Thompson's *International cyclopedia of music and musicians* (Q265).

—— —— American supplement, being the sixth volume of the complete work. Waldo Pratt, ed.; C. N. Boyd, assoc. ed. New ed. N.Y., Macmillan, 1928. 438p. il. $6.50.

Contains: (1) a compact historical introduction and a chronological register giving brief biographies of some 1700 persons; (2) main dictionary, in which about 700 names are given fuller treatment and other articles included. Includes United States, Canadian and some South American names.

The 1928 issue is a reprint of the 1920 issue with the addition of a supplement of 26 pages containing new material and cross references.

—— —— 4th ed. ed. by H. C. Colles. Lond., Macmillan, 1940. 6v. il. 30s.; $10 ea.

This English fourth edition includes slight plate revisions only, with cross references to volume 6, the new supplementary volume. The fourth edition was not published in this country but Volume 6 was issued as a *Supplementary volume* (*see* below).

A fifth edition to be edited by Eric Blom has been announced for publication, perhaps in 1951.

—— —— Supplementary volume. N.Y., Macmillan, 1940. 688p. il. $5.

Chronicles events since the third edition, amplifies and adds to material in that edition. Almost 80 per cent of the volume is devoted to biography. Particular attention is also paid to the broadcasting of music.

Historical Records Survey. District of Columbia. Bio-bibliographical index of musicians in the United States of America from colonial times. . . . Wash., Music Division, Pan American Union, 1941. 439p. (Pan American Union. Music Div. Music ser., no.2) $1. **Q255**

Sponsored by the Board of Commissioners of the District of Columbia; cosponsors, Pan American Union, Library of Congress.

Title, forewords, and introduction in English, Spanish, and Portuguese.

Indexes biographical material in about 65 books giving biographies of musicians in the United States. Names are given in as complete form as possible, followed by dates of birth and death when ascertainable and references to works in which biographical material is to be found.

"A list of special studies, biographies and autobiographies pertaining to the persons whose names appear in the Index," p.421-39.

Mayer-Serra, Otto. Música y músicos de Latinoamerica. Mexico, D.F., Ed. Atlante, 1947. 2v. il. **Q256**

An alphabetical encyclopedia covering history, biography (including living persons), folklore, religious music, musical instruments, terminology, legislation, etc.,

of all the countries of Spanish America. In some cases full bibliographies are given for composers. Includes portraits, musical examples, words and music of the national hymns of the various countries, etc.

Moser, Hans Joachim. Musik Lexikon. 2. völlig umgearb. Aufl. Berlin, Hesse, 1943. 1102p. il. **Q257**

An excellent small modern dictionary covering persons, terms, and subjects. Particularly useful for locating modern editions of old music.

Concise articles with well-selected bibliographies.

Palmer, Russell. British music. Lond., Skelton Robinson [1948]. 283p. il. 18s. **Q258**

A biographical index of British musicians and musical organizations.

Pratt, Waldo Selden. New encyclopedia of music and musicians. New ed. N.Y., Macmillan, 1929. 969p. il. $6; 12s. 6d. **Q259**

Planned originally as an abridgment of the second edition of *Grove's Dictionary* (Q254), but eventually developed as an independent work. First edition, 1924, 967p. the last edition differs only by the addition of a page and a half of death dates.

In three main parts, each alphabetically arranged: (1) Definitions and descriptions, including terms, topics, instruments, musical forms, about 1450 concise articles with references in some cases to fuller articles in Grove no bibliographies are appended to articles but there is a separate bibliography given as Appendix A; (2) Biographical dictionary of 7500 musicians from the year 1700, with briefer information about 1000 before 1700 given in Appendix B; (3) Places, institutions and organizations; Appendix C, List of operas and oratorios since 1900 with title and date of first presentation of each.

Reis, Claire. Composers in America; biographical sketches of contemporary composers with a record of their works, rev. and enl. ed. N.Y. Macmillan, 1947. 399p. $5. **Q260**

A revised edition of the work published in 1938 which included only living composers. This one includes composers who have written in America since 1915 whether or not they are still living. Brief biographical sketches are followed by lists of compositions, including unpublished manuscripts, with information about publishers, date, etc.

Riemann, Hugo. Hugo Riemanns Musik Lexikon. 11.Aufl., bearb. von Alfred Einstein. Berlin Hesse, 1929. 2v. il. **Q261**

—— —— 12. völlig neu bearb. Aufl. hrsg. von Josef Müller-Blattau. Mainz, Schott [1939?] v.1-2. il.

v.1-2, A-Beethoven.

—— Dictionnaire de musique. Tr. par George Humbert. 3. éd. entièrement refondue et augm sous la direction de A. Schaeffner, avec la collaboration de M. Pincherle, Y. Rokseth, A. Tessier. Paris, Payot, 1931. 1485p. il. **Q262**

The first French edition (1897) is a translation by Georges Humbert of the fourth German edition. The second (1913) and third French editions are not merely translations but are revisions as well. The present French edition (third) has kept to the original Riemann idea of a one-volume work as opposed to the eleventh German edition which has grown into two volumes. This French edition has taken over a good deal of material from the tenth German edition but has reduced the amount of space given to German subjects and has increased that for French, English and Italian musicians particularly of the sixteenth, seventeenth and eighteenth centuries, and the Spanish and Russian schools.

Scholes, Percy Alfred. The Oxford companion to music; self-indexed and with a pronouncing glossary. 7th ed. rev. with appendices. Lond., Ox. Univ. Pr., 1947. 1145p. il. (179pl.) 42s.; $15. **Q262**

Originally published in 1938 this useful compendium has gone through several editions in England, each one including some changes and corrections in the text. In the third British edition, Appendix I was added. This was enlarged in the fourth and included in the second American edition published in 1943. Appendix II was added in the fifth British edition and enlarged in the sixth and seventh editions: seventh edition, Appendix I, p.1095-1132; Appendix II, p.1133-45. Additions in the appendixes are cross-indexed from and to the main work.

A comprehensive alphabetical dictionary on all phases of music containing long encyclopedic articles, some short articles, and many definitions. Includes some 1500 biographical articles.

The second edition, 1940, included as an appendix the following bibliography which is also available separately:

—— A list of books about music in the English language, prepared as an appendix to The Oxford companion to music. Lond., N.Y., Ox. Univ. Pr., 1940. 64p. 3s. 6d.; 75c. **Q263**

Slonimsky, Nicolas. Music since 1900. 3d ed. rev. and enl. N.Y., Coleman-Ross, 1949. 759p. $7.50. **Q264**

Contents: Tabular views of stylistic trends in music, 1900-1948; Descriptive chronology, 1900-1948; Letters and documents.

Thompson, Oscar. International cyclopedia of music and musicians. 5th ed. rev. and enl. by Nicolas Slonimsky. N.Y., Dodd, Mead, 1949. 2380p. il. (music) $16. **Q265**

A very useful one-volume encyclopedia alphabetically arranged. Most of the articles are short but there are also included in the same alphabet signed monographs written by authorities on the more important composers and also on special subjects such as history of music, music criticisms, Negro music, folk music, opera, etc. Many of these articles are five to six pages in length and some run to as much as 15 to 20 pages. Each of the biographical articles is followed by a calendar of the composer's life and a classified list of his works. The work is strong in biography and many contemporary names are included. There are three appendixes: Plots of operas, p.2099-2243 (this section has been reprinted separately; *see* Q293); Pronunciation of names and titles by W. B. S. Smith, p.2247-67; and Bibliography, p.2297-2380, which is alphabetically arranged by author and

subject. There are also occasional bibliographies attached to articles in the main work.

First edition, 1939. Later editions show spotty revision, adding dates of death, some corrections and additional material in the appendixes.

Vannes, René. Dictionnaire des musiciens. (Compositeurs) Préface de Charles Van den Borren. Bruxelles, Larcier, 1947. 443p. 120fr.b. (Petits dictionnaires des lettres et des arts en Belgique) **Q266**

Bio-bibliographical notices of Belgian composers. Those dealing with persons before 1830 were done by Vannes, later ones by André Souris.

Dictionaries of terms

Apel, Willi. Harvard dictionary of music. Camb., Harvard Univ. Pr., 1944. 824p. il. $6. **Q267**

The emphasis is on the historical point of view. Omits biographical articles because other dictionaries cover that field. Contains definitions of all kinds including many used in musical performance, and articles on music history, esthetics, theory, etc. The bibliographies list books, periodical articles, and references to examples of music.

Baker, Theodore. Dictionary of musical terms . . . with a supplement containing an English-Italian vocabulary for composers. N.Y., Schirmer, 1923. 257p. music. **Q268**

Subtitle: Containing upwords of 9,000 English, French, German, Italian, Latin and Greek words and phrases used in the art and science of music, carefully defined, and with the accent of the foreign words marked; preceded by rules for the pronunciation of Italian, German and French.

"24th issue thoroughly revised, and augmented by an appendix of 700 additional words and phrases."

Bobillier, Marie. Dictionnaire pratique et historique de la musique par Michel Brenet [pseud.] 510 citations musicales, 140 figures. Paris, Colin 1926. 487p. il. **Q269**

Vannes, René. Essai de terminologie musicale. Dictionnaire universel comprenant plus de 15,000 termes de musique en italien, espagnol, portugais, français, anglais, allemand, latin et grec, disposés en un alphabet unique. Thann, "Alsatia," 1925. 230p. **Q270**

Annuals

Billboard encyclopedia of music. Ed. 8. 1946/47- . N.Y., Billboard Pub. Co., 1947- . il. (includes advertisements) Annual. $5. 1946/47 issued in 2v. **Q271**

1st-7th ed., 1939–1945/46, called *Billboard music yearbook.*

8th ed. in 2 pts.: v.1, sec. 1, Music today; sec. 2, Radio-Television; sec. 3, Films-Legit; sec. 4, Records;

sec. 5, Personal appearances; sec. 6, American folk music; sec. 7, Small bands; sec. 8, Music publishing.

v.2, Index to v.1, and Who's who in music with cross references to v.1 to all bands, singers, cocktail attractions, concert and opera artists, booking offices, etc.

9th ed., 1947/48, covers much the same ground but both parts are bound in one volume.

An annual record covering new books, records, "Hooperatings," disk jockeys, record companies, music publishers, film producers and directors, etc., with prolific advertising intermixed. The directory material is particularly useful.

Hinrichsen's Musical yearbook, v.1, 1944- . Lond., Hinrichsen, 1944- . Q272

v.1, 1944; v.2/3, 1945/46, ed. by Ralph Hill and Max Hinrichsen; v.4/5, 1947/48 ed. by Max Hinrichsen. v.4/5, 18s. 6d.

Volume 1 is devoted to "Music of our time" with articles by specialists. Includes information on educational institutions, music organizations of Great Britain, societies, clubs, press, etc. Obituary, Jan. 1942–Sept. 1943. Anniversary calendar, 1944. Bibliography, Jan. 1942–1943.

Volume 2/3 deals mainly with music in Great Britain (though not exclusively) and includes various regional surveys. Obituary, Oct. 1943–Mar. 1946. Bibliography, Oct. 1943–July 1945.

Volume 4/5 covers developments in Britain and other countries, with articles by specialists and includes Obituaries, Apr. 1946–Apr. 1947, and Bibliography Aug. 1945–Dec. 1946.

Pierre Key's Music year book, the standard music annual, 1924/25–38. N.Y., Pierre Key, Inc., 1925–38. 6v. il. (1938, $3) Q273

Contained general directory and current information, record of new works performed, obituaries, musical societies and schools, periodicals, publishers, etc. Covered musical interests in the United States and Canada.

No longer published but still useful for its period.

Year in American music, 1946/47- . ed. by Julius Bloom. N.Y., Allen, Towne and Heath, 1947- . v.1- . $5. Q274

An annual chronological record of events and personalities in the world of music in the United States. Appendixes in volume 1 include composers in America with indication of first performances and publications of the year; Orchestras; Opera companies; Books on music and musicians; Albums and recorded music; Awards; Obituaries.

History

Encyclopédie de la musique et dictionnaire du Conservatoire. Fondateur, Albert Lavignac, Directeur, Lionel de La Laurencie. Paris, Delagrave, 1913–31. pt.1, 5v.; pt.2, 6v. il. Q275

Not alphabetically arranged; as originally planned, to consist of three parts: part 1, History of music, arranged by countries; part 2, Technique, pedagogy and aesthetics; (part 3, Dictionary of subjects and names treated in parts 1-2, not published).

An important work for the historian, containing signed articles by specialists, bibliographical references, many good illustrations.

—— —— Partial index, comp. by Robert Bruce (In Music Library Assoc. Notes. v.1, no.4, May 1936)

Also published separately by the Eastman School of Music.

Handbuch der Musikwissenschaft, hrsg. von Ernst Bücken. Potsdam, Akad. Verlagsgesellschaft Athenaion, 1928–34. 13v. il. (Repr. by photolithography in black and white. N.Y., Musurgia, 1949. 13v. in 9. $150.30 per set; $18.50 per v.) Q276

Original set unnumbered. Musurgia set volumed as follows: (1) Sachs, C. Die Musik der Antike. 1930 (2) Besseler, H. Die Musik des Mittelalters und der Renaissance. 1931–34; (3) Haas, R. Die Musik des Barocks. 1929; (4) Bücken, E. Die Musik des Rokoko und der Klassik. 1931; (5) Bücken, E. Die Musik des neunzehnten Jahrhunderts bis zur Moderne. 1928; (6) Mersmann, H. Die moderne Musik seit der Romantik 1931; (7) Bücken, E. Geist und Form im musikalischen Kunstwerk. 1929; (8) Haas, R. Aufführungspraxis der Musik. 1931; (9) Ursprung, O. Die Katholische Kirchenmusik. 1931; (10) Blume, F. Die Evangelische Kirchenmusik. 1931; (11) Heinitz, W. Instrumentenkunde 1928; (12) Lachman, R. Die Musik der aussereuropäischen Natur- und Kulturvölker. 1931; (13) Panoff, P. Die Altslavische Volks- und Kirchenmusik. 1930.

A basic survey of European music, prepared by specialists with many bibliographies; lavishly illustrated, including colored plates, facsimiles and music. In the Musurgia edition the colored plates are reproduced in black and white.

Kinsky, Georg. History of music in pictures, ed by Georg Kinsky, with the cooperation of Robert Haas, Hans Schnoor and other experts, with an introd. by Eric Blom. Lond., Dent; N.Y., Dutton [1930]. 363p. 30s.; $15. Q277

A collection of approximately 1500 illustrations—portraits, instruments, facsimiles, etc.—forming a pictorial history of the subject from the earliest times to the present. The pictures constitute the main part of the work, the brief text consisting merely of (1) explanatory notes on each plate of illustrations, (2) indexes and contents and (3) introduction and foreword. Issued in three editions: (1) original German edition, with title *Geschichte der Musik in Bildern* (Leipzig, Breitkopf, 1930); (2) French edition with title *Album musical* (Paris, Delagrave, 1930) printed from same plates of pictures with notes, indexes, etc., translated into French and a new French introduction; and (3) the English edition listed above, also printed from the original German plates with translation of text.

Nef, Karl. An outline of the history of music. Tr. by Carl F. Pfatteicher. N.Y., Columbia Univ. Pr., 1935. 386p. music. $4. Q278

A well-documented one-volume survey.

[**Norton history of music.** N.Y., W. W. Norton 1940-] il. Q279

While the following volumes do not carry a series note, together they form a comprehensive historical survey.

Sachs, Curt. The rise of music in the ancient world, east and west. 1943. 324p. $5.50; Reese, Gustave. Music in the Middle Ages with an introduction on the music of ancient times. 1940. 502p. (Bibliography, p.425-63, Record list, p.465-80) $7.50; Bukofzer, Manfred F. Music in the Baroque era from Monteverdi to Bach. 1947. 489p. (Checklist of Baroque books on music, p.433-59) $6; Einstein, Alfred. Music in the Romantic era. 1947. 371p. $5; Salazar, A. Music in our time. 1946. 367p. $5.

Other volumes have been announced to cover the Renaissance and the classical era.

Oxford history of music. 2d ed. Ox. Univ. Pr., 1931–38. v.1-7 and introd. v. il. (incl. music) $6 ea. Q280

Contents: Introd. v. ed. by Percy C. Buck. Early history, Middle ages, Folk song, etc. 1929; v.1-2, Polyphonic period, by H. E. Wooldridge. 2d ed. rev. by Percy C. Buck. 1929–32; v.3, Music of the 17th century, by C. H. H. Parry, 2d ed. with revisions and introd. note by E. J. Dent. 1938; v.4, Age of Bach and Handel, by J. A. Fuller-Maitland. 2d ed. 1931; v.5, Viennese period, by Sir W. H. Hadow. 2d ed. 1931; v.6, Romantic period, by E. Dannreuther. 2d ed. 1931; v.7, Symphony and drama, 1850–1900, by H. C. Colles. 1934.

Originally published 1901–05, six volumes; volumes 1-3 revised and reissued, second edition, 1929–38; the new *Introductory volume* was issued with the second edition to serve as an introduction to the study of the history of music; volume 7 is new, but other volumes (i.e., volumes 4-6) though called second editions are virtual reprints of original editions, without revision.

Important reference history, indispensable in any library doing much reference work in musical history.

Musical forms

Operas

Loewenberg, Alfred. Annals of opera, 1597–1940; comp. from the original sources. Camb., Heffer, 1943. 879p. 84s.; $25. Q281

Lists nearly 4000 operas—arranged chronologically according to the dates of first performance, followed by the name of the composer and title of the opera (titles are given in the form in which they first appeared and in the original language; except for Italian, French, and German titles, a translation has been included), name of town where first performed, sometimes name of theater, and a history of performances. References to translations, revivals, etc.

Indexes: (1) Operas; (2) Composers, with dates of birth and death, giving the names of operas by each with dates; (3) Librettists; and (4) General index.

Riemann, Hugo. Opern-Handbuch. Repertorium der dramatisch-musikalischen Litteratur (Opern, Operetten, Ballette, Melodramen, Pantomimen, Oratorien, dramatische Kantaten, u.s.w.) Leipzig, H. Seemann Nachfolger [n.d.] 862p. Q282

Published in parts, 1881–86 (including first supplement) by C. A. Koch; second supplement, 1892.

Composers and titles given in one list; includes descriptive and historical information.

Seltsam, William H. Metropolitan opera annals; a chronicle of artists and performances. N.Y., Wilson, 1947. 751p. il. $7. Q283

A chronological record of the casts and of the operas performed from the first season of the Metropolitan in 1883/84 through 1946/47. Also gives excerpts from press reviews for each season, especially those covering important debuts and first performances.

Profusely illustrated with photographs of the leading singers in typical roles. The index traces all references to artists, performances, reviews, and portraits.

Towers, John. Dictionary-catalogue of operas and operettas which have been performed on the public stage. Morgantown, W. Va., Acme Pub. Co. [c1910]. 1045p. $7. Q284

pt.1, Dictionary of operas and operettas; pt.2, Composers and their operas in alphabetical order; pt.3, Libretti, with the number of times set to music for the public lyric stage.

A title-a-line list of 28,015 operas, giving for each title, composer's name and dates and whether ever publicly performed. The most comprehensive list, containing more titles than Clément (Q288) or Riemann (Q282), but lacking the descriptive and critical material included by them. Principally useful for ready reference for ascertaining name of composer of a given opera.

U. S. Library of Congress. Division of Music. Catalogue of opera librettos printed before 1800, prepared by O. G. T. Sonneck. Wash., Govt. Prt. Off., 1914. 2v. Q285

v.1, Title catalogue; v.2, Author list, composer list and aria index.

A detailed catalog giving for each libretto full cataloging information, date and place of first performance and valuable bibliographical and historical notes. Entry is first by original title, and then by replicas and translations, with reference from alternative, later and translated titles.

—— Dramatic music . . . catalogue of full scores, comp. by O. G. T. Sonneck. Wash., Govt. Prt. Off., 1908. 170p. Q286

PLOTS

☙ There are many books, old and new, giving plots or synopses of operas. They vary considerably in the operas covered and in general treatment: some have short notes, some long, some discuss the music, some the performances, etc. Only a few of the most comprehensive and more recent are listed here. However, various others will be found in many libraries.

Rieck, Waldemar. Opera plots. An index to the stories of operas, operettas, etc., from the 16th to the 20th century. N.Y., Public Lib., 1927. 102p. o.p. Q287

An index by composers' names, with added detailed index of titles, to the outlines of plots contained in over

200 books of synopses published in English, French, German, and Danish. The list of books indexed forms a useful bibliography of books of synopses.

Clément, Félix and **Larousse, Pierre.** Dictionnaire des opéras (Dictionnaire lyrique). . . . Rev. et mis à jour par Arthur Pougin. Paris, Larousse [1905]. 1293p. **Q288**

Subtitle: Contenant l'analyse et la nomenclature de tous les opéras, opéras-comiques, operettes et drames lyriques représentés en France et à l'étranger depuis l'origine de ces genres d'ouvrages jusqu'à nos jours.

First edition, 1869, had title *Dictionnaire lyrique.* This edition contains a supplement, p.1181-1293.

Arranged alphabetically by titles. Includes considerable descriptive, critical and historical matter.

Howard, John Tasker. The world's great operas. N.Y., Random House, 1948. 488p. $2.95. **Q289**

Gives plots of about 200 operas including some recent ones.

Appendixes: (1) Composers of the operas, with brief biographical sketches; (2) Librettists of the operas; (3) Sources and derivations of the plots; (4) Characters in the operas.

Kobbé, Gustav. Complete opera book; the stories of the operas together with 400 of the leading airs and motives in musical notation. Rev. and enl. ed. N.Y. and Lond., Putnam, 1935. 993p. il. $6. **Q290**

Discusses the development of opera, giving the stories of more than 200 operas, biographies of the composers, musical motives, etc.

McSpadden, Joseph Walker. Operas and musical comedies. N.Y., Crowell, 1946. 607p. il. $3.50. **Q291**

A revision of his *Opera synopses* and *Light opera and musical comedy.* Contains more than 350 plots including such recent ones as "Oklahoma" and "Carousel."

Martens, Frederick H. A thousand and one nights of opera. N.Y. and Lond., Appleton, 1926. 487p. o.p. **Q292**

The most comprehensive book of opera synopses, including some 1550 operas and ballets. Synopses vary in length, some being very brief.

Thompson, Oscar. Plots of the operas, as comp. for the International cyclopedia of music and musicians. N.Y., Dodd, 1940. 517p. **Q293**

Reprinted from the *International cyclopedia* (Q265).

Songs

INDEXES

Cushing, Helen Grant. Children's song index; an index to more than 22,000 songs in 189 collections comprising 222 volumes . . . N.Y., Wilson, 1936. xliip., 798p. Price on application. **Q295**

Collections indexed include 178 not indexed in Sears' *Song index* (Q297) and 11 indexed in Sears but rein-

dexed here partly because of their outstanding character and partly to supply subject indexing. In general, similar in plan to the *Song index* except that subject entries are added, containing titles, first lines, authors' and composers' names and subjects in one alphabet. Main entry with full information is under title, with *cross references* from alternate titles, different titles in different collections, translated titles, original titles in certain languages (e.g., Russian) and from first lines and sometimes first line of chorus, and *added entries* under composer of music, author of words, and subject.

Day, Cyrus Lawrence and **Murrie, Eleanore Boswell.** English song-books, 1651-1702; a bibliography with a first-line index of songs. Lond., pr. for the Bibliographical Soc. at the Univ. Pr., Oxford, 1940 (for 1937). 439p. il. music. 30s. members only. **Q296**

"The aim of this volume is to list, describe and index all the secular song-books published in England and Scotland between 1651 and 1702. The term secular song-book, as it is here somewhat arbitrarily used, means any publication containing the words and music of two or more secular songs."—*Introd.*

Contents: A detailed chronological bibliography of 252 numbered items, p.17-159; Indexes: First lines, p.163-400; Composers, p.401-08; Authors, p.409-15; Singers and actors, p.416-17; Tunes and airs, p.418-20; Sources, p.421-34; Song-books, p.435-37; Printers, publishers, and booksellers, p.438-39.

Sears, Minnie Earl. Song index. An index to more than 12,000 songs in 177 song collections comprising 262 volumes. Ed. by M. E. Sears, assisted by Phyllis Crawford. N.Y., Wilson, 1926. 650p. Service basis. **Q297**

—— —— Supplement; an index to more than 7,000 songs in 104 song collections comprising 124 volumes. Preface by I. G. Mudge. N.Y., Wilson, 1934. 367p. Service basis.

A most important index, useful in the public, college or school library, as well as in the music library. Contains titles, first lines, authors' names and composers' names in one alphabet. Each song is indexed fully under its title, with added entry under composer and author and cross references from first line and from variant or translated titles. Useful for finding (1) words and music of a wanted song, (2) lists of songs by a given author or composer, (3) authorship of a poem when only its title or first line is known, (4) whether or not a song has been translated, or is itself a translation, etc. The classified lists of song collections given at the beginning of each volume furnish useful buying lists of the best song books.

As many songs were originally poems which have been set to music, this index serves also as an index to poetry, especially for poems and translations not included in *Granger's Index to poetry* (R159).

❧ Various reference books listed elsewhere in this book, while not primarily concerned with songs, are frequently useful for supplementing the above indexes. *Notes and queries* (R52) notes more than 2500 songs under the heading "songs and ballads" in its indexes, and gives a considerable amount of information about these, including sometimes reference to their location in collections not included in the *Song index* (Q297). Larousse, *Grand dictionnaire universel* (D27) has separate articles on about 600 songs entered under the French title, usually giving some information about the song and its author, the words in French, and the music (air only). The fine catalog of the Allen A. Brown collection of the Boston Public Library (Q229) analyzes many songs included in song collections. Two printed catalogs of the British Museum are very useful: its *Catalogue of printed music . . . 1487–1800* (Q241) analyzes many songs printed in periodicals, and its *Catalogue of manuscript music* (Q240) has two important indexes, one of sacred vocal music and the other of secular vocal music which give title and first line indexing for many thousand songs. The Library of Congress *Catalogue of opera librettos* (Q285) has an aria index which serves as a key to songs included in operas.

Folk songs

BIBLIOGRAPHY

Henry, Mellinger Edward. A bibliography for the study of American folk songs, with many titles of folk songs (and titles that have to do with folk songs) from other lands. Lond., Mitre Pr., 1937. 142p. 25s.; $6. **Q299**

League of Nations. International Institute of Intellectual Co-operation. Folklore musical; répertoire international des collections et centres de documentation avec notices sur l'état actuel des recherches dans les différents pays et références bibliographiques. Paris, Département d'Art, d'Archéologie et d'Ethnologie, Institut International de Co-opération Intellectuelle [1939]. 332p. **Q300**

Forms the second part of "Musique et chanson populaires," results of an investigation undertaken at the request of the International Commission of Folk Arts. Includes data relating to collections of folk music in the possession of institutions, societies and individuals; methods and scope of research; lists of music recorded by musicians or by mechanical means; bibliographies, etc.

Lomax, Alan and **Cowell, Sidney Robertson.** American folk song and folk lore, a regional bibliography . . . [N.Y., Progressive Educ. Assoc., 1942] 59p. ([Progressive Education Assoc. Service Center] P.E.A. Service Center pamphlet, no.8) 25c. **Q301**

U. S. Library of Congress. Division of Music. Archive of American Folk Song. Check-list of recorded songs in the English language in the Archive of American Folk Song to July, 1940. Alphabetical list with geographical index. Wash., Library, 1942. 3v. **Q302**

Volume 3 is geographical index.

The Division of Music has also issued *Folk music of the United States and Latin America,* combined catalog of phonograph records (1948. 47p. 10c), which lists 107 records containing 341 titles which are for sale by the Library of Congress.

—— Bibliography of Latin American folk music, comp. by Gilbert Chase. Wash., Library, 1942. 141p. **Q303**

1143 numbered items arranged under country, with index of authors.

COLLECTIONS

Jackson, George Stuyvesant. Early songs of Uncle Sam. Bost., Humphries, 1933. 297p. il. $5. **Q304**

Bibliography: p.271-77.

Lomax, John Avery and **Lomax, Alan.** American ballads and folk songs, with a foreword by George Lyman Kittredge. N.Y., Macmillan, 1934. 625p. music. $5. **Q305**

Includes music and some comment on each song.

—— Our singing country; a second volume of American ballads and folk songs. . . . N.Y., Macmillan, 1941. 416p. $5. **Q306**

Classified, with song and first-line indexes.

Sharp, Cecil James. English folk songs from the southern Appalachians, comprising 273 songs and ballads with 968 tunes, including 39 tunes contributed by Olive Dame Campbell; ed. by Maud Karpeles. [2d and enl. ed.] Ox., Univ. Pr., 1932. 2v. 35s. ea.; $12. **Q307**

1st ed. 1917.

Instruments

Bessaraboff, Nicholas. Ancient European musical instruments; an organological study of the musical instruments in the Leslie Lindsey Mason Collection at the Museum of Fine Arts, Boston. Bost., pub. for the Museum of Fine Arts by Harvard Univ. Pr., 1941. 503p. il. $10. **Q308**

Includes a useful bibliography of books about musical instruments and catalogs of collections.

Sachs, Curt. History of musical instruments. N.Y., Norton, 1940. 505p. il. $6. **Q309**

—— Real-Lexikon der Musikinstrumente, zugleich ein Polyglossar für das gesamte Instrumentengebiet; mit 200 Abbildungen. Berlin, Bard, 1913. 442p. il. **Q310**

Recorded music

Barbour, Harriet Buxton and **Freeman, Warren S.** The Children's record book. N.Y., Oliver Durrell, Inc., 1947. 186p. $3.50.   **Q311**

Half title: An authoritative guide to the best recorded music for children from six months to sixteen years.

A graded list with historical, biographical and critical notes.

Bauer, Robert. The New catalogue of historical records, 1898–1908/09. Lond., Sidgwick and Jackson, 1947. 494p. 45s.   **Q312**

Delaunay, Charles. New hot discography; the standard directory of recorded jazz, ed. by Walter E. Schaap and George Avakian. N.Y., Criterion, 1948. 608p. $6.   **Q313**

In two parts: (1) the originators and pioneers of jazz; (2) alphabetical listing of the important artists and recording groups organized after 1930.

Gives detailed information about each record including the personnel, plan of recording, date of session, instruments involved, "discode" numbers, matrix numbers, company catalog numbers, etc. Alphabetical index to all names.

Eisenberg, Philip and **Krasno, Hecky.** A guide to children's records; a complete guide to recorded stories, songs and music for children. N.Y., Crown, 1948. 195p.   **Q314**

A well-organized list with evaluative notes.

Gramophone Shop, Inc., New York. The Gramophone shop encyclopedia of recorded music. 3d ed. rev. and enl. N.Y., Crown Pub., 1948. 639p. $5.   **Q315**

A basic and essential work. Earlier editions were published in 1936 and 1942.

Hall, David. The Record book; international edition. A guide to the world of the phonograph. N.Y., Durrell, 1948. 1394p. $7.50.   **Q316**

Contents: pt.1, General information, p.3-195; pt.2, Record reviews, p.199-1365; Index to pt.1; Index of composers in pt.2.

Part 1 includes general historical information, discussion of phonographs, recording, record catalogs, etc. Part 2 is arranged alphabetically by composers with critical notes on recordings.

This edition is not only much enlarged but is completely reorganized, and the material, which formerly was classified, is now arranged in one alphabet by composer. Folk songs, drama and poetry records, and children's music, previously included, have been dropped.

Kolodin, Irving. New guide to recorded music. Garden City, N.Y., Doubleday, Doran, 1947. 382p. $3.50.   **Q317**

An annotated guide giving an "estimate of the mechanical, the artistic and the economic elements" of worthwhile recordings of serious music.

This is the first revised edition of the *Guide to recorded music* originally published in 1941.

Index of record reviews, comp. by Kurtz Myers. Mar. 1948- . (In Notes. 2d ser. v.5, no.2-) Quarterly.   **Q318**

Indexes reviews in some 15 to 20 American and English periodicals with indication of the reviewer's opinion of the quality of the performance—excellent, adequate or inadequate.

Quarterly record-list, prepared by Philip L. Miller. (In Musical quarterly, Jan. 1935-)   **Q319**

Useful current listings.

SPORTS AND GAMES
Bibliography

Henry E. Huntington Library and Art Gallery, San Marino, Calif. Sporting books in the Huntington Library, comp. by Lyle H. Wright. San Marino, Calif., 1937. 132p. (Huntington Library lists, no.2)   **Q320**

A classed list with author and title index.

Greenwood, Frances Anderson. Bibliography of swimming. N.Y., Wilson, 1940. 308p. $4.25. **Q321**

A dictionary catalog of books and periodical articles on swimming and allied subjects, containing approximately 10,000 titles listed by authors and classified under 608 subjects. Includes material in various languages published up to June 1938.

Appendixes include organizations promoting swimming; sources for equipment and supplies; addresses of firms; films and film distributors; periodicals, etc.

Dictionaries and handbooks

Cummings, Parke. The dictionary of sports. N.Y., Barnes, 1949. 572p. il. $7.50.   **Q322**

A dictionary of terms used in sports.

Gomme, Alice Bertha. Traditional games of England, Scotland, and Ireland; with tunes, singing-rhymes and methods of playing according to the variants extant and recorded in different parts of the kingdom. Lond., Nutt, 1894–98. 2v. (Dictionary of British folk-lore, ed. by G. Laurence Gomme, pt.1)   **Q323**

Hunter's encyclopedia, ed. Raymond R. Camp. Harrisburg, Pa., Stackpole and Heck, 1948. 1152p. il.   **Q324**

A comprehensive work dealing with the game animals and birds of this continent, describing their appearance, characteristics, history, range, etc. Methods of hunting, firearms, game laws, etc. Arranged by groupings with a detailed index.

Contents: Big game; Small game; Animal predators; Winged predators; Small mammals; Upland game birds; Shorebirds; Waterfowl; Color section (colored plates of upland game birds and waterfowl); Firearms; Ammunition; Dogs; Miscellany (including chapters on camping, clothing, various methods of hunting, regulations and laws, etc.).

Menke, Frank Grant. New encyclopedia of sports. 3d ed. N.Y., Barnes, 1947. 1007p. $6.50. **Q325**

First edition 1939 and second edition 1944 have title: *Encyclopedia of sports.*

Covers a wide variety of sports giving history, description, and basic rules, names and records of champions, and financial statistics, with special attention to the United States. Includes more extensive data on championships than was given in the earlier editions.

Frey, Richard L. New complete Hoyle; an encyclopedia of rules, procedure, manners and strategy of games played with cards, dice, counters, boards, words, and numbers. Phila., McKay, 1947. 740p. $3.50. **Q326**

Morehead, Albert H. The Modern Hoyle; rules and instructions for all the most popular games. Phila., Winston, 1944. 308p. $2.50. **Q327**

Hargrave, Catherine Perry. History of playing cards and a bibliography of cards and gaming; comp. and il. from the old cards and books in the collection of the United States Playing Card Company in Cincinnati. Bost., Houghton; Lond., Allen and Unwin, 1930. 468p. il. **Q328**

Bibliography, p.369-449.

Annuals

Spalding's Official athletic almanac, 1893- . Founded by James E. Sullivan. N.Y., Amer. Sports Pub. Co., 1893- . (Spalding's Athletic library, no.1R) **Q329**

Gives world, Olympic and American track, field and swimming records for men and women; A.A.U. championships and records; All-America track and field teams, etc.

ETIQUETTE

Post, Emily Price. Etiquette; "The blue book of social usage," . . . illustrated with photographs and facsimiles of social forms. New ed., completely rewritten and reset, including military and post-war etiquette. N.Y. and Lond., Funk & Wagnalls, 1945. 645p. il. $5. **Q330**

Vogue. Book of etiquette, a complete guide to traditional forms and modern usage by Millicent Fenwick. N.Y., Simon and Schuster, [1948]. 658p. il. $5. **Q331**

LITERATURE
AND LANGUAGE

❦ In the general library many of the questions asked at the reference desk pertain to some phase of literature or language, *e.g.*, biographies of authors; reviews of books; quotations; identifications of partly remembered titles; characters; plots; location of poems, plays, short stories, essays; or the history and development of literature by form or by nationality. To answer these questions the general as well as the special reference works must be remembered. National bibliographies and biographical dictionaries, indexes to periodicals and book reviews, encyclopedias and dictionaries, are of basic importance. However, to supplement the general works there are a large number of special aids, some international in scope and others devoted to the literature of a particular country. The needs of libraries will vary but basic equipment for an average American library would include: for history and bibliography, the *Cambridge bibliography of English literature* (R258), the *Cambridge history of English literature* (R288), the *Cambridge history of American literature* (R197), and the *Literary history of the United States* (R198); bio-bibliography, Millett's *Contemporary American authors* (R186) and his *Contemporary British literature* (R274); dictionaries and handbooks, the *Columbia dictionary of modern*

European literature (R30), Kunitz and Haycraft, *Twentieth century authors* (R59), *American authors* (R202), and *British authors,* (R293), the *Oxford companion to American literature* (R194), and the *Oxford companion to English literature* (R281) or the *Concise Oxford dictionary of English literature* (R282); plots, Keller's *Reader's Digest of books* (R19); quotations and proverbs, *Bartlett's Familiar quotations* (R63), *Hoyt's New cyclopedia of practical quotations* (R67), the *Oxford dictionary of quotations* (R69), and the *Oxford dictionary of English proverbs* (R216), *Stevenson's Home book of quotations* (R70) and his *Home book of proverbs* (R127); and the various indexes to poetry, plays, short stories, essays, etc.

Anthologies and collections of poetry, plays, short stories and other forms of literature may be shelved in the reference room or may be made available elsewhere in the library. Materials in foreign literature should be acquired according to need. Libraries much used by students will need several of the annual bibliographical surveys, *e.g.*, *American bibliography* (R11), the *Annual bibliography* of the Modern Humanities Research Association (R262), and the *Year's Work in English studies* (R263), and many of the more specialized works.

GENERAL WORKS

Bibliography

Baldensperger, Fernand and **Friederich, Werner P.** Bibliography of comparative literature. Chapel Hill, Univ. of North Carolina Pr., 1950. 701p. (Univ. of North Carolina studies in comparative literature) **R1**

An extensive compendium attempting to cover literary influences from early to modern times. Arranged in four books, the first and third dealing with generalities (including themes, motifs, genres, international literary relations, etc.), the second and fourth with specific literatures

and their contributions listed according to country or author exerting influence.

Bibliographical citations are very brief. There is a detailed table of contents but no index.

Betz, Louis Paul. La littérature comparée. Essa bibliographique. Introduction par Joseph Texte 2. éd. augm., pub., avec un index méthodique par Fernand Baldensperger. Strasbourg, Trüb ner, 1904. 386 col., 389-410p. **R**

A bibliography of books and periodical articles on com parative literature from the Middle Ages through th nineteenth century.

Bibliographie linguistique des années 1939-

1947, publiée par le Comité International Permanent de Linguistes. Utrecht, Spectrum, 1949- . v.1- . $4; G12. **R3**

Added title page in English.

Volume 1 lists books, reviews, and periodical articles appearing 1939–47 in South Africa, Belgium (publications in Flemish), Czechoslovakia, Finland, France, Italy, the Netherlands, Norway, Poland, Spain, Switzerland, on various branches of linguistics. Contributions from other countries will be included in volume 2, with an author index to both volumes.

Materials are grouped under large classes, with subdivisions, e.g., General linguistics, Indo-European, Asianic and Mediterranean, Finno-Ugrian, Basque, Hamito-Semitic, Negro-African, Caucasian, Turkish and Mongolian, Eastern Asia [and others]. Continued by annual volumes.

Edwardes, Marian. Summary of the literatures of modern Europe (England, France, Germany, Italy, Spain) from the origins to 1400. Lond., Dent, 1907. 352p. **R4**

Arranged by countries and under each by centuries; for each century gives names of the principal writers with brief biographical data, list of works, notes about works, and bibliographical references to editions, translations, and critical works and articles. A useful manual for the older literatures, though not exhaustive.

Farrar, Clarissa Palmer and **Evans, Austin Patterson.** Bibliography of English translations from medieval sources. N.Y., Columbia Univ. Pr., 1946. 534p. (Records of civilization; sources and studies. Austin P. Evans, ed. No.xxxix) $7.50. **R5**

"Aims to include English translations of important literary sources produced during the period from Constantine the Great to the year 1500 within an area roughly inclusive of Europe, northern Africa and western Asia."— *Pref.* Lists works published through 1942 with a few items published later which were inserted in proof.

An outstanding work arranged alphabetically by author with many annotations describing content, translator's comment, editions or reprints of a given translation, etc. Extensive index to authors, translators, editors, titles, subjects, etc.

Istituto Nazionale per le Relazioni Culturali con l'Estero. Letterature straniere. Roma [I.R.C.E.] 1941. 455p. **R6**

On cover: "Bibliografie del ventennio."

List of works on the literature of foreign countries published in Italy, 1920–41.

Reuss, Jeremias David. Repertorium commentationum a societatibus litterariis editarum. Secundum disciplinarum ordinem . . . t.8-9. Gottingae, Dieterich, 1810. **R7**

Contents: t.8, Historia . . . Historia litteraria; t.9, Philologia, Linguae, Scriptores graeci, Scriptores latini, Litterae elegantiores, Poesis, Rhetorica, Ars antiqua, Pictura, Musica.

A valuable index to the publications of the learned societies of various countries up to 1800. Classed arrangement with author index.

For complete contents of volume 8 *see* V8; for description of complete set *see* N3.

Current

Progress of medieval and renaissance studies in the United States and Canada. Bull. no.1- . Boulder, Colo., 1923- . $1.50. **R8**

Title varies.

Renaissance studies added with number 15. Each number contains a list of medievalists and their publications and a list of doctoral dissertations. Bulletin 19, 1947, includes a list of "Continental publications on the Middle Ages and the Renaissance, 1940–1946."

Recent literature of the Renaissance, comp. by Hardin Craig [and others]. (In Studies in philology, v.14, 1917-) Annual. **R9**

Until 1938 covered works on the English Renaissance only. From 1939 covers English, French, Germanic, Italian, Neo-Latin and Spanish. Includes index of proper names.

Year's work in modern language studies, by a number of scholars. 1929/30–1938/39. Ox., Univ. Pr., 1931–40. v.1-10. **R10**

Publication discontinued?

Covers medieval Latin, Italian, French and Provençal, Hispanic, Rumanian, Germanic and Celtic studies, and in volume 2, International languages also. Slavonic studies are added in volume 3. Not all languages in all volumes.

American bibliography for 1921- . (In PMLA, v.39-) Annual. **R11**

Usually published in March as a supplement to the *Publications* of the Modern Language Association of America.

A very useful annual bibliography listing writings by Americans on the literatures of various countries, including, English, American, French, Italian, Spanish, Portuguese, and Germanic. Coverage varies. Classified arrangement. No cumulations, but for articles on American literature *see* R190.

Work in progress . . . in the modern humanities, 1938–42. Camb., Modern Humanities Research Assoc., 1938–42. 5v. (Its Bull. no.16A, 17A, 18A, 19A, 20A) **R12**

Publication suspended. Resumed in cooperation with the Modern Language Association of America as:

Research in progress in the modern languages and literatures, 1948- . (In PMLA, v.63, Suppl., pt.2, p.143-405, 1948-) **R13**

Lists work in progress in 29 countries. Classified with subject and author indexes. The author index also serves as an index to the addresses of the 3550 scholars in various countries.

General collections and anthologies

The Harvard classics, ed. by Charles W. Eliot. N.Y., Collier, 1909. 50 (i.e., 52)v. il.   **R14**

A collection of writings chosen as representations of the world's great literature in all fields. With a few exceptions such as the Bible and Shakespeare, the works are complete, not selections. Chronologically the material covers from ancient to modern times, from the sacred books of the early religions, through the literature of Greece and Rome, the Middle Ages in the Orient and Europe, the Renaissance, and the nineteenth century, in Europe and America.

Volume 50 contains an analytical author, subject, and title index to all of the material contained in the set, as well as an index to first lines of poems, songs and choruses, hymns and psalms. There are two additional unnumbered volumes: The Reading guide and Lectures on the Harvard Classics edited by William Allan Neilson.

The set is useful in libraries particularly for its comprehensive index, and also because it may provide additional copies of standard works.

Warner library . . . editors: John W. Cunliffe, Ashley H. Thorndike. N.Y., Warner Lib. Co., 1917. 30v. il.   **R15**

Contents: v.1-26, World's best literature (sketches and selections); v.27, Book of songs and lyrics; v.28, Reader's dictionary of authors, ed. by H. M. Ayres; v.29, Reader's digest of books, ed. by H. R. Keller; v.30, Students course in literature, by G. R. Lomer; General index, authors, titles, subjects, etc.

A useful popular collection of representative selections from writers of all periods and countries, with considerable popular reference material in the way of critical notices, biographies, synopses of books, etc. Issued in three different editions: the first edition, edited by Charles Dudley Warner (N.Y., Peale, 1896-97. 30v. o.p.), had title *Library of the world's best literature*. The 1917 edition is a reprint from plates of volumes 1-28 of the first edition with changes and the addition of considerable new material on new pages inserted throughout in their proper places and fitted into the original paging by the use of subletters a,b,c, etc.; volumes 28-30 of this edition are entirely reset. A later, entirely rearranged edition with the title *Columbia University course in literature, based on the World's best literature* utilized considerable material from the 1917 edition, was arranged by countries and periods rather than by authors, and added selections and notices, but omitted the three special reference volumes of the 1917 edition, i.e., *Dictionary of authors, Readers digest,* and *General index. The Readers digest* which forms volume 29 of the 1917 edition is also published separately by Macmillan; for new enlarged edition *see* R19. In addition to the general indexes included in the first edition and 1917 edition, the sets have been indexed as follows: for the first edition analytical cards (now o.p.) for insertion in a card catalog were printed by the American Library Association; the critical and biographical notices in volumes 1-26 of the 1917 edition and in the *Columbia University course in literature,* but not the selections, are indexed in the *Essay index* (N.Y., Wilson, 1934) (R167).

Bryant, William Cullen. New library of poetry and song; rev. and enl. with recent authors and

containing a dictionary of poetical quotations. N.Y., Baker [1903]. 1100p.   **R16**

Longfellow, Henry Wadsworth. Poems of places, ed. by H. W. Longfellow. Bost., Osgood, 1876-79. 31v.   **R17**

v.1-4, England and Wales; v.5, Ireland; v.6-8, Scotland, Denmark, Iceland, Norway and Sweden; v.9-10, France and Savoy; v.11-13, Italy; v.14-15, Spain, Portugal, Belgium and Holland; v.16, Switzerland and Austria; v.17-18, Germany; v.19, Greece and Turkey in Europe; v.20, Russia; v.21-23, Asia; v.24, Africa; v.25-30, America; v.31, Oceanica.

—— Poets and poetry of Europe. New ed., enl. Bost., Houghton, 1896 [c70]. 921p. o.p.   **R18**

Translations from the poetry of ten different nations of Europe, arranged chronologically under each country, with biographical notices of the authors and an author index.

Digests

❦ Various handbooks and compilations which give plots of novels and synopses and digests of well known books, should be represented in the general reference collection, although occasionally when a student asks for an outline to save the trouble of reading an assigned work, the librarian will need to exercise discretion in supplying or withholding material. Synopses are found in many author dictionaries and handbooks; in such works as the *Oxford companions* (R194 and R281) and Brewer's *Reader's handbook* (R39) (these are comparatively brief); and in some encyclopedias such as Larousse, *Grand dictionnaire* (D27). Critical reviews also often give outlines of the works reviewed. For other aids see the following:

Keller, Helen Rex. Reader's digest of books. New and greatly enl. ed. N.Y., Macmillan, 1929. 1447p. $6.   **R19**

Frequently reprinted.

Earlier edition, 1917, 941p., was also issued as volume 29 of the "Warner library" (R15). Separately published in 1922.

The most frequently useful of the books of synopses including the outstanding works, fiction and nonfiction of many countries and periods. In two alphabets, the supplementary alphabet, p.925-1423, contains the new material which was added in the 1929 edition, and is indexed in a separate index.

Haydn, Hiram and **Fuller, Edmund.** Thesaurus of book digests: Digests of the world's permanent writings from the ancient classics to current literature. N.Y., Crown Pub., 1949. 831p. $5.   **R20**

Very concise digests arranged by title, with an author index and an index to characters. In some cases where authors are remembered for the body of their work rather than for a particular title, discussion is given under the author's name.

Magill, Frank N. Masterplots; 510 plots in story form from the world's fine literature. Story ed., Dayton Kohler. N.Y., Salem Pr., 1949. 2v. $10. **R21**

Directories

Author's and writer's who's who and reference guide. Markets, publishers, legal and copyright formalities, agents, literary associations. Ed., L. G. Pine. Lond., Shaw Pub. Co., 1934- . Annual. (1948/49, 40s.) **R22**

The Literary market place, 1940- . The Complete directory of American book publishing. N.Y., Bowker, 1940- . Annual. (1949, $3.50) **R23**

Directory of names and organizations which might be useful in the promotion and advertising of literary property. Classified under such headings as: agents, artists and art services, book clubs, book publishers, book reviewers, columnists and commentators, magazines, motion picture studios, news services, news syndicates, radio and many others.

Literary prizes and their winners. [rev. and enl. ed] N.Y., Bowker, 1946. 119p. $3. **R24**

Former title: *Famous literary prizes and their winners,* edited by Bessie Graham, 1935 and 1939.

Includes brief introductory statements about each prize with list of the winners. In some cases, because of limitation of space, prizes awarded before 1939 are not listed but reference is made to the 1939 edition for names of winners to that date. Includes the Nobel prize, and prizes awarded in the United States, the British Empire, Czechoslovakia, France, Portugal, Sweden, the U.S.S.R. and Latin America. Also lists prize contests and fellowships open.

Literary year book, 1897–1923. Lond. and N.Y., 1897–[1923]. 25v. Annual. **R25**

Publication suspended 1918–19. Title 1920, *Literary who's who;* 1923 issue a supplement to 1922.

Discontinued in the above form after 1923 and continued by the "Literary yearbooks group," a series of four yearbooks including *Who's who in literature,* 1924–34; *What editors and publishers want,* 1924–32; *The librarian's guide,* 1923–32; and *British booksellers,* 1924.

Writers' and artists' year book, 1906- , a directory for writers, artists, playwrights, film writers, photographers and composers. Lond., Black; N.Y., Macmillan, 1906- . v.1- . (v.42, 1949, 7s. 6d.; $2.75) **R26**

Contains lists of English and American journals and magazines, with statement of kind of material accepted by each and rate of payment, lists of publishers, literary agents, classified index of magazines, list of editors, magazines controlled by the same firm, markets for writers, plays, films, broadcasting, artists, photographers, etc., and other kinds of directory material useful to writers desiring to place manuscripts.

Writer's handbook, 1936- . Bost., Writer, 1936- . Annual. $3.50. **R27**

In two parts: part 1 is made up of articles by various writers, which appeared originally in *The writer,* on various phases of professional writing including fiction, nonfiction and specialties. Many of the articles are carried over from earlier editions, some are new, none dated.

Part 2 is a market guide, mainly to the periodical field, giving for each periodical, address, editor, and type of material accepted with indication of rate of payment.

Writer's market for 1930, ed. by Aron M. Mathieu. Cincinnati, Writer's Digest, 1930- . $3. **R28**

Contains the names, addresses and editorial requirements of about 2500 markets for free-lance writers. Classified and indexed. Includes high class magazines, pulps and trade journals, but does not include many of the scholarly or professional journals.

Dictionaries and encyclopedias

Benét, William Rose. The reader's encyclopedia; an encyclopedia of world literature and the arts. N.Y., Crowell, 1948. 1242p. $6. **R29**

A comprehensive work containing brief articles on writers, scientists, philosophers, etc., of all nations and all periods, allusions, and literary expressions, terms, literary schools and movements, plots and characters, descriptions of musical compositions and works of art, etc.

The emphasis is primarily on literature, especially American and British, and reflects Mr. Benét's personal interest in modern poetry. Not a substitute for the *Oxford companions* (R194 and R281). Based on *Crowell's Handbook for readers and writers* by Henrietta Gerwig (N.Y., Crowell, 1925. 728p.).

Columbia dictionary of modern European literature. Horatio Smith, general ed. N.Y., Columbia Univ. Pr., 1947. 899p. $10. **R30**

"The intention of this Dictionary is to provide a record and signed evaluations of the chief books of the important literary artists of all continental Europe—in the twentieth century and the immediately preceding and closely related decades. . . ."—*Pref.*

A scholarly dictionary including biographical sketches with critical evaluations covering 200 French, 150 German, 100 Russian, 100 Italian, 100 Spanish, 50 Polish, 40 Czech writers, etc., and survey articles with bibliographies, of the 31 literatures of the Continent, each written and signed by an authority. Two hundred thirty-nine specialists have written the 1167 articles. For the most part careful editing has achieved a balance in choice and treatment of subjects, and in bibliographical form without formalizing the style of the individual writer, though as in any cooperative undertaking the result is sometimes uneven. In the survey articles titles of works are given both in the original and in English translation, with dates of publication of the original and of the translation if published in English.

Dizionario letterario Bompiani delle opere a dei personaggi di tutti i tempi e di tutte le letterature. Milan, Bompiani, 1947–50. 9v. **R31**

Contents: v.1-7, A-Z; v.8, a dictionary of literary characters; v.9, indexes.

A dictionary, listing and describing the works of all times and all countries in literature, art, and music. Although the emphasis is on literature, musical works and many famous pictures are described. The work is lavishly illustrated and includes many colored plates and black-and-white illustrations. The first half of volume 1 is devoted to 58 "movimenti spirituali," arranged alphabetically, e.g., dadaism, euphuism, mysticism. The main part of the work consists of signed articles arranged alphabetically by the Italian form of the title of the work. There are no cross references from the original titles although these are given in brackets following the Italian form. (The index volume includes a list of titles in the original languages with their Italian equivalents.) Brief biographical notes are usually included in the articles but there are no author entries.

Volume 8 is a dictionary of literary characters alphabetized according to the Italian form of the name. The scope is broad, ranging from Adam to Superman. Volume 9 includes synoptic tables showing literary development in all parts of the world; a list of titles in the original languages with their Italian equivalents; an index of authors, listing and thus bringing together their works, which are scattered through the first seven volumes in alphabetical title arrangement; and an index of illustrations by artist.

Eppelsheimer, Hanns Wilhelm. Handbuch der Weltliteratur. [2. Aufl.] Frankfurt am Main, Klostermann, 1947–50. 2v.   **R32**

The first edition, 1937, contained biographical information, critical comment, and bibliography (editions, translations, and criticism) concerning the major literary works of the world up to the first world war. This edition, in two volumes, retains the same format, arrangement, and subject content. Critical articles have not been rewritten, although some explicit references to National Socialism have been deleted. The major change in the second edition is the addition of post 1937 imprints in the bibliographies, primarily the works of German scholars produced between 1937 and 1943.

Handbuch der Literaturwissenschaft, hrsg. von Oskar Walzel. . . . Berlin-Neubabelsberg, Akademische Verlagsgesellschaft Athenaion [c1923–43] v.1- . il. (In progress)   **R33**

Issued in parts with covers supplied for completed volumes.

Contents: Walzel, Oskar. Gehalt und Gestalt im Kunstwerk des Dichters. [c1923]; Bethe, Erich. Die griechische Dichtung. [c1924]; Kappelmacher, Alfred. Die Literatur der Römer bis zur Karolingerzeit. [c1934]; Heusler, Andreas. Die altgermanische Dichtung. 2. Ausg. 1943; Schwietering, Julius. Die deutsche Dichtung des Mittelalters. [c1932–41]; Müller, Günther. Deutsche Dichtung von der Renaissance bis zum Ausgang des Barock. [c1927]; Walzel, Oskar. Deutsche Dichtung von Gottsched bis zur Gegenwart. [c1927–30] 2v.; Hecht, Hans and Schücking, Levin L. Die englische Literatur im Mittelalter. [c1927]; Keller, Wolfgang and Fehr, Bernhard. Die englische Literatur von der Renaissance bis zur Aufklärung. [c1928]; Fehr, Bernhard. Die englische Literatur des 19. und 20. Jahrhunderts mit einer Einführung in die englische Frühromantik. [c1923]; Fischer, Walther. Die englische Literatur der Vereinigten Staaten von Nordamerika. [c1929]; Borelius, Hilma. Die nordischen Literaturen. [c1931]; Olschki, Leonardo.

Die romanischen Literaturen des Mittelalters. [c1928]; Klemperer, Viktor, Hatzfeld, Helmut, and Neubert, Fritz. Die romanischen Literaturen von der Renaissance bis zur Französischen Revolution. [c1924]; Heiss, Hans. Romanischen Literaturen des 19. und 20. Jahrhunderts. [c1923] (incompl.); Sakulin, P. N. Die russische Literatur. [c1927]; Kleiner, Julius. Die polinsche Literatur. [c1929]; Novák, Arne. Die tschechische Literatur. [c1931]; Gesemann, Gerhard. Die serbokroatische Literatur. [c1930]; Glasenapp, Helmuth von. Die Literaturen Indiens von ihren Anfangen bis zur Gegenwart. [c1929]; Wilhelm, Richard. Die chinesische Literatur. [c1926]; Gundert, W. Die japanische Literatur. [c1929]; Pieper, Max. Die ägyptische Literatur. [c1927]; Meissner, Bruno. Die babylonisch-assyrische Literatur. [c1927]; Hempel, Johannes. Die althebräische Literatur und ihr hellenistisch-jüdisches Nachleben. [c1930]; Borelius, Hilma. Die nordischen Literaturen. [c1931].

Magnus, Laurie. Dictionary of European literature, designed as a companion to English studies. 2d impression, rev., with addenda. Lond., Routledge; N.Y., Dutton, 1927. 605p. 25s.; $7.   **R34**

Gives concise articles, with some bibliographical references to sources of fuller information, on writers, literary movements, motives, literary forms, anonymous classics, etc., of the literatures of the various European countries, including the British Isles, of all periods from the classics through the first part of the twentieth century excluding living authors (except Thomas Hardy and Georg Brandes). Articles on writers give some biographical data, but deal principally with the writer's literary position, attitude, influence, etc.

Shipley, Joseph Twadell. Dictionary of world literature; criticism, forms, technique. N.Y., Philosophical Lib. [1943]. 633p. $7.50.   **R35**

An alphabetical dictionary giving in compact form, definitions and descriptions of literary terms, criticism, forms, techniques and ideas, literary schools and movements, literary periodicals, etc., of all countries and periods. Many of the articles are signed. Uneven. There are fairly long articles on the literary criticism of various countries, e.g., French criticism, Polish criticism, Russian criticism. No biography. Bibliographies appended to many articles.

Vapereau, Gustave. Dictionnaire universel des littératures. Paris, Hachette, 1876. 2096p.   **R36**

Subtitle: Contenant, 1, Des notices sur les écrivains de tous les temps et de tous les pays . . . 2, La théorie et l'historique des différents genres de poésie et de prose . . . 3, La bibliographie générale et particulière.

Handbooks

Ackermann, Alfred Seabold Eli. Popular fallacies; a book of common errors explained and corrected, with copious references to authorities. 4th ed. Lond., Old Westminster Pr., 1950. 843p.   **R37**

An informative and sometimes amusing potpourri of facts arranged under broad headings, such as food, weather, literature, etc. Subject index.

Brewer, Ebenezer Cobham. Dictionary of phrase and fable. New ed., rev., cor. and enl. Lond., Cassell; Phila., Lippincott, 1923. 1157p. 25s.; $4. **R38**

Includes abbreviations, colloquial and proverbial phrases, mythological and biographical references, fictitious characters, titles, etc.

—— Reader's handbook of famous names in fiction, allusions, references, proverbs, plots, stories, and poems. New ed., rev. and greatly enl. Lond., Chatto; Phila., Lippincott, 1898. 1501p. **R39**

One of the best of these handbooks. Appendixes p.1245-1501 contain (1) List of English authors and their works, (2) Title list of dramas and operas, giving authors and dates.

Later issues omit the appendixes.

Century cyclopedia of names; a pronouncing and etymological dictionary of names in geography, biography, mythology, history, ethnology, art, archaeology, fiction, etc. rev. and enl. N.Y., Century [1911]. 1085p., 156p. o.p. **R40**

Also issued as volume 11 of the *Century dictionary* (M4).

A very useful reference book. Gives brief articles and indicates pronunciation. For the student of literature, particularly useful for sketches of authors of all periods and nationalities; also includes titles of works and characters in fiction. This edition contains two alphabets: (1) a reprint of the original list of names in the first edition, with some revisions and changes, (2) a reprint from the supplementary list of 3,000 new names and new matter about older names, appended to volume 2 of the 1909 supplement to the *Century dictionary*. Stars in the main alphabet refer to added information about the same name in the supplementary alphabet and vice versa. Appendixes: (1) Chronological table of historical events; (2) List of rulers; (3) Genealogical charts; (4) Chronological outlines of European and American literature.

Fournel, Victor. Dictionnaire encyclopédique d'anecdotes modernes et anciennes, françaises et étrangères, par Edmond Guérard [pseud.]. Paris, Dorbon [1926]. 2v. **R41**

Hyamson, Albert Montefiore. Dictionary of English phrases; phraseological allusions, catchwords . . . metaphors, nicknames, sobriquets, derivations from personal names. Lond., Routledge; N.Y., Dutton, 1922. 365p. **R42**

Killikelly, Sarah Hutchins. Curious questions in history, literature, art, and social life. Phila., McKay, 1886–1900. 3v. il. o.p. **R43**

Phyfe, William Henry Pinkney. 5000 facts and fancies . . . important, curious, quaint, and unique information in history, literature, sciences, art, and nature. N.Y., Putnam, 1901. 816p. o.p. **R44**

Shankle, George Earlie. American nicknames, their origin and significance. N.Y., Wilson, 1937. 599p. $5; $4.25 to libraries. **R45**

Not limited to nicknames of persons, but includes also those applied to places, institutions or objects, arranged by real names with cross references from nicknames. Information under the real names includes some explanation of the nicknames and their origin with reference to sources of information given in footnotes.

Walsh, William Shepard. Handy book of curious information comprising strange happenings in the life of men and animals, odd statistics, extraordinary phenomena and out-of-the-way facts. Phila. and Lond., Lippincott [1913]. 942p. $3.50; 25s. **R46**

—— Handy-book of literary curiosities. Phila. and Lond., Lippincott, 1893. 1104p. $6; 25s. **R47**

One of the most useful of these handbooks.

—— Heroes and heroines of fiction . . . famous characters and famous names in novels, romances, poems and dramas, classified, analyzed and criticised. Phila. and Lond., Lippincott, 1914–15. 2v. $6; 25s. **R48**

v.1, Classical, mediaeval and legendary. 1915. 379p.; v.2, Modern prose and poetry. 1914. 391p.

Wheeler, William Adolphus. Explanatory and pronouncing dictionary of the noted names of fiction; with an appendix by C. G. Wheeler. 22d ed. Bost., Houghton, 1893 [c65-89]. 440p. **R49**

—— Familiar allusions; a hand-book of miscellaneous information. 5th ed. Bost., Houghton, 1890 [c81]. 584p. o.p. **R50**

"Including the names of celebrated statues, paintings, palaces, country seats, ruins, churches, ships, streets, clubs, natural curiosities, and the like."

—— Who wrote it? ed. by C. G. Wheeler. Bost., Lee, 1887. 174p. o.p. **R51**

An alphabetical list of the titles of famous works in all literatures, including poems, songs, plays, first lines of poems, novels, short stories, fables, legends, romances, chronicles, and other works having distinctive titles. For each work, gives author's name and dates of birth and death.

❦ The above are popular handbooks, useful mainly as first aids. Important information will also often be found in periodicals of the "notes and queries" type. The following are especially useful:

Notes and queries, for readers and writers, collectors and librarians, 1849- . Lond., Ox. Univ. Pr., 1850- . v.1- . 32s. 6d. per v. **R52**

Imprint and title vary; earlier subtitle: A medium of communication for literary men, artists, antiquarians and genealogists.

Fortnightly (frequency varies), two volumes per year, formerly grouped in series of 12 volumes each but since the beginning of the thirteenth series (1923) volumed continuously. There is an index to each volume and a general index each six years. If it is not convenient to keep the whole set in the reference room the general indexes should be kept there.

Contains a large amount of interesting and often very valuable information on out-of-the-way questions, usually small points in general and local history and literature, bibliography, manners, customs, folklore, local observances, quotations, proverbs, etc. Much of the information is in the form of signed answers to questions from readers, and sources of information are given. Indexes are well made and detailed and should be used constantly as supplements to the handbooks of allusions, quotations, proverbs, etc.

❧ There are also local periodicals of this type which are useful for small points in the literature, biography, history, etc., of their special localities. For a list of English county "notes and queries" *see Bibliography of British history: Tudor period,* by Conyers Read, p.266-300 (V274).

American notes and queries; a journal for the curious. v.1, Apr. 1941- . No. Bennington, Vt. v.1- . Monthly. $2.50 per yr. **R53**

Annual and 5-year cumulative indexes announced.
Edited by Walter Pilkington and B. Alsterlund.

Intermédiaire des chercheurs et curieux, correspondance littéraire, historique et artistique, questions et réponses, lettres et documents inédits . . . 1864- . Paris, 1864- . v.1- . il. Semimonthly; frequency varies. 70fr. per yr.; foreign 100fr. **R54**

—— Table générale (t.1-34, 1864–96; t.35-82, 1897–1920; t.83-96, 1921–33). Paris, 1897, 1924, 1935. 3v.

Biographies of authors

❧ The main sources for biographical sketches of authors of any country are the encyclopedias and national biographical dictionaries of the country. For special dictionaries of authors of a particular country *see* the name of that country in this section. In the case of American Literature and British Literature *see* Dictionaries and Handbooks as well as Biographies of Authors. Following is a brief list of dictionaries which are international in scope:

Biographisches Jahrbuch für Altertumskunde, 1878- . Berlin, Calvary, 1879–98; Leipzig, Reisland, 1899- . v.1- . **R55**

Annual, except that no volume was published for 1912; issued as part of the *Jahresbericht über die Fortschritte der klassischen Altertumswissenschaft.*

Contains signed obituaries of classical philologists; articles are of some length, with bibliographies. More than 700 articles are included in volumes 1-50, 1899–1930.

Gubernatis, Angelo de. Dictionnaire international des écrivains du monde latin. Rome, l'Auteur, 1905–06. 1506p., 254p. **R56**

Includes contemporary writers of Latin nationality, i.e., Belgian, French, Italian, Latin-American, Portuguese, Rumanian, Spanish, whatever the subject of their works, and non-Latin authors who have written on Latin subjects. Especially full for Italian names.

His earlier works, *Dictionnaire international des écrivains du jour,* 1888–91, and *Dizionario biografico degli scrittori contemporanei,* 1879, are much out of date but occasionally useful. For descriptions of these *see* Mudge, I. G., *New Guide to reference books,* 1923, p.163.

Kunitz, Stanley Jasspon and **Haycraft, Howard.** Twentieth century authors, a biographical dictionary of modern literature; complete in one volume with 1850 biographies and 1700 portraits. N.Y., Wilson, 1942. 1577p. il. (The Authors ser.) $8.50. **R57**

Done in the same style and intended to supersede their *Living authors* (1931) and *Authors today and yesterday* (1933). Aims to give information on "writers of this century of all nations, whose books are familiar to readers of English. No attempt has been made to include foreign authors on the basis of their reputation in their native lands or tongues; the criterion, in general, has been the degree of acceptance of their translated works in the United States and England."—*Pref.* Includes bibliographies by and about the author.

Perdigão, Henrique. Dicionário universal de literatura (bio-bibliográfico e cronológico) 2d ed. Porto, 1940. 1038p. il. **R58**

Covers all countries and all periods but is especially strong in Portuguese and Brazilian.

Includes a chronological index by nationalities and an alphabetical index.

Sharp, Robert Farquharson. Short biographical dictionary of foreign literature. Lond., Dent; N.Y., Dutton [1933]. 302p. (Everyman's Library Reference. no.900) **R59**

A concise dictionary of some 550 "European-non-English" authors with brief biographical notes and lists of works with date of publication. Especially useful in libraries which do not have the larger foreign biographical dictionaries.

Who's who among living authors of older nations, covering the literary activities of living authors and writers of all countries of the world except the United States of America, Canada, Mexico, Alaska, Hawaii, Newfoundland, the Philippines, the West Indies and Central America. v.1, 1931-32; ed. by A. Lawrence. Los Angeles, Calif., Golden Syndicate Pub. Co. [c1931] 482p. $8.50. **R60**

Main list of biographies, p.1-437. Supplementary sections are: Press section, containing sketches of authors whose only output is in newspapers and magazines; Authors arranged by countries; Poets arranged by countries; Pen names.

Quotations and proverbs

❧ Books of quotations are important in any reference collection for (1) identifying a given quotation and verifying the wording; (2) suggesting quotations about a particular subject or suitable for a special occasion; (3) supplying quotable passages from the writings of a given author. The first is probably the most frequent need in libraries. As every book of quotations is necessarily selective and as each includes something not given in the others, the large library should keep the older works even when new and seemingly more comprehensive books are added to the reference collection. The small library, however, will find a much more limited supply quite adequate. If it has fairly recent editions of Bartlett's *Familiar quotations* (R63) as the best chronological author list, and Stevenson's *Home book of quotations* (R70), Hoyt's *New cyclopedia of practical quotations* (R67), and the *Oxford dictionary of quotations* (R69), as useful subject lists, it is well equipped for ordinary reference work for English as well as for a general selection of foreign quotations.

The reference value of a book of quotations depends upon three things: (1) the comprehensiveness of the collection and the care and judgment with which the quotations have been chosen; (2) the exactness of reference with which the quotations are given, i.e., the reference should be not merely to the author, but to the special work, and its chapter, section, stanza, etc.; and (3) the *completeness of the index*. As the most frequent use of such books is for the purpose of locating a given quotation, the index should include every word in each quotation which a reader is at all likely to remember.

Allibone, Samuel Austin. Poetical quotations from Chaucer to Tennyson. Phila. and Lond., Lippincott, 1891 [c73]. 788p. **R61**

Gives reference to author only. Includes indexes to authors, subjects, and first lines.

—— Prose quotations from Socrates to Macaulay. Phila., Lippincott, 1889 [c75]. 764p. **R62**

Subject list with an index of authors and an index of subjects. Quotations are brief.

Bartlett, John. Familiar quotations; a collection of passages, phrases and proverbs traced to their sources in ancient and modern literature. 12th ed., rev. and enl.; Christopher Morley, ed.; L. D. Everett, assoc. ed. Bost., Little, 1948. 1831p. $8. **R63**

1st ed., 1855; 10th ed., rev. by N. H. Dole, 1914; 11th ed., rev. by C. Morley and L. D. Everett, 1937.
Contents: Main list, chronological author list, p.3-1037; Addenda, p.1038-59; of unknown authorship, p.1060-70; Translations, p.1073-1219; Bible, etc., p.1223-54; Index, p.1257-1831.

A standard collection, comprehensive and well selected. Arranged by authors chronologically, with exact references. One of the best books of quotations with a long history. The eleventh edition almost doubled the size of the tenth edition, the twelfth edition is the same as the eleventh up to p.787, but after that it has been entirely re-edited to include new authors, particularly contemporary authors, additional quotations, etc. The miscellaneous section, Addenda, has also been enlarged by the inclusion of both old and new quotations. There are many interesting footnotes, tracing history or usage of analogous thoughts, the circumstances under which a particular remark was made, etc.

The index is especially fine, containing an average of four or five entries per quotation, and has been entirely remade to include all of the additional material in this twelfth edition.

There may be times when the tenth edition will still be useful as many quotations included there are omitted from the later editions.

Benham, Sir William Gurney. Benham's Book of quotations, proverbs, and household words. New and rev. ed. with supplement and with full indexes. N.Y., Putnam, 1949. 1384p. $7.50. **R64**

1st ed. 1907; 2d rev. ed. 1936.
Contains: Quotations, British and American, p.1-440; Bible and Book of Common Prayer, p.441-65; "Waifs and strays," e.g., political phrases, epitaphs, London street sayings, bell inscriptions, etc., p.466-512; Foreign (Greek, Latin, French, German, Italian, Spanish, Dutch), p.513-764; Proverbs, p.765-928; Index, p.929-1259.
Includes about 30,000 quotations.

Frequently reprinted with little change. In the 1949 edition, the main part of the work is substantially the same as in the 1936 edition with some errors corrected and dates of death added. A supplement with its own index has been added, p.1261-1322 (index p.1323-1384). . . . While this supplement includes a few recent quotations of modern authors it is largely devoted to additional quotations of authors included in the main work.

Dalbiac, Philip Hugh. Dictionary of quotations (English), with authors and subjects indexes. Lond., Sonnenschein; N.Y., Macmillan, 1908. 544p. **R65**

Gives references to exact source.

Day, Edward Parsons. Day's Collacon; an encyclopaedia of prose quotations with biographical index of authors. Lond., Low, 1883. 1216p. il. **R66**

Arranged alphabetically by subjects.

Hoyt, Jehiel Keeler. Hoyt's New cyclopedia of practical quotations drawn from the speech and literature of all nations, ancient and modern, classic and popular, in English and foreign text. With . . . copious indexes; comp. rev. and greatly enl. by Kate Louise Roberts. N.Y. and Lond., Funk, 1922. 1343p. $7.50. **R67**

1st ed. 1882; 2d ed. enl. 1896. Reissued in 1940 with a few corrections and the addition of death dates for some authors in the author list. The "New 1947 Edition" published by Somerset Books Inc., N.Y. ($4.95), is practically unchanged.

Contents: (1) Quotations, arranged alphabetically by general subjects; (2) Index of quoted authors, with brief biographical data; (3) Concordance of quotations.

A very comprehensive collection, the best indexed of the subject lists. Quotations are given with exact references, and the indexes are excellent. Though now more than 25 years old, still very useful except for contemporary writers.

Mencken, Henry Louis. A new dictionary of quotations on historical principles from ancient and modern sources. N.Y., Knopf, 1942. 1347p. $7.50. **R68**

A comprehensive collection with emphasis on the lesser known quotations. Includes many proverbs and some foreign quotations, mainly in English translation. Arranged by rubric with many cross references to allied headings. Quotations are dated whenever possible and arranged chronologically under rubric. An attempt has been made to trace each quotation to its earliest usage. There is no index. Gives name of author and title of work but not exact reference.

The Oxford dictionary of quotations, with an introd. by Carl Van Doren. Lond. and N.Y., Ox. Univ. Pr., 1941. 879p. 30s.; $6. **R69**

Contents: Authors writing in English, alphabetically arranged; Book of Common Prayer; Holy Bible; English literature; Foreign quotations; Addenda, Index.

A comprehensive collection of quotations chosen for their familiarity. Gives exact reference to source. Omits proverbs and phrases because these are given in the *Oxford dictionary of English proverbs* (R126). Indexed by key words. "The general plan has been to allow two words of index for each line of verse though it has been found impossible to limit the number to two in the most well-known quotations and to index the principal words in the prose passages." Foreign quotations have separate indexes.

Stevenson, Burton Egbert. Home book of quotations, classical and modern. 5th ed. rev. N.Y., Dodd, 1947. 2812p. $15. **R70**

1st ed. 1934.

A comprehensive and well-chosen collection of over 50,000 quotations arranged alphabetically by subject with subarrangement by smaller topics. Usually gives exact citation. Includes an index of authors, giving full name, identifying phrase, and dates of birth and death, with reference to all quotations cited; and a word index which indexes the quotation by leading words, usually nouns, though in some cases verbs and adjectives are also used. However black-letter entries are given for some of the smaller subjects. The quotations under these subjects carrying the subject word, e.g., accident, skill, are not indexed separately, and one must, therefore, turn to the subject and run through the entries. This practice must be remembered when using this index.

The fifth edition includes an appendix, p.2273-98g; p.2298a-g being new in this edition and including recent material. The quotations on these pages are indexed in a separate section at the end of the main index, p.2811-12.

The third edition (1937) is the most important edition of this work, being a thorough revision of the first two

editions with the addition of more than 1000 quotations, revision of notes, etc., and a much enlarged index. The later editions make some corrections, add dates of death in the author index and include some additional quotations in the Appendix. For many libraries, however, the third edition will be sufficient for most purposes.

Van Buren, Maud. Quotations for special occasions. N.Y., Wilson, 1938. 201p. $2.50. **R71**

Quotations selected for their appropriateness to certain days, e.g., Arbor day, Armistice day, Bird day, Book week, Christmas day, etc. Indication is given of the author of the quotation but not the source.

Walsh, William Shepard. International encyclopedia of prose and poetical quotations from the literature of the world, ancient and modern, classic and popular, including quotations from the writings and speeches of recent American and foreign poets, novelists, dramatists, statesmen. New ed. Phila., Winston [c1931]. 1029p. $3. **R72**

Wilstach, Frank Jenners. Dictionary of similes. Rev. ed. Bost., Little, 1924. 578p. $4. (cheap repr. $1) **R73**

Wood, James. Nuttall dictionary of quotations from ancient and modern, English and foreign sources . . . new ed., with supplement of over 1000 quotations including many from modern authors; comp. by A. L. Haydon. Lond. and N.Y., Warne, 1930. 659p., 28p. 7s. 6d.; $3. **R74**

Refers to author only, not to special work from which the quotation is taken. The added material in this edition, with its own index, is in the 28 pages at the end. There is no combined index to the main list and supplement.

Foreign and classical

✤ For some questions concerned with foreign and classical quotations the great dictionaries of the language, the special dialect or period dictionaries, and the dictionaries or concordances of individual authors are the most useful sources. For example the *Thesaurus linguae latinae* (M340) contains many more quotations than could be found in even a very comprehensive dictionary of Latin quotations; Merguet's *Lexikon zu den Schriften Cicero's* (R849) can be used to locate more Cicero quotations than would be found in a quotation book, etc. The books of foreign quotations listed below are the easy first aids but for material not found in them, dictionaries within the various fields should be consulted.

King, William Francis Henry. Classical and foreign quotations; a polyglot manual of historical and literary sayings, noted passages in poetry and prose, phrases, proverbs, and bon mots comp., ed. and told with their references, translations, and indexes. 3d ed. rev. and rewritten. Lond., Whitaker, 1904. 412p. o.p.   **R75**

> 1st ed. 1887.
> Gives reference to exact source.

Arabic and Persian

Field, Claud Herbert Alwyn Faure. Dictionary of oriental quotations (Arabic and Persian). Lond., Sonnenschein; N.Y., Macmillan, 1911. 351p.   **R76**

> Gives quotations in transliteration, arranged alphabetically by first word, with translations. Index of authors and index of subjects and catchwords; the latter not very full. Includes 85 authors.

Chinese

Ch'êng Yü K'ao. A manual of Chinese quotations, being a translation of the Ch 'êng Yü K'ao. With the Chinese text, notes, explanations and English and Chinese indices for easy reference by J. H. Stewart Lockhart. Hongkong, Kelly and Walsh, 1903. 645p., cxviip.   **R77**

Scarborough, William. Collection of Chinese proverbs, rev. and enl. by the addition of some six hundred proverbs, by C. Wilfrid Allan. Shanghai, Presbyterian Mission Pr., 1927. 381p.   **R78**

Dutch

Stoett, Frederik August. Nederlandsche spreekwoorden, spreekwijzen uitdrukkingen en gezegden. 3. druk. Zutphen, Thieme, 1915–16. 2v.   **R78a**

—— Nederlandsche spreekwoorden en gezegden, verklaard en vergeleken met die in het Fransch, Duitsch en Engelsch. 4. druk. Zutphen, Thieme, 1918. 392p.   **R78b**

French

Alexandre, Roger. Le musée de la conversation; répertoire de citations françaises, dictons modernes, curiosités littéraires, historiques et anecdotiques. Paris, Bouillon, 1902. 2v.   **R79**

> 1st ed., 1892; 3d ed., 1897, with supplement "Les mots qui restent," 1901; 4th ed., includes the material of the previous editions and some new material.
> Arranged alphabetically by catchwords; gives exact reference to source, and some discussion. Indexes: (1) proper names; (2) subjects.

Genest, Émile. Les belles citations de la littérature française, suggérées par les mots et les idées, à l'usage des élèves des hautes classes, des journalistes, des gens du monde. (1.-2. sér.) Paris, Nathan [c1923]–1927. 2v.   **R80**

—— Où est-ce donc? Dictionnaire des phrases, vers et mots célèbres employés dans le langage courant avec précision de l'origine, suivi d'un index alphabétique des auteurs cités. (1. sér.) Paris, Nathan [c1925]. 308p.   **R81**

Guerlac, Othon Goepp. Les citations françaises; recueil de passages célèbres, phrases familières, mots historiques. 2. ed. rev. et augm. Paris, Colin, 1933. 458p.   **R82**

> Arranged in main by authors, chronologically with two alphabetical indexes: (1) authors; (2) catchwords. Includes modern as well as older quotations, gives exact reference, not merely author's name, and has many footnotes giving additional facts, e.g., parallel passages in other writers, etc.
> The most generally useful of the French quotation books.

Harbottle, Thomas Benfield and **Dalbiac, P. H.** Dictionary of quotations (French and Italian). Lond., Sonnenschein; N.Y., Macmillan, 1901. 565p.   **R83**

> Allen and Unwin, 2v. 5s. ea.

Lecat, Maurice. Pensées sur la science, la guerre, et sur des sujets très variés. Bruxelles, Lamertin, 1919. 478p.   **R84**

> French quotations and quotations from other languages translated into French, arranged by subject with an author index and an analytical subject index. Reference is to authors only.

Porchère, Samuel. Dictionnaire poétique, recueil de poésies et pensées poétiques célèbres . . . acrostiches, anagrammes, boutades, épigraphes, épigrammes (100,000 vers sur 1,600 sujets, 1,000 auteurs cités). Saint-Etienne, L'Auteur, 1905. 3v. 2990p.   **R85**

> Arranged alphabetically by subject and catchword; many quotations given at considerable length, so that the work can serve to a certain extent as an anthology as well as a book of quotations.

Ramage, Craufurd Tait. Beautiful thoughts from French and Italian authors; with English translations. 4th ed. Lond., Routledge, 1884. 619p. o.p.   **R86**

> Also published under title *Familiar quotations from French and Italian authors.*

Vibraye, Henri, *conte de.* Trésor des proverbes français anciens et modernes. Paris, Hazan, 1934. 433p.   **R87**

> "Bibliographie parémiologique," p.11-14.

German

Büchmann, Georg. Geflügelte Worte; der Zitatenschatz des deutschen Volkes. Fortgesetzt von Walter Robert-tornow, Konrad Weidling [u.A.]. 28. Aufl. Neubearb. von Gunther Haupt und Werner Rust. Berlin, Max Paschke, 1937. 788p. **R88**

Arranged by country of origin with a name index and word indexes.

—— Geflügelte Worte und Zitatenschatz. Verbesserte Neuausgabe. Zürich, Werner Classen Verlag [1946]. 425p. Sw. Fr. 12.80; $4. **R89**

"Neu bearbeitet von dr. Paul Dorpert."
A shortened and modernized edition of the foregoing. Includes quotations from many languages.

Dalbiac, Lilian. Dictionary of quotations (German) with authors' and subjects' indexes. Lond., Sonnenschein; N.Y., Macmillan, 1906. 485p. **R90**

Krüger, Werner Adolf. Dichter und Denkerworte; 12,000 Zitate und Sentenzen aus der Weltliteratur. Basel, Munster [1945]. 1936 col. Sw. Fr. 20; $6. **R91**

Arranged by rubric. In most cases citation is not to exact source but only to author and title. Alphabetical list of authors but no index.

Lipperheide, Franz Joseph, *Freiherr von.* Spruchwörterbuch. Sammlung deutscher und fremder Sinnsprüche, Wahlsprüche, Inschriften an Haus und Gerät, Grabsprüche, Sprichwörter, Aphorismen, Epigramme, von Bibelstellen, Liederanfängen, von Zitaten. Berlin, Lipperheide, 1907. 1069p. **R92**

Ramage, Craufurd Tait. Beautiful thoughts from German and Spanish authors. New rev. ed. Lond., Routledge, 1884. 559p. o.p. **R93**

Also published under title *Familiar quotations from German and Spanish authors.*

Sanders, Daniel. Zitatenlexikon, eine Sammlung von über 12,000 Zitaten, Sprichwörtern, sprichwörtlichen Redensarten und Sentenzen. 3. verb. Aufl. Leipzig, Weber, 1911. 712p. **R94**

Singer, Samuel. Sprichwörter des Mittelalters. Bern, H. Lang, 1944–47. 3v. **R95**

Contents: v.1, Von den Anfängen bis ins 12. Jahrhundert; v.2, Das 13. Jahrhundert; v.3, Das 13. und 14. Jahrhundert.

Zoozmann, Richard. Zitatenschatz der Weltliteratur, eine Sammlung von Zitaten, Sentenzen, geflügelten Worten, Epigrammen und Sprichwörtern, nach Schlagworten geordnet. Neu bearb. von Karl Quenzel. Leipzig, Hesse und Becker, [1935?]. 950 col. **R96**

Greek

See Latin and Greek.

Italian

Finzi, Giuseppe. Dizionario di citazioni latine ed italiane. Milano, Sandron, 1902. 967p. **R97**

Fumagalli, Giuseppe. Chi l'ha detto? Tesoro di citazioni italiane e straniere. 9. ed. Milano, Hoepli, 1946. 841p. **R98**

1st ed. 1894.
Covers quotations in different languages, arranged by subject, with reference to exact source and some explanatory notes. Indexes: (1) authors; (2) quotations.

Harbottle, Thomas Benfield and **Dalbiac, P. H.** Dictionary of quotations, Italian. Lond., Sonnenschein; N.Y., Macmillan, 1909. (Allen and Unwin, 5s.) **R99**

A reprint of the Italian section of their *Dictionary of quotations (French and Italian)* (R83).

Ramage, Craufurd Tait. Beautiful thoughts from French and Italian authors. Lond., Routledge, 1884. 619p. **R99a**

For full record *see* R86.

Japanese

Akiyama, Aisaburo. Japanese proverbs and proverbial phrases. 3d ed. Yokohama, Yoshikawa Book Store, 1940. 305p. **R100**

Alphabetized by Japanese transliteration (Romanized). Gives Japanese characters, literal English translation and nearest equivalent English proverb.

Latin and Greek

Harbottle, Thomas Benfield. Dictionary of quotations (classical). Lond., Sonnenschein, 1906. 678p. o.p. **R101**

The best dictionary of Latin and Greek quotations. Gives each in the original, with exact reference to source, and an English translation with name of translator. Indexes: (1) authors; (2) subjects, Latin; (3) subjects, Greek; (4) subjects, English.
This edition includes an appendix, p.649-78.

—— Dictionary of quotations, Latin. Lond., Sonnenschein; N.Y., Macmillan, 1909. 389p. **R102**

A reprint of the Latin section of his *Dictionary of quotations (classical)* (R101), with an appendix of additional material.

Ramage, Craufurd Tait. Beautiful thoughts from Greek authors, with English translations. Lond., Routledge, 1895. 589p. o.p. **R103**

Also published under title *Familiar quotations from Greek authors.*

—— Beautiful thoughts from Latin authors, with English translations. Lond., Routledge, 1895. 855p. o.p. **R104**

Also published under title *Familiar quotations from Latin authors.*

Riley, Henry Thomas. Dictionary of Latin and Greek quotations, proverbs, maxims, and mottoes, classical and mediaeval. Including law terms and phrases. Lond., Bell, 1888. 622p. (Bohn library) **R105**

Sarasino, Ernesto. Flores sententiarum; raccolta di 5000 sentenze, proverbi e motti latini di uso quotidiano in ordine per materie, con le fonti indicate, schiarimenti e la traduzione italiana. Milano, Hoepli, 1926. 638p. **R106**

Scandinavian

Bonnevie, Margarete. Ord som lever; en samling av norske og utenlandske citater og slagord. Oslo, Some, 1928. 131p. **R108**

Langlet, Valdemar. Bevingade ord och slagord; efter olika källor sammanställda och förklarade. Stockholm, Geber, 1925–28. 2v. **R109**

v.1, Citat från främmande Sprak. 499p.; v.2, Svenska citat. 680p.

Spanish

Cejador y Frauca, Julio. Refranero castellano. Madrid, Hernando, 1928–29. 3v. **R110**

Correas, Gonzalo. Vocabulario de refranes y frases proverbiales y otras fórmulas comunes de la lengua castellana. . . . Madrid, Rev. de Archivos, Bibliotecas y Museos, 1924. 662p. **R111**

Published for the first time in 1906, by the Real Academia Española, from a copy made by Tomas Antonio Sánchez (completed in 1780) of the original manuscript.

Supplemented by the various collections by Rodríguez Marín (R115).

Echeverri, Elio Fabio. Diccionario del pensamiento, refranes, máximas, aforismos, sentencias. . . . Bogotá, Ed. Ferrini [1942]. 353p. il. **R112**

Does not indicate sources.

Harbottle, Thomas Benfield and **Hume, Martin.** Dictionary of quotations (Spanish) with subject and authors' index. Lond., Sonnenschein; N.Y., Macmillan, 1907. 462p. **R113**

Mir y Noguera, Juan. Diccionario de frases de los autores clásicos españoles. Buenos Aires, Gil, 1942. 1328p. **R114**

Previously published in Madrid in 1899, this Argentinian edition was revised and an index of authors and works from which the phrases were taken was added.

Ramage, Craufurd Tait. Beautiful thoughts from German and Spanish authors. Lond., Routledge, 1884. **R114a**

For full information *see* R93.

Rodríguez Marín, Francisco. Más de 21,000 refranes castellanos no contenidos en la copiosa colección del Maestro Gonzalo Correas. Madrid, Rev. de Archivos, Bibliotecas y Museos, 1926. 519p. **R115**

—— 12,600 refranes más. 1930. 344p.

—— Los 6,666 refranes. 1934. 198p.

—— Todavía 10,700 refranes más. 1941. 317p.

Sbarbi y Osuna, José María. Gran diccionario de refranes de la lengua española; refranes, adagios, proverbios, modismos, locuciones y frases proverbiales . . . cor. y publ. bajo la dirección de Manuel J. García. Buenos Aires, Gil, 1943. 1028p. **R116**

Published 1922 under title: *Diccionario de refranes, adagios [etc.].*

Proverbs

❧ Like books of quotations there are many types of books of proverbs. Many of the older works may still prove useful for historical purposes, but the very comprehensive Stevenson, *Home book of proverbs, maxims and familiar phrases* (R127) and the *Oxford dictionary of English proverbs* (R126) will now answer most of the general questions in this field. For books of proverbs of particular countries *see* Quotations of the country.

Bibliography

Stephens, Thomas Arthur. Proverb literature; a bibliography of works relating to proverbs, ed. by Wilfrid Bonser . . . comp. from materials left by the late T. A. Stephens. . . . Lond., W. Glaisher, 1930. 496p. ([Folk-lore Society. Pub.] 89) 21s. **R117**

An annotated bibliography of over 4000 works on the proverbs of all nations, including collections of particular localities and special subjects.

Collections

Apperson, George Latimer. English proverbs and proverbial phrases; a historical dictionary. . . . Lond., Dent; N.Y., Dutton, 1929. 721p. $8; 31s. 6d. **R118**

Traces the history of English proverbs and proverbial phrases, through references to the literature.

Arthaber, Augusto. Dizionario comparato di proverbi e modi proverbiali; italiani, latini, francesi, spagnoli, tedeschi, inglesi e greci antichi con relativi indici sistematico-alfabetici. . . . Milano, Hoepli, 1929. 892p.　　　**R119**

Bohn, Henry George. Handbook of proverbs. Lond., Bell, 1889. 583p. o.p.　　　**R120**

Includes John Ray's *Collection of English proverbs* (originally published in five editions, 1670-1813), with his additions from foreign languages, and a complete alphabetical index.

—— Polyglot of foreign proverbs. Lond., Bell, 1889. 579p. o.p.　　　**R121**

Comprises French, Italian, German, Dutch, Spanish, Portuguese and Danish proverbs, with English translations and a general index.

Champion, Selwyn Gurney. Racial proverbs; a selection of the world's proverbs arranged linguistically . . . with authoritative introductions to the proverbs of 27 countries and races. Lond., Routledge; N.Y., Macmillan, 1938. cxxixp., 767p. 35s.; $10.　　　**R122**

"Embodies the first and second series of [his] 'Wayside sayings.'"—*Introd.*
"Authorities consulted": p.cix-cxxix.
Arranged by country with the following four indexes: Linguistic and geographical, Subject-matter, Race, Alternative chief-word.
The introduction to the proverbs of each country or race is by a specialist.

Christy, Robert. Proverbs, maxims and phrases of all ages. N.Y., Putnam, 1905 [c1887]. 2v. in 1. 665p., 602p. $5.　　　**R123**

Arranged by subjects, giving sources of proverbs, etc., when known. Subject index.

Davidoff, Henry. A world treasury of proverbs, from twenty-five languages. N.Y., Random House, 1946. 526p. $3. (Garden City Pub. Co., 1948, $1.98)　　　**R124**

Over 15,000 proverbs and sayings from 25 languages arranged by rubric with subject and author indexes.

Lean, Vincent Stuckey. Lean's Collectanea; collections of proverbs, (English and foreign), folklore, and superstitions, also compilations towards dictionaries of proverbial phrases and words old and disused. Bristol, Arrowsmith; Lond., Simpkin, 1902–04. 4v. in 5. il. o.p.　　　**R125**

v.1, Local proverbs by countries, proverbs according to the calendar, proverbs relating to domestic life, etc.; v.2, pt.1-2, Folk-lore, superstitions, omens and popular customs; v.3, A compilation towards a dictionary of words and phrases with examples of their use; v.4, A list of authorities and general index.

Smith, William George. Oxford dictionary of English proverbs; introduction by Janet E. Heseltine. 2d ed. rev. throughout by Sir Paul Harvey. Ox., Clarendon Pr., 1948. 740p. $13.50; 35s. **R126**

The first edition (1935) contained about 10,000 proverbs, arranged alphabetically by first word, including, a, an, the. This edition has been somewhat enlarged and some earlier sources noted, but its main improvement lies in its new arrangement. Proverbs are now alphabetized under significant words (usually the first), with the preceding words, if any, transferred to the end or occasionally to an intermediate point. Liberal cross references are included from all other significant words, usually with enough of the phrase so that it is readily identifiable.
Dated references are given for each proverb to the earliest uses and sources found, with variant usages at succeeding times.

Stevenson, Burton. Home book of proverbs, maxims and familiar phrases. N.Y., Macmillan, 1948. 2957p. $20.　　　**R127**

Attempts to trace back to their sources proverbs, maxims, and familiar phrases in ordinary English and American use and to show their development.
Follows the pattern of his *Home book of quotations* (R70), with subject arrangement and detailed word index. Very comprehensive, including over 73,000 expressions from many languages and periods; many of them might be considered quotations as his interpretation of proverb and maxim is very broad. Dates for quotations are given, quotations from foreign sources are given in English translation followed by the original language (except for the Oriental). Indexed from at least one and sometimes more key words.

Taylor, Archer. The proverb. Camb., Harv. Univ. Pr., 1931. 223p. $2.　　　**R128**

—— —— Index. Helsinki, Suomalainen Tiedeakatemia, 1934. 105p. (FF communications no.113)

The main volume discusses the origin, content and style of proverbs. The index lists the proverbs mentioned with reference to page and also to its treatment in other collections of proverbs.

Tilley, Morris Palmer. A dictionary of the proverbs in England in the 16th and 17th centuries; a collection of the proverbs found in English literature and the dictionaries of the period. Ann Arbor, Univ. of Michigan Pr., 1950. 854p. **R128a**

Contains some 11,780 proverbs arranged by "catchword." Each proverb is followed by citations arranged chronologically. There is a bibliography of the works cited, an index of Shakespearean quotations appearing in the text, and an index of significant words in the proverbs.

Drama

See also Theater, p.344-45 and Drama, p.379, p.387-89, and p.409-10.

Bibliography

Baker, Blanch Merritt. Dramatic bibliography. N.Y., Wilson, 1933. 320p.　　　**R129**

Subtitle: An annotated list of books on the history and criticism of the drama and stage and on the allied arts of the theatre.

Boston. Public Library. Allen A. Brown Collection. Catalogue of the Allen A. Brown collection of books relating to the stage. Bost., 1919. 952p. **R130**

A dictionary catalog of a rich collection of works relating to the history of the stage, followed by an author list of works on the drama.

Clarence, Reginald. "The Stage" cyclopaedia; a bibliography of plays. Lond., "The Stage," 1909. 503p. **R131**

Subtitle: An alphabetical list of plays and other stage pieces of which any record can be found since the commencement of the English stage . . . with descriptions, authors' names, dates and places of production, and other useful information comprising in all nearly 50,000 plays and extending over a period of upwards of 500 years.

A title list with some subject entries (e.g., Greek plays), aiming to be complete for English drama and selective for the better known foreign plays.

Gilder, Rosamond and **Freedley, George.** Theatre collections in libraries and museums: An international handbook. N.Y., Theatre Arts, Inc., 1936. 182p. **R132**

Arranged geographically. Describes the theater collections in this country and abroad.

New York. Public Library. Foreign plays in English. A list of translations in the . . . library, comp. by D. C. Haskell. N.Y., 1920. 86p. **R133**

A list of plays from 30 different languages, arranged alphabetically by original language, and under language by author. Alphabetical index of English titles at end.

Indexes

American Library Association. Board on Library Service to Children and Young People. Subject index to children's plays, comp. by a Subcommittee, Elizabeth D. Briggs, chairman. Chic., Amer. Lib. Assoc., 1940. 277p. $3.50. **R134**

A subject index of plays found in 202 collections, suitable for children in grades 1 through 8.

Index to the Best plays series, 1899–1950. N.Y., Dodd, 1950. 147p. $2.75. **R134a**

For description *see* R211.

Dramatic index for 1909- , covering articles and illustrations concerning the stage and its players in the periodicals of America and England and including The Dramatic books of the year. Bost., Faxon, 1910- . v.1- . Annual. $7.50 per v. **R135**

Issued separately, and also as part two of the *Annual magazine subject index,* 1907- (E73). Contains the cumulation of the Dramatic index published in the quarterly numbers of the *Bulletin of bibliography.* Volumes 1-8, 11- , have appendix: *Dramatic books and plays (in English)* published 1912–16, 1919-

An annual subject index to articles about the drama, the theater, actors and actresses, playwrights, librettists, managers, etc., to synopses of plays, and to stage and dramatic portraits, scenes from plays and other theatrical illustrations contained in about 200 English and American periodicals, and to texts of plays whether published in book or magazine form. Magazine articles are entered under subject only, texts of plays under title or under the form heading "Dramas" with cross reference from author, costume portraits under both the actor and the character. All references are exact, i.e., to title of periodical, volume, date, and inclusive paging, and indication of illustrations, portraits, etc. While the index nominally begins with 1909 there is some retrospective indexing. From 1912 the dramatic books of the year are indexed both in the main index and in the appendix, Dramatic books and plays, which consists of (1) author list of books about the theater, (2) author list of play texts, (3) title list of texts. A useful index, necessary in any library which makes much use of dramatic material. Kept up to date by indexes in the *Bulletin of bibliography.*

Firkins, Ina Ten Eyck. Index of plays, 1800–1926. N.Y., Wilson, 1927. 307p. Service basis. **R136**

A comprehensive index of 7872 plays by 2203 authors, showing where the text of each can be found in collections or other publications. Indexes only plays in English but includes translations of foreign plays. In two parts: (1) author index, giving full bibliographical information about each play, and, in many cases, number of acts and brief characterizations, as, comedy, tragedy, social, domestic, etc.; (2) title and subject index, referring to the author list. Material indexed includes more than 100 collections, some 600 volumes of individual authors, periodicals, separately published plays.

—— —— Supplement, 1927–34. N.Y., Wilson, 1935. 140p.

Indexes 3284 plays by 1335 authors.

Hyatt, Aeola L. Index to children's plays. 3d ed., rev. and enl. Based on: Plays for children . . . by A. I. Hazeltine. Chic., Amer. Lib. Assoc., 1931. 214p. $2.50. o.p. **R137**

Index to plays, p.10-173, a title list with notes and references to works containing plays; Plays grouped by special days and subjects, p.174-88; Plays grouped by numbers of characters, p.189-206.

Logasa, Hannah and **Ver Nooy, Winifred.** Index to one-act plays. Bost., Faxon, 1924–50. 4v. (Useful reference ser., 30, 46, 68, 78) $6 ea. **R138**

Basic volume: Plays written in English or translated into English, published since 1900. 327p.; Supplement, 1924–31. 432p.; 2d Supplement, 1932–40. 556p.; 3d Supplement, 1941–48. 318p.

Title, author and subject indexes to one-act plays in collections, and also to separately published pamphlets. The third supplement includes radio plays.

Ottemiller, John H. Index to plays in collections; an author and title index to plays appearing in collections published between 1900 and 1942. N.Y., Wilson, 1943. 130p. $2.50. **R139**

Contents: (1) List of collections analyzed and key to symbols; (2) Author index, giving name and dates, title of play, date of first production, references from original titles and variant translated titles, references from joint authors, translators, etc.; (3) Title index, referring from all forms of titles, translated titles and subtitles.

Indexes 3844 plays by 890 authors in 329 collections appearing between 1900 and 1942 in England and the United States. Includes plays from ancient to modern times. All editions of the same collection have been included when the contents of successive editions vary. Does not include collections of children's plays, amateur plays, one-act plays, holiday and anniversary plays and pageants, but such plays are indexed if they appear in one of the collections that is included. Partial and selected texts are omitted.

Silk, Agnes K. and **Fanning, Clara E.** Index to dramatic readings. Bost., Faxon, 1925. 303p. (Useful reference ser., no.31) $5.   **R140**

Author, title, subject index in one alphabet to 25 collections published 1915–24. Also includes entries for types of selections, dialects, monologs, etc., and to occasions, Christmas, Thanksgiving Day, etc.

Includes an index to first lines and refrains.

Thomson, Ruth Gibbons. Index to full length plays, 1926–1944. Bost., Faxon, 1946. 305p. (Useful reference ser., no.71) $4.   **R141**

Title index gives author, translator, number of acts, number of characters, subject and scene. The author and subject indexes refer to the title index. These are followed by a bibliography giving publisher, date, etc. The subject approach would seem to be one of the most useful features of this work.

Handbooks

Clark, Barrett Harper. Study of the modern drama; a handbook for the study and appreciation of the best plays, European, English and American, of the last half century. New ed. N.Y., Appleton, 1928. 535p. $3.50.   **R142**

Melitz, Leo. Die Theaterstücke der Weltliteratur; ihrem Inhalte nach wiedergegeben. Berlin, Globus, 1904. 2v. in 1. o.p.   **R143**

3d ed.

Gives synopses, often very short, of more than 1000 plays.

Fiction

Bibliography

Aldred, Thomas. Sequels; incorporating Aldred and Parker's Sequel stories. Ed. by Frank M. Gardner. 3d ed. Lond., Assoc. of Asst. Librarians, 1947. 133p. 15s.; to members 12s.   **R144**

1st ed. 1922; 2d ed. 1928, ed. by W. H. Parker.

Incorporates and extends the original work and includes some nonfiction; particularly autobiographies.

Baker, Ernest Albert and **Packman, James.** Guide to the best fiction, English and American, including translations from foreign languages. New and enl. ed. Lond., Routledge; N.Y., Macmillan, 1932. 634p. 42s.; $10.50.   **R145**

1st ed., 1903; 2d ed., 1913. The third edition is much enlarged from the second by the addition of material since 1911, and differs from the second edition in arrangement, i.e., has one alphabetical list instead of national lists with chronological subdivisions.

A comprehensive and very useful work, with good annotations and a detailed and useful general index of authors, titles, subjects, historical names, allusions, places, characters, etc. Indispensable in any library that can afford it.

—— Guide to historical fiction. Lond., Routledge; N.Y., Macmillan, 1914. 566p. 25s.; $9.   **R146**

Lists about 5000 novels which in any way portray the life of the past, including medieval romances and novels of manners, as well as avowedly historical novels. Arrangement is first by country and then chronologically by the historical period, and descriptive notes indicate briefly the plot and scene of each story, its historical characters, etc. Full index (148p.) of authors, titles, historical names, places, events, allusions, etc.

Bethléem, Louis, *abbé.* Romans à lire et romans à proscrire. Essai de classification au point de vue moral des principaux romans et romanciers 1500–1932. 11. ed. Paris, Revue des Lectures, 1932. 620p.   **R147**

1st ed., 1905. A selection of the principal works of over 1600 authors, mostly French but including well-known names of other nationalities, with brief comment on subject and tone of each novel, and indication as to whether it is allowed or proscribed, and why. Contains six alphabetical lists: (1) books forbidden because on the *Index;* (2) books forbidden on moral grounds; (3) books for mature readers; (4) safe novels; (5) stories for younger readers; (6) juveniles. From the French Catholic point of view, but not limited to Catholic authors. Not of frequent use in the average American library, but occasionally useful for the point of view.

Fiction catalog, 1941 edition; a subject, author and title list of 5050 works of fiction in the English language with annotations, comp. by Dorothy E. Cook, Isabel S. Monro, assisted by Elizabeth S. Duvall. N.Y., Wilson, 1942. 789p. (Standard catalog ser.) Service basis.   **R148**

Annotated dictionary catalog of "the best works of fiction for library use which have been published in English through June 1941." Includes novels, mystery and detective stories, Western stories, collections of short stories, books for young people and translations from various languages. Titles are starred for first purchase and books for young people are indicated.

—— 1942–1946 Supplement. 1947. 205p.

A cumulation of annual supplements listing 1451 works of fiction.

Continued by annual supplements.

Gove, Philip Babcock. The imaginary voyage in prose fiction; a history of its criticism and a guide for its study, with an annotated check list of 215 imaginary voyages from 1700 to 1800. N.Y., Columbia Univ. Pr., 1941. 445p. (Columbia Univ. studies in English and comparative literature, no.152) $3.50. **R149**

Thesis (Ph.D.), Columbia University, 1940. Bibliography: p.[403]-20.

Part 2, p.180-402, is a detailed bibliography with full annotations of imaginary voyages in various languages, English, French, German, Dutch, Swedish, Danish, Latin, Japanese, etc. Locates copies.

Lenrow, Elbert. Reader's guide to prose fiction; an introductory essay, with bibliographies of 1500 novels selected, topically classified, and annotated for use in meeting the needs of individuals in general education . . . for the Commission on Secondary School Curriculum. N.Y., Lond., Appleton-Century, 1940. 371p. $3.50. **R150**

Divided into three main sections: pt.1, The individual's need for entertainment and escape; pt.2, The individual and his personal environment; pt.3, The individual and his social environment. Each of these is divided into topical classifications. Full annotations, and an author, title, and subject index.

Logasa, Hannah. Historical fiction and other reading references for classes in junior and senior high schools. 4th rev. and enl. ed. Phila., McKinley Pub. Co., 1949. 232p. $3.50. **R151**

A classified list with author and title index. This edition much revised, adds 900 new titles and omits 300. Adds sections on "Islands of the sea" and "World War II."

Nield, Jonathan. Guide to the best historical novels and tales. [5th ed.] Lond., Mathews; N.Y., Macmillan [1929]. 424p. **R152**

Chronological lists for pre-Christian era and first to twentieth centuries; Supplementary list of semi-historical novels; Bibliography of books and articles about historical fiction. Index of: (1) authors; (2) titles; (3) subjects.

A comprehensive list of 2392 titles mainly English but including some foreign material in English translation or original. Differs from the 1911 edition in the elimination of some 1400 titles and the addition of 1160 not previously included.

Indexes

Eastman, Mary Huse. Index to fairy tales, myths and legends. 2d ed., rev. and enl. Bost., Faxon, 1926. 610p. (Useful reference ser., 28) $6. **R153**

————— Supplement, 1937. 566p. $6.

A title index, with entry under best known title and cross references from variant titles, to the fairy tales and legends included in a large number of collections. Principally useful in public libraries and as a help to the children's librarian, but of some value also to the special student of folklore.

A second supplement is being published in preliminary form in the quarterly issues of *Bulletin of bibliography*, Jan./Apr. 1946- .

Firkins, Ina Ten Eyck. Index to short stories. 2d enl. ed. N.Y., Wilson, 1923. 537p. Service basis. **R154**

————— Supplement, 1929. 337p.; 2d supplement, 1936. 287p.

An alphabetical index of authors and titles with full information under author and cross references from titles. Indexes the short stories found in collected works, separate volumes, periodicals or composite collections. All material indexed is in English, but includes stories by many foreign writers (over 30 nationalities) whose works are accessible in English translations. The cross references from title to author serve to answer questions of authorship also.

A useful index, indispensable in college, public or school library.

Hannigan, Francis J. Standard index of short stories, 1900-1914. Bost., Small, 1918. 334p. $10. **R155**

An author and title index to stories published in 24 American magazines, 1900-14. Contains some 35,000 entries for stories by about 3000 authors, but duplicates much material available elsewhere, as more than half of the magazines covered are indexed in the *Readers' guide*. Its use is for the titles not covered by the *Readers' guide*, and for the convenience of a single list instead of three alphabets.

Poetry

Indexes

Brewton, John Edmund and **Brewton, Sara Westbrook.** Index to children's poetry; a title, subject, author, and first line index to poetry in collections for children and youth. N.Y., Wilson, 1942. 965p. Service basis. **R156**

"A dictionary index to 130 collections of poems for children and youth, with title, subject, author and first line entries. More than 15,000 poems by approximately 2500 different authors are classified under more than 1800 different subjects."—*Introd.*

A smaller work *Children's poetry index* by Maud R. Macpherson (Bost., Faxon, 1938. 453p.) indexes 50 collections, 18 of which are not included in Brewton, and therefore may occasionally be useful.

Bruncken, Herbert. Subject index to poetry; a guide for adult readers. Chic., Amer. Lib. Assoc., 1940. 201p. $3.25. **R157**

Indexes 215 anthologies of prose and poetry under specific subjects. "Attempts to supply material for (1) the location of poetry on specific subjects, (2) the location of a poem, the topical matter or dominant idea of which is known, but not author, title or first line, (3) the location of a poem whose author, title or first line is not known, but a line or fragment of a line of which is known."—Cf. *Pref.*

Cushing, Helen Grant. Children's song index. N.Y., Wilson, 1936. 798p. **R158**

Includes poems set to music. For full description *see* Q295.

Granger, Edith. Granger's Index to poetry and recitations; a practical reference book for librarians, teachers, booksellers, elocutionists, radio artists, etc. 3d ed., completely rev. and enl., covering 592 books and approximately 75,000 titles. Ed. by Helen Humphrey Bessey. Chic., McClurg, 1940. 1525p. **R159**

1st ed. pub. 1904; 2d ed. pub. 1918, with *Supplement,* 1919–1928, pub. 1934.

A very useful index, important in public, college and school libraries. Indexes standard and popular collections of poetry, recitations (both prose and verse), orations, drills, dialogues, selections from drama, etc., by (1) titles; (2) authors; (3) first lines.

This edition indexes anthologies which were indexed in the second edition and its supplement, that are still in print, and collections published 1928–37. However, earlier editions may sometimes need to be consulted for material in books dropped from this edition, and should therefore be preserved by those libraries which have them.

Appendixes contain: Suggested lists for special days; Choral readings, dialogues, and plays, readings and recitations; Miscellaneous selections on flowers, seasons, months, etc.

———— Supplement, 1938–1944. N.Y., Columbia Univ. Pr., 1945. 415p. $12.50.

The continuation of Granger has been taken over by the Columbia University Press, which plans to issue periodical supplements.

This one indexes 118 anthologies published 1938–44 including a few revised editions of anthologies indexed in the main work. Includes appendixes listing poems about famous men, seasons, special days, and "Poems by and about men in the armed services," which indexes five collections of war poems.

Ireland, Norma Olin. Index to monologs and dialogs. Rev. and enl. ed. Bost., Faxon, 1949. 171p. (Useful reference ser., no.77) $4.50. **R160**

1st ed. 1939.

An author, subject and title index to 140 collections, 51 more than in the first edition.

Sears, Minnie Earl. Song index. An index to more than 12,000 songs in 177 song collections. N.Y., Wilson, 1926–34. 2v. **R161**

Includes poems which have been set to music. Indexes many titles not included in Granger (R159), especially foreign poems in either original or translation.

For full description *see* Q297.

Romances and epics
Bibliography

British Museum. Dept. of Manuscripts. Catalogue of romances in the Department of Manu-

scripts in the British Museum. Lond., Trustees, 1883–1910. v.1–3. **R162**

v.1–2, by H. L. D. Ward; v.3, by J. A. Herbert.

The most important reference book in English on the subject. For each romance it gives, in addition to the description of the manuscript in the British Museum, some account of the tale, its outlines, different versions, other manuscripts, authorship, history, etc., and important bibliographical references both to printed texts and to critical comment.

Parry, John J. and **Schlauch, Margaret.** A bibliography of critical Arthurian literature . . . 1922–35. N.Y., Modern Language Assoc., 1931–36. 2v. **R163**

v.1, 1922–29; v.2, 1930–35.

Supplemented by lists appearing in the *Modern language quarterly,* the first covering 1936–39, annual thereafter.

See also Critical bibliography of French literature, v.1, The Mediaeval period, ch.6-11 (R570).

Handbooks

Guerber, Hélène Adeline. Book of the epic; the world's great epics told in story. Phila., Lippincott, 1913. 493p. $4.75. **R164**

Gives synopses of the stories of the great Dutch, English, Finnish, French, German, Greek, Italian, Latin, Portuguese, Scandinavian, and Spanish epics.

Spence, Lewis. Dictionary of mediaeval romance and romance writers. Lond., Routledge; N.Y., Dutton, 1913. 395p. o.p. **R165**

A list, in one alphabet, of the titles and characters of the principal British, Celtic, French, Italian, Scandinavian, Spanish and Teutonic romances from the eleventh to the fourteenth century, giving under title a fairly detailed synopsis of the story of the romance with some bibliographical references but no full list of editions, and under character a brief description of the character and the title of the romance in which it appears.

Essays

A. L. A. index . . . to general literature. 2d ed. enl. . . . Bost., Chic., A.L.A. Pub. Bd., 1901–14. 679p. and suppl. 223p. o.p. **R166**

Basic volume, covering material to Jan. 1, 1900. 679p. 1901; *Supplement,* 1900–10. 223p. 1914.

A subject index which attempts to do for books of essays and general literature what *Poole's Index* (E69) does for periodicals. Indexes books belonging to the following classes: (1) Essays and similar collections of critical, biographical and other monographs; (2) Books of travel and general history whose chapters or parts are worthy of separate reference; (3) Reports and publications of boards and associations dealing with sociological matters, and of historical and literary societies; (4) Miscellaneous books and some public documents.

Includes only books in English. Indexing is by catchword subject, not by modern catalog subject.

Continued by the *Essay index* (R167) which indexes collections published since 1900. Some of the books indexed in the *Supplement,* 1900–1910 have been taken over by the *Essay index,* but others, particularly those on travel, have not been re-indexed and therefore the *Supplement* has not been entirely superseded. For a more detailed discussion of the relationship of the two indexes *see* the preface to the *Essay index,* p.v-vi.

Essay and general literature index, 1900–1933; an index to about 40,000 essays and articles in 2,144 volumes of collections of essays and miscellaneous works, ed. by Minnie Earl Sears and Marian Shaw. N.Y., Wilson, 1934. 1952p. Service basis. **R167**

Frequently cited as the *Essay index.*
Index, p.1-1890; List of books indexed, p.1894-1952.
The basic volume is a detailed index, by authors, subjects and some titles, to essays and articles published 1900–33 and also to earlier essays if included in collections published since 1900. Indexing is given with exact reference, in the case of many essays first printed in periodicals the reference to the periodical is given also, and variant titles for the same essay are indicated.
A monumental work, useful in several departments of library service. In *cataloging* it provides a usable substitute for a large amount of analysis, the cost of which would be prohibitive in the average card catalog; as a *reference* aid it serves many purposes, showing, for example: (1) list of essays by a given author, (2) authorship of an essay when only title is known, (3) analytical material on a given subject, particularly small, unusual, or intangible subjects on which there may be no whole books, (4) biographical and critical matter about a person, (5) criticisms of individual books, (6) different places or collections in which an essay is printed (an important point in school or college libraries when it is necessary to supply many copies of some recommended reading). For purposes of *selection of books* the list of books indexed serves as a good guide to the worth-while essay and other composite-book material of the twentieth century; this *List of books indexed* is also issued separately in pamphlet form.
For a discussion of the relation of this work to similar analysis of books given in the *Standard catalog* (A551) and *Readers' guide* (E71) *see* its preface, p.v-vi.

—— 1934–1940; an index to 23,090 essays and articles in 1241 volumes of collections of essays and miscellaneous works, ed. by Marian Shaw. N.Y., Wilson, 1941. 1362p. Service basis.

—— 1941–1947; an index to 32,226 essays and articles in 2,023 volumes of collections of essays and miscellaneous works, ed. by Dorothy Herbert West and Estelle A. Fidell. N.Y., Wilson, 1948. 1908p.
Kept up to date by semiannual supplements, with annual, 3-year and 7-year cumulations.

Peabody Institute, Baltimore. Catalogue of the library. Balt., 1883–1905. **R168**

Contains so much author and subject analysis of parts of books and periodicals that it serves as an index as well as a catalog. For full description *see* A41.

Standard catalog for public libraries, 1940 ed. N.Y., Wilson, 1940- . **R169**

Primarily a catalog rather than an index, but serves as the latter also, as its index includes entries for analyzed material in hundreds of books of a composite character. For full description *see* A551.

Orations

Baird, A. Craig. Representative American speeches. 1937/38- . N.Y., Wilson, 1938- . Annual. $1.25-$1.50 per v. **R170**

Representative speeches of the year. Issued each year as one number of *The Reference shelf* (R180).

Brewer, David Josiah. World's best orations. St. Louis, Kaiser, 1899–1901. 10v. il. **R171**

Arranged alphabetically by authors. Gives for each a brief biographical sketch and selected orations. Indexes: (1) orators; (2) subjects; (3) chronological index of orators; (4) chronological index of periods and events; (5) chronological indexes of law, government and politics, of religion and philosophy, of literature; (6) general index of orators, subjects, events, etc.

Modern eloquence, ed. by Ashley H. Thorndike, rev. by Adam Ward. N.Y., Collier, 1941. 15v. il. $49. **R172**

A standard collection, frequently reprinted with some additional modern speeches.
v.1-3, After-dinner speeches; v.4-6, Business, industry, professions; v.7-9, Public affairs; v.10-12, Historical masterpieces (v.10, European; v.11, American; v.12, World war); v.13, Famous lectures; v.14, Anecdotes and epigrams; v.15, Public speaking (articles on the art of speaking, with selected debates); General index of authors, titles, subjects, occasions, etc.

Prochnow, Herbert V. The toastmaster's handbook. N.Y., Prentice-Hall, 1949. 374p. **R173**

Vital speeches of the day. v.1, Oct. 8, 1934- . N.Y., City News Pub. Co., 1934- . Monthly. $5 per yr. **R174**

Prints in full the important addresses of contemporary leaders of public opinion in the fields of economics, politics, education, sociology, business, labor, etc.

Indexes

Sutton, Roberta Briggs. Speech index; an index to 64 collections of world famous orations and speeches for various occasions. N.Y., Wilson, 1935. 272p. $1.50. **R175**

A dictionary catalog with entries for each oration under author, subject and type of speech.

Debating
Handbooks

Auer, John and **Ewbank, Henry L.** Handbook for discussion leaders. N.Y., Lond., Harper, 1947. 118p. $1.75. **R176**

Methods of organizing, conducting, and evaluating group discussions, panels, symposiums, lectures, debates, forums.

Garland, Jasper V. and **Phillips, Charles F.** Discussion methods explained and illustrated. N.Y., Wilson, 1938. 330p. (The Reference shelf. v.12, no.2) **R177**

Covers informal group discussion, committee discussion, panel discussion, colloquy, open forum, symposium, debate, and radio discussion.

Musgrave, George M. Competitive debate, rules and techniques. Rev. ed. N.Y., Wilson, 1946. 151p. $1.25. **R178**

1st ed., 1945, had title: *Competitive debate: Rules and strategy.*

Indexes

Debate index, comp. by Edith M. Phelps. New ed. rev. N.Y., Wilson, 1939. 130p. (The Reference shelf. v.12, no.9) **R179**

—— Supplement, comp. by Julia E. Johnsen. N.Y., Wilson, 1941. 90p. (The Reference shelf. v.14, no.9)

A subject index to debates, briefs, bibliographies, and collections of articles on public questions. Materials analyzed include the *Reference shelf* (R180) and *University debaters' annual* (R181).

Collections

Reference shelf. N.Y., Wilson, 1922- . v.1- . $7 per v. **R180**

Issued irregularly, 5-6 numbers to a volume.

Each number is devoted to a timely controversial question with reprints of selected articles from books and periodicals giving background information and pro and con arguments, followed by a comprehensive bibliography.

University debaters' annual; reports of debates and other forensic activities of American colleges and universities during the academic year 1914/15- . N.Y., Wilson, 1915- . v.1- . Annual. $2.50 ea. **R181**

v.3-32 ed. by E. M. Phelps; v.33 by E. M. Phelps and Ruth Ulman; v.34- by Ruth Ulman.

Includes bibliographies, and gives briefs for most debates.

School reading

Rue, Eloise. Subject index to books for intermediate grades. 2d ed. Chic., Amer. Lib. Assoc., 1950. 576p. $6. **R182**

1800 text and trade books commonly used throughout the country are analyzed under approximately 6500 subject headings. Each entry is graded and gives complete

source information. Makes it easy to locate quickly specific materials at specific grade levels. Practical also for setting up units of study.

—— Subject index to books for primary grades. Chic., Amer. Lib. Assoc., 1943. 236p. $2.50. **R183**

A revision and expansion of the compiler's *Subject index to readers,* published 1938.

This edition has added many new readers, bringing the number to 430, including 130 unit readers and has dropped many titles included in the earlier edition in favor of new editions and new titles. The scope has been expanded to include 250 books of the nonreader type, such as picture books, song books, easy books, etc. Intentionally avoids duplication of material in other indexes such as Brewton's *Index to children's poetry* (R156) and Rue's *Subject index to books for intermediate grades* (R182). Titles are starred for first and second purchase. Libraries are warned not to discard the first edition because it may be useful for indexing older titles still in use.

—— —— 1st supplement. 1946. 76p. $1.25.

The supplement adds over 225 titles published from late 1942 through early 1946.

ENGLISH LANGUAGE
American
Bibliography

❧ In addition to the bibliographies listed below, those listed under United States, p.19-23, should be used. Northup's *Register of bibliographies* (R256), Van Patten's *Index to bibliographies* (R257) and the *Bibliographic index* (A13) refer to many individual bibliographies, either issued separately or included in periodicals or other composite works.

Harwell, Richard Barksdale. Confederate belles-lettres; a bibliography and a finding list of the fiction, poetry, drama, songsters, and miscellaneous literature published in the Confederate States of America. Hattiesburg, Miss., Book Farm, 1941. 79p. (Heartman's Historical ser., no.56) $2.40. **R184**

Locates copies in 29 libraries. pt.1, List of works known to have been published with Confederate imprints and now in existence in a selected list of libraries, 105 entries; pt.2, List of works announced for publication or noticed as published in contemporary publications but which cannot now be located, 23 entries.

Literary history of the United States. v.3, Bibliography. N.Y., Macmillan, 1948. 817p. **R185**

For full description *see* R198.

Millett, Fred Benjamin. Contemporary American authors; a critical survey and 219 bio-bibliographies. N.Y., Harcourt, 1940. 716p. $3.75. **R186**

Based on *Contemporary American literature* by J. M Manly and Edith Rickert (1st ed., 1922, 2d ed., 1929) This edition has been completely revised and brought up to date. p.1-204 contain a critical survey of contemporary American literature since 1900; p.207-666 contain the bio-bibliographical sketches which give brief biographies followed by bibliographies of works by the author and a list of studies and articles about the author, to be found in books and periodicals. "107 authors have been dropped from the second edition; six authors who were dropped in the second edition have been restored; 30 authors who appeared for the first time in the second edition have been retained and 101 new authors have been added."—*Foreword.*

The older editions may still be useful for material omitted from this.

New York University. Washington Square Library. Index to early American periodical literature, 1728-1870. . . . N.Y., Pamphlet Distributing Co., 1941-43. pt.1-5. (In progress) **R187**

"A series of selected portions of the Index to early American periodical literature, a collection of materials in the New York University libraries."

Contents: pt.1, The list of periodicals indexed. 11p. 35c; pt.2, Edgar Allan Poe. 19p. $1; pt.3, Walt Whitman, 1819-1892. 18p. $1; pt.4, Ralph Waldo Emerson, 1803-1882. 39p. $1.50; pt.5, French fiction, comp. by Albert L. Rabinowitz. 45p. $1.50.

Rusk, Ralph Leslie. The literature of the middle western frontier. N.Y., Columbia Univ. Pr., 1925. 2v. $7.50. **R188**

v.1, History and survey; v.2, Bibliographies. Volume 2 classified according to the treatment in volume 1, covering cultural beginnings, travel, newspapers and magazines, controversial writings, scholarly writings and schoolbooks, fiction, poetry and drama. Locates copies.

Thompson, Ralph. American literary annuals and gift books, 1825-1865. N.Y., Wilson, 1936. 183p. $2.25. **R189**

Contents: History and discussion of representative American annuals, p.1-101; Catalog of gift books, p.102-163, describing, with fuller information than that given in Faxon, some 230 titles with detailed information as to the different editions of each, location of copies, indication as to whether the annual is for juvenile or adult readers, and many notes as to reprints under changed titles; index includes these variant titles.

Largely supersedes the earlier list by F. W. Faxon, *Literary annuals and gift books* (Bost. Bk. Co., 1912).

CURRENT

Leary, Lewis Gaston. Articles on American literature, appearing in current periodicals, 1920-1945; ed. from materials supplied by the Committee on Bibliography of the American Literature Group of the Modern Language Association of America, and the University of Pennsylvania Library. Durham, N.C., Duke Univ. Pr., 1947. 437p. $3.75. (Duke University pub.) **R190**

A very useful, though not exhaustive, annotated subject list. Compiled primarily from the bibliographies published quarterly since 1929 in *American literature* and annually since 1922 in *PMLA*. The range of periodicals

indexed is broad (mainly American with some English and scattered foreign titles), but the coverage is uneven.

Three fourths of the work is devoted to articles on individual writers, divided chronologically into four periods: 1607-1800; 1800-1870; 1870-1900; 1900-1945. The remainder touches on forms of literature and special subjects. There is no author index for articles cited, though there is an index of authors about whom articles are written.

Supplemented by the current lists appearing in *American literature* and *PMLA.*

American bibliography for 1921- . (In PMLA, v.39-) Annual. **R191**

For full description *see* R11.

See also Modern Humanities Research Association, *Annual bibliography of English language and literature* (R262).

Dictionaries and handbooks

Burke, William Jeremiah and **Howe, Will D.** American authors and books, 1640-1940. N.Y., Gramercy Pub. Co., 1943. 858p. $5. **R192**

"The purpose of this handbook is to present the most useful facts about the writing, illustrating, editing, publishing, reviewing, collecting, selling and preservation of American books from 1640 to 1940."—*Pref.* It includes in alphabetical order concise articles, with cross references to related subjects, on authors, books, periodicals, newspapers, characters, publishing firms, historical and literary societies, libraries, regions and localities, etc. Limited to the continental United States. Its biographical sketches, which include those of many minor writers, are brief and usually give complete dates of birth and death, principal occupations and titles of works; includes many titles of novels, plays, short stories, poems, essays, orations, songs, hymns, etc., with author and publication date and sometimes brief synopses; and information on some 700 magazines and 400 newspapers. Its coverage is larger but its articles much shorter than those in the *Oxford companion to American literature* (R194).

Duyckinck, Evert Augustus and **Duyckinck, G. L.** Cyclopaedia of American literature. Ed. to date by M. L. Simons. Phila., Baxter, 1875. 2v. il. **R193**

Standard collection containing biographies, criticism and selections arranged chronologically, 1626-1875. Still useful, especially for minor earlier writers.

Hart, James David. The Oxford companion to American literature. 2d ed. rev. and enl. Lond. and N.Y., Ox. Univ. Pr., 1948. 890p. $5. **R194**

"In alphabetical arrangement the work includes . . . short biographies, and bibliographies of American authors, with information regarding their style and subject matter; nearly 900 summaries and descriptions of the important American novels, stories, essays, poems and plays; definitions and historical outlines of literary schools and movements; and information on literary societies, magazines, anthologies, co-operative publications, literary awards, book collectors, printers, etc."—*Pref.* Includes some Canadian material. There are not so many entries, but the articles are longer than in Burke and Howe, *American authors and books* (R192); biographical sketches are longer and give more facts, but whereas Burke and Howe gives complete dates of birth and death, this gives years only; synopses are longer and more space is given to the social and cultural background of American literature and to biographies and discussions of men and movements, social, economic, scientific, military, political and religious, in their effects upon literature.

Chronological index giving in parallel columns the literary and social history of America from 1000 to 1947, p.863-90.

The second edition shows revision throughout, some new entries and additions to many old ones.

White's Conspectus of American biography; a tabulated record of American history and biography. 2d ed. N.Y., White, 1937. 455p. **R195**

Includes many lists relating to American literature, e.g., Americans in fiction, poetry and the drama, pseudonyms and sobriquets, recipients of awards, etc.

For full description *see* S35.

Outlines

Whitcomb, Selden L. Chronological outlines of American literature. N.Y., Macmillan, 1894. 286p. **R196**

Gives, in parallel columns, date, works, corresponding biographical dates, events in British literature, foreign history and political history.

History

Cambridge history of American literature, ed. by William Peterfield Trent, John Erskine, Stuart P. Sherman, Carl Van Doren. N.Y., Putnam, 1917–21. 4v. **R197**

v.1, Colonial and Revolutionary literature: Early national literature, pt.1; v.2, Early national literature, pt.2; Later national literature, pt.1; v.3-4, Later national literature, pt.2-3.

The most important history of American literature, necessary in all types of general libraries. Covers the early period with unusual thoroughness, treats the ordinary literary forms and subjects, standard writers, etc., with great detail, and includes adequate treatment of many subjects not covered in the ordinary literary histories, e.g., the accounts of the early travelers, explorers and observers, colonial newspapers, literary annuals and gift books, later magazines and newspapers, children's literature, oral literature, the English language in America, non-English writings, i.e., German, French, Yiddish, aboriginal. Each chapter is by a specialist and the bibliographies, arranged by chapters at the ends of volumes 1, 2 and 4, are very full and important; in all, the bibliography covers more than 500 pages. Author, title, and subject index in volume 1, volume 2, volume 4 (includes 3-4). The bibliographies are indexed in Northup's *Register* (R256).

Available in two different editions: (1) the complete edition, originally published by Putnam; and (2) an inexpensive reprint, complete as to text but lacking the bibliographies (Macmillan, 3v. in 1, $4.95). This reprint naturally lacks the reference value of the complete edition with the bibliographies, but is useful in the small library not able to afford the full edition, or in the larger library as an extra set for circulation.

Literary history of the United States; Robert E. Spiller, Willard Thorp [and others], eds. N.Y., Macmillan, 1948. 3v. $20. **R198**

The first comprehensive history since the *Cambridge history of American literature* (R197), volumes 1 and 2 present a survey from colonial times to the present day in a series of chapters written by various authorities and integrated into a whole by a board of editors. The chapters are not signed but a list of them with the name of the author of each is given in volume 2, p.1393-96. There are no footnotes.

Volume 3 is Bibliography, and consists of bibliographical essays organized to develop the treatment of the text. It is divided into four main divisions: Guide to resources; Literature and culture; Movements and influences; and Individual authors. While this comprehensive bibliography is very valuable it is difficult to use for many types of reference work because of its paragraph form and its inadequate index. The index lists names of literary authors treated, titles of periodicals, and some subject and form headings, e.g., Anthologies, Negro writers and writing, Regionalism and local color, etc. There seems to be no consistency in the indexing of authors of critical or bibliographical works; sometimes they are included, sometimes not.

The fourth section of the Bibliography furnishes information on 207 individual authors, usually listing separate and collected works, edited texts and reprints, biography and criticism, primary sources (including location of manuscripts) and bibliographies. These give valuable critical and evaluative comments on editions, biographies, etc.

Collections

Library of southern literature; comp. under the direct supervision of southern men of letters. E. A. Alderman, J. C. Harris, editors-in-chief. New Orleans, Martin and Hoyt [c1908–23]. 17v. il. **R199**

v.1-13, Biographical and critical sketches, and selected extracts arranged alphabetically by the authors discussed; v.14, Miscellanea: poems, anecdotes, letters, epitaphs and inscriptions, quotations, bibliography; v.15, Biographical dictionary, ed. by Lucian Lamar Knight, containing 3800 sketches; v.16, Historical side lights, 50 reading courses. Bibliography, references to bibliographies in v.1-13, and supplementary lists, index of authors, titles and subjects; v.17, Supplement.

Useful collection.

Stedman, Edmund Clarence and **Hutchinson E. M.** Library of American literature. N.Y., Webster, 1891 [c87-90]. 11v. il. **R200**

Gives selections which are characteristic examples of the work of the principal American writers 1607-1889, a biographical dictionary of the writers included is given in volume 11, p.467-614, and there is a general index of persons, subjects and some titles, the latter grouped under form headings such as poetry, essays, etc.; quotations are brought out in index under heading, Noted sayings.

Biographies of authors

See also Biographies of Authors, p.387.

In most cases the biographical directories listed on p.434-37 will give the best biographical sketches of American authors. The smaller ones listed below are sometimes helpful.

Hoehn, Matthew. Catholic authors; contemporary biographical sketches, 1930–1947. Newark, N.J., St. Mary's Abbey, 1948. 812p. il.　**R201**

Fairly long sketches of 620 Catholic authors, including both those who have died since 1930 and those still living.

Kunitz, Stanley J. and **Haycraft, Howard.** American authors, 1600–1900; a biographical dictionary of American literature, complete in one volume with 1300 biographies and 400 portraits. N.Y., Wilson, 1938. 846p. il.　**R202**

Popularly written biographies with brief bibliographies.

—— Junior book of authors; an introduction to the lives of writers and illustrators for younger readers from Lewis Carroll and Louisa Alcott to the present day. N.Y., Wilson, 1934. 400p., 30p. il. $4.　**R203**

Includes biographies or autobiographies of 265 writers living and deceased), with cross references to 95 other writers included in Kunitz and Haycraft's *Living authors*, 1931, and *Authors today and yesterday*, 1933. Articles are in simple style, for younger readers, but will be occasionally useful for older readers for names or information not given in other biographical dictionaries.

Drama

BIBLIOGRAPHY

Hill, Frank Pierce. American plays printed 1714–1830; a bibliographical record. Stanford Univ., Calif., Stanford Univ. Pr.; Ox., Univ. Pr., 1934. 152p. $3.50; 16s.　**R204**

Based primarily upon the second edition of Wegelin (R207) and upon the typewritten catalog prepared by T. W. Atkinson, 1918, of published plays in his library.

Roden, Robert F. Later American plays, 1831–1900; being a compilation of the titles of plays by American authors published and performed in America since 1831. N.Y., Dunlap Soc., 1900. 132p. (Pub. of the Dunlap Soc., n.s. 12) o.p.　**R205**

U. S. Copyright Office. Dramatic compositions copyrighted in the United States, 1870 to 1916. Wash., Govt. Prt. Off., 1918. 2v.　**R206**

A list of about 60,000 plays registered for copyright July 21, 1870–Dec. 31, 1916. The main list is arranged alphabetically by title and gives, for each title, number of acts, author's name, number of pages, place published

and date of a published play, or the word "typewritten" to indicate the typed manuscript of an unpublished play, date of copyright, holder of copyright, number of copies deposited, etc.; cross references from alternative, secondary and translated titles are given in the main alphabet. There is a supplementary alphabet of recent titles and a detailed author index containing names of authors, joint authors, editors, translators and copyright proprietors, pseudonyms, etc. A very useful list for questions as to authorship, publication, etc., of plays.

For titles of plays copyrighted later than 1916, the *Catalog of copyright entries* (A159) should be consulted.

Wegelin, Oscar. Early American plays, 1714–1830; a compilation of the titles of plays and dramatic poems written by authors born in or residing in North America previous to 1830. 2d ed., rev. N.Y., Literary Collector Pr., 1905. 94p.　**R207**

HISTORY

Odell, George Clinton Densmore. Annals of the New York stage. N.Y., Columbia Univ. Pr., 1927–49. v.1-15. il. (In progress) $10 per v. **R208**

v.1-15, approx. 1699–1894.

A very full account of the history of the stage in New York City, covering actors, plays, theaters, etc.

Quinn, Arthur Hobson. History of the American drama, from the beginning to the Civil war. 2d ed. N.Y., Crofts, 1943. 530p. $5.　**R209**

"A list of American plays," p.423-97. Bibliography, p.393-421.

—— A history of the American drama from the Civil war to the present day. [rev. ed.] N.Y. and Lond., Crofts, 1937. 2v. in 1. 296p., 432p. il. $5.　**R210**

General bibliography and list of American plays 1860–1936, p.305-402.

ANNUALS

Burns Mantle best plays of 1899/1909- and Year book of the drama in America. Bost., Small, 1920–25; N.Y., Dodd, 1926- . il. Annual. $4 ea. (1899/1909, 1909/19, $6)　**R211**

Title varies: 1899/1909–1946/47, *Best plays . . .*; 1947/48- , *Burns Mantle best plays*.

1899/1909 (pub. 1944) and 1909/19 (pub. 1933) are basic volumes edited by Burns Mantle and G. P. Sherwood, each covering ten years and giving (1) selected plays, (2) chronological lists of plays produced, with date, theater and cast.

Contents of the annual volumes vary somewhat but in general include: (1) Digests with critical comment of selected plays of the year; (2) Title list of plays produced in New York during the year, giving for each title, author, number of performances, theater, cast of characters and brief outline of plot; (3) Statistics of runs; (4) List of actors with place and date of birth of each; (5) Necrology; (6) Index of authors, Index of plays and casts.

—— Index, 1899–1950. N.Y., Dodd, 1950. 147p. $2.75

Includes an index to the plays appearing in the annual volumes, by title, and an index to authors, adapters, composers, and lyricists.

Fiction

BIBLIOGRAPHY

Coan, Otis Welton and **Lillard, Richard G.** America in fiction; an annotated list of novels that interpret aspects of life in the United States. 3d ed. Stanford, Calif., Stanford Univ. Pr., 1949. 196p. $2.25.   **R212**

1st ed. 1941; 2d ed. 1945.

In the second and third editions material has been revised, some titles dropped, and new titles added. There are very brief annotations, and recommended titles are starred.

Johnson, James Gibson. Southern fiction prior to 1860; an attempt at a first-hand bibliography. Charlottesville, Va., Michie Co., 1909. 126p.
R213

New York. Public Library. Beadle collection of dime novels given to the . . . library by Dr. Frank P. O'Brien. N.Y., Library, 1922. 99p. il. 50c.
R214

A list of some 1400 novels, arranged alphabetically by series, with indexes of: (1) authors; (2) titles.

Queen, Ellery, *pseud.* The Detective short story, a bibliography. Bost., Little, 1942. 146p. $4.
R215

Wegelin, Oscar. Early American fiction 1774–1830, a compilation of the titles of works of fiction by writers born or residing in North America, north of the Mexican border, and printed previous to 1831. 3d ed. cor. and enl. N.Y., P. Smith, 1929. 37p. $5.   **R216**

Wright, Lyle Henry. American fiction, 1774–1850; a contribution toward a bibliography. rev. ed. San Marino, Calif., 1948. 355p. (Huntington Lib. pub.) $6.   **R217**

1st ed. 1939. This edition has been thoroughly revised and enlarged by some 600 titles to a total of 2772 entries and a useful chronological index has been added. Lists novels, romances, short stories, fictitious biographies, travels, allegories and tract-like tales, written by Americans. Locates copies in 19 libraries and 2 private collections.

HISTORY

Quinn, Arthur Hobson. American fiction; an historical and critical survey. N.Y., Appleton, 1936. 805p. $5.   **R218**

A chronological treatment of the novel and short story from 1770–1935.

ANNUALS

Best American short stories of 1915- , and the Yearbook of the American short story. Bost., Houghton, 1915- . v.1- . Annual. $2.50 ea.
R219

Publisher varies. Title varies: 1915–41, *Best short stories;* 1942- , *Best American short stories.*

Editors: 1915–41, E. J. O'Brien; 1942- , Martha Foley. Each volume contains: (1) Text of selected short stories of the year and (2) Yearbook. Contents of yearbooks vary somewhat but include, in general, list of magazines which publish short stories, roll of honor of authors selected, with brief biographies, list of best books of short stories of year, list of articles on short stories (including reviews), index, by authors, of short stories published in books, index, by authors, of short stories in magazines. This latter index covers some magazines not indexed in the *Readers' guide.*

Poetry

BIBLIOGRAPHY

Brown University. Library. Anthony Memorial A catalogue of the Harris collection of American poetry, with biographical and bibliographical notes by J. C. Stockbridge. Providence, 1886. 320p.   **R220**

New York. Public Library. Early American poetry, 1610–1820. A list of works in the . . . library, comp. by J. C. Frank. N.Y., Library 1917. 58p.   **R22**

Porter, Dorothy Burnett. North American Negro poets, a bibliographical checklist of their writings 1760–1944. Hattiesburg, Miss., The Brook Farm 1945. 90p. [Heartman's Historical ser. no.70 $2.40.   **R22**

An expansion of *A Bibliographical checklist of American Negro poetry* by Arthur A. Schomburg, 1916.

U. S. Library of Congress. General Reference and Bibliographical Division. Sixty America poets, 1896–1944: Selected with preface an critical notes, by Allen Tate. A preliminary chec list by Frances Cheney. Wash., 1945. 188 (Free to libraries)   **R22**

Brief critical note about each author followed by titl of works with location in at least one American librar works edited; titles of books containing bibliographie location of manuscript collections, recordings, etc.

Wegelin, Oscar. Early American poetry; a com pilation of the titles of volumes of verse an broadsides by writers born or residing in Nort

America, north of the Mexican border. 2d ed. rev. and enl. N.Y., P. Smith, 1930. 2v. in 1. $10.
R224

Covers 1650–1820.

ANTHOLOGIES

See also Anthologies, p.390.

Braithwaite, William Stanley Beaumont. Anthology of magazine verse for 1913-   , and Yearbook of American poetry. N.Y., Gomme, 1913-   . Annual.
R225

Publisher varies.

Each volume consists of two parts: the anthology, and the yearbook. Contents of the yearbook vary somewhat, but in general include an author index to poems published in magazines, an author list of magazine reviews and articles on poetry, an author list of new volumes of poems, and a selected list of books about poets and poetry. The 1926 volume contains a separately paged *Biographical dictionary of poets in the United States.*

Oxford book of American verse, chosen and ed. by Bliss Carmen. Ox., Univ. Pr., 1928. 680p.
R226

Stedman, Edmund Clarence. American anthology, 1787–1900. Camb., Mass., Houghton, 1900. 878p. $5.50; students' ed. $3.50.
R227

Includes biographical notes.

Stevenson, Burton Egbert. Home book of verse, American and English, 1580–1918. N.Y., Holt, 1945]. 4009p.
R228

—— Home book of modern verse. N.Y., Holt, 1937. 1121p.
R229

For description of these two valuable anthologies *see* R340 and R341.

—— Poems of American history. Bost., Houghton, 1922. 720p. $4.50.
R230

1st ed. 1908. This edition adds poems of the first World War.

Untermeyer, Louis. Modern American poetry, a critical anthology. 6th rev. ed. N.Y., Harcourt, 1942. 712p. $3.25.
R231

Diaries and letters

Matthews, William. American diaries, an annotated bibliography of American diaries written prior to the year 1861. Berkeley and Los Angeles, Univ. of California Pr., 1945. 383p. (Univ. of California pub. in English, v.16, 1945) $4.
R232

A chronological list of diaries written prior to 1861 with annotations giving full name, occupation, dates, and name of author and brief notes as to subject content of diary and record of printed source. Manuscript diaries not included.

Weiss, Harry Bischoff. American letter-writers, 1698–1943. N.Y., N.Y. Public Library, 1945. 54p. 60c.
R233

"Reprinted from the *Bulletin* of the New York Public Library of Dec. 1944 and Jan. 1945."

A bibliography of handbooks of model letter writing for the "average" person. Locates copies.

Individual authors

❦ The following list is not complete for authors for whom there are separately published bibliographies. It includes only a selection of those writers for whom there are concordances, dictionaries, or handbooks as well as bibliographies. For additional titles consult the bibliographies listed under Literature and Language—American—Bibliography p.376-77.

CLEMENS

Johnson, Merle. A bibliography of the works of Mark Twain, Samuel Langhorne Clemens. Rev. and enl. N.Y., Harper, 1935. 274p.
R234

Subtitle: A list of first editions in book form and of first printings in periodicals and occasional publications of his varied literary activities.

Harnsberger, Caroline Thomas. Mark Twain at your fingertips. N.Y., Beechhurst Pr., 1948. 559p.
R235

Quotations from Mark Twain arranged alphabetically by subject matter, followed by a brief bibliography, a topical index with cross references, and a correlated subject index.

Ramsay, Robert L. and **Emberson, Frances Guthrie.** A Mark Twain lexicon. Columbia, Mo., Univ. of Missouri Pr., 1938. 278p. (Univ. of Missouri studies, v.13, no.1) $1.25.
R236

Includes a classification of Mark Twain's vocabulary: Americanisms, new words, archaisms, and miscellaneous groups; and a lexicon of words with exact references to his works.

EMERSON

Cooke, George Willis. Bibliography of Ralph Waldo Emerson. Bost., Houghton, 1908. 340p.
R237

Includes works both by and about Emerson.

Hubbell, George Shelton. Concordance to the poems of Ralph Waldo Emerson. N.Y., Wilson, 1932. 478p.
R238

Based on the text of volume 9 of the Centenary edition of Emerson (Houghton), and thus incomplete as it covers only the poems collected in that volume and does not include uncollected poems scattered through other volumes of the edition. Gives all occurrences of words listed except in the case of some 172 common words for which only selected references are given.

HAWTHORNE

Browne, Nina Eliza. Bibliography of Nathaniel Hawthorne. Bost., Houghton, 1905. 215p. **R239**

Includes material both by and about Hawthorne.

O'Connor, Evangeline M. Analytical index to the works of Nathaniel Hawthorne. Bost., Houghton [c1882]. 294p. **R240**

JEFFERSON

Foley, John P. The Jeffersonian cyclopedia; a comprehensive collection of the views of Thomas Jefferson. N.Y., Funk, 1900. 1009p. il. **R241**

Subtitle: Classified and arranged in alphabetical order under 9000 titles; relating to government, politics, law, education, political economy, finance, science, art, literature, religious freedom, morals, etc.

LANIER

Graham, Philip and **Jones, Joseph.** A concordance to the poems of Sidney Lanier, including the Poem outlines and certain uncollected items. Austin, Univ. of Texas Pr., 1939. 447p. $3.50. **R242**

"The texts used are (1) the *Poems of Sidney Lanier* ed. by Mary Day Lanier (N.Y. 1929), (2) *Poem outlines*, ed. by H. W. L[anier]. (N.Y., 1908), (3) texts for the uncollected items as listed on page vi of this work."—*Pref.*

POE

Heartman, Charles Frederick and **Canny, James R.** A bibliography of first printings of the writings of Edgar Allan Poe, together with a record of first and later printings of his contributions to annuals, anthologies, periodicals and newspapers issued during his lifetime, also some spurious Poeana and fakes. Rev. ed. Hattiesburg, Miss., The Book Farm, 1943. 294p. (Heartman's Historical ser. no.53 repr.) $10. **R243**

First published 1940, this is a revised edition of *A census of first editions and source materials by Edgar Allan Poe in American collections . . .* compiled by Charles F. Heartman and Kenneth Rede, published in 1932.—Cf. *Pref.* to 1940 edition.

Robertson, John W. Bibliography of the writings of Edgar A. Poe. San Francisco, Grabhorn, 1934. 2v. il. **R244**

v.1, Bibliography [works by Poe]; v.2, Commentary on the bibliography.

Booth, Bradford Allen and **Jones, Claude Edward.** A concordance of the poetical works of Edgar Allan Poe. Balt., Johns Hopkins Pr., 1941. 211p. $5.50. **R245**

ROOSEVELT

Roosevelt, Theodore. Theodore Roosevelt cyclopedia, ed. by Albert Bushnell Hart and Herbert Ronald Ferleger. N.Y., Roosevelt Memorial Assoc., 1941. 674p. $6. **R246**

A collection of approximately 4000 quotations from Roosevelt's writings, letters and speeches, arranged under subject with exact reference to source.

THOREAU

Allen, Francis H. A bibliography of Henry David Thoreau. Bost., Houghton, 1908. 201p. **R247**

Includes works both by and about Thoreau.
Supplemented by:

White, William. A Henry David Thoreau bibliography, 1908–1937. Bost., Faxon, 1939. 51p (Bulletin of bibliography pamphlets. no.35) **R248**

Stowell, Robert F. A Thoreau gazetteer. Calais Vt., The Poor Farm Pr., 1948. 5p. 8 maps. $1.50 **R249**

WHITMAN

Duke University, Durham, N. C. Library. Catalogue of the Whitman Collection in the Duke University Library being a part of the Trent collection given by Dr. and Mrs. Josiah C. Trent comp. by Ellen Frances Frey. . . . Durham, N.C. Duke Univ. Lib., 1945. 148p. il. **R250**

Includes material both by and about Whitman.

Wells, Carolyn and **Goldsmith, Alfred F.** A concise bibliography of the works of Walt Whitman with a supplement of fifty books about him. Bost., Houghton, 1922. 106p. **R251**

Allen, Gay Wilson. Walt Whitman handbook. Chic., Packard, 1946. 560p. $3. **R252**

Chapters discuss Whitman biography, the growth of *Leaves of grass*, the *Prose works*, Whitman's ideas and techniques, and his relation to world literature. Each chapter followed by a selected bibliography.

Eby, Edwin Harold. Concordance of Walt Whitman's Leaves of Grass and selected prose writings. Seattle, Univ. of Washington Pr., 1949- fasc. 1- . **R253**

fasc. 1, A-heart.
Subtitle: Including Democratic vistas; A backward glance o'er travel'd roads; Preface to the 1855 edition; Preface, 1872; Preface, 1876; and Preface note to 2nd Appendix.
Name on title page, Harold Edwin Eby corrected by errata slip to Edwin Harold Eby.

Australian

Miller, Edmund Morris. Australian literature from its beginnings to 1935; a descriptive and bibliographical survey of books by Australian authors in poetry, drama, fiction, criticism and anthology, with subsidiary entries to 1938 . . . initiated and commenced by the late Sir John Quick. . . . Melbourne, Melbourne Univ. Pr., in association with Ox. Univ. Pr., 1940. 2v. 42s.
R254

Historical treatment of the writers and literature of Australia with extensive bibliographies. Contains considerable biographical material.
Indexes: (1) Fiction: subject index; (2) Subjects and name-subjects, including non-Australian; (3) Australian authors including pseudonyms and anonyms.

Murdoch, Walter. Book of Australasian verse. Rev. ed. Ox., Univ. Pr., 1945. 284p. $3.   **R255**

First published in 1918 under title: *Oxford book of Australasian verse,* 1918.

British

Bibliography

In addition to the bibliographies listed below, those listed under Great Britain, p.34-39, should be used. The bibliographies in the *Dictionary of national biography* (S123) will also be helpful. Northup's *Register* (R256) and the *Bibliographic index* (A13) refer to many individual bibliographies, either issued separately or included in periodicals or other composite works.

Northup, Clark Sutherland. Register of bibliographies of the English language and literature. . . . New Haven, Yale Univ. Pr., 1925. 507p. (Cornell studies in English, 9)   **R256**

A very useful list of bibliographies both of those separately published and of those in periodicals, books, etc.

Van Patten, Nathan. Index to bibliographies and bibliographical contributions relating to the work of American and British authors, 1923–1932. Stanford Univ., Calif., Stanford Univ. Pr.; Lond., Milford, 1934. 324p. $6.   **R257**

Chronologically, this continues the work of Northup's *Register* (R256).

Cambridge bibliography of English literature, ed. by F. W. Bateson. . . . Camb., Univ. Pr., 1940; N.Y., Macmillan, 1941. 4v. $37.50.   **R258**

v.1-3, 600–1900; v.4, Index.
The most extensive and comprehensive bibliography in its field, covering with fullness and considerable detail, though avowedly not with actual completeness, the Old English, Middle English, modern English and Latin literature of the British Isles, with briefer treatment of the English literature of the Dominions and India; does not include American literature or the French literature of Canada, and gives only incidental inclusion of Welsh, Gaelic or Celtic material. Sections on the literatures of the Dominions are comparatively brief.

Arranged chronologically, and under periods by literary forms, e.g., Poetry, Drama, Periodicals, etc., and large class groups, such as History, Philosophy, etc., with further subdivision under forms and groups by special topics and by the individual authors treated. References given under each author vary according to his importance or to the amount of material available but include generally: *bibliographies* of that author, either separately published or included in some periodical or other work; *collected editions* of his works; *separate works,* with date of first edition and of subsequent editions within the next 50 years, with references to later editions having special features or editing; a selection of *biographical and critical* works about the author. Under the form group Drama a useful reference feature is the analytical reference to texts of separate plays as printed in the standard collections of plays, such as Dodsley, Bell, French, Lacy, etc., and a somewhat similar feature is the reference under some poets to anthologies containing examples of their work. Throughout, entries are given compactly and with considerable abbreviation, but there is no one complete list of the abbreviations used; a key to the most frequently used abbreviations is given at the beginning of volume 1, but other abbreviations used, particularly within certain sections, are explained only at the beginning of such sections. The index volume (287p.) includes *subject* entries for literary topics, *titles* of periodicals and anonymous books and *author names* in the case of authors treated as part of the subject matter of the bibliography but not in the case of authors of the biographical or critical references cited.

Indispensable as a first-aid reference bibliography in all college, university and large public libraries and also in medium-sized public libraries doing much work in English literature. For research work it will naturally need to be supplemented from various specialized works. Its value as a guide to the selection of books in the building up of library collections is obvious.

Cross, Tom Peete. Bibliographical guide to English studies. 9th ed., with an index. Chic., Univ. of Chic. Press, 1947. 73p.   **R259**

"Designed primarily . . . as a guide to graduate students in the Department of English of the University of Chicago."
First to sixth editions have title: *A list of books and articles, chiefly bibliographical, designed to serve as an introduction to the bibliography and methods of English literary history.*

Kennedy, Arthur Garfield. A bibliography of writings on the English language from the beginnings of printing to the end of 1922. Camb., Harv. Univ. Pr., 1927. 517p.   **R260**

A very comprehensive list of 13,402 numbered items. Classified with indexes to authors and reviewers and to subjects. A "Review with a list of additions and corrections" by Arvid Gabrielson was published in *Studia neophilologica,* v.2, p.117-68, 1929.

Körting, Gustav. Grundriss der Geschichte der englischen Literatur von ihren Anfängen bis zur

Gegenwart. 5. verm. und verb. Aufl. Münster i. W., Schöningh, 1910. 443p. (Sammlung von Kompendien für das Studium und die Praxis. 1. Ser. 1) **R261**

CURRENT

Modern Humanities Research Association. Annual bibliography of English language and literature, 1920- . Camb., Univ. Pr., 1921- . v.1- . Annual. (v.20, 1939, pub. 1948. 18s.) **R262**

An excellent annual bibliography of English and American literature, including books, pamphlets and periodical articles and referring to reviews of works listed.

The language section is arranged according to subject; the literature section is arranged chronologically. Name index.

Year's work in English studies, 1919/20- , ed. for the English Association. Ox., Univ. Pr., 1921- . v.1- . Annual. (v.28, 1947, pub. 1949, $2.50; 12s. 6d.) **R263**

Survey articles, excluding American literature but for British covering much the same ground as R262, listing fewer titles, but giving running comment on their importance or character.

See also Crane and Bredvold, *English literature, 1660–1800* (R275); Graham, *The Romantic movement* (R276); Templeman, *Bibliographies of studies in Victorian literature* (R277).

OLD AND MIDDLE ENGLISH

Heusinkveld, Arthur H. and **Bashe, Edwin J.** A bibliographical guide to Old English; a selective bibliography of the language, literature, and history of the Anglo-Saxons. Iowa City, Univ. of Iowa, 1931. 153p. (Univ. of Iowa humanistic studies, v.4, no.5) $1. **R264**

Loomis, Roger Sherman. Introduction to medieval literature chiefly in England; a reading list and bibliography. 2d ed. N.Y., Columbia Univ. Pr., 1948. 32p. 60c. **R265**

Wells, John Edwin. Manual of the writings in Middle English, 1050–1400, pub. under the auspices of the Connecticut Academy of Arts and Sciences. New Haven, Yale Univ. Pr., 1916–41. 941p. and suppl. 1-8. $5.50, suppl., 50c ea.; 7s. **R266**

Main work, covering bibliography to Sept. 1915, 941p.; Supplements 1-8. Additions and rectifications, Sept. 1915–July 1941, paged continuously with main work, p.947-1763. Suppl. 8, includes an index to pieces first treated in Suppl. 1-8.

"This manual makes the first attempt to treat all the extant writings in print, from single lines to the most extensive pieces, composed in English between 1050 and 1400. At times, as with the Romances, the Legends, and the Drama, a desire for greater completeness has led to the inclusion of pieces later than 1400.

"The work is not a history, but a handbook. It seeks to record the generally accepted views of scholars on pertinent matters, and does not pretend to offer new theories or investigations."—*Pref.*

Gives for each piece listed, its probable date, MS or MSS, form and extent, dialect in which first composed, source or sources when known, bibliography, and comment and abstract also, in case of the longer works.

An important handbook, indispensable in any library doing reference work in this field.

TO 1700

Hazlitt, William Carew. Handbook to the popular, poetical, and dramatic literature of Great Britain, from the invention of printing to the Restoration. Lond., J. R. Smith, 1867. 701p. o.p. **R267**

Supplemented by:

—— Bibliographical collections and notes on early English literature. 1474–1700. Lond., Quaritch, 1876–1903. 6v. **R268**

First series has title, *Collections and notes.*

1st ser. 498p. 1876; 2d ser. 717p. 1882; 3d ser. 315p. 1887; suppl. to 3d ser. 181p. 1889; 2d suppl. to 3d ser. 106p. 1892; 4th ser. 446p. 1903.

—— General index to Hazlitt's Handbook and his Bibliographical collections, by G. J. Gray. Lond., Quaritch, 1893. 866p. **R269**

Indexes the *Handbook* (R267) and all volumes of the *Bibliographical collections* (R268) except the fourth series and the second supplement to the third series.

Tannenbaum, Samuel A. and **Tannenbaum, Dorothy R.** Elizabethan bibliographies. [Concise bibliographies] N.Y., Author (601 W. 113 St.) 1937–47. no.1-39. **R270**

no.1, Christopher Marlowe. 1937. 95p. $3. Suppl. 1, 1937. [5]p. Suppl. 2, 1947. 99p.; no.2, Ben Jonson. 1938. 151p. $5; no.3, 4, 5, Beaumont and Fletcher. 1938. 94p., Philip Massinger. 1938. 39p., George Chapman. 1938. 40p. $5.50; Suppl. to no.3. 1946. 23p. $1.60. Suppl. to no.5. 1946. 17p. $1.25; no.6, 7, Thomas Heywood. 1939. 43p., Thomas Dekker. 1939. 46p. $4.25. Suppl. to no.7. 1945. 14p. $1; no.8, Robert Greene. 1939. 58p. $3.50. Suppl. to no.8, 1945. 23p. $1.50; no.9, Shakspere's Macbeth. 1939. 165p. $7; no.10, Shakspere's sonnets. 1940. 88p. $4; no.11, Thomas Lodge. 1940. 30p. $3; no.12, John Lyly. 1940. 38p. $3.35; no.13, Thomas Middleton. 1940. 35p. $3.25; no.14, John Marston. 1940. 34p. $3.25; no.15, George Peele. 1940. 36p. $3.25; no.16, Shakspere's King Lear. 1940. 101p. $5.50; no. 17, Shakspere's The Merchant of Venice. 1941. 140p. $6; no.18, Thomas Kyd. 1941. 34p. $3.25; no.19, John Webster. 1941. 38p. $3.25; no.20-21, John Ford. 1941. 26p., Thomas Nashe. 1941. 31p. $4.25; no.22, Michael Drayton. 1941. 54p. $3.50; no.23, Sir Philip Sidney. 1941. 69p. $6; no.24, Michel Eyquem de Montaigne. 1942. 137p. $9; no.25, Samuel

Daniel. 1942. 37p. $3.75; no.26, George Gascoigne. 1942. 22p. $3; no.27, Anthony Mundy, including the play of "Sir Thomas Moore." 1942. 36p. $3.75; no.28, Shakspere's Othello. 1943. 132p. $8.50; no.29, Shakspere's Troilus and Cressida. 1943. 44p. $4.50; no.30-32, Marie Stuart, Queen of Scots. 1944–46. 3v. v.1, $5.50, v.2, $4.75, v.3, $7.50; no.33, Cyril Tourner. 1946. 14p. $1.25; no.34, James Shirley. 1946. 42p. $3; no.35, George Herbert. 1946. 55p. $3.50; no.36, John Heywood. 1946. 31p. $2.50; no.37, Roger Ascham. 1946. 27p. $2; no.38, Thomas Randolph. 1946. 24p. $2; no.39, Nicholas Breton. 1947. 34p. $2.75.

Tucker, Lena Lucile and **Benham, Allen Rogers.** A bibliography of fifteenth century literature; with special reference to the history of English culture. Seattle, Wash., Univ. of Wash. Pr., 1928. 274p. (Univ. of Wash. pub. in language and literature, v.2, no.3) **R271**

1700-

Rochdieu, Charles Alfred. Bibliography of French translations of English works, 1700–1800. Chic., Univ. of Chic. Pr. [1948]. 387p. $5. **R272**

Lists the works of some 900 authors under the author's name and the English title, with cross reference from the French title. There is a classified index.

Tobin, James Edward. Eighteenth century English literature and its cultural background; a bibliography. N.Y., Fordham Univ. Pr., 1939. 190p. $2. **R273**

Contents: pt.1, Cultural and critical background, p.1-64; pt.2, Bibliographies of individual authors, p.67-180.

The individual bibliographies list works by the author in very brief form, and books and articles about the author. No annotations.

Millett, Fred Benjamin. Contemporary British literature; a critical survey and 232 author bibliographies. 3d rev. and enl. ed., based on the 2d rev. and enl. ed. by J. M. Manly and Edith Rickert. N.Y., Harcourt, 1935. 556p. $2.50; 10s. 6d. **R274**

This edition is brought up to date throughout, and adds new bibliographies of some 40 authors not included in the second edition; as it omits about 30 authors who were included in the second edition, that edition will still have a use for the omitted material.

Current

Crane, Ronald S., Bredvold, Louis I. [and others]. English literature, 1660–1800; a bibliography of modern studies comp. for Philological Quarterly. Princeton, Princeton Univ. Pr., 1950- . v.1- . **R275**

Volume 1 (575p.) includes reprints of the annual bibliographies published in the *Philological quarterly* 1926–38 covering studies published 1925–37; volume 2 is to continue the work to 1950 and will include an index to both volumes.

Continued annually in the *Philological Quarterly*.

Graham, Walter [and others]. The Romantic movement: A current selective and critical bibliography for 1936- . (In ELH, a journal for English literary history. v.4, 1937-) **R276**

Templeman, William Darby. Bibliographies of studies in Victorian literature for the thirteen years 1932–1944. Urbana, Univ. of Illinois Pr., 1945. 450p. $5. **R277**

A photoprint of bibliographies published originally in the May issues of *Modern philology*, 1933–1945, and therefore arranged by year. Includes an index of Victorian authors mentioned in Section IV of each year and in the first three sections of the bibliography for 1932 which was differently arranged.

Continued annually in *Modern philology*.

Dictionaries and handbooks

Adams, William Davenport. Dictionary of English literature . . . N.Y., Cassell, 1884. 776p. o.p. **R278**

Includes in one alphabet author's names, literary subjects, titles of literary works, famous passages, first lines, pseudonyms, fictitious characters, etc. Concise articles with a few bibliograpical notes. Useful for its indications of where poems, plays, etc., not published separately, can be found.

Allibone, Samuel Austin. Critical dictionary of English literature and British and American authors, living and deceased, from the earliest accounts to the latter half of the nineteenth century. Containing over 46,000 articles (authors), with forty indexes of subjects. Phila., Lippincott, 1858–91. 5v. **R279**

v.1-3, A-Z, v.4-5, suppl. by J. F. Kirk, A-Z.

A standard work very useful in spite of the fact that it is not entirely accurate and so must often be checked for important points, by reference to some other authority. Based in part upon Watt's *Bibliotheca Britannica* (A284) and reflects Watt's inaccuracies. Arranged alphabetically by authors, giving for each, brief biographical sketch, list of works with dates, and references to critical comments or reviews.

Chambers's Cyclopaedia of English literature. Ed. by David Patrick and rev. by J. L. Geddie. Lond., Chambers; Phila., Lippincott, 1922–38. 3v. il. 60s.; $22.50. **R280**

1st ed., 1844, 2v.; rev. ed., 1901, 3v.; v.1 rev. 1927, v.2 rev. 1938; v.3, 1922.

A chronological, not an alphabetical, encyclopedia, containing a large number of articles on individual writers and some articles on literary forms, periods, and subjects; for each writer treated gives biography, comment on his writings, some specimens of his works, a bibliography, and in many cases a portrait. Signed articles; general alphabetical index of authors and titles in volume 3.

The 1922 issue contains six additional pages at the end of volume 3, adding 143 new names, and shows some revision throughout, principally in the way of addition of dates of death in the case of authors who have died since the 1901 edition, and the inclusion of recent titles or editions in the bibliographies.

Harvey, Sir Paul. Oxford companion to English literature. 3d ed. Ox., Clarendon Pr., 1946. 931p. 25s.; $10.   **R281**

1st ed. 1932; 2d ed. 1937.

A very useful dictionary of brief articles on authors, literary works, characters in fiction, drama, etc., and literary allusions commonly met with in English literature. This edition has been revised and reset with some new and some rewritten articles.

—— The Concise Oxford dictionary of English literature. Ox., Clarendon Pr., 1939. 567p. 7s. 6d.; $2.50.   **R282**

An abridgement of the *Oxford companion to English literature* (R281), prepared by John Mulgan. It retains the entries which deal with the central matter of English literature, though often in shortened form. Articles have been added which summarize concisely periods of literary history and general literary subjects. Adds a number of entries dealing with contemporary writers, both English and American.—Cf. *Pref.*

Watt, Homer Andrew and **Watt, William Whyte.** A dictionary of English literature. N.Y., Barnes and Noble, 1945. 430p. $3. (College outline ser. pa. $1.25)   **R283**

Divided into five parts: Dictionary of authors (about 900); List of anonymous works; Glossary of literary terms; Note on versification; Chronological chart.

Outlines

[Ghosh, Jyotish Chandra] Annals of English literature, 1475–1925; the principal publications of each year with an alphabetical index of authors and their works. Ox., Clarendon Pr., 1935. 340p. $3; 8s. 6d.   **R284**

A chronological list giving under each year authors and brief titles of outstanding books published that year, with indication of character, e.g., whether prose, verse, drama, etc., and in parallel columns important literary or historical events of the same year. Detailed author index, p.268-340.

Ryland, Frederick. Chronological outlines of English literature. Lond., Macmillan, 1914. 351p. o.p.   **R285**

First published 1890. Frequently reprinted with slight alterations, but without any extension of the tables beyond the original date 1889.

A handbook which does for English literary history what the various "tabular views" do for political history. In two parts: part 1 presents in chronological arrangement the principal periods and events of English literature and shows in parallel columns contemporary events in foreign literatures, political history, and (after 1500) the principal biographical dates; part 2 is an alphabetical list of English authors with titles and dates of their principal works. For somewhat similar tables, *see* appendix to *Century cyclopedia of names* (R40).

Atlases

Briscoe, John D'Auby, Sharp, R. L. and **Borish, M. E.** A mapbook of English literature. N.Y., Holt, 1936. 47p. $1.   **R286**

Goode, Clement Tyson and **Shannon, E. F.** An atlas of English literature. N.Y., Century, 1925. 136p. $3.   **R287**

History

Cambridge history of English literature, ed. by A. W. Ward and A. R. Waller. Camb., Univ. Pr., 1907–27. 15v. $6.50 per v.; $85 per set.   **R288**

The most important general history of the literature, covering from the earliest times to the end of the nineteenth century; each chapter is by a specialist, and there are extended and very useful bibliographies. The bibliographies are indexed in Northup's *Register* (R256).

Available in different editions which show some variations in text and content. The English edition has made corrections in text from time to time and has issued errata sheets which contain further corrections and also additions to the bibliographies; the American edition (originally Putnam, now Macmillan) differs in paging and lacks the corrections in text and the errata lists of the English edition, except that some of these errata, but not the additions to the bibliographies, have been listed in the index volume published in 1933. Inexpensive reprints of both the English and the American editions (Macmillan, set, $45) are reprints of the full text and index but omit the bibliographies, thus losing much of their value for reference purposes. However these reprints are useful in the small library unable to afford either of the complete editions, and in the large library as an extra set for circulation.

Garnett, Richard and **Gosse, Edmund.** English literature, an illustrated record. Lond., Heinemann; N.Y., Macmillan, 1903. 4v. il. (Repr. 4v. in 2. 1935. $8.50)   **R289**

Gives literary history, biographical and critical sketches of authors, account and criticism of various works of literature, some illustrative extracts and quotations and many illustrations, in black and white and colors, largely from contemporary prints, illuminations, portraits, etc. The special reference value of the work is in these illustrations.

A new edition, 1923, differs only in having a supplementary chapter by John Erskine on the literature of 1902–22. This is the edition reprinted in 1935.

Oxford history of English literature, ed. by Frank Percy Wilson and Bonamy Dobree. Ox., Univ. Pr., 1945- . v.1- . (In progress)   **R290**

To be in 12 volumes. Includes extensive bibliographies.

Contents: v.2, pt.1, Bennett, H. S. Chaucer and the 15th century. 1947; v.2, pt.2, Chambers, E. K. English literature at the close of the middle ages. 1947; v.5, Bush, Douglas. English literature in the earlier 17th century, 1600–1660. 1946.

Collections

Moulton, Charles Wells. Library of literary criticism of English and American authors. Buffalo, Moulton Pub. Co., 1901–05. 8v. il. o.p.   **R291**

Reprint issued in 1934 by P. Smith at $8 per volume. A compilation of quoted material, not an encyclopedia of original articles. Covers 680–1904. For each author treated gives brief biographical data and then selected quotations from criticisms of his work grouped as (1) personal, (2) individual works, (3) general. Extracts are of some length and are given with exact reference, so that the work serves both as an encyclopedia of critical comment and an index of literary criticisms.

Biographies of authors

❦ In many cases the best biographical sketches of English authors will be found in the *Dictionary of national biography* (S123) and other works listed under Great Britain, p.443-44. In the absence of those works, or for names or information not included in them, the following smaller works are useful:

Allibone, Samuel Austin. Critical dictionary of English literature and British and American authors. Phila., Lippincott, 1858–91. 5v.   **R292**

For full description *see* R279.

Kunitz, Stanley J. British authors of the 19th century. . . . Complete in one volume with 1000 biographies and 350 portraits. N.Y., Wilson, 1936. 677p. il. $5; to libraries, $4.50.   **R293**

Popular reference book similar in plan to his *American authors* (R202). Most useful in libraries which do not have the *Dictionary of national biography* (S123).

Russell, Josiah Cox. Dictionary of writers of thirteenth century England. Lond. and N.Y., Longmans [1936]. 210p. (London. Univ. Inst. of Hist. Research. Bulletin. Special suppl. 3) 7s. 6d.; $2.   **R294**

Quite detailed sketches with many bibliographical references to sources.

Who's who in literature, 1924–34; a continuance of the bibliographical section of the Literary year book (founded 1897). Liverpool, Literary Year Bks. Pr., 1924–34. v.1-11. 1934. Annual.   **R295**

No more published.

Drama

BIBLIOGRAPHY

Coleman, Edward Davidson. The Bible in English drama; an annotated list of plays including translations from other languages. N.Y., N.Y. Public Library, 1931. 212p. $1.   **R296**

Classified with indexes of authors, plays, special topics and English translations of foreign plays.
Reprinted from the *Bulletin* of the N.Y. Public Library, Oct.–Dec. 1930 and Jan.–Mar. 1931.

——The Jew in English drama; an annotated bibliography . . . preface by Joshua Bloch. N.Y., N.Y. Public Library, 1943. 237p. $2.50.   **R297**

Edited by Daniel C. Haskell. A continuation of *The Bible in English drama*, 1931 (R296).
Reprinted with additions and revisions from the *Bulletin* of the N.Y. Public Library, 1938–40.

Greg, Walter Wilson. A bibliography of the English printed drama to the Restoration. v.1, Stationers' records, plays to 1616: nos. 1-349. Lond., pr. for the Bibliographical Soc. at the Univ. Pr., Oxford, 1939. 492p. Facsim. (Illustrated monographs issued by the Bibliographical Soc., no.24) To members only, 50s.   **R298**

Arranged according to the supposed date of the earliest surviving edition. Locates copies in British and American libraries.

——A list of English plays written before 1643 and printed before 1700. Lond., Bibl. Soc., 1900. 158p.   **R299**

——List of masques, pageants, etc., supplementary to a list of English plays. Lond., Bibl. Soc., 1902. 35p., cxxxip.   **R300**

List of masques, pageants, etc.; Index of authors; Index of titles; Appendixes; Advertisement lists; The Early play lists; A list of English plays (Addenda and corrigenda).

Harbage, Alfred. Annals of English drama, 975–1700; an analytical record of all plays, extant or lost, chronologically arranged and indexed by authors, titles, dramatic companies, etc. . . . Phila., Univ. of Penn. Pr., pub. in co-operation with the Modern Language Assoc. of America; Lond., Milford, Ox. Univ. Pr., 1940. 264p. $3; 14s.   **R301**

Chronologically arranged in tabular form indicating author, title, date of first performance, type, (i.e., mask, tragedy, tragi-comedy, etc.) auspices, first edition, and last edition. Indexes of playwrights, English plays, foreign plays translated or adapted, dramatic companies. List of theaters. Appendix: Extant play manuscripts, 975–1700, their location and catalog numbers.

Hazlitt, William Carew. Manual for the collector and amateur of old English plays. Ed. from the material formed by Kirkman, Langbaine, Downes, Oldys, and Halliwell-Phillipps, with extensive additions and corrections. Lond., Pickering and Chatto, 1892. 284p. o.p.   **R302**

Lowe, Robert William. Bibliographical account of English theatrical literature from the earliest times to the present day. N.Y., Nimmo, 1888. 384p.   **R303**

Macmillan, Dougald. Catalogue of the Larpent plays in the Huntington Library. San Marino, Calif., 1939. 442p. (Huntington Library lists, no.4) $4.25. **R304**

"The licensing act of 1737 required that copies of all plays and other entertainments designed to be performed on the stage in Great Britain be submitted . . . for license. . . ." John Larpent was appointed Examiner on Nov. 20, 1778 and "died in office on Jan. 18, 1824. The official copies of plays submitted to the Examiner between 1737 and Jan. 1824, in Larpent's possession at the time of his death were bought about 1832 by John Payne Collier and Thomas Amyot."—*Pref. note.* These are now in the Huntington Library.

The list is chronological with author and title indexes.

Sibley, Gertrude Marian. The Lost plays and masques, 1500–1642. Ithaca, N.Y., Cornell Univ. Pr., 1933. 205p. **R305**

Steele, Mary Susan. Plays and masques at court during the reigns of Elizabeth, James and Charles. New Haven, Yale Univ. Pr.; Lond., Milford, 1926. 300p. $4; 18s. **R306**

Summers, Montague. Bibliography of the Restoration drama. Lond., Fortune Pr. [1935]. 143p. **R307**

Alphabetical by author, no index.

Woodward, Gertrude Loop and **McManaway, James Gilmer.** A check list of English plays, 1641–1700. Chic., Newberry Library, 1945. 155p. $3. **R308**

"Its purpose is to record the plays and masques, with the variant editions and issues, printed in the English language in the British Isles or in other countries during the years 1641 to 1700, inclusive, and to give the location of copies in [15] American libraries."—*Pref.*

—— —— Supplement, comp. by Fredson Bowers. Charlottesville, Va., Univ. of Virginia, 1949. 22p. $1.

Locates copies.

HISTORY

Adams, William Davenport. Dictionary of the drama; a guide to the plays, playwrights, players and playhouses of the United Kingdom and America, from the earliest times to the present. v.1. Lond., Chatto; Phila., Lippincott, 1904. 627p. o.p. **R309**

v.1, A-G. No more published.

Baker, David Erskine. Biographia dramatica. . . . Lond., Longmans, 1812. 3v. in 4. o.p. **R310**

Subtitle: A companion to the playhouse: containing historical and critical memoirs, and original anecdotes, of British and Irish dramatic writers, from the commencement of our theatrical exhibitions; among whom are some

of the most celebrated actors. Originally comp. to the year 1764, by D. E. Baker. Continued to 1782, by Isaac Reed, and brought down to the end of November, 1811, with very considerable additions and improvements throughout, by Stephen Jones.

v.1, pts. 1-2, Authors and actors, A-Z; v.2, Names of dramas, A-L; v.3, Names of dramas, M-Z; Latin plays by English authors, Oratorios.

An older work but still important for its biographies of dramatists and long lists of their works.

Bentley, Gerald Eades. The Jacobean and Caroline stage; dramatic companies and players. Ox., Clarendon Pr., 1941. 2v. £2 2s.; $15. **R311**

Serves as a continuation of the detailed history of the English stage begun by E. K. Chambers in *The Mediaeval stage* (R312) and *The Elizabethan stage* (R313).

Chambers, Edmund Kerchever. The Mediaeval stage. Ox., Clarendon Pr., 1903. 2v. $15. **R312**

—— The Elizabethan stage. Ox., Clarendon Pr., 1923. 4v. il. $32.50. **R313**

—— —— Index, comp. by Beatrice White, to "The Elizabethan stage" and "William Shakespeare: A study of facts and problems." Ox., Clarendon Pr., 1934. 161p. $7.

Published by arrangement with the Shakespeare Association for whose members the index was made.

Fleay, Frederick Gard. Biographical chronicle of the English drama, 1559–1642. Lond., Reeves, 1891. 2v. **R314**

A list of authors, arranged alphabetically, giving for each, brief biographical data and a list of plays in the order of original production. Appendixes in volume 2 are: Plays by anonymous authors, Masques by anonymous authors, University plays in English, University plays in Latin, Translations.

Genest, John. Some account of the English stage, from the Restoration in 1660 to 1830. Bath, pr. by H. E. Carrington, 1832. 10v. o.p. **R315**

Nicoll, Allardyce. History of Restoration drama, 1660–1700. 3d ed. Camb., Univ. Pr., 1940. 412p. 18s.; $4.25. **R316**

—— History of early 18th century drama, 1700–1750. 2d ed. Camb., Univ. Pr., 1929. 431p. 18s.; $5.50. **R317**

—— History of late 18th century drama, 1750–1800. Camb., Univ. Pr., 1927. 387p. 16s.; $3.75. **R318**

—— History of early 19th century drama, 1800–1850. Camb., Univ. Pr., 1930. 2v. 30s.; $4.25 ea. **R319**

—— History of late 19th century drama, 1850–1900. Camb., Univ. Pr., 1946. 2v. v.1, $3.50; 15s.; v.2, $5.50; 25s. **R320**

Each of the above works is on the same general plan, giving (1) history, (2) appendixes, which contain useful reference material, i.e., Lists of theaters, and Hand-lists of plays produced during the period covered.

Ward, *Sir* **Adolphus William.** History of English dramatic literature to the death of Queen Anne. New and rev. ed. Lond. and N.Y., Macmillan, 1899. 3v. o.p. **R321**

Fiction

BIBLIOGRAPHY

Block, Andrew. The English novel, 1740–1850; a catalogue including prose romances, short stories, and translations of foreign fiction. Lond., Grafton, 1939. 367p. 63s. **R322**

Alphabetically arranged by author and by title for anonymous works, with title index for works listed under author. Indicates source of information.

Esdaile, Arundell. List of English tales and prose romances printed before 1740. Lond., Bibl. Soc., 1912. 329p. 10s. 6d. **R323**

Sold only to members of the society.
pt.1, 1475–1642; pt.2, 1643–1739. Each part is arranged alphabetically by author and title with plentiful cross references. Gives full titles and imprints, list of editions, libraries in which the copies included were seen, and bibliographies in which the work is described. Scope of list includes both English tales and English translations of foreign works. Notes are bibliographical, not critical. Of value to the specialist, the bibliographer and the cataloger.

Streeter, Harold Wade. The Eighteenth century English novel in French translation; a bibliographical study. N.Y., Institute of French Studies. 1936. 256p. o.p. **R324**

Summers, Montague. A Gothic bibliography. . . . Lond., Fortune Pr. [N.Y., Columbia Univ. Pr., 1941]. 621p. il. 42s.; $10. **R325**

Contents: Index of authors, p.1-219; Title index, p.220-568; Addenda, p.569-620.
A bibliography of the English romantic novel from 1728–1916. Usually omits the well-known writers for whom there are already standard bibliographies.

HISTORY

Baker, Ernest Albert. History of the English novel. Lond., Witherby, 1924–39. 10v. 16s. per v. **R326**

From the beginnings to the early twentieth century.

Singh, Bhupal. Survey of Anglo-Indian fiction. Ox., Univ. Pr., 1934. 344p. 12s. 6d.; $4.50. **R327**

ANNUALS

Best British short stories of 1922–1940. Bost., Houghton, 1922–40. v.1-19. Annual. $2.50 ea. **R328**

Publisher varies. Publication suspended.
Editors: 1922–25, E. J. O'Brien and John Cournos; 1926–40, E. J. O'Brien.
Each volume contains: (1) Text of selected short stories of the year, (2) Yearbook of the British and Irish short story. Contents of yearbooks vary somewhat but contain, in general, author list of best short stories, with references to periodicals containing the stories, list of articles on the short story contained in British and Irish magazines, list of volumes of short stories published in Great Britain and Ireland during the year, and a biographical dictionary of short story writers, this last included from 1926 on.

Poetry

BIBLIOGRAPHY

Boys, Richard Charles. A finding-list of English poetical miscellanies 1700–48 in selected American libraries. (Repr. from ELH, a journal of English literary history, v.7, p.144-62, June 1940) **R329**

Based on Case's *Bibliography* (R332), this is a chronological list showing location in 37 public and private American libraries.

Brown, Carleton Fairchild and **Robbins, Rossell Hope.** Index of Middle English verse. N.Y., pr. for the Index Society, Columbia Univ. Pr., 1943. 785p. $15; to members $10. **R330**

A scholarly index to all poems published in England before 1500. Designed to complete the work begun by Carleton Brown in the *Register of Middle English religious and didactic verse* (R331). The 2273 entries in the *Register* in about 1100 manuscripts have been increased in this *Index* to 4365 entries in over 2000 manuscripts.
Includes a subject and title index and a list of locations of privately owned manuscripts.

Brown, Carleton Fairchild. Register of Middle English religious and didactic verse. Ox., pr. for the Bibliographical Society at the Univ. Pr., 1916–20. 2v. [Bibl. Soc., London. Pub.] **R331**

pt.1, List of manuscripts; pt.2, Index of first lines and index of subjects and titles.

Case, Arthur Ellicott. Bibliography of English poetical miscellanies, 1521–1750. Ox., pr. for the Bibliographical Soc. at the Univ. Pr., 1935 (for 1929). 386p. Sold only to members. **R332**

Geddie, William. A bibliography of middle Scots poets; with an introduction on the history of their reputations. Edinburgh, pr. for the Soc. by Blackwood, 1912. 364p. (Scottish Text Soc. [pub. 61]) **R333**

HISTORY

Courthope, William John. History of English poetry. N.Y. and Lond., Macmillan, 1895–1910. 6v. $25.50. **R334**

ANTHOLOGIES

Arber, Edward. British anthologies. Lond., Frowde, 1900–01. 10v. o.p. **R335**

v.1, Dunbar anthology, 1401–1508; v.2, Surrey and Wyatt anthology, 1509–47; v.3, Spenser anthology, 1548–91; v.4, Shakespeare anthology, 1592–1616; v.5, Jonson anthology, 1617–37; v.6, Milton anthology, 1638–74; v.7, Dryden anthology, 1675–1700; v.8, Pope anthology, 1701–44; v.9, Goldsmith anthology, 1745–74; v.10, Cowper anthology, 1775–1800.

Includes about 2500 entire poems, by about 300 authors. Each volume has an author index, an index of first lines, with notes and a glossary; volume 10 has also a general index of first lines for the ten volumes.

Dixon, William Macneile. Edinburgh book of Scottish verse, 1300–1900. Lond., Meiklejohn, 1910. 938p. (N.Y., Ox. Univ. Pr., $3) **R336**

Bibliographical notes, glossary, index of authors, index of first lines and some titles.

Oxford book of Christian verse, chosen and ed. by Lord David Cecil. Ox., Clarendon Pr., 1940. 560p. 8s. 6d.; $4.75. **R337**

Covers from the thirteenth century to the early twentieth.

Oxford book of English verse, 1250–1918, chosen and ed. by Sir Arthur Quiller-Couch. New ed. Ox., Clarendon Pr., 1939. 1171p. 8s. 6d.; $4. **R338**

Includes 966 poems against 883 in the earlier edition which stopped with 1900. Many new poems have been included both for authors added and by adding to and in some cases changing the selections of poets included before.

Complemented by a series of *Oxford books* each devoted to a particular period or century, as follows: *English mystical verse,* chosen by D. H. S. Nicholson and A. H. E. Lee, 1916. 644p.; *Sixteenth century verse,* chosen by E. K. Chambers, 1932. 905p.; *Seventeenth century verse,* chosen by H. J. C. Grierson and G. Bullough, 1934. 974p.; *Eighteenth century verse,* chosen by David Nichol Smith, 1926. 727p.; *Regency verse,* 1798–1837, chosen by H. S. Milford, 1928. 888p.; *Victorian verse,* chosen by Arthur Quiller-Couch, 1912. 1023p.; *Modern verse,* chosen by W. B. Yeats. 1936. 454p.

Useful collections for the selection of poems though with little reference apparatus beyond indexes of authors and first lines.

Oxford book of light verse, chosen by W. H. Auden. Ox., Clarendon Pr., 1938. 553p. 8s. 6d.; $4. **R339**

"Three kinds of poetry have been included; (1) Poetry written for performance, to be spoken or sung before an audience, e.g., Folk-songs, the poems of Tom Moore, (2) Poetry intended to be read, but having for its subject matter the everyday social life of its period or the experiences of the poet as an ordinary human being, e.g., the poems of Chaucer, Pope, Byron, (3) Such nonsense poetry as, through its properties and technique, has a general appeal, e.g., Nursery rhymes, the poems of Edward Lear."—*Introd.*

To avoid overlapping it does not include poems which are in the *Oxford book of English verse* (R338).

Stevenson, Burton Egbert. Home book of verse, American and English; with an appendix containing a few well-known poems in other languages. 7th ed. N.Y., Holt [1945]. 2v. 4009p. $17.50. **R340**

Arranged by large subjects, with full indexes of authors, titles and first lines. A very useful collection; contains many of the modern poems omitted from most anthologies.

—— Home book of modern verse; an extension of the Home book of verse, being a selection from American and English poetry of the 20th century. 1st ed. rev. N.Y., Holt, 1937. 1121p. $8.50. **R341**

Untermeyer, Louis. Modern British poetry, a critical anthology. 5th rev. ed. N.Y., Harcourt, 1942. 506p. $4. **R342**

Published also in a combined edition with his *Modern American poetry* (R231) (1942. $3.25).

Includes biographical sketches of the authors.

—— A treasury of great poems, English and American, from the foundations of the English spirit to the outstanding poetry of our own time, with lives of the poets and historical settings selected and integrated. N.Y., Simon and Schuster, 1942. 1288p. $5. **R343**

An anthology of almost 1000 poems with interspersed comments on the poets, or the origin and source of a poem or an explanation of seeming obscurities, etc. Index of authors and titles. Index of first lines.

Ward, Thomas Humphrey. English poets; selections with critical introductions by various writers, and a general introduction by Matthew Arnold; ed. by Thomas Humphrey Ward. N.Y., Macmillan, 1894–1918. 5v. 7s. 6d. per v.; $2.75 per v. **R344**

Ballads

BIBLIOGRAPHY

[**Crawford, James Ludovic Lindsay,** *26th earl of*] Bibliotheca Lindesiana. Catalogue of a collection of English ballads of the xviith and xviiith centuries, printed for the most part in black letter. [Aberdeen] priv. pr. [Aberdeen Univ. Pr.], 1890. 686p. **R345**

London. Stationers' Company. An analytical index to the ballad-entries (1557–1709) in the

Registers of the Company of Stationers of London, comp. by Hyder E. Rollins. . . . Chapel Hill, N.C., Univ. of North Carolina Pr., 1924. 324p. $4.   **R346**

ANTHOLOGIES

Child, Francis James. English and Scottish popular ballads. Bost., Houghton, 1883–98. 5v. o.p.   **R347**

The great collection of English ballads. Contains 305 distinct ballads, each given in all its extant versions. For each ballad there is an historical and bibliographical introduction, with full account of parallels in other languages, account of the diffusion of the story, etc. Appendix in volume 5 contains: Glossary, Sources of the text, Index of published airs of English and Scottish ballads, Index of ballad titles, Titles of collections of ballads, Index of matters, Bibliography. For the large reference or university library; for the smaller library the following abridgement is sufficient:

—— English and Scottish popular ballads ed. from the collection of Francis James Child by Helen Child Sargent and George Lyman Kittredge. Bost., Houghton, 1904. 729p. Cambridge ed. $4.75; Students' ed. $3.75.   **R348**

An abridgement of the above sufficient for ordinary purposes. Gives each of the 305 ballads in one or more versions, without the apparatus criticus, and with briefer notes. Contains a briefer glossary, full list of sources, and an index of titles.

Oxford book of ballads chosen and ed. by Sir Arthur Thomas Quiller-Couch. Ox., Clarendon Pr., 1910. 871p. 8s. 6d.; $4.   **R349**

An anthology for reading rather than reference. Makes a selection of ballads and includes only one version of each, i.e., the one considered the best for the general reader. Index to first lines.

Parodies

Hamilton, Walter. Parodies of the works of English and American authors, collected and annotated. Lond., Reeves, 1884–99. 6v. il. o.p.   **R350**

The most comprehensive collection.

Jerrold, Walter and **Leonard, R. M.** Century of parody and imitation. Ox., Univ. Pr., 1913. 429p.   **R351**

Includes poems parodying some 92 authors; excludes the work of living parodists. The table of contents gives an alphabetical list of authors of parodies and there is an index of authors parodied and an index of first lines.

Wells, Carolyn. Parody anthology. N.Y., Scribner, 1904. 397p.   **R352**

Includes later parodies omitted by Jerrold (R351).

Diaries

Matthews, William. British diaries; an annotated bibliography of British diaries written between 1442 and 1942. Berkeley, Univ. of California Pr., 1950. 339p.   **R352a**

Diaries, both in published and manuscript form (and including those reproduced in periodicals), are listed chronologically by year of first entry. Brief annotations suggest the contents, religious, military, personal, social, etc. Author index. For unpublished items, owner or library location are given.

Individual authors

✥ The following list makes no pretense of being complete for authors for whom there are separately published bibliographies. It includes only a selection of those writers for whom there are concordances, dictionaries, or handbooks as well as bibliographies. For additional titles consult the bibliographies listed under Literature and Language—British—Bibliography p.383-85.

AUSTEN

Keynes, Geoffrey. Jane Austen; a bibliography. Lond., Nonesuch Pr., 1929. 289p.   **R353**

Apperson, George Latimer. A Jane Austen dictionary. [Lond.] C. Palmer [1932]. 151p. 5s.   **R354**

"A disappointing compilation."—*Times Literary Supplement*, 11 Aug. 1932, p.570.

A superficial and incomplete work which as the only separate dictionary of the subject may be of use for popular questions on Jane Austen; for questions calling for careful work the various reference appendixes in R. W. Chapman's fine edition of Jane Austen (Ox., Clarendon Pr., 1923. 5v.), which include notes, indexes of characters, scenes, real persons and places, literary allusions, etc., will be more useful.

BEOWULF

Tinker, Chauncey B. The translations of Beowulf; a critical bibliography. N.Y., Holt, 1903. 147p. (Yale studies in English, no.16)   **R355**

Cook, Albert Stanburrough. Concordance to Beowulf. Halle, Niemeyer, 1911. 436p.   **R356**

Based upon the text of Wyatt's second edition (Camb., 1898). Omits numerals, prepositions, many pronouns and 62 other common words.

BRONTË

Wise, Thomas J. A bibliography of the writings in prose and verse of the Brontë family. Lond., priv. circ., 1917. 255p. il.   **R357**

Wroot, Herbert E. Persons and places of the Brontë novels. Bradford, Eng., Brontë Soc., 1906. 237p. (Brontë Soc. Transactions, v.3)
R358

Not a formal dictionary, but gives for a selected list of characters and places the same kind of information as that given in regular author dictionaries. Covers only the four novels of Charlotte Brontë, giving for each: (1) places, with information about the originals of places described under fictitious names; (2) principal characters, with description, illustrative quotations and notes about originals; (3) alphabetical list of minor characters with briefer information; and (4) synopsis, which gives, not a connected story of the plot, but a list of the principal events chapter by chapter. No general index.

A reprint, with amplifications and corrections, has title, *Sources of Charlotte Brontë's novels; persons and places.* Shipley, Outhwaite, 1935. 214p. (Brontë Soc. Pub. v.8, no.4, Suppl. pt.) 5s.

BROWNING

Baylor University. Library. Browningiana in Baylor University, comp. by Aurelia Brooks. [Waco, Tex., Baylor Univ. Pr., 1921] 405p. **R359**

A bibliography of material about Browning, including references to periodicals.

Broughton, Leslie N. and **Stelter, Benjamin F.** Concordance to the poems of Robert Browning. N.Y., Stechert, 1924–25. 2v. **R360**

Complete, except in the case of 70 very common words which are either omitted altogether or represented by selected references. Based upon the text of the Globe edition with references to page and line of that edition, but can be used quickly with any edition which numbers the lines of each poem.

In libraries not having this complete concordance the smaller *Phrase book* by Marie Ada Molineux (Bost., Houghton, 1896. 520p.) is useful for the more familiar Browning quotations.

Berdoe, Edward. Browning cyclopaedia. 8th ed. Lond., Allen; N.Y., Macmillan, 1916. 577p. **R361**

1st ed. 1892. The eighth edition has appendix of 5 pages.

DeVane, William. Browning handbook. N.Y., Crofts, 1935. 533p. **R362**

Orr, Alexandra Leighton. Handbook to the works of Robert Browning. 6th ed., rev. Lond., Bell, 1892. 420p. **R363**

Frequently reprinted.

BURNS

Burns Exhibition, Glasgow, 1896. Memorial catalogue of the Burns Exhibition held in the galleries of the Royal Glasgow Institute of the Fine Arts . . . from 15th July till 31st October, 1896. Glasgow, W. Hodge, 1898. 505p. il. **R364**

Partial contents: Portraits and pictures; Relics; Manuscripts, inscribed books, and autographs; Books; Chronological list of dated editions of Burns; Index of writers on Burns; The Lamb collection; Index of lenders.

Cuthbertson, John. Complete glossary to the poetry and prose of Robert Burns. With upwards of three thousand illustrations from English authors. Paisley, Gardner, 1886. 464p. **R365**

Reid, J. B. Complete word and phrase concordance to the poems and songs of Robert Burns. Glasgow, Kerr, 1889. 561p. **R366**

Ross, John Dawson. Burns handbook. Stirling, Mackay [1931] 378p. **R367**

A popular dictionary of allusions, names, etc., either referred to in the poems or having some connection with the poet's life and works. A companion volume to the same author's *Who's who in Burns* (Stirling, Mackay, 1927). Has a map of the Burns country on the lining papers.

CHAUCER

Hammond, Eleanor Prescott. Chaucer: A bibliographical manual. N.Y., Macmillan, 1908. 579p. **R368**

Describes sources, manuscripts, editions, modernizations, translations, etc.

Griffith, Dudley David. Bibliography of Chaucer, 1908–1924. Seattle, Wash., 1926. 148p. (Univ. of Wash. pub. in language and literature, v.4, March 1926) $1. **R369**

"The articles and books which have appeared since the publication of Miss Eleanor P. Hammond's *Chaucer: A bibliographical manual,* Macmillan, 1908, have been gathered together and listed. . . . Some books and articles published before 1908 have been included because they have been significantly reviewed since that date and a few omissions from Miss Hammond's *Manual* have also been listed."—*Pref.*

Martin, Willard Edgar, Jr. Chaucer bibliography, 1925–1933. Durham, N.C., Duke Univ. Pr., 1935. 97p. (Duke Univ. pub.) **R370**

Spurgeon, Caroline Frances Eleanor. Five hundred years of Chaucer criticism and allusion (1357–1900). Lond., pub. for the Chaucer Soc. by K. Paul, 1914–[25]. 7v. (Chaucer Soc. [Pub.] Second ser., 48-50, 52-56) **R371**

Issued in seven parts: pt.I for the issue of 1908; pt.II for 1909–10; pt.III for 1913; pt.IV for 1914; pt.V for 1915; pt.VI for 1916; pt.VII for 1917.

Issued also in three volumes by the Cambridge University Press, 1925.

Contents: pt.1, Foreword to part I, Text of allusions (1357–1800); pt.2, Text of allusions (1801–1850); pt.3, Text of allusions (1851–1900); pt.4, Appendix A: Additional English and Latin references, with notes on the debt of some writers to Chaucer; pt.5, Appendices B and C: French and German allusions; [pt.6] Introductions; [pt.7] Index.

—— —— Supplement containing additional entries 1868–1900. Lond., priv. pr., 1920. 171p.

Corson, Hiram. Index of proper names and subjects to Chaucer's Canterbury tales, together with comparisons and similes, metaphors and proverbs, maxims, etc., in the same. [Lond.] pub. for the Chaucer Soc. by K. Paul, 1911, for the issue of 1884. 121p. (Chaucer Soc. [Pub.] 1st ser., 72)   **R372**

Tatlock, John Strong Perry and **Kennedy, Arthur G.** Concordance to the complete works of Geoffrey Chaucer and to the Romaunt of the Rose. Wash., Carnegie Inst., 1927. 1110p. (Carnegie Inst. Pub. 353) $20.   **R373**

Complete, except in the case of about 150 very common words for which only selected references are given. Based upon the text of the Globe edition.

French, Robert Dudley. A Chaucer handbook: 2d ed. N.Y., Crofts, 1947. 402p. $2.50.   **R374**

1st ed. 1929. The revision is mainly in the bibliography and in the footnotes, with occasional changes in the text. The bibliography has been increased from about 12 to 29 pages.

COLERIDGE

Kennedy, Virginia Wadlow and **Barton, Mary Neill.** Samuel Taylor Coleridge; a selected bibliography of the best available editions of his writings, of biographies and criticisms of him and of references showing his relations with contemporaries, for students and teachers. Balt., Enoch Pratt Free Library, 1935. 151p.   **R375**

Logan, Eugenia, *sister*. A concordance to the poetry of Samuel Taylor Coleridge. St. Mary-of-the-Woods, Ind., priv. pr., 1940. 901p. $10. **R376**

Based on the text edition by Ernest Hartley Coleridge (Ox., Univ. Pr., 1912. 2v.).

COLLINS

Booth, Bradford Allen and **Jones, Claude E.** Concordance of the poetical works of William Collins. Berkeley, Calif., Univ. of Calif. Pr., 1939. 126p. $1.25.   **R377**

Based on two texts: the Oxford "Standard authors" edition edited by A. L. Poole (3d ed. rev. Lond., 1937), which in turn was based on the edition by Christopher Stone (Lond., 1907), and also Edmund Blunden's edition (Lond., 1929) for material not included by Poole.

COWPER

Neve, John. Concordance to the poetical works of William Cowper. Lond., S. Low, 1887. 504p.   **R378**

Based upon the text of the Aldine edition. Omits translations, except the more important ones from Vincent Bourne, and most of the minor poems.

DEFOE

Payne, William L. Index to Defoe's Review. N.Y., Columbia Univ. Pr., 1948. 144p.   **R379**

DICKENS

Clark, William Andrews, Jr. The library of William Andrews Clark, Jr. Cruikshank and Dickens . . . Collated and comp. by R. E. Cowan and W. A. Clark, Jr. San Francisco, pr. by J. H. Nash, 1921–23. 2v.   **R380**

v.1, p.3-77, Cruikshank; v.1, p.81-142 and v.2, Dickens.

Eckel, John C. First editions of the writings of Charles Dickens and their values; a bibliography. . . . Lond., Chapman, 1913. 296p. il.   **R381**

Hatton, Thomas and **Cleaver, A. H.** Bibliography of the periodical works of Charles Dickens, bibliographical, analytical and statistical. Lond., Chapman, 1933. 384p. il.   **R382**

Miller, William. The Dickens student and collector; a list of writings relating to Charles Dickens and his works, 1836–1945. Camb., Harv. Univ. Pr., 1946. 351p. $7.50.   **R383**

A comprehensive bibliography of writings about Dickens and his works arranged by subject, and chronologically under subject. Chapter headings include, personal (biographical), critical, dramatic, musical, anthological, plagiaristic, topographical, and bibliographical. Detailed index.

Fyfe, Thomas Alexander. Who's who in Dickens. A complete Dickens repertory in Dickens' own words. Lond., Hodder; N.Y., Doran, 1912. 355p.   **R384**

Gives for each character included an illustrative quotation and the title of the story in which the character figures. No chapter references, full descriptions or analyses of characters, or synopses of plots. List of characters is selected, not complete.

Hayward, Arthur L. Dickens encyclopaedia; an alphabetical dictionary of references to every character and place mentioned in the works of fiction with explanatory notes on obscure allusions and phrases. Lond., Routledge; N.Y., Dutton, 1924. 174p. il.   **R385**

Includes in one alphabet synopses of plots, descriptions of characters and scenes with references to all chapters in which these occur, and articles on miscellaneous subjects, e.g., illustrators of Dickens' works. Includes fewer names of characters than Philip (R386), but is fuller for information about real persons and places. Good illustrations.

Philip, Alexander J. and **Gadd, W. L.** Dickens dictionary. 2d ed. rev. and greatly enl. Gravesend, "The Librarian," 1928. 375p. il. **R386**

Contains: (1) synopses of plots; (2) alphabetical list of characters and places; (3) index of originals. Includes names from all Dickens' works except the *Child's history of England*. Differs from Pierce's *Dickens dictionary* (R387) in having all names in one alphabetical list, instead of separate lists for each novel; in referring only to the first chapter in which a character appears, and in omitting quotations. Differs from the first edition in including all notes about originals in the Index.

Pierce, Gilbert Ashville. Dickens dictionary; a key to the characters and principal incidents in the tales of Charles Dickens, with additions by W. A. Wheeler. Bost., Houghton; Lond., Chapman [c1872, 1900]. 573p. il. **R387**

Arranged by books, not in one alphabet; an older work, but not superseded by more recent works. Gives description of each character, its connection with the plot, quotations, and exact chapter references for all chapters in which the character appears.

McSpadden, Joseph Walker. Synopses of Dickens's novels. N.Y., Crowell, 1904. 208p. **R388**

Good outlines of plots.

DONNE

Keynes, Geoffrey. A bibliography of Dr. John Donne. 2d ed. Camb., Univ. Pr., 1932. 195p. il. **R389**

Concerned chiefly with texts, although some critical and biographical works are included.

White, William. John Donne since 1900; a bibliography of periodical articles. Bost., Faxon, 1942. 23p. (Bulletin of Bibliography pamphlets, no.37) **R390**

Combs, Homer Carroll and **Sullens, Zay Rusk.** Concordance to the English poems of John Donne. Chic., Packard, 1940. 418p. $7.50. **R391**

Based on *Poetical works* of John Donne, edited by H. J. C. Grierson (rev. ed. Ox., Univ. Pr., 1929).

DOYLE

Christ, Jay Finley. An irregular guide to Sherlock Holmes of Baker Street. N.Y., Argus Books; Summit, N.J., The Pamphlet House, 1947. 118p. **R392**

An index to words, ideas, personal names, etc., with reference to the stories in which they appear.

ELIOT

Mudge, Isadore Gilbert and **Sears, M. E.** A George Eliot dictionary, the characters and scenes of the novels, stories and poems alpha-

betically arranged. Lond., Routledge; N.Y., Wilson, 1924. 260p. **R393**

Contains: (1) synopses, giving time and scene of the novels, short stories and poems, and outlines of the plots; (2) main dictionary of fictitious and historical characters, places, etc., with descriptions, illustrative quotations, notes as to originals, and many historical notes on the real characters and scenes, especially those in *Romola*; (3) list of books mentioned in the novels and stories, with identifications; (4) index of originals. Refers to all chapters in which a character appears and gives many bibliographical references to sources of information.

FITZGERALD

Tutin, John Ramsden. Concordance to Fitzgerald's translation of the Rubáiyát of Omar Khayyám. Lond. and N.Y., Macmillan, 1900. 169p. **R394**

Indexes every word in the last edition issued during Fitzgerald's lifetime, every word in the first edition, 1859, and all variations in the second, third and other editions, forming a practically complete index to the entire work in its distinct forms. References are to edition, quatrain and line.

GILBERT

Searle, Townley. Sir William Schwenck Gilbert; a topsy-turvey adventure. Lond., Alexander-Ousley, 1931. 105p. il. **R395**

A bibliography of the works of Gilbert and of the Gilbert and Sullivan operas.

Dunn, George E. A Gilbert and Sullivan dictionary. N.Y., Ox. Univ. Pr., 1936. 175p. **R396**

Includes obscure words, phrases, allusions, foreign and colloquial words, names of persons, places and incidents, characters, original creators, successors, etc. Lists the operas with dates and theaters of first productions, etc.

GOLDSMITH

Paden, William Doremus and **Hyder, Clyde Kenneth.** Concordance to the poems of Oliver Goldsmith. Lawrence, Kans., Author, 1940. 180p. $4. **R397**

Based exclusively on *Poetical works of Oliver Goldsmith* edited by Austin Dobson (Ox. Univ. Pr., 1906).

GRAY

Northup, Clark Sutherland. Bibliography of Thomas Gray. New Haven, Yale Univ. Pr., 1917. 296p. (Cornell studies in English, 1) **R398**

Cook, Albert Stanburrough. Concordance to the English poems of Thomas Gray. Bost., Houghton, 1908. 160p. **R399**

Omits 47 common words, but is otherwise complete. Based upon Gosse's edition.

HARDY

Webb, A. P. Bibliography of the works of Thomas Hardy, 1865–1915. Lond., Hollings, 1916. 127p. **R400**

Weber, Carl J. The First hundred years of Thomas Hardy, 1840–1940; a centenary bibliography of Hardiana. Waterville, Maine, Colby College Library, 1942. 276p. **R401**

Attempts to list everything published about Hardy, 1840–1940, including works in foreign languages.

Saxelby, F. Outwin. A Thomas Hardy dictionary; the characters and scenes of the novels and poems alphabetically arranged and described. Lond., Routledge; N.Y., Dutton, 1911. lxxviiip., 238p. **R402**

Contains: Biographical sketch; List of 1st editions; Bibliography of the novels; List of books about Hardy and Wessex; Map: "Heart of Wessex"; List of fictitious place names followed by real names; Synopses of the novels; Dictionary of characters and places. The dictionary gives brief account of each character and some illustrative quotations, and refers to all chapters in which the character appears.

HERRICK

MacLeod, Malcolm. Concordance to the poems of Robert Herrick. Ox., Univ. Pr., 1936. 299p. $4.50; 18s. **R403**

A comprehensive concordance, complete except for 11 very common words which are omitted altogether and about 110 others which are represented by selected examples only. Based upon the text of the edition of Herrick by F. W. Moorman (Ox. Univ. Pr., 1915).

HOUSMAN

Hyder, Clyde Kenneth. A concordance to the poems of A. E. Housman. Lawrence, Kans., Author, 1940. 133p. $3.50. **R404**

JONSON

Bradley, Jesse Franklin and **Adams, Joseph Quincy.** The Jonson allusion-book; a collection of allusions to Ben Jonson from 1597 to 1700. New Haven, Yale Univ. Pr., 1922. 466p. **R405**

KEATS

Baldwin, Dane Lewis, Broughton, L. N. [and others]. Concordance to the poems of John Keats. Wash., Carnegie Inst., 1917. 437p. **R406**

Based on the Buxton Forman editions of 1910 and 1914. Gives a complete record of all words used by Keats, except 59 common words omitted altogether and 10 others recorded only partially.

MacGillivray, J. R. Keats: A bibliography and reference guide with an essay on Keats' reputation. Toronto, Univ. of Toronto Pr., 1949. 210p. (Univ. of Toronto. Dept. of English. Studies and texts, no.3) **R407**

KEBLE

Concordance to "The Christian year." N.Y., Pott and Amery, 1871. 524p. **R408**

Omits "such words as would only enlarge the volume without adding to its usefulness."—*Pref.*

KIPLING

Livingston, Flora V. Bibliography of the works of Rudyard Kipling. N.Y., Edgar H. Wells, 1927. 523p. **R409**

—— —— Supplement. Camb., Harv. Univ. Pr., 1938. 333p.

Young, W. Arthur. Dictionary of the characters and scenes in the stories and poems of Rudyard Kipling, 1886–1911. Lond., Routledge; N.Y., Dutton [1911]. 231p. **R410**

Contains: Summary of the books (giving synopses of plots); Dictionary proper, which gives names of the characters and titles of books, stories and poems in one alphabet. Accounts of characters are brief, do not include illustrative quotations and do not refer exactly to all chapters in which characters occur.

KYD

Crawford, Charles. Concordance to the works of Thomas Kyd. Louvain, Uystpruyst, 1906–10. 690p. (Materialien zur Kunde des älteren Englischen Dramas, v.15) **R411**

Includes as an Appendix, p.472-690, a concordance to Edward Dowden's version of *Hamlet,* as printed in the Arden Shakespeare (Methuen, 1899).

MARLOWE

Crawford, Charles. The Marlowe concordance. Louvain, Uystpruyst, 1911–32. 1453p. (Materialien zur Kunde des älteren Englischen Dramas, begr. u. hrsg. von W. Bang, v.34, pts. 1-3; Materials for the study of the old English drama; ed. by Henry De Vocht, n.s. v.2-3, 6-7) **R412**

"Very few words have been omitted from the concordance, and only those which are of little aid to study, such as auxillary verbs, pronouns, and insignificant prepositions and conjunctions."—*Pref.*

MILTON

Stevens, David Harrison. Reference guide to Milton; from 1800 to the present day. Chic., Univ. of Chic. Pr., 1930. 302p.　　**R413**

Lists editions, translations, biography, criticism, etc., from 1800 to about 1928.

Fletcher, Harris Francis. Contributions to a Milton bibliography, 1800–1930, being a list of addenda to Stevens' Reference guide to Milton. Urbana, Univ. of·Illinois Pr., 1931. 166p. (Univ. of Illinois studies in language and literature. v.16, no.1)　　**R414**

Williamson, George Charles. Milton tercentenary; the portraits, prints and writings of John Milton . . . with an appendix and index by C. Sayle. Exhibited at Christ's College, Cambridge, 1908. [Camb., Univ. Pr., 1908] 167p. il.　**R415**

A reprint of the Milton tercentenary catalog, in which all the items in the list from pages 29 to 90 have been renumbered.

Bradshaw, John. Concordance to the poetical works of John Milton. Lond., Sonnenschein, 1894. 412p.　　**R416**

Based upon the Aldine edition (Bell, 1894), and includes all the poems except the Psalms and the translations in the prose works; omits the commoner pronouns, conjunctions, adverbs and prepositions.

Cooper, Lane. Concordance to the Latin, Greek and Italian poems of John Milton. Halle, Niemeyer, 1923. 212p.　　**R417**

Contents: (1) concordances of the Latin poems; (2) of the Greek poems; (3) of the Italian poems. Based mainly upon Beeching's reprint of 1900, with some use of the Oxford miniature edition and of two poems from Masson's edition.

Gilbert, Allan H. Geographical dictionary of Milton. New Haven, Yale Univ. Pr., 1919. 322p.　　**R418**

Gives all place names mentioned in all of Milton's prose and poetry (except the addresses of the *Letters of state* and the biblical quotations in *De Doctrina Christiana*) with exact reference to all passages where they occur, explanation of what they meant to Milton and illustrative quotations from books which Milton had read. References are to the Oxford edition of the *Poems*, edited by Beeching, and to the edition of the *Prose works* published by Pickering, 1851.

Lockwood, Laura Emma. Lexicon to the English poetical works of John Milton. Lond. and N.Y., Macmillan, 1907. 671p.　　**R419**

Based upon the text of the Globe edition. Defines words and refers to text. Records all occurrences of each word except in the case of very common words where each meaning, but not each occurrence, is recorded.

Patterson, Frank Allen. An index to the Columbia edition of the Works of John Milton, by Frank Allen Patterson assisted by French Rowe Fogle. N.Y., Columbia Univ. Pr., 1940. 2v. 2141p. $12.50.　　**R420**

Uniform with the Columbia *Milton* but sold separately. A detailed analytical index to the works of Milton, including references to names, ideas and subjects. Serves also as a word index. May be used with other editions of Milton, although the page references are to the Columbia *Milton*.

Hanford, James Holly. A Milton handbook; 4th ed. N.Y., Crofts, 1946. 465p. $2.50.　　**R421**

3d ed. pub. 1940. The fourth edition adds new appendixes, and revisions and additions in text, footnotes and bibliography.

A survey companion to Milton studies for the advanced student. Discusses Milton's life and works with reference to source materials. Bibliography, p.421-47.

POPE

Griffith, Reginald Harvey. Alexander Pope; a bibliography. Austin, Univ. of Texas, 1922–27. v.1, pts. 1-2.　　**R422**

v.1, pts. 1-2, Pope's own writings, 1709–51; v.2, to cover material about Pope, was never published.

Tobin, James Edward. Alexander Pope; a list of critical studies published from 1895 to 1944. N.Y., Cosmopolitan Science and Art Service Co., 1945. 30p. 75c.　　**R423**

Wise, Thomas James. Pope library, a catalogue of plays, poems, and prose writings by Alexander Pope. Lond., pr. for priv. circ. only, 1931. 112p. il.　　**R424**

pt.1, The Writings of Alexander Pope; pt.2, Popeiana.

Abbott, Edwin. Concordance to the works of Alexander Pope. N.Y., Appleton, 1875. 365p.　　**R425**

Based upon Warburton's edition, 1751; includes all words in poems in that edition except the translations from the Greek and Latin, the adaptations from Chaucer and the imitations of the English poets.

SCOTT

Corson, James Clarkson. Bibliography of Sir Walter Scott; a classified and annotated list of books and articles relating to his life and works, 1797–1940. Edinburgh, Oliver and Boyd, 1943. 428p. 32s.　　**R426**

Ruff, William. A bibliography of the poetical works of Sir Walter Scott, 1796–1832. Edinburgh, Edinburgh Bibl. Soc., 1938. p.99-239, 279-81. (Repr. from Edinburgh Bibliographical Soc., Transactions v.1, 1937–38)　　**R427**

Burr, Allston. Sir Walter Scott; an index placing the short poems in his novels and in his long poems and dramas. Camb., Harv. Univ. Pr., 1936. 130p.　　**R428**

Husband, M. F. A. Dictionary of the characters in the Waverley novels of Sir Walter Scott. Lond., Routledge; N.Y., Dutton, 1910. 287p. **R429**

Gives the characters and scenes of all the novels in one alphabetical list, but contains no outlines of plots. Differs from Rogers' *Waverley dictionary* (R431) in having the one list instead of a separate list for each novel and in referring only to the title of the story in which a character appears, not to specific chapters. In this latter respect less useful than Rogers, but lists more characters than the latter.

Redfern, Owen. The wisdom of Sir Walter; criticisms and opinions collected from the Waverley novels and Lockhart's Life of Sir Walter Scott. Lond., Black, 1907. 309p. **R430**

Not a complete concordance, but a selection of quotations of some length arranged alphabetically under subject word. Refers to title of work, chapter and page in Black's sixpenny edition of Scott and the 10-volume edition of Lockhart's *Life of Scott*.

Rogers, May. Waverley dictionary. 2d ed. Chic., Griggs, 1885 [c78]. 357p. **R431**

An alphabetical arrangement of all the characters in the Waverley novels with a descriptive analysis of each character and illustrative selections from the text. Gives exact chapter references.

McSpadden, Joseph Walker. Waverley synopses; a guide to the plots and characters of Scott's "Waverley novels." N.Y., Crowell [c1909]. 280p. o.p. **R432**

Arranges the novels in historical sequence and gives for each novel the date of the first edition, time and scene of the plot, cast of main characters and synopsis of plot. There is a general index of characters at the end. Useful in the small library which cannot afford the larger works by Rogers (R431) and Husband (R429), and in a larger library as a supplement to these two works, neither of which gives plots.

SHAKESPEARE

☙ For many questions on Shakespeare the elaborate notes given in the New Variorum edition (Phila., Lippincott, 1871–1944. v.1-25. $10 ea. In progress) furnish excellent reference material.

Bibliography

Jaggard, William. Shakespeare bibliography; a dictionary of every known issue of the writings of our national poet and of recorded opinion thereon in the English language, with historical introduction. Stratford-on-Avon, Shakespeare Pr., 1911. 729p. il. **R433**

Bartlett, Henrietta C. Mr. William Shakespeare; original and early editions of his quartos and folios, his source books and those containing contemporary notices. New Haven, Yale Univ. Pr., 1922. 217p. **R434**

——and **Pollard, Alfred W.** A census of Shakespeare's plays in quarto, 1594–1709, rev. and extended. New Haven, Yale Univ. Pr.; Lond., Milford, 1939. 165p. $10. **R435**

Records and describes all separate editions and issues before 1709. Every known copy of each edition and issue is described and its history from publication to January 1939 given as fully as possible. The index includes all names of owners, booksellers, auctioneers and binders found in the census.

Ebisch, Walther and **Schücking, Levin L.** Shakespeare bibliography. . . . Ox., Clarendon Pr., 1931. 294p. [Sächsische Forschungsinstitut in Leipzig. Forschungsinstitut für neuere Philologie. III. Anglistische Abt. Extra v.] **R436**

A selective bibliography of material about Shakespeare, his times, life, personality, texts, sources, literary influences, language, art, production, influence, individual plays, etc.

—— —— Supplement for the years 1930–35. Ox., Clarendon Pr., 1937. 104p.

Shakspere allusion-book: A collection of allusions to Shakspere from 1591 to 1700. Originally comp. by C. M. Ingleby, L. Toulmin Smith and by F. J. Furnivall, with the assistance of the New Shakspere Society: re-ed., rev. and re-arranged, with an introd. by John Munro (1909) and re-issued with a preface by Sir Edmund Chambers. Ox., Univ. Pr., 1932. 2v. il. (The Shakespeare Library) **R437**

A "combined edition" of the "Centurie of prayse" edited by C. M. Ingleby (second edition by Miss L. T. Smith) and "Some 300 fresh allusions to Shakspere," edited by Dr. Furnivall; with additions by the editor, John Munro.—Cf. *Introd.*

Shakespeare Association of America. Annual bibliography of Shaksperiana, 1925- . (In its Bulletin. v.1-) 50c per no. **R438**

An annual subject bibliography of book, pamphlet and periodical material, including much analysis of periodicals.

Raven, Anton Adolph. Hamlet bibliography and reference guide, 1877–1935. Chic., Univ. of Chic. Pr., 1936. 292p. $3.50. **R439**

Concordances

See also R411 for concordance to *Hamlet*.

Bartlett, John. New and complete concordance or verbal index to words, phrases, and passages in the dramatic works of Shakespeare with a supplementary concordance to the Poems. Lond., Macmillan, 1894. 1910p. **R440**

Based upon the text of the Globe edition; gives full context for each word listed, with exact reference to act, scene, and line as numbered in the Globe edition, 1891. The best and most comprehensive Shakespeare concordance.

Furness, Helen Kate Rogers. Concordance to Shakespeare's poems. 4th ed. Phila., Lippincott, 1916. 422p. **R441**

Stevenson, Burton Egbert. Home book of Shakespeare quotations, being also a concordance and a glossary of the unique words and phrases in the plays and poems. N.Y. and Lond., Scribner, 1937. 2055p. **R442**

Dictionaries

Baker, Arthur Ernest. A Shakespeare commentary . . . v.1. Taunton, Eng., Author, 1917–38. 965p. tables. **R443**

Subtitle: Dates of composition and first publication; sources of the plots and detailed outlines of the plays; together with the characters, place-names, classical, geographical, topographical and curious historical and folk allusions, with glosses; to which are added appendices, giving extracts from Holinshed, Plutarch, and the various romances, novels, poems and histories used by Shakespeare in the formation of the dramas.

Published in 15 parts. Parts 1-13 had title, *Shakespeare dictionary.*

Contents: pt.1, Julius Caesar; pt.2, As you like it; pt.3, Macbeth; pt.4, Tempest; pt.5, Hamlet; pt.6, King Lear; pt.7, King John; pt.8, Merchant of Venice; pt.9, King Richard II; pts. 10-11, King Henry IV; pt.12, King Henry V; pt.13, King Henry VI, pt.1; pt.14, King Henry VI, pt.2; pt.15, King Henry VI, pt.3.

A popular dictionary of characters, place names and allusions; each part in a separate alphabet.

Dyce, Alexander. Glossary to the works of William Shakespeare. The references made applicable to any edition of Shakespeare, the explanations revised and new notes added by Harold Littledale. Lond., Sonnenschein; N.Y., Dutton, 1902. 570p. **R444**

Kellner, Leon. Shakespeare Wörterbuch. Leipzig, Tauchnitz, 1922. 358p. (Engl. Bibliothek, hrsg. von Max Forster) **R445**

An English-German dictionary, with explanations of Shakespeare's words given in German.

Onions, Charles Talbut. Shakespeare glossary. 2d ed. rev. Ox., Clarendon Pr., 1919. 259p. **R446**

An excellent small dictionary, by a man who was for many years on the staff of the *New English dictionary* (M11). The aim of the glossary is to supply: (1) definitions or illustrations of words or senses now obsolete or surviving only in archaic or provincial use; (2) explanations of other words involving allusions not generally familiar; (3) explanations of proper names carrying with them some connotative significance or offering special interest or difficulty, and of idioms, or colloquial phrases, specialized uses of pronouns and particles and the rela-

tion of the poet's vocabulary to the midland area, especially Warwickshire. Includes also obsolete and technical terms which occur only in the stage directions.

Schmidt, Alexander. Shakespeare-lexicon; a complete dictionary of all the English words, phrases, and constructions in the works of the poet. 3d ed. rev. and enl. by Gregor Sarrazin. Berlin, Reimer; N.Y., Stechert, 1902. 2v. **R447**

Stokes, Francis Griffin. Dictionary of the characters and proper names in the works of Shakespeare, with notes on the sources and dates of the plays and poems. Lond., Harrap; Bost., Houghton, 1924. 359p. (Repr. N.Y., Peter Smith, 1949. $6.75) **R448**

Includes in one alphabet titles of Shakespeare's works, with brief account of first editions, sources, etc., names of all characters, historical, legendary and fictitious, with brief analysis of the dramatic action of each, names used as allusions, place names, and miscellaneous names such as seasons, planets, etc. Gives exact reference to play, act and line, and some bibliographical references to sources of further information.

Sugden, Edward Holdsworth. Topographical dictionary to the works of Shakespeare and his fellow dramatists. Manchester, Univ. Pr.; Lond. and N.Y., Longmans, 1925. 580p. il. maps. (Pub. of the University of Manchester, 168) **R449**

Lists all place names, i.e., countries, towns, rivers and streets, with brief article about each and exact reference to the play in which it occurs, and references to sources of further information. Includes also the place names of Milton and some references to Spenser.

Plots

Guerber, H. A. Stories of Shakespeare's comedies. N.Y., Dodd, 1910. 336p. **R450**

—— Stories of Shakespeare's tragedies. N.Y., Dodd, 1911. 349p. **R451**

—— Stories of Shakespeare's English history plays. N.Y., Dodd, 1912. 315p. **R452**

Three companion volumes, inferior in literary form to Lamb's *Tales from Shakespeare*, but useful for reference purposes because they give simple clear outlines, act by act, of the fourteen comedies, the twelve tragedies and the eight English history plays.

McSpadden, Joseph Walker. Shaksperian synopses; outlines or arguments of the plays of Shakspere. N.Y., Crowell [c1902]. 322p. **R453**

SHAW

Broad, C. Lewis and **Broad, V. M.** Dictionary to the plays and novels of Bernard Shaw, with bibliography of his works and of the literature concerning him, with a record of the principal

Shavian play productions. Lond., Black [1929]. 230p. **R454**

Heydet, X. Shaw-Kompendium; Verzeichnis und Analyse seiner Werke. Shaw-Bibliographie; Verzeichnis der Literatur über Shaw. Verzeichnis der Aufführungen seiner Werke in England und Deutschland. Paris, Didier, 1936. 224p. **R455**

SHELLEY

Wise, Thomas James. Shelley library, a catalogue of printed books, manuscripts and autograph letters by Percy Bysshe Shelley, Harriet Shelley and Mary Wollstonecraft Shelley. Lond., pr. for priv. circ., 1924. 164p. facsim. **R456**

Ellis, Frederick S. Lexical concordance to the poetical works of Percy Bysshe Shelley. Lond., Quaritch, 1892. 818p. **R457**

Based upon the text of the Forman edition, 1880.

SPENSER

Carpenter, Frederic Ives. Reference guide to Edmund Spenser. Chic., Univ. of Chic. Pr., 1923. 333p. **R458**

Atkinson, Dorothy F. Edmund Spenser, a bibliographical supplement. Balt., Johns Hopkins Pr.; Ox., Univ. Pr., 1937. 242p. $3; 13s. 6d. **R459**

Designed as a supplement to R458. Omits most allusions before 1800, which are to be included in the *Spenser allusion book* now in preparation, but includes allusions since 1800.—Cf. *Foreword.*

Johnson, Francis R. A critical bibliography of the works of Edmund Spenser printed before 1700. Balt., Johns Hopkins Pr., 1933. 61p. il. **R460**

Osgood, Charles Grosvenor. Concordance to the poems of Edmund Spenser. Wash., Carnegie Inst., 1915. 997p. **R461**

Complete, except in the case of 174 very common words for which only selected references are given; based upon the text of Morris' edition (Globe edition 1869) corrected by the text of R. E. Neil Dodge's edition (Cambridge edition 1908) with record of all variants in the Oxford edition 1909–10.

Whitman, Charles Huntington. Subject-index to the poems of Edmund Spenser, pub. under the auspices of the Connecticut Academy of Arts and Sciences. New Haven, Yale Univ. Pr., 1918. 261p. **R462**

A subject index of names of persons, places, animals and things, with some dictionary features also, as it includes brief allegorical and other explanations, when necessary. In the use of abbreviations, etc., conforms to Osgood's *Concordance* (R461), so that the two works

can be used together easily. Based upon the Cambridge text, edited by R. E. Neil Dodge, but as the table of abbreviations gives page references for each poem to the Cambridge, Globe, Smith, and de Selincourt editions the user can refer quickly to any of the four editions.

TENNYSON

Wise, Thomas James. Bibliography of the writings of Alfred, Lord Tennyson. Lond., pr. for priv. circ., 1908. 2v. il. **R463**

Baker, Arthur Ernest. Concordance to the poetical and dramatic works of Alfred, Lord Tennyson. Lond., K. Paul; N.Y., Macmillan, 1914. 1212p. **R464**

Complete except for about 250 common words; in four alphabets. Based upon the Macmillan edition (6v.) but covers also the poems included in the life of Tennyson by his son, and in the *Suppressed poems* edited by J. C. Thomson.

Supplemented by the same compiler's *Concordance to The devil and the lady, by Alfred Tennyson* (Lond., Golden Vista Pr., 1931. 247p.).

—— Tennyson dictionary, the characters and place-names contained in the poetical and dramatic works of the poet alphabetically arranged and described. Lond., Routledge; N.Y., Dutton [1916] 296p. **R465**

Contents: (1) Brief synopses of poems and plays; (2) Dictionary of characters and places, and of names referred to. Dictionary gives brief description of characters, occasional illustrative quotations and a general reference to work in which name appears; no specific references to line, stanza, etc.

Luce, Morton. Handbook to the works of Tennyson. Lond., Bell; N.Y., Macmillan, 1908. 454p. **R466**

THACKERAY

Van Duzer, Henry Sayre. Thackeray library; first editions and first publications, portraits, water colors, etchings, drawings and manuscripts . . . a few additional items are included, forming a complete Thackeray bibliography; with twenty-three illustrations. N.Y., priv. pr. [The De Vinne Pr.] 1919. 198p. il. **R467**

Mudge, Isadore Gilbert and **Sears, Minnie Earl.** A Thackeray dictionary; the characters and scenes of the novels and short stories alphabetically arranged. Lond., Routledge; N.Y., Dutton, 1910. xlvp., 304p. **R468**

Contains: (1) "Synopses" giving time and scene of the novels and short stories and outlines of the plots; (2) Main alphabetical list of historical and fictitious characters and place names; (3) Index of originals. Refers to all chapters in which a character appears, differentiates historical and fictitious names and gives authorities for originals.

TROLLOPE

Gerould, Winifred Gregory and **Gerould, James Thayer.** A guide to Trollope. Princeton, N.J., Princeton Univ. Pr., 1948. 256p. **R469**

"An alphabetical record of characters and places having a significant role in the novels and stories." Includes brief plots. References are to exact volume, chapter and page in the first edition with a conversion table to later editions.

WELLS

Wells, Geoffrey H. The works of H. G. Wells, 1887–1925. A bibliography, dictionary and subject-index. Lond., Routledge; N.Y., Wilson, 1926. 274p. **R470**

Connes, G. A. A dictionary of the characters and scenes in the novels, romances and short stories of H. G. Wells. Dijon, Maurice Darantière, 1926. 489p. **R471**

WORDSWORTH

Cornell University. Library. The Wordsworth collection formed by Cynthia Morgan St. John and given to Cornell University by Victor Emanuel; a catalogue, comp. by Leslie Nathan Broughton. Ithaca, Cornell Univ. Pr., 1931. 124p. **R472**

———— Supplement. 1942. 87p.

Logan, James Venable. Wordsworthian criticism; a guide and bibliography. Columbus, Ohio State Univ., 1947. 304p. (Graduate School monographs. Contributions in languages and literature, no.12) **R473**

Patton, Cornelius Howard. The Amherst Wordsworth collection; a descriptive bibliography. Amherst, Mass., pub. by the Trustees of Amherst College, 1936. 304p. **R474**

Wise, Thomas James. Bibliography of the writings in prose and verse of William Wordsworth. Lond., pr. for priv. circ., 1916. 268p. il. **R475**

Cooper, Lane. Concordance to the poems of William Wordsworth, ed. for the Concordance Society. Lond., Smith, Elder; N.Y., Dutton, 1911. 1136p. **R476**

Based upon the text of the Oxford *Wordsworth* edited by Hutchinson, 1907. Gives complete list of references for all words used by Wordsworth, except that all references for 52 of the most common words are omitted, and a selection is given for 195 other very common words.

Tutin, J. R. Wordsworth dictionary. Hull [Eng.], Tutin, 1891. 216p., and suppl. 20p. **R477**

(1) Dictionary of persons with indication of the poems in which they are mentioned; (2) Dictionary of places;

(3) Familiar quotations; (4) Chronological list of best poems; (5) Birds, trees and flowers of Wordsworth; Supplement: Index to the animal and vegetable kingdom of Wordsworth (Hull, 1892. 20p.).

WYATT

Hangen, Eva Catherine. Concordance to the complete poetical works of Sir Thomas Wyatt. Chic., Univ. of Chic. Pr., 1941. 527p. $5. **R478**

Based on Foxwell, A. K., *The poems of Sir Thomas Wiat* (Lond., Univ. of Lond. Pr., 1914).

Canadian

Garvin, John William. Canadian poets. Rev. ed. Toronto, McClelland [c1926]. 536p. il. $5; reissue $3.25. **R479**

Gives selections from poems of 75 authors with biography of each. Includes 28 poets (212 poems) not included in the 1916 edition.

Thomas, Clara. Canadian novelists, 1920–1945. Toronto, N.Y., Longmans [1946]. 129p. **R480**

Bio-bibliographical sketches of 122 contemporary authors, born in, or residents of Canada.

Wallace, William Stewart. Dictionary of Canadian biography. 2d ed. Toronto, Macmillan, 1945. 2v. **R481**

In this edition "an attempt has been made to extend the usefulness of the *Dictionary* as a guide to Canadian authors." For full description *see* S82.

Irish
Bibliography

Dublin. National Library of Ireland. Bibliography of Irish philology and of printed Irish literature. Dublin, H. M. Stat. Off., 1913. 307p. **R482**

Compiled by R. I. Best and supplemented by:

Best, Richard Irvine. Bibliography of Irish philology and manuscript literature; publication 1913–1941. Dublin, Dublin Inst. for Advanced Studies, 1942. 253p. 7s. 6d. **R483**

McCarthy, Justin. Irish literature. Phila., Morris [c1904]. 10v. il. **R484**

v.1-9, Irish authors who have written in English, and early Irish writers, in English translations, A-Y, biographies and selections; v.10, Gaelic authors; Biographies (1) of ancient Celtic authors in v.1-9 and (2) of modern Celtic authors in v.10; Glossary; General index, authors, titles, subjects.

For each author included gives brief biography, comment, list of works, illustrative selections.

Fiction

Brown, Stephen James. Ireland in fiction; a guide to Irish novels, tales, romances, and folk-lore

New ed. . . . Dublin and Lond., Maunsel, 1919. 362p. 10s. 6d. **R485**

"Includes all works of fiction published in volume form, and dealing with Ireland or with the Irish abroad, and such works only."—*Pref.*

An author list of 1713 novels, with descriptive annotations, and brief biographical notes. Appendixes are: Some useful works of reference, Publishers and series, Classified lists of novels (e.g., historical fiction, legends, Catholic clerical life, etc.), Irish fiction in periodicals. Index of titles and subjects. Has more titles, and about 550 more notes, than the edition of 1916.

An earlier work by the same author, entitled *Reader's guide to Irish fiction*, published 1910, was a classified list. It is practically superseded by the above.

Poetry

O'Donoghue, David James. Poets of Ireland; a biographical and bibliographical dictionary of Irish writers of English verse. Dublin, Figgis; Lond., Frowde, 1912. 504p. o.p. **R486**

Brooke, Stopford Augustus and **Rolleston, T. W.** Treasury of Irish poetry in the English tongue. Rev. and enl. N.Y., Macmillan, 1932. 610p. $3. **R487**

1st ed., 1900.

Gives 344 poems from the works of 119 authors, with biographical and bibliographical notes, occasionally of some length and signed, about each poet. This edition differs from the first edition in showing some revision of the biographical and bibliographical notes to include more recent information and in the addition, p.589-99, of selections from the poems of 12 writers not previously included.

Cooke, John. Dublin book of Irish verse, 1728–1909. Dublin, Hodges; Ox., Univ. Pr., 1909. 803p. 8s. 6d.; $3.75. **R488**

New Zealand

New Zealand Authors' Week Committee. Annals of New Zealand literature; being a preliminary list of New Zealand authors and their works with introductory essays and verses. [n.p.] Committee, 1936. 117p. il. **R489**

GERMANIC LANGUAGES

Paul, Hermann. Grundriss der germanischen Philologie. 2. verb. und verm. Aufl. Strassburg, Trübner, 1900–09. 3v. maps. **R490**

For advanced workers only. Not alphabetically arranged, but in chapters with detailed alphabetical indexes, and many important bibliographical references. Covers the fields of language, literature and allied subjects, e.g., myths, legends, manners and customs, etc.

A third edition has begun to appear, as follows:

—— Grundriss der germanischen Philologie unter Mitwirkung zahlreicher Fachgelehrter, begründet von Hermann Paul. Berlin, de Gruyter, 1913–43. v.1¹, 2-10, 11¹⁻³, 12¹⁻², 13¹, 14-16, 18¹. (In progress)

An extensive revision, each volume edited by a specialist and covering a particular period or phase of Germanic philology.

Jahresbericht über die Erscheinungen auf dem Gebiete der germanischen Philologie hrsg. von der Gesellschaft für Deutsche Philologie in Berlin, 1879–1935. Berlin, DeGruyter, 1880–1939. v.1-57. **R491**

Useful annual bibliography, listing the new book, pamphlet and dissertation literature, and also indexing articles in a large number of important periodicals.

Springer, Otto. Germanic bibliography, 1940–1945. p.251-326. (Repr. from the Journal of English and Germanic philology, July 1946) $1. **R492**

Subtitle: Books and articles in the field of Germanic philology published in Europe, especially in Germany and in the Scandinavian countries, during the war.

Dutch

Cauberghe, J. Nederlandsche taalschat. Turnhout, Belgium, Brepols, 1947. 4v. **R493**

Contents: (1) Spreuken en spreekwoorden; (2) Spreekwijzen; (3) Synoniemen; (4) Citaten.

Volumes 1 and 2, arranged by topics, include Dutch idioms and proverbs with citations from Dutch and Flemish authors and Dutch versions of such citations from German, French, English and Latin authors.

Volume 3 includes synonyms, antonyms, homonyms, and paronyms with its own index.

Coopman, Theophiel and **Scharpé, L.** Geschiedenis der vlaamsche letterkunde. Antwerpen, Smeding, 1910. 387p. il. **R494**

Frederiks, Johannes Godefridus and **Branden, F. J. van den.** Biografisch woordenboek der Noord-en Zuidnederlandsche letterkunde. 2. omgewerkte druk. Amsterdam, Veen, 1888–92. 918p. **R495**

Leopold, Lubbertus. Nederlandsche schrijvers en schrijfsters; proeven uit hun werken, met beknopte biographieen en portretten. 12. herziene druk door G. S. Overdiep en W. L. Brandsma. Groningen, Wolters, 1940. 903p. il. **R496**

Poelhekke, M. A. P. C., Vooys, C. G. N. de and **Brom, Gerard.** Platenatlas bij de nederlandsche literatuurgeschiedenis. 4. druk. Groningen, Wolters, 1933. 152p. il. **R497**

Winkel, Jan te. De ontwikkelingsgang der nederlandsche letterkunde. 2. druk. Haarlem, Bohn, 1922–27. 7v. **R498**

An important reference history, containing extensive bibliographies.

Flemish

Arents, Prosper. Flemish writers translated (1830–1931); bibliographical essay. The Hague, Nijhoff, 1931. 191p. **R499**

Ridder, Andre de and **Timmermans, Willy.** Anthologie des ecrivains flammands contemporains. Anvers, L. Opdebeek; Paris, Champion, 1926. 389p. **R500**

Includes prose and poetical selections, with biographies and bibliographies.

Roemans, Robert. Bibliographie van de moderne vlaamsche literatuur, 1893–1930. Kortrijk, Steenlandt, 1930–34. v.1$^{1-10}$. **R501**

1. deel, De Vlaamsche tijdschriften.

Friesian

Friesland. Provinciale Bibliotheek. Catalogus der Friesche taal- en letterkunde en overige Friesche geschriften. 1941. Leeuwarden, Noordnederlandsche Boekhandel, 1941. 859p. **R502**

Wumkes, G. A. Paden fen Fryslan; samle opstellen. Boalsert, A. J. Osinga, 1932–43. 4v. il. **R503**

German

Bibliography

Arnold, Robert Franz. Allgemeine Bücherkunde zur neueren deutschen Literaturgeschichte. 3. neu bearb. und stark verm. Aufl. Berlin, de Gruyter, 1931. 362p. **R504**

1st ed. 1910; 2d ed., 1919. The third edition is on the general plan of the second edition but extensively revised.

A useful small bibliography, covering more than the field of German literature as it is ordinarily understood. In addition to editions, histories, criticisms, etc., it takes up more general reference books such as encyclopedias, biographical dictionaries, special encyclopedias, and attempts to indicate their special value to the student of German literature.

Goedeke, Karl. Grundriss zur Geschichte der deutschen Dichtung aus den Quellen. 2. ganz neu bearb. Aufl. Dresden, Ehlermann, 1884–1934. v.1-10, 12-13. **R505**

v.1, Das Mittelalter; v.2, Reformationszeitalter; v.3, Vom Dreissigjährigen bis zum Siebenjährigen Kriege; v.4-5, Vom Siebenjährigen bis zum Weltkriege; v.6-7, Zeit des Weltkrieges; v.8-13, Vom Weltfrieden bis zur Französischen Revolution 1830.

The most complete bibliography of German literature, indispensable in the large reference library or for university work, but too exhaustive and special for the small library. Gives some biographical and critical comment on authors, critical and other notes on individual works, sources, etc., and exhaustive bibliographies of editions,

treatises, histories, biographical and critical articles, etc. Detailed index in each volume.

—— —— 3. neu bearb. Aufl. nach dem Tode des Verfassers in Verbindung mit Fachgelehrten fortgeführt von Edmund Goetze. Dresden, Ehlermann, 1906–12. v.4, pts. 1-4.

—— —— Neue Folge. (Fortführung von 1830 bis 1880) Im Auftrage der Preussischen Akademie der Wissenschaften, hrsg. von Georg Minde-Pouet. Dresden, Ehlermann, 1940- . Lfg. 1 (Bd.1, Bogen 1-13)- .

Lfg. 1, p.1-208, A-Amalia.

Johns Hopkins University. Library. Loewenberg Collection. Fifty years of German drama; a bibliography of modern German drama, 1880–1930, based on the Loewenberg Collection. Balt., Johns Hopkins Pr., 1941. 111p. $3.75. **R506**

Köhring, Hans. Bibliographie der Almanache, Kalender und Taschenbücher für die Zeit von ca. 1750–1860. Hamburg [Selbstverlag], 1929. 175p. **R507**

Körner, Josef. Bibliographisches Handbuch des deutschen Schrifttums. 3. völlig umgearb. und wesentlich verm. Aufl. Bern, Francke, 1949. 644p. **R508**

Previously published as an appendix to Scherer and Walzel, *Geschichte der deutschen Literatur* (R517) Lists books and periodical articles dealing with German literature and authors from ancient times to World War II. Arrangement is chronological by periods, each subdivided by subject. Subject and name indexes, though the latter lists only the names treated not the authors of articles.

In the research library will not be a substitute for Goedecke (R505) but will supplement it for recent materials. Should be useful in the smaller library not needing the wealth of detail given in Goedecke.

ANNUALS

Jahresberichte für neuere deutsche Literaturgeschichte, 1890–1915. Berlin, Behr, 1892–1919 v.1-26, pt.1. **R509**

An important annual survey, including books, pamphlets, theses and periodical articles. Continued by:

Jahresbericht über die wissenschaftlichen Erscheinungen auf den Gebiete der neueren deutschen Literatur, hrsg. von der Literaturarchiv gesellschaft in Berlin, 1921–35. Berlin, de Gruyter, 1924–39. n.F., v.1-15. **R510**

TRANSLATIONS INTO ENGLISH

Morgan, Bayard Quincy. A critical bibliography of German literature in English translation, 1481-

1927, with supplement embracing the years 1928–1935 . . . 2d ed. completely rev. and greatly augm. Stanford Univ., Calif., Stanford Univ. Pr.; Lond., Milford, Ox., Univ. Pr., 1938. 773p. $10. **R511**

1st ed. 1922.

The second edition has been completely revised and rearranged. "The works of a given author are now alphabetized by the original German titles instead of by those of the translations."—*Pref.*

The main list contains 10,797 numbered titles: followed by List A, Anonyms, 587 titles; List B, Bibliographies, 50 titles; List C, Collections, 577 titles; Index of translators, p.631-690; Supplement (1928–1935), p.693-773.

Davis, Edward Ziegler. Translations of German poetry in American magazines, 1741–1810; together with translations of other Teutonic poetry and original poems referring to the German countries. Phila., Americana Germanica Pr., 1905. 229p. **R512**

Goodnight, Scott Holland. German literature in American magazines prior to 1846. Madison, Wis., 1907. 264p. (Bull. of the Univ. of Wisconsin, no.188. Philology and literature ser. v.4, no.1) **R513**

Bibliography, arranged chronologically and by magazines, p.108-242; index of (1) authors, (2) magazines.

Haertel, Martin Henry. German literature in American magazines, 1846 to 1880. Madison, Wis., 1908. 188p. (Bull. of the Univ. of Wisconsin, no.263. Philology and literature ser. v.4, no.2) **R514**

Bibliography, p.95-178; index of (1) authors, (2) magazines.

Morgan, Bayard Quincy and **Hohlfeld, A. R.** German literature in British magazines, 1750–1860. Madison, Univ. of Wisconsin Pr., 1949. 364p. $5. **R515**

1750–1810 by Walter Roloff; 1811–1835 by Morton E. Mix, and 1836–1860 by Martha Nicolai.

A chronological list of magazine references with an alphabetical list of the German authors named. Preceded by an historical introduction giving a survey of magazine reflection of the British reception of German literature, 1750–1860.

History

Könnecke, Gustav. Bilderatlas zur Geschichte der deutschen Nationalliteratur. Eine Ergänzung zu jeder deutschen Literaturgeschichte. 2. verb. und verm. Aufl. Marburg, Elwert [1895]. 423p. il. **R516**

Scherer, Wilhelm and **Walzel, Oskar.** Geschichte der deutschen Literatur, mit einer Bibliographie von Josef Körner. 4. Aufl. Berlin, Askanischer Verlag, 1928. 942p. **R517**

A standard history with an excellent bibliography. For new edition of bibliography *see* R508.

Anthologies

Das Oxforder Buch deutscher Dichtung, vom 12ten bis zum 20sten Jahrhundert, hrsg. von H. G. Fiedler. Ox., Univ. Verlag, 1939. 647p. **R518**

2. Aufl. 1927, repr. 1939.

Dictionaries of authors and literature

Brümmer, Franz. Lexikon der deutschen Dichter und Prosaisten vom Beginn des 19. Jahrhunderts bis zur Gegenwart. 6. völlig neubearb. Aufl. Leipzig, Reclam, 1913. 8v. **R519**

A useful handbook containing brief biographical sketches and lists of works of some 9900 German, Austrian and Swiss authors. Very full for pseudonyms. Supplement in volume 8 brings the work down to end of 1912.

—— Lexikon der deutschen Dichter und Prosaisten von den ältesten Zeiten bis zum Ende des 18. Jahrhunderts. Leipzig, Reclam [1884]. 612p. (Reclam's Universal-Bibliothek, no.1941-45) **R520**

Geissler, Max. Führer durch die deutsche Literatur des zwanzigsten Jahrhunderts. Weimar, Duncker, 1913. 755p. **R521**

A biographical dictionary of modern German authors, principally of those living in 1913 but including names of a few who died after the beginning of the twentieth century. Gives only meager biographical data, but attempts to characterize each author and his work, to indicate his place in contemporary literature, and to give list of his writings.

Giebisch, Hans, Pichler, L. and **Vancsa, K.** Kleines österreichisches Literaturlexikon. Wien, Hollinek, 1948. 548p. (Buchreihe "Österreichische Heimat," Bd.8) **R522**

Biographical sketches of writers, titles of works, definitions and descriptions of literary expressions, etc., in one alphabet.

Kosch, Wilhelm. Deutsches Literatur-Lexikon; biographisches und bibliographisches Handbuch. 2. vollständig neu bearb. und stark erweiterte Aufl. Bern, Francke, 1947–49. v.1- . Sw. Fr. 1.20 per Lfg. (In progress) **R523**

Lfg. 1-9, A-Hasenauer (completes v.1).

Primarily a dictionary of German authors, emphasizing recent writers. Includes living persons. Bibliographies cite both original and critical works. Includes brief entries on literary forms, allusions, places, etc. First edition published 1927–30. This edition thoroughly revised and much enlarged.

Krüger, Hermann Anders. Deutsches Literatur-Lexikon; biographisches und bibliographisches Handbuch mit Motivübersichten und Quellennachweisen. München, Beck, 1914. 483p. **R524**

A useful dictionary of authors' names, titles of individual works, forms of literature, and topics, all in one alphabetical arrangement. Concise articles, some bibliographies.

Kürschners deutscher Literatur-Kalender hrsg. von Gerhard Lüdtke. Berlin, de Gruyter, 1879- . v.1- . Annual. (1949, DM. 16) **R525**

Title and imprint vary.

None published between volume 39, 1917, and volume 40, 1922. 1923 not published, 1924 being numbered volume 41. Beginning with volume 42, 1925, issued in two series: one continuing the *Literatur-Kalender*, the other becoming *Kürschners deutscher Gelehrten-Kalender* (S121).

A useful biographical record of German authors.

—— Nekrolog 1901–1935, hrsg. von Gerhard Lüdtke. Berlin, de Gruyter, 1936. 976 col. **R526**

Contents: Biographies reprinted from the *Literatur-Kalender* (R525), with date and place of death added, of some 3700 authors who have died since 1901; Two chronological lists arranged by years of (1) birth, (2) death.

Merker, Paul and **Stammler, Wolfgang.** Reallexikon der deutschen Literaturgeschichte, unter Mitwirkung zahlreicher Fachgelehrter. Berlin, de Gruyter, 1925–31. 4v. **R527**

An alphabetically arranged dictionary with signed articles and bibliographies on periods, types and kinds of German literature. No entries under personal names but there is an index by names to the articles in which they are mentioned.

Petry, Karl. Handbuch zur deutschen Literatur-Geschichte. Köln, B. Pick, 1949. 2v. **R528**

Contents: 1. Bd. Die deutsche Literatur von den Anfängen bis zum Ende des 16. Jahrhunderts; 2. Bd. Von der Barockdichtung bis zur Gegenwart.

—— —— Titel- und Namenregister, 27p. inserted at back of v.2.

Arranged chronologically by period. Includes biographical sketches which list works by an author as well as book and periodical material about him.

Schneider, Max. Deutsches Titelbuch. Ein Hilfsmittel zum Nachweis von Verfassern deutscher Literaturwerke. Berlin, Paschke, 1927. 798p. **R529**

Stammler, Wolfgang. Die deutsche Literatur des Mittelalters; Verfasserlexikon; unter Mitarbeit zahlreicher Fachgenossen. Berlin, de Gruyter, 1933–43. v.1-3. (In progress) **R530**

Issued in parts, v.1-3, A-R. v.3 completed by Karl Langosch.

Long scholarly articles signed by specialists. Detailed bibliographies. Treats German medieval authors, includes works in medieval Latin of significance in German literature and also anonymous works.

Individual authors

GOETHE

Berlin. Preussische Staatsbibliothek. Goethe. Berlin, Preussische Druckerei- und Verlags-Aktiengesellschaft, 1932. 10p., 224 col. **R531**

Fischer, Paul. Goethe-Wortschatz, ein sprachgeschichtliches Wörterbuch zu Goethes sämtlichen Werken. Leipzig, E. Rohmkopf, 1929. 905p. **R532**

Kippenberg, Anton. Katalog der Sammlung Kippenberg. 2. Ausg. Leipzig, Insel-Verlag, 1928. 2v. and index. il. **R533**

Includes manuscripts, editions, translations, etc.

Schmid, Günther. Goethe und die Naturwissenschaften; eine Bibliographie. Halle, Buchdruckerei des Waisenhauses, 1940. 620p. **R534**

Hrsg. im Namen der K. Leopoldnisch-Carolinisch Deutschen Akademie der Naturforscher von Emil Abderhalden.

Schmidt, Heinrich. Goethe-Lexikon. Leipzig, Kröner [1912]. 274p. **R535**

Yale University. Library. William A. Speck Collection of Goetheana. Goethe's works with the exception of Faust; a catalogue comp. by members of the Yale University Library Staff, ed., arr., and supplied with literary notes and preceded by an introduction and a biographical sketch of William A. Speck by Carl Frederick Schreiber. . . . New Haven, Yale Univ. Pr., 1940. 239p. facsim. $10. **R536**

The first volume of a comprehensive catalog of the William A. Speck collection of Goetheana. As planned, volume 2 will contain the record of the material on Faust, volume 3, biographical material, volume 4, addenda and general index.

Zeitler, Julius, *pseud.* Goethe-Handbuch; in Verbindung mit H. Bieber, A. v. Bloedau [u.A.]. Stuttgart, Metzler, 1916–18. 3v. **R537**

HEGEL

Glockner, Hermann. Hegel-Lexikon. . . . Stuttgart, Frommann, 1935–39. 4v. (Added title page: Georg Wilhelm Friedrich Hegel. Sämtliche Werke. Jubiläumsausgabe . . . 23.-26. Bd.) **R538**

KANT

Eisler, Rudolf. Kant-Lexikon; Nachschlagewerk zu Kants sämtlichen Schriften, Briefen und hand-

schriftlichen Nachlass. Hrsg. unter Mitwirkung der Kantgesellschaft. Berlin, Mittler, 1930. 642p.
R539

SCHILLER

Rudolph, Ludwig. Schiller-Lexikon; erläuterndes Wörterbuch zu Schiller's Dichterwerken, unter Mitwirkung von Karl Goldbeck. 2. Ausg. Berlin, Nicolay, 1890. 2v.
R540

Scandinavian

Bibliographie der nordischen Philologie, 1, 1925/26- . (Appears annually in Acta philologica scandinavica)
R541

Nordische bibliographie, hrsg. von dem Nordischen Institut der Universität Greifswald. Braunschweig, Westermann, 1928–31. v.1¹⁻³–2¹.   **R542**

   Contents: I. Reihe, Norwegen: 1. Hft. Ibsen-Bibliographie, bearb. von Fritz Meyen. 1928; 2. Hft. Norwegische Literatur (ausser Ibsen) bearb. von Fritz Meyen. 1928; 3. Hft., Knut Hamsun, bearb. von Fritz Meyen. 1931; II. Reihe, Schweden: 1. Hft. Selma Lagerlöf. 1930.

Oxford book of Scandinavian verse xvⅡth century to xxth century, chosen by Sir Edmund Gosse and W. A. Craigie. Ox., Clarendon Pr., 1925. 431p.
R543

Danish

Ehrencron-Müller, Holger. Forfatterlexikon omfattende Danmark, Norge og Island indtil 1814. København, Aschehoug, 1924–39. v.1-12; Suppl. 2. Kr. 15 per v.
R544

   v.1-8, A-Weg; v.9, Wei-Ø, Supplement; v.10-12, Bibliografi over Holbergs Skrifter; Supplement 2, includes corrections and additions to all volumes including the Holberg bibliography.
   An authoritative work, giving brief biographical data and full lists of writings for each author. Similar in plan to the dictionaries by Erslew (R546) and Halvorsen (R551) and linked to those two works by cross references in the case of many authors whose activity extended into the period after 1814.

Elkjaer, Kjeld, Haraldsted, Ib [and others]. Skønlitteratur i danske Tidsskrifter, 1913–1942; en Bibliografi. København, Folkebibliotekernes Bibliografiske Kontor, 1946. 236p.
R545

   Largely devoted to Danish literature but also includes references to articles that have appeared in Danish periodicals on foreign literatures.

Erslew, Thomas Hansen. Almindeligt Forfatter-Lexikon for Kongeriget Danmark med tilhørende Bilande, fra 1814 til 1840. Kjøbenhavn, Forlagsforeningens Forlag, 1843–53. 3v.
R546

―― ―― Supplement . . . indtil Utgangen of Aaret 1853. Kjøbenhavn, 1858–68. 3v.

Petersen, Carl Sophus and **Andersen, Vilhelm.** Illustreret dansk Litteraturhistorie. Kjøbenhavn, Gyldendal, 1924–34. 4v. il.
R547

   v.1, 1929; v.2, 1934; v.3, 1924; v.4, 1925. Issued in parts.
   Planned as a third revised edition of Peter Hansen's *Illustreret dansk Litteraturhistorie,* the standard illustrated history of Danish literature.

Woel, Cai Mogens. Dansk Forfatterleksikon; 338 Biografier over nulevende danske Forfattere. [København] Nordiske Landes Bogforlag, 1945. 360p. il. Kr. 30.
R548

Icelandic

See also Iceland, p.41.

Hermannsson, Halldór. Icelandic authors of today; with an appendix giving a list of works dealing with modern Icelandic literature. Ithaca, Cornell Univ. Lib., 1913. 69p. (Islandica v.6)
R549

   An excellent small biographical dictionary in English for living authors of some importance. Gives biographical data, list of works and references to books or periodicals containing fuller information.

Norwegian

Elster, Kristian. Illustreret Norsk litteratur historie. 2. utg. Oslo, Gyldendal, 1934–35. 6v. **R550**

Halvorsen, Jens Braage. Norsk forfatter-lexikon, 1814–1880. Paa grundlag af J. E. Krafts og Chr. Langes "Norsk forfatter-lexikon 1814–1856" samlet, redig. og udg. med understøttelse af statskassen af J. B. Halvorsen. Kristiania, Norske Forlagsforening, 1885–1908. 6v.
R551

Swedish

Ahlén, Bengt. Svenskt författarlexikon, 1900–1940: Biobibliografisk handbok till Sveriges moderna litteratur. . . . Stockholm, Svenskt Författarlexikons Förlag, 1942. 3v. ports. Kr. 40.
R552

   Volumes 1-2 are an alphabetical biographical dictionary with brief biographical sketches and lists of works by and about the authors. Volume 3 is a title index to works mentioned in the first two volumes.

Böök, Fredrik, Castren, Gunnar [and others]. Svenska litteraturens historia, under redaktion av Otto Sylwan. Stockholm, Norstedt, 1919–21. 3v. il.
R553

Schück, Henrik and **Warburg, Karl.** Illustrerad svensk litteratur-historia. 3. fullständigt omarb.

uppl. Stockholm, Geber, 1926–32. 7v. il. **R554**

Covers to 1914. Profusely illustrated. Includes a biographical section and a chronology.

Svensk litteraturhistorisk bibliografi, 1900–1935. Uppsala, Svenska Litteratursällskapet, 1939–47. Hft. 1-5. (Skrifter utg. af Svenska Litteratursällskapet) (In progress) Kr. 4 per hft. **R555**

Classed catalog. A cumulation of the material appearing in the following annual.

Svensk litteraturhistorisk bibliografi, no.1, 1880- . (Issued as a separately paged supplement to Samlaren: Tidskrift för svensk litteraturhistorisk forskning, 1880-) (no.64, 1945, pub. 1947) **R556**

Sveriges national-litteratur, 1500–1900, planlagdt af Oscar Levertin, utg. af Henrik Schück och Ruben G:son Berg. Stockholm, Bonnier [1907–19]. v.1-25$^{1-2}$. il. **R557**

An extensive collection of prose, poetical and dramatic selections, with biographies of authors represented. The arrangement is roughly chronological, some volumes being devoted to only one author, others including a number of authors. The lack of a general index makes the set difficult to use for quick reference.

ROMANCE LANGUAGES

Gröber, Gustav. Grundriss der romanischen Philologie. 1.-2. ed. Strassburg, Trübner, 1897–1906. v.1-2 in 4. o.p. **R558**

Volume 1 is second edition, 1904–06.
Important reference book, for advanced workers only. Not alphabetically arranged, but in chapters, with detailed indexes and many bibliographical references.

—————Neue Folge. Abt. 1. Geschichte der französischen Literatur. Berlin, de Gruyter, 1933–38. v.3-5.

Contents: Bd.3-4, Geschichte der mittelfranzöischen Literatur: I, Vers und Prosadichtung des 14. Jahrhunderts, Drama des 14. und 15. Jahrhunderts. 2. Aufl. bearb. von Stefan Hofer; II, Vers- und Prosadichtung des 15. Jahrhunderts. 2. Aufl. von Stefan Hofer; Bd.5, Frankreichs Literatur im XVI. Jahrhundert, von Walter Mönch.
v.1-2, to cover Altfranzöischen Dichtung; v.6- , 17. Jahrhundert- . (v.4, by Heinrich Morf, dropped from series.)

Palfrey, Thomas Rossman, Fucilla, Joseph Guerin and **Holbrook, William Collar.** A bibliographical guide to the romance languages and literature. 3d ed. Evanston, Ill., Chandler, 1947. 84p. **R559**

1st ed. 1939.
Contents: (1) General romance bibliography; (2) French language and literature (including Provençal, French-Swiss, Belgian); (3) Italian; (4) Portuguese and Brazilian; (5) Spanish, Catalan, Spanish-American; (6) Roumanian.

Kritischer Jahresbericht über die Fortschritte der romanischen Philologie, 1890–1912. Erlangen, Junge, 1892–1915. v.1-13. **R560**

An important bibliography of books and articles on Romance philology; i.e., language and literature. In chapters, not in list form, and so somewhat difficult to use for purposes of quick reference, but important for the large amount of material included and for the analysis of periodicals. Discontinued.

Jahrbuch für romanische und englische Sprache und Literatur. Berlin, Brockhaus, 1859–76. 15v. **R561**

None published 1872–73. Publisher varies. Contains a systematic bibliography of Romance languages and literatures.

—————"Verzeichniss der Mitarbeiter und ihrer Beiträge zu den ersten fünf Bänden." (In volume for 1863)

Zeitschrift für romanische Philologie. Supplement Heft: Bibliographie, 1875- . Halle, 1878- . (v.58/59, 1938/39, pub. 1943) **R562**

Volumes 39-43, 1914–23, never published.
An important current bibliography listing books and periodical articles on the language and literatures of the various romance languages.

Belgian writers (French)

Doutrepont, Georges. Histoire illustrée de la littérature française en Belgique; précis méthodique. Bruxelles, Didier, 1939. 398p. il. 45fr. **R563**

Includes many bio-bibliographies.

Dumont-Wilden, Louis. Anthologie des écrivains belges, poètes et prosateurs. Paris, Georges Crès, 1917. 2v. **R564**

Gives prose and poetical selections from Belgian authors who wrote in French, and biographies and bibliographies of authors included.

Hanlet, Camille. Les écrivains belges contemporains de langue française, 1800–1946. Liége, Dessain, 1946. 2v. 1302p. il. **R565**

An extensive survey of all Belgian authors writing in French from the eighteenth century to date. The length of the biography and critical annotation varies from a few lines to several pages. For many writers bibliographies of works about the person are included.

Liebrecht, Henri and **Rency, Georges.** Histoire illustrée de la littérature belge de langue française (des origines à 1925). Bruxelles, Vanderlinden, 1926. 454p. il. **R566**

Contains many illustrations, bibliographies and a general index of names.

Seyn, Eugène de. Dictionnaire des écrivains belges, bio-bibliographie. Bruges, Editions "Excelsior," 1930–31. 2v. il. **R567**

Includes writers born in modern Belgium, in ancient Flanders and Hainault and in the portions of Holland which once formed part of the duchy of Brabant, and, from 1830 on, naturalized as well as native citizens of Belgium and other persons of long residence there. Articles are of medium length, with lists of works *by* the writers included but little or no bibliography *about* them. Includes some names not included in de Seyn's *Dictionnaire biographique des sciences, des lettres et des arts en Belgique* (S73).

French
Bibliography

Alden, Douglas W., Jasper, G. R. and Waterman, R. P. Bibliography of critical and biographical references for the study of contemporary French literature. Books and articles published from 1940 to 1948. N.Y., Stechert-Hafner, 1949. 106p. (Modern Language Assoc. of Amer. French VII, Pub. no.1) $1.75. **R568**

A very useful bibliography of recent material. In two parts: pt.1, General subjects in a classified arrangement; pt.2, Author-subjects arranged alphabetically.

Includes both books and periodical articles.

To be continued by annual supplements.

Bady, René. Introduction à l'étude de la littérature française. Fribourg, Librairie de l'Univ. Fribourg, 1943. 155p. **R569**

A manual and guide to the basic materials for the study of French literature. Fairly elementary.

Critical bibliography of French literature; general ed., D. C. Cabeen. v.1, The Mediaeval period, ed. by Urban T. Holmes, Jr. Syracuse, Univ. Pr., 1947. 256p. **R570**

The first volume of what promises to be a valuable new series. Arranged as a chronological survey, each chapter is contributed by a specialist, and lists special references, bibliographies, outstanding editions, specific studies, etc. Reviews of many works are cited. Of first importance for its period.

Other volumes of the series are expected to cover from the sixteenth to the mid-twentieth centuries.

Dreher, Silpelitt and Rolli, Madeline. Bibliographie de la littérature française, 1930–1939. Complément à la Bibliographie de H. P. Thieme. Genève, Droz, 1948–49. 438p. **R571**

Appeared in fascicles. Includes material published 1930–39 on the authors treated by Thieme (R578).

Escoffier, Maurice. Le mouvement romantique, 1788–1850: Essai de bibliographie synchronique et méthodique. Paris, Maison du Bibliophile, 1934. 428p. **R572**

Arranged chronologically. Under each year works are listed by type: poetry, fiction, religion, philosophy, history, science, etc. Indexes of authors, anonymous works, collections and keepsakes, periodicals, binders.

Foulet, Lucien. Bibliography of medieval French literature for college libraries. Ed. by Albert Schinz and George Underwood. New Haven, Yale Univ. Pr.; Ox., Univ. Pr., 1915. 30p. **R573**

A useful brief list of the most worth-while works including both reference books and texts.

Giraud, Jeanne. Manuel de bibliographie littéraire pour les xvie, xviie, xviiie siècles français, 1921–1935. Paris, Vrin, 1939. 304p. (Publications de la Faculté des Lettres de l'Université de Lille, II) **R574**

Designed to serve as a supplement, for works published 1921–1935, to Lanson, *Manuel bibliographique* (R576) and to Thieme, *Bibliographie de la littérature française* (R578).

Lachèvre, Frédéric. Bibliographie sommaire des keepsakes et autres recueils collectifs de la période romantique, 1823–1848. Paris, Giraud-Badin, 1929. 2v. (Les Bibliographies nouvelles. Collection du Bulletin du bibliophile) **R575**

Lanson, Gustave. Manuel bibliographique de la littérature française moderne, 1500–1900. Nouv. éd., rev. et augm. Paris, Hachette, 1921. 1820p. **R576**

1st ed. in 5v. 1909–1912; rev. ed., with suppl., 1v. 1914. 1746p. The 1921 edition contains an additional section, "Littérature de la guerre."

An important bibliography of modern French literature, selective, not complete, including some 23,363 entries. Indexes a considerable amount of analytical material including articles from more than 800 periodicals.

For continuation *see* Giraud (R574).

Talvart, Hector and Place, Joseph. Bibliographie des auteurs modernes de langue française, 1928–49. v.1-9. (In progress) 2000fr. **R577**

v.1-9, A-Huysmans.

A new bibliography of French authors, planned on a large scale, which promises to be invaluable when completed, and is very useful even in its present state. Arranged alphabetically by authors, giving generally for each author: (1) a biographical sketch; (2) list of writings and editions; (3) minor literary works, i.e., addresses, prefaces, journals edited, etc.; (4) lists of biographical and critical works and articles about the author, including a large amount of analytical material.

Each volume includes material published up to the year of its publication, i.e., v.1, covers 1801–1927, v.9, 1801–1948.

Thieme, Hugo Paul. Bibliographie de la littérature française de 1800 à 1930. . . . Paris, E. Droz, 1933. 3v. **R578**

v.1-2, A-Z; v.3, Civilization.

A new edition of an important reference bibliography which includes both works by an author and extensive bibliographies of biographical and critical material about him. Greatly enlarged from the earlier edition (1907) in two ways: (1) by bringing up to date the lists by and about the authors included in the earlier edition, and (2) by the inclusion of many additional authors not treated in the earlier work; e.g., the first volume, A-K, includes about 700 authors not listed in the first edition.

For continuation *see* Dreher (R571) and Giraud (R574).

Will, Samuel F. A bibliography of American studies on the French renaissance (1500–1600). Urbana, Univ. of Illinois Pr., 1940. 151p. $1.50.
R579

Includes books and periodical articles published in America or by Americans from 1886–1937 on France in the sixteenth century. 1895 items.

Annuals

Almanach des lettres, 1947- . Paris, Éd. de Flore et La gazette des lettres, 1946- . Annual. (1949, 345fr.) **R580**

An annual survey of French literature in different fields with a brief biographical section of French and foreign authors, listing their works with dates of publication; lists of academies, societies, literary prizes, etc.

History

Bédier, Joseph and **Hazard, Paul.** Littérature française. Nouv. éd. ref. et augm. sous la dir. de Pierre Martino. Paris, Larousse, 1948–49. 2v. il. v.1, 3200fr.; v.2, 3300fr. **R581**

1st ed., 1923, had title: *Histoire de la littérature française illustrée.* This edition thoroughly revised and reset. Lavishly illustrated.

Calvet, J. Histoire de la littérature française. Paris, de Gigord, 1931–38. v.1-6, 8-9. il. **R582**

v.1, Le moyen age, par Robert Bossuat. 1931; v.2-3, La renaissance, par Raoul Morçay. 1933–35. 2v.; v.4, Les écrivains classiques, par H. Gaillard de Champris. 1934; v.5, La littérature religieuse de François de Sales à Fénelon, par J. Calvet. 1938; v.6, De Télémaque à Candide, par Albert Cherel. 1933; v.8, Le romantisme, par Pierre Moreau. 1932; v.9, Le réalisme, par René Dumesnil. 1936.

Godefroy, Frédéric Eugène. Histoire de la littérature française depuis le 16e siècle jusqu'à nos jours. 2. éd. Paris, Gaume, 1878–1881. 10v. **R583**

Histoire littéraire de la France; ouvrage commencé par des religieux bénédictins de la Congrégation de Saint Maur, et continué par des membres de l'Institut (Académie des Inscriptions et Belles-Lettres). Paris, Impr. Nationale, 1733–1941. v.1-38, fasc. 1. (In progress) **R584**

Title and imprint vary.

Twelve volumes of this work were published by the Maurists, 1733–1763. Volumes 11 and 12 were reprinted 1841 and 1830.

Index to v.9-15 in v.15; to v.16-23 in v.23; to v.25-32 in v.32.

The most detailed history of French literature, beginning with the earliest period and so full that the thirty-eighth volume has only advanced part way through the fourteenth century. Made up of signed contributions by specialists, containing very detailed information, and especially in the later volumes, very full bibliographical references. Contains some articles on literary subjects, forms, movements, etc., but consists in the main of biographical and critical articles on individual authors including many not treated in other histories.

Lanson, Gustave. Histoire illustrée de la littérature française; le moyen âge, du moyen âge à la renaissance, le xvie siècle, le xviie siècle, le xviiie siècle, époque contemporaine. Paris, Hachette [c1923]. 2v. il. **R585**

This edition profusely illustrated. Also frequently reprinted without the illustrations, in a one-volume edition. A standard work.

Petit de Julleville, Louis. Histoire de la langue et de la littérature française des origines à 1900. Paris, Colin, 1896–99. 8v. il. **R586**

An important history for reference use, chapters written by different authorities. Bibliographies, many good illustrations.

Wright, Charles Henry Conrad. History of French literature. Ox., Univ. Pr., 1925. 990p. **R587**

One of the best histories of French literature in English, especially useful for reference purposes because of the full, annotated bibliography, p.899-961, and the biographical dictionary of twentieth century authors, p.845-96.

See also Monglond, *La France révolutionnaire et impériale* (V230).

Anthologies

☙ Many anthologies of French poetry and prose are particularly useful for their bio-bibliographical notes on the authors included. Much of this information is not easily found elsewhere. Only a few of these collections are included here, others will be found listed in Thieme (R578), Lanson (R576), etc.

Ali-Bert. Anthologie des poètes néoclassiques; morceau choisis, précédés de notices bio-bibliographiques. Paris, Messein [1932–33]. 2v. **R588**

Anthologie des essayistes français contemporains. Paris, Éditions Kra [1934]. 550p. **R589**

Bio-bibliographical notes.

Association des Écrivains Combattants. Anthologie des écrivains morts à la guerre, 1914-1918. . . . Amiens, Malfère, 1924–26. 5v. **R590**

Gives biographies and bibliographies; includes many minor names.

Bever, Adolphe van. Poètes d'aujourd'hui, morceaux choisis, accompagnés de notices biographiques. Paris, Mercure de France, 1947. 3v. R591

Gives selected poems of modern poets, with useful biographical notes and bibliographies.

—— Poètes du terroir du xvᵉ siècle au xxᵉ siècle, textes choisis, accompagnés de notices biographiques, d'une bibliographie. Paris, Delagrave, 1914. 4v. R592

A useful regional anthology, grouped by the names of the old provinces. For each author represented there is given a biographical sketch, a bibliography and selected poems. The biographies and bibliographies are especially useful and there is a general index of authors and places in volume 4.

—— Anthologie littéraire de l'Alsace et de la Lorraine, xiiᵉ-xxᵉ siècles. Paris, Delagrave, 1920. 415p. R593

Mazade, Fernand. Anthologie des poètes français des origines à nos jours. Paris, Librairie de France [1928?]. 4v. R594

Includes biographical sketches.

Oxford book of French verse, 13th-20th century, chosen by St. John Lucas. Ox., Clarendon Pr., 1926. 553p. 8s. 6d.; $3. R595

Some biographical and bibliographical notes, indexes of writers and first lines.

Walch, Gérard. Anthologie des poètes français contemporains; le Parnasse et les écoles postérieures au Parnasse (1866-[1925/32]). Morceaux choisis, accompagnés de notices bio- et bibliographiques et de nombreux autographes. Nouv. éd. Paris, Delagrave, 1932-34. 4v. il. R596

v.1, 1866-1925; v.2, 1866-1926; v.3, 1866-1929; v.4, 1866-1932.

An earlier edition (Paris, Delagrave, 1906-14. 3v.) and its supplements, *Poètes d'hier et d'aujourd'hui* (Paris, Delagrave, 1919. 514p.) and *Poètes nouveaux* (Paris, Delagrave, 1923. 483p.) contain some poets omitted from this later edition.

Drama

Rondel, Auguste. La bibliographie dramatique et les collections de théâtre. Lille, Lefebvre-Ducrocq, 1913. 31p. R597

Reprinted from the *Bulletin* de la Société de l'Histoire du Théâtre, Jan.–Mar. 1913. Also in Association les Bibliothécaires Français, *Bibliothèques, livres et libraries,* 3. série, 1914.

Includes useful comments on the principal bibliographies and dictionaries of French drama.

Annales du théâtre et de la musique. 1.-39. année. 1875-1913. Paris, Charpentier, 1876-1914. 39v. R598

An annual survey of the work of the theaters, operas and concerts of Paris, giving for each theater a record,

with some comment, of the plays produced there during the year and, in case of new plays, cast of characters and synopses of plots.

Brenner, Clarence Dietz. A bibliographical list of plays in the French language, 1700-1789. Berkeley, Calif., 1947. 229p. R599

Lists more than 11,000 dramatic compositions by author and title. Analyzes many collections.

Champion, Édouard. La Comédie-Française, 1927-37. Nogent-le-Rotrou, Daupeley-Gouveneur, 1934-39. v.1-5. R600

1927-32; 1933-34; 1935; 1936; 1937.
A continuation of Joannidès (R601).

Joannidès, A. La Comédie-Française de 1680 à 1900. Dictionnaire général des pièces et des auteurs, avec une préface de Jules Claretie. Paris, Plon-Nourrit, 1901. 136p., 274p. 19 facsim. o.p. R601

Contents: (1) Alphabetical title list of plays, giving title, author's name, date of first performance; (2) Alphabetical list of authors with short title list of their works; (3) Chronological list, showing plays given each year and number of performances of each; (4) Appendixes giving plays of the Comédie Française presented at the Odéon, in the provinces, or at London, list of poems recited at the Comédie, etc.

—— La Comédie-Française, 1680-1920. Tableau des représentations par auteurs et par pièces. Paris, Plon-Nourrit, 1921. 138p. R602

Contents: (1) Author list giving short titles of plays, date of first performance and total number of times each has been played down to 1920; (2) Title index.

Lancaster, Henry Carrington. The Comédie Française, 1680-1701; plays, actors, spectators, finances. Balt., Johns Hopkins Pr.; Lond., Milford; Paris, Les Belles Lettres, 1941. 210p. R603

—— History of French dramatic literature in the 17th century. Balt., Johns Hopkins Pr.; Paris, Presses Universitaires, 1929-42. 5v. in 9. R604

A detailed history with lists of plays, bibliographical footnotes, etc. Volume 5 includes a subject index, a finding list of plays and a general index to all five volumes.

—— Sunset, a history of Parisian drama in the last years of Louis xiv, 1701-1715. Balt., Johns Hopkins Pr.; Lond., Milford; Paris, Belles-Lettres, 1945. 365p. R605

A sequel to the foregoing, compiled on the same plan, devoted primarily to plays acted or published in or near Paris. Includes additions and corrections to the *History . . . in the 17th century* (R604), and a list of plays acted at the Comédie Française, 1701-Sept. 1715, supplementing his work on the *Comédie Française,* 1680-1701 (R603).

Soleinne, Martineau de. Bibliothèque dramatique de Monsieur de Soleinne. Catalogue rédigé par

P. L. Jacob, bibliophile. Paris, Alliance des Arts, 1843–45. 7v. o.p. **R606**

t.1, Théâtre oriental; grec et romain; latin moderne; ancien théâtre français; théâtre français moderne depuis Jodelle jusqu'à Racine. Supplément; t.2, Théâtre français depuis Racine jusqu'à Victor Hugo. Théâtre des provinces. Théâtre français à l'étranger; t.3, Suite du théâtre français; recueils manuscrits; recueils divers; théâtre de la cour; ballets; répertoires des théâtres de Paris; théâtre burlesque; théâtre de société; proverbes dramatiques; théâtre d'éducation; pièces satiriques; pièces en patois; dialogues. Appendice. Autographes; t.4, Théâtre italien; espagnol et portugais; allemand; anglais; suédois, flamand et hollandais, russe et polonais, turc, grec et valaque; t.5, 1. pt., Écrits relatifs au théâtre. 2. pt., Estampes et dessins; [t.6], Livres doubles et livres omis; [t.7], Table générale.

The catalog of a very useful collection covering the theater from ancient times through the first part of the nineteenth century. Particularly strong in all forms of the French theater, including drama, ballets, burlesque, etc. Also includes works of the theater in many other European countries.

—— —— Table des pièces de théâtre décrites dans le catalogue de la bibliothèque de M. de Soleinne, par Charles Brunet. Pub. par Henri de Rothschild. Paris, D. Morgand, 1914. 491p.

Useful title index to over 5000 plays giving for each title brief information: whether prose or verse, kind of play (comedy, tragedy, etc.), number of acts, author's name, and reference to its number in the Soleinne catalog.

Fiction

DeJongh, William Frederick Jekel. A bibliography of the novel and short story in French from the beginning of printing till 1600. Albuquerque, N.Mex., Univ. of New Mexico Pr., 1944. 79p. (Univ. of New Mexico. Bull. Bibliographical ser. v.1, no.1) 25c. **R607**

336 items arranged chronologically.

Jones, Silas Paul. A list of French prose fiction from 1700–1750, with a brief introd. N.Y., Wilson, 1939. 150p. $3.50. **R608**

Chronological list with detailed index to authors, titles and pseudonyms. Locates copies.

Williams, Ralph Coplestone. Bibliography of the 17th-century novel in France. N.Y., Century, 1931. 355p. **R609**

An alphabetical list, followed by a chronological list. Additions and corrections are given in an article by F. P. Rolfe, "On the bibliography of 17th-century prose fiction" (*PMLA* 49:1071-86, Dec. 1934).

Poetry

Bédier, Joseph. Les légendes épiques; recherches sur la formation des chansons de geste . . . 3. éd. . . . Paris, Champion, 1926–29. 4v. **R610**

Gautier Léon. Bibliographie des chansons de geste. (Complément des Épopées françaises) Paris, Welter, 1897. 315p. **R611**

Forms volume 5 of his *Épopées françaises* (R612).

A comprehensive bibliography in two parts. The first part is a classed list of general works, the second is devoted to works about individual "Chansons."

—— Les épopées françaises. Étude sur les origines et l'histoire de la littérature nationale. 2d. éd., entièrement refondue. Paris, Palme, 1878–97. 5v. **R612**

Langlois, Ernest. Table des noms propres de toute nature compris dans les chansons de geste imprimées. Paris, Bouillon, 1904. 674p. **R613**

Lachèvre, Frédéric. Bibliographie des recueils collectifs de poésies du xvie siècle (du Jardin de plaisance, 1502, aux Recueils de Toussaint du Bray, 1609). . . . Paris, Champion, 1922. 613p. il. **R614**

Subtitles: Donnant: (1) La description et le contenu des recueils; (2) Une table générale des pièces anonymes ou signées d'initiales de ces recueils (titre et premier vers), avec l'indication du nom des auteurs pour celles qui ont pu être attribuées.

—— Bibliographie des recueils collectifs de poésies publiés de 1597 à 1700. . . . Paris, Leclerc, 1901–05. 4v. **R615**

Subtitle: Donnant: (1) La description et le contenu des recueils; (2) Les pièces de chaque auteur classées dans l'ordre alphabétique du premier vers, précédée d'une notice bio-bibliographique, etc.; (3) Une table générale des pièces anonymes ou signées d'initiales (titre et premier vers) avec l'indication des noms des auteurs pour celles qui ont pu leur être attribuées; (4) La reproduction des pièces qui n'ont pas été relevées par les derniers éditeurs des poètes figurant dans les recueils collectifs; (5) Une table des noms cités dans le texte et le premier vers des pièces des recueils collectifs. Etc., etc.

—— Les recueils collectifs de poésies libres et satiriques publiés depuis 1600 jusqu'à la mort de Théophile (1626). Bibliographie de ces recueils et bio-bibliographie des auteurs qui y figurent . . . Paris, Champion, 1914–22. 597p. and suppl. 95p. (His Le libertinage au xviie siècle—IV) **R616**

—— Bibliographie sommaire de l'Almanach des muses (1765–1833). . . . Paris, Giraud-Badin, 1928. 206p. (Les bibliographies nouvelles. Collection du Bulletin du bibliophile. no.12) **R617**

Subtitle: Description et collation de chaque année. Tables: 1e des auteurs et du nombre de leurs pièces (1550 environ); 2e des écrivains étrangers traduits ou imités (125 environ); 3e des principaux noms de personnes auxquelles les pièces sont adressées ou qui ont été l'objet de portraits, epigrammes, etc. (800 environ); des principaux sujets traités dans les poésies (200 e viron); 5° des airs gravés ou imprimés; 6° du titre et du premier vers des pièces d'un certain nombre d'auteurs.

Mendès, Catulle. Le mouvement poétique français de 1867 à 1900. Rapport . . . suivi d'un Dictionnaire bibliographique et critique et d'une Nomenclature chronologique de la plupart des poètes français du XIX° siècle. Paris, Impr. Nationale, E. Fasquelle, 1903. 218p., 340p. **R618**

The *Dictionnaire* is arranged alphabetically, listing for each poet the titles of his works and extracts from critical opinions with references to source.

Cooper, Clarissa Burnham. Women poets of the twentieth century in France, a critical bibliography. N.Y., King's Crown Pr., 1943. 317p. $2.50. **R619**

Contents: Introduction, p.3-55; Critical bibliography with biographical notes and specimens of poetry, p.59-11; General reference books and articles, p.313-17.

Individual authors

❧ The following list does not include all French authors for whom important reference bibliographies have been published. In the main, it includes authors for whom two types of reference aids are available, i.e., bibliographies and dictionaries. Bibliographies of many authors are listed in Lanson's *Manuel bibliographique* (R576), and the lists of works given under authors' names in the *Catalogue général* of the Bibliothèque Nationale (A35) serve as useful bibliographies especially in the cases of voluminous authors (e.g., Balzac, Dumas, etc.) for whom title indexes are given in that catalog. In many cases, these author bibliographies have been published as separates by the Bibliothèque Nationale and can be acquired by libraries which do not have the full catalog.

BALZAC

Royce, William Hobart. Balzac bibliography. . . . Chic., Univ. of Chic. Pr. [c1929–30]. 2v. $5. **R620**

v.1, Writings relative to the life and works of Balzac; 2, Indexes, (a) by periodicals, (b) topical index.

Cerfberr, Anatole and **Christophe, Jules.** Répertoire de la Comédie humaine de H. de Balzac. Paris, Lévy, 1887. 563p. **R621**

A dictionary of characters; gives for each character a brief description, indicates its connection with the plot of the story and refers to title of the novel or story in which the character appears; does not refer to chapters. Two English translations have been published as follows:

—— Repertory of the Comédie humaine tr. by W. McSpadden. Phila., Avil Pub. Co., 1902.

522p. (Balzac. Works. Popular Lib. ed. v.36) o.p. **R622**

—— Compendium, H. de Balzac's Comédie humaine, tr. and ed. by J. Rudd. Phila., Gebbie Pub. Co., 1899. 583p. o.p. **R623**

Gillette, Fredericka B. Title index to the works of Honoré de Balzac. Bost., Bost. Bk. Co., 1909. 24p. (Bull. of bibliography pamphlets, no.19) 50c. **R624**

Reprinted from the *Bulletin of bibliography*, v.5, nos. 6-8, July, October 1908, January 1909.

An index of all the titles to be found in two French editions and four English translations of Balzac's complete works. French and English titles are given in one alphabet and all references to any one story are given under each form of the title.

BAUDELAIRE

Bandy, William Thomas. A word index to Baudelaire's poems. Madison, Wis., 1939. 92p. **R625**

Based on volume 1 of Baudelaire's *Oeuvres complètes*, edited by Jacques Crépet (Paris, Conard, 1922).

BEYLE

Cordier, Henri. Bibliographie Stendhalienne. . . . Paris, Champion, 1914. 416p. il. (Half title: Oeuvres complètes de Stendhal, pub. sous la direction d'Édouard Champion) **R626**

Benedetto, Luigi Foscolo. Arrigo Beyle Milanese: Bilancio dello Stendhalismo italiano a cent' anni dalla morte dello Stendhal. Firenze, Sansoni, 1942. 723p. **R627**

Bibliografia critica degli scritti italiani relativi a Stendhal, p.19-691.

Bibliographie Stendhalienne, 1928/29- . Grenoble, Arthaud, 1930- . Biennial. (1944/46, pub. 1948. 250fr.) **R628**

1928/29–1936/37 ed. by Louis Royer; 1938/43- ed. by V. del Litto.

CORNEILLE

Picot, Émile. Bibliographie Cornélienne; ou, Description raisonnée de toutes les éditions des oeuvres de Pierre Corneille, des imitations ou traductions qui en ont été faites, et des ouvrages relatifs à Corneille et à ses écrits. Paris, Fontaine, 1876. 552p. **R629**

Le Verdier, Pierre and **Pelay, E.** Additions à la Bibliographie Cornélienne. Rouen, Lestringant, 1908. 251p. **R630**

Marty-Laveaux, Charles Joseph. Lexique de la langue de Pierre Corneille. Paris, Hachette, 1868. 2v. **R631**

Volumes 11-12 of the *Grands écrivains* edition of Corneille.

LA FONTAINE

Rochambeau, Achille Lacroix de Vimeur, *comte de*. Bibliographie des oeuvres de La Fontaine. Paris, Rouquette, 1911. 669p. **R632**

Regnier, Henri. Lexique de la langue de J. de La Fontaine avec une introduction grammaticale. Paris, Hachette, 1892. 2v. **R633**

Volumes 10-11 of the *Grands écrivains* edition of La Fontaine.

LA ROCHEFOUCAULD

Regnier, Henri. Lexique de la langue de La Rochefoucauld, avec une introduction grammaticale. Paris, Hachette, 1883. 464p. **R634**

Volume 3² of the *Grands écrivains* edition of La Rochefoucauld.

MOLIÈRE

Desfeuilles, Arthur. Notice bibliographique. Paris, Hachette, 1893. 326p. **R635**

Volume 11 of the *Grands écrivains* edition of Molière.

—— and Desfeuilles, Paul. Lexique de la langue de Molière, avec une introduction grammaticale. Paris, Hachette, 1900. 2v. **R636**

Volumes 12-13 of the *Grands écrivains* edition of Molière.

Fritsche, Hermann. Molière-studien; ein Namenbuch zu Molière's Werken, mit philologischen und historischen Erläuterungen. 2. verbesserte und vermehrte Ausg. Berlin, Weidmann, 1887. 235p. **R637**

Lacroix, Paul. Bibliographie Moliéresque. 2. éd. rev., corr. et considérablement augm. Paris, Fontaine, 1875. 412p. **R638**

Livet, Charles Louis. Lexique de la langue de Molière comparée à celle des écrivains de son temps, avec des commentaires de philologie historique et grammaticale. Paris, Impr. Nationale, 1895-97. 3v. **R639**

Saintonge, Paul Frédéric and **Christ, Robert Wilson.** Fifty years of Molière studies, a bibliography, 1892-1941. Balt., Johns Hopkins Pr.; Lond., Milford, 1942. 313p. (Johns Hopkins studies in Romance literatures and languages. Extra v. XIX) $3. **R640**

3316 numbered items.

MONTAIGNE

Richou, Gabriel. Inventaire de la collection des ouvrages et documents réunis par J. F. Payen et J. B. Bastide sur Michel de Montagne. . . . Paris, Téchener, 1878. 396p. **R641**

Villey-Desmeserets, Pierre. Lexique de la langue des Essais, et index des noms propres, . . . avec la collaboration de Grace Norton. Bordeaux, Impr. Nouvelle F. Pech, 1933. 727p. (Montaigne, M. E. de. Les essais . . . pub. d'après l'exemplaire de Bordeaux, 1933. v.5) **R642**

Contents: Lexique, p.5-697; Index du noms propres contenus dans les essais, p.699-727.

Forms volume 5 of the *Édition municipale de Bordeaux* of Montaigne.

RABELAIS

Plan, Pierre Paul. Bibliographie Rabelaisienne les éditions de Rabelais de 1532 à 1711. Catalogue raisonné descriptif et figuré, illustré de cent soixante-six facsimilés. . . . Paris, Impr. Nationale, 1904. 277p. **R643**

Săineanu, Lazar. La langue de Rabelais. Paris, Boccard, 1922-23. 2v. **R644**

Not in dictionary form. A discussion under types of words with an alphabetical index to words.

RACINE

Marty-Laveaux, Charles Joseph. Lexique de la langue de J. Racine, avec une introduction grammaticale, précédé d'une étude sur le style de Racine par P. Mesnard et suivi des tableaux des représentations de Corneille et de Racine par E. Despois. Paris, Hachette, 1873. cxlivp., 616p. **R645**

Volume 8 of the *Grands écrivains* edition of Racine.

Williams, Edwin E. Racine depuis 1885; bibliographie raisonnée des livres—articles—comptes rendus critiques relatifs à la vie et l'oeuvre de Jean Racine, 1885-1939. Balt., Johns Hopkins Pr.; Lond., Milford, 1940. 279p. (Johns Hopkins studies in Romance literatures and languages. Extra v.16) **R646**

SCARRON

Magne, Émile. Bibliographie générale des oeuvres de Scarron, documents inédits. . . . Paris, Giraud-Badin, 1924. 302p. **R647**

Richardson, Leonard T. Lexique de la langue des oeuvres burlesques de Scarron, avec un introduction grammaticale. Aix-en-Provence, Nicollet, 1930. 284p.   **R648**

Thèse, Université de Grenoble.

SÉVIGNÉ

Fitzgerald, Edward. Dictionary of Madame de Sévigné, ed. and annotated by Mary Eleanor Fitzgerald Kerrich. Lond. and N.Y., Macmillan, 1914. 2v. il. o.p.   **R649**

Sommer, Jean Édouard. Lexique de la langue de Madame de Sévigné. Paris, Hachette, 1866. 2v.   **R650**

Volumes 13-14 of the *Grands écrivains* edition of Madame de Sévigné's works.

ZOLA

Patterson, J. G. Zola dictionary; the characters of the Rougon-Macquart novels of Emile Zola, with a biographical and critical introduction, synopses of the plots, bibliographical note, map, genealogy, etc. Lond., Routledge; N.Y., Dutton, 1912. 232p.   **R651**

Contains note on the French editions and the English translations, short synopses of plots, the dictionary of characters, and an alphabetical list of principal scenes. The dictionary gives brief descriptions of each character but no illustrative quotations, and refers only to the title of the story in which a character appears, not to specific chapters.

Ramond, F. C. Les personnages des Rougon-Macquart pour servir à la lecture et à l'étude de l'oeuvre de Émile Zola. Paris, Fasquelle, 1901. 378p.   **R652**

Includes more names (e.g., names of the animals and inanimate characters) than Patterson's dictionary (R651), and the summaries of characters are fuller. Bracketed numbers refer to pages in the Fasquelle edition of Zola's novels.

Italian

Bibliography

Avola, Niccolò Domenico. Bibliografia degli studi sulla letteratura italiana, (1920-34). Milano, "Vita e pensiero," 1938-49. pt.1-5. (In progress)   **R653**

pt.1-5, A-Z.

Ferrari, Luigi. Onomasticon; repertorio biobibliografico degli scrittori italiani dal 1501 al 1850. Milano, Hoepli, 1947. 708p. (Bibliotheca veneta, collana di opere erudite a cura della Scuola Storico-Filologica delle Venezie . . . della R. Università di Padova. [v.1])   **R654**

An index to almost 50,000 individual biographies of authors contained in some 375 collections, general and local. The list of these collections, p.xxi-xliv, forms a bibliography of collected works of Italian biography with indication of location in some Italian library.

Fucilla, Joseph G. Universal author repertoire of Italian essay literature. N.Y., Vanni, 1941. 534p. $10.   **R655**

An index to biographical and critical articles on authors, primarily Italian, but also including non-Italian writers of many countries, contained in 1697 collections of Italian essays. Arranged alphabetically by subject.

Hall, Robert Anderson. Bibliography of Italian linguistics. Balt., Linguistic Soc. of Amer., 1941. 543p. (Special pub. of the Linguistic Soc. of America) $7.50.   **R656**

Aims to list "all material dealing with the scientific study of the history and description of the Italian language and dialects, and with the Romance language in general insofar as Italian and its dialects are involved." Includes material published since about 1860, arranged in four classes: History of the Italian language, Description of the Italian language, Italian dialectology, and History of Italian linguistics; and five indexes: Authors and titles, Regions and localities (dialects), Words, Etyma, and Technical subjects.

Mazzoni, Guido. Avvimento allo studio critico delle lettere italiane. 3. ed. emend. e accresciuta. Firenze, Sansoni, 1923. 342p.   **R657**

A bibliographical handbook, now out of date but still useful for its comment on older materials.

Prezzolini, Giuseppe. Repertorio bibliografico della storia e della critica della letteratura italiana dal 1902 al 1932, preparato nella Casa Italiana della Columbia University e con l'aiuto del Council on Research in the Humanities, New York, 1930-1936. Roma, Edizioni Roma, 1937-39. 2v. set, L450.   **R658**

Arranged alphabetically by names of authors written about or commented on, and by literary forms and subjects, with exact references to an enormous amount of critical and biographical material in books, periodicals, society publications, etc.

—— Repertorio bibliografico della storia e della critica della letteratura italiana dal 1933 al 1942. N.Y., Vanni, 1946-48. 2v. $12.50 ea.

This section follows the same general plan as the first two volumes, giving references under authors, literary forms, etc. Many form headings use geographical subdivisions.

Shields, Nancy Catchings. Italian translations in America. N.Y. [1931]. 410p. $4. (Institute of French Studies. Comparative literature series)   **R659**

Translations of Italian works arranged chronologically by date of publication, covering the period 1751-1928. Each title is located in one library or, if not found, the original source of entry is indicated.

Dictionaries and handbooks

Gardner, Edmund Garratt. Italy; a companion to Italian studies. Lond., Methuen, 1934. 274p. (Methuen's Companions to modern studies) 12s. 6d. **R660**

Bibliography at end of each chapter.
Chapters, by different writers, deal with Italian language, history, literature, fine arts; includes bibliographies.

Turri, Vittorio and **Renda, Umberto.** Dizionario storico-critico della letteratura italiana. Nuova ed. compl. rifatta. Torino, Paravia, 1941. 1143p. **R661**

1st ed. 1900.
A dictionary of authors, titles and literary forms in one alphabet; brief articles, with bibliographies.

History

Sanctis, Francesco de. Storia della letteratura italiana. Nuova ed. a cura di Francisco Flora. Milano, Vallardi, 1935. 437p. **R662**

A standard history published in many editions. English translation by Joan Redfern (N.Y., Harcourt, 1931. 2v.).

Storia illustrata della letteratura italiana, scritta da un gruppo di studiosi. Milano, Garzanti, 1942- . v.1- . il. (In progress) **R663**

Many illustrations. Each chapter signed by a specialist. Includes bibliography.

Storia letteraria d'Italia. . . . 3. ed. completamente rifatta. Milano, Vallardi, 1929–39. v.1-10. **R664**

[v.1] Giussani, C. Letteratura romana. [1897–99]; [v.2¹] Viscardi, Antonio. Le origini. 1939; [v.2²] Bertoni, Giulio. Il duecento. 3d ed. 1939; [v.3] Zingarelli, Nicola. La vita, i tempi e le opere di Dante. 1931. 2v.; [v.4] Sapegno, Natalino. Il trecento. 1934; [v.5] Rossi, Vitorio. Il quattrocento. 1933; [v.6] Toffanin, Giuseppe. Il cinquecento. 1929; [v.7] Belloni, Antonio. Il seicento. 1929; [v.8] Natali, Giulio. Il settecento. 1929. 2v.; [v.9] Mazzoni, Guido. L'ottocento. 1934. 2v.; [v.10] Galletti, Alfred. Il novecento. 1935.
Volume 1 is earlier edition.
The standard large history, with bibliographies at end of each chapter; index to each volume, but no general index.

Individual authors

D'ANNUNZIO

Falqui, Enrico. Bibliografia dannunziana. 2. ed. aumentata. Firenze, Le Monnier, 1941. 198p. **R665**

Forcella, Roberto. D'Annunzio, 1863–1886. Roma, Fond. Leonardo, 1926–36. v.1-3. **R666**

Contents: v.1, 1863–83; v.2, 1884–85; v.3, 1886.

Fucilla, Joseph G. and **Carrière, Joseph M.** D'Annunzio abroad; a bibliographical essay. N.Y., Inst. of French Studies, Columbia Univ., 1935–37. 2 pts. **R667**

The second part is supplementary to the first.

Passerini, Giuseppe Lando, *conte.* Il vocabolario dannunziano, con un autografo e un ritratto del poeta. Firenze, Sansoni [1928]. 971p. il. **R668**

1st ed., 1912–13, was in two alphabets, v.1, poetry, v.2, prose; 2d ed. rearranges the material in one alphabet.

DANTE

Bibliography

Cornell University. Library. Catalogue of the Dante collection presented by Willard Fiske, comp. by Theodore Wesley Koch. Ithaca, N.Y., Library, 1898–1921. 2v. and suppl. 152p. **R669**

v.1, Dante's works, Works on Dante (A-G); v.2, Works on Dante (H-Z), suppl., indexes, appendix; Suppl., additions 1898–1920.
Supplemented for some points by the following:

Koch, Theodore Wesley. Dante in America; a historical and bibliographical study. Bost., Ginn, 1896. 150p. **R670**

Repr. from the 15th *Annual report* of the Dante Society, Camb., Mass.

——— —— [Supplement] May 1896–May 1908. (In Dante Society. Camb., Mass. 28th Annual report, 1909. Bost., Ginn, 1910. p.11-35)

—— List of Danteiana in American libraries supplementing the catalogue of the Cornell collection. Bost., Ginn, 1901. 67p. **R671**

Repr. from the 18th *Annual report* of the Dante Society, Camb., Mass.

Evola, Niccolò Domenico. Bibliografia dantesca (1920–1930). Firenze, Olschki, 1932. 260p. (Giornale dantesco . . . v.33, n.s. 3. Annuario dantesco 1930. Supplemento) **R672**

Supplemented by *Bibliografia dantesca*, 1931/37–1938/39 published in *Il Giornale dantesco*, v.39-41.

Fucilla, Joseph Guerin. Forgotten Danteiana; a bibliographical supplement. Evanston and Chic. Northwestern Univ., 1939. 52p. (Northwestern Univ. studies in the humanities, no.5) **R673**

"Primarily the result of an attempt to keep a record of Dante studies from 1920 on . . . to supplement Fowler's additions to the . . . Cornell Dante collection."—*Pref.*
"Also published by the Dante Society of Cambridge Mass."—p.[2] of cover.

La Piana, Angelina. Dante's American pilgrimage; a historical survey of Dante studies in the United States, 1800–1944. New Haven, pub. fo

Wellesley College by Yale Univ. Pr., 1948. 310p.
$4. R674

Bibliography in footnotes. Author index.

Mambelli, Giuliano. Gli annali delle edizioni dantesche con XLVI tavole fuori testo; contributo ad una bibliografia definitiva. Bologna, Zanichelli, 1931. 424p. il. R675

Toynbee, Paget. Britain's tribute to Dante in literature and art; a chronological record of 540 years (c1380–1920). Lond., pub. for the British Academy by H. Milford [1921]. 212p. R676

Concordances

Fay, Edward Allen. Concordance of the Divina commedia. Camb. [Mass.] Dante Soc.; Ox., Univ. Pr., 1888. 819p. R677

Based upon the text of Witte's edition (Berlin, 1862) but adds variants from the edition of Niccolini (Capponi Borghi and Becchi, Florence, 1837). Includes all words used by Dante but omits context and reference for some of the commoner pronouns, prepositions, adverbs and conjunctions and the more frequently recurring forms of the verbs *avere* and *essere*.

Sheldon, Edward Stevens and White, A. C. Concordanza delle opere italiane in prosa e del Canzoniere di Dante Alighieri pubblicata per la Società Dantesca di Cambridge, Mass. Ox., Univ. Pr., 1905. 740p. R678

Gordon, Lewis H. Supplementary concordance to the minor Italian works of Dante. Camb., Mass., pub. for the Dante Society, Harv. Univ. Pr., 1936. 38p. R679

Supplementary to the *Concordanza* of Sheldon (R678).

Rand, Edward Kennard and Wilkins, Ernest Hatch. Dantis Alagherii opervm latinorvm concordantiae. Ox., Clarendon Pr., 1912. 577p. R680
Based on the text of the third Oxford edition, 1904.

Dictionaries

Gustarelli, Andrea. Dizionario Dantesco, per lo studio della Divina commedia. Milano, Malfasi, 1946. 253p. L580. R681

Alphabetical dictionary to names, places, some phrases, etc., with exact reference to source and biographical, historical, descriptive notes, etc.

Scartazzini, Giovanni Andrea. Enciclopedia Dantesca; dizionario critico e ragionato di quanto concerne la vita e le opere di Dante Alighieri. Milano, Hoepli, 1896–1905. 3v. R682

v.1-2, A-Z. v.3, Vocabolario-concordanza delle opere latine e italiane di Dante Alighieri, preceduto dalla biografia di G. A. Scartazzini.

Snell, Frederick John. Handbook to the works of Dante. Lond., Bell; N.Y., Macmillan, 1909. 378p. R683

A handbook, not a dictionary; useful for the more popular questions.

Toynbee, Paget. Dictionary of proper names and notable matters in the works of Dante. Ox., Clarendon Pr., 1898. 616p. R684

—— Concise dictionary of proper names and notable matters in the works of Dante. Ox., Clarendon Pr., 1914. 568p. R685

Based upon his larger work, 1898, but not a mere abridgement, as it includes some names and material not included in the earlier work, omits names in one point now known not to have been written by Dante and brings other matter in line with more recent information. Conciseness is attained by judicious condensation rather than by omission of anything vital.

PETRARCH

Cornell University. Library. Catalogue of the Petrarch collection bequeathed by Willard Fiske, comp. by Mary Fowler. Lond., Milford, 1916. 547p. R686

McKenzie, Kenneth. Concordanza delle rime di Francesco Petrarca. Ox., Univ. Pr.; New Haven, Yale Univ. Pr., 1912. 519p. R687

Based upon the text of the Salvo-Cozzo edition, 1904. Gives context and references for all important words, and references only for certain minor words of frequent occurrence.

Portuguese including Brazilian
Bibliography

Bell, Aubrey Fitz Gerald. Portuguese bibliography. Ox., Univ. Pr., 1922. 381p. (Hispanic notes and monographs; essays, studies, and brief biographies issued by the Hispanic Society of America. Bibliography ser. 1) R688

Ford, J. D. M., Whittem, A. F. and Raphael, M. I. Tentative bibliography of Brazilian belleslettres. Camb., Harv. Univ. Pr., 1931. 201p. (Harvard Council on Hispano-American Studies) R689

Garcia Péres, Domingo. Catalogo razonado biográfico y bibliográfico de los autores portugueses que escribieron en castellano. Madrid, Colegio Nacional de Sordo-Mudos y de Ciegos, 1890. 660p. R690

Simões dos Reis, Antônio. Bibliografia da História da literatura Brasileira de Sílvio Romero. Rio, Zélio Valverde, 1944- . v.1- . R691

Contents: Fatores da literatura brasileira: v.1, Trabalhos estrangeiros e nacionais sôbre a literatura brasileira.

Wogan, Daniel S. A literatura Hispano-Americana no Brasil: 1877–1944; bibliografia de crítica, história literária e traduções. Baton Rouge, Louisiana State Univ. Pr., 1948. 98p. $4. **R692**

An annotated bibliography of 822 items listing the contributions that Brazilians have made to the history and criticism of the literatures of Spanish America. Arranged by country, it includes books and articles published from 1877 to 1945. Portuguese translations of Spanish American novels, plays, short stories and poems are included under each country.

History

Forjaz de Sampaio, Albino. Historia da literatura portuguesa ilustrada, publicada . . . com a colaboração dos senhores Afonso Lopes Vieira, Agostinho de Campos [e outros]. Paris, Aillaud [1928–29]. v.1-2$^{1-3}$. il. **R693**

Lavishly illustrated.

Mendes dos Remedios, Joaquim. História da literatura portuguêsa desde as origens até a atualidade. 6. ed. Coimbra, "Atlântida," 1930. 710p. **R694**

Motta, Arthur. Historia da litteratura brasileira. . . . São Paulo, Companhia Editora Nacional, 1930. v.1-2. **R695**

v.1, Sixteenth-seventeenth centuries; v.2, Eighteenth century.

Anthologies

Campos, Humberto de. O conseito e a imagem na poesia brasileira; citações de poetas brasileiros dos seculos XVI, XVII, XVIII, XIX e XX. Rio de Janeiro, Leite Ribeiro, 1929. 333p. **R696**

Oxford book of Portuguese verse, XIIth century–XXth century, chosen by Aubrey F. G. Bell. Ox., Clarendon Pr., 1925. 320p. **R697**

Romansh

Ligia Romontscha. Bibliografia retoromontscha. Bibliographie des gedruckten bündnerromanischen Schrifttums von den Anfängen bis zum Jahre 1930. Chur, Schuller, 1938. 266p. **R698**

A comprehensive bibliography; locates copies in various Swiss and other libraries.

Maxfield, Mildred Elizabeth. Raeto-Romance bibliography; a selected bibliography of works on Raeto-Romance with special consideration of Romansh. Chapel Hill, 1941. 28p. (Univ. of

North Carolina studies in the Romance languages and literatures, no.2) **R699**

A selected annotated guide to this special field.

Rumanian

Adamescu, Gheorghe. Contribuțiune la bibliografia românească. fasc. 1-3. Bucureşti, Ed. Casei Scoalelor, 1921–28. 3 pts. **R700**

fasc. 1-3, Istoria literaturii române. Texte şi autori, 1500–1921/25.

Georgescu-Tistu, N. Bibliografia literară română. Bucureşti, Imprimeria Nationalǎ, 1932. 254p. il (Academia romǎnǎ, Studii şi cercetări, v.18) **R701**

Spanish
Bibliography

Bibliographie hispanique, 1905–17. N.Y., Hispanic Soc. [1909–19]. 13v. **R702**

Important annual bibliography including both books and periodical articles and covering the languages, literature, and history of the Spanish and Portuguese countries both in Europe and elsewhere.

No more published.

Coe, Ada May. Catálogo bibliográfico y crítico de las comedias anunciadas en los periódicos de Madrid desde 1661 hasta 1819. Balt., Johns Hopkins Pr.; Lond., Milford, 1935. 270p. $3.50; 16s (Johns Hopkins studies in Romance literature and languages, extra v.9) **R703**

Arranged alphabetically by titles, with author index.

Cotarelo y Mori, Emilio. Catálogo descriptivo de la gran colección de Comedias escogidas que consta de cuarenta y ocho volúmenes, impresos de 1652 a 1704. Madrid, Tip. de Archivos, 1932. 266p. **R70**

Contains full descriptions of each volume, with contents and author and title indexes.

Fitzmaurice-Kelly, James. Bibliographie de l'histoire de la littérature espagnole. Paris, Colin, 1913. 78p. (Histoires des littératures) **R70**

To accompany the second edition of the author's *Littérature espagnole* (Paris, 1913).

Foulché-Delbosc, Raymond. Manuel de l'hispanisant. N.Y., Putnam, 1920; Hispanic Soc. of America, 1925. v.1-2. **R70**

For full description see A490.

Millares Carlo, Augustín. Ensayo de una bibliografía de escritores naturales de las isla

Canarias (siglos XVI, XVII y XVIII). Madrid, Tip. de Archivos, 1932. 716p.   **R707**

Rogers, Paul Patrick. Spanish drama collection in the Oberlin College library; a descriptive catalogue. Oberlin, Ohio, Oberlin College, 1940. 468p. $4.50.   **R708**

Covers the period from the last quarter of the seventeenth century to the year 1924. Includes 7530 numbered items, arranged alphabetically by author.

———— ———— Supplementary volume, containing reference lists. 1946. 157p.

Vera, Francisco. La cultura española medieval. Datos bio-bibliográficos para su historia. Madrid, Victoriano Suárez, 1933–34. 2v.   **R709**

TRANSLATIONS INTO ENGLISH

Biaggi, Zelmira and **Sanchez y Escribano, F.** English translations from the Spanish, 1932 to April 1938. Stonington, Conn., Stonington Pub. Co., 1939. 18p. 50c.   **R710**

Pane, Remigio Ugo. English translations from the Spanish, 1484–1943, a bibliography. New Brunswick, N.J., Rutgers Univ. Pr., 1944. 218p. (Rutgers Univ. studies in Spanish, no.2) $2.50.   **R711**

An unannotated alphabetical list of 2682 items of peninsular Spanish literature and history. A review with corrections and additions by W. K. Jones was published in *Hispanic review* 13:174-77, Apr. 1945.

Dictionaries

Diccionario de literatura española. Madrid, Revista de Occidente, 1949. 641p.   **R712**

Includes biographies, articles on forms of literature, literary terms, etc. All articles are signed.

History

Cejador y Frauca, Julio. Historia de la lengua y literatura castellana. Madrid, "Rev. de Arch., Bibl. y Museos," 1915–22. 14v. il.   **R713**

t.1, Desde los orígenes hasta Carlos V; t.2, Época de Carlos V; t.3, Época de Felipe II; t.4, Época de Felipe III; t.5, Época de Felipe IV o de Lope y Calderón; t.6, Época del siglo XVIII: 1701–1829; t.7, Época romántica: 1830–1849; t.8, Primer período de la época realista: 1850–1869; t.9, Segundo período de la época realista: 1870–1887; t.10-12, Época regional y modernista: 1888–1907; t.13-14, Época contemporánea: 1908–1920.

Some volumes have appeared in a second edition, 1927- and some in a third edition, 1932- .

Includes bibliographies.

Fitzmaurice-Kelly, James. A new history of Spanish literature. Ox., Milford, 1926. 551p.   **R714**

The most useful history in English; contains considerable bibliography, including many bibliographical footnotes throughout and a brief general bibliography, p.520-28.

Rio, Angel del. Historia de la literatura española. N.Y., Dryden Pr., 1948. 2v.   **R715**

Extensive bibliography at the end of each chapter.

Salcedo y Ruiz, Angel. La literatura española; resumen de historia crítica. 2. ed. refundida y muy aumentada. Madrid, Calleja, 1915–17. 4v. il.   **R716**

v.1, La edad media; v.2, El siglo de oro; v.3, El clasicismo; v.4, Nuestros días.

Anthologies

Biblioteca de autores españoles, desde la formacion del languaje hasta nuestros dias. Madrid, Rivadeneyra, 1846–86. 71v.   **R717**

v.71, General indexes: (1) Index classified by literary forms; (2) Index to titles; (3) Index to first lines; (4) Author index.

De Onís, Federico. Antología de la poésia española e hispañoamericana (1882–1932). Madrid, Imp. Hernando, 1934. 1212p. (Revista de filología española, v.10)   **R718**

Includes selections from about 160 poets, with bibliography and biography for each.

Diego, Gerardo. Poesía española; antología (contemporáneos). . . . Madrid, Signo, 1934. 600p.   **R719**

Contains biographies and bibliographies of authors represented.

Oxford book of Spanish verse, 13th century to 20th century chosen by James Fitzmaurice-Kelly. 2d ed. by J. B. Trend. Ox., Clarendon; N.Y., Oxford, 1941. 522p. $3.   **R720**

1st ed., 1913.

In the second edition material through the eighteenth century in the main part of the work is unchanged. In the sections for the nineteenth and twentieth centuries, 11 names have been dropped, some changes have been made in selections and about 20 names have been added. Two new sections are included "Poesía de tipo tradicional," p.443-60; "Poesía barroac," p.461-75, which add selections for the sixteenth century.

Valera y Alcala Galiano, Juan. Florilegio de poesías castellanas del siglo XIX; con introducción y notas biográficas y críticas. . . . Madrid, F. Fé, 1902–03. 5v.   **R721**

v.1-4, Antología; v.5, Notas biográficas y críticas.

Walsh, Thomas. Hispanic anthology; poems translated from the Spanish by English and North American poets. N.Y., Putnam, 1920. 779p. il. (Hispanic notes and monographs. Peninsular series, iv)   **R722**

Individual authors

CERVANTES

Ford, Jeremiah Denis Matthias and **Lansing, Ruth.** Cervantes; a tentative bibliography of his works and of the biographical and critical materials concerning him. Camb., Harv. Univ. Pr., 1931. 239p. $5. **R723**

Grismer, Raymond Leonard. Cervantes: A bibliography. Books, essays, articles and other studies on the life of Cervantes, his works, and his imitators. N.Y., Wilson, 1946. 183p. $4.50. **R724**

Madrid. Biblioteca Nacional. Catálogo bibliográfico de la sección de Cervantes de la Biblioteca Nacional, por Gabriel-Martin del Rio y Rico. . . . Madrid, Tip. de la "Revista de Archivos, Bibliotecas y Museos," 1930. 915p. **R725**

Predmore, Richard L. An index to Don Quijote including proper names and notable matters. New Brunswick, N.J., Rutgers Univ. Pr., 1938. 102p. (Rutgers Univ. studies in Spanish, 1) $2. **R726**

Rius y de Llosellas, Leopoldo. Bibliografía crítica de las obras de Miguel de Cervantes Saavedra. Madrid, Murillo, 1895–1905. 3v. il. **R727**

Suñé Benages, Juan and **Suñé Fonbuena, Juan.** Bibliografía crítica de ediciones del Quijote, impresas desde 1605 hasta 1917 . . . continuado hasta 1937 por el primero de los citados autores y ahora redactada por J. D. M. Ford y C. T. Keller. Camb., Harv. Univ. Pr., 1939. 73p. $3.50. **R728**

Added title page in English.

Spanish American

Bibliography

Grismer, Raymond Leonard. A new bibliography of the literatures of Spain and Spanish America, including many studies on anthropology, archaeology, art, economics, education, geography, history, law, music, philosophy and other subjects. Dubuque, Iowa, Wm. C. Brown, 1941–46. v.1-7. (In progress) **R730**

v.1-7, A-Cez.

Publisher varies.

Will replace his two earlier volumes of bibliography on the literatures of Spain and Spanish America, published 1933 and 1935.

Arranged alphabetically by author and subject. Includes books and articles in periodicals and collections.

—— A reference index to twelve thousand Spanish American authors; a guide to the literature of Spanish America. N.Y., Wilson, 1939. 150p. (Inter-American Bibliographical and Library Association pub. ser. 3, v.1) $4.50. **R731**

"Bibliography of books on Spanish-American literature consulted for this index": p.[xii]-xvi.

Handbook of Latin American studies; a guide to the material published . . . in 1935- . Camb., Harv. Univ. Pr., 1936- . v.1- . Annual. **R732**

Each volume includes a section on literature. For full description *see* V367.

Harvard Council on Hispano-American Studies. Bibliographies of the belles-lettres of Hispanic America. Camb., Harv. Univ. Pr., 1947. 3v. **R733**

Reprints of some of its bibliographies, mainly the "tentative bibliographies of belles-lettres" of the various Latin American countries, originally published separately, 1931–35. The separate bibliographies are listed in this book under the name of the country by author.

Nichols, Madaline W. A bibliographical guide to materials on American Spanish. Camb., Harv. Univ. Pr., 1941. 114p. (Committee on Latin American studies, American Council of Learned Societies, Misc. pub., no.2) $1.50. **R734**

1201 annotated items on the philology of American Spanish including general material and material under each country. Records official philological academies and organizations and the learned journals.

Roberts, Sarah Elizabeth. José Toribio Medina; his life and works. Wash., Inter-American Bibl. and Library Assoc., 1941. 192p. (Inter-Amer. Bibl. and Library Assoc. pub., ser. 1, v.6) $1.50. **R735**

Yale University. Library. Spanish American literature in the Yale University Library; a bibliography [by] Frederick Bliss Luquiens. . . . New Haven, Yale Univ. Pr.; Lond., Milford, 1939. 335p. $10. **R736**

Contains 5668 numbered entries. "The word *literature* . . . is to be understood in the broad sense of 'good writing.'"—*Introd.* Arranged by the countries of Spanish America, with index to the whole.

TRANSLATIONS INTO ENGLISH

Granier, James Albert. Latin American belles-lettres in English translation; a selective and annotated guide. Wash., 1943. cover title, 38p. (U.S. Library of Congress. Hispanic Foundation Bibliographical ser., no.1. 2d rev. ed.) **R737**

Includes some 65 titles of prose fiction, poetry, drama and the essay with descriptive annotation and excerpts from published reviews.

Jones, Willis Knapp. Latin American writers in English translation; a tentative bibliography. Wash., Pan American Union, 1944. 141 (i.e., 142)

numb. 1. ([Pan American Union. Columbus Memorial Library] Bibliographic ser. no.30)
R738

"This bibliography is intended to list all Latin American writing from the time of Columbus and Cortes to the present, that has been translated into English."—*Introd.* Arranged by class with country subdivision. Includes history and travel, essays, poetry, drama, and fiction. Author index.

Leavitt, Sturgis E. Hispano-American literature in the United States; a bibliography of translations and criticisms. Camb., Harv. Univ. Pr., 1932. 54p. (Harvard Council on Hispano-American Studies)
R739

Anthologies

Antología de poetas hispano-americanos publicada por la Real Academia Española. Madrid, Rivadeneyra, 1893–95. 4v.
R740

Ed. by M. Menéndez y Pelayo.
v.1, México y América Central; v.2, Cuba, Santo Domingo, Puerto Rico, Venezuela; v.3, Colombia, Ecuador, Perú, Bolivia; v.4, Chile, República Argentina, Uruguay.

Fitts, Dudley. Anthology of contemporary Latin-American poetry. Norfolk, Conn., New Directions, 1947. 677p. $2.50.
R741

Added title page: Antología de la poesía americana contemporánea.
English and original text (Spanish, Portuguese, or French) on opposite pages.
"Biographical and bibliographical notes, by H. R. Hays": p.588-649.

Argentinian

Coester, Alfred. Tentative bibliography of the belles-lettres of the Argentine Republic. Camb., Harv. Univ. Pr., 1933. 94p. (Harvard Council on Hispano-American Studies)
R742

Leavitt, Sturgis E. Argentine literature; a bibliography of literary criticism, biography, and literary controversy. Chapel Hill, Univ. of North Carolina Pr., 1924. 92p. (Univ. of North Carolina studies in language and literature, no.1)
R743

Bolivian

Leavitt, Sturgis E. Tentative bibliography of Bolivian literature. Camb., Harv. Univ. Pr., 1933. 23p. (Harvard Council on Hispano-American Studies)
R744

Brazilian

See Portuguese.

Central American

Doyle, Henry Grattan. Tentative bibliography of the belles-lettres of the Republics of Central America. Camb., Harv. Univ. Pr., 1935. 136p. (Harvard Council on Hispano-American Studies)
R745

Chilean

Leavitt, Sturgis E. Chilean literature; a bibliography of literary criticism, biography and literary controversy. Balt., 1923. 89p. (Repr. from Hispanic American historical review, v.5, 1922)
R746

Rojas Carrasco, Guillermo. Filología chilena; guía bibliográfica y crítica . . . Ediciones de la Universidad de Chile. Santiago de Chile, Imp. y Lit. Universo, 1940. 300p.
R747

Solar, Hernán del. Indice de la poesía chilena contemporánea. Santiago de Chile, Ed. Ercilla, 1937. 298p.
R748

Anthology with bio-bibliographical notes.

Torres-Rioseco, Arturo and **Silva-Castro, Raúl.** Ensayo de bibliografía de la literatura Chilena. Camb., Harv. Univ. Pr., 1935. 71p. (Harvard Council on Hispano-American Studies)
R749

Colombian

Leavitt, Sturgis E. and **García-Prada, Carlos.** Tentative bibliography of Colombian literature. Camb., Harv. Univ. Pr., 1934. 80p. (Harvard Council on Hispano-American Studies)
R750

Ortega Torres y Gasset, José Joaquin. Historia de la literatura colombiana, con prólogos de Antonio Gomez Restrepo y de Daniel Samper Ortega. 2. ed. aumentada. . . . Bogotá, Ed. Cromos, 1935. 1214p. il. $5.
R751

Contains some general literary history, but the greater part of the history consists of biographies and bibliographies, with extracts from the works of some 180 Colombian authors.

Costa Rican

Sotela, Rogelio. Escritores de Costa Rica. San José, Lehmann, 1942. 876p.
R752

An anthology of prose and poetry with biographical notes.

Cuban

Arrom, José Juan. Historia de la literatura dramática cubana. New Haven, Yale Univ. Pr.,

1944. 132p. il. (Yale Romanic studies, v.23) $2.50.   **R752a**

Bibliografía general, p.93-94; Appéndice bibliográfico de obras dramáticas cubanos, p.95-127. This appendix is a useful bibliography of the Cuban theater. Locates copies in four libraries in this country and in five in Cuba.

Ford, J. D. M. and **Raphael, M. I.** Bibliography of Cuban belles-lettres. Camb., Harv. Univ. Pr., 1933. 204p. (Harvard Council on Hispano-American Studies)   **R753**

Remos y Rubio, Juan J. Historia de la literatura cubana. Habana, Cardenas, 1945. 3v.   **R754**

A comprehensive history of Cuban literature from its origin to the present day. Includes biographies and bibliographies.

Ecuadorian

Rivera, Guillermo. Tentative bibliography of the belles-lettres of Ecuador. Camb., Harv. Univ. Pr., 1934. 76p. (Harvard Council on Hispano-American Studies)   **R755**

Rolando, Carlos A. Las bellas letras en el Ecuador. Guayaquil, Imp. i Taleres Municipales, 1944. 157p.   **R756**

Running title: Bibliografia de autores nacionales-literatura.

A bibliography of literary works printed in Ecuador from colonial times to the present. Arranged by class including bibliography, library economy, periodicals, poetry, fiction, drama, essays, etc. Author index.

Mexican

Iguiniz, Juan Bautista. Bibliografía de novelistas mexicanos. Ensayo biográfico, bibliográfico y critico. Precedido de un estudio histórico de la novela mexicana por Francisco Monterde García Icazbalceta. Mexico, Impr. de la Secretaría de Relaciones Exteriores, 1926. 432p. (Monografías bibliograficas mexicanas, núm. 3)   **R757**

Bio-bibliographies of Mexican novelists.

Monterde García Icazbalceta, Francisco. Bibliografía del teatro en México. Mexico, Impr. de la Secretaría de Relaciones Exteriores, 1933, i.e., 1934. lxxxp., 649p. facsim. (Monografías bib. mexicanas, 28)   **R758**

Moore, Ernest Richard. Bibliografía de novelistas de la revolución mexicana. México [priv. pr.] 1941. 190p.   **R759**

Locates copies in Mexican, American, and European libraries.

Torres Rioseco, Arturo. Bibliografía de la novela mejicana. Camb., Harv. Univ. Pr., 1933. 58p.

(Harvard Council on Hispano-American Studies)   **R760**

——— and **Warner, R. E.** Bibliografía de la poesía mejicana. Camb., Harv. Univ. Pr., 1934. 86p. (Harvard Council on Hispano-American Studies)   **R761**

Panamanian

Doyle, Henry Grattan. Tentative bibliography of the belles-lettres of Panama. Camb., Harv. Univ. Pr., 1934. 21p. (Harvard Council on Hispano-American Studies)   **R762**

Paraguayan

Raphael, M. I. and **Ford, J. D. M.** Tentative bibliography of Paraguayan literature. Camb., Harv. Univ. Pr., 1934. 25p. (Harvard Council on Hispano-American Studies)   **R763**

Peruvian

Leavitt, Sturgis E. Tentative bibliography of Peruvian literature. Camb., Harv. Univ. Pr., 1932. 37p. (Harvard Council on Hispano-American Studies)   **R764**

Sanchez, Luis Alberto. Indice de la poesía peruana contemporánea (1900–1937). Santiago de Chile, Ed. Ercilla, 1938. 359p.   **R765**

Anthology with bio-bibliographical notes.

Puerto Rican

Rivera, Guillermo. Tentative bibliography of the belles-lettres of Porto Rico. Camb., Harv. Univ. Pr., 1931. 61p. (Harvard Council on Hispano-American Studies)   **R766**

Santo Dominican

Waxman, S. M. Bibliography of the belles-lettres of Santo Domingo. Camb., Harv. Univ. Pr., 1931. 31p. (Harvard Council on Hispano-American Studies)   **R767**

Uruguayan

Coester, Alfred. Tentative bibliography of Uruguayan literature. Camb., Harv. Univ. Pr., 1931. 22p. (Harvard Council on Hispano-American Studies)   **R768**

Venezuelan

Waxman, S. M. Bibliography of the belles-lettres of Venezuela. Camb., Harv. Univ. Pr., 1935. 145p. (Harvard Council on Hispano-American Studies)
R769

SLAVIC AND EAST EUROPEAN LANGUAGES

❧ Only a few works in these literatures can be listed here. For more detailed bibliographies, *see* Strakhovsky, *Handbook of Slavic studies*, (1949) (V441); *Columbia dictionary of modern European literature* edited by Horatio Smith (1947) (R30); Kerner, *Slavic Europe* (1918) (V439), etc. The *Slavonic review* includes many survey and bibliographical articles which are helpful.

Šafařík, Pavel Josef. Geschichte der südslawischen Literatur, hrsg. von Josef Jireček. Prag., Friedrich Tempsky, 1864–65. 4v. **R770**

Contents: v.1, Slowenisches und glagolitisches Schriftthum; v.2, Illirisches und kroatisches Schriftthum; v.3, Das serbische Schriftthum. 2v.

Strakhovsky, Leonid I. Handbook of Slavic studies. Camb., Harv. Univ. Pr., 1949. 753p. **R771**

Chapters by specialists on the history and literature of the various Slavic countries, each chapter followed by a bibliography. Bibliographies are largely of material in English and western European languages. For full description *see* V441.

U. S. Library of Congress. General Reference and Bibliography Division. The study and teaching of Slavic languages; a selected list of references, comp. by John T. Dorosh. Wash., 1949. 97p. **R772**

Lists periodicals, general works, grammars, readers, dictionaries, etc., for each Slavic language. Planned for teachers in American schools and colleges, for the study of the languages not the literatures.

Czech

Jelinek, Hanus. Histoire de la littérature tchèque. 4. ed. Paris, Éditions du Sagittaire, 1930–35. 3v. **R773**

v.1-3, Des origines à nos jours.

Kunc, Jaroslav. Slovník soudobých českých spisovatelú; krásné písemnictví v letech 1918–45. Praha, Orbis, 1945–46. 2v. il. **R774**

A dictionary of contemporary Bohemian writers, Oct. 28, 1918–May 5, 1945. Restricted to "belles-lettres."

Polish

Czachowski, Kasimierz. Obraz współczesnej literatury polskiej, 1884–1933. Lwów, Nakładem Państwowego Wydawnictwa Ksiązek Szkolnych, 1934–36. 3v. **R775**

Includes extensive bibliographies, chronology, and index.

—— Najnowsza twárczość literacka, 1935–37. Lwów, 1938. 273p. il.

Korbut, Gabrjel. Literatura polska od początków do wojny światowej; książka podręczna informacyjna dla studjujących naukowo dzieje rozwoju piśmiennictwa polskiego. . . . Wydanie 2., powiększone. Warszawa, Skład główny w kasie Im. Mianowskiego, 1929–31. 4v. **R776**

v.1, Tenth–seventeenth centuries; v.2, Eighteenth century—1820; v.3, 1820–63; v.4, 1864–1914.

Lorentowicz, Jan. La Pologne en France; essai d'une bibliographie raisonnée . . . avec la collaboration de A. M. Chmurski. . . . Paris, Champion, 1935–38. 2v. (v.2, Institut d'Études Slaves de l'Université de Paris. Bibliothèque Polonaise. IV) **R777**

v.1, Littérature, théâtre, beaux-arts; v.2, Encyclopédies, langue, voyages, histoire.
French writings concerning Poland including both book and periodical articles.
Classified with author and title indexes.

Russian

Bibliography

Adrianova-Peretts, Varavara Pavlovna and **Pokrovskaĭa, V. F.** Drevne-russkaĭa povest'. Moskva, Izdatel'stvo Akademiĭ nauk, 1940- . v.1- . (Akademiĭa Nauk, SSSR. Institut Literatury. Bibliografiĭa Istoriĭ Drevne-Russkoĭ Literatury) **R778**

Fomīn, Aleksandr Grīgor'evīch. Putevoditel' po bibliografiĭ, biobibliografiĭ, istoriografiĭ, khronologiĭ i entsiklopediĭ literatury. Sistematicheskiĭ, annotirovann'yĭ ukazatel' russkikh knig i zhurnal'nykh rabot, napechatannykh v 1736–1932 gg. Leningrad, Leningradskoe otdelenie, 1934. 335p. **R779**

Butchik, Vladimir. La littérature russe en France . . . [par] Vladimir Boutchik. Paris, Champion [1947]. 116p. **R780**

Intended as a companion volume to his bibliographies of translations from Russian into French (R783). Includes a classed list, with name index of 308 books about Russian literature appearing in France. Does not include periodical articles.

Olgin, Moissaye J. Guide to Russian literature, 1820–1917. N.Y., Harcourt, 1920. 323p. **R781**

A guide to a large number of writers, especially contemporary, describing their works and including extracts from comments by Russian critics.

Struve, Gleb. 25 years of Soviet Russian literature, 1918–1943. New and enl. ed. of Soviet Russian literature. Lond., Routledge, 1944. 347p. **R782**

Bibliography, p.321-32; Supplementary bibliography, p.333-41.

TRANSLATIONS

Butchik, Vladimir. Bibliographie des oeuvres littéraires russes traduites en français. Paris, Orobitg, 1935–36. 2v. **R783**

Volume 1 covers works published 1737–1934; volume 2 supplements volume 1, containing works omitted from it and those published Jan. 1, 1935—July 1, 1936.

————— Supplement, 1938- . Paris, Flory, 1938- . (In progress)

Contents: 1938 (July 1, 1936—Dec. 31, 1937), 16p.; 1941 (Jan. 1, 1938—June 1, 1941), 12p.

———— Bibliographie des oeuvres littéraires russes traduites en français: Tourguénev, Dostoevski, Léon Tolstoi. Paris, "Messages," 1949. 110p.

Ettlinger, Amrei and **Gladstone, Joan M.** Russian literature, theatre and art; a bibliography of works in English, published 1900–1945. Lond., Hutchinson [pref. 1945]. 96p. 7s. 6d. **R784**

Designed to supplement Philip Grierson's *Books on Soviet Russia*, 1917–42 (V424). Contains classified lists of books on studies in English on Russian literature, theater and art, and Russian literature in English translations from the nineteenth century to the present time. No index.

Dictionaries

Dobryv, A. P. Biografiĭ russkikh pisateleĭ sredniãgo i novago periodov. S alfavitnym ukazatelem proizvedeniĭ pisateleĭ. S.-Petersburg, Stolichnaĭa Tip., 1900. 534p., 49p. **R785**

Biographies of Russian writers with alphabetical index of their works.

Literaturnaĭa entsiklopediĭa, redaksionnaĭa kollegiĭa: P. I. Lebedev-Polĭanskiĭ, I. M. Nusinov. Moskva, "Khudozhestvennaĭa literatura," 1929–39. v.1-9, 11. il. (Repr. 1948. American Council of Learned Societies reprints. Russian ser. no.20 $50) **R786**

An extensive treatment of the history of world literature from the Marxist-Leninist standpoint, with special emphasis on the literatures of Russia and other portions of the U.S.S.R. Volumes 10 and 12 have not been distributed. For review by Dmitri von Mohrenschildt *see* the *Russian review* 8:358-60, Oct. 1949.

Snow, Valentine. Russian writers; a bio-bibliographical dictionary. N.Y., International Book Service, 1946- . $3.75. **R787**

Contents: [v.1] From the age of Catherine II to the October revolution of 1917. 222p.

Vengerov, S. A. Istochinki slovariĭa russkikh pisateleĭ. Sanktpeterburg, Tip. Imp. Akad. Nauk, 1900–17. v.1-4. **R788**

v.1-4, A-Nekrasov.

A dictionary of Russian writers with references to sources.

History

Gudziĭ, Nikolaĭ Kallinikovich. History of early Russian literature; tr. from the 2d Russian ed. by Susan Wilbur Jones; introd. by Gleb Struve. N.Y., Macmillan, 1949. 545p. $10. **R789**

A chronological survey from the eleventh through the seventeenth centuries with descriptions and analyses.

Mirsky, D. S. A history of Russian literature; comprising A history of Russian literature and Contemporary Russian literature, ed. and abridged by Frances J. Whitfield. N.Y., Knopf, 1949. 518p. **R790**

Anthologies

Ezhov, I. S. and **Shamurin, E. I.** Russkaĭa poeziĭa xx veka; antologiĭa russkoĭ liriki ot simbolizma do nashikh dneĭ. [Moskva] "Novaĭa Moskva," 1925. 671p. **R791**

The anthology includes representative poets of the symbolist, imagist and futurist schools, as well as those representing the realist revolutionary tendency, with a large representation of peasant and proletarian poetry with its decided communist ideology; many new and little known personages included. Contains a bibliographical guide, p.561-91, which gives authors' dates, works, etc. Well indexed.

Oxford book of Russian verse, chosen by Maurice Baring. 2d ed. supplemented by D. P. Costello. Ox., Clarendon Pr.; N.Y., Oxford Univ. Pr., 1949. 311p. 12s. 6d.; $4.75. **R792**

An enlargement, not a revision, of the first edition, 1924. In Russian.

Sobolevskiĭ, Alekseĭ Ivanovich. Veliko-russkiĭa narodnyĭa pĭesni. S.-Petersburg, 1895–1902. 7v. **R793**

A collection of Russian folk songs gathered from old and rare songsters and other collections of songs, from little known musical publications and from provincial publications of songs and songsters. The folk songs include those of family life, recruiting, soldiers, robbers, love songs, as well as humorous and satirical folk songs.

Wiener, Leo. Anthology of Russian literature from the earliest period to the present time. N.Y., Putnam, 1902–03. 2v. il.   **R794**

v.1, Tenth–eighteenth centuries; v.2, Nineteenth century.

Selections from prose and poetry, in English translation; with biographies and bibliographies.

Yarmolinsky, Avraham. A treasury of Russian verse. N.Y., Macmillan, 1949. 314p. $5.   **R795**

Primarily poems of the nineteenth and twentieth centuries, in translation with biographical notes.

CLASSICAL LANGUAGES
General works
Bibliography

Fabricius, Johann Albert. Bibliotheca graeca . . . Ed. 4 variorum curis emendatior atque auctior. Hamburgi, Bohn, 1790–1809. 12v.   **R796**

———— Index. Lipsiae, Cnobloch, 1838. 94p.

—— Bibliotheca Latina, mediae et infimae aetatis, cum supplemento Christiani Schoettgenii jam a p. Joanne Dominico Mansi. Florentiae, Baracchi, 1858–59. 6v. in 3.   **R797**

Engelmann, Wilhelm. Bibliotheca scriptorum classicorum; 8. Aufl. umfassend die Literatur von 1700 bis 1878, neu bearb. von E. Preuss. Leipzig, Engelmann, 1880–82. 2v.   **R798**

v.1, Greek; v.2, Latin.

The standard bibliography, useful for information about editions of collected works and separate works, translations, and works about. Of first importance in the large reference or college library. Continued for material since 1878 by the following:

Klussmann, Rudolf. Bibliotheca scriptorum classicorum et graecorum et latinorum. Die Literatur von 1878 bis 1896 einschliesslich umfassend. Leipzig, Reisland, 1909–13. 2v. in 4. o.p.
                          R799

v.1, Greek; v.2, Latin.

Also published as volumes 146, 151, 156, and 165 of *Jahresbericht über die Fortschritte der klassischen Altertumswissenschaft* (Berlin, 1873-).

Marouzeau, Jules. Dix années de bibliographie classique; bibliographie critique et analytique de l'antiquité gréco-latine pour la période 1914–1924. Paris, Soc. d'Édit. "Les belles lettres," 1927. 2v.   **R800**

v.1, Auteurs et textes; v.2, Matières et disciplines.

The subject volume covers the whole field of history and culture of the classical world.

Continued by *L'Année philologique* (R803).

Herescu, Niculae I. Bibliographie de la littérature latine. Paris, Société d'Édition "Les belles lettres," 1943. 426p. (Collection de bibliographie classique, pub. sous la direction de J. Marouzeau)
                          R801

An analytical, selective bibliography of materials on Latin subjects. Arranged by period with an alphabetical index to Latin authors. No index to secondary authors. Under each author, material is arranged under such subheadings as manuscripts, editions, extracts, translations, dictionaries and indexes, studies. In works of voluminous authors these may be further subdivided.

Useful because it brings together in a convenient form a large amount of material that is otherwise scattered. Covers to approximately 1940.

Ooteghem, J. van. Bibliotheca graeca et latina à l'usage des professeurs des humanités gréco-latine. 2. ed. rev. et aug. Namur, Éditions de la revue "Les études classiques" [1946]. 386p. 150fr.
                          R802

The first edition appeared in *Les études classiques* in April and October 1936. Compiled especially for teachers in the secondary schools and therefore treats mainly the authors taught in the schools, with other authors receiving less attention. Lists editions, translations, dictionaries, and critical studies under each author.

ANNUALS

L'Année philologique; bibliographie critique et analytique de l'antiquité gréco-latine, pub. sous la direction de J. Marouzeau, 1924/26- . Paris, Soc. d'Édition "Les belles lettres," 1928- . Annual. (v.18, 1947 (pub. 1949) 1500fr.)   **R803**

A very useful survey. Some volumes cover more than one year and all include additional references to previous years.

A continuation of Marouzeau (R800).

Bibliotheca philologica classica, 1874- . Leipzig, Reisland, 1875- . v.1- . Annual. (Beiblatt zum Jahresbericht über die Fortschritte der klassischen Altertumswissenschaft)   **R804**

Annual survey. Wider in scope than Engelmann (R798) or Klussmann (R799).

Klassieke bibliographie 1. jaarg., 1929- . Maandlijsten van tijdschriftartikelen met driemaandelijksche lijsten van nieuwe boekwerken in die Buma-Bibliotheek en in andere Nederlandsche bibliotheken. Utrecht, 1930- . Annual.   **R805**

Books and periodical articles, arranged by subject. Published also on cards.

Year's work in classical studies. v.1, 1906- , ed. for the Classical Journals Board. Lond., Arrowsmith, 1907- . Annual. (1939–45 pub. in 1v. 1948)   **R806**

Not as comprehensive as the *Bibliotheca philologica classica* (R804) or *L'Année philologique* (R803).

TRANSLATIONS INTO ENGLISH

Foster, Finley Melville Kendall. English translations from the Greek, a bibliographical survey. N.Y., Columbia Univ. Pr., 1918. 146p. (Columbia Univ. studies in English) $2. **R807**

A list of translations from 1476–1917.

Smith, F. Seymour. The classics in translation; an annotated guide to the best translations of the Greek and Latin classics into English. Lond., N.Y., Scribner, 1930. 307p. **R808**

Handbooks

Harsh, Philip Whaley. A handbook of classical drama. Stanford Univ., Calif., Stanford Univ. Pr., 1944. 526p. $5. **R809**

Discussions of Greek and Roman dramatists and their plays "designed to be a modern appreciation of the plays as literature and a convenient brief guide to further critical material."

Bibliography, p.497-511 lists texts in the original language and English translations. Recommended translations are starred.

Harvey, *Sir* Paul. Oxford companion to classical literature. Ox., Clarendon Pr., 1937. 468p. 7s. 6d.; $4. **R810**

A useful handbook of concise information on classical writers, literary forms and subjects, individual works, names and subjects in Greek and Roman history, institutions, religion, etc., about which the student or reader of classical literature may need information.

Thompson, *Sir* Edward Maunde. An introduction to Greek and Latin palaeography. Ox., Clarendon Pr., 1912. 600p. **R811**

An enlarged edition of his *Handbook of Greek and Latin palaeography* (3d ed. 1906).

Bibliography, p.571-83.

Collections

Loeb classical library, founded by James Loeb. Camb., Harv. Univ. Pr., 1912- . v.1- . $3 per v. **R812**

An extensive collection numbering in May 1950 more than 380 volumes, in two series, Greek and Latin.

Each volume gives parallel texts of original and English translation; has no general index as yet, but indexes to individual authors, though varying in kind and value, are frequently useful for locating a subject or specific passage.

Greek

Christ, Wilhelm von. Geschichte der griechischen Literatur. Unter Mitwirkung von Otto Stählin bearb. von Wilhelm Schmid. 6. Aufl. München, Beck, 1912–24. 2v. in 3. il. (Handbuch der klassischen Altertumswissenschaft, hrsg. von I. von Müller, 7. Bd.) **R813**

Bd.1, Die klassische Periode; Bd.2, 1. T., Die nachklassische Periode; 2. T., von 100 bis 530 nach Christus.

The standard German history, very detailed, with full general index and many bibliographical notes.

Croiset, Alfred and **Croiset, Maurice.** Histoire de la littérature grecque. 2.-4. ed. Paris, Boccard, 1899–1929. 5v. **R814**

v.1, 4th ed. 1928; v.2-3, 3d ed. 1914–1929; v.4, 2d ed. 1899; v.5, 3d ed. 1928.

Important reference history, many bibliographies.

Rose, Herbert Jennings. Handbook of Greek literature, from Homer to the age of Lucian. Lond., Methuen [1934]. 454p. **R815**

Anthologies

Oxford book of Greek verse, chosen by Gilbert Murray, Cyril Bailey, [and others]. Ox., Clarendon Pr., 1931. 608p. $4. **R816**

Oxford book of Greek verse in translation, ed. by T. F. Higham and C. M. Bowra. Ox., Clarendon Pr., 1938. 781p. 8s. 6d.; $5. **R817**

"Every piece in the *Oxford book of Greek verse* is here translated, and the same arrangement of authors and numeration is followed. . . . Wherever possible, we have used existing translations. . . ."—*Pref.*

Individual authors

AESCHYLUS

Dindorf, Wilhelm. Lexicon Aeschyleum. Leipzig, Teubner, 1876. 432p. **R818**

ARISTOPHANES

Dunbar, Henry. Complete concordance to the comedies and fragments of Aristophanes. Ox., Clarendon Pr., 1883. 342p. **R819**

Based upon the text of Dindorf's edition of Aristophanes (Oxford, 1835), and Meineke's edition of the Fragments (Berlin, 1840).

Todd, Otis Johnson. Index Aristophaneus. Camb., Harv. Univ. Pr.; Ox., Univ. Pr., 1932. 275p. $5; 21s. **R820**

ARISTOTLE

Bonitz, Hermann. Index Aristotelicus. Berlin, Reimer, 1870. 878p. **R821**

Forms part of volume 5 of the Bekker edition of Aristotle (Berlin, 1831–70).

Organ, Troy Wilson. An index to Aristotle in English translation. Princeton, N.J., Princeton Univ. Pr., 1949. 181p. $5. **R822**

Based on the translation by W. D. Ross and J. A. Smith (Ox., Univ. Pr., 1908–31. 11v.). Does not include the "Fragments" or the "Constitution of Athens."

EURIPIDES

Beck, Christian Daniel. Index Graecitatis Euripideae. Camb. [Eng.], Grant, 1829. [n.p.] **R823**

HERODOTUS

Powell, John Enoch. A lexicon to Herodotus. . . . Camb., Univ. Pr., 1938. 391p. 42s.; $12.50, Macmillan. **R824**

Based on the third Oxford text of Hude (1926).—Cf. *Pref.*

HOMER

Cunliffe, Richard John. Lexicon of the Homeric dialect. Lond., Blackie, 1924. 445p. **R825**

—— Homeric proper and place names. Lond., Blackie, 1931. 42p. **R826**

A supplement to the *Lexicon* (R825).

Dunbar, Henry. Complete concordance to the Odyssey and Hymns of Homer, to which is added a concordance to the parallel passages in the Iliad, Odyssey, and Hymns. Ox., Clarendon Pr., 1880. 419p. o.p. **R827**

A companion to Prendergast (R828), intended to form with that work a complete concordance to Homer. Based on Wolfgang Seber's *Index vocabularium in Homeri* (1604), and compiled from the text of Ameis' edition of the *Odyssey* and Baumeister's edition of the *Hymns, epigrams.*

Prendergast, Guy Lushington. Complete concordance to the Iliad of Homer. Lond., Longmans, 1875. 416p. o.p. **R828**

Compiled from Priestley's edition of Heyne's Homer, 1834.

JOSEPHUS

Thackeray, Henry St. John. Lexicon to Josephus . . . pub. for the Jewish Institute of Religion, New York, by the Alexander Kohut Memorial Foundation. Paris, Geuthner, 1930–34. pt.1–2. **R829**

pt. 1–2, A-dias.

PLATO

Apelt, Otto. Platon-index als Gesamtregister zu der Übersetzung in der Philosophischen Bibliothek. 2. verb. Aufl. Leipzig, Meiner, 1923. 158p. (Der Philosophischen Bibliothek. 182) **R830**

Ast, Friedrich. Lexicon Platonicum; sive, Vocum Platonicarum index. Lipsiae, Weidmann, 1835–38. 3v. **R831**

SOPHOCLES

Dindorf, Wilhelm. Lexicon Sophocleum. Leipzig, Teubner, 1870. 533p. **R832**

Latin

Labriolle, Pierre Champagne de. History and literature of Christianity from Tertullian to Boethius; from the French by Herbert Wilson, with introductory foreword by His Eminence Cardinal Gasquet. Lond., K. Paul; N.Y., Knopf, 1924. 555p. 25s.; $7.50. **R833**

Manitius, Maximilianus. Geschichte der lateinischen Literatur des Mittelalters. München, Beck, 1911–31. 3v. (Handbuch der klassischen Altertumswissenschaft . . . hrsg. von I. von Müller, 9. Bd. 2. Abt. 1.-3. Teil) **R834**

v.1, Von Justinian bis zur Mitte des 10. Jahrh.; v.2, Von der Mitte des 10. Jahrh. bis zum Ausbruch des Kampfes zwischen Kirche u. Staat; v.3, Vom Ausbruch des Kirchenstreites bis zum Ende des 12. Jahrh.

The standard history of medieval Latin literature, indispensable in the large reference library.

Schanz, Martin. Geschichte der römischen Literatur bis zum Gesetzgebungswerk des Kaisers Justinian. 1.-4. ganz umgearb. und stark verm. Aufl. München, Beck, 1911–35. 4v. in 5. (Handbuch der klassischen Altertumswissenschaft . . . hrsg. von I. von Müller. 8. Bd.) **R835**

v.1-2, 4th ed. 1927–35; v.3, 3d ed. 1912; v.4¹, 2d ed. 1914; v.4², 1st ed. 1920.

v.1, Die römische Literatur in der Zeit der Republik; v.2, Die römische Literatur in der Zeit der Monarchie bis auf Hadrian; v.3, Die Zeit von Hadrian 117 bis auf Constantin 324; v.4, Von Constantin bis zum Gesetzgebungswerk Justinians: 1. Hälfte, Die Literatur des vierten Jahrhunderts; 2. Hälfte, Die Literatur des fünften und sechsten Jahrhunderts.

Teuffel, Wilhelm Sigismund. History of Roman literature, rev. and enl. by Ludwig Schwabe. Authorized tr. from the 5th German ed. by George C. W. Warr. Lond., Bell, 1891–92. 2v. **R836**

Contents: v.1, The Republican period; v.2, The Imperial period.

Anthologies

Oxford book of Latin verse, from the earliest fragments to the end of the vth century A.D., chosen by H. W. Garrod. Ox., Clarendon Pr., 1912. 531p. 8s. 6d.; $4. **R837**

Oxford book of medieval Latin verse, chosen by Stephen Gaselee. Ox., Clarendon Pr., 1928. 250p. 8s. 6d.; $4. **R838**

Individual authors

See Paul Faider's *Répertoire des index et lexiques d'auteurs latins* (Paris, Soc. d'Édit. "Les Belle-lettres," 1926. 56p.) for titles of other dictionaries and indexes of Latin authors.

APULEIUS

Oldfather, William Abbott, Canter, Howard Vernon and **Perry, Ben Edwin.** Index Apuleianus. Middletown, Conn., Amer. Phil. Assoc., 1934. 490p. (Philological monographs. no.3) **R839**

BEDA VENERABILIS

Jones, Putnam Fennell. Concordance to the Historia ecclesiastica of Bede. Camb., Mass., pub. for the Concordance Soc. by the Mediaeval Acad. of America, 1929. 585p. (Mediaeval Acad. of America. Pub. 2) $6.50. **R840**

Based on the text of Charles Plummer's edition of Bede's *Opera historica* (Ox., Clarendon Pr., 1896).

Jones, Charles Williams. Bedae pseudepigrapha: Scientific writings falsely attributed to Bede. Ithaca, N.Y., Cornell Univ. Pr., 1939. 154p. $3. **R841**

BOETHIUS

Cooper, Lane. Concordance of Boethius; the five theological tractates and the Consolation of philosophy. Camb., Mass., Mediaeval Acad. of America, 1928. 467p. (Mediaeval Acad. of America. Pub. 1) $5. **R842**

CAESAR

Menge, Rudolf and **Preuss, Siegmund.** Lexicon Caesarianum. Leipzig, Teubner, 1890. 1428 col. **R843**

Meusel, Heinrich. Lexicon Caesarianum. Berlin, Weber, 1887–93. 2v. in 3. **R844**

Preuss, Siegmund. Vollständiges Lexikon zu den pseudo-cäsarianischen Schriftwerken. Erlangen, Deichertsche Universitätsbuchhandlung, 1884. 433p. **R845**

pt.1, bell. Gall. 8, und bell. Alex; pt.2, bell. Afr. und Hisp.

Sihler, Ernest Gottlieb. A complete lexicon of the Latinity of Caesar's Gallic war. Bost., Ginn, 1891. 188p. **R846**

CATULLUS

Wetmore, Monroe Nichols. Index verborvm Catvllianvs. New Haven, Yale Univ. Pr., 1912. 115p. $2.50. **R847**

A complete word index to the poems of Catullus, based upon Ellis edition, 1906, and including also the variants found in the editions of Baehrens-Schulze, 1893, of Haupt-Vahlen, 1904, of Riese, 1884, of Mueller, 1892, of Friedrich, 1908, and of Merrill, 1893.

CICERO

Merguet, Hugo. Handlexikon zu Cicero. Leipzig, Dieterich, 1905. 816p. **R848**

—— Lexikon zu den Schriften Cicero's mit Angabe sämtlicher Stellen. Jena, Fischer, 1877–94. 7v. **R849**

1. T., Lexikon zu den Reden. 1877–84. 4v.; 2. T., Lexikon zu den philosophischen Schriften. 1887–94. 3v.

Oldfather, William Abbott, Canter, Howard Vernon and **Abbott, Kenneth Morgan.** Index verborum Ciceronis Epistularum. Urbana, Univ. of Illinois Pr., 1938. 583p. **R850**

Based on the edition by L. C. Purser in Oxford Classical Texts, 1901–1903.

HORACE

Cooper, Lane. Concordance to the works of Horace. Wash., Carnegie Inst., 1916. 593p. $7. **R851**

Based on the text of Vollmer's *editio minor* (Leipzig, 1910), including also variant readings from his *editio major*, 1912, and other variants from Wickham's edition of the *Odes, Carmen saeculare* and *Epodes* (Oxford, 1904), and the *Satires* (Oxford, 1903).

LUCAN

Deferrari, Roy Joseph, Fanning, *Sister* **Maria Walburg** and **Sullivan,** *Sister* **Anne Stanislaus.** A concordance of Lucan. . . . Wash., Catholic Univ. of America Pr., 1940. 602p. $6. **R852**

"Based on the text of A. E. Housman (Oxford, Blackwell, 1927)."—*Pref.*

LUCRETIUS CARUS

Paulson, Johannes. Index Lucretianus continens copiam verborum quam exhibent editiones Lachmanni, Bernaysi, Munronis, Briegeri et Guissani. (Ut manu scriptus prelo datus) Gotoburgi, Zachrisson, 1911. 177p. **R853**

OVID

Deferrari, Roy Joseph, Barry, *Sister* **Inviolata and McGuire, Martin Rawson Patrick.** A concordance of Ovid. Wash., Catholic Univ. of America Pr., 1939. 2220p. $20. **R854**

"A combination of a concordance and an index verborum . . . based exclusively on the Teubner edition of Ovid."—*Pref.*

PLAUTUS

Lodge, Gonzalez. Lexicon Plavtinvm. Leipzig, Teubner, 1904–33. 2v. **R855**

PROPERTIUS

Phillimore, John S. Index verborum Propertianus. Ox., Clarendon Pr., 1905. 111p. **R856**

PRUDENTIUS CLEMENS

Deferrari, Roy Joseph and **Campbell, James Marshall.** Concordance of Prudentius. Camb., Mass., Mediaeval Acad. of America, 1932. 833p. (Mediaeval Acad. of America. Pub. 9) $5. **R857**

SENECA

Oldfather, William Abbott, Pease, Arthur Stanley and **Canter, Howard Vernon.** Index verborum quae in Senecae fabulis necnon in Octavia praetexta reperiunter. Urbana, Univ. of Illinois, 1918. 272p. (Univ. of Illinois studies in language and literature. v.4, no.2-4) **R858**

STATIUS

Deferrari, Roy Joseph and **Eagan,** *Sister* **M. Clement.** A concordance of Statius. Brookland, D.C., Author, 1943. 926p. $8. **R859**

SUETONIUS TRANQUILLUS

Howard, Albert Andrew and **Jackson, Carl Newell.** Index verborvm C. Svetoni Tranqvilli stiliqve eivs proprietatvm nonnvllarvm. Camb., Harv. Univ. Pr.; Ox. Univ. Pr., 1922. 273p. $4.50; 21s. **R860**

TACITUS

Fabia, Philippe. Onomasticon Tacitevm. Paris, Fontemoing, 1900. 772p. (Annales de l'Université de Lyon, n.s., t.2, fasc. 4) **R861**

Gerber, Arnold and **Greef, Adolf.** Lexicon Taciteum. U et V litteras confecit C. John. Leipzig, Teubner, 1903. 1802p. **R862**

TERENTIUS AFER

Jenkins, Edgar Bryan. Index verborum Terentianus. Chapel Hill, Univ. of North Carolina Pr., 1932. 187p. $2.50. **R863**

THOMAS À KEMPIS

Storr, Rayner. Concordance to the Latin original of the four books known as De imitatione Christi given to the world A.D. 1441 by Thomas à Kempis. Lond. and N.Y., Frowde, 1910. 599p. **R864**

Based on text of Karl Hirsch's second edition, 1891.

VERGIL

Mambelli, Giuliano. Gli studi Virgiliani nel secolo xx. Contributo ad una bibliografia generale. Firenze, Sansoni, 1940. 2v. (Guide bibliografiche dell' Istituto Nazionale di Cultura Fascista. VII) **R865**

An annotated bibliography of books and periodical articles in many languages.

Merguet, Hugo. Lexikon zu Vergilius, mit Angabe sämtlicher Stellen. Leipzig, Richard Schmidt, 1912. 786p. **R866**

Wetmore, Monroe Nichols. Index verborum Vergilianus. New Haven, Yale Univ. Pr., 1911. 554p. **R867**

A word index to the *Eclogues,* the *Georgics* and the *Aeneid* and to the poems usually included in the *Appendix Vergiliana.* Based upon Ribbeck's text edition of Vergil, 1895, but contains also the variants in Ribbeck's critical edition, 1894, and in the editions of Ladewig-Schaper-Deuticke, 1902–07, of Conington-Nettleship-Haverfield, 1883–1898, of Thilo, 1886, of Benoist, 1876–1880, and of Gossrau, 1876, and gives also readings from the edition of the *Appendix Vergiliana* by Ellis, 1907, and that of the *Culex* by Leo, 1891.

ORIENTAL LANGUAGES
Arabic

Chauvin, Victor. Bibliographie des ouvrages arabes ou relatifs aux arabes publiés dans l'Europe chrétienne de 1810 à 1885. Liége, Vaillant-Carmanne, 1892–1922. 12v. **R868**

Contents: (1) Préface. Table de Schnurrer. Les proverbes; (2) Kalîah; (3) Louqmâne et les fabulistes. Barlaam. 'Antar et les romans de chevalerie; (4-7) Les Milles et une nuits; (8) Syntipas; (9) Pierre Alphonse. Secundus. Recueils orientaux. Tables de Henning et de Mardrus. Contes occidentaux. Les maqâmes; (10) Le Coran et la tradition; (11) Mahomet; (12) Le Mahométisme.

No general index but some parts have alphabetical or subject indexes, some are arranged alphabetically.

Brockelmann, Carl. Geschichte der arabischen Litteratur. 2. den Supplementbände angepasste Aufl. Leiden, Brill, 1943–49. 2v. G20.　**R869**

Extensive bibliographies.
A new edition of this standard work "fitted to the *Supplementband*" (Leiden, Brill, 1936–42. 3v.).

Nicholson, Reynold A. Literary history of the Arabs. Camb., Univ. Pr., 1930. 506p. il.　**R870**

Chinese

Mayers, William Frederick. The Chinese reader's manual; a handbook of biographical, historical, mythological and general literary reference. Shanghai, Amer. Presbyterian Mission Pr., 1874. 440p.　**R871**

Legge, James. Chinese classics; with a translation, critical and exegetical notes, prolegomena and copious indexes. 2d ed. rev. Ox., Clarendon Pr., 1893–95. 5v. in 8. maps.　**R872**

Volumes 1-2, second edition, revised, 1893–95, printed at the Clarendon Press, Oxford; volumes 3-5, printed at the London Missionary Society's Printing Office, Hong-kong, are a reissue of the older edition with new title page and imprint: London, H. Frowde [n.d.].
The volumes originally planned were "to embrace all the books in 'The Thirteen king'" but volumes 6-7 were never published. English translations of the *Yih king* and the *Li ki* appeared respectively as volume 16 and volumes 27-28 of the series *Sacred books of the East.* A translation of the *Hsiao king* appeared in volume 3 of the same series.
v.1, Confucian analects, the Great learning, and the Doctrine of the mean; v.2, The works of Mencius; v.3, The Shoo king, or the Book of historical documents: pt.1, The first parts of the Shoo-king, or the Books of T'ang; the Books of Yu; the Books of Hea; the Books of Shang; and the Prolegomena; pt.2, The fifth part of the Shoo king, or the Books of Chow; and the indexes; v.4, The She-king, or the Book of poetry: pt.1, The first part of the She-king, or the Lessons from the states; and the Prolegomena; pt.2, The second, third, and fourth parts of the She-king, or the Minor odes of the kingdom, the Greater odes of the kingdom, the Sacrificial odes and praise-songs; and the indexes; v.5, The Ch'un ts'ew, with the Tso chuen: pt.1, Dukes Yin, Hwan, Chwang, Min, He, Wan, Seuen and Ch'ing; and the Prolegomena; pt.2, Dukes Seang, Ch'aou, Ting, and Gae, with Tso's appendix; and the indexes.

Schyns, Joseph. 1500 modern Chinese novels and plays. Peiping, Catholic Univ. Pr., 1948. 484p. $5.　**R873**

Study of contemporary Chinese literature, gives reviews in English of 1500 novels and plays and about 200 biographies. Names and titles are given in Anglicized form and in Chinese characters.
Subtitle: "Present day fiction and drama in China by Su Hsueh-Lin; Short biographies of authors by Chao Yen-Sheng."

Hebrew

Shunami, Shlomo. Bibliography of Jewish bibliographies. Jerusalem, Univ. Pr., 1936. 399p.　**R874**

For description *see* K240.

Benjacob, Isaac. Ozar Ha-Sepharim (Bücherschatz). Bibliographie der gesammten hebraeischen Literatur mit Einschluss der Handschriften (bis 1863). Wilna, Benjacob, 1880. 678p.　**R875**

Title pages in Hebrew, Russian, German, and Latin. Text in Hebrew. Arranged alphabetically. Includes entries for Hebrew books published up to 1863.

Frankfurt am Main. Stadtbibliothek. Katalog der Judaica und Hebraica. Frankfurt am Main, M. Lehrberger, 1932. v.1. 646p.　**R876**

Edited by A. Freimann.
v.1, Judaica.

Friedberg, B. Bet eked sepharim. Lexique bibliographique de tous les ouvrages de la littérature hébraïque et judéo-allemande . . . imprimés et publiés de 1475–1900. Anvers [Delplace, Koch] 1928–31. 844p.　**R877**

Includes Arabic, Greek, Italian, Persian, Samaritan, Spanish-Portuguese and Tartarian. Entirely in Hebrew.

Schwab, Moïse. Répertoire des articles relatifs à l'histoire et à la littérature juives, parus dans les périodiques, de 1665 à 1900. Paris, Geuthner, 1914–23. 539p.　**R878**

Reisen, Zalman. Leksikon fun der yidisher literatur. . . . Wilno, Kleckin, 1927–29. 4v. il.　**R879**

In Yiddish.

Waxman, Meyer. A history of Jewish literature from the close of the Bible to our own days. N.Y., Bloch, 1930–41. 4v. il.　**R880**

v.2, 4 pub. in 2d ed. enl. and corrected. 1943–47.

Japanese

Kokusai Bunka Shinkokai, Tokyo. Introduction to classic Japanese literature. Tokyo, Kokusai Bunka Shinkokai (The Society for International Cultural Relations), 1948. 443p.　**R881**

—— Introduction to contemporary Japanese literature. Tokyo, K.B.S. (The Society for International Cultural Relations), 1939. 485p.　**R882**

Bonneau, Georges. Bibliographie de la littérature japonaise contemporaine. Paris, Geuthner; Tôkyô, Mitsukoshi, 1938. 280p. (Bull. de la Maison Franco-Japonaise, t.9, nos. 1-4, 1937)　**R883**

"5ème supplement à la *Bibliographie des principales publications éditées dans l'Empire japonais.*"

A valuable bibliography. pt.1, Introduction: gives important sources, Japanese and western; list of translations from western works into Japanese; classification of authors as to type or school; pt.2, Bibliographie des oeuvres représentatives originales de la littérature japonaise contemporaine. Arranged alphabetically by author, gives English transliteration, Japanese characters, date and place of birth and death; subject arrangement of works with title in transliteration, Japanese characters and translation into French; place and date. Includes magazine articles; pt.3, Index to names in Introduction and Bibliographie.

Persian

Storey, Charles Ambrose. Persian literature; a bio-bibliographical survey. Lond., Luzac, 1927–39. v.1-2$^{1-3}$. **R884**

Sec. 1, Our'anic literature; sec. 2: fasc. 1, General history, the prophets and early Islam; fasc. 2, Special histories of Persia, Central Asia and the remaining parts of the world except India; fasc. 3, History of India.

Browne, Edward Granville. A literary history of Persia. Camb., Univ. Pr., 1928. 4v. il. **R885**

Contents: v.1, From the earliest times to Firdawsí; v.2, From Firdawsí to Sádi; v.3, The Tartar dominion (1265–1502); v.4, Modern times (1500–1924).

Reissue not new edition of volumes originally published separately, some with slightly different title.

BIOGRAPHY

❧ Dictionaries of biography are among the most used reference books in any collection and even a small library will need several works in this class. There are three main types of biographical dictionaries: (1) general; (2) national or regional; (3) professional or occupational. Each of these may be subdivided into (1) general or retrospective and (2) contemporary.

The basic works needed in almost any American library would include: the *Dictionary of American biography* (S32); the latest or at least a recent edition of *Who's Who in America* (S40); *Current biography* (S27) or the *Monthly supplement* to *Who's Who in America* (S29); and *Webster's Biographical dictionary* (S25). To these would probably be added the appropriate regional Who's who and where possible the *Biography index* (S2).

In examining biographical dictionaries, test them for the points enumerated in the general instructions for examining reference books, and in addition note carefully any evidence of lack of objectivity in the selection of names. Unscrupulous publishers will sometimes include "padded" or unduly eulogistic articles on comparatively unknown persons, with the expectation, or on condition, that these persons will pay for inclusion or will subscribe for the book. The inclusion of such articles puts the book in the "commercial" or "vanity" class and casts doubt upon the authority of all articles. Such books are not necessarily to be rejected if they happen to be the only ones in their field, but they must always be used with caution.

GENERAL WORKS

Indexes

Arnim, Max. Internationale Personalbibliographie, 1800–1943. 2. verb. und stark verm. Aufl. Leipzig, Hiersemann, 1944- . Bd.1- .   **S1**

Primarily an index to bibliographies of individuals, but, as many of the bibliographies indexed have accompanying biographical data, the work serves also as an index to biographical articles. For full description *see* (A10).

Biography index; a cumulative index to biographical material in books and magazines. N.Y., Wilson, 1947- . v.1- . (In progress) Service basis.   **S2**

A quarterly index to biographical material, published in September, December and March with annual cumulations in June. "It includes current books in the English language wherever published; biographical material from the 1500 periodicals now regularly indexed in the Wilson indexes, plus a selected list of professional journals in the fields of law and medicine; obituaries of national and international interest from the *New York Times*. All types of biographical material are covered: pure biography, critical material of biographical significance, autobiography, letters, diaries, memoirs, journals, genealogies, fiction, drama, poetry, bibliographies, obituaries, pictorial works and juvenile literature. Works of collective biography are fully analyzed. Incidental biographical material such as prefaces and chapters in otherwise non-biographical books is included. Portraits are indicated when they appear in conjunction with indexed material. . . ."—*Pref.*

Index is in two sections: (1) Name alphabet, giving for each biographee, insofar as possible, full name, dates, nationality, and occupation or profession with index references; (2) Index by profession and occupation. Large categories, such as authors, are divided by nationality.

The first volume indexes back to Jan. 1, 1946.

Chevalier, Cyr Ulysse. Répertoire des sources historiques du moyen âge; bio-bibliographique. Nouv. éd. refondue, corr. et augm. Paris, Picard, 1903–07. 2v.   **S3**

The most complete and important work for the medieval period, arranged alphabetically, giving under the French form of each name (1) brief biographical data, i.e., characterizing phrase and dates of birth and death, and (2) references to books, periodicals, society transactions, etc., where some account of the personage may be found. Very useful for out-of-the-way names, or for complete lists of references on more familiar names; less useful for quick reference work on more familiar names because too much material is given for the ordinary reader. For the large and university library.

For complete set *see* V85.

Hefling, Helen and **Richards, Eva.** Index to contemporary biography and criticism. New ed. rev. and enl. by Helen Hefling and Jessie W. Dyde . . . introd. by M. E. Hazeltine. Bost., Faxon, 1934. 229p. (Useful reference ser. 50) $4.   **S4**

An index to biographical material about persons born about 1850 or later. Some 417 collections of biography and criticism have been indexed, omitting such strictly reference works as the various Who's whos.

Logasa, Hannah. Biography in collections; suitable for junior and senior high schools. 3d ed. rev. and enl. N.Y., Wilson, 1940. 152p. $1.50.   **S5**

Based on the first two editions, this edition analyzes 334 collections including 41 additional books. It is an alphabetical list by biographee, with subject classifications.

Oettinger, Eduard Maria. Bibliographie biographique universelle. Dictionnaire des ouvrages relatifs à l'histoire de la vie publique et privée des personnages célèbres de tous les temps et de toutes les nations, depuis le commencement du monde jusqu'à nos jours . . . enrichi du répertoire des bio-bibliographies générales, nationales et spéciales. Bruxelles, Stienon, 1854. 2v. (Repr. Paris, Lacroix, 1866)   **S6**

Lists separately published works about a large number of eminent persons.

O'Neill, Edward Hayes. Biography by Americans, 1658–1936; a subject bibliography. Phila., Univ. of Penn. Pr.; Lond., Milford, 1939. 465p. $4.   **S7**

Attempts to record all known biographies written by Americans, except that in the case of particularly famous men only the more important books are listed. Arranged alphabetically by the subject of the biography. No index to authors. Locates copies in eight libraries.

Phillips, Lawrence Barnett. Dictionary of biographical reference; containing over 100,000 names; together with a classed index of the biographical literature of Europe and America. New ed. rev., cor. and augm. with supplement to date, by Frank Weitenkampf. [3d ed.] Lond., Low; Phila., Gebbie, 1889. 1038p.   **S8**

1st ed. 1871 (1020p.); 2d ed. under title *Great index of biographical reference*, 1881 (1036p.).

International in scope and covers all periods. Gives full name, identifying phrase, dates and reference to collections where biographical material can be found.

Riches, Phyllis M. Analytical bibliography of universal collected biography, comprising books published in the English tongue in Great Britain

and Ireland, America and the British dominions . . . with an introduction by Sir Frederic Kenyon. Lond., Lib. Assoc., 1934. 709p.   **S9**

An index to biographies in collected works, arranged alphabetically by the names of the persons, followed by a bibliography of the books analyzed; a chronological list of the biographees; and a list arranged by profession or trade.

Essay and general literature index. N.Y., Wilson, 1934- .   **S10**

Contains a large amount of analytical material for biography and criticism of individuals and so often serves as an index of biography. For full description *see* R167.

Sears, Minnie Earl. Standard catalog: Biography section. 2d ed., rev. and enl. About 1150 titles of the most representative, interesting and useful biographies. . . . N.Y., Wilson, 1927–32. 129p. and suppl., 67p.   **S11**

A selected bibliography of 1614 biographies (main list 1150, fifth supplement, 464), with analytical indexing of biographical material on about 1800 persons for whom no separate biographies are included. A revised edition, with additional analysis, is included in the combined edition of the *Standard catalog for public libraries* (A551).

Shaw, Thomas S. Index to profile sketches in New Yorker magazine. Bost., Faxon, 1946. 100p. $2. (Useful reference ser. no.72)   **S12**

Covers volume 1, Feb. 1925 to volume 16, Feb. 1940 when the *New Yorker* began to be indexed in the *Readers' guide to periodical literature*. The profiles are indexed by subjects, occupations of subjects, and authors.

Stauffer, Donald Alfred. The art of biography in 18th century England: Bibliographical supplement. Princeton, N.J., Princeton Univ. Pr., 1941. 293p. 2v. set $8.50; $5 ea.   **S13**

A subject and author index of biographies and autobiographies written or translated in England 1700–1800, with a "chronological table of the most important biographical works in England, 1700–1800." A supplement to his *The art of biography in 18th century England* (Princeton Univ. Pr., 1941).

Ungherini, Aglauro. Manuel de bibliographie biographique et d'iconographie des femmes célèbres. Turin, Roux; Paris, Nilsson, 1892–1905. 3v. i.e., main work, 896 col.; 1st suppl., 634 col.; 2d suppl., 758 col.   **S14**

A useful index to material about women of all countries and all periods. Gives an identifying phrase with dates of birth and death, and lists books, parts of books, periodical articles, portraits, autographs, etc. There is a cumulated index in the second supplement.

U. S. Library of Congress. General Reference and Bibliography Division. Biographical sources for foreign countries. Wash., 1944–45. no.1-4. Gratis to libraries.   **S15**

pt.1, General, comp. by Helen D. Jones; pt.2, Germany and Austria, comp. by Nelson R. Burr; pt.3, The Philippines, comp. by Helen D. Jones; pt.4, The Japanese Empire, comp. by Nelson R. Burr.

A very useful series of annotated bibliographies "designed to present a record of sources for biographical information on living persons in foreign countries. . . . In general . . . restricted to publications issued within the past twenty years."

In addition to general dictionaries of biography it includes a wide variety of sources, e.g., monographs, registers of national and local governments, official gazettes, city directories, yearbooks and membership lists of professional and technical associations, proceedings of conventions and congresses, school directories, etc.

Classed arrangement with author and subject indexes.

INTERNATIONAL

Biographie universelle (Michaud) ancienne et moderne. Nouv. éd., publiée sous la direction de M. Michaud, rev., corr. et considérablement augm. d'articles omis ou nouveaux; ouvrage rédigé par une société de gens de lettres et de savants. Paris, Mme. C. Desplaces, 1843–65. 45v. o.p. **S16**

Usually cited as *Michaud.*

The first edition, in 84 volumes including supplements, was published 1811–57. Issue of the new edition, revised and enlarged, was begun in 1843. Its publication was interrupted in 1852 by a law suit undertaken by Mme. Desplaces, its publisher, against the firm of Didot Frères, which had started a rival dictionary, the *Nouvelle biographie universelle ancienne et moderne,* edited by Hoefer (S21), and had incorporated in the first two volumes of the work 336 articles taken unchanged from *Michaud* and 69 taken with only slight alteration, besides others evidently based on *Michaud.* After various decisions and reversals the suit was finally won by Mme. Desplaces in 1855, Didot was forbidden to copy any more and the publication of *Michaud* was resumed. The Didot dictionary, under a changed title (*see* S21) and without the pirated articles, was also continued. For an interesting account of this famous suit, by R. C. Christie, *see Quarterly review,* 157:204-26; reprinted in his *Selected essays and papers* (Lond., Longmans, 1902).

The most important of the large dictionaries of universal biography, still very useful in spite of the fact that the articles are now more than 80 years old. While *Michaud* and the rival work by Hoefer cover much the same ground, there are definite and well recognized differences. In spite of various inaccuracies, *Michaud* is more carefully edited, its articles, which are signed with initials, are longer and often better than those in *Hoefer,* its bibliographies (except in one point) are better and it contains more names in the second half of the alphabet, N-Z. *Hoefer* contains more names, especially minor ones, in the part A-M, has some articles which are better than the corresponding articles in *Michaud,* and in the bibliographies gives titles in the original whereas *Michaud* translates into French.

Century cyclopedia of names; a pronouncing and etymological dictionary of names in geography, biography, mythology, history, ethnology, art,

archaeology, fiction, etc. ed. by Benjamin E. Smith. Rev. and enl. N.Y., Century [c1911]. 1085p. [158p.] (v.11 of the Century dictionary and cyclopedia [M4]) **S17**

A standard work very useful for biography. International in scope. Indicates pronunciation. This edition has a supplementary alphabet of 158 pages. For full description *see* R40.

Chambers's biographical dictionary; the great of all nations and all times, originally comp. by David Patrick and F. Hindes Groome. New ed., ed. by Wm. Geddie and J. L. Geddie. Lond., Chambers, 1949. 1006p. 21s.; $6. **S18**

A good small dictionary, first published in 1897 and reprinted several times with changes. This latest revision is not printed from new plates, but has minor corrections and additions to bring some of the information to date. Marks pronunciation of difficult foreign names. Index of selected pseudonyms and nicknames, p.996-1006.

Garollo, Gottardo. Dizionario biografico universale. Milano, Hoepli, 1907. 2v. **S19**

Gives only brief information, but useful because it includes a larger proportion of Italian names than other general biographical dictionaries.

Jöcher, Christian Gottlieb. Allgemeines Gelehrten-Lexicon, darinne die Gelehrten aller Stände sowohl männ-als weiblichen Geschlechts, welche vom Anfange der Welt bis auf ietzige Zeit gelebt, und sich der gelehrten Welt bekannt gemacht, nach ihrer Geburt, Leben, merckwürdigen Geschichten, Absterben und Schrifften aus den glaubwurdigsten Scribenten in alphabetischer Ordnung beschrieben werden. Leipzig, Gleditsch, 1750–51. 4v. o.p. **S20**

v.1-4, A-Z.

——— —— Fortsetzung und Ergänzungen. . . . Leipzig, Gleditsch, 1784–87; Delmenhorst, Jöntzen, 1810; Bremen, Heyse, 1813–19; Leipzig, Selbstverlag der Deutschen Gesellschaft, 1897. 7v. o.p.

v.1-7, A-Romuleus.

v.1-2 by J. C. Adelung; v.3-6 by H. W. Rotermund; v.7 by Otto Günther.

Comprehensive and very useful for biographies of persons living before 1750.

Nouvelle biographie générale depuis les temps plus reculés jusqu'à nos jours, avec les renseignements bibliographiques et l'indication des sources à consulter; publiée par MM. Firmin Didot Frères, sous la direction de M. le Dr. Hoefer. Paris, Firmin Didot, 1853–66. 46v. o.p. **S21**

Usually cited as *Hoefer.*

Begun in 1852 under the title *Nouvelle biographie universelle;* title later changed to *Nouvelle biographie générale.* There are three editions of volumes 1-2; (1) edition with the title *Nouvelle biographie universelle*

ncienne et moderne, containing the 405 pirated articles
om *Michaud* (*see* S16); (2) edition with title *Nouvelle
iographie universelle dépuis les temps les plus reculés*,
ith those articles omitted; (3) edition with title *Nou-
elle biographie générale*. This last is the one usually
und in libraries.

This work was planned to be more concise and more
omprehensive than *Michaud*, to include names of people
en living, and many minor names omitted in *Michaud*.
does include more names in the first part of the alpha-
et. For other points of comparison *see Biographie uni-
erselle* (S16).

ettinger, Eduard Maria. Moniteur des dates.
iographisch-genealogisch-historisches Welt-Re-
ister enthaltend die Personal-Akten der Mensch-
eit . . . von mehr als 100,000 geschichtlichen
ersönlichkeiten aller Zeiten und Nationen von
rschaffung der Welt bis auf den heutigen Tag.
. . Leipzig, Denicke, 1869–73; Hermann, 1873–
2. 9v. o.p. **S22**

v.1-6, A-Z; v.7-8, Supplément, A-W; v.9, Supplément
appendice, A-Z.

Volumes 1-6, edited by Oettinger, published in parts,
66–68, with title *Moniteur des dates, contenant un
illion de renseignements biographiques, généalogiques
historiques;* volumes 7-9 have title: *Moniteur des dates
. . Supplément;* commencé par Edouard-Marie Oet-
ger, considérablement augm. . . . réd. et éd. par
ugo Schramm.

Articles are very brief, usually three or four lines,
t work is very comprehensive and includes some names
t easily found elsewhere.

homas, Joseph. Universal pronouncing diction-
y of biography and mythology. Phila. and
nd., Lippincott [c1930]. 2550p. $12. **S23**

Usually cited as *Lippincott's Biographical dictionary.*
1st ed. 1870; 3d ed. 1901. Later editions are printed
m the plates of the third edition with alterations in
ne of the older articles to bring them up to date,
ission of some minor articles, and inclusion of new
mes.

As a first aid the most frequently useful of the general
graphical dictionaries in English. Comprehensive,
ludes men and women of all nations and periods,
d names from the Greek, Roman, Teutonic, Sanskrit
d other mythologies. Articles in general are brief,
ough there are some long articles; pronunciation is
rked and there is some bibliography, though this fea-
e is not important. Appendixes: (1) Vocabulary of
ristian (or first) names, with pronunciation, and
uivalents in the principal foreign languages; (2) Dis-
ed or doubtful pronunciations.

pereau, Gustave. Dictionnaire universel des
ntemporains contenant toutes les personnes
tables de la France et des pays étrangers . . .
uvrage rédigé et tenu à jour avec le concours
crivains de tous les pays. 6. éd. entièrement
ondue et considérablement augm. Paris,
chette, 1893. 1629p. **S24**

—— Supplément. Paris, Hachette, 1895.
p.

The supplement contains short notices of persons
treated in earlier editions, with references to the edition
containing the main article, in parallel alphabet at foot
of pages.

Webster's Biographical dictionary. 1st ed. A
Merriam-Webster. A dictionary of names of noteworthy persons, with pronunciations and concise
biographies. Springfield, Mass., Merriam [1943].
1697p. $7.50. **S25**

William Allan Neilson, ed.-in-chief.

A pronouncing biographical dictionary of "upwards of
40,000" names, not restricted by period, nationality, race,
religion or occupation. Includes living persons. Gives
brief, condensed biographical sketches and makes a particular point of giving syllabic division and pronunciation of all names. A pronouncing list of pre-names is
given, p.1628-68; p.1669-97 include tables of the presidents, vice-presidents, justices of the Supreme court,
cabinet officers, diplomatic agents, etc., of the United
States, rulers of the British Empire and some other countries, lists of popes, etc.

Who's who in Central and East Europe. 1933/34
ed. by R. P. D. Stephen Taylor. Zurich, Central
European Times Pub. Co. [1935]. 1163p. **S26**

Subtitle: A biographical dictionary containing . . .
biographies of prominent people from Albania, Austria,
Bulgaria, Czechoslovakia, Danzig, Estonia, Finland,
Greece, Hungary, Latvia, Liechtenstein, Lithuania, Poland, Rumania, Switzerland, Turkey and Yugoslavia.

Now much out of date but still useful for names difficult to find elsewhere.

Contemporary

Current biography; who's news and why. v.1,
1940- . N.Y., Wilson, 1940- . il. Monthly (except August). Monthly issues $4 per yr. to
individuals. Yearbooks, service basis ($5 to indi-
viduals). **S27**

Published monthly with a bound annual cumulation,
which includes all biographical sketches and obituary
notices, revised and brought up to date. Each issue carries a cumulative index for all issues of the current year,
and each volume includes a cumulated index to all preceding volumes.

This service includes an average of 400 biographies
annually of persons of various nationalities. Information
given generally includes: full name, pronunciation, dates
of birth and death, occupation and reason for news-
worthiness, address, a biographical sketch with portrait
and references to sources for further information. Length
of biographies averages three to four columns. Each
issue, including the cumulations, contains a classified list
by occupations.

International who's who, 1935- . Lond., Europa
Publications and Allen and Unwin, 1935- . $16.
Annual (slightly irregular in dating). **S28**

1947 contains about 13,000 short biographies often
only three or four lines in length, of persons prominent
in Europe, North and South America, Asia, Australia, etc.

Supersedes the loose-leaf *European who's who* formerly
published as volume 2 of *Europa* (L237).

Who's who in America. The Monthly supplement and international Who's who. Current biographical reference service. Dec. 1939-   . Chic., Marquis, 1939-   . v.1-   . Monthly. $4.50 per yr.   **S29**

Title varies.

A current supplementary service to *Who's who in America* (S40) and other Marquis publications, giving sketches of "Who's who in world news—and why," with cross references to the other works. International in scope, it includes some whose biographies will appear in the next issue of some Marquis publication; other persons in the news and authors of current books; selected sketches of deceased biographees from other Marquis works usually revised to date of death; current additions to sketches of Marquis biographees. Averages about 400 names per month in the established Who's who form.

Published monthly, with an index in each issue which cumulates from the beginning of the volume, the index in the December issue serving as the annual index. Biennial indexes are included in the appropriate volumes of *Who's who in America.*

Each issue includes an index to authorities, classed by specialty.

World biography, 1940-   . N.Y., Inst. for Research in Biography, 1940-   . v.1-   . (1948, $25)   **S30**

First three editions had title: *Biographical encyclopedia of the world.* The fourth edition 1948 in two volumes (5120p.) is arranged alphabetically and gives fairly long sketches of the Who's who type of some 40,000 persons from over 60 countries of the world.

UNITED STATES

Appleton's Cyclopaedia of American biography, ed. by J. G. Wilson and John Fiske. N.Y., Appleton, 1887–1900. 7v. il. o.p.   **S31**

v.1-6, A-Z, suppl. A-Z, analytical index; v.7, suppl. A-Z; Pen names, nicknames, sobriquets; List of deaths in v.1-6; Signers of the Declaration of Independence, presidents of the Continental Congress, presidents, vice-presidents, unsuccessful candidates for those offices, cabinets, 1789–1897; analytical index to v.7.

Includes names of native and adopted citizens of the United States, including living persons, from the earliest settlement. Also eminent citizens of Canada, Mexico, and all other countries of North and South America. Also names of men of foreign birth who are closely identified with American history.

Contains fairly long articles, little bibliography, many portraits, principally small cuts in the text, and many facsimiles of autographs. A peculiarity of arrangement to be remembered is that under each family name arrangement is not alphabetical but by seniority in the family. The analytical index is useful for subjects and for names not treated separately. Practically superseded by the *Dictionary of American biography* (S32) for names included in that work but still useful for other names and certain types of information not given there, e.g., illustrations, facsimiles of autographs. Not entirely accurate; for interesting accounts of some curious fictitious biographies *see* (1) Barnhart, J. H., "Some fictitious botanists," *Journal of the N.Y. Botanical Garden* 20:171-

81, Sept. 1919; (2) Schindler, Margaret Castle, "Fictitious biography," in *American historical review* 42:68-90, July 1937, an abstract of her essay for the Master degree at Columbia University entitled "Biograph imaginaria, an investigation of the fictitious element Appleton's Cyclopaedia of American biography," 193 117p. (Ms); and (3) "84 phonies" in *Letters* 3, no.1 Sept. 14, 1936, p.1-2. These three references point o some 84 fictitious articles but do not cover the who encyclopedia.

An edition entitled *Cyclopedia of American biograph new enl. ed. of Appleton's cyclopedia of American bio raphy . . .* (N.Y., Press Assoc. compilers, 1915, 6v.) printed from the same plates as the original edition w the omission of some of the older articles, the inclusion some new articles and the addition of a supplementa list at the end of each volume. Six supplementary (no alphabetical) volumes to this edition, numbered volumes 7-12, 1918–31, are sold separately.

No cumulated index.

Dictionary of American biography. Under t auspices of the American Council of Learned S cieties, ed. by Allen Johnson and Dumas Malon N.Y., Scribner; Lond., Milford, 1928–37. 20v. a Index. (Repr. N.Y., Scribner, 1943. 21v. o. 1946, 11v. on thin paper, $115)   **S**

The outstanding scholarly American biographical d tionary planned on the lines of the English *Diction of national biography* (S123) with signed articles a bibliographies. Does not include living persons. Plann to include noteworthy persons of all periods who liv in the territory that is now known as the United Stat excluding British officers serving in America after t colonies declared their independence.

As compared with the other principal dictionaries this field the DAB is narrower in scope than *Applet* (S31), which includes Canadian and Latin Americ names, and less inclusive than the *National cyclopae* (S34) which includes many more minor names. Ho ever it has articles of more distinction than either of th works and much more bibliography. In most cases articles are adequate but there are some inaccuracies, both articles and bibliographies.

In the reprint edition listed above there is a list errata, volume 1, p.xiii-xxxi, with this note: "In mak this reprinting of the *Dictionary of American biograp* such corrections as have so far come to the attention the editors have been made either in the plates or in following list."

—— Index. N.Y., Scribner, 1937. 613p.

Contains six separate indexes: (1) Names of subje of biographies, with authors; (2) Contributors, with s jects of their articles; (3) Birthplaces, arranged alp betically by (a) states, (b) foreign countries; (4) Scho and colleges attended by persons included in dictiona (5) Occupations; (6) Topics.

Prepared by the publishers, not by the editors, of dictionary.

—— Supplement 1 (to Dec. 31, 1935). N Scribner, 1944. 718p. $7.50.

Numbered volume 21.

Contains 652 sketches by 358 contributors. Inclu biographies of persons whose deaths occurred be Dec. 31, 1935, both of those who died between iginal publication date and 1935 and of some who ere not included in the main set, "although their inclu-on would have been appropriate."

amb's Biographical dictionary of the United tates, ed. by J. H. Brown. Bost., Federal Bk. o., 1900–03 [c1897–1903]. 7v. il. **S33**

Published also as *Twentieth century biographical dictionary of notable Americans;* ed. by Rossiter Johnson Bost., Biog. Soc., 1904. 10v.) with some corrections.

Alphabetically arranged. Includes some names not ven in *Appleton* (S31) or the *National cyclopaedia* S34).

ational cyclopaedia of American biography. .Y., White, 1892–1949. v.1–35. il. (In progress) 15 per v. Some v. issued in rev. ed. **S34**

The most comprehensive American work, less limited d selective than the *Dictionary of American biography* S32) and more up to date than either *Appleton* (S31) *Lamb* (S33). Articles are unsigned, in general being ritten by members of an office force from question-ires and other information supplied by families of the ographees. In general no bibliography is given with an ticle. However questionnaires, letters and other docu-ents on which an article is based have been preserved the office archives where they may be consulted by ialified persons. The special reference use of the *ational cyclopaedia* is in its comprehensiveness. Not phabetically arranged, so must be used through the neral indexes. Each volume is also separately indexed.

—— Current volumes A–G. N.Y., White, 1930– 3. il. (In progress)

Includes living persons only, the biographies given eing considerably longer than those in *Who's who in merica*. Each volume is separately indexed and all are mulatively indexed in part 3 of the General index.

—— Indexes. . . . N.Y., White, 1945- . $15. oose-leaf.

Subtitle: Personal and topical indexes to the pub-shed volumes of the National cyclopedia of American ography, including the first and revised editions. pt.1, v.1–30; pt.2, v.31 and subsequent volumes; pt.3, urrent volumes.

Loose-leaf. Parts 2–3 revised as new volumes appear. Indexes not only the main biographical articles but also mes, institutions, events and other subjects mentioned the articles.

White's Conspectus of American biography; a abulated record of American history and biogra-hy. 2d ed. A rev. and enl. edition of A con-pectus of American biography. Comp. by the ditorial staff of the National Cyclopaedia of merican Biography. N.Y., White, 1937. 455p. 15. **S35**

Based upon the Conspectus part of the Conspectus d index volume (1906) of the *National cyclopaedia of merican biography* (S34) but remade and much en-rged. Includes many chronological lists of office holders various kinds, e.g., presidents, cabinet members, bish-s, presidents of societies and colleges, recipients of terary and other awards and medals, and various alpha-etical lists, e.g., pseudonyms and sobriquets, Americans

in fiction, poetry and drama, etc. The pseudonym list includes names not given in Shankle (R45). Useful both as a classified index to the *National cyclopaedia* and as an independent handbook of information.

Preston, Wheeler. American biographies. N.Y. and Lond., Harper, 1940. 1147p. $7.50. **S36**

Includes concise biographies of 5257 Americans from early Colonial times to the present (excluding living persons) and a few non-Americans who have been promi-nent in the history of the nation. Includes almost no names not in the *Dictionary of American biography* (S32) except for persons who have died since the DAB was published. The information is usually very brief and the bibliographies are confined to two or three items of the type that would probably be in the average public library. This volume would probably add little to the works already available in a large library but might prove useful in the small library which does not have the larger sets.

Sabine, Lorenzo. Biographical sketches of loyal-ists of the American revolution, with an historical essay. Bost., Little, 1864. 2v. **S37**

Who was who in America; a companion volume to Who's who in America. v.1, 1897–1942. Biogra-phies of the non-living with dates of deaths ap-pended. Chic., Marquis, 1942. 1396p. $10. **S38**

Includes some 25,000 sketches removed because of death from the 21 volumes of *Who's who in America* (S40) published from 1897 to and including 1940/41, with dates of death appended. Usually gives day, month, and year of death, but sometimes only the year.

Willard, Frances Elizabeth and **Livermore, Mary A.** A woman of the century; 1470 biographical sketches accompanied by portraits of leading American women in all walks of life. Buffalo, N.Y., Charles Wells Moulton, 1893. 812p. il. **S39**

Useful for biographies of American women of the nineteenth century, many of whom do not appear in other biographical reference works.

Contemporary

❦ *Who's who in America* (S40) is the best known and generally the most useful of the current bio-graphical works for information about persons of national prominence. For persons not listed there or for whom additional information is desired, there are other compilations of various kinds only a few of which can be listed here. Most of these fall into one of the following categories:

1. NATIONAL. Other national works are of varying degrees of worth and usefulness. Some of them include longer more discursive biographies than *Who's who in America,* such as those in *Current biography* (S27). Others, such as *America's young men* (S43), treat persons not yet of suf-ficient prominence to be included widely in

Who's who in America. Still others of the "commercial" or "vanity" type must be used with caution.

2. LOCAL. These include both sectional and state. The A. N. Marquis Company is now publishing a series of sectional compilations to include *Who's who in the East* (S51); *Who's who in the Midwest* (S52); *Who's who in the South and Southwest;* and *Who's who on the Pacific coast* (S54). These are listed below. There are also various state publications, e.g., *Who's who in New York* (11th ed. 1947); *Who's who in Massachusetts* (v.2, 1942/43). These are not listed here but will be needed in libraries according to location.

3. PROFESSIONAL OR BUSINESS, e.g., *Who's who in commerce and industry* (L456); *Leaders in education* (L768); *American men of science* (N63). These will be found under their proper subject in this book.

4. FOREIGN-AMERICAN, e.g., *Italian-American who's who* (S44); *Who's who in Polish America* (S50). These should be acquired by libraries according to local need.

5. RELIGIOUS OR RACIAL, e.g., *American Catholic who's who* (S41); *Who's who in American Jewry* (S47); *Who's who in colored America* (S48); and various denominational works listed under Religion, p.131-41.

Who's who in America, a biographical dictionary of notable living men and women. Chic., Marquis, 1899- . v.1- . Biennial. (1948/49, $13.60)
                                                          S40

An excellent dictionary of contemporary biography, containing concise biographical data, with addresses and, in case of authors, lists of works. Issued biennially, and constantly expanded since 1899. The standards of admission are high aiming to include the "best-known men and women in all lines of useful and reputable achievement" including "(1) those selected on account of special prominence in creditable lines of effort . . . and (2) those included arbitrarily on account of official position."

Through volume 22, 1942/43, the subtitle read "A biographical dictionary of notable living men and women of the United States." Beginning with volume 23, a very few selected names from Canada and Latin America are included.

Volume 25, 1948/49, the "Fiftieth Anniversary Edition" includes over 40,000 sketches, some 5000 of them being entirely new. Each edition is thoroughly revised, new biographies added and others dropped.

For names of persons dropped because of death *see Who was who* (1942) (S38). Supplemented by Necrology lists in succeeding volumes. For discontinued biographies, dropped for reasons other than death, *see* volume 22, p.117-57; supplementary list for volumes 23-25, in volume 25, p.2820-25. Volumes up to volume 22, 1942/43, included geographical indexes (published separately thereafter). Biennial indexes to the *Monthly supplement* are included in volumes 22-25. Beginning with

volume 22, pronunciation of difficult names is indicate by diacritical marks.

For its *Monthly supplement see* S29.

American Catholic who's who, 1934/35- . De troit, Walter Romig [1934]- . Biennial. $6.5 per v.   S4

One earlier edition edited by G. P. Curtis was pub lished in 1911 by B. Herder in St. Louis.

American women; the standard biographical dic tionary of notable women. v.1, 1935/36—v. 1939/40. Ed., Durward Howes; assoc. eds., Mar L. Braun, Rose Garvey. Los Angeles, Amer. Pub lications, Inc., 1935-39. v.1-3. $10 ea.   S4

Subtitle varies.

Volume 3 contains 10,222 names, of which compara tively few appear in *Who's who in America* (S40) p.1023-1083, national organizations and sororities.

America's young men, the official who's wh among the young men of the nation, ed. b Durward Howes. v.1, 1934—v.3, 1938/39. Lc Angeles, Amer. Publications, Inc. 1934-38. $1 ea.   S4

Volume 3 contains 6532 names and cross reference to volume 2 for names omitted from this volume. Ir cludes men up to the age of 40.

Current biography. N.Y., Wilson, 1940- .

For full description *see* S27.

Italian-American who's who; a biographical dic tionary of Italian American leaders, ed. by Gic vanni Schiaro. v.1, 1935- . N.Y., Vigo P [1935]- . Annual (slightly irregular). $15 ea to libraries $10.   S4

Subtitle varies slightly.

Tewkesbury's Who's who in Alaska and Alask business index. v.1, 1947- . Juneau, Alask; Tewkesbury, 1947- . (v.1, $4.50)   S4

Subtitle: Containing a biographical index of person; sketches of prominent living Alaskans, an alphabetic; directory of business concerns and their owners, a con plete directory of the fur trade and of the fishing, minin and lumber industries, a list of federal and territori government agencies and welfare institutions, and muc information of a miscellaneous character.

According to announced plans, later editions will b issued separately, the *Who's who,* biennially, the *Bus ness index,* annually.

Who knows—and what, among authorities—ex perts—and the specially informed. 1st ed.- Chic., Marquis, 1949- . $15.70.   S4

A new work compiled as a companion volume Who's who in America* (S40). The main part of th work consists of biographical sketches of persons cor sidered authorities in their fields, arranged alphabeticall each with a "key-number." The "locator-index," p.xi-: lists "16,000 knowers keyed to 35,000 subjects." and is ; alphabetical listing of subjects with key-number referrir to sketch in main alphabet. In cases where the sketch is included in *Who's who in America* only the name is given, without even an indication of specialty. In this first edition, the use of subjects is not consistent and sometimes authorities in the same field are listed under quite different subject headings, even though the same wording for specialty is used in the sketches.

This edition omits members of the medical and legal professions.

Who's who in American Jewry; a biographical dictionary of living Jews of the United States and Canada, v.3, 1938–39. Ed. by John Simons. N.Y., Nat. News Assoc. [c1938]. 1177p. il. $9.85. **S47**

v.1, 1926; v.2, 1928. Publisher and subtitle vary.

Includes some 10,377 names of which 8477 are given with biographies and 1900 listed without biographical data but in most cases with references to biographies in earlier volumes. Comparatively few of the names included are also in *Who's who in America* (S40).

Contains a geographical index (p.xi-l), and an *Addenda* list (p.li-lv).

Who's who in colored America; a biographical dictionary of notable living persons of African descent in America. 1st ed., 1927- . Brooklyn, N.Y., Who's Who in Colored America, Thomas Yenser, ed. and pub., 1927- . v.1- . il. $10. **S48**

Published at irregular intervals. 6th ed. 1941–44.

Who's who in New England; a biographical dictionary of leading living men and women of the states of Maine, New Hampshire, Vermont, Massachusetts, Rhode Island and Connecticut. v.3, 1938, comp. and ed. under the direction of Albert Nelson Marquis. Chic., Marquis, 1938. 1411p. $15.25. **S49**

1st ed. 1909; 2d ed. 1915.

"The number of New Englanders sketched in *Who's who in America* is only slightly above 3000, whereas the total number sketched in *Who's who in New England* is 12,445."—*Pref.*

Who's who in Polish America; a biographical directory of Polish-American leaders and distinguished Poles resident in the Americas. 3d ed. Francis Bolek, ed.-in-chief. N.Y., Harbinger House, 1943. 579p. $5. **S50**

Includes biographies of some 5000 Polish Americans including prominent living Americans of Polish descent and historical figures whose contribution has been great. Includes a geographical index and a classified professional index.

Who's who in the East; a biographical dictionary of noteworthy men and women of the eastern United States. v.1, 1942/43- . Chic., Marquis, 1943- . v.1- . $15.25. **S51**

v.1, published by Larkin, Roosevelt; v.2, published by Marquis as the first of a new series of sectional and regional Who's whos. This includes over 27,000 biographies selected on the same principles of "reference usefulness" used for *Who's who in America*, and is intended to be supplemental to that work. Cross references are given both to *Who's who in America* (S40) and to *Who's who in commerce and industry* (L456).

Who's who in the Midwest; a biographical dictionary of noteworthy men and women of the central and midwestern states. 1st ed., 1949- . Chic., Marquis, 1949- . **S52**

Incorporates *Who's who in the central states.* Includes sketches for over 19,000 persons.

Who's who on the Pacific coast; a biographical dictionary of noteworthy men and women of the Pacific coast and the western states. [2d ed.]- . Chic., Marquis, 1949- . **S54**

Incorporates *Who's who on the Pacific coast.*
Includes some 14,000 sketches. A few copies, which were later withdrawn, were issued under the title *Who's who in the west.*

Bibliography

Dargan, Marion. Guide to American biography. Albuquerque, Univ. of New Mexico Pr., 1949- . v.1- . $2.50. (In progress) **S55**

pt.1, 1607–1815.

Arranged by chronological periods, subdivided by geographical regions. Under each person lists original sources, separately published biographies, references to collective biography, special aspects, etc. Includes only the outstanding names (179 in pt.1).

ARGENTINA

Muzzio, Julio A. Diccionario histórico y biográfico de la Républica Argentina. Buenos Aires, Roldán, 1920. 2v. **S56**

Covers all periods.

Parker, William Belmont. Argentines of to-day. Buenos Aires and N.Y., Hispanic Soc. of Amer., 1920. 2v. 1067p. il. (Hispanic notes and monographs. 5) **S57**

Udaondo, Enrique. Diccionario biográfico argentino. . . . Buenos Aires, Casa ed. "Coni," 1938. 1151p. **S58**

At head of title: Institución Mitre.

Contains some 3300 biographies in the period from 1800–1920. Little or no bibliography.

—— Diccionario biográfico colonial argentino. Obra prologada por Gregorio Araoz Alfaro. . . . Buenos Aires, Ed. Huarpes, 1945. 980p. il. **S59**

At head of title: Institución Mitre.

Covers the Colonial period of Argentina from the discovery and conquest of the Rio de la Plata to 1810. A companion volume to his *Diccionario biográfico argentino* (S58).

Yaben, Jacinto R. Biografías argentinas y sudamericanas; introducción del Juan B. Terán.

. . . Buenos Aires, Ed. "Metrópolis," 1938–40. 5v.
il. **S60**

Volumes 1, 2 and 4 contain lists of works used.
A large proportion of the subjects of these biographies
are military and naval men.
Volume 5 contains "un suplemento de nuevas biografías
y otro de agregados a las ya publicadas."

Contemporary

Quien es quien en la Argentina; biografías con-
temporaneas. 4. ed. 1947. Buenos Aires, Kraft,
1947. 969p. $20. **S61**

AUSTRALIA

Australian encyclopedia, ed. by A. W. Jose and
H. J. Carter. Sydney, Angus and Robertson,
1925–26. 2v. il. **S62**

Includes nearly 850 biographies of persons no longer
living. For full description *see* V152.

Mennell, Philip. Dictionary of Australasian biography; comprising notices of eminent colonists
1855–1892. Lond., Hutchinson, 1892. 542p. **S63**

Serle, Percival. Dictionary of Australian biography. Sydney, Angus and Robertson, 1949. 2v. **S64**

Patterned on the *Dictionary of national biography*
(S123), this new work contains "1030 biographies of
Australians, or men who were closely connected with
Australia, who died before the end of 1942." The
sketches average two to three columns in length and
include bibliographies of source material at the end of
each. Lists of works by writers usually give only title
and date without other bibliographical information.

Contemporary

Who's who in Australia, 13th ed. 1947. . . . Melbourne, Herald and Weekly Times, 1947. 925p.
Triennial. 31s. 6d. **S65**

Subtitle: Incorporating John's *Notable Australians,*
being a record of the careers of representative persons
who live or have lived in Australia, and including lists of
diplomats, the judiciary, federal and state ministries,
members of the federal and state parliaments, departmental officials, and winners of the Victoria Cross and
George Cross, together with an Australian register of
titled persons.
John's *Notable Australians* was published first in 1906.
Subsequent editions have appeared with varying titles
and at irregular intervals, now triennial. The thirteenth
edition contains approximately 7000 biographies, including more than 1000 new entries.

AUSTRIA

Wurzbach, Constantin von. Biographisches Lexikon des Kaiserthums Oesterreich, enthaltend die
Lebensskizzen der denkwürdigen Personen,

welche seit 1750 in den österreichischen Kron-
ländern geboren wurden oder darin gelebt und
gewirkt haben. Wien, Zamarski, 1856–91. 60v.
S66

Subtitle and imprint vary.
Covers the period from 1750. Contains 24,254 biographies of inhabitants of the various lands included in
the former Austrian empire. Gives biographies of some
length, and bibliographies.

———— Register zu den Nachträgen in Wurz-
bachs 'Biographischem Lexikon d. Kaiserthums
Österreich' . . . Wien, Gilhofer, 1923. 16p.

An index to the supplements included in volumes 9,
11, 14, 22, 23, 24, 26 and 28.

Neue österreichische Biographie, 1815–1918;
begr. von Anton Bettelheim, August Fournier,
Heinrich Friedjung [u. Anderen] geleitet von
Anton Bettelheim. Wien, Amalthea-Verlag,
1923–35. Abt. 1-2. **S67**

Abt. 1, Bd.1-8, Biographie; Abt. 2, Bd.1, Bibliographie.
Bd.8, ed. by Edwin Rollett.
The eight volumes of part 1 contain about 132 long
articles, signed, with bibliographies and in many cases
portraits; not alphabetically arranged, but with an alphabetical index at the end of volume 8. The second part
is a bibliography of Austrian biography, including biographical dictionaries and collective biography in two
sections: (1) by subject or specialty; (2) by geographical
divisions.

Krackowizer, Ferdinand and **Berger, Franz.**
Biographisches Lexikon des Landes Österreich
ob der Enns. Gelehrte, Schriftsteller und Künstler
Oberösterreichs seit 1800. Passau und Linz a.
Donau, Inst. für ostbairische Heimatforschung,
1931. 411p. **S68**

Contemporary

"Wer ist wer"; Lexikon österreichischer Zeitgenossen. Wien, Selbst-Verlag "Wer ist wer,"
1937. 420p. $7.50. **S69**

Contains about 1500 biographies with a subject index
by professions, specialties, etc.

BELGIUM

**Académie Royale des Sciences, des Lettres, et
des Beaux-arts de Belgique.** Biographie nationale.
Bruxelles, Bruylant-Christophe, 1866–1944. 28v.
S70

v.1-27, A-Z; v.28, Table générale.
Long, signed articles by specialists, bibliographies.
Includes no living personages and, as names were not
selected for inclusion until a person had been dead 10
years, the earlier volumes contain mainly persons who
died before 1850. For names of a later date this dictionary may be supplemented usefully by the long, signed
obituaries, with detailed bibliographies, often with portraits, in the *Annuaire* of the Académie Royale.

For these obituaries before 1914 the following general index is helpful.

—— Annuaire: Table des notices biographiques publiées dans l'Annuaire (1835–1914). Bruxelles, Hayez, 1919. 55p. **S71**

Also included in the issue of the *Annuaire* for 81°-85° années, 1915–1919, p.113-67; complément, 1915–1926, in *Annuaire* 92° année, 1926, p.129-33.

—— Notices biographiques et bibliographiques concernant les membres, les correspondants et les associés, 1.-5. éd. 1854–1909. Bruxelles, Hayez, 1855–1909. 5v. **S72**

Brief biographical sketches with long bibliographies. Each edition includes some names from the previous edition but also omits and adds other names.

Seyn, Eugène de. Dictionnaire biographique des sciences, des lettres et des arts en Belgique. Bruxelles, Editions L'Avenir, 1935–36. 2v. il. $15.25. **S73**

Articles are brief, with many portraits but little or no bibliography *about* the names included, although, in the case of articles about writers, lists of works by those writers are given. Many of the biographies of writers are adapted from the articles in the *Dictionnaire des écrivains belges*, by E. de Seyn (R567).

BOLIVIA

Parker, William Belmont. Bolivians of to-day. 2d ed. rev. and enl. Lond. and N.Y., Hispanic Soc. of America, 1922. 332p. (Hispanic notes and monographs, 3) **S74**

Quién es quién en Bolivia [La Paz?] Editorial Quién es quién en Bolivia, 1942. 257p. **S75**

BRAZIL

Segadas Machado-Guimarães, Argeu de. Dicionario bio-bibliographico Brasileiro, de diplomacia, politica externa e direito internacional, por Argeu Guimarães. Rio de Janeiro, Autor, 1938. 482p. **S76**

A biographical dictionary of Brazilian statesmen and bibliography of Brazilian foreign relations all in one alphabetical arrangement.

Velho Sobrinho, João Francisco. Dicionário bio-bibliográfico brasileiro. Rio de Janeiro, Ministério da educação e saude, 1937–40. v.1-2. il. (In progress) 30$. **S77**

v.1-2, A-Buxton.
Fairly long sketches with bibliographies. To be in about 16 volumes.

CANADA

Allaire, Jean Baptiste Arthur. Dictionnaire biographique du clergé canadien-français. St.-

Hyacinthe [Québec], Impr. de "La Tribune," 1908–20. 4v. il. **S78**

v.1, Les anciens; v.2, Les contemporains; v.3, Suppléments, 1-6; v.4, Le clergé canadien-français, revue mensuelle; Table générale des quatre volumes.
Consists of two main volumes, six supplements forming one volume, and 24 monthly numbers. The general index at the end of the fourth volume links together these 32 alphabets. Short articles, many small portraits.

Les Biographies françaises d'Amérique. Montréal, Journalistes Associés, 1942. 640p. il. $15. **S79**

Includes biographies of approximately 600 living persons outstanding in the French ethnic group in North America.

Morice, Adrien Gabriel. Dictionnaire historique des Canadiens et des Métis français de l'Ouest. Québec, Garneau, 1908. 329p. **S80**

Standard dictionary of Canadian biography; the Canadian who was who. Eds., Charles G. D. Roberts and Arthur L. Tunnell. Toronto, Trans-Canada Pr., 1934–38. 2v. v.1, $12.50; v.2, $15. **S81**

Contains fairly long biographies, with bibliographies, of Canadians who died 1875–1937. Articles are signed with initials.
Each volume is arranged alphabetically with a list in volume 2 of the sketches in volume 1.

Wallace, William Stewart. The dictionary of Canadian biography. 2d ed., rev. and enl. . . . Toronto, Macmillan Co. of Canada Ltd., 1945. 2v. $20. **S82**

Paged continuously. 729p.
An enlarged and revised edition of the work first published in 1926. The best general dictionary of Canadian biography of all periods and all classes, exclusive of living persons. Contains concise biographical sketches with bibliographies. In this edition particular emphasis has been placed on biographies of Canadian authors.

Contemporary

Canadian who's who. . . . v.1- . 1910, 1938- . Toronto, Trans-Canada Pr., [c1910- .] v.1- . (v.4, 1948. $20) **S83**

Subtitle: "Founded 1910, with which is incorporated 'Canadian men and women of the time.'" A handbook of Canadian biography of living characters, edited by Sir Charles G. D. Roberts and Arthur Leonard Tunnell.
Publisher varies.
v.1, 1910; v.2, 1936–37; v.3, 1938–39. Volume 2 incorporated from volume 1 and also from Morgan's *Canadian men and women of the time* (1912) biographies of persons still living and brought these up to date, but both of those works are still useful for names of persons now deceased. Includes biographies of some persons in *Who's who in Canada* (S84), but each work includes names not in the other.

Who's who in Canada, including the British possessions in the western hemisphere. An illustrated biographical record of men and women of the time, ed. by B. M. Greene. Toronto, Internat. Pr., 1922- . il. (v.36, 1947/48. $10)   **S84**

Subtitle varies.

Continues with same volume numbering *Who's who and why.* 1922 called sixteenth year of issue.

CHILE

Diccionario biográfico de Chile. Tercera edición. Editores, Empresa periodistica Chile. . . . Santiago, "La Nación," 1940. 1080p. P.300.   **S85**

1st ed. 1936; 2d ed. 1937–38.

Figueroa, Pedro Pablo. Diccionario biográfico de Chile. 4. ed. Santiago, Impr. y Encuadernación Barcelona, 1897–1902. 3v. il.   **S86**

1st ed. 1887; 2d ed. 1888; 3d ed. 1891.

Earlier editions include names dropped from later editions, and the later editions add new names as well as corrections and additional information to names previously included.

—— Diccionario biográfico de estranjeros en Chile. Santiago, Impr. Moderna, 1900. 258p.   **S87**

Figueroa, Virgilio. Diccionario histórico, biográfico y bibliográfico de Chile, por Virgilio Figueroa (Virgilio Talquino) 1800–1930. Santiago, "Balcells and Co.," 1925–31. 5v. in 4. il.   **S88**

Title varies: v.1 has title *Diccionario histórico y biográfico de Chile, 1800–1925.*

Arranged alphabetically by family name and then by seniority in the family rather than alphabetically.

Medina, José Toribio. Diccionario biográfico colonial de Chile. Santiago, Impr. Elzeviriana, 1906. 1004p. il.   **S89**

—— —— Muestras de errores y defectos del "Diccionario biográfico colonial de Chile por José Toribio Medina," [por] Luis Francisco Prieto. Santiago, Imprenta y Encuadernación Chile, 1907. 124p.

Parker, William Belmont. Chileans of to-day. Santiago de Chile and N.Y., Putnam, 1920. 633p. il. (Hispanic notes and monographs, 4)   **S90**

Contains 277 biographies of contemporaries.

CHINA

❧ Biographical sections are frequently included in the yearbooks listed under Social Science, e.g., *China year book* (L124), *China handbook* (L123), etc.

The following list includes some works on Chinese biography in languages other than Chinese:

Giles, Herbert Allen. A Chinese biographical dictionary. Lond., Quaritch, 1898; Shanghai, Kelly and Walsh (repr. 1939). 1022p.   **S91**

A standard dictionary in English, not completely superseded by the Library of Congress volumes listed below. May be supplemented and corrected on certain points by the use of the following: Zach, E. von. Einige Verbesserungen zu Giles' Chinese biographical dictionary. *Asia major* 3:545-68, 1926; Pelliot, Paul. A propos du "Chinese biographical dictionary" de M. H. Giles. *Ibid.* 4: 377-89, 1927; Pelliot, Paul. Les Yi nien lou. *T'oung pao* 25:65-81, 1927.

U. S. Library of Congress. Asiatic Division. Eminent Chinese of the Ch'ing period (1644–1912). Ed. by Arthur W. Hummel. Wash., Govt. Prt Off., 1943–44. 2v. v.1, $2.25; v.2, $2.   **S92**

v.1, A-O. 604p.; v.2, P-Y, p.605-1103.

Designed to include some 800 sketches of eminent Chinese of the last 300 years, primarily of the epoch ruled by the Ch'ing dynasty (1644–1912). A very useful reference work, with detailed, authoritative, signed articles with references to sources. "No independent sketches are included for persons who died after 1912; but it was found possible to incorporate information sometimes in considerable detail, of many men who lived after that date, and of not a few who are still living."—*Editor's note*

Who's who in China; biographies of Chinese leaders. Shanghai, China Weekly Review, 1918- v.1- . il.   **S9**

1st ed., 1918; 2d ed., 1920; 3d ed., 1925; 3d ed. suppl. [1928?]; 4th ed., 1932; 4th ed. suppl. 1933; 5th ed., 1936 5th ed. suppl. 1940.

The fifth edition is the first in the series to includ biographies of women.

COLOMBIA

Ospina, Joaquín. Diccionario biográfico y bibliográfico de Colombia. . . . Bogotá, Ed. de Cromo (v.2-3, Ed. Aguila), 1927–39. 3v. il.   **S9**

Subtitle: Comprendre desde la conquista hasta nuestros días. Figuran todos los gobernantes desde Jiméne de Quesada hasta el Dr. Miguel Abadía Méndez (v.: hasta el Dr. Alfonso Lopez); arzobispos y obispos; patriotas de la independencia; militares de rango en nuestra guerras civiles, literatos, poetas y artistas en genera médicos, jurisconsultos, ingenieros, académicos, magi trados, y todas aquellas personas que se han levantad sobre el nivel común por obras justificables.

Quien es quien en Colombia. 2. ed. con dat controlados hasta el 14 Mayo de 1948. Bogot Oliveiro Perry, 1948. 540p.   **S9**

1. ed. 1944.

Includes Who's who type of sketch for 1579 person Contains a professional directory by city and by professio

CUBA

Cuba en la mano: Enciclopedia popular ilustrad La Habana, Ucar, Garcia, 1940. 1302p. il. $6.5   **S**

Indice biográfico, p.787-1033.

For full description *see* V199.

Martinez Arango, Felipe. Proceres de Santiago de Cuba. (Indice biográfico-alfabético) La Habana, Imp. Univ. de la Habana, 1946. 215p. il.
S97

Parker, William Belmont. Cubans of to-day. N.Y. and Lond., Putnam, 1919. 684p. il. (Hispanic notes and monographs, 1)
S98

Pezuela y Lobo, Jacobo de la. Diccionario geográfico, estadístico, histórico, de la isla de Cuba. Madrid, Mellado, 1863–66. 4v.
S99
Includes biography.

DENMARK

Dansk biografisk Haandleksikon, redig. af Svend Dahl og P. Engelstoft. Kjøbenhavn, Gyldendal, 1920–26. 3v. il.
S100

Dansk biografisk Leksikon, grundlagt af C. F. Bricka, redig. af Povl Engelstoft under Medvirking af Svend Dahl; udg. med Støtte af Carlsbergfondet. København, Schultz, 1933–44. v.1-26. In progress) Kr. 18 per v.
S101
v.1-26, A-Østrup.
Long articles signed with writers' names, not initials; bliographies. Includes names of living persons. A re-sed, much enlarged edition of the following.

Bricka, Carl Frederik. Dansk biografisk Lexikon, tillige omfattende Norge for Tidsrummet, 1537–1814. Kjøbenhavn, Gyldendal, 1887–1905. 19v.
S102

Signed articles of medium length, bibliographies. Includes Danes of all periods, Norwegians, 1537–1814, Schleswig-Holsteiners before 1864, and inhabitants of Iceland and the Faroe Islands who had more than a local importance.

Contemporary

Kraks blaa Bog, nulevende danske maend og vinders Levnedsløb. København, Krak, 1910- . 1- . Annual. (v.41, 1950)
S103
The standard Danish "who's who." 1934 has a general index to the names included in volumes 1-25, 1910–34.

See also Vem är vem i Norden (S201).

Bibliography

Erichsen, Balder and Krarup, Alfred. Dansk Personalhistorisk Bibliografi; systematisk Fortegnelse over Bidrag til Danmarks Personalhistorie i Tilslutning til Bibliotheca danica). København, ads, 1917. 806p. (Dansk historisk Bibliografi. Bd.)
S104
Includes books and analytical material, indexing many articles in periodicals. Lists more than 15,000 references.

As it gives, in most cases, dates of birth or death and some characterizing phrase, it can be used for such direct biographical information, as well as for its bibliographical references.

Continued informally by the indexing of biographical articles, also with dates and characterizing phrases, given in the *Dansk Tidsskrift-Index*, 1915- , under the heading Personalhistorie. For description *see* E85.

ECUADOR

Pérez Marchant, Braulio. Diccionario biográfico del Ecuador. Quito, Escuela de Artes y Oficios, 1928. 515p. il.
S105

FINLAND

Finsk biografisk handbok, under medvärkan af fackmän utgifven af Tor Carpelan. Helsingfors, Edlunds Förlag, 1903. 2v.
S106
Issued in parts, 1895–1903.
Adequate signed biographies, little bibliography.

Contemporary

Vem och vad? Biografisk handbok, 1948. Under redaktion av J. O. Tallquist och Ola Zweygbergk. Helsingfors, H. Schildt, 1948. 879p.
S107
1st ed. 1920. Usually published every five years, but because of the war the volume due in 1946 was not published until 1948.
Earlier volumes edited by H. R. Söderström.

See also Vem är vem i Norden (S201).

FRANCE

Académie des Sciences, Paris. Index biographique des membres et correspondants de l'Académie des Sciences de 1666 à 1939. Paris, Gauthier-Villars, 1939. 477p.
S108

Biographie nouvelle des contemporains, ou, Dictionnaire historique et raisonné de tous les hommes qui, depuis la révolution française, ont acquis de la célébrité par leurs actions, leurs écrits, leurs erreurs, ou leurs crimes, soit en France, soit dans les pays étrangers, par A. V. Arnault, A. Jay [and others]. Paris, à la Librarie Historique, 1820–25. 20v. il.
S109

Dictionnaire de biographie française, sous la direction de J. Balteau, M. Barroux, M. Prevost. Paris, Letouzey, 1933–50. v.1-4, v.5 (incompl.). 40fr. per fasc. (In progress)
S110
v.1-5, fasc. 27, A-Bassot.
An important new dictionary of national biography which was projected before the outbreak of World War I, but was not brought to the point of beginning publication till 1929. Planned to be a much more extensive work than the corresponding dictionaries of English and American

biography. Articles, which in the main are shorter than those in the *Dictionary of national biography* (S123), are signed with the writers' names, not merely initials, and nearly all have bibliographies, some of which are very extensive.

Haag, Eugène. La France protestante; ou, Vies des protestants français qui se sont fait un nom dans l'histoire depuis les premiers temps de la réformation jusqu'à la reconnaissance du principe de la liberté des cultes par l'Assemblée Nationale. Paris, Genève, Cherbuliez, 1846–59. 10v. o.p. **S111**

There is a later edition of which only volumes 1-6 (A-Gasparen) were ever published (Paris, Sandoz, 1877–88).

Sketches vary in length from a few lines to several pages. Bibliographies consist largely of material by, rather than about, the biographee.

Jal, Auguste. Dictionnaire critique de biographie et d'histoire; errata et supplément pour tous les dictionnaires historiques, d'après des documents authentiques inédits. 2. éd. corr. et augm. d'articles nouveaux et renfermant 218 facsimiles d'autographes. Paris, Plon, 1872. 1357p. facsim. **S112**

Robert, Adolphe [and others]. Dictionnaire des parlementaires français, comprenant tous les membres des assemblées françaises et tous les ministres français depuis le 1er mai 1789 jusqu'au 1er mai 1889. Paris, Bourloton, 1891. 5v. il. **S113**

Continued by *Les Parlementaires français* by René Samuel and Georges Bonét-Maury. Intended to be published in two parts, 1889–1900 and 1900–1914, of which only the second was published (Paris, Roustan, 1914).

See also Biographie universelle (Michaud) (S16); *Nouvelle biographie générale (Hoefer)* (S21); Paris, Bibliothèque National, *Répertoire de l'histoire de la révolution française,* v.1, Personnes (V232).

Contemporary

Dictionnaire biographique français contemporain. Paris, Pharos, Centre International de Documentation, 1950. 498p. il. 300fr. **S114**

A new dictionary of contemporary French biography, which while largely of living persons also includes some who have died in recent years. Sketches vary from one-half to three or four columns. Bibliographies are usually given of works by a writer, but only occasionally are works about a person listed.

Dictionnaire national des contemporains, dirigé par Nath Imbert. Paris, Les éditions Lajeunesse, 1936–39. v.1-3. il. **S114a**

The three volumes include more than 3000 names. Volume 3 contains index to volumes 1-3.

Qui êtes-vous? Annuaire des contemporains notices biographiques, 1924. Paris, Ruffy, dépo à la librairie Delagrave, 1924. 806p. **S11**

1st issue, 1908; 2d, 1909.

The French "Who's who" now much out of date.

Regional

☙ There are many dictionaries of local biography titles of some of them may be found in Schneider *Handbuch der Bibliographie,* p.502-3 (A5).

GERMANY

Allgemeine deutsche Biographie; herausgegebe durch die Historische Commission bei der Akademie der Wissenschaften. Leipzig, Duncke 1875–1912. 56v. **S1**

v.1-45, A-Z; v.46-55, Nachträge bis 1899, Andr (A-Ad included in v.45); v.56, General register.

The outstanding German biographical dictionary, co taining long, signed articles, with bibliographies, on pe sons no longer living. As there are supplementary se tions in many volumes it is essential that the index used to find the complete record.

For biographies of persons deceased since the compil tion of this work the following may be used as inform supplements:

Biographisches Jahrbuch und deutscher Nekr log, 1896–1913; hrsg. von Anton Bettelheim. Be lin, Reimer, 1897–1917. v.1-18 and separate ind v. Annual. **S1**

Each volume contains: (1) section of long, signed ticles, with bibliographies, on prominent Germans w died during the year; (2) a necrology of briefer notic (3) index. The index volume is a combined index v.1-10 (1896–1905).

Deutsches biographisches Jahrbuch, hrsg. vo Verbande der deutschen Akademien, 1914–2 1928–29. Berlin, Deutsche Verlagsanstalt, 192 32. v.1-5, 10-11. **S1**

v.1, 1914–16; v.2, 1917–20; v.3, 1921; v.4, 1922; v 1923; v.10, 1928; v.11, 1929.

Kosch, Wilhelm. Das Katholische Deutschlan Biographisch-bibliographisches Lexikon. Au burg, Haas, 1933–37. v.1-2. il. (In progres **S1**

v.1-2, A-Rehbach.

Gives concise biographies, with appended bibli raphies in many cases, of German Catholics from sixteenth century to the present, including the names living persons.

Contemporary

Degeners Wer ist's. Eine Sammlung von ru 18,000 Biographien mit Angaben über Herkur Familie, Lebenslauf, Veröffentlichungen u

Verke, Lieblingsbeschäftigung, Mitgliedschaft
ei Gesellschaften, Anschrift und anderen Mit-
eilungen von allgemeinem Interesse. Auflösung
on ca. 5000 Pseudonymen. 10. Ausg. Berlin,
Degener, 1935. 1833p. **S120**

Published at irregular intervals; 1st ed. 1905; 9th, 1928.
Title varies. Previous editions had title *Wer ist's?*

Kürschners deutscher Gelehrten-Kalender, 1950,
. Ausg. Berlin, de Gruyter, 1950. 2534p. **S121**

1st ed. 1925; 2d ed. 1926; 3d ed. 1928; 4th ed. 1931;
th ed. 1935; 6th ed. 1940/41.

A biographical dictionary of German scholars in the
onliterary fields, an off-shoot of *Kürschners deutscher
Literatur-Kalender* (R525).

The editions vary considerably in size and content,
oth as to names included and as to supplementary infor-
nation.

Ver ist Wer? Berlin-Grunewald, Arani, 1948- .
.1- . DM. 9.50. **S122**

Connected in no way with the prewar Austrian publi-
ation of the same title or the German *Wer ist's?*, this is
he first volume of a proposed new series. 1100 entries
re included for persons in politics, industry, and culture,
rimarily from Western Germany. Coverage is spotty.

Regional

❦ There are many dictionaries and collections of
ocal biography which often contain names or information not given in the general dictionaries of German biography. A useful list of these regional works
s given in Schneider's *Handbuch der Bibliographie*,
.485-97 (A5).

GREAT BRITAIN

Dictionary of national biography, ed. by Leslie
Stephen and Sidney Lee. Reissue. Lond., Smith,
Elder, 1908–09. 22v. (1938 repr. 22v. $200) **S123**

v.1-21, A-Z; v.22, 1st suppl., Additional names, 1901.

——2d-5th supplements, Ox., Univ. Pr., 1912–
9. 4v.

2d suppl., 1901–11, ed. by Sir Sidney Lee. 1912.
8.50; 3d suppl., 1912–21, ed. by H. W. C. Davis and
. R. H. Weaver. 1927. $8.50; 4th suppl., 1922–30, ed.
y J. R. H. Weaver. 1937. $10; 5th suppl., 1931–40,
949. 50s.; $12.50.

——Index and epitome, ed. by Sir Sidney Lee.
Lond., Smith, Elder, 1903–13. 2v.

Contents: Index and epitome to main set and 1st suppl.
22v.) 1903. 1456p.; Index . . . to 2d suppl. 1913. 129p.

——The Concise dictionary from the beginnings
o 1921; being an epitome of the main work and
ts Supplement, to which is added an epitome of
he twentieth century volumes covering 1901–21.
Ox., Univ. Pr., 1930. 1456p., 142p. $11.50.

Binder's title: Concise dictionary of national biography,
complete to 1921.

History: Founded by George Smith of the London firm
of Smith, Elder and Co., and originally published by
that firm as follows: Main work and 1st suppl., 63v.,
1885–1901; Index and epitome to v.1-63, 1903. 1456p.;
Errata, for v.1-63, 1904. 299p.; 2d suppl. 3v. 1912;
Index and epitome to 2d suppl. 1913. 129p.; Reissue of
63v. ed., on thinner paper, with the incorporation in the
text of the material in the Errata volume, 22v. 1908–09.
Presented, 1917, by the heirs of George Smith, to the Oxford University Press, to be continued by that institution.
In 1920 that press reissued the second supplement, on
thin paper, in one volume and have continued the work
by publishing the third, fourth, and fifth supplements
and *The Concise dictionary*. Though the original work
is not being revised by the present publisher, an informal
revision of many articles is to be found in the important
Errata notes published in the *Bulletin* of the Institute of
Historical Research of London University, 1923- . These
notes are available also in separate form, printed on one
side of paper, for clipping and mounting. A library
wishing to make the best use of the *Dictionary of national
biography* should clip these Errata and mount them
alphabetically in a loose-leaf binder to form an additional
Errata volume.

Constitutes the most important reference work for
English biography, containing signed articles by specialists, and excellent bibliographies. Articles are adequate,
i.e., important names treated at great length, minor names
more briefly, and are generally reliable and scholarly.
Scope includes all noteworthy inhabitants of the British
Isles and the Colonies, exclusive of living persons; includes noteworthy Americans of the Colonial period. The
supplements bring the record down to 1940. *The Concise
dictionary* serves a double purpose, i.e., it is both an
index and also an independent biographical dictionary,
as it gives abstracts, each about one-fourteenth of the
length of the original article. It contains two alphabetical
lists: (1) The original Index and epitome (to v.1-66)
first published 1903 and reprinted here without change,
and (2) Concise dictionary of national biography, 20th
century 1901–1921. The fifth supplement includes an
index covering the years 1901–40 in one alphabetical
series.

❦ The following, though more limited in scope
than the *Dictionary of national biography*, are often
useful for either names or types of information not
given there:

Boase, Frederick. Modern English biography,
containing many thousand concise memoirs of
persons who have died since 1850, with an index
of the most interesting matter. Truro, Netherton,
1892–1921. 6v. **S124**

v.1-3, A-Z, Index; v.4-6 (suppl. v.1-3), A-Z.

A useful work, particularly for minor nineteenth century names not included in the *Dictionary of national
biography*. Good subject index, including lists of pseudonyms, fancy names, class lists, etc.

**Burke's Handbook to the most excellent Order
of the British Empire; containing biographies, a
full list of persons appointed to the order . . . ed.**

by A. Winton Thorpe. Lond., Burke, 1921. 703p.
il. **S125**

This order was established by Letters Patent on June 4, 1917, its members to be those who in either civil or military capacities rendered important services to the Empire. It is therefore a volume devoted primarily to the outstanding persons of the first world war.

Gillow, Joseph. Literary and biographical history, or, Bibliographical dictionary of the English Catholics from the breach with Rome in 1534 to the present time. Lond., Burns; N.Y., Catholic Pub. Soc. [1885–92]. 5v. **S126**

Gives 2000 biographies. Useful for names not given in the *Dictionary of national biography* and for fuller information about some names included there. Especially useful for the bibliographies which are very full.

Kirk, John. Biographies of English Catholics in the eighteenth century, by the Rev. John Kirk, being part of his projected continuation of Dodd's Church history, ed. by J. H. Pollen and Edwin Burton. Lond., Burns, 1909. 293p. **S127**

Includes some names not given in Gillow, *Literary and biographical history* (S126).

Ward, Thomas Humphry. Men of the reign; a biographical dictionary of eminent persons of British and colonial birth who have died during the reign of Queen Victoria. Lond., Routledge, 1885. 1020p. o.p. **S128**

Contains some names not included in either the *Dictionary of national biography* or Boase, *Modern English biography* (S124).

Wedgwood, Josiah Clement. History of Parliament, 1439–1509. Lond., Stat. Off., 1936–38. v.1-2. (In progress) col. coats of arms. 40s.; $10.25. **S129**

v.1, Biographies of members of the Commons House.
A list of 2600 men, out of a possible total of 3800 known to have been elected members of 29 Parliaments, 1439–1509, with biographical data about each and many bibliographical footnotes referring to sources. As only 60 of the 2600 names are included in the *Dictionary of national biography*, this work is important for British biography as well as for Parliamentary history.
For description of set *see* L274.

Who was who, 1897–1916, 1917–1928, 1929–1940; a companion to Who's who; containing the biographies of those who died during the period. Lond., Black, 1929–41. 3v. v.3, 40s.; $11. **S130**

1897–1916 was first published June 1920; new ed., with Addenda and Corrigenda, Dec. 1929; new ed. with rev. Corrigenda, 1935.
For the most part the original sketches as they last appeared in *Who's who* (S131) are reprinted with the date of death added, but in a few instances additional information has been added.

Contemporary

Who's who, an annual biographical dictionary with which is incorporated "Men and women of the time." Lond., Black; N.Y., Macmillan, 1849- v.1- . Annual. (1949, 85s.; $19) **S131**

The pioneer work of the "Who's who" type and still one of the most important. Until 1897, it was a hand book of titled and official classes and included lists of names rather than biographical sketches. With 1897 called "First year of new issue," it changed its character and became a biographical dictionary of prominent persons in many fields. It has been developed and enlarged along these lines ever since. It is principally British, but not completely, as a few prominent names of other nationalities are included. Biographies are reliable and fairly detailed; give main facts, addresses and, in case of authors, lists of works.

For a compilation of biographies of deceased persons selected from the volumes 1897–1940, *see Who was who* (S130).

Volumes before 1904 contained miscellaneous lists, e.g., clubs, colleges, peculiarly pronounced proper names, pseudonyms, etc. From 1904–17 these lists were omitted in the main work and issued in a supplementary volume entitled *Who's who year-book.*

Catholic who's who, 1908- . Lond., Burns, 1908- . Annual (slightly irregular). (1941. 7s. 6d.) **S132**

Until 1935, title was *Catholic who's who and yearbook.*

Kelly's Handbook to the titled, landed, and official classes, 1880- . Lond., Kelly Directories, 1880- . v.1- . Annual. (1949, 80s.; $20) **S133**

Brief biographical sketches arranged in alphabetical order. Includes those who have hereditary or honorary titles, members of Parliament, government officials, landed proprietors, distinguished members of the dramatic, literary and artistic worlds and leaders in commerce and industry.

Indexes

Index Society, London. An index to the biographical and obituary notices in the Gentleman's magazine, 1731–1780. Lond., British Record Soc., 1886–91. 677p. (Pub. of the British Record Soc. ... Index Society, v.15) **S134**

Musgrave, *Sir* William. Obituary prior to 1800 (as far as relates to England, Scotland, and Ireland) comp. by Sir William Musgrave ... and entitled by him "A general nomenclator and obituary, with reference to the books where the persons are mentioned, and where some account of their character is to be found." Ed. by Sir George J. Armytage. Lond., 1899–1901. 6v. (Pub. of the Harleian Society, v.44-49) 21s. per v. **S135**

An alphabetical index to a large number of obituaries and biographies.
Gives name, date of death, sometimes a characterizing word or phrase, and reference to the book or other pub

ication where a biography or obituary notice may be ound. Very useful, especially for names not included n the *Dictionary of national biography*. (S123)

Scotland

Anderson, William. The Scottish nation; or, The urnames, families, literature, honours and biographical history of the people of Scotland. Edinburgh, Fullarton, 1880. 3v. il. **S136**

Wales

Roberts, T. R. Eminent Welshmen. v.1 (1700–900). Cardiff, Educ. Publ. Co., 1908. 613p. **S137**

Subtitle: A short biographical dictionary of Welshmen who have attained distinction from the earliest times to he present.
A continuation of Williams, *Enwogion Cymru* (S139), including some earlier names omitted from that work and lso bringing it up to date.

Rowland, E. H. A biographical dictionary of minent Welshmen who flourished from 1700–900. By E. H. Rowland (Helen Elwy). Wrexam, Authoress, 1907. 295p. **S138**

Williams, Robert. Enwogion Cymru; a biographical dictionary of eminent Welshmen from the arliest times to the present and including every ame connected with the ancient history of Wales. Llandovery, Rees; Lond., Longman, 1852. 68p. o.p. **S139**

Contemporary

Who's who in Wales, 1937. 3d ed. Lond., Belravia Pub., [1937] 259p. il. 12s. 6d. **S140**
1st ed. 1921; 2d ed. 1933.

HUNGARY

[Jásznigi, Alexander] and **Parlagi, Imre.** Das eistige Ungarn, biographisches Lexikon, hrsg. on Oskar von Krücken [pseud.] u. Imre Parlagi. Vien, Braumüller [1918]. 2v. **S141**
Includes principally writers, artists and men in public fe.

zinnyei, József. Magyar írók élete és munkái a Iagyar tudományos akadémia megbizásából. udapest, Kiadja Hornyánszky V., 1891–1914. 4v. **S142**
Continued by the following:

Iagyar életrajzi lexikon; Szinnyei József Magyar ók élete és munkái kiegészíto sorozata, írja és zerkeszti dr. Gulyás Pál. Budapest, Lantos, 925–29. v.1¹⁻⁶. **S143**
v.1¹⁻⁶, A-Bacher.

See also Wurzbach's *Biographisches Lexikon des Kaiserthums Oesterreich* (S66) which includes biographies of 3344 Hungarians.

INDIA

Buckland, Charles Edward. Dictionary of Indian biography. Lond., Sonnenschein, 1906. 494p. **S144**
Contains 2600 concise biographies of persons—English, Indian, or foreign—noteworthy in the history, service, literature or science of India, since 1750.

Lethbridge, *Sir* Roper. The Golden book of India; a genealogical and biographical dictionary of the ruling princes, chiefs, nobles, and other personages, titled or decorated, of the Indian empire, with an appendix for Ceylon. Lond., S. Low, 1900. 366p. **S145**

Rao, C. Hayavadana. Indian biographical dictionary, 1915. Madras, Pillar [1915?]. 472p., 31p. **S146**
Brief biographies, of the "who's who" type, of both natives and Europeans. Supplements give warrant of precedence, New Year's and Birthday honors, list of clubs, etc.

Who's who in India, containing lives and portraits of ruling chiefs, nobles, titled personages and other eminent Indians. Popular ed. Lucknow, Newul Kishore Pr., 1911–14. 1610p. and 2 suppl. il. **S147**
Contains eight separate biographical lists, arranged by states and provinces, each list arranged in general order of precedence, not alphabetically. General alphabetical index at end. Many portraits. Only native Indians included.

Contemporary

Who's who in India, Burma and Ceylon, (illus.) ed. and comp. by Thomas Peters. Poona, Sun Pub. House [1938]. 818p., 48p., xxiiip. il. Rs. 15; 30s. **S148**
Contents: The Royal family and provincial governors, p.1-34; Indian princes and chiefs, p.37-122; General, p.125-818; Who's who in Indian industries and commerce, p.1-48; Index, p.i-xxiii.

See also Indian year book (L154).

IRELAND

Crone, John S. Concise dictionary of Irish biography. Rev. and enl. ed. N.Y., Longmans, 1937. 290p. **S149**
Originally published in 1928, this revised edition includes an appendix, p.271-90.

Ryan, Richard. Biographia Hibernica. A biographical dictionary of the worthies of Ireland, from the earliest periods to the present time. Lond., Ryan, 1819–21. 2v.   **S150**

ITALY

Enciclopedia biografica e bibliografica "Italiana." . . . Milano, Istituto ed. Ital., Bernardo Carlo Tosi, 1936- . ser. 4- . il. (In progress) L100 per v.   **S151**

Announced for publication in 48 series, each devoted to a special class, e.g., writers, soldiers, scientists, etc. Includes biographies of medium length unsigned but supplied with bibliographies and with many illustrations taken from contemporary sources. Planned on a large scale which, if all the projected series are carried to completion, should mean the provision of biographical information about a very large number of names.

Contents: ser. 4, Storici, teorici e critici delle arti figurative (1800–1940) di S. Lodovici. 1942. 412p.; ser. 6, Poetesse e scrittrici, a cura di Maria Bandini Buti. 1941–42. 2v.; ser. 7, Eroine, ispiratrici e donne di eccezione, diretta da Francesco Orestano. 1940. 399p.; ser. 9, Attori tragici, attori comici, di Nordo Leonelli. 1940–44. 2v.; ser. 19, Condottieri, capitani, tribuni, di Corrado Argegni. 1936–37. 3v.; ser. 20, Condottieri e generali del seicento, di Aldo Valori. 1943. 464p.; ser. 31, La medicina: v.1, Bibliografia di storia della medicina italiana, di Adalberto Pazzini. 1939. 455p.; ser. 38, Pedagogisti ed educatori, diretta da Ernesto Codignola. 1939. 451p.; ser. 41, Ceramisti, di Aurelio Minghetti. 1939. 451p.; ser. 42, Il risorgimento italiano: v.1, I Martiri, di Francesco Ercole. 1939; v.2-4, Gli uomini politici, di F. Ercole. 1941–42; v.5, I combattenti, di Almerico Ribera. 1943; ser. 43 Ministri deputati, senatori dal 1848 al 1922, di Alberto Malatesta. 1940–41. 3v.; ser. 50, Armi ed armaioli di Enzio Malatesta. 1939. 436p.

Savino, Edoardo. La nazione operante; albo d'oro del fascismo profili et figure . . . terza ed., riv. e amp. Novara, Istituto Geografico de Agostini, 1937. 784p. il.   **S152**

Contains some 2150 biographies of prominent Fascists in all fields.

Tipaldo, Emilio de. Biografia degli Italiani illustri nelle scienze, lettere ed arti del secolo XVIII, e de' contemporanei. . . . Venezia, Tip. di Alvisopoli, 1834–45. 10v.   **S153**

Not alphabetically arranged but has an alphabetical index in each volume. Indexed in Phillips' *Dictionary of biographical reference* (S8).

Contemporary

Chi è? Dizionario degli italiani d'oggi. 5. ed. Rome, Scarano, [1948] 1003p. L3500; foreign, L4000.   **S154**

1. ed., 1928. Suppl., 1929; 2. ed., 1931; 3. ed., 1936; 4. ed., 1940.

Another work with the same title was issued in 1908 by Guido Biagi.

Codignola, Arturo. L'Italia e gli italiani di ogg Genova, Nuovo Mondo, 1947. 751p. L2750. **S15**

A biographical work of the who's who type.

Bibliography

Pizzi, Francesco. Italica gens; repertori a stamp di biografia generale italiana. Cremona, Mas chetti, 1934. 131p.   **S15**

A bibliography of biographical works in three parts (1) general; (2) arranged by locality; (3) arranged b subject. Author index.

JAMAICA

Who's who, Jamaica, British West Indies. An i lustrated biographical record of outstanding Ja maicans and others connected with the island Kingston, B.W.I., Who's Who (Jamaica), 1935- v.1, 1934/35- . (1941–46, $16)   **S15**

Title varies: 1934/35–1939/40, *Who's who and why Jamaica;* 1941/46- , *Who's who, Jamaica, British We. Indies.*

Comp.: L. A. Thoywell-Henry.

JAPAN

Iseki, K. R. Who's who in "Hakushi" in gre: Japan. Tokyo, Hattensha [1921–30]. v.1-5.   **S15**

A dictionary of contemporary biography of Japanes who are "Hakushi" or holders of the doctor's degree various fields. Articles are in Japanese and English; t English version is often peculiarly expressed. Arrang by subjects: v.1, Pharmacology; v.2-4, Medicine; v. Engineering.

Contemporary

Who's who in Japan, 1912- , by Tsunesabu Kamesaka. Tokyo, Who's Who in Japan Pu Off., 1911- . v.1- . Annual (slightly irregular (v.21, 1940/41. $7)   **S1**

Editor varies.

In English on the general plan of the English *Wh who.*

Japan who's who and business directory. 1948- Tokyo, Tokyo News Service, 1948- .   **S1**

See also Ramming, *Japan-Handbuch* (V36 and the biographical sections in the *Japan ye book* (L163), the *Manchoukuo yearbook* (L164 and the *Orient yearbook* (L165).

LATIN AMERICA

See name of country for individual Latin Ame can country.

Who's who in Latin America; a biographical dictionary of notable living men and women of Latin America. Founded in 1935 by Percy Alvin Martin. (3d ed., rev. and enl.) . . . ed. by Ronald Hilton. . . . Stanford Univ., Calif., Stanford Univ. Pr.; Chic., Marquis [c1945–48]. pts. 1-2, 4, 6. (In progress) pt.1, $2.50; pt.2, $2.25; pt.4, $2.50; pt.6, $3.50.   **S161**

Contents: pt.1, Mexico; pt.2, Central America and Panama; pt.4, Bolivia, Chile and Peru; pt.6, Brazil.

The first two editions, 1935 and 1940, one volume each, were edited by P. A. Martin. This edition, revised and reorganized, aims to include 8000 biographies whereas the second edition included slightly over 1500. However, as each country is treated separately, the great disadvantage of this edition is the number of alphabets which must be checked if the country of the person searched for is not known. To be published in seven parts: pt.3, Colombia, Ecuador, and Venezuela; pt.5, Argentina, Paraguay, and Uruguay; pt.7, Cuba, Dominican Republic, and Haiti.

Bibliography

Jones, Cyril Knight. A bibliography of Latin American bibliographies. 2d ed. rev. and enl. by the author with the assistance of James A. Granier. Wash., Govt. Prt. Off., 1942. 311p. (U.S. Library of Congress. Latin American ser. no.2)   **S162**

Includes collective biographies. For full description see A398.

Toro, Josefina del. A bibliography of the collective biography of Spanish America. . . . Rio Piedras, P.R., Univ., 1938. 140p. (University of Puerto Rico bulletin, ser. IX, no.1, Sept. 1938)   **S163**

A very useful annotated list of 488 works of collective biography, arranged by country with author index.

MEXICO

See also Mexico, p.509-10.

Mestre Ghigliazza, Manuel. Efemérides biográficas (defunciones—nacimientos) México, D.F., Antigua Librería Robredo, J. Porrúa, 1945. 347p.   **S164**

A chronological arrangement by year of death of outstanding Mexicans who died between 1822 and 1945. Gives field of activity or title, place and date of birth and death. Alphabetical index.

Peral, Miguel Angel. Diccionario biográfico mexicano. México, D.F., Ed. P.A.C. [1944]. 2v. and Apéndice. P. 40.   **S165**

v.1-2, paged continuously, 894p.; Apéndice, 465p.

Covers 544 to 1944, and gathers much material in one place but with certain weaknesses, e.g., date of birth and death are frequently omitted and no bibliographical data or references to sources are given.

Sosa, Francisco. Biografías de Mexicanos distinguidos. Edición de la Secretaría de Fomento. México, Oficina Tipográfica de la Secretaría de Fomento, 1884. 1115p.   **S166**

Bibliography

Iguíniz, Juan B. Bibliografía biográfica mexicana: tomo 1. Repertorios biográficos. Mexico [Impr. de la Secretaría de Relaciones Exteriores] 1930. 546p. (Monografías bibliográficas mexicanas, núm. 18)   **S167**

A list of 703 works of collective biography with full contents notes including names of persons. Contains p.361-546, a full index to all names mentioned in notes which serves therefore as an index to biographical material on about 7000 Mexicans of all periods.

Beristain de Souza, J. M. Biblioteca hispano americana setentrional. Amecameca, 1883. **S168**

For full record see A407.

Includes bio-bibliographical information about 3217 authors.

MIDDLE EAST

Near and Middle East who's who. Jerusalem, Tel-Aviv, Haifa, Near and Middle East Who's Who Pub. Co., 1945- . v.1- . il.   **S169**

v.1, Palestine and Trans-Jordan, 1945–46 (in two sections: Who's who; Palestine at work, a social and economic survey).

Further volumes were announced as v.2, Syria and Lebanon; v.3, Egypt; v.4, Iraq; v.5, Iran.

NETHERLANDS

Aa, Abraham Jacobus van der. Biographisch woordenboek der Nederlanden. Nieuwe uitgaaf. Haarlem, Brederode, 1852–78. 12v. il.   **S170**

Biographisch woordenboek van protestantsche godgeleerden in Nederland onder redactie van J. P. De Bie en J. Loosjes. 'sGravenhage, Nijhoff, 1919–43. v.1-5. (In progress)   **S171**

v.1-5, A-Leyendecker.

Nieuw nederlandsch biografisch woordenboek, onder redactie van P. C. Molhuysen, P. J. Blok en Fr. K. H. Kossmann. Leiden, Sijthoff, 1911–37. v.1-10. (In progress) Fl. 15 per v.   **S172**

Each volume is arranged alphabetically, and the latest volume has a cumulated index to all volumes so far published. Adequate signed articles, bibliographies.

Persoonlijkheden in het koninkrijk der Nederlanden in woord en beeld; Nederlanders en hun werk met een inleidung van H. Brugmans; mede bevattende de biografieën van de leden van het koninklijk huis door N. Japikse. Amsterdam, Van Holkema & Warendorf, 1938. 1748p. il.   **S173**

Includes some 5000 biographies with portraits.

Contemporary

Wie is dat? Naamlijst van bekende personen op elk gebied in het Koninkrijk der Nederlanden met biografische aantekeningen . . . [5. uitg.] 'sGravenhage, Nijhoff, 1948. 581p. **S174**

1st ed., 1931; 2d ed., 1932; 3d ed., 1935; 4th ed., 1938. Subtitle varies.

NEW ZEALAND

Scholefield, Guy Hardy. A dictionary of New Zealand biography. Wellington, N.Z., Dept. of Internal affairs, 1940. 2v. 50s. **S175**

"Bibliography": v.1, p.xviii-xxix.
A national biographical dictionary, modeled on the *Dictionary of national biography* (S123), of persons who have distinguished themselves in the history of New Zealand since organized European migration began approximately 100 years ago. Includes bibliography.

Contemporary

Who's who in New Zealand and the western Pacific, ed. by G. H. Scholefield. (Established in 1908) 4th ed. Wellington, N.Z., Watkins, 1941. 366p. 22s. 6d. **S176**

The fourth edition contains preliminary directory material, including officials of government, church and education, diplomatic representatives, election returns, etc. Obituary lists, p.1-51; Biographies, p.52-365.

NORWAY

Illustrert biografisk leksikon over kjendte norske maend og kvinder; redigert av Nanna With. Kristiania, With and Co., [1916–20]. 969p. il. **S177**

Norsk biografisk leksikon. Redaktion: Edv. Bull, Anders Krogvig, Gerhard Gran. Oslo, Aschehoug, 1923–48. v.1-10 (hft. 49). (In progress) Kr. 6.80 per hft. **S178**

v.1-10 (hft. 49), A-Ore.
Long articles by specialists, signed with names, not initials; with bibliographies.

Norske kvinder; en oversigt over deres stilling og livsvilkaar i hundredeaaret 1814–1914, utgit av Marie Høgh under redaktion av Fredrikke Mørck. Kristiania, Berg, 1914–25. 3v. il. **S179**

Volume 3 has subtitle: En kort oversigt over deres stilling og livsvilkaar i tiaaret 1914–1924.

Contemporary

Hvem er hvem? 1948. [5. utg.] Oslo, Aschehoug, 1948. 615p. **S180**

1st ed., 1912; 2d ed., 1930; 3d ed., 1934; 4th ed., 1938. The Norwegian who's who.

See also Vem är vem i Norden (S201).

Bibliography

Andresen, Harald. Norsk biografisk oppslagslitteratur; katalog utarbeidet for Norsk Slektshistorisk Forening. [Oslo] Cammermeyer [1945]. 218p. [Slektshistorisk Bibliotek] **S181**

A bibliography of Norwegian sources for biographical materials arranged by fields of specialization.

Deichmanske Bibliothek. Register til Norges Tidsskrifter: v.2, Norsk biografi (til 31/12 1909). Kristiania, Cammermeyer, 1911. 599p. **S182**

Lists nearly 15,000 names giving for each dates of birth or death, some characterizing phrase, and references to biographical articles in Norwegian periodicals. Because of the dates and characterizing phrases it can be used for some direct biographical information as well as for its indexing.

Continued informally by the similar indexing, also with dates and characterizing phrases, given in the *Norsk tidsskriftindex*, 1921–30 (E95), under the heading "Personalhistorie" and from 1931–35 in:

Sommerfeldt, Wilhelm Preuss. Biografiske Artikler i norske Tidsskrifter, 1931–1935. Oslo, Fabritius, 1936. 106p. (Norsk bibliografisk bibliotek, bd.2, hft. 3) **S183**

A continuation of the indexing of biographical articles in periodicals formerly included in the *Norsk tidsskriftindex* (E95) under the heading "Personalhistorie."

ORIENT

Beale, Thomas William. Oriental biographical dictionary. New ed., rev. and enl. by H. G. Keene. Lond., Allen, 1894. 431p. 28s. **S184**

Omits Anglo-Indian and Chinese biographies; includes native Indian, Persian, Arabic, etc.

See also Encyclopaedia of Islam (K255).

PARAGUAY

Parker, William Belmont. Paraguayans of to-day. 2d ed. Lond., Hispanic Soc. of Amer., 1921. 317p. il. (Hispanic notes and monographs, 6) **S185**

Quien es quien en el Paraguay? Buenos Aires, Ed. F. Monte Domecq, 1941- . v.1- . il. Annual (slightly irregular). **S186**

Later volumes omit names included in earlier volumes and add others, making it necessary to consult all volumes. Includes commercial directories.

PERU

Diccionario biográfico del Perú . . . Raúl Garbin Diaz, Raúl Garbin, Jr., Julio Cárdenas Ramírez 1. ed. 1943–44. . . . [Lima, "Escuelas americanas," 1944] 977p. il. $15. **S187**

A combination who's who, commercial directory and government roster.

Mendiburu, Manuel de. Diccionario histórico-biográfico del Perú. 2d ed. con adiciones y notas bibliográficas publicada por Evaristo San Cristóval. . . . Lima, "Enrique Palacios," 1931–35. 11v. il. **S188**

"Catálogo de las obras y manuscritos que deben consultarse para la historia de la América latina y particularmente del Perú."—v.1, p.15-52.

Historical and biographical articles in one alphabet, with a subject index in each volume and a general index at the end. Includes fairly long articles with references to sources.

—— —— Apendice. Lima, Gil, 1935–36. v.1-3, A-N.

Parker, William Belmont. Peruvians of to-day. Lima, Peru, 1919. 616p. il. (Hispanic notes and monographs, 2) **S189**

Paz-Soldán, Juan Pedro. Diccionario biográfico de peruanos contemporáneos. Nueva ed. cor. y aum. Lima, Lib. e Impr. Gil, 1921. 449p. il. **S190**

PHILIPPINES

Who's who in the Philippines; a biographical dictionary of notable living men of the Philippine islands. v.1, 1936/1937- . Manila, McCullough Pr. Co., 1937- . v.1- . **S191**

v.1, ed. by Franz J. Weissblatt. Includes statistical section. Who's who section includes both native and foreign persons.

POLAND

Akademja Umiejetności, Krakow. Polski słownik biograficzny. Krakow, Nakładem Polskiej Akad. Umiejetności, 1935–48. v.1-7, pt.1. (In progress) **S192**

v.1-6, A-Firlej, H; v.7, pt.1, Firlej, J.-Frankowski.

A scholarly dictionary with signed articles and bibliographies.

Olszewicz, Bolesław. Lista strat kultury polskiej (1. IX. 1939–1. III. 1946) Warszawa, Wydawnictwo S. Arcta, 1947. 336p. **S193**

A useful necrology list covering the years from Sept. 1, 1939–March 1, 1946. Includes Poles who had contributed to Poland's cultural life—professors, writers, artists, etc. Information very brief.

PORTUGAL

Quem é alguém (Who's who in Portugal). Dicionário biográfico das personalidades em destaque do nosso tempo. 1947- . Lisboa, Portugália editora, [1947]- . v.1- . **S194**

PUERTO RICO

Quien es quien en Puerto Rico; diccionario biográfico de record personal. Dir. y ed., Conrado Asenjo. 4. ed. 1948–49. San Juan, Imp. Venezuela, 1947. 216p. $6. **S195**

1. ed. 1933–34; 2. ed. 1936–37; 3. ed. 1941–42.

RUSSIA

Akademiía Nauk, SSSR. Materialy dlía biograficheskago slovaría dieístvitel'nykh chlenov Imperatorskoi Akademii Nauk. Petrograd, 1915–17. 2v. (Imperatorskaía Akademiía Nauk, 1889–1914. v.3) **S196**

Fairly long sketches with detailed bibliographies.

Deíateli revoliútsionnogo dvizheniía v Rossii; bio-bibliograficheskii slovar'. Ot predshestvennikov dekabristov do padeniía tsarizma. Pod redaktsiei Vl. Vilenskogo-Sibiriakova, Feliksa Kona. Moskva, 1927–34. **S197**

v.1-2, 3¹⁻², 5¹⁻². il.

Vsesoíuznoe obshchestvo politicheskikh Katorzhan i ssyl'nopselentsev.

Biographical dictionary of the revolutionary movement.

Russkii biograficheskii slovar' . . . izdan pod nabliúdeniem predsiedatelía I. Russkago Istoricheskago Obshchestva A. A. Polovtsova. S.-Peterburg, "Kadima," 1896–1918. 25v. **S198**

Publisher varies.

Arranged alphabetically but not published in that order, some volumes in last of alphabet appearing before earlier letters; parts of the alphabet not yet covered when work was discontinued are the letters V, Gog-Gía, E, M, Nik-Nía, Tk-Tía, U; volumes after volume 2 are not numbered. Contains signed articles of some length with bibliographies; especially strong for material about the upper and ecclesiastical classes of pre-revolutionary Russia.

SALVADOR

García, Miguel Angel. Diccionario histórico-enciclopédico de la República de El Salvador. San Salvador, 1927–48. v.1-10. (In progress) **S199**

v.1-10, A-Car.

Includes biography. For full description see V436.

SCANDINAVIA

See name of country for individual Scandinavian country.

Vem är vem i Norden; biografisk handbok. Huvudredaktor: Gunnar Sjöström. Stockholm, Bonnier, 1941. 1544p. **S201**

Includes separate sections on Denmark, p.3-402; Finland, p.404-564; Iceland, p.567-90; Norway, p.593-926; Sweden, p.929-1544.

SOUTH AFRICA

South African who's who, an illustrated biographical sketch book of South Africans. Johannesburg, K. Donaldson, 1905- . Annual (slightly irregular). (v.33, 1949, 84s.)   **S202**

SPAIN

🌿 There is no general modern dictionary of national biography for Spain. The large Spanish encyclopedias, and especially the *Espasa* (D64), include many biographies of Spaniards and Spanish-Americans. For names and information not found there, works of collective biography and the numerous regional and special biographical dictionaries should be consulted. A useful bibliography of regional and special works is given in the following:

Foulché-Delbosc, Raymond and **Barrau-Dihigo, Louis.** Manuel de l'hispanisant. N.Y., Putnam, 1920–25. 2v.   **S203**

Volume 1 includes: List of general biographies, p.41-60; Regional biographies, arranged by place, p.60-81; List of biographical works on special classes, e.g., artists, etc., p.81-119.
For full description *see* A490.

SWEDEN

Biografiskt lexikon öfver namnkunnige svenske män. Ny reviderad upplaga. Stockholm, Beijers, 1874. 23v.   **S204**
Continued by the following:

Svenskt biografiskt lexikon. Ny följd. Örebro, N. M. Lindhs Boktryckeri, 1857–1907. 10v. **S205**
Publisher varies.

Hofberg, Herman. Svenskt biografiskt handlexikon; alfabetiskt ordnade lefnadsteckningar af sveriges namnkunniga män och kvinnor frän reformationen till nuvarande tid. Ny upplaga. Stockholm, Bonnier, 1906. 2v. il.   **S206**

Svenskt biografiskt lexikon. Redaktionskommitté: J. A. Almquist [o.a.] Redaktör: Bertil Boëthius. Stockholm, Bonnier, 1917–49. v.1-13, hft. 1. il. (In progress) Kr. 30 per v.   **S207**

v.1-12, A-Ekman; v.13, hft. 1, Ekman-Ekmark. A chronological index to v.1-10 is included in v.10, p.769-94.
Excellent work with long, signed articles, bibliographies, many portraits. Includes biographies of persons still living.

Svenska män och kvinnor; biografisk uppslagsbok. Stockholm, Bonnier, 1942–49. v.1-5. il. (In progress)   **S208**
v.1-5, A-O.
To be in eight volumes. Covers from the earliest times

to the present and includes living persons. Articles are brief but are signed. There is almost no bibliography except for the titles of books written by persons included. Differs from the *Svenskt biografiskt lexikon* (S207) in the brevity of its sketches and its lack of bibliography. Should be useful in libraries which do not need the extensive information given in the larger work.

Contemporary

Vem är det. Svensk biografisk handbok 1912- . Stockholm, Norstedt, 1912- . v.1- . Biennial. (3 years between 1920–1923) (1949. pub. 1948. 20kr.)   **S209**
Subtitle varies.

See also Vem är vem i Norden (S201).

Bibliography

Ägren, Sven. Svensk biografisk uppslagslitteratur; bibliografisk förteckning. Uppsala, Almquist, 1929. 423p. (Added title page: Svenska bibliotekariesamfundets skriftserie. I)   **S210**

Classified, with author and subject index.
Includes material dealing with Finland (to 1809) and other Swedish possessions, as well as with Swedes in foreign countries.
A comprehensive classified bibliography of more than 2000 titles of biographical dictionaries, registers, collective biographies, etc., which include Swedish biography.

SWITZERLAND

Dictionnaire historique et biographique de la Suisse. . . . Neuchâtel, Admïnistration du Dictionnaire, 1921–34. 7v. and suppl. il.   **S211**

Contains a large amount of genealogy and biography, including persons still living. For full description *see* V455.

Neue Schweizer Biographie; nouvelle biographie suisse; nuova biografia svizzera. Chefredaktion, A. Bruckner. Basel, Buchdruckerei sum Basler Berichthaus, 1938. 612p. il.   **S212**

Contains about 5000 biographies of contemporary native Swiss, the majority with pictures. The sketch is in the language of the subject, German, French, or Italian.

Schweizerisches Zeitgenossen-Lexikon. Lexique suisse des contemporains. Lessico svizzero dei contemporanei. Begründet und redigiert von Hermann Aellen. 2. Ausg. Bern und Leipzig, Gotthelf-Verlag [1932]. 1023p.   **S213**
1st ed. 1921. 764p.; Suppl., 1926. 200p.

Bibliography

Barth, Hans. Bibliographie der schweizer Geschichte. Basel, Geering, 1914–15. 3v.   **S214**

A very full bibliography of separately published biographies is given in volume 2, p.116-404. For full description *see* V452.

Bern. Schweizerische Landesbibliothek. Katalog . . . Personenkatalog, 1901–1920, 1921–1930. Bern, Huber, 1929–31. 2v. (In its Systematisches Verzeichnis der schweizerischen oder die Schweiz betreffenden Veröffentlichungen) **S215**

Lists of biographical works published in Switzerland during the period, arranged alphabetically by the name of the biographee.

For description of complete work *see* A520.

Bibliographie der Schweizergeschichte, Jahrg. 1913- . Zurich, Leemann, 1914- . Annual. **S216**

This current bibliography of Swiss history has a section *Personengeschichte* which, particularly in its earlier volumes, is very full in its indexing of biographical and obituary articles on natives and residents of Switzerland.

For full description *see* V453.

Repertorium über die in Zeit- und Sammelschriften der Jahre 1812–1890, 1891–1900, enthaltenen Aufsätze und Mitteilungen schweizergeschichtlichen Inhaltes. Basel, Geering, 1892–1906. 2v. **S217**

Each volume contains a list of biographical articles and obituaries in more than 300 periodicals and other collective works, which, as it gives dates of birth and death and in many cases a brief characterizing phrase, furnishes some direct information as well as the reference to the articles indexed. For full description *see* V454.

TURKEY

Türkiye teracimi ahval ansiklopedisi. Encyclopédie biographique de Turquie. Who is who in Turkey. v.3, 1930–32. Stamboul, Hamit Matbaasi [1932]. v.3, 943p. il. **S218**

Turkish and French in parallel columns; small portrait in text with each biographical sketch.

URUGUAY

Parker, William Belmont. Uruguayans of today. Lond. and N.Y., Hispanic Soc. of Amer., 1921. 575p. il. (Hispanic notes and monographs, 7) **S219**

Scarone, Arturo. Uruguayos contemporáneos; nuevo diccionario de datos biográficos y bibliográficos. Montevideo, Barreiro y Ramos, 1937. 610p. **S220**

1st ed. 1918. This edition completely revised and rewritten. Includes over 1280 names in the main alphabet and 71 in the appendix.

"Apéndice: Destacados compatriotas que han fallecido desde 1918—año de la primera publicación de esta obra—hasta la fecha de aparecer esta edición": p.[545]-610.

YUGOSLAVIA

Ko je ko u Jugoslaviji. Beograd, Izdanje "Jugoslovenskog godišnjaka," 1928. 168p. **S221**

GENEALOGY

❧ Genealogy is the study of family history and as such may require special techniques and the searching of records of many kinds. There are some guides and indexes which may be helpful but the average library will not find it possible to have available the materials necessary for detailed genealogical research, including the genealogies of individual families, local histories, etc. Some large libraries have special genealogical departments and there are also special libraries devoted to this work. When a local library cannot supply a reader with genealogical material it should refer him to one or more of the specialized libraries.

This section includes some of the bibliographies and guides useful for work in American genealogy; a selection of peerages and other compilations of European nobility; and reference works on heraldry, orders and decorations, flags, and personal names.

UNITED STATES
Guide

Doane, Gilbert Harry. Searching for your ancestors; the how and why of genealogy. [rev. ed.] Minneapolis, Univ. of Minnesota Pr., 1948. 176p. **T1**

1st ed. 1937.
A manual and guide to genealogical searching. Includes bibliographies, p.147-61.

Bibliography and indexes

American genealogical index; Fremont Rider, ed. . . . pub. by a committee representing the cooperating subscribing libraries. . . . Middletown, Conn., 1942–49. v.1-35. $10 ea. (In progress) **T2**

Begun in 1936 as a surname index printed on cards; now issued in book form giving full name entries.—Cf. *Pref.*
v.1-35, A-Sherly.

American genealogist, being a catalogue of family histories. . . . 5th ed. Albany, N.Y., Munsell, 1900. 406p. **T3**

Subtitle: A bibliography of American genealogy, or a list of the title pages of books and pamphlets on family history, published in America, from 1771 to date.
Earlier editions edited by W. H. Whitmore, 1862, 1868, 1875.

Index to American genealogies; and to genealogical material contained in all works such as town histories, county histories, historical society publications, biographies, historical periodicals, and kindred works, alphabetically arranged. 5th ed., rev., improved and enl. Albany, N.Y., Munsell, 1900–08. 352p. and suppl., 107p. **T4**

Basic volume (1900) indexes about 50,000 references; supplement continues indexing for 1900–1908.

Jacobus, Donald Lines. Index to genealogical periodicals. New Haven, Conn., Jacobus, 1932. [133]p. $12. **T5**

In two parts: (1) Name index; (2) Place and subject index. Indexes sets of 53 American periodicals.

Long Island Historical Society, Brooklyn, N.Y. Library. Catalogue of American genealogies in the library . . . prepared under the direction of the librarian, Emma Toedteberg. Brooklyn, Society, 1935. 660p. **T6**

Catalog, p.1-582 (items 1-7934); Supplement: Books received during printing of the catalog, p.583-603 (items 7935-8202); List of manuscripts, typewritten, multi-graphed, mimeographed and blueprint material, p.605-660 (849 items).

Stewart, Robert Armistead. Index to printed Virginia genealogies, including key and bibliography. Richmond, Va., Old Dominion Pr., 1930. 265p. **T7**

An index, begun by Dr. William G. Stannard, aided by Mrs. Rebecca Johnston, and completed in its present form by Robert Armistead Stewart, to the genealogies contained in some 750 historical, biographical and genealogical works. Arranged alphabetically by family name.

U. S. Library of Congress. American and English genealogies in the Library. . . . 2d ed. Wash., Govt. Prt. Off., 1919. 1332p. **T8**

Dictionaries

Hotten, John Camden. Original lists of persons of quality, emigrants, religious exiles, political rebels . . . and others who went from Great Britain to the American plantations. N.Y., Bouton; Lond., Chatto, 1874. 580p. (repr. N.Y., G. A. Baker, 1931) **T9**

Savage, James. Genealogical dictionary of the first settlers of New England showing three generations of those who came before May, 1692, on the basis of Farmer's Register. Bost., Little, 1860–62. 4v. o.p. **T10**

U. S. Bureau of the Census. Heads of families at the first census, 1790. Wash., Govt. Prt. Off., 1907–09. 12v. **T11**

Contents: Maine, New Hampshire, Vermont, Massachusetts, Rhode Island, Connecticut, New York, Pennsylvania, Maryland, Virginia, North Carolina, South Carolina. The statistics for Virginia are from the state census of 1782–85, those for all other states, from the federal census of 1790. For genealogical reference work, of great value, in that it shows in what towns families of any given surname were living in the year 1790, and so indicates what local records should be examined for further information.

Virkus, Frederick Adams. Compendium of American genealogy; the standard genealogical encyclopedia of the first families of America. Chic., Inst. of Amer. Genealogy, 1925–42. v.1-7. il. **T12**

Volumes 1-4 entitled *Abridged compendium of American genealogy.* Subtitle varies.

Periodicals

New England historical and genealogical register, v.1- . Bost., New England Historic Genealogical Soc., 1847- . Quarterly. $5 per yr. **T13**

Pub. varies.

Indexes, v.1-50: Index of persons. 1906–07. 3v.; Index of subjects. 1908. 296p.; Index of places. 1911. 123p.

New York genealogical and biographical record. Devoted to the interests of American genealogy and biography. v.1- . N.Y., N.Y. Genealogical and Biographical Soc., 1870- . il. Quarterly. $6 per yr. **T14**

—— Subject index. v.1-38. 1907. 47p.

CANADA

Tanguay, Cyprien. Dictionnaire généalogique des familles canadiennes, depuis la fondation de la colonie jusqu'à nos jours. Quebec, Eusèbe Senécal, 1871–90. 7v. **T15**

1st ser. v.1, 1608–1700; 2d ser. v.2-7, 1701–1763. The second series includes some entries later than 1763 belonging to a projected third series.

EUROPE

Ruvigny and Raineval, Melville Amadeus Henry Douglas Heddle de La Caillemotte de Massue de Ruvigny, *9th marquis of.* Titled nobility of Europe. An international peerage, or "Who's who," of the sovereigns, princes and nobles of Europe. Lond., Harrison, 1914. 1598p. il. (coats of arms) **T16**

Contains fairly full accounts of existing titles of nobility and biographies of living members (in 1914) of each family included in one international list arranged alphabetically under the chief title borne by the head of the house. There is a full index to surnames, variations in spelling, merged titles and to titled members of a family whose names differ from that of the head of the house. Claims to be fairly complete for all British, Spanish, Belgian and Portuguese titles, for French ducal titles, and for Austrian, German, Hungarian, Swedish, Dutch, Danish and Finnish titles above the rank of baron.

Almanach de Gotha, annuaire généalogique, diplomatique et statistique, 1763- . Gotha, Perthes, 1763- . Annual. **T17**

For full description *see* L246.

The first section is very useful for the genealogies of the royal and princely houses of Europe.

There have been many other annuals of the nobility of the various countries of Europe, most of which were suspended or discontinued before World War II. Some of the most important were: *Gothaisches genealogisches Taschenbuch der adeligen Häuser: Deutscher Uradel* (Gotha, Justus Perthes), 1900- . *Gothaisches genealogisches Taschenbuch der adeligen Häuser: Alten Adel und Briefadel* (Gotha, Justus Perthes), 1907- . *Gothaisches genealogisches Taschenbuch der freiherrlichen Häuser* (Gotha, Justus Perthes), 1848- . *Gothaisches genealogisches Taschenbuch der gräflicher Häuser* (Gotha, Justus Perthes), 1825- . *Annuaire de la noblesse de France* (Paris, Au Bureau de la Publication), 1843- . *Annuaire de la noblesse de Belgique* (Bruxelles), 1847- . *La noblesse belge* (Bruxelles), 1889- . *Annuario della nobilità italiana* (Bari), 1879- . *Libro d'oro della nobilità italiana* (Roma, Collegio Araldico), 1910- . *Nederland's adelsboeks* ('sGravenhage, VanStockum), 1903- . *Svensk adelskalender* (Stockholm, Norstedt), 1899- . *Danmarks adels Aarbog* (Kjøbenhavn, Vilk. Trydes), 1884- . *Annuaire de la noblesse de Russie* (St. Pétersbourg), 1889- . *Annuario de la nobleza de España* (Madrid), 1908- .

FRANCE

La Chesnaye-Desbois, François Alexandre Aubert de. Dictionnaire de la noblesse . . . de la France. . . . 3. éd. Paris, Schlesinger, 1863–77. 19v. **T18**

Subtitle: Contenant les généalogies, l'histoire & la chronologie des familles nobles de la France, l'explication de leurs armes et l'état des grandes terres du royaume. . . . On a joint à ce dictionnaire le tableau généalogique et historique des maisons souveraines de l'Europe et une notice des familles étrangères, les plus anciennes, les plus nobles et les plus illustres. 3. éd. entièrement refondue . . . & augm. d'une table générale de tous les noms de familles, de terres, de fiefs, d'alliances cités dans le cours de l'ouvrage, ainsi que d'un Armorial représentant les blasons de maisons dont les généalogies sont comprises dans cette édition.

v.1-19, A-Z.

Lorenz, volume 6, p.58 (A253), states that the work was to extend to 22 volumes, with an armorial; volumes 20-22 and the armorial were, however, never published.

Woelmont, Henri de. Notices généalogiques, 1.-7. sér. Paris, Champion, 1923–30. v.1-7 and suppl. v. **T19**

The seven series contain notices of 1078 noble French families, some still in existence and some extinct, giving, for each: description of the arms, bibliography, brief history of the family and the genealogy. Each volume is arranged alphabetically by family names. There is no general index, each volume having its own index to all names mentioned in articles as well as those used for headings. The supplementary volume contains "Additions et corrections" to series 1-5.

GERMANY

Familiengeschichtliche Bibliographie, hrsg. unter dem Schutze der Arbeitsgemeinschaft der deutschen Familien- und Wappenkundlichen Vereine, 1900- . . . . Leipzig, Zentralstelle f. Deut. Personen u. Familiengeschichte, 1928–39. v.1-6. **T20**

v.1, 1900–20, a basic volume for the twenty-year period, by Friedrich Wecken, containing 13,912 entries; v.2, 1921–26, by Friedrich Wecken, annual lists for each year, the six lists totalling 8033 entries; v.3, 1927–30, by Johannes Hohlfeld, annual lists for each of the four years; v.4, 1931/32, 1933, 1934. Register; v.5, pt.1, Bibliographie, 1935, by Johannes Hohlfeld; pt.2, Bibliographie, 1897–99, by Gunther Preuss-Tantzen; pt.3, Heraldischer Bibliographie, by Egon, Freiherr von Berchem; v.6, pt.1-2, Bibliographie, 1936/37, by Johannes Hohlfeld; pt.3, Gesamtregister zur familiengeschichtlichen Bibliographie 1897–1937 und zur Heraldischen Bibliographie, Bd.1, bearb. von Johannes Hohlfeld und Fritz Ranitzsch.

Heydenreich, Eduard Karl Heinrich. Handbuch der praktischen Genealogie. Leipzig, Degener, 1913. 2v. xi geneal. tab. **T21**

Kneschke, Ernst Heinrich. Neues allgemeines deutsches Adels-Lexicon im Vereine mit mehreren Historikern. Leipzig, Degener, 1929/30. 9v. **T22**

Unveränderter Abdruck des im Verlage von Friedrich Voigt zu Leipzig 1859–1870 erschienenen Werkes.

GREAT BRITAIN
Bibliography

Bridger, Charles. Index to printed pedigrees contained in county and local histories, the her-

alds' visitations, and in the more important genealogical collections. Lond., Smith, 1867. 384p. **T23**

Burke, Arthur Meredyth. Key to the ancient parish registers of England and Wales. Lond., Sackville Pr., 1908. 163p. **T24**

"The object of this work is to provide those who have reason to consult the Parish Registers with an easy and reliable guide to the accessibility or otherwise of these national records."—Pref.

An alphabetical list of all the parishes in England and Wales which have records beginning before 1813. For each register it gives the date of the earliest entry and notes all transcripts which have been printed. Useful.

Gatfield, George. Guide to printed books and manuscripts relating to English and foreign heraldry and genealogy, being a classified catalogue of works of those branches of literature. Lond., Mitchell & Hughes, 1892. 646p. **T25**

Stuart, Margaret. Scottish family history: A guide to works of reference on the history and genealogy of Scottish families. Edinburgh, Oliver, 1930. 386p. **T26**

Includes books, pamphlets and a large amount of analysis of periodicals, composite books, collections, etc.

Thomson, Theodore Radford. A catalogue of British family histories. Lond., Murray [1928]. 158p. **T27**

Dictionaries

Burke, Sir **John Bernard.** Genealogical and heraldic history of the peerage, baronetage, and knightage, Privy Council and order of precedence. Lond., Burke, 1826- . il. (coats of arms) Annual. (1949. £9 9s.) **T28**

Contents: Introductory lists, e.g., creations, obituaries, guide to relative precedence, degrees, styles and privileges of peerage and baronetage, etc.; Precedence; Orders of knighthood; Royal family; Peerage and baronetage, arranged alphabetically by title, giving brief account of present holder of title, names of wife, children, heir, lineage, date of creation, arms (both illustration and description), residence; Archbishops and bishops; Foreign titles of nobility held by British subjects; Knightage, companionage, and Privy Council.

The only one of the annual peerages which gives full lineage.

—— Genealogical and heraldic history of the landed gentry of Ireland. New ed., rev. by A. C. Fox-Davies. Lond., Harrison, 1912. 786p. il. (coats of arms) **T29**

—— Genealogical and heraldic history of the colonial gentry. Lond., Harrison, 1891–95. 2v. il. **T30**

—— Genealogical history of the dormant, abeyant, forfeited, and extinct peerages of the British empire. New ed. Lond., Harrison, 1883. 642p. **T31**

—— Burke's Genealogical and heraldic history of the landed gentry, founded by the late Sir Bernard Burke. Centenary (15th) ed., ed. by H. Pirie-Gordon. Lond., Shaw, 1937. lxxivp., 2756p. il. **T32**

History: 1st ed., *Burke's Commoners*, 1837, 2v.; 2d ed., *Landed gentry of Great Britain and Ireland*, with index of about 100,000 names, 1847–52, 3v.; 15th (Centenary) ed., 1937. After the ninth edition, Irish families were omitted and included, instead, in a separate work, *Landed gentry of Ireland* (1904, 1912) (T29). The fifteenth edition contains, p.2531-2716, an Irish supplement.

While the avowed purpose of the work is for genealogical and heraldic information, it is often very useful for biographical data on facts or names omitted in the biographical dictionaries.

Gives brief sketch of present head of family, names of wife and children, lineage, arms (both illustration and description), seat.

Cokayne, George Edward. Complete baronetage. Exeter, Pollard, 1900–09. 5v. and index v. **T33**

v.1, English baronetcies, 1611–25; and Irish, 1618–25; v.2, English, Irish and Scottish, 1625–49; v.3, English, Irish and Scottish, 1649–64; v.4, English, Irish and Scottish, 1665–1707; v.5, Great Britain and Ireland, 1707–1800; Index v.: Index and appendix.

—— The Complete peerage; or, A history of the House of Lords and all its members from the earliest times . . . rev. and much enl. ed. Lond., St. Catherine Pr., 1910–49. v.1-11, 13 (In progress) **T34**

Title and editors vary.

v.1-5 had title *Complete peerage of England, Scotland, Ireland, Great Britain, and the United Kingdom, extant, extinct, or dormant.*

v.1-11, A-Sisonby; v.13 (1940), Peerage creations and promotions from 22 Jan. 1901 to 31 Dec. 1938.

Gives full accounts, with bibliographical references to sources of information and many biographical details. Important as a supplement to biographical dictionaries as well as for genealogical information.

Debrett's Peerage, baronetage, knightage and companionage. Lond., Odhams Pr., 1713-   . il. Annual. (1949, 105s.) **T35**

Editors and publishers vary.

Subtitle 1949: Comprises information concerning persons bearing hereditary or courtesy titles, privy councillors, knights, companions of the various orders, and the collateral branches of peers and baronets.

Doyle, James William Edmund. Official baronage of England, showing the succession, dignities, and offices of every peer from 1066 to 1885. Lond., Longmans, 1886. 3v. il. **T36**

ITALY

Spreti, Vittorio, *marchese.* Enciclopedia storico-nobiliare italiana; famiglie nobili e titolate viventi riconosciute dal R. governo d'Italia compresi: città, comunità, mense vescovili, abazie, parrocchie ed enti nobili e titolati riconosciuti. Milano, Ed. Encic. Stor.-Nob. Ital., 1928–35. 8v. incl. appendix. il. (coats of arms) **T37**

—— and **Azzi Vitelleschi, Giustiniano degli.** Saggio di bibliografia araldica italiana. Supplemento a l'Enciclopedia storico-nobiliare italiana. Milano, Ed. Encic. Stor.-Nob., 1936. 230p. **T38**

FORMS OF ADDRESS

Titles and forms of address; a guide to their correct use. 7th rev. and enl. ed. Lond., Black, 1949. 176p. 7s. 6d.; $2.25. **T39**

A useful handbook to correct English usage. Helpful also for its table of abbreviations and its list of pronunciations of English proper names.

Revised every three or four years.

Early editions were by Armiger [pseud.].

❦ Somewhat similar lists, included in larger reference books, are: Modes of addressing persons of title, included regularly in the introductory parts of the lists and records of peers. "Forms of address" in *Webster's New international dictionary,* 2d ed., 1950, p.3012-14; "Forms of address" in *Century dictionary,* Supplement, under word, Forms. The *Webster* and *Century* lists include American forms, for government officials, etc., not given in the English lists.

Another useful list is found in Taintor, S. A. and Munro, K. M., *Secretary's handbook,* 1949, p.285-323.

HERALDRY

Bolton, Charles Knowles. Bolton's American armory; a record of coats of arms which have been in use within the present bounds of the United States. Bost., Faxon, 1927. 223p. (Useful reference ser.) **T40**

Boutell, Charles. Boutell's Manual of heraldry, rev. and illus. by V. Wheeler-Holohan. Lond., Warne [1931]. 332p. il. **T41**

"With 32 plates in colour and numerous line illustrations in the text."

Burke, *Sir* **John Bernard.** General armory of England, Scotland, Ireland, and Wales, comprising a registry of armorial bearings from the earliest to the present time. Lond., Harrison, 1884. 1185p. il. **T42**

An enlarged edition of *Encyclopaedia of heraldry or General armory of England, Scotland and Ireland,* published in many editions.

Fairbairn, James. Book of crests of the families of Great Britain and Ireland. 4th ed., rev. and enl. by A. C. Fox-Davies. Edinburgh, Jack, 1912. 2v. il.   **T43**

> v.1, text; v.2, plates.

Fox-Davies, Arthur Charles. Armorial families, a directory of gentlemen of coat-armour. 7th ed. Lond., Hurst and Blackett, 1929. 2v. il.   **T44**

—— Book of public arms, a complete encyclopaedia of all royal, territorial, municipal, corporate, official and impersonal arms. New ed., containing over 1300 drawings. Lond., Jack, 1915. 876p. il.   **T45**

—— Complete guide to heraldry. Rev. ed. Lond., Jack, 1929. 647p. il.   **T46**

> Founded upon his *Art of heraldry,* 1904.

Innes, Thomas. Scots heraldry, a practical handbook; the historical principles and modern application of the art and science . . . with 37 full-page plates, 10 in colour, and over 100 illustrations in the text. Edinburgh, Oliver and Boyd, 1934. 186p. il.   **T47**

Rietstap, Jean Baptiste. Armorial général; précédé d'un dictionnaire des termes du blason. 2. éd. Gouda, van Goor, 1884–87; Paris, Dupont, 1904; Institut héraldique, 1905–14; La Haye, Nijhoff, 1926–34. 2v. and suppl. (4v.)   **T48**

> v.1 (1884), A-K; v.2 (1887), L-Z and suppl., A-Z; Suppl. (1904–34): fasc. 1-4, each A-Z; v.1-2, A-Z; v.3, A-Z.
> Volume numbers of supplement as given in set not uniform. Volume numbering for supplement, volumes 1-3, as given above, is numbering as given on title pages. Table of contents in volume 2 uses different numbering.
> The two basic volumes are by J. B. Rietstap; the supplements by Victor and Henri Rolland.
> A general work useful for the heraldry of various countries. It deals only with families entitled to hereditary honours, so that in England, for instance, no families under the rank of a baronet are included.

—— —— Armoiries des familles contenues dans l'Armorial général. Paris, Institut Héraldique Universel, 1903–12; La Haye, Nijhoff, 1938. 6v.

> Plates of coats of arms (*blasons*) described in the basic volumes of the *Armorial général* (T48). Volumes 2-6 have title: *Planches de l'Armorial général.*

Ströhl, Hugo Gerard. Heraldischer Atlas; eine Sammlung von heraldischen Musterblättern für Künstler, Gewerbetreibende, sowie für Freunde der Wappenkunde. Stuttgart, Hoffmann, 1899. 23p., [158]p. 76 pl. (with descriptive text) **T49**

Woodward, John. Treatise on heraldry, British and foreign, with English and French glossaries. New and enl. ed. Edinburgh, Johnston, 1896. 2v. il.   **T50**

ORDERS AND DECORATIONS

American Numismatic Society. Numismatic notes and monographs nos. 11, 20, 31, 36, 51, 56, 89, 106. N.Y., Society, 1922–45. 8v. il.   **T51**

> no.11, *French* orders and decorations. 1922. 110p.; no.20, *Italian* orders of chivalry and medals of honor. 1923. 146p.; no. 31, *Spanish* orders of chivalry and decorations of honor. 1926. 165p.; no.36, Decorations and medals of the *French colonies* and protectorates. 1928. 62p.; no. 51, *Russian* imperial orders. 1932. 101p.; no.56, *South American* decorations and war medals. 1932. 178p.; no.89, *Mexican* decorations of honour. 1940. 53p.; no.106, *British* orders and decorations. 1945. 124p.
> no.51, by Alan W. Hazelton, no.106, by James C. Risk; the others by Harrold E. Gillingham.

Jocelyn, Arthur. Orders, decorations and medals of the world. . . . Lond., Nicholson & Watson, 1934. v.1. 91p. 14 pl.   **T52**

> v.1, British Empire.
> "This volume . . . is the first, it is hoped, of some twelve volumes to follow, comprising, in all, 73 countries."—*Pref.*
> Contains descriptions of the various orders and medals and fine colored plates of the ribbons, but not the medals.

Wyllie, Robert E. Orders, decorations and insignia, military and civil; with the history and romance of their origin and a full description of each . . . with 367 illustrations (over 200 in colour). N.Y. & Lond., Putnam [c1921]. 269p. il.   **T53**

Contains historical and descriptive information, with many excellent illustrations, of the medals, ribbons, badges, etc., of the United States, Great Britain, Belgium, China, Cuba, Czechoslovakia, France, Greece, Hawaii, Italy, Japan, Monaco, Montenegro, Panama, Poland, Portugal, Rumania, Russia and Serbia. Includes also information on shoulder insignia, insignia of rank, insignia and colors of arms of service.

❦ Information on orders and decorations is given in many genealogical annuals, such as the *Almanach de Gotha* (T17), Burke's *Peerage* (T28), etc., and in the older official registers, such as the French *Almanach national* (L262), the Belgian *Almanach royal* (L256), etc. The following monographs on the orders of special countries are useful:

Colleville, Ludovic, *comte de*, and Saint-Christo, François. Les ordres du roi; répertoire général contenant les noms et qualités de tous les chevaliers des ordres royaux militaires et chevaleresques, ayant existé en France de 1099 à 1830 (d'après les brevets originaux des Archives Nationales) avec une histoire des ordres du Saint-Esprit, de Saint-Michel, de Saint-Louis, etc. Paris, Jouve [1920]. 711p. **T54**

Hurley, Christopher. Russian orders, decorations and medals, including a historical résumé and notes, under the monarchy. Lond., Harrison, 1935. 90p. il. **T55**

Nicolas, *Sir* **Nicholas Harris.** History of the orders of knighthood of the British Empire; of the Order of the Guelphs of Hanover; and of the medals, clasps, and crosses, conferred for naval and military services. Lond., Hunter, 1842. 4v. il. **T56**

FLAGS

Brown, James LaSalle. The flag of the United States, its use in commerce. Wash., Govt. Prt. Off., 1941. 51p. (U.S. Bureau of Foreign and Domestic Commerce. Trade promotion ser., no.218) 10c. **T57**

This publication contains the text of the federal, state, and territorial laws on the use of the flag in the business world.—Cf. *Foreword.*

Gt. Brit. Admiralty. Drawings of the flags of all nations. Lond., Stat. Off., 1930. 30p. il. **T58**

—— **Colonial office.** Flags, badges and arms of His Majesty's dominions beyond the seas and of territories under His Majesty's protection. Lond., Stat. Off., 1932. 2v. **T59**

Contents: v.1, Flags and badges; v.2, Arms.

Moss, James Alfred. Flag of the United States; its history and symbolism. 3d ed. Wash., U.S. Flag Assoc., 1941. 272p. il. $2.50. **T60**

1st ed. 1930.

Shankle, George Earlie. State names, flags, seals, songs, birds, flowers, and other symbols; a study based on historical documents giving the origin and significance of the state names, nicknames, mottoes, seals, flags, flowers, birds, songs, and descriptive comments on the capitol buildings and on some of the leading state histories, with facsimiles of the state flags and seals. Rev. ed. N.Y., Wilson, 1938. 522p. il. **T61**

Smith, Cleveland H. and **Taylor, Gertrude R.** Flags of all nations. N.Y., Crowell, 1946. 152p. il. $2.50. **T62**

A small, popular handbook giving a very brief story of each flag with illustration in color.

U. S. Office of Naval Operations. Flags of the United States and other countries, 1938. . . . Wash., U.S. Navy Dept., Hydrographic Off., 1938. 1v. il. (Hydrographic Office. [Pub.] 89) $3. **T63**

Loose-leaf, to be kept up to date by new sheets. Colored plates.

". . . Supersedes the flag supplement to H.O.87 issued in 1933, and also chapter 28 of the Communication Instructions, 1929."

Wheeler-Holohan, Vincent. Flags of the world, past and present, their story and associations. Rev. and illus. Lond., N.Y., Warne, 1939. 254p. il. $3.50. **T64**

Comp. originally by F. E. Hulme, 1897, etc., rev. by W. J. Gordon, 1915–1933.

NAMES

Christian names

Withycombe, Elizabeth Gidley. Oxford dictionary of English Christian names. Ox., Clarendon Pr., 1945. 136p. 7s. 6d. **T65**

Gives sources for earliest usage.

Yonge, Charlotte Mary. History of Christian names. New ed., rev. Lond., Macmillan, 1884. 476p. **T66**

Contains a glossary of Christian names, pref. p.19-144, which gives the meaning and refers to the body of the book where a full description will be found with derivations, forms in various languages, etc.

❧ A list of Christian names, in English, with equivalent forms in the principal foreign languages, is given in *Lippincott's Biographical dictionary* (S23). The larger bilingual foreign dictionaries frequently give supplementary lists of Christian names in the languages of the dictionary.

Surnames

Weekley, Ernest. Surnames. [2d ed.] Lond., John Murray [1917]. 364p. Repr. 1927. **T67**

British

See also Kennedy, *Bibliography of writings on the English language,* p.328-37 (R260).

Bardsley, Charles Wareing. Dictionary of English and Welsh surnames, with special American instances. Lond., Frowde, 1901. 837p. **T68**

Black, George Fraser. The surnames of Scotland; their origin, meaning, and history. N.Y., N.Y. Pub. Lib., 1946. 838p. (Repr. from the Bulletin of the New York Public Library, Aug. 1943—Sept. 1946) $10. **T69**

A monumental work giving origin, meaning and history of Scotch surnames from the earliest times, with reference to sources.

Ewen, Cecil Henry L'Estrange. A history of surnames of the British isles; a concise account of their origin, evolution, etymology, and legal status. . . . Lond., K. Paul, 1931. 508p.   **T70**

"A short bibliography": p.429-36.

Fransson, Gustav. Middle English surnames of occupation, 1100–1350, with an excursus on toponymical surnames. Lund, Gleerup; Lond., Williams & Norgate, 1935. 217p. (Lund studies in English. no.3)   **T71**

Harrison, Henry. Surnames of the United Kingdom, a concise etymological dictionary. Lond., Morland Pr., 1912–18. 2v.   **T72**

Phillimore, William Phillimore Watts and **Fry, Edward A.** Index to changes of name under authority of act of Parliament or royal licence and including irregular changes from 1 George III to 64 Victoria, 1760 to 1901, with an introduction on the law of change of name. Lond., Phillimore, 1905. 357p.   **T73**

Canadian

Dionne, Narcisse Eutrope. Les Canadiens-Français. Origine des familles émigrées de France, d'Espagne, de Suisse, etc., pour venir se fixer au Canada, depuis la fondation de Québec jusqu'à ces derniers temps et signification de leurs noms. Québec, Garneau; Montréal, Granger, 1914. 611p.   **T74**

French

Chapuy, Paul. Origine des noms patronymiques français (donnant l'étymologie de 10,000 noms de famille) suivi d'une étude sur les noms de famille basques. Paris, Dorbon-Aîné, 1934. 350p.   **T75**

Larchey, Lorédan. Dictionnaire des noms contenant la recherche étymologique des formes anciennes de 20,200 noms relevés sur les Annuaires de Paris. Paris, l'Auteur, 1880. 511p. **T76**

German

Bach, Adolf. Deutsche Namenkunde. Berlin, de Gruyter, 1943- . v.1- . il. (Grundriss der germanischen Philologie, von Hermann Paul. 18)   **T77**

Contents: Bd.1, Die deutschen Personnennamen.

Gottschald, Max. Deutsche Namenkunde; unsere Familiennamen nach ihrer Entstehung und Bedeutung. München, J. F. Lehmann, 1932. 423p.   **T78**

Heintze, Albert. Heintze-Cascorbi. Die deutschen Familiennamen geschichtlich, geographisch, sprachlich. 7. sehr verb. u. verm. Aufl., hrsg. von Paul Cascorbi. Halle, Berlin, Buchh. d. Waisenhauses, 1933. 536p.   **T79**

Irish

Kelly, Patrick. Irish family names with origins, meanings, clans, arms, crests and mottoes; collected from the living Gaelic and from authoritative books, manuscripts and public documents and ed. with introd., notes and Gaelic script. 1st ed. Chic., O'Conner and Kelly, 1939. 136p. il.   **T80**

Matheson, *Sir* **Robert Edwin.** Special report on surnames in Ireland, with notes as to numerical strength, derivation, ethnology, and distribution; based on information extracted from the indexes of the General Register Office. Dublin, pr. for H. M. Stat. Off. by A. Thom & Co., 1909. 78p. incl. tables.   **T81**

Originally issued in 1894 as an appendix to the 29th *Annual report* of the Registrar-General for Ireland.
"Addendum. List of names of Irish septs as given in the *Book of arms,* comp. by Sir James Terry": p.76-78.

Woulfe, Patrick. Sloinnte gaedheal is gall; Irish names and surnames, collected and edited with explanatory and historical notes. Dublin, Gill, 1923. 696p.   **T82**

Italian

Bongioanni, Angelo. Nomi e cognomi; saggio di ricerche etimologiche e storiche. Torino, Bocca, 1928. 268p. (Piccola biblioteca di scienza moderne, no.367)   **T83**

Fumagalli, Giuseppe. Piccolo dizionario dei nomi propri italiani di persone, con le origini e i significati più probabili, le indicazioni degli onomastici, e accorciature più comuni nei classici e nell'uso volgare, con riscontri storici e letterari e altre notizie. Genova, A. Donath, 1901. 277p.   **T84**

Spanish

Gosnell, Charles Francis. Spanish personal names; principles governing their formation and use which may be presented as a help for catalogers and bibliographers. N.Y., Wilson, 1938. 112p.   **T85**

Bibliography: p.89-101.

GEOGRAPHY

❦ For answering questions in geography there are five principal types of reference books which are useful:

1. Bibliographies and indexes to the material published in books, periodicals, and the publications of learned societies
2. Gazetteers, both general and special, which serve to tell where a given place is and furnish descriptive information about it
3. Dictionaries of place names, which indicate the origin and meaning of such names, and the different forms which have been in use at different times
4. Atlases, which supply maps and through their indexes aid in the location of places
5. Guide books, which supply a different kind of descriptive material from that given in the gazetteers, and contain many maps, especially local maps and town plans, not given in the general atlases.

Wright and Platt's *Aids to geographical research* (U1) is a very valuable guide to geographical reference materials and should be consulted for aid in selecting books for the library and for discovering what books to use to answer particular reference questions.

The average library will need a comprehensive gazetteer such as: *Lippincott's new gazetteer* (U13) (now being revised by the Columbia University Press) or *Webster's geographical dictionary* (U16) and a general atlas such as: Rand, McNally's *Cosmopolitan world atlas* (U175), Hammond's *New world atlas* (U172) or the *Encyclopaedia Britannica world atlas* (U171). It should also be remembered that most of the general encyclopedias include maps, either gathered together in an atlas volume or scattered through the volumes with the articles on the regions covered.

Automobile road maps, furnished by gasoline dealers, are useful for certain types of questions.

GENERAL WORKS

Guides

Wright, John Kirtland and **Platt, Elizabeth T.** Aids to geographical research; bibliographies, periodicals, atlases, gazetteers, and other reference books. 2d ed. compl. rev. N.Y., pub. for the Amer. Geog. Soc. by the Columbia Univ. Pr., 1947. 331p. (Amer. Geog. Soc. Research ser. no.22) $4.50.   **U1**

1st ed. 1923.

A completely revised and rearranged edition of this invaluable manual. In three main sections; (1) General aids; (2) Topical aids; (3) Regional aids and general geographical periodicals. The coverage is comprehensive and includes materials in many languages. Author, subject and title index.

Includes as an appendix a "Classified index of American professional geographers, libraries of geographical utility, and institutions engaged in geographical research."

Bibliography

Cox, Edward Godfrey. A reference guide to the literature of travel, including voyages, geographical descriptions, adventures, shipwrecks and expeditions. Seattle, Univ. of Washington, 1935–49. v.1-3. (Univ. of Washington. Pub. in language and literature, v.9-10, 12) v.1, $3.50; v.2, $4.25; v.3, $10.   **U2**

v.1, The Old world, 401p.; v.2, The New world, 591p.; v.3, England, 732p.

Classified with author index.

Lists "in chronological order, from the earliest date ascertainable down to and including the year 1800, all the books on foreign travels, voyages and descriptions printed in Great Britain, together with translations from foreign tongues and continental renderings of English works. . . ."—*Pref.*

Engelmann, Wilhelm. Bibliotheca geographica. Verzeichnis der seit der Mitte des vorigen Jahrhunderts bis zu Ende des Jahres 1856 in Deutschland erschienenen Werke über Geographie und Reisen, mit Einschluss der Landkarten, Pläne und Ansichten. Leipzig, Engelmann, 1858. 1225p. **U3**

A comprehensive list arranged for the most part by geographical location. Subject index.

International catalogue of scientific literature: J, Geography, mathematical and physical, 1st-14th annual issues, 1901–14. Lond., 1902–19. v.1-14. **U4**

For description of full set *see* N6.

Istituto Nazionale per le Relazioni Culturali con l'Estero. Geografia e viaggi. Roma, 1941. 194p. (Bibliografie del Ventennio) **U5**

A record of the works published in Italy in the period between the two world wars.

Current surveys

American Geographical Society of New York. Current geographical publications; additions to the Research catalogue of the American Geographical Society. v.1, 1938- . N.Y., Amer. Geog. Soc., 1938- . v.1- . Monthly, except July and August. $3.75 per yr. **U6**

A classified index to current books, pamphlets, government publications and periodical articles in the field of geography. Volume 1 has no index; volumes 2 on have indexes by subject, author and regions.

Beginning with Oct. 1940, each issue contains a supplement listing photographs contained in publications received in the library of the American Geographical Society and indexed in its photograph catalog. (Supplement sold separately at $1 per yr.)

Bibliographie géographique internationale, 1891- . Paris, Colin, 1894- . v.1- . Annual. (v.57, 1947. pub. 1949) **U7**

Title varies slightly; v.1-24 issued with *Annales de geographie*.

A useful classified bibliography with alphabetical author index. Very full annotations, each signed.

The most important of the annual bibliographies.

Bibliotheca geographica; hrgs. von der Gesellschaft für Erdkunde zu Berlin, 1891/1892–1911/12. Berlin, Kuhl, 1895–1917. v.1-19. **U8**

Important annual bibliography of books and periodical articles, listing more titles than the French list noted above, but without annotations. Classified, with author index. No more published.

Geographisches Jahrbuch, 1866- . Gotha, Perthes, 1866- . v.1- . Annual (irregular). **U9**

—— Index, 1866–1925, in v.40, p.ix-xix.

A comprehensive and extensive series usually published annually, though sometimes there have been two volumes per year. Each volume includes surveys of the published

work in special geographical fields, the fields varying from year to year. For a convenient key to the reports in this series, *see* Wright and Platt, *Aids to geographical research*, p.52-57(U1).

GAZETTEERS

The gazetteer, or dictionary of places, is an interesting type of reference book in which the most recently revised work and the old work are of almost equal value, although for different questions. If the question calls for current information about a place —its present population, importance, industries, its political affiliations, i.e., the county, state, province, nation, within which it is located—only the most recent works in the field will serve, and the older works may be almost worthless or even misleading.

On the other hand, the old gazetteer is often very useful for historical information, for place names that have since changed, or for bits of local history that is difficult to find elsewhere. An old gazetteer which indicates the industries that flourished in a town a century ago may be a source for the economic or social history of the place, and, if the relative importance of the place has declined, may treat it at greater length than the more modern work can afford to do. For countries for which no good older gazetteer is available an old encyclopedia will sometimes serve this same purpose. The eighteenth century German encyclopedia by Zedler (D39) is often useful for place names not included in modern reference books.

General

Bertacchi, Cosimo. Nuovo dizionario geografico universale. Torino, Unione Tip. ed., 1904–12. 2v. **U10**

Chambers's Concise gazetteer of the world; pronouncing, topographical, statistical, historical, ed. by David Patrick assisted by William Geddie. New ed., rev. Lond., Chambers, 1914. 768p. **U11**

1st ed., 1895; rev. ed., 1906.

Chisholm, George Goudie. Longmans' Gazetteer of the world. New impression (1899). Lond., Longmans, 1902. 1788p. **U12**

First published 1895; re-issued by "The Times," 1899; re-issued by Longmans, July 1902.

Lippincott's New gazetteer; a complete pronouncing gazetteer or geographical dictionary of the world . . . ed. by Angelo Heilprin and Louis Heilprin. Phila. and Lond., Lippincott, 1906. 2053p. **U13**

1st ed. 1855. Latest revision is 1906 edition, reprinted after each decennial census of the United States with a conspectus covering that census. Latest is 1931 issue, with conspectus of the fifteenth census. New edition in preparation by the Columbia University Press.

Includes in one alphabet names of cities, towns, rivers, mountains, lakes and other geographical features, and gives for each the pronunciation of its name, information about other names by which the place was known, location, altitude, etc., and, in the case of towns, population figures, and brief information about local industries, finances, history, educational and other institutions, etc. Entry is under the modern form of the place name (in English), with cross references from ancient, medieval or other early and foreign forms.

This work is usually sufficient for ordinary gazetteer questions for which up-to-date information is not required. For out-of-the-way places omitted here, or for fuller information, the large foreign works or the special local gazetteers must often be consulted.

Ritters geographisch-statistisches Lexikon. 9. umbearb. Aufl. Leipzig, Wigand, 1905–06. 2v. **U14**

Vivien de Saint Martin, Louis and **Rousselet, Louis.** Nouveau dictionnaire de géographie universelle. Paris, Hachette, 1879–95. 7v. **U15**

—————— Supplément. Paris, Hachette, 1895–1900. 2v.

The most complete and important of the general gazetteers. The longer articles are by specialists and are of a high grade, information is much fuller than that given in either Lippincott (U13) or Chisholm (U12) and many names are included, especially minor European or Asiatic names, which are not given in the American and English works. Not now up to date, less useful for ordinary questions than Lippincott, but more useful than that work when very detailed or out-of-the-way information is needed. Includes names of tribes and races, as well as place names.

Webster's Geographical dictionary; a dictionary of names of places with geographical and historical information and pronunciations. Springfield, Mass., Merriam, 1949. 1293p. maps. $8.50. **U16**

A pronouncing dictionary of more than 40,000 geographical names, including not only current but also historical names from Biblical times, ancient Greece and Rome, medieval Europe, and World Wars I and II. Cross references are given for equivalent and alternative spellings of names that have been changed. Gives the usual gazetteer information, e.g., location, area, population, altitudes of mountains, etc., and for the largest cities, important countries, and each of the United States, also gives geographical features, historical monuments, and a concise history. Includes full-page and smaller, inset maps and an appendix of historical maps in color.

Ancient and medieval

Besnier, Maurice. Lexique de géographie ancienne. Paris, Klincksieck, 1914. 893p. **U17**

A compact handbook; gives only brief information about each place, but is full in its references to ancient writers in whose works the place is mentioned. Useful on account of these many references.

Deschamps, Pierre Charles Ernest. Dictionnaire de géographie ancienne et moderne. Paris, Firmin-Didot, 1870. 1592 col. **U18**

Also issued as volume 9 of Brunet's *Manuel du libraire* (A22).

Arranged alphabetically by the medieval name (Latin or Greek); gives, under each, an indication of the modern name and brief information about the place with special emphasis upon the history of printing in that place, establishment of presses, etc. Index of modern names.

Grässe, Johann Georg Theodor. Orbis latinus; oder, Verzeichnis der wichtigsten lateinischen Orts- und Ländernamen. Ein Supplement zu jedem lateinischen und geographischen Wörterbuch. 2. Aufl., mit besonderer Berücksichtigung der mittelalterlichen und neueren Latinität, neu bearb. von Friedrich Benedict. Berlin, Schmidt; N.Y., Steiger, 1909. 348p. (1922 repr.) **U19**

The first edition, 1866, was in two parts: (1) Latin names; (2) Modern names. The second edition includes only part 1; where part 2 is needed the first edition must still be used.

Smith, *Sir* **William.** Dictionary of Greek and Roman geography. Lond., Murray; Bost., Little, 1873–78. 2v. il. maps. **U20**

United States

❧ There is no geographical dictionary of the whole United States. Perhaps the most useful available substitute for such a work is Ayer's *Directory of newspapers* (E11) which gives brief up-to-date gazetteer information about each city or town for which a newspaper is listed. The *Postal guide* (L387) can be used to locate any town or village large enough to have a post office.

The following, though not formal gazetteers, are useful:

Douglas, Edward Morehouse. Boundaries, areas, geographic centers and altitudes of the United States and the several states, with a brief record of important changes in their territory and government. 2d ed. Wash., Govt. Prt. Off., 1930. 265p. il. maps. (U.S. Geological Survey. Bull. 817) 50c. **U21**

Gannett, Henry. Dictionary of altitudes in the United States. 4th ed. Wash., Govt. Prt. Off., 1906. 1072p. (U.S. Geological Survey. Bull. 274) **U22**

Arranged alphabetically by states and under states by cities; gives altitude and refers to authority.

Argentina

Latzina, Francisco. Diccionario geográfico argentino, con ampliaciones enciclopédicas rioplatenses. 3. ed. Buenos Aires, Peuser, 1899. 814p. **U23**

Belgium

Jourdain, Alfred and **Stalle, L. C. F. van.** Dictionnaire encyclopédique de géographie historique du royaume de Belgique. . . . Bruxelles, Bruylant-Christophe [pref. 1896]. 2v. il. **U24**

Subtitle: Description de ses neuf provinces et de ses 2,607 communes sous le rapport topographique, statistique, administratif, judiciaire, industriel, commercial, militaire, religieux, historique, littéraire, biographique et monumental, précédée d'un exposé historique et suivie d'une étude sur l'état indépendant du Congo.

Nouveau dictionnaire des communes, hameaux, charbonnages, carrières, mines, chateaux, fermes, etc., du Royaume de Belgique, rédigé sur les documents officiels. Bruxelles, Guyot [1913?]. 538p., and Addenda [1922], 12p. **U25**

Seyn, Eugène de. Dictionnaire historique et géographique des communes belges; histoire, géographie, archéologie, topographie, hypsométrie, administration, industrie, commerce. Bruxelles, Bieleveld, 1924–26. 2v. il. **U26**

Bolivia

Diccionario geográfico de la República de Bolivia. La Paz, Impr. "El Nacional" de I. V. Vila, 1890–1904. 4v. il. **U27**

v.2, 4, pub. by the Oficina Nacional de Immigración, Estadística y Propaganda Geográfica.

v.1, Ballivián, M. V. y Idiaquez, E. Departamento de La Paz. 1890; v.2, Blanco, F. Departamento de Cochabamba, 1901; v.3, Sociedad Geográfica Sucre. Departamento de Chuquisaca, 1903; v.4, Blanco, P. A. Departamento de Oruro, 1904.

No more published.

Brazil

Moreira Pinto, Alfredo. Apontamentos paro o Diccionario geographico do Brazil. Rio de Janeiro, Imp. Nacional, 1894–99. 3v. **U28**

Canada

Magnan, Hormisdas. Dictionnaire historique et géographique des paroisses, missions et municipalités de la Province de Québec. Arthabaska, Imp. d'Arthabaska, 1925. 738p. **U29**

White, James. Dictionary of altitudes in the Dominion of Canada. (2d ed.) Ottawa, Mortimer, 1916. 251p. **U30**

Published by the Conservation Commission.

Arranged by provinces, then alphabetically by place names. Supplementary to *Altitudes in Canada* (2d ed.

1915), by the same author, which gives altitudes arranged by railroad routes.

❦ There is no complete geographical dictionary of Canada. For complete gazetteer information several works need to be used. The *Dictionary of altitudes* locates many places (rivers, towns, mountains) with brief information about each. The reports of the Geographic Board (U82) supply additional information, and the *Postal guide* (L385) locates all places having post offices. Ayer's *Directory of newspapers* (E11) gives gazetteer information about all towns for which newspapers are listed.

Chile

Risopatrón Sanchez, Luis. Diccionario jeográfico de Chile. Santiago, Impr. Univ., 1924. 958p. **U31**

China

Playfair, George M. H. The cities and towns of China; a geographical dictionary. 2d ed. Shanghai, Kelly and Walsh, 1910. 582p., lxxvip. **U32**

Czechoslovakia

Czechoslovak Republic. Ministerstvo post a telegrafů. Dopravni místopisný lexikon Československé republiky. Praze, Tiskem České grafické, 1928. 873p. **U33**

France

Joanne, Paul Bénigne. Dictionnaire géographique et administratif de la France. Paris, Hachette, 1890–1905. 7v. il. **U34**

1st and 2d eds., 1865, 1869, included Alsace Lorraine.

The standard geographical dictionary of France, with long articles, many illustrations, but no bibliographies. Adequate for most questions, but for special work needs to be supplemented by the many regional dictionaries, i.e., dictionaries of the provinces, *départements,* etc.

Germany

Meyers Orts-und Verkehrs-Lexikon des Deutschen Reichs. 5. vollständig neubearb. und verm. Aufl. Auf grund amtlicher Unterlagen von Reichs-, Landes- und Gemeindebehörden hrsg. von E. Uetrecht. Mit 51 Stadtplänen, 19 Umgebungs- und Übersichtskarten, einer Verkehrs-Karte und vielen statistischen Beilagen. Leipzig, Bibliog. Inst., 1912–13. 2v. maps, plans. folded map in pocket. **U35**

The fifth edition is a gazetteer of prewar Germany. The sixth edition (Leipzig, 1935, 867p.) was also issued, much reduced in size, as Ergänz. Bd.1 of *Meyers Lexikon,* 7. Aufl. (D36).

Oesterley, Hermann. Historisch-geographisches Wörterbuch des deutschen Mittelalters. Gotha, Perthes, 1883. 806p. **U36**

Great Britain

Bartholomew, John George. Survey gazetteer of the British Isles, including summary of 1931 census and reference atlas. 8th ed. Edinburgh, Bartholomew, 1932. xxxiip., 47p., 748p. maps. **U37**

Gives in one alphabetical list brief accounts not only of all towns, villages and hamlets, but also of seats, shooting lodges, deer forests, fishing lochs, streams, grouse moors, etc., which have special names, but which would not be included in ordinary general gazetteers.

Groome, Francis Hindes. Ordnance gazetteer of Scotland; a graphic and accurate description of every place in Scotland. New ed., with census appendix 1901. Edinburgh, Jack, 1901. 1762p. il. map. **U38**

This edition contains all the printed matter of the large six volume edition, the revisions made in 1895 and subsequent partial revisions. –Cf. *Publishers' note.*

Johnston, W. and **Johnston, A. K.** Gazetteer of Scotland, including a glossary of the most common Gaelic and Norse names. Edinburgh and Lond., Johnston, 1937. 330p., 24p. maps. **U39**

Lewis, Samuel. Topographical dictionary of England. 5th ed. Lond., Lewis, 1845. 4v. il. and atlas, 55 maps. **U40**

Subtitle: Comprising the several counties, cities, boroughs, corporate and market towns, parishes, and townships, and the islands of Guernsey, Jersey, and Man, with historical and statistical descriptions: And embellished with engravings of the arms of the cities, bishoprics, universities, colleges, corporate towns, and boroughs; and of the seals of the various municipal corporations.

—— Topographical dictionary of Ireland . . . 2d ed. Lond., Lewis, 1846. 2v. il. and atlas, 32 maps. **U41**

—— Topographical dictionary of Scotland . . . Lond., Lewis, 1846. 2v. il. and atlas. **U42**

—— Topographical dictionary of Wales . . . 3d ed. Lond., Lewis, 1844. 2v. il. and atlas. **U43**

The Lewis gazetteers contain much fuller accounts than the smaller modern works and are still useful for historical information though out of date on other points.

Parliamentary gazetteer of England and Wales. . . . Lond., Fullarton, 1844. 3v. maps. **U44**

Subtitle: Adapted to the new poor-law, franchise, municipal and ecclesiastical arrangements, and comp. with a special reference to the lines of railroad and canal communication, as existing in 1840–44. Illustrated by a series of maps forming a complete county-atlas of Eng-

land, and by four large maps of Wales. With an appendix containing the results, in detail, of the census of 1841.

Parliamentary gazetteer of Ireland. . . . Dublin, Fullarton, 1846. 3v. il. maps. **U45**

Greece

Permanent Committee on Geographical Names for British Official Use. A gazetteer of Greece. Prepared for the Admiralty and War Office at the house of the Royal Geographical Society. Lond., pr. by W. Clowes, 1942. 161p. incl. maps. 7s. 6d. **U46**

Hawaii

Coulter, John Wesley. Gazetteer of the territory of Hawaii. Honolulu, Univ. of Hawaii, 1935. 241p. (Univ. of Hawaii. Research pub. 11) $2. **U47**

Honduras

Bonilla, Marcelina. Diccionario histórico-geográfico de las poblaciones de Honduras. Tegucigalpa, "Ariston," 1945. 256p. **U48**

India

Imperial gazetteer of India. New ed., pub. under the authority of His Majesty's Secretary of State for India in Council. Ox., Clarendon Pr., 1907–31. 26v. maps. **U49**

1st ed., 9v., 1881, and 2d ed., 14v., 1885–87, ed. by Sir William Wilson Hunter. The present may be considered as a new work, rather than a new edition.–Cf. *General pref.*

Editor for India: 1902–04, William Stevenson Meyer, 1905–09, Richard Burn; editor in England: James Sutherland Cotton.

v.1-4, Indian Empire: v.1, Descriptive; v.2, Historical; v.3, Economic; v.4, Administrative; v.5-24, Gazetteer; v.25, General index; v.26, Atlas. (Atlas, new rev. ed. 1931)

Includes historical, topographical, ethnical, agricultural, industrial, administrative and medical aspects of the various districts of British India.

Italy

Amati, Amato. Dizionario corografico dell'Italia. Opera illustrata da circa 1000 armi comunali colorate e da parecchie centinaia di incisioni intercalate nel testo rappresentanti i principali monumenti d'Italia. Milano, Vallardi [1875?–86?]. 8v. il. (coats of arms) **U50**

Fumagalli, Giuseppe. Lexicon typographicum Italiae. Dictionnaire géographique d'Italie pour

servir à l'histoire de l'imprimerie dans ce pays.
. . . Florence, Olschki, 1905. 587p. il.   **U51**

Subtitle: Contenant 1ᵉ l'indication de toutes les localités d'Italie géographique et politique, où l'imprimerie a été introduite jusqu'à nos jours, avec la synonymie latine, française, etc., et celle des lieux supposés d'impression; 2ᵉ des notices bibliographiques sur les éditions principes de chaque ville, bourg, château, etc., et sur les faits les plus remarquables se rapportant à l'histoire de l'art typographique dans ces localités; 3ᵉ des notices biographiques sur les plus célèbres imprimeurs italiens; 4ᵉ des notices statistiques sur l'état présent de l'imprimerie en Italie; 5ᵉ des renseignements historiques sur les arts auxiliares de l'imprimerie; lithographie, gravure, papeterie, fabrication des encres, des presses, des caractères, etc.

——— ——— Additions et corrections. Florence, Olschki, 1939. 84p.

Istituto Nazionale per le Relazioni Culturali con l'Estero. Geografia e viaggi. Roma, 1941. 194p. (Bibliografie del Ventennio)   **U52**

A record of the works published in Italy in the period between the two world wars.

La Nuova Italia; dizionario amministrativo, statistico, industriale, commerciale dei comuni del regno e dei principali paesi d'Italia oltre confine e colonie. Milano, Vallardi [1908?–10?]. 3v. il. and atlas of 26 col. pl. (coats of arms) **U53**

Valle, Antonio della. Dizionario dei comuni e delle frazioni di Comune del regno; guida completa di tutti gli organi della pubblica amministrazione; aggiornata a tutto agosto 1930. Livorno, Pasquini, 1930–31. 2v.   **U54**

v.1, Dizionario dei comuni; v.2, Dizionario delle frazioni di comune.

Japan

Gerr, Stanley. A gazetteer of Japanese place names in characters and in Rōmaji script giving latitudes and longitudes. Camb., Harvard Univ. Pr., 1942. 269p., 225p. $4.50.   **U55**

Two lists dealing with the same places, one in Rōmaji script (Latin alphabet), the other in Sino-Japanese character.

"Based on the map of the Japanese Empire published in 1937 by the Japanese Kokusai Bunka Shinkōkai (Society for International Cultural Relations). It contains about 4500 place names covering Japan proper, Korea, Formosa, Kwangtung leased territory, Saghalien, and the Japanese mandated islands, but does not include Manchuria or other territory recently occupied by Japan. . . ."—*Pref. note.*

U. S. Hydrographic Office. Gazetteer of the Japanese Empire, containing place names from the Japanese hydrographic charts and sailing directions on issue in 1936. Wash., 1943. 378p. (H.O. Pub. no.880. Repr. Aug. 1944 of H.O. Misc. no.10,947) $1.   **U56**

Latin America

American Geographical Society of New York. Index to map of Hispanic America; 1:1,000,000. Ed.-in-chief: Earl Parker Hanson; ass't ed.: Natalie Raymond. Wash., Govt. Prt. Off., 1945. 923p. il. (maps) (Its Map of Hispanic America, Pub. no.5)   **U57**

Also published in 12 separate volumes, 1943–44. Not for sale. Available to purchasers of the *Map* and to selected libraries.

An index by country of the names appearing on the "Millionth map" of the American Geographical Society. (*Map of Hispanic America* on the scale of 1:1,000,000.) Indexed by approximate latitudes and longitudes so that it can also be used with other maps of these regions on which Greenwich longitudes are shown. Also serves as an index to geographical names. Includes indexes to Mexico, Central America (by country), West Indies (by country), Argentina, Bolivia, Brazil, Chile, Colombia, Ecuador, The Guianas, Paraguay, Peru, Uruguay, Venezuela.

Netherlands

Laan, Kornelis ter. Aardrijkskundig woordenboek van Nederland. Tweede druk. 'sGravenhage, van Goor, 1948. 513p.   **U58**

Includes names of cities, villages, minor places, church groups, and geographical terms. Lists fewer names than the *Lijst der aardrijkskundige namen* (U134), but gives more information about each item and more up-to-date figures.

Oceanica

U. S. Hydrographic Office. Gazetteer . . . no.1–15. Wash., Govt. Prt. Off., 1943–45. no.1–15. maps.   **U59**

Contents: (1) Solomon Islands, Bismarck Archipelago and islands off the southeastern end of New Guinea, 2d ed. 1944; (2) New Guinea and nearby islands, 2d ed. 1944; (3) Lesser Sundas and Moluccas; (4) Hawaiian islands; (5) Celebes, 2d ed. 1944; (6) Caroline, Marianas, Marshall and Gilbert islands, 2d ed. 1944; (7) Islands of the central and south Pacific; (8) Borneo; (9) Java; (10) Sumatra; (11) Malay states; (12) French Indochina and South China sea; (13) Formosa; (14) Japan, including Karafuto, Chishima Retto, Nanpo Shoto and Nansei Shoto; (15) China coast.

Wise, H. and Co., Ltd. Wise's New Zealand index. 9th ed. Dunedin, Wise, 1945. 536p. il.   **U60**

1st ed., 1904?

A gazetteer of place names and geographical locations. Under names of places frequently gives history, legends, origin of name, etc., as well as usual gazetteer information.

Peru

Stiglich, Germán. Diccionario geográfico del Peru. Lima, Torres-Aguirre, 1922–23. 2 pts. in 4v.   **U61**

Philippines

U. S. Bureau of Insular Affairs. Pronouncing gazetteer and geographical dictionary of the Philippine Islands. Wash., Govt. Prt. Off., 1902. 933p. il. maps. **U62**

Poland

Słownik geograficzny królestwa polskiego i innych krajów słowiańskich; wydany pod redakcya Filipa Sulimierskiego, Bronisława Chlebowskiego, Władysława Walewskiego. Warszawa, nakładem Sulimierskiego i Walewskiego, 1880–1902. 15v. in 16. **U63**

v.15 is a supplement in 2v.

Salvador

Salvador. Dirección General de Estadistica. Diccionario geográfico de la república de El Salvador. San Salvador, Imp. Nacional, 1940. 360p. (Publicaciones de Ministerio de Hacienda) **U64**

Switzerland

Knapp, Charles, Borel, Maurice and **Attinger, V.** Dictionnaire géographique de la Suisse; publié sous les auspices de la Société Neuchâteloise de Géographie. . . . Neuchâtel, Attinger, 1902–10. 6v. il. maps. **U65**

One of the finest regional dictionaries, with authoritative articles and excellent illustrations. Articles contain more scientific geographical and geological information than is usual in local gazetteers.
Volume 6 includes Supplement, p.685-1136.

Uruguay

Araújo, Orestes. Diccionario geográfico del Uruguay. 2. ed., completamente reform. y aum. con más de 1,000 voces nuevas. Montevideo, Tipo-litografia Moderna, 1912. 528p. **U66**

GEOGRAPHICAL NAMES AND TERMS

Egli, Johann Jacob. Nomina geographica. Sprach- und Sacherklärung von 42,000 geographischen Namen aller Erdräume. 2. verm und verb. Aufl. Leipzig, Brandstetter, 1893. 1035p. **U67**

Knox, Alexander. Glossary of geographical and topographical terms and of words of frequent occurrence in the composition of such terms and of place-names. Lond., Stanford, 1904. 432p. (Stanford's Compendium of geography and travel, suppl. v.) 15s. **U68**

Kredel, Otto. Deutsch-fremdsprachiges (fremdsprachig-deutsches) Ortsnamen-Verzeichnis. Im Auftrage der Praktischen Abteilung der Deutschen Akademie in München, bearb. von Otto Kredel und Franz Thierfelder. Berlin, Deutsche Verlagsgesellschaft, 1931. 1172p. **U69**

Permanent Committee on Geographical Names for British Official Use. Glossaries, v.1-7. Lond., 1942–45. v.1-7. **U70**

Contents: v.1, Modern Greek. 1942. 2s. 6d.; v.2, Russian. 1942. 2s. 6d.; v.3, Albanian. 1943. 1s. 6d.; v.4, Serbo-Croat and Slovene. 1943. 2s. 6d.; v.5, Roumanian. 1944. 1s. 6d.; v.6, Thai (Siamese). 1944. 2s. 6d.; v.7, Turkish. 1945. 2s. 6d.

Not place names but glossaries of words, abbreviations and contractions found on official maps, charts and geographical texts of the country treated, with transliteration (if from a non-Roman alphabet), meaning and application.
More countries were covered but much more briefly in a series of *Short glossaries* published by the General Staff (Geographical Section, War Office, 1943–45. 23 nos.).

—— [Lists of names] Lond., Royal Geog. Soc., 1921–38. **U71**

An unnumbered series of pamphlets, in two main groups: (1) General lists (by continents); (2) National or regional lists, each giving the names of a country, dominion, protectorate, etc. A special pamphlet issued 1932 is: Rules for the spelling of geographical names.
Contents: (1) General lists: African names, 1st list, 1921; Asiatic names, 1st-2d lists, 1921–25, rev. 1930; European names, 1st-2d lists, [1921]–23, cor. and rev. 1929; Oceanic names, 1st-4th lists, 1922–35; (2) National lists: Abyssinia, 1st list, 1925; Albania, 1st list, 1938; Anglo-Egyptian Sudan, 1st list, 1927; Arabia, 1st list, 1931, 2d list, 1937; Belgium and Luxemburg, 1st list, 1938; Czechoslovakia, 1st-3d lists, 1924–30; Egypt (Upper), 1st list, 1929; Fiji, 1st list, 1925; Gold Coast and British Togo, 1st list, 1923; India, 1st list, 1924; Iraq (Mesopotamia), 1st list, 1922, rev. 1932; Nigeria and British Cameroons, 1st list, 1928; Palestine, 1st list, 1925, rev. 1937; Persia (South), 1st list, 1928; Persia (North), 2d list, 1929; Poland (West) and Danzig, 1st list, 1928; Poland (East), 2d list, 1930; Romania, 1st-2d lists, 1926–28; Somaliland Protectorate, 1st list, 1928; Syria, 1st list, 1927; Tanganyika territory, 1st list, 1926; Tonga, 1st list, 1927; Trans-Jordan, 1st list, 1927; Turkey (West), 1st list, 1935; Yugoslavia, 1st and 2d lists, 1928–31.
Gives brief information, including correct spelling and pronunciation of name, rejected forms of name, and location of place.

U. S. Board on Geographical Names. Sixth report, 1890–1932. Wash., Govt. Prt. Off., 1933. 834p. **U72**

(1) Geographic names, discussion of characteristics, problems, etc.; (2) The U.S. Geographic Board, its

method of work, history, etc.; (3) Decisions, arranged alphabetically by approved form of name, with cross references from other forms, p.76-834.

The Decisions form a dictionary of many thousand place names throughout the world, incorporating in one alphabetical list the material of the *Fifth report* (1921), subsequent decisions, the 2500 foreign place names included in the *First report on foreign geographic names* (1932) and the Philippine and Hawaiian names that were given in separate lists in the *Fifth report*. For each name gives approved form, locates the place, indicates rejected forms and, in some cases, marks pronunciation.

"This report contains, with the exception of a comparatively small number, all the decisions rendered by the Board from its organization in 1890 through June, 1932, and supersedes all previous reports. Not included . . . are such decisions as have either been vacated, or being revised, have been replaced by new decisions listed under the revised name or spelling."—*Foreword.*

Kept up to date by the following:

—— Decisions, nos. 20, Oct. 5, 1932- . Wash., 1932- . **U73**

Issued at frequent intervals in leaflets varying in size and form. Some of the leaflets contain general lists of decisions usually in annual cumulations; some are on special locations, e.g., National parks, or on specific foreign countries, e.g., Tibet, Mongolia, Italy, etc.

United States

❧ Because of the very full *Bibliography of place name literature* by Sealock and Seely listed below, works on place names of the United States, its individual states, Canada, Alaska and Newfoundland are not listed here.

Sealock, Richard Burl and **Seely, Pauline Augusta.** Bibliography of place name literature, United States, Canada, Alaska and Newfoundland. Chic., Amer. Lib. Assoc. [1948]. 331p. $4.50. **U74**

A comprehensive bibliography of books and articles dealing with particular types of names or the names of particular regions. Arranged by state under the United States and by province under Canada followed by a name and subject index.

U. S. Post-Office Dept. Street directory of the principal cities of the United States, embracing letter-carrier offices established to April 30, 1908. Rev. in the Division of Dead Letters. Wash. [Govt. Prt. Off.] 1908. 904p. **U75**

Indicates in what city or cities a street of any given name is to be found. Most frequently useful for questions about incomplete or illegible addresses.

Now much out of date.

Australia

Martin, A. E. One thousand and more place names in New South Wales. Sydney, Australia, N.S.W. Bookstall Co., 1943. 108p. (The romance of nomenclature) **U76**

—— Place names in Victoria and Tasmania. Sydney, Australia, N.S.W. Bookstall Co., 1944. 107p. il. (The romance of nomenclature) **U77**

—— Twelve hundred and more place names in South Australia, Western Australia and the Northern territory. Sydney, Australia, N.S.W. Bookstall Co., 1943. 109p. (The romance of nomenclature) **U78**

Austria

Schiffmann, Konrad. Historisches Ortsnamen-Lexikon des Landes Oberösterreich. München, Oldenbourg, 1935. 2v. **U79**

—— —— Ergänzungsbd.; Nachträge, Erklärung der Namen und Verweisungen. München, Oldenbourg, 1940. 556p.

Belgium

Carnoy, Albert Joseph. Dictionnaire étymologique du nom des communes de Belgique, y compris l'étymologie des principaux noms de hameaux et de rivières. Louvain, Editions Universitas, 1939–40. 2v. **U80**

Canada

See Sealock and Seely, *Bibliography of place name literature* (U74) for books of place names for particular provinces.

Armstrong, George Henry. Origin and meaning of place names in Canada. Toronto, Macmillan, 1930. 312p. $3. **U81**

Canada. Geographic Board. 18th-19th reports containing all decisions to July 31, 1927. Ottawa, 1924–27. 2v. **U82**

18th report, Decisions to March 1924; 19th report, Decisions, April 1924—July 1927.

Alphabetical lists of place names, with index by provinces, counties, etc. The main alphabet in each report gives form of name decided on, location of place, and origin of name when known, with cross references from superseded names. Supersedes the earlier reports of the Board except for certain appendixes which are still useful for fuller or special information which they contain. These appendixes (also issued as separates) are:

9th report, 1910: pt.2, Place-names in Quebec, by James White, p.153-219; pt.3, Place-names, Thousand Islands, St. Lawrence River, by James White, p.221-29; pt.4, Place-names in Northern Canada, by James White, p.229-455. o.p.

17th report, 1922: Meaning of Canadian city names, by R. Douglas, p.34-52; Place-names on Anticosti Island, by W. P. Anderson, p.53-65; Place-names on Magdalen islands, by R. Douglas, p.66-74.

Egypt

Gauthier, Henri. Dictionnaire des noms géographiques contenus dans les textes hiéroglyphiques. Caire, L'Impr. de l'Institut Français d'Archéologie Orientale pour la Société Royale de Géographie d'Égypte, 1925–31. 7v. **U83**

v.7 includes indexes and maps.

England and Wales

Charles, Bertie George. Non-Celtic place names in Wales. Lond., Univ. College, 1938. 326p. (London mediaeval studies: Monograph no.1) **U84**

Ekwall, Eilert. Concise Oxford dictionary of English place-names. 2d ed. Ox., Clarendon Pr., 1940. 524p. 17s. 6d.; $5.75. **U85**

Lists about 15,000 names, including many more than Johnston (U87) but giving briefer information and omitting some names given by Johnston.

"Embraces names of the country, of the counties, and other important divisions, towns (except those of late origin), parishes, villages, some names of estates and hamlets, or even farms whose names are old and etymologically interesting, rivers, lakes—also names of capes, hills, bays for which early material is available. Names of hundreds, as being no longer in use, have been omitted."

While the concise information given is considerably less full than that in the various volumes of the English Place-name Society it includes in general: modern form, location (in county), derivation or meaning, older forms with dates, and some references to sources. Pronunciation is given in some cases. 1st ed., 1936. 2d ed. includes some corrections in the text and a 4-page Addenda.

—— English river names. Ox., Clarendon Pr., 1928. 488p. **U86**

Gives detailed etymology for river names with references to sources.

Johnston, James B. Place-names of England and Wales. Lond., Murray, 1915. 532p. 18s. **U87**

The first comprehensive dictionary of English place names, including some 5000 names with explanation of their derivation and references to sources. Contains much useful information not accessible in any other one book, but is not always accurate in its etymologies, especially for Welsh names. For comment on this point *see* review by Henry Bradley in *English historical review* 30:558-61, July 1915.

English Place-name Society. Survey of English place-names. Camb., Univ. Pr., 1924- . v.1- . maps. 18s.–23s. 6d. ea. **U88**

v.1, pt.1, Introduction to the Survey of English place-names, by A. Mawer and F. M. Stenton. 1924. 201p.; t.2, Chief elements used in English place-names, by Allen Mawer. 1924. 67p.; v.2, Place-names of **Bucking-**

hamshire, by A. Mawer and F. M. Stenton. 1925. 274p.; v.3, Place-names of **Bedfordshire** and **Huntingdonshire,** by A. Mawer and F. M. Stenton. 1926. 316p.; v.4, Place-names of **Worcestershire,** by A. Mawer and F. M. Stenton. 1927. 420p.; v.5, Place-names of the **North Riding of Yorkshire,** by A. H. Smith. 1928. 352p.; v.6-7, Place-names of **Sussex,** by A. Mawer and F. M. Stenton. 1929–30. 2v.; v.8-9, Place-names of **Devon,** by J. E. B. Gover, A. Mawer and F. M. Stenton. 1931–32. 2v. and case of maps; v.10, Place-names of **Northamptonshire,** by J. E. B. Gover, A. Mawer and F. M. Stenton. 1933. 311p.; v.11, Place-names of **Surrey,** by J. E. B. Gover, A. Mawer and F. M. Stenton. 1934. 445p.; v.12, Place-names of **Essex,** by P. H. Reaney, 1935. 698p.; v.13, Place-names of **Warwickshire,** by J. E. B. Gover, A. Mawer, and F. M. Stenton. 1936. 409p.; v.14, Place-names of **East Riding of Yorkshire** and York, by A. H. Smith. 1937. 351p.; v.15, Place-names of **Hertfordshire,** by J. E. B. Gover, A. Mawer and F. M. Stenton. 1938. 342p.; v.16, Place-names of **Wiltshire,** by J. E. B. Gover, A. Mawer, and F. M. Stenton. 1939. 547p.; v.17, Place-names of **Nottinghamshire,** by J. E. B. Gover, A. Mawer and F. M. Stenton. 1933. 348p.; v.18, Place-names of **Middlesex,** apart from the city of London, by J. E. B. Gover, A. Mawer and F. M. Stenton. 1942. 235p.; v.19, Place-names of **Cambridgeshire** and the **Isle of Ely,** by P. H. Reaney. 1943. 396p.

❧ While largely superseded by the publications of the English Place-name Society the following regional lists are also occasionally still useful:

Skeat, W. W. Place-names of **Bedfordshire.** Camb., Antiquarian Soc., 1906. 74p. (Its *Pub.* no.42) **U89**; **Skeat,** W. W. Place-names of **Berkshire.** Ox., Clarendon Pr., 1911. 118p. **U90**; **Skeat,** W. W. Place-names of **Cambridgeshire.** 2d ed. Camb., Antiquarian Soc., 1911. 82p. **U91**; **Dexter,** T. F. G. **Cornish** names, an attempt to explain over 1600 Cornish names. Lond., Longmans, 1926. 89p. **U92**; **Sedgefield,** W. J. Place-names of **Cumberland** and Westmorland. Manchester, Univ. Pr., 1915. 208p. **U93**; **Walker,** B. Place-names of **Derbyshire.** Derbyshire, Arch. Soc., 1915. 310p. **U94**; **Blomé,** Bertil. Place-names of North **Devonshire.** Uppsala, Appelberg, 1929. 189p. **U95**; **Fägersten,** A. Place-names of **Dorset.** Uppsala, Appelberg, 1933. 334p. **U96**; **Jackson,** C. E. Place-names of **Durham.** Lond., Allen and Unwin, 1916. 114p. **U97**; (*See also* under Northumberland below); **Baddeley,** W. St. C. Place-names of **Gloucestershire.** Gloucester, Bellows, 1913. 185p. **U98**; **Bannister,** A. T. Place-names of **Herefordshire.** [Camb.] Author, 1916. 231p. **U99**; **Skeat,** W. W. Place-names of **Hertfordshire.** 1904. 109p. **U100**; **Horsley,** J. W. Place-names in **Kent.** Maidstone, "South Eastern Gazette" Newspaper Co., 1921. 84p. **U101**; **Wallenberg,** J. K. Place-names of **Kent.** Uppsala, Appelberg, 1934. 626p. **U102**; **Ekwall,** Eilert. Place-names of **Lancashire.** Manchester, Chetham Soc., 1922. 280p. (Chetham Society. Remains, historical and literary, connected with the Palatine counties of Lancaster and Chester, n.s. v.81) **U103**; SEPHTON, J. Handbook of **Lancashire** place-names. Liverpool, Young, 1913. 256p. **U104**; WYLD, H. C. and HIRST, T. O. Place-names of **Lancashire.** Lond., Constable, 1911. 400p. **U105**; EMINSON, T. B. F. Place and river names of the West Riding of Lindsey, **Lincolnshire.** Lincoln, Ruddock, 1934. 288p. **U106**; HARRISON, HENRY. Place-names of the **Liverpool** district. Lond., Stock, 1898. 104p. **U107**; KNEEN, J. J. Place-names of the Isle of **Man.** Douglas, Manx Soc., 1925–29. 2v. (645p.) **U108**; MOORE, A. W. **Manx** names. 2d ed., rev. Lond., Stock, 1903. 261p. **U109**; GOVER, J. E. B. Place-names of **Middlesex** (including those parts of the county of London formerly contained within the boundaries of the old county). Lond., Longmans, 1922. 114p. **U110**; MUNFORD, G. An attempt to ascertain the true derivation of the names of towns and villages and of rivers, and other great natural features . . . of **Norfolk.** Lond., Simpkin, 1870. 239p. **U111**; MAWER, A. Place-names of **Northumberland** and Durham. Camb., Univ. Pr., 1920. 270p. **U112**; MUTSCHMANN, H. Place-names of **Nottingham-shire.** Camb., Univ. Pr., 1913. 179p. **U113**; ALEXANDER, H. Place-names of **Oxfordshire.** Ox., Clarendon Pr., 1912. 251p. **U114**; BOWCOCK, E. W., **Shropshire** place-names. Shrewsbury, Wilding, 1923. 271p. **U115**; HILL, J. S. The place-names of **Somerset.** Bristol, St. Stephen's Pr., 1914. 373p. **U116**; DUIGNAN, W. H. Notes on **Staffordshire** place-names. Lond., Frowde, 1902. 178p. **U117**; SKEAT, W. W. Place-names of **Suffolk.** Camb., Antiquarian Soc., 1913. 132p. **U118**; HOPWOOD, DAVID. Place-names of the County of **Surrey,** including London in Surrey. Capetown, 1926. 101p. (Annals of the University of Stellenbosch, v.4, sect.B, no.2, Oct. 1926) **U119**; ROBERTS, R. G. Place-names of **Sussex.** Camb., Univ. Pr., 1914. 210p. **U120**; EMBLETON, D. A catalogue of place-names in **Teesdale.** [Lond., Williams and Norgate, 1887] 223p. **U121**; CHARLES, B. G. Non-Celtic place-names in **Wales.** Lond., Univ. College, 1938. 326p. **U122**; MORGAN, T. Place-names of **Wales.** 2d rev. ed. Newport, Mon., Southall, 1912. 262p. **U123**; DUIGNAN, W. H. **Warwickshire** place-names. Lond., Frowde, 1912. 130p. **U124**; **Westmorland,** *see* Cumberland above; EKBLOM, E. L. Place-names of **Wiltshire,** their origin and history. Uppsala, Appelberg, 1917. 187p. **U125**; DUIGNAN, W. H. **Worcestershire** place-names. Lond., Frowde, 1905. 185p. **U126**; GOODALL, A. Place-names of south-west **Yorkshire.** rev. ed. Camb., Univ. Pr., 1914. 313p. **U127**; MOORMAN,

F. W. Place-names of the West Riding of **York**shire. Leeds, Thoresby Soc., 1910. 218p. (Its Pub. v.18) **U128.**

France

Dictionnaire topographique de la France comprenant les noms de lieu anciens et modernes, publié par ordre du Ministère de l'Instruction Publique et sous la direction du Comité des Travaux Historiques et Scientifiques. Paris, Impr. Nat., 1861–1941. v.1-30.   **U129**

In process of publication, one volume for each *département*. A monumental work, the most complete study yet made of the place names of any country. Each volume lists all place names of its *département*, even names of farms, giving for each its location, derivation, variations in form from the earliest period to the present with date when each form was used and exact references to manuscripts or printed authorities, and, in the case of important names, a brief history and description of the place. Entry in the dictionary proper is under the modern form of name and cross references from old forms are given in a table of ancient forms at the end of the volume.

Volumes so far published are: **Ain,** by E. Philipon 1911; **Aisne,** by A. Matton, 1871; **Alpes (Hautes),** by J. Roman, 1884; **Aube,** by Th. Boutiot and E. Socard 1874; **Aude,** by the Abbé Sabarthès, 1912; **Calvados,** by C. Hippeau, 1883; **Cantal,** by E. Amé, 1897; **Cher,** by H. Boyer and R. Latouche, 1926; **Côte d'Or,** by A Roserot, 1924; **Dordogne,** by A. J. D. de Gourgues, 1873 **Drôme,** by J. Brun-Durand, 1891; **Eure,** by B. E. F de Blosseville, 1878; **Eure-et-Loir,** by L. Merlet, 1861 **Gard,** by E. Germer-Durand, 1868; **Hérault,** by F Thomas, 1865; **Loire (Haute),** by A. Chassaing an A. Jacotin, 1907; **Marne,** by A. Longnon, 1891; **Marn (Haute),** by A. Roserot, 1903; **Mayenne,** by L. Maître 1878; **Meurthe,** by H. Lepage, 1862; **Meuse,** by F. Lié nard, 1872; **Morbihan,** by L. Rosenzweig, 1870; **Mosell** by E. de Bouteiller, 1874; **Nièvre,** by J. H. G. R. de Sou trait, 1865; **Pas-de-Calais,** by A. C. H. Menche de Loisne 1908; **Pyrénnées (Basses),** by P. R. L. Raymond, 186; **Rhin (Haut),** by G. Stoffel, 1868; **Vienne,** by L. Réde 1881; **Vosges,** by P. Marichal, 1941; **Yonne,** by M Quantin, 1862.

Longnon, Auguste Honoré. Les noms de lieu d la France; leur origine, leur signification, leu transformations; résumé des conférences de t ponomastique générale faites à l'École Pratiqu des Hautes Études. . . . Pub. par Paul Marichal Léon Mirot. Paris, Champion, 1920–29. 831   **U1**

Ireland

Hogan, Edmund. Onomasticon Goedelicum l corum et tribuum Hiberniae et Scotiae; an inde with identifications, to the Gaelic names of plac and tribes. Dublin, Hodges, 1910. 695p. ma   **U1**

Joyce, Patrick W. Origin and history of Irish names of places. Lond. and N.Y., Longmans, 1898–1913. 3v. **U132**

The best dictionary of Irish place names, giving for each name its location, derivation, meaning, and an explanation of the meaning where necessary. Volumes 1-2, originally published 1869–71, are treatises, arranged in chapters with alphabetical indexes, but volume 3 is a regular dictionary list. As volume 3 does not duplicate many of the names in volumes 1-2, use must still be made of the earlier volumes.

Netherlands

Flou, Karel de. Woordenboek der toponymie van Westelijk Vlaanderen, Vlaamsch Artesië, het Land van den Hoek, de graafschappen Guines en Boulogne, en een gedeelte van het graafschap Ponthieu. Brugge, Poelvoorde, 1914–38. 18v. **U133**

Sponsored by the Vlaamsche Academie voor Taal en Letterkunde.

Nederlandsch Aardrijkskundig Genootschap, Amsterdam. Lijst der aardrijkskundige namen van Nederland. Leiden, Brill, 1936. 494p. **U134**

An extensive list which includes many names but gives very brief information about each, usually merely the location.

Wijer, H. J. van de. Bibliographie van de Vlaamsche plaatsnaamkunde (begin XIXe eeuw tot en met 1927). Den Haag, Nijhoff, 1928. 156p. (Nomina geographica Flandrica. I) **U135**

New Zealand

Andersen, Johannes Carl. Maori place-names, also personal names and names of colours, weapons, and natural objects. Wellington, Polynesian Soc., of New Zealand, 1942. 494p. [Polynesian Society memoir no.20] 18s. **U136**

Martin, A. E. Place names in Queensland, New Zealand and the Pacific. Sydney, Australia, N.S. W. Bookstall Co., 1944. [109]p. il. **U137**

New Zealand. Geographic Board. . . . Place-names in New Zealand; rules of nomenclature and lists of names approved or changed or expunged. Comp. by Johannes C. Andersen. Wellington, 1934. 47p. (Its Bulletin 1) 2s. **U138**

Scotland

Mackenzie, William Cook. Scottish place-names. Lond., K. Paul, 1931. 319p. 15s. **U139**

Johnston, James B. Place-names of Scotland [3d ed., enl.] Lond., Murray, 1934. 335p. 15s. **U140**

Watson, William J. History of the Celtic place-names of Scotland, being the Rhind lecture on Archaeology (expanded) delivered in 1916. Pub. under the auspices of the Royal Celtic Society. Edinburgh, Blackwood, 1926. 558p. 30s. **U141**

The following regional lists are also useful:

MACDONALD, J. Place-names of West **Aberdeenshire**. Aberdeen, New Spaulding Club, 1899. 374p. **U142**; MEIKLE, JAMES. Place-names around **Alyth**. Paisley, Gardner, 1925. 203p. **U143**; GILLIES, H. C. Place-names of **Argyll**. Lond., Nutt, 1906. 273p. **U144**; IRVING, JOHN. Place-names of **Dumbartonshire**. Dumbarton, Bennett and Thomson, 1928. 61p. **U145**; JOHNSON-FERGUSON, *Sir* EDWARD. Place-names of **Dumfriesshire**. Dumfries, Courier Pr., 1935. 140p. **U146**; MATHESON, D. Place-names of **Elginshire**. Stirling, Mackay, 1905. 208p. **U147**; MAXWELL, *Sir* HERBERT. Place-names of **Galloway**, their origin and meaning considered. Glasgow, Jackson, Wylie, 1930. 278p. **U148**; ELLICE, E. C. Place-names in **Glengarry** and **Glenquoich** and their associations. 2d ed. rev. Lond., Routledge, 1931. 163p. **U149**; ROBSON, W. S. **Hawick** place-names. Hawick, Hood, 1947. 82p. **U150**; MACIVER, DONALD. Place-names of **Lewis** and **Harris**. [Stornoway, "Gazette" Office] 1934. 102p. **U151**; MILNE, J. Gaelic place-names of the **Lothians**. Lond., McDougall's Educ. Co., 1912. 51p., 44p., 30p. **U152**; WATSON, W. J. Place-names of **Ross** and **Cromarty**. Inverness, Northern Counties Pr. and Pub. Co., 1904. 302p. **U153**; JAKOBSEN, JAKOB. Place-names of **Shetland**. Lond., Nutt, 1936. 273p. **U154**; FORBES, A. R. Place-names of **Skye** and adjacent islands, with lore mythical, traditional and historical. Paisley, Gardner. 1923. 495p. **U155**; MACDONALD, ANGUS. The place-names of **West Lothian**. Edinburgh, Oliver and Boyd, 1941. 179p. 15s. **U156**.

South Africa

Pettman, Charles. South African place-names, past and present. Queenstown, Daily Representative, Ltd., 1931. 194p. **U157**

Switzerland

Jaccard, Henri. Essai de toponymie; origine des noms de lieux habités et des lieux dits de la Suisse romande. Lausanne, Bridel, 1906. 558p. (Société d'Histoire de la Suisse Romande. Mémoires et documents, 2. ser. t.7) **U158**

Studer, Julius. Schweizer Ortsnamen; ein historisch-etymologischer Versuch. . . . Zürich, Schulthess, 1896. 288p. **U159**

ATLASES

❧ Atlases are important and necessary reference books in any library. As they are expensive and vary greatly in quality they should be chosen with care, after checking critical estimates by experts and examining the books themselves to note their suitability for the particular library in question. Atlases which are general in scope (i.e., cover the whole world) differ considerably in their contents according to the country in which they are published. An American atlas, for example, will include more or larger maps of American regions and cities than will be found in an English or French atlas, an English atlas will include more maps of British territory. As a general thing, the workmanship of the best foreign atlases is better than that of American atlases, and an American library should take that fact into account in forming its collection, including some British, French and German atlases for the quality of their maps and some American atlases for their more numerous maps of American regions. A useful survey of the principal modern atlases is given in Wright and Platt, *Aids to geographical research*, p.83-99 (U1). This gives a general discussion of the subject and special critical comment on most of the atlases listed below, as well as on others.

In studying atlases the student, in addition to following the general directions for examining reference books, should note the following special points:

I. Atlas as a whole
   A. Scope
      1. Does the atlas include all types of maps—political, physical, historical, economic, etc.?
   B. Country of origin—as indication both of quality of maps and emphasis of atlas
   C. Date—of publication, copyright, preface, revision
   D. Index
      1. Is there a general index for the whole atlas or are there separate indexes for each country or map?
      2. If there is a general index, is it in a separate volume or bound with the atlas?
      3. Does the index include population figures or other additional information, e.g., pronunciation, latitude and longitude, etc.?
      4. Does the index include only names printed on the maps or are other places included?
      5. How does the index refer to the location of a place on a given map?
         a) By locational squares indicated by marginal letters and figures?
         b) By a grid such as the *Times atlas* (U177) uses?
         c) By latitude and longitude?
   E. Supplementary material
      1. Does the atlas contain anything except maps and index, e.g., bibliographies, general descriptive, statistical, commercial or ethnographic information, lists of commercial products, gazetteer lists of places, etc.?

II. Maps
   A. Name and nationality of the maker—as indication of the quality of the work
   B. Date. (If map is undated, the name and address of the maker may show this approximately, or the date may be indicated by some kind of internal evidence such as inclusion or omission of new places, changed names, boundaries and explorations which were established or made at certain dates.)
   C. Method of indicating relief
      1. By hachuring?
      2. By layer method of altitude tints?
      3. By contour lines with altitude figures?
      4. By shading?
   D. Color
      1. Is the color definite and varied enough to be clear and at the same time not so dark as to obscure lettering?
      2. Does each map have a key, showing the meaning of the colors used?
   E. Scale
      1. Is the scale plainly indicated?
   F. Lettering and other details
      1. Is the lettering distinct and easily read?
      2. Are other details, e.g., rivers, railroads, boundaries, canals, etc., plain and well differentiated?
   G. Form of names
      1. Are geographical names in the vernacular or translated?
   H. Authority
      1. Are there bibliographical or other references to indicate the source and authority of the maps?
   I. Accuracy
      1. Are the maps accurate in detail? (The student who is not a specialist naturally cannot judge the whole atlas on this point, but he can examine some one map of a small region with which he is familiar and judge its accuracy and completeness on points known to him.)

See Atlases, p.481, for historical atlases.

Bibliography

Chubb, Thomas. Printed maps in the atlases of Great Britain and Ireland; a bibliography, 1579–1870 . . . with an introd. by F. P. Sprent and biographical notes on the map makers, engravers and publishers by T. Chubb assisted by J. W. Skells and H. Beharrell. . . . Lond., Homeland Assoc., 1927. 479p. il. **U160**

Claussen, Martin Paul and **Friis, Herman R.** Descriptive catalog of maps published by Congress, 1817–1843. Wash. [priv. pr.] 1941. 104p. $1.25. **U161**

"This is a catalog of the 503 maps that are scattered throughout v.1–429 of the 'Congressional series' . . . 15th through the 27th Congress, between 1817 and 1843."—*Introd.*

Arranged chronologically by Congress with index to area, place names that appear in title, names of persons, government agencies, and institutions involved in compiling maps.

Lowery, Woodbury. The Lowery collection. A descriptive list of maps of the Spanish possessions within the present limits of the United States, 1502–1820. Ed. with notes by P. L. Phillips. Wash., Govt. Prt. Off., 1912. 567p. $1. **U162**

Thiele, Walter. Official map publications; a historical sketch, and a bibliographical handbook of current maps and mapping services in the U.S., Canada, Latin America, France, Great Britain, Germany and certain other countries. Chic., Amer. Lib. Assoc., 1938. 356p. o.p. **U163**

"The primary purpose of this handbook is to serve as a guide to the map publications which are currently made available by national government mapping services."—*Pref.* pt.1, Historical sketch; pt.2, Current government maps and mapping services including reference lists of map publications issued by the various governments. Care of maps. Appendixes: (1) Tentative map classification outline by subject; (2) Map classification outline by areas; (3) State governments of the United States as map sources; (4) Public planning organizations in the United States and their map publications; (5) List of international maps.

U. S. Library of Congress. List of geographical atlases in the Library. . . . comp. by P. L. Phillips. Wash., Govt. Prt. Off., 1909–20. 4v. **U164**

The main part, volumes 1–2, is a catalog, arranged by locality, of 3265 atlases, giving for each full description and contents. Volume 2 contains an author list and a minute analytical index which, as it refers to single maps listed in the contents notes, is of great reference value for ascertaining in what atlases unusual or early maps are to be found. Volume 3 (1914) is a supplementary volume which lists the titles added to the collection since 1909 and contains also a minute alphabetical index and an author list, this latter including references to volumes 1–2 also, and forming a complete check list to the whole collection of some 4000 atlases. Volume 4 is another supplement which lists titles acquired 1914–20 and con-tains an index and a combined author list for the four volumes. This author list is also printed separately; *see* following entry.

—— Author list of the geographical atlases in the Library . . . enl. and rev. ed. comp. under the direction of P. L. Phillips. Wash., Govt. Prt. Off., 1920. clxiiip.

Reprinted from volume 4 of its *List of geographical atlases.*

—— List of maps of America in the Library . . . preceded by a list of works relating to cartography. Wash., Govt. Prt. Off., 1901. 1137p. **U165**

—— **Map Division.** United States atlases; a list of national, state, county, city, and regional atlases in the Library of Congress, comp. by Clara Egli Le Gear. Wash., Govt. Prt. Off., 1950. 445p. $2.25. **U165a**

General

Andree, Richard. Andrees Allgemeiner Handatlas in 231 Haupt- und 211 Nebenkarten. 8. neubear. u. verm. Aufl., 5. verb. u. verm. Abdruck. Hrsg. von Ernst Ambrosius. Bielefeld, Velhagen, 1930. 2v. 45cm., 29cm. **U166**

v.1, Atlas; v.2, Namenverzeichnis. 644p.

Atlante internazionale della Consociazione Turistica Italiana . . . sotto la direzione di L. V. Bertarelli, O. Marinelli, P. Corbellini. 5. ed. Milano, Consoc. Turist. Ital., 1938. 248 col. maps on 169 (i.e., 176) l. 231p. 49cm. **U167**

The fifth edition of the fine Italian atlas published by the Touring Club Italiano. This edition is published in uniform binding with the *Enciclopedia italiana* (D46). The abbreviation "A. T." after place names in the *Enciclopedia* refers to this atlas.

Bartholomew, John George. Citizen's atlas of the world, ed. by John Bartholomew. 8th ed. Edinburgh, Bartholomew, 1944. 192p., 160p. il. 158 maps. 37cm. 63s. **U168**

Bol'shoĭ sovetskiĭ atlas mira. Moskva, 1937–39. v.1–2. maps. 52cm. **U169**

Published according to the decision, of the Central Executive Committee and the Council of Peoples Commissars of the U.S.S.R., of Dec. 17, 1933 by the Scientific Publishing Institute of the Great Soviet atlas of the world at the Central Executive Committee of the U.S.S.R.

Under the general editorship of A. F. Gorkin, O. IŪ Shmidt, V. E. Motylev, M. V. Nikitin, B. M. Shaposhnikov.

Contents: v.1, pt.1, World maps; pt.2, Maps of the U.S.S.R.; v.2, pt.1, Political-administrative, survey, economic, and physical maps of the U.S.S.R.; pt.2, Historical maps of the Civil War in the U.S.S.R.; v.3, planned but not published.

An English translation of the text and legends for both parts of volume 1 was made by Andrew Perejda and Vera

471

Washburne (Syracuse Univ., Syracuse N.Y., 1940. 103p.)

Only two or three copies of the original of volume 2 were received in the United States but it was reproduced in color photography with an English translation of the table of contents by the U.S. Office of Strategic Services.

Century atlas of the world. N.Y., Century, 1914. 431p. 118 maps. 30cm. $15. **U170**

Also published as volume 12 of the *Century dictionary* (M4).

1st ed., 1897; revised several times, especially in 1899, 1901 and 1911. General index contains 185,000 names.

Encyclopaedia Britannica. Encyclopaedia Britannica world atlas; physical and political maps, geographical comparisons, a glossary of geographical terms, a gazetteer index, geographical summaries, world spheres of influence. G. Donald Hudson, geographical ed., under the direction of Walter Yust. Chic., Ency. Brit., Inc., 1949. 284p., 123p. 152 col. maps on 70 l. 42cm. $20; trade ed. $15. **U171**

Maps prepared by C. S. Hammond and Co. showing the state of the world as of Sept. 1, 1939. (Map of Germany shows zones of occupation as of Feb. 1947.)

Includes political and physical maps of the continents, countries, states, provinces, etc., of the world. The index includes names of cities and towns, rivers, mountains, lakes, etc., and gives population figures for cities and towns.

The "geographical summaries" give in tabular form statistics for seven continental regions of the world: North, Middle and South Americas, Europe, Asia, Africa, Australasia, and the Pacific Islands. Information is given by countries under each region on area and population, transportation, agricultural, mineral, forest and manufactured products, exports and imports, value of foreign trade, military service and personnel, military equipment and organization, etc.

Gives "world spheres of influence" for the United States, United Kingdom, France, Spain, Japan, Italy, Portugal, Belgium, and Netherlands as of Jan. 1, 1949.

Published also in a "trade edition" without geographical summaries and spheres of influence.

Hammond, C. S. and Co. New world atlas; containing new and complete historical, economic, political and physical maps of the entire world, in full colors, with complete indexes; and the races of mankind, illus. gazetteer of the world, illus. gazetteer of the U.S. and territories. Rev. ed. N.Y., Garden City Pub. Co., 1947. 344p. incl. maps. 52cm. $16.75. **U172**

Originally published by C. S. Hammond in loose-leaf form.

Philip, George. Philip's International atlas . . . 5th ed. Lond., Philip, 1945. 130p. 158 pl. 41cm. 73s. 6d. **U173**

Rand, McNally and Co. Rand McNally commercial atlas. 80th ed. N.Y., Rand McNally [1949]. 584p. incl. maps. 53cm. Yearly subscription service. **U174**

Primarily an atlas of America as more than three-quarters of the maps included are of that region, but includes world maps and a few maps of foreign countries. United States maps are indexed individually by states. There is a general index of foreign places and physical features at the back. Contains in cover pocket a "Road atlas of the United States, Canada, and Mexico."

—— **Cosmopolitan world atlas.** Chic., Rand McNally, 1949. 355p. maps. 37cm. $12.50. **U175**

In this new atlas the world has been mapped on a regional basis, centered around a major country or group of countries. Includes maps for individual states of the United States, with insets for regions of large cities. Maps are clear and up to date. Special tables include world political information, climatic and economic tables, and an historical gazetteer of geographical names. There is a gazetteer index.

A good, usable atlas for library and home.

Stieler, Adolf. Stieler's Atlas of modern geography; 263 maps on 114 sheets, engraved on copper. 10th ed. International ed., pub. by Dr. Hermann Haack, with the cooperation of Dr. Berthold Carlberg and Rudolf Schleifer. Gotha, Perthes, 1934–38. pt.1-34. 41cm. R.M.85.50. **U176**

Appearing in parts, to be completed in some 114 sheets. A thorough revision, with addition of various entirely new sheets, of the centenary edition of *Stieler's Handatlas* (Gotha, Perthes, 1925).

In the international edition, the maps are in the language of the country mapped, explanatory notes, etc. are in English, French, German, Italian, Portuguese and Spanish. Also published with French title.

Times, London. The Times survey atlas of the world. . . . Lond., "The Times," 1920–22. 112 double maps and index v., 259p. 48cm. o.p. **U177**

The original issue is a loose-leaf atlas, with index in a separate volume. A bound edition, with index in same volume with the atlas, was sold by Macmillan, New York. A good inexpensive issue, with the same maps but cheaper binding, was sold by Selfridge, London; now out of print.

Subtitle: A comprehensive series of new and authentic maps reduced from the national surveys of the world and the special surveys of travellers and explorers with general index of over two hundred thousand names. Prepared at the "Edinburgh Geographical Institute" under the direction of J. G. Bartholomew.

The index is particularly full and is all in one alphabet. Location indication is by means of a "grid" furnished with the atlas.

Världsatlas; en skildring av jorden och stjärnhimmeln i kartor, ord och bilder. Stockholm, Ahlén and Akerlands, (Bonnier) 1934. 248p. 50 double pl. 39cm. **U178**

Huvudredaktor: Axel Elvin.

New edition of *Nordisk världsatlas*, 1919–26.

Vidal de la Blache, P. Histoire et géographie: Atlas général Vidal-Lablache, 420 cartes et cartons, index alphabétique de 46,000 noms augm d'un supplément de 3,500 noms. Nouv. éd. conforme aux traités de paix. Paris, Colin, 1922. 131p. (i.e., 191) 47p. 38cm. **U179**

Vivien de Saint-Martin, Louis and **Schrader, Franz.** Atlas universel de géographie. Dressé sous la direction de F. Schrader d'après les sources originales et les documents le plus récents. Nouv. éd. [Paris] Hachette [1920–23]. 38p. 80 maps. 45cm. **U180**

School

Bartholomew, John George. Oxford advanced atlas. 6th ed. Ox., Univ. Pr., 1940. 36p., 96p. 12s. 6d. **U181**

Goode, John Paul. Goode's School atlas; physical, political, and economic, for American schools and colleges. 1946 ed. rev. and enl. N.Y. and Chic., Rand McNally, 1946. 286p. maps. 28cm. $5. **U182**

Includes, in addition to political and physical maps, maps showing population density, ocean depths, currents, des, climate, vegetation, communications, commercial roducts, etc., and plans of principal cities; "Pronouncing index of over 30,000 geographical names," p.177-286.
Perhaps the best, inexpensive small American atlas; frequently revised.

Sydow, Emil von. Sydow-Wagners Methodischer Schul-Atlas. 20. Aufl. neu bearb. von H. Haack und H. Lautensach. Gotha, Perthes, 1932. 62 pl. 1cm. **U183**

———— Namenverzeichnis. 39p.

China

Far Eastern Geographical Establishment. New tlas and commercial gazetteer of China. . . . hanghai, North-China Daily News [1917]. 374p. 6cm. **U184**

Subtitle: A work devoted to its geography and resources and economic and commercial development. Ed. y E. J. Dingle. Containing 25 bilingual maps with complete indexes and many colored graphs. Comp. and tr. om the latest and most authoritative surveys and records.

Hermann, Albert. Historical and commercial tlas of China. Camb., Harv. Univ. Pr., 1935. 112p. 119 maps. 33cm. (Harvard-Yenching Institute. Monograph ser. v.1) $5; 21s. **U185**

North-China Daily News. China provincial atlas nd geography; the provinces and outer territories of China (including the newly-formed provinces) with communications and key map, con-

tents and index. [2d ed.] Shanghai, North-China Daily News [1935]. 61p. il. maps. 37cm. **U186**

Ting, Wên-chiang, Wêng, Wên-hao and **Tsêng, Shih-ying.** Chung Kuo fên shêng hsin-t'u [New atlas of China]. 5th ed. Shanghai, Shên-pao, 1948. 58p., 94p. **U187**

A new edition of this standard atlas, with a useful index available in English as:

———— ———— Gazetteer of Chinese place names based on the index to V. K. Ting atlas, comp. by the U.S. Board on Geographical Names. June 1944. [Wash., Army Map Service 1944. lxxiixp., 229p. 38cm.] **U188**

Alphabetical romanized index to the atlas.

Czechoslovakia

Česká Akademie věd a Umění, Prague. Atlas Republiky Československé. Atlas de la République Tchécoslovaque. [Praze, Nákladem Akc. Spol. Orbis, 1935–36] 2v. 44cm. $55. **U189**

"Publié par l'Académie Tchèque sous les auspices du Ministère des Affaires Étrangères de la République Tchécoslovaque."
In two parts: (1) Atlas of 55 plates of maps (442 maps), 1935, forming a bound volume, and (2) accompanying text, 43p., 1936, unbound.
A very fine and detailed atlas, covering economic and physical geography, demography, political and cultural aspects, etc.

Egypt

Egypt. Survey Dept. Atlas of Egypt; a series of maps and diagrams with descriptive text illustrating the orography, geology, meteorology and economic conditions. Giza, Survey of Egypt, 1928. [11]p. 31 pl. 70x84cm. **U190**

Finland

Geografiska Sällskapet i Finland, Helsingfors. Atlas of Finland, 1925. Helsinski, Otava, 1929. 2v. text, 25cm; atlas of 38 maps. 46cm. **U191**

Explanatory headings in Finnish, Swedish and English. The text is issued separately in each of the three languages. Covers physical, economic, and social geography.

France

Comité National de Géographie. Atlas de France. . . . Paris, Editions Géographiques de France, 1945. 4p. 82 maps. 50cm. **U192**

Issued in parts, 1933- .
A regional atlas of the highest grade covering geomorphology, climatology, hydrography, biogeography, agriculture, industry, commerce, human and political geography.

Great Britain

Gt. Brit. Ordnance Survey. Ordnance survey atlas of England and Wales. Quarter inch to the mile. Southampton, Ordnance Survey Off., 1922. [21]p. 24 maps. 35x39cm. **U193**

—— Ordnance survey atlas of Scotland. Quarter inch to the mile. Southampton, Ordnance Survey Off., 1924. 18 maps. 35x39cm. **U193a**

Italy

Dainelli, Giotto. Atlante fisico-economico d'Italia; 82 tavole, 508 carte. Milan, Consociazione Turistica Italiana, 1940. xviip., 82 maps. 49cm. **U194**

—— —— Note illustrative, a cura del Aldo Sestini. 1940. 147p.

Japan

Fujita, Motoharu. New atlas of Japan (Shin Nippon Zucho). Wash., 1943. 34 pl. 241p. 26cm. (U.S. War Dept., Army Map Service. Corps of Engineers) **U195**

Philippines

Philippines (Commonwealth) Commission of the Census. Census atlas of the Philippines. Manila, 1941. 44 pl. 95p. 47cm. (Census of the Philippines, 1939. v.5) **U196**
Covers political, economic, physical geography as well as reproductions of some early maps of the Philippines.

GUIDE BOOKS

❦ The guide books prepared for the use of travelers are very useful in a reference department as they are fuller for certain kinds of local information than either the general or the special gazetteers and give more local maps, plans of cities, etc., than are given in the ordinary atlases. They are especially useful for information about the art museums, collections, etc., of any given place, its architectural and historical monuments, scenic features, railroad and other communications, hotels, literary and historical associations, etc.

Many guide books are now much out of date not having been published since World War II. A few titles in the "Blue guides" series have been published in postwar editions and there have been a few independent guides to other countries.

Some of the standard series of guide books are:
(1) **Muirhead's Blue guides (Guides bleues) U197** published in London by Benn, in Paris by Hachette.

This series includes mainly guides to European countries. Postwar editions include: *Short guide to London,* 1947; *Blue guide to Ireland,* 1949; *Blue guide to Scotland,* 1949; *Blue guide to Switzerland,* 1948 (2) the **Baedeker** series **U198** published in English, French and German editions, a standard series originating in Germany, most volumes of which are now quite out of date; (3) the **Murray** series **U199** (Lond., Murray) a nineteenth century series now largely out of date except for the *Handbook for India, Burma and Ceylon* (15th ed. 1939); (4) the **Terry** series **U200** (Hingham, Mass., Robert C Terry) including only three titles: *Cuba,* 1926; *Japan,* 1933; and *Mexico,* 1947 (rev. ed. $4.75).

Old guide books have a definite reference use and should not be discarded when a library acquires a later work or edition. For geographical and travel questions calling for up-to-date information the most recent work must be used, but the older books will often have historical information not given in the later—will show the location of an old street now done away with, give a description of a building no longer in existence, or furnish general descriptive information for an earlier period. For some such questions the older guide book is the most convenient first aid.

United States

American guide series, comp. by the Federal Writers' Project (later called Writers' Program) [pub. variously by different publishers] 1937–49. il. **U201**
Includes guides to each state, many cities and regions and some special subjects. The state guidebooks are particularly useful giving accurate information about points of interest with some historical and background material and side lights on the unusual.

Alsberg, Henry Garfield. The American guide; source book and complete travel guide for the United States. N.Y., Hastings House, 1949. 1348p. $7.50. **U202**
A much condensed guide covering the whole United States, arranged geographically by regions, with introductory essays. Within each region (except New England which is treated as a whole), each state is described by tours within that state, usually following U.S. highways. Information is very brief.

Jenkins, Elmer. Guide to America. Wash., Public Affairs Pr., 1949. 705p. $3.75. **U203**
Arranged alphabetically by state (with introduction) and then alphabetically by city. Information is very brief, emphasizes museums, historical monuments, etc.

Africa

Martens, Otto and **Karstedt, Oskar.** African handbook and traveller's guide; ed . . . for the Germa

African lines. Lond., Allen; N.Y., Macmillan, 1932. 948p. il. $2. **U204**

"The original German edition of this handbook—entitled *Afrika: ein Handbuch für Wirtschaft und Reise*—was issued in 1930."—*Pref.*

A general guidebook with a strong emphasis on economic information and statistics; bibliographies.

South and East African year book and guide, with atlas, town plans and diagrams. Lond., Sampson, Low, 1901- . Annual. **U204a**

For description *see* L207.

Latin America

Bullot, Ivan. Air travel guide to Latin America; including the U.S.A. territories of the Canal Zone, Puerto Rico and the Virgin Islands; Bermuda; and British, French, and Netherlands possessions in the West Indies and the Guianas. N.Y., Franklin Watts, 1946. 369p. il. $5. **U205**

Hanson, Earl Parker. The New world guides to the Latin American republics, sponsored by the Office of the U.S. Coordinator of Inter-American Affairs . . . Earl Parker Hanson, ed.-in-chief; Raye R. Platt, ed. rev. 2d ed. N.Y., Duell, Sloan and Pearce [1945]. 3v. il. (maps) $2.50 ea. **U206**

Contents: v.1, Mexico, Central America and the West Indies; v.2, Andes and west coast countries; v.3, East coast countries.

West Indies

Aspinwall, *Sir* **Algernon.** The Pocket guide to the West Indies. N.Y., Chemical Pub. Co., 1940. 425p. il. **U207**

Olley, Philip P. Guide to Jamaica. Kingston, Jamaica, Tourist Trade Development Bd., 1937. 83p. il. **U208**

Hotels

Official hotel red book and directory, 1886- . N.Y., Amer. Hotel Assoc. Directory Corp., 1886- . Annual. (1949, $5) **U209**

Timetables

❦ Timetables, schedules, etc., of trains, air lines, buses, etc., are frequently called for in libraries. The following are a selection of comprehensive monthly guides.

Official guide of the railways and steam navigation lines of the United States, Porto Rico, Canada, Mexico and Cuba, also time-tables of railroads in Central America. Air line schedules. N.Y., Nat'l Railway Pub. Co., 1868- . Monthly. Annual subscription $25; $3 per no. **U210**

Gives timetables, many maps, indexes of stations; the general index of stations shows on what road any given place is located.

Official steamship and airways guide. N.Y., Transportation Guides, Inc., 1932- . Monthly. $8 per yr. **U211**

Steamship and air line schedules and fares; entry requirements for international travel; lists of consulates, etc.

Russell's Official national motor coach guide. Cedar Rapids, Iowa, Russell's Guides, 1927- . Monthly. $7.50 per yr. **U212**

Schedules of bus lines.

Bradshaw's Guide to British railways and hotels, 1839- . Lond., Blacklock, 1839- . Monthly. 5s. each no.; 66s. per yr. **U213**

General guide to British railways.

Bradshaw's British and international air guide. no.1, Nov. 1934- . Lond., Blacklock, 1934- . Monthly. 41s. per yr. **U214**

Guide to commercial air services of the world.

HISTORY

❦ There are many approaches to the study of history which range from the school child with his textbook to the scholar searching for original sources. The first may want illustrative material to supplement his studies, the latter may need guides to the location of original manuscripts, and in between there will be numerous inquiries of other kinds. For many historical questions materials in other parts of this GUIDE must be used, the encyclopedias, the biographical dictionaries, atlases, gazetteers, and guidebooks, statistical compilations, national and special bibliographies, indexes to documents, newspapers, periodicals, and many others. This section includes

a selection of historical bibliographies, guides, hand books, dictionaries, and encyclopedias, and in som cases a few general histories which contain such de tailed bibliographies and indexes that they are usefi for reference purposes. For the most part histor texts are not included although in actual referenc work they must often be used. The first groups cov the chronological periods of history: archaeolog classical antiquities, medieval and modern times. Th later groups include material on individual countri and continents. These are arranged in alphabetic order with the exception of the United States whic is placed first.

GENERAL WORKS
Guides

Coulter, Edith Margaret and **Gerstenfeld, Melanie.** Historical bibliographies; a systematic and annotated guide. Berkeley, Calif., Univ. of California Pr., 1935. 206p. $2.50.　　　　　**V1**

Lists the important retrospective and current bibliographies of history for each country. A useful compilation, now, unfortunately, somewhat out of date.

Guide to historical literature, ed. by George Matthew Dutcher, Henry Robinson Shipman, Sidney Bradshaw Fay, Augustus Hunt Shearer, William Henry Allison. N.Y., Macmillan, 1931. xxviiip., 1222p. (Repr. N.Y., National Bibliophile Service, 1949. $12.50)　　　　　**V2**

Prepared by the Committee on Bibliography of the American Historical Association in cooperation with the American Library Association.–Cf. *Pref.*

Issued originally (the same year) with title, *A guide to historical literature,* edited by William Henry Allison, Sidney Bradshaw Fay, Augustus Hunt Shearer, and Henry Robinson Shipman; this title was later corrected by the issue of a revised title page for insertion in the original issue. Largely supersedes the older standard work *Manual of historical literature* by Charles Kendall

Adams (3d ed. 1889), noted for its selection and exce lent critical notes.

A selective bibliography of fundamental treatises ar source material, arranged in large subject and count groups, each group selected and described, or annotate by a specialist. Important as an aid to the building of a collection or for opinion on a particular work. I dispensable as a first aid and as a guide to the mo comprehensive bibliographies of individual countri which contain more analytical material.

Herre, Paul. Quellenkunde zur Weltgeschicht ein Handbuch, unter Mitwirkung von Adolf Ho meister und Rudolf Stübe; bearb. und hrsg. v Paul Herre. Leipzig, Koehler, 1910. 400p.　　**V**

A well-selected bibliography including books ar some periodical articles. Classed arrangement, with a thor and title index.

Langlois, Charles Victor. Manuel de bibliogr phie historique. Paris, Hachette, 1901–04. 2　　**V**

pt.1, Instruments bibliographiques. 2. ed. 1901; pt Histoire et organisation des études historiques, 1904.

A fundamental work, the first part giving valual commentary on bibliographies and other aids to histori research and the second surveying European historic raphy from the Renaissance to the end of the eighteer century.

Bibliography

Caron, Pierre and **Jaryc, Marc.** World list of historical periodicals and bibliographies. Ox., International Committee of Historical Sciences; N.Y., Wilson, 1939. 391p. $6.75; 30s. **V5**

Lists 3103 periodicals. Indexes: Editors, Abbreviations, Subjects. Broad interpretation of history to include allied subjects, e.g., palaeography, chronology, genealogy, sigillography, heraldry, numismatics, ethnography and folklore.

Koner, Wilhelm. Repertorium über die vom Jahre 1800 bis zum Jahre 1850 in Akademischen Abhandlungen, Gesellschaftsschriften und wissenschaftlichen Journalen auf dem Gebiete der Geschichte und ihrer Hülfswissenschaften erschienenen Aufsätze. Berlin, Nicolai, 1852–56. 2v. **V6**

A closely classified bibliography with subject index of articles on historical subjects appearing in some 500 periodicals and society publications in various languages. Includes some American publications. Volume 2, p.76–69, lists biographical articles arranged alphabetically by subject. These names do not appear in the index.

New York Library Association. Committee on Bibliographies and Surveys. A union list of printed collections of source materials on European history in New York state libraries. Preliminary ed. Lewis F. Stieg, editor. N.Y., New York Lib. Assoc., Committee on Bibliographies and Surveys, 1944. 112p. **V7**

Locates copies in 17 New York state libraries.

Reuss, Jeremias David. Repertorium commentationum a societatibus litterariis editarum. Secundum disciplinarum ordinem . . . t.8, Historia. . . Gottingae, Dieterich, 1810. 674p. **V8**

Contents: Historia; subsidia historica (geographia, chronologia, monumenta veterum populorum, inscriptiones, numi et res numaria, ars diplomatica, heraldica); Historia universalis; Historia generis humani; Historia mythica; Historia specialis: Asiae, Africae, Americae, Europae; Historia ecclesiastica; Historia litteraria.

A valuable index to the publications of the learned societies of various countries up to 1800. Classed arrangement with author index.

For description of complete set *see* N3.

Jahresberichte der Geschichtswissenschaft; im Auftrage der Historischen Gesellschaft zu Berlin. .-36. Jahrg., 1878–1913. Berlin, Mittler, 1880–1916. 36v. Annual. **V9**

Publisher varies.

International in scope, listing the historical works published in each year. A valuable record for the period covered.

Continued for Germany only by the *Jahresberichte der deutschen Geschichte*, v.1-7, 1918–1924 (Breslau, 1920–23) and continuation (V261).

Historical Association, London. Annual bulletin of historical literature. v.1, 1911- . Lond.,

1912- . Annual. (no.35, 1949. 2s. 7d.) **V10**

—— —— General index. v.1-12, 1911–22. Lond., 1923. 68p.

Survey articles by specialists on the annual production of historical works. Chiefly British, though other countries are included.

International bibliography of historical sciences, ed. for the International Committee of Historical Sciences . . . 1926- . Ox., Univ. Pr.; N.Y., Wilson, 1930- . v.1- . (v.16, 1947, pub. 1949. $10.65; 40s.) **V11**

Subtitle: Internationale Bibliographie der Geschichtswissenschaften; Bibliografia internacional de ciencias historicas; Bibliographie internationale des sciences historiques; Bibliografia internazionale delle scienze storiche.

Has also imprint: Paris, Colin; Rome, P. Maglione; Berlin, de Gruyter; Madrid, Edit. Hernando.

A very useful selected, classified list of historical publications, interpreted in a wide sense to include political, constitutional, religious, cultural, economic and social aspects, international relations, etc.

After volume 12, 1937, publication was delayed by the war. Volume 14 was published in France in a very limited edition in 1942, but few copies reached this country. Volume 15, to cover 1940–46, has not been published.

Meanwhile, material for the British section was published as:

Frewer, Louis Benson. Bibliography of historical writings published in Great Britain and the Empire, 1940–1945. Ox., B. Blackwell, 1947. 346p. 45s. **V12**

Edited for the British National Committee of the International Committee of Historical Sciences in the same manner and format as the *International bibliography of historical sciences* (V11). It includes a record of the books and periodical articles published in Great Britain and the Commonwealth 1940–45 inclusive, on all aspects of history.

Dissertations

List of doctoral dissertations in history now in progress at universities in the United States, 1909- . Wash., Carnegie Inst., 1909–39; N.Y., Macmillan, 1940–41; Wash., Govt. Prt. Off., 1943; Wash., Amer.-Hist. Assoc., 1947- . Annual. (irregular) (1949, $1) **V13**

Series originally edited by John Franklin Jameson and published by the Carnegie Institution of Washington, with the title *List of doctoral dissertations in history now in progress at the chief American universities*. The issues for 1939 and 1940 were published as supplements to the *American historical review*, projects from Canadian universities were included and a "List of research projects in history" was added. The 1941 issue was published as volume 3 of the *Annual report* of the American Historical Association and 1947 on are published as separates by the Association. Not published for 1942–46.

A very useful list arranged by field of history with author and university indexes.

Historiography

Fueter, Eduard. Geschichte der neueren Historiographie. 3., um einen Nachtrag vermehrte Aufl., besorgt von Dietrich Gerhard und Paul Sattler. München, Oldenbourg, 1936. 670p. (Handbuch der mittelalterlichen und neueren Geschichte. Abt. 1, Allgemeines) **V14**

Originally published in 1911.

Translated into French by E. Jeanmarie as *Histoire de l'historiographie moderne* (Paris, Alcan, 1914. 785p.) with some corrections and additions. The third edition includes only minor changes in the text and marginal cross references.

A basic work on historical writing from the time of the Renaissance to about 1870, giving biographical sketches of European and American historians with brief critical estimates of their work.

Garraghan, Gilbert Joseph. A guide to historical method . . . ed. by Jean Delanglez. N.Y., Fordham Univ. Pr., 1946. 482p. **V15**

A comprehensive guide written from the Catholic point of view.

With this is bound as issued: Appel, Livia, *Bibliographical citation in the social sciences* (Madison, Univ. of Wisconsin Pr., 1946. 30p.).

Gooch, George P. History and historians in the nineteenth century. 2d ed. Lond. and N.Y., Longmans, 1913. 604p. $5.50. **V16**

A scholarly critical survey of nineteenth century historians and historical method. Frequently reprinted.

Dictionaries, outlines, tables, etc.

Brewer, Ebenezer Cobham. Historic notebook; with an appendix of battles. Lond., Smith; Phila., Lippincott, 1896. 997p. **V17**

An alphabetical dictionary of historical information including events, expressions, societies, customs, etc.

Bouillet, Marie Nicolas. Dictionnaire universel d'histoire et de géographie. . . . Refondu sous la direction de L. G. Gourraigne. 33. éd., corr., complétée et augmentée d'un nouveau supplément. Paris, Hachette, 1908. 2216p. **V18**

Cambridge modern history. Genealogical tables and lists. (In Cambridge modern history, v.13, p.1-205 [V90]) **V19**

pt.1, Genealogical tables of ruling and royal houses; pt.2, List of spiritual princes, elected sovereigns, etc.; pt.3, List of Parliaments, presidents, governors of colonies, general councils, secularized bishoprics, leagues, alliances, universities since 1450, etc.

DeFord, Miriam Allen. Who was when? A dictionary of contemporaries. N.Y., Wilson, 1941. [162p.] $4.75. **V20**

Originally published 1940; reprinted with corrections and additions.

"Primary object is to ascertain who were the contemporaries of any celebrated person from 500 B.C. to 193 A.D." Tabular arrangement in columns under the following heads: Government and law; Military and naval affairs; Industry, commerce, economics, finance, invention, labor; Travel and exploration; Philosophy and religion; Science and medicine; Education, scholarship history; Literature; Painting and sculpture; Music; Miscellaneous.

Alphabetical index.

Delorme, Jean. Chronologie des civilisations Paris, Presses Universitaires de France, 1949 437p. (Clio: Introduction aux études historiques **V2**

Chronological tables from 3000 B.C. to 1945 A.D. with alphabetical index.

Fry, Edward Alexander. Almanacks for student of English history. Lond., Phillimore, 1915. 138p incl. tables. **V2**

Subtitle: A set of 35 almanacks arranged for every day upon which Easter can fall, together with a chronological list of years from A.D. 500 to A.D. 1751, old style, and A.D. 1752 to A.D. 2000, new style, also a list of regnal years of English sovereigns from the Norman conquest to the present time, lists of saints' days and other useful tables.

Much of the same material is included in revised form in Cheney, *Handbook of dates for students of English history* (V286).

George, Hereford Brooke. Genealogical table illustrative of modern history. 5th ed., rev. and enl., by J. R. H. Weaver. Ox., Clarendon Pr 1916. 55 tables. o.p. **V2**

1st ed., 1873. The fifth edition is revised and continued to 1915. Additions are: Belgium, Norway, Greece, Serbia Montenegro, Roumania, Bulgaria.

Gooch, G. P. Annals of politics and culture, 1492 1899. Camb., Univ. Pr.; N.Y., Macmillan, 1901 530p. o.p. **V2**

A parallel presentation of the principal events in political history and the history of culture, i.e., education literature, science, art.

Haydn, Joseph. Dictionary of dates and universal information relating to all ages and nations. 25th ed. . . . Lond., Ward, Locke, 1910; N.Y., Putnam 1911. 1614p. o.p. **V2**

1st ed. 1841.

A dictionary of history and general information alphabetically arranged, information under each heading given mainly in chronological lists. Convenient for the smaller facts of history and for lists, e.g., Lord mayors of London famous fires, inundations, etc. Addenda list include events to Oct. 1910.

Keller, Helen Rex. Dictionary of dates. N.Y Macmillan, 1934. 2v. $15. **V2**

v.1, Old World (Europe, Africa, Asia, and Australasia World War, Peace Conference, League of Nations, International Labor Organization, Permanent Court of Inte national Justice, international affairs generally; v.2, New World, including the Arctic and Antarctic.

An outline of events and a digest of information from many sources recording by dates the history of the world from the earliest times through 1930. Arranged by country and then chronologically. No index. Part 1 is based on Haydn's *Dictionary of dates* (V25).

Langer, William Leonard. An encyclopedia of world history; ancient, medieval and modern, chronologically arranged. Rev. ed. Bost., Houghton, 1948. 1270p. $7.50. **V27**

A new version of Ploetz's very useful *Manual of universal history* (Bost., Houghton, 1925), giving concise, accurate outlines, not tables. Each section has been revised and largely rewritten, old sections have been condensed and new ones added so that it is now an epitome of world history, whereas in Ploetz the emphasis was very largely on Europe. The chronological arrangement does not readily lend itself to general trends or to economic and cultural history and while some of these are given in brief summary, the main emphasis as before is on political, military and diplomatic history. Comprehensive index. First published in 1940. This revised edition includes a new section on the Second World War, 1939–1945, p.1135-71, and minor corrections throughout the work. Includes outline maps and genealogical tables.

Larned, Josephus Nelson. New Larned history for ready reference, reading and research; the actual words of the world's best historians, biographers and specialists . . . completely rev., enl. and brought up to date . . . by D. E. Smith . . . ed.-in-chief, Charles Seymour, A. H. Shearer, D. C. Knowlton, associate eds. Springfield, Mass., Nichols, 1922–24. 12v. il. **V28**

1st ed., with title *History for ready reference,* 1893–95, 5v.; rev. ed. with supplementary v. covering recent history, 1894–1900, 1901, 6v.; 2d supplement, covering recent history, 1901–10, 1910, v.7.

An alphabetical dictionary of universal history, with many cross references. Under each subject is given not an original article but one or more quoted articles or extracts from recognized authorities; as extracts are given with exact reference, the work serves the double purpose of encyclopedia and index. Interspersed with these are brief biographical sketches, definitions, etc.

Little, Charles Eugene. Cyclopedia of classified dates, with exhaustive index. N.Y., Funk, 1900. 1454p. o.p. **V29**

March of man; a chronological record of peoples and events from prehistoric times to the present day, comprising an historical atlas of 96 pages, comparative time charts in seven sections and 64 plates of illustration. American eds., Albert Bushnell Hart, Isaac J. Cox; English ed., Lawrence H. Dawson. N.Y. and Lond., Encyclopaedia Britannica, 1935. [v.p.] $12; 52s. **V30**

In three sections: Historical atlas; Comparative time charts of universal history; Historical illustrations. The atlas section is based on *Putnam's Historical atlas* (see V51). Includes an index to maps. The second section

contains seven folded charts showing comparative historical events, without index. The section of illustrations is relatively minor.

Mas-Latrie, Louis, *comte de.* Trésor de chronologie d'histoire et de géographie pour l'étude et l'emploi des documents du moyen âge. Paris, Palme, 1889. 2300 col. **V31**

An extremely useful compilation (though at times unreliable) including perpetual calendars, historical chronologies, lists of bishops and archbishops, rulers of many countries in Europe, Asia and Africa, etc.

Workers with medieval documents will also need the extensive work *L'art de vérifier les dates,* 1750 (4th rev. ed. 1818–44. 44v.) by Maur François Dantine, C. Clémencet and U. Durand, which appeared in various editions.

Morison, M. Time table of modern history, A.D. 400–1870. 2d ed. Westminster, Constable, 1908. 159p. o.p. **V32**

Parallel tables of the history of various countries, with genealogical tables of royal families, chronological lists of rulers, general chart of ancient and modern history, and seven historical maps; also full index.

Putnam, George Palmer and **Putnam, George Haven.** Dictionary of events; a handbook of universal history. . . . N.Y., Grosset and Dunlap, 1936. $1. 565p., [71]p. **V33**

Subtitle: A series of chronological tables presenting, in parallel columns, a record of the noteworthy events of history from the earliest times to the present day, together with an index of subjects and genealogical tables.

Earlier editions had titles *Tabular views of universal history, Putnam's Handbook of universal history,* and *Putnam's Dictionary of events.*

In this edition the record has been brought down through 1935, though the material from January 1927 on is not included in the index which is in two sections: (1) covering events up to Aug. 1, 1914; (2) Supplementary index covering Aug. 1, 1914 to Dec. 1926.

Steinberg, Sigfrid Heinrich. Historical tables, 58 B.C.—A.D. 1945, with a foreword by G. P. Gooch. 3d ed. Lond., Macmillan, 1949. 251p. 24s. **V34**

1st ed. 1939; 2d ed. 1947. A spot check of the third edition shows no noticeable change from the second edition.

A tabular chronology of world history arranged in parallel columns by period. Political history is subdivided by geographical areas with additional headings for constitutional history, economic history and natural science and cultural life. No index.

Stokvis, A. M. H. J. Manuel d'histoire, de généalogie et de chronologie de tous les états du globe, depuis les temps les plus reculés jusqu'à nos jours. Leide, Brill, 1888–93. 3v. **V35**

t.1, Asie, Afrique, Amérique, Polynésie; t.2-3, Les états de l'Europe et leurs colonies.

All the above are general in scope. The following deal only with military history:

Bodart, Gaston. Militär-historisches Kriegs-Lexikon. (1618–1905) Wien, Stern, 1908. 956p. **V36**

A dictionary of battles, chronologically arranged, useful for the statistics of forces engaged, losses, etc., on each side. More important than Harbottle's *Dictionary* (V37).

Harbottle, Thomas Benfield. Dictionary of battles from the earliest date to the present time. N.Y., Dutton; Lond., Sonnenschein, 1905. 298p. **V37**

Pictorial illustrations

Parmentier, André Émile Emmanuel. Album historique, publié sous la direction de Ernest Lavisse. Paris, Colin, 1907–10. 4v. il. **V38**

t.1, Le moyen âge (du 4ᵉ au 13ᵉ siècle) 4. éd. 1910; t.2, La fin du moyen âge (14ᵉ et 15ᵉ siècles) 3. éd. 1907; t.3, Le 16ᵉ et le 17ᵉ siècle. 4. éd. 1910; t.4, Le 18ᵉ et le 19ᵉ siècle. 1907.

Contains a large number of excellent illustrations of costume, furniture, civil and military life, manners and customs, dwellings, industries, etc.

Annuals and current surveys

Annual register; a review of public events at home and abroad, 1758- . Lond., 1761- . v.1- . Annual. (1948, 42s.; $15) **V39**

Originated with Robert Dodsley, at the suggestion of Edmund Burke, who was for some years editor and principal contributor. Some time after the year 1791, the copyright and stock were purchased by Otridge and other booksellers. Messrs. Rivington published a rival continuation, which lasted from 1791 to 1812, and again from 1820 to 1824, when the two were merged into one. Since 1890, published by Longmans.

Contents of each volume: English history (now the United Kingdom and the British Commonwealth), Foreign and imperial history, Chronicle of events, Retrospect of literature, science and art, Finance, Law, Public documents, Obituary, Index.

Includes some public documents, and many abstracts of political speeches. Gives English affairs with more fullness than those of other countries.

—— General index to Dodsley's Annual register, 1758 to 1819. Lond., Baldwin, 1826. 938p. o.p.

Les archives internationales "Pharos." Paris, Pharos, 1944- . Loose-leaf. **V40**

Issued weekly in separate leaflets including a biography, a chronology, and a number of factual articles or reproductions of documents (these usually are given in full). The biographies and documents are indexed together, the chronology has its own index. Indexes are issued monthly with periodic cumulations through the year culminating in annual cumulations. For the documents section there is now a 5-year index as follows:

—— Index general analytique et systématique, Oct. 1944–Mars 1950. 64p.

Facts on file; a weekly world news digest with cumulative index. v.1, Oct./Nov. 1940- . N.Y., Person's Index, Facts on File, Inc., 1940- . v.1- . (In progress) Subscription, $45 per yr. (Bound volumes 1941–48, $25 ea.) **V41**

Loose-leaf. Subtitle varies.

A weekly classified digest of news arranged under the following headings: World affairs, National affairs, Foreign affairs, Latin America, Finance and economics, Arts and science, Education and religion, Sports, Obituaries, Miscellaneous. (Headings vary slightly.) Biweekly, monthly, quarterly and annual cumulative indexes.

Keesing's Contemporary archives; weekly diary of world events with index continually kept up-to-date. v.1, July 1, 1931- . Lond., Keesing's Ltd., 1931- . il. (In progress) Loose-leaf (binders furnished for 3-yr. periods) **V42**

A weekly diary of important events in all countries, including texts of speeches and documents, obituaries, statistics, etc. Issued weekly with detailed indexes, cumulating fortnightly, quarterly, annually, and triennially, three years completing a volume.

Volume 1 preceded by Supplement: Synopsis of important events, 1918 (end of World War)–1931 (June), 35p.

Schulthess' Europäischer Geschichtskalender, 1861- . München, Beck, 1861- . v.1- . Annual. **V43**

Imprint varies, title varies.
Chronological survey by countries of the year's events.

Survey of international affairs, ed. by Arnold J. Toynbee. 1920/23- . Lond., Ox. Univ. Pr., 1925- . v.1- and 3 suppl. v. Price per v., 12s. 6d.–25s.; $4.25–$13. **V44**

Published under auspices of the Royal Institute of International Affairs.

Annual surveys of world politics and history, except that the first volume covers four years instead of one. Some years include extra volumes on special subjects. 1920/23–1927 issues contain appendixes of documents, but these are replaced (1928-) by the separate set, *Documents*, listed below (V45).

—— Consolidated index, 1920–1930 and supplementary volumes. Lond., Ox. Univ. Pr., 1932. 214p.

Indexes material in the *Survey* 1920–30, the *Documents*, 1928–30, and in the following supplements: *The world after the peace conference* and *The conduct of British Empire foreign relations*, both by A. J. Toynbee.

Documents on international affairs, 1928- . Lond., Ox. Univ. Pr., 1929- . v.1- . Annual. Price per v., 12s. 6d.–25s.; $5–$14. **V45**

"Prepared to accompany and supplement the annual *Survey of international affairs.*"

—— [Supplement] *Norway and the war*, Sept. 1939–Dec. 1940, ed. by Monica Curtis. Lond., Ox. Univ. Pr., 1941. 154p.

Atlases

For historical atlases of particular countries *see* the name of the country; for ancient history *see* Classical Antiquities p.484.

Treharne, Reginald Francis. Bibliography of historical atlases and hand-maps for use in schools. Lond., pub. for the Historical Assoc. by Bell, 1939. 24p. 21cm. (Historical Association pamphlet, no.114)   **V46**

A useful annotated bibliography listing historical atlases in various languages with pertinent comment.

Bartholomew, John George. Literary and historical atlas. Lond., Dent; N.Y., Dutton, 1913–36. 4v. 17cm. 2s. 6d. ea.   **V47**

A series of four small atlases, not volumed to form a set. Contents: Literary and historical atlas of Europe, 1936; America, 1930; Africa and Australasia, 1913; Asia, 1913.

Good, cheap atlases, each containing historical maps, plans of battles, a gazetteer of places having a literary or historical interest, and an account and plates of the coinage of the region.

Cambridge modern history atlas, ed. by A. W. Ward, G. W. Prothero, Stanley Leathes, assisted by E. A. Benians. 2d ed. Camb., Univ. Pr.; N.Y., Macmillan, 1926. 229p. 141 maps. 24cm. 40s.; $12.   **V48**

(1) Introduction (General survey of European territory, with marginal references to maps); (2) Index of local names in Introduction; (3) Maps; (4) Index to maps, including names of places, tribes and clans.

Covers period 1490–1910, inclusive. Published separately and also as volume 14 of the *Cambridge modern history* (V90).

Droysen, G. Allgemeiner historischer Handatlas. Leipzig, Velhagen, 1886. 88p., 92p. 103 col. maps. 43cm. o.p.   **V49**

Text at end. One of the best historical atlases.

March of man. . . . American eds., Albert Bushnell Hart and Isaac J. Cox. N.Y., Chic., and Lond., Encyclopaedia Britannica [1935]. 30cm.   **V50**

Includes an historical atlas which differs little from Muir and McElroy, *Putnam's Historical atlas* (*see* V51), though there are certain variations in cartography, some maps have been added, notably a section on ancient history, and some dropped. The index is fuller than in *Putnam's.*

For full description *see* V30.

Muir, Ramsay and **Philip, George** (with McElroy, R.) Philip's Historical atlas, ancient, medieval and modern. Lond., Philip, 1938. [n.p.] 19s. 6d.   **V51**

Covers 1500 B.C. to 1927 A.D.

Formed by combining *Philip's Atlas of ancient and classical history* (1935, 5s.) with *Philip's Historical atlas, medieval and modern* (1927, 16s.), omitting four duplicated plates.

These may be purchased separately. Both are very good atlases for college work.

The medieval and modern section was published in the United States as *Putnam's Historical atlas, medieval and modern* (N.Y., Putnam, 1927) with some changes and additions.

A good, cheap atlas for school use is *Philip's New school atlas of universal history,* 12th ed. (1935, 210 maps, 6s. 3d.).

Poole, Reginald Lane. Historical atlas of modern Europe, from the decline of the Roman Empire, comprising also maps of parts of Asia, Africa and the new world connected with European history. Ox., Clarendon Pr., 1896–1902. 30 pts. in 1v. 90 maps. 41cm. o.p.   **V52**

An excellent historical atlas, based to some extent on the German atlases of Spruner-Menke (V58) and Droysen (V49) but much fuller for the British Isles; has good maps, each accompanied by text and historical notes (signed), and, in some cases, by a bibliography. Contains 90 maps, distributed as follows: Europe in general, 14; British Isles, 17; various European countries, 39; Eastern Roman Empire, Asia, India, 14; exploration and colonization, 6. No index.

Putzger, Friedrich Wilhelm. Putzgers Historischer Schul-Atlas. Grosse Ausg. 50. Jubiläums-Aufl., bearb. und hrsg. von Max Pehle und Hans Silberborth. Bielefeld, Velhagen, 1931. 15p. 160 maps. 26cm.   **V53**

Robertson, Charles Grant and **Bartholomew, J. G.** Historical atlas of modern Europe, 1789–1922 with an historical and explanatory text. 2d ed., rev. and enl. Ox., Univ. Pr., 1924. 31p. 42 maps. 36cm.   **V54**

Schrader, Franz. Atlas de géographie historique par une réunion de professeurs et de savants . . . Nouv. éd. rev. Paris, Hachette, 1907. [110]p., 32p. incl. il. 55 maps. 38cm.   **V55**

Subtitle: Contenant 55 cartes doubles en couleurs accompagnées au verso d'un texte historique, d'un grand nombre de cartes de détail, figures, diagrammes et d'un index alphabétique d'environ 30,000 noms.

Shepherd, William Robert. Historical atlas. 7th ed., rev. and enl. N.Y., Holt, 1929. 216p., 115p. 26cm.   **V56**

The best of the smaller general historical atlases, covering the period from 1450 B.C. to the present time. Full general index of names.

—— Atlas of medieval and modern history. N.Y., Holt, 1932. 42p. 105 maps on 80p. 26cm. $3.   **V57**

A smaller work than the above, planned for college classes in medieval and modern history. Maps are identical with those in the *Historical atlas* (V56) but include European history only, omitting American maps. Covers 150 A.D. to 1929.

Spruner von Merz, Karl. Spruner-Menke. Handatlas für die Geschichte des Mittelalters und der neueren Zeit. 3. Aufl. neu bearb. von Th. Menke. Gotha, Perthes, 1880. 42p. 90 double maps. 39cm. o.p. **V58**

ARCHAEOLOGY AND PREHISTORY

Bibliography

Archäologisches Institut des Deutschen Reichs. Römische Zweiganstalt. Bibliothek. Katalog der Bibliothek des Kaiserlich deutschen archäologischen Instituts in Rom, von August Mau . . . Neu bearb. von Eugen von Mercklin und Friedrich Matz. Rome, Löscher, 1913–32. 2v. in 4. **V59**

Volume 1, issued in two parts, 1913–14, includes works published before 1911; volume 2 in two parts, 1932, works published before 1925.

—— —— 1. Supplement; Ergänzungen zu Band I für die Jahre 1911–1925, bearb. von Friedrich Matz. Berlin, de Gruyter, 1930. 516p.

—— Archäologische Bibliographie, 1913- ; Beilage zum Jahrbuch des Deutschen archäologischen Instituts. . . . Berlin, de Gruyter, 1914- . Annual. **V60**

1944–1948 published in one volume, 1950. 350p.

A very useful bibliography of books and periodical articles, broad in scope and international in coverage.

See also L'Année philologique (R803) for references to archaeological material.

Encyclopedias and handbooks

Dechelette, Joseph. Manuel d'archéologie préhistorique celtique et gallo-romaine. Paris, Picard, 1908–34. v.1-6, and apx. to v.2 in 2v. il. **V61**

v.1, Archéologie préhistorique. 1908; v.2, Archéologie celtique ou Protohistorique: Age du bronze. 1910; apx. to v.2, 2v.; v.3, Premier age du fer, ou Époque de Hallstatt. 1927; v.4, Second age du fer, ou Époque de La Tène. 1927; v.5-6, Manuel d'archéologie gallo-romaine, par Albert Grenier: pt.1, Généralités. Travaux militaires, pt.2, Archéologie du sol. 1931–34.

Ebert, Max. Reallexikon der Vorgeschichte, unter Mitwirkung zahlreicher Fachgelehrter hrsg. von Max Ebert. Berlin, de Gruyter, 1924–32. 15v. il. **V62**

v.1-14, A-Z; v.15, Register.
Signed articles by specialists, bibliographies, many illustrations.

Gay, Victor. Glossaire archéologique du moyen âge et de la renaissance. Paris, Soc. Bibliograph., 1887; Picard, 1928. 2v. il. **V63**

Volume 2 has title: Glossaire archéologique . . . par Victor Gay, texte revu et complété par Henri Stein, illustration dirigée par Marcel Aubert.

Handbuch der Archäeologie im Rahmen des Handbuchs der Altertumswissenschaft . . . hrsg. von Walter Otto. Munich, Beck, 1939- . (Müller, I. P. E. Handbuch der Altertumswissenschaft. 6. Abt.) **V64**

1. Textband. 873p.; 1. Tafelband. 204pl.

Schrader, Otto. Reallexikon der indogermanischen Altertumskunde. Grundzüge einer kultur- und völkergeschichtliche Alteuropas. 2. verm. u. umgearb. Aufl. Berlin, de Gruyter, 1917–26. 2v. **V65**

CLASSICAL ANTIQUITIES

See also Classical Languages, p.423-27.

Dictionaries and encyclopedias

Lübker, Friedrich. Reallexikon des klassischen Altertums. 8. vollst. umgearb. Aufl. hrsg. von J. Geffcken und E. Ziebarth. Leipzig, Teubner, 1914. 1152p. il. **V66**

Useful one-volume dictionary. Does not contain proper names.

Oxford classical dictionary, ed. by M. Cary, A. D. Nock [and others]. Ox., Clarendon Pr., 1949. 971p. **V67**

A scholarly dictionary with signed articles "designed to cover the same ground, though on a different scale, as the well-known dictionary by Sir William Smith." Covers biography, literature, mythology, philosophy, religion, science, geography, etc. Most of the articles are brief but there are also longer survey articles, e.g., Rome, music, scholarship, etc. Bibliographies are appended to most articles, usually limited to a few of the best works on the subject, in English and foreign languages. Bibliographies for the articles on the great classical writers usually include texts, commentaries, translations, lexicons, style, life, criticism, etc.

Unfortunately pronunciation is not indicated.

Peck, Harry Thurston. Harper's Dictionary of classical literature and antiquities. N.Y., Harper, 1897. 1701p. il. $8. **V68**

A popular work, useful for ready reference because it gives articles on topics in classical antiquities, biography, mythology, geography, art, history, etc., in one alphabet. Concise articles, brief bibliographies, good illustrations.

Smith, *Sir* William. Dictionary of Greek and Roman biography and mythology. Lond., Murray; Bost., Little, 1880. 3v. il. **V69**

A one-volume work based on this, but with some revisions, was edited by G. E. Marindin and published as *Classical dictionary of Greek and Roman biography* (Lond., Murray, 1894. 1018p.).

—— **Wayte, William** and **Marindin, G. E.** Dictionary of Greek and Roman antiquities, 3d ed., rev. and enl. Lond., Murray; Bost., Little, 1890–91. 2v. il. o.p. **V70**

1st ed., 1842. For many years a standard work and still useful for topics not affected by recent research, although for important work it is inferior to the great French and German dictionaries listed below.

A concise dictionary of Greek and Roman antiquities, edited by F. Warre Cornish (Lond., Murray, 1898. 829p.) is based on the larger work and incorporates some later information.

All of these works by Sir William Smith have been issued in many editions and reprints. Although now much out of date they are still very useful.

Walters, Henry Beauchamp. Classical dictionary of Greek and Roman antiquities, biography, geography, and mythology. Camb., Univ. Pr., 1916. 1103p. il. o.p. **V71**

❧ The dictionaries listed above are a few of the best authorities in English and are satisfactory for ordinary questions. There are also various other older works frequently found in libraries which may still be useful. The best foreign classical dictionaries are, however, superior to anything in English and should be used for scholarly reference work, for very detailed information, for full bibliographies, especially for reference work for graduate students in university libraries. The best foreign works are the French dictionary of Daremberg and Saglio (V72) and the German *Pauly-Wissowa* (V73). These two differ in scope and up-to-dateness but are about equal in authority.

Daremberg, Charles and **Saglio, Edmond.** Dictionnaire des antiquités grecques et romaines d'après les textes et les monuments. Paris, Hachette, 1873–1919. 5v. and index. il. **V72**

v.1-5, A-Z; separate index v., 166p.

A work of the highest authority, with long, signed articles by specialists and very detailed bibliographical references. Covers public and private life, manners and customs, institutions, arts, sciences, industries, religion, costume, furniture, military affairs, money, weights and measures, etc. Does not include biography and literature. Indexes of authors, Greek words, Latin words, and subjects.

Pauly, August Friedrich von. Pauly's Real-Encyclopädie der classischen Altertumswissenschaft; neue Bearb. begonnen von Georg Wissowa, unter Mitwirkungzahlreicher Fachgenossen hrsg. von Wilhelm Kroll und Karl Mittelhaus. Stuttgart, Metzler, 1894–1949. v.1-18$^{1-3}$, 19-20. 2. Reihe [v.1-7$^{1-2}$] also 7 suppl. v. maps. (In progress) **V73**

Bd.1-18$^{1-3}$, 19-20, A-Parant, Pech-Pignus; 2. Reihe (R-Z) [Bd.1-7$^{1-2}$] S-Tyr. Suppl.: (1) A-Dem.; (2) Herodes-Herodotos; (3) A-Juglandem; (4) A-Ledon; (5) A-Statilius; (6) A-Th; (7) A-Tr.

Volumes not published in straight alphabetical sequence but in two series.

The standard German work, covering the whole field of classical literature, history, antiquities, biography, etc. Long, signed articles by specialists, with bibliographies. Generally cited as *Pauly-Wissowa;* in German references sometimes cited as R.E.

Bd.15^{2}: mit Register der in Band 1-15 der ersten Reihe, Band 1-4 der zweiten Reihe und der Supplementbänden 1-5 enthaltenen Nachträge und Berichtigungen.

Manuals and source books

Botsford, George Willis and **Sihler, E. G.** Hellenic civilization. N.Y., Columbia Univ. Pr., 1915. 719p. (Records of civilization: Sources and studies, ed. by J. T. Shotwell) $4.50. **V74**

Source book with useful bibliographies.

Jones, Henry Stuart. Companion to Roman history. Ox., Clarendon Pr., 1912. 472p. il. 7s. 6d.; $7. **V75**

Laurand, Louis. Manuel des études grecques et latines. Paris, Picard, 1938–49. 4v. il. **V76**

Contents: t.1, Grèce. fasc. 1-3. 1939; t.2, Rome. fasc. 4-6. 1938; t.3, Compléments, atlas, tables. (fasc. 7) et appendices; t.4, Pour mieux comprendre l'antiquité classique.

Paged continuously. Arranged as a syllabus with bibliographies. Fasicules have appeared in various editions since 1914–19.

Volume 4 is a second edition of the supplement published in 1936 with the same title.

Sandys, *Sir* John Edwin. Companion to Latin studies. 3d ed. Camb., Univ. Pr.; N.Y., Macmillan, 1925. 891p. il. 25s.; $7.50. **V77**

1st ed. 1910; 2d ed. 1913.

Whibley, Leonard. Companion to Greek studies. 4th ed., rev. Camb., Univ. Pr., 1931. 790p. il. $8; 25s. **V78**

1st ed. 1905; 3d ed. 1916.

The two works by Sandys and Whibley are prepared on the same plan and similarly arranged. Each consists of a series of articles, by specialists, on topics of importance to the student of Greek and Roman history and literature, such as geography, ethnology, flora, science, chronology, coins, ships, buildings, population, slavery, etc. Articles are adequate, with useful bibliographies, and each volume has four indexes: (1) persons, deities and races; (2) places, rivers and mountains; (3) scholars and modern writers; (4) Latin (or Greek) words and phrases. Very useful as supplementing the various classical dictionaries.

❧ In addition to the above the worker in the university or large reference library will often need to refer to Iwan Müller's *Handbuch der Altertumswissenschaft* (Nördlingen, Beck), a series of scholarly treatises on subjects in classical literature, antiquities, etc., the various volumes of which have appeared in many different editions. Some of the volumes are the most comprehensive and definitive works in their fields, others are much briefer.

Atlases

Grundy, George Beardoe. Murray's Small classical atlas. 2d ed. Lond., Murray, 1917. xxiiip. 14 double maps. 36cm. $4.　　　　　　**V80**

Kiepert, Henry. Atlas antiquus; twelve maps of the ancient world for schools and colleges. Chic., Rand, McNally, 1900. 27p. 12 maps. 37cm. **V81**
Frequent reissues. Originally published in German.

Shepherd, William Robert. Atlas of ancient history. N.Y., Holt, 1913. 24p., 43p. 25cm.　**V82**

General histories

Cambridge ancient history. . . . Camb., Univ. Pr.; N.Y., Macmillan, 1923–39. 12v. and 5v. plates. maps. Price per v. varies, some v. o.p.
　　　　　　　　　　　　　　　　　　V83

v.1, Egypt and Babylonia to 1580 B.C.; v.2, Egyptian and Hittite empires to ca. 1000 B.C.; v.3, Assyrian empire; v.4, Persian empire and the West; v.5, Athens; v.6, Macedon; v.7, The Hellenistic monarchies and the rise of Rome; v.8, Rome and the Mediterranean, 218-133 B.C.; v.9, Roman Republic, 133-44 B.C.; v.10, Augustan Empire, 44 B.C.—A.D. 70; v.11, Imperial peace, A.D. 70-192; v.12, Imperial crisis and recovery, A.D. 193-324.
v.1-6 ed. by J. B. Bury, S. A. Cook, and F. E. Adcock; v.7-11 ed. by S. A. Cook, F. E. Adcock and M. P. Charlesworth; v.12 ed. by S. A. Cook, F. E. Adcock, M. P. Charlesworth and N. H. Baynes.
Excellent reference history, each chapter written by a specialist, with full bibliographies at end of each volume. The volumes of plates contain illustrations without comment.

MEDIEVAL AND MODERN HISTORY
Bibliographies and guides

American Council of Learned Societies devoted to Humanistic Studies. Committee on Renaissance Studies. Surveys of recent scholarship in the period of Renaissance. 1st ser. [Providence] 1945. v.p.　　　　　　　　　　　**V84**
"Published in various journals during . . . 1940–44."—*Pref.*
Bibliographical footnotes.
Contents: 1st ser.: Introduction, by L. B. Wright; Science, by F. R. Johnson and S. V. Larkey; Neo-Latin literature, by D. C. Allen; German literature, by J. G. Kunstmann; French literature, by S. F. Will; English literature, by Rosemond Tuve; Philosophy, by P. O. Kristeller and J. H. Randall, Jr.; Economic history, by F. L. Nussbaum; Political theory, by Felix Gilbert; The

Catholic Church, by R. M. Huber; The German Reformation, by Wilhelm Pauck; Classical and Biblical scholarship, by R. H. Bainton and D. P. Lockwood; Music, by C. S. Smith and William Dinneen.

Chevalier, Cyr Ulysse. Répertoire des sources historiques du moyen âge. Nouv. éd. refóndu, corr. et augm. Paris, Picard, 1894–1907. 2v. in 4.
　　　　　　　　　　　　　　　　　　V85
Publisher varies.
Contents: Bio-bibliographie, nouv. éd.; refondue, corr. et considérablement augm. 1905–07. 2v.; Topobibliographie, 1894–1903. 2v.
Of first importance for the literature of medieval history, the first part is arranged alphabetically by personal name (in the French form), the second by place and topic. Under each name references are given to sources. An immense mass of material is indexed but with no critical indication of value. For further information on the bio-bibliographical section *see* S3.

Paetow, Louis John. Guide to the study of medieval history . . . rev. ed. prepared under the auspices of the Mediaeval Academy of America. N.Y., Crofts, 1931. 643p. $6.　　　　　　**V86**
1st ed. 1917. 552p.
The most useful general guide to the literature of medieval history. Includes topical outlines and special recommendations for reading as well as bibliographies of original sources and secondary works. Critical and scholarly.

Potthast, August. Bibliotheca historica Medii Aevi. Wegweiser durch die Geschichtswerke des europäischen Mittelalters bis 1500. 2. verb. und verm. Aufl. Berlin, Weber, 1896. 2v.　　　**V87**
Subtitle: Vollständiges Inhaltsverzeichnis zu Acta Sanctorum Boll., Bouquet, Migne, Monum. Germ. Hist., Muratori, Rerum Britann. Scriptores, etc.
An indispensable work, though incomplete and sometimes inaccurate, listing medieval chronicles and analyzing many of the large source collections as indicated in the subtitle. The second part is an alphabetical list of medieval writers with, when possible, characterizing phrase and dates indicating manuscripts, editions and commentaries.

Progress of medieval and renaissance studies in the United States and Canada. Boulder, Colo., 1923- .　　　　　　　　　　　　**V88**
An annual survey. For full record *see* R8.

General histories

Cambridge mediaeval history, planned by J. B. Bury. . . . Camb., Univ. Pr.; N.Y., Macmillan, 1911–36. 8v. maps. v.1-2, $6.50 ea.; v.3-8, $9.50 ea.　　　　　　　　　　　　　　　**V89**
v.1, The Christian Roman empire and the foundation of the Teutonic kingdoms. 2d ed. 1924; v.2, Rise of the Saracens and the foundation of the Western empire; v.3, Germany and the Western empire; v.4, Eastern Roman empire; v.5, Contest of empire and papacy; v.6, Victory of the papacy; v.7, Decline of empire and papacy; v.8, Close of the middle ages.

Another excellent reference history written by specialists with full bibliographies at the end of each volume, similar to V83 and V90.

Cambridge modern history, planned by the late Lord Acton, ed. by A. W. Ward, G. W. Prothero, Stanley Leathes. Camb., Univ. Pr.; N.Y., Macmillan, 1902–26. 13v. and Atlas. v.1-13, £16 5s.; $6.75 ea. Atlas, 2d ed., 1926. 40s.; $14. **V90**

Cheaper reprint of v.1-13, text only, without the bibliographies, 1934, $32.

v.1, Renaissance; v.2, Reformation; v.3, Wars of religion; v.4, Thirty Years' War; v.5, Age of Louis XIV; v.6, Eighteenth century; v.7, United States; v.8, French Revolution; v.9, Napoleon; v.10, Restoration; v.11, Growth of nationalities; v.12, Latest age; v.13, Genealogical tables and general index; v.14, Atlas.

Contents of v.13: (1) pt.1, Genealogical tables of ruling and royal houses—British Empire, France, Empire and Austria, Netherlands, Italy, Spain, Portugal and Brazil, Sweden and Norway, Denmark, Poland, Hungary and Transylvania, Russia, Turkey, Balkan states, The East; pt.2, List of spiritual princes, elected sovereigns, etc.; pt.3, List of Parliaments, presidents, governors of colonies, general councils, secularized bishoprics, leagues, alliances, universities since 1450, etc.; (2) General index, p.207-542.

The most important general modern history, useful for reference purposes because of its high authority, bibliographies, its detailed general index and the miscellaneous tables included in the index volume.

UNITED STATES

Guides

Hockett, Homer Carey. Introduction to research in American history. 2d ed. with corrections and appendix. N.Y., Macmillan, 1948. 179p. $2.75. **V91**

A manual treating: Gathering of data; Criticism of data; Historical composition; Bibliography.

The second edition differs from the first (1931) only in the addition of an Appendix, p.169-79, which includes notes, comments, and corrections; a supplementary bibliography (of nine titles); and a Synopsis of historical criticism.

Bibliography

See also United States, p.19-23.

Beers, Henry Putney. Bibliographies in American history; guide to materials for research. N.Y., Wilson, 1942. 487p. $4.75. **V92**

"Published January 1938. Revised edition March 1942."

A classified list of over 11,000 bibliographies including separate works, analytics, compilations in progress and manuscript bibliographies, with author and subject index.

Covers many aspects of American history including political, diplomatic, religious, cultural, local, etc.

Bemis, Samuel Flagg and **Griffin, Grace Gardner.** Guide to the diplomatic history of the United States, 1775–1921. Wash., Govt. Prt. Off., 1935. 979p. $2.50. **V93**

An important bibliography and guide to printed works and manuscript sources, in two main parts: pt.1, Bibliography, p.3-779, listing 5318 items, with comment; pt.2, Remarks on the sources, p.781-942, including manuscript sources. Indexes of: Collections of personal papers, p.943-45; Authors, p.946-79.

Carnegie Institution, Washington. [Guides to manuscript materials for the history of the United States] Wash., Carnegie Inst., 1906–43. 23v. Price varies. **V94**

Contents: *American:* Guide to the archives of the government of the United States in Washington, by C. H. VanTyne and W. G. Leland. rev. ed. 1907. 327p.; Diplomatic archives of the Department of State, 1789–1840, by A. C. McLaughlin. rev. ed. 1906. 73p.; Inventory of unpublished material for American religious history in Protestant church archives and other repositories, by W. H. Allison. 1911. 254p.; Calendar of papers in Washington archives relating to the territories of the United States, by D. W. Parker. 1911. 476p.

British and British American: Guide to the manuscript materials for the history of the United States to 1783 in the British Museum, in minor London archives and in libraries of Oxford and Cambridge, by C. M. Andrews and F. G. Davenport. 1908. 499p.; Guide to the materials for American history, to 1783, in the Public Record Office of Great Britain, by C. M. Andrews: v.1, State papers, v.2, Departmental and miscellaneous papers, 1912–14. 2v.; Guide to materials in London archives . . . since 1783, by C. O. Paullin and F. L. Paxon. 1914. 642p.; Guide to British West Indian archive material in London and in the Islands, by H. C. Bell and D. W. Parker. 1926. 435p.; Guide to materials in Canadian archives, by D. W. Parker. 1913. 339p.

European (except Spanish): List of manuscripts concerning American history preserved in European libraries and noted in their published catalogues and similar printed lists, by D. M. Matteson. 1925. 203p.; Guide to the manuscript materials relating to American history in German state archives, by M. D. Learned. 1912. 352p.; Guide to materials for American history in the libraries and archives of Paris, by W. G. Leland. 1932–43. v.1-2; Guide to the materials for American history in Roman and other Italian archives, by C. R. Fish. 1911. 289p.; Guide to materials for American history in Russian archives, by F. A. Golder. 1917–37. 2v.; Guide to the materials for American history in Swiss and Austrian archives, by A. B. Faust. 1916. 299p.

Spanish and Spanish American: Guide to materials for American history in Cuban archives, by L. M. Perez. 1907. 142p.; Descriptive catalogue of the documents relating to the history of the United States in the Papeles Procedentes de Cuba, deposited in the Archivo General de Indias at Seville, by R. R. Hill. 1916. 594p.; Guide to materials for the history of the United States in the principal archives of Mexico, by H. E. Bolton. 1913. 553p.; List of documents in Spanish archives . . . which have been printed or of which transcripts are preserved in American libraries, by J. A. Robertson. 1910. 368p.; Guide to the materials . . . in Spanish archives, by W. R. Shepherd. 1907. 107p.

Channing, Edward, Hart, A. B. and **Turner, F. I.** Guide to the study and reading of American history. Rev. and augm. ed. Bost., Ginn, 1912. 650p. o.p.   **V95**

1st ed., 1896. A classified bibliography with author, title and subject index, not up to date but still useful as a guide to the best reading on all periods and aspects of the history of the United States. The last edition covers to 1910.

Greene, Evarts Boutell and **Morris, Richard B.** A guide to the principal sources for early American history (1600–1800) in the city of New York. N.Y., Columbia Univ. Pr., 1929. 357p. $7.50. **V96**

A guide to manuscript and printed sources not including secondary works.

Griffin, Appleton Prentiss Clark. Bibliography of American historical societies (the United States and the Dominion of Canada). 2d ed. rev. and enl. Wash., Govt. Prt. Off., 1907. 1374p. (In Amer. Hist. Assoc. Annual report, 1905. v.2)   **V97**

A useful index to material in the various publications of American historical societies, general and local, to 1905. Arranged by societies, with full contents of each volume and with two alphabetical indexes to the contents: (1) Authors and subjects index, (2) Biographical index. Continued, informally in the *Annual magazine subject index* (E73), and for material published 1906 on, by the analytical indexing in *Writings on American history* (V101).

Larned Josephus Nelson. The literature of American history, a bibliographical guide. Bost., Amer. Lib. Assoc. Pub. Bd., 1902. 596p. and suppl. v., 37p. o.p.   **V98**

An important annotated bibliography, not up to date but still useful for its indication of source material, for its selection of titles and for its critical notes which were prepared by specialists and are signed. The preliminary sections on original sources, colonial records, etc., are especially useful in a research library. Appendixes include selected lists for (1) a school library, (2) a larger town library, (3) a good working library. Classified, with alphabetical author and subject index.

U. S. Library of Congress. Division of Manuscripts. Guide to manuscripts relating to American history in British depositories reproduced for the Division of Manuscripts of the Library of Congress. Grace Gardner Griffin, ed. Wash., Govt. Prt. Off., 1946. 313p. $1.25.   **V99**

A record of reproductions in the Library of Congress, arranged by the library or other depository where the original is located; classified exactly as in the original depository. Detailed index.

The United States, 1865–1900; a survey of current literature, with abstracts of unpublished dissertations, ed. by Curtis Wiswell Garrison. v.1-3, Sept. 1941–Dec. 1944. Fremont, Ohio, Rutherford B. Hayes—Lucy Webb Hayes Foundation, 1943–45. v.1-3. $1 ea.   **V100**

Signed critiques of books and abstracts of periodical articles on history and life in the United States, 1865–1900, "appraised primarily as to . . . contribution to knowledge." Classed arrangement; contents of volumes vary slightly. Volume 3 includes such class headings as political and constitutional, international relations, social and economic, educational and intellectual, religion, literature and art, regional and state; textbooks, surveys and popular histories; abstracts of unpublished dissertations; indexes.

Writings on American history, 1902–[03] . . . books and articles on United States history published during the year 1902 and [1903], with some memoranda on other portions of America. . . . Princeton, N.J., Lib. Bk. Store, 1904; Wash., Carnegie Inst., 1905. 2v.   **V101**

1902 compiled by E. C. Richardson and A. E. Morse; 1903 compiled by A. C. McLaughlin, W. A. Slade and E. D. Lewis.

Writings on American history, 1906- . A bibliography of books and articles on United States history published during the years 1906- . comp. by Grace Gardner Griffin [and others]. N.Y., 1908–10; Wash., 1911–13; New Haven, 1914–19; Wash., 1921- . v.1- . Price varies; recent v., $1.75 ea. (In progress)   **V102**

Publisher varies: volumes 13 on, published as supplements or volume 2 of the *Annual report* of the American Historical Association for 1918 on.

Subtitle varies: 1906–1935, a bibliography of books and articles on United States and Canadian history . . . with some memoranda on other portions of America.

An excellent annual bibliography and index. Through 1935, included all books and articles, wherever published, which contained anything of value on the history of the United States and British North America, and all books published in the United States or Europe on Latin America and the Pacific islands.

Beginning with 1936 the scope was changed to include only writings on the history of the United States and its outlying possessions, omitting Canada and Latin America except for material dealing with the history of diplomatic relations of the United States and these countries and for the colonial history of those sections of the United States which were formerly a part of the overseas empire of Spain.

A classified arrangement, with author, title and subject index. Includes many contents and descriptive notes and refers to critical reviews. Indexes nearly 500 American and foreign periodicals.

The 1939/40 volume was the last volume to be prepared by Grace Gardner Griffin. The next volume, to cover 1948, is being prepared by James R. Masterson. If 1941–1947 are covered later it will probably be in abbreviated or condensed form.—Cf. *American historical review,* Oct. 1949, p.260.

Meynen, Emil. Bibliographie des Deutschtums der kolonialzeitlichen Einwanderung in Nordamerika, insbesondere der Pennsylvanien-Deutschen und ihrer Nachkommen, 1683–1933. Leipzig, Harrassowitz, 1937. 636p.   **V103**

Added title page: Bibliography on German settlements

in Colonial North America, especially on the Pennsylvania Germans and their descendants, 1683–1933.

Classified, with indexes of authors and surnames.

Regional

See Beers, *Bibliographies in American history* (V92), for bibliographies of individual states and specific regions, e.g., New England, Northwest, Southwest, South, etc.

Logasa, Hannah. Regional United States; a subject list. Bost., Faxon, 1942. 71p. (Useful reference ser., no.69) $2. **V104**

A selected subject list of books on regions of the United States, including fiction, travel, biography, memoirs, poetry, essays, short stories, etc., chosen as far as possible from material usually available in middle-sized libraries.

Peterson, Clarence Stewart. Bibliography of county histories of the 3111 counties in the 48 states. Balt., Author, Box 611, 1946. 126 numb. l. $2.75. **V105**

"Prepared in 1935 (2982 counties). First revision, 1944 (3050 counties). Second revision, 1946."

Societies

American Association for State and Local History. Historical societies in the United States and Canada. A handbook comp. and ed. by Christopher Crittenden, and Doris Godard. Wash., Assoc., 1944. 261p. $2.50; $1.75 to members. **V106**

Earlier edition published in 1936 listed 583 organizations, this lists 904. National and general societies are followed by local societies arranged by states.

Dunlap, Leslie Whittaker. American historical societies, 1790–1860. . . . Madison, Wis., priv. pr., 1944. 238p. $3.50. **V107**

Part 1 is a history of American historical societies before the Civil War with many bibliographical footnotes. Part 2 includes sketches describing the 65 societies organized within this period.

Dictionaries and handbooks

Dictionary of American history; James Truslow Adams, ed.-in-chief, R. V. Coleman, managing ed. 2d ed. rev. N.Y., Scribner, 1942. 5v. and index. $60. **V108**

v.1-5, A-Z; index, 258p. 1st ed. 1940; 2d ed. shows practically no change.

In general consists of brief, clear, compact articles each dealing with a separate and definite aspect of American history and each signed with full name of contributor. There are also a number of covering articles on broader subjects which include cross references to related articles on specific aspects.

Covers political, economic, social, industrial and cultural history but omits biography as this is considered the province of the *Dictionary of American biography* (S32). However, the activities of prominent persons may frequently be traced through the references under their names in the analytical index.

Includes many catchwords and popular names of bills and laws, etc., e.g., Hawley-Smoot act, Wade-Davis bill. There are numerous cross references, both in the covering articles and in the main alphabet.

The bibliographies are usually very brief, in most cases consisting of two or three items chosen "so far as possible, with a view to accessibility in the average library. References do not include volumes, chapters or page numbers if the subject may easily be found in the work referred to; but in those cases in which there might be difficulty, exact citations are provided." Author and title only are given, without place, publisher, date or number of volumes.

Dyer, Frederick Henry. Compendium of the war of the rebellion, comp. and arranged from official records of the Federal and Confederate armies, reports of the adjutant generals of the several states, the army registers, and other reliable documents and sources. Des Moines, Iowa, Dyer, 1908. 1796p. o.p. **V109**

pt.1, Number and organization of the armies of the United States; pt.2, Chronological record of the campaigns, battles, engagements, actions, combats, sieges, skirmishes, etc., in the United States, 1861 to 1865; pt.3, Regimental histories.

Harper's Encyclopaedia of United States history from 458 A.D. to 1912. New ed. entirely rev. and enl. based on the plan of B. J. Lossing. N.Y., Harper, 1912. 10v. il. **V110**

1st ed., 1902. This edition adds considerable new material on names and events since 1901. For popular use.

Harper's Popular cyclopaedia of United States history by Benson J. Lossing (new ed. N.Y., Harper, 1890 [c'81]. 2v.) was an early edition of this work.

Jameson, John Franklin. Dictionary of United States history; alphabetical, chronological, statistical, from the earliest explorations to the present time; based upon the original work prepared in 1893 by J. F. Jameson. Rev. ed. under the supervision of Albert E. McKinley. Phila., Hist. Pub. Co., 1931. 874p. $9.50. **V111**

Contents: Dictionary, p.1-569; Territorial development, p.571-591; Chronology, p.593-705; Analytical section, p.707-874.

U. S. General Staff. Second Section. American campaigns, by M. F. Steele. Wash., B. S. Adams, 1909. 731p. and atlas of xiip., 311 maps. (Its Pub. 13) o.p. **V112**

v.1, Text; v.2, Maps. Covers the period from the Colonial wars to the Spanish-American war.

White's Conspectus of American biography; a tabulated record of American history and biography. 2d ed. N.Y., White, 1937. 455p. $15. **V113**

Includes many chronological lists of office holders of various kinds, e.g., presidents, cabinet members, delegates to colonial and continental congresses, congressmen, ambassadors, governors, etc.

For full description *see* S35.

General histories

American nation: A history from original sources by associated scholars, ed. by Albert Bushnell Hart. . . . N.Y. and Lond., Harper, 1904–18. 28v. maps. $2.25 per v. **V114**

A standard history, each volume by a different author; its special reference features are the bibliography of sources and secondary works given at the end of each volume and the detailed separate index volume, volume 28 (first numbered 27).

Pageant of America; a pictorial history of the United States. Ralph Henry Gabriel, ed. New Haven, Yale Univ. Pr., 1925–29. 15v. il. Sold by subscription. **V115**

v.1, Adventures in the wilderness, by Clark Wissler, C. L. Skinner, William Wood; v.2, Lure of the frontier, by R. H. Gabriel; v.3, Toilers of land and sea, by R. H. Gabriel; v.4, March of commerce, by Malcolm Keir; v.5, Epic of industry, by Malcolm Keir; v.6, Winning of freedom, by William Wood and R. H. Gabriel; v.7, In defense of liberty, by William Wood and R. H. Gabriel; v.8, Builders of the Republic, by F. A. Ogg; v.9, Makers of a new nation, by J. S. Basset; v.10, American idealism, by L. A. Weigle; v.11, American spirit in letters, by S. T. Williams; v.12, American spirit in art, by F. J. Mather, Jr., C. R. Morey, William Henderson; v.13, American spirit in architecture, by T. F. Hamlin; v.14, American stage, by O. S. Coad and Edwin Mims, Jr.; v.15, Annals of American sport, by J. A. Krout.

Winsor, Justin. Narrative and critical history of America. . . . Bost., Houghton, 1884–89. 8v. il. **V116**

An older work still of reference importance for its many illustrations, maps, and especially its full bibliographical notes.

Source books

Commager, Henry Steele. Documents of American history. 5th ed. N.Y., Appleton-Century-Crofts, 1949. 450p., 759p. (Crofts American history ser.) $5. **V117**

This edition includes documents down to the North Atlantic Treaty, April 1949.

MacDonald, William. Select charters and other documents illustrative of American history, 1606–1775, ed. with notes. N.Y. and Lond., Macmillan, 1899. 401p. o.p. **V118**

—— Select documents illustrative of the history of the United States, 1776–1861, ed. with notes. N.Y. and Lond., Macmillan, 1898. 465p. $2.25. **V119**

—— Select statutes and other documents illustrative of the history of the United States, 1861–1898, ed. with notes. N.Y. and Lond., Macmillan, 1903. 442p. $2.25. **V120**

—— Documentary source book of American history, 1606–1926. 3d ed., rev. and enl. N.Y., Macmillan, 1926. 713p. $4. **V121**

Morison, Samuel Eliot. Sources and documents illustrating the American Revolution, 1764–1788, and the formation of the federal constitution. 2d ed. Ox., Clarendon Pr., 1929. 378p. $4.25; 10s. 6d. **V122**

Atlases

Adams, James Truslow. Atlas of American history; James Truslow Adams, ed.-in-chief; R. V. Coleman, managing ed. N.Y., Scribner, 1943. 360p. incl. maps. 26cm. $10. **V123**

Pages [1]-[296] numbered as plates 1-147.

A useful and usable atlas designed to accompany and supplement the *Dictionary of American history* (V108). Includes 147 black-and-white maps arranged chronologically with an alphabetical index of places mentioned on the maps. Index also has certain groupings such as Portages, Roads, Paths and trails, Boundaries, etc. The maps in their sequence are planned to show growth, expansion, military history, etc., and include, besides the names of places as they existed at the time, battles, roads and trails, railroads, canals, forts and in many cases, although not in all, important routes. This atlas shows little duplication with Paullin, *Atlas of the historical geography of the United States* (V126) or Fox, *Harper's Atlas of American history* (V124).

Fox, Dixon Ryan. Harper's Atlas of American history, selected from the American nation series with map studies. N.Y., Harper, 1920. 180p. maps. 25cm. o.p. **V124**

Lord, Clifford L. and **Lord, Elizabeth H.** Historical atlas of the United States. N.Y., Holt, 1944. 253p. maps. 28cm. $3. **V125**

A useful, inexpensive historical atlas with 312 outline maps mostly in black and white. Supplements but does note replace Paullin (V126) or Adams, *Atlas of American history* (V123). Divided into sections: General maps; Colonial period; 1775–1865; 1865–1941. Maps cover political and economic history including military campaigns, population, transportation, suffrage, education, slavery and abolition, agriculture, forests, labor, manufacturing, natural resources, etc.

Appendixes include statistical tables of population, presidential elections, immigration, imports and exports, railroad mileage, etc. Index of place names and subjects.

Paullin, Charles Oscar. Atlas of the historical geography of the United States, ed. by John K. Wright. [Wash. and N.Y.] Pub. jointly by Carnegie Inst. of Washington and the Amer. Geographical Soc., 1932. 162p. 688 maps. 36cm. [Carnegie Inst. Pub. 401] $15. **V126**

The first adequate atlas of American history with good maps and descriptive text for each; indispensable in any library doing much work in United States history. Maps cover the following main subjects: Natural environment; Cartography, 1492–1867; Indians, 1567–1930; Explorations; Settlement, population and towns, 1650–1790; States, territories and cities, 1790–1930; Population, 1790–1930; Colleges, universities and churches, 1773–1890; Boundaries, 1607–1927; Political parties and opinion, 1788–1930; Political, social and educational reforms, 1775–1931; Industries and transportation, 1620–1931; Foreign commerce, 1701–1929; Distribution of wealth, 1799–1928; Plans of cities, 1775–1803; Military history, 1689–1919; Possessions and territorial claims of the United States, also certain military operations and grounds formerly frequented (ca.1815–1860) by American whalers. Index.

"The first major historical atlas of the United States and probably the most comprehensive work of its kind that has yet been published for any country."—*Introd.* by J. K. Wright, Librarian of the American Geographical Society.

AFGHANISTAN

Akram, Mohammed. Bibliographie analytique de l'Afghanistan. Préface de René Grousset. Paris, Centre de Documentation Universitaire, 1947- . v.1- . **V127**

v.1, Ouvrages parus hors de l'Afghanistan. 504p.

AFRICA

See name of country for history of individual country in Africa.

Bibliography of African bibliographies, rev. to Feb. 1948. Cape Town, So. African Public Lib., 1948. 52p. (Grey bibliographies, no.2) **V128**

Originally compiled by P. Freer and D. H. Varley and published in the *South African libraries*, Oct. 1942 and Jan. 1943. Now revised and edited by A. M. Lewin Robinson.

Includes general, regional and subject bibliographies.

Bruel, Georges. Bibliographie de l'Afrique Equatoriale Française. Paris, Larose, 1914. 326p. **V129**

Fontán Lobé, Juan. Bibliografía colonial; contribucion à un indice de publicaciones africanas. Madrid, "Selecciones Gráficas," 1946. 669p. (Ediciones de la Direccion General de Marruecos y Colonias) **V130**

An alphabetical catalog of nearly 17,000 titles of books and periodical articles in various languages. Particularly rich in Spanish and Portuguese materials. Geographical and subject indexes.

France. État-Major de l'Armée. L'Afrique française du nord. Bibliographie militaire des ouvrages français ou traduits en français et des articles des principles revues françaises relatifs à l'Algérie, à la Tunisie et au Maroc de 1830 à 1926. Paris, Impr. Nat., 1930–35. 4v. **V131**

Joucla, Edmond A. Bibliographie de l'Afrique Occidentale Française. . . . Paris, Soc. d'Éditions Géographiques, Maritimes et Coloniales, 1937. 704p. (Bibliographie générale des colonies françaises par G. Grandidier et E. A. Joucla) **V132**

Lewin, Evans. Annotated bibliography of recent publications on Africa, south of the Sahara, with special reference to administrative, political, economic and sociological problems. Lond., Royal Empire Soc., 1943. 104p. (Royal Empire Soc. bibliographies, no.9) 5s. **V133**

In the main, covers material from 1930–43.

Royal Empire Society, London. Library. Subject catalogue of the library . . . by Evans Lewin. v.1, The British Empire generally, and Africa. [Lond., Society] 1930. 139p., 582p., cxxiiip. **V134**

A comprehensive bibliography of materials about Africa. For description of complete set *see* (V323).

Schnee, Heinrich. Deutsches Kolonial-Lexikon. Leipzig, Quelle [c1920]. 3v. il. **V135**

A very complete encyclopedia of everything about the former German colonies in Africa—their topography, history, biography, natural resources, agriculture, products, native races, religions, flora, fauna, etc. Many excellent illustrations, signed articles, bibliographies.

U. S. Library of Congress. Division of Bibliography. French colonies in Africa; a list of references, comp. by Helen F. Conover. Wash., Govt. Prt. Off., 1942. 89p. **V136**

ALBANIA

See also Balkans, p.491.

Kersopoulos, Jean G. Albanie; ouvrages et articles de revues parus de 1555 à 1934. (In Les Balkans 5:377-424, 651-712, 1934) (Série de bibliographies françaises sur les nations balkaniques, no.1) **V137**

Manek, F., Pekmezi, G. and **Stotz, A.** Albanesische Bibliographie. Wien, Vereines "Dija," 1909. 147p. **V138**

Covers 900–1909.

ARCTIC AND ANTARCTIC

Copenhagen. Marinens Bibliothek. Katalog. København, Levin, 1933–36. 2v. and annual suppl. **V139**

Rich in the field of polar explorations. For full description *see* L303.

Dutilly, Artheme. Bibliography of bibliographies on the Arctic. Wash., Catholic Univ. of America, 1945. 47p. (Arctic Inst. Dept. of Biology. Pub. no.1B) **V140**

Royal Empire Society, London. Library. Subject catalogue. Lond., v.2. 1931. **V141**

Includes a comprehensive bibliography on the Arctic and the Antarctic. For description of complete set *see* V323.

ARGENTINA

Carbia, Rómulo D. Historia crítica de la historiografía argentina (desde sus origenes en siglo XVI). La Plata, República Argentina [Buenos Aires, Imp. López] 1939. 483p. (Biblioteca Humanidades ed. por la Facultad de Humanidades y Ciencias de la Educación de la Universidad de La Plata, t.22) **V142**

"Indice bibliográfico," p.383-477.

A considerably enlarged and revised version of a book by the same author with almost the same title, published in 1925 as volume 2 of *Biblioteca humanidades.* "This volume of Dr. Carbia is unique in the bibliography of Latin-American history. For no other country have we a survey so complete, so authoritative, so consonant with the methods and ideals of modern historical science. The second version is a vast improvement over the first."— From a review by C. H. Haring in the *Hisp. Amer. hist. rev.* 20:581, Nov. 1940.

Nichols, Madaline Wallis. The gaucho, cattle hunter, cavalryman, ideal of romance. Durham, N.C., Duke Univ. Pr., 1942. 152p. (Inter-American Bibliographical and Library Assoc. Pub. ser. 1, v.7) **V143**

Bibliography, p.67-144, containing 1431 items.

Marrazzo, Javier. Nuevo diccionario geográfico histórico de la Republica Argentina. Buenos Aires, Radaelli, 1921. 550p. **V144**

Contains biography.

ARMENIA

Salmaslian, Armenag. Bibliographie de l'Arménie; préface de René Grousset. . . . Paris, l'Auteur, 1946. 195p. **V145**

A classed list with author index of some 1500 separately published works on Armenia from the sixteenth century to 1946. Includes material in French, German, English and some other European languages. Periodical articles are omitted.

ASIA

See name of country for history of individual country in Asia.

American Oriental Society. Library. Catalog of the library; ed. by Elizabeth Strout. New Haven, Yale Univ. Pr., 1930. 308p. **V146**

A list of about 5500 works.

Includes works, primarily in the western European languages, on all of Asia.

Embree, John Fee and **Dotson, Lillian Ota.** Bibliography of the peoples and cultures of mainland southeast Asia. New Haven, Yale Univ., 1950. 821p. (Yale Univ. Southeast Asia studies) $7.50. **V146a**

An extensive bibliography which includes books and periodical articles in English and the European languages ranging in date from the seventeenth century to the present. Material is grouped under broad areas with references on race, racial history, migration, ethnology, cultural history, social organization and law, religion, folklore, language, and writing. Many of the titles are annotated. There is a detailed table of contents but no author index.

Kerner, Robert Joseph. Northeastern Asia, a selected bibliography; contributions to the bibliography of the relations of China, Russia, and Japan, with special reference to Korea, Manchuria, Mongolia, and eastern Siberia, in oriental and European languages. . . . Berkeley, Calif., Univ. of Calif. Pr., 1939. 2v. (Publications of the Northeastern Asia seminar of the Univ. of California; ed. by R. J. Kerner) $26. **V147**

Classified, with full tables of contents and subject indexes. 14,000 titles, of which 10,000 are in Chinese, Japanese, Korean and Russian. Uneven. Covers material published through 1937, on all phases of life in Northeastern Asia, geographic, political, economic, social, historical, cultural, international, etc.

Contents: v.1: pt.1, Asia, The Far East, The Pacific; pt.2, China, including Manchuria, Manchukuo, Mongolia, Northwestern China, Tibet; v.2: pt.1, The Japanese Empire, including Korea; pt.2, The Russian Empire and the Soviet Union in Asia and on the Pacific.

Royal Asiatic Society of Great Britain and Ireland. Library. Catalogue of printed books published before 1932 in the library. Lond., Society, 1940. 541p. £3 3s. **V148**

Far eastern bibliography . . . Feb. 1936- . Wash., 1936- . v.1- . $2 ea. **V149**

Title and publisher vary: v.1-5, 1936-40, *Bulletin of far eastern bibliography,* published by the Committees on Far Eastern Studies of the American Council of Learned Societies; [v.6-], 1941- , *Far eastern bibliography* published by the Far Eastern Association in the *Far eastern quarterly.* Beginning with 1946, cumulated into annual issues with author index.

A classified bibliography appearing periodically, edited by Earl H. P. Pritchard and Gussie E. Gaskill. Volumes 1-5 have author indexes.

Orientalische bibliographie, 1887-1911, 1926. Berlin, Reuther, 1888-1922, 1928. v.1-26. **V150**

An important annual bibliography, including books, pamphlets, periodical articles and reviews in the whole field of oriental studies—language, literature, geography, ethnology, folklore, history, etc.

For material before 1887, the following should be consulted: Zenker's *Bibliotheca orientalis,* 1846–61; *Wissenschaftlicher Jahresbericht über die morgenländischen Studien,* 1859–81; Friederici, *Bibliotheca orientalis,* 1876–83; *Litteraturblatt für orientalische Philologie,* 1883–86.

ASSYRIA

Ebeling, Erich and **Meissner, Bruno.** Reallexikon der Assyriologie, unter Mitwirkung zahlreicher Fachgelehrter. Berlin, de Gruyter, 1932–38. v.1-2. il.   **V151**

v.1-2, A-Ezur.
Appeared in fasicles, 1929–38.
Signed articles with bibliographies.

AUSTRALIA

Australian encyclopedia; ed. by Arthur Wilberforce Jose and Herbert James Carter. Sydney, Angus and Robertson, 1925–26. 2v. il.   **V152**

Covers history, biography, geography, natural history, science, art, etc. Profusely illustrated.

Ferguson, John Alexander. Bibliography of Australia. Sydney and Lond., Angus and Robertson, 1941–45. 2v. 63s. ea.   **V153**

Contents: v.1, 1784–1830; v.2, 1831–1838.
2681 numbered entries arranged chronologically with alphabetical index. Locates copies in ten Australian libraries and the British Museum.

Royal Empire Society, London. Library. Subject catalogue of the library. v.2, Commonwealth of Australia, the Dominion of New Zealand, the South Pacific, general voyages and travels, and Arctic and Antarctic regions. Lond., 1931. 761p.   **V154**

For full description *see* V323.

AUSTRIA

See also Germany, p.499-500.

Charmatz, Richard. Wegweiser durch die Literatur der österreichischen Geschichte. Stuttgart, Cotta, 1912. 138p.   **V155**

A useful selected list with some brief annotations.

Krones, Franz Xaver. Grundriss der österreichischen Geschichte mit besonderer Rücksicht auf Quellen- und Literaturkunde. Wien, Hölder, 1882. 926p.   **V156**

A comprehensive survey covering to 1878 but especially strong for source material before 1700, now out of date but still useful.

Uhlirz, Karl. Handbuch der Geschichte Österreichs und seiner Nachbarländer Böhmen und Ungarn. Begonnen von Karl Uhlirz. Bearb. von Mathilde Uhlirz. Graz, Leuschner und Lubensky, 1927–30. v.1-2[1].   **V157**

A guide to research with extensive bibliographies.

BALKANS

Bengescu, George. Essai d'une notice bibliographique sur la question d'Orient: Orient Européen, 1821–1897. Paris, Le Soudier, 1897. 327p.   **V158**

Lists over 2100 separate works, historical, political and military, on the Balkans, published in France and Belgium from 1821–97. Arranged chronologically with author index and index to anonymous works.

Encyclopédie Balkanique permanente, publiée sous la direction de Léon Savadjian. Paris, Soc. Générale d'Imprimerie et d'Édition, 1936- . v.1- .   **V159**

Albanie, Bulgarie, Grèce, Roumanie, Turquie, Yougoslavie.
Each volume arranged alphabetically as a unit with index. Contains biography.

Savadjian, Léon. Bibliographie Balkanique, 1920- . Paris, Revue des Balkans, 1931; Société Générale d'Imprimerie et d'Édition, 1933- . v.1- .   **V160**

[v.1] 1920–30. 1931. 270p.; [v.2] 1931–32. 1933. 151p.; [v.3] 1933- . Annual.
1920–30 issued as *Revue des Balkans,* n.s., v.2-3, Avril–Sept. 1931.
Contains material concerning Albania, Bulgaria, Greece, Rumania, Turkey, and Jugoslavia in French, German, Italian and English.
Volumes 7 on include a section "Memento encyclopédique des Balkans" giving an annual survey of conditions in the Balkans.

BELGIUM

Grande encyclopédie de la Belgique et du Congo. t.1. Bruxelles, Wauthoz-Legrand, 1938. 676p. il. G60 for 3v.   **V161**

Nonalphabetical. Signed articles with some bibliography. Lavishly illustrated in black and white, and color. Maps. Contents: v.1, The Royal family, the geology, geography, demography and history of Belgium to the end of the war in 1918.
Announced contents: v.2, Les Beaux-arts, les sciences en Belgique; v.3, Le Congo, La Belgique economique, La Belgique administrative, La Belgique et la vie moderne.

Pirenne, Henri. Bibliographie de l'histoire de Belgique; catalogue méthodique et chronologique des sources et des ouvrages principaux relatifs à l'histoire de tous les Pays-Bas jusqu'en 1598 et à l'histoire de Belgique jusqu'en 1914. 3. éd., rev. et compl. avec la collaboration de

Henri Nowé et Henri Obreen. Bruxelles, Lamertin, 1931. 440p. **V162**

A revised and much enlarged edition of the standard
bibliography of Belgian history listing 4151 titles as
against the 2586 contained in the second edition, 1902.

Wachter, Leo de. Repertorium van de vlaamse
gouwen en gemeenten. Heemkundige documentatie, 1800–1940. Antwerpen, de Sikkel,
1942–48. 4v. **V163**

v.1, Algemeen gedeelte en gewesten; v.2-3, Gemeenten, A-S; v.4, Gemeenten, T-Z; Register.

A bibliography of book and periodical material on
Flemish local history. Indexes some 500 periodicals in
various languages.

BRAZIL
Bibliography

Borba de Moraes, Rubens. Manual bibliográfico
de estudos brasileiros. Rio de Janeiro, Souza,
1949. 895p. **V164**

An annotated bibliography of the origins and development of Brazilian culture, divided broadly by subject,
and covering mainly material published prior to 1942 in
the humanities and social sciences. The arrangement
generally followed is that of the *Handbook of Latin
American studies* (V367). Periodical articles are included. There is an author index. Each section was compiled under the direction of a specialist who also provided
an historical outline of Brazilian achievement in his field,
which precedes the actual bibliography.

**Brazil. Comissão de Estudo dos Textos da His-
toria do Brazil . . .** Bibliografia de história do
Brasil . . . 1943- . Rio de Janeiro, Imp. Nac.,
1944- . Semiannual. **V164a**

At head of title: Ministério das Relações Exteriores.
Reviews are included for most items.

Carvalho, Alfredo Ferreira de. Bibliotheca exo-
tico-brasileira, publicada em virtude de autori-
sação legislativa, no governo do Estacio de Albuquerque Coimbra, sob a direcção de Eduardo
Tavares de Mello. Rio de Janeiro, Paulo Pongetti,
1929–30. v.1-3. **V165**

v.1-3, A-M.
No more published.
Contains works of foreign authors on Brazil.

Garraux, Anatole Louis. Bibliographie brésilienne; catalogue des ouvrages français et latins
relatifs au Brésil (1500–1898). Paris, Chadenot,
1898. 400p. **V166**

Pierson, Donald. Survey of the literature on
Brazil of sociological significance published up
to 1940; ed. for the Joint Committee on Latin
American Studies of the National Research Council, the American Council of Learned Societies

and the Social Science Research Council. Camb.,
Harv. Univ. Pr., 1945. 60p. (Joint Committee
on Latin American Studies. Misc. pub. no.4.)
$1.50. **V167**

581 items, annotated.

Rodriguez, José Carlos. Bibliotheca brasiliense;
catalogo annotado dos livros sobre o Brasil e de
alguns autographos e manuscriptos. Parte 1,
Descobrimento da America: Brasil colonial,
1492–1822. Rio de Janeiro, Typographia do "Jor-
nal do commercio" de Rodrigues, 1907. 680p.
V168

Dictionaries

**Instituto Historico e Geographico Brasileiro,
Rio de Janeiro.** Diccionario historico, geogra-
phico e ethnographico do Brasil. Rio de Janeiro,
Imp. Nac., 1922. v.1-2. il. **V169**

Teixeira de Oliveira, José. Dicionário brasileiro
de datas históricas. Rio de Janeiro, Ed. Pan-
Americana, 1944. 653p. **V170**

Chronologically arranged with subject and author
indexes. Includes birth and death dates of many persons.

BULGARIA

See also Balkans, p.491, and Turkey, p.516-17.

Kersopoulos, Jean G. Bulgarie; ouvrages et articles de revues parus de 1613 à 1935. (In Les
Balkans, v.6-8, 1934–36) (Série de bibliographies françaises sur les nations balkaniques,
no.2) **V171**

Second edition of his *Bibliographie franco-bulgare*
(1911).

CANADA
Bibliography

McGill University. Library School. Bibliography of Canadian bibliographies; comp. by the
1929 and 1930 classes of the McGill University
Library School. Montreal, 1930. 45p. **V172**

A classified, selected list. For full record *see* A190.

Gagnon, Philéas. Essai de bibliographie cana-
dienne. Inventaire d'une bibliothèque comprenant imprimés, manuscrits, estampes, etc.,
relatifs à l'histoire du Canada et des pays ad-
jacents. . . . Québec, l'Auteur, 1895–1913. 2v. il.
V173

v.1, Books, pamphlets, periodicals, nos. 1-3747; Autographs and manuscripts, nos. 3748-4406; Prints, etc., nos.
4407-4745; Ex-libris, nos. 4746-5018; v.2, Additions to
the collection, 1895–1909.

Includes both English and French material. Information given for each book includes author, full title, place, publisher, date, paging, size, with occasional bibliographical notes, facsimiles of title pages, etc. The Gagnon collection was acquired in 1909 by the city of Montreal as a nucleus for the public library.

Review of historical publications relating to Canada. 1896–1917/18. Toronto, Briggs, 1897–1919. 22v. (Univ. of Toronto studies in history) Annual. **V174**

Annual volumes of book reviews with annual indexes and cumulated indexes for volumes 1-10, 11-20. Continued as the *Canadian historical review.*

Royal Empire Society, London. Library. Subject catalogue of the library: v.3, Dominion of Canada and its provinces, the Dominion of Newfoundland, the West Indies, and colonial America. Lond., 1932. 822p. **V175**

For full description *see* V323.

Trotter, Reginald George. Canadian history; a syllabus and guide to reading. New and enl. ed. Toronto, Macmillan, 1934. 193p. **V176**

Toronto. Public Library. Bibliography of Canadiana; being items in the Public Library . . . relating to the early history and development of Canada; ed. by Frances M. Staton and Marie Tremaine, with an introd. by George H. Locke. Toronto, Public Library, 1934. 828p. il. $5. **V177**

An author catalog of 4646 numbered items from the reference department of the library, described with full titles, collations, many contents notes, and references to bibliographical sources. Covers the period, 1534–1867.

Dictionaries and source books

Audet, Francis Joseph. Canadian historical dates and events, 1492–1915. Ottawa, Beauregard, 1917. 247p. **V178**

Burpee, Lawrence Johnstone and **Doughty, A. G.** Index and dictionary of Canadian history. Toronto, Morang, 1911. 446p. (Makers of Canada, v.21) **V179**

Serves the double purpose of furnishing in one alphabetical list: (1) an analytical index to all names and topics of Canadian history treated in the 20 volumes of the "Makers of Canada" series; and (2) brief encyclopedic articles, with bibliographies, on those topics and on related topics not treated in the volumes indexed. Includes also a list of the principal manuscript sources of Canadian history and a list of scarce maps and plans of Canada. For new edition *see* the following:

Burpee, Lawrence Johnstone. Oxford encyclopaedia of Canadian history. Ox., Univ. Pr., 1926. 699p. il. (Makers of Canada, anniversary ed. v.12) **V180**

Based on his *Index and dictionary* (V179), but differs from that work in the elimination of the index references and the addition of considerable new material.

Canada. Archives. Documents relating to the constitutional history of Canada, 1759–1791, selected and ed. by Adam Shortt and A. G. Doughty. 2d and rev. ed. by the Historical Documents Publication Board. Ottawa, J. de L. Taché, 1918. 2v. 1084p. maps. **V181**

—— —— 1791–1818, selected and ed. by A. G. Doughty and D. A. McArthur. Ottawa, C. H. Parmelee, 1914. 576p. maps. **V182**

—— —— 1819–1828, selected and ed. with notes by A. G. Doughty and Norah Story. Ottawa, Patenaude, 1935. 538p. **V183**

Encyclopedia of Canada; general ed., W. Stewart Wallace. Toronto, Univ. Associates of Canada, 1935–37. 6v. il. **V184**

A general encyclopedia of everything about Canada, including history, biography, place names. Reprinted (Toronto, Univ. Associates of Canada, 1948. 6v.) with almost no change except for the omission of 1934 population figures. More recent figures not substituted.

Innis, Harold Adams. Select documents in Canadian economic history, 1497–1783, 1783–1885. Toronto, Univ. of Toronto Pr., 1929–33. 2v. **V185**

1783–1885, ed. by H. A. Innis and A. R. M. Lower.

Kennedy, William Paul McClure. Statutes, treaties and documents of the Canadian constitution, 1713–1929. 2d ed. rev. and enl. Toronto, Ox. Univ. Pr., 1930. 752p. **V186**

LeJeune, Louis. Dictionnaire général de biographie, histoire, littérature, agriculture, commerce, industrie et des arts, sciences, moeurs, coutumes, institutions politiques et religieuses du Canada. Ouvrage orné de 187 photographies et de 56 gravures hors-texte. [Ottawa] Univ. d'Ottawa, 1931. 2v. il. **V187**

Bibliography at the end of most articles.

Shortt, Adam and **Doughty, A. G.** Canada and its provinces. A history of the Canadian people and their institutions, by 100 associates: v.23, General index, Documentary notes. Edinburgh, Constable, for the Pub. Assoc. of Canada, Toronto, 1914. 368p. **V188**

(1) General index, giving page references to volumes 1-22, and some direct information, e.g., dates of birth and death; (2) Manuscript sources of Canadian history; (3) Bibliography, arranged by volumes and chapters of the set; (4) Chronological outlines, giving Canadian and European events in parallel columns; (5) Historical tables.

The bibliographical section is particularly noteworthy.

Atlases

Burpee, Lawrence Johnstone. Historical atlas of Canada, with introd., notes, and chronological tables. Maps by John Bartholomew and Son. Toronto and N.Y., Nelson, 1927. 32p., 48p. incl. 31 maps. 28cm. **V189**

CHILE

Anrique Reyes, Nicolás and **Silva Arriagada, L. I.** Ensayo de una bibliografía histórica i jeográfica de Chile. Santiago de Chile, Imp. Barcelona, 1902. 679p. **V190**

A classified list of 2561 titles with author index.

CHINA

See also Asia, p.490.

Bibliography

Cordier, Henri. Bibliotheca sinica. Dictionnaire bibliographique des ouvrages relatifs à l'Empire chinois. 2. éd., rev., corr. et considérablement augm. Paris, Guilmoto, 1904–08. 4v. **V191**

———— Supplément. Paris, Geuthner, 1922–24.
Classified with "Table des matières" but no index. Includes books and periodical articles.

Fairbank, John King and **Liu, Kwang-Ching.** Modern China; a bibliographical guide to Chinese works, 1898–1937. Camb., Harv. Univ. Pr., 1950. 608p. (Harvard-Yenching Institute studies, v.1) **V192**

An annotated bibliography of Chinese works published 1898–1937, covering works of general reference, history, government and law, foreign affairs, economics, social problems, cultural movements, education, intellectual and literary history, selected newspapers and learned journals.

Author and title are given both in Chinese characters and in the Wade-Giles romanization, with English translation. Annotations are in English.

Gardner, Charles Sidney. A union list of selected western books on China in American libraries. 2d ed., rev., and enl. Wash., Committee on Chinese Studies, Amer. Council of Learned Societies, 1938. 111p. 75c. **V193**

371 numbered titles (including 21 periodicals) with locations in 76 American libraries. Arranged by subject with author index. In many cases includes citations to reviews of the books listed.

Skachkov, Petr Emel'íanovich. Bibliografiíã Kitaíã; sistematicheskiǐ ukazatel' knig i zhurnal'nykh stateǐ o Kitae na russkom íãzyke 1730–1930. Moskva, Gosudarst, 1932. 842p. (Repr. Ann Arbor, Mich., Edwards, 1948. $5.80) **V194**

A classed list of books and articles concerning China published in Russian from 1730–1930, with author index.

Dictionaries

Ball, James Dyer. Things Chinese; or Notes connected with China. 5th ed., rev. by E. Chalmers Werner. Shanghai, Kelly and Walsh, 1925. 766p. **V195**

An alphabetical dictionary by large subjects, with index of smaller subjects; some bibliographical references. For popular rather than scholarly use.

Couling, Samuel. Encyclopaedia sinica. Shanghai, Kelly and Walsh; Lond. and N.Y., Ox. Univ. Pr., 1917. 633p. 42s. **V196**

A useful encyclopedia of everything about China, its history, geography, literature, art, religions, institutions, flora, fauna, biography, etc. Most of the articles are by the editor, but there are articles by other authorities, some signed. Some bibliographies.

CHIOS

Argenti, Philip Pandely. Bibliography of Chios, from classical times to 1936 . . . with a preface by J. L. Myres. Ox., Clarendon Pr., 1940. 836p. 42s. **V197**

Contents: pt.1, Classified catalog, p.1-567; pt.2, Authors' catalog, p.571-801; pt.3, List of maps, 1422–1937, p.805-32. Alphabetical index of classifications, p.833-36.

COSTA RICA

Lines, Jorge A. Bibliografía antropológica aborigen de Costa Rica; incluye especialmente: arqueología, cartografía, etnología, geografía, historia y lingüística. San José, Costa Rica, 1943. 263p. **V198**

On cover: Universidad de Costa Rica. Facultad de Letras y Filosofía.
1262 numbered items including many analytics.

CUBA

Cuba en el mano; enciclopedia popular ilustrada. La Habana [Ucar, Garcia] 1940. 1302p. il. $6.50. **V199**

Includes sections on geographical names, natural history, history, printing, biography, education and culture, communications, politics, statistics, etc.

Pezuela y Lobo, Jacobo de la. Diccionario geográfico, estadístico, histórico, de la isla de Cuba. Madrid, Mellado, 1863–66. 4v. **V200**

Includes biography.

CZECHOSLOVAKIA

See also Slavic Europe, p.515.

Bibliografie česke historie za rok 1904- . Praha, Nákladem Klubu historického, 1905- . Annual. **V201**

Very comprehensive annual record of material in Czech and other languages on the history of Czechoslovakia.

1904–14 published as a supplement to *Český časopis historicky* (Prague). From 1915 published separately.

Čapek, Thomas and **Čapek, Anna V.** Bohemian (Čech) bibliography; a finding list of writings in English relating to Bohemia and the Čechs. N.Y., Revell [c1918]. 256p. il. **V202**

Includes both books and periodical articles.

Zibrt, Čenék. Bibliografie české historie. V Praze, Nákladem České akademie Cisaře Františka, 1900–12. 5v. **V203**

Very full for the period before 1679. For the large or special library.

DENMARK

Amsterdam. Universiteit. Bibliotheek. Catalogus van de Bibliotheca Danica en van de overige Deensche en Ijslandsche Werken aanwezig in de Universiteitsbibliotheek van Amsterdam. Amsterdam, Stadsdrukkerij, 1939. 522p. **V204**

Bay, Jens Christian. Denmark in English and American literature; a bibliography ed. for the Danish American Association. Chic., Assoc., 1915. 96p. **V205**

Includes books and periodical articles in English on Danish history and literature.

Erichsen, Balder Vermund Aage and **Krarup, Alfred.** Dansk historisk Bibliografi; systematisk Fortegnelse over Bidrag til Danmarks Historie til Udgangen af 1912 (i Tilslutning til Bibliotheca danica). Udgivet paa Carlsbergfondets Bekostning. Københaven, Gad, 1917–27. 3v. **V206**

v.1-2, history, topography, etc., a classified list of more than 20,000 references, with detailed indexes of authors and titles; v.3, biography.

A very full list, including books, pamphlets and many analytical references to articles in periodicals and other composite works. There are more than 35,000 numbered items, and as some numbers cover several titles the total number is much larger.

Volume 3 is a list of published biographies of persons living between 1830 and 1912 in continuation of a similar section in volume 3 of Bruun, *Bibliotheca danica* (A230) and including some names of the earlier period omitted in Bruun.

Historisk Tidsskrift . . . udgivet af den Danske historiske Forening. Kjøbenhavn, Luno, 1840- . **V207**

Since 1896, has contained an annual bibliography of Danish historical writings.

EGYPT

Annual Egyptological bibliography. Bibliographie Égyptologique annuelle. 1947- . comp. by Jozef M. A. Janssen. Leiden, Brill, 1948- . Annual. (International Association of Egyptologists) Fl. 16 **V208**

An alphabetical annotated list, started to fill the need of an annual bibliography caused by the cessation of the "Bibliografia metodica degli studi di egittologia e di papirologia," published in *Aegyptus,* 1920–43.

The war years are to be covered in:

Federn, Walter. Egyptian bibliography. Jan. 1, 1939–Dec. 31, 1947. (In Orientalia, n.s. v.17, 1948, p.467-89, and continuation) **V209**

Bachatly, Charles. Bibliographie de la préhistoire égyptienne, 1869–1938. Cairo, Soc. Royale de Géographie d'Egypte, 1942. 77p. **V210**

836 numbered entries.

Hill, Richard Leslie. A bibliography of the Anglo-Egyptian Sudan, from the earliest times to 1937. . . . Lond., Ox. Univ. Pr., Milford, 1939. 213p. 20s.; $6. **V211**

Classified, with indexes of persons and subjects.

Ibrahim-Hilmy, *prince.* Literature of Egypt and the Soudan from the earliest times to the year 1885, inclusive. A bibliography: comprising printed books, periodical writings and papers of learned societies; maps and charts; ancient papyri, manuscripts, drawings, etc. Lond., Trübner, 1886–88. 2v. **V212**

Lorin, Henri. Bibliographie géographique de l'Égypte. . . . [Cairo?] L'Impr. de l'Institut Français d'Archéologie Orientale du Caire pour la Société Royale de Géographie d'Égypte, 1928. v.1. 472p. **V213**

Contents: v.1, Géographie physique et géographie humaine.

Maunier, René. Bibliographie économique, juridique et sociale de l'Égypte moderne (1798–1916). . . . Le Caire, Impr. de l'Institut Français d'Archéologie Orientale, 1918. 372p. (Société Sultanieh d'Économie Politique, de Statistique et de Législation. Travaux spéciaux . . . no.1) **V214**

New York. Public Library. Ancient Egypt; sources of information in the New York Public Library, comp. by Ida A. Pratt under the direction of Richard Gottheil. [N.Y.] Library, 1925. 486p. $2.50. **V215**

"Reprinted with additions from the *Bulletin* of the New York Public Library, September 1923 to March and May 1924."

———— Supplement. 1925–1941. N.Y., Library, 1942. 340p. $2.50.

—— Modern Egypt; a list of references to material in the New York Public Library, comp. by Ida A. Pratt under the direction of Richard Gottheil. N.Y., Library, 1929. 320p. $2.50 **V216**

"Reprinted from the *Bulletin* of the New York Public Library, September 1928 to April 1929."

ETHIOPIA

Fumagalli, Giuseppe. Bibliografia etiopica. . . . Milano, Hoepli, 1893. 288p. **V217**

Subtitle: Catalogo descrittivo e ragionato degli scritti publicati dalla invenzione della stampa fino a tutto il 1891, intorno alla Etiopia e regioni limitrofe.

Zanutto, Silvio. Bibliografia etiopica, in continuazione alla "Bibliografia etiopica" di G. Fumagalli. Roma, Sindicato Italiano Arti Grafiche [1929–32]. v.1-2. il. **V218**

pt.1, Bibliografia; pt.2, Manoscritti etiopici.

FINLAND

Maliniemi, Aarno Henrik and **Kivikoski, Ella.** Suomen historiallinen bibliografia, 1901–1925. Finsk historisk bibliografi. Bibliographie historique findlandaise. Helsinki [Suomalaisen kirjallisuuden seuran kirjapainon oy], 1940. 2v. in 1. 527p., 107p. (Suomen historiallinen seura käsikirjoja. II: 1-2) **V219**

A comprehensive bibliography of Finnish historical works published 1901–25, including both books and periodical articles. Classed arrangement with author index. Headings are given in Finnish, Swedish and French. Most of the material is in Finnish, though some titles are in Swedish, German, and other languages.

History is interpreted in its broad sense to include not only political and economic history of all periods, but also allied interests, e.g., history of the church, education, literature, folklore, etc., and local history.

FRANCE
Bibliography

Franklin, Alfred Louis Auguste. Les sources de l'histoire de France. Notices bibliographiques et analytiques des inventaires et des recueils de documents relatifs à l'histoire de France. Paris, Firmin-Didot, 1877. 681p. **V220**

Langlois, Charles V. and **Stein, Henri.** Les archives de l'histoire de France. Paris, Picard,

1891–93. 3 pts. in 1v. (Manuels de bibliographie historique) **V221**

Guide to source materials in French and foreign archives. For a more complete record of the very valuable collection in the national archives consult: Schmidt, Charles, *Les sources de l'histoire de France depuis 1789 aux Archives Nationales* (Paris, 1907).

Paris. Bibliothèque Nationale. Dept. des Imprimés. Catalogue de l'histoire de France. Paris, Didot, 1855–95. 11v., index and 6 suppl. **V222**

A very comprehensive catalog of works, books, pamphlets, etc., printed before 1875 on the history of France prior to 1875. Classed (15 main and 904 subclasses) with author index.

Contents: t.1, Préliminaires et généralités. Histoire par époques. Histoire par règnes [à Louis XIII]; t.2, Louis XIV-Louis XVI; t.3, 1792–1848; t.4, 1848–1856. Journaux et publications périodiques; t.5, Histoire religieuse; t.6, Histoire constitutionnelle; t.7, Histoire constitutionnelle [suite]. Histoire administrative, diplomatique, militaire. Moeurs et coutumes. Archéologie; t.8, Histoire locale; t.9, Histoire locale [suite]. Biographie; t.10, Biographie [suite] supplément; t.11, Supplément [suite]. [Six additional supplements to special classes of the main work.]

———— Tables des auteurs. 1895. 798p.

———— Tables générale alphabétique des ouvrages anonymes. 1905. v.1-2.

Contents: Table des noms de personnes. 4v.; Table des noms de lieux: A-C.

Les Sources de l'histoire de France depuis les origines jusqu'en 1815, par A. Molinier, H. Hauser, E. Bourgeois, L. André, P. Caron. Paris, Picard, 1901–35. 1.-3. pt. (in 18v.) **V223**

Contents: 1. pt., Des origines aux guerres d'Italie (1494), par A. Molinier: t.1, Époque primitive, Mérovingiens et Carolingiens; t.2, Époque féodale, les Capétiens jusqu'en 1180; t.3, Les Capétiens, 1180–1328; t.4, Les Valois, 1328–1461; t.5, Introduction générale, Les Valois (suite), Louis XI et Charles VIII (1461–94); t.6, Table générale, par Louis Polain.

2. pt., Le XVIe siècle (1494–1600), par H. Hauser: t.1, Les premières guerres d'Italie, Charles VIII et Louis XII (1494–1515); t.2, François I et Henri II (1515–59); t.3, Les guerres de religion (1559–89); t.4, Henri IV (1589–1610).

3. pt., Le XVIIe siècle (1610–1715), par Émile Bourgeois et Louis André: t.1, Géographie et histoire générales; t.2, Mémoires et lettres; t.3, Biographies; t.4, Journaux et pamphlets; t.5, Histoire politique et militaire; t.6, Histoire maritime et coloniale, histoire religieuse; t.7, Histoire économique, Histoire administrative; t.8, Histoire provinciale et locale; Essai sur les sources étrangères; Additions et corrections; Table générale.

Early

Montandon, Raoul. Bibliographie générale des travaux palethnologiques et archéologiques (époques préhistorique, protohistorique et gallo-

romaine) France. . . . Genève, Georg, 1917–38.
v.1–5. **V224**

A comprehensive bibliography of books and periodical articles, arranged by geographical division.

—————— Supplément du t.1–3. 1921–29. v.1–3.

Répertoire archéologique de la France, publ. par ordre du Ministre de l'Instruction Publique et sous la direction du Comité des Travaux Historiques et des Sociétés Savantes. Paris, Impr. Nat., 1861–88. 8v. (Collection de documents inédits sur l'histoire de France, ser. vii, 7) **V225**

Contents: *Alpes (Hautes),* by Joseph Roman. 1888; *Aube,* by Henri d'Arbois de Jubainville. 1861; *Morbihan,* by Louis Rosensweig. 1863; *Nièvre,* by J. H. G. R. de Soultrait. 1875; *Oise,* by Emmanuel Woillez. 1862; *Seine-Inférieure,* by J. B. D. Cochet. 1872; *Tarn,* by Hippolyte Crozes, 1865; *Yonne,* by Maximilien Quantin. 1868.

To 1789

Du Peloux, Charles. Répertoire général des ouvrages modernes relatifs au dix-huitième siècle française (1715–1789). Paris, Grund, 1926. 306p. **V226**

—————— Supplément, table méthodique. 1927. 62p.

Lists books and periodical articles published since 1789 in French, English, German and Italian.

Monod, Gabriel. Bibliographie de l'histoire de France. Catalogue méthodique et chronologique des sources et des ouvrages relatifs à l'histoire de France depuis les origines jusqu'en 1789. Paris, Hachette, 1888. 420p. **V227**

Now largely superseded but still useful as a guide to older publications.

Saulnier, Eugène and **Martin, A.** Bibliographie des travaux publiés de 1866 à 1897 sur l'histoire de la France de 1500 à 1789. Paris, Presses Universitaires, 1932–38. v.1–2, fasc. 2. (Publication de la Société d'Histoire Moderne) (In progress) **V228**

v.1, Histoire intérieure, Histoire des institutions, Histoire diplomatique, Histoire militaire, Histoire de la marine militaire, Histoire religieuse; v.2, fasc. 1–2, Histoire économique et sociale; Histoire coloniale; Histoire des familles; Biographies.

Revolution

Caron, Pierre. Manuel pratique pour l'étude de la révolution française. Nouv. éd. mise à jour. Paris, Picard, 1947. 324p. 400fr. **V229**

Originally published in 1912, this edition has been revised and reorganized. A guide to the archival and manuscript sources, collections, bibliographical aids, etc.

Monglond, André. La France révolutionnaire et impériale; annales de bibliographie méthodique et description des livres illustrés. Grenoble, Arthaud, 1930–49. v.1–6 and index to v.1–2. il. **V230**

v.1–6, 1789–1805. Index to v.1–2, 91p.

A very detailed bibliography, including books, pamphlets and articles dealing with all phases of life and literature in France during this period.

Paris. Bibliothèque Nationale. Dept. des Imprimés. Catalogue de l'histoire de la révolution française, par André Martin et Gérard Walter. Paris, Éditions des Bibliothèques Nationales, 1936–43. v.1–3, 5. (In progress) **V231**

v.1–3, Écrits de la période révolutionnaire: A–Piis; v.5, Journaux et almanachs.

Complemented by:

—————— Répertoire de l'histoire de la révolution française par Gérard Walter: Travaux publiés de 1800 à 1940. Paris, Bibl. Nationale, 1941–43. v.1–2. (In progress) **V232**

t.1, Personnes; t.2, Lieux.

Tourneux, Maurice. Bibliographie de l'histoire de Paris pendant la révolution française. Paris, Impr. Nouv., 1890–1913. 5v. (Paris. Publications relative à la révolution française) **V233**

t.1, Préliminaires. Événements; t.2, Organisation et rôle politiques de Paris; t.3, Monuments, moeurs et institutions; t.4, Documents biographiques, Paris hors les murs, Additions et corrections; t.5, Table générale.

Since 1789

Caron, Pierre. Bibliographie des travaux publiés de 1866 à 1897 sur l'histoire de la France depuis 1789. Paris, Cornély, 1912. 831p. **V234**

A valuable bibliography including 13,496 titles of books, pamphlets and articles in periodicals, society publications and other composite works. Indicates book reviews and abstracts of important items included. Indexes the historical articles in some 394 French and 260 foreign periodicals. Classified arrangement with two indexes: (1) authors and persons, (2) places. Forms the main volume in Caron's series of indexes of the history of France since 1789, and is continued for the material published since 1897 by V235.

Annual bibliographies

Répertoire méthodique de l'histoire moderne et contemporaine de la France, pour les années 1898–1913. Paris, Rieder, 1899–1932. v.1–7, 9–11. **V235**

v.1–6, 1898–1903, ed. by G. Brière and P. Caron; v.7, 1904–06, ed. by G. Brière, P. Caron and J. Lépine; v.8, 1907–09, in preparation; v.9, 1910/11, ed. by P. Caron and R. Burnaud; v.10–11, 1911/12–1912/13, ed. by M. Bouteron, R. Burnaud and P. Caron; v.12, 1913–19, in preparation.

Répertoire bibliographique de l'histoire de France, par Pierre Caron et Henri Stein. Publication de la Société Française de Bibliographie, subventionnée par la Confédération des Sociétés Scientifiques Française, à l'aide des fonds alloués par le Parlement. Paris, Picard, 1923–38. v.1-6.
V236

v.1, 1920/21; v.2, 1922/23; v.3, 1924/25; v.4, 1926/27; v.5, 1928/29; v.6, 1930/31.

The standard current bibliography for France to 1914, listing historical writings in various languages, both books and periodical articles. Classified, with name and place indexes.

Bibliographie critique des principaux travaux parus sur l'histoire de 1600 à 1914 en 1932 et 1933- . Paris, Maison du Livre Français, 1935- . (Publications de la Société d'Histoire Moderne. Série des Instruments de Travail)
V237

"Publiée par le Comité de Direction de la Revue d'Histoire Moderne. Subventionnée par la Confédération des Sociétés Scientifiques Françaises, à l'aide des fonds alloués par le Parlement."

Ed. by Georges Pagès, Léon Cahen and Marc Jaryc. 1932/33, General; 1934–35, have subtitle, Travaux de langue française ou relatifs à l'histoire de France.

1934 includes in four sections: works in the French, English and German languages on the history of France, works in the French language on foreign countries.

1935 adds to these, works in Italian, Polish, and Russian languages on the history of France.

Local

☙ There are numerous bibliographies and dictionaries of local history. Many are listed in the general bibliographies noted above. A large number of bibliographies will be found in Besterman, *World bibliography of bibliographies* (A11). A useful list which includes bibliographies is given in the New York Public Library, *Provençal literature and language, including the local history of southern France,* comp. by Daniel C. Haskell. (N.Y., 1925. 885p.) p.189-660, 676-738.

Duportet, Maurice. Topobibliographie de la France. [Montluçon] 1937- . v.1- . Looseleaf.
V238

Allier: bulletins et revues (1763–1935); Creuse: mémoires, bulletins et revues (1823–1936); Indre: bulletins et revues (1801–1937).

Lasteyrie du Saillant, R. C. *comte de.* Bibliographie générale des travaux historiques et archéologiques publiés par les sociétés savantes de la France. Paris, Impr. Nat., 1888–1918. 6v. **V239**

For full description of this work and its continuations *see* C11.

A listing of French historical societies by *département* with full contents of their publications, though there is no author index to this analytical material.

Volumes 1-4 cover the literature published to 1885; volumes 5-6 cover 1886–1900. Continued by:

Bibliographie annuelle des travaux historiques et archéologiques publiés par les sociétés savantes de la France, 1901/04–1909/10. Paris, Impr. Nat., 1906–14. 9v. **V240**

An annual continuation on the same scale as the above. Continued by:

Bibliographie générale des travaux historiques et archéologiques, publiés par les sociétés savantes de la France . . . par René Gandilhon. 1910–1940. Paris, Impr. Nat., 1944- . **V241**

t.1, Ain-Creuse. 250fr.

A continuation of the above on the same general plan but with a somewhat enlarged scope. To the history and archaeology of the earlier works are added such related materials as geography, folklore, prehistoric studies, etc., and also obituaries.

Dictionaries, handbooks, etc.

Anderson, Frank Maloy. The constitutions and other select documents illustrative of the history of France, 1789–1907. 2d ed. rev. and enl. Minneapolis, H. W. Wilson, 1908. 693p. **V242**

A useful collection of translations from the original texts. Sources are indicated, and brief annotations with additional references are included.

Chéruel, Pierre Adolphe. Dictionnaire historique des institutions, moeurs et coutumes de la France. 10. éd. Paris, Hachette, 1910. 2v. il. **V243**

1st ed., 1885. Later editions unchanged.

Especially strong for material before the nineteenth century. Now much out of date but still useful.

France. Commission de la Topographie des Gaules. Dictionnaire archéologique de la Gaule, époque celtique. Pub. par la Commission instituée au Ministère de l'Instruction Publique et des Beaux-Arts. Paris, Impr. Nat., 1875–1923. 2v. il. (Collection de documents inédits sur l'histoire de France. sér. 6, t.20) **V244**

v.1, A-G, 1875; v.2, H-Z, 1878–1923.

Kuscinski, August. Dictionnaire des conventionnels. Paris, Au Siège de la Société, 1916–19. 615p. (Société de l'Histoire de la Révolution Française) **V245**

Lalanne, Ludovic. Dictionnaire historique de la France. 2. éd. Paris, Hachette, 1877. 2v. **V246**

A handbook for ready reference including brief articles on persons, places and institutions connected with the history of France through 1876.

Marion, Marcel. Dictionnaire des institutions de la France aux xviie et xviiie siècles. Paris, Picard, 1923. 564p. **V247**

Not as broad in coverage as the preceding work but includes some material not in that.

Robinet, Jean François Eugène [and others]. Dictionnaire historique et biographique de la révolution et de l'empire, 1789–1815. Paris, Lib. Hist. de la Révolution et de l'Empire, 1899. 2v. **V248**

Paris

Lazare, Félix and **Lazare, Louis.** Dictionnaire administratif et historique des rues et monuments de Paris. 2. éd. Paris, Lazare, 1855. 796p. **V249**

Pessard, Gustave. Nouveau dictionnaire historique de Paris. Paris, Rey, 1904. 1693p. **V250**

Alphabetically arranged by names of streets, places, churches, bridges, etc., with historical information.

General histories

Lavisse, Ernest. Histoire de France illustrée. Paris, Hachette, 1911–22. 19v. il. **V251**

Contents: Histoire de France illustrée, depuis les origines jusqu'à la révolution. 1911. 9v. in 18; Histoire de France contemporaine depuis la révolution jusqu'à la paix de 1919. 10v.–v.10, Tables générales des origines à la paix de 1919. 356p. (Table alphabétique des matières, p.3-242; Table alphabétique des gravures et des cartes, p.245-82)

A good reference history, important for both text and fine illustration. Published as two separate works which are volume numbered separately, but held together for reference use by a general index to the two works.

GERMANY
Bibliography

Dahlmann, Friedrich Christoph. Dahlmann-Waitz. Quellenkunde der deutschen Geschichte. 9. Aufl. unter Mitwirkung von Ernest Baasch, Max v. Bahrfeldt [u.A.], hrsg. von Hermann Haering. Leipzig, Koehler, 1931–32. 2v., i.e., 1292p. **V252**

v.1, Bibliography, 992p.; v.2, Index, p.993-1292.

The standard bibliography of German history in all its phases; covering through World War I; indispensable in any library where research work in that subject is done. The ninth edition contains 16,337 entries as against 13,380 in the eighth edition (1912).

Grundriss der Geschichtswissenschaft, zur Einführung in das Studium der deutschen Geschichte des Mittelalters und der Neuzeit, hrsg. von Aloys Meister. Leipzig, Teubner, 1908–27. 1. Reihe, Abt. 1-4a, 6-7; 2. Reihe, Abt. 1-6, 8. **V253**

1. Reihe: Historische Hilfswissenschaften u. Propädeutik; 2. Reihe: Historische Sonderwissenschaften.

—— Ergänzungsband. Bd.1, Die antiken Grundlagen der frühmittelalterlichen Privatkunde. 1927.

Loewe, Victor. Bücherkunde der deutschen Geschichte. Kritischer Wegweiser durch die neuere deutsche historische Literatur. 5. verb. u. verm. Aufl. Leipzig, Räde, 1919. 148p. **V254**

A brief selected bibliography, with critical annotations, convenient for the beginner.

To 1600

Lorenz, Ottokar. Deutschlands Geschichtsquellen im Mittelalter seit der Mitte des dreizehnten Jahrhunderts. 3. in Verbindung mit Arthur Goldmann umgearb. Aufl. Berlin, Hertz, 1886–87. 2v. **V255**

This and Wattenbach (V256) furnish comprehensive and critical guides to the historiography of medieval Germany.

Wattenbach, Wilhelm. Deutschlands Geschichtsquellen im Mittelalter bis zur Mitte des dreizehnten Jahrhunderts. 6. umgearb. Aufl. Berlin, Hertz, 1893–94. 2v. **V256**

7th ed., ed. by Ernst Dümmler. v.1 only, Stuttgart, Cotta, 1904.

—— Deutschlands Geschichtsquellen im Mittelalter; deutschen Kaizerzeit, hrsg. von Robert Holtzmann. . . . Berlin, Ebering, 1938–39. v.1, pts. 1-2. **V257**

Treats the "Zeitalter des Ottonischen Staates, 900–1050."

Schottenloher, Karl. Bibliographie zur deutschen Geschichte im Zeitalter der Glaubensspaltung 1517–1585. . . . Leipzig, Hiersemann, 1936–40. v.1-6. **V258**

Im Auftrag der Kommission zur Erforschung der Geschichte der Reformation und Gegenreformation.

Bd.1-2, Personen, A-Z; Orte u. Landschaften; Bd.3, Reich u. Kaiser; Territorien u. Landesherren; Bd.4, Gesamtdarstellungen der Reformationszeit; Stoffe; Bd.5, Nachträge und Ergänzungen; Zeittafel; Bd.6, Verfasser- und Titelverzeichnis.

A very comprehensive bibliography of books and periodical articles.

Current

Bibliographie des Deutschtums im Ausland, Jahrg. 1, 1937- . Stuttgart, Kohlhammer, 1937- . Monthly. **V259**

Title varies; 1937 is *Bibliographie des Auslandsdeutschtums.*

Bearb. von der Bücherei des Deutschtums in Ausland, Deutsches Ausland-Institut, Stuttgart.

An annotated bibliography arranged by country. Annual author and subject indexes.

Bibliographie zur deutschen Geschichte . . . 1889–1927. Leipzig, Teubner, 1889–1918; Dresden, Baensch, 1920–31. Annual. **V260**

No more published.

Issued as a supplement to the *Historische Vierteljahrschrift.*

A useful annual bibliography arranged by subjects with author index. Each issue lists books, pamphlets and periodical articles, with references to reviews of items listed.

Jahresberichte für deutsche Geschichte, 1.-15/16. Jahrg., 1925–39/40. . . . hrsg. von Albert Brackmann u. Fritz Hartung. Leipzig, Koehler, 1927–42. v.1-15/16. Annual. **V261**

Each volume is in two parts: (1) Bibliographie; (2) Forschungsberichte, with author and subject indexes.

A valuable annual survey preceded by the *Jahresberichte der Geschichtswissenschaft,* 1878–1913 (V9) and *Jahresberichte der deutschen Geschichte,* 1918–1924 (Breslau, 1920–26. 7v.).

Encyclopedias and handbooks

Gebhardt, Bruno. Gebhardts Handbuch der deutschen Geschichte . . . völlig neu Bearb. hrsg. von Robert Holtzmann. 7. Aufl. Stuttgart, Union Deutsche Verlagsgesellschaft, 1930–31. 2v. **V262**

A very useful compendium arranged chronologically. Includes bibliography. The work of several scholars, it originally appeared in 1891–92 and has been issued in several revised editions under various editors.

Grotefend, Hermann. Zeitrechnung des deutschen Mittelalters und der Neuzeit. Hannover, Hahn, 1891–98. 3 pts. in 2v. **V263**

1. Bd., Glossar und Tafeln. 1891; 2. Bd., 1. Abt., Kalendar der diöcesen Deutschlands, der Schweiz und Skandinaviens. 1892; 2. Abt., Ordenskalendar. Heiligenverzeichniss. Nachträge zum Glossar. 1898.

Hoops, Johannes. Reallexikon der Germanischen Altertumskunde, unter Mitwirkung zahlreicher Fachgelehrten. Strassburg, Trübner, 1911–19. 4v. il. **V264**

Lüdtke, Gerhard and **Mackensen, Lutz.** Deutscher Kulturatlas. Berlin, de Gruyter, 1928–38. 5v. il. **V265**

v.1, Vorzeit u. Frühzeit; bis zum Jahre 1000 N. Chr; v.2, Vom Ritter zum Patrizier; v.3, Vom Humanismus zum Rokoko; v.4, Vom Goethe bis Bismarck; v.5, Kaiserreich und Weltkrieg.

Petersen, Carl [and others]. Handwörterbuch des Grenz- und Auslanddeutschtums, unter Mitwirkung von etwa 800 Mitarbeitern und in Verbindung mit H. Aubin . . . M. Bierbaum [u.A.], hrsg. von Carl Petersen, Otto Scheel, Paul Hermann Ruth, Hans Schwalm. Breslau, Ferdinand Hirt, 1933–40. maps. v.1-3. (In progress) **V266**

v.1, A-Bütow; v.2¹⁻⁷, C-Finnland; v.3², G-Massachusetts; Nachtrag.

GOLD COAST

Cardinall, Allan Wolsey. Bibliography of the Gold Coast. Accra, Govt. Pr. [1932]. 384p. 12s. 6d. **V267**

Issued as a companion volume to the census report of 1931.

GREAT BRITAIN
Bibliography

Cannon, Henry Lewin. Reading references for English history. Bost., Ginn, 1910. 559p. **V268**

A chronological arrangement, with an author and subject index. Includes sources, modern accounts, poems and novels illustrative of English history, etc.

Gross, Charles. A bibliography of British municipal history, including gilds and parliamentary representation. N.Y., Lond., Longmans, 1897. 461p. (Harvard historical studies. v.5) **V269**

Early

Gomme, George Laurence. Index of archaeological papers, 1665–1890. Lond., Constable, 1907. 910p. **V270**

A useful author index to some 94 sets of English archaeological periodicals and transactions of local antiquarian societies. Gives for each article indexed author's name, full title, periodical, volume or date, and inclusive paging. Principally British archaeology, but includes also material on classical and other non-British antiquities. A subject index to the same material was contemplated but not published. Continued by the following:

Index of archaeological papers published in 1891–1910. Lond., Constable, 1892–1914. v.1-20. **V271**

An annual continuation of Gomme's *Index* (V270) indexing the same type of material and following the same plan as far as the author index is concerned, but differing from the main work in that each annual volume has a subject index to the author list. While each volume nominally covers one year, many cover a longer period since whenever a new periodical is added to the list it is indexed back to 1891.

Publication suspended after 1914. Most of the periodicals indexed are now included in the *Subject index to periodicals* (E75).

Medieval

Hall, Hubert. A select bibliography for the study, sources, and literature of English mediaeval economic history, comp. by a seminar of the London School of Economics under the supervision of

Hubert Hall. Lond., King, 1914. 350p. (Studies in economics and political science, ed. by the director of the London School of Economics and Political Science) **V272**

A well-selected list of sources and secondary works.

Gross, Charles. Sources and literature of English history from the earliest times to about 1485. 2d ed., rev. and enl. Lond. and N.Y., Longmans, 1915. 820p. **V273**

The best bibliography of English history for the period before 1485, valuable both for its selection of material and for the annotations. Includes more than 3234 closely classified titles (numbered to 3234, but actually more because of insertions) with general index.

Appendices: A. Reports of the deputy-keeper of the public records; B. The Historical Manuscripts Commission; C. Rolls series; D. Chronological tables of the principal sources.

Continued in period by the following:

16th and 17th centuries

Bibliography of British history: Tudor period 1485–1603, Stuart period 1603–1714. Issued under the direction of the American Historical Association and the Royal Historical Society of Great Britain. Ox., Univ. Pr., 1928–33. 2v. Tudor period, 30s.; $10. Stuart period, 21s.; $7. **V274**

Tudor period, 1485–1603, ed. by Conyers Read. 1933. 467p.; Stuart period, 1603–1714, ed. by Godfrey Davies. 1928. 459p.

In 1909 the Royal Historical Society and the American Historical Association undertook the compilation of a bibliography of British history from 1485. A joint committee of the two societies had the bibliography in hand for many years and the Tudor and Stuart volumes listed above are the results of their long intensive work. The original plan called for two more sections: (1) a bibliography of the modern period, 1715- ; and (2) a bibliography of general and allied material introductory to the whole. With Gross (V273), the two volumes already completed give a continuous bibliography from the earliest period to 1714.

The Tudor and Stuart volumes are alike in general plan, i.e., a select classified-subject list, with author indexes, of book, pamphlet and document material in the field, with a liberal inclusion of articles in periodicals and society transactions. They are useful as the most satisfactory bibliography of the periods yet produced but are, on the whole, less well done than Gross's monumental work, and the Tudor volume especially must be used with some caution as it shows many inaccuracies in titles; some of the inaccuracies are minor misprints, others are serious enough to cause real difficulty in finding the material or to be actually misleading.

For a list of some corrections *see* London, University Institute of Historical Research, *Bulletin* 11:80-84, 1933.

Abbott, Wilbur Cortez. A bibliography of Oliver Cromwell; a list of printed materials relating to Oliver Cromwell, together with a list of portraits and caricatures. Camb., Harv. Univ. Pr., 1929. 551p. $12.50. **V275**

Material on the Cromwell period published from 1597 to 1928.

New York (City). Union Theological Seminary. Library. Catalogue of the McAlpin collection of British history and theology; comp. and ed. by C. R. Gillett. N.Y., 1927–30. 5v. **V276**

Valuable for historical material published from 1500–1700. Arranged chronologically with alphabetical index.

18th and 19th centuries

Grose, Clyde Leclare. A select bibliography of British history, 1660–1760. Chic., Univ. of Chic. Pr., 1939. 507p. $9. **V277**

Divided by periods: General, 1660–1760; 1660–88; 1689–1714; 1715–60. Classified arrangement, detailed table of contents shows scheme. Includes some major collections of manuscripts as well as printed works. Annotated. Works considered exceptionally useful are starred.

Morgan, William Thomas and **Morgan, Chloe Siner.** Bibliography of British history (1700–1715) with special reference to the reign of Queen Anne. Bloomington, Ind. 1934–42. 5v. (Indiana Univ. studies nos. 94, 95, 114-116, 119-124) **V278**

Contents: v.1-2, Pamphlets and memoirs, 1700–1715; v.3, Source materials published in 1717 and later; Correspondence, autobiographies, diaries, and journals; Periodicals, including newspapers and annuals (1700–1715); Plays and other dramatic works; Secondary materials (to about June 1938); v.4, Unpublished manuscripts with index; v.5, Addenda and corrigenda; Supplements to v.1-3; Appendices; Comprehensive index to v.1,2,3, and 5.

Williams, Judith Blow. A guide to the printed materials for English social and economic history, 1750–1850. N.Y., Columbia Univ. Pr., 1926. 2v. (Records of civilization: Sources and studies, ed. by J. T. Shotwell) **V279**

A classed work, including sections on biography and local history. Alphabetical index.

Current

Guide to the historical publications of the societies of England and Wales; Suppl. 1, 1929- . Lond., Longmans, 1930- . pts. 1- . (Bulletin of the Institute of Historical Research, Suppl., Nov. 1930-) 2s. 6d. ea. **V280**

Prepared by a committee of the Institute and of the Congress of Archaeological Societies, the supplements appearing before the basic work which is still in preparation. Planned to do for the societies of England and Wales what Terry (V320) and Matheson (V321) do for those of Scotland and also to take the place of the discontinued *Index of archaeological papers* (V270). The supplements merely record issues for the years covered, leaving the historical information about the societies and the records of publication, index, etc., to be given in the basic volume.

A change of form was made beginning with the seventh supplement, 1935, to avoid overlapping with the *Writings on British history* (V281). Now contains only a list of the volumes and parts of volumes published during the year by societies whose work is primarily archaeological or historical in interest, including societies which are concerned with contemporary history and bibliographical societies. Contents are noted only in the case of volumes of miscellanies.—Cf. *Introd.*

Writings on British history, 1934- . . . . comp. by Alexander Taylor Milne. Lond., J. Cape, 1937- . [v.1- .] Annual. (1937, pub. 1949. 12s. 6d.; $3.75) **V281**

Subtitle: A bibliography of books and articles on the history of Great Britain from about 450 A.D. to 1914, published during the year 1934 [-37] with an appendix containing a select list of publications in 1934 [-37] on British history since 1914.

Guides to records

Galbraith, Vivian Hunter. Introduction to the use of the public records. Ox., Clarendon Pr., 1934. 112p. $2. **V282**

Gt. Brit. Historical Manuscripts Commission. Guide to the reports of the Royal Commission on Historical Manuscripts, 1870–1911. Lond., Stat. Off., 1914–38. 2v. in 3. **V283**

pt.1, Topographical index. 1914. 233p.; pt.2, v.1-2, Index of persons. 859p.

Part 2 is an alphabetical index of names, with reference under each to the report or reports of the Commission in which some letter or document connected with the person is listed or calendared.

Gt. Brit. Public Record Office. Guide to the manuscripts preserved in the Public Record Office, by M. S. Guiseppi. Lond., Stat. Off., 1923–24. 2v. **V284**

Volume 1 is "largely based" on the third edition of the *Guide to the various classes of documents preserved in the Public Record Office*, by S. R. Scargill-Bird (Lond., 1908).

Dictionaries and handbooks

Brendon, John Adams. Dictionary of British history. N.Y., Longmans; Lond., Edward Arnold, 1937. 603p. 15s.; $5. **V285**

Designed primarily for the use of the general reader; convenient for quick reference for brief information but not a substitute for longer articles in Low and Pulling (V287). Appendices include: Lists of English and Scottish sovereigns, (English) Princes of Wales, Chief ministers of the crown from the Norman conquest, Archbishops of Canterbury and York, Governors-general and viceroys of India, Statistical table of national revenue and expenditure and national debt from 1688.

Cheney, Christopher Robert. Handbook of dates for students of English history. Lond., Offices of the Royal Historical Soc., 1945. 164p. (Royal Historical Soc. Guides and handbooks, no.4) 6s. **V286**

Combines some of the useful features of various other handbooks. Four sections are reprinted, with some revision, from Powicke, *Handbook of British chronology* (V288), viz., Reckonings of time, Rulers of England, Saints' days and festivals, and Legal chronology. The 36 tables of calendars for all possible dates of Easter are based on Grotefend, Hermann, *Zeitrechnung* (Hannover, 1891–98. 2v.) and Fry, *Almanacks for students of English history* (V22). Seven-page bibliography.

Low, *Sir* Sidney and **Pulling, F. S.** Dictionary of English history. New ed., rev. and enl. by F. J. C. Hearnshaw, H. M. Chew and A. C. F. Beales. Lond. and N.Y., Cassell, 1928. 1154p. **V287**

1st ed., 1884; new ed., rev., 1896.
A compact, well-edited dictionary, with concise articles and some bibliographical references, on subjects, events and personages in English history.

Powicke, Frederick Maurice. Handbook of British chronology, ed. by F. M. Powicke, with the assistance of Charles Johnson, and W. J. Harte. Lond., Royal Historical Soc., 1939. 424p. (Royal Historical Soc. Guides and handbooks, no.2) 7s. 6d. **V288**

Partial contents: Chronological lists of rulers of England, Wales, Scotland and the Isle of Man; English officers of state; Chief governors of Ireland; Bishops of England, Wales, Scotland, Ireland; Dukes, Marquesses, and Earls, 1066–1603; English parliaments, 1258–1547; Provincial and national councils of the Church of England to 1536; Time reckonings, calendars, regnal years, Saints' days and festivals, legal chronology, etc. Some of the tables are brought down to 1939, but others stop at earlier dates. It is hoped that a revised edition may standardize the work and that an index may be added.—Cf. *Pref.* This would materially increase the usefulness of the book.

Some sections in revised form are included in Cheney, *Handbook of dates for students of English history* (V286).

General histories

Green, John Richard. Short history of the English people. Illus. ed. . . . N.Y., Harper, 1893–95. 4v. il. **V289**

History of England, ed. by Charles Oman. Lond., Methuen; N.Y., Putnam [1904]-48. [v.1, 1910] 8v. maps. 21s.; $6 per v. **V290**

v.1, England before the Norman Conquest, by Charles Oman. 1910; v.2, England under the Normans and Angevins, by H. W. C. Davis. 1905; v.3, England in the later Middle Ages, by K. H. Vickers. 1914; v.4, England under the Tudors, by A. D. Innes. [1905]; v.5, England under the Stuarts, by G. M. Trevelyan. [1904]; v.6, England under the Hanoverians, by C. G. Robertson. 15th ed. 1948; v.7, England since Waterloo, by J. A. R. Marriott. 4th ed. 1921; v.8, Modern England, 1885–1939, a history of my own times, by J. A. R. Marriott. rev. ed. 1944.

Includes maps, plans, genealogical charts and at end of each volume, a bibliography of sources. Each volume frequently reissued with varying edition numbers.

Less detailed than the *Political history of England* by Hunt and Poole (V292) and for the most part somewhat more readable.

Oxford history of England. . . . Ox., Clarendon Pr., 1936–43. v.1-2, 8-11, 13-14. (In progress)
V291

v.1, Roman Britain and the English settlements, by R. G. Collingwood and J. N. L. Myres. 1936. 515p. 12s. 6d., $6.50; v.2, Anglo-Saxon England, by F. M. Stenton. 1943. 748p. 21s., $7; v.8, Reign of Elizabeth, by J. B. Black. 1936. 448p. 12s. 6d., $6.50; v.9, Early Stuarts, 1603–60, by Godfrey Davies. 1937. 452p. 12s. 6d., $6.50; v.10, The Later Stuarts, 1660–1714, by C. N. Clark. 1934. 461p. 12s. 6d., $6.50; v.11, Whig supremacy, 1714–1760, by Basil Williams, 1939. 464p. 12s. 6d., $6.50; v.13, Age of reform, 1815–1870, by E. L. Woodward. 1938. 653p. 15s., $6.50; v.14, England, 1870–1914, by K. C. K. Ensor. 1936. 634p. 15s., $6.50.

Political history of England, ed. by William Hunt and R. L. Poole. Lond. and N.Y., Longmans, 1905–15. [v.1, 1906] 12v. maps. **V292**

v.1, From the earliest time to the Norman Conquest, by T. Hodgkin; v.2, From the Norman Conquest to the death of John (1066–1216), by G. B. Adams; v.3, From the accession of Henry III to the death of Edward III (1216–1377), by T. F. Tout; v.4, From the accession of Richard II to the death of Richard III (1377–1485), by C. Oman; v.5, From the accession of Henry VII to the death of Henry VIII (1485–1547), by H. A. L. Fisher; v.6, From the accession of Edward VI to the death of Elizabeth (1547–1603), by A. F. Pollard; v.7, From the accession of James I to the Restoration (1603–1660), by F. C. Montague; v.8, From the Restoration to the death of William III (1660–1702), by R. Lodge; v.9, From the accession of Anne to the death of George II (1702–1760), by I. S. Leadam; v.10, From the accession of George III to the close of Pitt's first administration (1760–1801), by W. Hunt; v.11, From Addington's administration to the close of William IV's reign (1801–1837), by C. C. Brodrick and J. K. Fotheringham; v.12, During the reign of Victoria (1837–1901), by S. J. Low and L. C. Sanders.

A standard history, a cooperative work by specialists, each volume forming a separate unit, the whole giving a complete and detailed survey of the history of England from the earliest times to the end of the nineteenth century. Includes several special reference features, e.g., maps, genealogical charts, lists of administrations with names of cabinet members and, especially, bibliographical lists of authorities which are given at end of each volume as Appendix 1.

Traill, Henry Duff and **Mann, J. S.** Social England, a record of the progress of the people in religion, laws, learning, arts, industry, commerce, science, literature and manners from the earliest times to the present day. [New illus. ed.] Lond., Cassell; N.Y., Putnam, 1909. 6v. il. **V293**

A very valuable illustrated record of cultural history to 1909.

Source books

Adams, George Burton and **Stephens, Henry Morse.** Select documents of English constitutional history. Lond. and N.Y., Macmillan, 1901. 555p. $4.50. **V294**

Bland, Alfred Edward, Brown, P. A. and **Tawney, R. H.** English economic history; select documents. Lond., Bell, 1914. 730p. **V295**

Gee, Henry and **Hardy, W. J.** Documents illustrative of English church history. Lond. and N.Y., Macmillan, 1896. 670p. **V296**

Stephenson, Carl and **Marcham, Frederick George.** Sources of English constitutional history . . . A.D. 600 to the present. N.Y. and Lond., Harper, 1937. 906p. $4.50. **V297**

Robertson, Agnes Jane. Anglo-Saxon charters, ed. with translation and notes. Camb., Univ. Pr., 1939. 555p. (Cambridge studies in English legal history) 25s. **V298**

Stubbs, William. Select charters and other illustrations of English constitutional history, from the earliest times to the reign of Edward the First. 9th ed., rev. throughout by H. W. C. Davis. Ox., Clarendon Pr., 1913. 528p. 10s. 6d.; $3.75. **V299**

Lodge, Eleanor Constance and **Thornton, Gladys A.** English constitutional documents, 1307–1485. Camb., Univ. Pr., 1935. 430p. 12s. 6d.; $3. **V300**

Tanner, Joseph Robson. Constitutional documents of the reign of James I, A.D. 1603–1625. Camb., Univ. Pr., 1930. 389p. 18s. **V301**

—— Tudor constitutional documents, A.D. 1485–1603. 2d ed. Camb., Univ. Pr., 1930. 636p. 21s.; $6. **V302**

Tawney, Richard Henry and **Power, Eileen.** Tudor economic documents; being select documents illustrating the economic and social history of Tudor England. Lond. and N.Y., Longmans, 1924. 3v. (Univ. of London hist. ser. no.4) **V303**

Prothero, Sir George Walter. Select statutes and other constitutional documents illustrative of the reigns of Elizabeth and James I. 4th ed. Ox., Clarendon Pr., 1913. 490p. 10s. 6d.; $3.50. **V304**

Gardiner, Samuel Rawson. Constitutional documents of the Puritan revolution, 1625–1660. 3d ed., rev. Ox., Clarendon Pr., 1906. 476p. $3.75. **V305**

Robertson, Charles Grant. Select statutes, cases and documents to illustrate English constitutional history, 1660–1832. 2d ed., rev. and enl.. Lond., Methuen, 1913. 591p. 15s. **V306**

Violette, Eugene Morrow. English constitutional documents since 1832. N.Y., Macmillan, 1936. 226p. $2; 8s. 6d. **V307**

"Supplementary to Adams and Stephens, *Select documents of English constitutional history*" (V294).

Regional history

Anderson, John Parker. The book of British topography; a classified catalogue of the topographical works in the library of the British Museum relating to Great Britain and Ireland. Lond., Satchell, 1881. 472p. **V308**

Humphreys, Arthur Lee. Handbook to county bibliography, being a bibliography of bibliographies relating to the counties and towns of Great Britain and Ireland. Lond., Strangeways, 1917. 501p. **V309**

Victoria history of the counties of England. Lond., Constable; Ox., Univ. Pr., 1901–49. il. (In progress) 63s. per v. Index v. 21s. ea. **V310**

First published by Constable, then by the St. Catherine Press, and later by the Oxford University Press for the University of London, Institute of Historical Research.

Contents: *Bedford,* ed. by H. Arthur Doubleday and William Page. 3v. and Index; *Berkshire,* ed. by P. H. Ditchfield and William Page. 4v. and Index; *Buckingham,* ed. by William Page. 4v. and Index; *Cambridge,* and the *Isle of Ely,* ed. by L. F. Salzman. v.1-2; *Cornwall,* ed. by William Page. v.1; *Cumberland,* ed. by James Wilson. v.1-2; *Derby,* ed. by William Page. v.1-2; *Devon,* ed. by William Page. v.1; *Dorset,* ed. by William Page. v.2; *Durham,* ed. by William Page. v.1-3; *Essex,* v.1, ed. by H. Arthur Doubleday and William Page, v.2, ed. by William Page and J. Horace Round. v.1-2; *Gloucester,* ed. by William Page. v.2; *Hampshire* and the *Isle of Wight,* v.1-2, ed. by H. Arthur Doubleday, v.3-4, ed. by G. Henniker Gotley and W. J. Hardy, v.5, ed. by William Page. 5v. and Index; *Hereford,* ed. by William Page. v.1; *Hertford,* ed. by William Page. 4v. and Index; *Huntingdon,* ed. by William Page. 3v. and Index; *Kent,* ed. by William Page. v.1-3; *Lancaster,* ed. by William Farrer and J. Brownbill. v.1-8; *Leicester,* ed. by William Page. v.1; *Lincoln,* ed. by William Page. v.2; *London,* ed. by William Page. v.1; *Middlesex,* ed. by William Page. v.2; *Norfolk,* v.1, ed. by H. Arthur Doubleday, v.2, ed. by William Page. v.1-2; *Northampton,* ed. by W. Ryland, D. Adkins and R. M. Serjeantson. v.1-4; *Nottingham,* ed. by William Page. v.1-2; *Oxford,* ed. by William Page. v.1-2; *Rutland,* ed. by William Page. 2v. and Index; *Shropshire,* ed. by William Page. v.1; *Somerset,* ed. by William Page. v.1-2; *Stafford,* ed. by William Page. v.1; *Suffolk,* ed. by William Page. v.1-2; *Surrey,* ed. by H. E. Malden. 4v. and Index; *Sussex,* ed. by William Page. v.1-3, 7, 9; *Warwick,* v.1-2, ed. by William Page, v.3-5 ed. by L. F. Salzman. v.1-5; *Worcester,* v.1, ed. by J. W. Willis-Bund and H. Arthur Doubleday, v.2, ed. by J. W. Willis-Bund and William Page. 4v. and Index; *York, North Riding,* ed. by William Page. 2v. and Index.

Of first importance for its large amount of detailed information on the natural history, archaeology, industries, religious history and religious houses, political and social history, manorial history, topography, biography and genealogy of each county; contains numerous excellent illustrations and maps and many references to sources of information. Indispensable in any library doing much research work in English local history.

London

Cunningham, George H. London, being a comprehensive survey of the history, tradition and historical associations of buildings and monuments, arranged under streets in alphabetical order. Lond., Dent; N.Y., Dutton, 1927. 887p. 25s. **V311**

Harben, Henry Andrade. Dictionary of London; being notes topographical and historical relating to the streets and principal buildings in the city of London. Lond., Jenkins, 1918. 641p. 42s. **V312**

Kent, William. Encyclopaedia of London. Lond., Dent; N.Y., Dutton, 1937. 772p. il. $3.25. **V313**

London. County Council. List of the streets and places within the administrative county of London. 3d ed. comp. by the superintending architect of metropolitan buildings and architect to the Council. Lond., County Council, 1929. 646p. **V314**

Subtitle: Including the names of blocks of dwellings, parks and open spaces, showing localities, postal districts . . . parishes, metropolitan and parliamentary boroughs, electoral divisions, ordnance and municipal map references, together with the alterations in street nomenclature and numbering since 1856, and the origins of certain of the names.

Wheatley, Henry Benjamin. London, past and present; its history, associations, and traditions. Based upon the *Handbook of London,* by the late Peter Cunningham. Lond., Murray; N.Y., Scribner, 1891. 3v. o.p. **V315**

Alphabetically arranged by name of place, house, street, etc.

Scotland

Livingstone, Matthew. Guide to the public records of Scotland deposited in H. M. General Register House, Edinburgh. Edinburgh, General Register House, 1905. 233p. **V316**

Thomson, John Maitland. Public records of Scotland. Glasgow, Maclehose, Jackson, 1922. 175p. **V317**

Mitchell, Arthur and **Cash, C. G.** A contribution to the bibliography of Scottish topography. Edinburgh, Univ. Pr., 1917. 2v. (Pub. of the Scottish Historical Soc. 2d ser., v.14-15) **V318**

v.1 indexes material by place; v.2 by subject.

New York. Public Library. A list of works relating to Scotland, comp. by George F. Black. N.Y., Public Library, 1916. 1233p. (Repr. with additions from its Bulletin, Jan.–Dec. 1914) **V319**

Terry, Charles Sanford. Catalogue of the publications of Scottish historical and kindred clubs and societies, and of the volumes relative to Scottish history, issued by His Majesty's Stationery Office, 1780–1908. Glasgow, Maclehose, 1909. 253p. **V320**

A useful though not complete work, on the same general plan as Griffin's *Bibliography of American historical societies* (V97).

Contents: (1) Catalog of the publications of over 50 Scottish historical and kindred clubs and societies arranged alphabetically by name of society, giving for each its corporate name, date of founding, purpose, list of its publications, and contents of each volume if several papers are included; (2) Author and subject index to the publications and contents notes. The index is often useful for analytic references on small or out-of-the-way points in Scottish history.

Matheson, Cyril. Catalogue of the publications of Scottish historical and kindred clubs and societies and of the papers relative to Scottish history issued by H. M. Stationery Office, including the reports of the Royal Commission on Historical MSS., 1908–27. Aberdeen, Milne and Hutchison, 1928. 232p. 10s. **V321**

A continuation of two works by C. S. Terry: (1) his *Catalogue,* described above (V320), and (2) his *Index to the papers relating to Scotland . . . in the Historical MSS. Commissions reports.*

Contents: (1) Catalog of the publications of societies, arranged alphabetically, continuing Terry's *Catalogue* from 1908 and referring to pages in Terry for earlier titles; (2) Author and subject index; (3) Index to Terry's *Catalogue;* (4) Index to papers relating to Scotland in Historical MSS. Commission's reports.

Wales

Wales. University. Guild of Graduates. Welsh History Section. Bibliography of the history of Wales; ed. for the section by R. T. Jenkins and William Rees. Cardiff, Univ. of Wales Pr., 1931. 218p. **V322**

British Empire

Royal Empire Society, London. Library. Subject catalogue of the library of the Royal Empire Society, formerly Royal Colonial Institute, by Evans Lewin. [Lond., Society] 1930–37. v.1-4. (In progress) **V323**

v.1, British Empire generally, and Africa; v.2, Commonwealth of Australia, Dominion of New Zealand, South Pacific, general voyages and travels, and Arctic and Antarctic regions; v.3, Dominion of Canada and its provinces, Dominion of Newfoundland, the West Indies, and colonial America; v.4, Mediterranean colonies, Middle East, Indian Empire, Burma, Ceylon, British Malaya, East Indian Islands, and the Far East.

A fine catalog, particularly for the history, description, etc., of certain regions for which no separate bibliographies exist.

Arranged geographically and by subject under each country. Entries are chronological under subject. Includes books, pamphlets, periodical articles, etc. Author index in each volume.

Cambridge history of the British Empire; general eds.: J. Holland Rose, A. P. Newton, E. A. Benians. N.Y., Macmillan; Camb., Univ. Pr., 1929–41. v.1-2, 4-8. (In progress) **V324**

v.1, The Old empire from the beginnings to 1783. 35s., $8; v.2, Growth of the new empire, 1783–1870. 50s., $10.50; v.4, British India, 1497–1858. 30s., $9; v.5, Indian Empire, 1858–1918 with chapters on the development of administration, 1818–58. 30s., $7; v.6, Canada and Newfoundland. 35s., $9.50; v.7, pt.1, Australia. 30s., $7; pt.2, New Zealand. 15s., $3.50; v.8, South Africa, Rhodesia, and the Protectorates. 42s., $11.

Volumes 4-5 published also as volumes 5-6 of the *Cambridge history of India* (V340) and furnished in binding to match either set.

Bibliographies at end of each volume.

GUAM

Reid, Charles Frederick. Bibliography of the island of Guam. N.Y., Wilson, 1939. 102p. $1.50. **V325**

Arranged alphabetically by subjects with no author index, and no cross references. Includes a large amount of analysis of periodicals, government publications and general works.

HUNGARY

Apponyi, Sándor. Hungarica. Ungarn betreffende im Auslande gedruckte Bücher und Flugschriften. München, Rosenthal, 1903–27. 4v. **V326**

Bd.1, 15. und 16. Jahrhundert; Bd.2, 17. und 18. Jahrhundert (bis 1720); Bd.3, Neue Sammlung. I. 15. und 16. Jahrhundert besorgt von L. Dézsi; Bd.4, 17. und 18. Jahrhundert besorgt von L. Dézsi.

Banner, János. Bibliographia archaeologica hungarica, 1793–1943. Szeged, Ed. Institutum Archaeologicum Universitatis de Nicolao Horthy, 1944. 558p. (Fontes rerum archaeologicarum hungaricarum. t.1) **V327**

Bibliographia Hungariae. Zusammengestellt vom Ungarischen Institut an der Universität Berlin. Verzeichnis der 1861–1921 erschienenen, Ungarn betreffenden Schriften in nichtungarischer Sprache. Berlin, de Gruyter, 1923–29. 4v. (Ungarische Bibliothek für das Ungarische Institut an der Universität Berlin. 3. Reihe) **V328**

Contents: (1) Historica; (2) Geographica. Politico-oeconomica; (3) Philologica. Periodica; (4) Register.

Kont, Ignace. Bibliographie française de la Hongrie (1521–1910) avec un inventaire sommaire des documents manuscrits. Paris, Leroux, 1913. 323p. **V329**

ICELAND

See also Denmark, p.29 and p.495; Iceland, p.41.

Afzelius, Nils. Svenska skrifter rörande Island; gava till Islands allting vid 1000-årsjubileet 1930 av Sveriges Riksdag. Uppsala, Almquist & Wiksell, 1930. 62p. (Kungl. Bibliotekets Handlingar. 42) **V330**

Covers literature and history.

Kiel. Universität. Bibliothek. Islandkatalog der Universitätsbibliothek Kiel und der Universitäts- und Stadtbibliothek Köln, bearb. von Olaf Klose. Kiel, 1931. 423p. (Kataloge der Universitätsbibliothek Kiel. I) **V331**

Classed with alphabetical index.

INDIA

Bibliography

Gt. Brit. High Commissioner for India. India House Library. India House Library; a short catalogue. Lond., Office of the High Com. for India, 1933. 533p. **V332**

Instituut Kern, Leyden. Annual bibliography of Indian archaeology, published with the aid of the government of Netherlands India and with the support of the Imperial Government of India 1926- . Leyden, Brill, 1928- . v.1- . Annual. (v.15, 1940–47, pub. 1950) **V333**

An annotated bibliography, including books and periodical articles and referring to reviews of items included.

Moraes, George M. Bibliography of Indological studies 1942- . Bombay, Examiner Pr., 1945- . (Konkan Inst. of Arts and Sciences) **V334**

Planned as an annual supplement to his projected *Bibliography of Indian history* which would cover through 1941. Includes material on all phases of Indian history and culture.

Royal Empire Society, London. Library. Subject catalogue of the library. v.4. Lond., 1937. **V335**

Includes India, p.112-491.
For description of complete set *see* V323.

Encyclopedias and handbooks

Balfour, Edward Green. Cyclopaedia of India and of eastern and southern Asia, commercial, industrial, and scientific; products of the mineral, vegetable and animal kingdoms, useful arts and manufactures. 3d ed. Lond., Quaritch, 1885. 3v. **V336**

Still valuable for its geographical and ethnographical material.

Mukherji, Panchanandas. Indian constitutional documents. (1600–1918) 2d ed. enl. Calcutta, Thacker, Spink, 1918. 2v. (Indian citizen ser.) **V337**

Chronology

Rickmers, C. Mabel Duff. The chronology of India, from the earliest times to the beginning of the sixteenth century. Westminster, Constable, 1899. 409p. **V338**

Burgess, James. The chronology of modern India for four hundred years from the close of the fifteenth century, A.D. 1494–1894. Edinburgh, Grant, 1913. 483p. **V339**

A list of historical events, in chronological order, with a minute alphabetical index; on the same general plan as Mrs. Rickmers' work (V338); the two together forming a continuous chronology of India from the earliest times to 1894.

General histories

Cambridge history of India. Camb., Univ. Pr.; N.Y., Macmillan, 1922–37. v.1, 3-6. il. 142s.; $48. (In progress) **V340**

v.1, Ancient India, by E. J. Rapson; v.3, Turks and Afghans, by Sir Wolseley Haig; v.4, The Mughal period, by Sir Wolseley Haig; v.5, British India, 1497–1858, by H. H. Dodwell; v.6, Indian Empire, 1858–1918, by H. H. Dodwell.

Volumes 5-6 published also as volumes 4-5 of the *Cambridge history of the British Empire* (V324) and furnished in binding to match either set.

Written by authorities; extensive bibliographies, chronologies, etc.

INDO-CHINA

Boudet, Paul and **Bourgeois, Remy.** Bibliographie de l'Indochine française, 1913–1926. Hanoi, Impr. d'Extrême-Orient, 1929. 271p., 75p. **V341**

Cordier, Henri. Bibliotheca indosinica; dictionnaire bibliographique des ouvrages relatifs à la péninsule Indochinoise. . . . Paris, Impr. Nat., Leroux, 1912–32. 4v. and index (309p.) (Publications de l'École française d'Extrême-Orient. v.15-18 bis) 750fr. **V342**

IRAN

Saba, M. Bibliographie de l'Iran: Bibliographie méthodique et raisonnée des ouvrages français parus depuis 1560 jusqu'à nos jours. Paris, Domat-Montchrestien, 1936. 227p. **V343**

Thèse - Univ. de Paris.

A comprehensive classed list of books and periodical articles with author index.

Wilson, *Sir* Arnold Talbot. Bibliography of Persia. Ox., Clarendon Pr., 1930. 253p. **V344**

Lists books and periodical articles in the principal European languages, arranged alphabetically except that anonymous works are grouped under general subject headings, such as, Letters, Journals, Routes, etc. Also includes translations into European languages of original Persian works.

IRELAND

Curtis, Edmund and **McDowell, Robert Brendon.** Irish historical documents, 1172–1922. Lond., Methuen, 1943. 331p. **V345**

Dublin. National Library of Ireland. Bibliography of Irish history, 1870–1911, 1912–1921, by James Carty. Dublin, Stat. Off., 1936–40. 2v. **V346**

1870–1911. 1940. 319p. 10s. 6d.; 1912–1921. 1936. 177p. 6s.

Ireland. Public Record Office. A guide to the records deposited in the Public Record Office of Ireland by Herbert Wood. Dublin, Stat. Off., 1919. 334p. **V347**

Kenney, James F. Sources for the early history of Ireland; an introduction and guide. N.Y., Columbia Univ. Pr., 1929- . v.1- . **V348**

v.1, Ecclesiastical.

Writings on Irish history, 1936- . (In Irish historical studies, v.1, 1936- . Annual) **V349**

Compiled in cooperation with the Bibliographical Subcommittee of the Irish Committee of Historical Sciences, 1936–37 by James Carty; 1939- by R. B. McDowell.

ITALY

See Bibliography, p.42, for bibliographies of general and local historical bibliography.

Bibliografia storica nazionale. Anno 1, 1939- . Giunto Centrale per gli Studi Storici. Roma, Tip. del Senato, 1942- . Annual. (Anno 9/10, 1947/48. pub. 1950) **V350**

A classified record of books and periodical articles, published in Italy about Italy. Name index. In many cases indicates location of reviews. Follows the general form of the *International bibliography of historical sciences* (V11).

Evola, Niccolò Domenico. Origini e dottrina del Fascismo. Firenze, Sansoni, 1935. 166p. (Guide bibliographiche dell' Istituto Nazionale Fascista di Cultura. I) **V351**

Hassall, W. O. A select bibliography of Italy: A thousand books about Italy, its geography, population, cities and regions, its language, literature and history, its social, economic and political life, its art and music. London, ASLIB, 1946. 82p. 6s. **V352**

A useful selected list planned for the English and American user. Includes the basic materials in Italian.

Lemmi, Francesco. Il risorgimento. Roma, Fondazione Leonardo, 1926. 320p. (Guide bibliografiche [23-24]) **V353**

Covers 1748–1870.

Lozzi, Carlo. Biblioteca istorica della antica e nuova Italia; saggio di bibliografia, analitico comparato e critico. . . . Imola, Galeati e Figlio, 1886–87. 2v. **V354**

A classified bibliography of more than 6500 archaeological and historical works on Italian municipalities. A third volume which should have contained the index was never published.

Gardner, Edmund G. Italy: A companion to Italian studies. Lond., Methuen, 1934. 274p. **V355**

Survey articles by specialists on the history and culture of Italy, with bibliographies.

See also Enciclopedia italiana, v.19, p.898-916 (D46), for a useful bibliography of the history of Italy compiled by F. Chabod.

JAPAN

See also Asia, p.490.

Bibliography

Borton, Hugh, Elisséeff, Serge and **Reischauer, Edwin O.** A selected list of books and articles on Japan in English, French and German. Wash., Committee on Japanese Studies, Amer. Council of Learned Societies, 1940. 142p. $1.50. **V356**

Includes bibliographies, reference works, periodicals, geography, history, economics, government and politics, sociology and ethnology, education and journalism, mythology, religion, philosophy, language, literature, art.

Cordier, Henri. Bibliotheca japonica; dictionnaire bibliographique des ouvrages relatifs à l'Empire japonais rangés par ordre chronologique jusqu'à 1870, suivi d'un appendice renfermant la liste alphabétique des principaux ouvrages parus de 1870 à 1912. Paris, Leroux, 1912. 762 col. (Publ. de l'École des Langues Orientales Vivantes, 5. sér., v.8) **V357**

Wenckstern, Friedrich von. A bibliography of the Japanese Empire; being a classified list of all books, essays and maps in European languages relating to Dai Nihon (Great Japan) published in Europe, America and in the East, 1859/93–1894/1906. Leiden, Brill, 1895; Tokyo, Maruya, 1907. 2v. **V358**

v.1, Literature published 1859–93, 338p.; Facsimile reprint of: Pagés, Leon. *Bibliographie japonaise*. Paris, 1859. 68p.; v.2, Literature published 1894–1906, 486p.; Supplement to Pagés' *Bibliographie japonaise*, 28p.; List of Swedish literature on Japan, by Vilfrid Palmgren, 21p.

Continued by the following:

Nachod, Oskar. Bibliographie von Japan, 1906–[1929]: Enthaltend ein ausführliches Verzeichnis der Bücher und Aufsätze über Japan, die seit der Ausgabe des zweiten Bändes von Wenckstern "Bibliography of the Japanese Empire" bis 1926 in europäischen Sprachen erschienen sind. . . . Leipzig, Hiersemann, 1928–40. v.1-6. **V359**

v.1-2 also published with English title: *Bibliography of the Japanese Empire*, 1906–26 (Lond., Goldston, 1928).

v.1-2, Books and articles. 1906–26; v.3, 1927–29. 1931; v.4, 1930–32, von Hans Praesent. 1935; v.5, 1933–35, von Hans Praesent und Wolf Haenisch. 1937; v.6, 1936–37, von Wolf Haenisch und Hans Praesent. 1940. Each volume includes some titles of earlier dates omitted from previous volumes.

A comprehensive classified list, including books, pamphlets and periodical articles; volumes 1-6 list a total of 33,621 items.

Watsuji, Tetsuró. A bibliography of representative writings on Japanese culture and science. Tokyo, Foreign Office, Cultural Affairs Division, Office of Public Relations, 1947. 122p., 11p. **V360**

Dictionaries and handbooks

Chamberlain, Basil Hall. Things Japanese; being notes on various subjects connected with Japan, for the use of travellers and others. 6th ed. rev. Lond., Kegan Paul, 1939. 584p. il. **V361**

An alphabetical dictionary by large subjects, with index of smaller subjects; bibliographical references. The sixth edition contains revisions, additions and supplementary material.

Some copies of this edition were censored by officials of the Imperial Japanese government, and p.11-12, 79-94, 247-252, 345-346 were deleted.

Papinot, E. Historical and geographical dictionary of Japan. Ann Arbor, Mich., Overbeck Co., 1948. 842p. il. $10. **V362**

Lithoprinted from the original edition published at Yokohama by Kelly and Walsh in 1910, that being a translation of the earlier *Dictionnaire d'histoire et de géographie du Japon*, 1906.

An alphabetical arrangement of names, places and events important in the history and geography of Japan.

Ramming, Martin. Japan-Handbuch; Nachschlagewerk der Japankunde. Im Auftrage des

Japaninstituts Berlin. Berlin, Steiniger [1941]. 740p. il. **V363**

An alphabetical dictionary of things Japanese, including biography.

KOREA

Courant, Maurice. Bibliographie coréenne: Tableau littéraire de la Corée, contenant la nomenclature des ouvrages publiés dans ce pays jusqu'en 1890 ainsi que la description et l'analyse détaillées des principaux d'entre ces ouvrages. Paris, Leroux, 1894–96. 3v. il. (Publ. de l'École des Langues Orientales Vivantes, 3. sér., v.18-20) **V364**

Contents: v.1, Enseignement, Étude des langues, Confucianisme, Littérature; v.2, Moeurs et coutumes, Histoire et géographie; v.3, Sciences et arts, religions, relationes exterieures. Index.

———— Supplément (jusqu'en 1899). Paris, 1901. 122p. (Publ. de l'École des Langues Orientales Vivantes. 3. sér., v.21)

LATIN AMERICA

See name of country for history of individual country in Latin America.

Bibliography

See also Latin America, p.43-44.

Barry, M. Elizabeth and **Goetz, Delia.** Children of the other Americas. Office of the Coordinator of Inter-American Affairs. Wash., Govt. Prt. Off., 1942. 170p. **V365**

"A guide to materials in English on the Other Americas suitable for the elementary and junior high school grades."

Behrendt, Richard F. Modern Latin America in social science literature. Albuquerque, Univ. of New Mexico Pr., 1949. 152p. **V366**

Subtitle: A selected annotated bibliography of books, pamphlets, and periodical articles in English in the fields of economics, politics, and sociology of Latin America.

Handbook of Latin American studies. Camb. Harv. Univ. Pr., 1936- . v.1- . Annual. **V367**

An extensive, annotated bibliography of material relating to Latin America, prepared by a group of scholars. Coverage varies. 1945 (published 1948) covers anthropology, archives, art, economics, education, folklore, cartography, geography, government, history, international relations, labor and social welfare, language and literature, law, libraries, music and philosophy.

Each volume also contains special articles on particular phases of life and culture or Inter-American relations.

Humphreys, Robin Arthur. Latin America: A selective guide to publications in English. Lond., Royal Inst. of International Affairs, 1949. 63p. 5s.
V368

A selective guide to some 900 books in English. Does not include periodical articles.

Keniston, Hayward. List of works for the study of Hispanic-American history. N.Y., Hispanic Soc. of Amer., 1920. 451p. (Hispanic notes and monographs, 5) **V369**

A valuable guide, still useful in spite of its date.

Wilgus, Alva Curtis. Histories and historians of Hispanic America. N.Y., Wilson, 1942. 144p. $1.75. **V370**

Revised, corrected and augmented edition of the work first appearing in 1936. Chronologically arranged by centuries and then grouped geographically by countries. Discusses the principal writings of over 1000 historians.

Encyclopedias and handbooks

Diccionario enciclopedico de las Americas; geografía, historia, economía, política, literatura, arte, música, deporte, cine, teatro, etnografía, fauna, flora, ciencias generales. 1. ed. Buenos Aires, Ed. Futuro, 1947. 711p. **V371**

A general encyclopedia with very brief articles, averaging four or five lines, with some longer ones, on all phases of life in the Americas including the United States. Includes biography.

Marchant, Alexander Nelson De Armand. Boundaries of the Latin American republics; an annotated list of documents, 1493–1943. (Tentative version) Wash., Govt. Prt. Off., 1944. 386p. (U.S. Dept. of State. Pub. 2082. Inter-American ser. 24) 40c. **V372**

Contents: pt.1, Documents arranged in chronological order, p.21-214; pt.2, Documents arranged according to boundary, p.215-351; Bibliography, p.355-86.

MADAGASCAR

Grandidier, Guillaume. Bibliographie de Madagascar. Paris, Comité de Madagascar, 1905–06. 405p. **V373**

—— and Joucla, E. Bibliographie de Madagascar, 1904–1933. Paris, Soc. d'Éditions Géographiques, Maritimes et Coloniales, 1935. p.759-850. (Bibliographie générale des colonies franaises)

Paged continuously with main part of the earlier volume, disregarding the supplement which appeared in that work.

MANCHURIA

Gibert, Lucien. Dictionnaire historique et géographique de la Mandchourie. Hongkong, Impr. de la Soc. des Missions Étrangères, 1934. 1040p. il. **V374**

MEXICO

Bibliography

California. State Library, Sacramento. Sutro Branch, San Francisco. Catalogue of Mexican pamphlets in the Sutro collection (1623-[1888]). Prepared by the personnel of the Works Progress Administration . . . A. Yedidia, supervisor. P. Radin, ed. Sponsored by the California State Library. San Francisco, 1939–40. 10 pts. (963 numb. l.) **V375**

—— —— Supplement (1605–1887). San Francisco, 1941. 290 numb. l. in 3 pts.

—— —— Author index. . . . San Francisco, 1941. 65 numb. l.

"In content and form the Supplement follows the *Catalogue* in all respects but two. First, while only part of the material relating to the Church was included in the *Catalogue,* all the material with the exception of prayers is included in the Supplement. Secondly an attempt has been made to present in the Supplement complete rather than short entries."—*Introd.*

The author index indexes both the main work and supplement.

Guzmán y Raz Guzmán, Jesús. Bibliografía de la independencia de México. México, Departamento Autónomo de Prensa y Publicidad, 1937–39. 3v. (Bibliografías Mexicanas, no.4-6) **V376**

"Indice alfabético de la 'Colección de documentos para la historia de la guerra de independencia de México de 1808 à 1821,' formada por J. E. Hernández y Davalos," por Genaro García, v.3, p.347-520.

—— Bibliografía de la reforma, la intervencion y el imperio. . . . Mexico, Impr. de la Secretaría de Relaciones Exteriores, 1930–31. 2v. (Monografias bibliográficas Mexicanas, núm. 17, 19) **V377**

Ramos, Roberto. Bibliografía de la revolución mexicana. México, Bibliografías Mexicanas, 1931–40. 3v. **V378**

Valle, Rafael Heliodoro. Bibliografía Maya. . . . Mexico, D.F., 1937–41. 404p. **V379**

At head of title: Instituto Panamericano de Geografía e Historia.

Issued in parts with the *Boletin bibliográfico de antropología americana,* v.1-5, 1937–41.

A comprehensive bibliography of materials about Mayan culture in various languages and of all periods.

Dictionaries

Garcia Cubas, Antonio. Diccionario geográfico, histórico y biográfico de los Estados Unidos Mexicanos. México, Oficina Tip. de la Secretaría de Fomento, 1888–91. 5v. il. **V380**

Leduc, Alberto, Lara y Pardo, Luis and **Roumagnac, Carlos.** Diccionario de geografía, historia y biografía mexicanas. Mexico [etc.], Bouret, 1910. 1109p. **V381**

Printed in Paris.

MOROCCO

Cenival, Pierre de, Funck-Brentano, C. and **Bousser, M.** Bibliographie marocaine, 1923–1933. Paris, Larose, 1937. 606p. **V382**

A reprinting of the annual bibliographies originally appearing in *Hespéris*.

NETHERLANDS

Repertorium der verhandelingen en bijdragen betreffende de geschiedenis des vaderlands, in tijdschriften en mengelwerken tot op 1900 verschenen. In opdracht van de Commissie voor Gescheid- en Oudheidkunde van de Maatschappij der Nederlandsche Letterkunde te Leiden bewerkt door L. D. Petit. Leiden, Brill, 1907. 1638 col. **V383**

Listing publications through 1900.

—— 2.-4. deel. Leiden, Brill, 1913–33.

2. deel, 1901–10. 884 col.; 3. deel, 1911–20. 904 col.; 4. deel, 1921–29. 1132 col.; 5. deel, 1930–39. (In progress)

A comprehensive classified bibliography of analytical material on all aspects of Dutch history, indexing articles on the subject in over 1000 periodicals, society transactions, composite books, etc., principally Dutch publications but including also some in other languages. List of titles indexed varies in the different volumes.

Continued by:

Repertorium van boeken en tijdschriftartikelen betreffende de geschiedenis van Nederland, door Aleida Gast. 1940- . Leiden, Brill, 1943- . v.1- . Annual. **V384**

Continues the *Repertorium der verhandelingen en bijdragen betreffende de geschiedenis des vaderlands* (V383) but on a smaller scale.

v.1, 1940. Groningen, Noordhoff, 1943; v.2, 1941–v.3, 1942–1944. Leiden, 1945–47.

Atlases

Geschiedkundige atlas van Nederland . . . Uitg. door de Commissie voor den Geschiedkundigen Atlas van Nederland en geteekend door het lid der Commissie. Dr. A. A. Beekman. 'sGraven hage, Nijhoff, 1913–38. v.1-19 (incompl.). 25cm and atlases, 50cm. **V38**

NETHERLANDS EAST INDIES

See also Oceanica, p.511-12.

Bibliography

Chijs, Jacobus Anne van der. Proeve eener Ned Indische bibliographie (1659–1870). . . . [Batavia, Bruining & Wijt, 1875–1903] 325p. and suppl. 93p., 64p. (Verhandelingen van het Bataviaasch Genootschap van Kunsten en Wetenschappen, deel 37, 55) **V38**

Basic list, 1659–1870, 325p.; the two supplements giv additions and corrections for the years 1720–1870.

Hague. Koloniale Bibliotheek. Catalogus de Koloniale Bibliotheek van het Kon. Instituut voo de Taal-, Land- en Volkenkunde van Ned. Indi en het Indisch Genootschap, door G. P. Rouffae en W. C. Muller. 'sGravenhage, Nijhoff, 1908–3 1053p. and 3 suppl. **V38**

Suppl. 1, 1915, 426p.; 2, 1927, 458p.; 3, 1937, 438

Hooykaas, J. C. Repertorium op de koloniaa litteratuur, of systematische inhoudsopgaaf va hetgeen voorkomt over de koloniën (beoosten d Kaap) in mengelwerken en tijdschriften 1595 1865 uitg. in Nederland en zijne overzeesche bi zittingen. . . . Amsterdam, van Kampen, 1874–8 2v. **V38**

Repertorium op de literatuur betreffende d Nederlandsche koloniën, voor zoover zij ve spreid is in tijdschriften en mengelwerken . . Samengesteld door A. Hartmann. 'sGravenhag Nijhoff, 1895–1935. 454p. and suppl. 1–8. **V38**

Basic volume, East Indies, 1866–93, West Indies, 184 93; supplements 1-8: v.1, 1894–1900. 1901. 224p v.2, 1901–05. 1906. 233p.; v.3, 1906–10. 1912. 271p v.4, 1911–15. 1917. 378p.; v.5, 1916–20. 1923. 508p v.6, 1921–25. 1928. 522p.; v.7, 1926–30. 1935. 712p v.8, 1931–32. 1934. 189p.

Suppl. 1-2, by A. Hartmann; 3-6, by W. J. P. Schalken and W. C. Muller; 7-8, by D. Sepp.

Includes a large amount of indexing of periodical a other analytical material, much of which is not eas available in other forms.

U. S. Library of Congress. General Referen and Bibliography Division. Netherlands Ea Indies: A bibliography of books published aft 1930, and periodical articles after 1932 availab in U.S. libraries. Wash., 1945. 208p. 55c. **V3**

Classified with author index. Locates copies in ov 90 libraries.

Encyclopedias and handbooks

Daniel, Hawthorne. Islands of the East Indies, with six maps by Lucien G. Picard. N.Y., Putnam [1944]. 266p. maps. $2.50. **V391**

A companion volume to his *Islands of the Pacific* (V406). Gives geographical information, including size, location, topography, climate, population, flora and fauna, and natural resources, of some 3000 islands that make up the Netherlands territories in the Far East, parts of New Guinea, Borneo, and Timor, and the Philippine Islands.

Encyclopaedie van Nederlandsch-Indië, 2. druk. met medewerking van verschillende geleerden ambtenaaren en officieren. 'sGravenhage, Nijhoff, 1917–40. v.1-8, 9 (incompl.). **V392**

v.1-4, A-Z; v.5-8, Suppl. 1-4. [v.9] Suppl. 5, Afl. 61-62.

An encyclopedia of everything about the region, its geography, inhabitants, products, etc., as well as its history; includes biography. An excellent work, with authoritative articles by specialists and good bibliographies.

An abridged edition based upon volumes 1-4 is: *Beknopte encyclopaedie van Nederlandsch-Indië . . . bewerkt door T. J. Bezemer* (Nijhoff, 1921. 632p.).

NEW ZEALAND

Hocken, Thomas M. Bibliography of the literature relating to New Zealand. Wellington, N.Z., Mackay, 1909. 619p. **V393**

Includes a Maori bibliography, p.499-547.

——— ———Supplement, comp. by A. H. Johnstone. Auckland, Whitcombe and Tomb, 1927. 73p.

Lists works published before 1909 not given in Hocken and some published 1909–26.

Chapple, Leonard James Bancroft. Bibliographical brochure containing addenda and corrigenda to extant bibliographies of New Zealand literature. Dunedin, N.Z., Reed, 1938. **V394**

Lists 116 items published in 1909 or earlier not found in Hocken or Johnstone (V393).

Royal Empire Society, London. Library. Subject catalogue. v.2. Lond., 1931. **V395**

Volume 2 includes a comprehensive bibliography on New Zealand. For description of complete set *see* V323.

Taylor, C. R. H. General bibliography. (In New Zealand official yearbook 55:979-98, 1947/49) **V396**

A list of some of the principal works dealing with New Zealand, Samoa, and the Cook Islands, issued since 1912. Earlier works are listed in the 1932 *Year-book.*

NORWAY

See also Denmark, p.495, and Sweden, p.515-16.

Schweigaard, Johan Elias. Norges topografi; bibliografisk fortegnelse over topografisk og lokal-historisk literatur. Kristiania, Grøndahl, 1918. 291p. **V397**

——— ———Tillegg, 1917–1927, ved W. P. Sommerfeldt. Oslo, Brøgger, 1930. 250p.

Skard, Sigmund. Bøker om norges kamp; bibliografiske samlingar. With an English summary. Wash., Royal Norwegian Information Service, 1945. 96p. **V398**

Lists books and pamphlets pertaining to Norway's part in the war printed outside of Norway since the German aggression, April 9, 1940.

Bibliografi til Norges historie, 1916–1925, 1926–1935, 1936- . . . . Utgitt av den Norske historiske forening. Oslo, Grondahl, 1927- . Annual. **V399**

Issued as annual supplements to *Historisk tidsskrift* (Oslo).

Full annual bibliography, including books, pamphlets and analytical material in periodicals, etc. General title pages and general author indexes are issued for ten-year periods, 1916–25, and 1926–35. Items are numbered consecutively throughout the ten-year period. With the issue of 1936 a new serial numbering of items begins, to form another volume not yet completed.

OCEANICA

Bibliography

Allied Forces. An annotated bibliography of the Southwest Pacific and adjacent areas. [n.p.] 1944. v.1-3. maps. **V400**

At head of title: Allied Geographical Section. Southwest Pacific Area.

Contents: v.1, The Netherlands and British East Indies and the Philippine Islands. 317p.; v.2, The Mandated territory of New Guinea, Papua, the British Solomon Islands, the New Hebrides and Micronesia. 274p.; v.3, Malaya, Thailand, Indo China, the China coast and the Japanese Empire. 256p.

Claremont Colleges, Claremont, Calif. Library. Materials on the Pacific area, in the Oriental library of Claremont Colleges Library and in the libraries of Pomona College and Scripps College, Claremont. . . . A preliminary checklist. Claremont, Calif., Claremont Colleges Lib., 1939. 141p. $2. **V401**

Issued under the auspices of Institute of Pacific Relations, American Council, Southern California Division.

Includes books, bound pamphlets and maps (about 2600 titles), and periodicals and serials (about 240 titles).

——— Materials on the Pacific area, in selected libraries of the Los Angeles region. A second checklist. . . . Claremont, Calif., Claremont Collegs Lib., 1943–44. 3 pts. **V402**

Supplementary to the preliminary checklist *Materials on the Pacific area* noted above (V401), and does not duplicate it.

Contents: pt.1, Books in western languages (predominantly Claremont but reports holdings of some other libraries). 289p. 5150 titles. $3.50; pt.2, Periodicals and serials in 36 California libraries (for Claremont libraries to January 1944, for others as reported in the *Union list of serials* to June 30, 1941). 90p. 1190 titles. $2.50; pt.3, Books in Chinese and Japanese languages (wholly Claremont in Chinese section but reports other holdings in Japanese section). 60p. 1100 titles. $2.

Lewin, Percy Evans. The Pacific region: A bibliography of the Pacific and East Indian islands, exclusive of Japan. Lond., Royal Empire Soc., 1944. 76p. 4s. (Royal Empire Soc. bibliographies, no.11) **V403**

Royal Empire Society, London. Library. Subject catalogue. v.2. Lond., 1931. **V404**

For description of complete set *see* V323.

U. S. Library of Congress. Division of Bibliography. Islands of the Pacific; a selected list of references, comp. by Helen F. Conover under the direction of Florence S. Hellman, chief bibliographer. Wash., Library, 1943. 181p. Free to libraries only. **V405**

"Intended to indicate modern and available sources for research on the islands of Melanesia, Polynesia and Micronesia. Most of the material is supplementary to that in the *Subject catalogue of the Royal Empire Society* (1931)."—*Foreword.*

———————— Supplement. Wash., 1945. 68p.

Includes a combined index to material in both parts.

Handbooks

Daniel, Hawthorne. Islands of the Pacific. N.Y., Putnam, 1943. 228p. maps. $2.75. **V406**

A description of the individual islands and the island groups of the Pacific. Gives location, size, topography, population, natural resources, products, etc.

Pacific islands handbook, 1944. North American ed. by Robert William Robson. N.Y., Macmillan, 1945. 371p. maps. $4. **V407**

A North American edition of the *Pacific islands yearbook,* published in Australia, last edition 1942 (reprinted without change 1944). This American edition has been revised, rewritten and rearranged. The islands of the Pacific are divided into five sections: Polynesian, Micronesian, Melanesian, Indonesian, and Non-Tropical. A brief note added as an introduction to each territory, describes how that territory was affected by the war. Includes a chronology of the Pacific war from Pearl Harbor to March 1944.

PALESTINE
Bibliography

Palestine and Zionism; a bibliography of books, pamphlets and periodicals. N.Y., Zionist Archives and Library, 1946- . v.1- . **V408**

Ed.: Sophie A. Udin.

Issued bimonthly. Cumulated annually and triennially.

Each issue is in two sections: index to current periodical material and a list of recently published books and pamphlets. The periodical section indexes Palestinian and Zionist periodicals in Hebrew, Yiddish, English and other languages, and pertinent articles in general periodicals. Author, title and subject entries in one alphabet.

The book list is also arranged by author, title and subject and includes publications in English, Hebrew, Yiddish and other languages. Titles in Hebrew and Yiddish are given in English.

Post-war bibliography of the Near Eastern mandates, 1919–1930. Stuart C. Dodd, General ed. Beirut, Syria, American Pr., 1932–36. 8 fascs. (American Univ. of Beirut. Pub. of the Faculty of Arts and Sciences. Social science series, no.1) **V409**

A preliminary survey of publications on the social sciences dealing with Iraq, Palestine and Trans-Jordan, and the Syrian states, from Nov. 11, 1918 to Dec. 31, 1929, arranged in an alphabetical list by authors, with a limited index by subject matter, presented in . . . eight fascicles by languages . . . (A) Arabic; (A P) Arabic periodicals; (E) English; (F) French; (G) German (never printed?); (H) Hebrew; (I) Italian; (M) Miscellaneous oriental languages; Armenian, Kurdish, Persian, Syriac, Turkish.

Royal Empire Society, London. Library. Subject catalogue. v.4. Lond., 1937. **V410**

For description of complete set *see* V323.

Thomsen, Peter. Die Palästina-Literatur; eine internationale Bibliographie in systematischer Ordnung mit Autoren-und Sachregister. . . . Leipzig, Hinrich, 1911–38. v.1-5. **V411**

v.1 (2. Ausg.), 1895–1904; v.2, 1905–09; v.3, 1910–14; v.4, 1915–24; v.5, 1925–34.

Published under the auspices of the Deutscher Verein zur Erforschung Palästinas, the Palestine exploration fund, Zionistisches Kommission zur Erforschung Palästinas, Gesellschaft zur Förderung der Wissenschaft des Judentums, and Notgemeinschaft der deutschen Wissenschaft.

1st ed. of v.1 (1908) has title: Systematische Bibliographie der Palästina-Literatur.

A very comprehensive index to book and periodical literature in many languages.

Encyclopedias and handbooks

Press, Isaiah. Eres yisrāēl. Topographical-historical encyclopaedia of Palestine. Jerusalem, Rubin Mass, 1946- . v.1- . il. (In progress) $9.50 per v. **V412**

v.1, A-G.

In Hebrew with added title page and introduction in English. A new encyclopedia treating the history of Palestine from ancient times to modern Israel and Arabic Palestine.

Luke, Harry Charles and **Keith-Roach, Edward.** The handbook of Palestine and Trans-Jordan. 2d ed. Lond., Macmillan, 1930. 505p. il. **V413**

Covers geography, history, archaeology, peoples and religions, government, commerce and industry, geology and natural history.

Palestine year book, 5706- , review of events Sept. 26, 1944/45- , ed. by Sophie A. Udin. N.Y., Zionist Organization of Amer., 1945- . v.1- . **V414**

Survey articles, bibliographies, organizational information, statistics, etc.

PERU

Mendiburu, Manuel de. Diccionario histórico-biográfico del Perú. Lima, Imp. "Enrique Palacios," 1931–35. 11v. **V415**

For full description *see* S188.

POLAND

See also Slavic Europe, p.515.

Finkel, Ludwik. Bibliografia historyi polskiej. Wspólnie z dr. Henrykiem Sawczyńskim i członkami Kółka historycznego uczniów Uniwersytetu lwowskiego zebrał i ułozył dr. Ludwik Finkel. W Krakowie, Nakładem Komisyi Historycznej Akademii Umiejętności w Krakowie, 1891–1906. 2150p. **V416**

Issued in seven parts.
2d ed., v.1, pts. 1-3, Lwów, Nakł. Polskiego towarzystwa historycznego, 1931–35.

———— Dodatek 1-2¹. Krakow, 1906–14.

An excellent bibliography listing works published down to 1900 on Polish history to 1815. The second supplement lists original sources published 1901–10. The second edition remains incomplete and with no index.
For works published after 1910 consult the periodical bibliography *Kwartalnik Historyczny* (1887-).

Comité des Publications Encyclopédiques sur la Pologne. Encyclopédie polonaise. Lausanne, 1916–20. il. v.1-4, pt.1. **V417**

v.1, Géographie et ethnographie; v.2, Territoire et population; v.3, Vie économique; v.4, pt.1, Régime politique et administratif dans la Pologne prussienne.

———— Atlas. Fribourg, 1920- .

Unfinished but an authoritative work as far as it goes. Partially published in an English edition as:

Polish encyclopaedia. . . . Published by the Committee for the Polish Encyclopaedic Publications at Fribourg and Geneva (Switzerland). Geneva, Atar, 1922–26. (v.1, 1926) 3v. maps. (Pub. of the Polish National Committee of America) **V418**

Contents: v.1, The Polish language; History of literature; History of Poland; v.2, Territory and population of Poland; v.3, Economic life of Poland.

PORTUGAL

Brito Aranha, Pedro W. de. Bibliographie des ouvrages Portugais pour servir à l'étude des villes, des villages, des monuments, des institutions, des moeurs et coutumes, etc., du Portugal, Açores, Madère et possessions d'outremer. Lisbonne, Imp. Nat., 1900. 90p. **V419**

Arranged alphabetically by place or subject with author index.

Costa Coutinho, Bernard Xavier da. Bibliographie franco-portugaise; essai d'une bibliographie chronologique de livres français sur le Portugal. Porto, Lopes da Silva, 1939. 409p. **V420**

"Publiée sous les auspices de l'Institut Français au Portugal et de l'Instituto para a Alta Cultura, avec le concours du Secrétariat de la Propagande Nationale."

Lisbon. Biblioteca Nacional. Subsidios para a bibliografia da história local Portuguêsa. Lisboa, Bib. Nac., 1933. 425p. **V421**

See also Foulché-Delbosc, *Manuel de l'hispanisant* (A490); and *Bibliographie hispanique* (R702).

RUMANIA

Crăciun, Ioachim. Bibliographie de la Transylvanie Roumaine, 1916–1936. Cluj, Roumanie, 1937. 366p. (Revue de Transylvanie, 3. année, no.4) **V422**

Rally, Alexandre and **Rally, Getta Hélène.** Bibliographie franco-roumaine. Paris, Leroux, 1930. 1.pt. t.1-2. **V423**

(1¹) Les oeuvres françaises des auteurs roumains; (1²) Les oeuvres françaises relatives à la Roumanie.
t.1, arranged alphabetically by authors; t.2, arranged by class with alphabetical index to names and places.
To a large extent supersedes the earlier work by Georges Bengescu, *Bibliographie franco-roumaine depuis le commencement du* xix *siècle jusqu'à nos jours* (Paris, 1907), of which only volume 1 was published (second edition with supplement, 1895–1906). The bibliographical descriptions in Bengescu are longer, but the coverage is less complete.

See also Enciclopedia Românieı (D58).

RUSSIA

See also Slavic Europe, p.515.

Bibliography

Grierson, Philip. Books on Soviet Russia, 1917–1942; a bibliography and a guide to reading. Lond., Methuen, 1943. 354p. 12s. 6d. **V424**

An annotated, classified guide to books and pamphlets on all phases of life in Soviet Russia, most of which were published in Great Britain. Includes a few works published in the United States and the Soviet Union and a few in languages other than English. Author index.

Kommunisticheskaĭa Akademiĭa. Biblioteka. Lenin i Leninism; alphabetno-predmetiyĭ ukazatel' literatury v Biblioteke Kommunisticheskoĭ Akademiĭ. Moskva, Kommunisticheskoĭ Akademiĭ, 1928. 365p. **V425**

Added title page in English.

An alphabetical and subject index to works by and about Lenin in the library of the Communist Academy.

Mazour, Anatole Grigorevich. An outline of modern Russian historiography. Berkeley, Univ. of Calif. Pr., 1939. 130p. **V426**

Mehnert, Klaus. Die Sovet-Union, 1917–1932. Systematische, mit Kommentaren versehene Bibliographie der 1917–1932 in deutscher Sprache ausserhalb der Sovet-Union veröffentlichten 1900 wichtigsten Bücher und Aufsätze über den Bolschewismus und die Sovet-Union. Königsberg, Ost-Europa Verlag, 1933. 186p. **V427**

Mezhov, Vladimir Izmaĭlovich. Russkaĭa istoricheskaĭa bibliografiĭa, 1800–54. St. Petersburg, Sibiriâkov, 1892–93. 3v. **V428**

Added title page in French; Bibliographie des livres et articles russe d'histoire et sciences auxiliaires de 1800–1854 incl.

Contents: v.1, Documents historiques et histoire politique de la Russie; v.2, Biographies. Sciences auxiliaires; généalogie, la science heraldique, chronologie, archéologie, paléographie, numismatique, sphragistique, mythologie; v.3, Géographie, hydrographie, orographie, cartographie, voyages, statistique, éthnographie, histoire des cultes et de l'église, agiologie, histoire de l'instruction publique.

34,994 entries. No index.

Continued by:

Lambin, Petr Petrovich and **Lambin, Boris Petrovich.** Russkaĭa istoricheskaĭa bibliografiĭa, 1855–64. St. Petersburg, Tip. Akad. nauk, 1861–84. 10v. Annual. **V429**

Continued by:

Mezhov, Vladimir Izmaĭlovich. Russkaĭa istoricheskaĭa bibliografiĭa, 1865–76. St. Petersburg, Imp. Akademiĭ nauk, 1882–90. 8v. **V430**

Classified with subject indexes.

U. S. Library of Congress. Division of Bibliography. Soviet Russia: A selected list of recent references, comp. by Helen F. Conover. Wash., 1943. 85p. **V431**

Designed to present a comprehensive picture of the Soviet Union during the third 5-year plan, 1938–1942. Lists books, pamphlets and periodicals primarily in the English language.

Viktorov-Toporov, Vladimir. Rossica et Sovietica. Bibliographie des ouvrages parus en français de 1917 à 1930 inclus relatifs à la Russie et à l'U.R.

S.S. Saint-Cloud, Éditions Documentaires et Bibliographiques, 1931. 130p. **V432**

See also the sections on Russia in *Foreign affairs bibliography*, 1919–1932, 1932–1942 (L223); and pt.4, The Russian Empire and the Soviet Union in Asia and on the Pacific, in Kerner, *Northeastern Asia*, v.2, p.271-609 (V147).

Encyclopedias and handbooks

Degras, Jane. Calendar of Soviet documents on foreign policy, 1917–1941. Lond. and N.Y., Royal Institute of International Affairs, 1948. 248p. **V433**

Chronological arrangement by periods and countries with reference to Russian and other sources.

Freund, Henry Alexander. Russia from A to Z; revolution, state and party, foreign relations, economic system, social principles, general knowledge. . . . Pub. under the auspices of the Australian Institute of International Affairs. Sydney, Lond., Angus and Robertson, 1945. 713p. 17s. 6d. **V434**

Alphabetical encyclopedic arrangement. Bibliography, p.603-65. Annotated.

Simmons, Ernest Joseph. USSR: A concise handbook. Ithaca, N.Y., Cornell Univ. Pr., 1947. 494p **V435**

Chapters were originally written by specialists for the *Encyclopedia Americana* and cover: pt.1, Geography; pt.2, Political science including history, foreign affairs, government and politics, jurisprudence, diplomatic relations; pt.3, Social sciences, including economics, banking and finance, agricultural development, industry, communications, medicine and health, education, religion, and the armed forces; pt.4, The humanities and science, including philosophy, language, literature, drama, music, art, architecture and the history of science. Indexes of names and places.

Each chapter has a bibliography including works in Russian, English and some other languages. In some sections Russian titles are given in English translation.

SALVADOR

García, Miguel Angel. Diccionario histórico-enciclopédico de la República de El Salvador. San Salvador, Tip. "La Luz," 1927–48. v.1-10. (In progress) **V436**

v.1-10, A-Car.

Historical and biographical articles in one alphabet. In some cases gives references to sources.

SERBIA

Petrovic, Nikola S. Essai de bibliographie française sur les Serbes et les Croates, 1544–1900. Belgrade, Imp. de l'État, 1900. 314p. **V437**

Éd. de l'Academie Royale de Serbie.
Title in Serbo-Croatian and French.

SIERRA LEONE

Luke, Harry Charles. Bibliography of Sierra Leone, preceded by an essay on the origin, character and peoples of the colony and protectorate. 2d enl. ed. Lond., Ox. Univ. Pr., 1925. 230p. il. 8s. 6d. **V438**

SLAVIC EUROPE

Kerner, Robert Joseph. Slavic Europe; a selected bibliography in the western European languages, comprising history, languages and literatures. Camb., Harv. Univ. Pr., 1918. 402p. (Harvard bibliographies. Library ser. v.1) **V439**

A selected list of basic works in the western European languages on all phases of life in Slavic Europe divided into six sections: (1) The Slavs; (2) The Russians (including the Great Russians, the Little Russians, and the White Russians); (3) The Poles; (4) The Slavs in Germany (not including the Poles); (5) The Bohemians (Čechs) and Slovaks; (6) The Southern Slavs including the Jugo-slavs or the Slovenes and Serbo-Croats and the Bulgarians and Macedonians. Author index.

Slavonic encyclopedia, ed. by Joseph S. Roucek. N.Y., Philosophical Library, 1949. 1445p. **V440**

Contains articles, usually brief, in various fields, but is more than half biographical. Some articles are signed. Treatment is uneven and cross references unreliable.

Strakhovsky, Leonid I. A handbook of Slavic studies. Camb., Harv. Univ. Pr., 1949. 753p. **V441**

A useful handbook for the reader unfamiliar with Slavic languages. Consists of survey chapters by specialists on the history and literature of the Slavs in Russia, Poland, Czechoslovakia, and the Balkans. Attached to each chapter is a bibliography of materials in western European languages. Source materials in the Slavic languages are sometimes included in footnotes. Comparative chronology, p.675-722.

SOUTH AFRICA

Mendelssohn, Sidney. Mendelssohn's South African bibliography. . . . Lond., K. Paul, 1910. 2v. il. 42s. **V442**

Subtitle: Being the catalogue raisonné of the Mendelssohn library of works relating to South Africa, including the full titles of the books, with synoptical, biographical, critical, and bibliographical notes on the volumes and their authors; together with notices of a large number of important works not as yet included in the collection . . . together with a bibliography of South African periodical literature, and of articles on South African subjects in periodical literature throughout the world; also a complete list of the British parliamentary blue-books on South Africa, a cartography of South Africa, etc.

Eybers, G. W. Select constitutional documents illustrating South African history, 1795–1910. Lond., Routledge, 1918. 582p. **V443**

Walker, Eric Anderson. Historical atlas of South Africa. Ox., Univ. Pr., 1922. 26p. 26 maps. 38cm. 10s. 6d. **V444**

SPAIN

Sánchez Alonso, B. Fuentes de la historia española e hispanoamericana . . . 2d ed. rev. y ampl. Madrid [Impr. Clásica Española] 1927. 2v. in. 1. 633p., 468p. (Publ. de la Revista de filología española, 8) **V445**

Subtitle: Ensayo de bibliografía sistemática de impresos y manuscritas que ilustran la historia política de España y sus antiguas provincias de ultramar.

The most comprehensive modern bibliography of Spanish history including over 13,000 titles arranged by chronological divisions. Volume 1 covers through the eighteenth century, and volume 2, the nineteenth with a few pages on the early twentieth century. Includes both books and periodical articles. There is an author index and three subject indexes: biographical, geographical and miscellaneous.

Ballester y Castell, Rafael. Bibliografía de la historia de España; catálogo metódico y cronológico de las fuentes y obras principales relativas a la historia de España desde los origenes hasta nuestros dias. Gerona, Barcelona, Sociedad General de Publ., 1921. 297p. **V446**

Sometimes useful as a complement to the more extensive Sánchez Alonso (V445). Section 1 lists bibliographies, collections, standard histories and periodical publications; section 2 covers history by chronological periods through the eighteenth century.

Muñoz y Romero, Tomás. Diccionario bibliográfico-histórico de los antiguos reinos, provincias, ciudades, villas, iglesias y santuarios de España. Madrid, Rivadeneyra, 1858. 329p. **V447**

A very useful bibliography of local history.

Menéndez Pidal, Ramón. Historia de España. Madrid, Espasa-Calpe, 1935- . [v.1, 1947] v.1- . il. (In progress) **V448**

Contents: t.1, España prehistórica. 1947; t.2, España Romana (218 B.C.—414 A.D.). 1935; t.3, España Visigoda (414–711). 1940.

A collaborative work by outstanding Spanish historians. Each chapter is followed by an extensive bibliography, and each volume is indexed. Well illustrated in black and white and in color.

SWEDEN

Augustana College and Theological Seminary. Denkmann Memorial Library. Guide to the material on Swedish history in the Augustana College Library, prepared by O. Frithof Ander. Rock Island, Ill., 1934. 75p. **V449**

Printed on one side of leaf only.

A useful collection of books in various languages.

Setterwall, Kristian. Svensk historisk bibliografi, 1875–1900, 1901–1920. . . . Stockholm, Norstedt, 1907; Uppsala, Appelberg, 1923. 2v. **V450**

A comprehensive classified bibliography of Swedish and some foreign material including books, pamphlets and articles in periodicals. Lists a total of 12,880 items (4636 in 1875–1900 volume, 8244 in 1901–1920 volume).

Continued by the following:

Svensk historisk bibliografi, 1880- . Stockholm, Norstedt, 1881- . Annual. **V451**

An annual bibliography of books and periodical articles, etc.; issued as an annual supplement to *Historisk tidskrift* (Stockholm).

SWITZERLAND

Barth, Hans. Bibliographie der schweizer Geschichte enthaltend die selbständig erschienenen Druckwerke zur Geschichte der Schweiz bis Ende 1912. Basel, Basler Buch- und Antiquariatshandlung, 1914–15. 3v. (Quellen zur schweizer Geschichte hrsg. von der Allgemeinen Geschichtforschenden Gesellschaft der Schweiz, n.F. 4. Abt. Handbücher) **V452**

v.1, General history, by periods; v.2-3, Special subjects, e.g., biography, religious history, etc.; author and title index.

A very comprehensive bibliography, including more than 32,000 entries. May be supplemented by the following: (1) for material after 1912 by the annual *Bibliographie der Schweizergeschichte* (V453); (2) for analytical material before 1900 by the two volumes of the *Repertorium* (V454).

Bibliographie der Schweizergeschichte, Jahrg. 1913- . Zurich, Leemann, 1914- . v.1- . Annual (some years combined). **V453**

1913–17 compiled by Felix Burckhardt; 1918–27, by Helen Wild; 1928–1937, by W. J. Meyer; 1938/40, compiled by Marcelle Klein and Paul Guyer; 1941- , compiled by Willy Vontobel and Walter Achtnich. Volumes for 1913–19 published as supplements to the *Anzeiger f. schweizerische Geschichte*, those for 1920–37 as supplements to the *Zeitschrift f. schweizerische Geschichte*.

Classed arrangement. Later volumes have author and subject indexes. Includes material on history, bibliography, biography, church, art, literature, music, customs, etc.

Repertorium über die in Zeit- und Sammelschriften der Jahre 1812–1890, 1891–1900, enthaltenen Aufsätze und Mitteilungen schweizergeschichtlichen Inhalts. Hrsg. von der Allgemeinen Geschichtforschenden Gesellschaft der Schweiz. Basel, Geering, 1892; Basler Buch- und Antiquariatshandlung, 1906. 2v. **V454**

1812–1890 compiled by J. L. Brandstetter; 1891–1900, by Hans Barth.

Classed lists arranged by small subjects, with alphabetical index of authors, to articles on Swiss history, biography, etc., in more than 300 periodicals and society transactions. The sections on biography, in each volume, give, in addition to the references to the articles, the dates of birth and death and a brief characterizing phrase, and so supply some direct biographical information.

Dictionnaire historique et biographique de la Suisse, publié avec la recommandation de la Société Générale Suisse d'Histoire. . . . Neuchâtel, Administration du Dictionnaire, 1921–34. 7v. and suppl. il. **V455**

Issued also in an edition in German: *Historisch-biographisches Lexikon der Schweiz.*

v.1-7, A-Z; suppl., A-Z, p.1-184; 2d suppl., A-Z, p.185-208. Table systématique.

May be considered a companion work to the *Dictionnaire géographique de la Suisse* (U65), published by Attinger. Covers the fields of general, political, local, economic and social history, topography, genealogy and biography of the country. Has adequate signed articles, bibliographies and many good illustrations, including portraits, local views, maps and plans, seals, coats of arms, colored plates of costumes, etc. The topographical articles cover the same places as are included in the *Dictionnaire géographique*, but do not duplicate information given in that work as the treatment and point of view are different. Many biographical articles, including some on persons still living.

SYRIA

Masson, Paul. Éléments d'une bibliographie française de la Syrie. Marseille, Barlatier, 1919. 528p. (Chambre de Commerce de Marseille, Congrès français de la Syrie) **V456**

Subtitle: Géographie, ethnographie, histoire, archéologie, langues, littératures, religions.

TURKEY

Mikhov, Nikola V. Bibliographie des articles de périodiques allemands, anglais, français et italiens sur la Turquie et la Bulgarie, [par] Nicholas V. Michoff. Sofia, Imp. de la Cour, 1938. 686p. 18fr.sw. **V457**

At head of title: Académie Bulgare des Sciences.

A comprehensive compilation of over 10,000 titles of articles appearing in the periodicals of western Europe from 1715 to 1880 (with some additional entries to 1891) arranged chronologically by year, with indexes by author and personal name and by subject and place name.

—— La population de la Turquie et de la Bulgarie au xviiie et xixe s. Recherches bibliographico-statistiques . . . avec une préface en français. Sofia, Imp. de la Cour Royale, 1915–35. 4v. **V458**

Volume 1 has added title page: Bulgarska Akademiia na Naukite. Sbornik. Kniga 4. Klon Istorikafilologichen i filosofsko-obshtestven, 3.

Title also in Bulgarian.

—— Sources bibliographiques sur l'histoire de la Turquie et de la Bulgarie. Sofia, Imp. de l'Etat, 1914–34. 4v. **V459**

Title also in Bulgarian.
Cumulated author and subject indexes in volume 4 to all four volumes.

URUGUAY

Araújo, Orestes. Diccionario popular de historia de la República o. del Uruguay, desde la época del descubrimiento de su territorio, hasta la de su independencia. Montevideo, Dornaleche y Reyes, 1901–03. 3v. **V460**

VENEZUELA

Silva Uzcátegui, Rafael Domingo. Enciclopedia larense; geografía, historia, cultura y lenguaje del estado Lara; obra profusamente documentada, editada por el gobierno del estado Lara. . . . Caracas, Impresores Unidos, 1941. v.1-2. il. **V461**

Contents: (1) Geografía; (2) Historia.
v.2, p.625-815, Dicionario de provincialismos.

WEST INDIES

Hiss, Philip Hanson. A selective guide to the English literature on the Netherlands West Indies; with a supplement on British Guiana. N.Y., Netherlands Information Bureau, 1943. 129p. (Netherlands Information Bureau booklets, no.9) 75c. **V462**

New York. Public Library. List of works relating to the West Indies. N.Y., 1912. 392p. (Repr. from the Bulletin of the New York Public Library, Jan.–Aug. 1912) **V463**

Ragatz, Lowell Joseph. A guide for the study of British Caribbean history, 1763–1834, including the abolition and emancipation movements. Wash., Govt. Prt. Off., 1932. 725p. $1.50. **V464**

Reid, Charles Frederick. Bibliography of the Virgin islands of the United States; Charles F. Reid, ed.; Nathan Habib, assoc. ed.; Florence D. Clark and Caroline Simonini, asst. eds. N.Y., Wilson, 1941. 225p. $3.50. **V465**

"Prepared with the assistance of the Federal Works Agency, Work Projects Administration for the City of New York, Division of Community Service Programs, 'Bibliographies of the territories and outlying possessions of the United States.'"
Classified and annotated, with alphabetical index.

Royal Empire Society, London. Library. Subject catalogue. v.3, Dominion of Canada . . . the West Indies, and colonial America. Lond., 1932. **V466**

For full description see V323.

Benjamins, H. D. and **Snelleman, J. F.** Encyclopaedie van Nederlandsch West-Indië. 'sGravenhage, Nijhoff, 1914–17. 782p. **V467**

An encyclopedia of everything about the region; includes biographies. Adequate signed articles, good bibliographies.

YUCATAN

Bolio Ontiveros, Edmundo. Diccionario histórico, geográfico y biográfico de Yucatán. México, D.F., I.C.D., 1944. 250p. **V468**

Enciclopedia yucatanense . . . publ. bajo la dirección del Carlos A. Echánove Trujillo. Ciudad de Mexico, Ed. Oficial del Gobierno de Yucatan, 1944–47. 8v. il. (v.8, 1944) **V469**

A classed encyclopedia aiming to cover all aspects of Yucatan history and life. Each section is written by an authority and most have bibliographies. Volume 7, *Biografías,* deals with only 14 individuals but more biographical material is included in articles throughout. Volume 8, *Bibliografía general yucatanense* (A542), is an extensive alphabetical list of works published in and on Yucatan. Indexes announced but not published.

INDEX

Dickens student and collector, W. Miller, R383

Dickinson, T. A. Plastics dictionary, P107

Dickons, J. N. Catalogue of books published at Bradford, A316

Dictionaries
  language, p.216-52
  polyglot, M384-M385: aeronautics, P93-P95; agriculture, P254; art, Q22; automotive engineering, P173; bacteriology, N438; banking, L550-L551; botany, N373-N374; business, L423-L425; chemistry, N205; commercial products, L345; dentistry, P350; forestry, P276; geology, N261, N264; insurance, L572-L573; library, B9; metallurgy, P211; military, P181; naval, P181; physics, N205; printing, A595, A598, A600, A602-A604; radio, P157; technical, P34-P38

  See also under names of languages, *e.g.* Arabic language: dictionaries; and under subjects, *e.g.* Geology, dictionaries: foreign terms

Dictionaries of printers and booksellers in England, Scotland, and Ireland, Bibliographical Society, London, A619

Dictionary for mining engineering and economics, H. J. Seebach, P212

Dictionary of aeronautics, L. Ahrens, P93

Dictionary of American biography, S32

Dictionary of American English, W. A. Craigie and J. R. Hulbert, M60

Dictionary of American history, V108

Dictionary of American medical biography, H. A. Kelly and W. L. Burrage, P337

Dictionary of American painters, sculptors and engravers, M. Fielding, Q53

Dictionary of anonymous and pseudonymous English literature, S. Halkett and J. Laing, A96

Dictionary of applied chemistry, J. F. Thorpe, N191

Dictionary of applied physics, *Sir* R. Glazebrook, N105

Dictionary of architecture and building, R. Sturgis, Q112

Dictionary of battles, T. B. Harbottle, V37

Dictionary of bio-chemistry, W. M. Malisoff, N187

Dictionary of biological equivalents, German-English, E. F. Artschwager, N333

Dictionary of books relating to America, J. Sabin, A145

Dictionary of botanical equivalents, E. F. Artschwager and E. M. Smiley, N373

Dictionary of British history, J. A. Brendon, V285

Dictionary of Canadian biography, W. S. Wallace, R481

Dictionary of Christ and the gospels, J. Hastings, K90

Dictionary of Christian antiquities, *Sir* W. Smith and S. Cheetham, K29

Dictionary of Christian biography, *Sir* W. Smith and H. Wace, K30

Dictionary of Christian biography, H. Wace and W. C. Piercy, K31

Dictionary of color, A. J. Maerz and M. R. Paul, N116

Dictionary of cooperation, E. S. Bogardus, L419

Dictionary of dates, J. Haydn, V25

Dictionary of dates, H. R. Keller, V26

Dictionary of dental science and art, W. B. Dunning and S. E. Davenport, Jr., P349

Dictionary of economics, H. S. Sloan and A. J. Zurcher, L338

Dictionary of education, C. V. Good, L723

Dictionary of English church history, S. L. Ollard and others, K120

Dictionary of English furniture, P. Macquoid and R. Edwards, Q145

Dictionary of English history, *Sir* S. Low and F. S. Pulling, V287

Dictionary of English literature, W. D. Adams, R278

Dictionary of English literature, H. A. Watt and W. W. Watt, R283

Dictionary of English phrases, A. M. Hyamson, R42

Dictionary of English plant-names, J. Britten and R. Holland, N363

Dictionary of European literature, L. Magnus, R34

Dictionary of events, G. P. Putnam and G. H. Putnam, V33

Dictionary of foreign trade, F. Henius, L354

Dictionary of genetics, R. L. Knight, N443

Dictionary of geological terms, C. M. Rice, N258

Dictionary of Greek and Roman antiquities, *Sir* W. Smith and others, V70

Dictionary of Greek and Roman biography and mythology, V69

Dictionary of heavy electrical engineering, G. W. Stubbings, P143

Dictionary of hymnology, J. Julian, K54

Dictionary of labor economics, B. Horton, L483

Dictionary of London, H. A. Harben, V312

Dictionary of mediaeval romance and romance writers, L. Spence, R165

Dictionary of metallography, R. T. Rolfe, P208

Dictionary of miniaturists, illuminators, calligraphers, and copyists, J. W. Bradley, Q87

Dictionary of modern American usage, H. W. Horwill, M26

Dictionary of modern economics, B. J. Horton and others, L335

Dictionary of modern English usage, H. W. Fowler, M25

Dictionary of modern music and musicians, Q250

Dictionary of music and musicians, *Sir* G. Grove, Q254

Dictionary of musical terms, T. Baker, Q268

Dictionary of musical themes, H. Barlow and S. Morgenstern, Q248

Dictionary of national biography, S123

Dictionary of non-classical mythology, M. Edwardes, K259

Dictionary of numismatic names, A. R. Frey, Q159

Dictionary of occupational titles, L464

Dictionary of organic compounds, I. M. Heilbron and H. M. Bunbury, N222

Dictionary of painters and engravers, M. Bryan, Q88

Dictionary of painters of miniatures, J. J. Foster, Q89

Dictionary of paper, American Paper and Pulp Association, A593

Dictionary of philosophy and psychology, J. M. Baldwin, H11

Dictionary of phrase and fable, E. C. Brewer, R38

Dictionary of plant names, H. L. Gerth van Wijk, N375

Dictionary of pronunciation of artists' names, G. E. Kaltenbach, Q54

Dictionary of psychology, H. C. Warren, J14

Dictionary of races or peoples, U. S. Immigration Commission 1907, N322

Dictionary of religion and ethics, S. Mathews and G. B. Smith, K6

Dictionary of social welfare, E. F. Young, L18

Dictionary of sociology, H. P. Fairchild, L12

Dictionary of statistics, M. G. Mulhall, L69

Dictionary of tariff information, U. S. Tariff Commission, L375

Dictionary of the American hierarchy, J. B. Code, K213

Eighteenth century English literature and its cultural background, J. E. Tobin, R273

Eighteenth century English novel in French translation, H. W. Streeter, R324

Eijkman, P. H. L'internationalisme médical, N41; L'internationalisme scientifique (sciences pures et lettres), N42

Einstein, A. Music in the Romantic era, Q279n

Eire *see* Ireland

Eiselen, F. C. and others. Abingdon Bible commentary, K97

Eisenberg, L. J. Grosses biographisches Lexikon, der deutschen Bühne im xix Jahrhundert, Q201

Eisenberg, P. and Krasno, H. A guide to children's records, Q314

Eisler, R. Handwörterbuch der Philosophie, H14; Kant-Lexikon, H16, R539; Philosophen-Lexikon, H21n; Wörterbuch der philosophischen Begriffe, H15

Eitner, R. Biographisch-bibliographisches Quellen-Lexikon der Musiker, Q231

Eitzen, F. W. Wörterbuch der Handelssprache, L427

Ekblom, E. L. Place-names of Wiltshire, U125

Ekklesia, K39

Ekwall, E. Concise Oxford dictionary of English place-names, U85; English river names, U86; Place-names of Lancashire, U103

Electrical engineering, p.306-08
abstract journals, P134-P135
bibliography, P130-P133
dictionaries, P142-P144
handbooks, P136-P141

Electrical engineering abstracts, P135

Electrical engineers' handbook, H. Pender and W. A. Del Mar, P137

Electricity: bibliography, P131-P132

Electronic engineering master index, P145

Electronic engineering patent index, P146

Electronics, P137; *see also* Radio

Electronics dictionary, N. M. Cooke and J. Markus, P156

Elektrotechnische Berichte, P134

Elementary teachers guide to free curriculum materials, J. G. Fowlkes and D. A. Morgan, L711

Elementos de bibliotecología, D. Buonocore, B44

Éléments d'un guide bibliographique du naturaliste, F. Bourlière, N325

Éléments d'une bibliographie française de la Syrie, P. Masson, V456

Eleutheroudakē enkyklopaidikon leksikon, D40

Eleven religions and their proverbial lore, S. G. Champion, K10

Elgueta de Ochsenius, H. Suplemento y adiciones a la Bibliografía de bibliografías chilenas, A198

Elias, E. A. Elias' Modern dictionary, English-Arabic, M93

Elias, E. E. Elias' Practical dictionary of the colloquial Arabic, M94

Eliot, C. W. Harvard classics, R14

Eliot, George: dictionary, R393

Elizabethan bibliographies, S. A. Tannenbaum and D. R. Tannenbaum, R270

Elizabethan stage, E. K. Chambers, R313

Elkjaer, K. and others. Skønlitteratur i danske Tidsskrifter, R545

Ellice, E. C. Place-names in Glengarry and Glenquoich, U149

Elliott, E. C. and Chambers, M. M. Charters of philanthropies, L16

Ellis, B. F. and Messina, A. R. Catalogue of foraminifera, N293

Ellis, E. T. Black's gardening dictionary, P255

Ellis, F. S. Lexical concordance to Shelley, R457

Ellis, J. C. Nature and its applications, Q15; Travel through pictures, Q16

Ellis, J. T. Select bibliography of the history of the Catholic church in the United States, K171

Elsbach, A. C. and others. Encyclopaedisch Handboek van het moderne Denken, H17

Elsevier's Encyclopaedia of organic chemistry, N223

Elster, K. Illustreret Norsk litteratur historie, R550

Elster, L. and others. Handwörterbuch der Staatswissenschaften, L229; Wörterbuch der Volkswirtschaft, L339

Elvin, A. Världsatlas, U178

Elwall, A. Dictionnaire anglais-français, M178

Elzinga, J. J. B. and Jong, A. J. de. Nieuw Nederlands woordenboek, M155

Emberson, F. G. and Ramsay, R. L. Mark Twain lexicon, R236

Embleton, D. A. Catalogue of place-names in Teesdale, U121

Embree, J. F. and Dotson, L. O. Bibliography of the peoples and cultures of mainland southeast Asia, V146a

Emeneau, M. B. and Steinen, D. v. d. Annamese-English dictionary, M90

Emerson, Ralph Waldo
bibliography, R187n, R237
concordance, R238

Eminent Chinese of the Ch'ing period, U. S. Library of Congress. Asiatic Division, S92

Eminent Welshmen, T. R. Roberts, S137

Eminson, T. B. F. Place and river names of the West Riding of Lindsey, Lincolnshire, U106

Emma Shearer Wood Library of Ornithology. An introduction to the literature of the vertebrate zoology, C. A. Wood, N397

Enamel bibliography and abstracts, E. H. McClelland, Q129

Enciclopedia biografica e bibliografica "Italiana," S151

Enciclopedia cattolica, K185

Enciclopedia di amministrazione, U. Monetti, L546

Enciclopedia ecclesiastica, A. Bernareggi, K24

Enciclopedia ilustrada Segui, D68

Enciclopedia italiana di scienze, lettere ed arti, D46

Enciclopedia Romániei, D58

Enciclopedia Sopena, D69

Enciclopedia storica delle scienze e delle loro applicazioni, A. Uccelli, N28

Enciclopedia storico-nobiliare italiana, V. Spreti, T37

Enciclopedia universal ilustrada Europeo-Americana, D64

Enciclopedia yucatenense, V469

Encyclicals of the Roman pontiffs, Guide, M. C. Carlen, K170

Encyclopaedia *see* Encyclopedia

Encyclopaedie van Nederlandsch-Indië, V392

Encyclopaedie van Nederlandsch West-Indië, H. D. Benjamins and J. F. Snelleman, V467

Encyclopaedisch Handboek van het moderne Denken, A. C. Elsbach and others, H17

Encyclopedia Americana, D1

Encyclopaedia and dictionary of education, F. Watson, L730

Encyclopaedia biblica, T. K. Cheyne and J. S. Black, K86

Encyclopaedia Britannica, D2; 10 eventful years, D3; World atlas, U171

Encyclopedia e diccionario internacional, D18

Encyclopaedia Hebraica, D42

Encyclopaedia Judaica, K241

Encyclopedia of American politics, E. V. Mitchell, L233

Encyclopedia of banking and finance, G. G. Munn, L547

Encyclopedia of Bible life, M. S. Miller and J. L. Miller, K94

García Péres, D. Catalogo razonado biográfico y bibliográfico de los autores portugueses que escribieron en castellano, R690

García-Prada, C. and Leavitt, S. E. Tentative bibliography of Colombian literature, R750

Garden dictionary *see* Taylor's Encyclopedia of gardening, P256

Gardening, P253, P255, P256, P258

Gardiner, S. R. Constitutional documents of the Puritan revolution, V305

Gardner, C. S. A union list of selected western books on China in American libraries, V193

Gardner, E. G. Italy, V355; Italy a companion to Italian studies, R660

Gardner, F. M. *see* Aldred, T. Sequels, R144

Gardner, H. Art through the ages, Q42

Gardner, W. Chemical synonyms and trade names, N197

Garland, J. V. and Phillips, C. F. Discussion methods, R177

Garnett, R. and Gosse, E. English literature, R289

Garnier, Ê. Dictionnaire de la céramique, Q135

Garnier, M. and Delamare, V. Dictionnaire des termes techniques de médecine, P305

Garnsey, H. E. F. History of botany, J. von Sachs, N377

Garollo, G. Dizionario biografico universale, S19; Piccola enciclopedia Hoepli, D47

Garraghan, G. J. A guide to historical method, V15

Garraux, A. L. Bibliographie brésilienne, V166

Garrison, C. W. The United States, 1865-1900; a survey of current literature, V100

Garrison, F. H. Introduction to the history of medicine, P329; A medical bibliography, P324

Garrison, J. J. and Robb, D. M. Art in the Western world, Q46

Garrod, H. W. Oxford book of Latin verse, R837

Garvin, J. W. Canadian poets, R479

Garzón, T. Diccionario argentino, M447

Gas, Natural: bibliography, P218

Gas chemists' handbook, American Gas Association, P103

Gas engineers' handbook, Pacific Coast Gas Association, P105

Gascogne: dialect, M209

Gascoigne, George: bibliography, R270

Gaselee, S. Oxford book of medieval Latin verse, R838

Gassner, J. Producing the play, Q200

Gast, A. Repertorium van boeken betreffende de geschiedenis van Nederland, V384

Gastren, G. and Böök, F. Svenska litteraturens historia, R553

Gastronomic bibliography, K. G. Bitting, P363

Gateways to readable books, R. Strang and others, A565

Gatfield, G. Guide to printed books and manuscripts relating to English and foreign heraldry and genealogy, T25

Gaucho, cattle hunter, cavalryman, ideal of romance, M. W. Nichols, V143

Gauthier, H. Dictionnaire des noms géographiques, U83

Gautier, L. Bibliographie des chansons de geste, R611; Les épopées françaises, R612

Gay, R. M. and Skillin, M. E. Words into type, A625

Gay, V. Glossaire archéologique du moyen âge, V63

Gayley, C. M. Classic myths, K260

Gaynor, F. International business dictionary in five languages, L423

GAZ. Gesamtverzeichnis der ausländischen Zeitschriften, E66

Gazetteers, p.460-65; *see also* Gazetteers under name of specific country

Gebhardt, B. Handbuch der deutschen Geschichte, V262

Geddie, J. L. Chambers's cyclopaedia of English literature, R280; Chambers's biographical dictionary, S18

Geddie, W. A bibliography of middle Scots poets, R333; Chambers's biographical dictionary, S18

Geden, A. S. and Moulton, W. F. Concordance to the Greek Testament, K84

Gee, H. and Hardy, W. J. Documents illustrative of English church history, K44, V296

Geflügelte Worte, G. Buchmann, R88-R89

Gehalt und Gestalt im Kunstwerk des Dichters, O. Walzel, R33n

Geiger, H. Handbuch der Physik, N107

Geissler, M. Führer durch die deutsche Literatur des zwanzigsten Jahrhunderts, R521

Geist und Form im musikalischen Kunstwerk, E. Bücken, Q276n

Genealogical and heraldic history of the colonial gentry, J. B. Burke, T30

Genealogical and heraldic history of the landed gentry, J. B. Burke, T32

Genealogical and heraldic history of the landed gentry of Ireland, J. B. Burke, T29

Genealogical and heraldic history of the peerage, baronetage, and knightage, J. B. Burke, T28

Genealogical history of the dormant, abeyant, forfeited, and extinct peerages of the British empire, J. B. Burke, T31

Genealogical tables and lists, Cambridge modern history, V19

Genealogical tables illustrative of modern history, H. B. George, V23

Genealogy, p.452-55
Canada, T15
Europe, T16-T17
France, T18-T19
Germany, T20-T22
Great Britain: bibliography, T23-T27; dictionaries, T28-T36
United States, T1-T14: bibliography and indexes, T2-T8; dictionaries, T9-T12; guides, T1; periodicals, T13-T14
See also History: genealogical tables

General basic English dictionary, C. K. Ogden, M20

General bibliographical dictionary, A. Browne, A23n

General catalogue of printed books, British Museum. Dept. of Printed Books, A33

General Council of Medical Education of the United Kingdom. Medical register, P321

General engineering handbook, C. E. O'Rourke, P29

Generic indexes *see* Zoology: generic indexes

Genest, É. Les belles citations de la littérature française, R80; Où est-ce donc?, R81

Genest, J. Some account of the English stage from the restoration in 1660 to 1830, R315

Genetics, N441-N443

Geneva. Université. Catalogue des ouvrages et des thèses, G43

Gennep, A. van. Bibliographie méthodique de folklore français, K274

Gentleman's magazine—index to biographical notices, S134

Geografia e viaggi, Istituto Nazionale per le Relazioni Culturali con l'Estero, U5, U52

Geografiska Sällskapet i Finland, Helsingfors. Atlas of Finland, U191

Geographical dictionary of Milton, A. H. Gilbert, R418

Geographical guide to the floras of the world, S. F. Blake, N352

Geographical names *see* Names, Geographical

Geographisches Jahrbuch, U9

Geography, p.459-75
bibliography, U2-U9

Modern English biography, F. Boase, S124

Modern English-Chinese chemical lexicon, Z. Zee and L. Cheng, N200

Modern home medical adviser, M. Fishbein, P300

Modern Hoyle, A. H. Morehead, Q327

Modern humanities: bibliography, R12

Modern Humanities Research Association. Annual bibliography of English language and literature, R262; Work in progress in the modern humanities, R12

Modern Language Association. American bibliography, R11; Reproductions of manuscripts and rare printed books, A50; Research in progress, R13

Modern language studies: bibliography, R10, R13

Modern Latin America in social science literature, R. F. Behrendt, V366

Modern marine engineer's manual, A. Osbourne, P162

Modern plastics encyclopedia, P108

Modern Spanish-English and English-Spanish technical and engineering dictionary, R. L. Guinle, P48

Moderne Musik seit der Romantik, Die H. Mersmann, Q276n

Moffatt, James. The Bible, K65

Moffatt Bible concordance, W. J. Grant, K72a

Mohammedanism
  bibliography, K251-K253
  encyclopedias, K255-K256
  handbooks, K254

Moisy, H. Dictionnaire de patois normand, M219

Molhuysen, P. J. [and others]. Nieuw nederlandsch biografisch woordenboek, S172

Molière, R635-R640

Molina Navarro, G. Indice para facilitar el manejo y consulta de los cátalogos de Salva y Heredia, A496

Molinier, A. Les Sources de l'histoire de France, V223

Møller, A. J. Dansk Bibliografier, A18

Monasticism see Roman Catholic church: religious orders

Monatliches Verzeichnis von Aufsätzen aus deutschen Zeitungen, E125

Monetti, U. Enciclopedia di amministrazione, L546

Money, L379-L383

Money manual, W. Tate, L382

Monglond, A. La France révolutionnaire et impériale, V230

Monier-Williams, Sir M. Sanskrit-English dictionary, M419

Moniteur des dates, E. M. Oettinger, S22

Monod, G. Bibliographie de l'histoire de France, V227

Monod, L. Aide-mémoire de l'amateur et du professionnel, Q33

Monologs and dialogs, Index, N. O. Ireland, R160

Monro, I. S. Fiction catalog, R148
—— and Monro, K. M. Index to reproductions of American paintings, Q75

·Monroe, P. Cyclopedia of education, L727

Monroe, W. S. Encyclopedia of educational research, L720; Ten years of educational research, L713
—— and Shores, L. Bibliography and summaries in education, L704

Monroy, G. and Manrique de Lara, J. Seudónimos, anagramas, iniciales, A113

Montague, F. C. From the accession of James I to the Restoration, V292n

Montaigne, Michel Eyquem de, R641-R642, R270n

Montandon, R. Bibliographie générale des travaux palethnologiques et archéologiques, V224

Monterde García Icazbalceta, F. Bibliografía del teatro en México, R758

Montesson, C. R. Vocabulaire du Haute-Maine, M215

Montessus de Ballore, F. de. Bibliografía general de temblores y terremotos, N270

Montevideo: bibliography, A532

Montgomery library of accountancy, Columbia University. Library, L531

Monthly catalog, United States public documents, F15n

Monthly checklist of state publications, U. S. Library of Congress. Processing Department, F24

Monthly evening sky map, N156

Monthly labor review, L476

Monthly list of Russian accessions, U. S. Library of Congress, A484

Monthly weather review, U. S. Weather Bureau, N287

Montt, L. Bibliografía chilena, A201

Moore, A. W. Manx names, U109; Vocabulary of the Anglo-Manx dialect, M372

Moore, E. R. Bibliografía de novelistas de la revolución mexicana, R759

Moore, F. J. and Hall, W. T. History of chemistry, N213

Moore, J. B. Digest of international law, L646

Moorhead, A. F. Australian blue book, L107

Moorman, R. W. Place-names of the West Riding of Yorkshire, U128

Mora, J. F. see Ferrater Mora, J.

Moraes, G. M. Bibliography of Indological studies, V334

Morales, A. Bachiller y see Bachiller y Morales, A.

Moran, A. V. see Vahid Moran, A.

Morante, J. and Miguel y Navas, R. Nuevo diccionario latino-español etimológico, M346

Morbihan, L. Rosensweig, V225n

Mørck, F. and Høgh, M. Norske Kvinder, S179

Morehead, A. H. The modern Hoyle, Q327

Moreira Pinto, A. Apontamentos paro o Diccionario geographico do Brazil, U28

Moreno, A. Dicionário complementar da lingua portuguesa, M388

Morgan, B. Q. A critical bibliography of German literature in English translation, R511
—— and Hohlfeld, A. R. German literature in British magazines, 1750-1860, R515

Morgan, D. A. and Fowlkes, J. G. Elementary teachers guide to free curriculum materials, L711

Morgan, E. M. and Dwyer, F. X. Introduction to the study of law, L582

Morgan, H. J. Bibliotheca canadensis, A194

Morgan, T. Place-names of Wales, U123

Morgan, W. T. and Morgan, C. S. Bibliography of British history, 1700-1715, A301, V278

Morgenstern, S. and Barlow, H. Dictionary of musical themes, Q248

Mori, E. Cotarelo y see Cotarelo y Mori, E.

Morice, A. G. Dictionnaire historique des Canadiens, S80

Morison, M. Time table of modern history, V32

Morison, S. English prayer books, K125

Morison, S. E. Sources and documents illustrating the American Revolution, 1764-1788, V122

Moritz, R. E. Memorabilia mathematica, N82

Morley, C. V. see Bartlett, J. Familiar quotations, R63

Morley, L. H. Contributions toward a special library glossary, B6
—— and Kight, A. C. Business books, 1920-26, L414; 2400 business books and guide to business literature, L413

Morocco
  history, V382
  statistics, L173

Morozov, P. O. Alfabetnyĭ ukazetel imen, A482n

New Testament literature, W. N. Lyons and M. M. Parvis, K69

New world atlas, C. S. Hammond, U172

New world guides to the Latin American republics, E. P. Hanson, U206

New York Academy of Medicine. Committee on Public Health Relations. Directory of convalescent homes in the United States, L21
—— Library. Dental bibliography, P347

New York (City). Union Theological Seminary. Library. Catalogue of the McAlpin collection of British history and theology, K15, V276

New York Daily Tribune index, E123

New York genealogical and biographical record, T14

New York Graphic Society, Inc. Fine art reproductions, old and modern masters, Q76

New York Library Association. Committee on Bibliographies and Surveys. A union list of printed collections of source materials on European history in New York state libraries, V7

New York. Public Library. Ancient Egypt, V215; Beadle collection of dime novels, R214; Check list of cumulative indexes to individual periodicals, E6; Checklist of newspapers and official gazettes, E100; Early American poetry, 1610-1820, R221; Foreign plays in English, R133; Guide to the reference collections, B36; History of aeronautics; selected list of references, P77; A list of works relating to Scotland, V319; List of works relating to the West Indies, V463; Modern Egypt, V216; New technical books, P13; Provençal literature and language, p.498

New York Times index, E122

New York University. Washington Square Library. Index to early American periodical literature, R187

New Yorker. Index to profile sketches, S12

New Zealand
biography, S175-S176
gazetteers, U60
history, V393-V396
reference books, A567
statistics, L176-L177

New Zealand. Authors' Week Committee. Annals of New Zealand literature, R489
—— Census and Statistics Dept. Local authorities handbook of

New Zealand, L298; New Zealand official year-book, L177
—— General Assembly. Library. Union catalogue of New Zealand newspapers, E121
—— Geographic Board. Place-names in New Zealand, U138

New Zealand literature, R489

New Zealand official year-book, New Zealand. Census and Statistics Dept., L177

New Zealand slang, S. J. Baker, M73

Newark, N. J. Free Public Library. Business Branch. Business books: 1920-26, L414; The business bookshelf, L411; Business information and its sources, L410; Business magazines, L412; 2400 business books and guide to business literature, L413

Newberry Library, Chicago. English books and books printed in England before 1641, A295

Newcastle, Eng.: bibliography, A337-A338

Newcastle upon Tyne. Central Public Library. Local catalogue of material concerning Newcastle and Northumberland, A337

Newmark, M. Dictionary of science and technology in English-French-German-Spanish, P34; Illustrated technical dictionary, P33

Newnes Engineer's reference book, F. J. Camm, P167

Newspaper press, J. Grant, E137

Newspaper press directory, E40

Newspapers, p.100-04
bibliography, foreign, E119-E127: Australia, E16; Canada, E17; Cuba, E19; Czechoslovakia, E20-E21; France, E22-E26; Germany, E27-E33; Great Britain, E34-E42, E120; Italy, E43; New Zealand, E121; Scotland, E39; Switzerland, E57-E60
bibliography, United States, E102-E118: Arkansas, E109; California, E110; Colorado, E111; Louisiana, E112; Massachusetts, E113; Mississippi, E114; Ohio, E115; Pennsylvania, E116; Texas, E117; Virginia, E118
indexes: Denmark, E124; Germany, E125; Great Britain, E126-E127; United States, E122-E123
union lists, E98-E101
See also Periodicals

Newspapers on microfilm, Association of Research Libraries, E98

Nicaragua
bibliography, A434-A435
statistics, L178

Nicaragua. Dirección General de Estadística. Anuario estadístico, L178

Nichols, M. W. A bibliographical guide to materials on American Spanish, M441, R734; The gaucho, cattle hunter, cavalryman, ideal of romance, V143

Nicholson, D. H. S. and Lee, A. H. E. Oxford book of English mystical verse, R338n

Nicholson, M. Manual of copyright practice, A626

Nicholson, R. A. Literary history of the Arabs, R870

Nickles, J. M. Bibliography of North American geology, N237; Geologic literature of North America, N236
—— and Miller, R. B. Bibliography and index of geology exclusive of North America, N238

Nicknames, R42, R45

Nicolas, F. J. General index to reports, [Canada. Geological Survey] 1885-1906, N246b; Index to memoirs, N246d; Index to paleontology (Geological publications), N246e; Index to separate reports, 1906-1910, and summary reports, 1905-1916, N246c

Nicolas, Sir N. H. History of the orders of knighthood of the British Empire, T56

Nicoll, A. History of early 18th century drama, 1700-1750, R317; History of early 19th century drama 1800-1850, R319; History of late 18th century drama, 1750-1800, R318; History of late 19th century drama, 1850-1900, R320; History of restoration drama, 1660-1700, R316

Nicoll, Sir W. R. Expositor's Bible, K98

Niederdeutsche Bibliographie, C. Borchling and B. Claussen, A261

Niederländisches Künstler-Lexikon, A. Wurzbach, Q61

Niedermann, M. and others. Wörterbuch der litauischen Schriftsprache, M365

Niederösterreichische Amtskalender, L255n

Nield, J. Guide to the best historical novels and tales, R152

Nielsen, F. Kirke-leksikon for Norden, K25

Nielsen, K. Sappisk ordbok, M339

Nielsen, L. M. Dansk bibliografi, A229

Nienaber, P. J. Bibliografie van afrikaanse boeke, A488

Nieuw nederlandsch biografisch woordenboek, S172

Phelps, E. M. Debate index, R179; University debaters' annual, R181

Philadelphia Bibliographical Center and Union Library Catalogue. Committee on Microphotography. Union list of microfilms, A51

Philately see Postage stamps

Philip, A. J. Index to the special collections in libraries in Great Britain and Ireland, B43

—— and Gadd, W. L. Dickens dictionary, R386

Philip, G. International atlas, U173

—— and Muir, R. Philip's Historical atlas, V51

Philippines
atlas, U196
bibliography, A450-A456
biography, S191: sources, S15
directories, L365
gazetteers, U62
statistics, L190

Philippines (Commonwealth). Commission of the Census. Census atlas of the Philippines, U196

—— (Republic). Bureau of the Census and Statistics. Yearbook of Philippine statistics, L190

Philip's Atlas of ancient and classical history, V51n

Philip's Historical atlas, R. Muir and G. Philip, V51

Philip's Historical atlas, medieval and modern, V51n

Philip's New school atlas of universal history, V51n

Phillimore, J. S. Index verborum Propertianus, R856

Phillimore, W. P. W. and Fry, E. A. Index to changes of name, T73

Phillippe, M. D. Aristoteles, H4n

Phillips, C. F. and Garland, J. V. Discussion methods, R177

Phillips, H. Étude du parler de la paroisse Évangeline, M211

Phillips, J. C. American game mammals and birds, N416

Phillips, L. B. Dictionary of biographical reference, S8

Phillips, P. L. Author list of the geographical atlases in the Library of Congress, U164; List of geographical atlases in the Library of Congress, U164; The Lowery collection: A descriptive list of maps of the Spanish possessions within the present limits of the United States, U162

Phillips, T. E. R. and Steavenson, W. H. Splendour of the heavens, N155

Phillips, W. A. History of the Church of Ireland, K128

Philobiblon; a quarterly review of Chinese publications, A208

Philo-Lexikon; Handbuch des judischen Wissens, K245

Philologists, classical: biography, R55

Philomath's quotation-book. R. E. Moritz, N82

Philosophen-Lexikon, H21

Philosophers
biography, H11, H18, H21, H23-H25: Renaissance, H24; Anglo-American, H25

Philosophisches Wörterbuch, W. Brugger, H13

Philosophy, p.116-18
bibliography, H1-H10
dictionaries and encyclopedias, H11-H21
history, H22

Phonograph records see Recorded music

Photo-lab-index, H. M. Lester, Q212

Photographic abstracts, Q210

Photography
annuals, Q215-Q216
bibliography, Q208-Q210
dictionaries, Q211-Q214

Photoprints: bibliography, A49

Photostats: bibliography, A49-A50

Phyfe, W. H. P. 5000 facts and fancies, R44

Physical Society of London. Reports on progress in physics, N104

Physicians: biography, P332-P344

Physics, p.263-65
abstract journals, N100-N104
bibliography, N96-N99
dictionaries, N108-N110
encyclopedias, N105-N107
guides, N95
tables, N111-N115

Physikalische Berichte, N100

Physikalisches Handwörterbuch, A. Berliner and K. Scheel, N109

Physiology: abstract journals, N330

Pianigiani, O. Vocabolario etimologico della lingua italiana, M324

Picardy: dialect, M223

Piccola enciclopedia Hoepli, G. Garollo, D47

Pichardo, E. Diccionario provincial casi razonado de vozes y frases cubanas, M457

Picken, M. B. The language of fashion, Q185

Picot, É. Bibliographie Cornélienne, R629

Pidal, R. Menéndez see Menéndez Pidal, R.

Pieper, M. Die Ägyptische Literatur, R33n

Pierce, G. A. Dickens dictionary, R387

Piercy, W. C. and Wace, H. Dictionary of Christian biography, K31

Pierre Key's music year book, Q273

Pierrehumbert, W. Dictionnaire historique du parler neuchâtelois et suisse romand, M229

Pierson, D. Survey of the literature on Brazil of sociological significance, V167

Pijóan y Soteras, J. History of art, Q44

—— and Cossío, M. B. Summa artis, Q39

Pikler, B. and Braun, R. List of all Hungarian books in trade, A372

Pilkington, W. American notes and queries, R53

Pincussen, L. and Oppenheimer, K. Tabulae biologicae, N346

Pine, L. G. Author's and writer's who's who and reference guide, R22

Pinson, K. S. Bibliographical introduction to nationalism, L225

Pinto, O. Le bibliografie nazionali, A135; Guida bibliografica, A570

Pinto de Mattos, R. Manual bibliographico portuguez de livros raros, A470

Pirenne, H. Bibliographie de l'histoire de Belgique, V162

Pirot, L. and Vigouroux, F. G. Dictionnaire de la Bible, K95

Pitrè, G. Bibliografia delle tradizioni popolari d'Italia, K283

Pivano, S. Annuario degli istituti scientifici italiani, N38

Pixley, F. W. Accountant's dictionary, L537

Pizzi, F. Italica gens, S156

Place, J. and Talvart, H. Bibliographie des auteurs modernes de langue française, R577

Place names see Names: geographical

Place names in Victoria and Tasmania, A. E. Martin, U77

Places, poetry of, R17-R18

Plan, P. P. Bibliographie Rabelaisienne, R643

Planat, P. Encyclopédie de l'architecture et de la construction, Q110

Planché, J. R. Cyclopaedia of costume, Q182

Planning and construction, Q122

Plant names, N362-N372, N375

Plant science literature see U. S. Dept. of Agriculture. Library. Bibliography of agriculture, P233

Plant sciences see Botany; Natural history

Planta, R. de and Melcher, F. Dicziunari rumantsch Grischun, M395

Plarr, V. G. Lives of the fellows of the Royal College of Surgeons of England, P342

Plastics, P107-P111
abstract journals, P109

Porter, H. P. Petroleum dictionary, P225

Porter, K. H. National party platforms, L299d

Porto Rico *see* Puerto Rico

Portrait index, A. L. A., Q13

Ports of the world, *Sir* A. Hurd, L356

Portugal
bibliography, A463-A473, A492: bibliography, A463, A490
biography, S194
history, V419-V421
statistics, L193

Portugal. Direcção Geral da Estatística. Anuário estatístico, L193

Portuguese language
dictionaries, M386-M392: etymology, M388, M392
dictionaries, special subjects: aeronautics, P98; business, L432; medicine, P312; military, P189; nautical, P185

Portuguese literature, p.415-16
bibliography, R688-R692

Portuguese poetry: anthologies, R696-R697

Pos, H. J. and others. Eerste nederlandse systematisch ingerichte encyclopaedie, D23

Posada, E. Bibliografia bogotana, A212

Post, C. R. History of European and American sculpture, Q100

—— and Chase, G. H. History of sculpture, Q99

Post office guide, Great Britain. Post Office Dept., L386

Post-war bibliography of the Near Eastern mandates, V409

Postage stamps, Q167-Q173

Postal guides, L385-L387

Potter, M. Index-catalogue of medical and veterinary zoology, N405

Potthast, A. Bibliotheca historica Medii Aevi. Wegweiser durch die Geschichtswerke des europäischen Mittelalters, V87

Poucher, W. A. Perfumes, cosmetics and soaps with especial reference to synthetics, L513

Powell, J. E. A lexicon to Herodotus, R824

Powell, W. H. List of officers of the army of the United States from 1779-1900, L321; Officers of the army and navy (volunteer) in the civil war, L322

—— and Shippen, E. Officers of the army and navy (regular) in the civil war, L323

Power, *Sir* D'A. *see* Plarr, V. G. Lives of the fellows of the Royal College of Surgeons of England, P342

Power, J. K. Salisbury, P169n

Powicke, F. M. Handbook of British chronology, V288

Powis Smith, J. M. The Old Testament, K66

Practical business statistics, F. E. Croxton and D. J. Cowden, L445

Practical guide to American book collecting, W. Bennett, A69

Practical petroleum engineers' handbook, J. Zaba and W. T. Doherty, P226

Prada, C. García *see* García Prada, C.

Praesant, H. and Haenisch, W. Bibliographie von Japan, V359

Prager, R. Geschichte und Literatur des Lichtwechsels, N124

Pratt, I. A. Ancient Egypt, V215; Modern Egypt, V216

Pratt, W. Grove's Dictionary of music and musicians, Q254; New encyclopedia of music and musicians, Q259

Prayer book dictionary, G. Harford and M. Stevenson, K124

Pražák, V. and Nosovský, K. Soupis československé literatury, A227

Précis de patrologie, B. Altaner, K216

Predmore, R. L. An index to Don Quijote, R726

Preisigke, F. Wörterbuch der griechischen Papyrusurkunden, M277

Preliminary guide to indexed newspapers in the United States, H. O. Brayer, E104

Preliminary list of libraries in the other American republics, R. O. Rivera, B29

Prendergast, G. L. Complete concordance to the Iliad of Homer, R828

Presbyterian church, K155-K158

Presbyterian Church in the United States. Minutes, K157

Presbyterian Church in the United States of America. Minutes, K156

Press, I. Eres yisrāēl, Topographical-historical encyclopaedia of Palestine, V412

Press directory of Australia and New Zealand, E16

Preston, W. American biographies, S36

Pretzsch, K. Verzeichnis der Breslauer Universitätsschriften, G26

Preuss, S. Vollständiges Lexikon zu den pseudo-cäsarianischen Schriftwerken, R845

—— and Menge, R. Lexicon Caesarianum, R843

Preussische Staatsbibliothek *see* Berlin. Preussische Staatsbibliothek

Prezzolini, G. Repertorio bibliografico della storia e della critica della letteratura italiana, R658

Price, A. L. The American nurses dictionary, P355

Price, H. T. Economic dictionary: English-German, German-English, L340

Price, M. O. Catalog for a law library of 15,000 volumes, B67

Price lists, U. S. Superintendent of Documents, F17

Prick van Wely, F. P. H. Engels handwoordenboek, M162

Prieto, L. F. Muestras de errores y defectos del "Diccionario biográfico colonial de Chile," S89

Primates, N404

Prime edizioni italiane, M. Parenti, A391

Princeton. Theological Seminary. Library. Bibliography of Bible study, K71

—— University. Industrial Relations Section. A trade union library, L477

—— —— Library. Alphabetical finding list, A42; Classed list, A42

Principles of bibliographical description, F. Bowers, A1

Prins, A. W. Winkler Prins' Algemeene encyclopaedie, D25

Print prices current, Q38

Printed maps in the atlases of Great Britain and Ireland, T. Chubb, U160

Printers,
France, A620-A621
Great Britain, A619
Spain, A505
See also Printing and publishing

Printers' and publishers' devices in England and Scotland, R. B. McKerrow, A82

Printers' ink directory of house organs, E13

Printers' marks, A80-A85

Printing and Allied Trades Research Association. Library. Classified lists of text books, reference books and periodicals, A587

Printing and promotion handbook, D. Melcher and N. Larrick, A589

Printing and publishing, p.60-63
bibliography, A583-A588
copy preparation, A622-A625
copyright, A626-A627
dictionaries, A590: terms, A593-A605
directories, A606-A615
encyclopedias, A591-A592
handbooks, A589
history, A617-A618
style manuals, A622, A624

Prisons, L34

Pritzel, G. A. Thesaurus literaturae botanicae omnium gentium, N350

Private book collectors in the United States and Canada, A74

Royal Institute of British Architects. London. Library. Catalogue of the . . . Library, Q106

Royal Irish Academy, Dublin. Contributions to a dictionary of the Irish language, M307; Dictionary of the Irish language, M306

Royal Meteorological Society, London. Bibliography of meteorological literature, N274

Royal Society of London. Catalogue of scientific papers, N4; Catalogue of scientific papers . . . Subject index, N4; Catalogue of scientific papers, Subject index, Mechanics, P11; Catalogue of scientific papers, Subject index, Physics, N98; Catalogue of scientific papers, Subject index, Pure mathematics, N74; Catalogue of the periodical publications, E2; Obituary notices of fellows, N66

Royce, W. H. Balzac bibliography, R620

Royer, L. Bibliographie Stendhalienne, R628

Rubio, D. La anarquia del lenguage en la America española, M443
—— and Sullivan, M. C. Glossary of technical library and allied terms in Spanish and English, A601, B10

Ruch, T. C. Bibliographia primatologica, N404

Rudd, J. see Cerfberr, A. and Christophe, J. Compendium, H. de Balzac's Comédie humaine, R623

Rudolph, L. Schiller-Lexikon, R540

Rue, E. Subject index to books for intermediate grades, R182; Subject index to books for primary grades, R183

Ruff, W. Bibliography of the poetical works of Sir Walter Scott, R427

Ruiz, A. Salcedo y see Salcedo y Ruiz, A.

Rumania
bibliography, A475-A477
history, V422-V423
statistics, L196-L197

Rumania. Directiunea Statisticei Generale. Anuarul statistic al Românieĭ, L196
—— Institut Central de Statistique. Bréviaire statistique, L197

Rumanian language: dictionaries, M397-M400

Rumanian literature, R700-R701

Rumball-Petre, E. A. America's first Bibles, K68

Runes, D. D. Who's who in philosophy, H25
—— and Schrickel, H. G. Encyclopedia of the arts, Q23

Runner, D. G. and Brown, V. J. Engineering terminology, P30

Rusk, R. L. The literature of the middle western frontier, R188

Russell, J. C. Dictionary of writers of thirteenth century England, R294

Russell Sage Foundation Library. List of directories of social agencies, p.150

Russell's Official national motor coach guide, U212

Russia
bibliography, A478-A484
biography, S196-S198
history: bibliography, V424-V432; encyclopedias and handbooks, V433-V435
statistics, L198-L202

Russia: a check list preliminary to a basic bibliography, U. S. Library of Congress. Reference Department, A483

Russia from A to Z, H. A. Freund, V434

Russia, U. S. S. R., P. N. Malevskiĭ-Malevich, L198

Russian books for college libraries, A552

Russian language
abbreviations, M313-M314
dictionaries, M401-M414: bibliography, M401
dictionaries, special subjects: chemistry, N208, P46; meteorology, N280; military, P189; technical, N208, P45-P46

Russian literature, p.421-23
bibliography, R778-R784
dictionaries, R785-R788
history, R789-R790

Russian poetry: anthologies, R791-R795

Russian writers: a bio-bibliographical dictionary, V. Snow, R787

Die russische Literatur, P. N. Sakulin, R33n

Russkaîa istoricheskaîa bibliografîâ, P. P. Lambin and B. P. Lambin, V429

Russkaîa istoricheskaîa bibliografîâ, V. I. Mezhov, V428

Russkaîa periodicheskaîa, N. M. Lisovskiĭ, E50

Russkiĭ biograficheskiĭ slovar, S198

Russo-Alesi, A. I. Martyrology pronouncing dictionary, K206

Rust, W. Verzeichnis von unklaren Titelkürzungen, E3

Ruvigny and Raineval, 9th marquis of. Titled nobility of Europe, T16

Ryan, R. Biographia Hibernica, S150

Ryland, F. Chronological outlines of English literature, R285

SAE handbook, Society of Automotive Engineers, P175

SPI handbook, Society of the Plastics Industry, Inc., P111

Saba, M. Bibliographie de l'Iran, V343

Sabin, J. Dictionary of books relating to America, A145

Sabine, L. Biographical sketches of loyalists of the American revolution, S37

Sacher, H. Staatslexikon, L230

Sachs, C. History of musical instruments, Q309; Die Musik der Antike, Q276n; Real-Lexikon der Musikinstrumente, Q310; The rise of music in the ancient world, Q279n

Sachs, J. von. History of botany, N377

Sachs, K. and Villatte, C. Encyklopädisches französisch-deutsches und deutsch-französisches Wörterbuch, M183

Sacra, M. and Berner, E. R. Basic book collection for junior high schools, A559

Sacramento Blake, A. V. A. do. Diccionario bibliographico brazileiro, A185

Sacred and legendary art, A. B. M. Jameson, Q71

Sacred books of China, the texts of Confucianism, J. Legge, K230n

Sacred books of China, the texts of Tâoism, J. Legge, K230n

Sacred books of the East, F. M. Müller, K230

Sacred laws of the Aryas, G. Buhler, K230n

Saddharma-pundarika, H. Kern, K230n

Šafařík, P. J. Geschichte der südslawischen Literatur, R770

Sag Harbor, L. I. imprints, D. C. McMurtrie, A163n

Sagas of Icelanders, H. Hermannsson, A376n

Sagas of the kings of Norway, H. Hermannsson, A376n

Saglio, E. and Daremberg, C. Dictionnaire des antiquités grecques et romaines, V72

Sáineanu, L. La langue de Rabelais, R644

Saint-Christo, F. and Colleville, L. Les ordres du roi, T54

St. John, Cynthia Morgan. Wordsworth collection, Cornell University Library, R472

Saint Romain, C. Du Peloux see Du Peloux de Saint Romain, C. Vicomte

Saintonge, P. F. and Christ, R. W. Fifty years of Molière studies, R640

Saintonge dialect, M224-M226

619

Tables of and annotated index to the congressional series . . . U. S. Superintendent of Documents, F12

Tables of computed altitude and azimuth, U. S. Hydrographic Office, N151

Tables of distances, L371-L373

Tables of physical and chemical constants, G. W. C. Kaye and T. H. Laby, N111

Tables of the higher mathematical functions, H. T. Davis, N92

Tabulae biologicae, K. Oppenheimer and L. Pincussen, N346

Tacitus, R861-R862

Taeuber, I. B. General censuses and vital statistics in the Americas, L83

—— and Beal, E. G., Jr. Guide to the official demographic statistics of Japan, L160

Taggart, A. F. Handbook of mineral dressing; ores and industrial minerals, P203

Talbot-Booth, E. Merchant ships, L402

Tallmadge, T. E. Story of architecture, Q127

Tallquist, J. O. Vem och vad?, S107

Talmudic Hebrew: dictionaries, M290, M292

Talvart, H. and Place, J. Bibliographie des auteurs modernes de langue française, R577

Tanger, G. and Schmidt, I. Flügel-Schmidt-Tanger, a dictionary of the English and German languages, M254

Tanguay, C. Dictionnaire généalogique des familles canadiennes, T15

Tannenbaum, S. A. and Tannenbaum, D. R. Elizabethan bibliographies, R270

Tanner, J. R. Constitutional documents of the reign of James I, V301; Tudor constitutional documents, V302

Taoism, texts, J. Legge, K320n

Tariff, L375-L378

Tariff, bibliography, U. S. Tariff Commission, L377

Tarn, H. Crozes, V225n

Taschenberg, O. Bibliotheca zoologica II, N402

Tate, A. Sixty American poets, 1896-1944, R223

Tate, W. Tate's Modern cambist, L381; Tate's Money manual, L382

Tatge, E. Bibliography and index of geology exclusive of North America, N238

Tatlock, J. S. P. and Kennedy, A. G. Concordance to Chaucer, R373

Tauro, A. Anuario bibliográfico peruano, A447

Tavera, T. H. Pardo de see Pardo de Tavera, T. H.

Tawney, R. H. Tudor economic documents, V303

Tax Foundation, Inc., New York. Facts and figures on government finance, L561

Tax systems, L562

Taylor, A. The proverb, R128

Taylor, A. M. The language of World War II, M51

Taylor, C. R. H. General bibliography on New Zealand, V396

Taylor, G. R. and Smith, C. H. Flags of all nations, T62

Taylor, N. Encyclopedia of gardening, P256

Taylor, R. P. D. S. Who's who in Central and East Europe, S26

Taylor's Encyclopedia of gardening, N. Taylor, P256

Tchemerzine, A. Bibliographie d'éditions originales, A250

Teacher-librarian's handbook, M. P. Douglas, B45

Teachers, L767-L769

certification, L733a

Teachers College. Institute of Adult Education. Handbook of adult education in the United States, L724

—— International Institute. Educational yearbook, L732

Teachers' directory, Association of American law schools, L626

Technical and scientific encyclopaedia, Hutchinson's, P27

Technical book review index, monthly, Carnegie Library of Pittsburgh, P16

Technical book review index, quarterly, P15

Technical data digest, P83

Technical schools: directories, L750

Technical terms used in bibliographies and by the book and printing trades, A. Moth, A604

Technologisches Wörterbuch, A. Schlomann, P37

Technology, p.295-314

abstract journals, P21-P24

bibliography, P5-P17

dictionaries, P30-P33: foreign terms, P34-P50

directories, P51-P54

encyclopedias, P27-P28

guides, P1-P4

handbooks, P25-P26, P29

indexes, P18-P20, P22-P23

periodicals, N13-N25

societies, P55-P56

yearbooks, P57

Teixeira de Oliveira, J. Dicionário brasileiro de datas históricas, V170

Tejada y Sainz, J. de D. Spanish and English legal and commercial dictionary, L607

Tekniikan sanasto, V. Airas and others, P38

Telang, K. T. Bhagavadgîtâ, with the Sanatsugâtîya and the Annugîtâ, K230n

Television, L404-L406, P154

Television encyclopedia, S. Kempner, L406

Television manual, J. F. Rider, P154

Temperance, L42

Templeman, W. D. Bibliographies of studies in Victorian literature, R277

10 eventful years, Encyclopaedia Britannica, D3

10,000 trade names, T. W. Lippert, P200

Ten years of educational research, W. S. Monroe, L713

Têng, S. and Biggerstaff, K. Annotated bibliography of selected Chinese reference works, A575

Tennessee imprints, 1793-1840, A163n; 1841-1850, A163n

Tennyson, Alfred, Lord

bibliography, R463

concordance, R464

dictionary, R465

handbook, R466

Téodorov-Balan, A. B'lgarski knigopis za sto godini, A188

Tercentenary handlist of English and Welsh newspapers, Times, London, E34

Terentius Afer, R863

Term catalogues, E. Arber, A296

Terman, F. E. Radio engineers' handbook, P149

Terminologia medica, L. Ferrio, P311

Terms commonly used in distribution and advertising, International Chamber of Commerce. International Distribution Commission and Committee on Advertising, L424

Terry, C. S. Catalogue of the publications of Scottish historical and kindred clubs, V320

Terry guide books, U200

Tests see Mental tests

Teuchert, H. and Wossidlo, R. Mecklenburgisches Wörterbuch, M263

Teuffel, W. S. History of Roman literature, R836

Tewkesbury's Who's who in Alaska and Alaska business index, L363, S45

Textile fabrics and their selection, I. B. Wingate, L518

Textile Mercury. Dictionary of textile terms, L521

Textiles, L515-L521

dictionaries, L519-L521

Thacher, J. American medical biography, p.325

Thackeray, H. J. Lexicon to Josephus, R829

Webster, John: bibliography, R270
Webster's Biographical dictionary, S25
Webster's Dictionary of synonyms, M59
Webster's Geographical dictionary, U16
Webster's New collegiate dictionary, M10
Webster's New international dictionary of the English language, M7
Wedgwood, J. C. History of Parliament, L274, S129
Weed, K. K. and Bond, R. P. British newspapers and periodicals from their beginning to 1800, E38
Weekley, E. Etymological dictionary of modern English, M24; Surnames, T67
Wegelin, O. Early American fiction, 1774-1830, R216; Early American plays, 1714-1830, R207; Early American poetry, R224
Wegweiser durch die Geschichtswerke des europäischen Mittelalters, A. Potthast, V87
Wegweiser durch die Literatur der österreichischen Geschichte, R. Charmatz, V155
Weights and measures, L379-L384
Weigle, L. A. American idealism, V115
Weiss, H. B. American letter-writers, R233
Welcher, F. Chemical solutions, N212
Weld, L. D. Glossary of physics, N110
Welding, P179-P180
Welding encyclopedia, P180
Welding handbook, American Welding Society, P179
Welford, R. Early Newcastle typography, A338
Weller, E. Die falschen und fingirten Druckorte, A131
Weller, E. O. Repertorium typographicum, A262n
Wells, C. Parody anthology, R352
—— and Goldsmith, A. F. Concise bibliography of Walt Whitman, R251
Wells, G. H. Works of H. G. Wells, a bibliography, R470
Wells, H. G.
bibliography, R470
dictionary, R471
Wells, J. E. Manual of the writings in Middle English, R266
Welsh Americana, H. Blackwell, A150
Welsh language: dictionaries, M498-M500
Wely, F. P. H. Prick van see Prick van Wely, F. P. H.
Wenckstern, F. von. A bibliography of the Japanese empire, V358

Wensinck, A. J. and Kramers, J. K. Handwörterbuch des Islam, K256
Wenström, O. E. Engelsk-svensk ordbok, M476
Wentworth, H. American dialect dictionary, M63
Wer ist Wer?, S122
"Wer ist wer," Lexikon österreichischer Zeitgenossen, S69
Werkgemeenschap van Wetenschappelijke Organisaties in Nederland. Natuurwetenschappelijk onderzoek in Nederland, N50
Werner, E. C. Things Chinese, V195
Werner, E. T. C. Dictionary of Chinese mythology, K263
Wessely, I. E. Swedish-English dictionary, M478
West, C. J. and Berolzheimer, D. D. Bibliography on chemistry and chemical technology, N173
West, D. H. and Cook, D. E. Standard catalog for public libraries, A551
West, E. W. Pahlavi texts, K230n
West Indies
biography, S157
dialect, M445
guide books, U207-U208
history, V462-V467
statistics, L218
West Indies year book, L218
West Virginia imprints, A163n
Western European painting of the Renaissance, F. J. Mather, Q82
Western words, R. F. Adams, M43
Westinghouse Electric Corporation. Industrial electronics reference book, P153
Westminster commentaries, W. Lock, K102
Westminster dictionary of the Bible, J. D. Davis, K87
Westminster historical atlas of the Bible, G. E. Wright and F. V. Filson, K105
Wetmore, M. N. Index verborvm Catvllianvs, R847; Index verborum Vergilianus, R867
Wetzer, H. J. Wetzer und Welte's Kirchenlexikon, K187
Wharton, J. J. S. Wharton's Law-lexicon, L598
What editors and publishers want, R25n
Wheatley, H. B. London, past and present, V315
Wheeler, C. G. see Wheeler, W. A. Who wrote it?, R51
Wheeler, M. T. Indexing, B71
Wheeler, W. A. Explanatory and pronouncing dictionary of the noted names in fiction, R49; Familiar allusions, R50; Who wrote it?, R51
Wheeler gift of books, American Institute of Electrical Engineers. Library, P130

Wheeler-Holohan, V. Flags of the world, T64
Wheelwright, W. B. Paper trade terms, A605
Where is the —— collection?, C. D. Sherborn, N343
Whibley, L. Companion to Greek studies, V78
Whig supremacy, B. Williams, V291
Whistling, K. F. Handbuch der musikalischen Literatur, Q232
Whitaker, J. Almanack, L148
Whitaker's Cumulative book list, A304
Whitaker's Cumulative book list, (current), A307
Whitby, Eng.: bibliography, A346
Whitcomb, S. L. Chronological outlines of American literature, R196
White, A. C. and Sheldon, E. S. Concordanza delle opere italiane in prosa e del canzoniere di Dante Alighiere, R678
White, B. see Chambers, E. K. The Elizabethan stage, Index, R313
White, J. Dictionary of altitudes in the Dominion of Canada, U30; Place-names in Northern Canada, U82; Place names in Quebec, U82n; Place names, Thousand Islands, U82n
White, J. M. The farmer's handbook, P259
White, W. Henry David Thoreau bibliography, R248; John Donne since 1900, R390
White, W. W. White's Political dictionary, L231
Whiteley, M. A. and Thorpe, J. F. Thorpe's Dictionary of applied chemistry, N191
White's Conspectus of American biography, R195, S35, V113
White's Political dictionary, W. W. White, L231
Whitfield, F. J. A history of Russian literature, D. S. Mirsky, R790
Whiting, G. Lace guide for makers and collectors, L510
Whitley, W. T. Baptist bibliography, K111
Whitlock, C. Abbreviations used in the Department of Agriculture for titles of publications, P250
Whitman, C. H. Subject-index to the poems of Edmund Spenser, R462
Whitman, Walt
bibliography, R187n, R250-R251
concordance, R253
handbook, R252
Whittle, W. C. M. The "Aeroplane" directory of British aviation, P101
Who is who in Turkey, S218
Who knows —— and what, S46

641